I want to say thank you, from a student here at UPEI...

I took the Organizational Behaviour course, and we used the book by McShane/Steen, 7th edition. This is the first textbook I've used that I actually enjoyed reading. I could follow, understand, and take away plenty from this book—something that textbooks typically do not offer me.

I am very impressed with this textbook, *and I received an outstanding mark in the course.*

Thank you for speaking to me like a person—a student—and not like someone who should already know all of this material.

Continue your great work—we, the students, appreciate it.

Chelsea Almeida, student using McShane/Steen, *Canadian Organizational Behaviour*
University of Prince Edward Island

CANADIAN ORGANIZATIONAL BEHAVIOUR

EIGHTH EDITION

STEVEN L. McSHANE

University of Western Australia

SANDRA L. STEEN

University of Regina

McGraw-Hill
Ryerson
Connect. Learn. Succeed.

Canadian Organizational Behaviour
Eighth Edition

ISBN-13: 978-0-07-040187-7
ISBN-10: 0-07-040187-X

1 2 3 4 5 6 7 8 9 10 DOW 1 9 8 7 6 5 4 3 2

Printed and bound in the United States.

Executive Sponsoring Editor: Kim Brewster
Marketing Manager: Cathie Lefebvre
Developmental Editors: Tracey Haggert and Lori McLellan
Senior Editorial Associate: Christine Lomas
Photo/Permission Research: Mary Rose MacLachlan, www.mrmassociates.ca
Supervising Editors: Joanne Limebeer and Kara Stahl
Copy Editor: Erin Moore
Production Coordinator: Lena Keating
Cover and Interior Design: Michelle Losier
Cover Image Credit: © Guido Daniele. Used with permission.
Page Layout: Laserwords Private Limited
Printer: R. R. Donnelley

Library and Archives Canada Cataloguing in Publication

McShane, Steven L. (Steven Lattimore)
    Canadian organizational behaviour/Steven L. McShane, Sandra L. Steen.—8th ed.

Includes bibliographical references and indexes.
ISBN 978-0-07-040187-7

    1. Organizational behavior—Canada—Textbooks.   2. Organizational behavior—
Canada—Case studies.   3. Teams in the workplace—Textbooks.   4. Corporate
culture—Textbooks.   I. Steen, Sandra   II. Title.
HD58.7.M32 2012   658.3   C98-300627-X

Dedicated with love and devotion to Donna,
and to our wonderful daughters,
Bryton and Madison—S.L.M.

For Aaron, Matt, and Jess—S.L.S.

ABOUT THE AUTHORS

STEVEN L. MCSHANE

Steven L. McShane is Winthrop Professor of Management at the University of Western Australia (UWA) Business School, where he receives high teaching ratings from students in Perth, Singapore, Manila, and other cities where UWA offers its programs. He previously taught in the business faculties at Simon Fraser University and Queen's University in Canada. Steve has conducted executive programs with Nokia, TÜV-SÜD, Wesfarmers Group, Main Roads WA, McGraw-Hill, ALCOA World Alumina Australia, and many other organizations. He is also a popular visiting speaker, having given numerous invited presentations over the past four years to faculty and students in the United States, China, India, Canada, the Philippines, Malaysia, and other countries.

Steve earned his Ph.D. from Michigan State University in organizational behaviour, human resource management, and labour relations. He also holds a Master of Industrial Relations from the University of Toronto, and an undergraduate degree from Queen's University in Canada. Steve is a past President of the Administrative Sciences Association of Canada (ASAC) and Director of Graduate Programs in the business faculty at Simon Fraser University.

Along with co-authoring *Canadian Organizational Behaviour*, Eighth Edition, Steve is co-author of *M: Organizational Behavior* (2012) and *Organizational Behavior*, Sixth Edition (2013) with Mary Ann Von Glinow (Florida International University); and *Organisational Behaviour on the Pacific Rim*, Third Edition (2010) with Mara Olekalns (University of Melbourne) and Tony Travaglione (Curtin University). Steve is also co-author of editions or translations of his organizational behaviour book in China, India, Quebec, Taiwan, and Brazil. Steve has published several dozen articles and conference papers on workplace values, training transfer, organizational learning, exit-voice-loyalty, employee socialization, wrongful dismissal, media bias in business magazines, and other diverse topics.

Steve enjoys spending his leisure time swimming, body board surfing, canoeing, skiing, and travelling with his wife and two daughters.

SANDRA L. STEEN

Sandra L. Steen teaches in the Paul J. Hill School of Business and the Kenneth Levene Graduate School of Business at the University of Regina. Sandra also leads executive education and professional development sessions with the Centre for Management Development, Faculty of Business Administration. Sandra has an integrated education and background in both organizational behaviour and human resource management. She received her MBA from the University of Regina and has more than 25 years of leading, managing, teaching, and consulting across a wide range of organizations in the private, public, and not-for-profit sectors. Sandra teaches in the undergraduate, MBA, and Executive MBA programs at the University of Regina. In addition to *Canadian Organizational Behaviour*, Eighth Edition, Sandra is co-author with Professors Raymond Noe (Ohio State University), John R. Hollenbeck (Michigan State University), Barry Gerhart (University of Wisconsin-Madison), and Patrick Wright (Cornell University) of *Human Resource Management*, Second Canadian Edition (2009).

Sandra holds the designation of Certified Human Resources Professional (CHRP) and she is a member of the Saskatchewan Association of Human Resource Professionals. She serves as a Commissioner of the Saskatchewan Public Service Commission, the central human resource agency for the Saskatchewan Provincial Government. Sandra has received recognition for her teaching accomplishments including "Inspiring Teacher Award—Business Administration." In her leisure time, Sandra enjoys time at the lake with her husband Aaron, and their children, Matt and Jess.

BRIEF CONTENTS

PART ONE

Introduction

1 Introduction to the Field of Organizational Behaviour   1

PART TWO

Individual Behaviour and Processes

2 Individual Behaviour, Personality, and Values   28

3 Perceiving Ourselves and Others in Organizations   63

4 Workplace Emotions, Attitudes, and Stress   92

5 Foundations of Employee Motivation   122

6 Applied Performance Practices   154

7 Decision Making and Creativity   181

PART THREE

Team Processes

8 Team Dynamics   211

9 Communicating in Teams and Organizations   245

10 Power and Influence in the Workplace   271

11 Conflict and Negotiation in the Workplace   297

12 Leadership in Organizational Settings   327

PART FOUR

Organizational Processes

13 Designing Organizational Structures   353

14 Organizational Culture   380

15 Organizational Change   407

ADDITIONAL CASES   432

APPENDIX A
Theory Building and Systematic Research Methods   453

APPENDIX B
Scoring Keys for Self-Assessment Exercises   461

GLOSSARY   477

ENDNOTES   483

NAME AND ORGANIZATION INDEX   544

SUBJECT INDEX   550

CONTENTS

Preface xiii
Acknowledgments xxiv

Self-Assessment Exercise 1.4: It All Makes Sense? 26

Self-Assessment Exercise 1.5: Are You a Good Telecommuter? 27

PART ONE

Introduction

CHAPTER 1
Introduction to the Field of Organizational Behaviour 1

Learning Objectives 1

Welcome to the Field of Organizational Behaviour 2

The Field of Organizational Behaviour 2

Historical Foundations of Organizational Behaviour 3

Why Study Organizational Behaviour? 3

Perspectives of Organizational Effectiveness 4

Open Systems Perspective 5

Organizational Learning Perspective 7

Connections 1.1: Duha Colour's Learning Organization Strategies 9

High-Performance Work Practices (HPWP) Perspective 10

Stakeholder Perspective 11

Connecting the Dots: Organizational Effectiveness and Organizational Behaviour 14

Contemporary Challenges for Organizations 14

Globalization 14

Increasing Workforce Diversity 15

Emerging Employment Relationships 18

Anchors of Organizational Behaviour Knowledge 19

The Multidisciplinary Anchor 19

The Systematic Research Anchor 20

The Contingency Anchor 20

The Multiple Levels of Analysis Anchor 21

The Journey Begins 21

Chapter Summary 22

Key Terms 22

Critical-Thinking Questions 23

Case Study 1.1: Hospitals are Driving toward a Leaner Organization 23

Team Exercise 1.2: Generational Myths and Realities 25

Web Exercise 1.3: Diagnosing Organizational Stakeholders 26

PART TWO

Individual Behaviour and Processes

CHAPTER 2
Individual Behaviour, Personality, and Values 28

Learning Objectives 28

MARS Model of Individual Behaviour and Performance 29

Employee Motivation 29

Ability 30

Role Perceptions 31

Situational Factors 32

Types of Individual Behaviour 32

Task Performance 32

Organizational Citizenship 33

Counterproductive Work Behaviours 33

Joining and Staying with the Organization 34

Maintaining Work Attendence 35

Personality in Organizations 35

Personality Determinants: Nature versus Nurture 36

Five-Factor Model of Personality 37

Jungian Personality Theory and the Myers-Briggs Type Indicator 39

Caveats about Personality Testing in Organizations 40

Values in the Workplace 41

Types of Values 42

Values and Individual Behaviour 42

Values Congruence 43

Ethical Values and Behaviour 45

Three Ethical Principles 45

Moral Intensity, Ethical Sensitivity, and Situational Influences 46

Supporting Ethical Behaviour 48

Values Across Cultures 48

Global Connections 2.1: Infosys Bridges the Cross-Cultural Divide 49

Individualism and Collectivism 49

Power Distance   50

Uncertainty Avoidance   51

Achievement-Nurturing Orientation   51

Caveats About Cross-Cultural Knowledge   51

Diversity of Canadian Cultural Values   52

Chapter Summary   53

Key Terms   54

Critical-Thinking Questions   54

Case Study 2.1: South Korea's SK Telecom Goes Egalitarian   54

Case Study 2.2: Pushing Papers Can Be Fun   55

Class Exercise 2.3: Test Your Knowledge of Personality   56

Team Exercise 2.4: Comparing Cultural Values   58

Team Exercise 2.5: Ethics Dilemma Vignettes   59

Self-Assessment Exercise 2.6: Are You Introverted or Extroverted?   61

Self-Assessment Exercise 2.7: What Are Your Dominant Values?   61

Self-Assessment Exercise 2.8: Individualism-Collectivism Scale   62

CHAPTER 3
Perceiving Ourselves and Others in Organizations   63

Learning Objectives   63

Self-Concept: How We Perceive Ourselves   64

Self-Concept Complexity, Consistency, and Clarity   64

Self-Enhancement   65

Self-Verification   66

Self-Evaluation   66

The Social Self   67

Self-Concept and Organizational Behaviour   68

Perceiving the World Around Us   69

Perceptual Organization and Interpretation   71

Specific Perceptual Processes and Problems   72

Stereotyping in Organizations   72

Attribution Theory   74

Self-Fulfilling Prophecy   76

Other Perceptual Effects   77

Improving Perceptions   79

Awareness of Perceptual Biases   79

Improving Self-Awareness   79

Meaningful Interaction   80

Global Connections 3.1: CEO Reality Check by Working on the Front Line   81

Global Mindset: Developing Perceptions Across Borders   81

Developing a Global Mindset   82

Chapter Summary   84

Key Terms   84

Critical-Thinking Questions   85

Case Study 3.1: Hy Dairies, Ltd.   85

Team Exercise 3.2: Who Am I?   86

Web Exercise 3.3: Diversity and Stereotyping on Display in Corporate Websites   88

Team Exercise 3.4: Do You Have a Global Mindset?   88

Self-Assessment Exercise 3.5: How Much Does Work Define Your Self-Concept?   89

Self-Assessment Exercise 3.6: Estimating Your Locus of Control   90

Self-Assessment Exercise 3.7: Identifying Your General Self-Efficacy   90

Self-Assessment Exercise 3.8: How Much Perceptual Structure Do You Need?   90

Self-Assessment Exercise 3.9: Assessing Your Perspective Taking (Cognitive Empathy)   91

Self-Assessment Exercise 3.10: Assessing Your Emotional Empathy   91

CHAPTER 4
Workplace Emotions, Attitudes, and Stress   92

Learning Objectives   92

Emotions in the Workplace   93

Types of Emotions   93

Emotions, Attitudes, and Behaviour   94

Managing Emotions at Work   98

Emotional Intelligence   99

Improving Emotional Intelligence   101

Job Satisfaction   102

Job Satisfaction and Work Behaviour   102

Global Connections 4.1: Happy Employees, Happy Customers   105

Organizational Commitment   106

Consequences of Affective and Organizational Commitment   106

Building Organizational Commitment   106

Work-Related Stress and Its Management   108

General Adaptation Syndrome   108

Consequences of Distress   109

Stressors: The Causes of Stress   110

Individual Differences in Stress   111

Managing Work-Related Stress   112

Chapter Summary   114

Key Terms   115

Critical-Thinking Questions   115

Case Study 4.1: Conestoga-Rovers and Associates   116

Class Exercise 4.2: Strengths-Based Coaching   116

Team Exercise 4.3: Ranking Jobs on Their Emotional Labour   117

Self-Assessment Exercise 4.4: How Do You Rate Your Emotional Intelligence?   118

Self-Assessment Exercise 4.5: Are You Committed to Your School?   120

Self-Assessment Exercise 4.6: What Is Your Emotional Personality?   120

Self-Assessment Exercise 4.7: Are You a Workaholic?   120

Self-Assessment Exercise 4.8: How Stressed Are You?   121

Self-Assessment Exercise 4.9: How Do You Cope with Stressful Situations?   121

CHAPTER 5
Foundations of Employee Motivation   122

Learning Objectives   122

Employee Engagement   123

Global Connections 5.1: Standard Chartered Gets Engaged   124

Employee Drives and Needs   125

Individual Differences in Needs   125

Maslow's Needs Hierarchy Theory   126

What's Wrong with Needs Hierarchy Models?   127

Learned Needs Theory   128

Four-Drive Theory   129

Expectancy Theory of Motivation   132

Expectancy Theory in Practice   133

Organizational Behaviour Modification and Social Cognitive Theory   134

Organizational Behaviour Modification   134

Social Cognitive Theory   136

Goal Setting and Feedback   137

Balanced Scorecard   138

Characteristics of Effective Feedback   138

Sources of Feedback   140

Evaluating Goal Setting and Feedback   141

Organizational Justice   141

Equity Theory   141

Procedural Justice   145

Chapter Summary   145

Key Terms   146

Critical-Thinking Questions   146

Case Study 5.1: Vêtements Ltée   147

Class Exercise 5.2: Needs Priority Exercise   148

Class Exercise 5.3: The Learning Exercise   149

Team Exercise 5.4: Bonus Decision Exercise   149

Self-Assessment Exercise 5.5: Need-Strength Questionnaire   151

Self-Assessment Exercise 5.6: Measuring Your Growth-Need Strength   152

Self-Assessment Exercise 5.7: Your Equity Sensitivity   153

CHAPTER 6
Applied Performance Practices   154

Learning Objectives   154

The Meaning of Money in the Workplace   155

Financial Reward Practices   156

Membership- and Seniority-Based Rewards   156

Job Status-Based Rewards   157

Competency-Based Rewards   157

Performance-Based Rewards   158

Improving Reward Effectiveness   160

Job Design Practices   161

Global Connections 6.1: When Rewards Go Wrong   162

Job Design and Work Efficiency   163

Job Design and Work Motivation   164

Job Design Practices that Motivate   166

Empowerment Practices   169

Supporting Empowerment   169

Self-Leadership Practices   170

Self-Leadership Strategies   171

Effectiveness of Self-Leadership   172

Self-Leadership Contingencies   173

Chapter Summary   173

Key Terms   174

Critical-Thinking Questions   174

Case Study 6.1: YakkaTech Ltd.   175

Case Study 6.2: And the Award for Best Commercial Goes To …   176

Team Exercise 6.3: Is Student Work Enriched?   177

Self-Assessment Exercise 6.4: What is Your Attitude Toward Money?   179

Self-Assessment Exercise 6.5: How Well Do You Practise Self-Leadership?   179

Self-Assessment Exercise 6.6: Are You Empowered As a Student?   180

CHAPTER 7
Decision Making and Creativity   181

Learning Objectives   181

Rational Choice Paradigm of Decision Making   182

Rational Choice Decision Making Process   183

Problems with the Rational Choice Paradigm   184

Identifying Problems and Opportunities   184

Problems with Problem Identification   184

Global Connections 7.1: Famous Missed Opportunities   186

Identifying Problems and Opportunities More Effectively   186

Searching for, Evaluating, and Choosing Alternatives   187

Problems with Goals   187

Problems with Information Processing   188

Problems with Maximization   189

Evaluating Opportunities   189

Emotions and Making Choices   190

Intuition and Making Choices   191

Making Choices More Effectively   191

Implementing Decisions   192

Evaluating Decision Outcomes   192

Escalation of Commitment   193

Evaluating Decision Outcomes More Effectively   194

Creativity   194

   The Creative Process 195

   Characteristics of Creative People   196

   Organizational Conditions Supporting Creativity   197

   Activities that Encourage Creativity   198

Employee Involvement in Decision Making   198

   Benefits of Employee Involvement   199

   Contingencies of Employee Involvement   200

Chapter Summary   201

Key Terms   202

Critical-Thinking Questions   202

   Case Study 7.1: Employee Involvement Cases   203

   Case Study 7.2: Going for WOW at Nottingham-Spirk 204

   Team Exercise 7.3: Where In the World Are We?   206

   Class Exercise 7.4: The Hopping Orange   208

   Class Exercise 7.5: Creativity Brainbusters   208

   Self-Assessment Exercise 7.6: Do You Have A Creative Personality?   209

   Self-Assessment Exercise 7.7: How Creative Are You?   210

   Self-Assessment Exercise 7.8: What Is Your Preferred Decision Making Style?   210

PART THREE

Team Processes

CHAPTER 8

Team Dynamics   211

Learning Objectives   211

Teams and Informal Groups   212

   Informal Groups   212

Advantages and Disadvantages of Teams   214

   The Challenges of Teams   215

A Model of Team Effectiveness   216

   Organizational and Team Environment   216

Team Design Elements   217

   Task Characteristics   217

   Team Size   219

   Team Composition   219

   GLOBAL Connections 8.1: Royal Dutch/Shell Finds Team Players in Gourami   220

Team Processes   222

   Team Development   222

   Team Norms   224

   Team Cohesion   225

   Team Trust   227

Self-Directed Teams   229

   Success Factors for Self-Directed Teams   229

   GLOBAL Connections 8.2: Reckitt Benckiser's Prescription for Productivity: Self-Directed Teams   230

Virtual Teams   230

   Success Factors for Virtual Teams   231

Team Decision Making   231

   Constraints on Team Decision Making   231

   Team Structures to Improve Decision Making   233

Chapter Summary   235

Key Terms   236

Critical-Thinking Questions   236

   Case Study 8.1: The Outstanding Faculty Award   236

   Case Study 8.2: The Philanthropic Team-Builder   238

   Team Exercise 8.3: Team Tower Power   238

   Team Exercise 8.4: Human Checkers   239

   Team Exercise 8.5: Mist Ridge   240

   Self-Assessment Exercise 8.6: What Team Roles Do You Prefer?   242

   Self-Assessment Exercise 8.7: Are You a Team Player?   243

   Self-Assessment Exercise 8.8: How Trusting Are You?   244

CHAPTER 9

Communicating in Teams and Organizations   245

Learning Objectives   245

The Importance of Communication   246

A Model of Communication   247

   Influences on Effective Encoding and Decoding   247

Communication Channels   248

   Web-Based Communication   249

   Problems with Email   249

   Workplace Communication through Social Media   250

   Global Connections 9.1: Goodbye Email, Hello Social Media!   251

   Nonverbal Communication   251

Choosing the Best Communication Channel   253

   Social Acceptance   253

   Media Richness   253

   Communication Channels and Persuasion   255

Communication Barriers (Noise)   256

   Information Overload   257

Cross-Cultural and Gender Communication   258

   Nonverbal Differences Across Cultures   258

   Gender Differences in Communication   258

Improving Interpersonal Communication   259

   Getting Your Message Across   259

   Connections 9.1: Gender Differences in Web-Based Communication   260

   Active Listening   260

Improving Communication Throughout the Hierarchy   261

   Workspace Design   261

   Web-Based Organizational Communication   262

   Direct Communication with Top Management   262

Communicating through the Grapevine 263

Grapevine Characteristics 263

Grapevine Benefits and Limitations 264

Chapter Summary 264

Key Terms 265

Critical-Thinking Questions 265

Case Study 9.1: Communicating with the Millenials 266

Team Exercise 9.2: Analyzing Blogs and Tweets 267

Team Exercise 9.3: Active Listening Exercise 267

Team Exercise 9.4: Cross-Cultural Communication Game 269

Self-Assessment Exercise 9.5: Are You An Active Listener? 269

CHAPTER 10
Power and Influence in the Workplace 271

Learning Objectives 271

The Meaning of Power 272

Sources of Power in Organizations 273

Legitimate Power 273

Reward Power 275

Coercive Power 276

Expert Power 276

Referent Power 277

Contingencies of Power 277

Substitutability 277

Centrality 278

Discretion 278

Visibility 278

The Power of Social Networks 279

Social Capital and Sources of Power 279

Global Connections 10.1: Powered by the Social Network 280

Gaining Power from Social Networks 280

Consequences of Power 282

Influencing Others 283

Types of Influence Tactics 283

Consequences and Contingencies of Influence Tactics 286

Influence and Organizational Politics 288

Conditions Supporting Organizational Politics 288

Chapter Summary 290

Key Terms 290

Critical-Thinking Questions 291

Case Study 10.1: NAB's Rogue Trader 291

Team Exercise 10.2: Impression Management in Employment Interviews 292

Team Exercise 10.3: Deciphering the Network 293

Team Exercise 10.4: Budget Deliberations 293

Self-Assessment Exercise 10.5: What's Your Approach to Influencing Co-workers? 294

Self-Assessment Exercise 10.6: Do You Have a Guanxi Orientation? 296

Self-Assessment Exercise 10.7: How Machiavellian Are You? 296

Self-Assessment Exercise 10.8: Does Your School Behave Politically? 296

CHAPTER 11
Conflict and Negotiation in the Workplace 297

Learning Objectives 297

The Meaning and Consequences of Conflict 298

Is Conflict Good or Bad? 298

The Emerging View: Constructive and Relationship Conflict 300

Conflict Process Model 301

Structural Sources of Conflict in Organizations 302

Incompatible Goals 302

Differentiation 303

Connections 11.1: Potential to Induce Generational Conflicts 303

Interdependence 304

Scarce Resources 305

Ambiguous Rules 305

Communication Problems 305

Interpersonal Conflict Handling Styles 305

Choosing the Best Conflict Handling Style 307

Cultural and Gender Differences in Conflict Handling Styles 308

Structural Approaches to Conflict Management 309

Emphasizing Superordinate Goals 309

Reducing Differentiation 309

Improving Communication and Mutual Understanding 309

Reducing Interdependence 310

Increasing Resources 311

Clarifying Rules and Procedures 311

Third-Party Conflict Resolution 311

Choosing the Best Third-Party Intervention Strategy 312

Resolving Conflict through Negotiation 313

Bargaining Zone Model of Negotiations 314

Strategies for Claiming Value 314

Strategies for Creating Value 315

Situational Influences on Negotiations 317

Chapter Summary 318

Key Terms 319

Critical-Thinking Questions 319

Case Study 11.1: Tamarack Industries 319

Class Exercise 11.2: The Contingencies of Conflict Handling 320

Team Exercise 11.3: Ugli Orange Role Play 325

Self-Assessment Exercise 11.4: What is Your Preferred Conflict Handling Style? 325

CHAPTER 12
Leadership in Organizational Settings   327

Learning Objectives   327
What is Leadership?   328
  Shared Leadership   329
Competency Perspective of Leadership   330
  Authentic Leadership   332
  Competency Perspective Limitations and Practical Implications   333
Behavioural Perspective of Leadership   333
  Choosing Directive versus Supportive Leadership   334
  Servant Leadership   334
Contingency Perspective of Leadership   335
  Path-Goal Theory of Leadership   335
  Global Connections 12.1: Leading With a Steel Fist in a Velvet Glove   337
  Other Contingency Theories   338
  Leadership Substitutes   339
Transformational Perspective of Leadership   340
  Transformational versus Transactional Leadership   340
  Transformational versus Charismatic Leadership   341
  Elements of Transformational Leadership   341
  Evaluating the Transformational Leadership Perspective   343
Implicit Leadership Perspective   344
  Prototypes of Effective Leaders   344
  The Romance of Leadership   344
Cross-Cultural and Gender Issues in Leadership   345
  Gender and Leadership   345
Chapter Summary   346
Key Terms   347
Critical-Thinking Questions   347
  Case Study 12.1: Profitel Inc.   348
  Case Study 12.2: The Staff Sergeant's Leadership Dilemma   349
  Team Exercise 12.3: Leadership Diagnostic Analysis   350
  Self-Assessment Exercise 12.4: Do You Think Leaders Make a Difference?   351
  Self-Assessment Exercise 12.5: What Kind of Leader Are You?   352

PART FOUR

Organizational Processes

CHAPTER 13
Designing Organizational Structures   353

Learning Objectives   353
Division of Labour and Coordination   354
  Division of Labour   354
  Coordinating Work Activities   355
Elements of Organizational Structure   357
  Span of Control   357
  Centralization and Decentralization   360
  Formalization   361
  Mechanistic versus Organic Structures   362
  Connections 13.1: Growing an Organic TAXI   363
Forms of Departmentalization   363
  Simple Structure   364
  Functional Structure   364
  Divisional Structure   365
  Team-Based Structure   367
  Matrix Structure   368
  Network Structure   370
Contingencies of Organizational Design   372
  External Environment   372
  Organizational Size   373
  Technology   374
  Organizational Strategy   374
Chapter Summary   375
Key Terms   375
Critical-Thinking Questions   376
  Case Study 13.1: Nokia's Evolving Organizational Structure   376
  Team Exercise 13.2: The Club Ed Exercise   377
  Self-Assessment Exercise 13.3: What Organizational Structure Do You Prefer?   378

CHAPTER 14
Organizational Culture   380

Learning Objectives   380
Elements of Organizational Culture   381
  Content of Organizational Culture   382
  Global Connections 14.1: BP's Espoused vs. Enacted Values   383
  Organizational Subcultures   384
Deciphering Organizational Culture through Artifacts   385
  Organizational Stories and Legends   386
  Rituals and Ceremonies   387
  Organizational Language   387
  Physical Structures and Symbols   387
Is Organizational Culture Important?   387
  Contingencies of Organizational Culture and Effectiveness   389
  Organizational Culture and Business Ethics   390
Merging Organizational Cultures   390
  Bicultural Audit   391
  Strategies for Merging Different Organizational Cultures   392
Changing and Strengthening Organizational Culture   393
  Actions of Founders and Leaders   394
  Aligning Artifacts   394
  Introducing Culturally Consistent Rewards   395
  Attracting, Selecting, and Socializing Employees   395

Organizational Socialization   396

   Organizational Socialization as a Learning
and Adjustment Process   396

   Organizational Socialization and Psychological Contracts   396

   Stages of Organizational Socialization   397

   Improving the Socialization Process   398

Chapter Summary   400

Key Terms   401

Critical-Thinking Questions   401

   Case Study 14.1: Hillton's Transformation   401

   Case Study 14.2: Separating the Steam from the Haze   403

   Team Exercise 14.3: Organizational Culture Metaphors   404

   Class Exercise 14.4: Diagnosing Corporate Culture
Proclamations   405

   Self-Assessment Exercise 14.5: Which Corporate Culture Do You
Prefer?   406

CHAPTER 15
Organizational Change   407

Learning Objectives   407

Lewin's Force Field Analysis Model   408

Understanding Resistance to Change   409

   Employee Resistance as a Resource for Change   410

   Global Connections 15.1: Not Hoppy about Change   411

   Why Employees Resist Change   412

Unfreezing, Changing, and Refreezing   413

   Creating an Urgency for Change   413

   Reducing the Restraining Forces   415

   Refreezing the Desired Conditions   417

Change Agents, Strategic Visions, and Diffusing Change   417

   Change Agents and Strategic Visions   417

   Diffusion of Change   418

Four Approaches to Organizational Change   419

   Action Research Approach   419

   Appreciative Inquiry Approach   421

   Large Group Interventions   423

   Parallel Learning Structures Approach   424

Cross-Cultural and Ethical Issues
in Organizational Change   424

Organizational Behaviour: The Journey Continues   425

Chapter Summary   425

Key Terms   426

Critical-Thinking Questions   426

   Case Study 15.1: TransAct Insurance Corporation   427

   Team Exercise 15.2: Strategic Change Incidents   429

   Self-Assessment Exercise 15.3: Are You Tolerant of Change?   430

ADDITIONAL CASES   432

Case 1: A Mir Kiss?   432

Case 2: Arctic Mining Consultants   434

Case 3: Barrie Super Subs   436

Case 4: Bridging the Two Worlds—The Organizational
Dilemma   437

Case 5: Chengdu Bus Group   439

Case 6: Going to the X-Stream   441

Case 7: Keeping Suzanne Chalmers   443

Case 8: Northwest Canadian Forest Products Limited   445

Case 9: The Regency Grand Hotel   447

Case 10: Resonus Corporation   448

Case 11: The Shipping Industry Accounting Team   450

Case 12: Treetop Forest Products   451

APPENDIX A

Theory Building and Systematic Research Methods   453

APPENDIX B

Scoring Keys for Self-Assessment Exercises   461

GLOSSARY   477

NOTES   483

NAME AND ORGANIZATION INDEX   544

SUBJECT INDEX   550

PREFACE

Welcome to the evolving world of organizational behaviour! Knowledge is replacing infrastructure. Social media and virtual teams are transforming the way accomplishments are achieved. Values and self-leadership are replacing traditional approaches to managing people. Companies are looking for employees with emotional intelligence and teamwork competencies, not just technical skills. Diversity and globalization pose competitive opportunities as well as challenges.

Canadian Organizational Behaviour, Eighth Edition, is written in the context of these emerging workplace realities. This edition explains how emotions shape employee motivation, attitudes, and decisions; how social networks shape power and communication; how self-concept influences individual outcomes, team cohesion, leadership, and behaviour; and how adopting a global mindset has become an important characteristic of employees in this increasingly interconnected world. This book also presents the reality that organizational behaviour is not just for managers; it is relevant and valuable to anyone who works in and around organizations.

CANADIAN AND GLOBAL FOCUS

Canadian Organizational Behaviour, Eighth Edition, is written by Canadians for Canadians. It includes several Canadian cases, is anchored by Canadian and global scholarship, and is filled with Canadian examples of organizational behaviour in practice.

For example you will read about how Steam Whistle Brewing in Toronto engages employees; how Telus encourages employees to telework; how Precision Metalcraft in Winnipeg improved performance through teamwork; how Loblaws demonstrates corporate social responsibility in Atlantic Canada; how TAXI Canada has thrived with an organic organizational structure; and how Great Little Box Company in British Columbia motivates employees.

Along with its Canadian focus, *Canadian Organizational Behaviour*, Eighth Edition, recognizes that we live in a world of increasing globalization. This emerging reality is discussed in the first chapter; several global and cross-cultural issues are also covered throughout the book. Every chapter includes global examples that illustrate OB concepts. Some of these appear in *Global Connections* features, but most are embedded in the text or found in captioned photos. For example, you will read how Malaysia Airlines trains employees to display desired emotions, how Royal Dutch/Shell uses a game to find team players in Europe, Asia, and North America; how Scotland's Clydesdale Bank has become a global role model for employee and customer satisfaction; how employees at Brazil's metal can company, Brasilata, have become inventors and the source of innovation; how Tokyo-based Hoppy Beverage Company overcame resistance to organizational change; and how executives at Atos Origin, the global information technology consulting firm headquartered in Paris, are turning to social media and saying goodbye to email.

CONNECTIONS 15.1

Not Hoppy about Change

Hoppy, a carbonated low-alcohol malt-and-hops beverage, was popular around Tokyo after World War II as a cheap alternative to expensive beer, but it fell out of favour as beer became affordable. Mina Ishiwatari (centre in photo), granddaughter of Hoppy Beverage Co.'s founder, was determined to improve Hoppy's image when she joined the company a decade ago. Unfortunately, the company's 30 employees—mostly men in their fifties who were family relatives—didn't want to disturb their cozy jobs.

"It was a turbulent decade of eliminating evils from the company and rebuilding a new organization from scratch," recalls Ishiwatari, who began as a rank-and-file employee and is now the company's executive vice-president. "I tried to take a new marketing approach to change the image of Hoppy...but no one would listen to me."

With limited support and budget, Ishiwatari developed a website that informed the public about the product, sold it online, and documented Ishiwatari's views in an early weblog. As the contemporary marketing caught the attention of health-conscious young people, Ishiwatari pushed for further changes. Most managers who opposed Ishiwatari's radical ideas eventually left the company.

But Ishiwatari experienced resistance even among those who remained. One day, the factory manager presented her with resignations from all of the factory workers. Ishiwatari resolved the dispute, acknowledging that she was pushing

Mina Ishiwatari (centre) faced—and overcame—resistance to change in the company that her grandfather founded. *Yoshiaki Miura Photo/Japan Times*

change through too quickly and without enough consideration of employee feelings.

In the seven years since Ishiwatari began introducing these changes, Hoppy's annual sales have increased fourfold to about CAD$42 million, even though it is sold mainly around Tokyo. The company's workforce has expanded to more than 50 people.[12]

LINKING THEORY WITH REALITY

Every chapter of *Canadian Organizational Behaviour*, Eighth Edition, is filled with examples to make OB knowledge more meaningful and reflect the relevance and excitement of this field. These stories about real people and organizations translate academic theories into relevant knowledge and real-life application. For example, you will read why Toronto-based Barrick Gold Corporation implemented a more decentralized approach to decision making to support global growth; why Cactus Club Café wants its teams of staff members to function like a school of fish; how a bitter year-long strike at Vale Inco strained relationships and negotiations; and what the Ottawa Fire Service is doing to recruit more female firefighters and change perceptions about women in the profession. Organizations, small and large, public and private were selected to illustrate key concepts.

CHAPTER 3

Perceiving Ourselves and Others in Organizations

LEARNING OBJECTIVES

After reading this chapter, you should be able to:

LO1 Describe the elements of self-concept and explain how they affect an individual's behaviour and well-being.

LO2 Outline the perceptual process and discuss the effects of categorical thinking and mental models in that process.

LO3 Discuss how stereotyping, attribution, self-fulfilling prophecy, halo, false-consensus, primacy, and recency influence the perceptual process.

LO4 Discuss three ways to improve perceptions, with specific application to organizational situations.

LO5 Outline the main features of a global mindset and justify its usefulness to employees and organizations.

Firefighting is a physically and psychologically demanding profession. The work is dangerous and demands availability during days, nights, and weekends. Although there has been a slight increase in the number of women working as firefighters, only about 3 percent of firefighters are women, according to the most recent Canadian Census data.

Regardless of the widely held perception that firefighting is an undesirable and unattainable job for women, Miranda Moir, at the age of 19, knows that she wants to spend her working life battling blazes and saving lives as a firefighter. She has applied to the Ottawa Fire Service and will face the demanding testing and training required for certification. In the meantime she is attending a five-day camp, sponsored by the Ottawa Fire Service and the Fire Service Women of Ontario to provide girls, aged 15 to 19 years of age with a chance to get a realistic glimpse into what it is like to be a firefighter.

Camp FFIT, which stands for female firefighters in training, requires participants to complete a wide variety of fire-training scenarios including forcing their way into a building using heavy tools, completing search and rescue missions while wearing air masks, and climbing a fire rig ladder leaning against a wall about 20 metres high.

Camp FFIT is part of the Ottawa Fire Service's campaign to recruit more female firefighters and change perceptions about women in the profession. Women firefighters have endured harassment at work according to veteran mediator Vince Ready in a report ordered by Richmond city council after all four of its remaining female firefighters took leaves of absence in 2006, over allegations of sexual harassment in the workplace. "I have observed a culture amongst members of the RFRD (Richmond Fire Rescue Department) characterized by juvenile and hostile behaviour towards firefighters, generally women in the RFRD specifically, which I find has contributed to the barriers to women's potential within the RFRD."

Annalee Lepp, head of the Women's Studies department at the Univer-

I Love Rewards Gets Media Rich Quick

Every day, employees at I Love Rewards Inc. meet face-to-face for 10 minutes to communicate priorities and coordinate their work. Each meeting at the Toronto-based incentive marketing company is brief and highly structured, but the richness of this communication event allows efficient transmission of information about "Today's Must-Do" and "Red Flags." For two minutes of the meeting, employees share a "Headline" summary of something important to them (e.g., a client meeting, last week's vacation). Each week has a new meeting facilitator, giving employees the chance to develop their communication and facilitation skills. I Love Rewards CEO Razor Suleman says these quick meetings provide a personal connection and highly interactive feedback.[12] © *Tim Fraser*

Keeping Drives in Balance Sparks Innovation at Radialpoint

At Montreal-based Radialpoint, innovation is key to keeping the company on the cutting edge of technology and meeting the needs of the world's biggest Internet providers including Bell Canada, Verizon, AT&T, and Virgin Media. Co-founder and executive chairman, Hamnett Hill offers a simple solution for Radialpoint's success—"People like working here." Hamnett adds, "We really rely on smart, dedicated folks and we need to help them understand what they can do to achieve that." The culture and work environment at Radialpoint provides a balance of opportunities for employees to fulfill their hardwired drives. Employees' self-concept is enhanced by knowing they work for an employer who seeks out the "best and brightest" and has been recognized as one of Canada's Best Managed Companies. In addition, top performers are rewarded through the company's partnership equity program and performance bonuses. Professional development programs are subsidized—"People definitely want to feel like they're moving forward, learning new skills," says Hill. "It's an opportunity to grow." Hill describes Radialpoint employees' desire to jump into challenges and solve big problems every day, "That has helped us in these difficult times." Radialpoint also encourages employees to develop social relationships and commitments to others. For example, off-site team-building events have brought employees together to build bikes for charity and finance an orphanage in Africa.[13] © *Pierre Obendrauf, Montreal Gazette*

These real-life stories appear in many forms. Every chapter of *Canadian Organizational Behaviour*, Eighth Edition, is filled with photo captions and in-text anecdotes about work life. Specific individuals are also featured to provide meaningful connections for students and instructors. For example, you will read about how one recent graduate chose the job offer that provided the best fit with his values, how a new Canadian developed confidence and a positive self-concept in her workplace, and how an ambitious Generation-Y employee plans to put in long hours, learn, and move to another firm.

Case studies in each chapter as well as video case studies associated with this book connect OB theories to emerging workplace realities. These stories represent a wide range of industries—from natural resources to government—and from small businesses to the largest global organizations.

ORGANIZATIONAL BEHAVIOUR KNOWLEDGE FOR EVERYONE

Another distinctive feature of *Canadian Organizational Behaviour*, Eighth Edition, is that it is written for everyone in organizations, not just "managers." The philosophy of this book is that everyone who works in and around organizations needs to understand and make use of organizational behaviour knowledge. The contemporary reality is that people throughout the organization—systems analysts, production employees, accounting professionals—are taking on more responsibilities as companies remove layers of management and give the rest of us more autonomy and accountability for our work outcomes. This book helps everyone to make sense of organizational behaviour, and provides the conceptual tools to work more effectively in the workplace.

CONTEMPORARY THEORY FOUNDATION

Canadian Organizational Behaviour, Eighth Edition, has a solid foundation of contemporary and classic research and writing. You can see this in the references. Each chapter is based on dozens of articles, books, and other sources. The most recent literature receives thorough coverage, resulting in what we believe is the most up-to-date organizational behaviour textbook available. These references also reveal that we reach out to marketing, information management, human resource management, and other disciplines for new ideas.

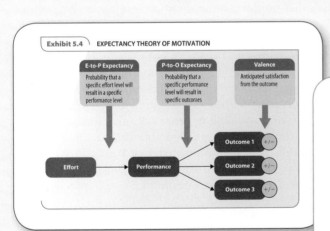

Exhibit 5.4 EXPECTANCY THEORY OF MOTIVATION

WORKPLACE COMMUNICATION THROUGH SOCIAL MEDIA

Email continues to dominate Web-based communication in organizations, but a few corporate leaders believe that it undermines productivity and well-being rather than supports these objectives. The opening vignette to this chapter described how Canadian companies such as Delta Hotels and Resorts are cautiously introducing social media into the workplace. As Global Connections 9.1 describes, Paris-based information technology consulting firm Atos Origin plans to replace email altogether with social media and other communication technologies.

Social media include Web-based tools (websites, applications, etc.) that allow users to generate and exchange information. This "user-generated content" is creative content (developed by the user), published on the Web (but may have restricted access), and produced outside of professional routines and practices.[23] Social media take many forms—blogs, wikis, instant messages, tweets, personal presentation sites (e.g., Facebook), viewer feedback forums, and the like. While earlier Web-based activity involved passively reading or watching content, these emerging Internet activities are more interactive and dynamic.

At the same time, this textbook is written for students, not the scholars whose work is cited. You won't find detailed methodologies of specific research studies; instead, we communicate the core knowledge from that research and integrate it with meaningful models and practices. Also, we take the view that students want to learn about ideas and practices, so this book rarely names researchers and their university affiliations. With a few classic exceptions, learning OB is not about remembering the "who's who" of the field.

Canadian Organizational Behaviour was the first textbook to discuss the self-concept model (not just core self-evaluation), workplace emotions, social identity theory, four-drive theory, appreciative inquiry, affective events theory (but without the jargon), somatic marker theory (also without the jargon), virtual teams, future search events, Schwartz's values model, employee engagement, learning orientation, workaholism, and several other groundbreaking topics. This edition continues this leadership by introducing the latest knowledge on global mindset, the elements of social networks (e.g., weak ties, centrality, and structural holes), communication strategies for social media, decision overload, the globally integrated enterprise, and mindfulness in ethical behaviour.

CONTINUOUS DEVELOPMENT

Canadian Organizational Behaviour is *not* a "Canadianized" adaptation of an American book. Steve also co-authors two successful organizational behaviour books in the United States and internationally (including several translations and adaptations in China, Taiwan, India, and Brazil) as well as the best-selling OB book in Australia and New Zealand. Still, all three books update each other in a virtuous cycle of continuous development. *Canadian Organizational Behaviour*, Eighth Edition, updates information from the current American and Pacific Rim editions, which will be incorporated into the next editions of these kindred publications. This global approach to textbook development ensures that *Canadian Organizational Behaviour* offers Canadians the latest organizational behaviour knowledge, issues, and examples at the time of publication.

ACTIVE LEARNING AND CRITICAL THINKING SUPPORT

We teach organizational behaviour, so we understand how important it is to use a textbook that offers deep support for active learning and critical thinking. Business school accreditation associations also emphasize the importance of the learning experience, which further reinforces our attention on classroom activities. *Canadian Organizational Behaviour*, Eighth Edition, includes more than two-dozen case studies in various forms and levels of complexity. It offers three-dozen self-assessments, most of which have been empirically tested and validated. This book is also a rich resource for in-class activities, some of which are not available in other organizational behaviour textbooks, such as Deciphering the (Social) Network, Test Your Knowledge of Personality, Impression Management in Employment Interviews, and the Cross-Cultural Communication Game.

KEY TERMS

anchoring and adjustment heuristic, p. 188
availability heuristic, p. 188
bounded rationality, p. 187
creativity, p. 194
decision making, p. 182

divergent thinking, p. 195
employee involvement, p. 199
escalation of commitment, p. 193
implicit favourite, p. 188
intuition, p. 191
prospect theory effect, p. 193

rational choice paradigm, p. 182
representativeness heuristic, p. 188
satisficing, p. 189
scenario planning, p. 192
subjective expected utility, p. 182

CRITICAL-THINKING QUESTIONS

1. A management consultant is hired by a manufacturing firm to determine the best site for its next production facility. The consultant has had several meetings with the company's senior executives regarding the factors to consider when making the recommendation. Discuss the decision-making problems that might prevent the consultant from recommending the best site location.

2. You have been asked to personally recommend a new travel agency to handle all airfare, accommodation, and related travel needs for your organization of 500 staff. One of your colleagues, who is responsible for the company's economic planning, suggests that the best travel agent could be selected mathematically by inputting the relevant factors for each agency and the weight (importance) of each factor. What decision making approach is your colleague recommending? Is this recommendation a good idea in this situation? Why or why not?

3. Intuition is both an emotional experience and an unconscious analytic process. One problem, however, is that not all emotions signal that there is a problem or opportunity. Explain how we would know if our "gut feelings" are intuition or not, and if not intuition, suggest what might be causing them.

4. A developer received financial backing for a new business financial centre along a derelict section of the waterfront, a few kilometres from the current downtown area of a large European city. The idea was to build several high-rise structures, attract large tenants to those sites, and have the city extend transportation systems out to the new centre. Over the next decade, the developer believed that others would build in the area, thereby attracting the regional or national offices of many financial institutions. Interest from potential tenants was much lower than initially predicted and the city did not build transportation systems as quickly as expected. Still, the builder proceeded with the original plans. Only after financial support was curtailed did the developer reconsider the project. Using your knowledge of escalation of commitment, discuss three possible reasons why the developer was motivated to continue with the project.

5. Ancient Book Company has a problem with new book projects. Even when others are aware that a book is far behind schedule and may engender little public interest, sponsoring editors are reluctant to terminate contracts with authors whom they have signed. The result is that

CHANGES TO THE EIGHTH EDITION

Canadian Organizational Behaviour, Eighth Edition, has benefited from reviews by several dozen organizational behaviour instructors and researchers in several countries over the past two years. The most significant structural change is that we have shifted some content across the first few chapters so topics fit logically together in the same chapter. This edition also substantially updates the section on negotiation (Chapter 11) and has developed a full section on social networks (Chapter 10). In addition, we have introduced "By the Numbers," a feature that presents interesting survey and statistical information related to the topic discussed on those pages. More generally, this edition updates topics in every chapter and provides fresh real-world examples to illustrate theories and concepts. The most notable improvements to this edition are as follows:

- *Chapter 1: Introduction to the Field of Organizational Behaviour*—The most significant change in this chapter is that the topic on the types of individual behaviour has been moved to Chapter 2, where it has a more logical link to other topics. This edition further develops the four perspectives of organizational effectiveness, which instructors are recognizing as the cornerstone of organizational behaviour. This chapter updates discussion on contemporary challenges in OB, adds more details about evidence-based management, and adds information about the historical foundations of OB.

- *Chapter 2: Individual Behaviour, Personality, and Values*—This edition inserts the types of individual behaviour after the MARS model of individual behaviour. We have also moved self-concept to Chapter 3. This edition has several small, yet meaningful changes, including new content on presenteeism, problems with cross-cultural knowledge, role perceptions, situational factors, relationship between Big 5 and performance, problems with personality testing, model of MBTI, the issue of mindfulness in ethics, and ways that companies support ethical behaviour.

- *Chapter 3: Perceiving Ourselves and Others in Organizations*—The previous edition was apparently the first to introduce the full model of self-concept and connect that model to various organizational behaviour topics. This edition further refines and clarifies the three characteristics as well as the four processes of self-concept. We moved the topic to this chapter because of the logical flow from self-perception (self-concept) to social perception (perceiving others). Another change in this chapter is that behaviour modification and social learning (social cognitive) theories have been moved to the motivation chapter (Chapter 5). Another development in this chapter is the section on global mindset—an important emerging topic that crosses cross-cultural thinking with the perceptual process.

- *Chapter 4: Workplace Emotions, Attitudes, and Stress*—This chapter has minor changes, particularly on cognitive dissonance, emotional labour across cultures, the relationship between job satisfaction and performance and customer service, and individual differences in stress.

- *Chapter 5: Foundations of Employee Motivation*—This chapter further refines discussion of drives, needs, and behaviour, which we believe is fundamental to understanding employee motivation. We also update our coverage of employee engagement, which continues to gain attention in the world of work. This chapter incorporates and condenses the topics of behaviour modification and social cognitive theory in the context of learning expectancies in expectancy theory. This edition also introduces the topics of balanced scorecard (previously in Chapter 6) and strengths-based feedback.

- *Chapter 6: Applied Performance Practices*—This edition has relatively minor updating to the topics on applied performance practices.

- *Chapter 7: Decision Making and Creativity*—This edition introduces three widely researched decision heuristic biases as well as the problems with having too much choice in decisions. Other topics have been revised, including the rational choice paradigm, stakeholder framing, characteristics of creative people, and aspects of employee involvement.

- *Chapter 8: Team Dynamics*—This edition has minor changes to a few team dynamics topics, including informal groups, team diversity, the effect of cohesion on performance (and vice versa), and brainstorming.

- *Chapter 9: Communicating in Teams and Organizations*—The previous edition introduced social media (Web 2.0); this edition further updates this important communication development, including a model on the functions of social media. Furthermore, this edition updates the topics of communication barriers, the importance of communication, persuasive communication, and the encoding-decoding process.

- *Chapter 10: Power and Influence in the Workplace*—You will find several new developments in this chapter. Most important is discussion of social networks, including strong ties, weak ties, centrality, and structural holes. We have also folded the two forms of information power into their respective sources of power (legitimate and expert). This edition also revises and updates writing on the meaning of power and the dependency model of power, legitimate power and the norm of reciprocity, the consequences of power, and exchange as an influence tactic.

- *Chapter 11: Conflict and Negotiation in the Workplace*—The most noticeable change in this chapter is that the negotiation section has been completely rewritten and updated. It is now organized around claiming value and creating value, and adds key negotiation concepts such as BATNA. The section on the benefits and problems with conflict has been improved, and the section on structural approaches to conflict management has been rewritten with more examples and clarification. This chapter also has some minor re-organization of topics.

- *Chapter 12: Leadership in Organizational Settings*—Two editions ago, we introduced the topic of shared leadership, which receives fuller attention in this edition. The previous edition introduced the emerging topic of authentic leadership, which also receives more emphasis in this edition. This chapter also devotes more attention to servant leadership. Other topics have been revised and updated, including managerial leadership, charismatic leadership, and romance of leadership.

- *Chapter 13: Designing Organizational Structures*—This chapter introduces the globally integrated enterprise as an extension of divisional structures. Other parts of the chapter have relatively minor updates and revisions, particularly on concurrent engineering, issues with flatter structures, and network structures.

- *Chapter 14: Organizational Culture*—This chapter introduces psychological contracts and provides fuller coverage of organizational socialization (e.g., information exchange conflicts, improving the socialization process). This edition also updates and has minor revisions on the organizational culture model, espoused versus enacted values, and contingencies of organizational culture strength.

- *Chapter 15: Organizational Change*—More than 15 years go, *Canadian Organizational Behaviour* became the first textbook in this field to discuss appreciative inquiry. Along with past updates on this important concept and practice, this edition adds new information about the five principles on which appreciative inquiry is based. In this edition, we also move future search and related large-scale change activities into a separate section representing one of the four approaches to organizational change. A few other topics on organizational change are also updated and rewritten in this edition, including Lewin's force field model, understanding resistance to change, and diffusion of change.

SUPPORTING THE OB LEARNING EXPERIENCE

The changes described above refer only to the text material. *Canadian Organizational Behaviour,* Eighth Edition also has improved technology supplements, cases, team exercises, and self-assessments.

CASE STUDY 6.2

And the Award for Best Commercial Goes To. . .

As the Canadian subsidiary of one of the world's largest consumer products companies, Procter & Gamble (P&G) Canada is continually on the lookout for the best ways to motivate its staff. One of these motivational highlights is the company's in-house awards night, in which P&G Canada's 100 marketing staff vie for 10 Canadian Business Building Marketing Awards—three for individual excellence and seven for team execution. The team awards include best initiative, best overall marketing plan, best product innovation, best marketing innovation, best turnaround brand, best test-and-learn (i.e., best learning either from success or failure), and best search-and-reapply (in which marketing from another country is applied successfully in Canada).

"Our objectives were to inspire, celebrate, and reward the organization," says Chris Laird, P&G Canada's associate marketing director of fabric and home care, who coordinated the most recent awards event. Laird and other associate marketing directors screened more than 60 marketing projects across the company's many brands, including Tide, Pampers, Swiffer, Crest, Gillette, Pringles, and Pantene. Eventually, they formed a list of three or four nominees for each of the 10 categories.

The three individual winners were chosen by a nine-member team of senior marketers. The seven team category winners, on the other hand, were determined during the awards night based on votes from the audience, which include P&G Canada marketing staff, nearly three dozen agency partners, and numerous senior executives from P&G's Canadian and global headquarters. Voting via text message, the audience mainly took

Case 6   Going to the X-Stream

By Roy Smollan, Auckland University of Technology

Gil Reihana was the chief executive officer of X-Stream, a company he launched in Auckland, New Zealand, six years ago at the age of 25, after graduating with a bachelor's degree in information technology and management. He had inherited $300,000 and had persuaded various family members to invest additional money. X-Stream assembled personal computers for the New Zealand and Australian markets and sold them through a number of chain stores and independent retailers. The company had soon established a reputation for quality hardware, customized products, excellent delivery times, and after-sales service. Six months ago it had started a software division, specializing in Web design and consulting on various applications for the development of electronic business.

CHAPTER CASES AND ADDITIONAL CASES

Every chapter includes at least one short case that challenges students to diagnose issues and apply ideas from that chapter. One dozen additional cases appear at the end of the book. Several cases are new to this book, many of which are written by Canadian instructors. Others, such as Arctic Mining Consultants, are classics that have withstood the test of time.

ADDITIONAL CASES

Case 1:	**A Mir Kiss?**
Case 2:	**Arctic Mining Consultants**
Case 3:	**Barrie Super Subs**
Case 4:	**Bridging the Two Worlds—The Organizational Dilemma**
Case 5:	**Chengdu Bus Group**
Case 6:	**Going to the X-Stream**
Case 7:	**Keeping Suzanne Chalmers**
Case 8:	**Northwest Canadian Forest Products Limited**
Case 9:	**The Regency Grand Hotel**
Case 10:	**Resonus Corporation**
Case 11:	**The Shipping Industry Accounting Team**
Case 12:	**Treetop Forest Products**

TEAM EXERCISES AND SELF-ASSESSMENTS

Experiential exercises and self-assessments represent an important part of the active learning process. *Canadian Organizational Behaviour,* Eighth Edition, facilitates that process by offering team/class exercises in every chapter. This edition also has three dozen self-assessments in the book. Self-assessments personalize the meaning of several organizational behaviour concepts, such as extroversion/introversion, self-leadership, empathy, stress, creative disposition, and tolerance of change. Additional and self-scoring, interactive self-assessments with detailed feedback can be found on *Connect.*

TEAM EXERCISE 7.3

Where In the World Are We?

Purpose   This exercise is designed to help you understand the potential advantages of involving others in decisions rather than making decisions alone.

Materials   Students require an unmarked copy of the map of Canada with grid marks (Exhibit 2). Students are not allowed to look at any other maps or use any other materials. The instructor will also provide a list of communities located somewhere on Exhibit 2. The instructor will also provide copies of the answer sheet after students have individually and in teams estimated the locations of communities.

Instructions   • *Step 1:* Write down in Exhibit 1 the list of communities identified by your instructor. Then, working alone, estimate the location in Exhibit 2 of these communities, all of which are in Canada. For example, mark a small "1" in Exhibit 2 on the spot where you believe the first community is located. Mark a small "2" where you think the second community is located, and so on. Please be sure to number each location clearly and with numbers small enough to fit within one grid space.

• *Step 2:* The instructor will organize students into approximately equal-sized teams (typically five or six people per team). Working with your team members, reach a consensus on the location of each community listed in Exhibit 1. The instructor might provide teams with a separate copy of this map, or each member can identify the team's numbers using a different coloured pen on their individual maps. The team's decision for each location should occur by consensus, not voting or averaging.

• *Step 3:* The instructor will provide or display an answer sheet, showing the correct locations of the communities. Using this answer sheet, students will count the minimum number of grid squares between the location they individually marked and the true location of each community. Write the number of grid squares in the second column of Exhibit 1, then add up the total. Next, count the minimum number of grid squares between the location the team marked and the true location of each community. Write the number of grid squares in the third column of Exhibit 1, then add up the total.

• *Step 4:* The instructor will ask for information about the totals and the class will discuss the implication of these results for employee involvement and decision making.

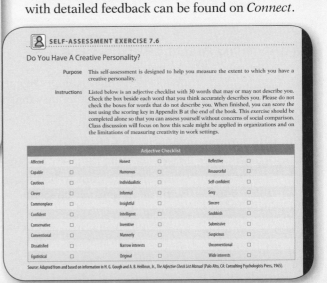

SELF-ASSESSMENT EXERCISE 7.6

Do You Have A Creative Personality?

Purpose   This self-assessment is designed to help you measure the extent to which you have a creative personality.

Instructions   Listed below is an adjective checklist with 30 words that may or may not describe you. Check the box beside each word that you think accurately describes you. Please do not check the boxes for words that do not describe you. When finished, you can score the test using the scoring key in Appendix B at the end of the book. This exercise should be completed alone so that you can assess yourself without concerns of social comparison. Class discussion will focus on how this scale might be applied in organizations and on the limitations of measuring creativity in work settings.

Adjective Checklist

Affected	☐	Honest	☐	Reflective	☐
Capable	☐	Humorous	☐	Resourceful	☐
Cautious	☐	Individualistic	☐	Self-confident	☐
Clever	☐	Informal	☐	Sexy	☐
Commonplace	☐	Insightful	☐	Sincere	☐
Confident	☐	Intelligent	☐	Snobbish	☐
Conservative	☐	Inventive	☐	Submissive	☐
Conventional	☐	Mannerly	☐	Suspicious	☐
Dissatisfied	☐	Narrow interests	☐	Unconventional	☐
Egotistical	☐	Original	☐	Wide interests	☐

Source: Adapted from and based on information in H. G. Gough and A. B. Heilbrun, Jr., *The Adjective Check List Manual* (Palo Alto, CA: Consulting Psychologists Press, 1965).

INDEXES, MARGIN NOTES, AND GLOSSARY

While minimizing unnecessary jargon, *Canadian Organizational Behaviour* assists the learning process by highlighting key terms in bold and providing brief definitions in the margin. These definitions are also presented in an alphabetical glossary at the end of the text. We have also developed comprehensive indexes of the content, names, and organizations described in this book. Also look for the Learning Objectives presented at the beginning of each chapter, and then linked to chapter content by numbered icons. An excellent study tool!

TEAMS AND INFORMAL GROUPS

L01

teams Groups of two or more people who interact and influence each other, are mutually accountable for achieving common goals associated with organizational objectives, and perceive themselves as a social entity within an organization.

Teams are groups of two or more people who interact and influence each other, are mutually accountable for achieving common goals associated with organizational objectives, and perceive themselves as a social entity within an organization.[4] This definition has a few important components worth repeating. First, all teams exist to fulfill some purpose, such as repairing electric power lines, assembling a product, designing a new healthcare program, or making an important decision. Second, team members are held together by their interdependence and need for collaboration to achieve common goals. All teams require some form of communication so that members can coordinate and share common objectives. Third, team members influence each other, although some members may be more influential than others regarding the team's goals and activities. Finally, a team exists when its members perceive themselves to be a team.

Exhibit 8.1 briefly describes various types of teams in organizations. Some teams are permanent, while others are temporary; some are responsible for making products or providing services, while others exist to make decisions or share knowledge. Each type of team has been created deliberately to serve an organizational purpose. Some teams, such as skunkworks teams, are not initially sanctioned by management, yet are called "teams" because members work toward an organizational objective.

CHAPTER 1

Introduction to the Field of Organizational Behaviour

LEARNING OBJECTIVES

After reading this chapter, you should be able to:

L01 Define organizational behaviour and organizations, and discuss the importance of this field of inquiry.

L02 Compare and contrast the four current perspectives of organizational effectiveness as well as the early goal attainment perspective.

L03 Debate the organizational opportunities and challenges of globalization, workforce diversity, and emerging employment relationships.

L04 Discuss the anchors on which organizational behaviour knowledge is based.

Cameron Heaps, Greg Taylor, and Gregory Cromwell took a canoe trip in Algonquin Park to rethink their future after the brewery where they worked was bought and then shut down by a competitor. Sitting around the campfire, the trio realized that they were still passionate about the beer industry, so they launched their own independent brewery. A dozen years later, Steam Whistle Brewing Co. has won numerous awards for the quality of its premium pilsner brew as well as for the quality of its workplace and leadership. The company was recently applauded as one of Canada's 50 best-managed companies, one of Canada's 10 most admired corporate cultures, one of Canada's greenest employers, and one of the top employers for young people.

How has Steam Whistle achieved such success? For a start, the founders decided to focus employees on one product—premium pilsner—and to strive for the vision to become Canada's favourite beer. "From day one, we set out to produce a really, really good beer that can compete in the premium segment of the market," says co-founder Cameron Heaps. "Steam Whistle demonstrates the power of engaging an entire organization in the pursuit of a single goal," suggests an industry observer.

Steam Whistle's success is also achieved through the quality of its employees. "The reason our product is so great is because of the hard work and skill of the people we've chosen to hire," explains co-founder Greg Taylor. The brewery achieves this quality partly through an inclusive culture. Half of the brewery's managers and many employees are new Canadians, bringing unique skills and knowledge about brewing from around the world. "If you're going to [produce] a pilsner that competes internationally, you need to have people capable of bringing that to the table," says Taylor. Steam Whistle also motivates employees through an ownership culture, which is nurtured through employee involvement, profit sharing, and the opportunity for employees to buy company shares. The company also rewards long service, such as the trip to Oktoberfest in Munich that the company recently paid for all employees with five or more years of service.

Another factor in Steam Whistle's success is its commitment to corporate social responsibility. The brewery operates out of one of Toronto's few green buildings, uses stronger bottles that can be refilled more often, consumes only wind and low-impact hydro electricity, uses Deep Lake Water for air conditioning, composts organic waste, and uses biofuel to power its delivery trucks. Steam Whistle pays its employees to deliver Meals on Wheels in brewery vehicles; it also distributes unused food from its events to street missions and women's shelters. "We've worked diligently to create an atmosphere that attracts people who are Good Beer Folks—people who are impassioned to work hard, are concerned about quality, and are also good people," says Taylor.[1]

Several organizational behaviour practices have contributed to Steam Whistle Brewing Co.'s success. *Photograph by Tanja Tiziana Burdi with permission of Steam Whistle Brewing and Adrian Joseph*

1

TEACHING AND LEARNING TOOLS

Available with *Canadian Organizational Behaviour*, Eighth Edition, is a comprehensive package of supplementary materials designed to enhance teaching and learning.

McSHANE CONNECT™

McGraw Hill connect™

McGraw-Hill Connect™ is a Web-based assignment and assessment platform that gives students the means to better connect with their coursework, with their instructors, and with the important concepts that they will need to know for success now and in the future.

With Connect, instructors can deliver assignments, quizzes, and tests online. Nearly all the questions from the text are presented in an auto-gradeable format and tied to the text's learning objectives. Instructors can edit existing questions and author entirely new problems. Track individual student performance—by question, assignment, or in relation to the class overall—with detailed grade reports. Integrate grade reports easily with Learning Management Systems (LMS) such as WebCT and Blackboard. And much more.

By choosing Connect, instructors are providing their students with a powerful tool for improving academic performance and truly mastering course material. Connect allows students to practise important skills at their own pace and on their own schedule. Importantly, students' assessment results and instructors' feedback are all saved online—so students can continually review their progress and plot their course to success.

Connect also provides 24/7 online access to an eBook—an online edition of the text—to aid them in successfully completing their work, wherever and whenever they choose.

KEY FEATURES

Simple Assignment Management

With Connect, creating assignments is easier than ever, so you can spend more time teaching and less time managing.

- Create and deliver assignments easily with selectable end-of-chapter questions and test bank material to assign online
- Streamline lesson planning, student progress reporting, and assignment grading to make classroom management more efficient than ever
- Go paperless with the eBook and online submission and grading of student assignments

Smart Grading

When it comes to studying, time is precious. Connect helps students learn more efficiently by providing feedback and practice material when they need it, where they need it.

- Automatically score assignments, giving students immediate feedback on their work and side-by-side comparisons with correct answers
- Access and review each response; manually change grades or leave comments for students to review
- Reinforce classroom concepts with practice tests and instant quizzes

Instructor Library

The Connect Instructor Library is your course creation hub. It provides all the critical resources you'll need to build your course, just how you want to teach it.

- Assign eBook readings and draw from a rich collection of textbook-specific assignments
- Access instructor resources, including ready-made PowerPoint® presentations and media to use in your lectures
- View assignments and resources created for past sections
- Post your own resources for students to use

eBook

Connect reinvents the textbook learning experience for the modern student. Every Connect subject area is seamlessly integrated with Connect eBooks, which are designed to keep students focused on the concepts key to their success.

- Provide students with a Connect eBook, allowing for anytime, anywhere access to the textbook
- Merge media, animation, and assessments with the text's narrative to engage students and improve learning and retention
- Pinpoint and connect key concepts in a snap using the powerful eBook search engine
- Manage notes, highlights, and bookmarks in one place for simple, comprehensive review

INSTRUCTOR'S RESOURCES

McShane Connect is a one-stop shop for instructor resources, including:

Instructor's Manual: Written by the text authors Steve McShane and Sandra Steen, the Instructor's Manual accurately represents the text's content and supports instructors' needs. Each chapter includes the learning objectives, glossary of key terms, a chapter synopsis, complete lecture outline with thumbnail images of corresponding Power-Point® slides, and solutions to the end-of-chapter discussion questions. It also includes teaching notes for the chapter case(s), team exercises, and self-assessments. Many chapters include supplemental lecture notes and suggested videos. The Instructor's Manual also includes teaching notes for the end-of-text cases.

Computerized Test Bank: Written by the McShane Connect author, Claude Dupuis from Athabasca University, this flexible and easy to use electronic testing program allows instructors to create tests from book specific items. The Test Bank contains a broad selection of multiple choice, true/false, and essay questions and instructors may add their own questions as well. Each question identifies the relevant page reference and difficulty level. Multiple versions of the test can be created and printed.

PowerPoint® Presentations: Written by the text co-authors, these robust presentations offer high quality visuals to bring key OB concepts to life.

Video Program: The accompanying video program is available to instructors through video streaming in Connect or on DVD. Teaching notes can be found in the Instructor's Resource section in Connect.

Management Asset Gallery: McGraw-Hill Ryerson, in conjunction with McGraw-Hill Irwin Management, is excited to provide a one-stop-shop for our wealth of assets, allowing instructors to quickly and easily locate specific materials to enhance their course. The Asset Gallery includes our non-text-specific management resources (Self-Assessments and Test Your Knowledge exercises).

Manager in the Hot Seat Resources (www.mhhe.com/mhs): In today's workplace, managers are confronted daily with issues such as ethics, diversity, working in teams, and the virtual workplace. The Manager's Hot Seat is an interactive online resource that allows students to watch as 15 real managers apply their years of experience to confront these issues.

McSHANE CONNECT™ FOR STUDENTS

By choosing McShane Connect, instructors are providing their students with a powerful tool for improving academic performance and truly mastering course material. McShane Connect allows students to study and practise important skills at their own pace and on their own schedule with online quizzing and matching exercises, study support, video streaming, a searchable glossary, Globe & Mail newsfeeds, and over 50 interactive self-assessment exercises.

SUPERIOR SERVICE

Service takes on a whole new meaning with McGraw-Hill Ryerson and *Canadian Organizational Behaviour*. More than just bringing you the textbook, we have consistently raised the bar in terms of innovation and educational research. These investments in learning and the education community have helped us to understand the needs of students and educators across the country, and allowed us to foster the growth of truly innovative, integrated learning.

INTEGRATED LEARNING

Your Integrated *i*Learning Sales Specialist is a McGraw-Hill Ryerson representative who has the experience, product knowledge, training, and support to help you assess and integrate any of our products, technology, and services into your course for optimal teaching and learning performance. Whether it's helping your students improve their grades, or putting your entire course online, your *i*Learning Sales Specialist is there to help you do it. Contact your *i*Learning Sales Specialist today to learn how to maximize all of McGraw-Hill Ryerson's resources!

*i*LEARNING SERVICES PROGRAM

McGraw-Hill Ryerson offers a unique *i*Services package designed for Canadian faculty. Our mission is to equip providers of higher education with superior tools and resources required for excellence in teaching. For additional information, visit www.mcgrawhill. ca/highereducation/iservices.

COURSE MANAGEMENT

McGraw-Hill Ryerson offers a range of flexible integration solutions for Blackboard, WebCT, Desire2Learn, Moodle, and other leading learning management platforms. Please contact your local McGraw-Hill Ryerson *i*Learning Sales Specialist for details.

BLACKBOARD

McGraw-Hill Higher Education and Blackboard have teamed up. Blackboard, the Web-based course-management system, has partnered with McGraw-Hill to better allow students and faculty to use online materials and activities to complement face-to-face teaching. Blackboard features exciting social learning and teaching tools that foster more logical, visually affective, and active learning opportunities for students. You'll transform your closed-door classrooms into communities where students remain connected to their educational experience 24 hours a day.

This partnership allows you and your students access to McGraw-Hill's Connect™ and Create™ right from within your Blackboard course—all with one single sign-on. Not only do you get single sign-on with Connect™ and Create™, you also get deep integration of McGraw-Hill content and content engines right in Blackboard. Whether you're choosing a book for your course or building Connect™ assignments, all the tools you need are right where you want them—inside of Blackboard. Gradebooks are now seamless. When a student completes an integrated Connect™ assignment, the grade for that assignment automatically (and instantly) feeds your Blackboard grade centre.

McGraw-Hill and Blackboard can now offer you easy access to industry-leading technology and content, whether your campus hosts it, or we do. Be sure to ask your local McGraw-Hill representative for details.

TEGRITY

Tegrity is a service that makes class time available all the time by automatically capturing every lecture in a searchable format for students to review when they study and complete assignments. With a simple one-click start-and-stop process, you capture all computer screens and corresponding audio. Students replay any part of any class with easy-to-use browser-based viewing on a PC or Mac. Educators know that the more students can see, hear, and experience class resources, the better they learn. With Tegrity, students quickly recall key moments by using Tegrity's unique search feature. This search helps students efficiently find what they need, when they need it across an entire semester of class recordings. Help turn all your students' study time into learning moments immediately supported by your lecture. To learn more about Tegrity watch a two-minute Flash demo at http://tegritycampus.mhhe.com.

CREATE ONLINE

McGraw-Hill's Create Online places the most abundant resource at your fingertips— literally. With a few mouse clicks, you can create customized learning tools simply and affordably. McGraw-Hill Ryerson has included many of its market-leading textbooks within Create Online for eBook and print customization as well as many licensed readings and cases. For more information, please visit www.mcgrawhillcreate.com.

COURSESMART

CourseSmart brings together thousands of textbooks across hundreds of courses in an eTextbook format providing unique benefits to students and faculty. By purchasing an eTextbook, students can save up to 50 percent off the cost of a print textbook, reduce their impact on the environment, and gain access to powerful Web tools for learning, including full text search, notes and highlighting, and email tools for sharing notes among classmates. For faculty, CourseSmart provides instant access to review and compare textbooks and course materials in their discipline area without the time, cost, and environmental impact of mailing print examination copies. For further details, contact your iLearning sales specialist or visit www.coursesmart.com.

ACKNOWLEDGMENTS

We have appreciated the privilege to work with an extraordinary team of professionals committed to the inspiring and shared goal of creating Canada's most engaging and authoritative introductory organizational behaviour textbook.

Executive sponsoring editor, Kim Brewster led the way. Her contributions included not only the executive insight that launched and sustained this major undertaking but also specific and tangible aspects such as securing the contemporary cover art. Kim's unwavering confidence and support sustained our team through the inevitable challenges and accomplishments along the way. We are also inspired by our developmental editor, Tracey Haggert, who smoothed the way at every turn by managing the entire writing process. Tracey anticipated our needs, shared her experience unconditionally and demonstrated an enviable work ethic through "it all." Thank you also to developmental editor Lori McLellan who so capably handled a full slate of key responsibilities including the instructor and student resources and video selections. Our thanks also to Christine Lomas, senior editorial associate, who managed all of those behind-the-scenes tasks that we may not even know about, but would certainly hear about if they didn't get done.

The keen copy editing skills and good humour provided by Erin Moore enriched the experience of the editing process and made *Canadian Organizational Behaviour*, Eighth Edition, incredibly error-free. Joanne Limebeer and Kara Stahl, our supervising editors, capably and confidently guided the project through a tight production schedule. Thanks also to Mary Rose MacLachlan for providing a wealth of diverse photo options to choose from and to Alison Derry for managing the photos and permission process so seamlessly. Also thank you to Michelle Losier for producing a refreshing elegant design.

As mentioned earlier, more than forty instructors around the world reviewed parts or all of *Canadian Organizational Behaviour*, Eighth Edition or related editions in the United States, Pacific Rim, and elsewhere over the past three years. Their feedback was energizing as well as thought-provoking and significantly improved the final product. The following people from Canadian colleges and universities are among those who provided the most recent feedback for improvements specifically for *Canadian Organizational Behaviour*, Eighth Edition. Thank you to all for your participation in the development and your commitment to learning and teaching excellence.

Stan Arnold	*Humber College*
Gordon Barnard	*Durham College*
Rhona Berengut	*York Schulich*
James Buchkowsky	*Saskatchewan Institute of Applied Science and Technology*
Bill Demarco	*University of Guelph*

Jane Deighan	*Southern Alberta Institute of Technology*
Cathy Denomme	*Algoma University*
Claude Dupuis	*Athabasca University*
Kelly Dye	*Acadia University*
Susan Fitzrandolph	*Ryerson University*
Thomas Foard	*Humber/Guelph at Humber*
Cynthia Freeman-King	*University of New Brunswick/Saint John*
Bill Fricker	*Northern Alberta Institute of Technology*
Jane Guzar	*Mohawk College*
Niran Harrison	*University of Saskatchewan*
Elizabeth Kelley	*Dalhousie University*
Alfred Jaeger	*McGill University*
Joanne Leck	*University of Ottawa*
Jody Merritt	*St. Clair College*
Dave Morrison	*Durham College*
Howard Muchnick	*Ryerson University*
Grace O'Farrell	*University of Winnipeg*
Kim Richter	*Kwantlen University*
Stephen Rose	*University of Ontario Institute of Technology*
Carol-Ann Samhaber	*Algonquin College*
Bonni Titgemeyer	*Sheridan College*
Amy Tucker	*Thompson Rivers University*
Debra Warren	*Centennial College*
Wendy Whitehead	*St. Lawrence College*
Kit Wilson	*Red River College*

We would also like to extend sincere thanks to the exceptional efforts of Claude Dupuis, Athabasca University, who championed and wrote *Connect*, and revised the test bank. Claude's enthusiasm and expertise in organizational behaviour teaching really comes through in his work on this project. We would also like to extend our sincerest thanks to the many instructors in Canada and abroad who contributed cases and exercises to this edition of *Canadian Organizational Behaviour*.

Steve would also like to extend special thanks to his students in Perth, Manila, and Singapore for sharing their learning experiences and assisting with the development of the three organizational behaviour textbooks in Canada, the United States, and the Pacific Rim, as well as their adaptations or translations in India, China, and Taiwan. Steve is also very grateful to his colleagues at the University of Western Australia for their support during challenging times. But more than anything else, Steve is forever indebted to his wife Donna McClement and to their wonderful daughters, Bryton and Madison. Their love and support give special meaning to Steve's life.

Sandra would like to extend appreciation to her students and colleagues at the University of Regina for sharing their passion for learning and teaching.

Introduction to the Field of Organizational Behaviour

Several organizational behaviour practices have contributed to Steam Whistle Brewing Co.'s success. *Photograph by Tanja Tiziana Burdi with permission of Steam Whistle Brewing and Adrian Joseph*

LEARNING OBJECTIVES

After reading this chapter, you should be able to:

LO1 Define organizational behaviour and organizations, and discuss the importance of this field of inquiry.

LO2 Compare and contrast the four current perspectives of organizational effectiveness as well as the early goal attainment perspective.

LO3 Debate the organizational opportunities and challenges of globalization, workforce diversity, and emerging employment relationships.

LO4 Discuss the anchors on which organizational behaviour knowledge is based.

Cameron Heaps, Greg Taylor, and Gregory Cromwell took a canoe trip in Algonquin Park to rethink their future after the brewery where they worked was bought and then shut down by a competitor. Sitting around the campfire, the trio realized that they were still passionate about the beer industry, so they launched their own independent brewery. A dozen years later, Steam Whistle Brewing Co. has won numerous awards for the quality of its premium pilsner brew as well as for the quality of its workplace and leadership. The company was recently applauded as one of Canada's 50 best-managed companies, one of Canada's 10 most admired corporate cultures, one of Canada's greenest employers, and one of the top employers for young people.

How has Steam Whistle achieved such success? For a start, the founders decided to focus employees on one product—premium pilsner—and to strive for the vision to become Canada's favourite beer. "From day one, we set out to produce a really, really good beer that can compete in the premium segment of the market," says co-founder Cameron Heaps. "Steam Whistle demonstrates the power of engaging an entire organization in the pursuit of a single goal," suggests an industry observer.

Steam Whistle's success is also achieved through the quality of its employees. "The reason our product is so great is because of the hard work and skill of the people we've chosen to hire," explains co-founder Greg Taylor. The brewery achieves this quality partly through an inclusive culture. Half of the brewery's managers and many employees are new Canadians, bringing unique skills and knowledge about brewing from around the world. "If you're going to [produce] a pilsner that competes internationally, you need to have people capable of bringing that to the table," says Taylor. Steam Whistle also motivates employees through an ownership culture, which is nurtured through employee involvement, profit sharing, and the opportunity for employees to buy company shares. The company also rewards long service, such as the trip to Oktoberfest in Munich that the company recently paid for all employees with five or more years of service.

Another factor in Steam Whistle's success is its commitment to corporate social responsibility. The brewery operates out of one of Toronto's few green buildings, uses stronger bottles that can be refilled more often, consumes only wind and low-impact hydro electricity, uses Deep Lake Water for air conditioning, composts organic waste, and uses biofuel to power its delivery trucks. Steam Whistle pays its employees to deliver Meals on Wheels in brewery vehicles; it also distributes unused food from its events to street missions and women's shelters. "We've worked diligently to create an atmosphere that attracts people who are Good Beer Folks—people who are impassioned to work hard, are concerned about quality, and are also good people," says Taylor.[1]

WELCOME TO THE FIELD OF ORGANIZATIONAL BEHAVIOUR!

The success of Steam Whistle Brewing Co. reveals some important truths about organizations that succeed and fail in today's turbulent environment. In every sector of the economy, organizations need to be innovative, have leaders with foresight and vision, employ people who are skilled and motivated, and make decisions that consider the interests of multiple stakeholders. In other words, the best companies succeed through the concepts and practices that we discuss in this book on organizational behaviour.

The purpose of this book is to help you understand what goes on in organizations, including the thoughts and behaviour of employees and teams. We examine the factors that make companies effective, improve employee well-being, and drive successful teams. We look at organizations from numerous and diverse perspectives, from the deepest foundations of employee thoughts and behaviour (personality, self-concept, commitment, etc.) to the complex interplay between the organization's structure and culture and its external environment. Along this journey, we emphasize why things happen and what you can do to predict and manage organizational events.

We begin in this chapter by introducing you to the field of organizational behaviour and why it is important to your career and to organizations. Next, this chapter describes the "ultimate dependent variable" in this field by presenting the four main perspectives of organizational effectiveness. This is followed by an overview of three challenges facing organizations: globalization, increasing workforce diversity, and emerging employment relationships. We complete this opening chapter by describing four anchors that guide the development of organizational behaviour knowledge.

THE FIELD OF ORGANIZATIONAL BEHAVIOUR

LO1

organizational behaviour (OB) The study of what people think, feel, and do in and around organizations.

organizations Groups of people who work interdependently toward some purpose.

Organizational behaviour (OB) is the study of what people think, feel, and do in and around organizations. It looks at employee behaviour, decisions, perceptions, and emotional responses. It examines how individuals and teams in organizations relate to each other and to their counterparts in other organizations. OB also encompasses the study of how organizations interact with their external environments, particularly in the context of employee behaviour and decisions. OB researchers systematically study these topics at multiple levels of analysis, namely, the individual, team (including interpersonal), and organization.[2]

The definition of organizational behaviour begs the question: What are organizations? **Organizations** are groups of people who work interdependently toward some purpose.[3] Notice that organizations are not buildings or government-registered entities. In fact, many organizations exist without either physical walls or government documentation to confer their legal status. Organizations have existed for as long as people have worked together. Massive temples dating back to 3500 BC were constructed through the organized actions of multitudes of people. Craftspeople and merchants in ancient Rome formed guilds, complete with elected managers. More than 1,000 years ago, Chinese factories were producing 125,000 tonnes of iron each year. The Hudson's Bay Company holds the distinction of being North America's oldest commercial enterprise. Founded in 1670, the once British-owned organization operated out of Winnipeg as a monopoly and semi-government over one-quarter of the continent for almost 200 years.[4]

Throughout history, these and other organizations have consisted of people who communicate, coordinate, and collaborate with each other to achieve common objectives. One key feature of organizations is that they are collective entities. They consist of human beings (typically, but not necessarily, employees), and these people interact with each other in an *organized* way. This organized relationship requires some minimal level of communication, coordination, and collaboration to achieve organizational objectives. As such, all organizational members have degrees of interdependence with each other; they accomplish goals by sharing materials, information, or expertise with co-workers.

A second key feature of organizations is that their members have a collective sense of purpose. This collective purpose isn't always well defined or agreed on. Furthermore, although most companies have vision and mission statements, these documents are sometimes out of date or don't describe what employees and leaders try to achieve in reality. Still, imagine an organization without a collective sense of purpose. It would consist of a collection of people without direction or unifying force. So, whether it's brewing premium pilsner at Steam Whistle Brewing Co. or providing patient care at Foothills Provincial General Hospital, people working in organizations do have some sense of collective purpose. "A company is one of humanity's most amazing inventions," said Apple Inc. CEO and co-founder Steven Jobs. "It's totally abstract. Sure, you have to build something with bricks and mortar to put the people in, but basically a company is this abstract construct we've invented, and it's incredibly powerful."[5]

HISTORICAL FOUNDATIONS OF ORGANIZATIONAL BEHAVIOUR

Organizational behaviour emerged as a distinct field around the 1940s, but organizations have been studied by experts in other fields for many centuries. The Greek philosopher Plato wrote about the essence of leadership. Around the same time, the Chinese philosopher Confucius discussed the virtues of ethics and leadership. In 1776, Adam Smith extolled the benefits of job specialization and division of labour. One hundred years later, German sociologist Max Weber wrote about rational organizations, the work ethic, and charismatic leadership. Soon after, industrial engineer Frederick Winslow Taylor proposed systematic ways to organize work processes and motivate employees through goal setting and rewards.[6]

In the early 1900s, before he became Canada's longest serving prime minister, William Lyon Mackenzie King was a pioneering consultant and advocate throughout North America of worker involvement and organizational reward systems. From the 1920s to the 1940s, Harvard professor Elton Mayo and his colleagues introduced the "human relations" school of management, which developed the study of employee attitudes and informal group dynamics in the workplace. Also during that time, political philosopher and social worker Mary Parker Follett described new ways of thinking about several OB topics, including constructive conflict, team dynamics, organizational democracy, power, and leadership. In the late 1930s, Chester Barnard wrote insightful views regarding organizational communication, coordination, leadership and authority, organizations as open systems, and team dynamics.[7] This brief historical tour indicates that OB has been around for a long time; it just wasn't organized into a unified discipline until around World War II.

WHY STUDY ORGANIZATIONAL BEHAVIOUR?

Organizational behaviour instructors face a challenge: Students who have not yet begun their careers tend to value courses related to specific jobs, such as accounting and marketing.[8] However, OB doesn't have a specific career path—there is no "vice-president of OB"—so students sometimes have difficulty recognizing the value that OB knowledge can offer to their future. Meanwhile, students with several years of work experience place OB near the top of their list of important courses. Why? Because they have directly observed that OB *does make a difference* to their career success. OB is important because it helps to fulfill the need to understand and predict the world in which we live.[9] OB theories help us to question and rebuild our personal theories that have developed through observation and experience. Some experts suggest that OB knowledge helps us to make sense of the world, not just what goes on inside organizations.[10]

But probably the greatest value of OB knowledge is that it helps people to get things done in organizations.[11] Everyone in the organization needs to work with other people, and OB provides the knowledge and tools for working with and through others. Building a high-performance team, motivating co-workers, handling workplace conflicts, influencing your boss, and changing employee behaviour are just a few of the areas of knowledge and skills offered in organizational behaviour. No matter what career path you choose, you'll find that OB concepts play an important role in performing your job and working more effectively within organizations.

Organizational Behaviour is for Everyone   Organizational behaviour is important for anyone who works in organizations, not just for managers. In fact, this book pioneered the notion that OB knowledge is for everyone. Whether you are a geologist, financial analyst, customer service representative, or chief executive officer, you need to understand and apply the many organizational behaviour topics that are discussed in this book. Yes, organizations will continue to have managers, and this book recognizes the relevance of OB knowledge in these vital roles. But this book also embraces the reality that all employees are increasingly expected to manage themselves and work effectively with each other in the workplace. In the words of one forward-thinking OB writer more than four decades ago: Everyone is a manager.[12]

OB and the Bottom Line   Up to this point, our answer to the question "Why study OB?" has focused on how organizational behaviour knowledge benefits you as an individual. However, OB knowledge is just as important for the organization's financial health. Steam Whistle Brewing Co. has flourished because it leverages human capital, employee commitment, creativity, visionary leadership, and corporate social responsibility. Numerous studies have reported that leadership, teamwork, employee engagement, and other OB ideas and practices discussed in this book tend to improve the organization's survival and success.[13]

For example, one investigation found that hospitals with higher levels of specific OB activities (e.g. training, staff involvement, reward and recognition) have lower patient mortality rates. Another study found that companies receiving "the best place to work" awards have significantly higher financial and long-term stock market performance. And as we will learn in Chapter 5, employee engagement is associated with significantly higher sales and profitability. The bottom-line value of organizational behaviour is also supported by human capital and investment portfolio studies. These investigations suggest that specific OB characteristics (employee attitudes, work-life balance, performance-based rewards, leadership, employee training and development, etc.) are important "positive screens" for selecting companies with the best long-term share appreciation.[14]

PERSPECTIVES OF ORGANIZATIONAL EFFECTIVENESS

LO2

organizational effectiveness A broad concept represented by several perspectives, including the organization's fit with the external environment, internal-subsystems configuration for high performance, emphasis on organizational learning, and ability to satisfy the needs of key stakeholders.

Almost all organizational behaviour theories have the implicit or explicit objective of making organizations more effective.[15] In fact, **organizational effectiveness** is considered the "ultimate dependent variable" in organizational behaviour.[16] This means that, whether stated or not, OB theories and practices ultimately try to improve the organization's effectiveness. One problem, though, is that "organizational effectiveness" has too many substitute labels—organizational performance, success, goodness, health, competitiveness, excellence—and almost as many definitions.

Over the next several pages, we will describe a coherent model of organizational effectiveness that incorporates four complementary perspectives. But first, we need to mention the now discredited "goal attainment" definition of organizational effectiveness. This view, which was popular for many years, states that companies are effective when they achieve their stated organizational objectives.[17] If western Canadian retailer London Drugs meets or exceeds its annual sales and profit targets, then it must be effective, according to this definition. Goal attainment is a poor way of viewing organizational effectiveness because any leadership team could set corporate goals that are easy to achieve but might still put the organization out of business. The goals might fall short of the more aggressive objectives of competitors, or they might aim the organization in the wrong direction.

Consider the following situation at a Canadian airline several years ago: The board gave the new CEO a mandate to reduce costs and dramatically improve profitability. The CEO accomplished these organizational goals by reducing the training budget and cancelling the purchase of new aircraft. Within a few years (after the CEO had taken a job elsewhere), the company was suffering from higher maintenance costs to keep the old planes flying safely and was losing customers to airlines with better-trained staff and more modern fleets. The airline never recovered and was eventually acquired by Air Canada. The CEO achieved the company's goals, but the result was a less effective organization in the long run.

This book takes the view that the best definition of organizational effectiveness is through a composite of four perspectives: open systems, organizational learning, high-performance work practices, and stakeholders.[18] Organizations are effective when they have a good fit with their external environment, are learning organizations, have efficient and adaptive internal subsystems (i.e. high-performance work practices), and satisfy the needs of key stakeholders. Let's examine each of these perspectives in detail.

> " Organizations are effective when they have a good fit with their external environment, are learning organizations, have efficient and adaptive internal subsystems, and satisfy the needs of key stakeholders. "

open systems A perspective which holds that organizations depend on the external environment for resources, affect that environment through their output, and consist of internal subsystems that transform inputs into outputs.

OPEN SYSTEMS PERSPECTIVE

The **open systems** perspective of organizational effectiveness is one of the earliest and well entrenched ways of thinking about organizations.[19] Indeed, the other major organizational effectiveness perspectives might be considered detailed extensions of the open systems model. The open systems perspective views organizations as complex organisms that "live" within an external environment, rather like the illustration in Exhibit 1.1. The word *open* describes this permeable relationship, whereas *closed systems* operate without dependence on or interaction with an external environment.

As open systems, organizations depend on the external environment for resources, including raw materials, job applicants, financial resources, information, and equipment.

Exhibit 1.1   **OPEN SYSTEMS PERSPECTIVE OF ORGANIZATIONS**

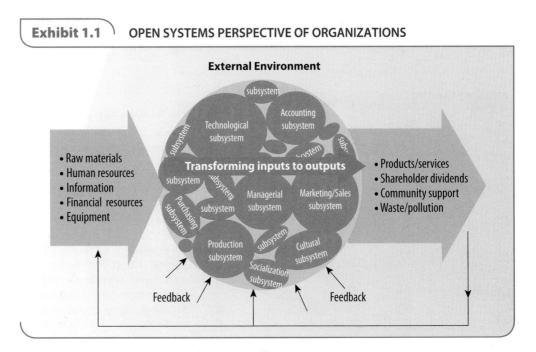

The external environment also consists of rules and expectations, such as laws and cultural norms, which place demands on how organizations should operate. Some environmental resources (e.g. raw materials) are transformed into outputs that are exported to the external environment, whereas other resources (e.g. job applicants, equipment) become subsystems in the transformation process.

Inside the organization are numerous subsystems, such as departments, teams, informal groups, work processes, technological configurations, and other elements. Rather like the Russian matryoshka dolls nested within each other, organizational subsystems are also systems with their own subsystems.[20] For example, the Canadian Tire store in Smiths Falls, Ontario, is a subsystem of the Canadian Tire chain, but the Smiths Falls store is also a system with its own subsystems of teams and work processes. An organization's subsystems are organized interdependently so they interact with each other to transform inputs into various outputs. Some outputs (e.g., products, services, community support) may be valued by the external environment, whereas other outputs (e.g., employee layoffs, pollution) are by-products that may have adverse effects on the environment and the organization's relationship with that environment. Throughout this process, organizations receive feedback from the external environment regarding the value of their outputs and the availability of future inputs.

Organization-Environment Fit   According to the open systems perspective, organizations are effective when they maintain a good "fit" with their external environment.[21] Good fit exists when the organization puts resources where they are most useful to adapt to and align with the needs of the external environment. For instance, Apple, Inc. has good fit with its many external environments—just look at the line-ups for iPads and the skyrocketing market share for Apple laptops and iPhones. In contrast, companies with a poor fit with the environment offer the wrong products and operate inappropriately in their environments.

Successful organizations maintain a good fit by anticipating change in the environment and fluidly reconfiguring their subsystems to become more consistent with that environment. To illustrate, food manufacturers have changed their ingredients and production processes to satisfy more health- and environment-conscious consumers. Companies also maintain a good fit by actively managing their external environment. For example, they might try to limit competitor access to critical resources (e.g. gaining exclusive rights), change consumer perceptions and needs (e.g. through marketing), or support legislation that strengthens their position in the marketplace. The third fit strategy is to move into different environments if the current environment is too challenging. For instance, Nokia started in 1865 as a pulp and paper company. The Finnish company entered the rubber and cable business in the 1920s, moved into electronics in the 1960s,

The Adaptive Apple

Apple, Inc. is rated as the world's most admired company. Yet just a dozen or so years ago the technology company was on life support, barely clinging on to a few percentage points of market share in the computer industry. Apple's incredible turnaround is a classic example of an organization that learned to anticipate and fluidly adapt to rapidly changing external environments. Under the guidance of Steve Jobs and his executive team, Apple designed more appealing products and invested more in laptops before that segment overtook desktop computers. The company launched the iPod and online music sales just as the consumer market was growing tired of music on CDs. Apple switched to Intel's new low-power chips when IBM's PowerPC chips failed to keep pace. With the foresight that computers would converge with cellphones (smartphones), Apple developed and launched the iPhone. And, sensing a between market (half computer, half mobile device), the computer launched the iPad, which has become the fastest growing technology in recent years.[22] *THE CANADIAN PRESS/Darryl Dyck*

and began producing cellphones a decade later. These strategic choices moved the company decisively into new external environments that seemed to be more appealing for Nokia's long-term survival and success.[23]

Internal Subsystems Effectiveness   The open systems perspective considers more than an organization's fit with the external environment. It also defines effectiveness by how well the company operates internally, that is, how well it transforms inputs into outputs. The most common indicator of this internal transformation process is **organizational efficiency** (also called *productivity*), which is the ratio of inputs to outcomes.[24] Companies that produce more goods or services with less labour, materials, and energy are more efficient. However, successful organizations not only have efficient transformation processes; they also have more *adaptive* and *innovative* transformation processes.[25] Apple's design, sales, accounting, and other subsystems likely operate fairly efficiently, but the company's success is due more to its adaptive and innovative capabilities. It has been able to develop unique products in markets it had just entered, while competitors scramble to catch up.

> **organizational efficiency** The amount of outputs relative to inputs in the organization's transformation process.

One last observation about the open systems perspective is that coordination is vital in the relationship among organizational subsystems, but this coordination is usually far from ideal.[26] Information gets lost, ideas are not shared, materials are hoarded, communication messages are misinterpreted, resources and rewards are distributed unfairly, and so forth. These coordination challenges are amplified as organizations grow, such as when employees are clustered into several departments and when departments are clustered into several organizational divisions. A slight change in work practices in one subsystem may ripple through the organization and undermine the effectiveness of other subsystems. For example, a new accounting procedure in the financial subsystem might unintentionally reduce sales staff motivation to sell high profit margin products.

ORGANIZATIONAL LEARNING PERSPECTIVE

The open-systems perspective has traditionally focused on physical resources that enter the organization and are processed into physical goods (outputs). This was representative of the industrial economy but not the "new economy," where the most valued input is knowledge. The **organizational learning** perspective (also called *knowledge management*) views knowledge as the main driver of competitive advantage. Through this lens, organizational effectiveness depends on the organization's capacity to acquire, share, use, and store valuable knowledge (see Exhibit 1.2).[27]

> **organizational learning** A perspective which holds that organizational effectiveness depends on the organization's capacity to acquire, share, use, and store valuable knowledge.

- *Knowledge acquisition.* This includes extracting information and ideas from the external environment as well as through insight. One of the fastest and most powerful ways to acquire knowledge is by hiring individuals or acquiring entire companies (i.e., grafting). Steam Whistle Brewery Co., described in the opening vignette to this chapter, uses this approach to secure better knowledge on how to brew premium pilsner. Knowledge also enters the organization when employees learn from external sources. As Connections 1.1 describes, Duha Colour in Winnipeg acquires knowledge by sending staff on training programs and by touring other companies to learn about their best practices. A third knowledge acquisition strategy is experimentation. Companies receive knowledge through insight as a result of research and other creative processes.

- *Knowledge sharing.* This aspect of organizational learning involves distributing knowledge to others across the organization. Knowledge sharing is often equated with computer intranets and digital repositories of knowledge. These systems are relevant, but knowledge sharing mainly occurs through structured and informal communication as well as various forms of learning (such as observation, experience, training, practice).[28]

- *Knowledge use.* The competitive advantage of knowledge comes from applying it in ways that add value to the organization and its stakeholders. To do this, employees

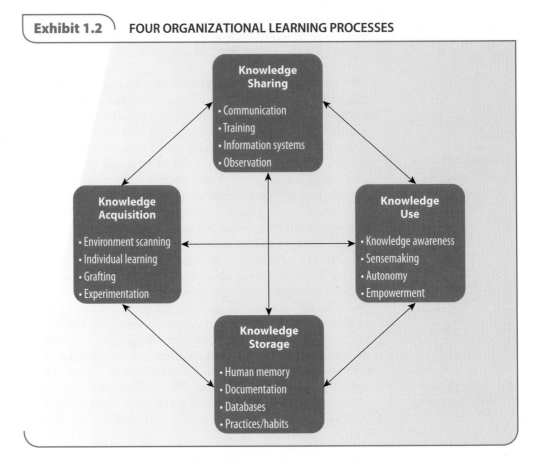

Exhibit 1.2   FOUR ORGANIZATIONAL LEARNING PROCESSES

Knowledge Sharing
- Communication
- Training
- Information systems
- Observation

Knowledge Acquisition
- Environment scanning
- Individual learning
- Grafting
- Experimentation

Knowledge Use
- Knowledge awareness
- Sensemaking
- Autonomy
- Empowerment

Knowledge Storage
- Human memory
- Documentation
- Databases
- Practices/habits

must realize that the knowledge is available and that they have enough autonomy to apply it. This requires a culture that supports the learning process.

- *Knowledge storage.* Knowledge storage includes any means by which knowledge is held for later retrieval. It is the process that creates organizational memory. Human memory plays a critical role here, as do the many forms of documentation and database systems that exist in organizations. Individual practices and habits hold less explicit (more tacit) knowledge.

absorptive capacity The ability to recognize the value of new information, assimilate it, and use it for value-added activities.	**Absorptive Capacity** An important prerequisite for acquiring, sharing, and using new knowledge is the amount and quality of knowledge already held within the organization. Just as students need to learn knowledge in core courses before they can understand content in more advanced courses, companies need to have employees with sufficient knowledge to receive and apply new knowledge. This knowledge prerequisite is known as the organization's **absorptive capacity**.[29] For example, many companies were slow to develop online marketing practices because no one in the organization had enough knowledge about the Internet to fathom its potential or apply that knowledge to the company's business. In some cases, companies had to acquire entire teams of people with the requisite knowledge to realize the potential of this marketing channel.

intellectual capital A company's stock of knowledge, including human capital, structural capital, and relationship capital.

human capital The stock of knowledge, skills, and abilities among employees that provides economic value to the organization.

Intellectual Capital: The Stock of Organizational Knowledge   Knowledge acquisition, sharing, use, and storage represent the flow of knowledge. The organizational learning perspective also considers the company's stock of knowledge, called its **intellectual capital**.[30] The most obvious form of intellectual capital is **human capital**—the knowledge, skills, and abilities that employees carry around in their heads. This is an important part of a company's stock of knowledge, and it is a huge risk in companies where knowledge is the main competitive advantage. When key people leave, they take

CONNECTIONS 1.1

Duha Colour's Learning Organization Strategies[31]

Nestled away in Winnipeg's industrial area is Duha Group, a role model for the learning organization. The global manufacturer, marketer, and supplier of paint fandecks (colour cards) and colour samples depends on lean manufacturing for quality and efficiency, and organizational learning practices enable it to continuously raise these standards. Duha's 290 Winnipeg employees (the company also has plants in New York, Mexico, Europe, Asia, and Australia) acquire external knowledge by touring other companies to learn about their best practices. Knowledge is also brought in through company-supported formal off-site training (such as health and safety officer training at a nearby college). In addition, Duha employees are encouraged to discover new knowledge through experimentation within their work area and through Kaizen Blitzes (where teams identify more effective ways to operate entire work areas). "We are encouraged to give our ideas a try even if they fail," says a Duha employee. "It's rewarding to apply new concepts that add value or improvement."

Duha Group employees engage in knowledge sharing through formal in-house training programs, mentoring arrangements, and informal hands-on training sessions. Also, detailed company operating manuals and other documents are centrally located with access to all staff. A popular form of knowledge sharing are Duha Group's lunch-and-learn sessions, where employees teach co-workers about lean management and specific production practices, as well as Health and Safety, Environmental, Quality, and Human Resources issues, while enjoying a hot meal paid for by the company. Knowledge sharing also occurs through departmental huddles held every day for five minutes. Employees

Duha Group applies organizational learning through Kaizen Blitzes, offsite training, lunch-and-learn sessions, and daily huddles. *Courtesy of the Duha Group*

congregate around a "huddle board" where they post suggestions for improvement, describe work process changes in their area, and hear about company news. "The huddles are a great idea," says a Duha employee. "I think that's one of our best outlets for communication."

Finally, Duha Group encourages employees to put knowledge to use by giving them plenty of autonomy and support. Indeed, every employee has a learning plan they review with management as well as a learning journal to maintain their focus on continuous learning. Knowledge use also occurs more readily because the huddle boards for each department show who has specific knowledge they might require.

with them some of the knowledge that makes the company effective. "Somebody with intellectual capital walking out the door could cause a team of 20 or 30 people to spend several weeks trying to re-study a particular piece of technology to come up with a solution," warns an executive at Ontario Power Generation.[32]

Even if every employee left the organization, intellectual capital would still remain in the form of **structural capital**. This includes the knowledge captured and retained in an organization's systems and structures, such as the documentation of work procedures and the physical layout of the production line. Structural capital also includes the organization's finished products because knowledge can be extracted by taking them apart to discover how they work and are constructed (i.e., reverse engineering). Finally, intellectual capital includes *relationship capital*, which is the value derived from an organization's relationships with customers, suppliers, and others who provide added mutual value for the organization.

> **structural capital**
> Knowledge embedded in an organization's systems and structures.

Organizational Memory and Unlearning
Corporate leaders need to recognize that they are the keepers of an *organizational memory*.[33] This unusual metaphor refers to the storage and preservation of intellectual capital. It includes knowledge that employees possess as well as knowledge embedded in the organization's systems and structures. It includes documents, objects, and anything else that provides meaningful information about how the organization operates.

How do organizations retain intellectual capital? One way is by keeping knowledgeable employees. Progressive companies achieve this by adapting their employment practices to become more compatible with emerging workforce expectations. A second organizational memory strategy is to systematically transfer knowledge to other employees. This occurs when newcomers apprentice with skilled employees, thereby acquiring knowledge that is not documented. A third strategy is to transfer knowledge into structural capital. This includes bringing out hidden knowledge, organizing it, and putting it in a form that can be available to others. Reliance Industries, India's largest business enterprise, applies this strategy by encouraging employees to document their successes and failures through a special intranet knowledge portal. One of these reports alone provided information that allowed others to prevent a costly plant shutdown.[34]

The organizational learning perspective states not only that effective organizations learn but also that they unlearn routines and patterns of behaviour that are no longer appropriate.[35] Unlearning removes knowledge that no longer adds value and, in fact, may undermine the organization's effectiveness. Some forms of unlearning involve replacing dysfunctional policies, procedures, and routines. Other forms of unlearning erase attitudes, beliefs, and assumptions. For instance, employees rethink the "best way" to perform a task and how to serve clients. Organizational unlearning is particularly important for organizational change, which we discuss in Chapter 15.

HIGH-PERFORMANCE WORK PRACTICES (HPWP) PERSPECTIVE

The open systems perspective states that successful companies are good at transforming inputs into outputs. However, it does not identify the subsystem characteristics that distinguish effective organizations from others. Consequently, an entire field of research has blossomed around the objective of determining specific "bundles" of organizational practices that offer competitive advantage. This research has had various labels over the years, but it is now most commonly known as **high-performance work practices (HPWP)**.[36]

high-performance work practices (HPWP) A perspective which holds that effective organizations incorporate several workplace practices that leverage the potential of human capital.

The HPWP perspective begins with the idea that *human capital*—the knowledge, skills, and abilities that employees possess—is an important source of competitive advantage for organizations.[37] Human capital is valuable, rare, difficult to imitate, and nonsubstitutable.[38] Employees are valuable because they help the organization to discover opportunities and to minimize threats in the external environment. They are rare and difficult to imitate, meaning that it is difficult to find talented people and they cannot be cloned like sheep. Finally, human capital is nonsubstitutable because it cannot be easily replaced by technology.

Organizations excel by introducing a bundle of systems and structures that leverage the potential of their workforce. Researchers have investigated numerous potential high-performance work practices, but we will focus on four that are recognized in most studies.[39] Two of these are employee involvement and job autonomy. Both activities tend to strengthen employee motivation as well as improve decision making, organizational responsiveness, and commitment to change. In high-performance workplaces, employee involvement and job autonomy often take the form of self-directed teams (see Chapter 8).

Another key variable in the HPWP model is employee competence. Specifically, organizations are more effective when they recruit and select people with relevant skills, knowledge, values, and other personal characteristics. Furthermore, successful companies invest in employee development through training and development. A fourth characteristic of high-performance organizations is that they link performance and skill development to various forms of financial and nonfinancial rewards valued by employees. Each of these four work practices—employee involvement, job autonomy, employee competence, and performance/skill-based rewards—individually improve organizational performance, but recent evidence suggests that they have a stronger effect when bundled together.[40]

PCL Invests in Employees' Skills and Knowledge: College of Construction

The PCL family of companies, Canada's largest construction organization and Top 100 Employer, retains its valued human capital for the long-term by investing heavily in employee learning and career development. Learning and development at PCL includes a range of offerings such as tuition and professional accreditation subsidies, apprenticeships, internships, online training, career planning services, and mentoring programs in addition to in-house training. At PCL, learning is rewarded as a never-ending process and the College of Construction was established to support PCL's status as a construction leader and employer of choice. The College of Construction offers programs and services to support and grow technical, personal, interpersonal, and leadership and management competence as well as skills for continuous improvement in a competitive, complex environment.[41]
Courtesy of PCL Families of Companies

Why are HPWPs associated with organizational effectiveness? Early studies were criticized for ignoring this question,[42] but OB experts are now building and testing more theoretical explanations.[43] The first reason is that HPWPs build human capital, which improves performance as employees develop the skills and knowledge to perform the work. A second explanation is that superior human capital may improve the organization's adaptability to rapidly changing environments. Employees respond better when they have a wide skill set to handle diverse tasks as well as confidence to handle unfamiliar situations. A third explanation why HPWPs improve organizational effectiveness is that these activities strengthen employee motivation and attitudes toward the employer. For instance, HPWPs represent the company's investment in and recognition of its workforce, which motivates employees to reciprocate through greater effort in their jobs and assistance to co-workers.

The HPWP perspective is still developing, but it already reveals important information about specific organizational practices that improve the input-output transformation process. Still, this perspective has been criticized for focusing on shareholder and customer needs at the expense of employee well-being.[44] This concern illustrates that the HPWP perspective offers an incomplete picture of organizational effectiveness. The remaining gaps are mostly filled by the stakeholder perspective of organizational effectiveness.

STAKEHOLDER PERSPECTIVE

stakeholders Individuals, organizations, and other entities who affect, or are affected by, the organization's objectives and actions.

The three organizational effectiveness perspectives described so far mainly consider processes and resources, yet they only minimally recognize the importance of relations with **stakeholders**. Stakeholders include anyone with a stake in the company—employees, shareholders, suppliers, labour unions, government, communities, consumer and environmental interest groups, and so on (see Exhibit 1.3). In other words, organizations are more effective when they consider the needs and expectations of any individual group, or other entity that affects, or is affected by, the organization's objectives and actions. This approach requires organizational leaders and employees to understand, manage, and satisfy the interests of their stakeholders.[45] The stakeholder perspective personalizes the open-systems perspective; it identifies specific people and social entities in the external environment as well as within the organization (the internal environment). It also recognizes that stakeholder relations are dynamic; they can be negotiated and managed, not just taken as a fixed condition.[46]

Exhibit 1.3 \ ORGANIZATIONAL STAKEHOLDERS

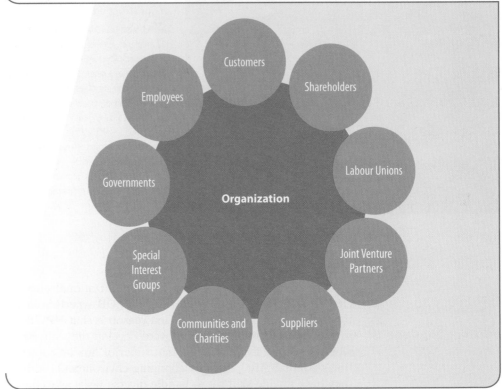

Note: This exhibit does not show the complete set of possible stakeholders.

Understanding, managing, and satisfying the interests of stakeholders is more challenging than it sounds because stakeholders have conflicting interests and organizations don't have the resources to satisfy every stakeholder to the fullest. Therefore, organizational leaders need to decide how much priority to give to each group. One commonly cited factor is to favour stakeholders with the most power.[47] This makes sense when one considers that the most powerful stakeholders hold the greatest threat and opportunity to the company's survival. Yet stakeholder power should not be the only factor to consider. Ignoring less powerful stakeholders might motivate them to form coalitions or seek government support, which would give them more power. Ignoring smaller stakeholders might also irritate the more powerful stakeholders if ignoring weaker interests violates the norms and standards of society.

Values, Ethics, and Corporate Social Responsibility   This brings us to one of the key strengths of the stakeholder perspective, namely, that it incorporates values, ethics, and corporate social responsibility into the organizational effectiveness equation.[48] The stakeholder perspective states that to manage the interests of diverse stakeholders, leaders ultimately need to rely on their personal and organizational values for guidance. **Values** are relatively stable, evaluative beliefs that guide our preferences for outcomes or courses of action in a variety of situations.[49] Values help us to know what is right or wrong, or good or bad, in the world. Chapter 2 explains how values anchor our thoughts and to some extent motivate our actions. Although values exist within individuals, groups of people often hold similar values, so we tend to ascribe these *shared values* to the team, department, organization, profession, or entire society. For example, Chapter 14 discusses the importance and dynamics of organizational culture, which includes shared values across the company or within subsystems.

Values have become a popular topic in corporate boardrooms because they replace command-and-control management, which involved top-down decisions with close

values Relatively stable, evaluative beliefs that guide a person's preferences for outcomes or courses of action in a variety of situations.

supervision of employees. The values-driven organization model guides employees with minimal supervision and formal rules. This values-based guidance is important where the environment is complex and changing rapidly because rules can't be created under these circumstances and supervision is too expensive. Bank of Montreal (BMO), which reviewed its organizational values a few years ago, is a case in point. "[BMO's values] provide a stable base for guiding employee decisions and actions in an otherwise rapidly changing workplace," explains a BMO executive. "Simply put, *values matter* and employees care that the organizations they work for and represent are ethical and walk the talk of their values."[50]

By linking values to organizational effectiveness, the stakeholder perspective also incorporates ethics and corporate social responsibility into the organizational effectiveness equation. In fact, the stakeholder perspective emerged out of earlier writing on ethics and corporate social responsibility. **Ethics** refers to the study of moral principles or values that determine whether actions are right or wrong and outcomes are good or bad. We rely on our ethical values to determine "the right thing to do." Ethical behaviour is driven by the moral principles we use to make decisions. These moral principles represent fundamental values. In a recent global survey of MBA students, almost 80 percent felt that a well-run company operates according to its values and code of ethics.[51] Chapter 2 provides more detail about ethical principles and related influences on moral reasoning.

Corporate social responsibility (CSR) consists of organizational activities intended to benefit society and the environment beyond the firm's immediate financial interests or legal obligations.[52] It is the view that companies have a contract with society, in which they must serve stakeholders beyond shareholders and customers. In some situations, the interests of the firm's shareholders should be secondary to those of other stakeholders.[53] As part of CSR, many companies have adopted the triple-bottom-line philosophy: They try to support or "earn positive returns" in the economic, social, and environmental spheres of sustainability. Firms that adopt the triple-bottom-line philosophy aim to survive and be profitable in the marketplace (economic), but they also intend to maintain or improve conditions for society (social) as well as the physical environment.[54] Companies are particularly keen on becoming "greener," that is, minimizing any negative effect they have on the physical environment.

Not everyone agrees that organizations need to cater to a wide variety of stakeholders. More than 30 years ago, economist Milton Friedman pronounced that "there is one and only one social responsibility of business—to use its resources and engage in activities designed to increase its profits."[55] Although few writers take this extreme view

ethics The study of moral principles or values that determine whether actions are right or wrong and outcomes are good or bad.

corporate social responsibility (CSR) Organizational activities intended to benefit society and the environment beyond the firm's immediate financial interests or legal obligations.

Loblaw's CSR Power

Quietly peeking over the rooftop of the Atlantic Superstore in Porters Lake, Nova Scotia, is a wind turbine that provides about 25 percent of the store's annual energy needs. The windy seaside community is a logical location to harness this environmentally friendly energy source. It is also one of many reasons why parent company Loblaw Companies Limited is rated as Canada's best company for corporate social responsibility. Canada's largest grocer is reducing its carbon footprint with this wind turbine, rooftop solar panels in Ontario, biofuel for its transport fleet from in-store cooking grease, and reduced-energy refrigeration systems. The company pioneered "green" grocery products and is now leading a commitment to source all seafood from sustainable sources. It has also diverted 1.3 billion plastic shopping bags from landfills and aims to reduce 70 percent of store waste. "Corporate social responsibility is not an add-on to our business; it is central to the way we conduct ourselves at Loblaw," says a company executive.[56] *Dan Kennedy Photography*

today, some point out that companies can benefit other stakeholders only if those with financial interests in the company receive first priority. Yet 93 percent of Canadians believe that CSR should be as important to companies as profit and shareholder value; 78 percent of Canadians say they would leave their current job if they found a more environmentally friendly employer. "Our company's position on corporate social responsibility and the environment is a significant part of what job candidates find attractive about HBC," acknowledges a senior executive at Hudson's Bay Co.[57] In short, leaders may put their organization at risk if they pay attention only to shareholders and ignore the broader corporate social responsibility.[58]

Capgemini discovered the importance of corporate social responsibility when the Netherlands-based information technology (IT) consulting firm tried to fill 800 IT and management consulting positions. Rather than offering a T-shirt for completing the 30-minute online survey on recruitment issues, Capgemini advised respondents (IT and management consultants) that for each completed survey it would provide funding for a street kid in Kolkata, India, to have one week of schooling and accommodation. The survey included an option for respondents to find out more about employment with the consulting firm. Far beyond its expectations, Capgemini received 10,000 completed surveys and 2,000 job inquiries from qualified respondents. The company filled its 800 jobs and developed a waiting list of future prospects. Furthermore, media attention about this initiative raised Capgemini's brand reputation for corporate social responsibility. The consulting firm supported 10,400 weeks of housing and education for children in Kolkata.[59]

CONNECTING THE DOTS: ORGANIZATIONAL EFFECTIVENESS AND ORGANIZATIONAL BEHAVIOUR

These four perspectives of organizational effectiveness—open systems, organizational learning, high-performance work practices, and stakeholders—provide a roadmap to guide the survival and success of organizations. They also provide a central source of links to the topics discussed throughout this book. The adaptive emphasis of the open systems perspective connects directly to leadership (Chapter 12) and organizational change (Chapter 15). The transformation process aspect of open systems relates to job design (Chapter 6), organizational structure (Chapter 13), relations between subunits in terms of conflict (Chapter 11), and power and influence (Chapter 10).

The organizational learning perspective highlights the importance of communication (Chapter 9) as well as creativity, employee involvement, and topics in decision making (Chapter 8). The high-performance work practices perspective of effectiveness directly casts a spotlight on team dynamics (Chapter 8), employee motivation (Chapter 5), rewards (Chapter 6), and most individual-level topics (Chapters 2 to 4). The stakeholder approach has direct relevance to values and ethics (Chapter 2), organizational culture (Chapter 14), and decision making (Chapter 7).

CONTEMPORARY CHALLENGES FOR ORGANIZATIONS

LO3

A message threaded throughout the previous section on organizational effectiveness is that organizations are deeply affected by the external environment. Consequently, they need to anticipate and adjust to environment changes to maintain a good organization–environment fit. The external environment is continuously changing, but some changes over the past decade and in the decade to come are more profound than others. These changes require corporate leaders and all other employees to make personal and organizational adjustments. In this section, we highlight three of the major challenges facing organizations: globalization, increasing workforce diversity, and emerging employment relationships.

GLOBALIZATION

PricewaterhouseCoopers LLP recently sent Maja Baiocco on a two-year international assignment in Zurich. For Baiocco, an asset management auditor in the accounting firm's Toronto office, it was a welcome chance to gain global experience and boost her career. "This company (PwC) is global and opportunities are global, and I know that international experiences are important to expand my experience and open new opportunities for advancement," she says.[60] Maja Baiocco is developing her career in a world of increasing globalization. **Globalization** refers to economic, social, and cultural connectivity with people in other parts of the world. Organizations globalize when they actively participate in other countries and cultures. Although businesses have traded goods across borders for centuries, the degree of globalization today is unprecedented because information technology and transportation systems allow a much more intense level of connectivity and interdependence around the planet.[61]

> **globalization** Economic, social, and cultural connectivity with people in other parts of the world.

Globalization offers numerous benefits to organizations in terms of larger markets, lower costs, and greater access to knowledge and innovation. At the same time, there is considerable debate about whether globalization benefits developing nations, and whether it is primarily responsible for increasing work intensification, as well as reducing job security and work-life balance in developed countries.[62] Globalization is now well entrenched, so the most important issue in organizational behaviour is how corporate leaders and employees alike can lead and work effectively in this emerging reality[63] Throughout this book, we will refer to the effects of globalization on teamwork, diversity, cultural values, organizational structure, leadership, and other themes. Each topic highlights that globalization has brought more complexity to the workplace, but also more opportunities and potential benefits for individuals and organizations. Globalization requires additional knowledge and skills that we will also discuss in this book, such as emotional intelligence, a global mindset, nonverbal communication, and conflict handling.

INCREASING WORKFORCE DIVERSITY

Walk into the offices of ProMation Engineering Ltd. and you might think you have entered a United Nations building. The Oakville, Ontario-based engineering firm employs 77 people who hail from Canada, Poland, India, China, Romania, Ukraine, Colombia, Peru, Serbia, Afghanistan, Angola, Belarus, Bosnia, Czech Republic, Croatia, England, Germany, Hong Kong, Hungary, Iran, Ireland, Italy, Jamaica, Macedonia, and the Philippines. "We take the best of all the people and try to find one common base for all of us in one small shop," says Promation's CEO Mark Zimny. He adds that the challenges of diversity require some patience but "the results are fantastic."[64]

ProMation is a reflection of Canada as a multicultural society that embraces diversity. Indeed, if Canada has a global "brand" image, it is as a trailblazer for multiculturalism and the benefits of this diversity. When describing multiculturalism, we are

Viterra's Globalized Growth

Viterra is Canada's largest agri-business and among the largest in Australia. This Saskatchewan-based company exports food ingredient products to more than 50 countries and has upwards of 5,500 employees around the world. Global operations are based in Australia, New Zealand, the United States, and Canada. In addition Viterra has offices located in Japan, Singapore, China, Switzerland, Italy, as well as a marketing joint venture in India. "Our whole ambition has been to move from a commodity organization to a food ingredient company that provides nutrition," says CEO and president, Mayo Schmidt. Keenly in tune with opportunities for global diversification and consolidation, Viterra recently acquired Australia's largest agri-business, ABB Grain as well as U.S.–based Dakota Growers Pasta Company. "That's the world today. Companies in all sectors, in all businesses, are constantly and continually assessing their opportunities to combine, to acquire and to grow. . . . You can't afford to stand on the sidelines."[65] *Courtesy of Viterra, Inc.*

surface-level diversity
The observable demographic or physiological differences in people, such as their race, ethnicity, gender, age, and physical capabilities.

deep-level diversity
Differences in the psychological characteristics of employees, including personalities, beliefs, values, and attitudes.

primarily referring to **surface-level diversity**—the observable demographic or physiological differences in people, such as their race, ethnicity, gender, age, and physical capabilities. Surface-level diversity has changed considerably in Canada over the past few decades. The percentage of Canadian residents identified as members of a visible minority jumped from less than 5 percent in 1981 to more than 13 percent in 2001 and will exceed 20 percent of the population by 2017. This increasing cultural diversity is most apparent in the City of Toronto where half of the population was born outside of Canada, one-quarter moved to Canada within the past 15 years, and 47 percent identify themselves as members of a visible minority group.[66]

Diversity also includes differences in the psychological characteristics of employees, including personalities, beliefs, values, and attitudes.[67] We can't directly see this **deep-level diversity**, but it is evident in a person's decisions, statements, and actions. A popular example is the apparent deep-level diversity across generations.[68] Exhibit 1.4 illustrates the distribution of the Canadian workforce by major generational cohort: 35 percent *Baby Boomers* (born from 1946 and 1964), 29 percent *Generation-X* (born from 1965 to 1980), and 27 percent *Millennials* (also called *Generation-Y*, born after 1980).

Do these generational cohorts have different attitudes and expectations, particularly regarding work? The answer is "yes," but some differences are smaller than depicted in the popular press, and some of these differences are due to age, not cohort (i.e., Boomers had the same attitudes as Millennials when they were that age). One recent investigation of 23,000 undergraduate college and university students from across Canada reported that Millennials expect rapid career advancement regarding promotions and pay increases.[69] These observations are consistent with other studies, which have also found that Millennials are more self-confident, are more narcissistic (self-centred), and have less work centrality (i.e., work is less of a central life interest) when compared to Boomers. Generation-X employees typically average somewhere between these two cohorts.[70]

One high quality study, which compared attitudes of senior U.S. high school students in 1976 (Boomers), 1991 (Gen-Xers), and 2006 (Millennials), reported that Gen-Xers prefer leisure significantly more than do Boomers, and Millennials prefer leisure

| **Exhibit 1.4** | **CANADA'S MULTIGENERATIONAL WORKFORCE**[71] |

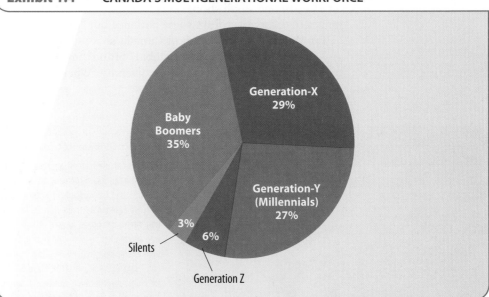

Note: Percentage of the Canadian workforce by age group, based on Statistics Canada 2010 estimates. "Silents" represent the generation of employees born before 1946. Generation Z employees are born after 1990, although some sources consider this group a subset of the Millennials.

Source: Based on Statistics Canada, Labour Force Characteristics by Age and Sex (2010). Ottawa: Statistics Canada, 2010.

significantly more than do Gen-Xers.[72] This longitudinal cohort study also revealed that Millennials and Gen-Xers value extrinsic rewards significantly more than do Boomers, Millennials value intrinsic motivation significantly less than do Boomers, and Millennials value social interaction significantly less than do Boomers or Gen-Xers. Of course, these results don't apply to everyone in each cohort, but they do suggest that deep level diversity exists across generations.

Consequences of Diversity   Diversity presents both opportunities and challenges in organizations.[73] Diversity is an advantage because it provides equally diverse knowledge, such as how to brew better pilsner at Steam Whistle Brewing Co. in Toronto. Furthermore, teams with some forms of diversity (particularly occupational diversity) make better decisions on complex problems than do teams whose members have similar backgrounds. There is also some evidence that diversity award-winning companies have higher financial returns, at least in the short run.[74] This is consistent with anecdotal evidence from many corporate leaders, namely that having a diverse workforce improves customer service and creativity. "If you want to serve a diverse client base, you have to have a diverse workforce," says John Taft, Royal Bank of Canada's head of U.S. wealth management. "If you don't do diversity well, they (high net-worth clients) won't give you their money."[75]

This information supports the popular refrain that workforce diversity is a sound business proposition. Unfortunately, it's not that simple. Most forms of diversity offer both advantages and disadvantages.[76] Teams with diverse employees usually take longer to perform effectively. Diversity brings numerous communication problems as well as "faultlines" in informal group dynamics. Diversity is also a source of conflict, which can lead to lack of information sharing and, in extreme cases, morale problems and higher turnover.

Whether or not workforce diversity is a business advantage, companies need to make it a priority because surface-level diversity is a moral and legal imperative. Ethically, companies that offer an inclusive workplace are, in essence, making fair and just decisions regarding employment, promotions, rewards, and so on. Fairness is a well-established influence on employee loyalty and satisfaction. "Diversity is about fairness; we use the term inclusive meritocracy," says a Bank of America New Jersey executive. "What it does for our workforce is build trust and assures that individual differences are valued."[77] In summary, workforce diversity is the new reality and organizations need to adjust to this reality both to survive and to experience its potential benefits for organizational success.

OB BY THE NUMBERS

Canada's Diversity Advantage[78]

83%
of Canadians agree that interacting with others from different ethnic backgrounds is enriching

79%
of Canadians believe that Canada's cultural diversity offers a distinct advantage when it comes to fostering innovation

68%
of younger Canadians (age 18–34) believe that multiculturalism has been good or very good for Canada

45%
of older Canadians (age 55+) believe that multiculturalism has been good or very good for Canada

65%
of Canadians believe visible minorities and Caucasians are treated equally at their place of work

57%
of Americans believe visible minorities and Caucasians are treated equally at their place of work

39%
of Canadians (all backgrounds) describe their workplace as very inclusive

28%
of visible minority Canadians describe their workplace as very inclusive

Note: All results are from national surveys involving at least 1,000 respondents.

 Companies that offer an inclusive workplace are, in essence, making fair and just decisions."

EMERGING EMPLOYMENT RELATIONSHIPS

Combine globalization with emerging workforce diversity, and then add in recent developments in information technology. The resulting concoction has created incredible changes in employment relationships. A few decades ago, most (although not all) employees in Canada and similar cultures would finish their workday after eight or nine hours and could separate their personal time from the workday. There were no Black-Berrys and no Internet connections to keep staff tethered to work on a 24/7 schedule. Even business travel was more of an exception due to its high cost. Most competitors were located in the same country, so they had similar work practices and labour costs. Today, work hours are longer (although arguably less than 100 years ago), employees experience more work-related stress, and there is growing evidence that family and personal relations are suffering.

Little wonder that one of the most important employment issues over the past decade has been **work-life balance**. Work-life balance occurs when people are able to minimize conflict between their work and nonwork demands.[79] Most employees lack this balance because they spend too many hours each week performing or thinking about their job, whether at the workplace, at home, or on vacation. This focus on work leaves too little time to fulfill nonwork needs and obligations. Recent surveys estimate that one-third of Canadians would take a pay cut to improve their work-life balance (although how much cut is unclear) and one-quarter cite lack of work-life balance as the main problem they currently face at work (second only to their level of pay).[80] Our discussion of work-related stress (Chapter 4) will examine work-life balance issues in more detail.

Another employment relationship trend is **virtual work**, whereby employees use information technology to perform their jobs away from the traditional physical workplace. The most common form of virtual work involves working at home rather than commuting to the office (often called *telecommuting* or *teleworking*, although experts use these terms less often now). Virtual work also includes employees connected to the office while travelling or at clients' offices. More than half of Canadian workers say they want to work at home some of the time, whereas less than 10 percent of Canadian employees actually do so. Several Canadian companies have developed opportunities for employees to work at home in response to this growing demand. "Like other employers, we're looking to respond to our changing workforce," says Peter McAdam, vice-president of employee experience at TD Bank. McAdam notes that newcomers to the workforce are particularly interested in telecommuting and other flexible work packages.[81]

work-life balance The degree to which a person minimizes conflict between work and nonwork demands.

virtual work Work performed away from the traditional physical workplace by means of information technology.

Welcome to My Office!

Meredith Forsythe kick starts her work day at sunrise in order to stay on top of her jam-packed schedule. The TELUS customer service agent has reports to complete and a team meeting to attend, and her goal is to exceed her customer service objectives. It is a good thing she has a very short commute. Meredith works out of her home in Barrie, Ontario as a TELUS At Home Agent. Telus has provided hundreds of these front-line employees with all the technical requirements they need to do their jobs from home. Telus communications manager Shawn Hall, says about half the company's employees have the ability to work at home using technologies such as teleconferencing and virtual private networks. Hall describes a "cultural shift in the Canadian workplace as more companies conclude that telecommuting can increase productivity, lessen workers' hours stuck in traffic, decrease greenhouse gas emissions, and allow workers more time with their families." "It's a triple bottom line," he added. "We're helping the environment. There's better morale and productivity. And we're helping the company by saving money [on office space] and keeping employees engaged."[82] © *Jim Craigmyle/Corbis*

Research indicates that offering the opportunity to work from home attracts job applicants, as well as improves the employee's work-life balance (which reduces stress) and productivity.[83] One recent study of 25,000 IBM employees found that employees who worked at home most of the time could perform 50 hours of work per week before experiencing work-life conflict compared to 46 hours per week for those who worked only at the office. Female telecommuters with children were able to work 40 hours per week, whereas non-telecommuters could only manage 30 hours before feeling work-life balance tension. Virtual work also offers environmental benefits. Cisco Systems recently estimated that telecommuting among its employees worldwide avoids almost 50,000 metric tonnes of greenhouse gas emission and saves employees $10 million in fuel costs each year.

Against these potential benefits, work-at-home employees face a number of real or potential challenges. Family relations may suffer rather than improve if employees lack sufficient space and resources for a home office. Some employees complain of social isolation and reduced promotion opportunities when they work away from the office most of the time. Telecommuting is clearly better suited to people who are self-motivated, organized, can work effectively with information technologies, and have sufficient fulfillment of social needs elsewhere in their life. This emerging employment arrangement is also more successful in organizations that evaluate employees by their performance outcomes rather than face time.[84]

ANCHORS OF ORGANIZATIONAL BEHAVIOUR KNOWLEDGE

L04

Globalization, increasing workforce diversity, and emerging employment relationships are just a few of the trends that challenge organizations and make the field of organizational behaviour more relevant than ever before. To understand these and other topics, the field of organizational behaviour relies on a set of basic beliefs or knowledge structures (see Exhibit 1.5). These conceptual anchors represent the principles on which OB knowledge is developed and refined.[85]

THE MULTIDISCIPLINARY ANCHOR

Organizational behaviour is anchored around the idea that the field should develop from theories and knowledge in other disciplines, not just from its own isolated research base. For instance, psychological research has aided our understanding of individual and interpersonal behaviour. Sociologists have contributed to our knowledge of team dynamics, organizational socialization, organizational power, and other aspects of the social system. OB knowledge has also benefited from knowledge in emerging fields such as communications, marketing, and information systems. This theory borrowing from other disciplines is inevitable. Organizations have central roles in society, so they are

Exhibit 1.5 | **ANCHORS OF ORGANIZATIONAL BEHAVIOUR KNOWLEDGE**

Multidisciplinary anchor	OB should import knowledge from many disciplines
Systematic research anchor	OB should study organizations using systematic research methods
Contingency anchor	OB theory should recognize that the effects of actions often vary with the situation
Multiple levels of analysis anchor	OB knowledge should include three levels of analysis: individual, team, organization

the subject of many social sciences. Furthermore, organizations consist of people who interact with each other, so there is an inherent intersection between OB and most disciplines that study human beings.

The field of organizational behaviour imports knowledge from other disciplines in various ways.[86] Many ideas are taken from different contexts. In Chapter 14, for instance, we discuss an organization's "culture" as well as its "artifacts," concepts that originate from anthropological studies of entire societies.[87] Borrowing theories from other disciplines has helped the field of OB to nurture a diversity of knowledge and perspectives about organizations, but there are a few concerns.[88] One issue is whether OB suffers from a "trade deficit"—importing far more knowledge from other disciplines than is exported to other disciplines. By relying on theories developed in other fields, OB knowledge necessarily lags rather than leads in knowledge production. In contrast, OB-bred theories allow researchers to concentrate on the quality and usefulness of the theory.

Finally, heavy reliance on theories borrowed from other disciplines may leave OB vulnerable to a lack of common identity. The field could potentially become a place for researchers who are raised in and mainly identify with the other disciplines (psychology, sociology, and so on) rather than with organizational behaviour. The lack of identification as an "OB scholar" might further challenge the field's ability to develop its own theory and may weaken its focus on practical relevance.

THE SYSTEMATIC RESEARCH ANCHOR

A critical feature of OB knowledge is that it should be based on systematic research, which typically involves forming research questions, systematically collecting data, and testing hypotheses against those data.[89] Appendix A at the end of this book provides a brief overview of these research methods. Systematic research investigation produces **evidence-based management**, which involves making decisions and taking actions based on this research evidence. It makes perfect sense, doesn't it, that management practice should be founded on the best available systematic knowledge? Yet many of us who study organizations using systematic methods are amazed at how often corporate leaders embrace fads, consulting models, and their own pet beliefs without bothering to find out if they actually work![90]

> **evidence-based management** The practice of making decisions and taking actions based on research evidence.

There are many reasons why people have difficulty applying evidence-based management. Leaders and other decision makers are bombarded with so many ideas from newspapers, books, consultant reports, and other sources that it is a challenge to figure out which ones are based on good evidence. Another problem is that good OB research is necessarily generic; it is rarely described in the context of a specific problem in a specific organization. Managers therefore have the difficult task of figuring out which theories are relevant to their unique situation.

A third reason why organizational leaders accept fads and other knowledge that lacks sufficient evidence is that consultants and popular book writers are rewarded for marketing their concepts and theories, not for testing to see if they actually work. Indeed, some management concepts have become popular—they are even found in some OB textbooks!—because of heavy marketing, not because of any evidence that they are valid. Finally, as we will discuss in Chapter 3, people form perceptions and beliefs quickly and tend to ignore evidence that their beliefs are inaccurate. To counter these opposing forces, OB experts have proposed a few simple suggestions to create a more evidence-based organization (see Exhibit 1.6).

THE CONTINGENCY ANCHOR

People and their work environments are complex, and the field of organizational behaviour recognizes this by stating that a particular action may have different consequences

Exhibit 1.6	**CREATING AN EVIDENCE-BASED MANAGEMENT ORGANIZATION**[91]

1. Stop treating old ideas as if they were brand-new.

2. Be suspicious of "breakthrough" ideas and studies.

3. Celebrate and develop collective brilliance.

4. Emphasize drawbacks as well as virtues.

5. Use success (and failure) stories to illustrate sound practices, but not in place of a valid research method.

6. Adopt a neutral stance toward ideologies and theories.

Source: J. Pfeffer and R. I. Sutton, *Hard Facts, Dangerous Half-Truths, and Total Nonsense* (Boston: Harvard Business School Press, 2006).

in different situations. In other words, no single solution is best all of the time.[92] Of course, it would be so much simpler if we could rely on "one best way" theories, in which a particular concept or practice has the same results in every situation. OB experts do search for simpler theories, but they also remain skeptical about sure fire recommendations; an exception is somewhere around the corner. Thus, when faced with a particular problem or opportunity, we need to understand and diagnose the situation and select the strategy most appropriate *under those conditions*.[93]

THE MULTIPLE LEVELS OF ANALYSIS ANCHOR

This textbook divides organizational behaviour topics into three levels of analysis: individual, team (including interpersonal), and organization. The individual level includes the characteristics and behaviours of employees as well as the thought processes that are attributed to them, such as motivation, perceptions, personalities, attitudes, and values. The team level of analysis looks at the way people interact. This includes team dynamics, team decisions, power, organizational politics, conflict, and leadership. At the organizational level, we focus on how people structure their working relationships and on how organizations interact with their environments.

Although an OB topic is typically pegged into one level of analysis, it usually relates to multiple levels.[94] For instance, communication is located in this book as a team (interpersonal) process, but we also recognize that it includes individual and organizational processes. Therefore, you should try to think about each OB topic at the individual, team, and organizational levels, not just at one of these levels.

THE JOURNEY BEGINS

This chapter gives you some background about the field of organizational behaviour. But it's only the beginning of our journey. Throughout this book, we will challenge you to learn new ways of thinking about how people work in and around organizations. We begin this process in Chapter 2 by presenting a basic model of individual behaviour, then introducing over the next few chapters various stable and mercurial characteristics of individuals that relate to elements of the individual behaviour model. Next, this book moves to the team level of analysis. We examine a model of team effectiveness and specific features of high-performance teams. We also look at team decision making, communication, power and influence, conflict, and leadership. Finally, we shift our focus to the organizational level of analysis, where the topics of organizational structure, organizational culture, and organizational change are examined in detail.

CHAPTER SUMMARY

 LO1 Define organizational behaviour and organizations, and discuss the importance of this field of inquiry.

Organizational behaviour is the study of what people think, feel, and do in and around organizations. Organizations are groups of people who work interdependently toward some purpose. OB theories help people to (a) make sense of the workplace, (b) question and rebuild their personal mental models, and (c) get things done in organizations. OB knowledge benefits everyone who works in organizations, not just managers. It is also very important for the organization's financial health.

 LO2 Compare and contrast the four current perspectives of organizational effectiveness as well as the early goal attainment perspective.

The goal attainment perspective, which states that organizations are effective if they achieve their stated objectives, is no longer accepted because (a) the goals set may be too easy, (b) goals may be too abstract to determine their accomplishment, and (c) achievement of some goals may threaten the company's survival.

The open systems perspective views organizations as complex organisms that "live" within an external environment. They depend on the external environment for resources, then use organizational subsystems to transform those resources into outputs, which are returned to the environment. Organizations receive feedback from the external environment to maintain a good "fit" with that environment. Fit occurs by adapting to the environment, managing the environment, or moving to another environment. According to the organizational learning perspective, organizational effectiveness depends on the organization's capacity to acquire, share, use, and store valuable knowledge. The ability to acquire and use knowledge depends on the firm's absorptive capacity. Intellectual capital consists of human capital, structural capital, and relationship capital. Knowledge is retained in the organizational memory; companies also selectively unlearn.

The high-performance work practices (HPWP) perspective identifies a bundle of systems and structures to leverage workforce potential. The most widely identified HPWPs are employee involvement, job autonomy, developing employee competencies, and performance/skill-based rewards. HPWPs improve organizational effectiveness by building human capital, increasing adaptability, and strengthening employee motivation and attitudes. The stakeholder perspective states that leaders manage the interests of diverse stakeholders by relying on their personal and organizational values for guidance. Ethics and corporate social responsibility (CSR) are natural extensions of values-based organizations because they rely on values to guide the most appropriate decisions involving stakeholders. CSR consists of organizational activities intended to benefit society and the environment beyond the firm's immediate financial interests or legal obligations.

 LO3 Debate the organizational opportunities and challenges of globalization, workforce diversity, and emerging employment relationships.

Globalization, which refers to various forms of connectivity with people in other parts of the world, has several economic and social benefits, but it may also be responsible for work intensification, reduced job security, and work-life balance. Workforce diversity is apparent at both the surface-level (observable demographic and other overt differences in people) and deep-level (differences in personalities, beliefs, values, and attitudes). There is some evidence of deep-level diversity across generational cohorts. Diversity may be a competitive advantage by improving decision making and team performance on complex tasks, yet it also brings numerous challenges such as team "faultlines," slower team performance, and interpersonal conflict. One emerging employment relationship trend is the call for more work-life balance (minimizing conflict between work and nonwork demands). Another employment trend is virtual work, particularly working from home. Working from home potentially increases employee productivity and reduces employee stress, but it may also lead to social isolation, reduced promotion opportunities, and tension in family relations.

LO4 Discuss the anchors on which organizational behaviour knowledge is based.

The multidisciplinary anchor states that the field should develop from knowledge in other disciplines (e.g. psychology, sociology, economics), not just from its own isolated research base. The systematic research anchor states that OB knowledge should be based on systematic research, which is consistent with evidence-based management. The contingency anchor states that OB theories generally need to consider that there will be different consequences in different situations. The multiple levels of analysis anchor states that OB topics should be viewed from the individual, team, and organization levels of analysis.

KEY TERMS

absorptive capacity, p. 8

corporate social responsibility (CSR), p. 13

deep-level diversity, p. 16

ethics, p. 13

evidence-based management, p. 20

globalization, p. 15

high-performance work practices (HPWP), p. 10

human capital, p. 8

intellectual capital, p. 8

open systems, p. 5

organizational behaviour (OB), p. 2

organizational effectiveness, p. 4

organizational efficiency, p. 7

organizational learning, p. 7
organizations, p. 2
stakeholders, p. 11

structural capital, p. 9
surface-level diversity, p. 16
values, p. 12

virtual work, p. 18
work-life balance, p. 18

CRITICAL-THINKING QUESTIONS

1. A friend suggests that organizational behaviour courses are useful only to people who will enter management careers. Discuss the accuracy of your friend's statement.

2. A number of years ago, employees in a city water distribution department were put into teams and encouraged to find ways to improve efficiency. The teams boldly crossed departmental boundaries and areas of management discretion in search of problems. Employees working in other parts of the began to complain about these intrusions. Moreover, when some team ideas were implemented, the managers discovered that a dollar saved in the water distribution unit may have cost the organization two dollars in higher costs elsewhere. Use the open systems perspective to explain what happened here.

3. After hearing a seminar on organizational learning, a mining company executive argues that this perspective ignores the fact that mining companies cannot rely on knowledge alone to stay in business. They also need physical capital (such as extracting and ore-processing equipment) and land (where the minerals are located). In fact, these two may be more important than what employees carry around in their heads. Evaluate the mining executive's comments.

4. A common refrain among executives is "People are our most important asset." Relate this statement to any two of the four perspectives of organizational effectiveness presented in this chapter. Does this statement apply better to some perspectives than to others? Why or why not?

5. Corporate social responsibility is one of the hottest issues in corporate boardrooms these days, partly because it is becoming increasingly important to employees and other stakeholders. In your opinion, why have stakeholders given CSR more attention recently? Does abiding by CSR standards potentially cause companies to have conflicting objectives with some stakeholders in some situations?

6. Look through the list of chapters in this textbook, and discuss how globalization could influence each organizational behaviour topic.

7. "Organizational theories should follow the contingency approach." Comment on the accuracy of this statement.

8. What does *evidence-based management* mean? Describe situations you have heard about in which companies have practised evidence-based management, as well as situations in which companies have relied on fads that lacked sufficient evidence of their worth.

 ## CASE STUDY 1.1

Hospitals are Driving toward a Leaner Organization

How is serving surgical patients similar to manufacturing a car? The answer is clear to staff at Sunderland Royal Hospital. The health facility in northern England borrowed several ideas from the nearby Nissan factory, one of the most efficient car plants in Europe, to improve its day surgery unit. "We took [Sunderland hospital staff] on a tour of our plant, showing them a variety of lean processes in action, and let them decide which ones could be applied back at the hospital," says a training manager at Nissan's factory in Sunderland.

Lean management involves seeking ways to reduce and remove waste from work processes. Employees are typically involved, where they map out the work process and identify ways to reduce steps, time, spaces, and other resources without threatening the work objectives. Sunderland's day surgery staff were actively involved in applying lean management to their work unit. After attending Nissan's two-day workshop, they mapped out the work processes, questioned assumptions about the value or relevance of some activities, and discovered ways to reduce the lengthy patient wait times (which were up to three hours). There was some initial resistance and skepticism, but the hospital's day surgery soon realized significant improvements in efficiency and service quality.

"By working with Nissan's staff, we have streamlined the patient pathway from 29 to 11 discrete stages," says Anne Fleming, who oversees Sunderland's 32-bed day case unit and its 54 staff. "We have done this by reducing duplication, halving the time that patients spend in the unit to three hours by giving them individual appointment times, and introducing the just-in-time approach to the patient pathway." Fleming also reports that Sunderland's operating theatres are now much more efficient.

Sunderland Royal Hospital is one of many healthcare centres around the world that are improving efficiency through lean thinking. After receiving training in Japan on lean practices, several teams of doctors, nurses, and other staff from Virginia Mason Medical Center in Seattle, Washington, redesigned work flows to cut out 54 kilometres of unnecessary walking each day. Park Nicollet Health Services in Minneapolis, Minnesota, improved efficiency at its ambulatory clinic to such an extent that the unit does not require a patient waiting area. One Park Nicollet team worked with orthopaedic surgeons to reduce by 60 percent the variety of instruments and supplies they ordered for hip and knee surgery.

Flinders Medical Centre also adopted lean management practices after the South Australian medical facility experienced severe congestion of patients in its emergency department. After mapping out the steps in the patient journey through the department, staff realized that the process was inefficient and stressful for everyone, particularly as lower priority patients got "bumped" down the queue when more serious cases arrived. Now, incoming emergency patients are immediately streamed to one of two emergency teams—those who will be treated and sent home and those who will be treated and admitted to hospital. This change immediately improved efficiency and the quality of patient care.

Bolton Hospitals NHS Trust in the U.K. is yet another illustration of how lean management practices improved the organization's efficiency and effectiveness. By involving employees in an analysis of procedures, the hospital reduced average wait times for patients with fractured hips by 38 percent (from 2.4 to 1.7 days), which also resulted in a lower mortality rate for these patients. By smoothing out the inflow of work orders and re-arranging the work process, Bolton's pathology department cut the time to process samples from 24–30 hours to just 2–3 hours and reduced the space used by 50 percent.

"We know that our case for extra funding will fall on deaf ears unless we cut out waste in the system," explains Dr Gill Morgan, chief executive of the U.K.'s NHS Confederation. "Lean works because it is based on doctors, nurses, and other staff leading the process and telling us what adds value and what doesn't. They are the ones who know."[95]

Discussion Questions

1. What perspective(s) of organizational effectiveness best describe the application of lean management practices? Describe how specific elements of that perspective relate to the interventions described in this case study.

2. Does lean management ignore some perspectives of organizational effectiveness? If so, what are the unintended consequences of these practices that might undermine rather than improve the organization's effectiveness?

3. In what situations, if any, would it be difficult or risky to apply lean management practices? What conditions make these practices challenging in these situations?

Sources: "NHS Chief Vows to Cut Waste and Look to Toyota in Efficiency Drive," *NHS Federation News Release* (London, UK: June 14, 2006); D. Jones and A. Mitchell, *Lean Thinking for the NHS* (London: NHS Confederation, 2006); M. McCarthy, "Can Car Manufacturing Techniques Reform Health Care," *Lancet* 367, no. 9507 (January 28, 2006), pp. 290–291; "Nissan 'Shot in the Arm' for Healthcare Sector," Newcarinfo.co.uk, February 13, 2007; I. Green, "Drive for Success," *Nursing Standard* 21, no. 38 (May 30, 2007): 62–63; A.-M. Kelly et al., "Improving Emergency Department Efficiency by Patient Streaming to Outcomes-Based Teams," *Australian Health Review* 31, no. 1 (2007), pp. 16–21.

 **TEAM EXERCISE 1.2**

Generational Myths and Realities

Purpose	This exercise is designed to help students examine and explore generational differences and similarities in the workplace.
Materials	Additional information will be provided by your instructor.
Instructions	*Step 1:* Form teams with five or six members.
	Step 2: With your team, brainstorm some of your dominant perceptions about workplace qualities of Baby Boomers (born 1945–1964), Generation-X (born 1965–1979), and Generation-Y (born 1980–1991*). Use the structure provided in the following table to organize your information.
	Step 3: Each team shares their list of perceptions with the rest of the class.
	Step 4: Instructor distributes a copy of Handout #1: Generational Myths and Realities. Teams examine the Generational Myths and Realities and discuss the accuracy of their perceptions from Step 2.
	Step 5: Instructor leads a class discussion using the following questions.
Discussion Questions	**1.** What are the main differences and similarities among the Baby Boomers, Generation-X, and Generation-Y cohorts of workers?
	2. How might these differences and similarities affect workplace performance?
	3. How can employers maximize the potential of a multigenerational workforce?

TABLE: Perceptions of Generations in the Workforce			
Workplace Qualities	Baby Boomers (Born 1945–1964)	Generation-X (Born 1965–1979)	Generation-Y (Born 1980–1991)
Teamwork *Is the ability to work with others.*			
Loyalty *Relates to a worker's commitment to his or her organization.*			
Manageability *Is the ability to accept authority and follow direction.*			
Adaptability *Includes characteristics such as openness to change, willingness to learn new things, and acceptance of diversity.*			
Balance *Is a measure of a worker's ability to achieve equilibrium between work and life.*			
Other Comments			

* Although this age cohort is defined as those born 1980–2000 this exercise is intended to focus on individuals participating in organizational workplaces.

Source: Based on Tim Krywulak and Martha Roberts, *Winning the 'Generation Wars': Making the Most of Generational Differences and Similarities in the Workplace* (Ottawa: The Conference Board of Canada), November 2009.

 **WEB EXERCISE 1.3**

Diagnosing Organizational Stakeholders

Purpose   This exercise is designed to help you understand how stakeholders influence organizations as part of the open-systems anchor.

Materials   Students need to select a company and prior to class, retrieve and analyze publicly available information over the past year or two about that company. This may include annual reports, which are usually found on the websites of publicly traded companies. Where possible, students should also scan full-text newspaper and magazine databases for recently published articles about the company.

Instructions   The instructor may have students work alone or in groups for this activity. Students will select a company and investigate the relevance and influence of various stakeholder groups on the organization. Stakeholders can be identified from annual reports, newspaper articles, website statements, and other available sources. Stakeholders should be rank-ordered in terms of their perceived importance to the organization.

Students should be prepared to present or discuss their rank-ordering of the organization's stakeholders, including evidence for this ordering.

Discussion Questions   1. What are the main reasons why certain stakeholders are more important than others for this organization?

2. On the basis of your knowledge of the organization's environmental situation, is this rank-order of stakeholders in the organization's best interest, or should other specific stakeholders be given higher priority?

3. What societal groups, if any, are not mentioned as stakeholders by the organization? Does this lack of reference to these unmentioned groups make sense?

Go to CONNECT to complete the following interactive self-assessments.

 SELF-ASSESSMENT EXERCISE 1.4

It All Makes Sense?

Purpose   This exercise is designed to help you comprehend how organizational behaviour knowledge can help you to understand life in organizations.

Instructions   (Note: Your instructor might conduct this activity as a self-assessment or as a team activity.) Read each of the statements below and circle whether each statement is true or false, in your opinion. The class will consider the answers to each question and discuss the implications for studying organizational behaviour.

Due to the nature of this activity, the instructor will provide the answers to these questions. There is no scoring key in Appendix B.

1. True	False	A happy worker is a productive worker.
2. True	False	A decision maker's effectiveness increases with the number of choices or alternatives available to her/him.
3. True	False	Organizations are more effective when they minimize conflict among employees.
4. True	False	Managers influence employees best by praising their skills and accomplishments.
5. True	False	Companies are more successful when they have strong corporate cultures.
6. True	False	Employees perform better without stress.
7. True	False	The best way to change people and organizations is by pinpointing the source of their current problems.
8. True	False	Female leaders involve employees in decisions to a greater degree than do male leaders.
9. True	False	The best decisions are made without emotion.
10. True	False	If employees feel they are paid unfairly, nothing other than changing their pay will reduce their feelings of injustice.

 SELF-ASSESSMENT EXERCISE 1.5

Are You a Good Telecommuter?

Some employees adapt better than others to telecommuting (also called *teleworking*) and other forms of virtual work. This self-assessment measures personal characteristics that seem to relate to telecommuting, and therefore it provides a rough indication of how well you would adapt to telework. The instrument asks you to indicate how much you agree or disagree with each of the statements provided. You need to be honest with yourself to get a reasonable estimate of your telework disposition. Please keep in mind that this scale considers only your personal characteristics. Other factors, such as organizational, family, and technological systems support, must also be taken into account.

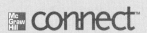 Practise and learn online with Connect. Connect resources include additional and interactive study exercises, videos, and practice quizzing, as well as additional material you won't find in the printed text.

CHAPTER 2

Individual Behaviour, Personality, and Values

LEARNING OBJECTIVES

After reading this chapter, you should be able to:

LO1 Describe the four factors that directly influence individual behaviour and performance.

LO2 Summarize the five types of individual behaviour in organizations.

LO3 Describe personality and discuss how the "Big Five" personality dimensions and four MBTI types relate to individual behaviour in organizations.

LO4 Summarize Schwartz's model of individual values and discuss the conditions under which values influence behaviour.

LO5 Describe three ethical principles and discuss four factors that influence ethical behaviour.

LO6 Review five values commonly studied across cultures and discuss the diverse cultures within Canada.

"We think it's awesome," says Becky Ferguson. "You can't beat having sand between your toes when you're having lunch," added Sherri Blake, another programmer at YTV, a division of Corus Entertainment. Corus recently moved to new headquarters at Corus Quay on Sugar Beach located along Toronto's Waterfront.

Corus Entertainment is a national media company that continues to thrive and remain profitable in an industry that has been facing layoffs in the midst of declining profits and vanishing sources of revenue. Spun off from parent company Shaw Communications, Corus holdings include 52 radio stations, three local television stations and specialty channels such as YTV, Treehouse, Nickelodeon, and TELETOON as well as Kids Can Press, Canada's leader in children's publishing. In the West, Corus provides pay television services including Movie Central, HBO Canada, and Encore Avenue.

"We firmly believe our success is based on the strong corporate culture we have created. Our people are engaged, empowered and have taken ownership of their jobs and their contribution to the corporation," says John Cassaday, president and CEO. "Employee commitment and engagement is shown in the number of employees that respond to the company's employee survey. About 89 percent participate, a figure that is extraordinarily high according to the experts, adds Cassaday.

John Cassaday is visible to employees throughout the year through both face-to-face and live electronic town hall meetings accessible to all staff. There is an annual leadership conference where yearly objectives are reviewed. Annual employee performance reviews "consist of five sections, each directly linked to one of the company's five core values."

Corus also established Corus U several years ago to ensure employees have the skills they need. In addition to providing more than 4,500 hours of in-class instruction each year Corus also provides an extensive online curriculum, and an in-house mentorship program.

Employee motivation is sustained at Corus through much more than direct access to a beach on Lake Ontario with rows of white Muskoka chairs and pink umbrellas. Corus provides a variety of formal awards recognizing organizational, team, and individual performance. Many of these awards are peer-nominated and recognize individuals, and teams or work groups. One of these major awards, The Samurai Award, recognizes individuals who "have gone above and beyond their work responsibilities, demonstrating the characteristics of the Corus core values of accountability, innovation, initiative, teamwork, and knowledge."

Giving back to the community also keeps motivation levels high at Corus. Last year Corus raised over $450,000 for the United Way and employees maintain their support throughout the year. For example,

Corus Entertainment's work environment includes new headquarters on Toronto's waterfront where employees enjoy their lunch at the beach. © *National Post/Brett Gundlock*

employees recently raffled off tickets for the chance to be the first employee to ride down the three-story tube slide, a focal point of the lobby in their new digs. Kathleen McNair, executive vice-president of human resources and corporate communications, describes the event that raised another $1,000 for the United Way: "(The winner) had a lot of fun and the employees loved the event too."[1]

Corus Entertainment is continually seeking ways to improve employee performance and well-being, so it has introduced training, rewards, and workplace conditions that improve employee knowledge, skills, motivation, role clarity, and resource support. Corus has created an environment that strengthens these direct predictors of individual behaviour, but we also need to understand the personal characteristics of employees that influence individual behaviour and results.

This chapter concentrates our attention on the role of individual differences in organizations. We begin by presenting the MARS model, which outlines the four direct drivers of individual behaviour and results. We also review the five types of individual behaviours and outcomes that represent the individual-level dependent variables found in most organizational behaviour research. The second half of this chapter looks closely at two of the most stable characteristics of individuals: personality and values. The section on personality specifically looks at personality development, personality traits, and how personality relates to behaviour in organizational settings. The section on values includes discussion of the various types of values, how values relate to individual behaviour, the dynamics of values congruence, ethical values and practices, and cross-cultural values and related differences.

MARS MODEL OF INDIVIDUAL BEHAVIOUR AND PERFORMANCE

L01

For most of the past century, experts have investigated the direct predictors of individual behaviour and performance.[2] One of the earliest formulas was *performance = person × situation*, where *person* includes individual characteristics and *situation* represents external influences on the individual's behaviour. Another frequently mentioned formula is *performance = ability × motivation*.[3] Sometimes known as the "skill-and-will" model, this formula elaborates two specific characteristics within the person that influence individual performance. Ability, motivation, and situation are by far the most commonly mentioned direct predictors of individual behaviour and performance, but in the 1960s researchers identified a fourth key factor: role perceptions (the individual's expected role obligations).[4]

Exhibit 2.1 illustrates these four variables—motivation, ability, role perceptions, and situational factors—which are represented by the acronym *MARS*.[5] All four factors are critical influences on an individual's voluntary behaviour and performance; if any one of them is low in a given situation, the employee would not perform the task as well. For example, motivated salespeople with clear role perceptions and sufficient resources (situational factors) will not perform their jobs as well if they lack sales skills and related knowledge (ability). Motivation, ability, and role perceptions are clustered together in the model because they are located within the person. Situational factors are external to the individual but still affect his or her behaviour and performance.[6] Let's look at each of these four factors in more detail.

EMPLOYEE MOTIVATION

motivation The forces within a person that affect his or her direction, intensity, and persistence of voluntary behaviour.

Motivation represents the forces within a person that affect his or her direction, intensity, and persistence of voluntary behaviour.[7] *Direction* refers to the path along which people engage their effort. People have choices about where they put their effort; they have a sense of what they are trying to achieve and at what level of quality, quantity, and so forth. In other words, motivation is goal-directed, not random. People are motivated

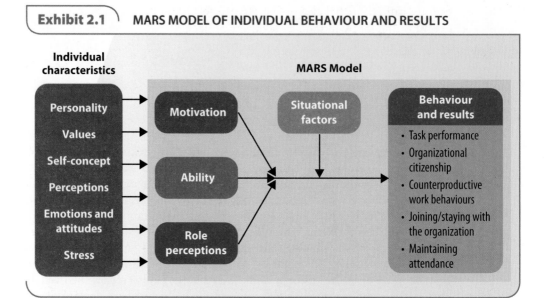

Exhibit 2.1   MARS MODEL OF INDIVIDUAL BEHAVIOUR AND RESULTS

to arrive at work on time, finish a project a few hours early, or aim for many other targets. The second element of motivation, called *intensity*, is the amount of effort allocated to the goal. Intensity is all about how much people push themselves to complete a task. For example, two employees might be motivated to finish their project a few hours early (direction), but only one of them puts forth enough effort (intensity) to achieve this goal.

Finally, motivation involves varying levels of *persistence*, that is, continuing the effort for a certain amount of time. Employees sustain their effort until they reach their goal or give up beforehand. To help remember these three elements of motivation, consider the metaphor of driving a car in which the thrust of the engine is your effort. Direction refers to where you steer the car, intensity is how much you put your foot down on the gas pedal, and persistence is for how long you drive towards that destination. Remember that motivation is a force that exists within individuals; it is not their actual behaviour. Thus, direction, intensity, and persistence are cognitive (thoughts) and emotional conditions that directly cause us to move.

ABILITY

ability The natural aptitudes and learned capabilities required to successfully complete a task.

Employee abilities also make a difference in behaviour and task performance. **Ability** includes both the natural aptitudes and learned capabilities required to successfully complete a task. *Aptitudes* are the natural talents that help employees learn specific tasks more quickly and perform them better. There are many physical and mental aptitudes, and our ability to acquire skills is affected by these aptitudes. For example, finger dexterity is an aptitude by which individuals learn more quickly and potentially achieve higher performance at picking up and handling small objects with their fingers. Employees with high finger dexterity are not necessarily better than others at first; rather, their learning tends to be faster and performance potential tends to be higher. *Learned capabilities* are the skills and knowledge that you currently possess. These capabilities include the physical and mental skills and knowledge you have acquired. Learned capabilities tend to wane over time when not in use.

competencies Skills, knowledge, aptitudes, and other personal characteristics that lead to superior performance.

Aptitudes and learned capabilities are closely related to *competencies*, which has become a frequently used term in business. **Competencies** are characteristics of a person that result in superior performance.[8] These characteristics include knowledge, skills, aptitudes, and behaviours. Some experts extend the meaning of competencies to include personality and values, while others suggest that competencies are action-oriented results of these characteristics, such as serving customers, coping with heavy workloads, and providing creative ideas. With any of these interpretations, the challenge is to match a person's competencies with the job's task requirements. A good person–job match not only produces higher performance; it also tends to increase the employee's well-being.

One way to match a person's competencies with the job's task requirements is to select applicants who already demonstrate the required competencies. For example, companies ask applicants to perform work samples, provide references for checking their past performance, and complete various selection tests. A second strategy is to provide training, which has a strong influence on individual performance and organizational effectiveness.[9] The third person–job matching strategy is to redesign the job so that employees are given tasks only within their current learned capabilities. For example, a complex task might be simplified—some aspects of the work are transferred to others—so that a new employee performs only tasks that he or she is currently able to perform. As the employee becomes more competent at these tasks, other tasks are added back into the job.

ROLE PERCEPTIONS

> **role perceptions** The extent to which people understand the job duties (roles) assigned to or expected of them.

Motivation and ability are important influences on individual behaviour and performance, but employees also require accurate **role perceptions** to perform their jobs well. Role perceptions refer to the extent to which people understand the job duties (roles) assigned to or expected of them. These perceptions are critical because they guide the employee's direction of effort and improve coordination with co-workers, suppliers, and other stakeholders. Employees who know they have poor role perceptions also tend to have lower motivation. Unfortunately, many employees do not have clear role perceptions. For instance, although 76 percent of Canadian employees polled said they understand the organization's business goals, only 39 percent said they understood how to achieve those goals in their own job.[10]

There are at least three ways in which employees are clear or unclear about their role obligations. First, employees have clear role perceptions when they understand the specific tasks assigned to them, that is, when they know the specific duties or consequences for which they are accountable. This may seem obvious, but employees are occasionally evaluated on job duties they were never told was within their zone of responsibility. For example, the metro transit system in Washington, D.C. experienced a serious train derailment a few years ago because the track department staff were not lubricating the tracks. An investigation revealed that the department had lubricated tracks several years earlier, but this work activity stopped after the previous department managers had transferred or retired. The incoming managers did not know about the department's

Best Buy Clarifies Employee Roles for Black Friday

Black Friday—the day after U.S. Thanksgiving—is the busiest shopping day of the year in that country because companies offer their best one-day bargains. Best Buy ensures that its employees are up to the challenge by giving them plenty of training and support. But the electronics retailer goes one step further; it also ensures that everyone has crystal clear role perceptions. In many Best Buy stores, employees hold special rehearsals where they practise their roles before Black Friday. For example, this photo shows customer assistance supervisor Aaron Sanford orchestrating a Black Friday practice run at a Best Buy store in Denver. These events help employees to understand their specific duties and responsibilities, the priority of those tasks, and the correct way to complete them. Some stores even have a huge floor plan that maps out exactly where each employee should be located on that busy day.[11] *Copyright © Judy Walgren*

track lubrication duties, so they didn't inform employees that lubricating tracks was part of their job.[12]

The second form of role perceptions refers to how well employees understand the *priority* of their various tasks and performance expectations. This is illustrated in the classic dilemma of prioritizing quantity versus quality, such as how many customers to serve in an hour (quantity) versus how well the employee should serve each customer (quality). It also refers to properly allocating time and resources to various tasks, such as how much time a manager should spend coaching employees each week versus spending time with suppliers and clients. The third form of role perceptions is understanding the *preferred behaviours* or procedures for accomplishing the assigned tasks. This refers to situations in which employees have the knowledge and skills to perform a particular task in more than one way. Employees with clear role perceptions know which of these methods is preferred or required by the organization.

Employees have accurate role perceptions when they *understand* the specific tasks assigned to them, the *priority* of those tasks, and the *preferred behaviours* or procedures for accomplishing the assigned tasks."

SITUATIONAL FACTORS

Employees' behaviour and performance also depend on the situation. This statement seems simple enough, but OB experts have been engaged in deep discussion about the meaning of "situation," including its dimensions and relevance to individual behaviour.[13] Most of the early writing focused on conditions beyond the employee's immediate control that constrain or facilitate behaviour and performance.[14] For example, employees who are motivated, skilled, and know their role obligations will nevertheless perform poorly if they lack time, budget, physical work facilities, and other situational conditions. Some situational constraints—such as consumer preferences and economic conditions—originate from the external environment and, consequently, are beyond the employee's and organization's control.

Along with situational constraints, situational factors also refer to the clarity and consistency of cues provided by the environment to employees regarding their role obligations and opportunities.[15] The importance of situational clarity and consistency is illustrated in workplace accidents. Let's say that you are motivated, able, and have a clear role obligation to act safely in your job. Even so, you are more likely to have an accident if the work setting does not clearly and consistently communicate a nearby electrical hazard or other safety risk. Your unsafe behaviour and accident are affected by the situation, namely the lack of signs and other indicators of the safety risk, or inconsistent placement of these warnings across the workplace.

TYPES OF INDIVIDUAL BEHAVIOUR

L02

The four elements of the MARS model—motivation, ability, role perceptions, and situational factors—affect all voluntary workplace behaviours and their performance outcomes. There are many varieties of individual behaviour, but most can be organized into the five categories described over the next few pages: task performance, organizational citizenship, counterproductive work behaviours, joining and staying with the organization, and maintaining work attendance (Exhibit 2.2).

TASK PERFORMANCE

Task performance refers to goal-directed behaviours under the individual's control that support organizational objectives. Task performance behaviours transform raw

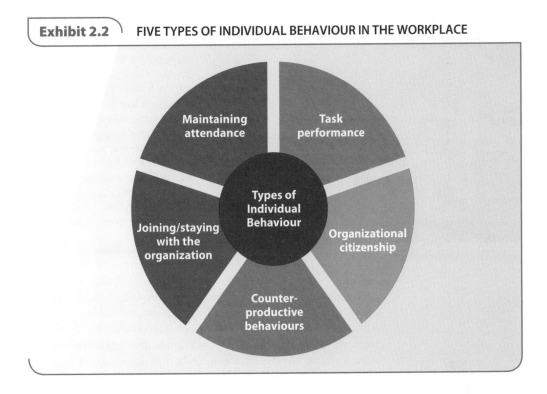

Exhibit 2.2   FIVE TYPES OF INDIVIDUAL BEHAVIOUR IN THE WORKPLACE

materials into goods and services or support and maintain these technical activities.[16] For example, foreign exchange traders at ScotiaBank make decisions and perform various tasks to buy and sell currencies. Most jobs consist of several tasks. For instance, foreign exchange traders at ScotiaBank must be able to identify profitable trades, work cooperatively with clients and co-workers in a stressful environment, assist in training new staff, and use specialized telecommunications technologies without error. More generally, tasks might involve working with data, people, or things; working alone or with other people; and degrees of influencing others.[17]

ORGANIZATIONAL CITIZENSHIP

organizational citizenship behaviours (OCBs) Various forms of cooperation and helpfulness to others that support the organization's social and psychological context.

Few companies could survive if employees performed only their formal job duties. They also need to engage in **organizational citizenship behaviours (OCBs)**—various forms of cooperation and helpfulness to others that support the organization's social and psychological context.[18] In other words, companies excel when employees go the "extra mile" beyond the required job duties. Organizational citizenship behaviours take many forms. Some are directed toward individuals, such as assisting co-workers with their work problems, adjusting your work schedule to accommodate co-workers, showing genuine courtesy toward co-workers, and sharing your work resources (supplies, technology, staff) with co-workers. Other OCBs represent cooperation and helpfulness toward the organization, such as supporting the company's public image, taking discretionary action to help the organization avoid potential problems, offering ideas beyond those required for your own job, attending voluntary functions that support the organization, and keeping up with new developments in the organization.[19]

COUNTERPRODUCTIVE WORK BEHAVIOURS

counterproductive work behaviours (CWBs) Voluntary behaviours that have the potential to directly or indirectly harm the organization.

Organizational behaviour is interested in all workplace behaviours, including those on the "dark side," collectively known as **counterproductive work behaviours (CWBs)**. CWBs are voluntary behaviours that have the potential to directly or indirectly harm the organization.[20] Some of the many types of CWBs include harassing co-workers, creating

Going the Extra Mile

Organizational citizenship behaviours are a significant source of competitive advantage to organizations. Consider, for example, the following recent incident at Procter & Gamble (P&G) in India. P&G was waiting for a shipment of materials needed to keep its production lines running. The shipment had arrived in customs, but due to heavy rains the government declared a holiday for all of its offices (including customs). Undeterred by the weather, a P&G plant engineer took the initiative of arranging transportation for a customs official from his house to the customs office and back to authorize clearance of the valuable materials. When the materials were cleared through customs, the engineer then made sure they were delivered to the plant the same day. By going beyond the call of duty, the engineer (with similar behaviour by the customs officer) was able to keep the production lines running.[21] *Dinodia Photo LLP*

unnecessary conflict, deviating from preferred work methods (e.g., shortcuts that risk work quality), being untruthful, stealing, sabotaging work, avoiding work obligations (tardiness), and wasting resources. CWBs are not minor concerns; research suggests that they can substantially undermine the organization's effectiveness. Furthermore, one recent study of Canadian and Chinese managers suggests that perceptions of counterproductive work behaviours are similar across cultures.[22]

JOINING AND STAYING WITH THE ORGANIZATION

Task performance, organizational citizenship, and the lack of counterproductive work behaviours are obviously important, but if qualified people don't join and stay with the organization, none of these performance-related behaviours would occur. Although staff shortages vary as the economy rises and falls, it seems that some employers never seem to get enough qualified staff. For instance, Alberta's two major cancer treatment centres have apparently delayed treatment for some patients due to a shortage of oncologists and other health professionals. Over the past three years, more than half of the nursing stations on northern Manitoba reserves operated with less than half of the required staff; two stations had to close temporarily because no qualified staff were available to operate the clinics. The Canadian hotel industry also suffers from a chronic lack of applicants. "I don't even run help-wanted ads anymore because there's no point. There's no one to hire," says the manager of a 120-room hotel in Alberta. The hotel, which pays thousands of dollars to bring in foreign help, sometimes lights up the 'no vacancy' sign when there are empty rooms and is offering a smaller restaurant menu because of the lack of staff.[23]

Companies survive and thrive not just by hiring people with talent or potential; they also need to ensure that these employees stay with the company. This threat is not trivial: even during the recent recession half of the employees polled in Canada and a dozen other countries said they would consider working elsewhere in a comparable job or were actively looking for another job.[24] Companies with high turnover suffer because of the high cost of replacing people who leave. More important, as was mentioned in the previous chapter, much of an organization's intellectual capital is the knowledge carried around in employees' heads. When people leave, some of this vital knowledge is lost, often resulting in lower productivity, poorer customer service, and so forth. Some employers attract job applicants and minimize turnover by nurturing an enjoyable work environment. For example, the opening vignette to this chapter described how Corus Entertainment employees enjoy the company's new headquarters at Sugar Beach on Toronto's waterfront. Career opportunities, extensive training, a fun culture, and high involvement also act as magnets to keep employees with the company.

MAINTAINING WORK ATTENDANCE

Along with attracting and retaining employees, organizations need everyone to show up for work at scheduled times. Statistics Canada reports that Canadian employees miss an average of almost 10 days of scheduled work each year, which is up from an average of 8.1 days lost a decade ago and is much higher than the average of 5 days absence in the United States and United Kingdom. However, Canadian absenteeism rates are modest compared to chronic absenteeism in some occupations and cultures. For instance, one study reported that more than 25 percent of primary and secondary school teachers in India, Uganda, and Indonesia are absent from work on any given work day.[25]

Most employees blame the situation for their absenteeism. They often point to the snowstorm, transit strike, flu epidemic, and family demands (e.g., children or parents require care). Indeed, Statistics Canada reports that employees in families with preschool children have four times as many days of absenteeism as those without any children. Also, a recent pandemic flu across Canada was responsible for one million cases of sick leave.[26] Even with these situational obstacles, some people still show up for work because of their strong motivation to attend work. In contrast, employees who experience job dissatisfaction or work-related stress are more likely to be absent or late for work because taking time off is a way to temporarily withdraw from stressful or dissatisfying conditions. Absenteeism is also higher in organizations with generous sick leave because this benefit minimizes the financial loss of taking time away from work. Some employees have poor attendance records because of their values and personality.[27] Studies have also found that absenteeism is higher in teams with strong absence norms, meaning that team members tolerate and even expect co-workers to take time off.[28]

presenteeism Attending scheduled work when one's capacity to perform is significantly diminished by illness or other factors.

Presenteeism   Along with attending work when expected, maintaining work attendance includes staying away from scheduled work when attendance would be dysfunctional for the individual and organization. In fact, OB experts warn that **presenteeism**—attending work when one's capacity to work is significantly diminished by illness, fatigue, personal problems, or other factors—may be more serious than being absent when capable of working.[29] Employees who attend work when they are unwell or unfit may worsen their own condition and increase the health risk of co-workers. These employees are also usually less productive and may reduce the productivity of co-workers.

Presenteeism is more common among employees with low job security (such as new and temporary staff), who lack sick leave pay or similar financial buffers, and whose absence would immediately affect many people (i.e., high centrality). Company or team norms about absenteeism also account for presenteeism. Personality also plays a role; some people possess traits that motivate them to show up for work when others would gladly recover at home. Personality is a widely cited predictor of most forms of individual behaviour. It is also the most stable personal characteristic, so we introduce this topic next.

PERSONALITY IN ORGANIZATIONS

L03

While applying for several jobs in the Canadian publishing industry, Christina was surprised that three of the positions required applicants to complete a personality test. "One page is a list of characteristics—sentimental, adventurous, attractive, compelling, helpful, etc.—and you check off the ones that best describe what others expect of you," Christina recalls of one personality test. "The second page is the same list, but you check off the ones that you think truly describe you." Christina didn't hear back from the first company after completing its personality test, so for the second company she completed the personality test "according to a sales personality" because that job was in sales. When writing a personality test at the third firm, she answered questions the way she thought someone would if they were "a good person, but honest" about what they thought. None of the applications resulted in a job offer, leaving Christina wondering what personality profile these companies were seeking and whether her strategy of guessing the best answer on these personality tests was a good idea.[30]

Personality is an important individual characteristic, which explains why many companies try to estimate the personality traits of job applicants and employees. Most of us also think about personality every day in our dealings with others. We use these traits (talkative, risk-oriented, thoughtful, etc.) to simplify our perception of each person and to predict their future behaviour. **Personality** is the relatively enduring pattern of thoughts, emotions, and behaviours that characterize a person, along with the psychological processes behind those characteristics.[31] It is, in essence, the bundle of characteristics that make us similar to or different from other people. We estimate an individual's personality by what they say and do, and we infer the person's internal states—including thoughts and emotions—from these observable behaviours.

A basic premise of personality theory is that people have inherent characteristics or traits that can be identified by the consistency or stability of their behaviour across time and situations.[32] For example, you probably have some friends who are more talkative than others. You might know some people who like to take risks and others who are risk-averse. This behaviour tendency is a key feature of personality theory because it attributes a person's behaviour to something within her or him—the individual's personality—rather than to purely environmental influences.

personality The relatively enduring pattern of thoughts, emotions, and behaviours that characterize a person, along with the psychological processes behind those characteristics.

> "A basic premise of personality theory is that people have inherent characteristics or traits that can be identified by the consistency or stability of their behaviour across time and situations."

Of course, people do not act the same way in all situations; in fact, such consistency would be considered abnormal because it indicates a person's insensitivity to social norms, reward systems, and other external conditions.[33] People vary their behaviour to suit the situation, even if the behaviour is at odds with their personality. For example, talkative people remain relatively quiet in a library where "no talking" rules are explicit and strictly enforced. However, personality differences are still apparent in these situations because talkative people tend to do more talking in libraries relative to how much other people talk in libraries.

People typically exhibit a wide range of behaviours, yet within that variety are discernible patterns that we refer to as *personality traits*. Traits are broad concepts that allow us to label and understand individual differences. Furthermore, traits predict an individual's behaviour far into the future. For example, studies report that an individual's personality in childhood predicts various behaviours and outcomes in adulthood, including educational attainment, employment success, marital relationships, illegal activities, and health-risk behaviours.[34]

PERSONALITY DETERMINANTS: NATURE VERSUS NURTURE

What determines an individual's personality? Most experts now agree that personality is shaped by both nature and nurture, although the relative importance of each continues to be debated and studied. *Nature* refers to our genetic or hereditary origins—the genes that we inherit from our parents. Studies of identical twins, particularly those separated at birth, reveal that heredity has a very large effect on personality; up to 50 percent of variation in behaviour and 30 percent of temperament preferences can be attributed to a person's genetic characteristics.[35] In other words, genetic code not only determines our eye colour, skin tone, and physical shape; it also significantly affects our attitudes, decisions, and behaviour.

Some similarities of twins raised apart are surreal. Consider Jim Springer and Jim Lewis, twins who were separated when only four weeks old and didn't meet each other until age 39. In spite of being raised in different families and communities in Ohio, the "Jim twins" held similar jobs, smoked the same type of cigarettes, drove the same make and colour of car, spent their vacations on the same Florida beach, had the same woodworking hobby, gave their first sons almost identical names, and had been married twice. Both their first and second wives also had the same first names![36]

Although personality is heavily influenced by heredity, it is also affected by *nurture*—the person's socialization, life experiences, and other forms of interaction with the environment. An individual's personality development and change occurs mainly when people are young; personality stabilizes by the time people reach 30 years of age, although some sources say personality development continues to occur through to age 50.[37]

The main explanation of why personality becomes more stable over time is that we form a clearer and more rigid self-concept as we get older. This increasing clarity of "who we are" serves as an anchor for our behaviour because the executive function—the part of the brain that manages goal-directed behaviour—tries to keep our behaviour consistent with our self-concept.[38] As self-concept becomes clearer and more stable with age, behaviour and personality therefore also become more stable and consistent. We discuss self-concept in more detail in the next chapter. The main point here is that personality is not completely determined by heredity; life experiences, particularly early in life, also shape each individual's personality traits.

FIVE-FACTOR MODEL OF PERSONALITY

five-factor model (FFM) The five abstract dimensions representing most personality traits: conscientiousness, agreeableness, neuroticism, openness to experience, and extroversion.

One of the most important elements of personality theory is that people possess specific personality traits. Traits such as sociable, anxious, cautious, and talkative represent clusters of thoughts, feelings, and behaviours that allow us to identify, differentiate, and understand people.[39] The most widely respected model of personality traits is the **five-factor model (FFM)**, also known as the "Big Five" personality dimensions. Several decades ago, personality experts identified more than 17,000 words that describe an individual's personality. These words were distilled down to five abstract personality dimensions. Similar results were found in studies of different languages, suggesting that the five-factor model is fairly robust across cultures.[40] These "Big Five" dimensions, represented by the handy acronym *CANOE*, are outlined in Exhibit 2.3 and described below.

Exhibit 2.3   FIVE-FACTOR MODEL'S "BIG FIVE" PERSONALITY DIMENSIONS

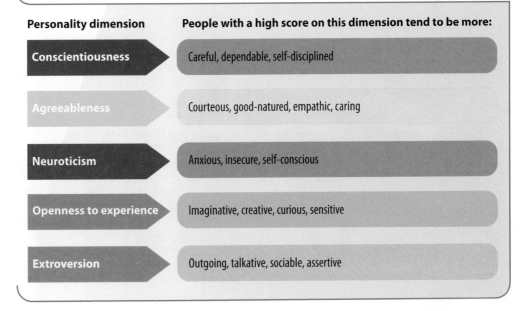

Personality dimension	People with a high score on this dimension tend to be more:
Conscientiousness	Careful, dependable, self-disciplined
Agreeableness	Courteous, good-natured, empathic, caring
Neuroticism	Anxious, insecure, self-conscious
Openness to experience	Imaginative, creative, curious, sensitive
Extroversion	Outgoing, talkative, sociable, assertive

conscientiousness
A personality dimension describing people who are careful, dependable, and self-disciplined.

neuroticism A personality dimension describing people with high levels of anxiety, hostility, depression, and self-consciousness.

extroversion A personality dimension describing people who are outgoing, talkative, sociable, and assertive.

- *Conscientiousness.* **Conscientiousness** characterizes people who are careful, industrious, reliable, goal-focused, achievement striving, dependable, organized, thorough, persistent, and self-disciplined. People with low conscientiousness tend to be careless, less thorough, more disorganized, and irresponsible.

- *Agreeableness.* This dimension includes the traits of being courteous, good-natured, empathic, and caring. Some scholars prefer the label "friendly compliance" for this dimension, with its opposite being "hostile noncompliance." People with low agreeableness tend to be uncooperative, short-tempered, and irritable.

- *Neuroticism.* **Neuroticism** characterizes people with high levels of anxiety, hostility, depression, and self-consciousness. In contrast, people with low neuroticism (high emotional stability) are poised, secure, and calm.

- *Openness to experience.* This dimension is the most complex and has the least agreement among scholars. It generally refers to the extent to which people are imaginative, creative, curious, and aesthetically sensitive. Those who score low on this dimension tend to be more resistant to change, less open to new ideas, and more conventional and fixed in their ways.

- *Extroversion.* **Extroversion** characterizes people who are outgoing, talkative, sociable, and assertive. The opposite is *introversion,* which characterizes those who are quiet, shy, and cautious. Extroverts get their energy from the outer world (people and things around them), whereas introverts get their energy from the internal world, such as personal reflection on concepts and ideas. Introverts do not necessarily lack social skills. Rather, they are more inclined to direct their interests to ideas than to social events. Introverts feel quite comfortable being alone, whereas extroverts do not.

These five personality dimensions influence employee motivation and role clarity in various ways.[41] Some experts suggest that agreeableness, conscientiousness, and emotional stability (low neuroticism) cluster around the broad characteristic of "getting along." People with high agreeableness are more sensitive to others (more empathy, less conflict), those with high conscientiousness are more dependable, and those with high emotional stability are more upbeat. Some writers suggest that extroversion also relates to getting along because extroverts are more motivated to interact with others. Openness to experience, extroversion, conscientiousness, and emotional stability cluster around the broad characteristic of "getting ahead." Those with high openness to experience are more eager to try out new ideas, extroverts are more ambitious (assertive), those with high conscientiousness are more achievement-oriented, and those with high emotional stability are more confident in their ability to perform well.

Scouting for Team Players Who Get Ahead, Not Just Get Along

Australian Rules Football (AFL) is to Australians what the National Hockey League (NHL) is to Canadians . . . a national passion. And just like in the NHL, scouting for new AFL team members is intensive and comprehensive. Gerard Ferrara, a registered psychologist, assists one of the leading AFL clubs to find the best players by assessing their personality characteristics. Although athletic capabilities are critical, Ferrara indicates that certain personality characteristics can lead to competitive advantage on the field. According to Ferrara, these traits include "persistence, strong attention to detail, high ambition, low to average concern for others, and an ability to tolerate a great deal of stress." One idea that surprises many people is that having a high concern for others could undermine the athlete's performance. "It is one thing to get along with and respect your teammates and other players, but it is another thing when a player strives too hard to be popular," Ferrara explains.[42]
© *Robert Colburn*

Studies report fairly strong associations between personality and several workplace behaviours and outcomes, even when employee ability and other factors are taken into account. Conscientiousness and emotional stability (low neuroticism) stand out as the personality traits that best predict individual performance in almost every job group.[43] Both are motivational components of personality because they energize a willingness to fulfill work obligations within established rules (conscientiousness) and to allocate resources to accomplish those tasks (emotional stability). Various studies have reported that conscientious employees set higher personal goals for themselves, are more motivated, and have higher performance expectations than do employees with low levels of conscientiousness. They also tend to have higher levels of organizational citizenship and work better in organizations that give employees more freedom than is found in traditional command-and-control workplaces.[44]

The other three personality dimensions predict more specific types of employee behaviour and performance.[45] Extroversion is associated with performance in sales and management jobs, where employees must interact with and influence people. Agreeableness is associated with performance in jobs where employees are expected to be cooperative and helpful, such as working in teams, customer relations, and other conflict-handling situations. People high on the openness-to-experience personality dimension tend to be more creative and adaptable to change. Finally, personality influences employee well-being in various ways.[46] For example, one recent study found that senior Canadians with higher conscientiousness enjoyed a longer life span. Generally, personality influences a person's general emotional reactions to her or his job, how well the person copes with stress, and what type of career path makes that person happiest.

JUNGIAN PERSONALITY THEORY AND THE MYERS-BRIGGS TYPE INDICATOR

> **Myers-Briggs Type Indicator (MBTI)** An instrument designed to measure the elements of Jungian personality theory, particularly preferences regarding perceiving and judging information.

The five-factor model of personality is the most respected and supported in research, but it is not the most popular in practice. That distinction goes to Jungian personality theory, which is measured through the **Myers-Briggs Type Indicator (MBTI)** (see Exhibit 2.4). Nearly a century ago, Swiss psychiatrist Carl Jung proposed that personality is primarily represented by the individual's preferences regarding perceiving and judging information.[47] Jung explained that perceiving, which involves how people prefer to gather information or perceive the world around them, occurs through two competing orientations: *sensing (S)* and *intuition (N)*. Sensing involves perceiving information directly through the five senses; it relies on an organized structure to acquire factual and preferably quantitative details. Intuition, on the other hand, relies more on insight and subjective experience to see relationships among variables. Sensing types focus on the here and now, whereas intuitive types focus more on future possibilities.

Jung also proposed that judging—how people process information or make decisions based on what they have perceived—consists of two competing processes: *thinking (T)* and *feeling (F)*. People with a thinking orientation rely on rational cause-effect logic and systematic data collection to make decisions. Those with a strong feeling orientation, on the other hand, rely on their emotional responses to the options presented, as well as to how those choices affect others. Jung noted that along with differing in the four core processes of sensing, intuition, thinking, and feeling, people also differ in their degrees of extroversion-introversion, which was introduced earlier as one of the Big Five personality traits.

Along with measuring the personality traits identified by Jung, the MBTI measures Jung's broader categories of *perceiving* and *judging*, which they say represents a person's attitude toward the external world. People with a perceiving orientation are open, curious, and flexible; prefer to adapt spontaneously to events as they unfold; and prefer to keep their options open. Judging types prefer order and structure and want to resolve problems quickly.

The MBTI is one of the most widely used personality tests in work settings as well as in career counselling and executive coaching.[48] For example, many staff at Southwest Airlines post their Myers-Briggs Type Indicator (MBTI) results in their offices. "You can walk by and see someone's four-letter [MBTI type] posted up in their cube," says Southwest's director of leadership development. Southwest began using the MBTI a

Exhibit 2.4   **JUNGIAN AND MYERS-BRIGGS TYPE INDICATOR TYPES**[49]

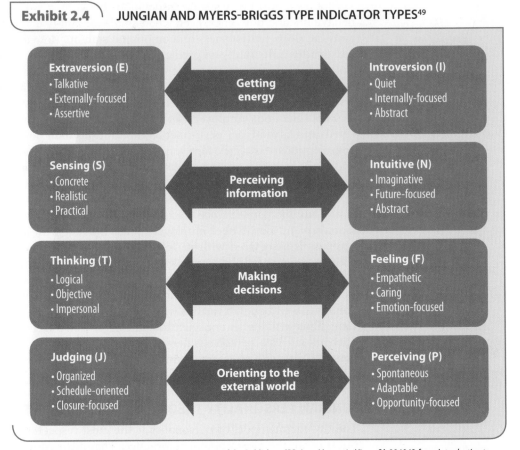

Source: Modified and reproduced by special permission of the Publisher, CPP, Inc., Mountain View, CA 994043 from *Introduction to Type and Careers* by Allen L. Hammer. Copyright 1993 by CPP, Inc. All rights reserved. Further reproduction is prohibited without the Publisher's written consent.

decade ago to help staff understand and respect co-workers' different personalities and thinking styles. "Behaviours that might have once caused misunderstanding and frustration now are viewed through a different filter," suggests the Southwest Airlines manager.[50]

In spite of its popularity, the MBTI and Jung's psychological types model have received uneven support.[51] On the one hand, MBTI seems to improve self-awareness for career development and mutual understanding. It also does a reasonably good job of representing Jung's psychological types. On the other hand, the MBTI poorly predicts job performance and is generally not recommended for employment selection or promotion decisions. For example, although one study found that intuitive types are more common in higher level than lower level management, other research has found no relationship between any MBTI types and effective leadership. One recent large-scale study also reported that the MBTI scores of team members is not useful for predicting the team's development. Finally, the MBTI overlaps with four of the five dimensions of the five-factor personality model, yet it does so less satisfactorily than existing Big Five personality measures.[52]

CAVEATS ABOUT PERSONALITY TESTING IN ORGANIZATIONS

Personality helps us to understand and predict workplace behaviour, but we need to urge moderation when applying this concept.[53] One concern is that although specific personality traits predict specific types of performance fairly well, personality is a relatively remote indicator of behaviour compared to other employment tests, such as work samples and past performance. Thus, personality test results could reject job applicants who would have performed well. A second concern is that many practitioners and personality experts tend to assume that more is better for each trait. They suggest, for instance, that high conscientiousness employees are better than low conscientiousness employees. However, the ideal range is probably closer to the middle than the extremes. For example, employees with high conscientiousness try to be thorough, which makes it difficult for them to give up quality for quantity. At extreme levels, this thoroughness becomes perfectionism, which can stifle rather than enhance job performance.[54]

A third worry is that too many companies have become enamoured with personality tests without recognizing their obvious limitations. Most personality tests are self-report scales, so applicants might fake their answers. Applicants might try to guess the "correct" answer on these tests, which Christina did in the opening story to this section. Consequently, the test scores might not represent the individual's personality or anything else meaningful because test takers often don't know what personality traits the company is looking for and may not know which statements are relevant to each trait.

A final concern is that personality testing might not convey a favourable image of the company. For example, the British operations of PricewaterhouseCoopers (PwC) required that applicants complete an online personality test early in the selection process. The accounting firm learned that the test discouraged female applicants from applying because the process was impersonal and the test could be faked. "Our personality test was seen to alienate women and so we had to respond to that," says PwC's head of diversity.[55] Overall, we need to understand personality in the workplace but also to be cautious about measuring and applying it too precisely and too often.

VALUES IN THE WORKPLACE

LO4

Growing up in Saskatchewan, Colleen Abdoulah developed a strong set of personal values from her parents. For example, her father emphasized that "No matter how much you earn, you're no better than anyone and they are no better than you," recalls Abdoulah. She also learned the importance of having the courage to do the right thing, and of forming relationships with people so they feel a sense of ownership. Abdoulah not only practises these values every day, she has instilled them at Wide Open West, the Denver-based Internet, cable, and phone provider where she is CEO to 1,300 employees. "[Our employees] display the courage to do the right thing, serve each other and our customers with humility, and celebrate our learnings and success with grace," says Abdoulah. "Anyone can set values, but we have operationalized our values so that they affect everything we do every day."[56]

Colleen Abdoulah and other successful people often refer to their personal values and the critical events that formed those values earlier in life. *Values,* a concept that we introduced in Chapter 1, are stable, evaluative beliefs that guide our preferences for outcomes or courses of action in a variety of situations.[57] They are perceptions about what is good or bad, right or wrong. Values tell us to what we "ought" to do. They serve as a moral compass that directs our motivation and, potentially, our decisions and actions.

People arrange values into a hierarchy of preferences, called a *value system.* Some individuals value new challenges more than they value conformity. Others value generosity more than frugality. Each person's unique value system is developed and reinforced through socialization from parents, religious institutions, friends, personal experiences, and the society in which he or she lives. As such, a person's hierarchy of values is stable and long-lasting. For example, one study found that value systems of a sample of adolescents were remarkably similar 20 years later when they were adults.[58]

Notice that our description of values has focused on individuals, whereas executives often describe values as though they belong to the organization. In reality, values exist only within individuals—we call them *personal values.* However, groups of people might hold the same or similar values, so we tend to ascribe these *shared values* to the team, department, organization, profession, or entire society. The values shared by people throughout an organization *(organizational values)* receive fuller discussion in Chapter 14 because they are a key part of corporate culture. The values shared across a society *(cultural values)* receive attention later in this chapter.

Values and personality traits are related to each other, but the two concepts differ in a few ways.[59] The most noticeable distinction is that values are evaluative—they tell us what we *ought* to do—whereas personality traits describe what we naturally *tend* to do. A second distinction is that personality traits have minimal conflict with each other (you can have high agreeableness and high introversion, for example), whereas some values are opposed to other values. For example, someone who values excitement and challenge would have difficulty also valuing stability and moderation. Third, although personality and values are both partly determined by heredity, values are influenced more by socialization whereas personality traits are more innate.

TYPES OF VALUES

Values come in many forms, and experts on this topic have devoted considerable attention to organizing them into clusters. Several decades ago, social psychologist Milton Rokeach developed two lists of values, distinguishing means (instrumental values) from end goals (terminal values). Although Rokeach's lists are still mentioned in some organizational behaviour sources, they were replaced by another model almost two decades ago. The instrumental-terminal values distinction was neither accurate nor useful, and it overlooks values that are now included in the current dominant model.

Today, the dominant model of personal values is the one developed and tested by social psychologist Shalom Schwartz and his colleagues.[60] Schwartz's list of 57 values builds on Rokeach's earlier work but does not distinguish instrumental from terminal values. Instead, research has found that human values are organized into the circular model (circumplex) shown in Exhibit 2.5.[61] This model clusters the 57 specific values into 10 broad values categories: universalism, benevolence, tradition, conformity, security, power, achievement, hedonism, stimulation, and self-direction. For example, conformity includes four specific values: politeness, honouring parents, self-discipline, and obedience.

These 10 broad values categories are further clustered into four quadrants. One quadrant, called *openness to change*, refers to the extent to which a person is motivated to pursue innovative ways. This quadrant includes the value categories of self-direction (creativity, independent thought), stimulation (excitement and challenge), and hedonism (pursuit of pleasure, enjoyment, gratification of desires). The opposing quadrant is *conservation*, which is the extent to which a person is motivated to preserve the status quo. The conservation quadrant includes the value categories of conformity (adherence to social norms and expectations), security (safety and stability), and tradition (moderation and preservation of the status quo).

The third quadrant in Schwartz's circumplex model, called *self-enhancement*, refers to how much a person is motivated by self-interest. This quadrant includes the value categories of achievement (pursuit of personal success), power (dominance over others), and hedonism (a values category shared with openness to change). The opposite of self-enhancement is *self-transcendence*, which refers to motivation to promote the welfare of others and nature. Self-transcendence includes the value categories of benevolence (concern for others in one's life) and universalism (concern for the welfare of all people and nature).

VALUES AND INDIVIDUAL BEHAVIOUR

Personal values guide our decisions and actions to some extent, but this connection isn't always as strong as most people believe. Habitual behaviour tends to be consistent with our values, but our everyday conscious decisions and actions apply our values much less consistently. The main reason for the "disconnect" between personal values and individual behaviour is that values are abstract concepts, so their relevance to specific situations is not obvious much of the time.

Three conditions strengthen the linkage between personal values and behaviour.[62] First, we tend to apply our values only when we can think of specific reasons for doing so. In other words, we need logical reasons for applying a specific value in a specific situation. Second, we tend to apply our values when the situation allows or encourages us to do so. Work environments influence our behaviour, at least in the short term, so they necessarily encourage or discourage values-consistent behaviour. Third, we are more likely to apply values when we actively think about them. This occurs naturally

Exhibit 2.5   SCHWARTZ'S VALUES CIRCUMPLEX

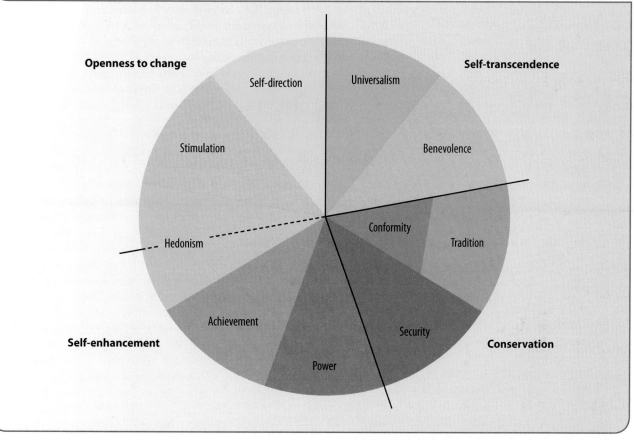

Source: S. H. Schwartz, "Universals in the Content and Structure of Values: Theoretical Advances and Empirical Tests in 20 Countries," *Advances in Experimental Social Psychology* 25 (1992), pp. 1–65; S. H. Schwartz and G. Sagie, "Value Consensus and Importance: A Cross-National Study," *Journal of Cross-Cultural Psychology* 31 (July 2000), pp. 465–497.

when confronted with situations that obviously violate our values. For example, you become aware that you value security when faced with a risky decision.

People also become more mindful of their values—and consequently act consistently with those values—when they are literally reminded of them by others. This effect was apparent in the following study:[63] Students were given a math test and paid for each correct answer. One group submitted their results to the experimenter for scoring, so they couldn't lie about their results. A second group could lie because they scored the test themselves and told the experimenter their test score. A third group was similar to the second (they scored their own test), but their test included the following statement and were required to sign their name to that statement: "I understand that this short survey falls under (the university's) honour system." (The university had no such honour system.) The researchers estimated that some students cheated when they scored their own test without the "honour system" statement, whereas no one given the "honour system" form lied about their results. Similar results occurred when, instead of an honour statement, the third group was first asked to recall the Ten Commandments. The message here is that people are more likely to apply their values (honesty, in this case) when explicitly reminded of those values.

VALUES CONGRUENCE

Values tell us what is right or wrong and what we ought to do. This evaluative characteristic affects how comfortable we are with specific organizations and individuals. The key concept here is *values congruence*, which refers to how similar a person's values hierarchy is to the values hierarchy of the organization, a co-worker, or another source of comparison. *Person-organization values congruence* occurs when a person's values are similar to the organization's dominant values. This form of values congruence increases (to some extent) the chance that employees will make decisions and act in ways consistent with organizational expectations. It also leads to higher job satisfaction, loyalty, and organizational citizenship as well as lower stress and turnover. "The most difficult but rewarding accomplishment in any career is 'living true' to your values and finding companies where you can contribute at the highest level while being your authentic self," says an executive at Japanese biopharmaceutical company Eisai Co. Ltd.[64]

Are organizations most successful when they have the highest levels of person-organization values congruence? Not at all! While a comfortable degree of values congruence is necessary for the reasons just noted, organizations also benefit from some level of incongruence. Employees with diverse values offer different perspectives, which potentially lead to better decision making. Also, too much congruence can create a "corporate cult" that potentially undermines creativity, organizational flexibility, and business ethics.

A second type of values congruence involves how consistent the values apparent in our actions (enacted values) are with what we say we believe in (espoused values). This *espoused-enacted values congruence* is especially important for people in leadership positions because any obvious gap between espoused and enacted values undermines their perceived integrity, a critical feature of effective leaders. One global survey reported recently that 55 percent of employees believe senior management behaves consistently with the company's core values.[65] Some companies try to

---

OB BY THE NUMBERS

Values Congruence on the Job[67]

94%
of 1,943 MBA students in Canada, the U.S., and U.K. believe conflicts between work obligations and their personal values would be stressful

65%
of 1,508 Canadian employees surveyed said there is a gap between their employer's values and their own personal values

83%
of 1,943 MBA students in Canada, the U.S., and U.K. believe their work obligations and personal values will sometimes conflict

36%
of employees at the *bottom* 10 Canadian organizations surveyed for the "Best Employers" award say their personal values were the same as those of their organization

83%
of employees at the *top* 10 Canadian "Best Employers" say their personal values were the same as those of their organization

Note: All survey results were conducted in 2007 and 2008. The Canadian best employer results were similar to a larger study by the same firm of 900 companies worldwide.

In Search of Congruent Values

Chad Hunt received two appealing job offers after graduating from university, one from a manufacturer of injection moulding equipment and the other from an automobile manufacturer. The car company offered a higher salary, but Hunt was also weighing these firms on another important factor. "I'm part of a generation that grew up knowing we had to reduce, reuse and recycle. So, it's important for me to work for a company that's also environmentally conscious," he says. Environmentalism is such an important part of Hunt's value system that he chose the offer from Husky Injection Molding Systems Ltd., of Bolton, Ontario, north of Toronto. Husky's environmental initiatives include an active recycling program, pesticide-free landscaping, and a head office that uses natural lighting. For Chad Hunt, the difference in starting salaries paled against the issue of values congruence. "It's not even an option," he explains. "I need to work for a company that shares my values, and that includes caring about our impact on the environment."[66] *Image courtesy of Husky Injection Molding Systems*

maintain high levels of espoused-enacted values congruence by surveying subordinates and peers about whether the manager's decisions and actions are consistent with the company's espoused values.

A third category, *organization-community values congruence,* refers to the similarity of an organization's dominant values with the prevailing values of the community or society in which it conducts business.[68] For example, an organization headquartered in one country that tries to impose its value system on employees and other stakeholders located in another culture may experience higher employee turnover and have more difficult relations with the communities in which the company operates. Thus, globalization calls for a delicate balancing act: Companies depend on shared values to maintain consistent standards and behaviours, yet they need to operate within the values of different cultures around the world.

ETHICAL VALUES AND BEHAVIOUR

L05

When 2,100 Canadians were recently asked to identify the most important attribute of a leader of this country, 48 percent chose honesty. The other attributes—intelligence, decisiveness, and compassion—were far less frequently mentioned. Similarly, employees typically choose honesty/ethics as the most important characteristic of effective corporate leaders.[69] *Ethics* refers to the study of moral principles or values that determine whether actions are right or wrong and outcomes are good or bad. People rely on their ethical values to determine "the right thing to do." The importance of ethical corporate conduct is almost constantly in the news, yet there doesn't seem to be any noticeable decline in wrongdoing. In one recent large-scale survey, almost half of the employees said they had witnessed misconduct on the job, such as abuse of company resources, abusive behaviour, lying to employees, e-mail or Internet abuse, conflicts of interest, discrimination, and lying to outside stakeholders.[70]

Canada is recognized around the world for its high ethical standards—it ranks eighth lowest on the global corruption index, for example[71]—yet it has its share of scandals involving unethical corporate behaviour. Consider the following small sample of very recent cases (some of which are still being investigated): (1) Air Canada and several other airlines have been found guilty by European regulators for participating for several years in a cartel that fixed the prices of cargo in Europe and elsewhere. (2) A forestry company in British Columbia housed workers in a remote camp that allegedly had no drinking water or toilets, offered subsistence-level food for breakfast and dinner, and failed to pay staff for their work. (3) Three Quebec construction companies have been charged and several others are still under investigation for allegedly rigging their bids for government contracts. (4) The Canadian mining industry's own investigation (leaked to the public) reported that Canadian mining firms have been implicated in nearly two-thirds of the global high profile environmental and human rights violations in that industry over the past decade. Canada is home to many of the world's mining companies, but some violations are so severe that governments have banned their pension plans from investing in these Canadian firms.[72]

THREE ETHICAL PRINCIPLES

To better understand business ethics, we need to consider three distinct types of ethical principles: utilitarianism, individual rights, and distributive justice.[73] While your personal values might sway you more towards one principle than the others, all three should be actively considered to put important ethical issues to the test.

- *Utilitarianism.* This principle advises us to seek the greatest good for the greatest number of people. In other words, we should choose the option that provides the highest degree of satisfaction to those affected. This is sometimes known as a *consequential principle* because it focuses on the consequences of our actions, not on how we achieve those consequences. One problem with utilitarianism is that it is

Mississauga Tied Up in Ethical Misconduct

The City of Mississauga recently faced two embarrassing lapses in ethical conduct. The first lapse was that employees in the city's Transportation and Works Department engaged in severe hazing, apparently over a few years. Some staff received "birthday spankings" with punches to the face or groin; others were tied up with duct tape and pelted with water balloons or sent through a car wash. One employee (who took extended stress leave) claimed he notified management about these incidents over this time, but no action was taken. When the employee filed a formal complaint, the city launched an independent investigation that confirmed his reports. The second ethical blunder occurred when, in spite of the formal complaint and investigation details, management concluded the events were "in the nature of horse play" and merely counselled the department manager (who supported the hazing) and staff about respectful behaviour. The city backtracked, however, after a video broadcast across Canada showing one hazing incident resulted in a "media storm and public outrage." The city quickly notified provincial labour officials and city police, and eventually suspended two supervisors without pay for these incidents. Alex Juani (shown in the photo) is the City of Mississauga employee who blew the whistle on harassment and hazing in the city's Works and Transit departments.[74] *Fred Loek/Mississauga.com*

almost impossible to evaluate the benefits or costs of many decisions, particularly when many stakeholders have wide-ranging needs and values. Another problem is that most of us are uncomfortable engaging in behaviours that seem unethical even though they attain results that are ethical.

- *Individual rights.* This principle reflects the belief that everyone has entitlements that let her or him act in a certain way. Some of the most widely cited rights are freedom of movement, physical security, freedom of speech, fair trial, and freedom from torture. The individual rights principle includes more than legal rights; it also includes human rights that everyone is granted as a moral norm of society. One problem with individual rights is that certain individual rights may conflict with others. Shareholders' rights to be informed about corporate activities may ultimately conflict with an executive's right to privacy, for example.

- *Distributive justice.* This principle suggests that people who are similar to each other should receive similar benefits and burdens; those who are dissimilar should receive different benefits and burdens in proportion to their dissimilarity. For example, we expect that two employees who contribute equally in their work should receive similar rewards, whereas those who make a lesser contribution should receive less. A variation of the distributive justice principle says that inequalities are acceptable when they benefit the least well off in society. Thus, employees in risky jobs should be paid more if their work benefits others who are less well off. One problem with the distributive justice principle is that it is difficult to agree on who is "similar" and what factors are "relevant."

MORAL INTENSITY, ETHICAL SENSITIVITY, AND SITUATIONAL INFLUENCES

Along with ethical principles and their underlying values, four other factors influence ethical conduct in the workplace: the moral intensity of the issue, the individual's ethical sensitivity, situational factors, and mindfulness.[75] **Moral intensity** is the degree to which an issue demands the application of ethical principles. Decisions with high moral intensity have greater importance, so the decision maker needs to more carefully apply ethical principles to resolve it. Several factors influence the moral intensity of an issue, including those listed in Exhibit 2.6. Keep in mind that this list represents the factors people tend to think about; some of them might not be considered morally acceptable when people are formally making ethical decisions.[76]

moral intensity The degree to which an issue demands the application of ethical principles.

Exhibit 2.6   FACTORS INFLUENCING PERCEIVED MORAL INTENSITY

Moral Intensity Factor	Moral Intensity Question	Moral Intensity Is Higher When:
Magnitude of consequences	How much harm or benefit will occur to others as a result of this action?	The harm or benefit is larger.
Social consensus	How many other people agree that this action is ethically good or bad?	Many people agree.
Probability of effect	(a) What is the chance that this action will occur?	The probability is higher.
	(b) What is the chance that this action will cause good or bad consequences?	
Temporal immediacy	How long after the action will the consequences occur?	The time delay is shorter.
Proximity	How socially, culturally, psychologically, and/or physically close to me are the people affected by this decision?	Those affected are close rather than distant.
Concentration of effect	(a) How many people are affected by this action?	Many people are affected.
	(b) Are the people affected by this action easily identifiable as a group?	Those affected are easily identifiable as a group.

Note: These are factors people tend to ask themselves about when determining the moral intensity of an issue. Whether some of these questions should be relevant is itself an ethical question.

Source: Based on information in T. J. Jones, "Ethical Decision Making by Individuals in Organizations: An Issue Contingent Model," *Academy of Management Review* 16 (1991), pp. 366–395.

---

ethical sensitivity A personal characteristic that enables people to recognize the presence of an ethical issue and determine its relative importance.

Even if an issue has high moral intensity, some employees might not recognize its ethical importance because they have low **ethical sensitivity**. Ethical sensitivity is a personal characteristic that enables people to recognize the presence of an ethical issue and determine its relative importance.[77] Ethically sensitive people are not necessarily more ethical. Rather, they are more likely to sense whether an issue requires ethical consideration; that is, they can more accurately estimate the moral intensity of the issue. Ethically sensitive people tend to have higher empathy. They also have more information about the specific situation. For example, accountants would be more ethically sensitive regarding the appropriateness of specific accounting procedures than would someone who has not received training in this profession.

The third important factor explaining why good people engage in unethical decisions and behaviour is the situation in which the conduct occurs. Employees say they regularly experience pressure from top management that motivates them to lie to customers, breach regulations, or otherwise act unethically. According to a global survey of managers and human resource managers, the leading cause of unethical corporate behaviour is pressure from top management or the board to meet unrealistic deadlines and business objectives.[78] Situational factors do not justify unethical conduct. Rather, we need to be aware of these factors so that organizations can reduce their influence in the future.

A final reason why people engage in unethical conduct is that they engage in mindless behaviour. In other words, they don't consciously think about whether their actions might be unethical.[79] Recall our discussion earlier in this chapter that people abide by their values only when they think about them. Yet, research suggests that people engage in almost automatic behaviour much of the time, so they seldom evaluate whether their actions violate personal values or ethical principles. This mindless behaviour is particularly true when (as often happens) employees are located away from the situation where their decisions have an impact (i.e., low moral intensity). Mindless behaviour is further supported by implicit assumptions that the company or its key decision makers have high moral standards. Employees quickly dismiss any ethical concerns about their work when they assume their boss who assigned that work is inherently ethical. For instance, one of the largest cases of accounting fraud occurred because the company's chief financial officer was highly respected in the industry, so employees assumed he was introducing innovative—and legal—accounting procedures. In reality, these activities were extreme forms of accounting fraud.[80]

SUPPORTING ETHICAL BEHAVIOUR

Large and medium-size organizations in Canada and several other countries apply one or more strategies to improve ethical conduct. The most common among these is the corporate code of ethics—a statement about codes of practice, rules of conduct, and philosophy about the organization's relationship to its stakeholders and the environment. The organization may have several ethical codes, ranging from corporate social responsibility to professional conduct.[81] These codes are supposed to motivate and guide employee behaviour, signal the importance of ethical conduct, and build the firm's trustworthiness to stakeholders. However, critics suggest that they do little to reduce unethical conduct. A glaring illustration is that Enron had a well-developed code of ethics, but that document didn't prevent senior executives from engaging in wholesale wrongdoing, resulting in the energy company's bankruptcy.[82]

Many firms supplement ethics codes with ethics training. At Texas Instruments, employees learn to ask the following questions as their moral compass: "Is the action legal? Does it comply with our values? If you do it, will you feel bad? How would it look in the newspaper? If you know it's wrong, don't do it! If you're not sure, ask. Keep asking until you get an answer." Molson Coors developed an award-winning online training program set up as an expedition: Employees must resolve ethics violations at each "camp" as they ascend a mountain. The first few camps present real scenarios with fairly clear ethical violations of the company's ethics code; later camps present much fuzzier dilemmas requiring more careful thought about the company's underlying values.[83]

Some companies also have ways to confidentially communicate wrongdoing. Toronto-based Rogers Cable Communications Inc., has an anonymous hotline as well as a weblink that employees can use to raise ethical issues or concerns about ethical conduct. Rogers employees can even call back to find out what actions have been taken to resolve the ethical issue.[84] A few companies employ ethics ombudspersons who receive information confidentially from employees and proactively investigate possible wrongdoing. Ethics audits are also conducted in some organizations, but are more common for evaluation of corporate social responsibility practices.[85]

These additional measures support ethical conduct to some extent, but the most powerful foundation is a set of shared values that reinforce ethical conduct. "If you don't have a culture of ethical decision making to begin with, all the controls and compliance regulations you care to deploy won't necessarily prevent ethical misconduct," warns a senior executive at British communications giant Vodafone. This culture is supported by the ethical conduct and vigilance of corporate leaders. By acting with the highest standards of moral conduct, leaders not only gain support and trust from followers; they role-model the ethical standards that employees are more likely to follow.[86]

VALUES ACROSS CULTURES

LO6

University of Western Ontario economics graduate Sean Billing had been working as Director of Rooms at Fairmont Hotels in Chicago when he casually asked his boss whether the Toronto-based hotel chain could use his skills and knowledge elsewhere. Soon after, Fairmont assigned Billing to a management position in Kenya, bringing the new properties in the African country up to world-class standards through training and technology without losing the distinctive Kenyan character. Billing jumped at the opportunity, but he also soon discovered the challenge of infusing Fairmont's deep values of customer service, environmentalism, and empowerment into another culture. "It's a little bit of hotel culture shock . . . things are quite different here," admits Billing, who is now a Fairmont manager in Canada.[87] Fairmont Hotels & Resorts operates world-class hotels in several countries and is eager to help Sean Billing and other employees develop and/or strengthen their cross-cultural competence. As Global Connections 2.1 describes, people think and act differently across cultures, and these differences are due to unique norms of behaviour as well as emphasis on different values.

CONNECTIONS 2.1

Infosys Bridges the Cross-Cultural Divide

Infosys Technologies, a technology outsourcing firm from India, was prepared for cross-cultural differences when it acquired an Australian company. Sean Fernando, Infosys general manager of human resources in Australia, provides a vivid example of one of these cultural differences: When asked to travel on business, Infosys employees in India would pack their bags without hesitation and be ready to go even though they lacked details about the trip. Australian staff, on the other hand, wanted to know about the accommodation, allowances, and project specifics before they felt at ease. In other words, employees from India had noticeably lower levels of uncertainty avoidance.

Another difference was that staff in India expect the boss to give them instructions on what to do, whereas Australian employees expect to be consulted. In other words, Australian employees have much lower power distance. Fernando recalls an incident where an Australian project manager met with a project team from India. He described the project, and then suggested that they share ideas about how to successfully complete the project. "They didn't know what he meant," says Fernando. "Then one of the people just said: 'We were wondering when you are going to tell us what the plan was.'"

Infosys is training its managers to be aware of cross-cultural differences when working with employees from other countries. *Dean Mitchell/Shutterstock*

To minimize cross-cultural conflict, Infosys Australia holds a three-hour session in which employees from both countries learn about their cultures and discuss how they can manage employees with these different values.[88]

INDIVIDUALISM AND COLLECTIVISM

individualism A cross-cultural value describing the degree to which people in a culture emphasize independence and personal uniqueness.

collectivism A cross-cultural value describing the degree to which people in a culture emphasize duty to groups to which they belong, and to group harmony.

Of the many values studied across cultures, the five summarized in Exhibit 2.7 are by far the most popular. This exhibit also lists countries that have high, medium, or low emphasis on these values. Two seemingly inseparable cross-cultural values are individualism and collectivism. **Individualism** is the extent to which we value independence and personal uniqueness. Highly individualist people value personal freedom, self-sufficiency, control over their own lives, and appreciation of the unique qualities that distinguish them from others. Canadians, Americans, Chileans, and South Africans generally exhibit high individualism, whereas Taiwan and Venezuela are countries with low individualism.[89] **Collectivism** is the extent to which we value our duty to groups to which we belong and to group harmony. Highly collectivist people define themselves by their group memberships, emphasize their personal connection to others in their in-groups, and value the goals and well-being of people within those groups.[90] Low collectivism countries include Canada, the United States, Japan, and Germany, whereas Israel and Taiwan have relatively high collectivism.

Contrary to popular belief, individualism is not the opposite of collectivism. In fact, an analysis of most previous studies reported that the two concepts are unrelated.[91] For example, cultures that highly value duty to one's group do not necessarily give a low priority to personal freedom and uniqueness. Generally, people across all cultures define themselves by both their uniqueness and their relationship to others. It is an inherent characteristic of everyone's self-concept, which we discuss in the next chapter. Some cultures clearly emphasize uniqueness or group obligations more than the other, but both have a place in a person's values and self-concept.

Also note that people in Japan have relatively low collectivism. This is contrary to many cross-cultural books, which claim that Japan is one of the most collectivist

Exhibit 2.7   FIVE CROSS-CULTURAL VALUES

Value	Sample Countries	Representative Beliefs/Behaviours in "High" Cultures
Individualism	High: Canada, South Africa Medium: Japan, Denmark Low: Taiwan, Venezuela	Defines self more by one's uniqueness; personal goals have priority; decisions have low consideration of effect on others; relationships are viewed as more instrumental and fluid.
Collectivism	High: Israel, Taiwan Medium: India, Denmark Low: Canada, Japan	Defines self more by one's in-group membership; goals of self-sacrifice and harmony have priority; behaviour regulated by in-group norms; in-group memberships are viewed as stable with a strong differentiation with out-groups.
Power distance	High: India, Malaysia Medium: Canada, Japan Low: Denmark, Israel	Reluctant to disagree with or contradict the boss; managers are expected and preferred decision makers; perception of dependence (versus interdependence) with the boss.
Uncertainty avoidance	High: Belgium, Greece Medium: Canada, Norway Low: Denmark, Singapore	Prefer predictable situations; value stable employment, strict laws, and low conflict; dislike deviations from normal behaviour.
Achievement orientation	High: Austria, Japan Medium: Canada, Brazil Low: Sweden, Netherlands	Focus on outcomes (versus relationships); decisions based on contribution (equity versus equality); low empathy or showing emotions (versus strong empathy and caring)

Sources: Individualism and collectivism descriptions and results are from the meta-analysis reported in D. Oyserman, H. M. Coon, and M. Kemmelmeier, "Rethinking Individualism and Collectivism: Evaluation of Theoretical Assumptions and Meta-Analyses," *Psychological Bulletin* 128 (2002), pp. 3–72. The other information is from G. Hofstede, *Culture's Consequences,* 2nd ed. (Thousand Oaks, CA: Sage, 2001).

countries on the planet! There are several explanations for the historical misinterpretation, ranging from problems defining and measuring collectivism to distorted reporting of early cross-cultural research. Whatever the reasons, studies consistently report that people in Japan have relatively low collectivism and moderate individualism (as indicated in Exhibit 2.7).[92]

POWER DISTANCE

power distance A cross-cultural value describing the degree to which people in a culture accept unequal distribution of power in a society.

Power distance refers to the extent to which people accept unequal distribution of power in a society.[93] Those with high power distance accept and value unequal power. They value obedience to authority and are comfortable receiving commands from their superiors without consultation or debate, and prefer to resolve differences through formal procedures rather than directly. In contrast, people with low power distance expect relatively equal power sharing. They view the relationship with their boss as one of interdependence, not dependence; that is, they believe their boss is also dependent on them, so they expect power sharing and consultation before decisions affecting them are made. People in India and Malaysia tend to have high power distance, whereas people in Denmark and Israel generally have low power distance. Canadians collectively have medium-low power distance.

To understand the effect of power distance, consider the experience of an engineer from Southeast Asia who immigrated to Canada. In his home country, the engineer generated data analysis reports and submitted them to his supervisor without recommendations. His boss would look at the factual information and make a decision. Including recommendations in those reports would have shown disrespect for the supervisor's higher position, which may have resulted in dismissal. But when the engineer moved to Canada, he was expected to propose recommendations along with the technical data. Excluding recommendations from an engineering report in Canada would be evidence of incompetence, which may result in dismissal. To remain employed, the engineer had to overcome a huge shift in expectations and power distance values.[94]

UNCERTAINTY AVOIDANCE

uncertainty avoidance
A cross-cultural value describing the degree to which people in a culture tolerate ambiguity (low uncertainty avoidance) or feel threatened by ambiguity and uncertainty (high uncertainty avoidance).

Uncertainty avoidance is the degree to which people tolerate ambiguity (low uncertainty avoidance) or feel threatened by ambiguity and uncertainty (high uncertainty avoidance). Employees with high uncertainty avoidance favour structured situations in which rules of conduct and decision making are clearly documented. They usually prefer direct rather than indirect or ambiguous communications. Uncertainty avoidance tends to be high in Belgium and Greece and very high in Japan. It is generally low in Denmark and Singapore. Canadians collectively have medium-low uncertainty avoidance.

ACHIEVEMENT-NURTURING ORIENTATION

achievement-nurturing orientation   A cross-cultural value describing the degree to which people in a culture emphasize competitive versus cooperative relations with other people.

Achievement-nurturing orientation reflects a competitive versus cooperative view of relations with other people.[95] People with a high achievement orientation value assertiveness, competitiveness, and materialism. They appreciate people who are tough, and they favour the acquisition of money and material goods. In contrast, people in nurturing-oriented cultures emphasize relationships and the well-being of others. They focus on human interaction and caring rather than competition and personal success. People in Sweden, Norway, and the Netherlands score very low on achievement orientation (i.e., they have a high nurturing orientation). In contrast, very high achievement orientation scores have been reported in Japan and Austria. Canada is placed around the middle of the range on achievement-nurturing orientation.

CAVEATS ABOUT CROSS-CULTURAL KNOWLEDGE

Cross-cultural organizational research has gained considerable attention over the past two decades, likely due to increased globalization and cultural diversity within organizations. Our knowledge of cross-cultural dynamics has blossomed, and many of these findings will be discussed throughout this book, particularly regarding leadership, conflict handling, and influence tactics. However, we also need to raise a few warning flags about cross-cultural knowledge. One problem is that too many studies have relied on small, convenient samples (such as students) to represent an entire culture.[96] The result is that many cross-cultural studies draw conclusions that might not generalize to the cultures they intended to study.

A second problem is that cross-cultural studies often assume that each country has one culture.[97] In reality, many countries (including Canada) have become culturally diverse. As more countries embrace globalization and multiculturalism, it becomes even less appropriate to assume that an entire country has one unified culture. For instance, Chinese Canadian attitudes toward money and materialism are more similar to people surveyed in China than to European Canadians. Studies also report that Javanese, Batik, and Chinese Indonesians have significantly different values even though they all live in the same country.[98]

A third concern is that cross-cultural research and writing continues to rely on a major study conducted almost four decades ago of 116,000 IBM employees across dozens of countries. That study helped to ignite subsequent cross-cultural research, but its findings are becoming out of date as values in some cultures have shifted over the years. For example, value systems seem to be converging across Asia as people in these countries interact more frequently with each other and adopt standardized business practices.[99] At least one recent review has recommended that future studies should no longer rely on the IBM study to benchmark values of a particular culture.[100]

DIVERSITY OF CANADIAN CULTURAL VALUES

You might think from reading some cross-cultural studies that Canada is a homogenous country where people hold identical or very similar values. Of course, anyone who lives here knows otherwise. But even Canadians may be surprised at how much cultural diversity exists within this country, even when excluding the incredible variety of new Canadians who grew up elsewhere in the world.[101]

Consider Canada's historical diversity of two cultural clusters—Anglophones and Francophones. At one time, Francophones were more religious, traditional, and deferent to authority, compared with Anglophones. Now, the situation is almost reversed. Francophones have lower scores than Anglophones on respect for patriarchal authority (i.e., the father should be the head of the household), and they tend to have more tolerant or morally permissive opinions regarding marriage, sexual activity, and nonmarried parenthood.[102] There is some evidence that Anglophone and Francophone values are converging, but these two sub-cultures within Canada are still easily identifiable as a form of deep-level diversity.[103]

Canada's cultural diversity is further evident in the values of Aboriginal (First Nations) people and their organizations.[104] Organizations with Aboriginal founders and leaders tend to have a strong collectivist value, low power distance, low uncertainty avoidance, and a relatively nurturing rather than achievement orientation. These values are evident from consensus-oriented decision making (low power distance), focus more on the group than individuals (high collectivism), fewer rules and procedures (low uncertainty avoidance), and emphasis on the holistic well-being of employees and community (nurturing more than achievement orientation).

Canadian versus American Values   Canadians increasingly shop at American stores and have close associations with friends and co-workers in the United States. Yet, the values held by people in these two countries are more divergent today than a few decades ago. "Canadians may like Americans, speak the same language, and consume more of their fast food and popular culture, but we embrace a different hierarchy of values," writes social policy researcher Michael Adams.[105] Another Canadian cultural expert is even more emphatic: the 49th parallel border is more than just an imaginary geographic division; it is a symbol of the widening ideological divide in North America.[106]

Canadians have significantly higher tolerance or moral permissiveness than do Americans. Canadians are also more willing to allow collective rights over individual rights and are less accepting of large wealth differences within society.[107] Another striking difference is that Canadians question authority and value autonomy from their institutions, whereas Americans have a relatively high deference to authority. Canadians are much less likely to be associated with a religious institution and to believe that these institutions should influence public policy. They are also much more likely than Americans to believe that organizations work better without a single leader. Perhaps the most significant difference is in the value of patriarchal authority. In the early 1980s, more than 40 percent of Canadians and Americans believed that the father should be the master of the home. Today, only 18 percent of Canadians hold this view, compared to almost 50 percent of Americans.[108]

Although there is strong evidence that Canadian and American values differ, we also need to take into account diversity of values within each country. For instance, one major study reported that the United States and Canada seem to consist of four cultural groups: the Southern U.S., Northern U.S., Anglophone (English-speaking) Canada, and Francophone (French-speaking) Canada. The Southern U.S. has the most conservative, hawkish, and deeply religious values of the four groups. Francophone Canadians, the second cluster, hold the most tolerant or morally permissive values. This leaves Anglophone Canadians and Americans residing in the northern U.S. Research suggests that these two groups have very similar cultural values.[109] Overall, these findings confirm that clusters of people across Canada and the United States differ in their dominant values.

CHAPTER SUMMARY

 LO1 Describe the four factors that directly influence individual behaviour and performance.

Four variables—motivation, ability, role perceptions, and situational factors—which are represented by the acronym MARS, directly influence individual behaviour and performance. Motivation represents the forces within a person that affect his or her direction, intensity, and persistence of voluntary behaviour; ability includes both the natural aptitudes and the learned capabilities required to successfully complete a task; role perceptions are the extent to which people understand the job duties (roles) assigned to them or expected of them; situational factors include conditions beyond the employee's immediate control that constrain or facilitate behaviour and performance.

LO2 Summarize the five types of individual behaviour in organizations.

There are five main types of workplace behaviour. Task performance refers to goal-directed behaviours under the individual's control that support organizational objectives. Organizational citizenship behaviours consist of various forms of cooperation and helpfulness to others that support the organization's social and psychological context. Counterproductive work behaviours are voluntary behaviours that have the potential to directly or indirectly harm the organization. Joining and staying with the organization refers to agreeing to become an organizational member and remaining with the organization. Maintaining work attendance includes minimizing absenteeism when capable of working and avoiding scheduled work when not fit (i.e., low presenteeism).

LO3 Describe personality and discuss how the "Big Five" personality dimensions and four MBTI types relate to individual behaviour in organizations.

Personality is the relatively enduring pattern of thoughts, emotions, and behaviours that characterize a person, along with the psychological processes behind those characteristics. Personality traits are broad concepts about people that allow us to label and understand individual differences. Personality is developed through hereditary origins (nature) as well as socialization (nurture). The "Big Five" personality dimensions include conscientiousness, agreeableness, neuroticism, openness to experience, and extroversion. Conscientiousness and emotional stability (low neuroticism) predict individual performance in most job groups. Extroversion is associated with performance in sales and management jobs, whereas agreeableness is associated with performance in jobs requiring cooperation and openness to experience is associated with performance in creative jobs. Based on Jungian personality theory, the Myers-Briggs Type Indicator (MBTI) identifies competing orientations for getting energy (extroversion vs. introversion), perceiving information (sensing vs. intuiting), processing information and making decisions (thinking vs. feeling), and orienting to the external world (judging vs. perceiving). The MBTI improves self-awareness for career development and mutual understanding but is more popular than valid. Overall, it is useful to understand an individual's personality, but testing for personality in organizations raises a few concerns.

LO4 Summarize Schwartz's model of individual values and discuss the conditions under which values influence behaviour.

Values are stable, evaluative beliefs that guide our preferences for outcomes or courses of action in a variety of situations. Compared to personality traits, values are evaluative (rather than descriptive), more likely to conflict with each other, and are formed more from socialization than heredity. Schwartz's model organizes 57 values into a circumplex of 10 dimensions along two bipolar dimensions: openness to change to conservation and self-enhancement to self-transcendence. Values influence behaviour under three conditions: (1) we can think of specific reasons for doing so, (2) when the situation supports those values, and (3) when we actively think about them. Values congruence refers to how similar a person's values hierarchy is to the values hierarchy of another source (organization, person, etc.).

LO5 Describe three ethical principles and discuss four factors that influence ethical behaviour.

Ethics refers to the study of moral principles or values that determine whether actions are right or wrong and outcomes are good or bad. Three ethical principles are utilitarianism, individual rights, and distributive justice. Ethical behaviour is influenced by the degree to which an issue demands the application of ethical principles (moral intensity), the individual's ability to recognize the presence and relative importance of an ethical issue (ethical sensitivity), situational forces, and the extent to which people actively evaluate their decisions and actions against ethical and personal values (i.e., mindfulness). Ethical conduct at work is supported by codes of ethical conduct, ethics training, mechanisms for communicating ethical violations, the organization's culture, and the leader's behaviour.

LO6 Review five values commonly studied across cultures and discuss the diverse cultures within Canada.

Five values that are often studied across cultures are individualism (valuing independence and personal uniqueness); collectivism (valuing duty to in-groups and to group harmony); power distance (valuing unequal distribution of power); uncertainty avoidance (tolerating or feeling threatened by ambiguity and uncertainty); and achievement-nurturing orientation (valuing competition vs. cooperation). Although cross-cultural knowledge is valuable, we need to be concerned that some of this knowledge is based on non-representative samples, old information, and lack of sensitivity to cultural differences within countries. Canada consists of several cultures in addition to those brought by new Canadians. Anglophones and Francophones differ in their values, although these values have almost reversed over the past several decades. Aboriginal values also differ from others in Canada. Canadians and Americans also have noticeably different values, although North America might be divided into four clusters that cross national boundaries.

KEY TERMS

ability, p. 30

achievement-nurturing
    orientation, p. 51

collectivism, p. 49

competencies, p. 30

conscientiousness, p. 38

counterproductive work
    behaviours (CWBs), p. 33

ethical sensitivity, p. 47

extroversion, p. 38

five-factor model
    (FFM), p. 37

individualism, p. 49

moral intensity, p. 46

motivation, p. 29

Myers-Briggs Type
    Indicator (MBTI), p. 39

neuroticism, p. 38

organizational citizenship
    behaviours (OCBs), p. 33

personality, p. 36

power distance, p. 50

presenteeism, p. 35

role perceptions, p. 31

uncertainty avoidance, p. 51

CRITICAL-THINKING QUESTIONS

1. An insurance company has high levels of absenteeism among the office staff. The head of office administration argues that employees are misusing the company's sick leave benefits. However, some of the mostly female staff members have explained that family responsibilities interfere with work. Using the MARS model, as well as your knowledge of absenteeism behaviour, discuss some of the possible reasons for absenteeism here and how it might be reduced.

2. You notice that the sales representative for Eastern Ontario made 20 percent fewer sales to new clients over the past quarter than salespeople located elsewhere in Canada. Use the MARS model of individual behaviour to explain why his or her performance was lower than the performance of other salespeople.

3. Studies report that heredity has a strong influence on an individual's personality. What are the implications of this in organizational settings?

4. Suppose you give all candidates applying for a management trainee position a personality test that measures the five dimensions in the five-factor model. Which personality traits would you consider to be the most important for this type of job? Explain your answer.

5. Compare and contrast personality with personal values, and identify values categories in Schwartz's values circumplex that likely relate to one or more personality dimensions in the five-factor personality model.

6. This chapter discussed values congruence mostly in the context of an employee's personal values versus the organization's values. But values congruence also relates to the juxtaposition of other pairs of value systems. Explain how values congruence is relevant with respect to organizational versus professional values (i.e., values of a professional occupation, such as physician, accountant, pharmacist).

7. "All decisions are ethical decisions." Comment on this statement, particularly by referring to the concepts of moral intensity and ethical sensitivity.

8. People in a particular South American country have high power distance and high collectivism. What does this mean, and what are the implications of this information when you (a senior executive) visit employees working for your company in that country?

 ## CASE STUDY 2.1

South Korea's SK Telecom Goes Egalitarian

Until recently, Hur Jae-hoon could end debate with junior staff members just by declaring that the discussion was over. Employed at the fourth tier in SK Telecom Co.'s five-tier management/professional hierarchy, the 33-year-old strategist held the corresponding title of "Hur Daeri" and received plenty of respect from people in lower positions. No one below Hur was allowed to question his decisions, and Hur was expected to silently comply with requests from above. South Korea's culture of deferring to people in higher positions was deeply ingrained in the telecommunications company. In some South Korean companies, such as Samsung, junior staff members aren't even allowed to initiate conversations with anyone above their boss.

Now, in spite of South Korea's strong hierarchical culture, SK Telecom wants to support more egalitarian values. It has already removed its five management ranks and their differentiated titles and status. The English word "Manager" is now used to address anyone employed throughout the five former ranks. (Hur Jae-hoon's title has changed from Hur Daeri to "Hur Manager"). Only vice-presidents and above retain their previous status titles. People in charge of projects or people are also called "Team Leader." Furthermore, the company is assigning project leadership responsibilities to employees in their twenties, whereas these roles were previously held only by people with much more seniority. As an added change, the company is allowing a more casual dress code at work.

Through this dramatic shift in values and practices, SK Telecom's senior executives hope that junior staff will speak up more freely, thereby improving creativity and decision making. They particularly want to avoid incidents such as one that occurred several years ago in which an excellent idea from younger employees was initially shot down by their bosses. The junior staff suggested that allowing customers to change their cellphone ringtones to music chosen by the friend they've phoned would generate revenue through music licensing. Fortunately, the idea was introduced several months later, after a few persistent employees proposed the idea again.

SK Telecom's initiative is not completely new to South Korea. Small high-tech companies already embrace egalitarian values and flatter corporate structures. But SK Telecom is among the first large firms in the country to attempt this culture shift, and it has met with resistance along the way. SK Telecom executives were initially divided over how quickly and to what extent the company should distance itself from South Korea's traditional hierarchical culture. "There were ideas for gradual versus all-out reforms," recalls chief executive Kim Shin-bae. "But the word 'gradually' means 'not now' to some people. So we decided to go all-out."

According to a company survey, 80 percent of employees support the changes. However, even with the changes in titles, many still look for subtle evidence of who has higher status and, therefore, should receive more deference. Some also rely on what positions managers held under the old five-tier hierarchy. "I know what the old titles were," says an LG Electronics Co. manager who supplies cellphones to SK Telecom. "So unconsciously, I keep that in mind."

Hur Jae-hoon admits there are times when he prefers a more hierarchical culture, but he believes that SK Telecom's more egalitarian values and practices are already showing favourable results. In one recent meeting, a younger colleague sparred with Hur over the better way to complete a strategy project. "For a moment, I wished it was back in the old days when I could have shut that guy down," Hur recalls. "But I had to admit his opinion was better than mine, and I adjusted. So the system worked."

Discussion Questions

1. SK Telecom is attempting to distance itself from which South Korean cultural value? What indicators of this value are identified in this case study? What other artifacts of this cultural value would you notice while visiting a South Korean company that upheld this national culture?

2. In your opinion, why is this particular value so strong in South Korea? What are the advantages and disadvantages of this value in societies?

3. Do you think SK Telecom will be successful in integrating a more egalitarian culture, even though it contrasts with South Korea's culture? What are some of the issues that may complicate or support this transition?

Source: Adapted from E. Ramstad, "Pulling Rank Gets Harder at One Korean Company," *Wall Street Journal*, August 20, 2007, p. B1.

 CASE STUDY 2.2

Pushing Papers Can Be Fun

A large city government was putting on a number of seminars for managers of various departments throughout the city. At one of these sessions, the topic discussed was motivation—how we can get public servants motivated to do a good job. The plight of a police captain became the central focus of the discussion:

I've got a real problem with my officers. They come on the force as young, inexperienced rookies, and we send them out on the street, either in cars or on a beat. They seem to like the contact they have with the public, the action involved in crime prevention, and the apprehension of criminals. They also like helping people out at fires, accidents, and other emergencies.

The problem occurs when they get back to the station. They hate to do the paperwork, and because they dislike it, the job is frequently put off or done inadequately. This lack of attention hurts us later on when we get to court. We need clear, factual reports. They must be highly detailed and unambiguous. As soon as one part of a report is shown to be inadequate or incorrect, the rest of the report is suspect. Poor reporting probably causes us to lose more cases than any other factor.

I just don't know how to motivate them to do a better job. We're in a budget crunch and I have absolutely no financial rewards at my disposal. In fact, we'll probably have to lay some people off in the near future. It's hard for me to make the job interesting and challenging because it isn't—it's boring, routine paperwork, and there isn't much you can do about it.

Finally, I can't say to them that their promotions will hinge on the excellence of their paperwork. First of all, they know it's not true. If their performance is adequate, most are more likely to get promoted just by staying on the force a certain number of years than for some specific outstanding act. Second, they were trained to do the job they do out in the streets, not to fill out forms. All through their career it is the arrests and interventions that get noticed.

Some people have suggested a number of things, like using conviction records as a performance criterion. However, we know that's not fair—too many other things are involved. Bad paperwork increases the chance that you lose in court, but good paperwork doesn't necessarily mean you'll win. We tried setting up team competitions based upon the excellence of the reports, but the officers caught on to that pretty quickly. No one was getting any type of reward for winning the competition, and they figured why should they bust a gut when there was no payoff.

I just don't know what to do.

Discussion Questions

1. What performance problems is the captain trying to correct?

2. Use the MARS model of individual behaviour and performance to diagnose the possible causes of the unacceptable behaviour.

3. Has the captain considered all possible solutions to the problem? If not, what else might be done?

Source: T. R. Mitchell and J. R. Larson, Jr., *People in Organizations*, 3rd ed. (New York: McGraw-Hill, 1987), p. 184. Used with permission.

 CLASS EXERCISE 2.3

Test Your Knowledge of Personality

Purpose   This exercise is designed to help you think about and understand the effects of the Big Five personality dimensions on individual preferences and outcomes.

Instructions Below are several questions relating to the Big Five personality dimensions and various
(Large Class) preferences or outcomes. Answer each of these questions relying on your personal experience or best guess. Later, the instructor will show you the answers based on scholarly results. You will *not* be graded on this exercise, but it may help you to better understand the effect of personality on human behaviour and preferences.

Instructions (Small Class)

1. The instructor will organize students into teams. Members of each team work together to answer each of the questions below relating to the Big Five personality dimensions and various preferences or outcomes.

2. The instructor will reveal the answers based on scholarly results. (Note: The instructor might create a competition to see which team has the most answers correct.)

Personality and Preferences Questions

1. You have been asked to select job applicants for a nine-month over-winter assignment working in an Antarctic research station with a dozen other people. Assuming that all candidates have equal skills, experience, and health, identify the level of each personality dimension that would be best for people working in these remote, confined, and isolated conditions.

Personality Dimension	Low	Below Average	Average	Above Average	High
Conscientiousness	☐	☐	☐	☐	☐
Agreeableness	☐	☐	☐	☐	☐
Neuroticism	☐	☐	☐	☐	☐
Openness to experience	☐	☐	☐	☐	☐
Extroversion	☐	☐	☐	☐	☐

2. Listed below are several jobs. Please check no more than two personality dimensions that you believe are positively associated with preferences for each occupation.

	Personality Dimensions				
Job	Extroversion	Conscientiousness	Agreeableness	Neuroticism	Openness to Experience
Budget analyst	☐	☐	☐	☐	☐
Corporate executive	☐	☐	☐	☐	☐
Engineer	☐	☐	☐	☐	☐
Journalist	☐	☐	☐	☐	☐
Life insurance agent	☐	☐	☐	☐	☐
Nurse	☐	☐	☐	☐	☐
Physician	☐	☐	☐	☐	☐
Production supervisor	☐	☐	☐	☐	☐
Public relations director	☐	☐	☐	☐	☐
Research analyst	☐	☐	☐	☐	☐
Sculptor	☐	☐	☐	☐	☐
Teacher	☐	☐	☐	☐	☐

3. On which two personality dimensions should team members have the highest scores, on average, to produce the best team performance?

☐ Conscientiousness

☐ Agreeableness

☐ Neuroticism

☐ Openness to experience

☐ Extroversion

4. Rank-order (1 = highest, 5 = lowest) the Big Five personality dimensions in terms of how much you think they predict a person's degree of life satisfaction. (Note: Personality dimensions are ranked by their absolute effect, so ignore the negative or positive direction of association.)

_____ Conscientiousness

_____ Agreeableness

_____ Neuroticism

_____ Openness to experience

_____ Extroversion

5. Which two Big Five personality dimensions are positively associated with enjoyment of workplace humour?

☐ Conscientiousness

☐ Agreeableness

☐ Neuroticism

☐ Openness to experience

☐ Extroversion

 TEAM EXERCISE 2.4

Comparing Cultural Values

Purpose This exercise is designed to help you determine the extent to which students hold similar assumptions about the values that dominate in other countries.

Instructions (Small Class) The terms in the left column represent labels that a major consulting project identified with businesspeople in a particular country, based on its national culture and values. These terms appear in alphabetical order. In the right column are the names of countries, also in alphabetical order, corresponding to the labels in the left column.

1. Working alone, connect the labels with the countries by relying on your perceptions of these countries. Each label is associated with only one country, so each label should be connected to only one country, and vice versa. Draw a line to connect the pairs, or put the label number beside the country name.

2. The instructor will form teams of four or five members. Members of each team will compare their results and try to reach consensus on a common set of connecting pairs.

3. Teams or the instructor will post the results so that all can see the extent to which students hold common opinions about businesspeople in other cultures. Class discussion can then consider the reasons why the results are so similar or different, as well as the implications of these results for working in a global work environment.

Instructions (Large Class)

1. Working alone, connect the labels with the countries by relying on your perceptions of these countries. Each label is associated with only one country, so each label should be connected to only one country, and vice versa. Draw a line to connect the pairs, or put the label number beside the country name.

2. Asking for a show of hands, the instructor will find out which country is identified by most students with each label. The instructor will then post the correct answers.

Values Labels and Country Names	
Values label (Alphabetical)	Country name (Alphabetical)
1. Affable humanists	Australia
2. Ancient modernizers	Brazil
3. Commercial catalysts	Canada
4. Conceptual strategists	China
5. Efficient manufacturers	France
6. Ethical statesmen	Germany
7. Informal egalitarians	India
8. Modernizing traditionalists	Netherlands
9. Optimistic entrepreneurs	New Zealand
10. Quality perfectionists	Singapore
11. Rugged individualists	Taiwan
12. Serving merchants	United Kingdom
13. Tolerant traders	United States

Source: Based on R. Rosen, P. Digh, M. Singer, and C. Phillips, *Global Literacies* (New York: Simon & Schuster, 2000).

 TEAM EXERCISE 2.5

Ethics Dilemma Vignettes

Purpose   This exercise is designed to make you aware of the ethical dilemmas people face in various business situations, as well as the competing principles and values that operate in these situations.

Instructions (Small Class)   The instructor will form teams of four or five students. Team members will read each case below and discuss the extent to which the company's action in each case was ethical. Teams should be prepared to justify their evaluation using ethical principles and the perceived moral intensity of each incident.

Instructions (Large Class)   Working alone, read each case below and determine the extent to which the company's action in each case was ethical. The instructor will use a show of hands to determine the extent to which students believe the case represents an ethical dilemma (high or low moral intensity) and the extent to which the main people or company in each incident acted ethically.

Case One

A large European bank requires all employees to open a bank account with that bank. The bank deposits employee paycheques to those accounts. The bank explains that this is a formal policy which all employees agree to at the time of hire. Furthermore, failure to have an account with the bank shows disloyalty, which could limit the employee's career advancement opportunities with the bank. Until recently, the bank has reluctantly agreed to deposit paycheques to accounts at other banks for a small percentage of employees. Now, bank executives want to reinforce the policy. They announced that employees have three months to open an account with the bank or face disciplinary action.

Case Two

A 16-year-old hired as an office administrator at a small import services company started posting her thoughts about the job on her Facebook page. After her first day, she wrote: "first day at work. omg!! So dull!!" Two days later, she complained "all i do is shred holepunch n scan paper!!! omg!" Two weeks later she added "im so totally bord!!!" These comments were intermixed with the other usual banter about her life. Her Facebook page did not mention the name of the company where she worked. Three weeks after being hired, the employee was called into the owner's office, where he fired her for the comments on Facebook, then had her escorted from the building. The owner argues that these comments put the company in a bad light, and her "display of disrespect and dissatisfaction undermined the relationship and made it untenable."

Case Three

Computer printer manufacturers usually sell printers at a low margin over cost and generate much more income from subsequent sales of the high-margin ink cartridges required for each printer. One global printer manufacturer now designs its printers so that they work only with ink cartridges made in the same region. Ink cartridges purchased in Canada will not work with the same printer model sold in Europe, for example. This "region coding" of ink cartridges does not improve performance. Rather, it prevents consumers and grey marketers from buying the product at a lower price in another region. The company says this policy allows it to maintain stable prices within a region rather than continually changing prices due to currency fluctuations.

Case Four

Judy Price is a popular talk show radio personality and opinionated commentator on the morning phone-in show of a Toronto radio station. Ms. Price is married to John Tremble, a lawyer who was recently elected for the first time to the parliament of Ontario. He also became Minister of the Environment and Conservation in the newly formed government that defeated the previous government. The radio station's board of directors is very concerned that the station's perceived objectivity will be compromised if Ms. Price remains on air as a commentator and talk show host while her husband holds such a public position in the province. For example, the radio station manager believes that Ms. Price gave minimal attention to the Environment Ministry's slow response to a leakage of toxic chemicals a week ago at a large manufacturing company. Ms. Price denied that her views are biased and that the incident didn't merit as much attention as other issues that particular day. To ease the board's concerns, the station manager has transferred Ms. Price from a talk show host and commentator to the hourly news reporting position, where most script is edited by others. Although technically a lower position, Ms. Price's total salary package remains the same. Ms. Price is now seeking professional advice to determine whether the radio station's action represents a form of discrimination on the basis of marital status.

Case Five

For the past few years, the design department of a small (40-employee) company has been using a particular software program, but the three employees who use the software have been complaining for more than a year that the software is out of date and is slowing down their performance. The department agreed to switch to a competing software program, costing several thousand dollars. However, the next version won't be released for six months and buying the current version will not allow much discount on the next version. The company has put in advance orders for the next version. Meanwhile, one employee was able to get a copy of the current version of the software from a friend in the industry. The company has allowed the three employees to use this current version of the software even though they did not pay for it.

Go to CONNECT to complete the following interactive self-assessments.

 SELF-ASSESSMENT EXERCISE 2.6

Are You Introverted or Extroverted?

Purpose	This self-assessment is designed to help you estimate the extent to which you are introverted or extroverted.
Instructions	The statements in the scale below refer to personal characteristics that might or might not be characteristic of you. Check the box indicating the extent to which the statement accurately or inaccurately describes you. Then use the scoring key in Appendix B at the end of this book to calculate your results. This exercise should be completed alone so that you can assess yourself honestly without concerns of social comparison. Class discussion will focus on the meaning and implications of extroversion and introversion in organizations.

IPIP Introversion-Extroversion Scale					
How accurately does each of the statements listed below describe you?	Very Accurate Description of Me	Moderately Accurate	Neither Accurate nor Inaccurate	Moderately Inaccurate	Very Inaccurate Description of Me
1. I feel comfortable around people.	☐	☐	☐	☐	☐
2. I make friends easily.	☐	☐	☐	☐	☐
3. I keep in the background.	☐	☐	☐	☐	☐
4. I don't talk a lot.	☐	☐	☐	☐	☐
5. I would describe my experiences as somewhat dull.	☐	☐	☐	☐	☐
6. I know how to captivate people.	☐	☐	☐	☐	☐
7. I don't like to draw attention to myself.	☐	☐	☐	☐	☐
8. I am the life of the party.	☐	☐	☐	☐	☐
9. I am skilled in handling social situations.	☐	☐	☐	☐	☐
10. I have little to say.	☐	☐	☐	☐	☐

Source: Adapted from instruments described and/or presented in L. R. Goldberg, J. A. Johnson, H. W. Eber, R. Hogan, M. C. Ashton, C. R. Cloninger, and H. C. Gough, "The International Personality Item Pool and the Future of Public-Domain Personality Measures," *Journal of Research in Personality* 40 (2006), pp. 84–96.

 SELF-ASSESSMENT EXERCISE 2.7

What are Your Dominant Values?

Values have taken centre stage in organizational behaviour. Increasingly, OB experts are realizing that our personal values influence our motivation, decisions, and attitudes. This self-assessment is designed to help you estimate your personal values and value system. The instrument consists of several words and phrases, and you are asked to indicate whether each word or phrase is highly opposite or highly similar to your personal values or is at some point between these two extremes. As with all self-assessments, you need to be honest with yourself when completing this activity in order to get the most accurate results.

 SELF-ASSESSMENT EXERCISE 2.8

Individualism-Collectivism Scale

Two of the most important concepts in cross-cultural organizational behaviour are individualism and collectivism. This self-assessment measures your levels of individualism and collectivism with one of the most widely adopted measures. This scale consists of several statements, and you are asked to indicate how well each statement describes you. You need to be honest with yourself to receive a reasonable estimate of your level of individualism and collectivism.

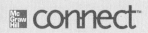 Practise and learn online with Connect. Connect resources include additional and interactive study exercises, videos, and practice quizzing, as well as additional material you won't find in the printed text.

CHAPTER 3

Perceiving Ourselves and Others in Organizations

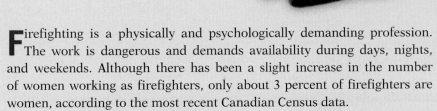

LEARNING OBJECTIVES

After reading this chapter, you should be able to:

LO1 Describe the elements of self-concept and explain how they affect an individual's behaviour and well-being.

LO2 Outline the perceptual process and discuss the effects of categorical thinking and mental models in that process.

LO3 Discuss how stereotyping, attribution, self-fulfilling prophecy, halo, false-consensus, primacy, and recency influence the perceptual process.

LO4 Discuss three ways to improve perceptions, with specific application to organizational situations.

LO5 Outline the main features of a global mindset and justify its usefulness to employees and organizations.

Firefighting is a physically and psychologically demanding profession. The work is dangerous and demands availability during days, nights, and weekends. Although there has been a slight increase in the number of women working as firefighters, only about 3 percent of firefighters are women, according to the most recent Canadian Census data.

Regardless of the widely held perception that firefighting is an undesirable and unattainable job for women, Miranda Moir, at the age of 19, knows that she wants to spend her working life battling blazes and saving lives as a firefighter. She has applied to the Ottawa Fire Service and will face the demanding testing and training required for certification. In the meantime she is attending a five-day camp, sponsored by the Ottawa Fire Service and the Fire Service Women of Ontario to provide girls, aged 15 to 19 years of age with a chance to get a realistic glimpse into what it is like to be a firefighter.

Camp FFIT, which stands for female firefighters in training, requires participants to complete a wide variety of fire-training scenarios including forcing their way into a building using heavy tools, completing search and rescue missions while wearing air masks, and climbing a fire rig ladder leaning against a wall about 20 metres high.

Camp FFIT is part of the Ottawa Fire Service's campaign to recruit more female firefighters and change perceptions about women in the profession. Women firefighters have endured harassment at work according to veteran mediator Vince Ready in a report ordered by Richmond city council after all four of its remaining female firefighters took leaves of absence in 2006, over allegations of sexual harassment in the workplace. "I have observed a culture amongst members of the RFRD (Richmond Fire Rescue Department) characterized by juvenile and hostile behaviour towards firefighters, generally women in the RFRD specifically, which I find has contributed to the barriers to women's potential within the RFRD."

Annalee Lepp, head of the Women's Studies department at the University of Victoria describes a "chill factor" for women. "Oftentimes . . . the assumption is they can't do the job as well," Lepp said. "The first challenge is always getting in. And the next question is, do women want to work in that environment where there could be hostility toward them?"

"The opinion out there is that this is a male-only profession. We're trying to change that," explains Ottawa Fire Chief, John de Hooge. Although the small number of women in firefighting can be attributed to few women applying for the job, deHooge says, "It has nothing to do with ability to do the job. . .women can do the job just as well as men can." deHooge also says that women add an element of empathy to the fire service and people in distress may find women easier to talk to than men.

Camp FFIT coordinator, Louise Hine-Schmidt changed careers and became a firefighter after many years spent thinking that women weren't even allowed to be in the profession. "Lots of women can do this job," she said. "We just need to let them know that."[1]

Felice Perron, left, and Meagan Elliott are taking part in a week-long camp intended to give girls a taste of the firefighting life. *Jean Levac/Ottawa Citizen. Reprinted by permission.*

Firefighting services around Canada and internationally face two challenges in attracting and keeping women in this occupation: (1) the self-concept women have about themselves versus their image of firefighters and (2) perceptions that others have about firefighters and of women in these roles. We discuss both of these related topics in this chapter. First, we examine how people perceive themselves—their self-concept—and how that self-perception affects their decisions and behaviour. Next, we focus on perceptions in organizational settings, beginning with how we select, organize, and interpret information, and then reviewing several specific perceptual processes such as stereotyping, attribution, and self-fulfilling prophecy. We then identify potentially effective ways to improve perceptions, such as corporate volunteering. The final section of this chapter reviews the main elements of global mindset, a largely perceptual process valued in this increasingly globalized world.

SELF-CONCEPT: HOW WE PERCEIVE OURSELVES

LO1

Why are there only 900 women among the 30,000 or so firefighters in Canada? The opening vignette to this chapter offers a few reasons, one of which is that women do not see themselves as firefighters and have doubts about doing that job. "I don't think women automatically think they can be a firefighter," admits Kate Bailey, who entered this line of work a few years ago in southeastern England. This self-concept incompatibility is further reinforced by genderized perceptions of firefighters held by family, friends, and the media. "My family told me they thought I'd be an interior designer or something," recalls Maria Dominguez, a firefighter in Odessa, Texas. "They would say, 'Why's she doing that (becoming a firefighter), it's a man's job?'"[2]

self-concept An individual's self-beliefs and self-evaluations.

We begin this chapter by looking at how people perceive themselves, that is, their self-concept. **Self-concept** refers to an individual's self-beliefs and self-evaluations. It is the "Who am I?" and "How do I feel about myself?" that people ask themselves and that guide their decisions and actions. Whether contemplating a career as a firefighter or a financial analyst, we compare our images of that job with our current (perceived self) and desired (ideal self) images of ourselves. We also evaluate our current and desired competencies to determine whether there is a good fit with that job. A growing number of OB writers are discovering that how people perceive themselves helps to explain their attitudes, motivation, decisions, and behaviour in the workplace.

SELF-CONCEPT COMPLEXITY, CONSISTENCY, AND CLARITY

Self-concepts vary in their complexity, consistency, and clarity (see Exhibit 3.1).[3] First, self-concepts have varying degrees of *complexity*, that is, the number of distinct and important roles or identities that people perceive about themselves. Everyone has some degree of complexity because they see themselves in more than one role (student, friend, daughter, sports enthusiast, etc). Complexity is determined not only by the number of selves but also by the separation of those selves.[4] A self-concept has low complexity when the individual's most important identities are highly interconnected, such as when they are all work-related (manager, engineer, family income-earner).

A second characteristic of self-concept is its internal *consistency*. People have high internal consistency when most of their self-perceived roles require similar personality traits, values, and other attributes. Low consistency occurs when some self-perceptions require personal characteristics that conflict with characteristics required for other aspects of self. Low self-concept consistency would exist if you see yourself as a very exacting engineer, yet also a cavalier and risk-oriented skier. *Clarity*, the third characteristic of self-concept, is the degree to which you have a clear, confidently defined, and stable self-concept. Clarity occurs when we are confident about "who we are," can

Exhibit 3.1	**SELF-CONCEPT DIMENSIONS**
Self-Concept Dimension	**Description**
Complexity	How many distinct and important roles or identities does a person think about to define him/herself?
Consistency	How compatible are the person's self-concept identities with each other and with the person's personality, values, and other attributes?
Clarity	To what extent does the person define him/herself clearly, confidently, and consistently over time?

describe our important identities to others, and provide the same description of ourselves across time. Self-concept clarity increases with age as well as with the consistency of the person's multiple selves.[5]

Self-concept complexity, consistency, and clarity are important because they influence a person's well-being, behaviour, and performance. People tend to have psychological well-being when they have multiple selves (complexity) that are well established (clarity), and are similar to each other and compatible with personal traits (consistency). Complexity is important because it protects our self-evaluation when some roles are threatened or damaged.[6] A complex self-concept is rather like a ship with several compartments that can be sealed off from each other. If one compartment is damaged, it can be secured so most of the ship remains intact. People with low complexity, on the other hand, suffer severe loss when they experience failure because these events affect a large part of themselves.

A person's well-being also increases to some extent when his or her multiple selves are in harmony with each other (consistency).[7] Some self-concept diversity helps people to adapt, but too much variation causes internal tension and conflict. Finally, well-being tends to increase with self-concept clarity. When we lack confidence in ourselves, we are more easily influenced by others, experience more stress when making decisions, and feel more threatened by social forces that undermine our self-confidence and self-esteem.[8]

Self-concept complexity, consistency, and clarity have more varied effects on behaviour and performance.[9] On the one hand, people who define themselves mainly by their work (i.e., low complexity) tend to have lower absenteeism and turnover. They also potentially perform better due to more investment in skill development, longer hours, more concentration on work, and so forth. On the other hand, low complexity commonly results in higher stress and depression when the main self aspect is damaged or threatened, which further undermines individual performance. Self-concept clarity tends to improve performance and is considered vital for leadership roles.[10] However, people with very high clarity may have role inflexibility such that they cannot adapt to changing job duties.

Complexity, consistency, and clarity describe characteristics of a person's self-concept. In addition to these characteristics are four processes that shape self-concept and influence a person's decisions and behaviour. Let's look at each of these four "selves": self-enhancement, self-verification, self-evaluation, and social self (social identity).

SELF-ENHANCEMENT

self-enhancement
A person's inherent motivation to have a positive self-concept (and to have others perceive him/her favourably), such as being competent, attractive, lucky, ethical, and important.

People across most (and likely all) cultures are inherently motivated to perceive themselves (and to be perceived by others) as competent, attractive, lucky, ethical, and important.[11] This **self-enhancement** is observed in many ways. Individuals tend to rate themselves above average, believe that they have a better than average probability of success, and attribute their successes to personal motivation or ability while blaming the situation for their mistakes. For instance, a recent U.S. government survey reported that 69 percent of government workers rated their performance above average compared to other co-workers in their unit; only 1 percent rated their performance below average. Even more extreme is that 94 percent of university professors in one study rated themselves as above-average teachers compared with others at their university; two-thirds rated themselves in the top quartile![12] People don't see themselves as above average in all circumstances, but this bias is apparent for conditions that are common rather than rare and that are important to them.[13]

Self-enhancement has both positive and negative consequences in organizational settings.[14] On the positive side, individuals tend to experience better mental and physical health and adjustment when they view their self-concept in a positive light. On the negative side, self-enhancement can result in bad decisions. For example, some studies report that self-enhancement causes managers to overestimate the probability of success in investment decisions. Other research suggests that self-enhancement is a factor in high accident rates among novice drivers. Generally, though, successful companies strive to help employees feel that they are valued and integral members of the organization.

SELF-VERIFICATION

> **self-verification** A person's inherent motivation to confirm and maintain his/her existing self-concept.

Along with being motivated by self-enhancement, people try to confirm and maintain their existing self-concept.[15] This process, called **self-verification**, stabilizes an individual's self-concept, which, in turn, provides an important anchor that guides his or her thoughts and actions. Employees actively communicate their self-concept so co-workers can provide feedback that reinforces the self-concept. For example, you might let co-workers know that you are a very organized person; later, they point out situations where you have indeed been very organized. Unlike self-enhancement, self-verification occurs when we seek out feedback that supports our self-view, even when it isn't flattering (e.g., I'm a numbers person, not a people person). Social scientists continue to debate whether and under what conditions people prefer information that supports self-enhancement or self-verification.[16] In other words, do we prefer compliments rather than accurate critique about known weaknesses?

Self-verification has several implications for organizational behaviour.[17] First, it affects the perceptual process because employees are more likely to remember information that is consistent with their self-concept and screen out information that seems inconsistent with it. Second, the clearer the individual's self-concept, the less he/she will accept feedback that contradicts that self-concept. Third, employees are motivated to interact with others who affirm their self-concept, and this affects how well they get along with their boss and team members.

SELF-EVALUATION

Almost everyone strives to have a positive self-concept, but some people have a more positive evaluation of themselves than do others. This *self-evaluation* is mostly defined by three concepts: self-esteem, self-efficacy, and locus of control.[18]

Self-Esteem   *Self-esteem*—the extent to which people like, respect, and are satisfied with themselves—represents a global self-evaluation. Some experts also believe that self-esteem is a person's rating of his/her success at social inclusion. In other words, people have higher self-esteem when they believe they are connected to and accepted by others. People with high self-esteem are less influenced by others, tend to persist in spite of failure, and think more rationally. Self-esteem regarding specific aspects of self (e.g., a good student, a good driver, a good parent) predicts specific thoughts and behaviours, whereas a person's overall self-esteem predicts only large bundles of thoughts and behaviours.[19]

Supporting a Positive Self-Concept at Fairmont Hotels and Resorts

Yasmeen Youssef's self-confidence was a bit shaky when she and her husband moved from Egypt to Canada a few years ago. "I was worried no one would take a chance on me, would believe in me," she recalls. But any self-doubts slowly disappeared after taking an entry-level job with Fairmont Hotels & Resorts corporate offices in Toronto. "Everything changed when I started working at Fairmont," says Youssef, who is now on Fairmont's human resources team and recently trained new staff in Cairo. "I can't believe the amount of value, care, respect everyone has extended to me." Yasmeen now influences the confidence and well-being of other Fairmont employees by serving as an executive and mentor in the company's Toastmasters club. One of the key ingredients to employee performance and well-being at Fairmont is supporting the individual's self-concept. "People want to feel valued and they stay where they feel valued," says Carolyn Clark, Fairmont's senior vice-president of human resources.[20] ©*National Post/Nathan Denette*

---

self-efficacy A person's belief that he or she has the ability, motivation, correct role perceptions, and favourable situation to complete a task successfully.

Self-Efficacy **Self-efficacy** refers to a person's belief that he or she can successfully complete a task.[21] Those with high self-efficacy have a "can do" attitude. They believe they possess the energy (motivation), resources (situational factors), understanding of the correct course of action (role perceptions), and competencies (ability) to perform the task. In other words, self-efficacy is an individual's perception regarding the MARS model in a specific situation. Although originally defined in terms of specific tasks, self-efficacy is also a general trait related to self-concept.[22] General self-efficacy is a perception of one's competence to perform across a variety of situations. The higher the person's general self-efficacy, the higher is his or her overall self-evaluation.

locus of control A person's general belief about the amount of control he or she has over personal life events.

Locus of Control **Locus of control** is defined as a person's general beliefs about the amount of control he or she has over personal life events.[23] Individuals with more of an internal locus of control believe that their personal characteristics (i.e., motivation and competencies) mainly influence life's outcomes. Those with more of an external locus of control believe that events in their life are due mainly to fate, luck, or conditions in the external environment. Locus of control is a generalized belief, so people with an external locus can feel in control in familiar situations (such as performing common tasks). However, their underlying locus of control would be apparent in new situations in which control over events is uncertain.

People with a more internal locus of control have a more positive self-evaluation. They also tend to perform better in most employment situations, are more successful in their careers, earn more money, and are better suited for leadership positions. Internals are also more satisfied with their jobs, cope better in stressful situations, and are more motivated by performance-based reward systems.[24] One worrisome observation is that young people significantly shifted from an internal to more of an external locus of control over the four decades since the early 1960s.[25]

THE SOCIAL SELF

Everyone has a self-concept that includes at least a few identities (manager, parent, golfer, etc.) and each identity is defined by a set of attributes. These attributes highlight both the person's uniqueness (personal identity) or association with others (social identity).[26] *Personal identity* (also known as internal self-concept) consists of attributes that make us unique and distinct from people in the social groups to which we have a connection. For instance, an unusual achievement that distinguishes you from other people typically becomes a personal identity characteristic. Personal identity refers to something about you as an individual without reference to a larger group.

At the same time, human beings are social animals; they have an inherent drive to be associated with others and to be recognized as part of social communities. This drive to belong is reflected in self-concept by the fact that all individuals define themselves to some degree by their relationships.[27] This *social identity* (also called external self-concept) is the central theme of **social identity theory**, which says that people define themselves by the groups to which they belong or have an emotional attachment. For instance, someone might have a social identity as a Canadian, a graduate of the Southern Alberta Institute of Technology, and an employee at Potash Corp. (see Exhibit 3.2). Social identity is a complex combination of many memberships arranged in a hierarchy of importance. One factor determining importance is how easily we are identified as members of the reference group, such as by our gender, age, and ethnicity. A second factor is your minority status in a group. It is difficult to ignore your gender in a class where most other students are the opposite gender. For example, in that context, gender tends to become a stronger defining feature of your social identity than it is in social settings where there are many people of the same gender.

Along with demographic characteristics, the group's status is an important factor in determining whether we include it in our social identity because this association makes us feel better about ourselves (i.e., self-enhancement). Medical doctors usually define themselves by their profession because of its high status. Some people describe themselves by where they work ("I work at Research In Motion") because their employer has a good reputation. Others never mention where they work because their employer is noted for poor relations with employees or has a poor reputation in the community.[28]

Everyone tries to balance their personal and social identities, but the priority for uniqueness (personal identities) versus relatedness (social identities) differs from one person to the next. People whose self-concepts are heavily defined by social rather than personal identities are more motivated to abide by team norms and more easily influenced by peer pressure. Those who place more emphasis on personal identities, on the other hand, speak out more frequently against the majority and are less motivated to follow the team's wishes. Furthermore, expressing disagreement with others is a sign of distinctiveness and can help employees form a clearer self-concept, particularly when that disagreement is based on differences in personal values.[29]

social identity theory A theory that explains that people define themselves by the groups to which they belong or have an emotional attachment.

 People whose self-concepts are heavily defined by social rather than personal identities are more motivated to abide by team norms and more easily influenced by peer pressure.**"**

SELF-CONCEPT AND ORGANIZATIONAL BEHAVIOUR

Self-concept has become a hot topic in several disciplines and is now gaining attention in organizational behaviour as a valuable set of theories to explain employee attitudes and behaviour. For instance, recent studies have revealed that self-concept is a valuable concept for understanding leadership, team dynamics, employee motivation, decision making, influence, organizational commitment, and other topics that we will discuss in this book.[30] Consequently, self-concept and its specific elements will be mentioned in several topics throughout this book, including later parts of this chapter.

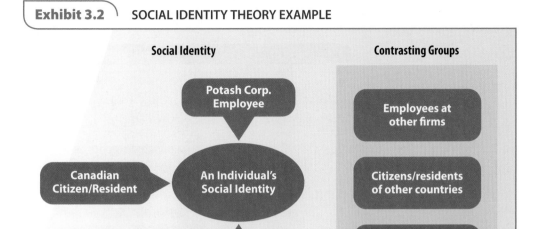

Exhibit 3.2   SOCIAL IDENTITY THEORY EXAMPLE

PERCEIVING THE WORLD AROUND US

L02

perception The process of receiving information about and making sense of the world around us.

selective attention The process of attending to some information received by our senses and ignoring other information.

We spend more time perceiving ourselves (thinking about our self-concept) than anyone else. Nevertheless, our perceptual energy is directed toward the outer world most of the time. Whether as a structural engineer, forensic accountant, or senior executive, you need to pay attention to how to make sense of the world around you, including the conditions that challenge the accuracy of those perceptions. **Perception** is the process of receiving information about and making sense of the world around us. It entails determining which information to notice, how to categorize this information, and how to interpret it within the framework of our existing knowledge. This perceptual process generally follows the steps shown in Exhibit 3.3. Perception begins when environmental stimuli are received through our senses. Most stimuli that bombard our senses are screened out; the rest are organized and interpreted.

The process of attending to some information received by our senses and ignoring other information is called **selective attention**. Selective attention is influenced by characteristics of the person or object being perceived, particularly size, intensity, motion, repetition, and novelty. For example, a small, flashing red light on a nurses' station console is immediately noticed because it is bright (intensity), flashing (motion), a rare event (novelty), and has symbolic meaning that a patient's vital signs are failing. Notice that selective attention is also influenced by the context in which the target is perceived. The selective attention process is triggered by things or people who might be out of context, such as someone with a foreign accent in a setting where most people have Canadian accents.

Characteristics of the perceiver also influence selection attention, usually without the perceiver's awareness.[31] When information is received through the senses, our brain quickly and nonconsciously assesses whether it is relevant or irrelevant to us and then attaches emotional markers (worry, happiness, boredom) to that information. These emotional markers help us to store information in memory; they also reproduce the same emotions when we are subsequently thinking about this information.[32] The selective attention process is far from perfect, however. The Greek philosopher Plato acknowledged this imperfection long ago when he wrote that we see reality only as shadows reflecting against the rough wall of a cave.[33]

One perceptual bias in selective attention is the effect of our assumptions and conscious anticipation of future events. You are more likely to notice a co-worker's email among the daily bombardment of messages when you expect to receive that email

Exhibit 3.3   MODEL OF THE PERCEPTUAL PROCESS

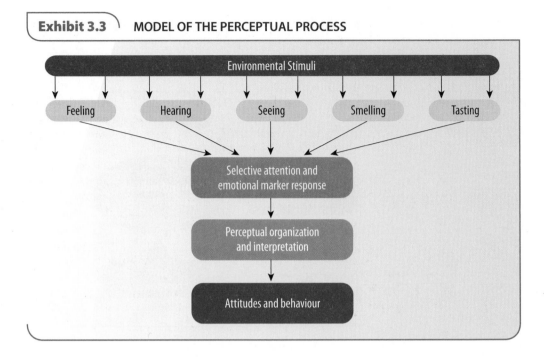

Environmental Stimuli

Feeling | Hearing | Seeing | Smelling | Tasting

Selective attention and emotional marker response

Perceptual organization and interpretation

Attitudes and behaviour

(particularly when it is important to you). Unfortunately, expectations and assumptions also cause us to screen out potentially important information. In one study, students were asked to watch a 30-second video clip in which several people passed around two basketballs. Students who were instructed just to watch the video clip easily noticed someone dressed in a gorilla suit walking among the players for nine seconds and stopping to thump his/her chest. But only half of the students who were asked to count the number of times one basketball was passed around noticed the intruding gorilla.[34]

Another selective attention problem, called **confirmation bias**, is the tendency for people to screen out information that is contrary to their decisions, beliefs, values, and assumptions, whereas confirming information is more readily accepted through the perceptual process.[35] This bias occurs, for instance, when we form an opinion or theory about something, such as a consumer trend or an employee's potential. The preconception causes us to select information that is consistent with the theory and to ignore contrary or seemingly irrelevant information. Studies have reported that this faulty selective attention occurs when police detectives and other forensic experts quickly form theories about what happened.[36]

confirmation bias The tendency to screen out information that is contrary to our decisions, beliefs, values, and assumptions, and to more readily accept confirming information.

Perceptually Blinded by Theory

"It is a capital mistake to theorize before you have all the evidence," warned the mythical detective Sherlock Holmes in *A Study in Scarlet*. "It biases the judgment." Law enforcement agencies around the world have been following Holmes' advice to reduce the risk of wrongful conviction. Rather than test theories about a crime, detectives do their best to *avoid* forming or at least paying attention to any theories too early in the investigation. "We have to be extremely careful not to have tunnel vision and not to come up with a theory and start to go down that road," advises an RCMP spokesperson during investigation of a mass murder in British Columbia. Vernon Geberth echoes this view. "At times, investigators may close their minds to other possibilities once they've developed a theory," says the retired lieutenant commander of the New York City police department's Homicide division. "Then they begin to try to make the evidence fit their theory instead of allowing the evidence to lead you to the suspect."[37] *The Canadian Press Images/Charles-Antoine Auger*

There are many examples of confirmation bias in scientific research, where scientists have ignored or removed evidence that contradicts their prized theories. One classic case occurred in the 1970s when nuclear particle researchers at CERN in Europe found an unusual dip in the pattern formed by a colliding particle. This was an exciting discovery, until a growing chorus of nuclear researchers elsewhere reported that they could not replicate that dip in their data. CERN vigorously defended the existence of the dip until the contrary evidence was overwhelming. What happened? CERN's researchers looked closely at batches of data that did not show any dip. They were convinced that the missing dip was due to bad data, so they invariably found enough justification to discard batches that didn't have any dip. Meanwhile, batches of confirming data were accepted without scrutiny. In effect, CERN discarded the evidence that opposed their exciting, but short-lived, discovery![38]

PERCEPTUAL ORGANIZATION AND INTERPRETATION

categorical thinking Organizing people and objects into preconceived categories that are stored in our long-term memory.

People make sense of information even before they become aware of it. This sense making partly includes **categorical thinking**—the mostly nonconscious process of organizing people and objects into preconceived categories that are stored in our long-term memory.[39] Categorical thinking relies on a variety of automatic perceptual grouping principles. Things are often grouped together based on their similarity or proximity to others. If you notice that a group of similar-looking people includes several professors, for instance, you will likely assume that the others in that group are also professors. Another form of perceptual grouping is based on the need for cognitive closure, such as filling in missing information about what happened at a meeting that you didn't attend (e.g., who was there, where it was held). A third form of grouping occurs when we think we see trends in otherwise ambiguous information. Several studies have found that people have a natural tendency to see patterns that really are random events, such as presumed winning streaks among sports stars or in gambling.[40]

The process of "making sense" of the world around us also involves interpreting incoming information. This happens as quickly as selecting and organizing because the previously mentioned emotional markers are tagged to incoming stimuli, which are essentially quick judgments about whether that information is good or bad for us. To give you an idea of how quickly and systematically this nonconscious perceptual interpretation process occurs, consider the following study:[41] After viewing video clips of university instructors teaching an undergraduate class, eight observers rated the instructors on several personal characteristics (optimistic, likeable, anxious, active, etc.). The observers had never met the instructors and they rated the instructors without communicating with each other. Yet their scores showed considerable agreement about which instructors were better or worse on each attribute. Equally important, these ratings were very similar to the ratings completed by students who attended the class in person.

You might find these results interesting, but they are really remarkable when you consider that the observers formed their perceptions from as little as *six seconds* of video—three segments of two seconds each selected randomly from the one-hour class! Furthermore, the video didn't have any sound. In other words, perceptions are formed from very thin slices of information, and those perceptions are similar to views formed by people with much more detail about the perceived object. Other studies have reported similar findings for observations of high school teachers, courtroom judges, and physicians. Collectively, these "thin slice" studies reveal that selective attention, perceptual organization, and interpretation operate very quickly and to a large extent without our awareness.

mental models Visual or relational images in our mind that represent the external world.

Mental Models   To achieve our goals with some degree of predictability and sanity, we need road maps of the environments in which we live. These road maps, called **mental models**, are internal representations of the external world.[42] They consist of visual or relational images in our mind, such as what the classroom looks like or what happens when we submit an assignment late. Mental models partly rely on the process of perceptual grouping to make sense of things; they fill in the missing pieces, including the causal connection among events. For example, you have a mental model about attending a class lecture or seminar, including assumptions or expectations about where the instructor and students arrange themselves in the room, how they ask and answer questions, and so forth. We can create a mental image of a class in progress.

Mental models play an important role in sense making, yet they also make it difficult to see the world in different ways. For example, accounting professionals tend to see corporate problems from an accounting perspective, whereas marketing professionals see the same problems from a marketing perspective. Mental models also block our recognition of new opportunities. How do we change mental models? That's a tough challenge. After all, we developed models from several years of experience and reinforcement. The most important way to minimize the perceptual problems with mental models is to constantly question them. We need to ask ourselves about the assumptions we make. Working with people from diverse backgrounds is another way to break out of existing mental models. Colleagues from different cultures and areas of expertise tend to have different mental models, so working with them makes our own assumptions more obvious.

SPECIFIC PERCEPTUAL PROCESSES AND PROBLEMS

LO3

Within the perceptual process described on the previous pages are specific sub-processes and associated errors that have received considerable attention by OB experts. Over the next several pages, we will examine several of these perceptual processes and biases as well as their implications for organizational behaviour. We begin with the most widely known perceptual process and bias: stereotyping.

STEREOTYPING IN ORGANIZATIONS

One reason why few women become firefighters is that they, along with family and friends, usually depict fightfighters as rugged, risk-oriented, physically very strong, and male. Although this image has kernels of truth (firefighting requires above average physical strength and has above average risk), many features of the occupation such as helping others, teamwork, and focus on safety, are seldom mentioned. In other words, people have a stereotype of firefighters that is neither accurate nor desirable for most women.

> **stereotyping** The process of assigning traits to people on the basis of their membership in a social category.

Stereotyping is the perceptual process of adopting and applying beliefs about the characteristics of identifiable groups.[43] These characteristics might be personality traits, physical characteristics, expected behaviours, or a host of other qualities. For instance, most people recognize the stereotype that professors are intelligent and absentminded. Stereotypes are formed to some extent from personal experience, but they are mainly provided to us through media images (e.g., movie characters) and other cultural prototypes. In other words, stereotypes are collective beliefs—often held across an entire society and sometimes across several cultures—rather than beliefs held uniquely by each person. Stereotypes are typically generalizations because they assume everyone in the group has the group's traits. In other words, stereotyping involves assigning a group's perceived attributes—particularly personality and other nonobservable features—to individuals known or believed to be members of that group. If we learn that someone is a professor, for example, we implicitly assume the person is also intelligent and absentminded. Historically, researchers also defined stereotypes as exaggerations or falsehoods. This is often true, but some stereotypes can be fairly accurate.

Why People Stereotype   One reason why people engage in stereotyping is that, as a form of categorical thinking, it is a natural and mostly nonconscious "energy-saving" process that simplifies our understanding of the world. It is easier to remember features of a stereotype than the constellation of characteristics unique to everyone we meet.[44] A second reason is that we have an innate need to understand and anticipate how others will behave. We don't have much information when first meeting someone, so we rely heavily on stereotypes to fill in the missing pieces. The higher the perceiver's need for cognitive closure, the higher the reliance on stereotypes.

Professional Accountants Break the Stereotype

Samantha Merritt (shown in photo) spent five years flying small planes for an air charter company in Canada's rugged Yukon. She flew to more than 300 bush locations, delivering everything from snowmobiles to caribou carcasses. With this background, it might be difficult to believe that Merritt is now an accountant. Research indicates that films, literature, and other cultural sources paint a fairly consistent and somewhat negative stereotype of accountants: typically white males who are boring, monotonous, cautious, unromantic, and antisocial. Fortunately, according to one recent survey, most people think this traditional stereotype is mostly inaccurate. Professional accountants also have much more diverse backgrounds than the stereotype depicts. "A CA is no longer a guy in a dark suit," says an executive at the Chartered Accountants of Ontario. "Now almost anything goes. . . . There is no stereotype that can describe a CA student today."[45] *Jiri Herman/KlixPix*

A third reason is that stereotyping enhances our self-concept. Earlier in this chapter we explained that people define themselves by the groups to which they belong or have an emotional attachment. They are also motivated to maintain a positive self-concept. This combination of social identity and self-enhancement occurs through categorization, homogenization, and differentiation:[46]

- *Categorization.* Social identity is a comparative process, and the comparison begins by categorizing people into distinct groups. By viewing someone (including yourself) as a Ontarian, for example, you remove that person's individuality and, instead, see him or her as a prototypical representative of the group "Ontarians." This categorization then allows you to distinguish Ontarians from people who live in, say, Alberta or Newfoundland.

- *Homogenization.* To simplify the comparison process, we tend to think that people within each group are very similar to each other. For instance, we think Ontarians collectively have similar attitudes and characteristics, whereas Albertans collectively have their own set of characteristics. Of course, every individual is unique, but we tend to lose sight of this fact when thinking about our social identity and how we compare to people in other social groups.

- *Differentiation.* Social identity fulfills our inherent need to have a distinct and positive self-concept. To achieve this, we do more than categorize and homogenize people; we also differentiate them by assigning more favourable characteristics to people in our groups than to people in other groups. This differentiation is often subtle, but it can escalate into a "good guy–bad guy" contrast when groups are in conflict with each other.[47] In other words, when out-group members threaten our self-concept, we are particularly motivated (often without our awareness) to assign negative stereotypes to them.

Problems with Stereotyping   Everyone engages in stereotyping, but it distorts our perceptions in various ways. First, although stereotypes are not completely fictional, neither do they accurately describe every person in a social category. For instance, the widespread "bean counter" stereotype may be true of some accountants, but it is certainly not characteristic of all—or even many—people in this profession. Even so, once we categorize someone as an accountant, the features of accountants in general rather than the features of the specific person get recalled, even when the person does not possess many of the stereotypic traits.

Another problem with stereotyping is that it lays the foundation for discriminatory attitudes and behaviour. Forty-one percent of Canadians say they have experienced discrimination in employment within the past five years, with age and race discrimination being the most common. Similarly, Statistics Canada reports that the majority of visible minorities in Canada say they feel or experience discrimination in the workplace.[48] This perceptual bias usually occurs as *unintentional (systemic) discrimination*, whereby decision makers rely on stereotypes to establish notions of the "ideal" person in specific roles. A person who doesn't fit the ideal tends to receive a less favourable evaluation. This subtle discrimination often shows up in age discrimination claims, such as the case in which Ryanair's recruitment advertising said it was looking for "young dynamic" employees. Recruiters at the Irish discount airline probably didn't intentionally discriminate against older people, but the tribunal concluded that systemic discrimination did occur because none of the job applicants were over 40 years old.[49]

The more serious form of stereotype bias is *intentional discrimination* or *prejudice*, in which people hold unfounded negative attitudes toward people belonging to a particular stereotyped group.[50] Is overt prejudice less common today? Perhaps, but there are plenty of examples to remind us that it still exists. Quebec's Human Rights Tribunal was shocked to discover that one of Canada's largest vegetable farms prevented black employees from eating in the regular cafeteria. Instead, they were relegated to a "blacks only" eating area that lacked heat, running water, proper toilets, and refrigeration.[51] A French study of 2,300 help-wanted ads revealed that job applicants with French-sounding names were much more likely to get job interviews than were applicants with North African or sub-Saharan African names, even though the study sent employers the same résumés for both names! Furthermore, when applicants personally visited human resource staff, those with foreign names were often told the job had been filled, whereas few of the applicants with French names received this message (even when visiting afterwards).[52]

If stereotyping is such a problem, shouldn't we try to avoid this process altogether? Unfortunately, it's not that simple. Most experts agree that categorical thinking (including stereotyping) is an automatic and nonconscious process. Specialized training programs can minimize stereotype activation to some extent, but for the most part the process is hardwired in our brain cells.[53] Also remember that stereotyping helps us in several valuable (although fallible) ways described earlier: minimizing mental effort, filling in missing information, and supporting our social identity. The good news is that while it is very difficult to prevent the *activation* of stereotypes, we can minimize the *application* of stereotypic information. Later in this chapter, we identify ways to minimize stereotyping and other perceptual biases.

ATTRIBUTION THEORY

attribution process The perceptual process of deciding whether an observed behaviour or event is caused largely by internal or external factors.

Another widely discussed perceptual phenomenon in organizational settings is the **attribution process**. Attribution involves deciding whether an observed behaviour or event is caused mainly by the person (internal factors) or by the environment (external factors).[54] Internal factors include the person's ability or motivation, whereas external factors include lack of resources, other people, or just luck. If a co-worker doesn't show up for an important meeting, for instance, we infer either internal attributions (the co-worker is forgetful, lacks motivation, etc.) or external attributions (traffic, a family emergency, or other circumstances prevented the co-worker from attending).

People rely on the three attribution rules shown in Exhibit 3.4 to determine whether someone's behaviour mainly has an internal or external attribution. Internal attributions are made when the observed individual behaved this way in the past (high consistency), he or she behaves like this toward other people or in different situations (low distinctiveness), and other people do not behave this way in similar situations (low consensus). On the other hand, an external attribution is made when there is low consistency, high distinctiveness, and high consensus.

Exhibit 3.4   **RULES OF ATTRIBUTION**

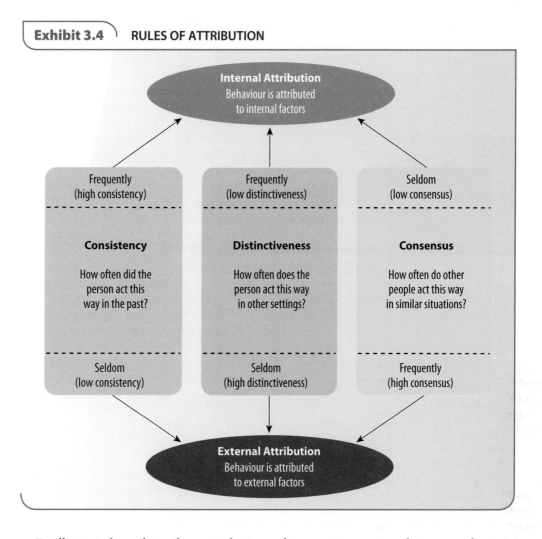

To illustrate how these three attribution rules operate, suppose that an employee is making poor-quality products one day on a particular machine. We would probably conclude that there is something wrong with the machine (an external attribution) if the employee has made good-quality products on this machine in the past (low consistency), the employee makes good-quality products on other machines (high distinctiveness), and other employees have recently had quality problems on this machine (high consensus). We would make an internal attribution, on the other hand, if the employee usually makes poor-quality products on this machine (high consistency), other employees produce good-quality products on this machine (low consensus), and the employee also makes poor-quality products on other machines (low distinctiveness).[55]

Attribution is a necessary process; we need to form cause-effect relationships to survive in our environment. How we react to a co-worker's poor performance depends on our internal or external attribution of that performance. Students who make internal attributions about their poor performance are more likely to drop out of their programs, for instance.[56] However, as we see next, people distort their perceptions through various attribution errors.

Attribution Errors   Attribution is the source of a few perceptual errors, the two most common of which are fundamental attribution error and self-serving bias. **Fundamental attribution error** refers to our tendency to perceive another person's actions caused mainly by internal attributions, whereas we recognize both internal and external causes of our own actions.[57] We tend to identify a co-worker's motivation as the main reason why he or she is late for work (e.g., doesn't like the job), whereas we attribute our own lateness

fundamental attribution error The tendency to see the person rather than the situation as the main cause of that person's behaviour.

partly or mostly to external factors such as traffic jams, failed alarm clocks, or unexpected emergencies (e.g., getting the kids ready for school). Fundamental attribution error occurs because observers can't easily see the external factors that constrain the person's behaviour. We didn't see the traffic jam that caused the person to be late, for instance. Research suggests that fundamental attribution error is more common in Western countries than in Asian cultures, where people are taught from an early age to pay attention to the context in interpersonal relations and to see everything as being connected in a holistic way.[58]

self-serving bias The tendency to attribute our favourable outcomes to internal factors and our failures to external factors.

Nearly a century ago, fictional New York crime investigator Philo Vance quipped, "Bad luck is merely a defensive and self-consoling synonym for inefficiency." Vance was referring to an attribution error known as **self-serving bias**, which is the tendency to attribute our failures to external causes (such as bad luck) more than internal causes (e.g., inefficiency), while successes are due more to internal than external factors.[59] Simply put, we take credit for our successes and blame others or the situation for our mistakes. In annual reports, for example, executives mainly refer to their personal qualities as reasons for the company's successes and to external factors as reasons for the company's failures. Similarly, entrepreneurs in one recent study overwhelmingly cited situational causes for their business failure (funding, economy) whereas even in interviews they noticeably understated lack of vision, social capital skills, and other personal causes.[60] Philo Vance's comment about bad luck points out that self-serving bias is associated with self-enhancement. By relying on external causes of failure and internal causes of success, people generate a more positive (and self-consoling) self-concept.

SELF-FULFILLING PROPHECY

self-fulfilling prophecy The perceptual process in which our expectations about another person cause that person to act in a way that is consistent with those expectations.

Self-fulfilling prophecy is the perceptual process in which our expectations about another person cause that person to act in a way that is consistent with those expectations. In other words, our perceptions can influence reality. Exhibit 3.5 illustrates the four steps in the self-fulfilling-prophecy process using the example of a supervisor and an employee.[61] The process begins when the supervisor forms expectations about the employee's future behaviour and performance. These expectations are sometimes inaccurate, because first impressions are usually formed from limited information.

Exhibit 3.5   THE SELF-FULFILLING-PROPHECY CYCLE

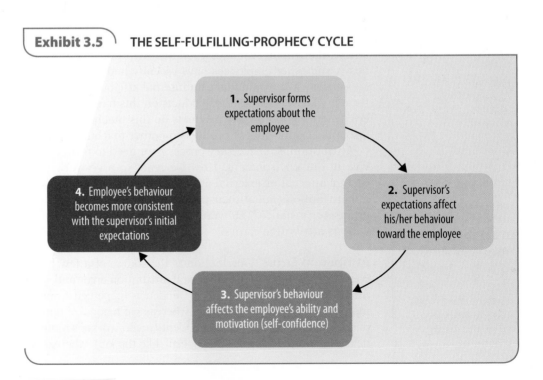

1. Supervisor forms expectations about the employee

2. Supervisor's expectations affect his/her behaviour toward the employee

3. Supervisor's behaviour affects the employee's ability and motivation (self-confidence)

4. Employee's behaviour becomes more consistent with the supervisor's initial expectations

The supervisor's expectations influence his or her treatment of employees. Specifically, high-expectancy employees (those expected to do well) receive more emotional support through nonverbal cues (e.g., more smiling and eye contact), more frequent and valuable feedback and reinforcement, more challenging goals, better training, and more opportunities to demonstrate good performance.

The third step in self-fulfilling prophecy includes two effects of the supervisor's behaviour on the employee. First, through better training and more practise opportunities, a high-expectancy employee acquires more skills and knowledge than a low-expectancy employee. Second, the employee becomes more self-confident, which results in higher motivation and willingness to set more challenging goals.[62] In the final step, high-expectancy employees have higher motivation and better skills, resulting in better performance, while the opposite is true of low-expectancy employees.

There are many examples of self-fulfilling prophecies in work and school settings.[63] Research has found that women perform less well on math tests after being informed that men tend to perform better on them. Women perform better on these tests when they are not exposed to this negative self-fulfilling prophecy. Similarly, people over 65 years of age receive lower results on memory tests after hearing that mental ability declines with age. Another study reported that the performance of Israeli Defence Force trainees was influenced by their instructor's expectations regarding the trainee's potential in the program. Self-fulfilling prophecy was at work here because the instructor's expectations were based on a list provided by researchers showing which recruits had high and low potential, even though the researchers had actually listed these trainees randomly.

Contingencies of Self-Fulfilling Prophecy   Self-fulfilling prophecies are more powerful under some conditions than others. The self-fulfilling-prophecy effect is stronger at the beginning of a relationship, such as when employees are first hired. It is also stronger when several people (rather than just one person) hold the same expectations of the individual. In other words, we might be able to ignore one person's doubts about our potential but not the collective doubts of several people. The self-fulfilling-prophecy effect is also stronger among people with a history of low achievement. High achievers can draw on their past successes to offset low expectations, whereas low achievers do not have past successes to support their self-confidence. Fortunately, the opposite is also true: Low achievers respond more favourably than high achievers to positive self-fulfilling prophecy. Low achievers don't receive this positive encouragement very often, so it probably has a stronger effect on their motivation to excel.[64]

The main lesson from the self-fulfilling-prophecy literature is that leaders need to develop and maintain a positive, yet realistic, expectation toward all employees. This recommendation is consistent with the emerging philosophy of **positive organizational behaviour**, which suggests that focusing on the positive rather than negative aspects of life will improve organizational success and individual well-being. Communicating hope and optimism is so important that it is identified as one of the critical success factors for physicians and surgeons. Training programs that make leaders aware of the power of positive expectations seem to have minimal effect, however. Instead, generating positive expectations and hope depend on a corporate culture of support and learning. Hiring supervisors who are inherently optimistic toward their staff is another way of increasing the incidence of positive self-fulfilling prophecies.

positive organizational behaviour   A perspective of organizational behaviour that focuses on building positive qualities and traits within individuals or institutions as opposed to focusing on what is wrong with them.

OTHER PERCEPTUAL EFFECTS

Self-fulfilling prophecy, attribution, and stereotyping are among the most common perceptual processes and biases in organizational settings, but there are many others. Four of them which have received attention in organizational settings are briefly described below.

halo effect   A perceptual error whereby our general impression of a person, usually based on one prominent characteristic, distorts our perception of other characteristics of that person.

Halo Effect   The **halo effect** occurs when our general impression of a person, usually based on one prominent characteristic, distorts our perception of other characteristics of that person.[65] If a supervisor who values punctuality notices that an employee is sometimes late for work, the supervisor might form a negative image of the employee and evaluate that person's other traits unfavourably as well. The halo effect is most likely to occur when concrete information about the perceived target is missing or we are not sufficiently motivated to search for it. Instead, we use our general impression of the person to fill in the missing information.

false-consensus effect
A perceptual error in which we overestimate the extent to which others have beliefs and characteristics similar to our own.

False-Consensus Effect

The **false-consensus effect** (also called *similar-to-me effect*) occurs when people overestimate the extent to which others have similar beliefs or behaviours to our own.[66] Employees who are thinking of quitting their jobs overestimate the percentage of co-workers who are also thinking about quitting, for example. There are several explanations for false-consensus effect. One is that we are comforted by the belief that others are similar to us, particularly regarding less acceptable or divisive behaviour. Put differently, we perceive "everyone does it" to reinforce our self-concept regarding behaviours that do not have a positive image (quitting, parking illegally, etc.). A second explanation is that we interact more with people who have similar views and behaviours, which causes us to overestimate how common those views/behaviours are in the entire organization or society. Third, as noted earlier in this chapter, we are more likely to remember information that is consistent with our own views and selectively screen out communication that is contrary to our beliefs. Finally, our social identity process homogenizes people within groups, so we tend to think that everyone in that group has similar opinions and behaviour, including the false-consensus topic.

primacy effect A perceptual error in which we quickly form an opinion of people on the basis of first information we receive about them.

Primacy Effect

The **primacy effect** is our tendency to quickly form an opinion of people on the basis of the first information we receive about them.[67] It is the notion that first impressions are lasting impressions. This rapid perceptual organization and interpretation occurs because we need to make sense of the world around us. The problem is that first impressions—particularly negative first impressions—are difficult to change. After categorizing someone, we tend to select subsequent information that supports our first impression and screen out information that opposes that impression.

recency effect A perceptual error in which the most recent information dominates our perception of others.

Recency Effect

The **recency effect** occurs when the most recent information dominates our perceptions.[68] This perceptual bias is most common when people (especially those with limited experience) are making an evaluation involving complex information. For instance, auditors must digest large volumes of information in their judgments about financial documents, and the most recent information received prior to the decision tends to get weighted more heavily than information received at the beginning of the audit. Similarly, when supervisors evaluate the performance of employees over the previous year, the most recent performance information dominates the evaluation because it is the most easily recalled.

IMPROVING PERCEPTIONS

L04

We can't bypass the perceptual process, but we should try to minimize perceptual biases and distortions. Three potentially effective ways to improve perceptions include awareness of perceptual biases, self-awareness, and meaningful interaction.

AWARENESS OF PERCEPTUAL BIASES

One of the most obvious and widely practised ways to reduce perceptual biases is by knowing that they exist. For example, diversity awareness training tries to minimize discrimination by making people aware of systemic discrimination as well as prejudices that occur through stereotyping. This training also attempts to dispel myths about people from various cultural and demographic groups. Awareness of perceptual biases can reduce these biases to some extent by making people more mindful of their thoughts and actions. However, awareness training has only a limited effect.[69] One problem is that teaching people to reject incorrect stereotypes has the unintended effect of reinforcing rather than reducing reliance on those stereotypes. Another problem is that diversity training is ineffective for people with deeply held prejudices against those groups.

Self-fulfilling-prophecy awareness training has also failed to live up to expectations.[70] This training approach informs managers about the existence of the self-fulfilling-prophecy effect and encourages them to engage in more positive rather than negative self-fulfilling prophecies. Unfortunately, research has found that managers continue to engage in negative self-fulfilling prophecies after they complete the training program.

IMPROVING SELF-AWARENESS

A more powerful way to minimize perceptual biases is to help people discover biases in their own decisions and behaviour.[71] We need to understand our beliefs, values, and attitudes to be more open-minded and nonjudgmental toward others. Self-awareness is equally important in other ways. For instance, the emerging concept of authentic leadership emphasizes self-awareness as the first step in a person's ability to effectively lead others (see Chapter 12). Essentially, we need to understand our own values, strengths, and biases as a foundation for building a vision and leading others toward that vision.[72]

But how do we become more self-aware? One approach is to complete formal tests that indicate any implicit biases you might have towards others. One such test (the accuracy of which is currently being hotly debated by scholars) is the Implicit Association Test (IAT). The IAT attempts to detect subtle racial, age, and gender bias by associating positive and negative words with specific demographic groups.[73] Many people are much more cautious about their stereotypes and prejudices after discovering that their test results show a personal bias against older people or individuals from different ethnic backgrounds.[74]

Another way to increase self-awareness and thereby reduce perceptual biases is by applying the **Johari Window**.[75] Developed by Joseph Luft and Harry Ingram (hence the name "Johari"), this model of self-awareness and mutual understanding divides information about you into four "windows"—open, blind, hidden, and unknown—based on whether your own values, beliefs, and experiences are known to you and to others (see Exhibit 3.6). The *open area* includes information about you that is known both to you and to others. The *blind area* refers to information that is known to others but not to you. For example, your colleagues might notice that you are self-conscious and awkward when meeting the company chief executive, but you are unaware of this fact. Information known to you but unknown to others is found in the *hidden area.* Finally,

Johari Window A model of mutual understanding that encourages disclosure and feedback to increase our own open area and reduce the blind, hidden, and unknown areas.

Exhibit 3.6 \ JOHARI WINDOW MODEL OF SELF-AWARENESS AND MUTUAL UNDERSTANDING

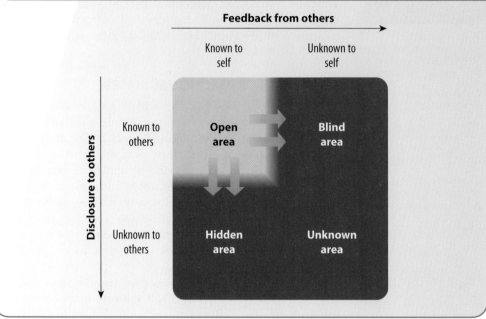

Source: Based on J. Luft, *Of Human Interaction* (Palo Alto, CA: National Press Books, 1969).

the *unknown area* includes your values, beliefs, and experiences that aren't known to you or others.

The main objective of the Johari Window is to increase the size of the open area so that both you and colleagues are aware of your perceptual limitations. This is partly accomplished by reducing the hidden area through *disclosure*—informing others of your beliefs, feelings, and experiences that may influence the work relationship.[76] The open area also increases through *feedback* from others about your behaviour. This information helps you to reduce your blind area, because co-workers often see things in you that you do not see. Finally, the combination of disclosure and feedback occasionally produces revelations about information in the unknown area.

MEANINGFUL INTERACTION

While the Johari Window relies on dialogue, self-awareness and mutual understanding can also improve through *meaningful interaction*.[77] Meaningful interaction is founded on the **contact hypothesis**, which states that, under certain conditions, people who interact with each other will be less prejudiced or perceptually biased against each other. Simply spending time with members of other groups can improve your understanding and opinion of that person to some extent. However, meaningful interaction is strongest when people work closely and frequently with each other on a shared goal that requires cooperation and reliance on each other. Everyone should have equal status in that context and should be engaged in a meaningful task. Global Connections 3.1 describes several examples of meaningful interaction where CEOs and other executives work beside front-line staff.

Meaningful interaction reduces dependence on stereotypes to understand others because we gain better knowledge about that individual and experience the unique attributes of that person in action. Meaningful interaction also potentially improves empathy toward others. **Empathy** refers to understanding and being sensitive to the feelings,

contact hypothesis A theory stating that the more we interact with someone, the less prejudiced or perceptually biased we will be against that person.

empathy A person's understanding of and sensitivity to the feelings, thoughts, and situation of others.

CONNECTIONS 3.1

CEO Reality Check by Working on the Front Line

If the meal service seems a bit slower than usual on your next Air New Zealand flight, it might be that CEO Rob Fyfe is doing the serving while chatting with passengers. Every month, Fyfe and his top executive team fill the roster as flight attendants, check-in counter staff, or baggage handlers. (The executives had to pass tests to work as cabin crew.) Helmut Wieser, an executive vice-president at Alcoa, also works beside front-line staff on the shop floor of several plants four times a year. As part of a television series on CEOs in front-line jobs, Herschend Family Entertainment CEO Joel Manby worked incognito alongside employees at the entertainment company in jobs ranging from waiting tables to window-washing gigantic aquarium fish tanks.

Working in these front-line jobs gives executives a reality check about the business and its employees. For example, along with getting to know staff, Joel Manby discovered that Herschend's benefits and services for employees could be better aligned with employee needs. He also realized that he had become a bit too recluse. "Working with [these employees] helped me realize that during the recession, I had become withdrawn and detached, affected by difficult business decisions," Manby acknowledges. "They showed me the importance of getting back in touch with people."

Working in front-line jobs also gives new executives a better understanding about how the business works. When Moya Greene joined Canada Post as CEO a few years ago, she spent six months travelling around the country and working in a large sample of positions. "I knew I didn't know anything about the operation. I wanted to understand what it takes for the whole thing to run," says Greene, who recently became the first foreigner to lead Britain's Royal Mail. She spent hot summer nights working with mail sorters. She delivered mail with a carrier in Pointe-Claire, Quebec. Greene also got first-hand experience with the poor state of Canada Post's infrastructure in downtown Winnipeg. "It was

Air New Zealand CEO Rob Fyfe and other executives keep their perceptions in focus by working beside frontline staff. *Photograph by Brett Phibbs/New Zealand Herald*

a real eye-opener," Greene recalls. "The building was literally falling down. It was being held up with metal netting."

Some companies have extended this front-line experience by giving professional and administrative staff face-to-face time with customers. Every non-customer-contact employee at WideOpenWest spends time every quarter working at the Denver-based telecommunication company's call centre or travelling to work sites with technology staff. Everyone at Domino's head office in Ann Arbor, Michigan, attends Pizza Prep School, where they learn how to make pizzas and run a pizza store. New hires at 1-800-GOT-JUNK?, North America's largest rubbish removal company, spend an entire week on a junk removal truck to better understand how the business works. "How can you possibly empathize with someone out in the field unless you've been on the truck yourself?" asks Brian Scudamore, founder and CEO of the Vancouver-based company.[78]

thoughts, and situations of others.[79] People empathize when they cognitively transpose themselves into the other person's place as if they are the other person. This perceptual experience is both cognitive and emotional, meaning that empathy is about understanding as well as feeling what the other person experiences in that context. Empathizing with others improves our sensitivity to the external causes of another person's performance and behaviour, thereby reducing fundamental attribution error. A supervisor who imagines what it's like to be a single mother, for example, would become more sensitive to the external causes of lateness and other events among such employees.

GLOBAL MINDSET: DEVELOPING PERCEPTIONS ACROSS BORDERS

L05

Anne Connelly had previously worked outside Canada, but her current job at Médecins Sans Frontières (Doctors Without Borders) pushed her even further onto the global stage. Connelly was sent to the Central African Republic to help the government with some of its financial programs. The setting wasn't for the fainthearted. "There has been civil unrest in the country for a while, mainly caused by poor government and warring rebel tribes coming in from neighbouring countries," Connelly explains. But the experience of working in other lands with people who have different perceptions and experiences is exactly what Connelly had been seeking. "DeGroote taught me to develop a global mindset of how businesses operate at the international level," says the McMaster University's (DeGroote) MBA graduate. "By learning the culture, the languages, the people, the climate, everything, you can develop more holistic solutions to any given problem."[80]

There has been a groundswell of interest among corporate leaders in employees such as Anne Connelly who are developing a global mindset. A **global mindset** refers to an individual's ability to perceive, know about, and process information across cultures. It includes (a) an awareness of, openness to, and respect for other views and practices in the world, (b) the capacity to empathize and act effectively across cultures, (c) ability to process complex information about novel environments, and (d) the ability to comprehend and reconcile intercultural matters with multiple levels of thinking.[81]

Let's look at each of these features. First, global mindset occurs as people develop more of a global than local/parochial frame of reference about their business and its environment. They also have more knowledge and appreciation of many cultures and do not judge the competence of others by their national or ethnic origins. Second, global mindset includes understanding the mental models held by colleagues from other cultures as well as their emotional experiences in a given situation. Furthermore, this empathy translates into effective use of words and behaviours that are compatible with the local culture. Third, people with a strong global mindset are able to process and analyze large volumes of information in new and diverse situations. Finally, global mindset involves the capacity to quickly develop accurate mental models of situations, particularly at both a local and global level of analysis.

As you imagine, employees offer tremendous value to organizations as they develop a global mindset.[82] They develop better relationships across cultures by understanding and showing respect to distant colleagues and partners. They can sieve through huge volumes of ambiguous and novel information transmitted in multinational relationships. They have a capacity to form networks and exchange resources more rapidly across borders. They also develop greater sensitivity and respond more quickly to emerging global opportunities. "Today's business leaders must learn to develop a global mindset that enables them to leverage the diverse perspectives necessary to drive innovation and renew economic growth," advises Trent Henry, chairman and chief executive officer of Ernst & Young Canada.

> **global mindset** An individual's ability to perceive, appreciate, and empathize with people from other cultures and to process complex cross-cultural information.

> " A global mindset enables people to develop better relationships across cultures by understanding and showing respect to distant colleagues and partners."

DEVELOPING A GLOBAL MINDSET

Developing a global mindset involves improving one's perceptions, so the practices described earlier on self-awareness and meaningful interaction are relevant. As with most perceptual capabilities, a global mindset begins with self-awareness—understanding one's own beliefs, values, and attitudes. Through self-awareness, people are more open-minded and nonjudgmental when receiving and processing complex information for decision making. In addition, employees develop a global mindset when they are given opportunities to compare their own mental models with those of co-workers

Gaining a Global Mindset Beyond the Comfort Zone

John Leiter spends most of his time helping companies conduct internal investigations of financial wrongdoing. But for three months the Boston-based Ernst & Young manager was transplanted to Montevideo, Uruguay, assisting a young information technology company with its first real five-year strategic plan. Leiter (shown in this photo with staff at the Uruguayan firm) was performing different work in a different country with a different culture and language. "I worked out of my comfort zone the entire time," he recalls. Ernst & Young has sent Leiter and many other high-performing employees to work with entrepreneurs in South America to gain a better understanding of themselves and of people from different cultures. "We need people with a global mindset, and what better way to develop a global mindset, and what more realistic way, than for somebody to have an immersion experience with just enough safety net," says Deborah K. Holmes, Ernst & Young Americas director of corporate responsibility.[83] *Courtesy of John Leiter*

or partners from other regions of the world. For example, employees might engage in virtual dialogues about how well the product's design or marketing strategy is received in Canada versus India or Chile. When companies engage in regular discussions about global competitors, suppliers, and other stakeholders, they eventually move the employee's sphere of awareness more toward that global stratum.

A global mindset develops through better knowledge of people and cultures. Some of that knowledge is acquired through formal programs, such as diversity training, but deeper absorption results from immersion in those cultures. Just as executives need to experience front-line jobs to better understand their customers and employees, so too do they and other employees need to have meaningful interaction with colleagues from other cultures in those settings. The more people embed themselves in the local environment (such as following local practices, eating local food, and using the local language), the more they tend to understand the perspectives and attitudes of their colleagues in those cultures.

Several companies have introduced special programs to accelerate global mindset development by sending teams of employees on social responsibility missions in developing countries for one or two months. IBM's Corporate Service Corps program is one of the leading examples. Each year about 500 IBMers, including two dozen Canadian employees, are dispatched to other countries where they are responsible for assisting local people on an economic or social development project. One such program helped Tanzania's largest university to introduce an online learning management system. Another team of six IMBers, including one from Canada, helped officials in Ho Chi Minh City in Vietnam to identify sustainable solutions for water, transportation, food, and other resources.

IBM CEO Sam Palmisano explains that employees in the Corporate Service Corps program will develop a better global mindset because "these people actually go out and work in emerging markets, to work in NGOs (nongovernment organizations), to work in these other kinds of environments, so they can get a perspective and learn . . . how to think about problems from another perspective, from another point of view." Dave Robitaille, manager of corporate citizenship and corporate affairs for IBM Canada, adds that "what we're aiming to do is train the next generation of global leaders and the way we're doing that is by exposing them to diverse cultures, different policy environments."[84]

CHAPTER SUMMARY

 LO1 Describe the elements of self-concept and explain how they affect an individual's behaviour and well-being.

Self-concept includes an individual's self-beliefs and self-evaluations. It has three structural dimensions: complexity, consistency, and clarity, all of which influence employee well-being, behaviour, and performance. People are inherently motivated to promote and protect their self-concept (self-enhancement) and to verify and maintain their existing self-concept (self-verification). Self-evaluation consists of self-esteem, self-efficacy, and locus of control. Self-concept also consists of both personality identity and social identity. Social identity theory explains how people define themselves in terms of the groups to which they belong or have an emotional attachment.

 LO2 Outline the perceptual process and discuss the effects of categorical thinking and mental models in that process.

Perception involves selecting, organizing, and interpreting information to make sense of the world around us. Perceptual organization engages categorical thinking—the mostly nonconscious process of organizing people and objects into preconceived categories that are stored in our long-term memory. Mental models—internal representations of the external world—also help us to make sense of incoming stimuli.

 LO3 Discuss how stereotyping, attribution, self-fulfilling prophecy, halo, false-consensus, primacy, and recency influence the perceptual process.

Stereotyping occurs when people assign traits to others based on their membership in a social category. This economizes mental effort, fills in missing information, and enhances our self-concept, but it also lays the foundation for prejudice and systemic discrimination. The attribution process involves deciding whether an observed behaviour or event is caused mainly by the person (internal factors) or the environment (external factors). Attributions are decided by perceptions of the consistency, distinctiveness, and consensus of the behaviour. This process is subject to fundamental attribution error and self-serving bias. Self-fulfilling prophecy occurs when our expectations about another person cause that person to act in a way that is consistent with those expectations. This effect is stronger when employees first join the work unit, when several people hold these expectations, and when the employee has a history of low achievement. Four

other perceptual errors commonly noted in organizations are the halo effect, false-consensus effect, primacy effect, and recency effect.

 LO4 Discuss three ways to improve perceptions, with specific application to organizational situations.

One way to minimize perceptual biases is to become more aware of their existence. Awareness of these biases makes people more mindful of their thoughts and actions, but this training sometimes reinforces rather than reduces reliance on stereotypes and tends to be ineffective for people with deeply held prejudices. A second strategy is to become more aware of biases in our own decisions and behaviour. Self-awareness increases through formal tests such as the AIT and by applying the Johari Window, which is a process in which others provide feedback to you about your behaviour and you offer disclosure to them about yourself. The third strategy is meaningful interaction, which applies the contact hypothesis that people who interact with each other will be less prejudiced or perceptually biased against each other. Meaningful interaction is strongest when people work closely and frequently with each other in relatively equal status on a shared meaningful task that requires cooperation and reliance on each other. Meaningful interaction helps to improve empathy, which is a person's understanding and sensitivity to the feelings, thoughts, and situations of others.

 LO5 Outline the main features of a global mindset and justify its usefulness to employees and organizations.

A global mindset is a multidimensional competency that includes the individual's ability to perceive, know about, and process information across cultures. This includes (a) an awareness of, openness to, and respect for other views and practices in the world, (b) the capacity to empathize and act effectively across cultures, (c) ability to process complex information about novel environments, and (d) the ability to comprehend and reconcile intercultural matters with multiple levels of thinking. A global mindset enables people to develop better cross-cultural relationships, to digest huge volumes of cross-cultural information, and to identify and respond more quickly to emerging global opportunities. Employees develop a global mindset through self-awareness, opportunities to compare their own mental models with people from other cultures, through formal cross-cultural training, and through immersion in other cultures.

KEY TERMS

attribution process, p. 74

categorical thinking, p. 71

confirmation bias, p. 70

contact hypothesis, p. 80

empathy, p. 80

false-consensus effect, p. 78

fundamental attribution error, p. 75

global mindset, p. 82

halo effect, p. 77

Johari Window, p. 79

locus of control, p. 67

mental models, p. 71

perception, p. 69

positive organizational
    behaviour, p. 77

primacy effect, p. 78   self-efficacy, p. 67   self-verification, p. 66
recency effect, p. 78   self-enhancement, p. 65   social identity theory, p. 68
selective attention, p. 69   self-fulfilling prophecy, p. 76 stereotyping, p. 72
self-concept, p. 64   self-serving bias, p. 76

CRITICAL-THINKING QUESTIONS

1. You are manager of a district that has just hired several recent university and college graduates. Most of these people are starting their first full-time job, although most or all have held part-time and summer positions in the past. They have general knowledge of their particular skill area (accounting, engineering, marketing, etc.) but know relatively little about specific business practices and developments. Explain how you would nurture the self-concepts in these new hires to strengthen their performance and maintain their psychological well-being. Also explain how you might reconcile the tendency for self-enhancement while preventing them from forming a negative self-evaluation.

2. Do you define yourself in terms of the university you attend? Why or why not? What are the implications of your answer for your university or college?

3. Several years ago, senior executives at energy company CanOil wanted to acquire an exploration company (HBOG) that was owned by another energy company, AmOil. Rather than face a hostile takeover and unfavourable tax implications, CanOil's two top executives met with the CEO of AmOil to discuss a friendly exchange of stock to carry out the transaction. AmOil's chief executive was previously unaware of CanOil's plans, and as the meeting began, the AmOil executive warned that he was there merely to listen. The CanOil executives were confident that AmOil wanted to sell HBOG because energy legislation at the time made HBOG a poor investment for AmOil. AmOil's CEO remained silent for most of the meeting, which CanOil executives interpreted as an implied agreement to proceed to buy AmOil stock on the market. But when CanOil launched the stock purchase a month later, AmOil's CEO was both surprised and outraged. He thought he had given the CanOil executives

the cold shoulder, remaining silent to show his disinterest in the deal. The misunderstanding nearly bankrupted CanOil because AmOil reacted by protecting its stock. What perceptual problem(s) likely occurred that led to this misunderstanding?

4. What mental models do you have about attending a college or university lecture? Are these mental models helpful? Could any of these mental models hold you back from achieving the full benefit of the lecture?

5. During a diversity management session, a manager suggests that stereotypes are a necessary part of working with others. "I have to make assumptions about what's in the other person's head, and stereotypes help me do that," she explains. "It's better to rely on stereotypes than to enter a working relationship with someone from another culture without any idea of what they believe in!" Discuss the merits of and problems with the manager's statement.

6. Describe how a manager or coach could use the process of self-fulfilling prophecy to enhance an individual's performance.

7. Self-awareness is increasingly recognized as an important ingredient for effective leadership. Suppose that you are responsible for creating a leadership development program in a government organization. What activities or processes would you introduce to help participants in this program to constructively develop a better self-awareness of their personality, values, and personal biases?

8. Almost everyone in a college or university business program has developed some degree of global mindset. What events or activities in your life have helped to nurture the global mindset you have developed so far? What actions can you take now, while still attending school, to further develop your global mindset?

  ## CASE STUDY 3.1

Hy Dairies, Ltd.

Syd Gilman read the latest sales figures with a great deal of satisfaction. The vice-president of marketing at Hy Dairies, Ltd., a large Canadian milk products manufacturer, was pleased to see that the marketing campaign to improve sagging sales of Hy's gourmet ice cream brand was working. Sales volume and market share of the product had increased significantly over the past two quarters compared with the previous year.

The improved sales of Hy's gourmet ice cream could be credited to Rochelle Beauport, who was assigned to the gourmet ice cream brand last year. Beauport had joined Hy less than two years ago as an assistant brand manager after leaving a similar job at a food products firm. She was one of the few visible minority employees in marketing management at Hy Dairies and had a promising career with the company. Gilman was pleased with Beauport's work and tried to let her know this in the annual performance reviews. He now had an excellent opportunity to reward her by offering the recently vacated position of market research coordinator. Although technically only a lateral transfer with a modest salary increase, the marketing research coordinator job would give Beauport broader experience in some high-profile work, which would enhance her career with Hy Dairies. Few people were aware that Gilman's own career had been boosted by working as marketing research coordinator at Hy several years before.

Rochelle Beauport had also seen the latest sales figures on Hy's gourmet ice cream and was expecting Gilman's call to meet with her that morning. Gilman began the conversation by briefly mentioning the favourable sales figures, and then explained that he wanted Beauport to take the marketing research coordinator job. Beauport was shocked by the news. She enjoyed brand management and particularly the challenge involved with controlling a product that directly affected the company's profitability. Marketing research coordinator was a technical support position—a "backroom" job— far removed from the company's bottom-line activities. Marketing research was not the route to top management in most organizations, Beauport thought. She had been sidelined.

After a long silence, Beauport managed a weak "Thank you, Mr. Gilman." She was too bewildered to protest. She wanted to collect her thoughts and reflect on what she had done wrong. Also, she did not know her boss well enough to be openly critical.

Gilman recognized Beauport's surprise, which he naturally assumed was her positive response to hearing of this wonderful career opportunity. He, too, had been delighted several years earlier about his temporary transfer to marketing research to round out his marketing experience. "This move will be good for both you and Hy Dairies," said Gilman as he escorted Beauport from his office.

Beauport was preoccupied with several tasks that afternoon, but was able to consider the day's events that evening. She was one of the top women and few visible minority employees in brand management at Hy Dairies and feared that she was being sidelined because the company didn't want women or visible minority employees in top management. Her previous employer had made it quite clear that women "couldn't take the heat" in marketing management and tended to place women in technical support positions after a brief term in lower brand management jobs. Obviously Syd Gilman and Hy Dairies were following the same game plan. Gilman's comments that the coordinator job would be good for her was just a nice way of saying that Beauport couldn't go any further in brand management at Hy Dairies.

Beauport now faced the difficult decision of whether to confront Gilman and try to change Hy Dairies' practices or to leave the company.

Discussion Questions

1. Apply your knowledge of stereotyping and social identity theory to explain what went wrong here.

2. What other perceptual error is apparent in this case study?

3. What can organizations do to minimize misperceptions in these types of situations?

 TEAM EXERCISE 3.2

Who Am I?

Purpose   This exercise is designed to help you understand the elements and implications of self-concept and social identity theory.

Materials   None.

Instructions   • *Step 1:* Working alone (no discussion with other students), use the space provided below or a piece of paper to write down 12 words or phrases that answer the question "Who am I?" Write your words or phrases describing you as they come to mind; don't worry about their logical order here. Please be sure to fill in all 12 spaces.

a) I am _____	S	P
b) I am _____	S	P
c) I am _____	S	P
d) I am _____	S	P
e) I am _____	S	P
f) I am _____	S	P
g) I am _____	S	P
h) I am _____	S	P
i) I am _____	S	P
j) I am _____	S	P
k) I am _____	S	P
l) I am _____	S	P

• *Step 2:* Circle an "S" beside the items that define you in terms of your social identity, such as your demographics and formal or informal membership in a social group or institution (school, company, religious group). Circle a "P" beside the items that define you in terms of your personal identity; that is, something unique about you, such as an accomplishment, trait, or skill that few around you possess. Next, underline one or more items that you believe will still be a strong characteristic of you 10 years from now.

• *Step 3:* Form small groups. If you have a team project for this course, your project team would work well for this exercise. Compare your list with the lists that others in your group wrote about themselves. Discuss the following questions in your group and prepare notes for class discussion and possible presentation of these questions:

Discussion Questions   1. Among members of this team, what was the typical percentage of items representing the person's social versus personal identity? Did some team members have many more or less social identity items compared to other team members? Why do you think these large or small differences in emphasis on social or personal identity occurred?

2. What characteristics did people in your group underline as being the most stable (i.e., remaining the same in 10 years from now)? Were these underlined items mostly social or personal identity features? How similar or different were the underlined items among team members?

3. What do these lists say about the dynamics of your group as a team (whether or not your group for this activity is actually involved in a class project for this course)?

Sources: M. H. Kuhn and T. S. McPartland, "An Empirical Investigation of Self-Attitudes," *American Sociological Review* 19 (February 1954), 68–76; C. Lay and M. Verkuyten, "Ethnic Identity and Its Relation to Personal Self-Esteem: A Comparison of Canadian-Born and Foreign-Born Chinese Adolescents," *Journal of Social Psychology* 139 (1999), 288–299; S. L. Grace and K. L. Cramer, "The Elusive Nature of Self-Measurement: The Self-Construal Scale versus the Twenty Statements Test," *Journal of Social Psychology* 143 (2003), 649–668.

WEB EXERCISE 3.3

Diversity and Stereotyping on Display in Corporate Websites

Purpose   This exercise is designed to help you diagnose evidence of diversity and stereotyping in corporate websites.

Materials   Students need to complete their research for this activity prior to class, including selecting one or more medium-large sized public or private organizations and retrieving sample images of people from the organization's website.

Instructions   The instructor may have students work alone or in groups for this activity. Students will select one or more medium-large sized public or private organizations. Students will closely examine images in the selected company's website in terms of how women, visible minorities, people with disabilities, Aboriginal peoples, and older employees and clients are portrayed. Specifically, students should be prepared to discuss and provide details in class regarding:

1. The percentage of images showing (i.e., visual representations of) women, visible minorities, people with disabilities, Aboriginal peoples, and older employees and clients. Students should also be sensitive to the size and placement of these images in the website or documents therein.

2. The roles in which women, visible minorities, people with disabilities, Aboriginal peoples, and older employees and clients are depicted. For example, are women shown more in traditional or non-traditional occupations and roles in these websites?

3. Pick one or more of the best examples of diversity on display and one stereotypic image you can find from the website to show in class, either in printed form, or as a weblink that can be displayed in class.

TEAM EXERCISE 3.4

Do You Have a Global Mindset?

Purpose   This exercise is designed to help students examine and explore their global experiences and perspectives acquired while travelling, working, or studying in countries outside Canada.

Materials   Students require an unmarked copy of a world map (Exhibit 1).

Exhibit 1   **WORLD MAP**

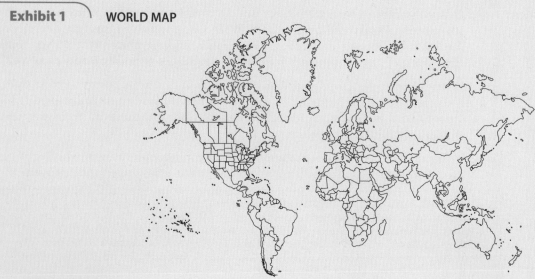

Natural Warp/iStockphoto

Instructions
- *Step 1:* Working alone, place a dot to mark locations (outside Canada) that you recall visiting or residing in at some point in your life. Did you spend one consecutive month or more at any of these locations? If yes—mark those locations with a triangle.
- *Step 2:* Form teams with four or five members. Take another unmarked copy of the world map and compile your team's composite results. Within your team, discuss interactions and experiences you have had while travelling, working, or studying globally. For example: Were you able to carry on a conversation in more than one language? Did you routinely eat local foods? Had meaningful direct contact with locals? Did you ever feel outside your "comfort zone"?
- *Step 3:* Instructor leads a class discussion including the following questions.

Discussion Questions
1. How would you characterize your knowledge and appreciation of other cultures?
2. What kinds of things have you done while travelling, working, or studying in another country that have contributed to your knowledge and appreciation of other cultures?
3. How have your experiences travelling, working, or studying globally influenced your attitudes, beliefs, and/or perceptions?
4. How can employers benefit from employees with a global mindset?

Go to CONNECT to complete the following interactive self-assessments.

 SELF-ASSESSMENT EXERCISE 3.5

How Much Does Work Define Your Self-Concept?

Work is an important part of our lives, but some people view it as secondary to other life interests whereas others view work as central to their identity as individuals. The following scale estimates the extent to which you view work as a central or not-so-central life interest. Read each of the statements below and decide how accurate each one is in describing your focus in life. Then use the scoring key in Appendix B at the end of this book to calculate your results. Remember that there are no right or wrong answers to these questions. Also, this self-assessment should be completed alone so that you can rate yourself honestly without concerns of social comparison. Class discussion will focus on the meaning of this scale and its relevance to self-concept and perceptions.

Work Centrality Scale						
Please indicate the extent to which you agree or disagree with each statement below in describing *your focus in life.*	Strongly Disagree	Moderately Disagree	Slightly Disagree	Slightly Agree	Moderately Agree	Strongly Agree
1. The most important things that happen in my life involve my work.	☐	☐	☐	☐	☐	☐
2. Work is something people should get involved in most of the time.	☐	☐	☐	☐	☐	☐
3. Work should be only a small part of one's life.	☐	☐	☐	☐	☐	☐
4. Work should be considered central to life.	☐	☐	☐	☐	☐	☐
5. In my view, an individual's personal life goals should be work-oriented.	☐	☐	☐	☐	☐	☐
6. Life is worth living only when people get absorbed in work.	☐	☐	☐	☐	☐	☐

Source: R. N. Kanungo, *Work Alienation: An Integrative Approach* (New York: Praeger, 1982).

CHAPTER 4

Workplace Emotions, Attitudes, and Stress

LEARNING OBJECTIVES

After reading this chapter, you should be able to:

LO1 Explain how emotions and cognition (conscious reasoning) influence attitudes and behaviour.

LO2 Discuss the dynamics of emotional labour and the role of emotional intelligence in the workplace.

LO3 Summarize the consequences of job dissatisfaction as well as strategies to increase organizational (affective) commitment.

LO4 Describe the stress experience and review three major stressors.

LO5 Identify five ways to manage workplace stress.

After being hit on the head by a piece of luggage and being cursed at by a passenger who refused to remain in his seat, career flight attendant Steven Slater snapped.

It has been some time since flight attendant was a glamorous job title. There are many stressors in the work environment that place physical and emotional demands on the person. The work is tedious. Passengers with feelings of entitlement collide with new no-frills policies. Babies wail. Security precautions irritate.

After a dispute with a passenger who stood up too soon to fetch his luggage on a full flight, Steven Slater had had enough. He got on the intercom and called the passenger a 12-letter adjective beginning with 'm' and then told everyone, "I've been in the business 28 years. I've had it. That's it." He then activated the emergency inflatable slide, grabbed two beers from the beverage cart and exited the passenger-filled plane and presumably his career with JetBlue airlines.

In the days following the incident, passengers on the flight described Slater as "disturbed and agitated" during the 90-minute flight. Passengers recalled him repeatedly opening and slamming shut serving doors and overhead bins during the flight.

People who knew him seemed hard-pressed to explain Slater's rash actions in the wake of a fairly typical stress experience for a flight attendant. It has been reported that Slater had been spending a lot of his non-work time caring for his mother. "It could be the pressure of his mother's illness because that's not the type of behaviour or conduct that Steve exhibits," said a neighbour.

Adding to his woes, authorities cited concerns that employing the emergency slide could have injured workers on the ground. Slater was charged with a variety of criminal offences including reckless endangerment, criminal mischief, and trespassing. Ensuing social support for Slater has taken the form of a legal defence fund popping up on Facebook backed up by a PayPal account. As for the public outpouring of support he has received, Mr. Slater said: "It's all been very, very appreciated . . . it seems like something here has resonated with people. That's kind of neat."

Despite Slater's newly minted folk hero status, Professor Westhues, a sociology professor at the University of Waterloo, concludes "employers should recognize that such meltdowns say more about the company and situation than they do about the employee's character."[1]

Flight attendants like Steven Slater are expected to manage their emotions on the job even when faced with significant stressors.
Peter Kramer/NBC/NBC Newswire

teven Slater's outburst and final exit from a JetBlue flight illustrates several topics covered in this chapter. It dramatically shows the effects of strong emotions and job dissatisfaction on employee behaviour and customer service. It shows how employees are expected to manage their emotions and to display specific types of emotions, even in difficult situations. This vignette also highlights the effects of work-related stress, which Steven Slater was experiencing due to work and nonwork challenges. This chapter begins by defining and describing emotions and explaining why researchers are so eager to discover how emotions influence attitudes and behaviour. Next, we consider the dynamics of emotional labour, followed by the popular topic of emotional intelligence. The specific work attitudes of job satisfaction and organizational commitment are then discussed, including their association with various employee behaviours and work performance. The final section looks at work-related stress, including the stress experience, three prominent stressors, individual differences in stress, and ways to combat excessive stress.

EMOTIONS IN THE WORKPLACE

LO1

Emotions influence almost everything we do in the workplace. This is a strong statement, and one that you would rarely find a dozen years ago among organizational behaviour experts. Most OB theories still assume that a person's thoughts and actions are governed primarily or exclusively by logical thinking (called *cognition*).[2] Yet groundbreaking neuroscience discoveries have revealed that our perceptions, attitudes, decisions, and behaviour are influenced by emotions as well as cognitions.[3] In fact, emotions may have a greater influence because they often occur before cognitive processes and, consequently, influence the latter. By ignoring emotionality, many theories have overlooked a large piece of the puzzle about human behaviour in the workplace.

emotions Physiological, behavioural, and psychological episodes experienced toward an object, person, or event that create a state of readiness.

Emotions are physiological, behavioural, and psychological episodes experienced toward an object, person, or event that create a state of readiness.[4] These "episodes" are very brief events that typically subside or occur in waves lasting from milliseconds to a few minutes. Emotions are directed toward someone or something. For example, we experience joy, fear, anger, and other emotional episodes toward tasks, customers, or a software program we are using. This differs from *moods*, which are not directed toward anything in particular and tend to be longer-term emotional states.[5]

Emotions are experiences. They represent changes in our physiological state (e.g., blood pressure, heart rate), psychological state (e.g., thought process), and behaviour (e.g., facial expression). Most of these emotional reactions are subtle and occur without our awareness. This is an important point because the topic of emotions often conjures up images of people "getting emotional." In reality, most emotions occur fleetingly, nonconsciously, and with low intensity. Finally, emotions put us in a state of readiness. When we get worried, for example, our heart rate and blood pressure increase to make our body better prepared to engage in fight or flight. Strong emotions also trigger our conscious awareness of a threat or opportunity in the external environment.[6]

TYPES OF EMOTIONS

People experience many emotions as well as various combinations of emotions, but all of them have two common features. First, emotions generate a global evaluation (called *core affect*) that something is good or bad, helpful or harmful, to be approached or to be avoided. In other words, all

"Biosensors. The whole company knows instantly when I'm displeased."

emotions communicate that the perceived object or event is either positive or negative. Second, all emotions produce some level of activation; that is, they generate some level of energy within us. Some emotional experiences are strong enough that they make us consciously motivated to do something. Most are much more subtle, but they still energize us enough to become more aware of our environment. These two dimensions of emotions are the foundation of the circumplex model shown in Exhibit 4.1.[7] For instance, fearful is a negative emotion that generates a high level of activation, whereas relaxed is a pleasant emotion that has fairly low activation.

EMOTIONS, ATTITUDES, AND BEHAVIOUR

attitudes The cluster of beliefs, assessed feelings, and behavioural intentions toward a person, object, or event (called an *attitude object*).

To understand how emotions influence our thoughts and behaviour in the workplace, we first need to know about attitudes. **Attitudes** represent the cluster of beliefs, assessed feelings, and behavioural intentions toward a person, object, or event (called an *attitude object*).[8] Attitudes are *judgments*, whereas emotions are *experiences*. In other words, attitudes involve conscious logical reasoning, whereas emotions operate as events, usually without our awareness. We also experience most emotions briefly, whereas our attitude toward someone or something is more stable over time.

Until recently, experts believed that attitudes could be understood just by the three cognitive components illustrated on the left side of Exhibit 4.2: beliefs, feelings, and behavioural intentions. Now evidence suggests that a parallel emotional process is also at work, shown on the right side of the exhibit.[9] Using attitude toward mergers as an example, let's look more closely at this model, beginning with the traditional cognitive perspective of attitudes.

Exhibit 4.1   **CIRCUMPLEX MODEL OF EMOTIONS**

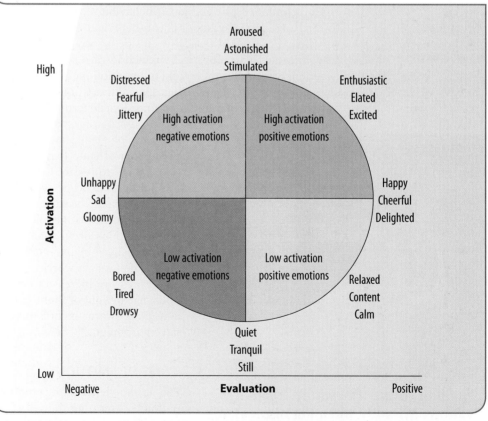

Source: Adapted from J. Larson, E. Diener, and R. E. Lucas, "Emotion: Models, Measures, and Differences," in R. G. Lord, R. J. Klimoski, and R. Kanfer (Eds.), *Emotions in the Workplace* (San Francisco: Jossey-Bass, 2002), pp. 64–113; J. A. Russell, "Core Affect and the Psychological Construction of Emotion," *Psychological Review* 110, no. 1 (2003): 145–172.

Exhibit 4.2   MODEL OF EMOTIONS, ATTITUDES, AND BEHAVIOUR

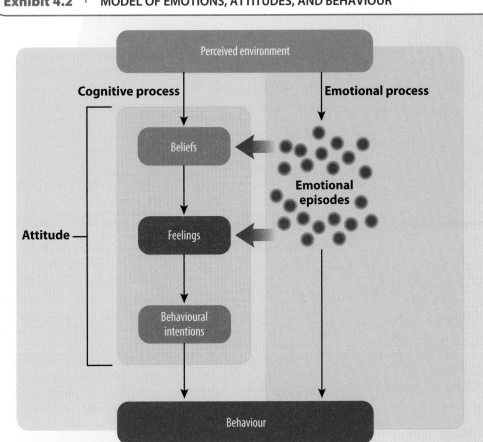

- *Beliefs.* These are your established perceptions about the attitude object—what you believe to be true. For example, you might believe that mergers reduce job security for employees in the merged firms, or that mergers increase the company's competitiveness in this era of globalization. These beliefs are perceived facts that you acquire from experience and other forms of learning.

- *Feelings.* Feelings represent your conscious positive or negative evaluations of the attitude object. Some people think mergers are good; others think they are bad. Your like or dislike of mergers represents your assessed feelings. According to the traditional cognitive perspective of attitudes (left side of the model), feelings are calculated from your beliefs about mergers. If you believe that mergers typically have negative consequences such as layoffs and organizational politics, you will form negative feelings toward mergers in general or about a specific planned merger in your organization.

- *Behavioural intentions.* Intentions represent your motivation to engage in a particular behaviour regarding the attitude object.[10] Upon hearing that the company will merge with another organization, you might become motivated to look for a job elsewhere or possibly to complain to management about the merger decision. Your feelings toward mergers motivate your behavioural intentions, and which actions you choose depends on your past experience, personality, and social norms of appropriate behaviour.

Exhibit 4.2 illustrates that behavioural intentions directly predict behaviour. However, whether your intentions translate into behaviour depends on the situation and possibly other elements of the MARS model. For example, you might intend to quit after hearing about the merger, but do not do so because of lack of better job opportunities (situation). Attitudes are also more likely to influence behaviour when they are strong, meaning that they are anchored by strong emotions.

How Emotions Influence Attitudes and Behaviour   As we mentioned, emotions play a central role in forming and changing employee attitudes.[11] The right side of Exhibit 4.2 illustrates this process, which (like the cognitive process) also begins with perceptions of the world around us. Our brain tags incoming sensory information with emotional markers based on a quick and imprecise evaluation of whether that information supports or threatens our innate drives. These markers are not calculated feelings; they are automatic and nonconscious emotional responses based on very thin slices of sensory information.[12]

Consider your attitude toward mergers. You might experience worry, nervousness, or relief upon learning that your company intends to merge with a competitor. The fuzzy dots on the right side of Exhibit 4.2 illustrate the numerous emotional episodes you experience upon hearing the merger announcement, subsequently thinking about the merger, discussing the merger with co-workers, and so on. These emotions are transmitted to the reasoning process, where they are logically analyzed along with other information about the attitude object.[13] Thus, while you are consciously evaluating whether the merger is good or bad, your emotions are already sending normative (good–bad) signals, which then sways your conscious evaluation. In fact, we often deliberately "listen in" on our emotions to help us consciously decide whether to support or oppose something.[14]

The influence of both cognitive reasoning and emotions on attitudes is most apparent when they disagree with each other. People occasionally experience this mental tug-of-war, sensing that something isn't right even though they can't think of any logical reason to be concerned. This conflicting experience indicates that the person's logical analysis of the situation (left side of Exhibit 4.2) can't identify reasons to support the automatic emotional reaction (right side of Exhibit 4.2).[15] Should we pay attention to our emotional response or our logical analysis? This question is not easy to answer, but some studies indicate that while executives tend to make quick decisions based on their gut feelings (emotional response), the best decisions tend to occur when executives spend time logically evaluating the situation.[16] Thus, we should pay attention to both the cognitive and emotional sides of the attitude model, and hope they agree with each other most of the time!

Generating Positive Emotions at Work   Some companies seem to be well aware of the dual cognitive-emotional attitude process because they try to inject more positive experiences in the workplace. For instance, employees at Vancouver-based Suntech

Having Fun Is Part of the Culture at Hill & Knowlton

Communications consulting firm, Hill & Knowlton provides public affairs and corporate communications services to an impressive list of clients that includes well-known companies such as Virgin Mobile, Motorola, and the Royal Canadian Mint. To celebrate the end of each week a travelling beer cart winds through the office on Friday afternoons, much to the delight and enjoyment of employees. Fun at work? It sounds like an oxymoron. But in order to attract, engage, and keep valuable talent, companies are finding creative ways to generate positive emotions in the workplace. "I am personally committed to creating an engaging, fun and enjoyable workplace to attract and retain this country's top communications professionals," says Michael Coates, president and CEO, Hill & Knowlton Canada. "Ultimately, this means staff at H&K stay longer—and our clients benefit from steady account teams, and the continued learning and knowledge that results. When people enjoy their work—it shows," he adds.[17] *Courtesy of Hill & Knowlton Canada*

Optics enjoy impromptu fun activities (solving puzzles co-workers have placed on their desks) and scheduled events (pumpkin carving at Halloween). "We try to infuse having fun into our whole corporate culture," says a Suntech manager. "It's one of our core strategies. It's part of our life." Similarly, employees at Razer, the Singapore-based gaming peripherals company, zoom around on scooters and pit their gaming skills against each other on the state-of-the-art online gaming console. "Sometimes I can't believe that I have been here for seven months already," admits one Razer employee. "I guess you don't feel the time passing when you are having so much fun."[18]

These deliberate "fun" activities can improve employee attitudes in many situations, but the main focus should be on ensuring that employees experience positive emotions through the job itself as well as everyday natural occurrences such as supportive co-workers and polite customers. Furthermore, contrived fun events at work can backfire.[19] They may produce negative emotions either because employees resent having fun forced on them or because the activity evokes negative emotions in some people (such as when the activity seems silly or too competitive). Still, most people perform work that produces some negative emotions, and research has found that humour and fun at work—whether natural or contrived—can potentially offset some of the negative experiences.[20] Overall, corporate leaders need to keep in mind that emotions shape employee attitudes and, as we will discuss later, attitudes influence various forms of work-related behaviour.

One last comment about Exhibit 4.2: Notice the arrow from the emotional episodes to behaviour. It indicates that emotions directly (without conscious thinking) influence a person's behaviour. This occurs when we jump suddenly if someone sneaks up on us. It also occurs in everyday situations because even low-intensity emotions automatically change our facial expressions. These actions are not carefully thought out. They are automatic emotional responses that are learned or hardwired by heredity for particular situations.[21]

Cognitive Dissonance   Emotions and attitudes usually lead to behaviour, but the opposite sometimes occurs through the process of **cognitive dissonance**.[22] Cognitive dissonance is a condition that occurs when we perceive an inconsistency between our beliefs, feelings, and behaviour. This inconsistency generates emotions (such as feeling hypocritical) that motivate us to create more consistency by changing one or more of these elements. Suppose that you think of yourself as someone who supports environmentalism. You also work at an oil sands company that seemed to be environmentally friendly until news reports accuse the company and others in Alberta's oil sands of creating environmental damage. This internal tension occurs because your "green" self-concept (beliefs) and positive regard for environmentalism (feelings) are inconsistent with your employment at a company with a poor environmental record (behaviour). People experience an internal tension because they want to see themselves as rational creatures, which requires some alignment between their thoughts and actions.[23] Working for a company that has a poor environmental reputation seems inconsistent with your beliefs and attitudes about environmentalism, so you would be motivated to reduce that discrepancy.

cognitive dissonance A condition that occurs when we perceive an inconsistency between our beliefs, feelings, and behaviour.

How do people reduce cognitive dissonance? Changing behaviour is one option, but it is more difficult and often more costly than changing beliefs and feelings. You might be very reluctant to quit your job with the oil sands company, for instance. Changing behaviour is particularly difficult when others know about the behaviour, you performed the behaviour voluntarily, and the consequence of the behaviour can't be undone. Although you could quit your job, you can't hide the fact that you work for an oil sands company or claim someone forced you to work there.

When it is difficult to undo or change behaviour, people instead reduce cognitive dissonance by changing their beliefs and feelings. As an employee at an oil sands company, you might convince yourself that problems with the company's environmental record have been exaggerated or that they fail to take into account the company's most recent environmental initiatives. Research suggests that people sometimes reduce cognitive dissonance by rebalancing their self-concept indirectly. So, rather than deny the company's environmental record, you might reduce the inconsistency by emphasizing your personal environmental behaviours (e.g., using public transport to work and composting food waste at home). Overall, these mental acrobatics maintain some degree of consistency between your behaviour (working for the oil sands company) and your beliefs and attitudes toward environmentalism.

Emotions and Personality   Our coverage of the dynamics of workplace emotions wouldn't be complete unless we mention that emotions are also partly determined by a person's personality, not just workplace experiences.[24] Some people experience positive emotions as a natural trait. People with more positive emotions typically have higher emotional stability and are extroverted (see Chapter 2). Those who experience more negative emotions tend to have higher neuroticism (lower emotional stability) and are introverted. Positive and negative emotional traits affect a person's attendance, turnover, and long-term work attitudes.[25] While positive and negative personality traits have some effect, other research concludes that the actual situation in which people work has a noticeably stronger influence on their attitudes and behaviour.[26]

MANAGING EMOTIONS AT WORK

L02

The Elbow Room Café is packed and noisy on this Saturday morning. A customer at the downtown Vancouver restaurant half shouts across the room for more coffee. A passing waiter scoffs: "You want more coffee, get it yourself!" The customer laughs. Another diner complains loudly that he and his party are running late and need their food. This time, restaurant manager Patrick Savoie speaks up: "If you're in a hurry, you should have gone to McDonald's." The diner and his companions chuckle. To the uninitiated, the Elbow Room Café is an emotional basket case, where staff turn rudeness into a fine art. But it's all a performance—a place where guests can enjoy good food and play out their emotions about dreadful customer service. "It's almost like coming to a theatre," says Savoie, who spends much of his time inventing new ways to insult the clientele.[27]

Whether giving the most insulting service at Elbow Room Café in Vancouver or the best treatment one could imagine at Four Seasons Hotels & Resorts, people are expected to manage their emotions in the workplace. They must conceal their frustration when serving an irritating customer, display compassion to an ill patient, and hide their boredom in a long meeting with senior management. These are all forms of **emotional labour**—the effort, planning, and control needed to express organizationally desired emotions during interpersonal transactions.[28] Almost everyone is expected to abide by *display rules*—norms requiring us to display specific emotions and to hide

emotional labour The effort, planning, and control needed to express organizationally desired emotions during interpersonal transactions.

Learning to Show Correct Emotions at Malaysia Airlines

Malaysia Airlines flight attendants receive extensive training on the essentials of safety and medical emergencies, but they also learn how to remain composed and pleasant even in difficult conditions. "Are they presentable? Respectable? Do they make you feel comfortable? Do they seem approachable?" asks Madam Choong Lee Fong, Malaysia Airlines' cabin crew training and standards manager. Students at the Malaysia Airlines Academy in Petaling Jaya learn the fine art of smiling, making eye contact, and keeping their chin up at a level that displays confidence without arrogance. The academy even has large mirrors on the walls of its grooming room so students constantly see how their facial expressions appear to others. Students receive training in voice enrichment and public speaking. They also learn about personal grooming as well as different formalities of behaviour in countries where the airline flies.[29] *Xinhua/Landov*

other emotions. Emotional labour demands are higher in jobs requiring a variety of emotions (e.g., anger as well as joy) and more intense emotions (e.g., showing delight rather than smiling weakly), as well as in jobs where interaction with clients is frequent and longer. Emotional labour also increases when employees must precisely rather than casually abide by the display rules.[30] This particularly occurs in the service industries, where employees have frequent face-to-face interaction with clients.

Emotional Display Norms Across Cultures   Not long ago, *L'Express* published a special series of articles about living in Canada. Among other things, the Paris-based magazine warned that French managers might find Canadians somewhat more abrupt and less apologetic in their correspondence. Another article commented that Canadian waiters provide "hyper-friendly, always smiling" service, which can seem a bit too insincere to many Europeans. "It's too much. It's too friendly," explains Laurence Pivot, who edited the special edition of *L'Express*.[31]

The French magazine's description highlights cultural differences regarding emotional display norms.[32] In some countries—such as Kuwait, Egypt, Spain, and Russia—cultural norms allow or encourage open display of one's true emotions. People are expected to be transparent in revealing their thoughts and feelings, dramatic in their conversational tones, and animated in their use of nonverbal behaviours to get their message across. In other countries—particularly Ethiopia, Japan, and Austria—people are expected to follow emotional display norms more precisely. In these cultures, emotional expression also tends to be more subdued and physical contact with others is minimal in professional settings. Even voice intonation tends to be monotonic. One major study reported that 81 percent of Ethiopians and 74 percent of Japanese agreed that overtly expressing their personal emotions is unprofessional, whereas 49 percent of Canadians, 33 percent of Italians, and only 19 percent of Spaniards, Cubans, and Egyptians agreed with this statement.[33]

Emotional Dissonance   Emotional labour can be challenging for most of us because it is difficult to conceal true emotions and to display the emotions required by the job. Joy, sadness, worry, and other emotions automatically activate a complex set of facial muscles that are difficult to prevent and equally difficult to fake. Pretending to be cheerful or concerned requires adjustment and coordination of several specific facial muscles and body positions. Meanwhile, our true emotions tend to reveal themselves as subtle gestures, usually without our awareness. More often than not, observers see when we are faking and sense that we feel a different emotion.[34]

emotional dissonance
The conflict between required and true emotions.

Emotional labour also creates conflict between required and true emotions, called **emotional dissonance**. The larger the gap, the more employees tend to experience stress, job burnout, and psychological separation from self.[35] This problem can be minimized through deep acting rather than surface acting.[36] *Surface acting* involves pretending to show the required emotions but continue to hold different internal feelings. *Deep acting* involves changing true emotions to match the required emotions. In other words, you train yourself to actually feel the emotion you are supposed to express. Deep acting also requires considerable emotional intelligence, which we discuss next.

EMOTIONAL INTELLIGENCE

Air Canada is looking beyond flying skills when choosing new pilots. All new pilots are also evaluated by their scores on an emotional intelligence test. Pilots are team leaders of the on-board crew and need to work effectively with staff on the ground, so they must have the ability to understand and manage their own emotions as well as the emotions of others. "If you have to interact well with other people, these [emotional intelligence tests] are instruments that we can use during the selection process to identify people that have these enhanced skills," says Air Canada's vice-president of flight operations. "At the end of the day, we want to have a better idea of who we're hiring."[37]

**emotional intelligence
(EI)** A set of abilities
to perceive and express
emotion, assimilate emotion
in thought, understand and
reason with emotion, and
regulate emotion in oneself
and others.

Air Canada is among the growing crowd of companies that are paying attention to **emotional intelligence (EI)** as a factor in the organization's effectiveness. Emotional intelligence includes a set of *abilities* to perceive and express emotion, assimilate emotion in thought, understand and reason with emotion, and regulate emotion in oneself and others.[38] Although several emotional intelligence dimensions have been proposed over the past decade, the research findings seem to be converging around the four quadrant model shown in Exhibit 4.3.[39] This model organizes EI into four dimensions representing the recognition of emotions in ourselves and in others, as well as the regulation of emotions in ourselves and in others.

- *Self-awareness of emotions.* This is the ability to perceive and understand the meaning of your own emotions. You are more sensitive to subtle emotional responses to events and understand their message. Self-aware people are better able to listen in on their emotional responses to specific situations and to use this awareness as conscious information.[40]

- *Self-management of emotions.* Emotional intelligence includes the ability to manage your own emotions, something that we all do to some extent. We keep disruptive impulses in check. We try not to feel angry or frustrated when events go against us. We try to feel and express joy and happiness toward others when the occasion calls for these emotional displays. We try to create a second wind of motivation later in the workday. Notice that management of your own emotions goes beyond displaying behaviours that represent desired emotions in a particular situation. It includes generating or suppressing emotions. In other words, the deep acting described earlier requires high levels of the self-management component of emotional intelligence.

- *Awareness of others' emotions.* This dimension refers to the ability to perceive and understand the emotions of other people. To a large extent, awareness of other people's emotions is represented by *empathy*—having an understanding of and sensitivity to the feelings, thoughts, and situations of others (see Chapter 3). This ability includes understanding the other person's situation, experiencing his or her emotions, and knowing his or her needs even though unstated. Social awareness extends beyond empathy to include being organizationally aware, such as sensing office politics and understanding social networks.

Exhibit 4.3   **DIMENSIONS OF EMOTIONAL INTELLIGENCE**

	Yourself	**Others**
Recognition of Emotions	Self-awareness of one's own emotions	Awareness of others' emotions
Regulation of Emotions	Self-management of one's own emotions	Management of others' emotions

(**Abilities**)

Sources: D. Goleman, "An EI-Based Theory of Performance," in *The Emotionally Intelligent Workplace,* (Eds.), C. Cherniss and D. Goleman (San Francisco: Jossey-Bass, 2001), p. 28; Peter J. Jordan and Sandra A. Lawrence, "Emotional Intelligence in Teams: Development and Initial Validation of the Short Version of the Workgroup Emotional Intelligence Profile (WEIP-S)," *Journal of Management & Organization* 15 (2009): 452–469.

- *Management of others' emotions.* This dimension of EI involves managing other people's emotions. This includes consoling people who feel sad, emotionally inspiring your team members to complete a class project on time, getting strangers to feel comfortable working with you, and managing dysfunctional emotions among staff who experience conflict with customers or other employees.

These four dimensions of emotional intelligence form a hierarchy.[41] Awareness of your own emotions is lowest because you need awareness to engage in the higher levels of emotional intelligence. You can't manage your own emotions if you don't know what they are (i.e., low self-awareness). Managing other people's emotions is the highest level of EI because this ability requires awareness of our own and others' emotions. To diffuse an angry conflict between two employees, for example, you need to understand the emotions they are experiencing and manage your emotions (and display of emotions). To manage your own emotions, you also need to be aware of your current emotions.

Most jobs involve social interaction with co-workers or external stakeholders, so employees need emotional intelligence to work effectively. Emotional intelligence is particularly important for managers because their work requires management of their own emotions and the emotions of others. Research indicates that people with high EI are better at interpersonal relations, perform better in jobs requiring emotional labour, are superior leaders, make better decisions involving social exchanges, are more successful in many aspects of job interviews, and are better at organizational learning activities. Teams whose members have high emotional intelligence initially perform better than teams with low EI.[42] However, emotional intelligence does not improve some forms of performance, such as tasks that require minimal social interaction.[43]

IMPROVING EMOTIONAL INTELLIGENCE

Emotional intelligence is associated with some personality traits, as well as with the emotional intelligence of one's parents. For this reason, Air Canada and other companies *try* to measure EI in job applicants. (We emphasize the word "try" because a high quality test of emotional intelligence remains elusive.) Emotional intelligence can also be learned. One study reported that business students had higher emotional intelligence scores after taking an undergraduate interpersonal skills course. Sony Europe incorporates EI training in its executive development program, including an exercise in which leaders keep a journal of their emotional experiences throughout a week of work. At orthopaedic device manufacturer Exactech Inc., two dozen leadership development participants learn how to improve their EI skills in self-awareness and interaction with other staff members.[44] Personal coaching, plenty of practise, and frequent feedback are particularly effective at developing EI. Emotional intelligence also increases with age; it is part of the process called maturity.[45]

Hiring for Emotional Intelligence

Most of the 900 employees at Softchoice Corp. need to have technical skills. Even so, this Toronto-based IT services company also recognizes the importance of emotional intelligence. "When I am interviewing somebody, I am definitely looking for clues that this person is a relationship-builder," says Maria Odoardi, Softchoice vice-president of people. "It's just really important that you are going to get along with people." Brad Beveridge, who heads the Canadian practice of executive search firm Knightsbridge Human Capital Solutions, observes that emotional intelligence abilities are becoming a priority among Canadian employers. "We are finding much more emphasis on people who can relate to their co-workers, so it ties into the EQ (emotional intelligence)," Beveridge notes. "They can inspire others to participate in team-related activities and, really, when necessary, mitigate any conflict among their co-workers."[46] *Jim Powell/GetStock*

Before leaving this topic, we should mention an ongoing debate about the usefulness of emotional intelligence as a concept.[47] The concept has not been as clear as some would hope. Even the label "intelligence" is inappropriate because EI is a skill, not a form of intelligence. Critics also suggest that general intelligence and personality traits overlap with most of EI's contribution to knowledge. These criticisms are serious, yet the meaning of EI is becoming clearer and several studies (cited over the previous pages) suggest that EI is relevant to workplace behaviour. Overall, emotional intelligence offers considerable potential, but we also have a lot to learn about its measurement and effects on people in the workplace.

So far, this chapter has introduced the model of emotions and attitudes, as well as emotional intelligence as the means by which we manage emotions in the workplace. The next two sections look at two specific attitudes: job satisfaction and organizational commitment. These two attitudes are so important to our understanding of workplace behaviour that some experts suggest the two combined should be called "overall job attitude."[48]

JOB SATISFACTION

L03

job satisfaction A person's evaluation of his or her job and work context.

Job satisfaction, a person's evaluation of his or her job and work context, is probably the most studied attitude in organizational behaviour.[49] It is an *appraisal* of the perceived job characteristics, work environment, and emotional experiences at work. Satisfied employees have a favourable evaluation of their jobs, based on their observations and emotional experiences. Job satisfaction is best viewed as a collection of attitudes about different aspects of the job and work context. You might like your co-workers but be less satisfied with your workload, for instance.

How satisfied are employees at work? The answer depends on the person, the workplace, and the country. Global surveys indicate with some consistency that job satisfaction tends to be highest in the Nordic countries (Denmark, Sweden, Norway, and Finland) as well as in India and the United States. The lowest levels of overall job satisfaction are usually recorded in Hungary and several Asian countries (e.g., Mainland China, Hong Kong, and South Korea).[50] Job satisfaction in Canada is usually above the global average but usually a little below the typical American scores.[51]

It's probably fair to conclude that employees in Denmark, the United States, and Canada are more satisfied than those in some other parts of the world, but we also need to be somewhat cautious about these and other job satisfaction surveys. One problem is that surveys often use a single direct question, such as "How satisfied are you with your job?" Many dissatisfied employees are reluctant to reveal their feelings in a direct question because this is tantamount to admitting that they made a poor job choice and are not enjoying life. For instance, although most Canadian employees say they are satisfied with their job, almost half also admit they would consider working elsewhere in a comparable job or are actively looking for another job.[52] Another indication is that employees rate almost all aspects of the job lower than their overall satisfaction.

A second problem is that cultural values make it difficult to compare job satisfaction across countries. People in China and Japan tend to subdue their emotions in public, and there is evidence that they also avoid extreme survey ratings such as "very satisfied." A third problem is that job satisfaction changes with economic conditions. Employees with the highest job satisfaction in current surveys tend to be in countries where the economies are chugging along quite well.[53]

JOB SATISFACTION AND WORK BEHAVIOUR

Brad Bird pays a lot of attention to job satisfaction. "In my experience, the thing that has the most significant impact on a budget—but never shows up in a budget—is morale," advises Bird, who directed *Ratatouille* and other award-winning films at Pixar Animation Studios. "If you have low morale, for every dollar you spend, you get 25 cents of value. If you have high morale, for every dollar you spend, you get about 3 dollars of value."[54]

Brad Bird's opinion about the importance of job satisfaction is consistently reflected in the actions of leaders in many companies. Many companies carefully monitor job satisfaction and related employee attitudes and they actively compete to win best-workplace awards. In some firms, executive bonuses depend partly on employee satisfaction ratings. The reason for this attention is simple: Job satisfaction affects many of the individual behaviours introduced in Chapter 2 (task performance, organizational citizenship, quitting, absenteeism, etc.). A useful template for organizing and understanding the consequences of job dissatisfaction is the **exit-voice-loyalty-neglect (EVLN) model**. As the name suggests, the EVLN model identifies four ways that employees respond to dissatisfaction:[55]

> **exit-voice-loyalty-neglect (EVLN) model** The four ways, as indicated in the name, that employees respond to job dissatisfaction.

- *Exit.* Exit includes leaving the organization, transferring to another work unit, or at least trying to get away from the dissatisfying situation. The traditional theory is that job dissatisfaction builds over time and is eventually strong enough to motivate employees to search for better work opportunities elsewhere. This is likely true to some extent, but the most recent opinion is that specific "shock events" quickly energize employees to think about and engage in exit behaviour. For example, the emotional reaction you experience to an unfair management decision or a conflict episode with a co-worker motivates you to look at job ads and speak to friends about job opportunities where they work. This begins the process of re-aligning your self-concept more with another company than with your current employer.[56]

- *Voice.* Voice is any attempt to change, rather than escape from, the dissatisfying situation. Voice can be a constructive response, such as recommending ways for management to improve the situation, or it can be more confrontational, such as filing formal grievances or forming a coalition to oppose a decision.[57] In the extreme, some employees might engage in counterproductive behaviours to get attention and force changes in the organization.

- *Loyalty.* In the original version of this model, loyalty was not an outcome of dissatisfaction. Rather, it determined whether people chose exit or voice (i.e., high loyalty resulted in voice; low loyalty produced exit).[58] More recent writers describe loyalty as an outcome, but in various and somewhat unclear ways. Generally, they suggest that "loyalists" are employees who respond to dissatisfaction by patiently waiting—some say they "suffer in silence"—for the problem to work itself out or be resolved by others.[59]

- *Neglect.* Neglect includes reducing work effort, paying less attention to quality, and increasing absenteeism and lateness. It is generally considered a passive activity that has negative consequences for the organization.

Which of the four EVLN alternatives do employees use? It depends on the person and situation.[60] One determining factor is the person's self-concept. Some people avoid the self-image of being a complainer, whereas others view themselves very much as taking action when they dislike a work situation. Self-concept relates to personal and cultural values as well as personality. For example, people with a high-conscientiousness personality are less likely to engage in neglect and more likely to engage in voice. Past experience also influences which EVLN action is applied. Employees who were unsuccessful with voice in the past are more likely to engage in exit or neglect when experiencing job dissatisfaction in the future. Another factor is loyalty, as it was originally intended in the EVLN model. Specifically, employees are more likely to quit when they have low loyalty to the company, and they are more likely to engage in voice when they have high loyalty. Finally, the response to dissatisfaction depends on the situation. Employees are less likely to use the exit option when there are few alternative job prospects, for example.

Job Satisfaction and Performance   Is a happy worker a more productive worker? Most corporate leaders likely think so. Yet, for most of the past century, organizational behaviour scholars have challenged this happy-productive employee belief, concluding that job satisfaction minimally affects job performance. Now OB experts believe that maybe the popular saying is correct after all; there is a *moderately* positive relationship between job satisfaction and performance. In other words, workers tend to be more productive *to some extent* when they have more positive attitudes toward their job and workplace.[61]

Why isn't the job satisfaction-performance relationship even stronger? One reason is that general attitudes (such as job satisfaction) don't predict specific behaviours very well. As the EVLN model explained, dissatisfaction might lead to turnover, complaining, or patiently waiting rather than reduced performance (a form of neglect). A second reason is that dissatisfaction might affect performance only when employees have considerable control over their job performance. People working on an assembly line, for example, would produce about the same quantity and quality output no matter what they think about their job. A third consideration is that job performance might cause job satisfaction, rather than vice versa.[62] Higher performers receive more rewards (including recognition) and, consequently, are more satisfied than low-performing employees who receive fewer rewards. The connection between job satisfaction and performance isn't stronger because many organizations do not reward good performance very well.

Job Satisfaction and Customer Satisfaction   Wegmans Food Markets in the United States and HCL Technologies in India have the same unusual motto: Employees first, customers second. Both firms definitely put employees on top of stakeholder lists, but why not customers first? Their rationale is that customer satisfaction is a natural outcome of employee satisfaction. Put differently, it is difficult to keep customers happy if employee morale is low. "It just seems common sense to me that if you start with a happy, well-motivated workforce, you're much more likely to have happy customers," suggests Virgin Group founder Sir Richard Branson.[63]

This employee-customer relationship is illustrated in the **service profit chain model**, shown in Exhibit 4.4. Specifically, workplace practices affect job satisfaction, which influence employee retention, motivation, and behaviour. These employee

> **service profit chain model**   A theory explaining how employees' job satisfaction influences company profitability indirectly through service quality, customer loyalty, and related factors.

Exhibit 4.4   SERVICE PROFIT CHAIN MODEL

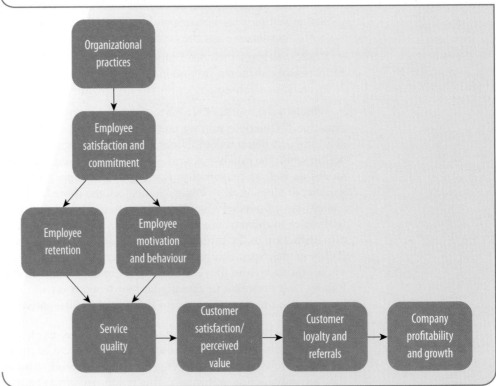

Source: This model is based on: J. I. Heskett, W. E. Sasser, and L. A. Schlesinger, *The Service Profit Chain* (New York: Free Press, 1997); A. J. Rucci, S. P. Kirn, and R. T. Quinn, "The Employee-Customer-Profit Chain At Sears," *Harvard Business Review* 76 (1998): 83–97; S. P. Brown and S. K. Lam, "A Meta-Analysis of Relationships Linking Employee Satisfaction to Customer Responses," *Journal of Retailing* 84, no. 3 (2008): 243–255.

CONNECTIONS 4.1

Happy Employees, Happy Customers

A few years ago, contact centre employees at Clydesdale Bank were not a happy group. Up to 12 percent of the 300 staff at the major Scottish bank were absent each day. Employee turnover was around 65 percent annually—a level so high that managers spent much of their time hiring and inducting replacements for those who quit. Kevin Page, head of Clydesdale's contact centre at the time, quipped: "We were a professional recruitment and training company." Customer service suffered, operating costs were 25 percent above the industry average in Europe, and employee productivity was substantially below average.

Two years later, Clydesdale's contact centre had become a global role model. Job satisfaction and commitment improved substantially. Absenteeism dropped to 4 percent each day; employee turnover was cut in half. Customers were much more satisfied with their contact centre calls. Due to this dramatic improvement, Clydesdale Bank was awarded the best contact centre in the region (including Europe, the Middle East, and Africa). A few months later, it was named the best large contact centre in the world, beating 1,000 entrants across all industries.

How did Clydesdale Bank achieve this amazing turnaround? According to Kevin Page, now Clydesdale Bank's operations director, the answer is treating employees well

Jim Allan/Alamy

so they treat customers well. Page and his management team listened to and acted on employee concerns, spruced up the work environment, introduced career development programs, provided better coaching, and gave staff more freedom to decide how to serve clients. "Our staff started to treat their jobs more seriously," says Page. "They felt their role was important and felt better about themselves."[64]

outcomes affect service quality, which then influence customer satisfaction and perceptions of value, customer referrals, and ultimately the company's profitability and growth.[65]

Behind the service profit chain model are two key explanations why satisfied employees cause customers to be more satisfied.[66] First, employees are usually in a more positive mood when they feel satisfied with their jobs and working conditions. Employees in a good mood display friendliness and positive emotions more naturally and frequently, and this causes customers to experience positive emotions, which translate into a more positive service experience (i.e., higher service quality). Second, satisfied employees are less likely to quit their jobs, so they have better knowledge and skills to serve clients. Lower turnover also enables customers to have the same employees serve them, so there is more consistent service. Some evidence indicates that customers build their loyalty to specific employees, not to the organization, so keeping employee turnover low tends to build customer loyalty. Global Connections 4.1 presents a dramatic example of how the service profit chain model has helped the bottom line at Clydesdale Bank.

Job Satisfaction and Business Ethics   Before leaving the topic of job satisfaction, we should mention that job satisfaction is also an ethical issue that influences the organization's reputation in the community. People spend a large portion of their time working in organizations, and many societies now expect companies to provide work environments

Job satisfaction is also an ethical issue that influences the organization's reputation in the community. "

that are safe and enjoyable. Indeed, employees in several countries closely monitor ratings of the best companies to work for, an indication that employee satisfaction is a virtue worth considerable goodwill to employers. This virtue is apparent when an organization has low job satisfaction. The company tries to hide this fact, and when morale problems become public, corporate leaders are usually quick to improve the situation.

ORGANIZATIONAL COMMITMENT

organizational (affective) commitment The employee's emotional attachment to, identification with, and involvement in a particular organization.

continuance commitment An employee's calculative attachment to the organization, whereby an employee is motivated to stay only because leaving would be costly.

Organizational commitment represents the other half (with job satisfaction) of what some experts call "overall job attitude." **Organizational commitment**—or more specifically **affective commitment**—is the employee's emotional attachment to, identification with, and involvement in a particular organization.[67] Affective commitment is a person's feeling of loyalty to the place where he or she works.

Affective commitment differs from **continuance commitment**, which is a calculative attachment to the organization. Employees have high continuance commitment when they feel bound to remain with the organization because it would be too costly to quit. In other words, they choose to stay because the calculated (typically financial) value of staying is higher than the value of working somewhere else. You can tell an employee has high calculative commitment when he or she says: "I hate this place but can't afford to quit!" This reluctance to quit may exist because the employee would lose a large bonus by leaving early or is well established in the community where he or she works.[68]

CONSEQUENCES OF AFFECTIVE AND CONTINUANCE COMMITMENT

Affective commitment can be a significant competitive advantage.[69] Loyal employees are less likely to quit their jobs and be absent from work. They also have higher work motivation and organizational citizenship, as well as somewhat higher job performance. Organizational commitment also improves customer satisfaction because long-tenure employees have better knowledge of work practices and because clients like to do business with the same employees. One warning is that employees with very high loyalty tend to have high conformity, which results in lower creativity. There are also cases of dedicated employees who violated laws to defend the organization. However, most companies suffer from too little rather than too much employee loyalty.

In contrast to the benefits of affective commitment, employees with high levels of continuance commitment are more likely to have *lower* performance and are *less* likely to engage in organizational citizenship behaviours. Furthermore, unionized employees with high continuance commitment are more likely to use formal grievances, whereas employees with high affective commitment engage in less formal problem solving when employee-employer relations sour.[70] Although some level of financial connection may be necessary, employers should not confuse continuance commitment with employee loyalty. Employers still need to win employees' hearts (affective commitment) beyond tying them financially to the organization (continuance commitment).

BUILDING ORGANIZATIONAL COMMITMENT

There are almost as many ways to build organizational loyalty as there are topics in this textbook, but the following list is most prominent in the literature:

- *Justice and support.* Affective commitment is higher in organizations that fulfill their obligations to employees and abide by humanitarian values, such as fairness, courtesy, forgiveness, and moral integrity. These values relate to the concept of organizational justice, which we discuss in the next chapter. Similarly, organizations that support employee well-being tend to cultivate higher levels of loyalty in return.[71]

- *Shared values.* The definition of affective commitment refers to a person's identification with the organization, and that identification is highest when employees believe

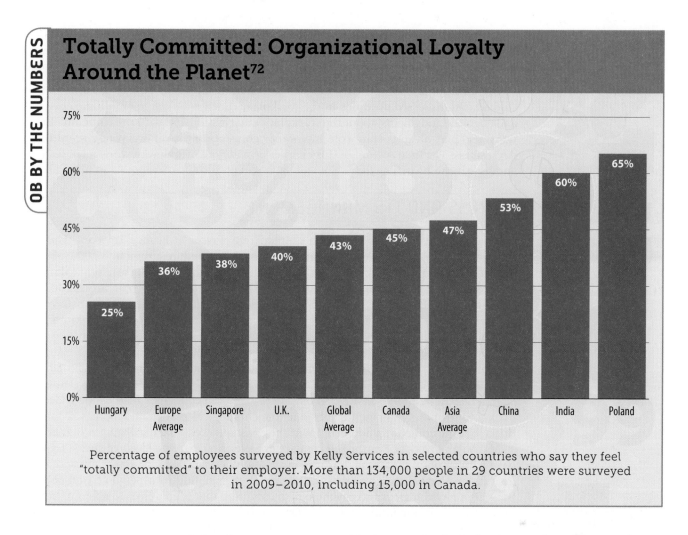

Totally Committed: Organizational Loyalty Around the Planet[72]

Percentage of employees surveyed by Kelly Services in selected countries who say they feel "totally committed" to their employer. More than 134,000 people in 29 countries were surveyed in 2009–2010, including 15,000 in Canada.

their values are congruent with the organization's dominant values. Also, employees experience more comfort and predictability when they agree with the values underlying corporate decisions. This comfort increases their motivation to stay with the organization.[73]

trust Refers to positive expectations one person has toward another person or group in situations involving risk.

- *Trust.* **Trust** refers to positive expectations one person has toward another person or group in situations involving risk.[74] Trust means putting faith in the other person or group. It is also a reciprocal activity: To receive trust, you must demonstrate trust. Employees have stronger commitment to the organization when they trust its leaders. This explains why layoffs are one of the greatest blows to employee loyalty; when employees have less job security, they feel less trust in their employer and the employment relationship.[75]

- *Organizational comprehension.* Organizational comprehension refers to how well employees understand the organization, including its strategic direction, social dynamics, and physical layout.[76] This awareness is a necessary prerequisite to affective commitment because it is difficult to identify with or feel loyal to something that you don't know very well. Furthermore, lack of information produces uncertainty, and the resulting stress can distance employees from that source of uncertainty (i.e., the organization). The practical implication here is to ensure that employees develop a reasonably clear and complete mental model of the organization. This occurs by giving staff information and opportunities to keep up to date with organizational events, interact with co-workers, discover what goes on in different parts of the organization, and learn about the organization's history and future plans.[77]

- *Employee involvement.* Employee involvement increases affective commitment by strengthening the employee's psychological ownership and social identity with the organization.[78] Employees feel that they are part of the organization when they participate in decisions that guide the organization's future. Employee involvement also builds loyalty because giving this power is a demonstration of the company's trust in its employees.

Organizational commitment and job satisfaction represent two of the most often studied and discussed attitudes in the workplace. Each is linked to emotional episodes and cognitive judgments about the workplace and relationship with the company. Emotions also play an important role in another concept that is on everyone's mind these days: stress. The final section of this chapter provides an overview of work-related stress and how it can be managed.

WORK-RELATED STRESS AND ITS MANAGEMENT

LO4

The past few years have been rough on many employees at France Telecom. The former state-owned company was privatized and restructured, resulting in 22,000 job cuts (about 20 percent of the company's workforce) through layoffs or attrition. Management developed a "time to move" doctrine of regularly shifting people around to new locations and different types of jobs. Several telecom engineers have been transferred to call centres, for example. The stress has been overwhelming for some staff. More than two dozen France Telecom employees took their own lives and another dozen attempted to do so over the past two years. Several left notes saying they couldn't stand the pressure any longer or blamed management for terrorizing them. The CEO who led the transition resigned over this matter. Stephane Richard, France Telecom's current CEO, claims he will be more sensitive to employee stress. "The former management needed to change the nature of peoples' jobs due to technological change and increased competition, but the company underestimated the consequences," Richard acknowledges."[79]

stress An adaptive response to a situation that is perceived as challenging or threatening to a person's well-being.

Many employees at France Telecom are experiencing extreme levels of stress. Experts have trouble defining **stress**, but it is most often described as an adaptive response to a situation that is perceived as challenging or threatening to a person's well-being.[80] Stress is a physiological and psychological condition that prepares us to adapt to hostile or noxious environmental conditions. Our heart rate increases, muscles tighten, breathing speeds up, and perspiration increases. Our body also moves more blood to the brain, releases adrenaline and other hormones, fuels the system by releasing more glucose and fatty acids, activates systems that sharpen our senses, and conserves resources by shutting down our immune system. One school of thought suggests that stress is a negative evaluation of the external environment. However, critics of this cognitive appraisal perspective point out that stress is more accurately described as an emotional experience, which may occur before or after a conscious evaluation of the situation.[81]

Whether stress is a complex emotion or a cognitive evaluation of the environment, it has become a pervasive experience in the daily lives of most people. More than one-third of Canadians report that their work makes them ill or unhealthy. That recent survey of 115,000 employees in 33 countries, identified Canadians as having the second highest level of stress-related health complaints (Japan topped the list), followed by the Ukraine, Finland, and Hong Kong. In another major multi-country poll, 76 percent of Canadians said they frequently or sometimes feel stress in their daily lives, with their job accounting for the single greatest cause of that stress.[82]

Stress is typically described as a negative experience. This is known as *distress*—the degree of physiological, psychological, and behavioural deviation from healthy functioning. However, a positive form of stress—called *eustress*—is a necessary part of life because it activates and motivates people to achieve goals, change their environments, and succeed in life's challenges.[83] Our focus is on the causes and management of distress, because it has become a chronic problem in many societies.

GENERAL ADAPTATION SYNDROME

More than 500 years ago, people began using the word *stress* to describe the human response to harsh environmental conditions. However, it wasn't until the 1930s that

Montreal researcher Hans Selye (often described as the father of stress research) first documented the stress experience, called the **general adaptation syndrome**. Selye determined (initially by studying rats) that people have a fairly consistent and automatic physiological response to stressful situations, which helps them to cope with environmental demands.

general adaptation syndrome A model of the stress experience, consisting of three stages: alarm reaction, resistance, and exhaustion.

The general adaptation syndrome consists of the three stages shown in Exhibit 4.5.[84] The *alarm reaction* stage occurs when a threat or challenge activates the physiological stress responses that were noted above. The individual's energy level and coping effectiveness decrease in response to the initial shock. The second stage, *resistance,* activates various biochemical, psychological, and behavioural mechanisms that give the individual more energy and engage coping mechanisms to overcome or remove the source of stress. To focus energy on the source of the stress, the body reduces resources to the immune system during this stage. This explains why people are more likely to catch a cold or some other illness when they experience prolonged stress. People have a limited resistance capacity, and if the source of stress persists, the individual will eventually move into the third stage, *exhaustion.* Most of us are able to remove the source of stress or remove ourselves from that source before becoming exhausted. However, people who frequently reach exhaustion have increased risk of long-term physiological and psychological damage.[85]

CONSEQUENCES OF DISTRESS

Stress takes its toll on the human body.[86] Many people experience tension headaches, muscle pain, and related problems mainly due to muscle contractions from the stress response. Studies have found that high stress levels also contribute to cardiovascular disease, including heart attacks and strokes, and may be associated with some forms of cancer. Stress also produces various psychological consequences, such as job dissatisfaction, moodiness, depression, and lower organizational commitment. Furthermore, various behavioural outcomes have been linked to high or persistent stress, including lower job performance, poor decision making, and increased workplace accidents and aggressive behaviour. Most people react to stress through "fight or flight," so increased absenteeism is another outcome because it is a form of flight.[87]

job burnout The process of emotional exhaustion, cynicism, and reduced personal accomplishment that results from prolonged exposure to stressors.

Job Burnout   **Job burnout** is a particular stress consequence that refers to the process of emotional exhaustion, cynicism, and reduced feelings of personal accomplishment.[88] *Emotional exhaustion,* the first stage, is characterized by a lack of energy,

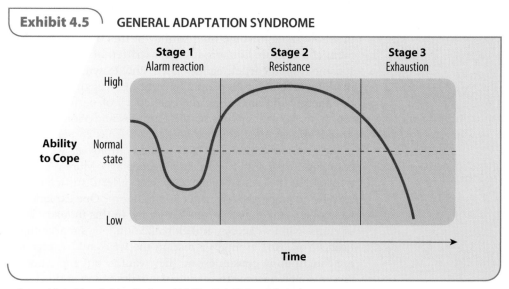

Exhibit 4.5   **GENERAL ADAPTATION SYNDROME**

Source: Adapted from H. Selye, *The Stress of Life* (New York: McGraw-Hill, 1956).

tiredness, and a feeling that one's emotional resources are depleted. This is followed by *cynicism* (also called *depersonalization*), which is an indifferent attitude toward work, emotional detachment from clients, a cynical view of the organization, and a tendency to strictly follow rules and regulations rather than adapt to the needs of others. The final stage of burnout, called *reduced personal accomplishment,* entails feelings of diminished confidence in one's ability to perform the job well. In such situations, employees develop a sense of learned helplessness as they no longer believe that their efforts make a difference.

STRESSORS: THE CAUSES OF STRESS

stressors Any environmental conditions that place a physical or emotional demand on a person.

Before identifying ways to manage work-related stress, we must first understand its causes, known as stressors. **Stressors** include any environmental conditions that place a physical or emotional demand on a person.[89] There are numerous stressors in the workplace and in life in general. In this section, we'll highlight three of the most common stressors: harassment and incivility, work overload, and low task control.

psychological harassment Repeated and hostile or unwanted conduct, verbal comments, actions, or gestures that affect an employee's dignity or psychological or physical integrity and that result in a harmful work environment for the employee.

Harassment and Incivility   One of the fastest-growing sources of workplace stress is **psychological harassment**. Psychological harassment includes repeated hostile or unwanted conduct, verbal comments, actions, and gestures that undermine an employee's dignity or psychological or physical integrity. This covers a broad landscape of behaviours, from threats and bullying to subtle yet persistent forms of incivility.[90] Psychological harassment permeates the corporate landscape. The Quebec government, which passed the first workplace anti-harassment legislation in North America, received more than 2,500 complaints in the first year alone! A survey of more than 100,000 employees in Asia reported that between 19 percent (China) and 46 percent (Korea) of employees experience incivility monthly or more often. Two-thirds of Americans think people are less civil today than 20 years ago; 10 percent say they witness incivility daily in their workplaces and are targets of that abuse at least once each week.[91]

sexual harassment Unwelcome conduct of a sexual nature that detrimentally affects the work environment or leads to adverse job-related consequences for its victims.

Sexual harassment is a type of harassment in which a person's employment or job performance is conditional and depends on unwanted sexual relations (called *quid pro quo* harassment) and/or the person experiences sexual conduct from others (such as posting pornographic material) that unreasonably interferes with work performance or creates an intimidating, hostile, or offensive working environment (called *hostile work environment* harassment).[92]

Work Overload   "We just keep rushing along in a confused state of never having time to do the things that seem to be pressing upon us." Sound familiar? Most Canadians probably thought something similar to this over the past year. But although this comment comes from Canada, it wasn't written in the past year or even in the past decade. It came from an article called "Let's Slow Down!" in a Royal Bank of Canada newsletter in 1949![93] The fact is, people have been struggling for more than a half-century with the pace of life, including the challenges of performing too many tasks and working too many hours. Surveys by the Families and Work Institute report that 44 percent of Americans say they are overworked, up from 28 percent who felt this way a few years earlier. Almost 25 percent of Canadian employees work more than 50 hours per week, compared with only 10 percent a decade ago. More recently, Canadians identified work overload as the second highest stressor, after insufficient salary.[94]

Why do employees work such long hours? One explanation is the combined effects of technology and globalization. "Everyone in this industry is working harder now because of email, wireless access, and globalization," says marketing executive Christopher Lochhead. "You can't even get a rest on the weekend." A second factor is that many people are caught up in consumerism; they want to buy more goods and services, and doing so requires more income through longer work hours. A third reason, called the "ideal worker norm," is that professionals expect themselves and others to work longer hours. For many,

Smartphone Addiction Begins

The "BlackBerry has become so addictive to many of its users that it has been given the nickname CrackBerry." Nick Salaysay admits that his work routinely gets mixed in with his personal time. "I have a BlackBerry, so I check my email a lot when I'm supposed to be on vacation," says the Calgary lawyer. Salaysay also acknowledges that having work spill over into his time off "really annoys my girlfriend." Research indicates that the increased workload and work preoccupation caused by smartphones of all types can result in the additional stress of relationship and marital problems. The term "BlackBerry thumb" describes how these devices contribute to arthritis when used excessively and one law report recently warned that employers who issue BlackBerrys could also incur liability of stress-related illnesses as the devices keep employees on an "electronic leash." And even if the organization is not issuing the employee's smartphone, workers of all ages and occupations are increasingly making time on company time to check for the latest ping, flashing light, or icon to signal a new text, email, Facebook or Twitter message, or even the outdated missed call.[95] *David Young-Wolff/PhotoEdit*

toiling away far beyond the normal workweek is a badge of honour, a symbol of their superhuman capacity to perform above others.[96] This badge of honour is particularly serious in several (but not all) Asian countries, to the point where "death from overwork" is now part of the common language (*karoshi* in Japanese and *guolaosi* in Chinese).[97]

 For many, toiling away far beyond the normal workweek is a badge of honour, a symbol of their superhuman capacity to perform above others. "

Low Task Control   An increasingly popular model of job burnout suggests that emotional exhaustion depends on both job demands and job resources.[98] *Job demands* are aspects of work that require sustained physical or psychological effort. High workload is one of the more significant job demands in the contemporary workplace. At the same time, the effect of job demands on burnout (or stress in general) depends on the individual's job resources. *Job resources* represent aspects of the job that help employees to achieve work goals, reduce job demands, and/or stimulate personal growth and development.

An important job resource is autonomy or control over the pace of work. Low task control increases the risk of job burnout because employees face high workloads without the ability to adjust the pace of the load to their own energy, attention span, and other resources. Furthermore, the degree to which low task control is a stressor increases with the burden of responsibility the employee must carry.[99] Assembly-line workers have low task control, but their stress can be fairly low if their level of responsibility is also low. In contrast, sports coaches are under immense pressure to win games (high responsibility), yet they have little control over what happens on the playing field (low task control).

INDIVIDUAL DIFFERENCES IN STRESS

People experience different stress levels when exposed to the same stressor. One factor is the employee's physical health. Regular exercise and a healthy lifestyle produce a larger store of energy to cope with stress. A second individual difference are the coping strategies employees use to ward off a particular stressor.[100] People sometimes figure out ways to remove the stressor or to minimize its presence. Some other coping mechanisms include seeking support from others, reframing the stressor in a more positive light, blaming others for the stressor, and denying the stressor's existence. Some coping strategies work better for specific stressors and some work well for all stressors.[101] Thus, someone who uses a less effective coping mechanism in a particular situation may continue to experience stress in response to that situation. People have a tendency to rely on one or two coping strategies, and those who rely on generally poor coping strategies (such as denying the stressor exists) will continue to experience stress.

Personality is the third and possibly the most important reason why people experience different levels of stress when faced with the same stressor.[102] Individuals with low neuroticism (high emotional stability) usually experience lower stress levels because, by definition, they are less prone to anxiety, depression, and other negative emotions. Extroverts also tend to experience lower stress than do introverts, likely because extroversion includes a degree of positive thinking and extroverts interact with others, which helps buffer the effect of stressors. People with a positive self-concept—high self-esteem, self-efficacy, and internal locus of control (see Chapter 3)—feel more confident and in control when faced with a stressor. In other words, they tend to have a stronger sense of optimism.[103]

While positive self-concept protects us from stress, workaholism attracts more stressors and weakens the capacity to cope with them. The classic **workaholic** (also called *work addict*) is highly involved in work, feels compelled or driven to work because of inner pressures, and has a low enjoyment of work. Workaholics are compulsive and preoccupied with work, often to the exclusion and detriment of personal health, intimate relationships, and family.[104]

workaholic A person who is highly involved in work, feels compelled to work, and has a low enjoyment of work.

MANAGING WORK-RELATED STRESS

L05

Many people deny the existence of their stress until it has more serious outcomes. This avoidance strategy creates a vicious cycle because the failure to cope with stress becomes another stressor on top of the one that created the stress in the first place. To prevent this vicious cycle, employers and employees need to apply one or more of the stress management strategies described below: remove the stressor, withdraw from the stressor, change stress perceptions, control stress consequences, and receive social support.[105]

Remove the Stressor   There are many ways to remove the stressor, but some of the more common actions involve assigning employees to jobs that match their skills and preferences, reducing excessive workplace noise, having a complaint system and taking corrective action against harassment, and giving employees more control over the work process. Another important way that companies can remove stressors is by facilitating better work-life balance. Work-life balance initiatives minimize conflict between the employee's work and nonwork demands (see Chapter 1). Five of the most common work-life balance initiatives are flexible and limited work time, job sharing, teleworking, personal leave, and child care support.[106]

- *Flexible and limited work time.* An important way to improve work-life balance is limiting the number of hours that employees are expected to work and giving them flexibility in scheduling those hours. For example, Vancouver-based Propaganda Games stands out in the overworked electronic games industry because it keeps work hours within reasonable limits. American electronics retailer Best Buy has also become a role model in work-life balance by giving employees very flexible work hours.[107]

- *Job sharing.* Job sharing splits a career position between two people so that they experience less time-based stress between work and family. They typically work different parts of the week, with some form of communication arrangement to coordinate activities. This strategy gives employees the ability to work part-time in jobs that are naturally designed for full-time responsibilities.

- *Teleworking.* Teleworking reduces the time and stress of commuting to work and makes it easier to fulfill family obligations, such as temporarily leaving the home office to pick the kids up from school. Consequently, teleworkers tend to experience better work-life balance.[108] However, teleworking may increase stress for those who crave social interaction and who lack the space and privacy necessary to work at home.

- *Personal leave.* Employers with strong work-life values offer extended maternity, paternity, and personal leave for employees to care for a new family member or take advantage of a personal experience. Most countries provide 12 to 16 weeks of paid leave, with some offering one year or more of fully or partially paid family leave.[109]
- *Child care support.* Many large and medium-sized companies in Canada provide on-site or subsidized child care facilities. Child care support reduces stress because employees are less rushed to drop off children and less worried during the day about how well their children are doing.[110]

Withdraw from the Stressor Removing the stressor may be the ideal solution, but it is often not feasible. An alternative strategy is to permanently or temporarily remove employees from the stressor. Permanent withdrawal occurs when employees are transferred to jobs that are a better fit for their competencies and values. Temporarily withdrawing from stressors is the most frequent way that employees manage stress. Vacations and holidays are important opportunities for employees to recover from stress and re-energize for future challenges. A small number of companies offer paid or unpaid sabbaticals. "Sabbaticals result in happier, healthier employees," says Colliers managing director Mark Synnott, who has taken four sabbaticals during his career. "People recharge their batteries and come back clear-headed and motivated."[111] Many firms also provide innovative ways for employees to withdraw from stressful work throughout the day, such as games rooms, karaoke rooms, ice cream cart breaks, nap rooms, and cafeterias that include live piano recitals.

Change Stress Perceptions Earlier, we learned that employees experience different stress levels because they have different levels of positive self-evaluation and optimism. Consequently, another way to manage stress is to help employees improve their self-concept so that job challenges are not perceived as threatening. Personal goal setting and self-reinforcement can also reduce the stress that people experience when they enter new work settings. Research also suggests that some (but not all) forms of humour can improve optimism and create positive emotions by taking some psychological weight off the situation.[112]

Control Stress Consequences Regular exercise and maintaining a healthy lifestyle is an effective stress management strategy because it controls stress consequences. Research indicates that physical exercise reduces the physiological consequences of stress by helping employees moderate their breathing and heart rate, muscle tension, and stomach acidity.[113] Many Canadian companies offer pilates, yoga, and other exercise and meditation classes during the workday. Research has found that various forms of meditation reduce anxiety, reduce blood pressure and muscle tension, and moderate breathing and heart rate.[114] Wellness programs can also help control the consequences of stress. These programs inform employees about better nutrition and fitness, regular sleep, and other good health habits. Many large employers offer *employee assistance programs (EAPs)*—counselling services that help employees resolve marital, financial, or work-related troubles, but some counselling also varies with the industry. For instance, Vancouver City Savings Credit Union has an award-winning program that counsels employees following a bank robbery. There are more than 200 bank robberies in Vancouver each year, and VanCity's program dramatically reduces the time employees require for recovery compared to employees in other financial institutions.[115]

Receive Social Support Social support occurs when co-workers, supervisors, family members, friends, and others provide emotional and/or informational support to buffer an individual's stress experience. For instance, one recent study found that employees

Do You Have a Work Spouse?

Every morning (just like the couple in the photo), Nita Ossi and her co-worker Steve carpool to their office near Prince George in British Columbia. They seek out each other's advice throughout the day and enjoy time together in the break room. Co-workers joke that Nita and Steve are like a married couple, even though their friendship is platonic. A more accurate label is that they are work spouses. "We lean on each other for everything," says Ossie. "I don't know what I'd do without him." Estimates vary widely on the percentage of employees with work spouses, but these close non-sexual partnerships with co-workers seem to help manage workplace stress. For example, soon after they joined Ketchum Public Relations Canada in Toronto a few years ago, Linsey Nogueira and Erin Manning formed a close friendship that has since helped them through many stressful work and nonwork issues. "It certainly makes it more enjoyable to come to work and have someone here who understands you and the office and the stresses of everyday life," says Nogueira. "Erin is honest and funny and supportive. And we trust each other."[116] © *Image Source/Alamy*

whose managers are good at empathizing experienced fewer stress symptoms than did employees whose managers were less empathetic. Social support potentially (but not always) improves the person's optimism and self-confidence because support makes people feel valued and worthy. Social support also provides information to help the person interpret, comprehend, and possibly remove the stressor. For instance, to reduce a new employee's stress, co-workers could describe ways to handle difficult customers. Seeking social support is called a "tend and befriend" response to stress, and research suggests that women often follow this route rather than the "fight-or-flight" response mentioned earlier.[117]

Employee emotions, attitudes, and stress influence employee behaviour mainly through motivation. Recall, for instance, that behavioural intentions are judgments or expectations about the motivation to engage in a particular behaviour. The next chapter introduces the prominent theories of employee motivation.

CHAPTER SUMMARY

 LO1 Explain how emotions and cognition (conscious reasoning) influence attitudes and behaviour.

Emotions are physiological, behavioural, and psychological episodes experienced toward an object, person, or event that create a state of readiness. Emotions differ from attitudes, which represent a cluster of beliefs, feelings, and behavioural intentions toward a person, object, or event. Beliefs are a person's established perceptions about the attitude object. Feelings are positive or negative evaluations of the attitude object. Behavioural intentions represent a motivation to engage in a particular behaviour toward the target.

Attitudes have traditionally been described as a purely rational process in which beliefs predict feelings, which predict behavioural intentions, which predict behaviour. We now know that emotions have an influence on behaviour that is equal to or greater than that of cognition. This dual process is apparent when we internally experience a conflict between what logically seems good or bad and what we emotionally feel is good or bad in a situation.

Emotions also affect behaviour directly. Behaviour sometimes influences our subsequent attitudes through cognitive dissonance.

 LO2 Discuss the dynamics of emotional labour and the role of emotional intelligence in the workplace.

Emotional labour consists of the effort, planning, and control needed to express organizationally desired emotions during interpersonal transactions. It is more common in jobs requiring a variety of emotions and more intense emotions, as well as in jobs where interaction with clients is frequent and has a long duration. Cultures also differ regarding the norms of displaying or concealing a person's true emotions. Emotional dissonance occurs when required and true emotions are incompatible with each other. Deep acting can minimize this dissonance, as can the practice of hiring people with a natural tendency to display desired emotions.

Emotional intelligence is the ability to perceive and express emotion, assimilate emotion in thought, understand and reason with emotion, and regulate emotion in oneself and others. This concept includes four components arranged in a hierarchy: self-awareness, self-management, social awareness, and relationship management. Emotional intelligence can be learned to some extent, particularly through personal coaching.

 L03   Summarize the consequences of job dissatisfaction as well as strategies to increase organizational (affective) commitment.

Job satisfaction represents a person's evaluation of his or her job and work context. Four types of job dissatisfaction consequences are quitting or otherwise getting away from the dissatisfying situation (exit), attempting to change the dissatisfying situation (voice), patiently waiting for the problem to sort itself out (loyalty), and reducing work effort and performance (neglect). Job satisfaction has a moderate relationship with job performance and with customer satisfaction. Affective organizational commitment (loyalty) is the employee's emotional attachment to, identification with, and involvement in a particular organization. This contrasts with continuance commitment, which is a calculative bond with the organization. Companies

build loyalty through justice and support, shared values, trust, organizational comprehension, and employee involvement.

 L04   Describe the stress experience and review three major stressors.

Stress is an adaptive response to a situation that is perceived as challenging or threatening to a person's well-being. The stress experience, called the general adaptation syndrome, involves moving through three stages: alarm, resistance, and exhaustion. Stressors are the causes of stress and include any environmental conditions that place a physical or emotional demand on a person. Three stressors that have received considerable attention are harassment and incivility, work overload, and low task control.

L05   Identify five ways to manage workplace stress.

Many interventions are available to manage work-related stress, including removing the stressor, withdrawing from the stressor, changing stress perceptions, controlling stress consequences, and receiving social support.

KEY TERMS

affective commitment, p. 106

attitudes, p. 94

cognitive dissonance, p. 97

continuance commitment, p. 106

emotional dissonance, p. 99

emotional intelligence (EI), p. 100

emotional labour, p. 98

emotions, p. 93

exit-voice-loyalty-neglect (EVLN) model, p. 103

general adaptation syndrome, p. 109

job burnout, p. 109

job satisfaction, p. 102

organizational (affective) commitment, p. 106

psychological harassment, p. 110

service profit chain model, p. 104

sexual harassment, p. 110

stress, p. 108

stressors, p. 110

trust, p. 107

workaholic, p. 112

CRITICAL-THINKING QUESTIONS

1. A recent study reported that university instructors are frequently required to engage in emotional labour. Identify the situations in which emotional labour is required for this job. In your opinion, is emotional labour more troublesome for university instructors or for 911 emergency service operators?

2. "Emotional intelligence is more important than cognitive intelligence in influencing an individual's success." Do you agree or disagree with this statement? Support your perspective.

3. Describe a time when you effectively managed someone's emotions. What happened? What was the result?

4. "Happy employees create happy customers." Explain why this statement might be true, and identify conditions in which it might not be true.

5. What factors influence an employee's organizational loyalty?

6. Is being a full-time college or university student a stressful role? Why or why not? Contrast your response with other students' perspectives.

7. Two university graduates recently joined the same major newspaper as journalists. Both work long hours and have tight deadlines for completing their stories. They are under constant pressure to scout out new leads and be the first to report new controversies. One journalist is increasingly fatigued and despondent and has taken several days of sick leave. The other is getting the work done and seems to enjoy the challenges. Use your knowledge of stress to explain why these two journalists are reacting differently to their jobs.

8. A senior official of a labour union stated: "All stress management does is help people cope with poor management. [Employers] should really be into stress reduction." Discuss the accuracy of this statement.

CASE STUDY 4.1

Conestoga-Rovers and Associates

At first glance, the thick, hardcover books featured prominently in the reception area of Conestoga-Rovers and Associates in Waterloo, Ontario, have the appearance of dry legal volumes. Then you notice the word "Yearbook" inscribed in large, gold letters across their covers; a peek inside reveals a vividly photographed encapsulation of the company's unspoken, but well understood, work hard–play hard mantra. Within their pages, hundreds of photographs capture smiling, laughing, and often zanily dressed Conestoga-Rovers employees engaged in any number of social events, clubs, and activities that play an integral role in the company's culture.

There are plenty of events to choose from. Hardly a weekend goes by when a group of employees is not engaged in some social event, be it jet-boating on the Niagara River, taking a bus trip to a Buffalo Bills football game, celebrating Roverfest (a massive annual bash for employees and their families), or indulging in a death-by-chocolate night.

Conestoga-Rovers and Associates has forged an exemplary reputation for its expertise in the fields of engineering, the environment, construction, and information technology. But its employees, some 450 in Waterloo alone, will tell you the company's dynamic social side, along with a range of unique employee perks, also makes it a great place to work and grow, both professionally and socially. Not surprisingly, Conestoga-Rovers has been identified as one of the best places to work in the Waterloo Region.

In addition to an extremely active social committee, the company boasts an on-site day-care centre—The Butterfly Learning Centre—that was launched just months after Dianne Freeman, a senior project manager with the company's air quality group, suggested it. "You always go in and ask for the whole dream but you usually only get a window," says Freeman. "[Company president Ed Roberts] offered the whole dream and it was overwhelming."

Another valued Conestoga-Rovers perk is company-paid vacations for employees and their families after 10 years of service. Freeman and her family went to New Zealand, courtesy of the company, five years ago. Last year alone, 44 other 10-year employees were rewarded with similarly ambitious vacations.

"The only thing we have is our employees," says Conestoga-Rovers vice-president Ian Richardson. "Without happy, engaged employees we don't have anything." Richardson also acknowledges that creating a positive work environment helps to recruit top talent: "Our employees know the kind of place they work in. We wanted to let others know a little more about what goes on here."

Discussion Questions

1. Why do Conestoga-Rovers and Associates and other companies try to create a positive work environment?

2. How does this company manage to provide events and perks that employees value?

3. Is it possible that employees can have too much fun at work?

Source: Gary Nyp, "Where Dreams Sometimes Come True," *Kitchener-Waterloo Record*, October 13, 2007, p. E1.

 CLASS EXERCISE 4.2

Strengths-Based Coaching

Purpose   To help students practise a form of interpersonal development built on the dynamics of positive emotions.

Materials   None.

Background   Several chapters in this book introduce and apply the emerging philosophy of *positive organizational behaviour,* which suggests that focusing on the positive rather than negative aspects of life will improve organizational success and individual well-being. An application of positive OB is strengths-based or appreciative coaching, in which the coach focuses on the person's strengths rather than weaknesses, and helps to realize the person's potential. As part of any coaching process, the coach listens to the employee's story and uses questions and suggestions to help that person redefine her or his self-concept and perceptions of the environment. Two important skills in effective coaching are active listening and probing for information (rather than telling the person a solution or direction). The instructions below identify specific information and issues that the coach and coachee will discuss.

Instructions   • *Step 1:* Form teams of four people. One team can have six people if the class does not have multiples of four. For odd-numbered class sizes, one person may be an observer. Divide into pairs in which one person is coach and the other coachee. Ideally for this exercise, the coach and coachee should have little knowledge of each other.

• *Step 2:* Coachees will describe something about themselves in which they excel and for which they like to be recognized. This competency might be work-related, but not necessarily. It would be a personal achievement or ability that is close to their self-concept (how they define themselves). The coach mostly listens, but also prompts more details from the coachee using "probe" questions ("Tell me more about that." "What did you do next?" "Could you explain that further, please?" "What else can you remember about that event?"). As the coachee's story develops, the coach will guide the coachee to identify ways to leverage this strength. For example, the pair would explore situational barriers to practising the coachee's strength as well as aspects of this strength that require further development. The strength may also be discussed as a foundation for the coachee to develop strengths in other, related ways. The session should end with some discussion of the coachee's goals and action plans. The first coaching session can be any length of time specified by the instructor, but 15 to 25 minutes is typical for each coaching session.

• *Step 3:* After completing the first coaching session, regroup so that each pair consists of different partners than those in the first pair (i.e., if pairs were A-B and C-D in session 1, pairs are A-C and B-D in session 2). The coaches become coachees to their new partners in session 2.

• *Step 4:* The class will debrief regarding the emotional experience of discussing personal strengths, the role of self-concept in emotions and attitudes, the role of managers and co-workers in building positive emotions in people, and the value and limitations of strengths-based coaching.

Note: For further information about strengths-based coaching, see Sara L. Orem, Jacqueline Binkert, and Ann L. Clancy, *Appreciative Coaching* (San Francisco: Jossey-Bass, 2007); Marcus Buckingham and C. Coffman, *First, Break All the Rules* (New York: Simon & Schuster, 1999).

 TEAM EXERCISE 4.3

Ranking Jobs on Their Emotional Labour

Purpose   This exercise is designed to help you understand the jobs in which people tend to experience higher or lower degrees of emotional labour.

Instructions   • *Step 1:* Individually rank-order the extent that the jobs listed below require emotional labour. In other words, assign a "1" to the job you believe requires the most effort, planning, and control to express organizationally desired emotions during interpersonal transactions. Assign a "10" to the job you believe requires the least amount of emotional labour. Mark your rankings in column 1.

- *Step 2:* The instructor will form teams of four or five members and each team will rank-order the items on the basis of consensus (not simply averaging the individual rankings). These results are placed in column 2.

- *Step 3:* The instructor will provide expert ranking information. This information should be written in column 3. Then students calculate the differences in columns 4 and 5.

- *Step 4:* The class will compare the results and discuss the features of jobs with high emotional labour.

Occupational Emotional Labour Scoring Sheet				
Occupation	(1) Individual Ranking	(2) Team Ranking	(3) Expert Ranking	(4) Absolute Difference of 1 and 3	(5) Absolute Difference of 2 and 3
Bartender					
Cashier					
Dental hygienist					
Insurance adjuster					
Lawyer					
Librarian					
Postal clerk					
Registered nurse					
Social worker					
Television announcer					
			TOTAL		
			(The lower the score, the better)	Your score	Team score

Go to CONNECT to complete the following interactive self-assessments.

 SELF-ASSESSMENT EXERCISE 4.4

How Do You Rate Your Emotional Intelligence?

Purpose   This self-assessment is designed to help you understand the meaning and dimensions of emotional intelligence and to estimate your perceptions of your emotional intelligence.

Overview   Emotional intelligence has become an important concept and ability in the workplace. It is a skill that people develop throughout their lives to help them interact better with others, make better decisions, and manage the attitudes and behaviour of other people.

Although emotional intelligence is best measured as an ability test, this scale offers you an opportunity to estimate your perceptions and self-awareness of this ability in yourself.

Instructions   Read each of the statements below and select the response that best describes you. Then use the scoring key in Appendix B of this book to calculate your results. This self-assessment is completed alone so that students rate themselves honestly without concerns of social comparison. However, class discussion will focus on the meaning and dimensions of emotional intelligence, its application in the workplace, and the best ways to measure emotional intelligence.

Emotional Intelligence Self-Assessment					
To what extent do you agree or disagree with each of these statements?	Strongly Agree	Moderately Agree	Slightly Agree	Slightly Disagree	Moderately Disagree	Strongly Disagree
1. I tend to describe my emotions accurately.	☐	☐	☐	☐	☐	☐
2. I show respect for others' opinions, even when I think those opinions are wrong.	☐	☐	☐	☐	☐	☐
3. I know how others are feeling, even when they try to hide their feelings.	☐	☐	☐	☐	☐	☐
4. I am good at getting people enthusiastic and motivated.	☐	☐	☐	☐	☐	☐
5. When I get worried or angry, I have difficulty suppressing those emotions such that others do not notice them.	☐	☐	☐	☐	☐	☐
6. I have a talent for gauging from their body language a person's true feelings.	☐	☐	☐	☐	☐	☐
7. I usually know when I am feeling frustrated.	☐	☐	☐	☐	☐	☐
8. I tend to have difficulty getting people in the right emotional frame of mind.	☐	☐	☐	☐	☐	☐
9. I am very much aware of my own emotions.	☐	☐	☐	☐	☐	☐
10. I am able to understand all sides of a disagreement before forming an opinion.	☐	☐	☐	☐	☐	☐
11. I can easily cheer people up when they are feeling discouraged or sad.	☐	☐	☐	☐	☐	☐
12. I am sometimes unaware when I get emotional about an issue.	☐	☐	☐	☐	☐	☐
13. I can tell when others do not mean what they say.	☐	☐	☐	☐	☐	☐
14. I am good at controlling my own emotions when the situation requires such control.	☐	☐	☐	☐	☐	☐
15. I sometimes don't realize how others are feeling about an issue.	☐	☐	☐	☐	☐	☐
16. I have a talent for getting others to share my keenness for an idea.	☐	☐	☐	☐	☐	☐

Sources: Copyright © 2011 Steven L. McShane. This self-assessment was inspired by similar instruments, particularly: P. J. Jordan and S. A. Lawrence, "Emotional Intelligence in Teams: Development and Initial Validation of the Short Version of the Workgroup Emotional Intelligence Profile (WEIP-S)," *Journal of Management & Organization* 15 (2009): 452–469; C.-S. Wong and K. S. Law, "The Effects of Leader and Follower Emotional Intelligence on Performance and Attitude: An Exploratory Study," *Leadership Quarterly* 13 (2002): 243–274; N. S. Schutte, J. M. Malouff, L. E. Hall, D. J. Haggerty, J. T. Cooper, C. J. Golden, and L. Dornheim, "Development and Validation of a Measure of Emotional Intelligence," *Personality and Individual Differences* 25, no. 2 (1998): 167–177.

SELF-ASSESSMENT EXERCISE 4.5

Are You Committed to Your School?

This self-assessment is designed to help you understand the concept of organizational commitment and to assess your commitment to an organization where you currently or recently worked. Read each of the statements and circle the response that best fits your personal belief. This self-assessment should be completed alone so that you can rate yourself honestly without concerns of social comparison. However, class discussion will focus on the meaning of the different types of organizational commitment and how well this scale applies to the commitment of students toward the college or university they are attending.

SELF-ASSESSMENT EXERCISE 4.6

What is Your Emotional Personality?

This self-assessment is designed to help you understand mood states or personality traits of emotions and to assess your own mood or emotional personality. This self-assessment consists of several words representing various emotions that you might have experienced. For each word presented, indicate the extent to which you have felt this way generally across all situations *over the past six months.* You need to be honest with yourself to receive a reasonable estimate of your mood state or personality trait on these scales. The results provide an estimate of your level on two emotional personality scales. This instrument is widely used in research, but it is only an estimate. You should not assume that the results are accurate without a more complete assessment by a trained professional.

SELF-ASSESSMENT EXERCISE 4.7

Are You a Workaholic?

This self-assessment is designed to help you identify the extent to which you are a workaholic. This instrument presents several statements and asks you to indicate the extent to which each statement is true of your work habits. You need to be honest with yourself for a reasonable estimate of your level of workaholism.

SELF-ASSESSMENT EXERCISE 4.8

How Stressed Are You?

This self-assessment is designed to help you estimate your perceived general level of stress. The items in this scale ask you about your feelings and thoughts during the last month. In each case, please indicate how often you felt or thought a certain way. You need to be honest with yourself for a reasonable estimate of your general level of stress.

 SELF-ASSESSMENT EXERCISE 4.9

How Do You Cope with Stressful Situations?

This self-assessment is designed to help you identify the type of coping strategy you prefer to use in stressful situations. This scale lists a variety of things you might do when faced with a stressful situation. You are asked how often you tend to react in these ways. You need to be honest with yourself for a reasonable estimate of your preferred coping strategy.

 Practise and learn online with Connect. Connect resources include additional and interactive study exercises, videos, and practice quizzing, as well as additional material you won't find in the printed text.

CHAPTER 5

Foundations of Employee Motivation

LEARNING OBJECTIVES

After reading this chapter, you should be able to:

LO1 Define employee engagement.

LO2 Explain the role of human drives and emotions in employee motivation and behaviour.

LO3 Summarize Maslow's needs hierarchy, McClelland's learned needs theory, and four-drive theory and discuss their implications for employee motivation.

LO4 Discuss the expectancy theory model, including its practical implications.

LO5 Outline organizational behaviour modification (OB Mod) and social cognitive theory and explain their relevance to employee motivation.

LO6 Describe the characteristics of effective goal setting and feedback.

LO7 Summarize equity theory and describe ways to improve procedural justice.

Robert Meggy understands the importance of employee motivation and engagement for business success. "When I set out . . . to turn around a box manufacturing company in receivership, the focus quickly became the employees," explains Meggy, who has transformed Vancouver-based Great Little Box Company Ltd. (GLBC) into a strong competitor in the corrugated box and point-of-purchase display industry. "It is clear that happy and motivated employees are the key to success and longevity."

To keep staff motivated, Meggy relies on a combination of challenging goals, open-book feedback, valued rewards that are distributed fairly, and plenty of appreciation and recognition in between. The company has a "Big Outrageous eXtranvaganza (BOX)" goal representing a stretch profit target for the coming year. If the BOX goal is achieved, all of GLBC's 180 employees receive an all-expense-paid vacation to a sunny location. GLBC employees have enjoyed seven such trips in 13 years, the most recent being Cabos San Lucas, Mexico. Employees are also motivated more frequently through open-book meetings where they see the company's financial results for the previous month and receive a bonus cheque representing a share of that month's profits. The same amount of bonus is distributed to everyone, which most staff say is fair. "I certainly believe in fair pay," says Meggy. "You don't have to be the best paying but you do have to be fair."

Meggy also rewards employee suggestions and cost-saving ideas. Employees receive a share of the financial savings to the company when their idea is implemented. For example, one employee recently earned $2,000 for a cost-saving suggestion. The $10'ers program distributes $10 rewards for small day-to-day ideas and mistakes caught. Equally important, anyone can participate in one of several task forces focused on improving sales, reducing costs, or improving employee well-being. "We are always into improving what we do, and this motivates middle management and sales people to put ideas on the table," Meggy explains. "It has really helped our growth."

GLBC subsidizes an active social calendar for employees. Events include summer barbeques, golf tournament, paintball competition, bowling nights, boat cruises, as well as annual celebrations including the employee Christmas party, Chinese New Year, and the Sikh festival of Vaisakhi. Altogether, these activities have produced a workforce that is motivated and highly engaged in their work. It has also contributed to GLBC's standing as one of Canada's Top 100 Employers and British Columbia's Top Employers. "Over the years we have made it a priority to engage employees, provide them with the information they need and empower them to make decisions," says Meggy.[1]

Great Little Box Company motivates its employees through goal setting, fair pay, and recognition, resulting in a highly engaged workforce. "It is clear that happy and motivated employees are the key to success and longevity," says CEO Robert Meggy. *Ron Sangha Photography*

The $10'ers program distributes $10 rewards for small day-to-day ideas and mistakes caught. Equally important, anyone can participate in one of several task forces focused on improving sales, reducing costs, or improving employee well-being. "We are always into improving what we do, and this motivates middle management and sales people to put ideas on the table," Meggy explains. "It has really helped our growth."

motivation The forces within a person that affect his or her direction, intensity, and persistence of voluntary behaviour.

Goal setting, open-book feedback, rewards, and various social bonding events are designed to maintain and improve employee motivation at Vancouver's Great Little Box Company. This motivation has sustained the company's performance in a highly competitive market and has ranked it as one of the best places to work in Canada. **Motivation** refers to the forces within a person that affect his or her direction, intensity, and persistence of voluntary behaviour.[2] Motivated employees are willing to exert a particular level of effort (intensity), for a certain amount of time (persistence), toward a particular goal (direction). Motivation is one of the four essential drivers of individual behaviour and performance (see Chapter 2).

This chapter introduces the core theories of employee motivation. We begin by introducing employee engagement, an increasingly popular concept associated with motivation. Next, we explain how drives and emotions are the prime movers of employee motivation. Three theories that focus on drives and needs—Maslow's needs hierarchy, McClelland's learned needs theory, and four-drive theory—are introduced and evaluated. Next, we turn our attention to the popular rational decision model of employee motivation: expectancy theory. Organizational behaviour modification and social cognitive theory are then introduced, which relate to learning the expectancies that motivate employees through the expectancy theory model. Next, we look at goal setting and feedback, which are considered the most robust and practical motivational concepts and practices in organizations. This chapter closes with the topic of motivation through organizational justice, including the dimensions and dynamics of equity theory and procedural justice.

EMPLOYEE ENGAGEMENT

LO1

employee engagement Individual's emotional and cognitive motivation, particularly a focused, intense, persistent, and purposive effort toward work-related goals.

When executives discuss employee motivation these days, they are just as likely to use the phrase *employee engagement*. This concept, which has become popular in everyday language, is closely connected to employee motivation. Although its definition is still being debated,[3] we cautiously define **employee engagement** as an individual's emotional and cognitive (rational) motivation, particularly a focused, intense, persistent, and purposive effort toward work-related goals. It is typically described as an emotional involvement in, commitment to, and satisfaction with the work. Employee engagement also includes a high level of absorption in the work—the experience of focusing intensely on the task with limited awareness of events beyond that work. Finally, employee engagement is often described in terms of self-efficacy—the belief that you have the ability, role clarity, and resources to get the job done (see Chapter 3).

Employee engagement is a hot topic because various reports suggest that it has a strong effect on employee and work unit performance. British retailer Marks & Spencer claims that a 1 percent improvement in the engagement levels of its workforce produces a 2.9 percent increase in sales per square foot. American electronics retailer Best Buy reports that a 0.1 increase (on a 5.0 point scale) in a store's engagement score is associated with a $100,000 increase in that store's profitability for the year. At JC Penney, stores with the top 25 percent engagement scores generate 36 percent greater operating income than similar-size stores with the lowest 25 percent of scores. Standard Chartered Bank, which is described in Global Connections 5.1, estimates that branches with highly engaged employees produce 20 percent higher returns than branches with lower engagement scores. Other research indicates that employee engagement is associated with higher organizational citizenship and lower turnover intentions. Unfortunately, it isn't clear whether employee engagement makes companies more successful, or whether company success makes employees more engaged. However, the interventions at Standard Chartered, Best Buy, and some other companies suggest that employee engagement scores cause the company outcomes more than vice versa.[4]

The challenge facing organizational leaders is that most employees aren't very engaged. The numbers vary, but generally only about 20 percent of employees in

CONNECTIONS 5.1

Standard Chartered Gets Engaged

Standard Chartered Bank's operations in Hong Kong recently won the Gallup Great Workplace Award for two consecutive years and was named Employer of Choice at the Hong Kong HR Awards. The company's businesses in India (Scope International-India) and Korea (First Bank Korea Ltd.) were also recognized as two of the top-rated employers in those countries. These major achievements are outcomes of a journey that began eight years ago to improve employee engagement and motivation. Employee engagement scores among Standard Chartered employees worldwide (75 percent of whom work in Asia) have more than doubled over this time. Almost half of the bank's employees are now highly engaged, whereas at most large organizations only 25–30 percent are highly engaged.

How has Standard Chartered boosted employee engagement and motivation? First, managers receive training to establish clear key performance indicators (KPIs) for teams and individuals, coach employees frequently, and provide constructive feedback regarding those goals. Employees also receive several days of training and development each year. As a result, almost all the bank's employees say they understand their role and have confidence in performing those objectives. Second, the bank rewards performance, particularly through career development opportunities, and offers a share ownership program so employees can benefit from the company's financial performance. Third, Standard Chartered supports fun activities in the workplace and encourages employees to be involved in community events.

Finally, Standard Chartered focuses on employee strengths rather than shortcomings. "We deliberately build on strengths to help people understand their talents, how to develop these into strengths, and how to work around what they are not so good at," explains Laura

Standard Chartered Bank has significantly improved employee engagement and motivation throughout Asia. *Photo by Servais Mont/Pictobank/ABACAPRESS.COM*

Wilson, Standard Chartered's project leader and manager of performance and engagement. Dustin Woods describes how the strengths-based approach motivates employees. "It's all in the dialogue," says Woods, who is Standard Chartered's organizational learning manager in Pakistan. "Through sharing stories of 'Me at My Best,' individuals build a common understanding of what they want from the workplace."

"Using this focus (employee engagement), we have seen spectacular results," says Tim Miller, Standard Chartered's director of people, property and assurance and non-executive chairman of the company's operations in Korea (SC First Bank). "Our most engaged bank branches [have] significantly higher deposit growth, better cost income ratios, and lower employee attrition than less engaged branches."[5]

Canada are highly engaged, about 60 percent are somewhat engaged, and the remainder have low engagement or are actively disengaged. Actively disengaged employees tend to be disruptive at work, not just disconnected from work. Employees in several Asian countries (notably Japan, China, and South Korea) and a few European countries (notably Italy, Netherlands, and France) have the lowest levels of employee engagement, whereas the highest scores are usually found in the United States, Brazil, and India.[6]

This leads to the question: What are the drivers of employee engagement? Goal setting, employee involvement, organizational justice, communication about the business, employee development opportunities, sufficient resources, and an appealing company vision are some of the more commonly mentioned influences on employee engagement.[7] In other words, building an engaged workforce calls on most topics in this book, such as the MARS model (Chapter 2), the ways to build affective commitment (Chapter 4), motivation practices (Chapter 5), and leadership (Chapter 12).

EMPLOYEE DRIVES AND NEEDS

L02

drives Hardwired characteristics of the brain that correct deficiencies or maintain an internal equilibrium by producing emotions to energize individuals.

To figure out how to create a more engaged and motivated workforce, we first need to understand the motivational "forces" or prime movers of employee behaviour.[8] Our starting point is **drives** (also called *primary needs*), which we define as hardwired characteristics of the brain that attempt to keep us in balance by correcting deficiencies. Drives accomplish this task by producing emotions that energize us to act on our environment.[9] Drives are receiving increasing attention because recent neuroscience (brain) research has highlighted the central role of emotions in human decisions and behaviour. A few human drives that are consistently identified in research include the drive for social interaction, understanding the environment, competence or status, and defending oneself against physiological and psychological harm.[10]

Drives are innate and universal, which means that we are born with them and everyone has them. Furthermore, drives are the "prime movers" of behaviour because they generate emotions, which put people in a state of readiness to act on their environment. Emotions play a central role in motivation.[11] In fact, both words *(emotion* and *motivation)* originate from the same Latin word, *movere*, which means "to move."

needs Goal-directed forces that people experience.

As Exhibit 5.1 illustrates, drives (and, in particular, the emotions produced by these drives) produce human needs. We define **needs** as goal-directed forces that people experience. They are the motivational forces of emotions channelled toward particular goals to correct deficiencies or imbalances. As one leading neuroscientist explained: "drives express themselves directly in background emotions and we eventually become aware of their existence by means of background feelings."[12]

The following example illustrates this process of drives, emotions, needs, and behaviour. Suppose you arrive at work to discover a stranger sitting at your desk. Seeing this situation produces emotions (worry, curiosity) that motivate you to act. These emotions are generated from drives, such as the drive to defend and drive to know. When strong enough, they motivate you to do something about this situation, such as finding out who that person is and possibly seeking reassurance from co-workers that your job is still safe. In this case, you have a need to know what is going on, to feel secure, and possibly to correct a sense of personal violation. Notice that your emotional reactions to seeing the stranger sitting at your desk represent the forces that move you, but you channel those emotions towards specific goals.

INDIVIDUAL DIFFERENCES IN NEEDS

Everyone has the same drives; they are hardwired in us through evolution. However, the type and intensity of emotions formed in a particular situation varies from one person to the next. Exhibit 5.1 explains why this difference occurs. The left side of the

Exhibit 5.1   DRIVES, NEEDS, AND BEHAVIOUR

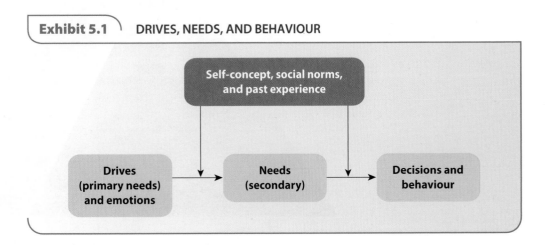

model shows that the individual's self-concept (as well as personality and values), social norms, and past experience amplify or suppress drive-based emotions, thereby resulting in stronger or weaker needs.[13] People who define themselves as very sociable typically experience a stronger need for social interaction if alone for a while, whereas people who view themselves as less sociable would experience a less intense need to be with others over that time. These individual differences also explain why needs can be "learned" to some extent. Socialization and reinforcement may cause people to alter their self-concept somewhat, resulting in a stronger or weaker need for social interaction, achievement, and so on. We will discuss learned needs later in this chapter.

Self-concept, social norms, and past experience also regulate a person's motivated decisions and behaviour, as the right side of Exhibit 5.1 illustrates. Consider the earlier example of the stranger sitting at your desk. You probably wouldn't walk up to the person and demand that he or she leave; such blunt behaviour is contrary to social norms in most cultures. Employees who view themselves as forthright would tend to approach the stranger directly, whereas those who have a different self-concept or have had negative experiences with direct confrontation in the past are more likely to first gather information from co-workers before approaching the intruder. In short, your drives (drive to know, to defend, to bond, etc.) and resulting emotions energize you to act, and your self-concept, social norms, and past experience direct that energy into goal-directed behaviour.

Exhibit 5.1 provides a useful template for understanding how drives and emotions are the prime sources of employee motivation and how individual characteristics (self-concept, experience, values) influence goal-directed behaviour. You will see pieces of this theory when we discuss four-drive theory, expectancy theory, goal setting, and other concepts in this chapter. The remainder of this section describes theories that try to explain the dynamics of drives and needs.

MASLOW'S NEEDS HIERARCHY THEORY

By far, the most widely known theory of human motivation is **Maslow's needs hierarchy theory** (see Exhibit 5.2). Developed by psychologist Abraham Maslow in the 1940s, the

> **Maslow's needs hierarchy theory** A motivation theory of needs arranged in a hierarchy, whereby people are motivated to fulfill a higher need as a lower one becomes gratified.

L03

| **Exhibit 5.2** | **MASLOW'S NEEDS HIERARCHY** |

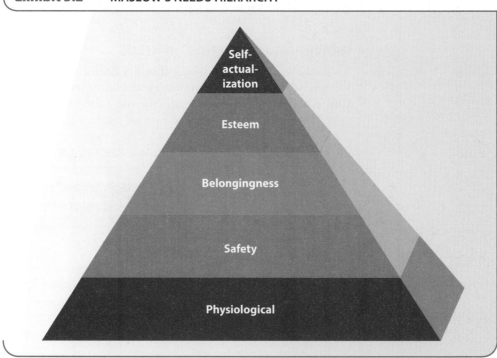

Source: Based on information in A. H. Maslow, "A Theory of Human Motivation," *Psychological Review* 50 (1943), pp. 370–396.

model condenses and integrates the long list of needs that had been studied previously into a hierarchy of five basic categories (from lowest to highest):[14] *physiological* (need for food, air, water, shelter, etc), *safety* (need for security and stability), *belongingness/ love* (need for interaction with and affection from others), *esteem* (need for self-esteem and social esteem/status), and *self-actualization* (need for self-fulfillment, realization of one's potential). Along with developing these five categories, Maslow identified the desire to know and the desire for aesthetic beauty as two innate drives that do not fit within the hierarchy. According to Maslow, we are motivated simultaneously by several needs but the strongest source is the lowest unsatisfied need at the time. As the person satisfies a lower-level need, the next higher need in the hierarchy becomes the primary motivator and remains so even if never satisfied.

Limitations and Contributions of Maslow's Work   In spite of its popularity, Maslow's needs hierarchy theory has been dismissed by most motivation experts.[15] Research found that people do not progress through the hierarchy as the theory predicts. There is also an issue about how quickly and for how long people fulfill their needs. Although needs hierarchy theory has failed the reality test, Maslow deserves credit for bringing a more holistic, humanistic, and positive approach to the study of human motivation.[16]

> Maslow deserves credit for bringing a more holistic, humanistic, and positive approach to the study of human motivation. "

- *Holistic perspective.* Maslow explained that the various needs should be studied together (holistically) because human behaviour is typically initiated by more than one need at the same time. Previously, motivation experts had splintered needs or drives into dozens of categories, each studied in isolation.[17]

- *Humanistic perspective.* Maslow introduced the then-novel idea that higher-order needs are influenced by personal and social influences, not just instincts.[18] In other words, he was among the first to recognize that human thoughts (including self-concept, social norms, past experience) play a role in motivation. Previous motivation experts had focused almost entirely on human instincts without considering that motivation could be shaped by human thought.

- *Positive perspective.* Maslow popularized the previously developed concept of *self-actualization*, suggesting that people are naturally motivated to reach their potential and that organizations and societies need to be structured to help people continue and develop this motivation.[19] This positive view of motivation contrasted with the dominant position that needs become activated by deficiencies such as hunger. Indeed, Maslow is considered a pioneer in *positive organizational behaviour.* Positive OB says that focusing on the positive rather than negative aspects of life will improve organizational success and individual well-being (see Chapter 3). In other words, this approach advocates building positive qualities and perspectives within individuals or institutions as opposed to focusing on trying to fix what might be wrong with them.[20]

WHAT'S WRONG WITH NEEDS HIERARCHY MODELS?

Maslow's theory ultimately failed to explain human motivation because people don't fit into a one-size-fits-all needs hierarchy. There is growing evidence that people have different hierarchies. Some place social status at the top of their personal hierarchy; others view personal development and growth above social relations or status. Employee needs are strongly influenced by self-concept, personal values, and personality.[21] If your most important values lean toward stimulation and self-direction, you probably pay more attention to self-actualization needs. If power and achievement are at the top of your value system, status needs will likely be at the top of your needs hierarchy. This connection between values and needs suggests that a needs hierarchy is unique to each person and can possibly change over time, just as values change over a lifetime.[22]

LEARNED NEEDS THEORY

Earlier in this chapter we stated that drives (primary needs) are innate whereas needs are shaped, amplified, or suppressed through self-concept, social norms, and past experience. Maslow noted this when he wrote that individual characteristics influence the strength of higher-order needs, such as the need to belong. Psychologist David McClelland further investigated the idea that need strength can be altered through social influences. In particular, he recognized that a person's needs can be strengthened through reinforcement, learning, and social conditions. McClelland examined three "learned" needs: achievement, power, and affiliation.[23]

need for achievement (nAch) A need in which people want to accomplish reasonably challenging goals, and desire unambiguous feedback and recognition for their success.

Need for Achievement   People with a strong **need for achievement (nAch)** want to accomplish reasonably challenging goals through their own effort. They prefer working alone rather than in teams, and they choose tasks with a moderate degree of risk (i.e., neither too easy nor impossible to complete). High-nAch people also desire unambiguous feedback and recognition for their success. Money is a weak motivator, except when it provides feedback and recognition.[24] In contrast, employees with a low nAch perform their work better when money is used as an incentive. Successful entrepreneurs tend to have a high nAch, possibly because they establish challenging goals for themselves and thrive on competition.[25]

need for affiliation (nAff) A need in which people seek approval from others, conform to their wishes and expectations, and avoid conflict and confrontation.

Need for Affiliation   **Need for affiliation (nAff)** refers to a desire to seek approval from others, conform to their wishes and expectations, and avoid conflict and confrontation. People with a strong nAff try to project a favourable image of themselves. They tend to actively support others and try to smooth out workplace conflicts. High nAff employees generally work well in coordinating roles to mediate conflicts and in sales positions where the main task is cultivating long-term relations. However, they tend to be less effective at allocating scarce resources and making other decisions that potentially generate conflict. People in decision-making positions must have a relatively low need for affiliation so that their choices and actions are not biased by a personal need for approval.[26]

need for power (nPow) A need in which people want to control their environment, including people and material resources, to benefit either themselves (personalized power) or others (socialized power).

Need for Power   People with a high **need for power (nPow)** want to exercise control over others and are concerned about maintaining their leadership position. They frequently rely on persuasive communication, make more suggestions in meetings, and tend to publicly evaluate situations more frequently. McClelland pointed out that there are two types of nPow. Individuals who enjoy their power for its own sake, use it to advance personal interests, and wear their power as a status symbol have a high need for *personalized power*. Others mainly have a high need for *socialized power* because they desire power as a means to help others.[27] McClelland argues that effective leaders should have a high need for socialized rather than personalized power. They must have a high degree of altruism and social responsibility and be concerned about the consequences of their actions on others.

Learning Needs   McClelland believed that needs can be learned (more accurately, strengthened or weakened), and the training programs he developed supported that proposition. In his achievement motivation program, trainees wrote achievement-oriented stories and practised achievement-oriented behaviours in business games. They also completed a detailed achievement plan for the next two years and formed a reference group with other trainees to maintain their new-found achievement motivation.[28] Participants attending these achievement motivation programs subsequently started more new businesses, had greater community involvement, invested more in expanding their businesses, and employed twice as many people compared with a matched sample of non-participants. These training programs increased achievement motivation by altering participant self-concept and reinforced experiences such that they amplified related emotions generated by innate drives. When writing an achievement plan, for example, participants were encouraged (and supported by other participants) to experience the anticipated thrill of succeeding.

FOUR-DRIVE THEORY

One of the central messages of this chapter is that emotions play a central role in employee motivation. This view is supported by a groundswell of research in neuroscience, but slow to gain recognition in organizational behaviour theories. Also, social scientists in several fields (psychology, anthropology, etc.) increasingly agree that human beings have several hardwired drives, including social interaction, learning, and getting ahead. One of the few theories to apply this emerging knowledge is **four-drive theory**.[29] Developed by Harvard Business School professors Paul Lawrence and Nitin Nohria, four-drive theory states that everyone has the drive to acquire, bond, learn, and defend:

> **four-drive theory** A motivation theory that is based on the innate drives to acquire, bond, learn, and defend, and that incorporates both emotions and rationality.

- *Drive to acquire.* This is the drive to seek, take, control, and retain objects and personal experiences. The drive to acquire extends beyond basic food and water; it includes enhancing one's self-concept through relative status and recognition in society.[30] Thus, it is the foundation of competition and the basis of our need for esteem. Four-drive theory states that the drive to acquire is insatiable because the purpose of human motivation is to achieve a higher position than others, not just to fulfill one's physiological needs.

- *Drive to bond.* This is the drive to form social relationships and develop mutual caring commitments with others. It explains why people form social identities by aligning their self-concept with various social groups (see Chapter 3). It may also explain why people who lack social contact are more prone to serious health problems.[31] The drive to bond motivates people to cooperate and, consequently, is a fundamental ingredient in the success of organizations and the development of societies.

- *Drive to learn.* This is the drive to satisfy our curiosity, to know and understand ourselves and the environment around us.[32] When observing something that is inconsistent with or beyond our current knowledge, we experience a tension that motivates us to close that information gap. In fact, studies have revealed that people who are removed from any novel information will crave even boring information; the drive to learn generated such strong emotions that the study participants eventually craved month-old stock reports![33] The drive to learn is related to the higher-order needs of growth and self-actualization described earlier.

- *Drive to defend.* This is the drive to protect ourselves physically and socially. Probably the first drive to develop, it creates a "fight-or-flight" response in the face of personal danger. The drive to defend goes beyond protecting our physical self. It includes defending our relationships, our acquisitions, and our belief systems.

These four drives are innate and universal, meaning that they are hardwired in our brains and are found in all human beings. They are also independent of each other. There is no hierarchy of drives, so one drive is neither dependent on nor inherently inferior or superior to another drive. Four-drive theory also states that these four drives are a complete set—there are no fundamental drives excluded from the model. Another key feature is that three of the four drives are proactive—we regularly try to fulfill them. Only the drive to defend is reactive—it is triggered by threat. Thus, any notion of fulfilling drives is temporary, at best.

How Drives Influence Employee Motivation
Four-drive theory is derived from recent neuroscience research regarding the emotional marker process and how emotions are channelled into decisions and behaviour. As we described in previous chapters,

our perceptions of the world around us are quickly and nonconsciously tagged with emotional markers.[34] According to four-drive theory, the four drives determine which emotions are tagged to incoming stimuli. If you arrive at work one day to see a stranger sitting in your office chair, you might quickly experience worry, curiosity, or both. These emotions are automatically created by one or more of the four drives. In this example, the emotions produced are likely strong enough to demand your attention and motivate you to act on this observation.

Most of the time, we aren't aware of our emotional experiences because they are subtle and fleeting. However, emotions do become conscious experiences when they are sufficiently strong or when we experience conflicting emotions. Under these circumstances, our mental skill set relies on social norms, past experience, and personal values to direct the motivational force of our emotions to actions that deal with that situation (see Exhibit 5.3). In other words, our mental skill set chooses courses of action that are acceptable to society, consistent with our own moral compass, and seem to correct any problems or opportunities.[35] This is the process described at the beginning of this chapter, namely, that drives produce emotions; our self-concept, social norms, and past experience translate these emotions into goal-directed needs, and these individual characteristics also translate needs into decisions and behaviour.

Evaluating Four-Drive Theory   Although four-drive theory was introduced very recently, it is based on a deep foundation of research that dates back more than three decades. The drives have been identified from psychological and anthropological studies. Shalom Schwartz recently reported that four-drive theory maps well onto the 10 dimensions in his circumplex model of personal values (see Chapter 2).[36] The translation of drives into goal-directed behaviour originates from considerable research on emotions and neural processes. The theory explains why needs vary from one person to the next, but avoids the assumption that everyone has the same needs hierarchy. Notice, too, that four-drive theory satisfied two of Maslow's criteria for motivation theory: it is holistic (it relates to all drives, not just one or two) and humanistic (it acknowledges the role of human thought and social influences, not just instinct). Four-drive theory also provides a much clearer understanding of the role of emotional intelligence in employee motivation and behaviour. Employees with high emotional intelligence are more sensitive to competing demands from the four drives, are better able to avoid impulsive behaviour from those drives, and can judge the best way to act to fulfill those drive demands in a social context.

Exhibit 5.3   **FOUR-DRIVE THEORY OF MOTIVATION**

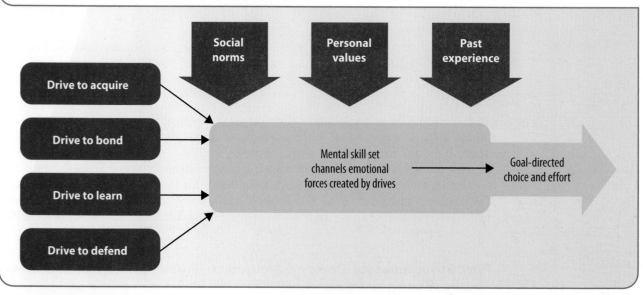

Source: Based on information in P. R. Lawrence and N. Nohria, *Driven: How Human Nature Shapes Our Choices* (San Francisco: Jossey-Bass, 2002).

Even with its well-researched foundations, four-drive theory is far from complete. Most experts would argue that one or two other drives exist that should be included. Furthermore, social norms, personal values, and past experience probably don't represent the full set of individual characteristics that translate emotions into goal-directed effort. For example, personality and self-concept likely also play a significant role in translating drives into needs and needs into decisions and behaviour.

Practical Implications of Four-Drive Theory   The main recommendation from four-drive theory is to ensure that individual jobs and workplaces provide a balanced opportunity to fulfill the drives to acquire, bond, learn, and defend.[37] There are really two recommendations here. The first is that the best workplaces for employee motivation and well-being offer conditions that help employees fulfill all four drives. Employees continually seek fulfillment of their innate drives, so successful companies provide sufficient rewards, information about organizational events, social interaction, and so forth, for all employees.

The second recommendation is that fulfillment of the four drives must be kept in balance; that is, organizations should avoid too much or too little opportunity to fulfill each drive. The reason for this advice is that the four drives counterbalance each other. The drive to bond counterbalances the drive to acquire; the drive to defend counterbalances the drive to learn. An organization that energizes the drive to acquire without the drive to bond may eventually suffer from organizational politics and dysfunctional conflict. Change and novelty in the workplace will aid the drive to learn, but too much of it will trigger the drive to defend to such an extent that employees become territorial and resistant to change. Thus, the workplace should offer enough opportunity to keep all four drives in balance.

These recommendations help explain why Vancouver-based Great Little Box Company Ltd., described at the beginning of this chapter, has a motivated workforce and is rated as one of the best places to work in Canada. The company motivates employees to achieve challenging goals (drive to acquire), yet balances this with social events and egalitarian rewards. The company encourages innovation, yet also tries to maintain some degree of stability in everyone's work lives and seeks out ways to improve employee well-being.

Keeping Drives in Balance Sparks Innovation at Radialpoint

At Montreal-based Radialpoint, innovation is key to keeping the company on the cutting edge of technology and meeting the needs of the world's biggest Internet providers including Bell Canada, Verizon, AT&T, and Virgin Media. Co-founder and executive chairman, Hamnett Hill offers a simple solution for Radialpoint's success—"People like working here." Hamnett adds, "We really rely on smart, dedicated folks and we need to help them understand what they can do to achieve that." The culture and work environment at Radialpoint provides a balance of opportunities for employees to fulfill their hardwired drives. Employees' self-concept is enhanced by knowing they work for an employer who seeks out the "best and brightest" and has been recognized as one of Canada's Best Managed Companies. In addition, top performers are rewarded through the company's partnership equity program and performance bonuses. Professional development programs are subsidized—"People definitely want to feel like they're moving forward, learning new skills," says Hill. "It's an opportunity to grow." Hill describes Radialpoint employees' desire to jump into challenges and solve big problems every day, "That has helped us in these difficult times." Radialpoint also encourages employees to develop social relationships and commitments to others. For example, off-site team-building events have brought employees together to build bikes for charity and finance an orphanage in Africa.[38] *Pierre Obendrauf, Montreal Gazette*

EXPECTANCY THEORY OF MOTIVATION

expectancy theory A motivation theory based on the idea that work effort is directed toward behaviours that people believe will lead to desired outcomes.

The theories described so far mainly explain the internal origins of employee motivation. But how do these drives and needs translate into specific effort and behaviour? Four-drive theory recognizes that social norms, personal values, and past experience direct our effort, but it doesn't offer any more detail. **Expectancy theory**, on the other hand, offers an elegant model based on rational logic to predict the chosen direction, level, and persistence of motivation. Essentially, the theory states that work effort is directed toward behaviours that people believe will lead to desired outcomes. In other words, we are motivated to achieve the goals with the highest expected payoff.[39] As illustrated in Exhibit 5.4, an individual's effort level depends on three factors: effort-to-performance (E-to-P) expectancy, performance-to-outcome (P-to-O) expectancy, and outcome valences. Employee motivation is influenced by all three components of the expectancy theory model. If any component weakens, motivation weakens.

- *E-to-P expectancy.* This is the individual's perceived probability that his or her effort will result in a particular level of performance. In some situations, employees may believe that they can unquestionably accomplish the task (a probability of 1.0). In other situations, they expect that even their highest level of effort will not result in the desired performance level (a probability of 0.0). In most cases, the E-to-P expectancy falls somewhere between these two extremes.

- *P-to-O expectancy.* This is the perceived probability that a specific behaviour or performance level will lead to a particular outcome. In extreme cases, employees may believe that accomplishing a particular task (performance) will definitely result in a particular outcome (a probability of 1.0), or they may believe that successful performance will have no effect on this outcome (a probability of 0.0). More often, the P-to-O expectancy falls somewhere between these two extremes.

- *Outcome valences.* A *valence* is the anticipated satisfaction or dissatisfaction that an individual feels toward an outcome. It ranges from negative to positive. (The actual range doesn't matter; it may be from –1 to +1 or from –100 to +100.) An outcome valence represents a person's anticipated satisfaction with the outcome.[40] Outcomes have a positive valence when they are consistent with our values and satisfy our needs; they have a negative valence when they oppose our values and inhibit need fulfillment.

Exhibit 5.4   **EXPECTANCY THEORY OF MOTIVATION**

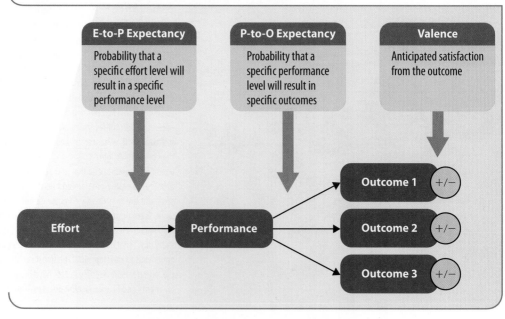

EXPECTANCY THEORY IN PRACTICE

One of the appealing characteristics of expectancy theory is that it provides clear guidelines for increasing employee motivation.[41] Several practical applications of expectancy theory are listed in Exhibit 5.5 and described below.

Increasing E-to-P Expectancies   E-to-P expectancies are influenced by the individual's belief that he or she can successfully complete the task. Some companies increase this can-do attitude by assuring employees that they have the necessary competencies, clear role perceptions, and necessary resources to reach the desired levels of performance. An important part of this process involves matching employees' competencies to job requirements and clearly communicating the tasks required for the job. Similarly, E-to-P expectancies are learned, so behavioural modelling and reinforcement (which we discuss next) typically strengthen the individual's belief that he or she is able to perform the task.

Increasing P-to-O Expectancies   The most obvious ways to improve P-to-O expectancies are to measure employee performance accurately and distribute more valued rewards to those with higher job performance. P-to-O expectancies are perceptions, so employees also need to believe that higher performance will result in higher rewards. Furthermore, they need to know how that connection occurs, so leaders should use examples, anecdotes, and public ceremonies to illustrate when behaviour has been rewarded.

Increasing Outcome Valences   One size does not fit all in the business of motivating and rewarding people. Organizational leaders need to find ways to individualize rewards or, where standard rewards are necessary, to identify rewards that do not have a negative valence for some staff. Consider the following story: Top-performing employees in one Canadian organization were rewarded with a one-week Caribbean cruise with the company's executive team. Many were likely delighted, but at least one top-performer was aghast at the thought of going on a cruise with senior management. "I don't like schmoozing, I don't like feeling trapped. Why couldn't they just give me the money?" she complained. The employee went on the cruise, but spent most of her time working in her stateroom.[42]

Exhibit 5.5   PRACTICAL APPLICATIONS OF EXPECTANCY THEORY

Expectancy Theory Component	Objective	Applications
E→P expectancies	To increase the belief that employees are capable of performing the job successfully	• Select people with the required skills and knowledge. • Provide required training and clarify job requirements. • Provide sufficient time and resources. • Assign simpler or fewer tasks until employees can master them. • Provide examples of similar employees who have successfully performed the task. • Provide coaching to employees who lack self-confidence.
P→O expectancies	To increase the belief that good performance will result in certain (valued) outcomes	• Measure job performance accurately. • Clearly explain the outcomes that will result from successful performance. • Describe how the employee's rewards were based on past performance. • Provide examples of other employees whose good performance has resulted in higher rewards.
Outcome valences	To increase the expected value of outcomes resulting from desired performance	• Distribute rewards that employees value. • Individualize rewards. • Minimize the presence of countervalent outcomes.

One more recommendation for increasing outcome valences: Watch out for countervalent outcomes that might cancel any positive outcomes. For example, several employees in one work unit were individually motivated to perform well because this achievement gave them a feeling of accomplishment and rewarded them with higher pay. But their performance was considerably lower when they worked together with others because peer pressure discouraged performance above a fairly low standard. In this situation, the positively valent outcomes (feeling of accomplishment, higher pay) were offset by the negatively valent outcome of peer pressure.

Overall, expectancy theory is a useful model that explains how people rationally figure out the best direction, intensity, and persistence of effort. It has been tested in a variety of situations and predicts employee motivation in different cultures.[43] However, critics have a number of concerns with how the theory has been tested. Another concern is that expectancy theory ignores the central role of emotions on employee effort and behaviour. The valence element of expectancy theory captures some of this emotional process, but only peripherally.[44] Finally, expectancy theory outlines how expectancies (probability of outcomes) affect motivation, but it doesn't explain how employees develop these expectancies. Two theories that provide this explanation are organizational behaviour modification and social cognitive theory, which we describe next.

ORGANIZATIONAL BEHAVIOUR MODIFICATION AND SOCIAL COGNITIVE THEORY

L05

Expectancy theory explains how motivation is impacted by employee beliefs and knowledge about outcome probabilities as well as the probability that a certain level of performance can be achieved. But how do employees learn these expectancies? The answer to this question directs us to two prominent perspectives of learning: organizational behaviour modification (OB Mod) and social cognitive theory. Although these theories explain how people learn what to expect from their actions, they are also theories of motivation because, as expectancy theory explained, the learned expectancies affect the person's direction, intensity, and persistence of effort.

ORGANIZATIONAL BEHAVIOUR MODIFICATION

For most of the first half of the 1900s, the dominant paradigm about managing individual behaviour was *behaviourism,* which argues that a good theory should rely exclusively on behaviour and the environment and ignore nonobservable cognitions and emotions.[45] Although behaviourists don't deny the existence of human thoughts and attitudes, they view them as unobservable and, therefore, irrelevant to scientific study. A variation of this paradigm, called **organizational behaviour modification** or OB Mod, eventually entered organizational studies of motivation and learning.[46]

organizational behaviour modification A theory that explains employee behaviour in terms of the antecedent conditions and consequences of that behaviour.

A-B-Cs of OB Mod   The A-B-C model shown in Exhibit 5.6 represents OB Mod's core elements. Essentially, OB Mod attempts to change behaviour (B) by managing its antecedents (A) and consequences (C).[47] *Consequences* are events following a particular behaviour that influence its future occurrence, such as the compliments or teasing received from co-workers when the employee wears safety goggles. Consequences also include no outcome at all, such as when no one says anything about how well you have been serving customers. *Antecedents* are events preceding the behaviour, informing employees that a particular action will produce specific consequences. An antecedent may be a sound from your computer signalling that an email has arrived or a request from your supervisor asking you to complete a specific task by tomorrow. Notice that antecedents do not cause behaviour. The computer sound doesn't cause us to open our email. Rather, the sound (antecedent) is a cue telling us that if we check our email (behaviour), we are certain to find a new message (consequence).

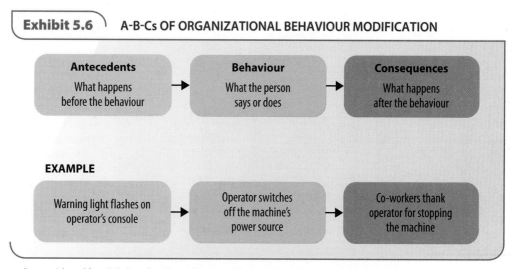

Exhibit 5.6   A-B-Cs OF ORGANIZATIONAL BEHAVIOUR MODIFICATION

Sources: Adapted from T. K. Connellan, *How to Improve Human Performance* (New York: Harper & Row, 1978), p. 50; F. Luthans and R. Kreitner, *Organizational Behaviour Modification and Beyond* (Glenview, IL: Scott, Foresman, 1985), pp. 85–88.

OB Mod identifies four types of consequences.[48] *Positive reinforcement* occurs when the *introduction* of a consequence *increases or maintains* the frequency or future probability of a specific behaviour. This occurs, for example, when receiving praise after completing a project. *Punishment* occurs when a consequence decreases the frequency or future probability of a behaviour. Most of us would consider being demoted or being ostracized by our co-workers as forms of punishment. *Negative reinforcement* occurs when the removal or avoidance of a consequence increases or maintains the frequency or future probability of a specific behaviour. Supervisors apply negative reinforcement when they stop criticizing employees whose substandard performance has improved. (Note that negative reinforcement is not punishment.) Finally, *extinction* occurs when the target behaviour decreases because no consequence follows it. For instance, research suggests that performance tends to decline when managers stop congratulating employees for their good work.[49]

Which contingency of reinforcement works best? In most situations, positive reinforcement should follow desired behaviours and extinction (do nothing) should follow undesirable behaviours. This approach is preferred because punishment and negative reinforcement generate negative emotions and attitudes toward the punisher (e.g., supervisor) and organization. However, some form of punishment (dismissal, suspension, demotion, etc.) may be necessary for extreme behaviours, such as deliberately hurting a co-worker or stealing inventory. Indeed, research suggests that, under certain conditions, punishment maintains a sense of fairness.[50]

Along with the types of reinforcement, the frequency and timing of the reinforcers also influence employee behaviours.[51] The most effective reinforcement schedule for learning new tasks is *continuous reinforcement*—providing positive reinforcement after every occurrence of the desired behaviour. The best schedule for reinforcing learned behaviour is a *variable ratio schedule* in which employee behaviour is reinforced after a variable number of times. Salespeople experience variable ratio reinforcement because they make a successful sale (the reinforcer) after a varying number of client calls. The variable ratio schedule makes behaviour highly resistant to extinction because the reinforcer is never expected at a particular time or after a fixed number of accomplishments.

Evaluating OB Mod   Everyone uses organizational behaviour modification principles in one form or another to motivate others. We thank people for a job well done, are silent when displeased, and sometimes try to punish those who go against our plans. OB Mod also occurs in various formal programs to reduce absenteeism, improve task performance, encourage safe work behaviours, and have a healthier lifestyle.[52] At Montana's

Reinforcing the Long (and Healthy) Walk

Walking to work is starting to look much more appealing to city employees in Stoke-on-Trent, Staffordshire. The British municipality issued pedometers to its staff (see photo) and encouraged them to develop a regimen of daily walking. The goal is to get sedentary employees walking at least 10,000 steps each day for five days a week. The pedometers provide instant feedback, thereby reinforcing longer walks. The city also introduced support groups to further encourage people to walk regularly.[53] *Courtesy of Stoke-on-Trent City Council*

Cookhouse (owned by Toronto-based Cara Operations Ltd.), for example, employees reinforce co-worker behaviours such as safety, customer service, and collegiality through online feedback. "We want to create a culture of celebrating good behaviour and ignoring behaviour we don't want," explains Montana's president Andy O'Brien.

Organizational behaviour modification has a number of limitations. One limitation is "reward inflation," in which the reinforcer is eventually considered an entitlement. For this reason, most OB Mod programs must run infrequently and for a short duration. Another concern is that the variable ratio schedule of reinforcement tends to create a lottery-style reward system, which might be viewed as too erratic for formal rewards and is unpopular to people who dislike gambling. Probably the most significant problem is OB Mod's radical view that behaviour is learned only through personal interaction with the environment.[54] This view is no longer accepted; instead, experts recognize that people also learn and are motivated by observing others and inferring possible consequences of their actions. This learning process is explained by social cognitive theory.

SOCIAL COGNITIVE THEORY

social cognitive theory A theory that explains how learning and motivation occur by observing and modelling others as well as by anticipating the consequences of our behaviour.

Social cognitive theory states that much learning and motivation occurs by observing and modelling others as well as by anticipating the consequences of our behaviour.[55] Although the learning and motivation value of observation and modelling (imitation) have been noted for many years, Canadian-born social scientist Albert Bandura reframed these ideas within a cognitive (internal thoughts) perspective as an alternative to the behaviourist approach. There are several pieces to social cognitive theory, but the three most relevant to employee motivation are learning behaviour consequences, behavioural modelling, and self-regulation.

Learning Behavioural Outcomes   People learn the consequences of behaviour by observing or hearing about what happened to other people, not just by directly experiencing the consequences.[56] Hearing that a co-worker was fired for being rude to a client increases your perception that rude behaviour will result in being fired. In other words, learning behaviour consequences changes a person's perceived P-to-O probability used in expectancy theory. Furthermore, people logically anticipate consequences in related situations. For instance, the story about the fired employee might also strengthen your P-to-O expectancy about getting fired if you are rude toward co-workers and suppliers.

Behaviour Modelling   People learn not only by observing others but also by imitating and practising those behaviours.[57] Direct sensory experience helps to acquire tacit knowledge and skills, such as the subtle person-machine interaction while driving a vehicle. Behavioural modelling also increases self-efficacy because people gain more self-confidence after observing others and performing the task successfully themselves. Self-efficacy particularly improves when observers identify with the role model, such as someone who is similar in age, experience, gender, and related features.

Self-Regulation   An important feature of social cognitive theory is that human beings set goals and engage in other forms of intentional, purposive action. They establish their own short and long-term objectives, choose their own standards of achievement, work out a plan of action, consider back-up alternatives, and have the forethought to anticipate the consequences of their goal-directed behaviour. Furthermore, people self-regulate by engaging in **self-reinforcement**; that is, they reward and punish themselves for exceeding or falling short of their self-set standards of excellence.[58] For example, you might have a goal of completing the rest of this chapter, after which you reward yourself by having a snack. Raiding the refrigerator is a form of self-induced positive reinforcement for completing this reading assignment.

Self-regulation has become an important topic in the social sciences. It is also the cornerstone of motivation through goal setting and feedback, which we discuss next.

> **self-reinforcement**
> Reinforcement that occurs when an employee has control over a reinforcer but doesn't 'take' it until completing a self-set goal.

GOAL SETTING AND FEEDBACK

L06

Walk into almost any customer contact centre (i.e., call centre) in Canada—whether it's Intuit Canada's centre in Edmonton or Rogers' customer care centre in Moncton—and you will notice that work activities are dominated by goal setting and plenty of feedback.[59] Contact-centre performance is judged on several *key performance indicators (KPIs),* such as average time to answer the call, average handle time, and abandon rates (customers who hang up before the call is handled by a customer service representative). Some contact centres have large electronic boards showing how many customers are waiting, the average time they have been waiting, and the average time before someone talks to them. A few even have "emotion detection" software, which translates words and voice intonation into a measure of the customer's level of happiness or anger during the telephone conversation.[60]

> **goal setting** The process of motivating employees and clarifying their role perceptions by establishing performance objectives.

Goal setting is the process of motivating employees and clarifying their role perceptions by establishing performance objectives. It potentially improves employee performance in two ways: (1) by amplifying the intensity and persistence of effort and (2) by giving employees clearer role perceptions so that their effort is channelled toward behaviours that will improve work performance. Goal setting is more complex than simply telling someone to "do your best." It requires several specific characteristics. Some consultants refer to these as "SMART goals," but the acronym doesn't quite capture all the key ingredients identified by goal-setting research. The six key characteristics are specific goals, relevant goals, challenging goals, goal commitment, participation in goal formation (sometimes), and goal feedback.[61]

- *Specific goals.* Employees put more effort into a task when they work toward specific goals with specific time deadlines rather than "do your best" targets. Specific goals have measurable levels of change over a specific and relatively short time frame, such as "reduce patient wait time by 25 percent over the next three months." Specific goals communicate more precise performance expectations, so employees can direct their effort more efficiently and reliably.

- *Relevant goals.* Goals must also be relevant to the individual's job and be within his or her control. For example, a goal to reduce waste materials would have little value if employees don't have much control over waste in the production process.

- *Challenging goals.* Challenging goals (rather than easy ones) tend to raise the employee's intensity and persistence of work effort and to think through information more actively. They also fulfill a person's achievement or growth needs when the goal is achieved.

- *Goal commitment.* Ideally goals should be challenging without being so difficult that employees lose their motivation to achieve them.[62] This is the same as the E-to-P expectancy that you learned about in the section on expectancy theory. The lower the E-to-P expectancy that the goal can been accomplished, the less committed (motivated) the employee is to the goal.

- *Goal participation* (sometimes). Goal setting is usually (but not always) more effective when employees are involved in setting the goals.[63] Participation potentially creates a higher level of goal commitment than is found when goals are set alone by the supervisor. It may also improve goal quality, because employees have valuable information and knowledge that may not be known to those who initially formed the goal.

- *Goal feedback.* Feedback is another necessary condition for effective goal setting.[64] Feedback is any information that lets us know whether we have achieved the goal or are properly directing our effort toward it. Feedback redirects our effort, but it potentially also fulfills our growth needs.

BALANCED SCORECARD

balanced scorecard (BSC) A goal-setting and reward system that translates the organization's vision and mission into specific, measurable performance goals related to financial, customer, internal, and learning/growth (i.e., human capital) processes.

Balanced scorecard (BSC) represents an organization-level form of goal setting and feedback that attempts to represent objectives across various stakeholders and processes. It translates the organization's vision and mission into specific, measurable performance goals related to financial, customer, internal, and learning/growth (i.e., human capital) processes. These goals cascade down to departments and to employees within those departments. For example, an airline might include on-time performance as one of its customer process goals and number of hours of safety training per employee as a learning and growth process goal. These specific goals are linked to various work units and employees (such as department managers). BSC goals are often weighted and scored to create a composite measure of results across the organization.

Balanced scorecards have been introduced in a variety of organizations across Canada, such as the Children's Aid Society of Brant, Royal Bank of Canada, Royal Canadian Mounted Police, the City of Edmonton, and several public health agencies and centres across Canada.[65] In spite of their popularity, BSCs present a number of challenges. As with most goal setting and feedback systems, the quality of the process is only as good as the goals established and the feedback available. Some companies choose goals that are easily measured rather than valuable. Others go to great lengths to measure internal processes, but these measures create a bureaucracy that raises overhead costs and employee resentment for diverting resources from the company's main functions. One recent report from the Royal Canadian Mounted Police (RCMP), which has a highly regarded BSC, warned that people get caught up on the measures whereas they need discipline to focus on achieving BSC goals. The RCMP report also noted that BSC systems suffer when they become overburdened with too many goals and when those goals don't resonate with employees.

CHARACTERISTICS OF EFFECTIVE FEEDBACK

Feedback is just as important as goal setting in employee motivation and performance. Along with clarifying role perceptions and improving employee skills and knowledge, feedback motivates when it is constructive and when employees have strong self-efficacy.[66] Effective feedback has many of the same characteristics as effective goal setting. It should be *specific* and *relevant;* that is, the information should refer to specific metrics (e.g., sales increased by 5 percent last month) and to the individual's behaviour or outcomes within his or her control. Feedback should also be *timely;* the information should be available soon after the behaviour or results occur so that employees see a clear association between their actions and the consequences. Effective feedback is also *credible.* Employees are more likely to accept feedback from trustworthy and credible sources.

The final characteristic of effective feedback is that it should be *sufficiently frequent.* How frequent is "sufficiently"? The answer depends on at least two things. One consideration is the employee's knowledge and experience with the task. Feedback is a form of reinforcement, so employees working on new tasks should receive more frequent feedback because they require more behaviour guidance and reinforcement. Employees who perform repetitive or familiar tasks can receive less frequent feedback. The second factor is how long it takes to complete the task. Feedback is necessarily less frequent in jobs with a long cycle time (e.g., executives and scientists) than in jobs with a short cycle time (e.g., grocery store cashiers).

Feedback through Strengths-Based Coaching   Forty years ago, Peter Drucker recognized that leaders are more effective when they focus on strengths rather than weaknesses. "The effective executive builds on strengths—their own strengths, the strengths of superiors, colleagues, subordinates; and on the strength of the situation," wrote the late management guru.[67] Standard Chartered Bank, which was described earlier in this chapter, has adopted this positive OB approach to improve employee engagement. It gives employees opportunities to develop their strengths rather than requiring them to focus on areas where they have limited interest or skill.

This is the essence of **strengths-based coaching** (also known as *appreciative coaching*)—maximizing employee potential by focusing on their strengths rather than weaknesses.[68] In strengths-based coaching, the employee describes areas of work where they excel or demonstrate potential. The coach guides this discussion by asking exploratory questions and by helping the employee to discover ways of leveraging these strengths. For example, the pair would explore situational barriers to practising the coachee's strength as well as aspects of this strength that require further development.

Strengths-based coaching can potentially motivate employees because they inherently seek feedback about their strengths, not their flaws. Thus, strengths-based feedback is consistent with the process of self-enhancement (see Chapter 3). Strengths-based

> **strengths-based coaching** A positive organizational behaviour approach to coaching and feedback that focuses on building and leveraging the employee's strengths rather than trying to correct his or her weaknesses.

Sony Europe Builds on Strengths

To compete more effectively, Sony Europe chose to leverage the power of employee strengths rather than battle against weaknesses. Each employee was asked to identify activities in which he/she excels, enjoys the work, and feels at ease. This information helped Sony Europe to redesign jobs around these strengths. For example, when the performance of a Sony Europe employee dropped after he moved to another sales position, the company compared the individual's strengths against the job requirements. It discovered that the employee enjoyed and was best at face-to-face communication, whereas his new job required very little social interaction. Rather than pushing the employee to deliver higher performance in the existing job, Sony created a new role for the employee that leveraged his strengths around social interaction. Within a year, the employee's team had delivered record sales and increased profits at a lower cost. Strengths-based coaching "ensures that everybody in Sony is focusing on what they do best," says Ray White, Sony Europe's vice-president of human resources.[69] *Jens Kalaene/DPA/Landov*

coaching also makes sense because personality becomes quite stable by the time of a person's early career and this limits the flexibility of the person's interests, preferences, and competencies.[70] In spite of these research observations, most companies focus goal setting and feedback on tasks that employees are performing poorly. After the initial polite compliments, many coaching or performance feedback sessions analyze the employee's weaknesses, including determining what went wrong and what the employee needs to do to improve. These inquisitions sometimes produce so much negative feedback that employees become defensive; they can also undermine self-efficacy, thereby making the employee's performance worse rather than better. By focusing on weaknesses, companies fail to realize the full potential of the employee's strengths.

SOURCES OF FEEDBACK

Feedback can originate from nonsocial or social sources. Nonsocial sources provide feedback without someone communicating that information. Employees at contact centres view electronic displays showing how many callers are waiting and the average time they have been waiting. Nova Chemicals operators in Alberta receive feedback from a computer screen that monitors in real time the plant's operational capacity, depicted as a gently flowing green line, and actual production output, shown as a red squiggly line. Soon after Nova installed the feedback system, employees engaged in friendly bouts of rivalry to determine who could keep the actual production output as close as possible to the plant's maximum capacity.[71]

Corporate intranets allow many executives to receive feedback instantaneously on their computer, usually in the form of graphic output on an executive dashboard. Almost half of Microsoft's employees use a dashboard to monitor project deadlines, sales, and other metrics. Microsoft CEO Steve Ballmer regularly reviews dashboard results in one-on-one meetings with his division leaders. "Every time I go to see Ballmer, it's an expectation that I bring my dashboard with me," says the head of the Microsoft Office division.[72]

multisource (360-degree) feedback Information about an employee's performance collected from a full circle of people, including subordinates, peers, supervisors, and customers.

Multisource (360-Degree) Feedback   **Multisource (360-degree) feedback** is a social form of feedback that has been widely used in organizations. As the name implies, multisource feedback is information about an employee's performance collected from a full circle of people, including subordinates, peers, supervisors, and customers. Multisource feedback tends to provide more complete and accurate information than feedback from a supervisor alone. It is particularly useful when the supervisor is unable to observe the employee's behaviour or performance throughout the year. Lower-level employees also feel a greater sense of fairness and open communication when they are able to provide upward feedback about their boss's performance.[73]

However, multisource feedback also creates challenges. Having several people review so many other people can be expensive and time-consuming. With multiple opinions, the 360-degree process can also produce ambiguous and conflicting feedback, so employees may require guidance to interpret the results. A third concern is that peers may provide inflated rather than accurate feedback to avoid conflicts during the forthcoming year. A final concern is that employees experience a stronger emotional reaction when they receive critical feedback from many people rather than from just one person (such as the boss). "Initially you do take it personally," admits a manager at software maker Autodesk. "[360-degree feedback] is meant to be constructive, but you have to internally battle that."[74]

Choosing Feedback Sources   With so many sources of feedback—multisource feedback, executive dashboards, customer surveys, equipment gauges, nonverbal communication from your boss—which one works best under which conditions? The preferred feedback source depends on the purpose of the information. To learn about their progress toward goal accomplishment, employees usually prefer nonsocial feedback sources, such as computer printouts or feedback directly from the job. This is because information from nonsocial sources is considered more objective than information from social sources. Performance feedback from nonsocial sources is also less damaging to self-esteem. In contrast, social sources tend to delay negative information, leave some of it out, and distort the bad news in a positive way.[75] When employees want to improve their self-image, they seek out positive feedback from social sources. It feels better to have co-workers say that you are performing the job well than to discover this from a computer screen.

EVALUATING GOAL SETTING AND FEEDBACK

Goal setting represents one of the "tried-and-true" theories in organizational behaviour, so much so that it is rated by experts as one of the top OB theories in terms of validity and usefulness.[76] In partnership with goal setting, feedback also has an excellent reputation for improving employee motivation and performance. At the same time, putting goal setting into practice can create problems.[77] One concern is that goal setting tends to focus employees on a narrow subset of measurable performance indicators while ignoring aspects of job performance that are difficult to measure. The saying, "What gets measured, gets done" applies here. A second problem is that when goal achievement is tied to financial rewards, many employees are motivated to set easy goals (while making the boss think they are difficult) so that they have a higher probability of the bonus or pay increase. As a former CEO at Ford once quipped: "At Ford, we hire very smart people. They quickly learn how to make relatively easy goals look difficult!"[78] A third problem is that setting performance goals is effective in established jobs but seems to interfere with the learning process in new, complex jobs. Thus, we need to be careful not to apply goal setting where an intense learning process is occurring.

> " Goal setting is rated by experts as one of the top OB theories in terms of validity and usefulness. "

ORGANIZATIONAL JUSTICE

L07

distributive justice
Perceived fairness in the individual's ratio of outcomes to contributions compared with a comparison to other's ratio of outcomes to contributions.

procedural justice
Perceived fairness of the procedures used to decide the distribution of resources.

When Robert Meggy first introduced a profit sharing plan at Great Little Box Company, he felt that the size of a profit sharing bonus should correspond to the person's position and seniority in the organization. "It used to be a program based on seniority and a number of other variables but there were a number of complaints about that," Meggy recalls. "Now that it's equal across the board, we don't have that problem." In other words, employees felt that the original bonus distribution system lacked fairness, a condition that Meggy considers vital to a successful company. "I certainly believe in fair pay," says Meggy. "You don't have to be the best paying but you do have to be fair."[79]

Most organizational leaders know that treating employees fairly is both morally correct and good for employee motivation, loyalty, and well-being. Yet feelings of injustice and inequity are regular occurrences in the workplace. To minimize these incidents, we need to first understand that there are two forms of organizational justice: distributive justice and procedural justice.[80] **Distributive justice** refers to perceived fairness in the outcomes received compared to our contributions and the outcomes and contributions of others. **Procedural justice**, on the other hand, refers to perceived fairness of the procedures used to decide the distribution of resources.

EQUITY THEORY

At its most basic level, the employment relationship is about exchanging an employee's time and services for various things in return, such as pay, opportunities to develop skills and knowledge, fulfilling work, and so forth. What is considered "fair" in this exchange relationship varies with each person and situation. We apply an *equality principle* when we believe that everyone in the group should receive the same outcomes, such as when everyone gets subsidized meals in the company cafeteria. The *need principle* is applied when we believe that those with the greatest need should receive more outcomes than others with less need. The *equity principle* infers that people should be paid in proportion to their contribution. The equity principle is the most common distributive justice rule in organizational settings, so let's look at it in more detail.

> **equity theory** A theory explaining how people develop perceptions of fairness in the distribution and exchange of resources.

Feelings of equity are explained by **equity theory**, which says that employees develop perceptions of fairness by comparing their own outcome/input ratio to the outcome/input ratio of some other person.[81] As Exhibit 5.7 illustrates, the *outcome/input ratio* is the value of the outcomes you receive divided by the value of the inputs you provide in the exchange relationship. Inputs include such things as skill, effort, reputation, performance, experience, and hours worked. Outcomes are what employees receive from the organization, such as pay, promotions, recognition, interesting jobs, and opportunities to improve one's skills and knowledge.

Equity theory states that we compare our outcome/input ratio with that of a *comparison other*.[82] The comparison other might be another person or group of people in other jobs (e.g., comparing your pay with the CEO's pay) or another organization. Some research suggests that employees frequently collect information on several referents to form a "generalized" comparison other.[83] For the most part, however, the comparison other varies from one person to the next and is not easily identifiable.

The comparison of our own outcome/input ratio with the ratio of someone else results in perceptions of equity, underreward inequity, or overreward inequity. In the equity condition, people believe that their outcome/input ratio is similar to the ratio of the comparison other. In the underreward inequity situation, people believe their outcome/input ratio is lower than the comparison other's ratio. In the overreward inequity condition, people believe their ratio of outcomes/inputs is higher than the comparison other's ratio.

Inequity and Employee Motivation   How do perceptions of equity or inequity affect employee motivation? The answer is illustrated in Exhibit 5.8. When people believe they

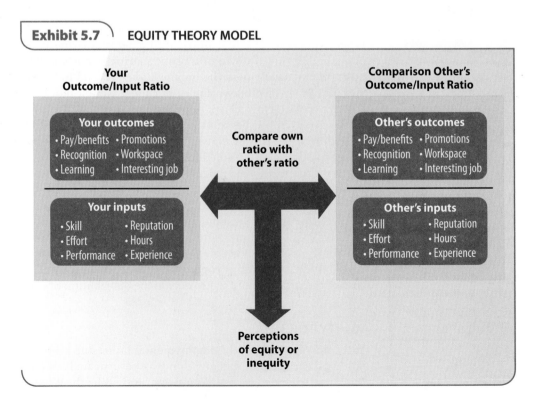

Exhibit 5.7   **EQUITY THEORY MODEL**

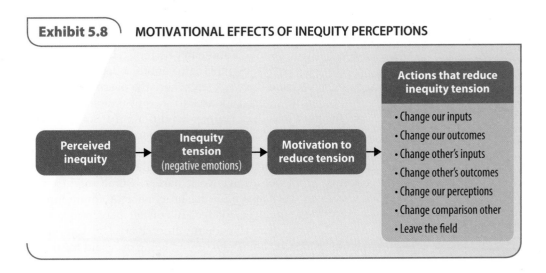

Exhibit 5.8   MOTIVATIONAL EFFECTS OF INEQUITY PERCEPTIONS

are underrewarded or overrewarded, they experience negative emotions (called inequity tension). As we have pointed out throughout this chapter, emotions are the engines of motivation. In the case of inequity, people are motivated to reduce the emotional tension. Imagine the following: You discover that a co-worker earns slightly more than you do, even though he or she began the job at the same time you did, has the same background, and doesn't seem to perform any better. Most people have a strong emotional response to this information, and this emotion nags them until they take some sort of action to correct the perceived inequity.

There are many other ways that people might try to reduce the inequity tension.[84] Let's consider each of these in the context of underreward inequity. One action would be to reduce our inputs so the outcome/input ratio is similar to the higher-paid co-worker. Some employees do this by working more slowly, offering fewer suggestions, and engaging in less organizational citizenship behaviour. A second action might be to increase our outcomes. Some people who think they are underpaid ask for a pay raise. Others make unauthorized use of company resources. A third behavioural response is to increase the comparison other's inputs. You might subtly ask the better-paid co-worker to do a larger share of the work, for instance. A fourth action would be to reduce the comparison other's outcomes. This might occur by ensuring that the co-worker gets less desirable jobs or working conditions. Another action, although unlikely, would be to ask the company to reduce the co-worker's pay so it is the same as yours.

A fifth action is perceptual rather than behavioural. It involves changing our beliefs about the situation. For example you might believe that the co-worker really is doing more (e.g., working longer hours) for that higher pay. Alternatively, we might change our perceptions of the value of some outcomes. Although initially upset that a co-worker gets more travel opportunities than you do, you eventually believe the travel is more a nuisance than desirable feature of the job. A sixth action to reduce the inequity tension would be to change the comparison other. You

OB BY THE NUMBERS

Not Paid What They're Worth[85]

46%
of Canadians polled believe they are paid less than they deserve

4.5%
of Canadians polled believe they are paid more than they deserve

43%
of Americans polled say they are underpaid for the work they do

4%
of Americans polled say they are overpaid for the work they do

39%
of banking/financial services employees polled in Asia Pacific countries believe their current salary package is unfair and not in line with the market

Note: These surveys, which were conducted in 2009 and 2010, suggest that employees are much more likely to believe they are underrewarded than overrewarded.

might compare yourself more with a friend or neighbour who works in a similar job rather than use the higher-paid co-worker as the comparison. Finally, if the inequity tension is strong enough and can't be reduced through other actions, you might leave the field. This occurs by moving to another department, joining another company, or keeping away from the work site where the overpaid co-worker is located.

Although the seven responses to inequity remain the same, people who feel overreward inequity would, of course, act differently. Some overrewarded employees reduce their feelings of inequity by working harder. "What helps motivate me is that I look around the office and I see people who are working as hard or harder than I am. You feel guilty if you're not pulling your weight," says one accountant. However, many overrewarded employees don't work harder. Some might encourage the underrewarded co-worker to work at a more leisurely pace. A common reaction, however, is that the overrewarded employee changes his or her perceptions to justify the more favourable outcomes. As the late Canadian author Pierre Burton once said: "I was underpaid for the first half of my life. I don't mind being overpaid for the second half."[86]

Individual Differences: Equity Sensitivity   People vary in their **equity sensitivity**, that is, how strongly they feel about outcome/input ratios with others.[87] At one end of the equity sensitivity continuum are people who are tolerant of situations where they are underrewarded. They might still prefer equal outcome/input ratios, but they don't mind if others receive more than they do for the same inputs. In the middle are people who fit the standard equity theory model; they want their outcome/input ratio to be equal to the outcome/input ratio of the comparison other. At the other end of the equity sensitivity continuum are people who feel more comfortable when they receive proportionately more than others. They might accept having the same outcome/input ratio as others, but they would prefer receiving more than others performing the same work.

> **equity sensitivity** An individual's outcome/input preferences and reaction to various outcome/input ratios.

Evaluating Equity Theory   Equity theory is widely studied and quite successful at predicting various situations involving feelings of workplace injustice.[88] However, equity theory isn't so easy to put into practice because it doesn't identify the comparison other and doesn't indicate which inputs or outcomes are most valuable to each employee. The best solution here is for leaders to know their employees well enough to minimize the risk of inequity feelings. Open communication is also a key, enabling employees to let decision makers know when they feel decisions are unfair. A second problem is that equity theory accounts for only some of our feelings of fairness or justice in the workplace. Experts now say that procedural justice is at least as important as distributive justice.

Fired Subway Worker Hired by Quiznos

Heidi Heise was fired by a Dartmouth, Nova Scotia Subway restaurant four days after giving six-inch sandwiches to two neighbours left homeless by an apartment fire. Company policy permitted Heise to have one free 12-inch sub during her shift but instead she split it for her neighbours. However, she violated the required procedure by not recording the sub taken. "I was going to do it before I left and I forgot," she said. "But everybody in the store gives out their employee subs. So I don't understand why it was a big problem for me and nobody else." "They didn't give me any verbal warnings, they didn't give me any written warnings it was just an automatic firing because they considered it theft." Rival Quiznos moved quickly to give Heidi a new job and restore her sense of fairness. "Heidi is a person who was trying to do the right thing," said Quiznos franchisee Steve Webber. "These are the kind of people Quiznos likes to have working in our stores." Webber also committed to donate $1 plus a matching amount from every sub sold during the week to help out people left homeless by the fire.[89] *Copyright © 2011 BellMedia. All rights reserved.*

PROCEDURAL JUSTICE

Recall that *procedural justice* refers to fairness of the procedures used to decide the distribution of resources. How do companies improve procedural justice?[90] A good way to start is by giving employees "voice" in the process; encourage them to present their facts and perspectives on the issue. Voice also provides a "value-expressive" function; employees tend to feel better after having an opportunity to speak their mind. Procedural justice is also higher when the decision maker is perceived as unbiased, relies on complete and accurate information, applies existing policies consistently, and has listened to all sides of the dispute. If employees still feel unfairness in the allocation of resources, those feelings tend to subside when they have the opportunity to appeal the decision to a higher authority.

Finally, people usually feel less injustice when they are given a full explanation of the decision and their concerns are treated with respect. If employees believe a decision is unfair, refusing to explain how the decision was made could fuel their feelings of inequity. For instance, one Canadian study found that visible minority nurses who experienced racism tended to file grievances only after experiencing disrespectful treatment in their attempt to resolve the racist situation. Another study reported that employees with repetitive strain injuries were more likely to file workers' compensation claims after experiencing disrespectful behaviour from management. A third recent study noted that employees have stronger feelings of injustice when the manager has a reputation of treating people unfairly most of the time.[91]

Consequences of Procedural Injustice   Procedural justice has a strong influence on a person's emotions and motivation. Employees tend to experience anger toward the source of the injustice, which generates various response behaviours that scholars categorize as either withdrawal or aggression.[92] Notice how these response behaviours are similar to the fight-or-flight responses described earlier in the chapter regarding situations that activate our drive to defend. Research suggests that being treated unfairly threatens our self-concept and social status, particularly when others see that we have been unjustly treated. Employees retaliate to restore their self-concept and reinstate their status and power in the relationship with the perpetrator of the injustice. Employees also engage in these counterproductive behaviours to educate the decision maker, thereby trying to minimize the likelihood of future injustices.[93]

CHAPTER SUMMARY

LO1   Define employee engagement.

Employee engagement is defined as an individual's emotional and cognitive (rational) motivation, particularly a focused, intense, persistent, and purposive effort toward work-related goals. It is emotional involvement in, commitment to, and satisfaction with the work, as well as a high level of absorption in the work and sense of self-efficacy about performing the work.

LO2   Explain the role of human drives and emotions in employee motivation and behaviour.

Motivation consists of the forces within a person that affect his or her direction, intensity, and persistence of voluntary behaviour in the workplace. Drives (also called primary needs) are neural states that energize individuals to correct deficiencies or maintain an internal equilibrium. They are the "prime movers" of behaviour, activating emotions that put us in a state of readiness to act.

Needs—goal-directed forces that people experience—are shaped by the individual's self-concept (including personality and values), social norms, and past experience.

LO3   Summarize Maslow's needs hierarchy, McClelland's learned needs theory, and four-drive theory and discuss their implications for employee motivation.

Maslow's needs hierarchy groups needs into a hierarchy of five levels and states that the lowest needs are initially most important but higher needs become more important as the lower ones are satisfied. Although very popular, the theory lacks research support because it wrongly assumes that everyone has the same hierarchy. The emerging evidence suggests that needs hierarchies vary from one person to the next according to their personal values.

McClelland's learned needs theory argues that needs can be strengthened through learning. The three needs studied in this respect are need for achievement, need for power, and need for affiliation. Four-drive theory states that everyone has four innate drives—the drive to acquire, bond, learn, and defend. These drives activate emotions that people regulate through a skill set that considers social norms, past experience, and personal values. The main recommendation from four-drive theory is to ensure that individual jobs and workplaces provide a balanced opportunity to fulfill the four drives.

L04   Discuss the expectancy theory model, including its practical implications.

Expectancy theory states that work effort is determined by the perception that effort will result in a particular level of performance (E-to-P expectancy), the perception that a specific behaviour or performance level will lead to specific outcomes (P-to-O expectancy), and the valences that the person feels for those outcomes. The E-to-P expectancy increases by improving the employee's ability and confidence to perform the job. The P-to-O expectancy increases by measuring performance accurately, distributing higher rewards to better performers, and showing employees that rewards are performance-based. Outcome valences increase by finding out what employees want and using these resources as rewards.

L05   Outline organizational behaviour modification (OB Mod) and social cognitive theory and explain their relevance to employee motivation.

Organizational behaviour modification states that the environment teaches people to alter their behaviour so that they maximize positive consequences and minimize adverse consequences. Antecedents are environmental stimuli that provoke (not necessarily cause) behaviour. Consequences are events following behaviour that influence its future occurrence. Consequences include positive reinforcement, punishment, negative reinforcement, and extinction. The schedules of reinforcement also influence behaviour.

Social cognitive theory states that much learning and motivation occurs by observing and modelling others as well as by anticipating the consequences of our behaviour. It suggests that people typically infer (rather than only directly experience) cause-effect relationships, anticipate the consequences of their actions, develop self-efficacy in demonstrating behaviour, exercise personal control over their behaviour, and reflect on their direct experiences. The theory emphasizes self-regulation of individual behaviour, including self-reinforcement, which is the tendency of people to reward and punish themselves as a consequence of their actions.

L06   Describe the characteristics of effective goal setting and feedback.

Goal setting is the process of motivating employees and clarifying their role perceptions by establishing performance objectives. Goals are more effective when they are specific, relevant, and challenging; have employee commitment; and are accompanied by meaningful feedback. Participative goal setting is important in some situations. Effective feedback is specific, relevant, timely, credible, and sufficiently frequent. Strengths-based coaching (also known as *appreciative coaching*) maximizes employee potential by focusing on strengths rather than weaknesses. Employees usually prefer nonsocial feedback sources to learn about their progress toward goal accomplishment.

L07   Summarize equity theory and describe ways to improve procedural justice.

Organizational justice consists of distributive justice (perceived fairness in the outcomes we receive relative to our contributions and the outcomes and contributions of others) and procedural justice (fairness of the procedures used to decide the distribution of resources). Equity theory has four elements: outcome/input ratio, comparison other, equity evaluation, and consequences of inequity. The theory also explains what people are motivated to do when they feel inequitably treated. Companies need to consider not only equity of the distribution of resources but also fairness in the process of making resource allocation decisions.

KEY TERMS

balanced scorecard (BSC), p. 138

distributive justice, p. 141

drives, p. 125

employee engagement, p. 123

equity sensitivity, p. 144

equity theory, p. 142

expectancy theory, p. 132

four-drive theory, p. 129

goal setting, p. 137

Maslow's needs hierarchy theory, p. 126

motivation, p. 123

multisource (360-degree) feedback, p. 140

need for achievement (nAch), p. 128

need for affiliation (nAff), p. 128

need for power (nPow), p. 128

needs, p. 125

organizational behaviour modification, p. 134

procedural justice, p. 141

self-reinforcement, p. 137

social cognitive theory, p. 136

strengths-based coaching, p. 139

CRITICAL-THINKING QUESTIONS

1. Four-drive theory is conceptually different from Maslow's needs hierarchy in several ways. Describe these differences. At the same time, needs are based on drives, so the four drives should parallel the seven needs that Maslow identified (five in the hierarchy and two additional needs). Map Maslow's needs onto the four drives in four-drive theory.

2. Learned needs theory states that needs can be strengthened or weakened. How might a company strengthen the achievement needs of its management team?

3. Two friends who have just completed an organizational behaviour course at another university inform you that employees must fulfill their need for self-esteem and social esteem before they can reach their full potential through self-actualization. What theory are these friends referring to? How does their statement differ from what you learned about that theory in this chapter?

4. Use all three components of expectancy theory to explain why some employees are motivated to show up for work during a severe snowstorm whereas others make no effort to leave their home.

5. Describe a situation in which you used organizational behaviour modification to influence someone's behaviour. What specifically did you do? What was the result?

6. Using your knowledge of the characteristics of effective goals, establish two meaningful goals related to your performance in this class.

7. Several service representatives are upset that the newly hired representative with no previous experience will be paid $3,000 a year above the usual starting salary in the pay range. The department manager explained that the new hire would not accept the entry-level rate, so the company raised the offer by $3,000. All five reps currently earn salaries near the top of the scale ($15,000 higher than the new recruit), although they all started at the minimum starting salary a few years earlier. Use equity theory to explain why the five service representatives feel inequity in this situation.

8. A large organization has hired you as a consultant to identify day-to-day activities for middle managers to minimize distributive and procedural injustice. The company explains that employees have complained about distributive injustice because they have different opinions about what is fair (equity, equality, need) and what outcomes and inputs have the greatest value. They also experience procedural injustice due to misperceptions and differing expectations. Given these ambiguities, what would you recommend to middle managers?

 CASE STUDY 5.1

Vêtements Ltée

By Steven L. McShane, The University of Western Australia

Vêtements Ltée is a chain of men's retail clothing stores located throughout Quebec. Two years ago, the company introduced new incentive systems for both store managers and sales employees. Store managers in each store receive a salary with annual merit increases based on sales above targeted goals, store appearance, store inventory management, customer complaints, and several other performance measures. Some of this information (e.g., store appearance) is gathered during visits by senior management, while other information is based on company records (e.g., sales volume).

Sales employees are paid a fixed salary plus a commission based on the percentage of sales credited to that employee over the pay period. The commission represents about 30 percent of a typical paycheque and is intended to encourage employees to actively serve customers and to increase sales volume. Because returned merchandise is discounted from commissions, sales employees are discouraged from selling products that customers do not really want.

Soon after the new incentive systems were introduced, senior management began to receive complaints from store managers regarding the performance of their sales staff. They observed that sales employees tended to stand near the store entrance waiting to "tag" customers as their own. Occasionally, sales staff would argue over "ownership" of the customer. Managers were concerned that this aggressive behaviour intimidated some customers. It also tended to leave some parts of the store unattended by staff.

Many managers were also concerned about inventory duties. Previously, sales staff would share responsibility for restocking inventory and completing inventory reorder forms. Under the new compensation system, however, few employees were willing to do these essential tasks. On several occasions, stores have faced stock shortages because merchandise was not stocked or reorder forms were not completed in a timely manner. Potential sales have suffered from empty shelves when plenty of merchandise was available in the back storeroom or at the warehouse. The company's new automatic inventory system could reduce some of these problems, but employees must still stock shelves and assist in other aspects of inventory management.

Store managers have tried to correct the inventory problem by assigning employees to inventory duty, but this has created resentment among the employees selected. Other managers have threatened sales staff with dismissals if they do not do their share of inventory management. This strategy has been somewhat effective when the manager is in the store, but staff members sneak back onto the floor when the manager is away. It has also hurt staff morale, particularly relations with the store manager.

To reduce the tendency of sales staff to hoard customers at the store entrance, some managers have assigned employees to specific areas of the store. This has also created some resentment among employees stationed in areas with less traffic or lower-priced merchandise. Some staff have openly complained of lower paycheques because they have been placed in a slow area of the store or have been given more than their share of inventory duties.

Discussion Questions

1. What symptom(s) in this case suggest that something has gone wrong?

2. What are the main causes of these symptoms?

3. What actions should Vêtements executives take to correct these problems?

 CLASS EXERCISE 5.2

Needs Priority Exercise

Purpose   This class exercise is designed to help you understand employee needs in the workplace.

Instructions (Small Class)

- *Step 1:* The table on the next page lists in alphabetical order 16 characteristics of the job or work environment. Working alone, use the right column to rank-order the importance of these characteristics to you personally. Write in "1" beside the most important characteristic, "2" for the second most important, and so on through to "16" for the least important characteristic on this list.

- *Step 2:* Identify any three of these work attributes that you believe have the largest score differences between Generation-Y (Millennial) male and female postsecondary students across Canada (i.e., those born in 1980 or after). Indicate which gender you think identifies that attribute as more important.

- *Step 3:* Students are assigned to teams, where they compare each other's rank-order results as well as perceived gender differences in needs. Note reasons for the largest variations in rankings and be prepared to discuss these reasons with the entire class. Students should pay close attention to different needs, self-concepts, and various forms of diversity (culture, profession, age, etc.) within your class to identify possible explanations for any variation of results across students.

- *Step 4:* The instructor will provide results of a recent large-scale survey of Canadian Generation-Y/Millennial postsecondary students (i.e., born in 1980 or after). When these results are presented, identify the reasons for any noticeable differences in the class. Relate the differences to your understanding of the emerging view of employee needs and drives in work settings. For gender differences, discuss reasons why men and women might differ on these work-related attributes.

Instructions (Large Class)

- *Step 1 and Step 2:* Same as above.

- *Step 3:* The instructor will ask students, by a show of hands (or use of classroom technology), to identify their top-ranked attributes as well as the attributes believed to have the greatest gender differences among Generation-Y Canadians.

- *Step 4:* Same as above.

Personal Ranking of Work-Related Attributes	
Attributes of Work (listed alphabetically)	**Your Ranking (1 = most important ; 16 = least important)**
Challenging work	_____
Commitment to social responsibility	_____
Good health and benefits plan	_____
Good initial salary level	_____
Good people to report to	_____
Good people to work with	_____
Good training opportunities/developing new skills	_____
Good variety of work	_____
Job security	_____
Opportunities for advancement in position	_____
Opportunities to have a personal impact	_____
Opportunities to have a social impact	_____
Opportunity to travel	_____
Organization is a leader in its field	_____
Strong commitment to employee diversity	_____
Work-life balance	_____

CLASS EXERCISE 5.3

The Learning Exercise

Purpose   This exercise is designed to help you understand how learning and motivation are influenced by the contingencies of reinforcement in organizational behaviour modification.

Materials   Any objects normally available in a classroom will be acceptable for this activity.

Instructions   The instructor will ask for three volunteers, who are then briefed outside the classroom. The
(Small or   instructor will spend a few minutes describing the exercise to students in the class about
Large Class)   their duties. Then, one of the three volunteers will enter the room to participate in the exercise. When completed, the second volunteer enters the room and participates in the exercise. When completed, the third volunteer enters the class and participates in the exercise.

   For students to gain the full benefit of this exercise, no other information will be provided here. However, the instructor will have more details at the beginning of this fun activity.

 TEAM EXERCISE 5.4

Bonus Decision Exercise

By Steven L. McShane, The University of Western Australia

Purpose   This exercise is designed to help you understand the elements of equity theory and how people differ in their equity perceptions.

Instructions

Four managers in a large national insurance company are described below. The national sales director of the company has given your consulting team (first individually, then together) the task of allocating $100,000 in bonus money to these four managers. It is entirely up to your team to decide how to divide the money among these people. The only requirements are that all of the money must be distributed and that no two branch managers can receive the same amount. The names and information are presented in no particular order. You should assume that economic conditions, client demographics, and other external factors are very similar for these managers.

- *Step 1:* Working alone, read information about the four managers. Then fill in the amount you would allocate to each manager in the "Individual Decision" column.

- *Step 2:* Still working alone, fill in the "Equity Inputs Form." First, in the "Input Factor" column, list in order of importance the factors you considered when allocating these bonus amounts (e.g., seniority, performance, age, etc.). The most important factor should be listed first and the least important last. Next, in the "Input Weight" column estimate the percentage weight that you assigned to this factor. The total of this column must add up to 100 percent.

- *Step 3:* Form teams (typically four to six people). Each team will compare their results and note any differences. Then, for each job, team members will reach a consensus on the bonus amount that each manager should receive. These amounts will be written in the "Team Decision" column.

- *Step 4:* The instructor will call the class together to compare team results and note differences in inputs and input weights used by individual students. The class will then discuss these results using equity theory.

Instructions
(Large Class)

- *Step 1 and Step 2:* Same as above.

- *Step 3:* The instructor will ask students, by a show of hands (or use of classroom technology), to identify which manager would receive the highest bonus, then how much should be allocated to that manager. Repeat with the manager receiving the lowest bonus. (Some classroom technology allows students to directly indicate their bonus amount to that manager.) The class will then discuss these results using equity theory.

Bonus Decision
Making Manager
Profiles

Bob B. Bob has been in the insurance business for over 27 years and has spent the past 21 years with this company. A few years ago, Bob's branch typically made the largest contribution to regional profits. More recently, however, it has brought in few new accounts and is now well below average in terms of its contribution to the company. Turnover in the branch has been high and Bob doesn't have the same enthusiasm for the job as he once did. Bob is 56 years old and is married with five children. Three children are still living at home. Bob has a high school diploma as well as a certificate from a special course in insurance management.

Edward E. In the two years that Edward has been a branch manager, his unit has brought in several major accounts and now stands as one of the top units in the country. Edward is well respected by his employees. At 29, he is the youngest manager in the region and one of the youngest in the country. The regional director initially doubted the wisdom of giving Edward the position of branch manager because of his relatively young age and lack of experience in the insurance industry. Edward received an undergraduate business degree from a regional college and worked for five years as a sales representative before joining this company. Edward is single and has no children.

Lee L. Lee has been with this organization for seven years. The first two years were spent as a sales representative in the office that she now manages. According to the regional director, Lee rates about average as a branch manager. She earned an undergraduate degree in geography from a major university and worked as a sales representative for four years with another insurance company before joining this organization.

Lee is 40 years old, divorced, and has no children. She is a very ambitious person but sometimes has problems working with her staff and other branch managers.

Sandy S. Sandy is 47 years old and has been a branch manager with this company for 17 years. Seven years ago, her branch made the lowest contribution to the region's profits, but this has steadily improved and is now slightly above average. Sandy appears to lack a sense of urgency in performing key duties of her job but is well liked by her staff and other branch managers. Her experience in the insurance industry has been entirely with this organization. She previously worked in non-sales positions, and it is not clear how she became a branch manager without previous sales experience. Sandy is married and has three school-aged children. Several years ago, Sandy earned a diploma in business from a nearby community college by taking evening courses.

Bonus Allocation Form		
Name	**Individual Decision**	**Team Decision**
Bob B.	$_____	$_____
Edward E.	$_____	$_____
Lee L.	$_____	$_____
Sandy S.	$_____	$_____
TOTALS:	$100,000	$100,000

Equity Inputs Form	
Input Factor*	**Input Weight****
_____	_____%
_____	_____%
_____	_____%
_____	_____%
_____	_____%
TOTAL:	100%

* List factors in order of importance, with most important factor listed first.

** The weight of each factor is a percentage ranging from 1 to 100. All factor weights together must add up to 100 percent.

Copyright © 2000, 1983 Steven L. McShane

Go to CONNECT to complete the following interactive self-assessments.

 SELF-ASSESSMENT EXERCISE 5.5

Need-Strength Questionnaire

Although everyone has the same innate drives, secondary or learned needs vary from one person to the next in the same situation. This self-assessment provides an estimate of your needs strength on selected secondary needs. Read each of the statements below and check the response that you believe best reflects your position regarding each statement. Then use the scoring key in Appendix B at the end of the book to calculate your results. To receive a meaningful estimate of your need strength, you need to answer each item honestly and with reflection on your personal experiences. Class discussion will focus on the meaning of the needs measured in this self-assessment as well as their relevance in the workplace.

Personal Needs Questionnaire					
How accurately do each of the following statements describe you?	Very Accurate Description of Me	Moderately Accurate	Neither Accurate nor Inaccurate	Moderately Inaccurate	Very Inaccurate Description of Me
1. I would rather be myself than be well thought of.	☐	☐	☐	☐	☐
2. I'm the type of person who never gives up.	☐	☐	☐	☐	☐
3. When the opportunity occurs, I want to be in charge.	☐	☐	☐	☐	☐
4. I try not to say things that others don't like to hear.	☐	☐	☐	☐	☐
5. I find it difficult to talk about my ideas if they are contrary to group opinion.	☐	☐	☐	☐	☐
6. I tend to take control of things.	☐	☐	☐	☐	☐
7. I am not highly motivated to succeed.	☐	☐	☐	☐	☐
8. I usually disagree with others only if I know my friends will back me up.	☐	☐	☐	☐	☐
9. I try to be the very best at what I do.	☐	☐	☐	☐	☐
10. I seldom make excuses or apologize for my behaviour.	☐	☐	☐	☐	☐
11. If anyone criticizes me, I can take it.	☐	☐	☐	☐	☐
12. I try to outdo others.	☐	☐	☐	☐	☐
13. I seldom change my opinion when people disagree with me.	☐	☐	☐	☐	☐
14. I try to achieve more than what others have accomplished.	☐	☐	☐	☐	☐
15. To get along and be liked, I tend to be what people expect me to be.	☐	☐	☐	☐	☐

Sources: Adapted from instruments described and/or presented in L. R. Goldberg, J. A. Johnson, H. W. Eber, R. Hogan, M. C. Ashton, C. R. Cloninger, and H. C. Gough, "The International Personality Item Pool and the Future of Public-Domain Personality Measures," *Journal of Research in Personality* 40 (2006), pp. 84–96; H. J. Martin, "A Revised Measure of Approval Motivation and Its Relationship to Social Desirability," *Journal of Personality Assessment* 48 (1984), pp. 508–519.

 SELF-ASSESSMENT EXERCISE 5.6

Measuring Your Growth-Need Strength

Abraham Maslow's need hierarchy theory distinguished between deficiency needs and growth needs. Deficiency needs become activated when unfulfilled, such as the need for food or belongingness. Growth needs, on the other hand, continue to develop even when temporarily fulfilled. Maslow identified self-actualization as the only category of growth needs. Although research found little support for Maslow's needs hierarchy theory, people do have growth needs. This self-assessment is designed to estimate your level of growth-need strength. This instrument asks you to consider what it is about a job that is most important to you. Please indicate which of the two jobs you personally would prefer if you had to make a choice between them. In answering each question, assume that everything else about the jobs is the same. Pay attention only to the characteristics actually listed.

SELF-ASSESSMENT EXERCISE 5.7

Your Equity Sensitivity

Some people experience stronger or weaker feelings of unfairness in specific situations. This self-assessment estimates your level of equity sensitivity. Read each of the statements in this questionnaire, and indicate the response that you believe best reflects your position regarding each statement. This exercise should be completed alone so that you assess yourself honestly, without concerns of social comparison. Class discussion will focus on equity theory and the effect of equity sensitivity on perceptions of fairness in the workplace.

Practise and learn online with Connect. Connect resources include additional and interactive study exercises, videos, and practice quizzing, as well as additional material you won't find in the printed text.

LEARNING OBJECTIVES

After reading this chapter, you should be able to:

LO1 Discuss the meaning of money and identify several individual, team, and organizational-level performance-based rewards.

LO2 Describe five ways to improve reward effectiveness.

LO3 List the advantages and disadvantages of job specialization.

LO4 Diagram the job characteristics model and describe three ways to improve employee motivation through job design.

LO5 Define empowerment and identify strategies that support empowerment.

LO6 Describe the five elements of self-leadership and identify specific personal and work environment influences on self-leadership.

By any measure, Spruceland Millworks is a high-performance workplace that leverages employee potential through rewards, job design, empowerment, and self-leadership. The Acheson, Alberta, manufacturer of mouldings, decking, and other niche lumber products organizes employees into teams, which are responsible for their own production. Team members earn a bonus for exceeding the daily objectives and can take the rest of the day off when their goals have been achieved. Along with team performance, management encourages individual initiative and innovation by handing out gift certificates on the spot to deserving employees. The company also puts owners and staff "on the same page" through an employee share ownership plan, giving everyone a financial stake in the company's success. Spruceland even rewards long service; employees receive an engraved Rolex watch after 20 years with the company.

The company's most popular motivator is probably the all-expense paid trip to a resort destination when employees achieve a challenging annual production and profitability target. For example, the company recently flew every employee and many family members to Puerto Vallarta, Mexico, for a week. Each employee receives up to four tickets for the trip, depending on their years of service with the company. "I've always strongly believed my job is to recognize people and reward their efforts, and that they go home at night feeling significant," says Spruceland founder Ben Sawatzky.

Spruceland Millworks has received numerous employment awards and recognition over the years. Sawatzky attributes this success to the rewards, empowerment, and strong relationships formed in a small company. "It's more of a personal feel. It's more of a relationship-based business, rather than a number on a time card," he suggests. Even so, Spruceland struggles to compete for skilled tradespeople against the high wages offered by companies in the oil and gas industry. "Hardly am I able to hold on to them long enough to indoctrinate them with our corporate culture, which shows them that there's a lot more to working at Spruceland than working eight to five," explains Sawatzky.[1]

Spruceland Mills has survived and thrived in the turbulent woods products industry through the bene[fit] of applied performance management practices. *Bruce Edwards/The Edmonton Journal*

Spruceland Millworks is a Canadian beacon for enhancing employee performance through rewards, job design, empowerment, and self-leadership. Employees receive a variety of rewards to motivate their performance. Teams have considerable autonomy and employees feel empowered to achieve their goals. With reliance on teams rather than supervision, the company also depends on the self-leadership of its workforce. This chapter looks at each of these applied performance practices. The chapter begins with an overview of financial reward practices, including the different types of rewards and how to implement rewards effectively. Next, we look at the dynamics of job design, including specific job design strategies to motivate employees. We then consider the elements of empowerment as well as conditions that support empowerment. The final part of this chapter explains how employees manage their own performance through self-leadership.

THE MEANING OF MONEY IN THE WORKPLACE

LO1

Rewarding people with money is one of the oldest and certainly the most widespread applied performance practice. At the most basic level, money and other financial rewards represent a form of exchange; employees provide their labour, skill, and knowledge in return for money and benefits from the organization. From this perspective, money and related rewards align employee goals with organizational goals. This concept of economic exchange can be found across cultures. The word for *pay* in Malay and Slovak means "to replace a loss"; in Hebrew and Swedish it means "making equal."[2]

However, money is much more than an object of compensation for an employee's contribution to organizational objectives. Money relates to our needs, our emotions, and our self-concept. It is a symbol of achievement and status, a reinforcer and motivator, and a source of enhanced or reduced anxiety.[3] According to one source, "Money is probably the most emotionally meaningful object in contemporary life: only food and sex are its close competitors as common carriers of such strong and diverse feelings, significance, and strivings."[4]

The meaning of money varies considerably from one person to the next.[5] Studies report that money is viewed as a symbol of status and prestige, as a source of security, as a source of evil, or as a source of anxiety or feelings of inadequacy. It is considered a "taboo" topic in many social settings. It has been described both as a "tool" (i.e., money is valued because it is an instrument for acquiring other things of value) and as a "drug" (i.e., money is an object of addictive value in itself). One large-scale study revealed that money generates a variety of emotions, most of which are negative, such as anxiety, depression, anger, and helplessness.[6] A widely studied model of money attitudes suggests that people have a strong "money ethic" when they believe that money is not evil; that it is a symbol of achievement, respect, and power; and that it should be budgeted carefully. These attitudes toward money influence an individual's ethical conduct, organizational citizenship, and many other behaviours and attitudes.[7]

The meaning of money seems to differ between men and women. One large-scale survey revealed that in almost all 43 countries studied, men attach more importance or value to money than do women. Men particularly tend to view money as a symbol of power and status.[8] Personal and cultural values influence the meaning of money. People in countries with high power distance (such as China and Japan) tend to have a high respect and priority for money, whereas people in countries with a strong egalitarian culture (such as Denmark, Austria, and Israel) are discouraged from openly talking about money or displaying their personal wealth. One study suggests that Swiss culture values saving money whereas Italian culture places more value on spending it.[9]

Many experts now believe that money is a much more important motivator than was previously believed, more because of its inherent or symbolic value than because of what it can buy.[10] Philosopher John Stuart Mill made this observation 150 years ago when he wrote: "The love of money is not only one of the strongest moving forces of human life, but money is, in many cases, desired in and for itself."[11] People who are more highly paid tend to have higher job performance because the higher paycheque makes them feel more valued in the organization (i.e., they have a more positive self-concept). Others have noted that the symbolic value of money and other rewards is particularly motivational when few people receive this reward. In these situations, the reward gives beneficiaries a degree of social distinction, which is consistent with the drive to acquire (see Chapter 5).

Overall, current organizational behaviour knowledge indicates that money is much more than a means of exchange between employer and employee. It fulfills a variety of needs, influences emotions, and shapes or represents a person's self-concept. This is important to remember when the employer is distributing financial rewards in the workplace. Over the next few pages, we look at various reward practices and how to improve the implementation of performance-based rewards.

FINANCIAL REWARD PRACTICES

Financial rewards come in many forms, which can be organized into the four specific objectives identified in Exhibit 6.1: membership and seniority, job status, competencies, and task performance.

MEMBERSHIP- AND SENIORITY-BASED REWARDS

Membership-based and seniority-based rewards (sometimes called "pay for pulse") represent the largest part of most paycheques. Some employee benefits, such as free or discounted meals in the company cafeteria, remain the same for everyone, whereas others increase with seniority. For example, employees at Better Beef Ltd. (one of Canada's largest meat processing companies) receive an additional $1,000 for each year of seniority. As the opening vignette to this chapter mentioned, Spruceland Millworks rewards employees for their long service with an expensive watch. Many Asian companies distribute a "13th month" bonus, which every employee expects to receive each

Exhibit 6.1   REWARD OBJECTIVES, ADVANTAGES, AND DISADVANTAGES

Reward Objective	Sample Rewards	Advantages	Disadvantages
Membership/seniority	• Fixed pay • Most employee benefits • Paid time off	• May attract applicants • Minimizes stress of insecurity • Reduces turnover	• Doesn't directly motivate performance • May discourage poor performers from leaving • "Golden handcuffs" may undermine performance
Job status	• Promotion-based pay increase • Status-based benefits	• Tries to maintain internal equity • Minimizes pay discrimination • Motivates employees to compete for promotions	• Encourages hierarchy, which may increase costs and reduce responsiveness • Reinforces status differences • Motivates job competition and exaggerated job worth
Competencies	• Pay increase based on competency • Skill-based pay	• Improves workforce flexibility • Tends to improve quality • Is consistent with employability	• Relies on subjective measurement of competencies • Skill-based pay plans are expensive
Task performance	• Commissions • Merit pay • Gainsharing • Profit sharing • Share options	• Motivates task performance • Attracts performance-oriented applicants • Organizational rewards create an ownership culture • Pay variability may avoid layoffs during downturns	• May weaken job content motivation • May distance reward giver from receiver • May discourage creativity • Tends to address symptoms, not underlying causes of behaviour

year no matter how well the company performed over the previous year. Although many Japanese firms have shifted to performance-based pay, others have retained or returned to wage scales based on the employee's age. "Even during that period [when the employee's performance is below expectations], we raise salaries according to their age," says the president of Tokai Rubber Industries Ltd., which returned to age-based salaries after discarding a short-lived performance-based pay plan.[12]

These membership and seniority-based rewards potentially attract job applicants (particularly those who desire predictable income) and reduce turnover. However, they do not directly motivate job performance; on the contrary, they discourage poor performers from seeking work better suited to their abilities. Instead, the good performers are lured to better-paying jobs. Some of these rewards are also "golden handcuffs"— they discourage employees from quitting because of deferred bonuses or generous benefits that are not available elsewhere. However golden handcuffs potentially weaken job performance because they generate continuance rather than affective commitment (see Chapter 4).

JOB STATUS-BASED REWARDS

job evaluation
Systematically rating the worth of jobs within an organization by measuring their required skill, effort, responsibility, and working conditions.

Almost every organization rewards employees to some extent on the basis of the status or worth of the jobs they occupy. In some parts of the world, companies measure job worth through **job evaluation**. Most job evaluation methods give higher value to jobs that require more skill and effort, have more responsibility, and have more difficult working conditions.[13] The higher worth assigned to a job, the higher the minimum and maximum pay for people in that job. Along with receiving higher pay, employees with more valued jobs sometimes receive larger offices, company-paid vehicles, and other perks.

> Almost every organization rewards employees to some extent on the basis of the status or worth of the jobs they occupy. "

Job status-based rewards try to improve feelings of fairness, such as that people in higher-valued jobs should get higher pay. These rewards also motivate employees to compete for promotions. However, at a time when companies are trying to be more cost-efficient and responsive to the external environment, job status-based rewards potentially do the opposite by encouraging a bureaucratic hierarchy. These rewards also reinforce a status mentality, whereas Generation-X and Generation-Y employees expect a more egalitarian workplace. Furthermore, status-based pay potentially motivates employees to compete with each other for higher-status jobs and to raise the value of their own jobs by exaggerating job duties and hoarding resources.[14]

COMPETENCY-BASED REWARDS

Almost one-quarter of Canadian organizations reward employees for their competencies that lead to superior performance.[15] The most common competency-based practices identify specific competencies within a broad group of jobs as well as core competencies that are relevant across all job groups. Employees progress through the pay range within that job group based on how well they demonstrate each of those competencies.[16] For example, the RCMP has eight core competencies (common to all jobs), including client-centred service, interpersonal skills, and continuous learning. Job incumbents receive higher pay as they master these competencies as well as those specific to their job group. The second form of competency-based rewards are *skill-based pay* plans that reward employees based on their mastery of specific skill blocks. Each skill block represents a different piece of machinery or technical skill in the production process. Although employees work on only one machine at a time, they earn higher pay with the number of machines they are qualified to operate.

The main problem with ESOPs, share options, and profit sharing is that employees often perceive a weak connection between individual effort and corporate profits or the value of company shares. Even in small firms, the company's stock price or profitability is influenced by economic conditions, competition, and other factors beyond the employee's immediate control. This low individual performance-to-outcome expectancy weakens employee motivation. Another concern is that some companies (notably in the United States) use ESOPs as a replacement for employee pension plans. This is a risky strategy because the superannuation funds lack diversification. If the company goes bankrupt, employees lose both their jobs and a large portion of their retirement nest egg.[30]

IMPROVING REWARD EFFECTIVENESS

L02

Performance-based rewards have come under attack over the years for discouraging creativity, distancing management from employees, distracting employees from the meaningfulness of the work itself, and being quick fixes that ignore the true causes of poor performance. While these issues have kernels of truth under specific circumstances, they do not necessarily mean that we should abandon performance-based pay. On the contrary, top-performing companies are more likely to have performance-based rewards, which is consistent with evidence that these rewards are one of the high-performance work practices (see Chapter 1).[31] Reward systems do motivate most employees, but only under the right conditions. Here are some of the more important strategies for improving reward effectiveness.

Link Rewards to Performance   Organizational behaviour modification theory and expectancy theory (Chapter 5) both recommend that employees with better performance should be rewarded more than those with poorer performance. Unfortunately, this simple principle seems to be unusually difficult to apply. Few employees see a relationship between job performance and the amount of pay they and co-workers receive. Only one-quarter of 10,000 Canadian employees surveyed said they regularly receive rewards for a job well done. This is consistent with another survey, which reported that only 27 percent of Canadian employees say there is a clear link between their job performance and pay.[32]

How can companies improve the pay–performance linkage? Inconsistencies and bias can be minimized through gainsharing, ESOPs, and other plans that use objective performance measures. Where subjective measures of performance are necessary, companies should rely on multiple sources of information. Companies also need to apply rewards soon after the performance occurs, and in a large-enough dose (such as a bonus rather than a pay increase), so that employees experience positive emotions when they receive the reward.[33]

Ensure that Rewards are Relevant   Companies need to align rewards with performance within the employee's control. The more employees see a "line of sight" between their daily actions and the reward, the more they are motivated to improve performance. BHP Billiton applies this principle by rewarding top executives with bonuses based on the company's overall performance, whereas front-line mining staff earn bonuses based on the production output, safety performance, and other local indicators. Reward systems also need to correct for situational factors. Salespeople in one region may have higher sales because the economy is stronger there than elsewhere, so sales bonuses need to be adjusted for such economic factors.

Use Team Rewards for Interdependent Jobs   Team rewards are better than individual rewards when employees work in highly interdependent jobs because it is difficult to measure individual performance in these situations. Spruceland Millworks, described in the opening vignette to this chapter, relies on team-based bonuses for this reason; manufacturing lumber products is a team effort, so employees earn bonuses based on team performance. Team rewards also encourage cooperation, which is more important when work is highly interdependent. A third benefit of team rewards is that they tend to support employee preferences for team-based work. One concern, however, is that employees (particularly the most productive employees) in Canada and many other low-collectivism cultures prefer rewards based on their individual performance rather than team performance.[34]

Ensure that Rewards are Valued   It seems obvious that rewards work best when they are valued. Yet companies sometimes make false assumptions about what employees want, with unfortunate consequences. For instance, a manager in one Canadian company honoured an employee's 25th year of service by buying her a box of Timbits. The employee was insulted. She privately complained later to co-workers that she would rather receive nothing than "a piddling box of doughnuts."[35] The solution, of course, is to ask employees what they value. Campbell Soup did this a few years ago at its distribution centres in Canada. Executives thought the employees would ask for more money in a special team reward program. Instead, distribution staff said the most valued reward was a leather jacket with the Campbell Soup logo on the back. The leather jackets cost much less yet were worth much more than the financial bonus the company had intended to distribute.[36]

Watch Out for Unintended Consequences   Performance-based reward systems sometimes have an unexpected—and undesirable—effect on employee behaviours. Consider the pizza company that decided to reward its drivers for on-time delivery. The plan got more hot pizzas to customers on time, but it also increased the accident rates of the company's drivers because the incentive motivated them to drive recklessly.[37] Global Connections 6.1 describes a few other examples in which reward systems had unintended consequences. The solution here is to carefully think through the consequences of rewards and, where possible, test incentives in a pilot project before applying them across the organization.

Financial rewards come in many forms and, as was mentioned at the outset of this section, influence employees in complex ways. But money isn't the only thing that motivates people to join an organization and perform effectively. In one recent survey, 58 percent of the 7,000 Canadians polled said they are prepared to accept a lesser role or lower wage to perform work that is more meaningful to them or their organization. "The reward of doing a job well is in having done the job," says Richard Currie, who built Loblaws into one of the top 10 mass retailing companies in the world and is currently Chancellor of the University of New Brunswick. "The money is a by-product."[38] In other words, companies motivate employees mainly by designing interesting and challenging jobs, which is the topic we discuss next.

JOB DESIGN PRACTICES

L03

job design   The process of assigning tasks to a job, including the interdependency of those tasks with other jobs.

How do you build a better job? That question has challenged organizational behaviour experts as well as psychologists, engineers, and economists for a few centuries. Some jobs have very few tasks and usually require very little skill. Other jobs are immensely complex and require years of experience and learning to master them. From one extreme to the other, jobs have different effects on work efficiency and employee motivation. The challenge, at least from the organization's perspective, is to find the right combination so that work is performed efficiently but employees are motivated and engaged.[39] This objective requires careful **job design**—the process of assigning tasks to a job, including the interdependency of those tasks with other jobs. A *job* is a set of tasks performed by one person. To understand this issue more fully, let's begin by describing early job design efforts aimed at increasing work efficiency through job specialization.

CONNECTIONS 6.1

When Rewards Go Wrong

There is an old saying that "what gets rewarded gets done." But what companies reward isn't always what they had intended their employees to do. Here are a few dramatic examples of how performance-based rewards produce unintended consequences:

- Until recently, most public transit bus drivers in Santiago, Chile, were paid by the number of fare-paying passengers. This incentive system motivated drivers to begin their route on time, take shorter breaks, and drive efficiently, but it also had horrendous unintended consequences. To take on more passengers, bus drivers aggressively raced with competing buses to the next passenger waiting area, sometimes cutting off each other and risking the safety of people in nearby vehicles. Drivers reduced time at each stop by speeding off before passengers were safely on board. They also left the bus doors open, resulting in many passenger injuries and fatalities during the journey. Some drivers drove past waiting areas if there was only one person waiting. According to one study, Santiago's transit buses caused one fatal accident every three days. Another study found that drivers paid per-passenger caused twice as many traffic accidents as drivers paid per hour. Santiago now pays drivers partly by the distance travelled. Unfortunately, drivers are no longer motivated to ensure that passengers pay the fare (about one-third are freeloaders) and they sometimes skip passenger stops altogether when they are behind schedule.[40]

- UBS AG lost more than $37 billion (yes, *billion*) during the first year of the recent global financial meltdown because of its exposure to high-risk mortgage securities. The massive loss forced Switzerland's largest bank to lay off staff, close down a hedge fund business, borrow from foreign governments, and suffer an exodus of clients. Many financial institutions suffered severe losses and a few went bankrupt during the subprime mortgage crisis, but UBS openly acknowledged that a faulty reward system was partly responsible. Specifically, its bonus plan motivated its traders to generate short-term revenue without penalizing them for exposing the bank to high-risk investments. "Essentially, bonuses were measured against gross revenue with no formal account taken of the quality or sustainability of those earnings," says a UBS report submitted to the Swiss banking regulator.[41]

- Share options are supposed to motivate executives to improve corporate performance. Instead, they seem to motivate some leaders to use dodgy accounting practices to distort or misrepresent the company's performance. One study found that financial misrepresentation was associated with executive share options but not with bonuses or other forms of executive compensation. Another report estimated that for every 25 percent increase in share options awarded to executives, the risk of fraud rises by 68 percent. Companies with the largest corporate frauds in

When transit bus drivers in Santiago, Chile, were paid for each passenger they took on board, the unintended consequence was higher traffic fatalities and passenger accidents because drivers engaged in dangerous driving to receive as many passengers as possible. © *Megapress/Alamy*

recent years had, on average, eight times as many options as similar companies that did not experience fraud.[42]

- Integrated steel companies often rewarded managers for increased labour efficiency. The lower the labour-hours required to produce a tonne of steel, the larger the manager's bonus. Unfortunately, steel firms usually didn't count the work of outside contractors in the formula, so the reward system motivated managers to hire expensive contractors in the production process. By employing more contractors, the true cost of production increased, not decreased.[43]

- Donnelly Mirrors (now part of Canada's Magna International empire) introduced a gainsharing plan that motivated employees to reduce labour but not material costs. Employees at the automobile parts manufacturer knew they worked faster with sharp grinding wheels, so they replaced the expensive diamond wheels more often. This action reduced labour costs, thereby giving employees the gainsharing bonus. However, the labour savings were easily offset by much higher costs for diamond grinding wheels.[44]

JOB DESIGN AND WORK EFFICIENCY

In her first job at a toy factory in China's Pearl River Delta, Li Mei used four pens to paint the eyes on dolls. The 18-year-old had exactly 7.2 seconds to paint each doll—about 4,000 every day. Eventually, the paint fumes made Li Mei too faint to work, so she was moved to another department that stamped out plastic doll parts. Again, the work was repetitive: open the machine, insert the plastic, press the machine, remove the plastic. Li Mei repeated this cycle 3,000 times each day. White collar jobs (whether in China or elsewhere) can also be highly repetitive. For Melody Zou, who works as an accountant for a media company in Shanghai, the novelty of her work wore off after the first six months. "I do the same thing day by day, month by month, year by year," complains Zou.[45]

job specialization The result of division of labour in which each job includes a subset of the tasks required to complete the product or service.

Li Mei and Melody Zou perform jobs with a high degree of **job specialization**. Job specialization occurs when the work required to make a toy—or any other product or service—is subdivided into separate jobs assigned to different people. Each resulting job includes a narrow subset of tasks, usually completed in a short cycle time. *Cycle time* is the time required to complete the task before starting over with a new work unit. Li Mei had an average cycle time of 7.2 seconds, which means she repeats the same set of tasks at least 450 times each hour.

Why would companies divide work into such tiny bits? The simple answer is that job specialization potentially improves work efficiency. One reason for this higher efficiency is that employees spend less time changing activities because they have fewer tasks to juggle. Even when people can change tasks quickly, their mental attention lingers on the previous task, which slows down performance on the new task.[46] A second reason for increased work efficiency is that specialized jobs require fewer physical and mental skills to accomplish the assigned work, so less time and fewer resources are needed for training. A third reason is that shorter work cycles give employees more frequent practise with the task, so jobs are mastered more quickly. A fourth reason why specialization tends to increase work efficiency is that employees with specific aptitudes or skills can be matched more precisely to the jobs for which they are best suited.[47]

The benefits of job specialization were noted more than 2,300 years ago by the Chinese philosopher Mencius and Greek philosopher Plato. In the 1400s and 1500s, the Arsenal of Venice employed up to 4,000 people in specialized jobs (caulkers, paymasters, division managers, carpenters, iron workers, warehouse supervisors, etc.) to build ships and many accessories such as cannons, ropes, oars, and armour. The state-owned organization became so efficient that in 1570 it built 100 ships in two months. After construction, the galleons travelled along a waterway where workers apportioned food, ammunition, cordage, and other supplies from specially designed warehouses. This assembly line could outfit 10 galleons in just six hours.[48]

Scottish economist Adam Smith wrote 250 years ago about the advantages of job specialization. Smith described a small factory where 10 pin makers collectively produced as many as 48,000 pins per day because they performed specialized tasks, such as straightening, cutting, sharpening, grinding, and whitening the pins. In contrast, Smith explained that if these 10 people worked alone producing complete pins, they would collectively manufacture no more than 200 pins per day.[49]

scientific management The practice of systematically partitioning work into its smallest elements and standardizing tasks to achieve maximum efficiency.

Scientific Management   One of the strongest advocates of job specialization was Frederick Winslow Taylor, an American industrial engineer who introduced the principles of **scientific management** in the early 1900s.[50] Scientific management consists of a toolkit of activities. Some of these interventions—employee selection, training, goal setting, and work incentives—are common today but were rare until Taylor popularized them. However, scientific management is mainly associated with high levels of job specialization and standardization of tasks to achieve maximum efficiency.

According to Taylor, the most effective companies have detailed procedures and work practices developed by engineers, enforced by supervisors, and executed by employees. Even the supervisor's tasks should be divided: One person manages operational efficiency, another manages inspection, and another is the disciplinarian. Taylor and other industrial engineers demonstrated that scientific management significantly improves work efficiency. No doubt, some of the increased productivity can be credited to the training, goal setting, and work incentives, but job specialization quickly became popular in its own right.

Problems with Job Specialization   Frederick Taylor and his contemporaries focused on how job specialization reduces labour "waste" by improving the mechanical efficiency of work (i.e., matching skills, faster learning, less switchover time). Yet they didn't seem to notice how this extreme job specialization adversely affects employee attitudes and motivation. Some jobs—such as painting eyes on dolls—are so specialized that they soon become tedious, trivial, and socially isolating. Employee turnover and absenteeism tend to be higher in specialized jobs with very short time cycles. Companies sometimes have to pay higher wages to attract job applicants to this dissatisfying, narrowly defined work.[51]

Job specialization often reduces work quality because employees see only a small part of the process. As one observer of an automobile assembly line reports: "Often [employees] did not know how their jobs related to the total picture. Not knowing, there was no incentive to strive for quality—what did quality even mean as it related to a bracket whose function you did not understand?"[52]

Equally important, job specialization can undermine the motivational potential of jobs. As work becomes specialized, it tends to become easier to perform but less interesting. Work motivation increases (to a point) as jobs become more complex, but complex jobs also take much longer to master. Maximum job performance occurs somewhere between these two extremes, where most people can eventually perform the job tasks efficiently yet the work is interesting.

JOB DESIGN AND WORK MOTIVATION

LO4

Industrial engineers may have overlooked the motivational effect of job characteristics, but it is now the central focus of many job design changes. Organizational behaviour scholar Frederick Herzberg is credited with shifting the spotlight when he introduced **motivator-hygiene theory** in the 1950s.[53] Motivator-hygiene theory proposes that employees experience job satisfaction when they fulfill growth and esteem needs (called *motivators*) and they experience dissatisfaction when they have poor working conditions, job security, and other factors categorized as lower-order needs (called *hygienes*). Herzberg argued that only characteristics of the job itself motivates employees, whereas the hygiene factors merely prevent dissatisfaction. It might seem obvious to us today that the job itself is a source of motivation, but the concept was radical when Herzberg proposed the idea.

motivator-hygiene theory   Herzberg's theory stating that employees are primarily motivated by growth and esteem needs, not by lower-level needs.

Motivator-hygiene theory has been soundly rejected by research studies, but Herzberg's ideas generated new thinking about the motivational potential of the job itself.[54] Out of subsequent research emerged the **job characteristics model**, shown in Exhibit 6.2. The job characteristics model identifies five core job dimensions that produce three psychological states. Employees who experience these psychological states tend to have higher levels of internal work motivation (motivation from the work itself), job satisfaction (particularly satisfaction with the work itself), and work effectiveness.[55]

job characteristics model   A job design model that relates the motivational properties of jobs to specific personal and organizational consequences of those properties.

Core Job Characteristics   The job characteristics model identifies five core job characteristics. Under the right conditions, employees are more motivated and satisfied when jobs have higher levels of these characteristics:

skill variety   The extent to which employees must use different skills and talents to perform tasks within their jobs.

- *Skill variety.* **Skill variety** refers to the use of different skills and talents to perform tasks within their jobs. For example, sales clerks who normally only serve customers might be assigned the additional duties of stocking inventory and changing storefront displays.

task identity   The degree to which a job requires completion of a whole or an identifiable piece of work.

- *Task identity.* **Task identity** is the degree to which a job requires completion of a whole or identifiable piece of work, such as assembling an entire broadband modem rather than just soldering in the circuitry.

Exhibit 6.2 \   **THE JOB CHARACTERISTICS MODEL**

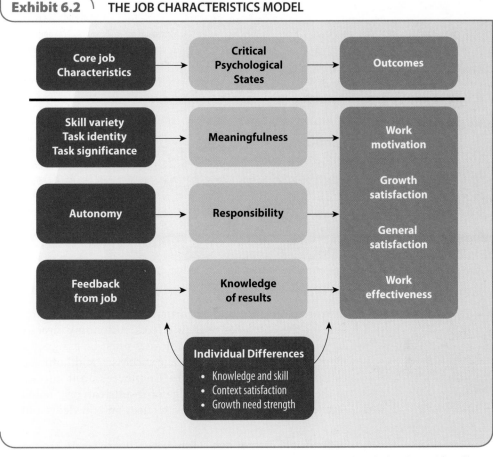

Source: J. R. Hackman and G. Oldham, *Work Redesign*, p. 90. Copyright © 1980 by Addison-Wesley Publishing Co., Inc. Adapted by permission of Pearson Education, Inc. Upper Saddle River, NJ.

<table>
<tr><td>

task significance The degree to which a job has a substantial impact on the organization and/or larger society.

</td><td>

- *Task significance.* **Task significance** is the degree to which a job affects the organization and/or larger society. It is an observable characteristic of a job (you can see how it benefits others) as well as a perceptual awareness. For instance, to make employees more aware of the task significance of their jobs, Rolls Royce Engine Services in Oakland, California invited customer representatives to talk to production staff about why the quality of these engines is important to them.

</td></tr>
<tr><td>

autonomy The degree to which a job gives employees the freedom, independence, and discretion to schedule their work and to determine the procedures used in completing it.

</td><td>

- *Autonomy.* Jobs with high levels of **autonomy** provide freedom, independence, and discretion in scheduling the work and in determining the procedures to be used to complete the work. In autonomous jobs, employees make their own decisions rather than relying on detailed instructions from supervisors or procedure manuals.

- *Job feedback.* Job feedback is the degree to which employees can tell how well they are doing on the basis of direct sensory information from the job itself. Airline pilots can tell how well they land their aircraft, and road crews can see how well they have prepared the roadbed and laid the asphalt.

</td></tr>
</table>

Critical Psychological States   The five core job characteristics affect employee motivation, satisfaction, and work effectiveness through three critical psychological states, shown in Exhibit 6.2. One of these psychological states is *experienced meaningfulness*—the belief that one's work is worthwhile or important. Skill variety, task identity, and task significance directly contribute to the job's meaningfulness. If the job has high levels of all three characteristics, employees are likely to feel that their jobs are highly meaningful. The meaningfulness of a job drops as one or more of these characteristics declines.

Work motivation and performance increase when employees feel personally accountable for the outcomes of their efforts. Autonomy directly contributes to this feeling of *experienced responsibility*. Employees must be assigned control of their work environment to feel responsible for their successes and failures. The third critical psychological state is *knowledge of results*. Employees want information about the consequences of their work effort. Knowledge of results can originate from co-workers, supervisors, or clients. However, job design focuses on knowledge of results from the work itself.

Individual Differences   Job design doesn't increase work motivation for everyone in every situation. Employees must have the required skills and knowledge to master the more challenging work. Otherwise, job design tends to increase stress and reduce job performance. The original model also suggests that increasing the motivational potential of jobs will not motivate employees who are dissatisfied with their work context (e.g., working conditions, job security) or who have a low growth-need strength. However, research findings have been mixed, suggesting that employees might be motivated by job design no matter how they feel about their job context or how high or low they score on growth needs.[57]

JOB DESIGN PRACTICES THAT MOTIVATE

Three main strategies can increase the motivational potential of jobs: job rotation, job enlargement, and job enrichment. This section also identifies several ways to implement job enrichment.

job rotation The practice of moving employees from one job to another.

Job Rotation   Most Chrysler assembly-line employees in Canada and the United States have a high degree of specialization. According to one estimate, these production workers have an average cycle time of about 65 seconds. Chrysler executives are aware of the motivational and physiological problems that this repetitive work can create, so they have introduced **job rotation**, whereby employees work in teams and rotate to a different workstation within that team every few hours. "The whole idea of job rotation makes a big difference," says one Chrysler executive. "The job naturally gets better, quality improves, throughput improves." Chrysler reported significant improvements in productivity and morale within the first year of its job rotation program. Job rotation offers "important ergonomic benefits to workers, improvements in product quality, and higher employee satisfaction," says a senior manager at Chrysler's plant in Toledo, Ohio.[58]

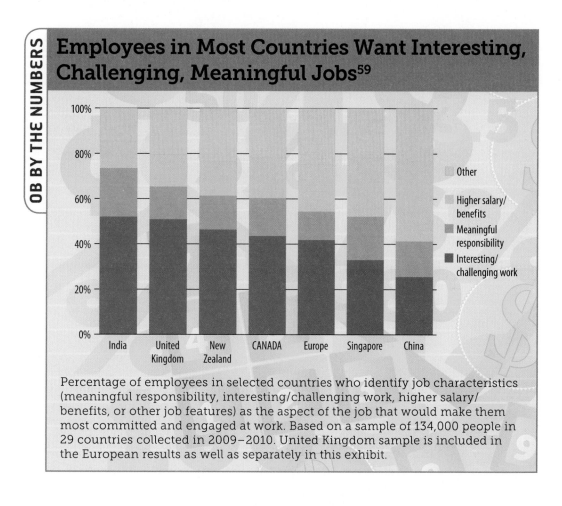

Employees in Most Countries Want Interesting, Challenging, Meaningful Jobs[59]

Percentage of employees in selected countries who identify job characteristics (meaningful responsibility, interesting/challenging work, higher salary/benefits, or other job features) as the aspect of the job that would make them most committed and engaged at work. Based on a sample of 134,000 people in 29 countries collected in 2009–2010. United Kingdom sample is included in the European results as well as separately in this exhibit.

From the experience at Chrysler and many other companies, we can identify three potential benefits of job rotation. First, it minimizes health risks from repetitive strain and heavy lifting because employees use different muscles and physical positions in the various jobs. Second, it supports multi-skilling (employees learn several jobs), which increases workforce flexibility in staffing the production process and in finding replacements for employees on vacation. A third benefit of job rotation is that it potentially reduces the boredom of highly repetitive jobs. However, organizational behaviour experts continue to debate whether job rotation really is a form of job redesign because the jobs remain the same; they are still highly specialized. Critics argue that job redesign requires changes within the job, such as job enlargement.

job enlargement The practice of adding more tasks to an existing job.

Job Enlargement   **Job enlargement** adds more tasks to an existing job. This might involve combining two or more complete jobs into one or just adding one or two more tasks to an existing job. Either way, skill variety increases because there are more tasks to perform. Video journalist is an example of an enlarged job. As Exhibit 6.3 illustrates, a traditional news team consists of a camera operator, a sound and lighting specialist, and the journalist who writes and presents or narrates the story. One video journalist performs all of these tasks.

Job enlargement significantly improves work efficiency and flexibility. However, research suggests that simply giving employees more tasks won't affect motivation, performance, or job satisfaction. These benefits result only when skill variety is combined with more autonomy and job knowledge.[60] In other words, employees are motivated when they perform a variety of tasks *and* have the freedom and knowledge to structure their work to achieve the highest satisfaction and performance. These job characteristics are at the heart of job enrichment.

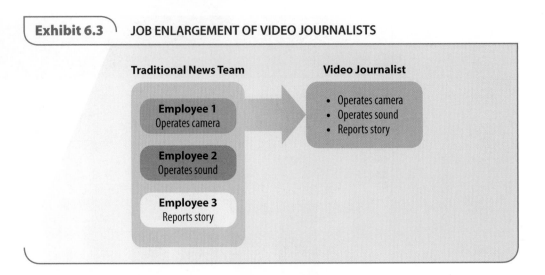

Exhibit 6.3   JOB ENLARGEMENT OF VIDEO JOURNALISTS

---

job enrichment The practice of giving employees more responsibility for scheduling, coordinating, and planning their own work.

Job Enrichment   **Job enrichment** occurs when employees are given more responsibility for scheduling, coordinating, and planning their own work.[61] Generally, people in enriched jobs experience higher job satisfaction and work motivation, along with lower absenteeism and turnover. Productivity is also higher when task identity and job feedback are improved. Product and service quality tend to improve because job enrichment increases the jobholder's felt responsibility and sense of ownership over the product or service.[62]

One way to increase job enrichment is by combining highly interdependent tasks into one job. This *natural grouping* approach is reflected in the video journalist job. Video journalist was earlier described as an enlarged job, but it is also an example of job enrichment because it naturally groups tasks together to complete an entire product (i.e., a news story). By forming natural work units, jobholders have stronger feelings of responsibility for an identifiable body of work. They feel a sense of ownership and, therefore, tend to increase job quality. Forming natural work units increases task identity and task significance because employees perform a complete product or service and can more readily see how their work affects others.

A second job enrichment strategy, called *establishing client relationships*, involves putting employees in direct contact with their clients rather than using the supervisor as a go-between. By being directly responsible for specific clients, employees have more information and can make decisions affecting those clients.[63] Establishing client relationships also increases task significance because employees see a line-of-sight connection between their work and consequences for customers. City Telecom in Hong Kong redesigned customer service jobs around customers for this reason. "We introduced a one-stop service for our customers," explains Ellis Ng, City Telecom's head of learning and development. "Each of our staff in the special duty unit (SDU) can handle all inquiries including sales, customer service, and simple troubleshooting. They are divided into small working units and serve a set number of customers so they have the chance to build a rapport and create a personalized service."[64]

Forming natural task groups and establishing client relationships are common ways to enrich jobs, but the heart of the job enrichment philosophy is to give employees more autonomy over their work. This basic idea is at the core of one of the most widely mentioned—and often misunderstood practices—empowerment.

EMPOWERMENT PRACTICES

L05

empowerment A psychological concept in which people experience more self-determination, meaning, competence, and impact regarding their role in the organization.

Fairmont Hotels and Resorts is one of the world's most respected hotel groups and is ranked as one of Canada's best places to work. One of the company's objectives is for employees to "turn moments into memories" for their guests, that is, for guests to have pleasant memorable experiences while staying at the hotel. Creating memories doesn't occur through command-and-control management. It demands that employees have sufficient discretion, skill, commitment, and identification with the organization's vision. In other words, Fairmont depends on the empowerment of its workforce to turn moments into memories. This feeling of empowerment also happens to be one of the company's core values.[66]

Fairmont Hotels and Resorts is a role model for organizations that want to nurture employee **empowerment**. Empowerment is a term that has been loosely tossed around in corporate circles and has been the subject of considerable debate among academics. However, the most widely accepted definition is that empowerment is a psychological concept represented by four dimensions: self-determination, meaning, competence, and impact of the individual's role in the organization.[67]

- *Self-determination.* Empowered employees feel that they have freedom, independence, and discretion over their work activities.
- *Meaning.* Employees who feel empowered care about their work and believe that what they do is important.
- *Competence.* Empowered people are confident about their ability to perform the work well and have a capacity to grow with new challenges.
- *Impact.* Empowered employees view themselves as active participants in the organization; that is, their decisions and actions have an influence on the company's success.

SUPPORTING EMPOWERMENT

Chances are that you have heard leaders say they are "empowering" the workforce. Yet empowerment is a state of mind, so what these executives really mean is that they are changing the work environment to support the feeling of empowerment.[68] Numerous individual, job design, and organizational or work-context factors support empowerment. At the individual level, employees must possess the necessary competencies to be able to perform the work as well as handle the additional decision-making requirements.[69] Job characteristics clearly influence the degree to which people feel

Empowering Handelsbanken

One of Europe's most successful banks doesn't believe in budgets or central-ized financial targets. Executives at Svenska Handelsbanken AB learned decades ago that these costly controls from the head office stifle rather than motivate employees. Instead, the Swedish bank gives its 10,000 employees and managers across 450 branches in 21 countries (mostly Nordic countries and the United King-dom) considerable autonomy to run the local branches as their own businesses. Branches have the freedom to prepare their own action plans as well as decide how to advertise products, how much to pay for property leases, how many staff to hire, and so forth. "The culture of our company is based on entrusting employees and allowing those who are closest to the customer and who know the customer best to make decisions," says a Handelsbanken's executive in Northern Britain. "Being empowered and having this trust leads to better decisions and higher satisfac-tion."[71] © Stuwdamdorp/Alamy

empowered.[70] Employees are much more likely to experience self-determination when working in jobs with a high degree of autonomy and minimal bureaucratic control. They experience more meaningfulness when working in jobs with high levels of task identity and task significance. They experience more self-confidence when working in jobs that allow them to receive feedback about their performance and accomplishments.

Several organizational and work-context factors also influence empowerment. Employees experience more empowerment in organizations where information and other resources are easily accessible. Empowerment also requires a learning orienta-tion culture. In other words, empowerment flourishes in organizations that appreciate the value of employee learning and that accept reasonable mistakes as a natural part of the learning process. Furthermore, as mentioned above in describing Handelsbanken, empowerment requires corporate leaders who trust employees and are willing to take the risks that empowerment creates."[72]

With the right individuals, job characteristics, and organizational environment, empow-erment can substantially improve motivation and performance. For instance, a study of bank employees concluded that empowerment improved customer service and tended to reduce conflict between employees and their supervisors. A study of nurses reported that empowerment is associated with higher trust in management, which ultimately influences job satisfaction, belief and acceptance of organizational goals and values, and effective orga-nizational commitment. Empowerment also tends to increase personal initiative because employees identify with and assume more psychological ownership of their work.[73]

SELF-LEADERSHIP PRACTICES

L06

What is the most important characteristic that companies look for in their employees? Leadership potential, ability to work in a team, and good communication skills are important, but they don't top the list in a survey of 800 British employers. Instead, the most important employee characteristic is self-motivation. Philip Deck can identify with these survey results. The chief executive officer of MKS, a Waterloo, Ontario, soft-ware developer, looks for people who can work effectively without supervision or other external sources of motivation and behaviour management. "We need a workforce that is highly intelligent, and self-motivated, and independent and creative," says Deck.[74]

self-leadership The process of influencing oneself to establish the self-direction and self-motivation needed to perform a task.

Most of the concepts introduced in this chapter and in Chapter 5 have assumed that leaders do things to motivate employees. Certainly, these theories and practices are valuable, but they overlook the fact that the most successful employees ultimately motivate and manage themselves. In other words, they engage in self-leadership. **Self-leadership** refers to the process of influencing oneself to establish the self-direction and self-motivation needed to perform a task.[75] This concept includes a toolkit of behav-ioural activities borrowed from social cognitive theory and goal setting. It also includes

Sonny Pham—Self-Leadership

Sonny Pham, entrepreneur and owner of Oodle Noodle restaurants has always had "oodles of optimism." After spending two years in Vietnam refugee camps, Sonny arrived in Canada and worked two jobs as he established himself. Sonny's positive and enthusiastic focus, hard work and "can-do" belief have been the foundation for the success of his quick service restaurants, Oodle Noodle, which have grown from one to four restaurants in Edmonton. He has attracted a loyal following of customers drawn to the fun atmosphere generated from motivated and long-term employees. For example, the Whyte Avenue location is famous for staff who can be seen dancing as they prepare the dishes. But Sonny envisions even bigger accomplishments ahead. He has set a specific and challenging goal to "reach 50 franchises across Western Canada." "I've been working at this for a long time, and I'm very excited about taking this next step," says Sonny.[76] *Candace Elliott, The Edmonton Journal*

constructive thought processes that have been extensively studied in sports psychology. Overall, self-leadership suggests that individuals mostly regulate their own actions through these behavioural and cognitive (thought) activities.

SELF-LEADERSHIP STRATEGIES

Although self-leadership consists of several processes, the five main activities are identified in Exhibit 6.4. These elements, which generally follow each other in a sequence, are personal goal setting, constructive thought patterns, designing natural rewards, self-monitoring, and self reinforcement.[77]

Personal Goal Setting   The first step in self-leadership is to set goals for your own work effort. This applies the ideas learned in Chapter 5 on goal setting, such as identifying goals that are specific, relevant, and challenging. The main difference is that self-leadership involves setting goals alone, rather than having them assigned by or jointly decided with a supervisor. Research suggests that employees are more focused and perform better when they set their own goals, particularly in combination with other self-leadership practices.[78] Personal goal setting also requires a high degree of self-awareness, because people need to understand their current behaviour and performance before establishing meaningful goals for personal development.

Constructive Thought Patterns   Before beginning a task and while performing it, employees should engage in positive (constructive) thoughts about that work and its accomplishment. In particular, employees are more motivated and better prepared to accomplish a task after they have engaged in positive self-talk and mental imagery.

> " Positive self-talk increases motivation by raising our self-efficacy and reducing anxiety about challenging tasks. "

self-talk The process of talking to ourselves about our own thoughts or actions.

Positive Self-talk.   Do you ever talk to yourself? Most of us do, according to a major study of Canadian university students.[79] **Self-talk** refers to any situation in which we talk to ourselves about our own thoughts or actions. The problem is that most self-talk is negative; we criticize much more than encourage or congratulate ourselves. Negative self-talk undermines our confidence and potential to perform a particular task. In contrast, positive self-talk creates a "can-do" belief and thereby increases motivation by raising our self-efficacy and reducing anxiety about challenging tasks.[80] We often hear that professional athletes "psyche" themselves up before an important event. They tell themselves that they can achieve their goal and that they have practised enough to reach that goal. They are motivating themselves through self-talk.

Exhibit 6.4   ELEMENTS OF SELF-LEADERSHIP

Personal goal setting → Constructive thought patterns → Designing natural rewards → Self-monitoring → Self-reinforcement

mental imagery The process of mentally practising a task and visualizing its successful completion.

Mental Imagery.   You've probably heard the phrase "I'll cross that bridge when I come to it!" Self-leadership takes the opposite view. It suggests that we need to mentally practise a task and imagine successfully performing it beforehand. This process, known as **mental imagery**, has two parts. One part involves mentally practising a task, anticipating obstacles to goal accomplishment, and working out solutions to those obstacles before they occur. By mentally walking through the activities required to accomplish a task, we begin to see problems that may occur. We can then imagine what responses would be best for each contingency.[81]

While one part of mental imagery helps us to anticipate things that could go wrong, the other part involves visualizing successful completion of a task. You might imagine the experience of completing a task and the positive results that follow, such as being promoted, receiving a prestigious award, or taking time off work. This visualization increases goal commitment and motivates people to complete a task effectively. This is the strategy that Tony Wang applies to motivate himself. "Since I am in sales, I think about the reward I get for closing new business—the commission cheque—and the things it will allow me to do that I really enjoy," explains Wang. "Or I think about the feeling I get when I am successful at something and how it makes me feel good, and use that to get me going."[82]

Designing Natural Rewards   Self-leadership recognizes that employees actively craft their jobs. To varying degrees, they can alter tasks and work relationships to make the work more motivating.[83] One way to build natural rewards into the job is to alter the way a task is accomplished. People often have enough discretion in their jobs to make slight changes to suit their needs and preferences. "In 28 years I do not think I have ever had a bad job—it is about the attitude that you bring to your work," says Steve Collier, National Australia Bank's General Manager of Sales & Distribution Services. "Self motivation has meant that even in tough times I have changed the job or changed the way I did it." Collier's advice seems to work; he was recently awarded top honours for best contact centre leader in the world.[84]

Self-Monitoring   Self-monitoring is the process of keeping track at regular intervals of one's progress toward a goal by using naturally occurring feedback. Some people can receive feedback from the job itself, such as members of a lawn maintenance crew who can see how they are improving the appearance of their client's property. But many of us are unable to observe our work output so readily. Instead, many people need to design feedback systems. Salespeople might arrange to receive weekly reports on sales levels in their territory. Production staff might have gauges or computer feedback systems installed so that they can see how many errors are made on the production line. Research suggests that people who have control over the timing of performance feedback perform their tasks better than do those with feedback assigned by others.[85]

Self-Reinforcement   Self-leadership includes engaging in *self-reinforcement*, which is part of social cognitive theory described in Chapter 5. Self-reinforcement occurs whenever an employee has control over a reinforcer but doesn't "take" the reinforcer until completing a self-set goal.[86] A common example is taking a break after reaching a predetermined stage of your work. The work break is a self-induced form of positive reinforcement. Self-reinforcement also occurs when you decide to do a more enjoyable task after completing a task that you dislike. For example, after slogging through a difficult report, you might decide to spend time doing a more pleasant task, such as catching up on industry news by scanning websites.

EFFECTIVENESS OF SELF-LEADERSHIP

Self-leadership is shaping up to be a valuable applied performance practice in organizational settings. A respectable body of research shows consistent support for most elements of self-leadership. Self-set goals and self-monitoring increased the frequency of wearing safety equipment among employees in a mining operation. Airline employees who received constructive thought training experienced better mental performance, enthusiasm, and job satisfaction than co-workers who did not receive this training. Mental imagery helped supervisors and process engineers in a pulp-and-paper mill to transfer what they learned in an interpersonal communication skills class back to the job.[87] Studies in Canada and elsewhere also indicate that constructive thought processes improve individual performance in cycling, hockey goaltending, ice skating, soccer, and other sports. Indeed, studies show that almost all Olympic athletes rely on mental rehearsal and positive self-talk to achieve their performance goals.[88]

SELF-LEADERSHIP CONTINGENCIES

As with most other forms of organizational behaviour, self-leadership is more or less likely to occur depending on the person and the situation. With respect to individual differences, preliminary research suggests that self-leadership behaviours are more frequently found in people with higher levels of conscientiousness and extroversion. Some writers also suggest that people with a positive self-concept evaluation (i.e., self-esteem, self-efficacy, and internal locus of control) are more likely to apply self-leadership strategies.[89]

Although the research is still sparse, the work environment also seems to influence the extent to which employees engage in self-leadership strategies. In particular, employees require some degree of autonomy to engage in some or most aspects of self-leadership. They probably also feel more confident with self-leadership when their boss is empowering rather than controlling and where there is a high degree of trust between them. Employees are also more likely to engage in self-monitoring in companies that emphasize continuous measurement of performance.[90] Overall, self-leadership promises to be an important concept and practice for improving employee motivation and performance.

CHAPTER SUMMARY

 LO1 Discuss the meaning of money and identify several individual, team, and organizational-level performance-based rewards.

Money (and other financial rewards) is a fundamental part of the employment relationship, but it also relates to our needs, our emotions, and our self-concept. It is viewed as a symbol of status and prestige, as a source of security, as a source of evil, or as a source of anxiety or feelings of inadequacy. Money is both a "tool" (instrument for acquiring other things) and a "drug" (addictive value in itself). People have a strong "money ethic" when they believe that money is not evil; that it is a symbol of achievement, respect, and power; and that it should be budgeted carefully. The meaning and value of money also varies between men and women and across cultures.

Organizations reward employees for their membership and seniority, job status, competencies, and performance. Membership-based rewards may attract job applicants and seniority-based rewards reduce turnover, but these reward objectives tend to discourage turnover among those with the lowest performance. Rewards based on job status try to maintain internal equity and motivate employees to compete for promotions. However, they tend to encourage a bureaucratic hierarchy, support status differences, and motivate employees to compete and hoard resources.

Competency-based rewards are becoming increasingly popular because they improve workforce flexibility and are consistent with the emerging idea of employability. However, they tend to be subjectively measured and can result in higher costs as employees spend more time learning new skills.

Awards and bonuses, commissions, and other individual performance-based rewards have existed for centuries and are widely used. Many companies are shifting to team-based rewards such as gainsharing plans and to organizational rewards such as employee share ownership plans (ESOPs), share options, and profit sharing. ESOPs and share options create an ownership culture, but employees often perceive a weak connection between individual performance and the organizational reward.

LO2 Describe five ways to improve reward effectiveness.

Financial rewards have a number of limitations, but reward effectiveness can be improved in several ways. Organizational leaders should ensure that rewards are linked to work performance, rewards are aligned with performance within the employee's control, team rewards are used where jobs are interdependent, rewards are valued by employees, and rewards have no unintended consequences.

L03 List the advantages and disadvantages of job specialization.

Job design is the process of assigning tasks to a job, including the interdependency of those tasks with other jobs. Job specialization subdivides work into separate jobs for different people. This increases work efficiency because employees master the tasks quickly, spend less time changing tasks, require less training, and can be matched more closely with the jobs best suited to their skills. However, job specialization may reduce work motivation, create mental health problems, lower product or service quality, and increase costs through discontentment, absenteeism, and turnover.

L04 Diagram the job characteristics model and describe three ways to improve employee motivation through job design.

The job characteristics model is a template for job redesign that specifies core job dimensions, psychological states, and individual differences. The five core job dimensions are skill variety, task identity, task significance, autonomy, and job feedback. Contemporary job design strategies try to motivate employees through job rotation, job enlargement, and job enrichment. Organizations introduce job rotation to reduce job boredom, develop a more flexible workforce, and reduce the incidence of repetitive strain injuries. Job enlargement involves increasing the number of tasks within the job. Two ways to enrich jobs are clustering tasks into natural groups and establishing client relationships.

L05 Define empowerment and identify strategies that support empowerment.

Empowerment is a psychological concept represented by four dimensions: self-determination, meaning, competence, and impact regarding the individual's role in the organization. Individual characteristics seem to have a minor influence on empowerment. Job design is a major influence, particularly autonomy, task identity, task significance, and job feedback. Empowerment is also supported at the organizational level through a learning orientation culture, sufficient information and resources, and corporate leaders who trust employees.

L06 Describe the five elements of self-leadership and identify specific personal and work environment influences on self-leadership.

Self-leadership is the process of influencing oneself to establish the self-direction and self-motivation needed to perform a task. This includes personal goal setting, constructive thought patterns, designing natural rewards, self-monitoring, and self-reinforcement. Constructive thought patterns include self-talk and mental imagery. Self-talk occurs in any situation in which a person talks to himself or herself about his or her own thoughts or actions. Mental imagery involves mentally practising a task and imagining successfully performing it beforehand. People with higher levels of conscientiousness, extroversion, and a positive self-concept are more likely to apply self-leadership strategies. It also increases in workplaces that support empowerment and have high trust between employees and management.

KEY TERMS

autonomy, p. 165

employee share ownership plans (ESOPs), p. 159

empowerment, p. 169

gainsharing plans, p. 159

job characteristics model, p. 164

job design, p. 161

job enlargement, p. 167

job enrichment, p. 168

job evaluation, p. 157

job rotation, p. 166

job specialization, p. 163

mental imagery, p. 172

motivator-hygiene theory, p. 164

profit-sharing plans, p. 159

scientific management, p. 163

self-leadership, p. 170

self-talk, p. 171

share options, p. 159

skill variety, p. 164

task identity, p. 164

task significance, p. 165

CRITICAL-THINKING QUESTIONS

1. As a consultant, you have been asked to recommend either a gainsharing plan or a profit-sharing plan for employees who work in the four regional distribution and warehousing facilities of a large retail organization. Which reward system would you recommend? Explain your answer.

2. You are a member of a team responsible for developing a reward system for your college or university faculty unit. Assume that the faculty is nonprofit, so profit sharing is not an option. What other team or organization-level rewards might work in this situation? Describe specific measures that could be used to calculate the amount of bonus.

3. Okanagan Tire Corporation redesigned its production facilities around a team-based system. However, the company president believes that employees will not be motivated unless they receive incentives based on their individual performance. Give three explanations why Okanagan Tire should introduce team-based rather than individual rewards in this setting.

4. What can organizations do to increase the effectiveness of financial rewards?

5. Most of us have watched pizzas being made while waiting in a pizzeria. What level of job specialization do you usually notice in these operations? Why does this high or low level of specialization exist? If some pizzerias have different levels of specialization than others, identify the contingencies that might explain these differences.

6. Can a manager or supervisor "empower" an employee? Discuss fully.

7. Describe a time when you practised self-leadership to successfully perform a task. With reference to each step in the self-leadership process, describe what you did to achieve this success.

8. Can self-leadership replace formal leadership in an organizational setting?

 CASE STUDY 6.1

YakkaTech Ltd.

By Steven L. McShane, The University of Western Australia

YakkaTech Ltd. is an information technology services firm employing 1,500 people across Canada. YakkaTech has a consulting division, which mainly installs and upgrades enterprise software systems and related hardware on the client's site. YakkaTech also has a customer service division, which consists of four customer contact centres serving clients within each region.

Each customer contact centre consists of a half-dozen departments representing functional specializations (computer systems, intranet infrastructure, storage systems, enterprise software systems, customer billing, etc.). These centres typically have more than two dozen employees in each department. When a client submits a problem to the centre by email or telephone, the message or call is directed to the department where the issue best applies. The query is given a "ticket" number and is assigned to the next available employee in that department. Individual employees are solely responsible for the tickets assigned to them. The employee investigates and corrects the issue, and the ticket is "closed" when the problem has been resolved. If the client experiences the same problem again, even a few days later, a new ticket is issued and sent to whichever employee is available to receive the ticket. A client's problems are almost always handled by different employees each time, even when the issue is sent to the same department. Furthermore, when a customer centre department is heavily backlogged, clients are redirected to the same department at another regional centre where their problem can be addressed more quickly.

At one time, YakkaTech operated more than a dozen small customer contact centres in each city because client problems had to be diagnosed and resolved on-site. Today, employees can investigate most software and hardware system faults from the centre through remote monitoring systems, rather than personally visit the client. Consequently, eight years ago, YakkaTech amalgamated its customer service operations into four large regional centres. Customer service staff work entirely within the centre. When a client visit is required, the ticket is transferred to an individual or team in the consulting business, who then visits the client.

YakkaTech's customer service business has nearly doubled over the past five years, but with this growth has come increasing customer complaints regarding poor quality service. Many say that employees seem indifferent to the client's problems. Others have commented on the slow response to their problems where the issue requires involvement of more than one department. Several clients have also complained that they are continually educating YakkaTech's customer service employees about details of their unique IT systems infrastructure.

Another concern is that until 18 months ago, YakkaTech's voluntary employee turnover rates in the contact centres had risen above the industry average. This increased labour costs due to the cost of recruiting new technical staff as well as lower productivity of new employees. According to results of an employee survey two years ago (as well as informal comments since then), many employees felt that their work is monotonous. Some also said that they felt disconnected from the consequences of their work. A few also complained about ongoing conflicts with people in other departments and the stress of serving dissatisfied clients.

Eighteen months ago, YakkaTech's executive team decided to raise pay rates for its customer service staff to become among the highest in the industry. The assumption was that the high pay rates would improve morale and reduce turnover, thereby reducing hiring costs and improving productivity. In addition, YakkaTech introduced a vested profit-sharing plan, in which employees received the profit-sharing bonus only if they remained with the company for two years after the bonus was awarded. Employees who quit or were fired for just cause before the vesting period forfeited the bonus.

Employee turnover rates dropped dramatically, so the executive team concluded that customer service quality and productivity would improve. Instead, customer complaints and productivity remain below expectations and, in some cases, have worsened. Experienced employees continue to complain about the work. There are a few disturbing incidents where employees are careless at solving client problems or do not bother to forward tickets that belong in another department. Employee referrals (where staff recommend friends to join the company) have become rare events, whereas at one time they represented a significant source of qualified job applicants. Furthermore, a few executives have recently overheard employees say that they would like to work elsewhere but can't afford to leave YakkaTech.

Discussion Questions   1. What symptom(s) in this case suggest that something has gone wrong?

2. What are the main causes of these symptoms?

3. What actions should YakkaTech executives take to correct these problems?

 CASE STUDY 6.2

And the Award for Best Commercial Goes To. . .

As the Canadian subsidiary of one of the world's largest consumer products companies, Procter & Gamble (P&G) Canada is continually on the lookout for the best ways to motivate its staff. One of these motivational highlights is the company's in-house awards night, in which P&G Canada's 100 marketing staff vie for 10 Canadian Business Building Marketing Awards—three for individual excellence and seven for team execution. The team awards include best initiative, best overall marketing plan, best product innovation, best marketing innovation, best turnaround brand, best test-and-learn (i.e., best learning either from success or failure), and best search-and-reapply (in which marketing from another country is applied successfully in Canada).

"Our objectives were to inspire, celebrate, and reward the organization," says Chris Laird, P&G Canada's associate marketing director of fabric and home care, who coordinated the most recent awards event. Laird and other associate marketing directors screened more than 60 marketing projects across the company's many brands, including Tide, Pampers, Swiffer, Crest, Gillette, Pringles, and Pantene. Eventually, they formed a list of three or four nominees for each of the 10 categories.

The three individual winners were chosen by a nine-member team of senior marketers. The seven team category winners, on the other hand, were determined during the awards night based on votes from the audience, which include P&G Canada marketing staff, nearly three dozen agency partners, and numerous senior executives from P&G's Canadian and global headquarters. Voting via text message, the audience mainly took into account each project's business results (share growth and return on investment). However, they were also treated to two-minute video presentations that each shortlisted team created with their agencies over the previous two months to showcase their project during the awards event.

"The winners just get the glory and a statue, but it's a pretty big deal," Laird emphasizes. "It's really our one shot a year to get the whole marketing organization together outside of the typical training sessions and celebrate the great work that's been done." Laird adds that these awards motivate staff to be more innovative. "It's a big company that can at times be siloed, and the awards are a great way to share and reapply and get everybody's creative juices going."

Source: Adapted from Mary Dickie, "The (Real) Best Work of the Year," *Strategy*, January 2, 2008, p. 14.

Discussion Questions

1. In what ways would Procter & Gamble Canada's awards event likely improve the organization's effectiveness?

2. Evaluate P&G's awards event against the five strategies for improving reward effectiveness.

 TEAM EXERCISE 6.3

Is Student Work Enriched?

Purpose   This exercise is designed to help you learn how to measure the motivational potential of jobs and evaluate the extent that jobs should be further enriched.

Instructions (Small Class)   Being a student is like a job in several ways. You have tasks to perform, and someone (such as your instructor) oversees your work. Although few people want to be students most of their lives (the pay rate is too low!), it may be interesting to determine how enriched your job is as a student.

1. Students are placed into teams (preferably four or five people).

2. Working alone, each student completes both sets of measures in this exercise. Then, using the guidelines below, each student individually calculates the score for the five core job characteristics as well as the overall motivating-potential score for the job.

3. Members of each team compare their individual results. The group should identify differences of opinion for each core job characteristic. They should also note which core job characteristics have the lowest scores and recommend how these scores could be increased.

4. The entire class will then meet to discuss the results of the exercise. The instructor may ask some teams to present their comparisons and recommendations for a particular core job characteristic.

Instructions (Large Class)

1. Working alone, each student completes both sets of measures in this exercise. Then, using the guidelines below, each student individually calculates the score for the five core job characteristics as well as the overall motivating-potential score for the job.

2. Using a show of hands or classroom technology, students indicate their results for each core job characteristic. The instructor will ask for results for several bands across the range of the scales. Alternatively, students can complete this activity prior to class and submit their results through online classroom technology. Later, the instructor will provide feedback to the class showing the collective results (i.e., distribution of results across the range of scores).

3. Where possible, the instructor might ask students with very high or very low results to discuss their views with the class.

Job Diagnostic Survey

Circle the number on the right that best describes student work.	Very Little		Moderately			Very Much	
1. To what extent does student work permit you to decide on your own how to go about doing the work?	1	2	3	4	5	6	7
2. To what extent does student work involve doing a whole or identifiable piece of work, rather than a small portion of the overall work process?	1	2	3	4	5	6	7
3. To what extent does student work require you to do many different things, using a variety of your skills and talents?	1	2	3	4	5	6	7
4. To what extent are the results of your work as a student likely to significantly affect the lives and well-being of other people (e.g., within your school, your family, society)?	1	2	3	4	5	6	7
5. To what extent does working on student activities provide information about your performance?	1	2	3	4	5	6	7

Circle the number on the right that best describes student work.	Very Inaccurate		Uncertain			Very Accurate	
6. Being a student requires me to use a number of complex and high-level skills.	1	2	3	4	5	6	7
7. Student work is arranged so that I do *not* have the chance to do an entire piece of work from beginning to end.	7	6	5	4	3	2	1
8. Doing the work required of students provides many chances for me to figure out how well I am doing.	1	2	3	4	5	6	7
9. The work students must do is quite simple and repetitive.	7	6	5	4	3	2	1
10. The work of a student is the type where a lot of other people can be affected by how well the work gets done.	1	2	3	4	5	6	7
11. Student work denies me any chance to use my personal initiative or judgment in carrying out the work.	7	6	5	4	3	2	1
12. Student work provides me the chance to completely finish the pieces of work I begin.	1	2	3	4	5	6	7
13. Doing student work by itself provides very few clues about whether I am performing well.	7	6	5	4	3	2	1
14. As a student, I have considerable opportunity for independence and freedom in how I do the work.	1	2	3	4	5	6	7
15. The work I perform as a student is *not* very significant or important in the broader scheme of things.	7	6	5	4	3	2	1

Source: Adapted from the Job Diagnostic Survey, developed by J. R. Hackman and G. R. Oldham. The authors have released any copyright ownership of this scale (see J. R. Hackman and G. Oldham, *Work Redesign* (Reading, MA: Addison-Wesley, 1980), p. 275).

Calculating The Motivating-Potential Score

Scoring Core Job Characteristics: Use the following set of calculations to estimate the motivating-potential score for the job of being a student. Use your answers from the Job Diagnostic Survey that you completed above.

Skill Variety (SV) $\dfrac{\text{Questions } 3 + 6 + 9}{3} = \underline{\hspace{1cm}}$ *Autonomy* $\dfrac{\text{Questions } 1 + 11 + 14}{3} = \underline{\hspace{1cm}}$

Task Identity (TI) $\dfrac{\text{Questions } 2 + 7 + 12}{3} = \underline{\hspace{1cm}}$ *Job Feedback* $\dfrac{\text{Questions } 5 + 8 + 13}{3} = \underline{\hspace{1cm}}$

Task Significance (TS) $\dfrac{\text{Questions } 4 + 10 + 15}{3} = \underline{\hspace{1cm}}$

Calculating Motivating-Potential Score (MPS): Use the following formula and the results above to calculate the motivating-potential score. Notice that skill variety, task identity, and task significance are averaged before being multiplied by the score for autonomy and job feedback.

$$\left(\frac{SV + TI + TS}{3}\right) \times \text{Autonomy} \times \text{Job Feedback}$$

$$\left(\frac{\underline{\hspace{1cm}} + \underline{\hspace{1cm}} + \underline{\hspace{1cm}}}{3}\right) + \underline{\hspace{1cm}} + \underline{\hspace{1cm}} = \underline{\hspace{1cm}}$$

Go to CONNECT to complete the following interactive self-assessments.

 SELF-ASSESSMENT EXERCISE 6.4

What is Your Attitude Toward Money?

Purpose   This exercise is designed to help you understand the types of attitudes toward money and assess your attitude toward money.

Instructions   Read each of the statements below and circle the response that you believe best reflects your position regarding each statement. Then use the scoring key in Appendix B at the end of the book to calculate your results. This exercise should be completed alone so that you can assess yourself honestly without concerns of social comparison. Class discussion will focus on the meaning of money, including the dimensions measured here and other aspects of money that may have an influence on behaviour in the workplace.

Money Attitude Scale					
To what extent do you agree or disagree that...	Strongly Agree	Agree	Neutral	Disagree	Strongly Disagree
1. I sometimes purchase things because I know they will impress other people.	5	4	3	2	1
2. I regularly put money aside for the future.	5	4	3	2	1
3. I tend to get worried about decisions involving money.	5	4	3	2	1
4. I believe that financial wealth is one of the most important signs of a person's success.	5	4	3	2	1
5. I keep a close watch on how much money I have.	5	4	3	2	1
6. I feel nervous when I don't have enough money.	5	4	3	2	1
7. I tend to show more respect to people who are wealthier than I am.	5	4	3	2	1
8. I follow a careful financial budget.	5	4	3	2	1
9. I worry about being financially secure.	5	4	3	2	1
10. I sometimes boast about my financial wealth or how much money I make.	5	4	3	2	1
11. I keep track of my investments and financial wealth.	5	4	3	2	1
12. I usually say "I can't afford it," even when I can afford something.	5	4	3	2	1

Sources: Adapted from J. A. Roberts and C. J. Sepulveda, "Demographics and Money Attitudes: A Test of Yamauchi and Templer's (1982) Money Attitude Scale in Mexico," *Personality and Individual Differences* 27 (July 1999), pp. 19–35; K. Yamauchi and D. Templer, "The Development of a Money Attitudes Scale," *Journal of Personality Assessment* 46 (1982), pp. 522–528.

 SELF-ASSESSMENT EXERCISE 6.5

How Well Do You Practise Self-Leadership?

This exercise is designed to help you understand self-leadership concepts and assess your self-leadership tendencies. Self-leadership is the process of influencing oneself to establish the self-direction and self-motivation needed to perform a task. Indicate the extent to which each statement in this instrument describes you very well or does not describe you at all. Complete each item honestly to get the best estimate of your score on each self-leadership dimension.

 SELF-ASSESSMENT EXERCISE 6.6

Are You Empowered As a Student?

Empowerment is a concept that applies to people in a variety of situations. This instrument is specifically adapted to your position as a student at this college or university. Indicate the extent to which you agree or disagree with each statement in this instrument; then request the results, which provide an overall score as well as scores on each of the four dimensions of empowerment. Complete each item honestly to get the best estimate of your level of empowerment.

 Practise and learn online with Connect. Connect resources include additional and interactive study exercises, videos, and practice quizzing, as well as additional material you won't find in the printed text.

Decision Making and Creativity

After reading this chapter, you should be able to:

LO1 Describe the rational choice paradigm.

LO2 Explain why people refrain from applying the rational choice paradigm when identifying problems/opportunities, evaluating/choosing alternatives, and evaluating decision outcomes.

LO3 Discuss the roles of emotions and intuition in decision making.

LO4 Describe employee characteristics, workplace conditions, and specific activities that support creativity.

LO5 Describe the benefits of employee involvement and identify four contingencies that affect the optimal level of employee involvement.

BP's blown out deep-sea Macondo well, subsequent explosion, and fire on the Deepwater Horizon drilling platform in the Gulf of Mexico killed 11 workers and caused one of the most devastating oil spills in history.

BP investigators concluded a "complex and interlinked series of mechanical failures, human judgments, engineering design, operational implementation and team interfaces came together to allow the initiation and escalation of the accident."

During the months of media reports and hearings, BP's deep water drilling engineer, John Guide has emerged as one of the critical decision makers in BP's deep-water drilling operations. Guide was "in charge of vetting each step in the drilling process" aboard the Deepwater Horizon rig.

Just four days before the explosion, Guide issued an email that overruled recommendations from a BP engineer and a Halliburton technician to more than triple the number of centralizers used to keep the drilling pipe centred in the well while the cement casing was being installed. Halliburton's report to BP warned that failure to use more centralizers would leave the well susceptible to "severe gas flow potential."

But despite accepting some responsibility, BP continued to point the finger at Transocean Ltd., the company that BP leased the drilling platform from and oil services giant, Halliburton, which cemented the well. "Over a 40-minute period, the Transocean rig crew failed to recognize and act on the influx of hydrocarbons into the well," BP said.

Halliburton's vice-president of cementing, Thomas Roth, disputed BP's allegation that his company's casing of the well was improperly done. Roth told investigators that "BP's well design and operational decisions compromised well integrity" and BP workers ignored "multiple red flags" that the well was improperly sealed and that natural gas could escape. When asked why Halliburton didn't take a decisive role in demanding that operations be suspended, Roth explained that although the drilling operation was "challenging," BP had "ultimate decision responsibility."

David Sims, BP's drilling and completion operations manager who had only been on the job for 18 days before the disaster, explained other factors that may have contributed to problems going undetected. "BP workers were struggling with converting to an electronic system from paper," and "reorganization of the engineering unit also led to confusion about who was an approver and who was a reviewer during the decision-making process." Critics have also suggested that BP's incentive system encouraged managers to put cost-cutting shortcuts ahead of safety.[1]

Reports blame the devastating rig blast and Gulf oil spill on bad decision making by BP and its contractors. *USCG/Landov*

BP's oil rig disaster in the Gulf of Mexico reveals the complexities, ambiguities, and importance of decision making in organizations. All businesses, governments, and not-for-profit agencies depend on employees to foresee and correctly identify problems, to survey alternatives and pick the best one based on a variety of stakeholder interests, and to execute those decisions effectively. Decision making is such a vital function for an organization's health that it might be equated with the importance of breathing to a human being. Indeed, great leaders typically resuscitate organizations by encouraging and teaching employees at all levels to make decisions more efficiently and effectively.

> **decision making** The conscious process of making choices among alternatives with the intention of moving toward some desired state of affairs.

Decision making is the conscious process of making choices among alternatives with the intention of moving toward some desired state of affairs.[2] The decision making process can be viewed from three paradigms, and this chapter investigates all three of them. The chapter begins by outlining the rational choice paradigm of decision making. Next, the limitations of this paradigm are discussed, including the human limitation of rational choice. We also examine the emerging paradigm that decisions consist of a complex interaction of logic and emotion. The latter part of this chapter focuses on two activities that are found in most decisions: creativity and employee involvement. We present these topics separately rather than within any stage of decision making because they deserve more detailed inspection and, in the case of creativity, because it occurs throughout the decision making process.

RATIONAL CHOICE PARADIGM OF DECISION MAKING

LO1

How should people make decisions in organizations? Most business leaders would likely answer this question by saying that effective decision making involves identifying, selecting, and applying the best possible alternative. In other words, the best decisions use pure logic and all available information to choose the alternative with the highest value—such as highest expected profitability, customer satisfaction, employee well-being, or some combination of these outcomes. These decisions sometimes involve complex calculations of data to produce a formula that points to the best choice.

> **rational choice paradigm** The view in decision making that people should—and typically do—use logic and all available information to choose the alternative with the highest value.

In its extreme form, this calculative view of decision making represents the **rational choice paradigm**, which has dominated decision making philosophy in Western societies for most of written history.[3] It was established 2,500 years ago when Plato and his contemporaries in ancient Greece raised logical debate and reasoning to a fine art. A few centuries later, Greek and Roman Stoics insisted that one should always "follow where reason leads" rather than fall victim to passion and emotions. About 400 years ago, Descartes and other European philosophers emphasized that the ability to make logical decisions is one of the most important accomplishments of human beings. In the 1700s, Scottish philosophers proposed that the best choice is the one that offers the "greatest good for the greatest number." This eventually evolved into the ethical principle of utilitarianism (described in Chapter 2), as well as maximization, which is at the heart of contemporary economics. By the 1900s, social scientists and mathematicians had developed elegant rational choice models and formulae that are now embedded in operations research, economics, and other decision sciences.

> **subjective expected utility** The probability (expectation) of satisfaction (utility) resulting from choosing a specific alternative in a decision.

The ultimate principle of the rational choice paradigm is to choose the alternative with the highest **subjective expected utility**.[4] Subjective expected utility is the probability (expectation) of satisfaction (utility) for each specific alternative in a decision. Rational choice assumes that decision makers naturally select the alternative that offers the greatest level of happiness (i.e., maximization), such as highest returns for stockholders and highest satisfaction for customers, employees, government, and other stakeholders. The maximum subjective expected utility depends on the value (utility) of outcomes resulting from that choice and the probability of those outcomes occurring.

Consider the role of subjective expected utility in BP's decision not to triple the number of centralizers, as Halliburton experts had recommended (see the opening vignette to this chapter). BP's executives undoubtedly knew that failure of the cement casing would have disastrous consequences (i.e., a high negative utility). However, they likely believed the probability of a cement casing failure was so low that installing more centralizers was unnecessary. At the same time, centralizers are expensive and might take more time to install; both of these outcomes (cost and delays) are negative outcomes and have high probabilities (i.e., installing more centralizers will almost certainly cost more and delay the project). The key point from this example is that all decisions rely to some degree on (a) the expected value of the outcomes (utility) and (b) the probability of those good or bad outcomes occurring (expectancy).

RATIONAL CHOICE DECISION MAKING PROCESS

Along with the principle of making decisions based on subjective expected utility, the rational choice paradigm assumes that decision makers follow the systematic process illustrated in Exhibit 7.1.[5] The first step is to identify the problem or recognize an opportunity. A *problem* is a deviation between the current and the desired situation—the gap between "what is" and "what ought to be." This deviation is a symptom of more fundamental causes that need to be corrected.[6] An *opportunity* is a deviation between current expectations and a potentially better situation that was not previously expected. In other words, decision makers realize that some decisions may produce results beyond current goals or expectations.

The second step involves deciding how to decide; that is, what processes to apply to make the decision.[7] One issue is whether the decision maker has enough information or needs to involve others in the process. Later in this chapter, we'll examine the contingencies of employee involvement in the decision. Another issue is whether the decision is programmed or nonprogrammed. *Programmed decisions* follow standard operating procedures; they have been resolved in the past, so the optimal solution has already been identified and documented. In contrast, *nonprogrammed decisions* require all steps in the decision model because the problems are new, complex, or ill-defined. The third step is to discover and develop a list of possible solutions. This usually begins by searching for ready-made solutions, such as practices that have worked well on

Exhibit 7.1   RATIONAL CHOICE DECISION MAKING PROCESS

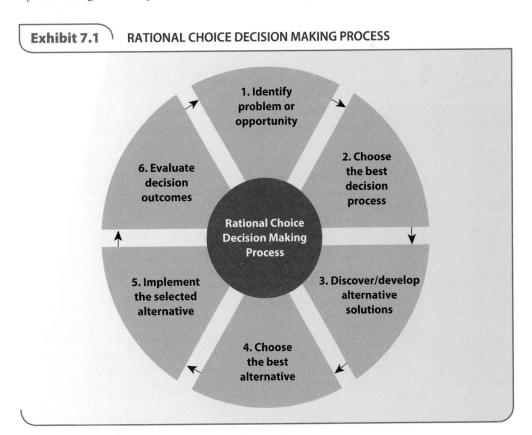

similar problems. If an acceptable solution cannot be found, then decision makers need to design a custom-made solution or modify an existing one.

The fourth step in the rational choice decision process is to choose the alternative with the highest subjective expected utility. This calls for all possible information about all possible alternatives and their outcomes, but the rational choice paradigm assumes this can be accomplished with ease. The fifth step in the rational choice decision process is to implement the selected alternative. Rational choice experts have little to say about this step because they assume implementation occurs without any problems. This is followed by the sixth step, evaluating whether the gap has narrowed between "what is" and "what ought to be." Ideally, this information should come from systematic benchmarks so that relevant feedback is objective and easily observed.

PROBLEMS WITH THE RATIONAL CHOICE PARADIGM

The rational choice paradigm seems so logical, yet it is impossible to apply in reality. One reason is that the model assumes people are efficient and logical information processing machines. In reality, people have difficulty recognizing problems; they cannot (or will not) simultaneously process the huge volume of information needed to identify the best solution; and they have difficulty recognizing when their choices have failed. The second reason why the rational model doesn't fit reality is that it focuses on logical thinking and completely ignores the fact that emotions also influence—perhaps even dominate—the decision making process. As we shall discover in this chapter, emotions both support and interfere with our quest to make better decisions.[8] With these points in mind, let's look again at each step in the rational choice decision making process, but with more detail about what really happens.

> " The rational choice paradigm seems so logical, yet it is impossible to apply in reality. "

IDENTIFYING PROBLEMS AND OPPORTUNITIES

When Albert Einstein was asked how he would save the world in one hour, he replied that the first 55 minutes should be spent defining the problem and the last 5 minutes solving it.[9] Einstein's point is that problem identification is not just the first step in decision making; it is arguably the most important step. But problems and opportunities are not clearly labelled objects that magically appear on our desks or computer screens. Instead, they are conclusions that we form from ambiguous and conflicting information.[10]

PROBLEMS WITH PROBLEM IDENTIFICATION

The problem identification stage is, itself, filled with problems. Below are five of the most widely recognized concerns.[11]

Stakeholder Framing   Employees, suppliers, customers, and other stakeholders have vested interests when bringing good or bad news to corporate decision makers. Often unwittingly, they filter information to amplify or suppress the seriousness of the situation. By framing the situation, stakeholders throw a spotlight on specific causes of the symptoms and away from other possible causes. Stakeholders also frame problems in ways that raise the value of resources they can provide to help the organization solve those problems.

Decision makers easily fall prey to these constructed realities because it is challenging for any individual or small executive team to make sense of the overwhelming volume of complex and often ambiguous information in the external environment. Consequently, as one popular management theory emphasizes, organizational decisions and actions are influenced mainly by what attracts management's attention, rather than by what is truly important in the external or internal environment.[12] This attention process is subject to a variety of cognitive biases, such as the decision maker's perceptual process, specific circumstances, and (as mentioned) the ways that stakeholders shape or filter incoming information.

Mental Models   Even if stakeholders don't frame information, our mind creates its own framing through preconceived mental models. Mental models are visual or relational images in our mind of the external world; they fill in information that we don't immediately see, which helps us understand and navigate in our surrounding environment (see Chapter 3). Many mental images are also prototypes—they represent models of how things should be. Unfortunately, these mental models also blind us from seeing unique problems or opportunities because they produce a negative evaluation of things that are dissimilar to the mental model. If an idea doesn't fit the existing mental model of how things should work, then it is quickly dismissed as unworkable or undesirable. Examples of missed opportunities and mistaken problems dot the corporate landscape, as Global Connections 7.1 illustrates.

Decisive Leadership   According to various studies, employees believe that decisiveness is a characteristic of effective leaders.[13] Being decisive includes quickly forming an opinion of whether an event signals a problem or opportunity. Consequently, eager to look effective, many leaders quickly announce problems or opportunities before having a chance to logically assess the situation. The result, according to research, is more often a poorer decision than would result if more time had been devoted to identifying the problem and evaluating the alternatives.

Solution-Focused Problems   Decision makers have a tendency to define problems as veiled solutions.[14] For instance, someone might say: "The problem is that we need more control over our suppliers." This statement doesn't describe the problem; it is really a slightly rephrased presentation of a solution to an ill-defined problem. Decision makers engage in solution-focused problem identification because it provides comforting closure to the otherwise ambiguous and uncertain nature of problems. People with a strong need for cognitive closure (those who feel uncomfortable with ambiguity) are particularly prone to solution-focused problems. Some decision makers take this solution focus a step further by seeing all problems as solutions that have worked well for them in the past, even though they were applied under different circumstances. As Abraham Maslow once quipped, "When the only tool you have is a hammer, all problems begin to resemble nails."[15] Again, the familiarity of past solutions makes the current problem less ambiguous or uncertain.

Perceptual Defence   People sometimes block out bad news as a coping mechanism. Their brain refuses to see information that threatens their self-concept. This phenomenon is not true for everyone. Some people inherently overlook negative information, whereas others are more aware of it. Recent studies also report that people are more likely to disregard danger signals when they have limited control over the situation.[16]

For example, an investigation of the space shuttle *Columbia* disaster in 2003 revealed that NASA managers were in denial that the shuttle and its seven crew members were in trouble. NASA management almost immediately rejected a proposal by a team of engineers to have military satellites take photos of Columbia's exterior to determine if any damage was visible. Managers also criticized tests suggesting that damage could have occurred, yet quickly accepted a faulty test indicating that the shuttle was in trouble. In one meeting, *Columbia*'s lead flight director candidly admitted: "I don't think there is much we can do, so you know it's not really a factor during the flight because there isn't much we can do about it."[17]

CONNECTIONS 7.1

GLOBAL

Famous Missed Opportunities

Mental models create road maps that guide our decisions. Unfortunately, these maps also potentially block our ability to see emerging problems and opportunities. Here are a few famous examples:

- Even though Harry Potter books were becoming the world's best sellers, Hollywood filmmakers were reluctant to produce film versions unless the Hogwarts School of Witchcraft was set in the United States or, at least, that Harry was an American at the British academy. Some filmmakers insisted that all the main characters had to be Americans for the films to have any degree of success. Fortunately, after considerable persuasion, Hollywood decision makers reluctantly agreed to keep the location and characters all British.[18]

- The late Thomas Bata, who rebuilt Bata Ltd. from Toronto into the world's largest shoemaker, acknowledged that preconceived mental models caused a famous missed opportunity. Bata decided against investing in an upstart running shoe company that approached him because he didn't know the owner and thought Bata could build its own running shoe business. The upstart was Reebok International Ltd., which subsequently gained considerable success in sports footwear and is now owned by Adidas Group. Bata was never able to grow market share in this highly profitable sector of the footwear business.[19]

- One of the most famous commercials in history—the Apple Macintosh "1984" ad—almost never got aired because the computer maker's external board members thought it was the worst commercial they had ever seen. They complained that the commercial mentioned the product and company only in the last few seconds. The company asked the creative agency that produced the commercials to sell the two Super Bowl time slots where they would have been shown, but the agency's CEO claimed that he could not find a buyer for the 60-second slot. The single 60-second ad shown during the Super Bowl became one of the top news stories over the next week and has since been rated as the best commercial in history. Apple's board members subsequently apologized for their misjudgment of the "1984" commercial and applauded the Macintosh team for a successful launch.[20]

Due to their preconceived mental models of a successful film, Hollywood filmmakers were reluctant to produce Harry Potter films unless they had an American location and characters. They believed the films would fail if they emphasized the British culture apparent in the books. © *Warner Bros./Courtesy Everett Collection*

- Graphical user interfaces, mice, windows, pull-down menus, laser printing, distributed computing, and Ethernet technologies weren't invented by Apple, Microsoft, or IBM. These essential elements of contemporary personal computing originated in the 1970s from researchers at Xerox PARC. Unfortunately, Xerox executives were focused on their photocopier business and didn't recognize the value of the Xerox PARC inventions, many of which never got patented. The lost value of Xerox PARC's discoveries is much larger than the entire photocopier industry today.[21]

IDENTIFYING PROBLEMS AND OPPORTUNITIES MORE EFFECTIVELY

Recognizing problems and opportunities will always be a challenge, but one way to improve the process is by becoming aware of the five problem identification biases just described. For example, by recognizing that mental models restrict a person's perspective of the world, decision makers are more motivated to consider other perspectives of reality. Along with increasing their awareness of problem identification flaws, leaders require considerable willpower to resist the temptation of looking decisive when a more thoughtful examination of the situation should occur.

A third way to improve problem identification is for leaders to create a norm of "divine discontent." They are never satisfied with the status quo, and this aversion to complacency creates a mindset that more actively searches for problems and opportunities.[22] Finally, employees can minimize problem identification errors by discussing the situation with colleagues. It is much easier to discover blind spots in problem identification when listening to how others perceive the situation. Opportunities also become apparent when outsiders explore this information from their different mental models.

SEARCHING FOR, EVALUATING, AND CHOOSING ALTERNATIVES

According to the rational choice paradigm of decision making, people rely on logic to evaluate and choose alternatives. This paradigm assumes that decision makers have well-articulated and agreed-on organizational goals, efficiently and simultaneously process facts about all alternatives and the consequences of those alternatives, and choose the alternative with the highest payoff.

bounded rationality The view that people are bounded in their decision-making capabilities, including access to limited information, limited information processing, and tendency toward satisficing rather than maximizing when making choices.

Nobel Prize–winning organizational scholar Herbert Simon questioned these assumptions a half century ago. He argued that people engage in **bounded rationality** because they process limited and imperfect information and rarely select the best choice.[23] Simon and other OB experts demonstrated that people evaluate and choose alternatives differently from the rational choice paradigm in several ways, as illustrated in Exhibit 7.2. These differences are so significant that many economists are now shifting from rational choice to bounded rationality assumptions in their theories. Let's look at these differences in terms of goals, information processing, and maximization.

PROBLEMS WITH GOALS

The rational choice paradigm assumes that organizational goals are clear and agreed-on. In fact, these conditions are necessary to identify "what ought to be" and, therefore, provide a standard against which each alternative is evaluated. Unfortunately, organizational goals are often ambiguous or in conflict with each other.

Exhibit 7.2   RATIONAL CHOICE ASSUMPTIONS VERSUS ORGANIZATIONAL BEHAVIOUR FINDINGS ABOUT CHOOSING ALTERNATIVES

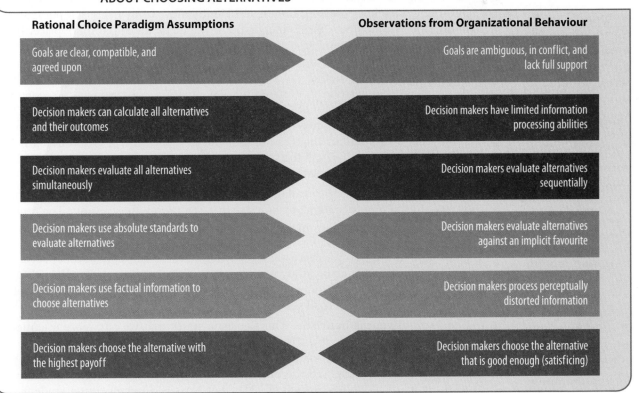

Rational Choice Paradigm Assumptions	Observations from Organizational Behaviour
Goals are clear, compatible, and agreed upon	Goals are ambiguous, in conflict, and lack full support
Decision makers can calculate all alternatives and their outcomes	Decision makers have limited information processing abilities
Decision makers evaluate all alternatives simultaneously	Decision makers evaluate alternatives sequentially
Decision makers use absolute standards to evaluate alternatives	Decision makers evaluate alternatives against an implicit favourite
Decision makers use factual information to choose alternatives	Decision makers process perceptually distorted information
Decision makers choose the alternative with the highest payoff	Decision makers choose the alternative that is good enough (satisficing)

PROBLEMS WITH INFORMATION PROCESSING

The rational choice paradigm also makes several assumptions about the human capacity to process information. It assumes that decision makers can process information about all alternatives and their consequences, whereas this is not possible in reality. Instead, people evaluate only a few alternatives and only some of the main outcomes of those alternatives.[24] For example, there may be dozens of computer brands to choose from and dozens of features to consider, yet people typically evaluate only a few brands and a few features.

A related problem is that decision makers typically evaluate alternatives sequentially rather than all at the same time. This sequential evaluation occurs partly because all alternatives are not usually available to the decision maker at the same time.[25] Consequently, as a new alternative comes along, it is immediately compared to an **implicit favourite**—an alternative that the decision maker prefers and that is used as a comparison with other choices. When choosing a new computer system, for example, people typically have an implicit favourite brand or model in their heads that they use to compare with the others. This sequential process of comparing alternatives with an implicit favourite occurs even when decision makers aren't consciously aware that they are doing this.[26]

Although the implicit favourite comparison process seems to be hardwired in human decision making (i.e., we naturally compare things), it often undermines effective decision making because people distort information to favour their implicit favourite over the alternative choices. They tend to ignore problems with the implicit favourite and advantages of the alternative. Decision makers also overweight factors on which the implicit favourite is better and underweight areas in which the alternative is superior.[27]

Biased Decision Heuristics   Subjective expected utility is the cornerstone of rational choice decision making, yet psychologists Amos Tversky and Daniel Kahneman discovered that human beings have built-in *decision heuristics* that automatically distort either the probability of outcomes or the value of those outcomes. Three of the most widely studied heuristic biases are anchoring and adjustment, availability, and representativeness:[28]

- **Anchoring and adjustment heuristic**. This heuristic states that we are influenced by an initial anchor point and do not sufficiently move away from that point as new information is provided.[29] The anchor point might be an initial offer price, initial opinion of someone, or initial estimated probability that something will occur. This bias affects the value we assign to choices and their outcomes. For example, suppose you ask one person whether the population of Chile is above or below 50 million, then you ask that person to estimate Chile's population. Next, you ask a second person whether the population of Chile is above or below 10 million, then you ask him or her to estimate that country's actual population. If these two people don't actually know Chile's population, chances are that the first person will give a much higher population estimate than will the second person. The initial anchor point (50 million vs. 10 million) biases their estimate.

- **Availability heuristic**. The availability heuristic is the tendency to estimate the probability of something occurring by how easily we can recall those events. The problem is that how easily we recall something is due to more than just its frequency (probability).[30] For instance, we easily remember emotional events (such as earthquakes and shark attacks), so we overestimate how often these emotional events occur. We also have an easier time recalling recent events. If the media reports about the poor condition of several roads or bridges, we likely give more pessimistic estimates of the quality of the province's road system than if there have been no recent reports.

- **Representativeness heuristic**. This heuristic states that we pay more attention to whether something resembles (is representative of) something else than on more precise statistics about its probability.[31] Suppose that one-fifth of the students in your class are in engineering and the others are business majors. Objectively, there is a 20 percent chance that any individual in that class is an engineering student. Yet,

---

implicit favourite A preferred alternative that the decision maker uses repeatedly as a comparison with other choices.

anchoring and adjustment heuristic A natural tendency for people to be influenced by an initial anchor point such that they do not sufficiently move away from that point as new information is provided.

availability heuristic A natural tendency to assign higher probabilities to objects or events that are easier to recall from memory, even though ease of recall is also affected by nonprobability factors (e.g., emotional response, recent events).

representativeness heuristic A natural tendency to evaluate probabilities of events or objects by the degree to which they resemble (are representative of) other events or objects rather than on objective probability information.

if one student looks and acts like a stereotype of an engineer, we tend to believe the person is an engineer even though there is much stronger and more reliable statistical evidence that he/she is a business major. Another form of the representativeness heuristic, known as the *clustering illusion,* is the tendency to see patterns from a small sample of events when those events are, in fact, random. For example, most players and coaches believe that players are more likely to have a successful shot on the net when their previous two or three shots have been successful. The representativeness heuristic is at work here because players and coaches believe these sequences are causally connected (representative) when, in reality, they are random events.

PROBLEMS WITH MAXIMIZATION

One of the main assumptions of the rational choice paradigm is that people want to—and are able to—choose the alternative with the highest payoff (i.e., the highest "utility" in subjective expected utility). Yet rather than aiming for maximization, people engage in **satisfising**—they select an alternative that is satisfactory or "good enough."[32] People satisfice when they select the first alternative that exceeds a standard of acceptance for their needs and preferences. Satisficing partly occurs because alternatives present themselves over time, not all at once. For example, it is impossible to choose the best job candidate because people apply over a period of time and the best candidate might not apply until next month, after earlier candidates have found other jobs. Consequently, as we mentioned earlier, decision makers rely on sequential evaluation of new alternatives against an implicit favourite. This necessarily calls for a satisficing decision rule— choose the first alternative that is "good enough."

A second reason why people engage in satisficing rather than maximization is that they lack the capacity and motivation to process the huge volume of information required to identify the best choice. Studies have found that people like to have choices, but when exposed to many alternatives, they become cognitive misers by engaging in satisficing.[33] When faced with numerous alternatives, decision makers also discard alternatives based on easily identifiable factors (i.e., colour, size) and by evaluating alternatives using only a handful of factors. Studies also report that making decisions when there are many alternatives can be cognitively and emotionally draining.

Satisficing is the main response to complex choices, but there is a more extreme response. When presented with a large number of choices, people often choose the least cognitively challenging alternative—they don't make any decision at all! For example, one American study found that many employees don't sign up for the company's pension plan when they face dozens of investment options, even though signing up would give them tax benefits, company contributions to that plan, and long-term financial security. The company pension plan registration rate increases dramatically when employees are given only two or three initial investment options, such as a growth fund, balanced fund, and capital stable investment. The dozens of other investment choices are available after the employee has signed up.[34] Four decades ago, futurist Alvin Toffler warned about the increasing risk of choice overload: "People of the future may suffer not from an absence of choice, but from a paralyzing surfeit of it. They may turn out to be victims of that peculiarly super-industrial dilemma: overchoice."[35]

> **satisfising** Selecting an alternative that is satisfactory or "good enough," rather than the alternative with the higher value (maximization).

 When presented with a large number of choices, people often choose the least cognitively challenging alternative—they don't make any decision at all! "

EVALUATING OPPORTUNITIES

Opportunities are just as important as problems, but what happens when an opportunity is "discovered" is quite different from the process of problem solving. Research suggests that decision makers do not evaluate several alternatives when they find an opportunity; after all, the opportunity *is* the solution, so why look for others! An opportunity is usually experienced as an exciting and rare revelation, so decision makers tend to have an emotional attachment to the opportunity. Unfortunately, this emotional preference motivates decision makers to apply the opportunity and short-circuit any detailed evaluation of it.[36]

EMOTIONS AND MAKING CHOICES

L03

Herbert Simon and many other experts have presented plenty of evidence that people do not evaluate alternatives nearly as well as is assumed by the rational choice paradigm. However, they neglected to mention another glaring weakness with rational choice: It completely ignores the effect of emotions in human decision making. Just as both the rational and emotional brain centres alert us to problems, they also influence our choice of alternatives.[37] Emotions affect the evaluation of alternatives in three ways.

Emotions Form Early Preferences   The emotional marker process described in previous chapters (Chapters 3 through 5) determines our preferences for each alternative before we consciously think about those alternatives. Our brain very quickly attaches specific emotions to information about each alternative, and our preferred alternative is strongly influenced by those initial emotional markers.[38] Of course, logical analysis also influences which alternative we choose, but it requires strong logical evidence to change our initial preferences (initial emotional markers). Yet even logical analysis depends on emotions to sway our decision. Specifically, neuroscientific evidence says that information produced from logical analysis is tagged with emotional markers that motivate us to choose or avoid a particular alternative. Ultimately, emotions, not rational logic, energize us to make the preferred choice. In fact, people with damaged emotional brain centres have difficulty making choices.

Emotions Change the Decision Evaluation Process   A considerable body of literature indicates that moods and specific emotions influence the *process* of evaluating alternatives.[39] For instance, we pay more attention to details when in a negative mood, possibly because a negative mood signals that there is something wrong that requires attention. When in a positive mood, on the other hand, we pay less attention to details and rely on a more programmed decision routine. This phenomenon explains why executive teams in successful companies are often less vigilant about competitors and other environmental threats.[40] Research also suggests that decision makers rely on stereotypes and other shortcuts to speed up the choice process when they experience anger. Anger also makes them more optimistic about the success of risky alternatives, whereas the emotion of fear tends to make them less optimistic. Overall, emotions shape *how* we evaluate information, not just which choice we select.

Emotions Serve as Information When We Evaluate Alternatives   The third way that emotions influence the evaluation of alternatives is through a process called "emotions as information." Marketing experts have found that we listen in on our emotions to gain guidance when making choices.[41] This process is similar to having a temporary improvement in emotional intelligence. Most emotional experiences remain below the level of conscious awareness, but people actively try to be more sensitive to these subtle emotions when making a decision.

When buying a new car, for example, you not only logically evaluate each vehicle's features; you also try to gauge your emotions when visualizing what it would be like to own each of the cars on your list of choices. Even if you have solid information about the quality of each vehicle on key features (purchase price, fuel efficiency, maintenance costs, resale value, etc.), you are swayed by your emotional reaction and actively try to sense that emotional response when thinking about it. Some people pay more attention to these gut feelings, and personality tests such as the Myers-Briggs Type Indicator (see

Chapter 2) identify individuals who listen in on their emotions more than others.[42] But all of us use our emotions as information to some degree. This phenomenon ties directly into our next topic, intuition.

INTUITION AND MAKING CHOICES

Greg McDonald felt uneasy about a suspicious-looking crack in the rock face, so the veteran Potash Corp. of Saskatchewan miner warned a co-worker to stay away from the area. "There was no indication there was anything wrong—just a little crack," McDonald recalled. A few minutes later, the ceiling in the mine shaft 1,000 metres underground caved in. Fortunately, the co-worker had heeded McDonald's advice. "If he had been there, he would be dead," McDonald said in an interview following a near-sleepless night after the incident.[43]

The gut instinct that helped Greg McDonald save his co-worker's life is known as **intuition**—the ability to know when a problem or opportunity exists and to select the best course of action without conscious reasoning.[44] Intuition is both an emotional experience and a rapid nonconscious analytic process. As mentioned in the previous section, the gut feelings we experience are emotional signals that have enough intensity to make us consciously aware of them. These signals warn us of impending danger, such as a dangerous mine wall, or motivate us to take advantage of an opportunity. Some intuition also directs us to preferred choices relative to other alternatives in the situation.

All gut feelings are emotional signals, but not all emotional signals are intuition. The key distinction is that intuition involves rapidly comparing our observations with deeply held patterns learned through experience.[45] These templates represent tacit knowledge that has been implicitly acquired over time. They are mental models that help us to understand whether the current situation is good or bad, depending on how well that situation fits our mental model. When a template fits or doesn't fit the current situation, emotions are produced that motivate us to act. Greg McDonald's years of experience produced mental templates of unsafe rock faces that matched what he saw on that fateful day. Studies have also found that chess masters receive emotional signals when they sense an opportunity through quick observation of a chessboard. When given the opportunity to think about the situation, chess masters can explain why they see a favourable move on the chessboard. However, their intuition signals the opportunity long before this rational analysis takes place.

As mentioned, some emotional signals are not intuition. As a result, some experts warn that we should not trust our gut feelings. The problem is that emotional responses are not always based on well-grounded mental models. Instead, they occur when we compare the current situation to more remote templates, which may or may not be relevant. A new employee might feel confident about relations with a supplier, whereas an experienced employee senses potential problems. The difference is that the new employee relies on templates from other experiences or industries that might not work well in this situation. Thus, whether the emotions we experience in a situation represent intuition or not depends largely on our level of experience in that situation.

So far, we have described intuition as an emotional experience (gut feeling) and a process in which we compare the current situation with well-established templates of the mind. Intuition also relies on *action scripts*—programmed decision routines that speed up our response to pattern matches or mismatches.[46] Action scripts effectively shorten the decision-making process by jumping from problem identification to selection of a solution. In other words, action scripting is a form of programmed decision making. Action scripts are generic, so we need to consciously adapt them to the specific situation.

MAKING CHOICES MORE EFFECTIVELY

It is very difficult to get around the human limitations of making choices, but a few strategies help to minimize these concerns. One important discovery is that decisions tend to have a higher failure rate when leaders are decisive rather than contemplative

intuition The ability to know when a problem or opportunity exists and to select the best course of action without conscious reasoning.

What If...?

Scenario planning has long been recognized as a potentially effective way to help decision makers figure out the best solutions to crises before those crises occur. One Norwegian company has created a variation of scenario planning as a board game for shipping, IT security, and other industries. The game, called "What If," teaches employees to make better decisions when facing risky situations. Participants first review several dozen scenarios and collectively determine which of these events pose the greatest risk. For example, one scenario in the shipping exercise is a situation where a fire knocks out all engines, resulting in a collision with another vessel. Next, the team examines drills or exercises associated with the highest risk scenarios. Finally, they determine what actions are required to prepare their company or ship for these high-risk scenarios.[47] *Courtesy of Dryer Kompetense*

about the available options. Of course, decisions can also be ineffective when leaders take too long to make a choice, but research indicates that a lack of logical evaluation of alternatives is a greater concern. By systematically assessing alternatives against relevant factors, decision makers minimize the implicit favourite and satisficing problems that occur when they rely on general subjective judgments. This recommendation does not suggest that we ignore intuition; rather, it suggests that we use it in combination with careful analysis of relevant information.[48]

A second piece of advice is to remember that decisions are influenced by both rational and emotional processes. With this awareness, some decision makers deliberately revisit important issues later so that they look at the information in different moods and have allowed their initial emotions to subside. For example, if you sense that your team is feeling somewhat too self-confident when making an important competitive decision, you might decide to have the team members revisit the decision a few days later when they are thinking more critically. Another strategy is **scenario planning,** which is a disciplined method for imagining possible futures. It typically involves thinking about what would happen if a significant environmental condition changed and what the organization should do to anticipate and react to such an outcome.[49] Scenario planning is a useful vehicle for choosing the best solutions under possible scenarios long before they occur. Alternative courses of action are evaluated without the pressure and emotions that occur during real emergencies.

scenario planning A systematic process of thinking about alternative futures and what the organization should do to anticipate and react to those environments.

IMPLEMENTING DECISIONS

Implementing decisions is often skipped over in most writing about the decision-making process. Yet leading business writers emphasize that execution—translating decisions into action—is one of the most important and challenging tasks of leaders. "When assessing candidates, the first thing I looked for was energy and enthusiasm for execution," says Larry Bossidy, the former CEO of Honeywell and Allied Signal.[50]

EVALUATING DECISION OUTCOMES

Contrary to the rational choice paradigm, decision makers aren't completely honest with themselves when evaluating the effectiveness of their decisions. One problem is *confirmation bias* (also known as *post-decisional justification* in the context of decision evaluation), which is the "unwitting selectivity in the acquisition and use of evidence."[51] When evaluating decisions, people with confirmation bias ignore or downplay the negative outcomes of the selected alternative and overemphasize its positive outcomes.

Confirmation bias gives people an excessively optimistic evaluation of their decisions, but only until they receive very clear and undeniable information to the contrary. Unfortunately, it also inflates the decision maker's initial evaluation of the decision, so reality often comes as a painful shock when objective feedback is finally received.

ESCALATION OF COMMITMENT

escalation of commitment The tendency to repeat an apparently bad decision or allocate more resources to a failing course of action.

Another reason why decision makers don't evaluate their decisions very well is due to **escalation of commitment**—the tendency to repeat an apparently bad decision or allocate more resources to a failing course of action.[52] For example, the British Columbia Ferry Services ordered the design and construction of three catamaran-style ferries for its route between the city of Vancouver and Vancouver Island. These "PacifiCats" were supposed to travel faster than conventional ferries and cost $210 million "right down to the toilet paper." Not only did costs balloon to nearly $500 million, the ferries were almost unusable due to their damaging wake, maintenance problems, poor manoeuvrability, and high fuel costs. The three ferries were eventually auctioned off for $20 million. Another classic incident of escalation is the Taurus project at the London Stock Exchange. The Taurus information technology system originally had a £6 million budget, but the Exchange eventually spent more than £400 million before the project was abandoned.[53]

A third example is the Darlington nuclear power plant in Ontario, which had an estimated cost of $2.5 billion (although some say it was originally $5 billion) and was eventually completed a decade late at a cost of more than $14 billion. This debt is still being paid off through a special levy on Ontario electricity bills. The Darlington debacle prompted the Ontario government to deregulate the electricity industry and split Ontario Hydro into two operating companies (Hydro One and Ontario Power Generation). Ironically, a former CEO of Ontario Hydro warned that Darlington and other megaprojects invite escalating commitment because "once you commit to them, there's very little you can do to reverse that commitment."[54]

Causes of Escalating Commitment Why are decision makers led deeper and deeper into failing projects? Several explanations have been identified and discussed over the years, but the four main influences are self-justification, prospect theory effect, perceptual blinders, and closing costs.

- *Self-justification*—Decision makers typically want to appear rational and effective. One such impression management tactic is to demonstrate the importance of a decision by continuing to invest in it, whereas pulling the plug symbolizes the project's failure and the decision maker's incompetence. This self-justification effect is particularly evident when decision makers are personally identified with the project, have staked their reputations to some extent on the project's success, and have low self-esteem.[55]

prospect theory effect A natural tendency to feel more dissatisfaction from losing a particular amount than satisfaction from gaining an equal amount.

- *Prospect theory effect*—Escalation of commitment is partly fuelled by the **prospect theory effect.** This is a natural tendency to experience stronger negative emotions when losing something of value than the positive emotions when gaining something of equal value. This prospect theory effect motivates us to avoid losses, which typically occurs by taking the risk of investing more in that losing project. Stopping a project is a certain loss, which is more painful to most people than the uncertainty of success associated with continuing to fund the project. Given the choice, decision makers choose the less painful option.[56]

- *Perceptual blinders*—Escalation of commitment sometimes occurs because decision makers do not see the problems soon enough.[57] They nonconsciously screen out or explain away negative information to protect self-esteem. Serious problems initially look like random errors along the trend line to success. Even when decision makers see that something is wrong, the information is sufficiently ambiguous that it can be misinterpreted or justified.

- *Closing costs*—The financial, reputational, and other costs of terminating the failing project can also be a powerful incentive to continue investing in that project. Some projects involve considerable penalties to others involved with the project as well as loss of goodwill with those groups. Closing costs are particularly important in political situations because closing the project is acknowledgement that the decision makers made a grave mistake in their previous decisions. This effect was apparent when a former premier of Ontario was asked why he didn't shut down the Darlington nuclear plant project. "I don't think anybody can look at a situation with . . . $7 billion in the ground and just cavalierly write it off," he replied.[58]

Escalation of commitment is usually framed as poor decision making, but some experts argue that throwing more money into a failing project is sometimes a logical attempt to further understand an ambiguous situation. This strategy is essentially a variation of testing unknown waters. By adding more resources, the decision maker gains new information about the effectiveness of these funds, which provides more feedback about the project's future success. This strategy is particularly common where the project has high closing costs.[59]

EVALUATING DECISION OUTCOMES MORE EFFECTIVELY

One of the most effective ways to minimize escalation of commitment and confirmation bias is to ensure that the people who made the original decision are not the same people who later evaluate that decision. This separation of roles minimizes the self-justification effect because the person responsible for evaluating the decision is not connected to the original decision. However, the second person might continue to escalate the project if he or she empathizes with the decision maker, has a similar mindset, or has similar attributes such as age. A second strategy is to publicly establish a preset level at which the decision is abandoned or re-evaluated. This is similar to a stop-loss order in the stock market, whereby the stock is sold if it falls below a certain price. The problem with this solution is that conditions are often so complex that it is difficult to identify an appropriate point to abandon a project.[60]

A third strategy is to find a source of systematic and clear feedback.[61] At some point, even the strongest escalation and confirmation bias effects deflate when the evidence highlights the project's failings. A fourth strategy to improve the decision evaluation process is to involve several people in the evaluation. Co-workers continuously monitor each other and might notice problems sooner than someone working alone on the project.

CREATIVITY

LO4

creativity The development of original ideas that make a socially recognized contribution.

The entire decision-making process described over the preceding pages depends on **creativity**—the development of original ideas that make a socially recognized contribution.[62] Creativity is at work when imagining opportunities, such as how a company's expertise might be redirected to untapped markets. Creativity is present when developing alternatives, such as figuring out new places to look for existing solutions or working out the design of a custom-made solution. Creativity also helps us choose alternatives because we need to visualize the future in different ways and to figure out how each choice might be useful or a liability in those scenarios. In short, creativity is an essential component of decision making as well as a powerful resource for corporate competitive advantage and individual career development.

The value of creativity in decision making is evident at Google. Google's creative culture includes a natural practice of experimenting with ideas and seeking out different uses of technology. Perhaps most famous is the company's policy of giving engineers 20 percent of their time to develop projects of their choosing. "Almost everything that is interesting which Google does started out as a 20 percent time idea," explains a Google executive. Google News and the photos linked to Google Maps were two projects developed from the 20 percent time rule.[63]

THE CREATIVE PROCESS

How does creativity occur? This question has puzzled experts for hundreds of years and has been the fascination of dozens of scientists (Einstein, Poincaré) who have reflected on their own creative experience that produced important discoveries. More than a century ago, German physicist Hermann von Helmholtz gave a public talk on the process that led to his many discoveries (energy physics, instruments for examining eyes, and many others). A few decades later, London School of Economics professor Graham Wallas built on Helmholtz's ideas as well as many others to construct the four-stage model shown in Exhibit 7.3.[64] Although there are other ways of viewing the creative process, many of them overlap with Wallas's model, which remains the most reputable and influential.

The first stage is *preparation*—the process of investigating the problem or opportunity in many ways. Preparation involves developing a clear understanding of what you are trying to achieve through a novel solution and then actively studying information seemingly related to the topic. It is a process of developing knowledge and possibly skills about the issue or object of attention. The second stage, called *incubation*, is the period of reflective thought. We put the problem aside, but our mind is still working on it in the background.[65] The important condition here is to maintain a low-level awareness by frequently revisiting the problem. Incubation does not mean that you forget about the problem or issue.

divergent thinking
Reframing a problem in a unique way and generating different approaches to the issue.

Incubation assists **divergent thinking**—reframing a problem in a unique way and generating different approaches to the issue. This contrasts with *convergent thinking*—calculating the conventionally accepted "right answer" to a logical problem. Divergent thinking breaks us away from existing mental models so that we can apply concepts or processes from completely different areas of life. The discovery of Velcro is a case in point. In the 1940s, Swiss engineer Georges de Mestral had just returned home from a walk with his dog through the countryside when he noticed that his clothing and the dog's fur were covered in burrs. While struggling to remove the barbed seeds, de Mestral engaged in divergent thinking by developing an idea that the adhesion used by burrs could be used to attach other things together. It took another dozen years of hard work, but de Mestral eventually perfected the hook-and-loop fastener, which he trademarked as Velcro.[66]

Illumination, the third stage of creativity, refers to the experience of suddenly becoming aware of a unique idea.[67] Illuminations is often visually depicted as a light bulb, but a better image would be a brief flash of light or perhaps a briefly flickering candle because these bits of inspiration are fleeting and can be quickly lost if not documented. For this reason, many creative people keep a journal or notebook nearby so that they can jot down their ideas before they disappear. Also, flickering ideas don't keep a particular schedule; they might come to you at any time of day or night.

Illuminations are merely rough ideas. Their usefulness still requires verification through detailed logical evaluation, experimentation, and further creative insight. Thus, although *verification* is labelled the final stage of creativity, it is really the beginning of a long process of creative decision making toward development of an innovative product or service.

Exhibit 7.3   **THE CREATIVE PROCESS MODEL**

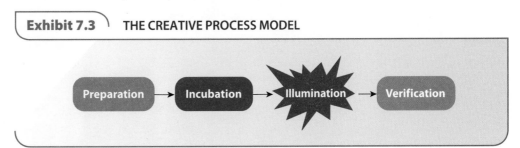

Source: Based on Graham Wallas, *The Art of Thought* (London: Jonathan Cape, 1926).

CHARACTERISTICS OF CREATIVE PEOPLE

Everyone is creative, but some people have a higher potential for creativity. Four of the main characteristics that give individuals more creative potential are intelligence, persistence, knowledge and experience, and a cluster of personality traits and values representing independent imagination (see Exhibit 7.4).

- *Cognitive and practical intelligence.* Creative people have above-average intelligence to synthesize information, analyze ideas, and apply their ideas.[68] Like the fictional sleuth Sherlock Holmes, creative people recognize the significance of small bits of information and are able to connect them in ways that few others can imagine. They also have *practical intelligence*—the capacity to evaluate the potential usefulness of their ideas.

- *Persistence.* Creative people have persistence, which is based on a higher need for achievement, a strong motivation from the task itself, and a moderate or high degree of self-esteem. In support of this, one study reported that Canadian inventors have higher levels of confidence and optimism than do people in the general population, and these traits motivate inventors to continue working on and investing in a project after receiving diagnostic advice to quit.[69]

- *Knowledge and experience.* Creative people require a foundation of knowledge and experience to discover or acquire new knowledge (the idea of *absorptive capacity* that was discussed in Chapter 1).[70] However, this expertise is a double-edge sword. As people acquire knowledge and experience about a specific topic, their mental models tend to become more rigid. They are less adaptable to new information or rules about that knowledge domain. Some writers suggest that expertise also increases "mindless behaviour" because expertise reduces the tendency to question why things happen.[71] To overcome the limitations of expertise, some corporate leaders like to hire people from other industries and areas of expertise. For instance, when Geoffrey Ballard, founder of Vancouver-based Ballard Power Systems, hired a chemist to develop a better battery, the chemist protested that he didn't know anything about batteries. Ballard replied: "That's fine. I don't want someone who knows batteries. They know what won't work."[72]

- *Independent imagination.* Creative people possess a cluster of personality traits and values that support an independent imagination: high openness to experience, moderately low need for affiliation, and strong values around self-direction and

Exhibit 7.4 CHARACTERISTICS OF CREATIVE PEOPLE

Independent Imagination
- High openness to experience
- Moderately low need for affiliation
- Strong self-direction value
- Strong stimulation value

Cognitive and Practical Intelligence
- Ability to synthesize, analyze, and apply ideas
- Ability to evaluate potential usefulness of ideas

Characteristics of Creative People

Knowledge and Experience
- Prerequisite knowledge and experience (absorptive capacity)
- Not locked into a fixed knowledge mindset

Persistence
- High need for achievement
- Strong task motivation
- Moderately high self-esteem and optimism

Generating a Creative Lightwave

When it comes to creative thinking, Alex Beim sees the light almost all the time. The founder and chief creative technologist of Tangible Interaction Design in Vancouver invents enticing interactive displays. He designed the illuminated lightweight orbs that change colour when touched (called zygotes) at the Vancouver Olympics. He also created digital graffiti walls at Chanel and Converse outlets in the United States. The insight for Beim's first invention, the zygotes, came to him a few years ago as a mental picture of colour-changing balls floating above a crowd at a music festival. He says his creativity is fuelled by the fun and challenge of designing something that touches people. "I get ideas all the time for designs I want to create," says Beim, who now employs a team of people. "I may not initially know how to build them, but I love researching the idea, seeing it come to life and watching the happiness it brings to people."[73] *Rob Newell Photography*

stimulation.[74] Openness to experience is a Big Five personality dimension representing the extent to which a person is imaginative, curious, sensitive, open-minded, and original (see Chapter 2). Creative people have a moderately low need for affiliation so they are less embarrassed when making mistakes. Self-direction includes the values of creativity and independent thought; stimulation includes the values of excitement and challenge. Together, these values form openness to change—representing the motivation to pursue innovative ways (see Chapter 2).

ORGANIZATIONAL CONDITIONS SUPPORTING CREATIVITY

Intelligence, persistence, expertise, and independent imagination represent a person's creative potential, but the extent to which they translate into more creative output depends on a work environment that supports the creative process.[75] Several job and workplace characteristics have been identified in the literature, and different combinations of situations can equally support creativity; there isn't one best work environment.[76]

One of the most important conditions that supports creative practice is that the organization has a *learning orientation;* that is, leaders recognize that employees make reasonable mistakes as part of the creative process. "Creativity comes from failure," recently retired Samsung Electronics CEO Yun Jong-yong advised employees. "We should reform our corporate culture to forgive failure if workers did their best."[77] Motivation from the job itself is another important condition for creativity.[78] Employees tend to be more creative when they believe their work benefits the organization and/or larger society (i.e., task significance) and when they have the freedom to pursue novel ideas without bureaucratic delays (i.e., autonomy). Creativity is about changing things, and change is possible only when employees have the authority to experiment. More generally, jobs encourage creativity when they are challenging and aligned with the employee's competencies.

Along with supporting a learning orientation and intrinsically motivating jobs, companies foster creativity through open communication and sufficient resources. They also provide a comfortable degree of job security, which explains why creativity suffers during times of downsizing and corporate restructuring.[79] Some companies also support creativity by designing nontraditional workspaces, such as unique building design or unconventional office areas.[80] Canadian Tire has gone one step further: It set up an innovation room featuring a canoe, sun deck, Lego building blocks, crayons, and a tree that looks like it has sprouted ski poles, skateboards, and other Canadian Tire products. Creative teams use the innovation room to design new products. "It's really about unlocking and unleashing creativity and getting people to just let loose and dream a little and have fun," explains a Canadian Tire executive. "It's a process that usually ends up with some very unique and different products and concepts."[81]

To some degree, creativity also improves with support from leaders and co-workers. One study reported that effective product champions provide enthusiastic support for new ideas. Other studies suggest that co-worker support can improve creativity in some situations whereas competition among co-workers improves creativity in other situations.[82] Similarly, it isn't clear how much pressure should be exerted on employees to produce creative ideas. Extreme time pressures are well-known creativity inhibitors, but lack of pressure doesn't seem to produce the highest creativity either.

ACTIVITIES THAT ENCOURAGE CREATIVITY

Hiring people with strong creative potential and providing a work environment that supports creativity are two cornerstones of a creative workplace. The third cornerstone consists of various activities that help employees think more creatively. One set of activities involves redefining the problem. Employees might be encouraged to revisit old projects that have been set aside. After a few months of neglect, these projects might be seen in new ways.[83] Another strategy involves asking people unfamiliar with the issue (preferably with different expertise) to explore the problem with you. You would state the objectives and give some facts and then let the other person ask questions to further understand the situation. By verbalizing the problem, listening to questions, and hearing what others think, you are more likely to form new perspectives on the issue.[84]

A second set of creativity activities, known as *associative play*, ranges from art classes to impromptu storytelling and acting. For example, British media giant OMD sends employees to two-day retreats in the countryside, where they play grapefruit croquet, chant like medieval monks, and pretend to be dog collars. "Being creative is a bit like an emotion; we need to be stimulated," explains Harriet Frost, one of OMD's specialists in building creativity. "The same is true for our imagination and its ability to come up with new ideas. You can't just sit in a room and devise hundreds of ideas."[85] Another associative play activity, called *morphological analysis*, involves listing different dimensions of a system and the elements of each dimension and then looking at each combination. This encourages people to carefully examine combinations that initially seem nonsensical.

A third set of activities that promote creative thinking falls under the category of *cross-pollination*.[86] Cross-pollination occurs when people from different areas of the organization exchange ideas or when new people are brought into an existing team. Mother, the London-based creative agency, has unusual policies and working conditions that apply this creative process. The company's 100 or so employees perform their daily work around one monster-size table—a 2.5-metre-wide reinforced-concrete slab that extends 91 metres like a skateboard ramp around the entire floor. Every three weeks, employees are asked to relocate their laptop, portable telephone, and trolley to another area around the table. Why the musical-chairs exercise? "It encourages cross-pollination of ideas," explains Stef Calcraft, one of Mother's founding partners. "You have people working on the same problem from different perspectives. It makes problem-solving much more organic."[87]

Cross-pollination highlights the fact that creativity rarely occurs alone. Some creative people may be individualistic, but most creative ideas are generated through teams and informal social interaction. "This whole thing about the solitary tortured artist is nonsense I think," says John Collee, the screenwriter who penned such films as *Happy Feet* and *Master and Commander*. "All the great creative people I know have become great precisely because they know how to get along with people and swim around in the communal unconscious."[88] This notion of improving creativity through social interaction leads us to the final section of this chapter: employee involvement in decision making.

EMPLOYEE INVOLVEMENT IN DECISION MAKING

L05

Nishith Desai Associates (NDA) isn't your typical law firm. About 60 percent of decisions at the 100-member Mumbai, India-based organization occur through consensus. Another 25 percent are reached through majority vote of the partners, and the remainder are determined by the executive committee or the CEO. The law firm also has representative committees. The compensation committee, for example, consists of staff voted into the position and who have three or more years of professional experience. Overall, NDA strives to become a democratic organization by relying on various levels and forms of employee involvement in decision making.[89]

employee involvement
The degree to which employees influence how their work is organized and carried out.

Employee involvement (also called *participative management*) refers to the degree to which employees influence how their work is organized and carried out.[90] Employee involvement has become a natural process in every organization, but the level of involvement varies with the situation. In some organizations, such as NDA, almost everyone has a high degree of involvement in some corporate-wide decisions during a given year, whereas other organizations might give employees only low levels of involvement. The main levels of involvement (from lowest to highest) include:[91]

- *Decide alone.* The decision maker relies on personal knowledge and insight to complete the entire decision process without conferring with anyone else.
- *Receive information from individuals.* The decision maker asks individuals for information. These individuals do not make recommendations and might not even know what the problem is about.
- *Consult with individuals.* The decision maker describes the problem to selected individuals and seeks both their information and recommendations. The final decision is made by the decision maker, who may or may not take the advice from others into account.
- *Consult with the team.* The decision maker brings together a team of people (such as all staff in the department), who are told about the problem and provide their ideas and recommendations. The decision maker makes the final decision, which may or may not reflect the team's information.
- *Facilitate the team's decision.* The entire decision making process is handed over to the team, where the original decision maker serves only as a facilitator to guide the team's decision process and keep everyone on track. The team identifies the problem, discovers alternative solutions, chooses the best alternative, and implements their choice.

BENEFITS OF EMPLOYEE INVOLVEMENT

For the past half century, organizational behaviour experts have advised that employee involvement potentially improves decision making quality and commitment.[92] Involved employees can help improve decision quality by recognizing problems more quickly and defining them more accurately. Employees are, in many respects, the sensors of the organization's environment. When the organization's activities misalign with customer expectations, employees are usually the first to know. Employee involvement ensures that everyone in the organization is quickly alerted to such problems.[93] Employee involvement can also potentially improve the number and quality of solutions generated. In a well-managed meeting, team members create synergy by pooling their knowledge to form new alternatives. In other words, several people working together can potentially generate better solutions than the same people working alone.

A third benefit of employee involvement is that, under specific conditions, it improves the evaluation of alternatives. Numerous studies on participative decision making, constructive conflict, and team dynamics have found that involvement brings out more diverse perspectives, tests ideas, and provides more valuable knowledge, all of which help the decision maker to select the best alternative.[94] A mathematical theorem introduced in 1785 by the Marquis de Condorcet states that the alternative selected by the team's majority is more likely to be correct than is the alternative selected by any team member individually.[95]

Along with improving decision quality, employee involvement tends to strengthen employee commitment to the decision. Rather than viewing themselves as agents of someone else's decision, staff members who participate in a decision feel personally responsible for its success. Involvement also has positive effects on employee motivation, satisfaction, and turnover. It also increases skill variety, feelings of autonomy, and task identity, all of which potentially increase job enrichment and employee motivation.

Participation is also a critical practice in organizational change because employees are more motivated to implement the decision and less likely to resist changes resulting from the decision.[97] Brian Scudamore, CEO of Vancouver-based 1-800-GOT-JUNK?, explains: "Everybody at 1-800-GOT-JUNK? has an opportunity to express their ideas for growth and improvement of our business and we all share best practices. As a result, our people take pride in the work they do every day, and our customers reap the benefits."[98]

CONTINGENCIES OF EMPLOYEE INVOLVEMENT

If employee involvement is so wonderful, why don't leaders leave all decisions to employees? The answer is that the optimal level of employee involvement depends on the situation. The employee involvement model shown in Exhibit 7.5 lists four contingencies: decision structure, source of decision knowledge, decision commitment, and risk of conflict in the decision process.[99]

- *Decision structure.* At the beginning of this chapter, we stated that some decisions are programmed, whereas others are nonprogrammed. Programmed decisions are less likely to need employee involvement because the solutions are already worked out from past incidents. In other words, the benefits of employee involvement increase with the novelty and complexity of the problem or opportunity.

- *Source of decision knowledge.* Employees should be involved in some level of decision making when the leader lacks sufficient knowledge and employees have additional information to improve decision quality. In many cases, employees are closer to customers and production activities, so they often know where the company can save money, improve product or service quality, and realize opportunities. This is particularly true for complex decisions where employees are more likely to possess relevant information.

- *Decision commitment.* Participation tends to improve employee commitment to the decision. If employees are unlikely to accept a decision made without their involvement, some level of participation is usually necessary.

| Exhibit 7.5 | MODEL OF EMPLOYEE INVOLVEMENT IN DECISION MAKING |

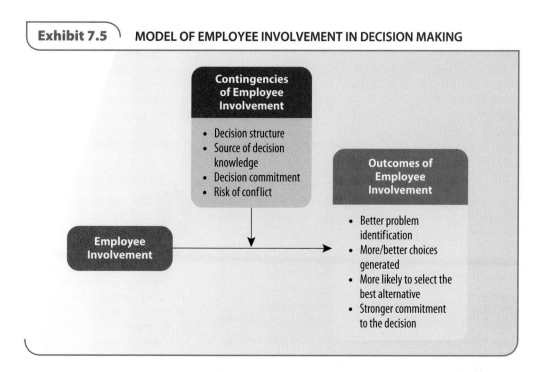

- *Risk of conflict.* Two types of conflict undermine the benefits of employee involvement. First, if employee goals and norms conflict with the organization's goals, only a low level of employee involvement is advisable. Second, the degree of involvement depends on whether employees will agree on the preferred solution. If conflict is likely to occur, high involvement (i.e., employees make the decision alone) would be difficult to achieve.

Employee involvement is an important component of the decision making process. To make the best decisions, we need to involve people who have the most valuable information and who will increase commitment to implement the decision. Employee involvement is a formative stage of team dynamics, so it carries many of the benefits and challenges of working in teams. The next chapter provides a closer look at team dynamics, including processes for making decisions in teams.

CHAPTER SUMMARY

 LO1 Describe the rational choice paradigm.

Decision making is a conscious process of making choices among one or more alternatives with the intention of moving toward some desired state of affairs. The rational choice paradigm relies on subjective expected utility to identify the best choice. It also follows the logical process of identifying problems and opportunities, choosing the best decision style, discovering and developing alternative solutions, choosing the best solution, implementing the selected alternative, and evaluating decision outcomes.

LO2 Explain why people refrain from applying the rational choice paradigm when identifying problems/opportunities, evaluating/choosing alternatives, and evaluating decision outcomes.

Stakeholder framing, mental models, decisive leadership, solution-focused problems, and perceptual defence affect

our ability to objectively identify problems and opportunities. We can minimize these challenges by being aware of the human limitations and discussing the situation with colleagues.

Evaluating and choosing alternatives is often challenging because organizational goals are ambiguous or in conflict, human information processing is incomplete and subjective, and people tend to satisfice rather than maximize. Decision makers also short-circuit the evaluation process when faced with an opportunity rather than a problem. People generally make better choices by systematically evaluating alternatives. Scenario planning can help to make future decisions without the pressure and emotions that occur during real emergencies.

Confirmation bias and escalation of commitment make it difficult to accurately evaluate decision outcomes. Escalation is mainly caused by self-justification, the prospect theory effect, perceptual blinders, and closing costs. These problems are minimized by separating decision choosers from decision evaluators, establishing a preset level at which the decision is abandoned or re-evaluated, relying on more systematic and clear feedback about the project's success, and involving several people in decision making.

 LO3   Discuss the roles of emotions and intuition in decision making.

Emotions shape our preferences for alternatives and the process we follow to evaluate alternatives. We also listen in to our emotions for guidance when making decisions. This latter activity relates to intuition—the ability to know when a problem or opportunity exists and to select the best course of action without conscious reasoning. Intuition is both an emotional experience and a rapid unconscious analytic process that involves both pattern matching and action scripts.

 LO4   Describe employee characteristics, workplace conditions, and specific activities that support creativity.

Creativity is the development of original ideas that make a socially recognized contribution. The four creativity stages are preparation, incubation, illumination, and verification. Incubation assists divergent thinking, which involves reframing the problem in a unique way and generating different approaches to the issue.

Four of the main features of creative people are intelligence, persistence, expertise, and independent imagination. Creativity is also strengthened for everyone when the work environment supports a learning orientation, the job has high intrinsic motivation, the organization provides a reasonable level of job security, and project leaders provide appropriate goals, time pressure, and resources. Three types of activities that encourage creativity are redefining the problem, associative play, and cross-pollination.

 LO5   Describe the benefits of employee involvement and identify four contingencies that affect the optimal level of employee involvement.

Employee involvement refers to the degree that employees influence how their work is organized and carried out. The level of participation may range from an employee providing specific information to management without knowing the problem or issue, to complete involvement in all phases of the decision process. Employee involvement may lead to higher decision quality and commitment, but several contingencies need to be considered, including the decision structure, source of decision knowledge, decision commitment, and risk of conflict.

KEY TERMS

anchoring and adjustment heuristic, p. 188

availability heuristic, p. 188

bounded rationality, p. 187

creativity, p. 194

decision making, p. 182

divergent thinking, p. 195

employee involvement, p. 199

escalation of commitment, p. 193

implicit favourite, p. 188

intuition, p. 191

prospect theory effect, p. 193

rational choice paradigm, p. 182

representativeness heuristic, p. 188

satisficing, p. 189

scenario planning, p. 192

subjective expected utility, p. 182

CRITICAL-THINKING QUESTIONS

1. A management consultant is hired by a manufacturing firm to determine the best site for its next production facility. The consultant has had several meetings with the company's senior executives regarding the factors to consider when making the recommendation. Discuss the decision-making problems that might prevent the consultant from recommending the best site location.

2. You have been asked to personally recommend a new travel agency to handle all airfare, accommodation, and related travel needs for your organization of 500 staff. One of your colleagues, who is responsible for the company's economic planning, suggests that the best travel agent could be selected mathematically by inputting the relevant factors for each agency and the weight (importance) of each factor. What decision making approach is your colleague recommending? Is this recommendation a good idea in this situation? Why or why not?

3. Intuition is both an emotional experience and an unconscious analytic process. One problem, however, is that not all emotions signal that there is a problem or opportunity. Explain how we would know if our "gut feelings" are intuition or not, and if not intuition, suggest what might be causing them.

4. A developer received financial backing for a new business financial centre along a derelict section of the waterfront, a few kilometres from the current downtown area of a large European city. The idea was to build several high-rise structures, attract large tenants to those sites, and have the city extend transportation systems out to the new centre. Over the next decade, the developer believed that others would build in the area, thereby attracting the regional or national offices of many financial institutions. Interest from potential tenants was much lower than initially predicted and the city did not build transportation systems as quickly as expected. Still, the builder proceeded with the original plans. Only after financial support was curtailed did the developer reconsider the project. Using your knowledge of escalation of commitment, discuss three possible reasons why the developer was motivated to continue with the project.

5. Ancient Book Company has a problem with new book projects. Even when others are aware that a book is far behind schedule and may engender little public interest, sponsoring editors are reluctant to terminate contracts with authors whom they have signed. The result is that

editors invest more time with these projects than on more fruitful projects. As a form of escalation of commitment, describe two methods that Ancient Book Company can use to minimize this problem.

6. Think of a time when you experienced the creative process. Maybe you woke up with a brilliant (but usually sketchy and incomplete) idea, or you solved a baffling problem while doing something else. Describe this incident to your class and explain how the experience followed the creative process.

7. Two characteristics of creative people are that they have relevant experience and are persistent in their quest. Does this mean that people with the most experience and the highest need for achievement are the most creative? Explain your answer.

8. Employee involvement applies just as well to the classroom as to the office or factory floor. Explain how student involvement in classroom decisions typically made by the instructor alone might improve decision quality. What potential problems may occur in this process?

 CASE STUDY 7.1

Employee Involvement Cases

Scenario 1: Social Media Decision for the Provincial Government

You are the director of training, learning, and development for the provincial government. Faced with shrinking budgets you are particularly concerned about your ability to attract and retain recent hires that include many young, well-educated, high-potential employees who seem to be particularly motivated by opportunities to learn, develop, and collaborate with their co-workers.

Last week you were the guest speaker for an HR class at one of the local colleges and received some candid feedback from business students. Student comments included:

- "I would love to work for government for a year or two to get some experience."

- "The work environment in government is soooo old-fashioned. I have a friend who works at one of the ministries and her boss told her that she needs to keep her phone turned off during work hours."

- "I heard that only managers in government ever get the chance to go on training."

You are interested and intrigued by the potential of social media platforms such as Facebook, LinkedIn, Twitter, and Google+ as well as tools such as blogs and wikis to support informal learning, collaboration, and information sharing. You have discussed your interest to implement a "pilot" with a few of your most experienced colleagues but have found that several of your direct reports view these tools as "just entertainment fads" that are likely to diminish in popularity over time. However, you are confident several employees, including recent hires, would be eager to explore the possibilities of how these technologies could be used as learning tools and perhaps even enhance the image of the provincial government as a great place to work in the process.

You are mindful that you are not the best role model for use of technology. You have a BlackBerry and recently created a Twitter account but have not even joined Facebook despite receiving a few requests to "friend" some of the younger employees in your area.

Scenario 2: The Sugar Substitute Research Decision

You are the head of research and development (R&D) for a major beer company. While working on a new beer product, one of the scientists in your unit seems to have tentatively identified a new chemical compound that has few calories but tastes closer to sugar than current sugar substitutes. The company has no foreseeable need for this product, but it could be patented and licensed to manufacturers in the food industry.

The sugar-substitute discovery is in its preliminary stages and would require considerable time and resources before it would be commercially viable. This means that it would necessarily take some resources away from other projects in the lab. The sugar-substitute project is beyond your technical expertise, but some of the R&D lab researchers are familiar with that field of chemistry. As with most forms of research, it is difficult to determine the amount of research required to further identify and perfect the sugar substitute. You do not know how much demand is expected for this product. Your department has a decision process for funding projects that are behind schedule. However, there are no rules or precedents about funding projects that would be licensed but not used by the organization.

The company's R&D budget is limited, and other scientists in your work group have recently complained that they require more resources and financial support to get their projects completed. Some of these R&D projects hold promise for future beer sales. You believe that most researchers in the R&D unit are committed to ensuring that the company's interests are achieved.

Scenario 3: Coast Guard Cutter Decision Problem

You are the captain of a 72-metre Coast Guard cutter, with a crew of 16, including officers. Your mission is general at-sea search and rescue. At 2:00 this morning, while en route to your home port after a routine 28-day patrol, you received word from the nearest Coast Guard station that a small plane had crashed 100 kilometres offshore. You obtained all the available information concerning the location of the crash, informed your crew of the mission, and set a new course at maximum speed for the scene to commence a search for survivors and wreckage.

You have now been searching for 20 hours. Your search operation has been increasingly impaired by rough seas, and there is evidence of a severe storm building. The atmospherics associated with the deteriorating weather have made communications with the Coast Guard station impossible. A decision must be made shortly about whether to abandon the search and place your vessel on a course that would ride out the storm (thereby protecting the vessel and your crew, but relegating any possible survivors to almost certain death from exposure) or to continue a potentially futile search and the risks it would entail.

Before losing communications, you received an update weather advisory concerning the severity and duration of the storm. Although your crew members are extremely conscientious about their responsibility, you believe that they would be divided on the decision of leaving or staying.

Discussion Questions (for all three scenarios)

1. To what extent should your employees be involved in this decision? Select one of the following levels of involvement:

   • *Decide alone.* The decision maker relies on personal knowledge and insight to complete the entire decision process without conferring with anyone else.

   • *Receive information from individuals.* The decision maker asks individuals for information. These individuals do not make recommendations and might not even know what the problem is about.

   • *Consult with individuals.* The decision maker describes the problem to selected individuals and seeks both their information and recommendations. The final decision is made by the decision maker, who may or may not take the advice from others into account.

   • *Consult with the team.* The decision maker brings together a team of people (such as all staff in the department), who are told about the problem and provide their ideas and recommendations. The decision maker makes the final decision, which may or may not reflect the team's information.

   • *Facilitate the team's decision.* The entire decision making process is handed over to the team, where the original decision maker serves only as a facilitator to guide the team's decision process and keep everyone on track. The team identifies the problem, discovers alternative solutions, chooses the best alternative, and implements their choice.

2. What factors led you to choose this level of employee involvement rather than the others?

3. What problems might occur if less or more involvement occurred in this case (where possible)?

Sources: Social Media Decision for the Provincial Government is written by Sandra. L. Steen, copyright © 2011. The Sugar Substitute Research Decision is written by Steven L. McShane, copyright © 2002. The Coast Guard Cutter Decision Problem is adapted from V. H. Vroom and A. G. Jago, *The New Leadership: Managing Participation in Organizations* (Englewood Cliffs, NJ: Prentice Hall, 1988), copyright © 1987 V. H. Vroom and A. G. Jago. Used with permission of the authors.

 CASE STUDY 7.2

Going for WOW at Nottingham-Spirk

You might say that creativity is a religious experience at Nottingham-Spirk Design Associates, Inc. A few years ago, the industrial-design company moved into an old church in Cleveland's university park area. Perched atop an escarpment on two hectares of property, the 1920s octagon-shaped limestone building looks like a Roman temple. Inside, employees work in a large rotunda below a domed ceiling supported by 20 columns. Symbols of the original church remain, including a choir loft and soaring pipe organ. "You can't help but walk in here and say, 'I want to create something new,'" says John Nottingham, who co-founded Nottingham-Spirk with John Spirks three decades ago.

Along with an inspiring church building, Nottingham-Spirk supports creativity through its risk-tolerant learning orientation culture. "We stick our necks out," says Nottingham. "If we fail, we go down the wrong path, we dust ourselves off and go the other way. We understand that's innovation." The co-founders and their 70 employees also discover ideas by looking around store shelves. "We're trying to figure out what consumers will want two years down the road," explains Spirk. "We look and see what's not there," Nottingham adds. "We literally visualize an innovation sitting on the shelf next to the competition at a price point."

These activities produce sparks of insight, but they are only the starting point in the creative process. "Anyone can have a good idea," he says. "The difficult thing is to get it to market. You've got to make the idea work and prove its feasibility as a product." To transform ideas to profitable products, Nottingham-Spirk forms teams of up to 10 employees who hold two types of meetings. In the first meeting, called a *diverging session,* team members brainstorm ideas. "We start with a creative session, people from our team that can complement each other, and we come up with as many ideas as you can," says Nottingham. These ideas are documented as scribbles and sketches on slips of paper; up to 100 of them plaster the walls by the end of the session.

In the second round of meetings, called a *converging session,* each idea is systematically evaluated by the team. "I pass around notecards, each with a word or phrase on it that says, WHO CARES, NICE, or WOW" Nottingham explains. The person who introduced an idea can explain it further, then each person judges the idea by selecting one of the three cards. "If everyone holds up a WOW card, you know you've got something," says Nottingham. The WHO CARES ideas get tossed. Some of the NICE ideas are developed further by an idea champion. For example, the SwivelStraight one-minute Christmas tree stand, received mainly NICE ratings when it was first proposed, but co-workers gave it WOW ratings after Nottingham-Spirk designer Craig Saunders refined it further. Almost one million SwivelStraight stands were sold in its first five years on the market.

Diverging and converging sessions are complemented by focus group meetings and client feedback to improve prototypes. Nottingham-Spirk's redesign of the round metal paint can, which has changed little over the past century, is a case in point. Employees knew from experience the frustration of working with traditional paint cans. "We couldn't think of another consumer product that you need a screwdriver to open and a hammer to close," says designer Craig Saunders. So Saunders and his co-workers created a paint can with a twist top and built-in no-drip pour spout. When shown an early prototype, potential users claimed the container wouldn't stack well in warehouses and stores, so the revised prototype was made wider and more stackable. Next, users were concerned that the plastic container would break if it was dropped. "So we took a bunch of them up on ladders and dropped them," says Nottingham. "They bounced." This feedback made the Twist and Pour paint can an instant success; Sherwin-Williams tripled sales of its Dutch Boy paint in the first six months.

Thanks to its creative work environment and innovation process, Nottingham-Spirk has registered close to 500 patents and helped clients achieve more than $30 billion sales over the past three decades. Its most visible innovations include the Crest Spin-Brush®, Invacare Corp. wheelchairs, Swiffer SweeperVac®, wide oval-shaped antiperspirant containers, MRI scanner design, and the Twist and Pour paint can.[100]

Discussion Questions

1. What organizational conditions seem to support creative thinking at Nottingham-Spirk? Why do these conditions support creativity?

2. Explain how the converging–diverging sessions at Nottingham-Spirks aid employee and team creativity.

TEAM EXERCISE 7.3

Where In the World Are We?

Purpose   This exercise is designed to help you understand the potential advantages of involving others in decisions rather than making decisions alone.

Materials   Students require an unmarked copy of the map of Canada with grid marks (Exhibit 2). Students are not allowed to look at any other maps or use any other materials. The instructor will provide a list of communities located somewhere on Exhibit 2. The instructor will also provide copies of the answer sheet after students have individually and in teams estimated the locations of communities.

Instructions
- *Step 1:* Write down in Exhibit 1 the list of communities identified by your instructor. Then, working alone, estimate the location in Exhibit 2 of these communities, all of which are in Canada. For example, mark a small "1" in Exhibit 2 on the spot where you believe the first community is located. Mark a small "2" where you think the second community is located, and so on. Please be sure to number each location clearly and with numbers small enough to fit within one grid space.

- *Step 2:* The instructor will organize students into approximately equal-sized teams (typically five or six people per team). Working with your team members, reach a consensus on the location of each community listed in Exhibit 1. The instructor might provide teams with a separate copy of this map, or each member can identify the team's numbers using a different coloured pen on their individual maps. The team's decision for each location should occur by consensus, not voting or averaging.

- *Step 3:* The instructor will provide or display an answer sheet, showing the correct locations of the communities. Using this answer sheet, students will count the minimum number of grid squares between the location they individually marked and the true location of each community. Write the number of grid squares in the second column of Exhibit 1, then add up the total. Next, count the minimum number of grid squares between the location the team marked and the true location of each community. Write the number of grid squares in the third column of Exhibit 1, then add up the total.

- *Step 4:* The instructor will ask for information about the totals and the class will discuss the implication of these results for employee involvement and decision making.

Exhibit 1	**LIST OF SELECTED COMMUNITIES IN CANADA**		
Number	Community	Individual distance in grid units from the true location	Team distance in grid units from the true location
1			
2			
3			
4			
5			
6			
7			
8			
		Total:	Total:

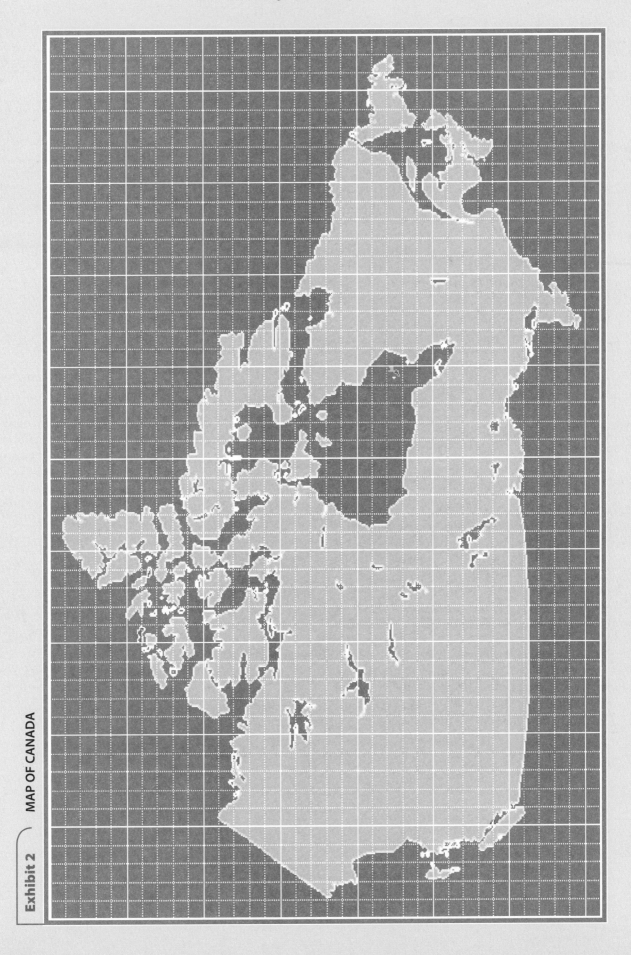

Exhibit 2   MAP OF CANADA

CLASS EXERCISE 7.4

The Hopping Orange

Purpose   This exercise is designed to help students understand the dynamics of creativity and team problem solving.

Instructions   You will be placed in teams of six students. One student serves as the official timer for the team and must have a watch, preferably with a stopwatch timer. The instructor will give each team an orange (or similar object) with a specific task involving use of the orange. The objective is easily understood and nonthreatening, and it will be described by the instructor at the beginning of the exercise. Each team will have a few opportunities to achieve the objective more efficiently. To maximize the effectiveness of this exercise, no other information is provided here.

 CLASS EXERCISE 7.5

Creativity Brainbusters

Purpose   This exercise is designed to help students understand the dynamics of creativity and team problem solving.

Instructions   (Large or Small Class)   The instructor describes the problem, and students are asked to figure out the solution working alone. When enough time has passed, the instructor may then ask specific students who think they have the solution to describe or show their answer. The instructor will review the solutions and discuss the implications of this exercise. In particular, be prepared to discuss what you needed to solve these puzzles and what may have prevented you from solving them more quickly

1. *Double-circle problem.* Draw two circles, one inside the other, with a single line and with neither circle touching the other (as shown below). In other words, you must draw both of these circles without lifting your pen (or other writing instrument).

2. *Nine-dot problem.* Below are nine dots. Without lifting your pencil, draw no more than four straight lines that pass through all nine dots.

● ● ●

● ● ●

● ● ●

3. *Nine-dot problem revisited.* Referring to the nine-dot exhibit above, describe how, without lifting your pencil, you could pass a pencil line through all dots with three or fewer straight lines.

4. *Word search.* In the following line of letters, cross out five letters so that the remaining letters, without altering their sequence, spell a familiar English word.

CFRIVEELATETITEVRSE

5. *Burning ropes.* You have two pieces of rope of unequal lengths and a box of matches. In spite of their different lengths, each piece of rope takes one hour to burn; however, parts of each rope burn at unequal speeds. For example, the first half of one piece might burn in 10 minutes. Use these materials to accurately determine when 45 minutes has elapsed.

Go to CONNECT to complete the following interactive self-assessments.

 SELF-ASSESSMENT EXERCISE 7.6

Do You Have A Creative Personality?

Purpose   This self-assessment is designed to help you measure the extent to which you have a creative personality.

Instructions   Listed below is an adjective checklist with 30 words that may or may not describe you. Check the box beside each word that you think accurately describes you. Please do not check the boxes for words that do not describe you. When finished, you can score the test using the scoring key in Appendix B at the end of the book. This exercise should be completed alone so that you can assess yourself without concerns of social comparison. Class discussion will focus on how this scale might be applied in organizations and on the limitations of measuring creativity in work settings.

Adjective Checklist					
Affected	☐	Honest	☐	Reflective	☐
Capable	☐	Humorous	☐	Resourceful	☐
Cautious	☐	Individualistic	☐	Self-confident	☐
Clever	☐	Informal	☐	Sexy	☐
Commonplace	☐	Insightful	☐	Sincere	☐
Confident	☐	Intelligent	☐	Snobbish	☐
Conservative	☐	Inventive	☐	Submissive	☐
Conventional	☐	Mannerly	☐	Suspicious	☐
Dissatisfied	☐	Narrow interests	☐	Unconventional	☐
Egotistical	☐	Original	☐	Wide interests	☐

Source: Adapted from and based on information in H. G. Gough and A. B. Heilbrun, Jr., *The Adjective Check List Manual* (Palo Alto, CA: Consulting Psychologists Press, 1965).

SELF-ASSESSMENT EXERCISE 7.7

How Creative Are You?

This self-assessment takes the form of a self-scoring quiz. It consists of 12 questions that require divergent thinking to identify the correct answers. For each question, type in your answer in the space provided. When finished, look at the correct answer for each question, along with the explanation for that answer.

 SELF-ASSESSMENT EXERCISE 7.8

What Is Your Preferred Decision Making Style?

People have different styles of decision making that are reflected in how they identify problems or opportunities and make choices. This self-assessment estimates your decision making style through a series of statements describing how individuals go about making important decisions. Please indicate whether you agree or disagree with each statement. Answer each item as truthfully as possible so that you get an accurate estimate of your decision making style. This exercise should be completed alone so that you can assess yourself honestly without concerns of social comparison. Class discussion will focus on the decision making style that people prefer in organizational settings.

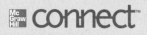 Practise and learn online with Connect. Connect resources include additional and interactive study exercises, videos, and practice quizzing, as well as additional material you won't find in the printed text.

CHAPTER 8

Team Dynamics

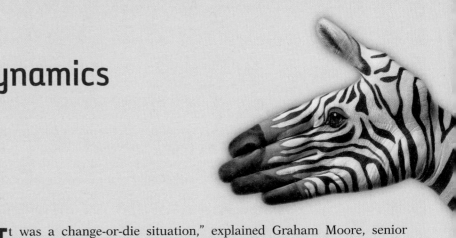

After reading this chapter, you should be able to:

LO1 Explain why employees join informal groups, and discuss the benefits and limitations of teams.

LO2 Outline the team effectiveness model and discuss how task characteristics, team size, and team composition influence team effectiveness.

LO3 Discuss how the four team processes—team development, norms, cohesion, and trust—influence team effectiveness.

LO4 Discuss the characteristics and factors required for success of self-directed teams and virtual teams.

LO5 Identify four constraints on team decision making and discuss the advantages and disadvantages of four structures aimed at improving team decision making.

"**I**t was a change-or-die situation," explained Graham Moore, senior vice-president of operations at Precision Metalcraft. Faced with plummeting revenues in a difficult and changing business environment, the Winnipeg-based manufacturer of metal cabinets, consoles, and enclosures for diverse industries including health care, telecommunications, air traffic control, food service, defence, and consumer electronics, restructured the entire operation. Reorganizing employees into high-performance teams was one ingredient in the company's successful turnaround.

The restructure included replacing 10 to 15 percent of its employees with new workers who were good communicators and had the experience and ability to perform more than one job. When the plant manager job became available, Moore recognized four young employees who had been taking on roles of informal team leaders, by making them his top choice to manage the plant. They had learned their jobs quickly, taken on additional responsibilities, were active in making improvement suggestions, and were a source of encouragement to other employees. So Moore offered Leah Labossiere, Sandy Stadnyk, Mike Sidoryk, and Katie Butler (pictured below) the opportunity to become a self-managed leadership team with shared accountability for running the entire plant. Each of these new team leaders was assigned a primary area aligned with strengths and interests. For example, Labossiere is accountable for human resource tasks, Stadnyk for scheduling and operational systems, Sidoryk for managing and expediting changing priorities, and Butler for manufacturing process improvement.

Each day starts with the four team leaders holding an employee meeting to discuss production issues and scheduling. As situations arise, this leadership team gets together quickly to collaborate and make decisions needed to ensure resources are deployed in the most efficient way to meet changing needs and priorities.

The restructuring and leadership team approach appears to be paying off for Precision Metalcraft. Moore reports that sales are almost back to pre-recession levels and that many new customers have been added. "The accomplishments achieved by this young team and their ability to quickly facilitate organizational change are proof that self-managed teams are the way to go," says Precision Metalcraft president Kingsley Bowes. "Their pride shows through their smiles, their voice, their body language and, of course, through the hard number results they have been able to achieve."[1]

Winnipeg-based Precision Metalcraft relies on a self-managed leadership team to run its manufacturing plant. *Ruth Bonneville/Winnipeg Free Press*

Winnipeg-based Precision Metalcraft discovered how teamwork can improve employee engagement and performance. Indeed, teams have become one of the main ingredients of successful contemporary organizations. More than half of the organizations polled in a recent survey use teams to a high or very high extent to conduct day-to-day business. Furthermore, 77 percent of those firms rely on teams for one-time projects and 67 percent rely on teams for ongoing projects. By comparison, a decade ago only 50 percent of executives said their work is done in teams. Two decades ago, only 20 percent of those executives said they worked in teams.[2] Teamwork has also become more important in scientific research. A recent study of almost 20 million research publications reported that the percentage of journal articles written by teams rather than individuals has increased substantially over the past five decades. Team-based articles also had a much higher number of subsequent citations, suggesting that journal articles written by teams are superior to articles written by individuals.[3]

Why are teams becoming so important, and how can organizations strengthen their potential for organizational effectiveness? We find the answers to these (and other) questions in this chapter on team dynamics. This chapter begins by defining *teams* and examining the reasons why organizations rely on teams and why people join informal groups in organizational settings. A large segment of this chapter examines a model of team effectiveness, which includes team and organizational environment, team design, and the team processes of development, norms, cohesion, and trust. We then turn our attention to two specific types of teams: self-directed teams and virtual teams. The final section of this chapter looks at the challenges and strategies for making better decisions in teams.

TEAMS AND INFORMAL GROUPS

L01

teams Groups of two or more people who interact and influence each other, are mutually accountable for achieving common goals associated with organizational objectives, and perceive themselves as a social entity within an organization.

Teams are groups of two or more people who interact and influence each other, are mutually accountable for achieving common goals associated with organizational objectives, and perceive themselves as a social entity within an organization.[4] This definition has a few important components worth repeating. First, all teams exist to fulfill some purpose, such as repairing electric power lines, assembling a product, designing a new healthcare program, or making an important decision. Second, team members are held together by their interdependence and need for collaboration to achieve common goals. All teams require some form of communication so that members can coordinate and share common objectives. Third, team members influence each other, although some members may be more influential than others regarding the team's goals and activities. Finally, a team exists when its members perceive themselves to be a team.

Exhibit 8.1 briefly describes various types of teams in organizations. Some teams are permanent, while others are temporary; some are responsible for making products or providing services, while others exist to make decisions or share knowledge. Each type of team has been created deliberately to serve an organizational purpose. Some teams, such as skunkworks teams, are not initially sanctioned by management, yet are called "teams" because members work toward an organizational objective.

INFORMAL GROUPS

For the most part, this chapter focuses on formal teams, but employees also belong to informal groups. All teams are groups, but many groups do not satisfy our definition of teams. Groups include people assembled together, whether or not they have any interdependence or organizationally focused objective. The friends you meet for lunch are an *informal group,* but they wouldn't be called a team because they have little or no interdependence (each person could just as easily eat lunch alone) and no organizationally mandated purpose. Instead, they exist primarily for the benefit of their members. Although the terms are used interchangeably, "teams" has largely replaced "groups" in the language of business when referring to employees who work together to complete organizational tasks.[5]

Exhibit 8.1 \ **TYPES OF TEAMS IN ORGANIZATIONS**

Team type	Description
Departmental teams	Teams that consist of employees who have similar or complementary skills and are located in the same unit of a functional structure; usually minimal task interdependence because each person works with clients or employees in other departments.
Production/service/leadership teams	Typically multiskilled (employees have diverse competencies), team members collectively produce a common product/service or make ongoing decisions; production/service teams typically have an assembly-line type of interdependence, whereas leadership teams tend to have tight interactive (reciprocal) interdependence.
Self-directed teams	Similar to production/service teams except (1) they are organized around work processes that complete an entire piece of work requiring several interdependent tasks and (2) they have substantial autonomy over the execution of those tasks (i.e., they usually control inputs, flow, and outputs with little or no supervision).
Advisory teams	Teams that provide recommendations to decision makers; include committees, advisory councils, work councils, and review panels; may be temporary, but often permanent, some with frequent rotation of members.
Task force (project) teams	Usually multiskilled, temporary teams whose assignment is to solve a problem, realize an opportunity, or design a product or service.
Skunkworks	Multiskilled teams that are usually located away from the organization and are relatively free of its hierarchy; often initiated by an entrepreneurial team leader who borrows people and resources *(bootlegging)* to design a product or service.
Virtual teams	Teams whose members operate across space, time, and organizational boundaries and are linked through information technologies to achieve organizational tasks; may be a temporary task force or permanent service team.
Communities of practice	Teams (but often informal groups) bound together by shared expertise and passion for a particular activity or interest; main purpose is to share information; often rely on information technologies as the main source of interaction.

Why do informal groups exist? One reason is that human beings are social animals. Our drive to bond is hardwired through evolutionary development, creating a need to belong to informal groups.[6] This is evident by the fact that people invest considerable time and effort forming and maintaining social relationships without any special circumstances or ulterior motives. A second reason why people join informal groups is provided by social identity theory, which states that individuals define themselves by their group affiliations (see Chapter 3). Thus, we join groups—particularly those that are viewed favourably by others and that have values similar to our own—because they shape and reinforce our self-concept.[7]

A third reason why people are motivated to form informal groups is that such groups accomplish tasks that cannot be achieved by individuals working alone. For example, employees will sometimes create a group to oppose organizational changes because the group collectively has more power than individuals who try to bring about change alone. These informal groups, called coalitions, are discussed in Chapter 10. A fourth explanation for informal groups is that we are comforted by the mere presence of other people and are therefore motivated to be near them in stressful situations. When in danger, people congregate near each other even though doing so serves no protective purpose. Similarly, employees tend to mingle more often after hearing rumours that the company might be acquired by a competitor. As Chapter 4 explained, this social support minimizes stress by providing emotional and/or informational support to buffer the stress experience.[8]

Informal Groups and Organizational Outcomes   Informal groups are not created to serve organizational objectives. Nevertheless, they have a profound influence on organizations and individual employees. Informal groups potentially minimize employee stress because, as mentioned above, group members provide emotional and informational social support. This stress-reducing capability of informal groups improves employee well-being, thereby improving organizational effectiveness. Informal groups are also the backbone of *social networks*, which are important sources of trust building, information sharing, power, influence, and employee well-being in the workplace.[9] Chapter 9 describes the growing significance of social networking sites similar to Facebook and LinkedIn to encourage the formation of informal groups and associated communication. Chapter 10 explains how social networks are a source of influence in organizational settings. Employees with strong informal networks tend to have more power and influence because they receive better information and preferential treatment from others and their talent is more visible to key decision makers.

 Informal groups are not created to serve organizational objectives, yet they have a profound influence on organizations and individual employees. "

ADVANTAGES AND DISADVANTAGES OF TEAMS

Many organizational leaders are convinced that teams make a difference. Hotel Dieu Grace Hospital in Windsor is one of many hospitals throughout Canada that have organized medical staff into cross-functional teams to improve emergency and specialized services. Rackspace Hosting, Inc., organizes most of its 2,700 employees into teams of 12 to 20 people. The Texas-based global provider of enterprise-level Web infrastructure assigns every customer to one of these dedicated teams, which provides around-the-clock service. New Zealand Post's largest delivery branch was the poorest performing branch in the country until employees were re-organized into teams. Now, it is the company's model operation measured by performance and morale.[10]

Why are teams so important in so many organizations around the world? The answer to this question has a long history.[11] Early research on British coal mining in the 1940s, the Japanese economic miracle of the 1970s, and a huge number of investigations since then, have revealed that *under the right conditions,* teams make better decisions, develop better products and services, and create a more engaged workforce than do employees working alone.[12] Similarly, team members can quickly share information and coordinate tasks, whereas these processes are slower and prone to more errors in traditional departments led by supervisors. Teams typically provide superior customer service because they provide more breadth of knowledge and expertise to customers than individual "stars" can offer.

In many situations, people are potentially more motivated when working in teams than when working alone.[13] One reason for this motivation is that, as we mentioned

Cactus Club Café Maintains the Teamwork Rhythm

Most Canadian restaurants try to become successful by using quality ingredients, hiring talented staff, and creating the right ambience. Cactus Club Café does all of these things, but the Western Canadian restaurant chain believes that its team culture is also a key ingredient. "This achievement is a direct result of tremendous teamwork," said Cactus Club president and founder Richard Jaffray after recently receiving an award as one of the best places to work in British Columbia. Chief operating officer Andrew Latchford explains that Cactus Club staff members are organized into teams "to function like a school of fish. An effective team has to be able to respond quickly." This quick and highly coordinated response is possible through "meeting rhythms," which are structured and routinized gatherings held twice each day as well as weekly and monthly. The meetings particularly focus on building team trust and mutual agreement on priorities and role responsibilities. "We call it collective intelligence," says Latchford.[14] *Photo courtesy of Cactus Club Cafe, www.cactusclubcafe.com*

Recognizing the Benefits of Teams[19]

86%
of 1,760 Canadian professionals believe that working in teams is more important to business success today than it was five years ago

68%
of 1,000 working Canadians sampled believe that teams contribute to their own creativity

70%
of 278 American human resource professionals believe that teams encourage diverse thinking

62%
of 278 American human resource professionals believe that teams result in higher productivity

a few paragraphs ago, employees have a drive to bond and are motivated to fulfill the goals of groups to which they belong. This motivation is particularly strong when the team is part of the employee's social identity. "Our employees really value teamwork," says Lucie Bennett, a manager at Ergon Energy, which supplies electricity throughout most of Queensland, Australia. "It is a real key to our success and there's a real family culture, a sort of feeling that everyone is your mate."[15]

Second, people are more motivated in teams because they are accountable to fellow team members, who monitor performance more closely than a traditional supervisor. This is particularly true where the team's performance depends on the lowest performer, such as on an assembly line, where how fast the product is assembled depends on the speed of the slowest employee. Third, under some circumstances, performance improves when employees work near others because co-workers become benchmarks of comparison. Employees are also motivated to work harder because of apprehension that their performance will be compared to others' performance.

THE CHALLENGES OF TEAMS

In spite of their many benefits, teams are not always as effective as individuals working alone.[16] Teams are usually better suited to complex work, such as designing a building or auditing a company's financial records. Under these circumstances, one person rarely has all the necessary knowledge and skills. Instead, complex work is performed better by dividing its tasks into more specialized roles, with people in those specialized jobs coordinating with each other. In contrast, work is typically performed more effectively by individuals alone when they have all the necessary knowledge and skills and the work cannot be divided into specialized tasks or is not complex enough to benefit from specialization. Even where the work can and should be specialized, a team structure might not be necessary if the tasks performed by several people require minimal coordination.

process losses Resources (including time and energy) expended toward team development and maintenance rather than the task.

The main problem with teams is that they have additional costs called **process losses**—resources (including time and energy) expended toward team development and maintenance rather than the task.[17] It is much more efficient for an individual to work out an issue alone than to resolve differences of opinion with other people. For a team to perform well, team members need to agree and have mutual understanding of their goals, the strategy for accomplishing those goals, their specific roles, and informal rules of conduct.[18] Team members need to divert time and energy away from performing the work so they can develop and maintain these team requirements. The process-loss problem is particularly apparent when more people are added or replace others on the team. Team performance suffers when a team adds members, because those employees need to learn how the team operates and how to coordinate efficiently with other team members. Process losses also occur because the workload often needs to be redistributed.

Brooks's law The principle that adding more people to a late software project only makes it later. Also called the *mythical man-month*.

The software industry even has a name for the problems of adding people to a team: **Brooks's law** (also called the *mythical man-month*) says that adding more people to a late software project only makes it later! According to some sources, Apple Computer may have fallen into this trap in the recent development of its professional photography software program, called Aperture. When the project started to fall behind schedule, the manager in charge of the Aperture project increased the size of the team—some sources say it ballooned from 20 to almost 150 engineers and quality assurance staff within a few weeks. Unfortunately, adding so many people further bogged down the project.

The result? When Aperture was finally released, it was nine months late and considered one of Apple's buggier software offerings.[20]

social loafing The problem that occurs when people exert less effort (and usually perform at a lower level) when working in teams than when working alone.

Social Loafing   Perhaps the best-known limitation of teams is the risk of productivity loss due to **social loafing**. Social loafing is the problem that occurs when people exert less effort (and usually perform at a lower level) when working in teams than when working alone.[21] Social loafing tends to be more serious when the individual's performance is less likely to be noticed, such as when people work together in very large teams. The individual's output is also less noticeable where the team produces a single output (rather than each team member producing output), such as finding a single solution to a customer's problem. There is less social loafing when each team member's contribution is more noticeable; this can be achieved by reducing the size of the team, for example, or measuring each team member's performance. Strategic Investments & Holdings Inc., a buyout firm in Buffalo, New York, deliberately restricts the number of company directors for this reason. "When the group is smaller, there's nowhere to hide," explains Strategic Investments principal David Zebro. "You have to pull your weight."[22]

Social loafing also depends on the employee's motivation to perform the work. Social loafing is less prevalent when the task is interesting, because individuals are more motivated by the work itself to perform their duties. For example, one recent study revealed that student apathy explains some of the social loafing that occurs in university student teams. Social loafing is also less common when the team's objective is important, possibly because individuals experience more pressure from co-workers to perform well. Finally, social loafing occurs less frequently among members who value team membership and believe in working toward the team's objectives.[23]

In summary, teams can be very powerful forces for competitive advantage, or they can be much more trouble than they are worth, so much so that job performance and morale decline when employees are placed in teams. To understand when teams are better than individuals working alone, we need to more closely examine the conditions that make teams effective or ineffective. The next few sections of this chapter discuss the model of team effectiveness.

A MODEL OF TEAM EFFECTIVENESS

LO2

Why are some teams effective while others fail? To answer this question, we first need to clarify the meaning of team effectiveness. A team is effective when it benefits the organization, its members, and its own survival.[24] First, most teams exist to serve some organizational purpose, so effectiveness is partly measured by the achievement of those objectives. Second, a team's effectiveness relies on the satisfaction and well-being of its members. People join groups to fulfill their personal needs, so effectiveness is partly measured by this need fulfillment. Finally, team effectiveness includes the team's viability—its ability to survive. It must be able to maintain the commitment of its members, particularly during the turbulence of the team's development. Without this commitment, people leave and the team will fall apart. The team must also secure sufficient resources and find a benevolent environment in which to operate.

Researchers have developed several models over the years to identify the features or conditions that make some teams more effective than others.[25] Exhibit 8.2 integrates the main components of these team effectiveness models. We will closely examine each component over the next several pages. This model is best viewed as a template of several theories because each component (team development, team cohesion, etc.) includes its own set of theories and models to explain how that component operates.

ORGANIZATIONAL AND TEAM ENVIRONMENT

The organizational and team environment represents all conditions beyond the team's boundaries that influence its effectiveness. Team members tend to work together more effectively when they are at least partly rewarded for team performance.[26] Another

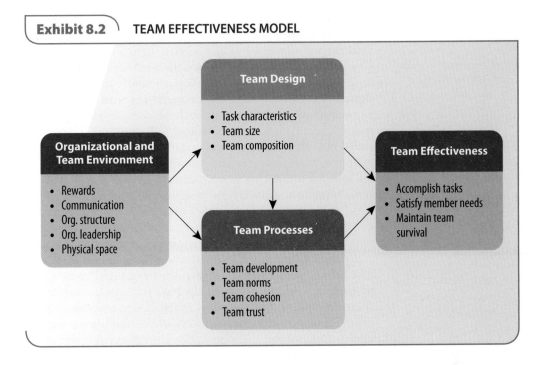

Exhibit 8.2   **TEAM EFFECTIVENESS MODEL**

environmental factor is the organizational structure. Teams flourish when organized around work processes because this structure increases interaction and interdependence among team members and reduces interaction with people outside the team. High-performance teams also depend on organizational leaders who provide support and strategic direction while team members focus on operational efficiency and flexibility.[27] The physical layout of the team's workspace can also make a difference. This was evident at Celestica, Inc., the Toronto-based electronic equipment manufacturer. The company found that one of the best ways to support teams and lean manufacturing (minimize waste) was by replacing the straight-line assembly line with a clustered production arrangement in which members of each team work more closely in U-shaped work cells.[28]

TEAM DESIGN ELEMENTS

Along with setting up a team-friendly environment, leaders need to carefully design the team itself, including task characteristics, team size, team composition, and team roles.

TASK CHARACTERISTICS

What type of work is best for teams? Recall that teams operate better than individuals working alone on work that is sufficiently complex, such as launching the business in a new market, developing a computer operating system, or constructing a bridge. Complex work requires skills and knowledge beyond the competencies of one person. Teams are particularly well suited when the complex work can be divided into more specialized roles and the people in the specialized roles require frequent coordination with each other. Some evidence also suggests that teams work best with well-structured tasks because it is easier to coordinate such work among several people.[29]

For example, La-Z-Boy, Inc., previously organized production staff around their respective trades. "You would have a group of upholsterers in one place, the sewing people in another section, the framing people in another area, and everyone would just work in the same place all day," recalls Jovie Dabu, general manager of La-Z-Boy's manufacturing facility in Redlands, California. Now, the company organizes one or two people from each trade into teams of five to seven employees who work side by side to build an entire piece of furniture. La-Z-Boy executives say the new team structure has improved coordination, communication, and team bonding. "The idea is to help make workers accountable, but also to give them a sense of ownership of what they do," said Greg Bachman, Redlands's production manager.[30]

task interdependence
The extent to which team members must share materials, information, or expertise in order to perform their jobs.

One task characteristic that is particularly important for teams is **task interdependence**—the extent to which team members must share materials, information, or expertise to perform their jobs.[31] Apart from complete independence, there are three levels of task interdependence, as illustrated in Exhibit 8.3. The lowest level of interdependence, called *pooled interdependence,* occurs when an employee or work unit shares a common resource, such as machinery, administrative support, or a budget, with other employees or work units. This would occur in a team setting where each member works alone but shares raw materials or machinery to perform her or his otherwise independent tasks. Interdependence is higher under *sequential interdependence,* in which the output of one person becomes the direct input for another person or unit. Sequential interdependence occurs where team members are organized in an assembly line.

Reciprocal interdependence, in which work output is exchanged back and forth among individuals, produces the highest degree of interdependence. People who design a new product or service would typically have reciprocal interdependence because their design decisions affect others involved in the design process. Any decision made by the design engineers would influence the work of the manufacturing engineer and purchasing specialist, and vice versa. Employees with reciprocal interdependence should be organized into teams to facilitate coordination in their interwoven relationship.

As a rule, the higher the level of task interdependence, the greater the need to organize people into teams rather than have them work alone. A team structure improves interpersonal communication and thus results in better coordination. High task interdependence also motivates most people to be part of the team. However, the rule that a team should be formed when employees have high interdependence applies when team members have the same task goals, such as serving the same clients or collectively assembling the same product. When team members have different goals (such as serving different clients) but must depend on other team members to achieve those unique goals, teamwork might create excessive conflict. Under these circumstances, the company should

Exhibit 8.3   LEVELS OF TASK INTERDEPENDENCE

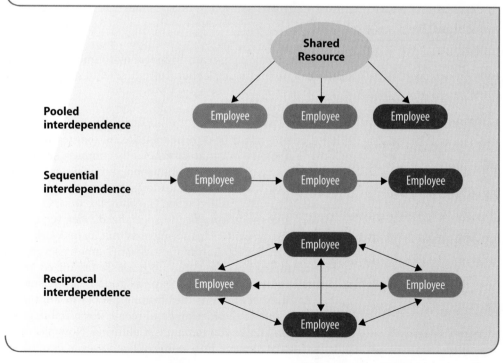

try to reduce the level of interdependence or rely on supervision as a buffer or mediator among employees.

TEAM SIZE

What is the ideal size for a team? Online retailer Amazon relies on the "two-pizza team" rule, namely that a team should be small enough to be fed comfortably with two large pizzas. This works out to between five and seven employees. At the other extreme, a few experts suggest that tasks are becoming so complex that many teams need to have more than 100 members.[32] Unfortunately, the former piece of advice (two-pizza teams) is excessively simplistic, and the latter seems to have lost sight of the meaning and dynamics of real teams.

Generally, teams should be large enough to provide the necessary competencies and perspectives to perform the work, yet small enough to maintain efficient coordination and meaningful involvement of each member.[33] "You need to have a balance between having enough people to do all the things that need to be done, while keeping the team small enough so that it is cohesive and can make decisions effectively and speedily," says Jim Hassell, a senior executive at NBN Co. who previously worked at Sun and IBM.[34] Small teams (say, less than a dozen members) operate effectively because they have less process loss. Members of smaller teams also tend to feel more engaged because they get to know the other team members (which improves trust), have more influence on the group's norms and goals, and feel more responsible for the team's success and failure.

Should companies have 100-person teams if the task is highly complex? The answer is that a group this large probably isn't a team, even if management calls it one. A team exists when its members interact and influence each other, are mutually accountable for achieving common goals associated with organizational objectives, and perceive themselves as a social entity within an organization. It is very difficult for everyone in a 100-person work unit to influence each other and experience enough cohesion to perceive themselves as team members. Executives at Whole Foods Market were aware that real teams are much smaller than 100 people when the food retailer opened its huge store in New York City's Columbus Circle. The store had 140 cashiers—far too many people for one cashier team—so Whole Foods Market divided the group into teams with a dozen employees each. All cashiers meet as one massive group every month to discuss production issues, but the smaller teams work effectively on a day-to-day basis.[35]

TEAM COMPOSITION

To work effectively in a team, employees must have more than technical skills to perform their own work; they must also be able and willing to perform that work in a team environment. Royal Dutch/Shell is serious about selecting job applicants who have excellent team skills. As Global Connections 8.1 describes, the global energy giant hosts a special five-day exercise in Europe, North America, Asia, and the Middle East to observe how well participants work under pressure with others from diverse backgrounds.

The most frequently mentioned characteristics or behaviours of effective team members are depicted in the "five C's" model illustrated in Exhibit 8.4 (see page 221): cooperating, coordinating, communicating, comforting, and conflict resolving. The first three competencies are mainly (but not entirely) task-related, while the last two primarily assist team maintenance:[36]

- *Cooperating.* Effective team members are willing and able to work together rather than alone. This includes sharing resources and being sufficiently adaptive or flexible to accommodate the needs and preferences of other team members, such as rescheduling use of machinery so that another team member with a tighter deadline can use it.

- *Coordinating.* Effective team members actively manage the team's work so that it is performed efficiently and harmoniously. For example, effective team members keep the team on track and help to integrate the work performed by different members. This typically requires that effective team members know the work of other team members, not just their own.

CONNECTIONS 8.1

GLOBAL

Royal Dutch/Shell Finds Team Players in Gourami

Royal Dutch/Shell (Shell) relies on teams to accomplish its extremely complex work. For example, Shell Canada's website states that in addition to achievement-orientation, intelligence, and technical skills, the energy company is seeking people with "the character and ability to work effectively with others in a diverse team." Shell managers learned long ago that traditional job interviews don't test an applicant's team skills, so the company launched the Shell Gourami Business Challenge a decade ago in Europe and more recently in North America, Asia, and the Middle East to examine team skills in action.

Shell's five-day Gourami Business Challenge involves several dozen engineering and business students who are split into teams representing different departments (exploration, refining, manufacturing, finance, etc.). Teams initially develop a business plan for their own department; later, they must merge the departmental plans into an organization-wide business strategy. On the final day, the multi-team's strategy is presented to Gourami's board of directors, which consists of senior level executives from Shell.

Shell leaders emphasize that the Gourami event is more like an audition than a competition because the company hires as many participants as it thinks are qualified. Throughout the event, Shell assessors evaluate students' technical knowledge and skills, but equally observe how effectively they worked in diverse teams. The need for team skills is quickly apparent to most participants. "Coming from a business background, it's most difficult to understand the engineering aspect of the oil industry," admitted Arpan Shah, a University of Texas finance student who attended

Royal Dutch/Shell has found a better way to identify the team skills of prospective job applicants by observing business and engineering students in the Shell Gourami Business Challenge. *AP Images/Michael Stravato/The Canadian Press*

the Gourami exercise in Rancho Mirage, California. "We have to work together so that both sides understand each other."

Claire Gould, a mechanical engineering student at Imperial College, London, who attended the European session, also noticed the challenges and potential of teamwork with people from other disciplines. "Dealing with the 'real-life' challenges of Gourami made us all aware of the value of other skills and aptitudes and the need to work as a team," says Gould.[37]

- *Communicating.* Effective team members transmit information freely (rather than hoarding), efficiently (using the best channel and language), and respectfully (minimizing arousal of negative emotions). They also listen actively to co-workers.

- *Comforting.* Effective team members help co-workers to maintain a positive and healthy psychological state. They show empathy, provide psychological comfort, and build co-worker feelings of confidence and self-worth.

- *Conflict resolving.* Conflict is inevitable in social settings, so effective team members have the skills and motivation to resolve dysfunctional disagreements among team members. This requires effective use of various conflict-handling styles as well as diagnostic skills to identify and resolve the structural sources of conflict.

These characteristics of effective team members are associated with conscientiousness and extroversion personality traits, as well as with emotional intelligence. Furthermore, the old saying "One bad apple spoils the barrel" seems to apply to teams; one team member who lacks these teamwork competencies may undermine the dynamics of the entire team.[38]

Team Diversity   Another important dimension of team composition is diversity. Team diversity seems to have both positive and negative effects on team effectiveness.[39] Let's first look at the benefits of team diversity. Research suggests that, in specific situations, diverse teams are better than homogeneous teams at making decisions. One reason is that people from different backgrounds tend to see a problem or opportunity from

| **Exhibit 8.4** | **FIVE C's OF TEAM MEMBER COMPETENCY** |

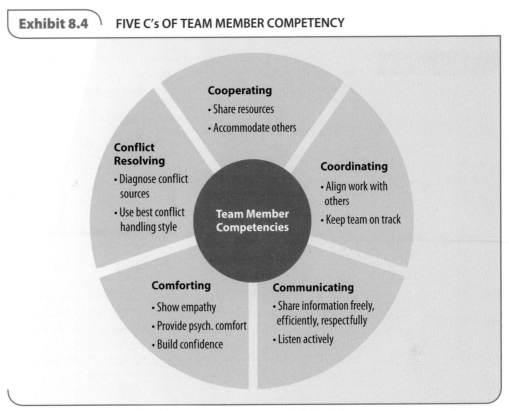

Sources: Based on information in V. Rousseau, C. Aubé, and A. Savoie, "Teamwork Behaviours: A Review and an Integration of Frameworks," *Small Group Research* 37, no. 5 (2006), pp. 540–570; M.L. Loughry, M.W. Ohland, and D. D. Moore, "Development of a Theory-Based Assessment of Team Member Effectiveness," *Educational and Psychological Measurement* 67, no. 3 (2007), pp. 505–524.

different angles. Team members have different mental models, so they are more likely to identify viable solutions to difficult problems.

A second reason why diverse teams tend to make better decisions is that they have a broader pool of technical competencies. Consider the diverse management team at Precision Metalcraft, which was described at the beginning of this chapter. The Winnipeg-based management team included members with backgrounds in human resources, operations, manufacturing processes, and strategic planning. Precision Metalcraft requires people with these diverse skills and experiences to effectively lead the plant through complex problems and opportunities. A third reason favouring teams with diverse members is that they provide better representation of the team's constituents, such as other departments or clients from similarly diverse backgrounds. A team responsible for designing and launching a new service, for instance, should have representation from the organization's various specializations so that people in those work units will support the team's decisions.

Team diversity offers many advantages, but it also presents a number of opposing challenges.[40] Specifically, employees with diverse backgrounds take longer to become a high-performing team. This partly occurs because team members take longer to bond with people who are different from them, particularly when others hold different perspectives and values (i.e., deep-level diversity). Diverse teams are susceptible to "fault lines"—hypothetical dividing lines that may split a team into subgroups along gender, ethnic, professional, or other dimensions. These fault lines reduce team effectiveness by reducing the motivation to communicate and coordinate with teammates on the other side of the hypothetical divisions. In contrast, members of teams with minimal diversity experience higher satisfaction, less conflict, and better interpersonal relations. Consequently, homogeneous teams tend to be more effective on tasks requiring a high degree of cooperation and coordination, such as emergency response teams.

TEAM PROCESSES

L03

The third set of elements in the team effectiveness model, collectively known as *team processes,* includes team development, norms, cohesion, and trust. These elements represent characteristics of the team that continuously evolve.

TEAM DEVELOPMENT

Team members must resolve several issues and pass through several stages of development before emerging as an effective work unit. They need to get to know and trust each other, understand and agree on their respective roles, discover appropriate and inappropriate behaviours, and learn how to coordinate with each other. The longer that team members work together, the better they develop common or complementary mental models, mutual understanding, and effective performance routines to complete the work.

A popular model that captures many team development activities is shown in Exhibit 8.5.[41] The model shows teams moving systematically from one stage to the next, while the dashed lines illustrate that teams might fall back to an earlier stage of development as new members join or other conditions disrupt the team's maturity. *Forming,* the first stage of team development, is a period of testing and orientation in which members learn about each other and evaluate the benefits and costs of continued membership. People tend to be polite, will defer to authority, and try to find

Exhibit 8.5   **STAGES OF TEAM DEVELOPMENT**

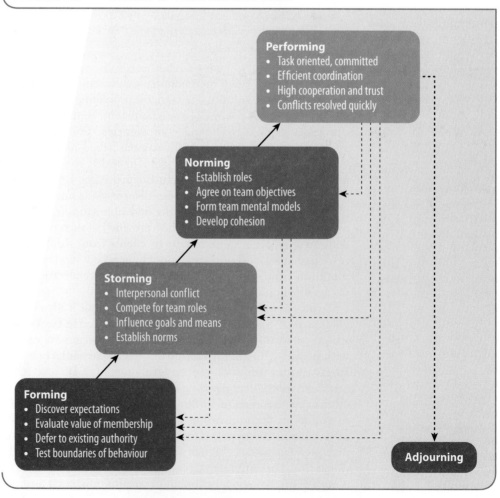

Performing
- Task oriented, committed
- Efficient coordination
- High cooperation and trust
- Conflicts resolved quickly

Norming
- Establish roles
- Agree on team objectives
- Form team mental models
- Develop cohesion

Storming
- Interpersonal conflict
- Compete for team roles
- Influence goals and means
- Establish norms

Forming
- Discover expectations
- Evaluate value of membership
- Defer to existing authority
- Test boundaries of behaviour

Adjourning

out what is expected of them and how they will fit into the team. The *storming* stage is marked by interpersonal conflict as members become more proactive and compete for various team roles. Members try to establish norms of appropriate behaviour and performance standards.

During the *norming* stage, the team develops its first real sense of cohesion as roles are established and a consensus forms around group objectives and a common or complementary team-based mental model. By the *performing* stage, team members have learned to efficiently coordinate and resolve conflicts. In high-performance teams, members are highly cooperative, have a high level of trust in each other, are committed to group objectives, and identify with the team. Finally, the *adjourning* stage occurs when the team is about to disband. Team members shift their attention away from task orientation to a relationship focus.

The five-stage model is consistent with what students experience on team projects (as one Canadian study found), but it is far from a perfect representation of the team development process. For instance, it does not show that some teams remain in a particular stage longer than others. The five-stage model also masks two distinct processes during team development: developing team identity and developing team competence.[42]

- *Developing team identity*—This process involves the transition that individuals make from viewing the team as something "out there" to something that is part of themselves. In other words, team development occurs when employees shift their view of the team from "them" to "us." Developing team identity relates to becoming familiar with the team, making it part of their social identity, and shaping the team to better fit their prototype of an ideal team.

- *Developing team competence*—This process includes developing habitual routines with teammates and forming shared or complementary mental models.[43] Team mental models are visual or relational mental images that are shared by team members. For example, members of a newly formed team might have different views about customer service (quality of interaction, speed of service, technical expertise provided, etc.). As the team develops, these views converge into more of a shared mental model of customer service. One recent meta-analysis reported that teams are more effective when their members share common mental models of the work.[44]

Team Roles   An important part of the team development process is forming and reinforcing team roles. A **role** is a set of behaviours that people are expected to perform because of the positions they hold in a team and organization.[45] In a team setting, some roles help the team achieve its goals; other roles maintain relationships within the team. Some team roles are formally assigned to specific people. For example, team leaders are usually expected to initiate discussion, ensure that everyone has an opportunity to present his or her views, and help the team reach agreement on the issues discussed.

role A set of behaviours that people are expected to perform because of the positions they hold in a team and organization.

Team members are assigned specific roles within their formal job responsibilities. Yet, team members also assume informal roles that suit their personality and values as well as the wishes of other team members. These informal roles, which are negotiated throughout the team development process, range from supporting others to initiating new ideas. Informal team roles are shared, but many are eventually associated with one or two people on the team.[46]

team building A process that consists of formal activities intended to improve the development and functioning of a work team.

Accelerating Team Development through Team Building   **Team building** is a process that consists of formal activities intended to improve the development and functioning of a work team.[47] To a large extent, team building attempts to speed up the team development process. This process may be applied to new teams, but it is more commonly introduced for existing teams that have regressed to earlier stages of team development due to membership turnover or loss of focus.

Some team-building interventions are task-focused. They clarify the team's performance goals, increase the team's motivation to accomplish these goals, and establish a mechanism for systematic feedback on the team's goal performance. A second type of

The Amazing Chase Team Building Challenge

One of the most popular team building activities offered by Calgary-based, Canadian Outback Adventures & Events is the "Amazing Chase." The Amazing Chase combines planning, strategy, communication, and teamwork in a race against the clock. Courses can be custom-designed, set up outdoors or even indoors with creative use of covered walkways and public transit. The overall goal is for teams to work together to navigate route markers, deal with road blocks and detours, and finish the race in the least amount of time. "One of my favourite things was the way that people were able to get creative and have some fun problem solving," says a Bentall Capital spokesperson. "For the teams themselves I think getting exposure to others in our department that they do not work with day-to-day was a key! It proved the old adage, "no one is good at everything, but everyone is good at something."[48]
Courtesy Canadian Outback Adventures & Events, www.canadianoutback.com

team building tries to improve the team's problem-solving skills. A third category clarifies and reconstructs each member's perceptions of her or his role as well as the role expectations that a member has of other team members. Role definition team building also helps the team to develop shared mental models—common internal representations of the external world, such as how to interact with clients, maintain machinery, and engage in meetings. Research studies indicate that team processes and performance depend on how well team members share common mental models about how they should work together.[49]

A fourth—and likely the most common—type of team building is aimed at improving relations among team members. Its objective is to help team members learn more about each other, build trust in each other, and develop ways to manage conflict within the team. Popular interventions such as wilderness team activities, paintball wars, and obstacle-course challenges are typically offered to build trust. "If two colleagues hold the rope for you while you're climbing 10 metres up, that is truly team building," suggests a partner in a German communications consulting firm who participated in that team-building event.[50]

Although team-building activities are popular, their success is less certain.[51] One problem is that team-building activities are used as general solutions to general team problems. A better approach is to begin with a sound diagnosis of the team's health and then select team-building interventions that address weaknesses.[52] Another problem is that team building is applied as a one-shot medical inoculation that every team should receive when it is formed. In truth, team building is an ongoing process, not a three-day jump start.[53] Finally, we must remember that team building occurs on the job, not just on an obstacle course or in a national park. Organizations should encourage team members to reflect on their work experiences and to experiment with just-in-time learning for team development.

TEAM NORMS

norms The informal rules and shared expectations that groups establish to regulate the behaviour of their members.

Norms are the informal rules and shared expectations that groups establish to regulate the behaviour of their members. Norms apply only to behaviour, not to private thoughts or feelings. Furthermore, norms exist only for behaviours that are important to the team.[54] Norms are enforced in various ways. Co-workers grimace if we are late for a meeting, or they make sarcastic comments if we don't have our part of the project completed on time. Norms are also directly reinforced through praise from high-status members, more access to valued resources, or other rewards available to the team. But team members often conform to prevailing norms without direct reinforcement or punishment because they identify with the group and want to align their behaviour with the team's values. The more closely the person's social identity is connected to the group, the more the individual is motivated to avoid negative sanctions from that group.[55]

How Team Norms Develop   Norms develop when teams form because people need to anticipate or predict how others will act. Even subtle events during the team's formation, such as how team members initially greet each other and where they sit in the first few meetings, can initiate norms that are later difficult to change. Norms also form as team members discover behaviours that help them function more effectively (such as the need to respond quickly to email). In particular, a critical event in the team's history can trigger formation of a norm or sharpen a previously vague one. A third influence on team norms are the experiences and values that members bring to the team. If members of a new team value work-life balance, norms are likely to develop that discourage long hours and work overload.[56]

Preventing and Changing Dysfunctional Team Norms   Team norms often become deeply anchored, so the best way to avoid norms that undermine organizational success or employee well-being is to establish desirable norms when the team is first formed. One way to do this is to clearly state desirable norms when the team is created. Another approach is to select people with appropriate values. If organizational leaders want their teams to have strong safety norms, they should hire people who already value safety and who clearly identify the importance of safety when the team is formed.

The suggestions so far refer to new teams, but how can organizational leaders maintain desirable norms in older teams? One solution comes from a recent Canadian study, namely that leaders often have the capacity to alter existing norms.[57] By speaking up or actively coaching the team, they can often subdue dysfunctional norms while developing useful norms. A second suggestion is to introduce team-based rewards that counter dysfunctional norms. However, studies report that employees might continue to adhere to a dysfunctional team norm (such as limiting output) even though this behaviour reduces their paycheque. Finally, if dysfunctional norms are deeply ingrained and the previous solutions don't work, it may be necessary to disband the group and replace it with people having more favourable norms.

> " By speaking up or actively coaching the team, leaders can often subdue dysfunctional norms while developing useful norms."

TEAM COHESION

team cohesion The degree of attraction people feel toward the team and their motivation to remain members.

Team cohesion refers to the degree of attraction people feel toward the team and their motivation to remain members. It is a characteristic of the team, including the extent to which its members are attracted to the team, are committed to the team's goals or tasks, and feel a collective sense of team pride.[58] Thus, team cohesion is an emotional experience, not just a calculation of whether to stay or leave the team. It exists when team members make the team part of their social identity. Team development tends to improve cohesion because members strengthen their identity to the team during the development process.

Influences on Team Cohesion   Several factors influence team cohesion: member similarity, smaller team size, member interaction, difficult entry, team success, and external competition or challenges. For the most part, these factors reflect the individual's social identity with the group and beliefs about how team membership will fulfill personal needs.

- *Member similarity.* Teams have higher cohesion or become cohesive more quickly when members are similar to each other. This influence on cohesion is due to the similarity–attraction effect, which states that people with similar backgrounds and values are more comfortable with and attracted to each other. Generally, it is more difficult or takes longer for teams with diverse members to become cohesive, but this depends on the form of diversity. For example, teams consisting of people from different job groups seem to gel together just as well as teams of people from the same job.[59]

- *Team size.* Smaller teams tend to have more cohesion than larger teams because it is easier for a few people to agree on goals and coordinate work activities. However, small teams have less cohesion when they lack enough members to perform the required tasks.

- *Member interaction.* Teams tend to have more cohesion when team members interact with each other fairly regularly. This occurs when team members perform highly interdependent tasks and work in the same physical area.

- *Somewhat difficult entry.* Teams tend to have more cohesion when entry to the team is restricted. Elite teams confer more prestige upon their members, which increases the value of being a team member. At the same time, research suggests that severe initiations can weaken team cohesion because of the adverse effects of humiliation, even for those who successfully endure the initiation.[60]

- *Team success.* Cohesion is both emotional and instrumental, with the latter referring to the notion that people feel more cohesion to teams that fulfill their needs and goals. Consequently, cohesion increases with the team's level of success.[61] Furthermore, individuals are more likely to attach their social identity to successful teams than to those with a string of failures.[62]

- *External competition and challenges.* Team cohesion tends to increase when members face external competition or a valued objective that is challenging. This might include a threat from an external competitor or friendly competition from other teams. Employees value their membership on the team because of its ability to overcome the threat or competition and as a form of social support. However, cohesion can dissipate when external threats are severe because these threats are stressful and cause teams to make less effective decisions.[63]

Consequences of Team Cohesion   Every team must have some minimal level of cohesion to maintain its existence. People who belong to high-cohesion teams are motivated to maintain their membership and to help the team achieve its mutually agreed objectives. Compared to low-cohesion teams, high-cohesion team members spend more time together, share information more frequently, and are more satisfied with

A Lighthouse Built on High Cohesion

The staff at Lighthouse Publishing in Bridgewater, Nova Scotia, are a highly cohesive group that successfully keeps its much larger competitors off-guard. "Lighthouse staff members [have] kept us independent in the face of stiff competition and corporate takeovers," says Lighthouse president Lynn Hennigar. Its weekly newspaper, the *Bridgewater Bulletin*, has received more than 200 newspaper industry awards. Lighthouse's mostly female staff often demonstrate their cohesion when faced with new challenges. For instance, the team performed above any reasonable expectations when the press broke down, which threatened to delay getting the paper out on time. On another occasion, when putting together an interactive presentation promoting Nova Scotia tourism, Lighthouse staff displayed skills that Hennigar admits she didn't even know about. "Lighthouse succeeds because of its multi-talented, highly dedicated team of employees," says Hennigar. "It's a team that embraces change."[64] *Courtesy of Atlantic Business Magazine and Lighthouse Publishing*

each other. They provide each other with better social support in stressful situations.[65] Members of high-cohesion teams are generally more sensitive to each other's needs and develop better interpersonal relationships, thereby reducing dysfunctional conflict. When conflict does arise, members tend to resolve their differences swiftly and effectively. With better cooperation and more conformity to norms, high-cohesion teams usually perform better than low-cohesion teams.[66]

There are two important matters that need to be discussed regarding the cohesion–performance relationship, however. First, although we typically assume that higher cohesion leads to higher team performance, we earlier explained that team performance (success) is a predictor of cohesion. Indeed, one recent study estimated that team performance has a stronger effect on cohesion than vice versa. In other words, a team's performance will likely affect its cohesion, whereas a team's cohesion has less of an effect on its performance.

The second matter might explain why cohesion has less of an effect on performance than vice versa. Specifically, as Exhibit 8.6 illustrates, team cohesion increases team performance only when the team's norms are compatible with organizational values and objectives. When team norms are counterproductive (such as when norms encourage absenteeism or discourage employees from working more productively), a cohesive team will typically perform worse than if the team has low cohesion. This effect occurs because cohesion motivates employees to perform at a level more consistent with team norms. When team norms undermine the organization's performance, high cohesion will motivate employees to reduce team performance.[67]

TEAM TRUST

trust The positive expectations one person has toward another person or group in situations involving risk.

Any relationship—including the relationship among team members—depends on a certain degree of trust.[68] **Trust** refers to the positive expectations one person has toward another person or group in situations involving risk (see Chapter 4).[69] A high level of trust occurs when others affect you in situations where you are at risk but you believe they will not harm you. Trust includes both your beliefs and conscious feelings about the relationship with other team members. In other words, you both logically evaluate a person as trustworthy and feel that she or he is trustworthy.[70] Trust is built on three foundations: calculus, knowledge, and identification (see Exhibit 8.7).

Exhibit 8.6 \ EFFECT OF TEAM COHESION ON TASK PERFORMANCE

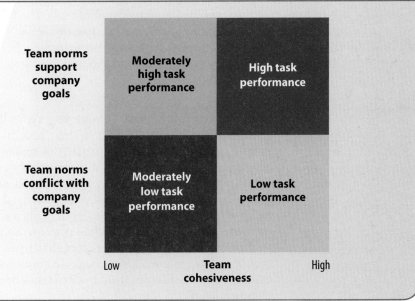

	Low — Team cohesiveness — High
Team norms support company goals	Moderately high task performance / High task performance
Team norms conflict with company goals	Moderately low task performance / Low task performance

Exhibit 8.7 \ **THREE FOUNDATIONS OF TRUST IN TEAMS**

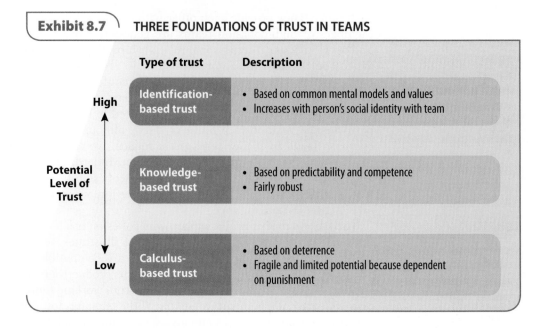

- *Calculus-based trust* represents a logical calculation that other team members will act appropriately because they face sanctions if their actions violate reasonable expectations.[71] It offers the lowest potential trust and is easily broken by a violation of expectations. Generally, calculus-based trust alone cannot sustain a team's relationship, because it relies on deterrence.

- *Knowledge-based trust* is based on the predictability of another team member's behaviour. Even if we don't agree with a particular team member's actions, his or her consistency generates some level of trust. Knowledge-based trust also relates to confidence in the other person's ability or competence, such as the confidence that exists when we trust a physician.[72] Knowledge-based trust offers a higher potential level of trust and is more stable because it develops over time.

- *Identification-based trust* is based on mutual understanding and an emotional bond among team members. It occurs when team members think, feel, and act like each other. High-performance teams exhibit this level of trust because they share the same values and mental models. Identification-based trust is potentially the strongest and most robust of all three types of trust. The individual's self-concept is based partly on membership in the team and he or she believes the members' values highly overlap, so any transgressions by other team members are quickly forgiven. People are more reluctant to acknowledge a violation of this high-level trust because it strikes at the heart of their self-concept.

Dynamics of Team Trust   Employees typically join a team with a moderate or high level—not a low level—of trust in their new co-workers. The main explanation for the initially high trust (called *swift trust*) in organizational settings is that people usually believe fellow team members are reasonably competent (knowledge-based trust) and they tend to develop some degree of social identity with the team (identification-based trust). Even when working with strangers, most of us display some level of trust, if only because it supports our self-concept of being a good person.[73] However, trust is fragile in new relationships because it is based on assumptions rather than well-established experience. Consequently, studies report that trust tends to decrease rather than increase over time. This is unfortunate because employees become less forgiving and less cooperative toward others as their level of trust decreases, and this undermines team and organizational effectiveness.[74]

The team effectiveness model is a useful template for understanding how teams work—and don't work—in organizations. With this knowledge in hand, let's briefly investigate two types of teams that have received considerable attention among OB experts and practitioners: self-directed teams and virtual teams.

SELF-DIRECTED TEAMS

LO4

self-directed teams (SDTs) Cross-functional work groups that are organized around work processes, that complete an entire piece of work requiring several interdependent tasks, and that have substantial autonomy over the execution of those tasks.

When Whole Foods Market opens new stores, the organic food retailer isn't just looking for employees with good customer service skills. It is looking for people who also work well in self-directed teams. Every Whole Foods Market store is divided into about 10 teams, such as the prepared-foods team, the cashier/front-end team, and the seafood team. Teams are "self-directed" because team members make the decisions about their work unit with minimal interjection from management. "Each team is . . . responsible for managing its own business," explains Whole Foods Market co-founder John Mackey. "It gets a profit-and-loss statement, it's responsible for managing inventory, labour productivity, gross margins; and its members are responsible for many of the product-placement decisions."[75]

Whole Foods Market operates with self-directed teams. **Self-directed teams (SDTs)** are cross-functional groups that are organized around work processes, that complete an entire piece of work requiring several interdependent tasks, and that have substantial autonomy over the execution of those tasks.[76] From this definition are two distinct features of SDTs. First, these teams complete an entire piece of work requiring several interdependent tasks. This type of work arrangement clusters the team members together while minimizing interdependence and interaction with employees outside the team. The result is a close-knit group of employees who depend on each other to accomplish their individual tasks. For example, Whole Foods Market employees responsible for a store's fish department would naturally work more closely with each other than with members of other teams. Another example is Reckitt Benckiser Healthcare's manufacturing facility in the United Kingdom, which is described in Global Connections 8.2.

The second distinctive feature of SDTs is that they have substantial autonomy over the execution of their tasks. In particular, these teams plan, organize, and control work activities with little or no direct involvement of a higher-status supervisor. The teams at Whole Foods Market, for instance, are called self-directed because they have considerable autonomy and responsibility for decisions in their work area, including managing inventory, profitability, scheduling, and hiring.

Self-directed teams are found in several Canadian industries, ranging from petrochemical plants to aircraft parts manufacturing. Some sources estimate that most of the top-rated manufacturing firms in North America rely on SDTs.[77] Indeed, self-directed teams have become such a popular way to organize employees in manufacturing, services, and government work that many companies don't realize they have them. The popularity of SDTs is consistent with research indicating that they potentially increase both productivity and job satisfaction. For instance, one study found that car dealership service shops that organize employees into SDTs are significantly more profitable than shops where employees work without a team structure. Another study reported that both short- and long-term measures of customer satisfaction increased after street cleaners in a German city were organized into SDTs.[78]

SUCCESS FACTORS FOR SELF-DIRECTED TEAMS

The successful implementation of self-directed teams depends on several factors.[79] SDTs should be responsible for an entire work process, such as making an entire product or providing a service. This structure keeps each team sufficiently independent from other teams, yet it demands a relatively high degree of interdependence among employees within the team.[80] SDTs should also have sufficient autonomy to organize and coordinate their work. Autonomy allows them to respond more quickly and effectively to client and stakeholder demands. It also motivates team members through feelings of

CONNECTIONS 8.2

Reckitt Benckiser's Prescription for Productivity: Self-Directed Teams

Through teamwork and lean manufacturing practices, Reckitt Benckiser Healthcare has become one of the most productive pharmaceutical operations in Europe. In fact, teamwork is one of the company's four core values. At its facility in Hull, United Kingdom, for example, every line is operated by a dedicated self-directed team.

"The people on the lines decide how they are going to run over the next three to four weeks," says Lisa Adams, team leader of the area that packages products in sachets and tubes. Mark Smith, a crew leader of one line, proudly notes that his team has become "one of the most efficient in northern Europe" because "we were given the opportunity to take ownership of the line."

The benefits of self-directed teams were apparent at Reckitt Benckiser Healthcare when the team responsible for producing Gaviscon antacid tablets tackled a problem with the delivery of tablets in the production process. The team changed the tablet-feed angle and, after a few trials, found a solution. That production line hasn't experienced any further tablet-feed problems, and this has significantly reduced costs and improved efficiency due to fewer down-times and less wasted product.[81]

Reckitt Benckiser relies on self-directed teams to operate its pharmaceutical plants in Europe more productively. *Dean Smith camera crew*

empowerment. Finally, SDTs are more successful when the work site and technology support coordination and communication among team members and increase job enrichment.[82] Too often, management calls a group of employees a "team," yet the work layout, assembly-line structure, and other technologies isolate the employees from each other.

VIRTUAL TEAMS

Denis Chamberland admits that he had trouble recognizing most of his colleagues when he worked at Accenture. That's because Chamberland was chief legal counsel in Toronto for the global consulting firm, whereas his boss and co-workers operated out of London, Chicago, and other far-flung locations. "There were many people who I worked with for years and never actually met. In many cases, I never even talked to them on the phone," says Chamberland, who is now a partner at a Toronto law firm.[83]

Denis Chamberland has had plenty of experience with the growing trend toward **virtual teams**. Virtual teams are teams whose members operate across space, time, and organizational boundaries, and are linked through information technologies to achieve organizational tasks.[84] Virtual teams differ from traditional teams in two ways: (1) They are not usually co-located (do not work in the same physical area), and (2) due to their lack of co-location, members of virtual teams depend primarily on information technologies rather than face-to-face interaction to communicate and coordinate their work effort.

Virtual teams have spread throughout most organizations, and this trend will continue. Two-thirds of human resource managers estimate that reliance on virtual teams will grow rapidly over the next few years.[85] In global companies such as IBM, almost everyone in knowledge work is part of a virtual team. One reason why virtual teams have become so widespread is that information technologies have made it easier than ever before to communicate and coordinate with people at a distance.[86] The shift from production-based to knowledge-based work is a second reason why virtual teamwork is

virtual teams Teams whose members operate across space, time, and organizational boundaries, and are linked through information technologies to achieve organizational tasks.

feasible. It isn't yet possible to make a product when team members are located apart, but most of us are now in jobs that mainly process knowledge.

Information technologies and knowledge-based work make virtual teams *possible,* but organizational learning and globalization are two reasons why they are increasingly *necessary.* Virtual teams represent a natural part of the organizational learning process because they encourage employees to share and use knowledge where geography limits more direct forms of collaboration. Globalization makes virtual teams increasingly necessary because employees are spread around the planet rather than around one building or city. Thus, global businesses depend on virtual teamwork to leverage their human capital. Indeed, one consortium of chief information officers listed managing virtual teams as the top-ranked challenge of globalization.[87]

SUCCESS FACTORS FOR VIRTUAL TEAMS

Virtual teams have all the challenges of traditional teams, along with the complications of distance and time. Fortunately, OB researchers have been keenly interested in virtual teams, and their studies are now yielding ways to improve virtual-team effectiveness.[88] First, along with having the team competencies described earlier in this chapter, members of successful virtual teams must have good communication technology skills, strong self-leadership skills to motivate and guide their behaviour without peers or bosses nearby, and higher emotional intelligence so that they can decipher the feelings of other team members from email and other limited communication media. For example, one survey reported that twice as many employees believe workplace relationship problems (such as missing work deadlines) occur more frequently in virtual than face-to-face teams. They also believe virtual teams take considerably longer to resolve these problems than when employees work in the same building.[89]

A second recommendation is that virtual teams should have a toolkit of communication channels (email, virtual whiteboards, video conferencing, etc.) as well as the freedom to choose the channels that work best for them. This may sound obvious, but unfortunately senior management tends to impose technology on virtual teams, often based on advice from external consultants, and expects team members to use the same communication technology throughout their work. In contrast, research suggests that specific communication channels gain and lose importance over time, depending on the task and level of trust.

Third, virtual teams need plenty of structure. In one recent review of effective virtual teams, many of the principles for successful virtual teams related mostly to creating these structures, such as clear operational objectives, documented work processes, and agreed upon roles and responsibilities.[90] The final recommendation is that virtual-team members should meet face-to-face fairly early in the team development process. This idea may seem contradictory to the entire notion of virtual teams, but so far, no technology has replaced face-to-face interaction for high-level bonding and mutual understanding.

TEAM DECISION MAKING

L05

Self-directed teams, virtual teams, and practically all other groups are expected to make decisions. Under certain conditions, teams are more effective than individuals at identifying problems, choosing alternatives, and evaluating their decisions. To leverage these benefits, however, we first need to understand the constraints on effective team decision making. Then, we look at specific team structures that try to overcome these constraints.

CONSTRAINTS ON TEAM DECISION MAKING

Anyone who has spent enough time in the workplace can rhyme off several ways in which teams stumble in decision making. The four most common problems are time constraints, evaluation apprehension, pressure to conform, and some elements of groupthink.

Time Constraints   There's a saying that committees keep minutes and waste hours. This reflects the fact that teams take longer than individuals to make decisions.[91] Unlike individuals, teams require extra time to organize, coordinate, and maintain relationships. The larger the group, the more time is required to make a decision. Team members need time to learn about each other and build rapport. They need to manage an imperfect communication process so that there is sufficient understanding of each other's ideas. They also need to coordinate roles and rules of order within the decision process.

Another time-related constraint found in most team structures is that only one person can speak at a time.[92] This problem, known as **production blocking**, undermines idea generation in several ways. First, team members need to listen in on the conversation to find an opportune time to speak up, and this monitoring makes it difficult for them to concentrate on their own ideas. Second, ideas are fleeting, so the longer they wait to speak up, the more likely these flickering ideas will die out. Third, team members might remember their fleeting thoughts by concentrating on them, but this causes them to pay less attention to the conversation. By ignoring what others are saying, team members miss other potentially good ideas as well as the opportunity to convey their ideas to others in the group.

production blocking A time constraint in team decision making due to the procedural requirement that only one person may speak at a time.

Evaluation Apprehension   Team members are often reluctant to mention ideas that seem silly because they believe (often correctly) that other team members are silently evaluating them.[93] This **evaluation apprehension** is a decision making problem that is based on the individual's desire to create a favourable self-presentation and need to protect self-esteem. It is most common when meetings are attended by people with different levels of status or expertise or when members formally evaluate each other's performance throughout the year (as in 360-degree feedback). Creative ideas often sound bizarre or illogical when first presented, so evaluation apprehension tends to discourage employees from mentioning them in front of co-workers.

evaluation apprehension A decision making problem that occurs when individuals are reluctant to mention ideas that seem silly because they believe (often correctly) that other team members are silently evaluating them.

Pressure to Conform   Team cohesion leads employees to conform to the team's norms. This control keeps the group organized around common goals, but it may also cause team members to suppress their dissenting opinions, particularly when a strong team norm is related to the issue. When someone does state a point of view that violates the majority opinion, other members might punish the violator or try to persuade him or her that the opinion is incorrect. Conformity can also be subtle. To some extent, we depend on the opinions that others hold to validate our own views. If co-workers don't agree with us, we begin to question our own opinions even without overt peer pressure.

Groupthink   **Groupthink** refers to the tendency of highly cohesive groups to value consensus at the price of decision quality.[94] The concept includes the dysfunctional effects of conformity on team decision making, which we just described. It also includes the dysfunctional consequences of trying to maintain harmony within the team. This desire for harmony exists as a group norm and is most apparent when team members have a strong social identity with the group. Groupthink supposedly occurs most often when the team is isolated from outsiders, the team leader is opinionated (rather than impartial), the team is under stress due to an external threat, the team has experienced recent failures or other decision-making problems, and the team lacks clear guidance from corporate policies or procedures.

groupthink The tendency of highly cohesive groups to value consensus at the price of decision quality.

The term *groupthink* is now part of everyday language, but most experts have dismissed the concept. The main problem with the groupthink concept is that it consists of several elements that don't cluster together very well, and some of those elements actually improve rather than undermine decision making in some situations. Also, almost all support for the groupthink effect comes from case studies, most of which are flawed.[95]

Although the groupthink concept is on its last legs, there are specific elements that remain relevant as problems with team decision making. One of these elements, conformity, was identified earlier as a problem with team decision making. Overconfidence is another groupthink element that also deserves continued attention as a problem. Studies consistently report that highly confident teams have a false sense of invulnerability, which makes them less attentive in decision making than are moderately confident teams.[96] This overconfidence effect is related to problems with self-enhancement described in Chapter 3 and with the adverse effects of positive moods and emotions on the quality of decision making (see Chapter 7).

TEAM STRUCTURES TO IMPROVE DECISION MAKING

Team decision making is fraught with problems, but several solutions also emerge from these bad-news studies. Team members need to be confident in their decision making but not so confident that they collectively feel invulnerable. This calls for team norms that encourage critical thinking as well as team membership with sufficient diversity. Checks and balances need to be in place to prevent one or two people from dominating the discussion. The team should also be large enough to possess the collective knowledge to resolve the problem yet small enough that the team doesn't consume too much time or restrict individual input. One recent view is that executive teams have difficulty reaching consensus on many decisions because the problems are ill-defined and executives on the team see themselves as representatives of their constituents (divisions, departments, regions, etc.). Consequently, executive teams might work best by identifying everyone's preferences, have them vigorously debated, create a few plausible options and, in most cases, allow the CEO or team leader to make the final decision where consensus is too difficult.[97]

Team structures also help to minimize the problems described over the previous few pages. Four structures potentially improve team decision making in team settings: constructive conflict, brainstorming, electronic brainstorming, and nominal group technique.

Constructive Conflict   A popular way to improve team decision making at Corning Inc. is to assign promising ideas to two-person teams, who spend up to four months analyzing the feasibility of their assigned idea. The unique feature about this process is that the team is always composed of one person with marketing expertise and another person with technical expertise. This oil-and-water combination sometimes ruffles feathers, but it seems to generate better ideas and evaluations. "We find great constructive conflict this way," says Deborah Mills, who leads Corning's early-stage marketing team.[98]

constructive conflict A type of conflict in which people focus their discussion on the issue while maintaining respect for people having other points of view.

Constructive conflict is a type of conflict in which people focus their discussion on the issue while maintaining respect for people having other points of view. This conflict is called "constructive" because it encourages people to present their divergent viewpoints so ideas and recommendations can be clarified, redesigned, and tested for logical soundness. This critical thinking and analysis helps participants to re-examine their assumptions and logic. The main challenge with constructive conflict is that people get defensive when their ideas are questioned, even when those critiques are polite and logical. Consequently, constructive conflict often degenerates into defensive behaviour and personal attacks. This tendency may explain why constructive conflict has not been consistently beneficial for team decision making across studies.[99] We explore this issue further in Chapter 11, along with specific strategies for minimizing the emotional effects of conflict while maintaining constructive debate.

brainstorming A freewheeling, face-to-face meeting where team members aren't allowed to criticize, but are encouraged to speak freely, generate as many ideas as possible, and build on the ideas of others.

Brainstorming   **Brainstorming** is a team event where participants try to think up as many ideas as possible. The process, which was invented by advertising executive Alex Osborn in 1939, has four simple rules to maximize the number and quality of ideas presented: (1) Speak freely—describe even the craziest ideas; (2) don't criticize others or their ideas; (3) provide as many ideas as possible—the quality of ideas increases with the quantity of ideas; and (4) build on the ideas that others have presented. These rules are supposed to encourage divergent thinking while minimizing evaluation apprehension and other team dynamics problems.[100]

Although brainstorming became immensely popular when first introduced, it lost credibility over the years—for the wrong reasons. First, a business magazine article in

Brainstorming with Second City

IBM Canada wanted to sign up more retailers for its customer service offerings and turned to Second City, well-known for sketch comedy to lend a hand. "We started with something pretty basic—a panel of talking heads discussing customer service," says IBM Canada marketing manager, Dave Rodgerson. Current and prospective clients along with experts from the retail industry such as Elizabeth Evans, director of the Ted Rogers School of Retail Management at Ryerson were invited to Second City's location in downtown Toronto for a brainstorming session moderated by Lee Smart, a creative director at Second City. Second City injected its brand of humour to get participants thinking in new and creative ways.[101] *The Canadian Press/Steve White*

the 1950s misrepresented and lampooned the process.[102] Second, numerous psychology studies using college and university students concluded that brainstorming isn't very effective, mainly because production blocking and evaluation apprehension still interfere with team dynamics.[103]

These studies and the magazine article were unfortunate because subsequent work has found that brainstorming tends to be effective in real-world work settings.[104] Many of the old lab studies were flawed because student teams lacked the supportive learning orientation norms found in organizations where brainstorming has been successful. Indeed, companies that use brainstorming point out that it takes skill to facilitate effective brainstorming sessions to minimize evaluation apprehension and production blocking. The lab studies also measured brainstorming effectiveness by the number of ideas generated, whereas recent investigations within companies indicate that brainstorming results in more *creative* ideas (not more ideas).

The lab studies also overlooked other benefits of brainstorming reported by companies that swear by these events. The positive focus of brainstorming (no criticizing) tends to increase team cohesion and participant commitment to the eventual decision. Brainstorming sessions also tend to spread enthusiasm—a condition that often generates more creativity. Overall, while brainstorming might not always be the best team structure, it seems to be more valuable than the earlier research studies indicated.

electronic brainstorming
A form of brainstorming that relies on networked computers for submitting and sharing creative ideas.

Electronic Brainstorming   **Electronic brainstorming** is a form of brainstorming that relies on networked computers for submitting and sharing creative ideas. After receiving the question or issue, participants enter their ideas using special computer software. The ideas are distributed anonymously to other participants, who are encouraged to piggyback on those ideas. Team members eventually vote electronically on the ideas presented. Face-to-face discussion usually follows. Electronic brainstorming can be quite effective at generating creative ideas with minimal production blocking, evaluation apprehension, or conformity problems.[105] Despite these numerous advantages, electronic brainstorming seems to be too structured and technology-bound for some executives. Some leaders may also feel threatened by the honesty of statements generated through this process and by their limited ability to control the discussion.

nominal group technique
A variation of brainstorming consisting of three stages: participants (1) silently and independently document their ideas, (2) collectively describe these ideas to the other team members without critique, and (3) silently and independently evaluate the ideas presented.

Nominal Group Technique   **Nominal group technique** is another variation of traditional brainstorming that tries to combine the benefits of team decision making without the problems mentioned earlier.[106] The method is called "nominal" because participants form a group in name only during two of its three stages. After the problem is described, team members silently and independently document their ideas. In the second stage, participants collectively describe these ideas to the other team members, usually in a round-robin format. As with brainstorming, there is no criticism or debate, although members are encouraged to ask for clarification of the ideas presented. In the third stage, participants silently and independently evaluate the ideas presented.

Nominal group technique has been applied in numerous laboratory and real-world settings, such as identifying issues that affect the development of agri-tourism in Nova Scotia.[107] For the most part, these studies endorse the use of this structured form of team decision making. It tends to generate a higher number of ideas and better-quality ideas than do traditional interacting and possibly brainstorming groups.[108] Due to its high degree of structure, nominal group technique usually maintains a high task orientation and relatively low potential for conflict within the team. However, production blocking and evaluation apprehension still occur to some extent. At least one study also reports that participants require training to apply this structured approach to team decision making.[109]

CHAPTER SUMMARY

 LO1   Explain why employees join informal groups, and discuss the benefits and limitations of teams.

Teams are groups of two or more people who interact and influence each other, are mutually accountable for achieving common goals associated with organizational objectives, and perceive themselves as a social entity within an organization. All teams are groups, because they consist of people with a unifying relationship; not all groups are teams, because some groups do not exist to serve organizational objectives.

People join informal groups (and are motivated to be on formal teams) for four reasons: (1) People have an innate drive to bond, (2) group membership is an inherent ingredient in a person's self-concept, (3) some personal goals are accomplished better in groups, and (4) individuals are comforted in stressful situations by the mere presence of other people. Teams have become popular because they tend to make better decisions, support the knowledge management process, and provide superior customer service. People also tend to be more motivated working in teams. However, teams are not always as effective as individuals working alone. Process losses and social loafing are two particular concerns that drag down team performance.

LO2   Outline the team effectiveness model and discuss how task characteristics, team size, and team composition influence team effectiveness.

Team effectiveness includes the team's ability to achieve its objectives, fulfill the needs of its members, and maintain its survival. The model of team effectiveness considers the team and organizational environment, team design, and team processes. Three team design elements are task characteristics, team size, and team composition. Teams tend to be better suited for situations in which the work is complex and the tasks among employees have high interdependence. Teams should be large enough to perform the work yet small enough for efficient coordination and meaningful involvement. Effective teams are composed of people with the competencies and motivation to perform tasks in a team environment. Team member diversity has advantages and disadvantages for team performance.

 LO3   Discuss how the four team processes—team development, norms, cohesion, and trust—influence team effectiveness.

Teams develop through the stages of forming, storming, norming, performing, and eventually adjourning. Within these stages are two distinct team development processes: developing team identity and developing team competence. Team development can be accelerated through team building—any formal activity intended to improve the development and functioning of a work team. Teams develop norms to regulate and guide member behaviour. These norms may be influenced by initial experiences, critical events, and the values and experiences that team members bring to the group.

Team cohesion—the degree of attraction people feel toward the team and their motivation to remain members—increases with member similarity, smaller team size, higher degree of interaction, somewhat difficult entry, team success, and external challenges. Cohesion increases team performance when the team's norms are congruent with organizational goals. Trust is a psychological state comprising the intention to accept vulnerability on the basis of positive expectations of the intent or behaviour of another person. People trust others on the basis of three foundations: calculus, knowledge, and identification.

LO4   Discuss the characteristics and factors required for success of self-directed teams and virtual teams.

Self-directed teams (SDTs) complete an entire piece of work requiring several interdependent tasks, and they have substantial autonomy over the execution of their tasks. Members of virtual teams operate across space, time, and organizational boundaries and are linked through information technologies to achieve organizational tasks. Virtual teams are more effective when the team members have certain competencies, the team has the freedom to choose the preferred communication channels, and the members meet face-to-face fairly early in the team development process.

LO5 Identify four constraints on team decision making and discuss the advantages and disadvantages of four structures aimed at improving team decision making.

Team decisions are impeded by time constraints, evaluation apprehension, conformity to peer pressure, and groupthink (specifically overconfidence). Four structures potentially improve decision making in team settings: constructive conflict, brainstorming, electronic brainstorming, and nominal group technique.

KEY TERMS

brainstorming, p. 233
Brooks's law, p. 215
constructive conflict, p. 233
electronic brainstorming, p. 234
evaluation apprehension, p. 232
groupthink, p. 232
nominal group technique, p. 234

norms, p. 224
process losses, p. 215
production blocking, p. 232
role, p. 223
self-directed teams (SDTs), p. 229
social loafing, p. 216
task interdependence, p. 218

team building, p. 223
team cohesion, p. 225
teams, p. 212
trust, p. 227
virtual teams, p. 230

CRITICAL-THINKING QUESTIONS

1. Informal groups exist in almost every form of social organization. What types of informal groups exist in your classroom? Why are students motivated to belong to these informal groups?

2. The late management guru Peter Drucker said: "The now-fashionable team in which everybody works with everybody on everything from the beginning rapidly is becoming a disappointment." Discuss three problems associated with teams.

3. You have been put in charge of a cross-functional task force that will develop enhanced Internet banking services for retail customers. The team includes representatives from marketing, information services, customer service, and accounting, all of whom will move to the same location at headquarters for three months. Describe the behaviours you might observe during each stage of the team's development.

4. You have just been transferred from the Regina office to the Vancouver office of your company, a national sales organization of electrical products for developers and contractors. In Regina, team members regularly called customers after a sale to ask whether the products arrived on time and whether they are satisfied. But when you moved to the Vancouver office, no one seemed to make these follow-up calls. A recently hired co-worker explained that other co-workers discouraged her from making those calls. Later, another co-worker suggested that your follow-up calls were making everyone else look lazy. Give three possible reasons why the norms in Vancouver might be different from those in the Regina office, even though the customers, products, sales commissions, and other characteristics of the workplace are almost identical.

5. You have been assigned to a class project with five other students, none of whom you have met before. To what extent would team cohesion improve your team's performance on this project? What actions would you recommend to build team cohesion among student team members in this situation?

6. Suppose that you were put in charge of a virtual team whose members are located in different cities around the country or region. What tactics could you use to build and maintain team trust, as well as minimize the decline in trust that often occurs in teams?

7. You are responsible for convening a major event in which senior officials from several provincial governments will try to come to an agreement on environmental issues. It is well known that some officials posture so that they appear superior, whereas others are highly motivated to solve the environmental problems that cross adjacent provinces. What team decision making problems are likely to be apparent in this government forum, and what actions can you take to minimize these problems?

8. Chatham Technologies wants to use brainstorming with its employees and customers to identify new uses for its technology. Advise Chatham's president about the potential benefits of brainstorming, as well as its potential limitations.

 CASE STUDY 8.1

The Outstanding Faculty Award

Adapted from a case by David J. Cherrington, Brigham Young University

I recently served on the Outstanding Faculty Award committee for the College of Business. This award is our college's highest honour for a faculty member, which is bestowed at a special reception ceremony. At the first meeting, our committee discussed the nomination process and decided to follow our traditional practice of inviting nominations from both the faculty and students. During the next month, we received six completed files with supporting documentation. Three of the nominations came from department chairs, two from faculty who recommended their colleagues, and one from a group of 16 graduate students.

At the second meeting, we agreed that we didn't know the six applicants well enough to make a decision that day, so we decided that we would read the applications on our own and rank them. There was no discussion about ranking criteria; I think we assumed that we shared a common definition of the word "outstanding."

During the third meeting, it quickly became apparent that each committee member had a different interpretation of what constitutes an "outstanding" faculty member. The discussion was polite, but we debated the extent to which this was an award for teaching, or research, or service to the college, or scholarly textbook writing, or consulting, or service to society, or some other factor. After three hours, we agreed on five criteria that we would apply to independently rate each candidate using a five-point scale.

When we reconvened the next day, our discussion was much more focused as we tried to achieve a consensus regarding how we judged each candidate on each criterion. After a lengthy discussion, we finally completed the task and averaged the ratings. The top three scores had an average rating (out of a maximum of 25) of 21, 19.5, and 18.75. I assumed the person with the highest total would receive the award. Instead, my colleagues began debating over the relevance of the five criteria that we had agreed on the previous day. Some committee members felt, in hindsight, that the criteria were incorrectly weighted or that other criteria should be considered. Although they did not actually say this, I sensed that at least two colleagues on the committee wanted the criteria or weights changed because their preferred candidate didn't get the highest score using the existing formula. When we changed the weights in various ways, a different candidate among the top three received the top score. The remaining three candidates received lower ratings every time. Dr. H always received the lowest score, usually around 12 on the 25-point range.

After almost two hours, the Associate Dean turned to one committee member and said, "Dolan, I sure would like to see Dr. H in your department receive this honour. He retires next year and this would be a great honour for him and no one has received this honour in your department recently."

Dolan agreed, "Yes, this is Dr. H's last year with us and it would be a great way for him to go out. I'm sure he would feel very honoured by this award."

I sat there stunned at the suggestion while Dolan retold how Dr. H had been active in public service, his only real strength on our criteria. I was even more stunned when another committee member, who I think was keen to finish the meeting, said, "Well, I so move." and Dolan seconded it.

The Associate Dean, who was conducting the meeting, said, "Well, if the rest of you think this is a good idea, all in favour say Aye." A few members said Aye and he quickly proceeded to explain what we needed to do to advertise the winner and arrange the ceremony without calling for Nays.

During my conversations with other committee members over the next two weeks, I learned that everyone—including the two who said Aye—were as shocked as I was at our committee's decision. I thought we made a terrible decision and I was embarrassed to be a member of the committee. A few weeks later, we were appropriately punished when Dr. H gave a 45-minute acceptance speech that started poorly and got worse.

Discussion Questions

1. What problems in team decision making likely caused the committee to select for the award the worst applicant on their list?

2. What would you recommend to future committees so they avoid the problems identified in this case?

3. Discuss what happened in this case using concepts and theories of individual decision making (see Chapter 7).

CASE STUDY 8.2

. . . .

The Philanthropic Team-Builder

To kick off the post-merger integration of Molson and Coors breweries, the top dozen executives from both companies wanted to accelerate their team development. But rather than the usual team building in the woods or a challenging in-house activity, the Molson Coors leaders spent a full day helping build a house for Habitat for Humanity. "We quickly got past the idea of a ropes course or golf outing," recalls Samuel D. Walker, Molson Coors' chief legal officer. "We really wanted something where we would give back to one of the communities where we do business." According to Walker, the volunteering experience exceeded everyone's expectations. "We had to unload this truck full of cement roof tiles. We actually had to figure out how to have kind of a bucket line, handing these very heavy tiles from one person to the next. That's the ultimate teambuilding exercise."

The Molson Coors executive team's experience with team building through volunteerism has since spread throughout the company. In particular, Molson Canada's operations have changed how they support communities and how they engage employees in team building to support that process. "Traditionally, you have someone in charge of philanthropy [who made decisions about] donating money," says Scott Ewart, chief of legal and public affairs at Molson Canada. "We wanted our customers and employees to feel that we were doing the right thing." A survey of customers and staff revealed that Molson should be donating more to help young adults to develop active lifestyles, new skills, and healthy communities.

Along with aligning corporate donations more closely to stakeholder preferences, Molson now actively encourages employee involvement in these philanthropic projects through an in-house volunteer program. Rather than meeting on the golf course or a corporate retreat, employees participate in team building exercises such as painting youth hostels and refurbishing cabins at children's cancer camps in Quebec and Alberta.

This movement toward team building through volunteerism has not only helped Molson Coors employees to form more functional teams; it has also had a positive effect on morale. The percentage of employees who said they were 'extremely satisfied' with Molson as a place to work increased from 62 percent to 78 percent in the year after the volunteering initiative was introduced. "The results were swift and positive," Ewart recalls. This initiative has also made the company a more attractive employer of choice. "To attract and retain the right people today, you simply can't say we're going to train you or we're going to give you a good salary, or whatever," explains Molson Coors CEO Kevin Boyce. "They are looking for more. They are looking for a company they can feel good about."

Discussion Questions

1. What type of team building best describes these volunteering activities?

2. Explain how the corporate social responsibility element of volunteering contributes to team building.

3. Along with team building, in what other ways do these volunteering activities improve organizations?

Sources: Martha C. White, "Doing Good on Company Time," *New York Times,* May 8, 2007; Hollie Shaw, "Doing the Right Thing," *National Post,* June 15, 2007; Michael Kane, "Companies Find New Ways to Celebrate," *Vancouver Sun,* December 1, 2007.

TEAM EXERCISE 8.3

. . . .

Team Tower Power

Purpose   This exercise is designed to help you understand team roles, team development, and other issues in the development and maintenance of effective teams.

Materials   The instructor will provide enough Lego pieces or similar materials for each team to complete the assigned task. All teams should have identical (or very similar) amounts and types of pieces. The instructor will need a measuring tape and stopwatch. Students may use writing materials during the design stage (Step 2, below). The instructor will distribute a "Team Objectives Sheet" and "Tower Specifications Effectiveness Sheet" to all teams.

Instructions   **1.** The instructor will divide the class into teams. Depending on class size and space availability, teams may have between four and seven members, but all should be approximately equal size.

2. Each team is given 20 minutes to design a tower that uses only the materials provided, is freestanding, and provides an optimal return on investment. Team members may wish to draw their tower on paper or a flipchart to facilitate the tower's design. Teams are free to practise building their tower during this stage. Preferably, teams are assigned to their own rooms so that the design can be created privately. During this stage, each team will complete the Team Objectives Sheet distributed by the instructor. This sheet requires the Tower Specifications Effectiveness Sheet, also distributed by the instructor.

3. Each team will show the instructor that it has completed its Team Objectives Sheet. Then, with all teams in the same room, the instructor will announce the start of the construction phase. The time allowed for construction will be closely monitored, and the instructor will occasionally call out the time elapsed (particularly if there is no clock in the room).

4. Each team will advise the instructor as soon as it has completed its tower. The team will write down the time elapsed that the instructor has determined. It may be asked to assist the instructor by counting the number of blocks used and measuring the height of the tower. This information is also written on the Team Objectives Sheet. Then the team calculates its profit.

5. After presenting the results, the class will discuss the team dynamics elements that contribute to team effectiveness. Team members will discuss their strategy, division of labour (team roles), expertise within the team, and other elements of team dynamics.

Source: Several published and online sources describe variations of this exercise, but there is no known origin to this activity.

 TEAM EXERCISE 8.4

Human Checkers

Purpose   This exercise is designed to help students understand the importance and application of team dynamics and decision making.

Materials   None, but the instructor has more information about the team's task.

Instructions   **1.** Form teams of eight students. If possible, each team should have a private location where team members can plan and practise the required task without being observed or heard by other teams.

2. All teams receive special instructions in class about their assigned task. All teams have the same task and have the same amount of time to plan and practise the task. At the end of this planning and practise, each team will be timed while completing the task in class. The team that completes the task in the least time wins.

3. No special materials are required or allowed (see rules below) for this exercise. Although the task is not described here, students should learn the following rules for planning and implementing the task:

    a. You cannot use any written form of communication or any props to assist in the planning or implementation of this task.

    b. You may speak to other students in your team at any time during the planning and implementation of this task.

c. When performing the task, you can only move forward, not backward. (You are not allowed to turn around.)

d. When performing the task, you can move forward to the next space, but only if it is vacant. In Exhibit 1, the individual (black dot) can move directly into an empty space (white dot).

e. When performing the task, you can move forward two spaces if that space is vacant. In other words, you can move around a person who is one space in front of you to the next space if that space is vacant. (In Exhibit 2, two people occupy the black dots, and the white dot is an empty space. A person can move around the person in front to the empty space.)

Exhibit 1   Exhibit 2

4. When all teams have completed their task, the class will discuss the implications of this exercise for team dynamics and decision making.

Discussion Questions

1. Identify team dynamics and decision making concepts that the team applied to complete this task.

2. What personal theories of people and work teams were applied to complete this task.

3. What other organizational behaviour issues occurred, and what actions were (or should have been) taken to solve them.

 TEAM EXERCISE 8.5

Mist Ridge

By Richard Field and Nicola Sutton

It is approximately 9 a.m. on August 23, and you and four friends are about to set off on an all-day hike in the mountains of southwestern Alberta. Having driven southwest from Calgary, Alberta, you have arrived at Kananaskis Provincial Park, located on the boundary between British Columbia and Alberta. Just off Highway 40, you turn into the Mist Creek day-use area and have just parked the car. You can see a sign indicating the beginning of the Mist Ridge trail, which you have selected for your hike, but you know that from there on the trail proceeds along unmarked paths and logging roads. You can also see another sign that allows campfires only in designated rest areas.

Since it is mid-week, few others should be on the Mist Ridge trail. You and your friends are looking forward to an enjoyable day walking the long grass and rock ridge as it is usually dry and sunny at this time of year, when a mere few kilometres away across the valley, Mist Mountain can be covered in rain clouds. Hiking from the parking lot to the ridge, then along the whole top of the ridge to Rickert's Pass, and then returning at ground level alongside the Mist Creek, is, at minimum, an eight-hour trip. In guidebooks it is classified as a long day hike covering a total distance of 23 kilometres with a height gain of 808 metres and a maximum elevation of 2,515 metres.

The weather at the moment is cool but not cold, and the sun is beaming down, beginning to heat the air. In general, the climate of southwestern Alberta is cold continental, having long cold winters and cool summers, though summers do have brief hot spells. Annual precipitation peaks in the summer and thunderstorms occur regularly. Hikers at this time of year must be prepared for rain or cold weather. Snow has been known to fall by the middle of August in this area, with accumulations on the ground of up to 20 centimetres. Also, the weather can be somewhat changeable and unpredictable. What starts out as a warm, sunny morning could easily change into a cold, snowy afternoon. Therefore, experienced hikers will make sure that they have adequate reserve clothing for the rain or snow that could develop. It is also known that temperatures are expected to be cooler at the top of the ridge, as temperatures decrease, in general, 2 degrees Celsius for ever 300 metres of altitude.

There are a few dangers to watch out for during your hike. If you get soaked crossing a river, loss of body heat may result in hypothermia, even when temperatures are above freezing. Death from hypothermia is quite possible within a few hours of the first symptoms if proper care is not taken. On the other hand, the exertions of walking and climbing will probably cause you to sweat. Dehydration can increase your chance of sunstroke and hypothermia. In terms of animals, you may encounter a bear looking for berries. While bear attacks on humans are not common, they are not unusual either. It is also possible that elk or moose may be encountered. These large plant eaters are not usually dangerous to humans, but may become aggressive during the mating season. There are also some insects to be considered. Ticks can carry Rocky Mountain Spotted Fever, which can be fatal if left untreated. Bees can also be dangerous if the person stung has a strong allergic reaction.

You are all currently dressed in warm clothes including wool socks and sturdy hiking boots, and each person has a day pack in which to carry those items that you deem necessary.

Part I: Individual Decision

There are 15 items listed below. Before you set out on your hike your task is to rank these items according to their general importance for a hiker, not for you specifically. Rank the items from 1, the most important, to 15, the least important. No ties are allowed. You might want to consider "If a hiker was allowed to take only one item, what would it be?" That item would be ranked number 1. Then, "If a hiker was allowed only one more item, what would it be?" That item would rank number 2. Write your rankings in the item titled "Your Ranking." It is important to remember that the decisions you are making are for your group as a whole and should not be influenced by factors affecting you as an individual.

Items	Your Ranking	Group Ranking	Expert Ranking	Your Score	Group Score
Canteen with water					
Matches					
Compass					
Hat					
Repair kit (includes short length of cord, string, duct tape, and shoelaces)					
First aid kit (includes blister protection and aspirin)					
Five sleeping bags					
Sunglasses					
Topographic map and *Kananaskis Country Trail* guide book					
Food					
5-person tent with waterproof fly					
Sunscreen					
Rain gear					
Insect repellent					

Part II: Group Decision   Now form into groups. Take a few minutes to examine and discuss your individual assumptions before you begin to discuss how to rank specific items. Use constructive controversy decision rules to guide your decision method and rank the 15 items again. To refresh your memory, they are: (1) be critical of ideas, not people; (2) focus on making the best possible decision, not winning; (3) encourage everyone to participate in the discussion; (4) listen to everyone's ideas, even if you do not agree; (5) restate what someone has said if their point is not clear to you; (6) bring out the ideas and facts supporting both sides of the argument and then try to integrate them; (7) try to understand both sides of the issue under discussion; and (8) change your mind if the evidence clearly indicates that you should do so.[110]

Write your group's answers in the "Group Ranking" column.

Part III: Scoring   Your instructor will inform you of how experts have ranked these 15 items. Write these rankings into the column titled "Expert Ranking." To calculate your personal score, calculate for each of the 15 items the absolute difference between your ranking and the expert's ranking, then sum these 15 absolute value differences. Determine your group's score in the same manner. Write these scores and summary statistics into the spaces below.

Your total score _____

Average of the individual scores in your group _____

Your group's total score _____

Number of individuals in your group having a lower score than your group's total score _____

Go to CONNECT to complete the following interactive self-assessments.

 SELF-ASSESSMENT EXERCISE 8.6

What Team Roles Do You Prefer?

Purpose   This self-assessment is designed to help you identify your preferred roles in meetings and similar team activities.

Instructions   Read each of the statements below and circle the response that you believe best reflects your position regarding each statement. Then use the scoring key in Appendix B at the end of the book to calculate your results for each team role. This exercise should be completed alone so that you can assess yourself honestly without concerns of social comparison. Class discussion will focus on the roles that people assume in team settings. This scale assesses only a few team roles.

Team Roles Preferences Scale					
Circle the number that best reflects your position regarding each of these statements.	Does Not Describe Me at All	Does Not Describe Me Very Well	Describes Me Somewhat	Describes Me Well	Describes Me Very Well
1. I usually take responsibility for getting the team to agree on what the meeting should accomplish.	1	2	3	4	5
2. I tend to summarize to other team members what the team has accomplished so far.	1	2	3	4	5
3. I'm usually the person who helps other team members overcome their disagreements.	1	2	3	4	5
4. I try to ensure that everyone gets heard on issues.	1	2	3	4	5
5. I'm usually the person who helps the team determine how to organize the discussion.	1	2	3	4	5
6. I praise other team members for their ideas more than do others in the meetings.	1	2	3	4	5
7. People tend to rely on me to keep track of what has been said in meetings.	1	2	3	4	5
8. The team typically counts on me to prevent debates from getting out of hand.	1	2	3	4	5
9. I tend to say things that make the group feel optimistic about its accomplishments.	1	2	3	4	5
10. Team members usually count on me to give everyone a chance to speak.	1	2	3	4	5
11. In most meetings, I am less likely than others to criticize the ideas of teammates.	1	2	3	4	5
12. I actively help teammates to resolve their differences in meetings.	1	2	3	4	5
13. I actively encourage quiet team members to describe their ideas about each issue.	1	2	3	4	5
14. People tend to rely on me to clarify the purpose of the meeting.	1	2	3	4	5
15. I like to be the person who takes notes or minutes of the meeting.	1	2	3	4	5

 SELF-ASSESSMENT EXERCISE 8.7

Are You a Team Player?

How much do you like working in teams? Some of us avoid teams whenever possible; others tolerate teamwork; still others thrive in team environments. This exercise is designed to help you estimate the extent to which you are positively predisposed to work in teams. Read each statement in the scale and indicate the extent to which you agree or disagree with the statement. This exercise should be completed alone so that you can assess yourself honestly without concerns of social comparison. Class discussion will focus on the characteristics of individuals who are more or less compatible with working in teams.

SELF-ASSESSMENT EXERCISE 8.8

How Trusting Are You?

Trust is a psychological state comprising the intention to accept vulnerability on the basis of positive expectations of the intent or behaviour of another person. While trust varies from one situation to the next, some people have a higher or lower propensity to trust. In other words, some people are highly trusting of others, even when first meeting them, whereas others have difficulty trusting anyone, even over a long time. This self-assessment provides an estimate of your propensity to trust. Indicate your preferred response to each statement, being honest with yourself for each item. This self-assessment should be completed alone, although class discussion will focus on the meaning of propensity to trust, why it varies from one person to the next, and how it affects teamwork.

 Practise and learn online with Connect. Connect resources include additional and interactive study exercises, videos, and practice quizzing, as well as additional material you won't find in the printed text.

CHAPTER 9

Communicating in Teams and Organizations

LEARNING OBJECTIVES

After reading this chapter, you should be able to:

LO1 Explain why communication is important in organizations and discuss four influences on effective communication encoding and decoding.

LO2 Compare and contrast the advantages of and problems with electronic mail, other verbal communication media, and nonverbal communication.

LO3 Explain how social acceptance and media richness influence the preferred communication channel.

LO4 Discuss various barriers (noise) to effective communication, including cross-cultural and gender-based differences in communication.

LO5 Explain how to get your message across more effectively, and summarize the elements of active listening.

LO6 Summarize effective communication strategies in organizational hierarchies, and review the role and relevance of the organizational grapevine.

Canadians love using social media and organizations are increasingly turning to communication platforms similar to Facebook, Twitter, and YouTube to share information, and engage and support employee collaboration.

Delta Hotels and Resorts promotes a work style referred to as "casual professionalism" where employees are encouraged to relax, be themselves, and provide welcoming service that is straight from the heart. To encourage community and communication among employees across Canada, Delta developed its own social network in partnership with Google. Like Facebook, each of Delta's 7,000 employees can create and personalize their own profile, post photos and videos, and connect to people with similar interests. Delta's social network was developed to replace their traditional intranet with a corporate communication platform that relies heavily on user-generated information. The site also provides Delta employees with access to a people directory, chat functions, and corporate resources including training videos.

Bayer Inc. is another Canadian company with a "social media style intranet" that encourages employees to communicate with one another. Bayer's social networking platform is also home to a blog from president and CEO Philip Blake, company information, as well as an RSS feed from Bayer Inc.'s global parent company. Bayer Inc.'s approach to employee communication is one of the key factors that came into play in being recognized as one of "North America's 50 Most Engaged Workplaces."

Like Delta Hotels and Resorts and Bayer Inc., electronic networking giant, Cisco Systems, has a "Facebook-like internal directory" that encourages employees to collaborate and share information needed to respond to a customer or find a lunch partner. Cisco Systems has also devised an internal YouTube-like video-sharing site called "C-vision" that lets employees share product reports, engineering updates, and sales ideas.

Delta Hotels and Resorts, Bayer Inc., and Cisco Systems are all companies recognized as great places to work and may be considered useful role models for employee communication using social media. "The culture of the organization has to be right to get these kinds of things to work," explains Mark Bower, CTO for Connectegrity, a company that specializes in the use of social software and knowledge management. "In some organizations, it's very much a culture of 'knowledge is power'. . . in other organizations, it's very much about sharing."[1]

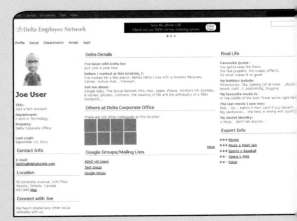

Delta Hotels and Resorts is embracing the use of social networks and has created its own online community for employees.
Copyright 2011 Delta Hotels and Resorts. All Rights Reserved.

Communication is the lifeblood of all organizations, so Delta Hotels and Resorts, Bayer Inc., Cisco Systems, and other organizations remain effective by incorporating social media and other emerging channels into their communication toolkit. Certainly, social media technologies such as Facebook, Twitter, and LinkedIn have transformed how we communicate in society, yet we may still be at the beginning of this revolution. Wire cablegrams and telephones introduced a century ago are giving way to email, instant messaging, Weblogs, and now social media sites. Each of these inventions creates fascinating changes in how people communicate with each other in the workplace, as well as new opportunities to improve organizational effectiveness and employee well-being.

> **communication** The process by which information is transmitted and *understood* between two or more people.

Communication refers to the process by which information is transmitted and *understood* between two or more people. We emphasize the word 'understood' because transmitting the sender's intended meaning is the essence of good communication. This chapter begins by discussing the importance of effective communication, outlining the communication process model, and discussing factors that improve communication coding and decoding. Next, we identify types of communication channels, including email and social media sites, followed by factors to consider when choosing a communication medium. This chapter then identifies barriers to effective communication. The latter part of this chapter offers an overview of ways to communicate in organizational hierarchies and offers insight about the pervasive organizational grapevine.

THE IMPORTANCE OF COMMUNICATION

LO1

Effective communication is vital to all organizations, so much so that no company could exist without it. The reason? Recall from Chapter 1 that organizations are defined as groups of people who work interdependently toward some purpose. People work interdependently only when they can communicate with each other. Although organizations rely on a variety of coordinating mechanisms (which we discuss in Chapter 13), frequent, timely, and accurate communication remains the primary means through which employees and work units effectively synchronize their work.[2] Chester Barnard, a telecommunications CEO and a respected pioneer in organizational behaviour theory, stated this point back in 1938: "An organization comes into being when there are persons able to communicate with each other."[3]

In addition to coordination, communication plays a central role in organizational learning. It is the means through which knowledge enters the organization and is distributed to employees.[4] A third function of communication is decision making. Imagine the challenge of making a decision without any information about the decision context, the alternatives available, the likely outcomes of those options, or the extent to which the decision is achieving its objectives. All of these ingredients require communication from co-workers as well as from stakeholders in the external environment. For example, airline cockpit crews make much better decisions—and thereby cause far fewer accidents—when the captain encourages the crew to openly share information.[5]

A fourth function is to change behaviour. When communicating to others, we are often trying to alter their beliefs and feelings and ultimately their behaviour. This influence process might be passive, such as merely describing the situation more clearly and fully. Sometimes, the communication event is a deliberate attempt to change someone's thoughts and actions. We will discuss this under the topic of persuasion later in this chapter.

Finally, communication supports employee well-being.[6] Informationally, communication conveys knowledge that helps employees to better manage their work environment. For instance, research shows that new employees adjust much better to the organization when co-workers communicate subtle nuggets of wisdom, such as how to avoid office politics, complete work procedures correctly, find useful resources, handle difficult customers, and so on.[7] Emotionally, the communication experience itself is a soothing balm. Indeed, people are less susceptible to colds, cardiovascular disease, and other physical and mental illnesses when they have regular social interaction.[8]

In essence, people have an inherent drive to bond, to validate their self-worth, and to maintain their social identity. Communication is the means through which these drives and needs are fulfilled.

A MODEL OF COMMUNICATION

To understand the key interpersonal features of effective communication, let's examine the model presented in Exhibit 9.1, which provides a useful "conduit" metaphor for thinking about the communication process.[9] According to this model, communication flows through channels between the sender and receiver. The sender forms a message and encodes it into words, gestures, voice intonations, and other symbols or signs. Next, the encoded message is transmitted to the intended receiver through one or more communication channels (media). The receiver senses the incoming message and decodes it into something meaningful. Ideally, the decoded meaning is what the sender had intended.

In most situations, the sender looks for evidence that the other person received and understood the transmitted message. This feedback may be a formal acknowledgment, such as "Yes, I know what you mean," or indirect evidence from the receiver's subsequent actions. Notice that feedback repeats the communication process. Intended feedback is encoded, transmitted, received, and decoded from the receiver to the sender of the original message. This model recognizes that communication is not a free-flowing conduit. Rather, the transmission of meaning from one person to another is hampered by *noise*—the psychological, social, and structural barriers that distort and obscure the sender's intended message. If any part of the communication process is distorted or broken, the sender and receiver will not have a common understanding of the message.

INFLUENCES ON EFFECTIVE ENCODING AND DECODING

The communication process model suggests that communication effectiveness depends on the ability of sender and receiver to efficiently and accurately encode and decode information. There are four main factors that influence the effectiveness of the encoding-decoding process.[10]

Exhibit 9.1   **THE COMMUNICATION PROCESS MODEL**

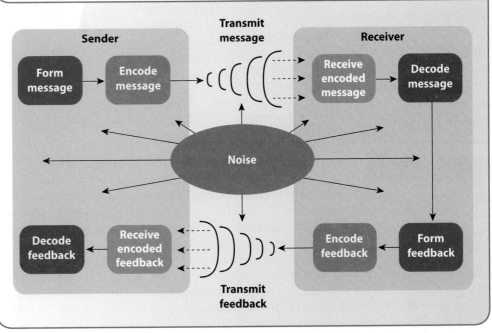

Communication effectiveness depends on the ability of sender and receiver to efficiently and accurately encode and decode information. "

1. *Communication channel proficiency*—Communication effectiveness improves when the sender and receiver are both motivated and able to communicate through the communication channel. Some people are better and more motivated to communicate through face-to-face conversations. Others are awkward in conversations, yet are quite good at communicating using a smartphone. Generally, the encoding-decoding process is more effective when both parties are skilled and enjoy using the selected communication channel.[11]

2. *Similar codebooks*—The sender and receiver rely on "codebooks," which are dictionaries of symbols, language, gestures, idioms, and other tools used to convey information. With similar codebooks, the communication participants are able to encode and decode more accurately because they both have the same or similar meaning. Communication efficiency also improves because there is less need for repetition (such as saying the same thing in different ways) and less need for confirmation feedback ("So, you are saying that . . .?").

3. *Shared mental models of the communication context*—Mental models are internal representations of the external world that allow us to visualize elements of a setting and relationships among those elements (see Chapter 3). When sender and receiver have shared mental models, they have a common understanding of the environment relating to the information, so less communication is necessary to clarify meaning about that context. Notice that sharing the same codebook differs from sharing the same mental models of the topic context. Codebooks are symbols used to convey message content, whereas mental models are knowledge structures of the communication setting. For example, a Russian cosmonaut and Canadian astronaut might have shared mental models about the design and technology onboard the International Space Station (communication context), yet they experience poor communication because of language differences (i.e., different codebooks).

4. *Experience encoding the message*—As people gain experience with the subject matter, they become more proficient at using the codebook of symbols to convey the message. For example, after speaking to several groups of employees about the company's new product development, you learn which words and phrases help to communicate that particular message better to the audience. This is similar to the effect of job training or sports practise. The more experience and practise gained at communicating a subject, the more people learn how to effectively transmit that information to others.

COMMUNICATION CHANNELS

LO2

A critical part of the communication model is the channel or medium through which information is transmitted. There are two main types of channels: verbal and nonverbal. Verbal communication uses words and occurs through either spoken or written channels. Nonverbal communication is any part of communication that does not use words. Spoken and written communication are both verbal (i.e., they both use words), but they are quite different from each other and have different strengths and weaknesses in communication effectiveness, which we discuss later in this section. Also, written communication has traditionally been much slower than spoken communication at transmitting messages, although electronic mail, Twitter "tweets," and other Internet-based communication channels have significantly improved written communication efficiency.

WEB-BASED COMMUNICATION

In the early 1960s, with funding from the U.S. Department of Defense, university researchers began discussing how to collaborate better by connecting their computers through a network. Their rough vision of connected computers became a reality in 1969 as the Advanced Research Projects Agency Network (ARPANET). ARPANET initially had only a dozen or so connections and was very slow and expensive by today's standards, but it marked the birth of the Internet. Two years later, a computer engineer developing ARPANET sent the first electronic mail (email) message between different computers on a network. By 1973, most communication on ARPANET was through email. ARPANET was mostly restricted to U.S. Defense-funded research centres, so in 1979 two graduate students at Duke University developed a public network system, called Usenet. Usenet allowed people to post information that could be retrieved by anyone else on the network, making it the first public computer-mediated social network.[12]

We have come a long way since the early days of ARPANET and Usenet. The most popular form of Web-based communication in organizational settings today is email. Email has become the medium of choice in most workplaces because messages are quickly written, edited, and transmitted. Information can be appended and conveyed to many people with a simple click to send. It is asynchronous (messages are sent and received at different times), so there is no need to coordinate a communication session. With advances in computer search technology, email software has also become an efficient filing system.[13]

Email tends to be the preferred medium for coordinating work (e.g., confirming deadlines with a co-worker's schedule) and for sending well-defined information for decision making. It often increases the volume of communication and significantly alters the flow of that information within groups and throughout the organization.[14] Specifically, it reduces some face-to-face and voice communication but increases communication with people further up the hierarchy. Some social and organizational status differences still exist with email,[15] but they are somewhat less apparent than in face-to-face communication. By hiding age, race, and other features, email reduces stereotype biases. However, it also tends to increase reliance on stereotypes when we are already aware of the other person's personal characteristics.[16]

OB BY THE NUMBERS

Communicating Across the Internet[18]

294 billion
emails transmitted globally *per day*

80%
of emails transmitted are spam or viruses

2.64 billion
tweets sent globally in one month

163 million
text messages Canadians send *per day*

17.4 million
average number of Canadians use Facebook each month (8th highest country per capita)

5.6
average hours per week Canadians spend viewing social media websites (3rd highest country)

23.1
average hours per month people globally spend online

43.5
average hours per month Canadians spend online (highest hours in the world)

3,349
average number of Web pages Canadians view each month

PROBLEMS WITH EMAIL

In spite of the wonders of email, anyone who has used this communication medium knows that it has its limitations. Here are the top four complaints:

Poor Medium for Communicating Emotions People rely on facial expressions and other nonverbal cues to interpret the emotional meaning of words; email lacks this parallel communication channel. Indeed, people consistently and significantly underestimate the degree to which they understand the emotional tone of email messages.[17] Senders try to clarify the emotional tone of their messages by using expressive language

("Wonderful to hear from you!"), highlighting phrases in boldface or quotation marks, and inserting graphic faces and symbols (called emoticons) representing the desired emotion. Recent studies suggest that writers are getting better at using these emotional markers. Still, they do not replace the full complexity of real facial expressions, voice intonation, and hand movements.[19]

Reduces Politeness and Respect   Email messages are often less diplomatic than written letters, so much so that the term "flaming" refers mainly to email and other electronic messages. People who receive email are partly to blame because they tend to infer a more negative or neutral interpretation of the email than was intended by the sender.[20] Even so, email flame wars occur mostly because senders are more likely to send disparaging messages by email than other communication channels. One reason is that individuals can post email messages before their emotions subside, whereas the sender of a traditional memo or letter would have time for sober second thoughts. A second reason is the low social presence (impersonal) of email; people are more likely to write things that they would never say in face-to-face conversation. Fortunately, research has found that flaming decreases as teams move to later stages of development and when explicit norms and rules of communication are established.[21]

Poor Medium for Ambiguous, Complex, and Novel Situations   Email is usually fine for well-defined situations, such as giving basic instructions or presenting a meeting agenda, but it can be cumbersome in ambiguous, complex, and novel situations. As we will describe later in this section, these circumstances require communication channels that transmit a larger volume of information with more rapid feedback. In other words, when the issue gets messy, stop emailing and start talking, preferably face-to-face.

Contributes to Information Overload   Email contributes to information overload.[22] Approximately 20 trillion emails (excluding spam) are now transmitted annually around the world, up from just 1.1 trillion in 1998. The email glut occurs because messages are created and copied to many people without much effort. The number of email messages will probably decrease as people become more familiar with it; until then, email volume continues to rise.

WORKPLACE COMMUNICATION THROUGH SOCIAL MEDIA

Email continues to dominate Web-based communication in organizations, but a few corporate leaders believe that it undermines productivity and well-being rather than supports these objectives. The opening vignette to this chapter described how Canadian companies such as Delta Hotels and Resorts are cautiously introducing social media into the workplace. As Global Connections 9.1 describes, Paris-based information technology consulting firm Atos Origin plans to replace email altogether with social media and other communication technologies.

Social media include Web-based tools (websites, applications, etc.) that allow users to generate and exchange information. This "user-generated content" is creative content (developed by the user), published on the Web (but may have restricted access), and produced outside of professional routines and practices.[23] Social media take many forms—blogs, wikis, instant messages, tweets, personal presentation sites (e.g., Facebook), viewer feedback forums, and the like. While earlier Web-based activity involved passively reading or watching content, these emerging Internet activities are more interactive and dynamic.

One recent Canadian model suggests that social media serve several functions: presenting the individual's identity, enabling conversations, sharing information, sensing the presence of others in the virtual space, maintaining relationships, revealing reputation or status, and supporting communities (see Exhibit 9.2).[24] For instance, Facebook has a strong emphasis on maintaining relationships but relatively low emphasis

CONNECTIONS 9.1

Goodbye Email, Hello Social Media!

Atos Origin is at war with email. Executives at the Paris-based global information technology consulting firm believe the volume of email transmitted around the company has created "information pollution" that stifles productivity and undermines employee well-being. "We are producing data on a massive scale that is fast polluting our working environments and also encroaching into our personal lives," says Atos Origin chief executive Thierry Breton. The company estimates that reading and writing emails consume up to half of their managers' workweek. Furthermore, email messages are irrelevant to about 70 percent of the people who receive them, according to a survey by Salesforce.com.

Many other companies have fought email overload by banning them for one day each week. Unfortunately, these "email-free Fridays" often produce "email-overload Mondays." Atos Origin's strategy is more radical: it plans to ban all email among the company's 50,000 staff within the next couple of years. The company will encourage staff to share ideas, engage in communities, and have virtual team meetings through instant messaging, Web conferences, and an enterprise-strength social media site.

"It is clearly going to be a big challenge for us because email is everywhere," admits Atos Origin vice-president for

European information technology company Atos Origin plans to replace email completely with other Internet-based communication tools within the next couple of years. *Christopher Lee/Getty Images for Atos Origin*

global innovation Marc-Henri Desportes. Desportes notes, however, that this transformation is less difficult for the company's Generation-Y employees. "These people do not use email any more. They use social media tools."[25]

---

on sharing information or forming communities (circles). Wikis, on the other hand, focus on sharing information or forming communities but have much lower emphasis on presenting the user's identity or reputation.

A few studies conclude (with caution) that social media offer considerable versatility and potential in the workplace.[26] Even so, few companies have introduced these communication tools, mainly because they lack knowledge, staff/resources, and technical support to put them into practice.[27] However, a common practice is to simply ban employee access to social media (usually after discovering excess employee activity on Facebook) without thinking through its potential. One exception is Serena Software, which has made Facebook its new corporate intranet. The Californian company introduced "Facebook Fridays" sessions in which teenagers are hired to teach older staff how to use Facebook. Most Serena employees now have Facebook pages, and the company's Facebook site links employees to confidential documents behind the company's firewall.[28]

NONVERBAL COMMUNICATION

Nonverbal communication includes facial gestures, voice intonation, physical distance, and even silence. This communication channel is necessary where noise or physical distance prevents effective verbal exchanges and the need for immediate feedback precludes written communication. But even in face-to-face meetings, most information is communicated nonverbally. Rather like a parallel conversation, nonverbal cues signal subtle information to both parties, such as reinforcing their interest in the verbal conversation or demonstrating their relative status in the relationship.[29]

Nonverbal communication differs from verbal (i.e., written and spoken) communication in a couple of ways. First, it is less rule-bound than verbal communication. We

Exhibit 9.2   FUNCTIONS OF COMMUNICATING THROUGH SOCIAL MEDIA

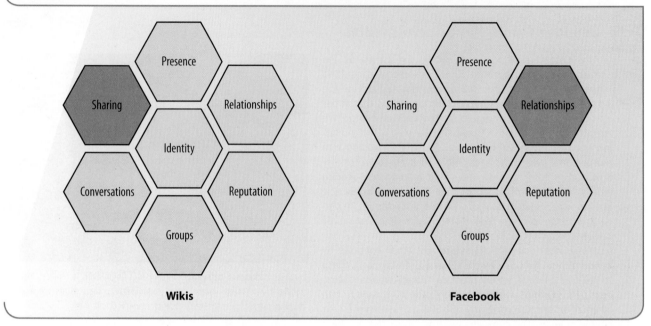

Source: Based on J. H. Kietzmann, K. Hermkens, I. P. McCarthy, and B. S. Silvestre, "Social Media? Get Serious! Understanding the Functional Building Blocks of Social Media," *Business Horizons* 54 (2011), pp. 241–251.

receive considerable formal training on how to understand spoken words, but very little on how to understand the nonverbal signals that accompany those words. Consequently, nonverbal cues are generally more ambiguous and susceptible to misinterpretation. At the same time, many facial expressions (such as smiling) are hardwired and universal, thereby providing the only reliable means of communicating across cultures.

The other difference between verbal and nonverbal communication is that the former is typically conscious, whereas most nonverbal communication is automatic and nonconscious. We normally plan the words we say or write, but we rarely plan every blink, smile, or other gesture during a conversation. Indeed, as we just mentioned, many of these facial expressions communicate the same meaning across cultures because they are hardwired nonconscious responses to human emotions.[30] For example, pleasant emotions cause the brain centre to widen the mouth, whereas negative emotions produce constricted facial expressions (squinting eyes, pursed lips, etc.).

Emotional Contagion   One of the most fascinating effects of emotions on nonverbal communication is the phenomenon called **emotional contagion**, which is the nonconscious process of 'catching' or sharing another person's emotions by mimicking that person's facial expressions and other nonverbal behaviour. Technically, human beings have brain receptors that cause them to mirror what they observe. In other words, to some degree our brain causes us to act as though we are the person we are watching.[31]

Consider what happens when you see a co-worker accidentally bang his or her head against a filing cabinet. Chances are, you wince and put your hand on your own head as if you had hit the cabinet. Similarly, while listening to someone describe a positive event, you tend to smile and exhibit other emotional displays of happiness. While some of our nonverbal communication is planned, emotional contagion represents nonconscious behaviour—we automatically mimic and synchronize our nonverbal behaviours with other people.[32]

Emotional contagion serves three purposes. First, mimicry provides continuous feedback, communicating that we understand and empathize with the sender. To consider the significance of this, imagine employees remaining expressionless after watching a co-worker bang his or her head! The lack of parallel behaviour conveys a lack of

emotional contagion
The nonconscious process of 'catching' or sharing another person's emotions by mimicking that person's facial expressions and other nonverbal behaviour.

understanding or caring. Second, mimicking the nonverbal behaviours of other people seems to be a way of receiving emotional meaning from those people. If a co-worker is angry with a client, your tendency to frown and show anger while listening helps you to experience that emotion more fully. In other words, we receive meaning by expressing the sender's emotions as well as by listening to the sender's words.

The third function of emotional contagion is to fulfill the drive to bond that was described in Chapter 5. Social solidarity is built out of each member's awareness of a collective sentiment. Through nonverbal expressions of emotional contagion, people see others share the same emotions that they feel. This strengthens relations among team members as well as between leaders and followers by providing evidence of their similarity.[33]

CHOOSING THE BEST COMMUNICATION CHANNEL

L03

Which communication channel is most appropriate in a particular situation? Two important sets of factors to consider are (a) social acceptance and (b) media richness.

SOCIAL ACCEPTANCE

Social acceptance refers to how well the communication medium is approved and supported by the organization, teams, and individuals.[34] One factor in social acceptance is organizational and team norms regarding the use of specific communication channels. Norms partly explain why telephone conversations are more common among staff in some firms, whereas email or text messaging is the medium of choice in other organizations. Some companies expect employees to meet face-to-face, whereas meetings and similar conversations are rare events elsewhere. This effect extends to cultural norms. One recent study reported that when communicating with people further up the hierarchy, Koreans are much less likely than Americans to use email because this medium is less respectful of the superior's status.[35] A second social acceptance factor is individual preferences for specific communication channels.[36] You may have noticed that some co-workers ignore (or rarely check) voice mail, yet they quickly respond to text messages or tweets. These preferences are due to personality traits as well as previous experience and reinforcement with particular channels.

A third social acceptance factor is the symbolic meaning of a channel. Some communication channels are viewed as impersonal whereas others are more personal; some are considered professional whereas others are social; some are succinct whereas others may be long-winded. In one recent survey, 60 percent of employees say they use email to arrange meetings whereas less than 10 percent use this channel to communicate with their boss about problems.[37] The importance of a channel's symbolic meaning is perhaps most apparent in stories about managers who use emails or text messages to inform employees that they are fired or laid off. These communication events make headlines because email and text messages are considered inappropriate (too impersonal) for transmission of that particular information.[38]

MEDIA RICHNESS

media richness
A medium's data-carrying capacity, that is, the volume and variety of information that can be transmitted during a specific time.

Along with social acceptance, people select communication media based on their **media richness**. Media richness refers to a medium's data-carrying capacity—the volume and variety of information that can be transmitted during a specific time.[39] Exhibit 9.3 illustrates various communication channels arranged in a hierarchy of richness, with face-to-face interaction at the top and lean data-only reports at the bottom. A communication channel has high richness when it is able to convey multiple cues (such as both verbal and nonverbal information), allows timely feedback from receiver to sender, allows the sender to customize the message to the receiver, and makes use of complex symbols (such as words and phrases with multiple meanings). Face-to-face communication is at the top of media richness because it allows us to communicate both verbally

Exhibit 9.3   MEDIA RICHNESS HIERARCHY

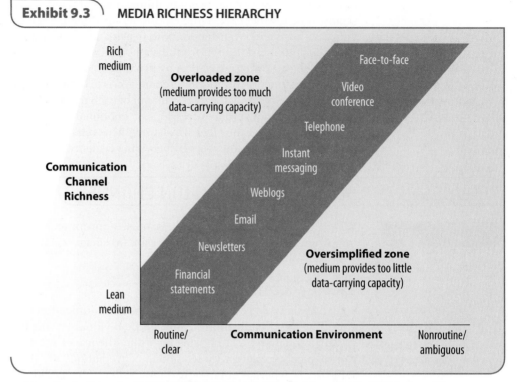

Sources: Based on R. Lengel and R. Daft, "The Selection of Communication Media as an Executive Skill," *Academy of Management Executive* 2, no. 3 (August, 1988), p. 226; R. L. Daft and R. H. Lengel, "Information Richness: A New Approach to Managerial Behaviour and Organization Design," *Research in Organizational Behaviour,* 1984, p. 199.

and nonverbally at the same time, to receive feedback almost immediately from the receiver, to quickly adjust our message and style, and to use complex language such as metaphors and idioms (e.g., "scratch the surface").

According to media richness theory, rich media are better than lean media when the communication situation is nonroutine and ambiguous. In nonroutine situations (such as an unexpected and unusual emergency), the sender and receiver have little common experience, so they need to transmit a large volume of information with immediate feedback. Lean media work well in routine situations because the sender and receiver have common expectations through shared mental models. Ambiguous situations also require rich media because the parties must share large amounts of information with immediate feedback to resolve multiple and conflicting interpretations of their observations and experiences.[40] Choosing the wrong medium reduces communication effectiveness. When the situation is routine or clear, using a rich medium—such as holding a special meeting—would seem like a waste of time. On the other hand, if a unique and ambiguous issue is handled through email or another lean medium, then issues take longer to resolve and misunderstandings are more likely to occur.

Exceptions to Media Richness Theory   Research generally supports the relevance of media richness for traditional channels (face-to-face, written memos, etc.). However, the model doesn't fit reality nearly as well when electronic communication channels are studied. Three factors seem to override or blur the medium's richness:

1. *Ability to multi-communicate*—It is usually difficult (as well as rude) to communicate face-to-face with someone while simultaneously transmitting messages to someone else using another medium. Most information technologies, on the other hand, require less social etiquette and attention, so employees can easily engage in two or more communication events at the same time. In other words, they can multi-communicate.[41] For example, people routinely scan Web pages while carrying on

I Love Rewards Gets Media Rich Quick

Every day, employees at I Love Rewards Inc. meet face-to-face for 10 minutes to communicate priorities and coordinate their work. Each meeting at the Toronto-based incentive marketing company is brief and highly structured, but the richness of this communication event allows efficient transmission of information about "Today's Must-Do" and "Red Flags." For two minutes of the meeting, employees share a "Headline" summary of something important to them (e.g., a client meeting, last week's vacation). Each week has a new meeting facilitator, giving employees the chance to develop their communication and facilitation skills. I Love Rewards CEO Razor Suleman says these quick meetings provide a personal connection and highly interactive feedback.[42] © *Tim Fraser*

telephone conversations. Some send text messages to a client while simultaneously listening to a discussion at a large meeting. People don't multitask as efficiently as they believe, but some are good enough that they likely exchange as much information through two or more lean media as through one high media richness channel.

2. *Communication proficiency*—Earlier in this chapter we explained that communication effectiveness is partially determined by the sender's competency with the communication channel. People with higher proficiency can "push" more information through the channel, thereby increasing the channel's information flow. Experienced smartphone users, for instance, can whip through messages in a flash, whereas new users struggle to type notes and organize incoming messages. In contrast, there is less variation in the ability to communicate through casual conversation and other natural channels because most of us develop good levels of proficiency throughout life and possibly through hardwired evolutionary development.[43]

3. *Social presence effects*—Channels with high media richness tend to have more social presence, that is, the participants experience a stronger physical presence of each other.[44] However, high social presence also sensitizes both parties to their relative status and self-presentation, which can distort or divert attention away from the message.[45] Face-to-face communication has very high media richness, yet its high social presence can disrupt the efficient flow of information through that medium. During a personal meeting with the company's CEO, for example, you might concentrate more on how you come across than on what the CEO is saying to you. In other words, the benefits of channels with high media richness may be offset by their social presence distractions, whereas lean media have much less social presence to distract or distort the transmitted information.

COMMUNICATION CHANNELS AND PERSUASION

Media richness as well as social acceptance lay the foundation for understanding which communication channels are more effective for **persuasion**, that is, changing another person's beliefs and attitudes. Recent studies support the long-held view that spoken communication, particularly face-to-face interaction, is more persuasive than emails, websites, and other forms of written communication. There are three main reasons for this persuasive effect.[46] First, spoken communication is typically accompanied by nonverbal communication. People are often persuaded more when they receive both emotional and logical messages, and the combination of spoken with nonverbal communication provides this dual punch. A lengthy pause, raised voice tone, and (in face-to-face interaction) animated hand gestures can amplify the emotional tone of the message, thereby signalling the vitality of the issue.

Second, spoken communication offers the sender high quality immediate feedback whether the receiver understands and accepts the message (i.e., is being persuaded).

persuasion The use of facts, logical arguments, and emotional appeals to change another person's beliefs and attitudes, usually for the purpose of changing the person's behaviour.

This feedback allows the sender to adjust the content and emotional tone of the message more quickly than with written communication. Third, people are persuaded more under conditions of high social presence than low social presence. The sender can more easily monitor the receiver's listening in face-to-face conversations (high social presence), so listeners are more motivated to pay attention and consider the sender's ideas. When people receive persuasion attempts through a website, email, or other source of written communication, on the other hand, they experience a higher degree of anonymity and psychological distance from the persuader. These conditions reduce the motivation to think about and accept the persuasive message.

Although spoken communication tends to be more persuasive, written communication can also persuade others to some extent. Written messages have the advantage of presenting more technical detail than can occur through conversation. This factual information is valuable when the issue is important to the receiver. Also, people experience a moderate degree of social presence in written communication when they are exchanging messages with close associates, so messages from friends and co-workers can be persuasive.

COMMUNICATION BARRIERS (NOISE)

LO4

In spite of the best intentions of sender and receiver to communicate, several barriers (called "noise" earlier in Exhibit 9.1) inhibit the effective exchange of information. As author George Bernard Shaw wrote, "The greatest problem with communication is the illusion that it has been accomplished." One barrier is the imperfect perceptual process of both sender and receiver. As receivers, we don't listen as well as senders assume, and our needs and expectations influence what signals get noticed and ignored. We aren't any better as senders, either. Some studies suggest that we have difficulty stepping out of our own perspectives and stepping into the perspectives of others, so we overestimate how well other people understand the message we are communicating.[47]

Language issues can be huge sources of communication noise because sender and receiver might not have the same "codebook." They might not speak the same language, or might have different meanings for particular words and phrases. For example, a French executive might call an event a "catastrophe" as a casual exaggeration, whereas someone in Germany usually interprets this word literally as an earth-shaking event.[48] The English language (among others) also has built-in ambiguities that cause misunderstandings. Consider the question "Can you close the door?" You might assume the sender is asking whether shutting the door is permitted. However, the question might be asking whether you are physically able to shut the door or whether the door is designed such that it can be shut. In fact, this question might not be a question at all; the person could be politely *telling* you to shut the door.[49]

The ambiguity of language isn't always dysfunctional noise.[50] Corporate leaders are sometimes purposely obscure to reflect the ambiguity of the topic or to avoid using precise language that carries unwanted emotional responses. They might use metaphors to represent an abstract vision of the company's future, or use obtuse phrases such as "rightsizing" and "restructuring" to obscure the underlying message that people would be fired or laid off. One study reported that people rely on more ambiguous language when communicating with people who have different values and beliefs. In these situations, ambiguity minimizes the risk of conflict.[51]

Jargon—specialized words and phrases for specific occupations or groups—is usually designed to improve communication efficiency. However, it is a source of communication noise when transmitted to people who do not possess the jargon codebook. Furthermore, people who use jargon excessively put themselves in an unflattering light. For example, former Chrysler CEO Robert Nardelli announced: "I'm blessed to have individuals with me who can take areas of responsibility and do vertical dives to really get the granularity and make sure that we're coupling horizontally across those functions so that we have a pure line of sight toward the customer." Business journalists weren't impressed, even if they did figure out what Nardelli meant.[52]

Another source of noise in the communication process is the tendency to filter messages. Filtering may involve deleting or delaying negative information or using less harsh words so the message sounds more favourable.[53] Filtering is less likely to occur when corporate leaders create a "culture of candour." This culture develops when leaders themselves communicate truthfully, seek out diverse sources for information, and protect and reward those who speak openly and truthfully.[54]

INFORMATION OVERLOAD

Start with a daily avalanche of email, then add in phone calls, text messages, posted videos and photos, file downloads, Web pages, hard copy documents, tweets, blogs, wikis, and other sources of incoming information. Altogether, you have created a perfect recipe for **information overload**.[55] As Exhibit 9.4 illustrates, information overload is a condition in which the volume of information received exceeds the person's capacity to process it. Employees have a certain *information processing capacity*—the amount of information that they are able to process in a fixed unit of time. At the same time, jobs have a varying *information load*—the amount of information to be processed per unit of time. Information overload creates noise in the communication system because information gets overlooked or misinterpreted when people can't process it fast enough. The result is poorer quality decisions as well as higher stress.[56]

Information overload problems can be minimized by increasing our information processing capacity, reducing the job's information load, or through a combination of both. Studies suggest that employees often increase their information processing capacity by temporarily reading faster, scanning through documents more efficiently, and removing distractions that slow information processing speed. Time management also increases information processing capacity. When information overload is temporary, information processing capacity can increase by working longer hours. Information load can be reduced by buffering, omitting, and summarizing. Buffering involves having incoming communication filtered, usually by an assistant. Omitting occurs when we decide to overlook messages, such as using software rules to redirect emails from distribution lists to folders that we never look at. An example of summarizing would be where we read executive summaries rather than the full report.

information overload
A condition in which the volume of information received exceeds the person's capacity to process it.

Exhibit 9.4   **DYNAMICS OF INFORMATION OVERLOAD**

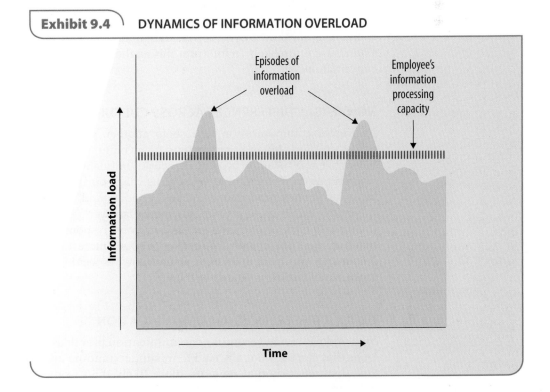

CROSS-CULTURAL AND GENDER COMMUNICATION

Increasing globalization and cultural diversity have no doubt brought more cross-cultural communication issues.[57] As mentioned earlier, language is an obvious cross-cultural communication challenge. Words are easily misunderstood in verbal communication, either because the receiver has a limited vocabulary or the sender's accent distorts the usual sound of some words. Voice intonation is another cross-cultural communication barrier. How loudly, deeply, and quickly people speak vary across cultures, and these voice intonations send secondary messages that have different meaning in different cultures.

Communication includes silence, but its use and meaning varies from one culture to another.[58] One study estimated that silence and pauses represented 30 percent of conversation time between Japanese doctors and patients, compared to only 8 percent of the time between American doctors and patients. Why is there more silence in Japanese conversations? One reason is that interpersonal harmony and saving face are more important in Japanese culture, and silence is a way of disagreeing without upsetting that harmony or offending the other person.[59] In addition, silence symbolizes respect and indicates that the listener is thoughtfully contemplating what has just been said.[60] Empathy is very important in Japan, and this shared understanding is demonstrated without using words. In contrast, most people in Canada and the United States and many other cultures view silence as a *lack* of communication and often interpret long breaks as a sign of disagreement.

> Communication includes silence, but its use and meaning vary from one culture to another. "

Conversational overlaps also send different messages in different cultures. Japanese people usually stop talking when they are interrupted, whereas talking over the other person's speech is more common in Brazil, France, and some other countries. The difference in communication behaviour is, again, due to interpretations. Talking while someone is speaking to you is considered quite rude in Japan, whereas Brazilians and French are more likely to interpret this as the person's interest and involvement in the conversation.

NONVERBAL DIFFERENCES ACROSS CULTURES

Nonverbal communication represents another potential area for misunderstanding across cultures. Many nonconscious or involuntary nonverbal cues (such as smiling) have the same meaning around the world, but deliberate gestures often have different interpretations. For example, most of us shake our head from side to side to say "No," but a variation of head shaking means "I understand" to many people in India. Filipinos raise their eyebrows to give an affirmative answer, yet Arabs interpret this expression (along with clicking one's tongue) as a negative response. Most Americans are taught to maintain eye contact with the speaker to show interest and respect, whereas some First Nations peoples learn at an early age to show respect by looking down when an elder or more senior person is talking to them.[61]

GENDER DIFFERENCES IN COMMUNICATION

Men and women have similar communication practices, but there are subtle distinctions that can occasionally lead to misunderstanding and conflict (see Exhibit 9.5).[62] One distinction is that men are more likely than women to view conversations as

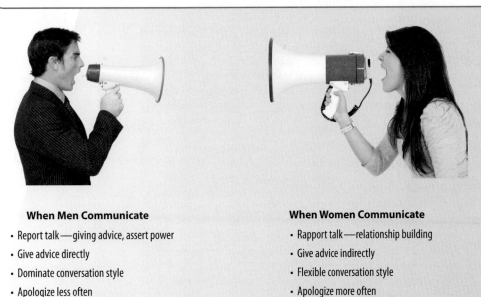

Exhibit 9.5   GENDER DIFFERENCES IN COMMUNICATION

When Men Communicate

- Report talk—giving advice, assert power
- Give advice directly
- Dominate conversation style
- Apologize less often
- Less sensitive to nonverbal cues

When Women Communicate

- Rapport talk—relationship building
- Give advice indirectly
- Flexible conversation style
- Apologize more often
- More sensitive to nonverbal cues

wavebreakmedia ltd/Shutterstock (left); Andresr/Shutterstock (right)

negotiations of relative status and power. They assert their power by directly giving advice to others (e.g., "You should do the following") and using combative language. There is also evidence that men dominate the talk time in conversations with women, as well as interrupt more and adjust their speaking style less than do women.

Men engage in more "report talk," in which the primary function of the conversation is impersonal and efficient information exchange. Women also do report talk, particularly when conversing with men, but conversations among women have a higher incidence of relationship building through "rapport talk." Women make more use of indirect requests ("Do you think you should . . ."), apologize more often, and seek advice from others more quickly than do men. Finally, research fairly consistently indicates that women are more sensitive than men to nonverbal cues in face-to-face meetings.[63] Together, these conditions can create communication conflicts. Women who describe problems get frustrated that men offer advice rather than support, whereas men become frustrated because they can't understand why women don't appreciate their advice. As Connections 9.1 describes, these gender differences are also apparent in Web-based communication.

IMPROVING INTERPERSONAL COMMUNICATION

L05

Effective interpersonal communication depends on the sender's ability to get the message across and the receiver's performance as an active listener. In this section, we outline these two essential features of effective interpersonal communication.

GETTING YOUR MESSAGE ACROSS

This chapter began with the statement that effective communication occurs when the other person receives and understands the message. This is more difficult to accomplish than most people believe. To get your message across to the other person, you first need

CONNECTIONS 9.1

Gender Differences in Web-Based Communication

According to a recent report from online Web tracking firm comScore Inc., women are more active users of various online communication media than men. Women are more likely to visit social networking sites like Facebook and Twitter, spend more time online, and click on more Web pages than their male counterparts. The report offered data to compare gender differences in online communication patterns. Although women made up 47.9 percent of visitors who accessed a social networking site during the month the study was conducted, they accounted for almost 57 percent of the Web pages accessed and total minutes spent on the sites. "Understanding gender-specific differences in Web usage is valuable to any digital stakeholder looking to successfully reach and engage both women and men in the online environment," said Linda Boland Abraham, comScore chief marketing officer and executive vice-president for global development.

When it comes to sharing photos using sites like Flickr, women are more likely than men to post pictures to the Web. Globally, women are signing up for Twitter faster than men and their reasons differ from men. Women appear to be particularly interested in learning about promotions tweeted by shopping sites. They are more likely than men

Women are engaging in more online communication than men. *Fancy/Alamy*

to use Twitter as a conversation medium. Women were also reported to be more active on Facebook than men. Overall the study noted that women spent an average of 24.8 hours per month online compared to men who spent 22.9 hours per month.[64]

to empathize with the receiver, such as being sensitive to words that may be ambiguous or trigger the wrong emotional response. Second, be sure that you repeat the message, such as by rephrasing the key points a couple of times. Third, your message competes with other messages and noise, so find a time when the receiver is less likely to be distracted by these other matters. Finally, if you are communicating bad news or criticism, focus on the problem, not the person.

ACTIVE LISTENING

Almost 2,000 years ago Greek philosopher Epictetus wrote: "Nature gave us one tongue, but two ears, so we may listen twice as much as we speak."[65] This sage advice suggests that we need to recognize the value of active listening by actively sensing the sender's signals, evaluating them accurately, and responding appropriately. These three components of listening—sensing, evaluating, and responding—reflect the listener's side of the communication model described at the beginning of this chapter. Listeners receive the sender's signals, decode them as intended, and provide appropriate and timely feedback to the sender (see Exhibit 9.6). Active listeners constantly cycle through sensing, evaluating, and responding during the conversation and engage in various activities to improve these processes.[66]

Sensing   Sensing is the process of receiving signals from the sender and paying attention to them. Active listeners improve sensing in three ways. First, they postpone evaluation by not forming an opinion until the speaker has finished. Second, they avoid interrupting the speaker's conversation. Third, they remain motivated to listen to the speaker.

Evaluating   This component of listening includes understanding the message meaning, evaluating the message, and remembering the message. To improve their evaluation

Exhibit 9.6   **ACTIVE LISTENING PROCESS AND STRATEGIES**

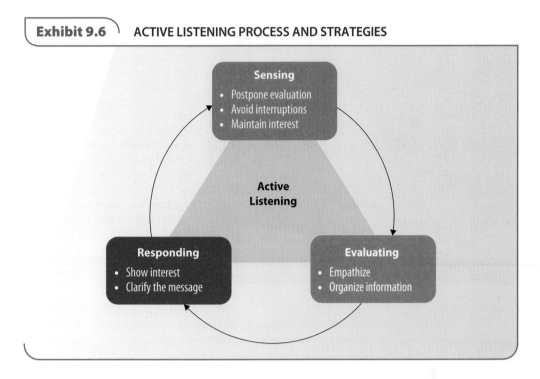

of the conversation, active listeners empathize with the speaker—they try to understand and be sensitive to the speaker's feelings, thoughts, and situation. Evaluation also improves by organizing the speaker's ideas during the communication episode.

Responding   Responding, the third component of listening, is feedback to the sender, which motivates and directs the speaker's communication. Active listeners accomplish this by maintaining sufficient eye contact and sending back channel signals (e.g., "I see"), both of which show interest. They also respond by clarifying the message—rephrasing the speaker's ideas at appropriate breaks ("So you're saying that . . . ?").

IMPROVING COMMUNICATION THROUGHOUT THE HIERARCHY

L06

So far, we have focused on micro-level issues in the communication process, namely, the dynamics of sending and receiving information between two employees or the informal exchanges of information across several people. But in this era where knowledge is competitive advantage, corporate leaders also need to maintain an open flow of communication up, down, and across the organization. In this section, we discuss three communication strategies: workspace design, Web-based communication, and direct communication with top management.

WORKSPACE DESIGN

Some organizations are improving communication among staff by tearing down walls.[67] The location and design of hallways, offices, cubicles, and communal areas (cafeterias, elevators) all shape whom we speak to as well as the frequency of that communication. Some firms are replacing traditional offices with an open space where all employees (including management) work together. "We do not have doors," explains an executive at Continuum, the Boston-based design and innovation firm. "It's structured that way to stimulate conversation and to allow people to work collaboratively."[68] Although these open space arrangements increase communication, they also potentially increase noise, distractions, and loss of privacy.[69] The challenge is to increase social interaction without these stressors.

Another workspace strategy is to cloister employees into team spaces, but also encourage sufficient interaction with people from other teams. Pixar Animation Studios constructed its campus in Emeryville, California with these principles in mind. The buildings encourages communication among team members. At the same time, the campus encourages happenstance interactions with people on other teams. Pixar executives call this the "bathroom effect," because team members must leave their isolated team pods to fetch their mail, have lunch, or visit the restroom.[71]

WEB-BASED ORGANIZATIONAL COMMUNICATION

For decades, employees received official company news through hard copy newsletters and magazines. Some firms still use these communication devices, but most have supplemented or replaced them completely with Web-based sources of information. The traditional company magazine is now typically published on Web pages or distributed in PDF format. The advantage of these *e-zines* is that company news can be prepared and distributed quickly.

Employees are increasingly skeptical of information that has been screened and packaged by management, so a few companies such as IBM are encouraging employees to post their own news on internal blogs and wikis. **Wikis** are collaborative Web spaces where anyone in a group can write, edit, or remove material from the website. Wikipedia, the popular online encyclopedia, is a massive public example of a wiki. IBM's WikiCentral now hosts more than 20,000 wiki projects involving 100,000 employees. The accuracy of wikis depends on the quality of participants, but IBM experts say that errors are quickly identified by IBM's online community. Wikis lack employee involvement in some firms, however, likely because they require time and the company does not reward or recognize those who provide this time to wiki development.[72]

wikis Collaborative Web spaces where anyone in a group can write, edit, or remove material from the website.

DIRECT COMMUNICATION WITH TOP MANAGEMENT

"The best fertilizer in any field is that of the farmer's footsteps!" This old Chinese saying suggests that farmers have greater success when they spend more time in the fields directly observing the crop's development. Translated into an organizational context, this means that senior executives will understand their business better if they meet directly with employees and other stakeholders. Four decades ago, people at Hewlett-Packard coined a phrase for this communication strategy: **management by walking around (MBWA)**. Brian Scudamore, founder and CEO of Vancouver-based 1-800-Got-Junk?, takes this practice further. "I don't have my own office, and I very often move around to different departments for a day at a time," says Scudamore.[73]

management by walking around (MBWA) A communication practice in which executives get out of their offices and learn from others in the organization through face-to-face dialogue.

Open Communication at Zappos

Tony Hsieh likes to tweet. Even as CEO of Zappos, one of the world's largest online retailers, Hsieh discovered that tweeting is a powerful way to connect with his staff and the wider community. "What I found was that people really appreciated the openness and honesty (of tweets), and that led people to feel more of a personal connection with Zappos and me," Hsieh wrote in one of his Weblogs. Tweeting is so important at Zappos that new employees receive training on how to use the technology and are free to tweet to the public. But if tweeting the top boss seems too impersonal, Hsieh has the ultimate open-door policy. His desk is located in an open office setting in an area called "the jungle" (complete with fake vines hanging from the ceiling) where anyone can speak with him.[74] *Jared McMillen/Aurora Photos*

Along with MBWA, executives communicate more directly with employees through "town hall meetings." Some executives also conduct employee roundtable forums to hear opinions from a small representation of staff about various issues. At the departmental level, some companies (including I Love Rewards, described earlier) hold daily or weekly "huddles"—brief stand-up meetings in which staff and their manager discuss goals and hear good news stories. These direct communication strategies potentially minimize filtering because executives listen directly to employees. They also help executives acquire a deeper meaning and quicker understanding of internal organizational problems. A third benefit of direct communication is that employees might have more empathy for decisions made further up the corporate hierarchy.

COMMUNICATING THROUGH THE GRAPEVINE

grapevine An unstructured and informal network founded on social relationships rather than organizational charts or job descriptions.

No matter how much organizational leaders try to get messages to employees quickly through any and all of the various media available, employees still use the oldest communication channel: the corporate **grapevine**. The grapevine is an unstructured and informal network founded on social relationships rather than organizational charts or job descriptions. What do employees think about the grapevine? Surveys of employees in two firms—one in Florida, the other in California—found that almost all employees use the grapevine, but very few of them prefer this source of information. The Californian survey also reported that only one-third of employees believe grapevine information is credible. In other words, employees turn to the grapevine when they have few other options.[75]

GRAPEVINE CHARACTERISTICS

Research conducted several decades ago reported that the grapevine transmits information very rapidly in all directions throughout the organization. The typical pattern is a cluster chain, whereby a few people actively transmit rumours to many others. The grapevine works through informal social networks, so it is more active where employees have similar backgrounds and are able to communicate easily. Many rumours seem to have at least a kernel of truth, possibly because they are transmitted through media-rich communication channels (e.g., face-to-face) and employees are motivated to communicate effectively. Nevertheless, the grapevine distorts information by deleting fine details and exaggerating key points of the story.[76]

Some of these characteristics might still be true, but the grapevine almost certainly has changed as email, social networking sites, and tweets have replaced the traditional water cooler as sources of gossip. For example, several Facebook sites are themed around specific companies, allowing employees and customers to vent their complaints about the organization. Along with altering the speed and network of corporate grapevines, the Internet has expanded these networks around the globe, not just around the next cubicle.

GRAPEVINE BENEFITS AND LIMITATIONS

Should the grapevine be encouraged, tolerated, or quashed? The difficulty in answering this question is that the grapevine has both benefits and limitations.[77] One benefit, as was mentioned earlier, is that employees rely on the grapevine when information is not available through formal channels. It is also the main conduit through which organizational stories and other symbols of the organization's culture are communicated. A third benefit of the grapevine is that this social interaction relieves anxiety. This explains why rumour mills are most active during times of uncertainty.[78] Finally, the grapevine is associated with the drive to bond. Being a recipient of gossip is a sign of inclusion, according to evolutionary psychologists. Trying to quash the grapevine is, in some respects, an attempt to undermine the natural human drive for social interaction.[79]

While the grapevine offers these benefits, it is not a preferred communication medium. Grapevine information is sometimes so distorted that it escalates rather than reduces employee anxiety. Furthermore, employees develop more negative attitudes toward the organization when management is slower than the grapevine in communicating information. What should corporate leaders do with the grapevine? The best advice seems to be to listen to the grapevine as a signal of employee anxiety, then correct the cause of this anxiety. Some companies also listen to the grapevine and step in to correct blatant errors and fabrications. Most important, corporate leaders need to view the grapevine as a competitor, and meet this challenge by directly informing employees of news before it spreads throughout the grapevine.

CHAPTER SUMMARY

LO1 Explain why communication is important in organizations and discuss four influences on effective communication encoding and decoding.

Communication refers to the process by which information is transmitted and *understood* between two or more people. Communication supports work coordination, organizational learning, decision making, changing others' behaviour, and employee well-being. The communication process involves forming, encoding, and transmitting the intended message to a receiver, who then decodes the message and provides feedback to the sender. Effective communication occurs when the sender's thoughts are transmitted to and understood by the intended receiver. Four ways to improve this process is for both sender and receiver to be proficient with the communication channel, have similar codebooks, have shared common mental models of the communication context, and for the sender to be experienced at sending that message.

LO2 Compare and contrast the advantages of and problems with electronic mail, other verbal communication media, and nonverbal communication.

The two main types of communication channels are verbal and nonverbal. Various forms of Web-based communication are widely used in organizations, with email the most popular. Although efficient and a useful filing cabinet, email is relatively poor at communicating emotions;

it tends to reduce politeness and respect; it is an inefficient medium for communicating in ambiguous, complex, and novel situations; and it contributes to information overload. Facebook-like websites, wikis, virtual reality platforms, and other forms of social media are gaining popularity in the workplace. Social media include Web-based tools (websites, applications, etc.) that allow users to generate and exchange information. They serve several functions, including presenting the individual's identity, enabling conversations, sharing information, sensing the presence of others in the virtual space, maintaining relationships, revealing reputation or status, and supporting communities. Nonverbal communication includes facial gestures, voice intonation, physical distance, and even silence. Unlike verbal communication, nonverbal communication is less rule-bound and is mostly automatic and nonconscious. Some nonverbal communication is automatic through a process called emotional contagion.

LO3 Explain how social acceptance and media richness influence the preferred communication channel.

The most appropriate communication medium partly depends on its social acceptance and media richness. Social acceptance refers to how well the communication medium is approved and supported by the organization, teams, and individuals. This contingency includes organization and team norms, individual preferences for specific communication channels, and the symbolic meaning of a channel. A communication medium should also be chosen for its data-carrying capacity (media richness). Non-routine and ambiguous situations require rich media. However, technology-based lean media might be almost as effective as rich media for transferring information. This particularly occurs where users can multi-communicate and have high proficiency with that technology, and where social distractions of high media richness channels reduce the efficient processing of information through those channels. These contingencies are also considered when selecting the best channels for persuasion.

 L04 Discuss various barriers (noise) to effective communication, including cross-cultural and gender-based differences in communication.

Several barriers create noise in the communication process. People misinterpret messages because of misaligned codebooks due to different languages, jargon, and use of ambiguous phrases. Filtering messages and information overload are two other communication barriers. These problems are often amplified in cross-cultural settings where the above problems occur along with differences in meaning of nonverbal cues, silence, and conversational overlaps. There are also some communication differences between men and women, such as the tendency for men to exert status and engage in report talk in conversations, whereas women use more rapport talk and are more sensitive than are men to nonverbal cues.

 L05 Explain how to get your message across more effectively, and summarize the elements of active listening.

To get a message across, the sender must learn to empathize with the receiver, repeat the message, choose an appropriate time for the conversation, and be descriptive rather than evaluative. Listening includes sensing, evaluating, and responding. Active listeners support these processes by postponing evaluation, avoiding interruptions, maintaining interest, empathizing, organizing information, showing interest, and clarifying the message.

 L06 Summarize effective communication strategies in organizational hierarchies, and review the role and relevance of the organizational grapevine.

Some companies try to encourage communication through workspace design, as well as through Web-based communication channels. Some executives also meet directly with employees, such as through management by walking around (MBWA) and town hall meetings, to facilitate communication across the organization.

In any organization, employees rely on the grapevine, particularly during times of uncertainty. The grapevine is an unstructured and informal network founded on social relationships rather than organizational charts or job descriptions. Although early research identified several unique features of the grapevine, some of these features may be changing as the Internet plays an increasing role in grapevine communication.

KEY TERMS

communication, p. 246
emotional contagion, p. 252
grapevine, p. 263

information overload, p. 257
management by walking around
   (MBWA), p. 262

media richness, p. 253
persuasion, p. 255
wikis, p. 262

CRITICAL-THINKING QUESTIONS

1. You have been hired as a consultant to improve communication between engineering and marketing staff in a large high-technology company. Use the communication model and the four ways to improve that process to devise strategies to improve communication effectiveness among employees between these two work units.

2. A company that operates in a developing country intends to introduce electronic mail (email) for office staff at its three buildings located throughout the city. Describe two benefits as well as two potential problems that employees will likely experience with this medium.

3. Senior management at a consumer goods company wants you to investigate the feasibility of using a video calling application (such as Skype) for monthly online meetings involving its three-dozen sales managers located in several cities and countries. Use the social acceptance and media richness factors described in this chapter to identify information you need to consider when conducting this evaluation.

4. Wikis are collaborative websites where anyone in the group can post, edit, or delete any information. Where might this communication technology be most useful in organizations?

5. Under what conditions, if any, do you think it is appropriate to use email to notify an employee that he or she has been laid off or fired? Why is email usually considered an inappropriate channel to convey this information?

6. Suppose that you are part of a virtual team and must persuade other team members on an important matter (such as switching suppliers or altering the project deadline). Assuming that you cannot visit these people in person, what can you do to maximize your persuasiveness?

7. Explain why men and women are sometimes frustrated with each other's communication behaviours.

8. In your opinion, has the use of email and other information technologies increased or decreased the amount of information flowing through the corporate grapevine? Explain your answer.

CASE STUDY 9.1

Communicating with the Millennials

The Millennials (including Gen-Ys) have arrived in the workplace, and they are bringing new ways to communicate. Surveys report that this generation lives by computer and cellphone communication. Three out of four Gen-Ys use instant messaging (including tweets); 15 percent of them are logged on to IM 24/7! Most Gen-Ys either have a space on a social network site such as Facebook, or frequent these sites where they have friends. These digital natives also get most of their news from the Internet rather than from TV or printed newspapers.

"Employers are going to find this generation communicates differently. They IM (Instant Message), send text messages, and can't live without a cellphone," says Dave O'Brien, regional manager of Berbee, a company that helps businesses with their information technology needs. Frank Albi, president of Inacom, a technology and business consulting firm, agrees. "The way they (Millennials) exchange information is vastly different. It's all about IMs and text messages—nice and short."

Albi also notes that Millennials are much more active in multi-communicating. "You can be on the phone with someone and easily instant message someone who you see is online to answer a question or share an idea with," Albi says. However, managers also worry that too much of this multi-communication isn't work-related. "There's a fine line about what can be allowed at work and what can't," suggests Steve Hoeft, a recruiting manager at Time Warner Cable. "Instant messaging is very popular, but if it's affecting their work, that's when there's a problem."

Corporate leaders at BT, Britain's largest telecommunications company, are also aware that Millennials (and to some extent Gen-X employees) live in different communication channels from Baby Boomers. "Young people in BT communicate much more informally and in real-time," says Richard Dennison, BT's intranet and channel strategy manager. "They're not intimidated by hierarchy or status; to them BT is flat." Dennison adds that Gen-Y employees want bit-size information, not long treatises.

Dennison also emphasizes that, more than previous generations, Millennials demand authentic communication, not marketing hype. "Corporate speak won't cut it anymore," Dennison warns. "First, people won't read it—if they ever did—and second, people won't believe it—if they ever did." Dennison also notices that if Gen-Ys get corporate babble, they find ways to let the source know that it lacks authenticity. Remember, this is the generation that has always had a place to write comments after reading the original message.

From these observations, you might think that executive blogs are the answer to Gen-Y communication needs. Not so, argues Dennison. "Force all our senior managers to blog? My experience is that the more senior a manager is, the less likely they'll be able to blog successfully." He adds that executives have too little time to nurture a blog, and they tend to have communication experts who want to meddle (thereby undermining the blog's authenticity).

So how can the company's top dogs communicate effectively with Millennial employees? At BT, the chief executive has held 90-minute online Web chats with BT staff every six weeks. This medium works well for young BT employees because the communication is in real time and authentic—the questions aren't screened and the CEO's answers aren't edited. "Thousands of people participate in these chats and it has helped to build up a significant amount of trust" in the CEO, says Dennison. These online Web chats also work well with BT executives because they represent a fixed chunk of time and provide direct contact with the concerns and issues facing employees throughout the hierarchy.

Discussion Questions 1. Take a poll of your class (at least, the Gen-X and Gen-Y members). At school or work, how many regularly (e.g., daily or every few days) send or receive information (not entertainment) using (a) email, (b) instant messaging, (c) text messaging, (d) reading/writing blogs or microblogs (e.g., Twitter), (e) video calling (e.g., Skype), (f) visiting/posting to social networking sites (e.g., Facebook), (g) watching/creating online videos (e.g., YouTube)?

2. Even within this generation, there are different preferences for communication media. After conducting the poll above, ask students who don't regularly use one or more of these methods why they don't like that particular communication medium. Ask those who very often use these sources to give their point of view.

3. Companies have been slow and reluctant to adopt social media channels, online videos, and similar forms of communication. If you were a senior manager, how would you introduce these communication technologies in the workplace to share information and knowledge more effectively?

Sources: MaryBeth Matzek, "R U on 2 Gen Y?" *Marketplace*, September 4, 2007, p. 10; Richard Dennison, "Encouraging BT's Authentic Voice of Leadership," *Strategic Communication Management* 12, no. 2 (2008), p. 12.

 TEAM EXERCISE 9.2

Analyzing Blogs and Tweets

Purpose   This exercise is designed to help you understand the dynamics of corporate blogs & microblogs as a way to communicate around organizations.

Instructions   This exercise is usually conducted between classes as an assignment. The instructor will divide the class into teams (although this can also be conducted with individuals). Each team will identify a Canadian executive who communicates using a corporate blog or microblog (e.g., Twitter) aimed for customers, employees, or the wider community. (See www.ceocouncil.ca/en/about/members.php for a sample list of the names of some Canadian CEOs.)

The team will analyze content from the selected blog or microblog and answer the following questions in class (preferably with brief samples where applicable).

1. Who is the main intended audience of the selected blog or microblog?

2. What are the main topics in recent postings/tweets about this organization?

3. To what extent do you think this blog/microblog attracts the interest of its intended audience? Explain.

 TEAM EXERCISE 9.3

Active Listening Exercise

By Mary Gander, Winona State University

Purpose   This exercise is designed to help you understand the dynamics of active listening in conversations and to develop active listening skills.

Instructions   For each of the four vignettes presented here, student teams (or students working individually) will compose three statements that demonstrate active listening. Specifically, one statement will indicate that you show empathy for the situation; the second will ask for clarification and detail in a nonjudgmental way; and the third statement will provide nonevaluative feedback to the speaker. Here are details about each of these three types of responses:

- *Showing empathy: acknowledge feelings.* Sometimes it sounds like a speaker wants you to agree with him or her, but in reality the speaker mainly wants you to understand how he or she feels. "Acknowledging feelings" involves taking in the speaker's statements while looking at the "whole message" including body language, tone of voice, and level of engagement, and trying to determine what emotion the speaker is conveying. Then you let the speaker know that you realize what he or she is feeling by acknowledging it in a sentence.

- *Asking for clarification and detail while withholding your judgment and own opinions.* This conveys that you are trying to understand and not just trying to push your opinions onto the speaker. To formulate a relevant question in asking for more clarification, you will have to listen carefully to what the speaker says. Frame your question as someone trying to understand in more detail; often asking for a specific example is useful. This also helps the speaker evaluate his or her own opinions and perspective.

- *Providing nonevaluative feedback: feeding back the message you heard.* This will allow the speaker to determine if he or she conveyed the message to you and will help prevent troublesome miscommunication. It will also help the speaker become more aware of how he or she is coming across to another person (self-evaluation). Just think about what the speaker is conveying; paraphrase it in your own words, and say it back to the speaker (without judging the correctness or merit of what was said), asking him or her if that is what was meant.

After teams (or individual students) have prepared the three statements for each vignette, the instructor will ask them to present their statements and explain how these statements satisfy the active listening criteria.

Vignette #1

A colleague stops by your desk and says, "I am tired of the lack of leadership around here. The boss is so wishy-washy, he can't get tough with some of the slackers around here. They just keep milking the company, living off the rest of us. Why doesn't management do something about these guys? And you are always so supportive of the boss; he's not as good as you make him out to be."

Develop three statements that respond to the speaker in this vignette by (a) showing empathy, (b) seeking clarification, and (c) providing nonevaluative feedback.

Vignette #2

Your co-worker stops by your cubicle; her voice and body language show stress, frustration, and even some fear. You know she has been working hard and has a strong need to get her work done on time and done well. You are trying to concentrate on some work and have had a number of interruptions already. She abruptly interrupts you and says, "This project is turning out to be a mess. Why can't the other three people on my team quit fighting with each other?"

Develop three statements that respond to the speaker in this vignette by (a) showing empathy, (b) seeking clarification, and (c) providing nonevaluative feedback.

Vignette #3

One of your direct reports is working on an important project. He is an engineer who has good technical skills and knowledge and was selected for the project team because of that. He stops by your office and appears to be quite agitated: His voice is loud and strained, and his face has a look of bewilderment. He says, "I'm supposed to be working with four other people from four other departments on this new project, but they never listen to my ideas and seem to hardly know I'm at the meeting!"

Develop three statements that respond to the speaker in this vignette by (a) showing empathy, (b) seeking clarification, and (c) providing nonevaluative feedback.

Vignette #4

One of your direct reports comes into your office in a state of agitation, asking if she can talk to you. She is polite and sits down. She seems calm and does not have an angry look on her face. However, she says, "It seems like you consistently make up lousy schedules;

you are unfair and unrealistic in the kind of assignments you give certain people, me included. Everyone else is so intimidated they don't complain, but I think you need to know that this isn't right and it's got to change."

Develop three statements that respond to the speaker in this vignette by (a) showing empathy, (b) seeking clarification, and (c) providing nonevaluative feedback.

 TEAM EXERCISE 9.4

Cross-Cultural Communication Game

Purpose   This exercise is designed to develop and test your knowledge of cross-cultural differences in communication and etiquette.

Materials   The instructor will provide one set of question/answer cards to each pair of teams.

Instructions
- *Step 1:* The class is divided into an even number of teams. Ideally, each team would have three students. (Two- or four-student teams are possible if matched with an equal-sized team.) Each team is then paired with another team and the paired teams (Team "A" and Team "B") are assigned a private space away from other matched teams.

- *Step 2:* The instructor will hand each pair of teams a stack of cards with the multiple choice questions face down. These cards have questions and answers about cross-cultural differences in communication and etiquette. No books or other aids are allowed.

- *Step 3:* The exercise begins with a member of Team A picking up one card from the top of the pile and asking the question on that card to the members of Team B. The information given to Team B includes the question and all alternatives listed on the card. Team B has 30 seconds after the question and alternatives have been read to give an answer. Team B earns one point if the correct answer is given. If Team B's answer is incorrect, however, Team A earns that point. Correct answers to each question are indicated on the card and, of course, should not be revealed until the question is correctly answered or time is up. Whether or not Team B answers correctly, it picks up the next card on the pile and reads it to members of Team A. In other words, cards are read alternatively to each team. This procedure is repeated until all of the cards have been read or time has expired. The team receiving the most points wins.

Important note: The textbook provides very little information pertaining to the questions in this exercise. Rather, you must rely on past learning, logic, and luck to win.

Copyright © 2011, 2001 Steven L. McShane

Go to CONNECT to complete the following interactive self-assessment.

 SELF-ASSESSMENT EXERCISE 9.5

Are You An Active Listener?

Purpose   This self-assessment is designed to help you estimate your strengths and weaknesses on various dimensions of active listening.

Instructions   Think back to face-to-face conversations you have had with a co-worker or client in the office, hallway, factory floor, or other setting. Indicate the extent that each item below describes your behaviour during those conversations. Answer each item as truthfully as possible so that you get an accurate estimate of where your active listening skills need improvement. Then use the scoring key in Appendix B to calculate your results for each scale. This exercise is completed alone so students assess themselves honestly without concerns of social comparison. However, class discussion will focus on the important elements of active listening.

Active Listening Skills Inventory

When listening to others in face-to-face, phone, or similar conversations, how often do you do the following?	Never or Rarely	Seldom	Sometimes	Often	Almost always
1. I keep an open mind when others describe their ideas.	☐	☐	☐	☐	☐
2. I organize the speaker's ideas while she or he is talking to me.	☐	☐	☐	☐	☐
3. I ask questions to show I understand and am focused on the speaker's message.	☐	☐	☐	☐	☐
4. I interrupt before the speaker sufficiently presents his or her views.	☐	☐	☐	☐	☐
5. While listening, I mentally sort out the speaker's ideas so she or he makes sense to me.	☐	☐	☐	☐	☐
6. I use gestures and words (nodding, agreeing) to show I am listening.	☐	☐	☐	☐	☐
7. I let my mind wander when listening to people.	☐	☐	☐	☐	☐
8. I try to visualize and feel the speaker's experience while she or he is describing those events.	☐	☐	☐	☐	☐
9. I summarize the speaker's ideas to confirm that I understand him or her correctly.	☐	☐	☐	☐	☐
10. I focus on what the speaker is saying to me even when it doesn't sound interesting.	☐	☐	☐	☐	☐
11. I see the topic from my perspective rather than from the speaker's perspective.	☐	☐	☐	☐	☐
12. I show interest while listening to others.	☐	☐	☐	☐	☐

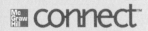

Practise and learn online with Connect. Connect resources include additional and interactive study exercises, videos, and practice quizzing, as well as additional material you won't find in the printed text.

CHAPTER 10

Power and Influence in the Workplace

LEARNING OBJECTIVES

After reading this chapter, you should be able to:

LO1 Describe the dependence model of power and describe the five sources of power in organizations.

LO2 Discuss the four contingencies of power.

LO3 Explain how people and work units gain power through social networks.

LO4 Describe eight types of influence tactics, three consequences of influencing others, and three contingencies to consider when choosing an influence tactic.

LO5 Identify the organizational conditions and personal characteristics that support organizational politics, as well as ways to minimize organizational politics.

Former RCMP Commissioner William Elliott was hired to right the wrongs of recent scandals involving the alleged abuse of power by his predecessor. However, Williams has been described as "a cure much worse than the disease." Elliott, the first ever civilian to head the RCMP, has faced harsh criticism for behaviours described as "brutal, disrespectful, intimidating, and careless." Elliott has also been accused of abusing his power and being "vindictive" in his motivation for a recent shakeup in the RCMP senior management team. For example, one of his critics, deputy commissioner Raf Souccar, was "stripped of his responsibilities of overseeing federal and international policing" during a recent round of promotions and retirements.

The 14 senior officials of the RCMP who went over the commissioner's head to complain about his behaviour worried that "the deck was stacked" against them when the invitation to discuss their concerns with Reid Morden, former director of CSIS (Canadian Security Intelligence Service), came from Commissioner Elliott's executive office. Subsequent meetings were held in the Commissioner's boardroom. Despite fears they would be "putting their careers on the line," they appeared before Morden as part of the workplace assessment.

Controversy has also surrounded Elliott with the reassignment of Chief Superintendent Marty Cheliak, who was formerly responsible for overseeing the politically charged long-gun registry. Questions about political influence were "absolute and positive fiction" said Elliott. "There is not one iota of truth in that. The media and others just made this up. It's not true, it's not true, it's not true."

In the wake of this "mutiny in the ranks" Commissioner Elliott maintains that he has had discussions with his internal critics. "We all said we were committed to working together, to working on our issues and to move the force forward." David McAusland, chair of the independent council who recently released his report providing recommendations to guide RCMP reforms, said in an interview that creating an external civilian management board could have helped to prevent the work issues arising between Elliott and his senior managers. In an interview, McAusland explained, "There is a risk of the people involved becoming insular, talking the same language, living the same reality and not being in a position to be exposed to or influenced by ideas from the outside."[1]

Former RCMP Commissioner William Elliott has faced high-profile accusations of subversive power, influence and politics. *THE CANADIAN PRESS/Darryl Dyck*

As this opening story illustrates, power and influence are never far from the actions of leaders and followers. Some senior officers concluded that Commissioner Elliott abused his power by sidelining people and being assertive toward others. These officers may have been particularly sensitive to Elliott's actions because his predecessor had used similar tactics. Elliott, in turn, might have quietly thought that these officers were using dysfunctional influence tactics—airing their complaints publicly to undermine Elliott's credibility as head of the RCMP. The opening story might paint the RCMP as an organization mired in abuses of power and organizational politics, but every organization faces similar challenges to some degree. Although this story illustrates the dark side of power and influence, these concepts are equally relevant to ethical conduct and organizational performance. In fact, some OB experts point out that power and influence are inherent in all organizations. They exist in every business and in every decision and action.

This chapter unfolds as follows: First, we define power and present a basic model depicting the dynamics of power in organizational settings. The chapter then discusses the five bases of power, as well as information as a power base. Next, we look at the contingencies necessary to translate those sources into meaningful power. Our attention then turns to social networks and how they provide power to members through social capital. The latter part of this chapter examines the various types of influence in organizational settings as well as the contingencies of effective influence strategies. The final section of this chapter looks at situations in which influence becomes organizational politics, as well as ways of minimizing dysfunctional politics.

THE MEANING OF POWER

LO1

power The capacity of a person, team, or organization to influence others.

Power is the capacity of a person, team, or organization to influence others.[2] There are a few important features of this definition. First, power is not the act of changing someone's attitudes or behaviour; it is only the *potential* to do so. People frequently have power they do not use; they might not even know they have power. Second, power is based on the target's *perception* that the powerholder controls (i.e., possesses, has access to, or regulates) a valuable resource that can help them achieve their goals.[3] People might generate power by convincing others that they control something of value, whether or not they actually control that resource. Thus, power exists when others believe the powerholder controls resources that will help them. Notice, too, that power is not a personal feeling of power. You might feel powerful or think you have power over others, but this is not power unless others believe you have that capacity.

Third, power involves asymmetric (unequal) *dependence* of one party on another party.[4] This dependent relationship is illustrated in Exhibit 10.1. The line from Person B to the goal shows that he or she believes Person A controls a resource that can help or hinder Person B in achieving that goal. Person A—the powerholder in this illustration—might have power over Person B by controlling a desired job assignment, useful information, rewards, or even the privilege of being associated with him or her! For example, if you believe a co-worker has expertise (the resource) that would substantially help you to write a better report (your goal), then that co-worker has some power over you because you value that expertise to achieve your goal. Whatever the resource is, Person B is *dependent* on Person A (the powerholder) to provide the resource so Person B can reach his or her goal.

countervailing power The capacity of a person, team, or organization to keep a more powerful person or group in the exchange relationship.

Although dependence is a key element of power relationships, we use the phrase "asymmetric dependence" because the less powerful party still has some degree of power—called **countervailing power**—over the powerholder. In Exhibit 10.1, Person A dominates the power relationship, but Person B has enough countervailing power to keep Person A in the exchange relationship and ensure that person or department uses its dominant power judiciously. For example, although managers have power over employees in many ways (e.g., controlling job security, preferred work assignments), employees have countervailing power by possessing skills and knowledge to keep production humming and customers happy, something that management can't accomplish alone.

Finally, the power relationship depends on some minimum level of trust. Trust indicates a level of expectation that the more powerful party will deliver the resource.

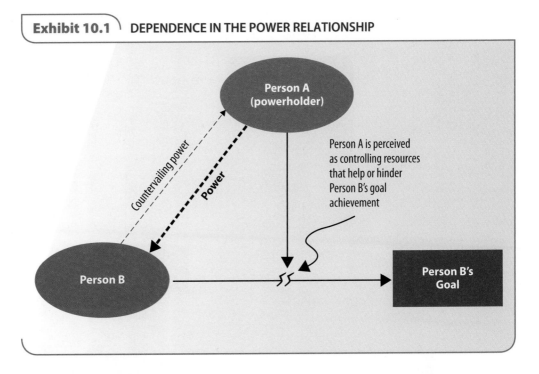

Exhibit 10.1 DEPENDENCE IN THE POWER RELATIONSHIP

For example, you trust your employer to give you a paycheque at the end of each pay period. Even those in extremely dependent situations will usually walk away from the relationship if they lack a minimum level of trust in the more powerful party.

The dependence model reveals only the core features of power dynamics in organizations. We also need to learn about the specific sources of power and contingencies that allow that power to be effectively applied as influence. As Exhibit 10.2 illustrates, power is derived from five sources: legitimate, reward, coercive, expert, and referent. The model also identifies four contingencies of power: the employee's or department's substitutability, centrality, discretion, and visibility. Over the next few pages, we will discuss each of these sources and contingencies of power in the context of organizations.

SOURCES OF POWER IN ORGANIZATIONS

Why do some people have more power than others in the workplace? A half-century ago, social scientists John French and Bertrand Raven identified five sources of power found in organizations. Although variations of this list have been proposed over the years, the original list remains surprisingly intact.[5] Three sources of power—legitimate, reward, and coercive—originate mostly (but not completely) from the powerholder's formal position or informal role. In other words, the person is granted these sources of power formally by the organization or informally by co-workers. Two other sources of power—expert and referent—originate mainly from the powerholder's own characteristics; in other words, people carry these power bases around with them. However, even personal sources of power are situational to some extent because they depend on how others perceive the individual.

legitimate power An agreement among organizational members that people in certain roles can request certain behaviours of others.

LEGITIMATE POWER

Legitimate power is an agreement among organizational members that people in certain roles can request certain behaviours of others. This perceived right or obligation originates from formal job descriptions as well as informal rules of conduct. The most obvious example of legitimate power is a manager's right to tell employees what tasks to perform, who to work with, what office resources they can use, and so forth. Employees agree to the boss's requests because there is mutual agreement that employees will follow a range

Exhibit 10.2 \ SOURCES AND CONTINGENCIES OF POWER

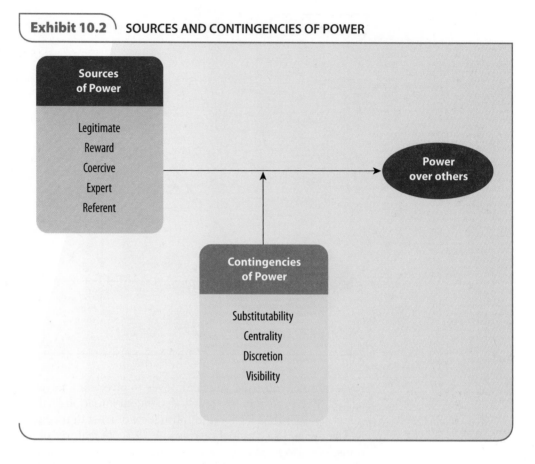

of directives from people in these positions of authority. Employees defer to this authority whether or not they will be rewarded or punished for complying with those requests.

Notice that legitimate power has restrictions; it only gives the powerholder the right to ask for a *range* of behaviours from others. This range—known as the "zone of indifference"—is the set of behaviours that individuals are willing to engage in at the other person's request.[6] Although most employees accept the boss's right to deny them access to Facebook during company time, some might draw the line when the boss asks them to work several hours beyond the regular workday. There are also occasions where employees actively oppose the boss's actions. In the opening vignette to this chapter, for example, several RCMP executives publicly complained that Commissioner William Elliott's reassignment of two senior management staff went beyond his legitimate power. Elliott's position allows him to reassign people, and the two executives involved didn't refuse their new reassignment. However, other executives claim Commissioner Elliott stepped beyond the zone of indifference because they believe his actions were political rather than in the best interests of the organization and society.

 Legitimate power only gives the powerholder the right to ask for a *range* of behaviours from others. "

The size of the zone of indifference (and, consequently, the magnitude of legitimate power) increases with the level of trust in the powerholder. Some people are also more obedient to authority, particularly those who value conformity and tradition. People in high power distance cultures (i.e., they accept an unequal distribution of power) also tend to have higher deference to authority compared with people in low power distance cultures. The organization's culture represents another influence on the willingness of

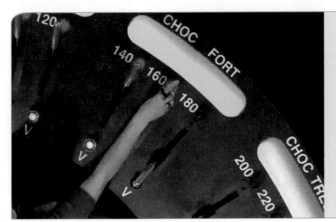

Legitimate Power Takes People to the Extreme

French reality television recently revealed how far people are willing to follow orders. As a variation of the 1960s experiments conducted by Stanley Milgram, 80 contestants administered electric shocks whenever a volunteer (an actor who didn't receive the shocks at all) answered a question incorrectly. Shocks increased in 20-volt increments, from 20 volts for the first mistake through to 460 volts (lethal if passed through the body). Most contestants who hesitated to administer further shocks (after hearing loud screams from the volunteer) continued the treatment after the host reminded them that their job is to administer the shocks. Audience support also encouraged contestants to continue giving shocks. Only 16 of the 80 contestants refused to administer the strongest shocks. Eighty percent followed orders . . . to the end.[7] *"Le jeu de la mort" by Christopher Nick, courtesy of Metropole Films*

employees to follow orders. A 3M scientist might continue to work on a project after being told by superiors to stop working on it because the 3M culture supports an entrepreneurial spirit, which includes ignoring your boss's authority from time to time.[8]

Managers are not the only people with legitimate power in organizations. Employees also have legitimate power over their bosses and co-workers through legal and administrative rights as well as informal norms.[9] For example, an organization might give employees the right to request information that is required for their job. Laws give employees the right to refuse work in unsafe conditions. More subtle forms of legitimate power also exist. Human beings have a **norm of reciprocity**—a feeling of obligation to help someone who has helped you.[10] If a co-worker previously helped you handle a difficult client, that co-worker has power because you feel an obligation to help the co-worker on something of similar value in the future. The norm of reciprocity is a form of legitimate power because it is an informal rule of conduct that we are expected to follow.

One final observation is that a particularly potent form of legitimate power occurs where people have the right to control the information that others receive.[11] These information gatekeepers gain power in two ways. First, information is a resource, so those who need that information are dependent on the gatekeeper to provide that resource. For example, the maps department of a mining company has incredible power when other departments are dependent on the map department to deliver maps required for exploration projects. Information gatekeepers also gain power by selectively distributing information so those receiving the information perceive the situation differently.[12] Executives depend on middle managers and employees to provide an accurate picture of the company's operations. Yet, as we learned in the previous chapter on communication, information is often filtered as it flows up the hierarchy. Middle managers and employees filter information so it puts them in a more positive light and allows them to steer the executive team toward one decision rather than another. In other words, these information gatekeepers can potentially influence executive decisions by framing their reality through selective distribution of information.

norm of reciprocity A felt obligation and social expectation of helping or otherwise giving something of value to someone who has already helped or given something to you.

REWARD POWER

Reward power is derived from the person's ability to control the allocation of rewards valued by others and to remove negative sanctions (i.e., negative reinforcement). Managers have formal authority that gives them power over the distribution of organizational rewards such as pay, promotions, time off, vacation schedules, and work assignments. Employees also have reward power over their bosses through their feedback and ratings in 360-degree feedback systems. These ratings affect supervisors' promotions and other rewards, so supervisors pay more attention to employee requests after 360-degree feedback is introduced.

COERCIVE POWER

Coercive power is the ability to apply punishment. For many of us, the first thought is managers threatening employees with dismissal. Yet, employees also have coercive power, such as being sarcastic toward co-workers or threatening to ostracize them if they fail to conform to team norms. Many firms rely on this coercive power to control co-worker behaviour in team settings. Nucor is one such example: "If you're not contributing with the team, they certainly will let you know about it," says Dan Krug, manager of HR and organizational development at the Charlotte, N.C. steelmaker. "The few poor players get weeded out by their peers." Similarly, when asked how AirAsia maintained attendance and productivity after the Malaysian discount airline removed the time clocks, chief executive Tony Fernandes replied: "Simple. Peer pressure sees to that. The fellow employees, who are putting their shoulders to the wheel, will see to that."[13]

EXPERT POWER

For the most part, legitimate, reward, and coercive power originate from the position.[14] Expert power, on the other hand, originates from within the powerholder. It is an individual's or work unit's capacity to influence others by possessing knowledge or skills valued by others. One important form of expert power is the (perceived) ability to manage uncertainties in the business environment. Organizations are more effective when they operate in predictable environments, so they value people who can cope with turbulence in the consumer trends, societal changes, unstable supply lines, and so forth.

A groundbreaking study of Canadian breweries and container companies identified three types of expertise that cope with uncertainty. These coping strategies are arranged in a hierarchy of importance, with prevention being the most powerful:[15]

- *Prevention*—The most effective strategy is to prevent environmental changes from occurring. For example, financial experts acquire power by preventing the organization from experiencing a cash shortage or defaulting on loans.

- *Forecasting*—The next best strategy is to predict environmental changes or variations. In this respect, trendspotters and other marketing specialists gain power by predicting changes in consumer preferences.

- *Absorption*—People and work units also gain power by absorbing or neutralizing the impact of environmental shifts as they occur. An example is the ability of maintenance crews to come to the rescue when machines break down.

DeCourcy's Expert Power

Toronto-born Colleen DeCourcy has developed a reputation as "one of the most brilliant digital people," explains David Jones, global CEO of Euro RSCG Worldwide. "Historically in our business the competitive difference among agencies has been talent." DeCourcy wields considerable expert power in the advertising industry. Until recently, DeCourcy held the post of global chief digital officer with ad agency giant Omnicom Group's TBWA. Tom Carroll, TBWA's worldwide president, described DeCourcy's expertise: "her knowledge of the digital landscape, grounded in creativity, make her an invaluable addition." For example, Decourcy recognized that traditional media no longer reach teenagers and led the advertising industry by developing "MediaJamming"—communicating the advertising message through many sources scattered across the Web (videos, ringtones, games, and music) so the audience is surrounded by the message. DeCourcy is currently heading up Socialistic, a new social media firm creating content and applications for innovative social platform applications.[16] *Photo used with permission of Nielsen Business Media, Inc.*

The power of expertise is similar to the power of authority (legitimate power) because many people tend to follow the guidance of these experts without careful thought.[17] In one classic study, for example, a researcher posing as a hospital physician telephoned on-duty nurses to prescribe a specific dosage of medicine to a hospitalized patient. None of the nurses knew the person calling, and hospital policy forbade them from accepting treatment by telephone. Furthermore, the medication was unauthorized and the prescription was twice the maximum daily dose. Yet, almost all 22 nurses who received the telephone call followed the "doctor's" orders until stopped by researchers.

This doctor–nurse study is a few decades old, but the power of expertise remains strong today, sometimes with tragic consequences. Most recently, the Canadian justice system discovered that the expert testimony of a famous Canadian pathologist was far from accurate in more than a dozen cases, resulting in the conviction of innocent people. The pathologist's reputation as a renowned authority was the main reason why his often-weak evidence was rarely questioned. "Experts in a courtroom—we give great deference to experts," says the chairman of the Canadian Council of Criminal Defence Lawyers when explaining why the pathologist's testimony was so readily accepted.[18]

referent power The capacity to influence others on the basis of an identification with and respect for the powerholder.

REFERENT POWER

People have **referent power** when others identify with them, like them, or otherwise respect them. As with expert power, referent power originates within the powerholder. It is largely a function of the person's interpersonal skills and tends to develop slowly. Referent power is also associated with **charisma**. Experts have difficulty agreeing on the meaning of charisma, but it is most often described as a form of interpersonal attraction whereby followers ascribe almost magical powers to the charismatic individual.[19] Some writers describe charisma as a special "gift" or trait within the charismatic person, while others say it is mainly in the eyes of the beholder. However, all agree that charisma produces a high degree of trust, respect, and devotion towards the charismatic individual.

charisma A personal characteristic or special "gift" that serves as a form of interpersonal attraction and referent power over others.

CONTINGENCIES OF POWER

LO2

Let's say that you have expert power because of your ability to forecast and possibly even prevent dramatic changes in the organization's environment. Does this expertise mean that you are influential? Not necessarily. As Exhibit 10.2 shown earlier illustrates, sources of power generate power only under certain conditions. Four important contingencies of power are substitutability, centrality, discretion, and visibility.[20]

SUBSTITUTABILITY

substitutability A contingency of power referring to the availability of alternatives.

Substitutability refers to the availability of alternatives. Power is strongest when someone has a monopoly over a valued resource. Conversely, power decreases as the number of alternative sources of the critical resource increases. If you—and no one else—has expertise across the organization on an important issue, you would be more powerful than if several people in your company possess this valued knowledge. Substitutability refers not only to other sources that offer the resource, but also to substitutions of the resource itself. For instance, labour unions are weakened when companies introduce technologies that replace the need for their union members. Technology is a substitute for employees and, consequently, reduces union power.

Nonsubstitutability is strengthened by controlling access to the resource. Professions and labour unions gain power by controlling knowledge, tasks, or labour to perform important activities. For instance, the medical profession is powerful because it controls who can perform specific medical procedures. Labour unions that dominate an industry effectively control access to labour needed to perform key jobs. Employees become nonsubstitutable when they possess knowledge (such as operating equipment or serving clients) that is not documented or readily available to others. Nonsubstitutability also occurs when people differentiate their resource from the alternatives. Some people claim that consultants use this tactic—take skills and knowledge that many other consulting firms can provide and wrap them into a package so that it looks like a service that no one else can offer.

CENTRALITY

centrality A contingency of power pertaining to the degree and nature of interdependence between the powerholder and others.

Centrality refers to the powerholder's importance based on the degree and nature of interdependence between the powerholder and others.[21] Centrality increases with the number of people dependent on you as well as how quickly and severely they are affected by that dependence. Think about your own centrality for a moment: If you decided not to show up for work or school tomorrow, how many people would have difficulty performing their jobs because of your absence? How soon after they arrive at work would these co-workers notice that you are missing and would have to adjust their tasks and work schedule as a result? If you have high centrality, most people in the organization would be adversely affected by your absence, and they would be affected quickly.

The extent to which centrality leverages power is apparent in well-timed labour union strikes, such as the New York City transit strike during the busy Christmas shopping season a few years ago. The illegal three-day work stoppage clogged roads and caused half the city workers to miss or arrive very late for work. "[The Metropolitan Transit Authority] told us we got no power, but we got power," said one striking transit worker. "We got the power to stop the city."[22]

DISCRETION

The freedom to exercise judgment—to make decisions without referring to a specific rule or receiving permission from someone else—is another important contingency of power in organizations. Consider the plight of first-line supervisors. It may seem that they have legitimate, reward, and coercive power over employees, but this power is often curtailed by specific rules. The lack of discretion makes supervisors less powerful than their positions would indicate. "Middle managers are very much 'piggy-in-the-middle,'" complains a middle manager at Britain's National Health System. "They have little power, only what senior managers are allowed to give them."[23] More generally, research indicates that managerial discretion varies considerably across industries, and that managers with an internal locus of control are viewed as more powerful because they act as though they have considerable discretion in their job.[24]

VISIBILITY

Power does not flow to unknown people in the organization. Those who control valued resources or knowledge will yield power only when others are aware of these sources of power, in other words, when they are visible. One way to increase visibility is to take people-oriented jobs and work on projects that require frequent interaction with senior executives. "You can take visibility in steps," advises an executive at a pharmaceutical firm. "You can start by making yourself visible in a small group, such as a staff meeting. Then when you're comfortable with that, seek out larger arenas."[25]

Employees also gain visibility by being, quite literally, visible. Some people strategically locate themselves in more visible offices, such as those closest to the elevator or staff coffee room. People often use public symbols as subtle (and not-so-subtle) cues to make their power sources known to others. Many professionals display their educational diplomas and awards on office walls to remind visitors of their expertise. Medical professionals wear white coats with a stethoscope around their neck to symbolize their legitimate and expert power in hospital settings. Other people play the game of "face time"—spending more time at work and showing that they are working productively.

THE POWER OF SOCIAL NETWORKS

LO3

social networks Social structures of individuals or social units that are connected to each other through one or more forms of interdependence.

"It's not what you know, but who you know that counts!" This often-heard statement reflects the idea that employees get ahead not just by developing their competencies, but by locating themselves within **social networks**—social structures of individuals or social units (e.g., departments, organizations) that are connected to each other through one or more forms of interdependence.[26] Some networks are held together due to common interests, such as when employees who love fancy cars spend more time together. Other networks form around common status, expertise, kinship, or physical proximity. For instance, employees are more likely to form networks with co-workers located near them as well as with co-workers who are relatives or close neighbours.[27]

Social networks exist everywhere because people have a drive to bond. However, there are cultural differences in the norms of active network involvement. Several writers suggest that social networking is more of a central life activity in Asian cultures that emphasize *guanxi*, a Chinese term referring to an individual's network of social connections. Guanxi is an expressive activity because being part of a close-knit network of family and friends reinforces one's self-concept. Guanxi is also an instrumental activity because it is a strategy for receiving favours and opportunities from others. People across all cultures rely on social networks for both expressive and instrumental purposes, but these activities seem to be somewhat more explicit in Confucian cultures.[28]

SOCIAL CAPITAL AND SOURCES OF POWER

social capital The knowledge and other resources available to people or social units (teams, organizations) from a durable network that connects them to others.

Social networks generate power through **social capital**—the goodwill and resulting resources shared among members in a social network.[29] Social networks produce trust, support, sympathy, forgiveness, and similar forms of goodwill among network members, and this goodwill motivates and enables network members to share resources with each other.[30]

Social networks offer a variety of resources, each of which potentially enhances the power of its members. Probably the best-known resource is information from other network members, which improves the individual's expert power.[31] The goodwill of social capital opens communication pipelines among those within the network. Network members receive valuable knowledge more easily and more quickly from fellow network members than do people outside that network.[32] With better information access and timeliness, members have more power because their expertise is a scarce resource; it is not widely available to people outside the network.

Increased visibility is a second way that social networks increase one's power. When asked to recommend someone for valued positions, other network members more readily think of you than people outside the network. Similarly, they are more likely to mention your name when asked to identify people with expertise in your areas of knowledge. A third source of power from networks is referent power. People tend to gain referent power because network members identify more with or at least have greater trust in network members, thereby gaining access to more resources controlled by those members. Referent power is also apparent by the fact that reciprocity increases among network members as they become more embedded in the network.[33]

A common misperception is that social networks are free spirits that cannot be orchestrated by corporate leaders. In reality, company structures and practices can shape these networks to some extent.[34] But even if organizational leaders don't try to manage social networks, they need to be aware of them. Indeed, people gain power in organizations through accurate perception of social networks.[35] As Global Connections 10.1 describes, some leaders are discovering the hidden dynamics of these networks and tapping into their potential.

CONNECTIONS 10.1

Powered by the Social Network

Engineering and environmental consulting firm MWH Global reorganized its information technology (IT) operations into a single global division and located its main service centre in New Zealand. Ken Loughridge was transferred from England to manage the new service centre, but he didn't know who were the key players in his New Zealand team. "By and large, the staff I'd adopted were strangers," he says.

Fortunately, Loughridge was able to consult a report displaying the informal social network of relationships among his staff. MWH Global had surveyed its IT employees a few months earlier about who they communicated with most often for information. These data produced a web-like diagram of nodes (people) connected by a maze of lines (relationships). From this picture, Loughridge could identify the employees who others depend on for information. "It's as if you took the top off an ant hill and could see where there's a hive of activity," he says of the map. "It really helped me understand who the players were."

Social network analysis has gained a following among some executives as they discover that visual displays of relationships and information flows can help them to tap into employees with expertise and influence. "You look at an org chart within a company and you see the distribution of power that should be," says Eran Barak, global head of marketing strategies at Thomson Reuters. "You look at the dynamics in the social networks [to] see the distribution of power that is. It reflects where information is flowing—who is really driving things."

Karl Arunski, director of Raytheon's engineering centre in Colorado, can appreciate these words. The defence and technology company's organizational chart didn't show how mission management specialists influenced people across departmental boundaries. So Arunski asked two executives to identify the names of up to 10 experts who didn't fit squarely in a particular department, then he conducted social network analysis to see how these people collaborated with engineers throughout the organization.

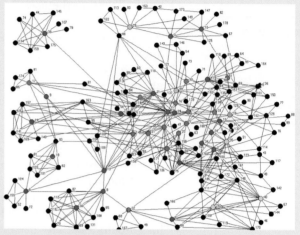

This is one of several social network analysis diagrams that helped Ratheon engineering director Karl Arunski to determine who has the most social network power. *Courtesy of Karl J. Arunski, Raytheon*

The resulting maps (one of which is shown here), showed Arunski the influence and knowledge flow of various experts. It also highlighted problems where a cluster of employees is almost completely disconnected from the rest of the engineering group (such as the top left side of this diagram). One team's isolation was worrisome because its members were experts in systems architecture, an important growth area for Raytheon. To increase the team's social network, Arunski encouraged the team leader to hold meetings where engineers could share information about systems architecture. The number of people attending eventually grew to 75 people and subsequently reduced the team's isolation from others. "Social network analysis helped Rocky Mountain Engineering understand how organizations develop architectures, and it enabled us to know how engineers become architects," says Arunski.[36]

GAINING POWER FROM SOCIAL NETWORKS

How do individuals (and teams and organizations) gain the most social capital from social networks? To answer this question, we need to consider the number, depth, variety, and centrality of connections that people have in their networks.

Strong Ties, Weak Ties, Many Ties   Social capital tends to increase with the number of network ties. The more people connected to you, the more resources (information, favours, etc.) will be available. Some people have an amazing capacity to maintain their connectivity with many people, and emerging communication technologies (Facebook, LinkedIn, etc.) have increased this capacity to gain social capital.[37] At the same time, the more people you know, the less time and energy you have to form "strong ties." These are close-knit relationships evident from how often we interact with people, how much we share resources with them, and whether we have multiple or singular relationships with them (e.g., friend, co-worker, sports partner). The main advantages of having strong ties are that they offer resources more quickly and sometimes more plentifully than are available in weak ties (i.e., acquaintances).

Some minimal connection strength is necessary to remain in any social network, but strong connections aren't necessarily the most valuable ties. Instead, having weak ties (i.e., being merely acquaintances) with people from diverse networks can be more valuable than having strong ties (i.e., having close friendships) with people in similar networks.[38] Why is this so? Close ties—our close-knit circle of friends—tend to be similar to us, and similar people tend to have the same information and connections that we already have.[39] Weak ties, on the other hand, are acquaintances who are usually different from us and therefore offer resources we do not possess. Furthermore, by serving as a "bridge" across several unrelated networks, we receive unique resources from each network rather than more of the same resources.

The strength of weak ties is most apparent in job hunting and career development.[40] People with diverse networks tend to be more successful job seekers because they have a wider net to catch new job opportunities. In contrast, people who belong to similar overlapping networks tend to receive the fewer leads, many of which you already knew about. As careers require more movement across many organizations and industries, you need to establish connections with people across a diverse range of industries, professions, and other spheres of life.

Social Network Centrality   Earlier in this chapter, we explained that centrality is an important contingency of power. This contingency also applies to social networks.[41] The more central a person (or team or organization) is located in the network, the more social capital and therefore more power he or she acquires. Centrality is your importance in that network. What conditions give you more centrality than others in social networks? One key factor is your "betweenness," which literally refers to the extent to which you are located between others in the network. The more betweenness you have, the more you control the distribution of information and other resources to people on either side of you. In Exhibit 10.3, Person A has high betweenness centrality because

Exhibit 10.3   **CENTRALITY IN SOCIAL NETWORKS**

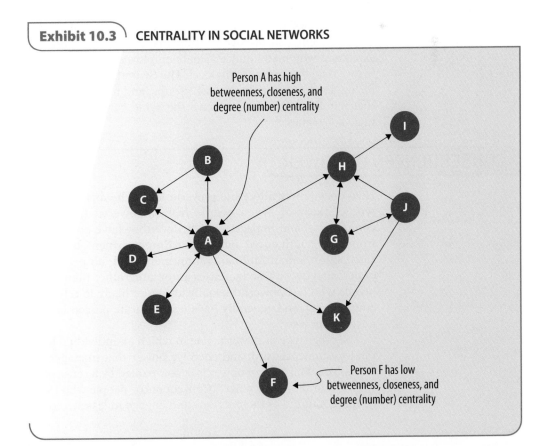

Person A has high betweenness, closeness, and degree (number) centrality

Person F has low betweenness, closeness, and degree (number) centrality

he or she is a gatekeeper who controls the flow of information to and from many other people in the network. Person H has less betweenness, and most other network members have no betweenness.

Another factor in centrality is the number or percentage of connections you have to others in the network (called "degree centrality"). Recall that the more people connected to you, the more resources (information, favours, etc.) will be available. The number of connections also increases centrality because you are more visible to other members of the network. Although being a member of a network gives you access to resources in that network, having direct connections to people make that resource sharing more fluid. Finally, centrality is a function of the "closeness" of the relationship. High closeness occurs when a member has shorter, more direct, and efficient paths or connections with others in the network. For example, Person A has fairly high closeness centrality because he or she has direct paths to most of the network, and many of these paths are short (implying efficient and high quality communication links).

One last observation is that Exhibit 10.3 reveals two clusters of people in the network. The gap between these two clusters is called a **structural hole**.[42] Notice that Person A provides the main bridge across this structural hole (connecting to H and K in the other cluster). This bridging role gives Person A additional power in the network. By bridging this gap, Person A becomes a broker—someone who connects two independent networks and controls information flow between them. Research shows that the more brokering relationships you have, the more likely you are to get early promotions, higher pay, and bonuses.

structural hole An area between two or more dense social network areas that lacks network ties.

The Dark Side of Social Networks

Social networks are natural elements of all organizations, yet they can create a formidable barrier to those who are not actively connected to it.[43] Women are often excluded from informal management networks if they do not participate in golf games and other male-dominated social events. Nina Smith, who leads Sage Software's Business Management Division, has had several conversations with female executives about these power dynamics. "I'm still trying to knock down the Boys' Club and I still have women at Sage coming to me and saying, 'Nina, that's the boys' network and I can't get in.'"[44] Several years ago, executives at Deloitte Touche Tohmatsu discovered that inaccessibility to powerful social networks partly explained why many junior female employees left the accounting and consulting firm before reaching partnership level. The Swiss-based accounting firm now relies on mentoring, formal women's network groups, and measurement of career progress to ensure that female staff members have the same career development opportunities as their male colleagues.[45]

CONSEQUENCES OF POWER

How does power affect the powerholder? The answer depends to some extent on the type of power.[46] When people feel empowered (high self-determination, meaning, competence, and impact), they believe they have power over themselves and freedom from being influenced by others. Empowerment tends to increase motivation, job satisfaction, organizational commitment, and job performance. However, this feeling of personal power also increases automatic rather than mindful thinking. In particular, people who feel powerful usually are more likely to rely on stereotypes, have difficulty empathizing, and generally have less accurate perceptions compared with people who have less power.[47]

The other type of power is one in which an individual has power over others, such as the legitimate, reward, and coercive power that managers have over employees in the workplace. This type of power is accompanied by a sense of responsibility for the people over whom they have power. Consequently, people who have power over others tend to be more mindful of their actions and engage in less stereotyping.

INFLUENCING OTHERS

LO4

influence Any behaviour that attempts to alter someone's attitudes or behaviour.

We have focused on the sources and contingencies of power as well as power derived from social networks. But power is only the *capacity* to influence others. It represents the potential to change someone's attitudes and behaviour. **Influence**, on the other hand, refers to any behaviour that attempts to alter someone's attitudes or behaviour.[48] Influence is power in motion. It applies one or more sources of power to get people to alter their beliefs, feelings, and activities. Consequently, our interest in the remainder of this chapter is on how people use power to influence others.

Influence tactics are woven throughout the social fabric of all organizations. This is because influence is an essential process through which people coordinate their effort and act in concert to achieve organizational objectives. Indeed, influence is central to the definition of leadership. Influence operates down, across, and up the corporate hierarchy. Supervisors ensure that employees complete required tasks. Employees influence co-workers to help them with their job assignments. Employees engage in upward influence tactics so corporate leaders make decisions compatible with employees' needs and expectations.

TYPES OF INFLUENCE TACTICS

Organizational behaviour researchers have devoted considerable attention to the various types of influence tactics found in organizational settings. They do not agree on a definitive list, but the most commonly identified influence tactics are documented in Exhibit 10.4 and described over the next few pages.[49] The first five are known as "hard" influence tactics because they force behaviour change through position power (legitimate, reward, and coercion). The latter three—persuasion, ingratiation and impression management, and exchange—are called "soft" tactics because they rely more on personal sources of power (referent, expert) and appeal to the target person's attitudes and needs.

Silent Authority   The silent application of authority occurs where someone complies with a request because of the requester's legitimate power as well as the target person's role expectations.[50] This deference occurs when you comply with your boss's request to complete a particular task. If the task is within your job scope and your boss has the right to make this request, then this influence strategy operates without negotiation, threats, persuasion, or other tactics. Silent authority is the most common form of influence in high power distance cultures.[51]

Exhibit 10.4   TYPES OF INFLUENCE TACTICS IN ORGANIZATIONS

Influence Tactic	Description
Silent authority	Influencing behaviour through legitimate power without explicitly referring to that power base
Assertiveness	Actively applying legitimate and coercive power by applying pressure or threats
Information control	Explicitly manipulating someone else's access to information for the purpose of changing their attitudes and/or behaviour
Coalition formation	Forming a group that attempts to influence others by pooling the resources and power of its members
Upward appeal	Gaining support from one or more people with higher authority or expertise
Persuasion	Using logical arguments, factual evidence, and emotional appeals to convince people of the value of a request
Ingratiation/impression management	Attempting to increase liking by, or perceived similarity to, some targeted person
Exchange	Promising benefits or resources in exchange for the target person's compliance

Assertiveness   In contrast to silent authority, assertiveness might be called "vocal authority" because it involves actively applying legitimate and coercive power to influence others. Assertiveness includes persistently reminding the target of his or her obligations, frequently checking the target's work, confronting the target, and using threats of sanctions to force compliance. Assertiveness typically applies or threatens to apply punishment if the target does not comply. Explicit or implicit threats range from job loss to losing face by letting down the team. Extreme forms of assertiveness include blackmailing colleagues, such as by threatening to reveal the other person's previously unknown failures unless he or she complies with your request.

Information Control   Earlier in this chapter we explained that people with centrality in social networks have the power to control information. This power translates into influence when the powerholder selectively distributes information such that it reframes the situation and causes others to change their attitudes and/or behaviour. Controlling information might include withholding information that is more critical or favourable, or by distributing information to some people but not to others. According to one major survey, almost half of employees believe co-workers keep others in the dark about work issues if it helps their own cause. Another study found that CEOs influence their board of directors by selectively feeding and withholding information.[52]

coalition   A group that attempts to influence people outside the group by pooling the resources and power of its members.

Coalition Formation   When people lack sufficient power alone to influence others in the organization, they might form a **coalition** of people who support the proposed change. A coalition is influential in three ways.[53] First, it pools the power and resources of many people, so the coalition potentially has more influence than any number of people operating alone. Second, the coalition's mere existence can be a source of power by symbolizing the legitimacy of the issue. In other words, a coalition creates a sense that the issue deserves attention because it has broad support. Third, coalitions tap into the power of the social identity process introduced in Chapter 3. A coalition is an informal group that advocates a new set of norms and behaviours. If the coalition has a broad-based membership (i.e., its members come from various parts of the organization), then other employees are more likely to identify with that group and, consequently, accept the ideas the coalition is proposing.

upward appeal   A type of influence in which someone with higher authority or expertise is called on (in reality or symbolically) to support the influencer's position.

Upward Appeal   **Upward appeal** is a type of influence in which someone with higher authority or expertise is called on (in reality or symbolically) to support the influencer's position. It occurs when someone says: "The boss likely agrees with me on this matter; let's proceed!" Upward appeal also occurs when relying on the authority of the firm's policies or values. By reminding others that your request is consistent with the organization's overarching goals, you are implying support from senior executives without formally involving them. The opening vignette to this chapter illustrates how this upward appeal influence tactic occurs even at the highest levels of management. Several members of the RCMP executive "went over the head" of the RCMP Commissioner to complain about the Commissioner's behaviour. Specifically, they complained to the elected minister responsible for the RCMP about the Commissioner's actions.

persuasion   The use of facts, logical arguments, and emotional appeals to change another person's beliefs and attitudes, usually for the purpose of changing the person's behaviour.

Persuasion   **Persuasion** is one of the most effective influence strategies for career success. The ability to use facts, logical arguments, and emotional appeals to change another person's beliefs and attitudes, usually for the purpose of changing the person's behaviour, is not just an acceptable way to influence others; in many societies, it is a noble art and a quality of effective leaders. The effectiveness of persuasion as an influence tactic depends on characteristics of the persuader, message content, communication medium, and the audience being persuaded (see Exhibit 10.5).[54] People are more persuasive when listeners believe they have expertise and credibility, such as when the persuader does not seem to profit from the persuasion attempt and states a few points against the position.

Exhibit 10.5 ⟍ ELEMENTS OF PERSUASION

Persuasion Element	Characteristics of Effective Persuasion
Persuader characteristics	• Expertise • Credibility • No apparent profit motive • Appears somewhat neutral (acknowledges benefits of the opposing view)
Message content	• Multiple viewpoints (not exclusively supporting the preferred option) • Limited to a few strong arguments (not many arguments) • Repeat arguments, but not excessively • Use emotional appeals in combination with logical arguments • Offers specific solutions to overcome the stated problems • Inoculation effect— audience warned of counter-arguments that opposition will present
Communication medium	• Media-rich channels are usually more persuasive
Audience characteristics	• Lower self-esteem • Lower intelligence • Self-concept is not tied to the opposing view

The message is more important than the messenger when the issue is important to the audience. Persuasive message content acknowledges several points of view so the audience does not feel cornered by the speaker. The message should also be limited to a few strong arguments, which are repeated a few times, but not too frequently. The message should use emotional appeals (such as graphically showing the unfortunate consequences of a bad decision), but only in combination with logical arguments and specific recommendations to overcome the threat. Finally, message content is more persuasive when the audience is warned about opposing arguments. This **inoculation effect** causes listeners to generate counter-arguments to the anticipated persuasion attempts, which makes the opponent's subsequent persuasion attempts less effective.[55]

Two other considerations when persuading people are the medium of communication and characteristics of the audience. Generally, persuasion works best in face-to-face conversations and through other media-rich communication channels. The personal nature of face-to-face communication increases the persuader's credibility, and the richness of this channel provides faster feedback that the influence strategy is working. With respect to audience characteristics, it is more difficult to persuade people who have high self-esteem and intelligence, as well as a self-concept that is strongly tied to the opposing viewpoint.[56]

Ingratiation and Impression Management   Silent authority, assertiveness, information control, coalitions, and upward appeals are somewhat (or very!) forceful ways to influence other people. In contrast, a very "soft" influence tactic is **ingratiation**—any attempt to increase liking by, or perceived similarity to, some targeted person.[57] Ingratiation comes in several flavours. Employees might flatter their boss in front of others, demonstrate that they have similar attitudes as their boss (e.g., agreeing with the boss's proposal), and ask their boss for advice. Ingratiation is one of the more effective influence tactics at boosting a person's career success (i.e., performance appraisal feedback, salaries, and promotions).[58] However, people who engage in high levels of ingratiation are less (not more) influential and less likely to get promoted.[59] The explanation for the contrasting evidence is that those who engage in too much ingratiation are viewed as insincere and self-serving. The terms "apple polishing" and "brown-nosing" are applied to those who ingratiate to excess or in ways that suggest selfish motives for the ingratiation.

inoculation effect A persuasive communication strategy of warning listeners that others will try to influence them in the future and that they should be wary about the opponent's arguments.

ingratiation Any attempt to increase liking by, or perceived similarity to, some targeted person.

impression management
The practice of actively shaping our public images.

Ingratiation is part of a larger influence tactic known as impression management. **Impression management** is the practice of actively shaping our public images.[60] These public images might be crafted as being important, vulnerable, threatening, or pleasant. For the most part, employees routinely engage in pleasant impression management behaviours to satisfy the basic norms of social behaviour, such as the way they dress and how they behave toward colleagues and customers.

Impression management is a common strategy for people trying to get ahead in the workplace. In fact, career professionals encourage people to develop a personal "brand;" that is, to demonstrate and symbolize a distinctive competitive advantage.[61] Furthermore, people who master the art of personal branding rely on impression management through distinctive personal characteristics such as black shirts, tinted hair, or unique signatures. "Every piece of career advice I ever heard was that you are your own brand," says Josh Orzech, director of communications for Direct Energy Marketing Ltd. in Toronto. "You have to be constantly selling yourself and looking for that next job, even as you start a new job."[62]

"Our task is to find out what management thinks we should be doing, and then to make management think we're doing it."

© Copyright Ted Goff 2007. www.tedgoff.com. Used with permission.

Unfortunately, a few individuals carry impression management beyond ethical boundaries by exaggerating their credentials and accomplishments. For instance, a Lucent Technologies executive lied about having a PhD from Stanford University and hid his criminal past involving forgery and embezzlement. Ironically, the executive was Lucent's director of recruiting![63] One of the most elaborate misrepresentations occurred a few years ago when a Singaporean entrepreneur sent out news releases claiming to be a renowned artificial intelligence researcher, the author of several books, and the recipient of numerous awards from MIT and Stanford University (one of the awards was illustrated on his website). These falsehoods were so convincing that the entrepreneur almost received a real award, the "Internet Visionary of the Year" at the Internet World Asia Industry Awards.[64]

Exchange   Exchange activities involve the promise of benefits or resources in exchange for the target person's compliance with your request. Negotiation is an integral part of exchange influence activities. For instance, you might negotiate with your boss for a day off in return for working a less desirable shift at a future date. Exchange also includes applying the norm of reciprocity that we described earlier, such as reminding the target of past benefits or favours with the expectation that the target will now make up for that debt. Earlier in this chapter we explained how people gain power through social networks. They also use norms of reciprocity to influence others in the network. Active networkers build up "exchange credits" by helping colleagues in the short-term for reciprocal benefits in the long term.

CONSEQUENCES AND CONTINGENCIES OF INFLUENCE TACTICS

Faced with a variety of influence strategies, you are probably asking: Which ones are best? The best way to answer this question is to describe how people react when others try to influence them: resistance, compliance, or commitment.[65] *Resistance* occurs when people or work units oppose the behaviour desired by the influencer by refusing, arguing, or delaying engagement in the behaviour. *Compliance* occurs when people are motivated to implement the influencer's request at a minimal level of effort and for purely instrumental reasons. Without external sources to prompt the desired behaviour, compliance would not occur. *Commitment* is the strongest outcome of influence, whereby people identify with the influencer's request and are highly motivated to implement it even when extrinsic sources of motivation are no longer present.

Generally, people react more favourably to "soft" tactics than to "hard" tactics (see Exhibit 10.6). Soft influence tactics rely on personal sources of power (expert and referent power), which tend to build commitment to the influencer's request. In contrast, hard tactics rely on position power (legitimate, reward, and coercion), so they tend to produce compliance or, worse, resistance. Hard tactics also tend to undermine trust, which can hurt future relationships.

> Soft influence tactics tend to build commitment to the influencer's request, whereas hard tactics tend to produce compliance or, worse, resistance. "

Apart from the general preference for soft rather than hard tactics, the most appropriate influence strategy depends on a few contingencies. One obvious contingency is which sources of power are strongest. Those with expertise tend to have more influence using persuasion, whereas those with a strong legitimate power base are usually more successful applying silent authority.[66] A second contingency is whether the person being influenced is higher, lower, or at the same level in the organization. As an example, employees may face adverse career consequences by being too assertive with their boss. Meanwhile, supervisors who engage in ingratiation and impression management tend to lose the respect of their staff.

Finally, the most appropriate influence tactic depends on personal, organizational, and cultural values.[67] People with a strong power orientation might feel more

Exhibit 10.6   **CONSEQUENCES OF HARD AND SOFT INFLUENCE TACTICS**

Commitment		
	Persuasion	
	Ingratiation and	**Soft**
	impression mgt.	**Influence**
	Exchange	**Tactics**
Compliance		
	Silent authority	
	Upward appeal	**Hard**
	Coalition formation	**Influence**
	Information control	**Tactics**
Resistance	Assertiveness	

comfortable using assertiveness, whereas those who value conformity might feel more comfortable with upward appeals. At an organizational level, firms with a competitive culture might foster more use of information control and coalition formation, whereas companies with a learning orientation would likely encourage more influence through persuasion. The preferred influence tactics also vary across societal cultures. Research indicates that ingratiation is much more common among managers in Canada than in Hong Kong, possibly because this tactic disrupts the more distant roles that managers and employees expect in high power distance cultures.

INFLUENCE AND ORGANIZATIONAL POLITICS

L05

organizational politics
Behaviours that others perceive as self-serving tactics for personal gain at the expense of other people and possibly the organization.

You might have noticed that organizational politics has not been mentioned yet, even though some of the practices or examples described over the past few pages are usually considered political tactics. The phrase was carefully avoided because, for the most part, organizational politics is in the eye of the beholder. You might perceive a co-worker's attempt to influence the boss as acceptable behaviour for the good of the organization, whereas someone else might perceive the co-worker's tactic as brazen organizational politics.

This perceptual issue explains why OB experts increasingly discuss influence tactics as behaviours and organizational politics as perceptions.[68] The influence tactics described earlier are perceived as **organizational politics** when they seem to be self-serving behaviours at the expense of others and possibly contrary to the interests of the entire organization. Of course, some tactics are so blatantly selfish and counterproductive that almost everyone correctly sees them as organizational politics. In other situations, however, a person's behaviour might be viewed as political or in the organization's best interest, depending on your point of view.

Employees who experience organizational politics have lower job satisfaction, organizational commitment, organizational citizenship, and task performance, as well as higher levels of work-related stress and motivation to leave the organization.[69] And because political tactics serve individuals rather than organizations, they potentially divert resources away from the organization's effective functioning and potentially threaten its survival.

CONDITIONS SUPPORTING ORGANIZATIONAL POLITICS

Employees are more likely to engage in organizational politics (that is, use influence tactics for personal gain) under certain conditions.[70] One of those conditions is scarce resources. When budgets are slashed, people rely on political tactics to safeguard their resources and maintain the status quo. Office politics also flourishes when resource allocation decisions are ambiguous, complex, or lack formal rules. This occurs because decision makers are given more discretion over resource allocation, so potential recipients of those resources use political tactics to influence the factors that should be considered in the decision. Organizational change encourages

Office Politics by the Numbers[71]

36%
of Canadian employees polled recently say that office politics is one of the biggest roadblocks to productivity

19%
of Canadian employees polled 10 years ago said that office politics is one of the biggest roadblocks to productivity

47%
of American employees polled say that office politics cuts into productive time (2nd highest cause, after fixing someone else's work)

58%
of Canadian employees polled say a co-worker has taken credit for one of their ideas

29%
of American employees polled say a co-worker has taken credit for one of their ideas

53%
of British managers polled feel that organizational politics is a major cause of stress at work (top-ranked cause of stress)

Coming up Next, Philadelphia's Top Political Story . . .

Over a two-year period, Philadelphia news co-anchor Alycia Lane was subject to malicious news stories from anonymous sources about her off-air behaviour. Lane's co-anchor, Larry Mendte showed concern when these stories emerged but, Lane claims, he suggested that the best solution would be for her to move to another city. Soon after she lost her job (partly due to the rumours), Lane discovered why Mendte offered this advice: he was likely the person who fed private information about Lane to the media. The FBI found that Mendte used keystroke software to gain access to Lane's email, and that he looked at her email at least 500 times. Lane's attorney claims that Mendte sent Lane's emails to newspapers because "[Alycia Lane's] star was climbing, while his was not climbing. . . . His conduct was designed to undermine her." Mendte's email tampering surprised most people, but not everyone who knew him. One former colleague claims that "[Mendte] was great to my face and manipulative and destructive behind my back." Another TV insider suggests that "Larry worked hard to take Alycia down."[72] *Photo by April Saul/Philadelphia Inquirer*

political behaviours for this reason. Change creates uncertainty and ambiguity as the company moves from an old set of rules and practices to a new set. During these times, employees apply political strategies to protect their valued resources, position, and self-concept.[73]

Personal Characteristics   Several personal characteristics affect an individual's motivation to engage in self-serving behaviour.[74] This includes a strong need for personal as opposed to socialized power. Those with a need for personal power seek power for its own sake and try to acquire more power. Some individuals have strong **Machiavellian values**. Machiavellianism is named after Niccolò Machiavelli, the sixteenth-century Italian philosopher who wrote *The Prince*, a famous treatise about political behaviour. People with high Machiavellian values are comfortable with getting more than they deserve, and they believe that deceit is a natural and acceptable way to achieve this goal. They seldom trust co-workers and tend to use cruder influence tactics, such as bypassing one's boss or being assertive, to get their own way.[75]

> **Machiavellian values**
> The belief that deceit is a natural and acceptable way to influence others and that getting more than one deserves is acceptable.

Minimizing Organizational Politics and its Consequences   The conditions that fuel organizational politics also give us some clues about how to control dysfunctional political activities.[76] One strategy to keep organizational politics in check is to introduce clear rules and regulations that specify the use of scarce resources. Organizational politics can become a problem during times of organizational change, so politics can be minimized through effective organizational change practices. Leaders also need to actively manage group norms to curtail self-serving influence activities. In particular, they can support organizational values that oppose political tactics, such as altruism and customer-focus. One of the most important strategies is for leaders to become role models of organizational citizenship rather than symbols of successful organizational politicians.

Along with minimizing organizational politics, companies can limit the adverse effects of political perceptions by giving employees more control over their work and keeping them informed of organizational events. Research has found that employees who are kept informed of what is going on in the organization and who are involved in organizational decisions are less likely to experience organizational politics, which results in less stress, job dissatisfaction, and absenteeism.

CHAPTER SUMMARY

 LO1 Describe the dependence model of power and describe the five sources of power in organizations.

Power is the capacity to influence others. It exists when one party perceives that he or she is dependent on the other for something of value. However, the dependent person must also have countervailing power—some power over the dominant party—to maintain the relationship and the parties must have some level of trust.

There are five power bases. Legitimate power is an agreement among organizational members that people in certain roles can request certain behaviours of others. This power has restrictions represented by the target person's zone of indifference. It also includes the norm of reciprocity (a feeling of obligation to help someone who has helped you) as well as control over the flow of information to others. Reward power is derived from the ability to control the allocation of rewards valued by others and to remove negative sanctions. Coercive power is the ability to apply punishment. Expert power is the capacity to influence others by possessing knowledge or skills that they value. An important form of expert power is the (perceived) ability to manage uncertainties in the business environment. People have referent power when others identify with them, like them, or otherwise respect them.

LO2 Discuss the four contingencies of power.

Four contingencies determine whether these power bases translate into real power. Individuals and work units are more powerful when they are non-substitutable, that is, there is a lack of alternatives. Employees, work units, and organizations reduce substitutability by controlling tasks, knowledge, and labour, and by differentiating themselves from competitors. A second contingency is centrality. People have more power when they have high centrality, that is, the number of people affected is large and people are quickly affected by their actions. Discretion, the third contingency of power, refers to the freedom to exercise judgment. Power increases when people have freedom to use their power. The fourth contingency, visibility, refers to the idea that power increases to the extent that a person's or work unit's competencies are known to others.

LO3 Explain how people and work units gain power through social networks.

Social networks are social structures of individuals or social units (e.g., departments, organizations) that are connected to each other through one or more forms of interdependence. People receive power in social networks through social capital, which is the goodwill and resulting resources shared among members in a social network. Three main resources from social networks are information, visibility, and referent power.

Employees gain social capital through their relationship in the social network. Social capital tends to increase with the number of network ties. Strong ties (close-knit relationships) can also increase social capital because these connections offer more resources and offer them more quickly. However, having weak ties with people from diverse networks can be more valuable than having strong ties with people in similar networks. Weak ties provide more resources that we do not already possess. Another influence on social capital is the person's centrality in the network. Network centrality is determined in several ways, including the extent to which you are located between others in the network (betweenness), how many direct ties you have (degree), and the closeness of these ties. People also gain power by bridging structural holes—linking two or more clusters of people in a network.

 LO4 Describe eight types of influence tactics, three consequences of influencing others, and three contingencies to consider when choosing an influence tactic.

Influence refers to any behaviour that attempts to alter someone's attitudes or behaviour. The most widely studied influence tactics are silent authority, assertiveness, information control, coalition formation, upward appeal, ingratiation and impression management, persuasion, and exchange. "Soft" influence tactics such as friendly persuasion and subtle ingratiation are more acceptable than "hard" tactics such as upward appeal and assertiveness. However, the most appropriate influence tactic also depends on the influencer's power base; whether the person being influenced is higher, lower, or at the same level in the organization; and personal, organizational, and cultural values regarding influence behaviour.

LO5 Identify the organizational conditions and personal characteristics that support organizational politics, as well as ways to minimize organizational politics.

Organizational politics refers to influence tactics that others perceive to be self-serving behaviours at the expense of others and sometimes contrary to the interests of the organization. It is more common when ambiguous decisions allocate scarce resources and when the organization tolerates or rewards political behaviour. Individuals with a high need for personal power and strong Machiavellian values have a higher propensity to use political tactics. Organizational politics can be minimized by providing clear rules for resource allocation, establishing a free flow of information, using education and involvement during organizational change, supporting team norms and a corporate culture that discourage dysfunctional politics, and having leaders who role model organizational citizenship rather than political savvy.

KEY TERMS

centrality, p. 278

charisma, p. 277

coalition, p. 284

countervailing power, p. 272

impression management, p. 286

influence, p. 283

ingratiation, p. 285

inoculation effect, p. 285

legitimate power, p. 273

Machiavellian values, p. 289

norm of reciprocity, p. 275

organizational politics, p. 288

persuasion, p. 284

power, p. 272

referent power, p. 277

social capital, p. 279

social networks, p. 279

structural hole, p. 282

substitutability, p. 277

upward appeal, p. 284

CRITICAL-THINKING QUESTIONS

1. What role does countervailing power play in the power relationship? Give an example of your own encounter with countervailing power at school or work.

2. Several years ago, the Major League Baseball Players Association (MLBPA) went on strike in September, just before the World Series started. The players' contract expired at the beginning of the season (May), but they held off the strike until September when they would lose only one-sixth of their salaries. In contrast, a September strike would hurt the owners financially because they earn a larger portion of their revenue during the play-offs. As one player explained: "If we strike next spring, there's nothing stopping [the club owners] from letting us go until next June or July because they don't have that much at stake." Use your knowledge of the sources and contingencies of power to explain why the MLBPA had more power in negotiations by walking out in September rather than March.

3. You have just been hired as a brand manager of toothpaste for a large consumer products company. Your job mainly involves encouraging the advertising and production groups to promote and manufacture your product more effectively. These departments aren't under your direct authority, although company procedures indicate that they must complete certain tasks requested by brand managers. Describe the sources of power you can use to ensure that the advertising and production departments will help you make and sell toothpaste more effectively.

4. How does social networking increase a person's power? What social networking strategies could you initiate now to potentially enhance your future career success?

5. List the eight influence tactics described in this chapter in terms of how they are used by students to influence their university teachers. Which influence tactic is applied most often? Which is applied least often, in your opinion? To what extent is each influence tactic considered legitimate behaviour or organizational politics?

6. How do cultural differences affect the following influence factors: (a) silent authority and (b) upward appeal?

7. Many years ago, the CEO of Apple Computer invited Steve Jobs (who was not associated with the company at the time) to serve as a special adviser and raise morale among Apple employees and customers. While doing this, Jobs spent more time advising the CEO on how to cut costs, redraw the organization chart, and hire new people. Before long, most of the top people at Apple were Jobs's colleagues, who began to systematically evaluate and weed out teams of Apple employees. While publicly supporting Apple's CEO, Jobs privately criticized him and, in a show of nonconfidence, sold 1.5 million shares of Apple stock he had received. This action caught the attention of Apple's board of directors, who soon after decided to replace the CEO with Steve Jobs. The CEO claimed Jobs was a conniving back-stabber who used political tactics to get his way. Other suggest that Apple would be out of business today if he hadn't taken over the company. In your opinion, were Steve Jobs's actions examples of organizational politics? Justify your answer.

8. This book frequently emphasizes that successful companies engage in organizational learning. How do political tactics interfere with organizational learning objectives?

 CASE STUDY 10.1

NAB's Rogue Trader

For three long days, junior trader Dennis Gentilin received the cold shoulder from his boss, Luke Duffy. Duffy, who ran National Australia Bank's (NAB) foreign currency options desk in Melbourne, had discovered that Gentilin complained to Duffy's boss, Gary Dillon, that Duffy was altering transaction records to "smooth" his group's profits. Smoothing (which includes carrying forward trading losses) was apparently common at one time, but traders had recently been warned to stop the practice.

On the fourth day, Duffy called Gentilin into a private meeting and, according to Gentilin, launched into a tirade: "I felt like . . . killing someone the other day," Duffy said pointedly to Gentilin. "If you want to stay in the team, I demand loyalty and don't want you going to Dillon about what's happening in the team."

Duffy was apparently accustomed to getting his way. Gentilin explained that Duffy, Dillon, and a few other senior traders were "untouchables" who were given free rein at NAB due to their expertise. "They just created this power base where they were laws unto themselves," claims Gentilin.

Anyone who interfered with Duffy's plans was apparently mocked into submission. For example, Duffy taunted a co-worker in London who he thought was too skeptical and conservative. Duffy called him "the London stench boy" because he "was always making a stink about things whether they were going on both good and bad, and you could smell the stink coming from London," Duffy admitted in court. Duffy's actions kept the London employee compliant with Duffy's activities.

Soon after his private meeting with Duffy, Gentilin was transferred to NAB's London office, still working in the foreign exchange group. Duffy's unit in Melbourne continued to fudge the numbers so upper management wouldn't notice any problems with the trading results. But when the group bet the wrong way against a rising Australian dollar, the cover-ups escalated, including creation of fictitious trades to offset the losses. The idea was that they could recover the losses and receive their cherished bonuses by year end.

Fatefully, Gentilin got wind of the problems from London, so he asked Vanessa McCallum, a junior NAB trader in Melbourne, to have other people look into Duffy's transactions. McCallum later acknowledged that she was terrified about asking for the audit. "My greatest fear was, if nothing is wrong I'm going to have to leave the desk (move to a different division) because you had to be loyal to Luke [Duffy]," explained McCallum, who no longer works at the bank.

What senior NAB executives discovered shook the Australian bank to its core. Duffy and other senior traders had become a rogue team that amassed $350 million in losses in one year. They managed to keep everyone in line, resulting in countless transaction record irregularities and over 800 breaches of the bank's trading limits. Duffy and a few other traders were jailed for securities violations. Several executives, including both NAB's chief executive and chairman, lost their jobs due to these events.

Discussion Questions

1. What were the main sources of power that Luke Duffy used to keep everyone in line with his irregular business practices? Describe how he applied these power sources to influence employees and senior executives.

2. What contingencies strengthened Luke Duffy's power at NAB's foreign currency options desk?

3. What can companies do to minimize this sort of abuse of power and influence?

Sources: R. Gluyas, "Fear and Loathing in NAB's Forex Fiasco," *The Australian*, August 6, 2005, p. 35; E. Johnston, "'Anything Goes,' Ex-Trader Says," *Australian Financial Review*, August 2, 2005, p. 3; E. Johnston, "Expletives and Stench in Hothouse of NAB Dealers," *Australian Financial Review*, August 6, 2005, p. 3.

 TEAM EXERCISE 10.2

Impression Management in Employment Interviews

Purpose   This exercise is designed to help students examine impression management as it relates to employment interviews.

Instructions   *Step 1:* Form teams with four or five members.

a) Identify specific *principles/rules* to help an interviewee guide the best response to each interviewer questions.

b) Provide possible *statements* the interviewee should say in the interview to represent that principle/rule in action.

For example:

Interview Question: Why are you leaving your current job?

Principle/Rule: Keep positive, don't criticize your current employer.

Possible Statement: "I enjoyed working at XYZ, but I was looking for more personal growth and development, which your company has a great reputation for."

Interview Questions
- What interests you about this job?
- What are your greatest weaknesses?
- Describe a time when you had to deal with a professional disagreement or conflict with a co-worker?
- Is there anything you would like to avoid in your next job?
- How many times do a clock's hands overlap in a day?

Step 2: Instructor leads a class discussion for each of the interview questions.

1. What was your ideal answer?
2. What impression of your knowledge or skills were you attempting to create with your ideal answer?
3. What is an example of an unsuitable interview response?

Discussion Question   1. Why is it important that the personal brand you cultivate in an employment interview is an authentic representation of your knowledge and skills?

 TEAM EXERCISE 10.3

Deciphering the Network

Purpose
This exercise is designed to help students interpret social network maps, including their implications for organizational effectiveness.

Materials
The instructor will distribute several social network diagrams to each student.

Instructions (Smaller Classes)
The instructor will organize students into teams (typically four to seven people, depending on class size). Teams will examine each social network diagram to answer the following questions:

1. What aspects of this diagram suggest that the network is not operating as effectively as possible?
2. Which people in this network seem to be most powerful? Least powerful? What information or features of the diagram lead you to this conclusion?
3. If you were responsible for this group of people, how would you change this situation to improve their effectiveness?

After teams have diagnosed each social network map, the class will debrief by hearing each team's assessments and recommendations.

Instructions (Larger Classes)
This activity is also possible in large classes by projecting each social network diagram on a screen and giving students a minute or two to examine the diagram. The instructor can then ask specific questions to the class, such as pointing to a specific individual in the network and asking whether he or she has high or low power, what level of centrality is apparent, and whether the individual's connections are mainly strong or weak ties. The instructor might also ask which quadrant on the map indicates the most concern and then allow individual students to provide their explanation why.

 TEAM EXERCISE 10.4

Budget Deliberations

By Sharon Card

Purpose
This exercise is designed to help you understand some of the power dynamics and influence tactics that occur across hierarchical levels in organizations.

Materials   This activity works best where one small room leads to a larger room, which leads to a larger area.

Instructions   These exercise instructions are based on a class size of about 30 students. The instructor may adjust the size of the first two groups slightly for larger classes. The instructor will organize students as follows: A few (three–four) students are assigned the position of executives. They are preferably located in a secluded office or corner of a large classroom. Another six–eight students are assigned positions as middle managers. These people will ideally be located in an adjoining room or space, allowing privacy for the executives. The remaining students represent the nonmanagement employees in the organization. They are located in an open area outside the executive and management rooms.

Rules   Members of the executive group are free to enter the space of either the middle management or nonmanagement groups and to communicate whatever they wish, whenever they wish. Members of the middle management group may enter the space of the nonmanagement group whenever they wish, but must request permission to enter the executive group's space. The executive group can refuse the middle management group's request. Members of the nonmanagement group are not allowed to disturb the top group in any way unless specifically invited by members of the executive group. The nonmanagement group does have the right to request permission to communicate with the middle management group. The middle management group can refuse the lower group's request.

Task   Your organization is in the process of preparing a budget. The challenge is to balance needs with the financial resources. Of course, the needs are greater than the resources. The instructor will distribute a budget sheet showing a list of budget requests and their costs. Each group has control over a portion of the budget and must decide how to spend the money over which they have control. Nonmanagement has discretion over a relatively small portion and the executive group has discretion over the greatest portion. The exercise is finished when the organization has negotiated a satisfactory budget, or until the instructor calls time. The class will then debrief with the following questions and others the instructor might ask.

Discussion Questions   1. What can we learn from this exercise about power in organizational hierarchies?

2. How is this exercise similar to relations in real organizations?

3. How did students in each group feel about the amount of power they held?

4. How did they exercise their power in relations with the other groups?

Go to CONNECT to complete the following interactive self-assessments.

 SELF-ASSESSMENT EXERCISE 10.5

What's Your Approach to Influencing Co-workers?

Purpose   This exercise is designed to help you understand different forms of influence when working with co-workers (i.e., people at the same organizational level), as well as estimate your preference for each influence tactic in this context.

Instructions   Think about the occasions when a co-worker disagreed with you, opposed your preference, or was reluctant to actively support your point of view about something at work. These conflicts might have been about company policy, assignment of job duties, distribution of resources, or any other matter. What did you do to try to get the co-worker to support your preference?

The statements below describe ways that people try to influence co-workers. Thinking about your own behaviour *over the past six months,* how often did you engage in each of these behaviours to influence co-workers (i.e., people at a similar level in the organization)?* Circle the most accurate number for each statement. When done, use the scoring key in Appendix B to calculate your results. This exercise is completed alone so students assess themselves honestly without concerns of social comparison. However, class discussion will focus on the types of influence in organizations and which influence tactics are most and least successful or popular when influencing co-workers.

Co-worker Influence Scale					
Over the past six months, how often did you use the following tactics to influence co-workers?	Rarely/ Never	Seldom	Sometimes	Often	Almost Always
1. Gave the co-worker logical reasons why the matter should be decided in my favour.	1	2	3	4	5
2. Made my authority or expertise regarding the issue known without being obvious about it.	1	2	3	4	5
3. Tried to negotiate a solution, where I would offer something in return for the co-worker's support.	1	2	3	4	5
4. Demanded that the matter should be resolved in my favour.	1	2	3	4	5
5. Avoided showing the co-worker information that opposed my preference.	1	2	3	4	5
6. Enlisted the support of other employees so the co-worker would see that I have the more popular preference.	1	2	3	4	5
7. Claimed or demonstrated that my preference has management support.	1	2	3	4	5
8. Said something positive about the co-worker, hoping this would increase his or her support for my views.	1	2	3	4	5
9. Tried to convince the co-worker using factual information and logic.	1	2	3	4	5
10. Subtly let the co-worker know about my expertise on the matter.	1	2	3	4	5
11. Offered to support or assist the co-worker on something if he or she would agree with me on this matter.	1	2	3	4	5
12. Showed impatience or frustration with the co-worker's opposition to my preference.	1	2	3	4	5
13. Presented information in a way that looked better for my preference.	1	2	3	4	5
14. Claimed that other staff support my position on this matter.	1	2	3	4	5
15. Suggested or threatened to have the issue resolved by higher management.	1	2	3	4	5
16. Became friendlier towards the co-worker, hoping this would create a more favourable opinion of my viewpoint.	1	2	3	4	5
17. Helped the co-worker to see the benefits of my preference and/or the negative outcomes of other choices.	1	2	3	4	5
18. Quietly or indirectly showed the co-worker my authority, expertise, or right to have this matter decided in my favour.	1	2	3	4	5
19. Mentioned that I had helped the co-worker in the past, hoping that he or she would reciprocate by supporting me now.	1	2	3	4	5
20. Let the co-worker know that I might be disagreeable or uncooperative in the future if he or she did not support me now.	1	2	3	4	5
21. Framed and selected information that mainly agreed with (rather than opposed) my preference.	1	2	3	4	5
22. Made sure that at least a few other people were on my side of this issue.	1	2	3	4	5
23. Pointed out that my view was consistent with the company's values or policies.	1	2	3	4	5
24. Showed more respect toward the co-worker, hoping this would encourage him or her to support me.	1	2	3	4	5

*Note: If you have not been in the workforce recently, complete this self-assessment exercise thinking about influencing another student instead of a co-worker.

SELF-ASSESSMENT EXERCISE 10.6

Do You Have a Guanxi Orientation?

Guanxi, which is translated as interpersonal connections, is an important element of doing business in China and some other Asian countries with strong Confucian cultural values. Guanxi is based on traditional Confucian values of helping others without expecting future repayment. This instrument estimates your guanxi orientation; that is, the extent to which you accept and apply guanxi values. This self-assessment is completed alone so that students rate themselves honestly without concerns of social comparison. However, class discussion will focus on the meaning of guanxi and its relevance for organizational power and influence.

 SELF-ASSESSMENT EXERCISE 10.7

How Machiavellian Are You?

Machiavellianism is named after Niccolo Machiavelli, the sixteenth-century Italian philosopher who wrote *The Prince,* a famous treatise about political behaviour. Out of Machiavelli's work emerged this instrument that estimates the degree to which you have a Machiavellian personality. Indicate the extent to which you agree or disagree that each statement in this instrument describes you. Complete each item honestly to get the best estimate of your level of Machiavellianism.

 SELF-ASSESSMENT EXERCISE 10.8

Does Your School Behave Politically?

Organizations have been called "political arenas"—environments where political tactics are common because decisions are ambiguous and resources are scarce. This instrument estimates the degree to which you believe the school where you attend classes has a politicized culture. This scale consists of several statements that might or might not describe the school where you are attending classes. These statements refer to the administration of the school, not the classroom. Please indicate the extent to which you agree or disagree with each statement.

 Practise and learn online with Connect. Connect resources include additional and interactive study exercises, videos, and practice quizzing, as well as additional material you won't find in the printed text.

Conflict and Negotiation in the Workplace

LEARNING OBJECTIVES

After reading this chapter, you should be able to:

LO1 Define conflict and debate its positive and negative consequences in the workplace.

LO2 Distinguish constructive from relationship conflict and describe three strategies to minimize relationship conflict during constructive conflict episodes.

LO3 Diagram the conflict process model and describe six structural sources of conflict in organizations.

LO4 Outline the five conflict handling styles and discuss the circumstances in which each would be most appropriate.

LO5 Apply the six structural approaches to conflict management and describe the three types of third-party dispute resolution.

LO6 Describe the bargaining zone model and outline strategies skilled negotiators use to claim value and create value in negotiations.

The bitter year-long strike by 3,100 members of United Steelworkers Local 6500 at Vale Inco's Sudbury operations was one of Canada's longest strikes. During the strike the company took the union to court over a variety of alleged picket line incidents while the union accused Vale of bad faith bargaining.

The conflict escalated when the company introduced replacement workers as well as non-striking technical, office, and clerical employees to resume partial operations. The strike had a heavy cost for both the company and union members. Workers lost wages for a year and it is estimated the Brazilian mining giant lost billions in nickel and copper production. Contentious issues included Vale Inco's move to make changes to the pension plan and cap a bonus that rewarded miners when nickel prices are high.

Relationship conflict between the union and company occurred well before the strike. The United Steelworkers alleged the dispute was rooted in a cultural clash and that Inco's owners wanted to "install a foreign brand of subservient labour relations." Vale Inco responded by saying the "union's statements smack of racism and the company rejects the idea that cultural differences" had anything to do with the strike. The company also accused the union of misleading its members by refusing to accept that significant operational changes are needed to be internationally competitive and profitable.

The strike dragged on as both Vale Inco and the Steelworkers retained their positions and attempted to force the other party back to bargaining. The union staged rallies in Toronto and even took its fight against the company overseas, lobbying customers in Australia and Europe to boycott the company. It was reported these actions inflamed Vale senior executives. Cory McPhee, Vale Inco's vice-president of corporate affairs responded: "rather than staging protests in Toronto and London, England, union officials should spend their time working out a deal."

An agreement to end the strike was finally reached when both sides reduced their demands amid environmental pressures such as falling nickel prices and concerns about ongoing global economic worries. The settlement reached was not far off from the offer the union rejected several months earlier and included a relatively modest wage increase, a signing bonus, stricter worker conditions, and a less desirable pension plan for new employees. A compromise was reached on the once lucrative nickel bonus and both sides agreed to drop all of the lawsuits against each other.[1]

The lengthy Vale Inco strike was characterized by bitter conflicts and strained negotiations between the union and company. *Marg Seregelyi/Northern Life, www.northernlife.ca*

Labour strikes may be more severe than most workplace disputes, but every type of conflict includes similar key elements. The Vale Inco strike certainly has these telltale features. Many executives and employees perceived that the other side wanted to undermine their objectives. Both sides developed negative attitudes toward the other and clung to rigid stereotypes that reinforced those negative opinions. The origins of the Vale Inco dispute can be traced back to fundamental sources of conflict that we will discuss in this chapter, such as goal incompatibility, differentiation, and interdependence. The Vale Inco strike also illustrates the dynamics of negotiation to resolve conflict, including how the negotiators used their power and (in this case overestimated) their best alternatives to a negotiated settlement. Finally, although conflict can be beneficial, the negative consequences of the Vale Inco conflict were enormous for both sides.

This chapter investigates the dynamics of conflict in organizational settings. The chapter begins by defining conflict and discussing the age-old question: Is conflict good or bad? Next, we look at the conflict process and examine in detail the main factors that cause or amplify conflict. The five styles of handling conflict are then described, including important contingencies of conflict handling as well as gender and cross-cultural differences. Next, we look at the role of managers and others in third-party conflict resolution. The final section of this chapter reviews key issues in negotiating conflict resolution.

THE MEANING AND CONSEQUENCES OF CONFLICT

LO1

One of the facts of life is that organizations are continuously changing. Recall that from an open systems perspective (Chapter 1), organizations need to regularly adapt to their external environment and to introduce better methods of transforming resources into outputs. There is no clear road map on how the company should change, and employees and other stakeholders rarely agree completely on the direction or form of these adjustments. How should the firm's products and services be designed and marketed to the younger generation? What is the best safety practice for new workplace technology? How much should purchasing decisions be centralized or decentralized? These and many other questions inevitably cause disagreements because people form preferences and are motivated by diverse values, beliefs, and experiences about the "right way" of doing things. Employees also have divergent personal and work goals, which leads them to prefer different directions the organization should take.

> **conflict** A process in which one party perceives that his or her interests are being opposed or negatively affected by another party.

These differences in goals and viewpoints, along with a few other key factors described in this chapter, lead to conflict. **Conflict** is a process in which one party perceives that his or her interests are being opposed or negatively affected by another party.[2] It may occur when one party obstructs another's goals in some way, or just from one party's perception that the other party is going to do so. Conflict is ultimately based on perceptions; it exists whenever one party *believes* that another might obstruct its efforts, whether the other party actually intends to do so. This perceptual characteristic highlights the fact that conflict exists as a threshold level of awareness regarding the risk that others may interfere with their needs and objectives.

IS CONFLICT GOOD OR BAD?

One of the oldest debates in organizational behaviour is whether conflict is good or bad—or, more recently, what forms of conflict are good or bad—for organizations.[3] The dominant view over most of this time has been that conflict is dysfunctional.[4] At the turn of the previous century, European administrative theorists Henri Fayol and Max Weber independently recommended organizational structures that depended on harmonious relations and systematically discouraged conflict. Elton Mayo, who founded Harvard University's human relations school and is considered one of the founders of organizational behaviour, was convinced that employee conflict with management undermines organizational effectiveness. These and other critics warn that even moderately low levels of disagreement tatter the fabric of workplace relations and sap energy away from productive activities. Disagreement with one's supervisor, for example, wastes productive time, violates the hierarchy of command, and questions the efficient assignment of authority (where managers made the decisions and employees followed them).

Although the "conflict-is-bad" perspective is now considered too simplistic, it can indeed have negative consequences under some circumstances (see Exhibit 11.1).[5] Conflict has been criticized for consuming otherwise productive time. For instance, almost one-third of the 5,000 employees recently surveyed across nine countries reported that they are frequently or always dealing with workplace conflict. More than half of the employees in Germany complained that conflict was consuming their workday.[6]

Conflict can undermine job performance in other ways.[7] It is often stressful, which distracts employees from their work and consumes energy. Conflict discourages people from sharing resources and coordinating with others engaged in the dispute. It can reduce job satisfaction, resulting in higher turnover and lower customer service. Conflict fuels organizational politics, such as motivating employees to find ways to undermine the credibility of their opponents. Decision making suffers because people are less motivated to communicate valuable information. Ironically, with less communication, the feuding parties are more likely to escalate their disagreement because each side relies increasingly on distorted perceptions and stereotypes of the other party. Finally, conflict among team members may undermine team cohesion.

In the 1920s, when most organizational scholars viewed conflict as inherently dysfunctional, educational philosopher and psychologist John Dewey praised its benefits: "Conflict is the gadfly of thought. It stirs us to observation and memory. It instigates to invention. It shocks us out of sheeplike passivity, and sets us at noting and contriving."[8] Three years later, political science and management theorist Mary Parker Follett similarly remarked that the "friction" of conflict should be put to use rather than treated as an unwanted consequence of differences.[9]

It wasn't until the 1970s, however, that conflict management experts began to embrace the "optimal conflict" perspective, which states that organizations are most effective when employees experience some level of conflict, but become less effective with high levels of conflict.[10] What are the benefits of conflict? As Dewey, stated, conflict energizes people to debate issues and evaluate alternates more thoroughly. The debate tests the logic of arguments and encourages participants to re-examine their basic assumptions about the problem and its possible solution. It prevents individuals and groups from making inferior decisions. As individuals and teams strive to reach agreement, they learn more about each other and come to understand the underlying issues that need to be addressed. This helps them to develop more creative solutions that reflect the needs of multiple stakeholders. By generating active thinking, conflict also potentially improves creativity.[11]

A second potential benefit is that moderate levels of conflict prevent organizations from stagnating and becoming nonresponsive to their external environment. Through conflict, employees continuously question current practices and become more sensitive to dissatisfaction from stakeholders. In other words, conflict generates more vigilance.[12] Conflict offers a third positive consequence when team members have a dispute

Exhibit 11.1 \ CONSEQUENCES OF WORKPLACE CONFLICT

Negative Consequences	Positive Consequences
Uses otherwise productive time	Better decision making
Less information sharing	—tests logic of arguments
Higher stress, dissatisfaction, and turnover	—questions assumptions
Increases organizational politics	More responsive to changing environment
Wastes resources	Stronger team cohesion (conflict between the team and outside opponents)
Weakens team cohesion (conflict among team members)	

or competition with external sources. This form of conflict represents an external challenge which, as was noted in the team dynamics chapter (Chapter 8), potentially increases cohesion within the team. People are more motivated to work together when faced with an external threat, such as conflict with people outside the team.

THE EMERGING VIEW: CONSTRUCTIVE AND RELATIONSHIP CONFLICT

L02

constructive conflict
A type of conflict in which people focus their discussion on the issue while maintaining respect for people having other points of view.

Although many writers still adhere to the "optimal conflict" perspective, an emerging school of thought is that there are two types of conflict with opposing consequences: constructive conflict and relationship conflict.[13] **Constructive conflict** (also called *task-related conflict*) is a type of conflict in which people focus their discussion on the issue while maintaining respect for people having other points of view. This conflict is called "constructive" because different positions are encouraged so ideas and recommendations can be clarified, redesigned, and tested for logical soundness. By keeping the debate focused on the issue, participants calmly re-examine their assumptions and beliefs without their drive to defend triggering hostile emotions and ego-defence mechanism behaviours. Research indicates that teams and organizations with very low levels of constructive conflict are less effective.[14] At the same time, there is likely an upper limit to the intensity of any disagreement, above which it would be difficult to remain constructive.

relationship conflict
Type of conflict in which people focus on the characteristics of other individuals, rather than on the issues, as the source of conflict.

In contrast to constructive conflict, **relationship conflict** (also known as *socioemotional conflict*) focuses on the characteristics of other individuals, rather than on the issues, as the source of conflict. The parties refer to "personality clashes" and other interpersonal incompatibilities rather than legitimate differences of opinion regarding tasks or decisions. They try to undermine the other person's argument by questioning their competency. Attacking a person's credibility or displaying an aggressive response toward him or her triggers defence mechanisms and a competitive orientation. Relationship conflict also reduces trust because the strong negative emotions that typically accompany this conflict undermine any identification with the other person, leaving the relationship held together mainly by calculus-based trust.[15] The conflict more easily escalates because the adversaries become less motivated to communicate and share information, making it more difficult for them to discover common ground and ultimately resolve the conflict. Instead, they rely more on distorted perceptions and stereotypes which, as we noted earlier, tend to further escalate the conflict.

Separating Constructive from Relationship Conflict   If there are two types of conflict, as recent studies suggest, then the obvious advice is to encourage constructive conflict and minimize relationship conflict. This recommendation sounds good in

Constructive Confrontation Inside Intel

Until a few years ago, Intel engineers were obsessed with designing computer processors that were faster, smaller, and ultimately hotter and more power hungry. But key people at Intel's Israeli operations saw trouble brewing. Almost weekly, they would fly from Haifa to Intel's headquarters in California, "pestering" top executives with data and arguments that the company would soon hit the limits of chip speed. The Israeli crew also warned that Intel would lose out to competitors for cooler and more power efficient "mobility" chips for laptops and other mobility devices. The conflict may have rankled some Intel bosses, but the Israeli staff convinced Intel to change direction. Their persistent arguing also demonstrated the value of "constructive confrontation"—the art of argument and respectful debate that Intel co-founder Andy Grove encouraged long ago. The practice is so important that new Intel employees are taught the fine art of confrontation through supervised debates and role plays. "The goal of a leader should be to maximize resistance—in the sense of encouraging disagreement and dissent," says Dov Frohman, founder of Intel Israel.[16] *John Davis/Photolibrary*

theory, but separating these two types of conflict isn't easy. Research indicates that we experience some degree of relationship conflict whenever we are engaged in constructive debate.[17] No matter how diplomatically someone questions our ideas and actions, they potentially trigger our drive to defend our ideas, our sense of competence, and our public image. The stronger the level of debate and the more the issue is tied to our self-concept, the higher the chance that the constructive conflict will evolve into (or mix with) relationship conflict.

> Most of us experience some degree of relationship conflict whenever we are engaged in constructive debate. "

Fortunately, three strategies or conditions potentially minimize the level of relationship conflict during constructive conflict episodes.[18]

- *Emotional Intelligence.* Relationship conflict is less likely to occur, or is less likely to escalate, when team members have high levels of emotional intelligence. Employees with higher emotional intelligence are better able to regulate their emotions during debate, which reduces the risk of escalating perceptions of interpersonal hostility. People with high emotional intelligence are also more likely to view a co-worker's emotional reaction as valuable information about that person's needs and expectations, rather than as a personal attack.

- *Cohesive Team.* Relationship conflict is suppressed when the conflict occurs within a highly cohesive team. The longer people work together, get to know each other, and develop mutual trust, the more latitude they give to each other to show emotions without being personally offended. Strong cohesion also allows each person to know about and anticipate the behaviours and emotions of their teammates. Another benefit is that cohesion produces a stronger social identity with the group, so team members are motivated to avoid escalating relationship conflict during otherwise emotionally turbulent discussions.

- *Supportive Team Norms.* Various team norms can hold relationship conflict at bay during constructive debate. When team norms encourage openness, for instance, team members learn to appreciate honest dialogue without personally reacting to any emotional display during the disagreements.[19] Other norms might discourage team members from displaying negative emotions toward co-workers. Team norms also encourage tactics that diffuse relationship conflict when it first appears. For instance, research has found that teams with low relationship conflict use humour to maintain positive group emotions, which offsets negative feelings team members might develop toward some co-workers during debate.

CONFLICT PROCESS MODEL

L03

Now that we have outlined the history and current knowledge about conflict and its outcomes, let's look at the model of the conflict process, shown in Exhibit 11.2.[20] This model begins with the sources of conflict, which we will describe in the next section. At some point, the sources of conflict lead one or both parties to perceive that conflict exists. They become aware that one party's statements and actions are incompatible with their own goals. These perceptions usually interact with emotions experienced about the conflict.[21] Conflict perceptions and emotions manifest themselves in manifest conflict—the decisions and behaviours of one party toward the other. These *conflict episodes* may range from subtle nonverbal behaviours to warlike aggression. Particularly when people experience high levels of conflict-generated emotions, they have difficulty finding the words and expressions that communicate effectively without further

Exhibit 11.2 \ MODEL OF THE CONFLICT PROCESS

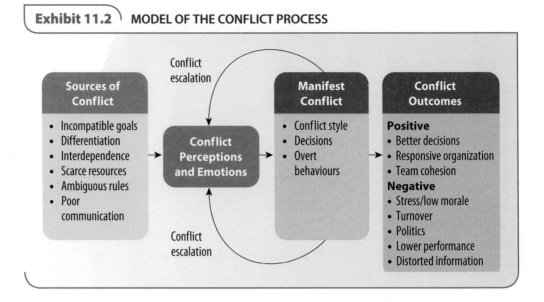

irritating the relationship.[22] Conflict is also manifested by the style each side uses to resolve the conflict. Some people tend to avoid the conflict whereas others try to defeat those with opposing views.

Exhibit 11.2 shows arrows looping back from manifest conflict to conflict perceptions and emotions. These arrows illustrate that the conflict process is really a series of episodes that potentially cycle into conflict escalation.[23] It doesn't take much to start this conflict cycle—just an inappropriate comment, a misunderstanding, or action that lacks diplomacy. These behaviours cause the other party to perceive that conflict exists. Even if the first party did not intend to demonstrate conflict, the second party's response may create that perception.

STRUCTURAL SOURCES OF CONFLICT IN ORGANIZATIONS

The conflict model starts with the sources of conflict, so we need to understand these sources to effectively diagnose conflict episodes and subsequently resolve the conflict or occasionally to generate conflict where it is lacking. The six main conditions that cause conflict in organizational settings are incompatible goals, differentiation, interdependence, scarce resources, ambiguous rules, and communication problems.

INCOMPATIBLE GOALS

Goal incompatibility occurs when the goals of one person or department seem to interfere with another person's or department's goals.[24] For example, the production department strives for cost efficiency by scheduling long production runs whereas the sales team emphasizes customer service by delivering the client's product as quickly as possible. If the company runs out of a particular product, the production team would prefer to have clients wait until the next production run. This infuriates sales representatives who would rather change production quickly to satisfy consumer demand.

Goal incompatibility partly explains some of the "intense struggles" reported at Microsoft in recent years. One former executive recounted how competition among Microsoft divisions effectively killed many great products because accepting another division's inventions was tantamount to giving them more budget. One example was ClearType, an innovative technology that makes screens more readable. Microsoft divisions gave questionable reasons why they wouldn't adopt the technology. Only the pocket devices group agreed to use ClearType, but only if the program and engineers were transferred to their division! A few years earlier, Microsoft's MSN group fought against the Microsoft Office Group over MSN's desire to connect their online calendar with the calendar in Office. The Office group balked because "then MSN could canni-balize Office," says an employee who left Microsoft. "Windows and Office would never let MSN have more budget or more control."[25]

DIFFERENTIATION

Another source of conflict is differentiation—differences among people and work units regarding their training, values, beliefs, and experiences. Differentiation can be distin-guished from goal incompatibility; two people or departments may agree on a com-mon goal (serving customers better) but have different beliefs about how to achieve that goal (e.g., standardize employee behaviour versus give employees autonomy in cus-tomer interactions). Consider the opening story to this chapter. The Vale Inco strike was partly due to incompatible goals (higher pay versus lower labour costs), but it was just as much caused by the divergent backgrounds and expectations of the two groups. The company's new owners came from a different culture, which may have caused both sides to develop an "us–them" mindset and to act in ways that aggravated the other party more than expected. Even without cultural differences, labour union and com-pany leaders often have divergent work experiences and values, so they see different routes to the company's survival and success.

Intergenerational conflicts are also attributed to differentiation. As Connections 11.1 describes, younger and older employees have different needs, different expectations, and different workplace practices, which sometimes produces conflicting preferences and actions. Recent studies suggest that these intergenerational differences occur because people develop social identities around technological developments and other pivotal social events that are unique to their era.[26]

Differentiation also produces the classic tension between employees from two com-panies brought together through a merger. Even though everyone wants the company to succeed, they fight over the "right way" to do things because of their unique experi-

---

CONNECTIONS 11.1

Potential to Induce Generational Conflicts

"I'm not going to be the type of person who's going to sit around and do nothing if there's nothing to do," says Ten-nyson Cho. Although Cho is willing to put in the long hours that his job demands, he has no qualms about acknowledg-ing that he plans to "learn as much as I can" and then move on to another firm. A commerce graduate from Queen's University, Cho recently left his former firm and is now an Associate at Richardson Capital Partners according to his LinkedIn profile.

Highly confident organizational newcomers sometimes find their enthusiasm receives skepticism or even hostility from older employees. Baby boomer managers also have work expectations that sometimes clash with expectations held by their younger employees. One oft-cited complaint is that younger employees demand clear assignments as well as frequent task clarification and feedback, whereas their baby boomer bosses expect new hires to take initia-tive without close supervision. Ambiguous rules can also result in conflict between younger and more seasoned employees.[27]

Technologically savvy and ambitious, Generation-Y employees' attributes and attitudes toward work have the potential to induce generational conflicts in the workplace. © J.P. Moczulaki

ences in the separate companies. A mid-sized Canadian retail clothing chain experienced another variation of differentiation-based conflict when the founder and CEO hired several senior managers from large organizations to strengthen the experience levels of its senior management group. The newly hired managers soon clashed with long-time executives at the clothing chain. "We ended up with an old team and a new team and they weren't on the same wavelength," explains the company owner, who eventually fired most of the new managers.

INTERDEPENDENCE

Conflict tends to increase with the level of task interdependence. Task interdependence refers to the extent to which employees must share materials, information, or expertise to perform their jobs (see Chapter 8). This interdependence includes sharing common resources, exchanging work or clients back and forth, and receiving outcomes (such as rewards) that are partly determined by the performance of others.[28] Higher interdependence increases the risk of conflict because there is a greater chance that each side will disrupt or interfere with the other side's goals.[29]

Aside from complete independence, employees tend to have the lowest risk of conflict when working with others in a pooled interdependence relationship. Pooled interdependence occurs where individuals operate independently except for reliance on a common resource or authority. The potential for conflict is higher in sequential interdependence work relationships, such as an assembly line. The highest risk of conflict tends to occur in reciprocal interdependence situations. With reciprocal interdependence, employees have high mutual dependence on each other and, consequently, have a higher probability of interfering with each other's work and personal goals.

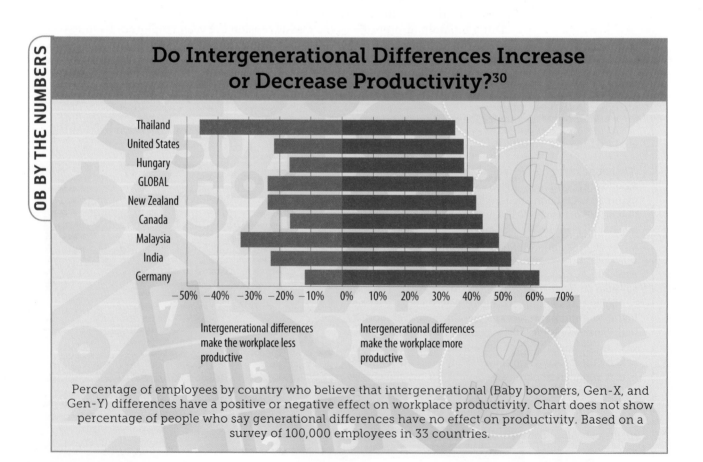

OB BY THE NUMBERS

Do Intergenerational Differences Increase or Decrease Productivity?[30]

Intergenerational differences make the workplace less productive

Intergenerational differences make the workplace more productive

Percentage of employees by country who believe that intergenerational (Baby boomers, Gen-X, and Gen-Y) differences have a positive or negative effect on workplace productivity. Chart does not show percentage of people who say generational differences have no effect on productivity. Based on a survey of 100,000 employees in 33 countries.

SCARCE RESOURCES

Resource scarcity generates conflict because each person or unit requiring the same resource necessarily undermines others who also need that resource to fulfill their goals. Most labour strikes, including the Vale Inco dispute described in the opening vignette, occur because there aren't enough financial and other resources for employees and company owners to each receive the outcomes they seek, such as higher pay (employees) and higher investment returns (shareholders). The more resources one group receives, the fewer resources other stakeholders will receive. Fortunately, these interests aren't perfectly opposing in complex negotiations, but limited resources are typically a major source of friction.

AMBIGUOUS RULES

Ambiguous rules—or the complete lack of rules—breed conflict. This occurs because uncertainty increases the risk that one party intends to interfere with the other party's goals. Ambiguity also encourages political tactics and, in some cases, employees enter a free-for-all battle to win decisions in their favour. This explains why conflict is more common during mergers and acquisitions. Employees from both companies have conflicting practices and values, and few rules have developed to minimize the manoeuvring for power and resources.[31] When clear rules exist, on the other hand, employees know what to expect from each other and have agreed to abide by those rules.

COMMUNICATION PROBLEMS

Conflict often occurs due to the lack of opportunity, ability, or motivation to communicate effectively. Let's look at each of these causes. First, when two parties lack the opportunity to communicate, they tend to rely more on stereotypes to understand the other party in the conflict. Unfortunately, stereotypes are sufficiently subjective that emotions can negatively distort the meaning of an opponent's actions, thereby escalating perceptions of conflict. Second, some people lack the necessary skills to communicate in a diplomatic, nonconfrontational manner. When one party communicates its disagreement arrogantly, opponents are more likely to heighten their perception of the conflict. This may lead the other party to reciprocate with a similar response, which further escalates the conflict.[32]

A third problem is that relationship conflict is uncomfortable, so people are less motivated to communicate with others in a disagreement. Unfortunately, less communication can further escalate the conflict because each side has less accurate information about the other side's intentions. To fill in the missing pieces, they rely on distorted images and stereotypes of the other party. Perceptions are further distorted because people in conflict situations tend to engage in more differentiation with those who are different from them (see Chapter 3). This differentiation creates a more positive self-concept and a more negative image of the opponent. We begin to see competitors less favourably so our self-concept remains positive during these uncertain times.[33]

INTERPERSONAL CONFLICT HANDLING STYLES

L04

The six structural conditions described in the previous section lead to conflict perceptions and emotions which, in turn, motivate people to take some sort of action to address the conflict. Mary Parker Follett, who we identified earlier as one of the first scholars to suggest the benefits of conflict, was also among the first to identify the different ways that people respond to conflict. Conflict management experts subsequently expanded and refined this taxonomy of conflict handling styles, with most of them adapting variations of the five-category model shown in Exhibit 11.3 and described below. This model recognizes that how people approach a conflict situation depends on the relative importance they place on maximizing their outcomes and preserving the relationship with the other person.[34]

Exhibit 11.3   INTERPERSONAL CONFLICT HANDLING STYLES

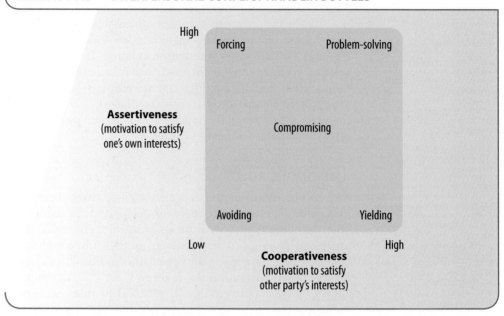

Source: C. K. W. de Dreu, A. Evers, B. Beersma, E. S. Kluwer, and A. Nauta, "A Theory-based Measure of Conflict Management Strategies in the Workplace," *Journal of Organizational Behaviour* 22 (2001), pp. 645–68. For other variations of this model, see: T. L. Ruble and K. Thomas, "Support For a Two-Dimensional Model of Conflict Behaviour," *Organizational Behaviour and Human Performance* 16 (1976), p. 145; R. R. Blake, H. A. Shepard, and J. S. Mouton, *Managing Intergroup Conflict in Industry* (Houston: Gulf Publishing, 1964); and M. A. Rahim, "Toward a Theory of Managing Organizational Conflict," *International Journal of Conflict Management* 13, no. 3 (2002), pp. 206–235.

> **win–win orientation**
> The belief that the parties will find a mutually beneficial solution to their disagreement.

> **win–lose orientation**
> The belief that conflicting parties are drawing from a fixed pie, so the more one party receives, the less the other party will receive.

- *Problem solving*—Problem solving tries to find a solution that is beneficial for both parties. This is known as the **win–win orientation** because people using this style believe the resources at stake are expandable rather than fixed if the parties work together to find a creative solution. Information sharing is an important feature of this style because both parties collaborate to identify common ground and potential solutions that satisfy everyone involved.

- *Forcing*—Forcing tries to win the conflict at the other's expense. People who use this style typically have a **win–lose orientation**—they believe the parties are drawing from a fixed pie, so the more one party receives, the less the other party will receive. Consequently, this style relies on some of the "hard" influence tactics described in Chapter 10, particularly assertiveness, to get one's own way.

- *Avoiding*—Avoiding tries to smooth over or avoid conflict situations altogether. It represents a low concern for both self and the other party; in other words, avoiders try to find ways to avoid thinking about the conflict.[35] Some employees rearrange their work area or tasks to minimize interaction with certain co-workers. According to one recent large survey across several countries, 67 percent of employees go out of their way to avoid seeing co-workers with whom they have a disagreement. A smaller number (14 percent) have missed a day of work to avoid workplace conflict.[36]

- *Yielding*—Yielding involves giving in completely to the other side's wishes, or at least cooperating with little or no attention to your own interests. This style involves making unilateral concessions and unconditional promises, as well as offering help with no expectation of reciprocal help.

- *Compromising*—Compromising involves looking for a position in which your losses are offset by equally valued gains. It involves matching the other party's concessions, making conditional promises or threats, and actively searching for a middle ground between the interests of the two parties.

CHOOSING THE BEST CONFLICT HANDLING STYLE

Chances are that you have a preferred conflict handling style. You might typically engage in avoiding or yielding because disagreement makes you feel uncomfortable and is contrary to your self-view as someone who likes to get along with everyone. Or perhaps you prefer the compromising and forcing strategies because they reflect your strong need for achievement and to control your environment. People usually gravitate toward one or two conflict handling styles that match their personality, personal and cultural values, and past experience. However, the best style depends on the situation, so we need to understand and develop the capacity to use each style for the appropriate occasions.[37]

Exhibit 11.4 summarizes the main contingencies, as well as problems with using each conflict handling style. Problem solving is widely recognized as the preferred conflict handling style, whenever possible. Why? This approach calls for dialogue and clever thinking, both of which help the parties discover a win-win situation. In addition, the problem solving style tends to improve long-term relationships, reduce stress, and minimize emotional defensiveness and other indications of relationship conflict.[38]

However, problem solving assumes there are opportunities for mutual gains, such as when the conflict is complex with multiple elements. If the conflict is simple and perfectly opposing (each party wants more of a single fixed pie), then this style will waste time and increase frustration. The problem solving approach also takes more time and requires a fairly high degree of trust, because there is a risk that the other party will take advantage of the information you have openly shared. As one Canadian study recently found, the problem solving style is more stressful when people experience strong feelings of conflict, likely because these negative emotions undermine trust in the other party.[39]

The conflict avoidance style is often ineffective because it doesn't resolve the conflict and may increase the other party's frustration. However, avoiding may be the best strategy where conflict has become emotionally charged or where conflict resolution would cost more than its benefits.[40] The forcing style is usually inappropriate because research indicates that it commonly generates relationship conflict more quickly or intensely

Exhibit 11.4   CONFLICT HANDLING STYLE CONTINGENCIES AND PROBLEMS

Conflict Handling Style	Preferred Style When ...	Problems with this Style
Problem solving	• Interests are not perfectly opposing (i.e., not pure win-lose) • Parties have trust, openness, and time to share information • The issues are complex	• Sharing information that the other party might use to their advantage
Forcing	• You have a deep conviction about your position (e.g., believe other person's behaviour is unethical) • Dispute requires a quick solution • The other party would take advantage of more cooperative strategies	• Highest risk of relationship conflict • May damage long-term relations, reducing future problem solving
Avoiding	• Conflict has become too emotionally charged • Cost of trying to resolve the conflict outweighs the benefits	• Doesn't usually resolve the conflict • May increase other party's frustration
Yielding	• Other party has substantially more power • Issue is much less important to you than to the other party • The value and logic of your position isn't as clear	• Increases other party's expectations in future conflict episodes
Compromising	• Parties have equal power • Time pressure to resolve the conflict • Parties lack trust/openness for problem solving	• Sub-optimal solution where mutual gains are possible

than other conflict handling styles. However, forcing may be necessary where you know you are correct (e.g., the other party's position is unethical or based on obviously flawed logic), the dispute requires a quick solution, or the other party would take advantage of a more cooperative conflict handling style.

The yielding style may be appropriate when the other party has substantially more power, the issue is not as important to you as to the other party, and you aren't confident that your position has the superior logical or ethical justification. On the other hand, yielding behaviours may give the other side unrealistically high expectations, thereby motivating them to seek more from you in the future. In the long run, yielding may produce more conflict rather than resolve it. The compromising style may be best when there is little hope for mutual gains through problem solving, both parties have equal power, and both are under time pressure to settle their differences. In particular, compromising occurs rather than problem solving when it appears that the parties have perfectly opposing interests. Therefore, entering a conflict with the compromising style may cause the parties to overlook better solutions because they have not attempted to share enough information and creatively look for win–win alternatives.

CULTURAL AND GENDER DIFFERENCES IN CONFLICT HANDLING STYLES

Cultural differences are more than just a source of conflict. They also influence the preferred conflict handling style.[41] Some research suggests that people from collectivist cultures—where group goals are valued more than individual goals—are motivated to maintain harmonious relations and, consequently, are more likely than those from low collectivism cultures to manage disagreements through avoidance or problem solving. However, this view may be somewhat simplistic because people in some collectivist cultures are also more likely to publicly shame those whose actions oppose their own.[42] Cultural values and norms influence the conflict handling style used most often in a society, but they also represent an important contingency when outsiders choose the preferred conflict handling approach. For example, people who frequently use the conflict avoidance style might have more problems in cultures where the forcing style is common.

According to some writers, men and women tend to rely on different conflict handling styles.[43] They suggest that, compared to men, women pay more attention to the relationship between the parties. Consequently, women tend to adopt a compromising or occasionally problem solving style in business settings and are more willing to compromise to protect the relationship. Men tend to be more competitive and take a short-term orientation to the relationship. In low collectivism cultures, men are more likely than women to use the forcing approach to conflict handling. However, we must be cautious about these observations because gender has a weak influence on conflict handling style.

Asia's Influence on Conflict Handling in Western Canada's Energy Sector

Chinese, Korean, and Thai companies have been making significant acquisitions in Western Canada's energy sector and this growing Asian presence could result in a significant shift in conflict handling style between organizations, communities, and governments, as well as between individuals within organizations. In western cultures, conflict is considered acceptable and a normal part of life and a variety of conflict handling styles may be used. However, Asian executives prefer avoiding conflict, part of the values of shame and honour and the concept of "face." Gordon Houlden, former long-time Canadian diplomat in China and director of the University of Alberta's China Institute suggests that adaptations of business practices including conflict resolution will occur. "The oil patch in Calgary will have to become more sensitive to Asian business practices."[44] *Dan Bannister/Tetra Images/Alamy*

STRUCTURAL APPROACHES TO CONFLICT MANAGEMENT

L05

Conflict handling styles describe how we approach the other party in a conflict situation. But conflict management also involves altering the underlying structural causes of potential conflict. The main structural approaches are emphasizing superordinate goals, reducing differentiation, improving communication and understanding, reducing task interdependence, increasing resources, and clarifying rules and procedures.

EMPHASIZING SUPERORDINATE GOALS

One of the oldest recommendations for resolving conflict is to refocus the parties' attention around superordinate goals and away from the conflicting subordinate goals.[45] **Superordinate goals** are broad goals that all parties to a dispute value and agree are important, and whose attainment requires the joint resources and effort of those parties.[46] These goals are called superordinate because they are higher-order aspirations such as the organization's strategic objectives rather than objectives specific to the individual or work unit. Research indicates that the most effective executive teams frame their decisions as superordinate goals that rise above each executive's departmental or divisional goals. Similarly, a recent Canadian study reported that leaders reduce conflict through an inspirational vision that unifies employees and makes them less preoccupied with their subordinate goal differences.[47]

> **superordinate goal** A broad goal that all parties to a dispute value and agree is important.

Suppose that marketing staff want a new product released quickly whereas engineers want more time to test and add new features. Leaders can potentially reduce this interdepartmental conflict by reminding both groups of the company's mission to serve customers, or by pointing out that competitors currently threaten the company's leadership in the industry. By increasing commitment to corporate-wide goals (customer focus, competitiveness), engineering and marketing employees pay less attention to their competing departmental-level goals, which reduces their perceived conflict with co-workers. Superordinate goals also potentially reduce the problem of differentiation because they establish feelings of a shared social identity (work for the same company).[48]

REDUCING DIFFERENTIATION

Another way to minimize dysfunctional conflict is to reduce the differences that generate conflict. As people develop a shared repository of experiences and beliefs, they become more motivated to coordinate activities and resolve their disputes through constructive discussion.[49]

One way to reduce differentiation is by creating common experiences. SAP, the German enterprise software company, applied this approach when it recently acquired Business Objects, a French company with a strong American presence. Immediately after the merger, SAP began intermingling people from the two organizations. "In the first six months after the acquisition, more than 35 percent of senior managers transferred from SAP while all the original Business Objects corporate services people are now a part of a global shared services team," says Business Objects CEO John Schwarz. "We also encourage cross-border, cross-functional teamwork on projects such as major product releases. In this way team members come to depend on each other."[50] Essentially, SAP provided opportunities for managers and technical employees in the acquired firm to develop common experiences with their SAP counterparts by moving staff across the two companies or having them work together on joint projects.

IMPROVING COMMUNICATION AND MUTUAL UNDERSTANDING

A third way to resolve dysfunctional conflict is to give the conflicting parties more opportunities to communicate and understand each other. This recommendation applies two principles and practices introduced in Chapter 3: the Johari Window model and contact hypothesis. Although both were previously described as ways to improve self-awareness, they are equally valuable to improve other-awareness. In the Johari Window process, you disclose more about yourself so others have a better understanding of the underlying causes of your behaviour. The contact hypothesis is the theory stating that the more we interact with someone, the less prejudiced or perceptually biased we will be against that person.[51] Through meaningful interaction, we develop a more person-specific and accurate understanding of others.

Montreal-based L'Oréal Canada introduced a program to improve mutual understanding as soon as they saw signs of intergenerational conflict brewing. "When we saw (generational differences), we realized we could be faced with an interesting problem" recalls Marjolaine Rompré, L'Oréal's director of learning for development. The half-day seminar, called Valorize Generational Differences, enables employees across all generations to share their perceptions, values, and expectations with each other. In one activity, employees organized into generational cohorts ask questions to employees in the other cohorts. "Each group is interested and surprised to see what's important to the other group," says Rompré, adding that the program has been both successful and popular. "The (Gen)-Ys told us they were so happy to learn why the baby boomers were so conservative and why Gen-X didn't want to share information with them."[52]

Although communication and mutual understanding can work well, there are two important warnings. First, these interventions should be applied only where differentiation is sufficiently low or *after* differentiation has been reduced. If perceived differentiation remains high, attempts to manage conflict through dialogue might escalate rather than reduce relationship conflict. The reason is that when forced to interact with people who we believe are quite different and in conflict with us, we tend to select information that reinforces that view.[53] The second warning is that people in collectivist and high power distance cultures are less comfortable with the practice of resolving differences through direct and open communication.[54] As noted earlier, people in Confucian cultures prefer an avoidance conflict management style because it is the most consistent with harmony and face saving. Direct communication is a high-risk strategy because it easily threatens the need to save face and maintain harmony.

REDUCING INTERDEPENDENCE

Conflict occurs when people are dependent on each other, so another way to reduce dysfunctional conflict is to minimize the level of interdependence between the parties. Here are three strategies to reduce interdependence among employees and work units.

Create Buffers   A buffer is any mechanism that loosens the coupling between two or more people or work units. By decoupling the relationship, buffers help to reduce the potential for conflict. Building up inventories between people in an assembly line would be a buffer, for example, because each employee is less dependent in the short term on

Mutual Understanding Get CN and CWB Back on Track

Strained relations between Canadian National Railways (CN) and the Canadian Wheat Board (CWB) recently changed to cooperation when Claude Mongeau became CN's chief executive. Mongeau implemented a plan where the two companies share information so CN can provide hopper cars to grain elevators when they are needed. This information exchange alone dramatically gave each party a better understanding of the other's situation. But CN and CWB also tackled their longstanding conflicts by having executives and staff talk to each other more often about their needs and perceptions. "Under Claude, CN has quickly moved to a more collaborative model," says CWB chief operating officer Ward Weisensel. "That's not to say we agree on every issue, but with Claude we are able to discuss and explore and both parties are better able to understand each other."[55] *Sherman Hines/Alamy*

the previous person along that line. In contrast, a just-in-time inventory system (where supplies are provided just before they are needed) has tight coupling, which increases the potential for conflict.

Use Integrators   *Integrators* are employees who coordinate the activities of differentiated work units toward the completion of a common task. For example, an individual might be responsible for coordinating the efforts of the research, production, advertising, and marketing departments in launching a new product line. In some respects, integrators are human buffers; they reduce the frequency of direct interaction among work units with diverse goals and perspectives. Integrators rarely have direct authority over the departments they integrate, so they must rely on referent power and persuasion to manage conflict and accomplish the work. Integrators need to work effectively with each unit, so they must possess sufficient knowledge of each area.

Combine Jobs   Combining jobs is both a form of job enrichment and a way to reduce task interdependence. Consider a toaster assembly system where one person inserts the heating element, another adds the sides, and so on. By combining these tasks so that each person assembles an entire toaster, the employees now have a pooled rather than sequential form of task interdependence and the likelihood of dysfunctional conflict is reduced.

INCREASING RESOURCES

An obvious way to reduce conflict caused by resource scarcity is to increase the amount of resources available. Corporate decision makers might quickly dismiss this solution because of the costs involved. However, they need to carefully compare these costs with the costs of dysfunctional conflict arising out of resource scarcity.

CLARIFYING RULES AND PROCEDURES

Conflicts that arise from ambiguities can be minimized by establishing rules and procedures. If two departments are fighting over the use of a new laboratory, a schedule might be established which allocates the lab exclusively to each team at certain times of the day or week. Armstrong World Industries, Inc., applied the clarifying rules and procedures strategy when consultants and information systems employees clashed while working together on development of a client–server network. Information systems employees at the flooring and building materials company thought they should be in charge, whereas consultants believed they had the senior role. Also, the consultants wanted to work long hours and take Friday off to fly home, whereas Armstrong employees wanted to work regular hours. The company reduced these conflicts by having both parties agree on specific responsibilities and roles. The agreement also assigned two senior executives at the companies to establish rules if future disagreements arose.[56]

THIRD-PARTY CONFLICT RESOLUTION

third-party conflict resolution   Any attempt by a relatively neutral person to help conflicting parties resolve their differences.

Most of this chapter has focused on people directly involved in a conflict, yet many disputes among employees and departments are resolved with the assistance of a manager. **Third-party conflict resolution** is any attempt by a relatively neutral person to help conflicting parties resolve their differences. There are three main third-party dispute resolution activities: arbitration, inquisition, and mediation. These interventions can be classified by their level of control over the process and control over the decision (see Exhibit 11.5).[57]

- *Arbitration*—Arbitrators have high control over the final decision, but low control over the process. Executives engage in this strategy by following previously agreed rules of due process, listening to arguments from the disputing employees, and making a binding decision. Arbitration is applied as the final stage of grievances by unionized employees in many countries, but it is also becoming more common in nonunion conflicts.

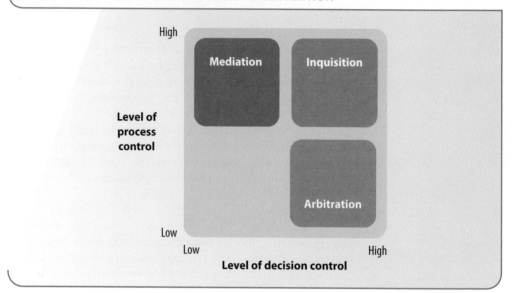

Exhibit 11.5   TYPES OF THIRD-PARTY INTERVENTION

- *Inquisition*—Inquisitors control all discussion about the conflict. Like arbitrators, they have high decision control because they choose an action that will resolve the conflict. However, they also have high process control because they choose which information to examine and how to examine it, and they generally decide how the conflict resolution process will be handled.

- *Mediation*—Mediators have high control over the intervention process. In fact, their main purpose is to manage the process and context of interaction between the disputing parties. However, the parties make the final decision about how to resolve their differences. Thus, mediators have little or no control over the conflict resolution decision. Some organizations, including Shell Canada, TD Canada Trust, and Royal Bank of Canada (RBC), have an ombuds officer to mediate conflicts between management and employees, such as allegations of employment discrimination and other unfair decisions.

CHOOSING THE BEST THIRD-PARTY INTERVENTION STRATEGY

Team leaders, executives, and co-workers regularly intervene in workplace disputes. Sometimes they adopt a mediator role; at other times they serve as arbitrators. Occasionally, they begin with one approach then switch to another. However, research suggests that people in positions of authority (e.g., managers) usually adopt an inquisitional approach whereby they dominate the intervention process as well as make a binding decision.[58]

Managers tend to rely on the inquisition approach because it is consistent with the decision-oriented nature of managerial jobs, gives them control over the conflict process and outcome, and tends to resolve disputes efficiently. However, inquisition is usually the least effective third-party conflict resolution method in organizational settings.[59] One problem is that leaders who take an inquisitional role tend to collect limited

Managers tend to rely on the inquisition approach, yet it is usually the least effective third-party conflict resolution method in organizational settings.

RBC's Ombuds Office

RBC, Canada's largest financial institution, employs more than 8,000 people who manage other people throughout the organization. They have an important role in maintaining employee morale and engagement, which includes addressing conflicts when they occur. But what happens when the manager is part of the conflict or doesn't provide the level of assistance an employee expects? RBC's solution is an Employee Ombudsman, who serves as a confidential and impartial resource to help employees manage and resolve workplace conflicts. Each year, more than 1,000 RBC employees contact the employee ombudsman for coaching and mediation to solve workplace problems.[60] *Toronto Star/GetStock.com*

information about the problem, so their imposed decision may produce an ineffective solution to the conflict. Another problem is that employees often view inquisitional procedures and outcomes as unfair because they have little control over this approach. In particular, the inquisitional approach potentially violates several practices required to support procedural justice (see Chapter 5).

Which third-party intervention is most appropriate in organizations? The answer partly depends on the situation, such as the type of dispute, the relationship between the manager and employees, and cultural values such as power distance.[61] But generally speaking, for everyday disagreements between two employees, the mediation approach is usually best because this gives employees more responsibility for resolving their own disputes. The third-party representative merely establishes an appropriate context for conflict resolution. Although not as efficient as other strategies, mediation potentially offers the highest level of employee satisfaction with the conflict process and outcomes.[62] When employees cannot resolve their differences through mediation, arbitration seems to work best because the predetermined rules of evidence and other processes create a higher sense of procedural fairness.[63] Arbitration is also preferred where the organization's goals should take priority over individual goals.

RESOLVING CONFLICT THROUGH NEGOTIATION

L06

negotiation The process whereby two or more conflicting parties attempt to resolve their divergent goals by redefining the terms of their interdependence.

Think back through yesterday's events. Maybe you had to work out an agreement with other students about what tasks to complete for a team project. Chances are that you shared transportation with someone, so you had to clarify the timing of the ride. Then perhaps there was the question of who made dinner. Each of these daily events created potential conflict, and they were resolved through negotiation. **Negotiation** occurs whenever two or more conflicting parties attempt to resolve their divergent goals by redefining the terms of their interdependence. In other words, people negotiate when they think that discussion can produce a more satisfactory arrangement (at least for them) in their exchange of goods or services.

As you can see, negotiation is not an obscure practice reserved for labour and management bosses when hammering out a collective agreement. Everyone negotiates, every day. Most of the time, you don't even realize that you are in negotiations. Negotiation is particularly evident in the workplace because employees work interdependently with each other. They negotiate with their supervisors over next month's work assignments, with customers over the sale and delivery schedules of their product, and with co-workers over when to have lunch. And yes, they occasionally negotiate with each other in labour disputes and collective agreements.

BARGAINING ZONE MODEL OF NEGOTIATIONS

One way to view the negotiation process is that each party moves along a continuum in opposite directions with an area of potential overlap called the *bargaining zone*.[64] Exhibit 11.6 displays one possible bargaining zone situation. This linear diagram illustrates a purely win–lose situation—one side's gain will be the other's loss. However, the bargaining zone model can also be applied to situations in which both sides potentially gain from the negotiations. As this model illustrates, the parties typically establish three main negotiating points. The *initial offer point* is the team's opening offer to the other party. This may be its best expectation or a pie-in-the-sky starting point. The *target point* is the team's realistic goal or expectation for a final agreement. The *resistance point* is the point beyond which the team will make no further concessions.

The parties begin negotiations by describing their initial offer point for each item on the agenda. In most cases, the participants know that this is only a starting point that will change as both sides offer concessions. In win–lose situations, neither the target nor the resistance point is revealed to the other party. However, people try to discover the other side's resistance point because this knowledge helps them determine how much they can gain without breaking off negotiations.

The bargaining zone model implies that the parties compete against each other to reach their target point. Competition does exist to varying degrees because constituents expect the negotiator to *claim value*, that is, to get the best possible outcomes for themselves. Yet, the hallmark of successful negotiations is a combination of competition and cooperation. Negotiators need to cooperate with each other to *create value*, that is, to discover ways to achieve mutually satisfactory outcomes for both parties.[65] Cooperation maintains a degree of trust necessary to share information. To some degree, it may also improve concessions so the negotiations are resolved more quickly and with greater mutual gains.

STRATEGIES FOR CLAIMING VALUE

Claiming value involves trying to obtain the best possible outcomes for yourself and your constituents. A purely competitive approach, in which you forcefully persuade the other party and assert your power (such as threatening to walk away from the negotiation), typically leads to failure because it generates negative emotions and undermines trust. Even so, some degree of value claiming is necessary to achieve a favourable outcome. Here are four skills to effectively claim value in negotiations.

Exhibit 11.6 BARGAINING ZONE MODEL OF NEGOTIATIONS

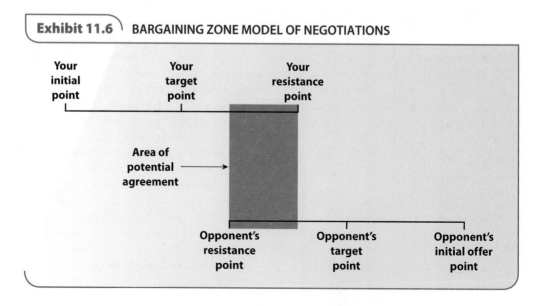

Prepare and Set Goals   People negotiate more successfully when they carefully think through their three key positions in the bargaining zone model (initial, target and resistance), consider alternative strategies to achieve those objectives, and test their underlying assumptions about the situation.[66] Equally important, they need to research what the other party wants from the negotiation. "You have to be prepared every which way about the people, the subject, and your fallback position," advises Paul Tellier, chairman of Vancouver-based Global Container Terminals and the former president of Canadian National Railway and Bombardier, Inc. "Before walking into the room for the actual negotiation, I ask my colleagues to throw some curve balls at me."[67]

Know Your BATNA   To determine whether the opponent's offers are favourable, negotiators need to understand what outcome they might achieve through some other means (such as negotiating with someone else). This comparison is called the **best alternative to a negotiated agreement (BATNA)**. BATNA estimates your power in the negotiation because it represents the estimated cost of walking away from the relationship. If others are willing to negotiate with you for the product or service you need, then you have a high BATNA and considerable power in the negotiation because it would not cost you much to walk away from the current negotiation. A common problem in negotiations, however, is that people overestimate their BATNA; they wrongly believe there are plenty of other ways to achieve their objective rather than through this negotiation.

> **best alternative to a negotiated agreement (BATNA)** The best outcome you might achieve through some other course of action if you abandon the current negotiation.

Manage Time   Negotiators make more concessions as the deadline gets closer.[68] This can be a liability if you are under time pressure, or it can be an advantage if the other party alone is under time pressure. Negotiators with more power in the relationship sometimes apply time pressure through an "exploding offer" whereby they give their opponent a very short time to accept their offer.[69] These time-limited offers are frequently found in consumer sales ("on sale today only!") and in some job offers. They produce time pressure, which can motivate the other party to accept the offer and forfeit the opportunity to explore their BATNA. Another time factor is that the more time someone has invested in the negotiation, the more committed they become to ensuring an agreement is reached. This commitment increases the tendency to make unwarranted concessions so that the negotiations do not fail.

Manage First Offers and Concessions   Negotiators who make the first offer have the advantage of creating a position around which subsequent negotiations are anchored. As we explained in Chapter 7, people tend to adjust their expectations around the initial point, so a high/low first bid tends to push the other party more quickly toward their resistance point along the bargaining zone.[70] It may even cause opponents to lower their resistance point.

After the first offer, negotiators need to make concessions. Concessions serve at least three important purposes: (1) they enable the parties to move toward the area of potential agreement, (2) they symbolize each party's motivation to bargain in good faith, and (3) they tell the other party of the relative importance of the negotiating items.[71] However, concessions need to be clearly labelled as such and should be accompanied by an expectation that the other party will reciprocate. They should also be offered in instalments because people experience more positive emotions from a few smaller concessions than from one large concession.[72] Generally, the best strategy is to be moderately tough and give just enough concessions to communicate sincerity and motivation to resolve the conflict.[73]

STRATEGIES FOR CREATING VALUE

An opposing objective to claiming value in negotiations is creating value, which involves cooperating to help both negotiators obtain the best possible outcomes.

In other words, negotiators need to apply the problem-solving approach to conflict handling. Information exchange is a critical feature of creating value, but it is also a potential pitfall. Information is power in negotiations, so information sharing gives the other party more power to leverage a better deal if the opportunity occurs.[74] Skilled negotiators address this dilemma by adopting a cautious problem-solving style at the outset. They begin by sharing information slowly and determining whether the other side will reciprocate. In this way, they try to establish trust with the other party. Here are several ways that skilled negotiators reap the benefits of problem-solving and value creation.

Gather Information   Information is the corner stone of effective value creation.[75] Therefore, skilled negotiators heed the advice of management guru Stephen Covey: "Seek first to understand, then to be understood."[76] This means that we should present our case only after spending more time listening closely to the other party and asking for details. It is particularly important to look beyond the opponent's stated justifications to the unstated motivation for their claims. Probing questions (such as asking "why") and listening intently can reveal better solutions for both parties. Negotiating in teams can also aid the information gathering process because some team members will hear information that others have ignored.

Discover Priorities Through Offers and Concessions   Some types of offers and concessions are better than others at creating value. The key objective is to discover and signal which issues are more and less important to each side. Suppose another division is "seconding" (temporarily transferring) some of your best staff to their projects, whereas you need these people on site for other assignments and to coach junior staff. Through problem-solving negotiation, you discover that the other division doesn't need those staff at their site; rather the division head mainly needs some guarantee that these people will be available. The result is that your division keeps the staff (important to you) while the other division has some guarantee these people will be available at specific times for their projects (important to them).

One way to figure out the relative importance of the issues to each party is to make multi-issue offers rather than discussing one issue at a time.[77] You might offer a client a specific price, delivery date, and guarantee period, for example. The other party's counteroffer to multiple items signals which are more and which are less important to them. Your subsequent concessions similarly signal how important each issue is to your group.

Build the Relationship   Trust is critical for the problem-solving style of conflict handling as well as in the value creation objective of negotiations.[78] How do you build trust in negotiations? One approach is to discover common backgrounds and interests, such as places you have lived, favourite hobbies and sports teams, and so forth. If there are substantial differences between the parties (age, gender, etc.), consider having team members who more closely match the backgrounds of the other party. First impressions are also important. Recall from earlier chapters in this book that people attach emotions to incoming stimuli in a fraction of a second. Therefore, you need to be sensitive to your nonverbal cues, appearance, and initial statements.

Signalling that we are trustworthy also helps strengthen the relationship. We can do this by demonstrating that we are reliable and will keep our promises as well as by identifying shared goals and values. Trustworthiness also increases by developing a shared understanding of the negotiation process, including its norms and expectations about speed and timing.[79] Finally, relationship building demands emotional intelligence.[80] This includes managing the emotions you display to the other party, particularly avoiding an image of superiority, aggressiveness, or insensitivity. Emotional intelligence also involves managing the other party's emotions. We can use well-placed

Disney's Patient Negotiating Builds Relationships

Global negotiations are complex and require highly skilled negotiators. Often they involve negotiations with governments, who bring both social and economic interests to the negotiation table. Task-oriented and time pressured westerners also need to remember the importance of relationship building not to mention the very different timeframes over which agreement is reached. A key skill for the Walt Disney Co., who have been negotiating with the Shanghai Municipal Government about the construction of the first Disneyland in mainland China, has been patience. When Shanghai's mayor Han Zheng announced that agreement had been reached he added that "the government has been in talks with Disney for more than 10 years, and the two sides have kept smooth communication."[81] *ALY SONG/ Reuters/Landov*

flattery, humour, and other methods to keep everyone in a good mood and to break unnecessary tension.[82]

SITUATIONAL INFLUENCES ON NEGOTIATIONS

The effectiveness of negotiating depends to some extent on the environment in which the negotiations occur. Three key situational factors are location, physical setting, and audience.

Location   It is easier to negotiate on your own turf because you are familiar with the negotiating environment and are able to maintain comfortable routines.[83] Also, there is no need to cope with travel-related stress or depend on others for resources during the negotiation. Of course, you can't walk out of negotiations as easily when on your own turf, but this is usually a minor issue. Considering these strategic benefits of home turf, many negotiators agree to neutral territory. Phone calls, videoconferences, and other forms of information technology potentially avoid territorial issues, but skilled negotiators usually prefer the media richness of face-to-face meetings. Frank Lowy, co-founder of retail property giant Westfield Group, says that telephones are "too cold" for negotiating. "From a voice I don't get all the cues I need. I go by touch and feel and I need to see the other person."[84]

Physical Setting   The physical distance between the parties and formality of the setting can influence their orientation toward each other and the disputed issues. So can the seating arrangements. People who sit face to face are more likely to develop a win–lose orientation toward the conflict situation. In contrast, some negotiation groups deliberately intersperse participants around the table to convey a win–win orientation. Others arrange the seating so that both parties face a white board, reflecting the notion that both parties face the same problem or issue.

Audience Characteristics   Most negotiators have audiences—anyone with a vested interest in the negotiation outcomes, such as executives, other team members, or the general public. Negotiators tend to act differently when their audience observes the negotiation or has detailed information about the process, compared to situations in which the audience sees only the end results.[85] When the audience has direct surveillance over the proceedings, negotiators tend to be more competitive, less willing to make concessions, and more likely to engage in political tactics against the other party. This "hardline" behaviour shows the audience that the negotiator is working for their interests. With their audience watching, negotiators also have more interest in saving face.

CHAPTER SUMMARY

 LO1 Define conflict and debate its positive and negative consequences in the workplace.

Conflict is the process in which one party perceives that its interests are being opposed or negatively affected by another party. The earliest view of conflict was that it was dysfunctional for organizations. Even today, we recognize that conflict sometimes or to some degree consumes productive time, increases stress and job dissatisfaction, discourages coordination and resource sharing, undermines customer service, fuels organizational politics, and undermines team cohesion. But conflict can also be beneficial. It is known to motivate more active thinking about problems and possible solutions, encourage more active monitoring of the organization in its environment, and improve team cohesion (where the conflict source is external).

 LO2 Distinguish constructive from relationship conflict and describe three strategies to minimize relationship conflict during constructive conflict episodes.

Constructive conflict occurs when people focus their discussion around the issue while showing respect for people with other points of view. Relationship conflict exists when people view each other, rather than the issue, as the source of conflict. It is apparent when people attack each other's credibility and display aggression towards the other party. It is difficult to separate constructive from relationship conflict. However, three strategies or conditions that minimize relationship conflict during constructive debate are: (1) emotional intelligence of the participants, (2) team cohesion, and (3) supportive team norms.

 LO3 Diagram the conflict process model and describe six structural sources of conflict in organizations.

The conflict process model begins with the five structural sources of conflict: incompatible goals, differentiation (different values and beliefs), interdependence, scarce resources, ambiguous rules, and communication problems. These sources lead one or more parties to perceive a conflict and to experience conflict emotions. This, in turn, produces manifest conflict, such as behaviours toward the other side. The conflict process often escalates through a series of episodes.

 LO4 Outline the five conflict handling styles and discuss the circumstances in which each would be most appropriate.

There are five known conflict handling styles: problem solving, forcing, avoiding, yielding, and compromising. People who use problem solving have a win-win orientation. Others, particularly forcing, assume a win-lose orientation. In general, people gravitate toward one or two preferred conflict handling styles that match their personality, personal and cultural values, and past experience.

The best style depends on the situation. Problem solving is best when interests are not perfectly opposing, the parties trust each other, and the issues are complex. Forcing works best when you strongly believe in your position, the dispute requires quick action, and the other party would take advantage of a cooperative style. Avoiding is preferred when the conflict has become emotional or the cost of resolution is higher than its benefits. Yielding works well when the other party has substantially more power, the issue is less important to you, and you are not confident in the logical soundness of your position. Compromising is preferred when the parties have equal power, they are under time pressure, and they lack trust.

 LO5 Apply the six structural approaches to conflict management and describe the three types of third-party dispute resolution.

Structural approaches to conflict management include emphasizing superordinate goals, reducing differentiation, improving communication and understanding, reducing interdependence, increasing resources, and clarifying rules and procedures.

Third-party conflict resolution is any attempt by a relatively neutral person to help the parties resolve their differences. The three main forms of third-party dispute resolution are mediation, arbitration, and inquisition. Managers tend to use an inquisition approach, although mediation and arbitration are more appropriate, depending on the situation.

 LO6 Describe the bargaining zone model and outline strategies skilled negotiators use to claim value and create value in negotiations.

Negotiation occurs whenever two or more conflicting parties attempt to resolve their divergent goals by redefining the terms of their interdependence. The bargaining zone model identifies three strategic positions for each party (initial, target, resistance) and shows how each party moves along a continuum in opposite directions with an area of potential overlap. All negotiations consist of two divergent objectives: claiming value (getting the best personal outcome) and creating value (discover ways to achieve mutually satisfactory outcomes for both parties). Skilled negotiators claim more value by preparing and setting goals, knowing their alternatives to the negotiation (BATNA), managing time to their advantage, and managing first offers and concessions. Skilled negotiators create more value by gathering information, using offers and concessions to discover issue priorities, and building relationships with the other party. The situation is also an important consideration in negotiations, including location, physical setting, and audience characteristics.

KEY TERMS

best alternative to a negotiated
   agreement (BATNA), p. 315
conflict, p. 298
constructive conflict, p. 300

negotiation, p. 313
relationship conflicts, p. 300
superordinate goal, p. 309
third-party conflict resolution, p. 311

win–lose orientation, p. 306
win–win orientation, p. 306

CRITICAL-THINKING QUESTIONS

1. Distinguish constructive conflict from relationship conflict and explain how to apply the former with minimal levels of the latter.

2. The chief executive officer of Creative Toys, Inc. read about cooperation in Japanese companies and vowed to bring this same philosophy to the company. The goal is to avoid all conflict, so that employees would work cooperatively and be happier at Creative Toys. Discuss the merits and limitations of the CEO's policy.

3. Conflict among managers emerged soon after a French company acquired a Swedish firm. The Swedes perceived the French management as hierarchical and arrogant, whereas the French thought the Swedes were naive, cautious, and lacking an achievement orientation. Describe ways to reduce dysfunctional conflict in this situation.

4. This chapter describes three levels of interdependence that exist in interpersonal and intergroup relationships. Identify examples of these three levels in your work or school activities. How do these three levels affect potential conflict for you?

5. You are a special assistant to the commander-in-chief of a peacekeeping mission to a war-torn part of the world. The unit consists of a few thousand peacekeeping troops from Canada, France, India, and four other countries. The troops will work together for approximately one year. What strategies would you recommend to improve mutual understanding and minimize conflict among these troops?

6. The chief operating officer (COO) has noticed that production employees in the company's Mexican manufacturing operations are unhappy with some of the production engineering decisions made by engineers in the company's headquarters in Toronto. At the same time, the engineers complain that production employees aren't applying their engineering specifications correctly and don't understand why those specifications were put in place. The COO believes that the best way to resolve this conflict is to have a frank and open discussion between some of the engineers and employees representing the Mexican production crew. This open dialogue approach worked well recently among managers in the company's Toronto headquarters, so should work equally well between the engineers and production staff. Based on your knowledge of communication and mutual understanding as a way to resolve conflict, discuss the COO's proposal.

7. Describe the inquisitional approach to resolve disputes between employees or work units. Discuss its appropriateness in organizational settings including the suitability of its use with a multigenerational workforce.

8. Jane has just been appointed as purchasing manager of Sechelt Technologies Ltd. The previous purchasing manager, who recently retired, was known for his "winner-take-all" approach to suppliers. He continually fought for more discounts and was skeptical about any special deals that suppliers would propose. A few suppliers refused to do business with Sechelt Technologies, but senior management was confident that the former purchasing manager's approach minimized the company's costs. Jane wants to try a more collaborative approach to working with suppliers. Will her approach work? How should she adopt a more collaborative approach in future negotiations with suppliers?

 CASE STUDY 11.1

Tamarack Industries

By David J. Cherrington, Brigham Young University

Tamarack Industries manufactures motor boats primarily used for water skiing. During the summer months, a third production line is normally created to help meet the heavy summer demand. This third line is usually created by assigning the experienced workers to all three lines and hiring college and university students who are home for summer vacation to complete the crews. In the past, however, experienced workers resented having to break up their teams to form a third line. They also resented having to work with a bunch of college and university kids and complained that the kids were slow and arrogant.

   The supervisor, Dan Jensen, decided to try a different strategy this summer and have all the students work on the new line. He asked Mark Allen to supervise the new crew because Mark claimed that he knew everything about boats and could perform every job "with my eyes closed." Mark was happy to accept the new job and participated in selecting his own crew. Mark's crew was called "The Geek Team" because the students were always talking about computer technology.

Mark spent many hours in training to get his group running at full production. The students learned quickly, and by the end of June their production rate was up to standard, with an error rate that was only slightly above normal. To simplify the learning process, Dan Jensen assigned the Geek Team long production runs that generally consisted of 30 to 40 identical units. Thus the training period was shortened and errors were reduced. Shorter production runs were assigned to the experienced teams.

By the middle of July, a substantial rivalry had been created between the Geek Team and the older workers. At first, the rivalry was good-natured. But after a few weeks, the older workers became resentful of the remarks made by the students. The Geek Team often met its production schedules with time to spare at the end of the day for goofing around. It wasn't uncommon for someone from the Geek Team to go to another line pretending to look for materials just to make demeaning comments. The experienced workers resented having to perform all the shorter production runs and began to retaliate with sabotage. They would sneak over during breaks and hide tools, dent materials, install something crooked, and in other small ways do something that would slow production for the Geek Team.

Dan felt good about his decision to form a separate crew of students, but when he heard reports of sabotage and rivalry, he became very concerned. Because of complaints from the experienced workers, Dan equalized the production so that all of the crews had similar production runs. The rivalry, however, did not stop. The Geek Team continued to finish early and flaunt their performance in front of the other crews.

One day the Geek Team suspected that one of their assemblies was going to be sabotaged during the lunch break by one of the experienced crews. By skillful deception, they were able to substitute an assembly from the other experienced line for their's. By the end of the lunch period, the Geek Team was laughing wildly because of their deception, while one experienced crew was very angry with the other one.

Dan Jensen decided that the situation had to be changed and announced that the job assignments between the different crews would be shuffled. The employees were told that when they appeared for work the next morning, the names of the workers assigned to each crew would be posted on the bulletin board. The announcement was not greeted with much enthusiasm, and Mark Allen decided to stay late to try to talk Dan out of his idea. Mark didn't believe the rivalry was serious enough for this type of action, and he suspected that many of the students would quit if their team was broken up.

Discussion Questions

1. What are the signs (symptoms) of conflict in this case?

2. Use the conflict model to (a) identify the structural causes of conflict and (b) discuss the escalation of conflict described in this case.

3. If you were Dan Jensen, what action would you take in this situation?

 CLASS EXERCISE 11.2

The Contingencies of Conflict Handling

By Gerard A. Callanan and David F. Perri, West Chester University of Pennsylvania

Purpose   This exercise is designed to help you understand the contingencies of applying conflict handling styles in organizational settings.

Instructions
- *Step 1:* Participants will read each of the five scenarios presented below and select the most appropriate response from among the five alternatives. Each scenario has a best response for that situation.

- *Step 2 (Optional):* The instructor may ask each student to complete the conflict handling self-assessment exercise in this chapter (Self-Assessment Exercise 11.4) or a similar instrument. This instrument will provide an estimate of your preferred conflict handling style.

- *Step 3:* As a class, participants give their feedback on the responses to each of the scenarios, with the instructor guiding discussion on the contextual factors embodied in each scenario. For each scenario, the class should identify the response selected by the majority. In addition, participants will discuss how they decided on the choices they made and the contextual factors they took into account in making their selections.

- *Step 4:* Students will compare their responses to the five scenarios with their results from the conflict handling self-assessment. Discussion will focus on the extent to which each person's preferred conflict handling style influenced their alternatives in this activity, and the implications of this style preference for managing conflict in organizations.

Scenario #1

Setting   You are a manager of a division in the accounting department of a large Canadian bank. Nine exempt-level analysts and six nonexempt clerical staff report to you. Recently, one of your analysts, Jane Wilson, has sought the bank's approval for tuition reimbursement for the cost of an evening MBA program specializing in organizational behaviour. The bank normally encourages employees to seek advanced degrees on a part-time basis. Indeed, through your encouragement, nearly all of the members of your staff are pursuing additional schoolwork. You consult the bank's policy manual and discover that two approvals are necessary for reimbursement—yours and that of the manager of training and development, Kathy Gordon. Further, the manual states that approval for reimbursement will only be granted if the coursework is "reasonably job related." Based on your review of the matter, you decide to approve Jane's request for reimbursement. However, Kathy Gordon rejects it outright by claiming that coursework in organizational behaviour is not related to an accounting analyst position. She states that the bank will only reimburse the analyst for a degree in either accounting or finance. In your opinion, however, the interpersonal skills and insights to be gained from a degree in organizational behaviour are job related and can also benefit the employee in future assignments. The analyst job requires interaction with a variety of individuals at different levels in the organization, and it is important that interpersonal and communication skills be strong.

After further discussion it becomes clear that you and Kathy Gordon have opposite views on the matter. Since both of you are at the same organization level and have equal status, it appears that you are at an impasse. Although the goal of reimbursement is important, you are faced with other pressing demands on your time. In addition, the conflict has diverted the attention of your work group away from its primary responsibilities. Because the school term is about to begin, it is essential that you and Kathy Gordon reach a timely agreement to enable Jane to pursue her coursework.

Action Alternatives for Scenario #1   Please indicate your first (1) and second (2) choices from among the following alternatives by writing the appropriate number in the space provided.

Action Alternative	Ranking (1st & 2nd)
1. You go along with Kathy Gordon's view and advise Jane Wilson to select either accounting or finance as a major for her MBA.	_____
2. You decide to withdraw from the situation completely, and tell Jane to work it out with Kathy Gordon on her own.	_____
3. You decide to take the matter to those in higher management levels and argue forcefully for your point of view. You do everything in your power to ensure that a decision will be made in your favour.	_____
4. You decide to meet Kathy Gordon halfway in order to reach an agreement. You advise Jane to pursue her MBA in accounting or finance, but also recommend she minor in organizational behaviour by taking electives in that field.	_____
5. You decide to work more closely with Kathy Gordon by attempting to get a clear as well as flexible policy written that reflects both of your views. Of course, this will require a significant amount of your time.	_____

Scenario #2

Setting   You are the vice-president of a relatively large division (80 employees) in a medium-sized consumer products company. Due to the recent turnover of visible minority staff, your division has fallen behind in meeting the company's goal for employment equity hiring. Because of a scarcity of qualified visible minority candidates, it appears that you may fall further behind in achieving stated employment equity goals.

Although you are aware of the problem, you believe that the low level of visible minority hiring is due to increased attrition in visible minority staff as well as the lack of viable replacement candidates. However, the employment equity officer believes that your hiring criteria are too stringent, resulting in the rejection of visible minority candidates with the basic qualifications to do the job. You support the goals and principles of employment equity; however, you are concerned that the hiring of less-qualified candidates will weaken the performance of your division. The employment equity officer believes that your failure to hire visible minority employees is damaging to the company in the short term because corporate goals will not be met, and in the long term because it will restrict the pool of visible minority candidates available for upward mobility. Both of you regard your concerns as important. Further, you recognize that both of you have the company's best interests in mind and that you have a mutual interest in resolving the conflict.

Action Alternatives for Scenario #2   Please indicate your first (1) and second (2) choices from among the following alternatives by writing the appropriate number in the space provided.

Action Alternative	Ranking (1st & 2nd)
1. You conclude that the whole problem is too complex an issue for you to handle right now. You put it on the "back burner" and decide to reconsider the problem at a later date.	_____
2. You believe that your view outweighs the perspective of the employment equity officer. You decide to argue your position more vigorously and hope that your stance will sway the employment equity officer to agree with your view.	_____
3. You decide to accept the employment equity officer's view. You agree to use less stringent selection criteria and thereby hire more visible minority employees.	_____
4. You give in to the employment equity officer somewhat by agreeing to relax your standards a little bit. This would allow slightly more visible minority hiring (but not enough to satisfy the employment equity goal) and could cause a small reduction in the overall performance of your division.	_____
5. You try and reach a consensus that addresses each of your concerns. You agree to work harder at hiring more visible minority applicants and request that the employment equity officer agree to help find the most qualified visible minority candidates available.	_____

Scenario #3

Setting   You are the manager in charge of the financial reporting section of a large insurance company. It is the responsibility of your group to make periodic written and oral reports to senior management regarding the company's financial performance. The company's senior management has come to rely on your quick and accurate dissemination of financial data as a way to make vital decisions in a timely fashion. This has given you a relatively high degree of organizational influence. You rely on various operating departments to supply you with financial information according to a pre-established reporting schedule.

In two days, you must make your quarterly presentation to the company's board of directors. However, the Claims department has failed to supply you with several key pieces of information that are critical to your presentation. You check the reporting schedule and realize that you should have had the information two days ago. When you call Bill Jones, the Claims department manager, he informs you that he cannot possibly have the data to you within the next two days. He states that other pressing work has a higher priority. Although you explain the critical need for this data, he is unwilling to change his position. You believe that your presentation is vital to the company's welfare and explain this to Bill Jones. Although Bill has less status than you, he has been known to take advantage of individuals who are unwilling or unable to push their point of view. With your presentation less than two days away, it is critical that you receive information from the Claims department within the next 24 hours.

Action Alternatives for Scenario #3

Action Alternatives for Scenario #3

Please indicate your first (1) and second (2) choices from among the following alternatives by writing the appropriate number in the space provided.

Action Alternative	Ranking (1st & 2nd)
1. Accept the explanation from Bill Jones and try to get by without the figures by using your best judgment as to what they would be.	_____
2. Tell Bill Jones that unless you have the data from his department on your desk by tomorrow morning, you will be forced to go over his head to compel him to give you the numbers.	_____
3. Meet Bill Jones halfway by agreeing to receive part of the needed figures and using your own judgment on the others.	_____
4. Try to get your presentation postponed until a later date, if possible.	_____
5. Forget about the short-term need for information and try to achieve a longer term solution, such as adjusting the reporting schedule to better accommodate your mutual needs.	_____

Scenario #4

Setting

You are the production manager of a medium-sized building products company. You control a production line that runs on a three-shift basis. Recently, Ted Smith, the materials handling manager, requested you to accept a different packaging of the raw materials for the production process than what has been customary. He states that new machinery he has installed makes it much easier to provide the material in 45-kilogram sacks instead of the 22-kilogram bags that you currently receive. Ted further explains that the provision of the material in the 22-kilogram bags would put an immense strain on his operation, and he therefore has a critical need for you to accept the change. You know that accepting materials in the new packaging will cause some minor disruption in your production process, but should not cause long-term problems for any of the three shifts. However, you are a little annoyed by the proposed change because Ted did not consult with you before he installed the new equipment. In the past, you and he have been open in your communication. You do not think that this failure to consult you represents a change in your relationship.

Because you work closely with Ted, it is essential that you maintain the harmonious and stable working relationship that you have built over the past few years. In addition, you may need some help from him in the future, since you already know that your operation will have special material requirements in about two months. You also know that Ted has influence at higher levels of the organization.

Action Alternatives for Scenario #4

Please indicate your first (1) and second (2) choices from among the following alternatives by writing the appropriate number in the space provided.

Action Alternative	Ranking (1st & 2nd)
1. Agree to accept the raw material in the different format.	_____
2. Refuse to accept the material in the new format because it would cause a disruption in your operation.	_____
3. Propose a solution where you accept material in the new format during the first shift, but not during the second and third.	_____
4. Tell Ted Smith that you do not wish to deal with the issue at this time, but that you will consider his request and get back to him at a later date.	_____
5. You decide to tell Ted Smith of your concern regarding his failure to consult with you before installing new equipment. You inform him that you wish to find longer term solutions to the conflict between you.	_____

Scenario #5

Setting   You are employed as supervisor of the compensation and benefits section in the human resources department of a medium-sized pharmaceutical company. Your staff of three clerks is responsible for maintaining contacts with the various benefits providers and answering related questions from the company's employees. Your section shares support staff and copier resources with the training and development section of the department. Recently, a disagreement has arisen between you and Beth Hanson, the training and development supervisor, over when the support staff should take their lunch break. Beth would like the support staff to take their lunches an hour later to coincide with the time most of her people go to lunch. You know that the support staff do not want to change their lunch times. Further, the current time is more convenient for your staff.

At this time, you are hard-pressed to deal with the situation. You have an important meeting with the provider of dental insurance in two days. It is critical that you are well prepared for this meeting, and these other tasks are a distraction.

Action Alternatives for Scenario #5   Please indicate your first (1) and second (2) choices from among the following alternatives by writing the appropriate number in the space provided.

Action Alternative	Ranking (1st & 2nd)
1. Take some time over the next day and propose a solution whereby three days a week the support staff take their lunch at the earlier time and two days at the later.	_____
2. Tell Beth Hanson you will deal with the matter in a few days, after you have addressed the more pressing issues.	_____
3. Let Beth Hanson have her way by agreeing to a later lunch hour for the support staff.	_____
4. Flat out tell Beth Hanson that you will not agree to a change in the support staff's lunchtime.	_____
5. Devote more time to the issue. Attempt to achieve a broad-based consensus with Beth Hanson that meets her needs as well as yours and those of the support staff.	_____

Source: Based on G. A. Callanan and D. F. Perri, "Teaching Conflict Management Using a Scenario-Based Approach," *Journal of Education for Business* 81 (January/February 2006), pp. 131–139.

 **TEAM EXERCISE 11.3**

Ugli Orange Role Play

Purpose This exercise is designed to help you understand the dynamics of interpersonal and intergroup conflict as well as the effectiveness of negotiation strategies under specific conditions.

Materials The instructor will distribute roles for Dr. Roland, Dr. Jones, and a few observers. Ideally, each negotiation should occur in a private area away from other negotiations.

Instructions
- *Step 1:* The instructor will divide the class into an even number of teams of three people each, with one participant left over for each team formed (e.g., six observers if there are six teams). One-half of the teams will take the role of Dr. Roland and the other half will be Dr. Jones. The instructor will distribute roles after these teams have been formed.

- *Step 2:* Members within each team are given 10 minutes (or other time limit stated by the instructor) to learn their roles and decide negotiating strategy.

- *Step 3:* After reading their roles and discussing strategy, each Dr. Jones team is matched with a Dr. Roland team to conduct negotiations. Observers will receive observation forms from the instructor, and two observers will be assigned to watch the paired teams during prenegotiations and subsequent negotiations.

- *Step 4:* As soon as Roland and Jones reach agreement or at the end of the time allotted for the negotiation (which ever comes first), the Roland and Jones teams report to the instructor for further instruction.

- *Step 5:* At the end of the exercise, the class will congregate to discuss the negotiations. Observers, negotiators, and the instructor will then discuss their observations and experiences and the implications for conflict management and negotiation.

Note: This exercise was developed by Robert J House, Wharton Business School, University of Pennsylvania. A similar activity is also attributed to earlier writing by R. R. Blake and J. S. Mouton.

....

Go to CONNECT to complete the following interactive self-assessment.

 SELF-ASSESSMENT EXERCISE 11.4

What is Your Preferred Conflict Handling Style?

Purpose This self-assessment is designed to help you identify your preferred conflict management style.

Instructions Read each of the statements below and select the response that best indicates how often you handled conflict in the way described in that statement. Then use the scoring key in Appendix B to calculate your results for each conflict management style. This exercise is completed alone so students assess themselves honestly without concerns of social comparison. However, class discussion will focus on the different conflict management styles and the situations in which each is most appropriate.

Conflict Handling Scale					
Over the past SIX MONTHS, how often did you do the following to handle conflicts?	Never/Rarely	Seldom	Sometimes	Often	Almost Always
1. I went along with the other party's wishes rather than my own.	☐	☐	☐	☐	☐
2. I compromised by accepting a middle ground solution.	☐	☐	☐	☐	☐
3. I tried to creatively find the best solution for everyone.	☐	☐	☐	☐	☐
4. I avoided differences of opinion as much as possible.	☐	☐	☐	☐	☐
5. I pushed my own ideas and preferences.	☐	☐	☐	☐	☐
6. I tried to make the dispute seem less important.	☐	☐	☐	☐	☐
7. I accommodated the other party's wishes.	☐	☐	☐	☐	☐
8. I did my best to get what I wanted.	☐	☐	☐	☐	☐
9. I tried to figure out how to satisfy both my interests and the other party's.	☐	☐	☐	☐	☐
10. I made sure that both sides gave in a little.	☐	☐	☐	☐	☐
11. I worked toward a 50–50 compromise.	☐	☐	☐	☐	☐
12. I fought for my own position.	☐	☐	☐	☐	☐
13. I searched for a solution that satisfied both parties.	☐	☐	☐	☐	☐
14. I delayed or avoided solving the disagreement.	☐	☐	☐	☐	☐
15. I held my position.	☐	☐	☐	☐	☐
16. I let the other side have its way.	☐	☐	☐	☐	☐
17. I tried to settle the conflict with a half-way compromise.	☐	☐	☐	☐	☐
18. I tried to find a solution that benefited both sides.	☐	☐	☐	☐	☐
19. I avoided communicating with the people I had the conflict.	☐	☐	☐	☐	☐
20. I gave the other party what they wanted.	☐	☐	☐	☐	☐

Sources: This scale was created by Steven L. McShane based on information or previous instruments in: R. R. Blake, H. A. Shepard, and J. S. Mouton, *Managing Intergroup Conflict in Industry* (Houston: Gulf Publishing, 1964); K. W. Thomas, "Conflict and Negotiation Processes in Organizations," in *Handbook of Industrial and Organizational Psychology,* edited by M. D. Dunnette and L. M. Hough, pp. 651–718, 2nd ed. (Palo Alto, CA: Consulting Psychologists Press, 1992); C. K. W. de Dreu, A. Evers, B. Beersma, E. S. Kluwer, and A. Nauta, "A Theory-based Measure of Conflict Management Strategies in the Workplace," *Journal of Organizational Behavior* 22 (2001), pp. 645–68; and M. A. Rahim, *Managing Conflict in Organizations,* 4th ed. (New Brunswick, NJ: Transaction Publishers, 2011).

Practise and learn online with Connect. Connect resources include additional and interactive study exercises, videos, and practice quizzing, as well as additional material you won't find in the printed text.

CHAPTER 12

Leadership in Organizational Settings

After reading this chapter, you should be able to:

LO1 Define leadership and shared leadership.

LO2 Identify eight competencies associated with effective leaders and describe authentic leadership.

LO3 Describe the key features of directive, supportive, and servant leadership, and discuss their effects on followers.

LO4 Discuss the key elements of path-goal theory, Fiedler's contingency model, and leadership substitutes.

LO5 Describe the four elements of transformational leadership and distinguish this theory from transactional and charismatic leadership.

LO6 Describe the implicit leadership perspective.

LO7 Discuss cultural and gender similarities and differences in leadership.

Moya Greene, former president and chief executive of Canada Post has taken on a new leadership challenge as CEO of Britain's Royal Mail. Early in her career Greene's reputation as an effective leader was recognized as she moved through the ranks in Canada's federal public service. Barbara McDougall who was minister of Human Resources Development Canada at the time recalls Greene as "intelligent, conscientious, creative." Mount Allison University president, Robert Campbell describes Greene's approach to leadership as: "She's got a good kind of Newfoundland toughness to her."

This toughness, which included cost-cutting, not replacing many retiring workers, and taking on high levels of employee absenteeism did not always sit well with the Canadian Union of Postal Workers. But Greene's confidence, drive, and willingness to learn all she could about the mail delivery business put her out on the front lines with Canada Post employees. She delivered mail with letter carriers, sorted mail during hot summer night shifts, and experienced first hand what it was like to work in a crumbling Canada Post building in downtown Winnipeg. Despite declining revenues brought on by the worldwide reduction of mail volumes due to alternatives such as email and online banking, Greene kept Canada Post profitable. Under her leadership Canada Post also reduced accident rates, maintained labour stability, and transformed facilities through a $2.1 billion investment in aging infrastructure.

Known for her energy and decisiveness, Greene is the first woman and first foreigner to head Britain's 350 year-old mail service. Her leadership style is likely a good fit for Royal Mail. Britain's new coalition government plans to sell off up to 49 percent of Royal Mail requiring a leader able to deliver on "postal transformation," an accomplishment Greene is credited with during her five year service to Canada Post.

Greene's new boss, Royal Mail chairman Donald Brydon, says she brings "energy, clear thinking and a proven leadership track record." In her new job, Greene is Britain's highest paid female public servant, earning approximately $800,000 a year. In her characteristic matter-of-fact style she describes the challenge and opportunity: "Hopefully I won't walk in too many cow pies," Greene says.[1]

Moya Greene brings her leadership qualities from Canada Post to the top job at Britain's Royal Mail. *Reuters/Canada Post/ Royal Mail/Landov*

The world is changing, and so is our concept of leadership. Yesteryear's command-and-control boss has become more of a liability than an asset. Also disappearing—but much more slowly—is the notion that leaders are charismatic heroes who stand in front of and far above their followers. Instead, as we learn in this chapter, leaders influence, motivate, and facilitate the performance and well-being of a group of people. The opening vignette to this chapter describes this emerging image of leadership in Moya Greene, who led Canada Post through substantial change.

WHAT IS LEADERSHIP?

L01

leadership Influencing, motivating, and enabling others to contribute toward the effectiveness and success of the organizations of which they are members.

A few years ago, 54 leadership experts from 38 countries reached a consensus that **leadership** is about influencing, motivating, and enabling others to contribute toward the effectiveness and success of the organizations of which they are members.[2] This definition has two key components. First, leaders motivate others through persuasion and other influence tactics. They use their communication skills, rewards, and other resources to energize the collective to achieve challenging objectives. Second, leaders are enablers. They arrange the work environment—such as allocating resources and altering communication patterns—so employees can achieve organizational objectives more easily.

Leadership is one of the most researched and discussed topics in the field of organizational behaviour. Google returns a whopping 724 million Web pages where either "leader" or "leadership" is mentioned (24 million of them have one of these words in the title). Google Scholar lists 173,000 journal articles and books that have one or both words in the title. Amazon, the online retailer, currently lists more than 55,000 printed leadership books. As Exhibit 12.1 illustrates, the number of leadership books and materials added to Library and Archives Canada's catalogue has grown exponentially over the past half-century. Why does the topic of leadership command so much attention? Possibly because leadership does make a difference to an organization's effectiveness. Furthermore, we are awed by individuals who influence and motivate others beyond expectations and build commitment to a better future.

Exhibit 12.1   **FILLING LIBRARY AND ARCHIVES CANADA WITH LEADERSHIP MATERIALS[3]**

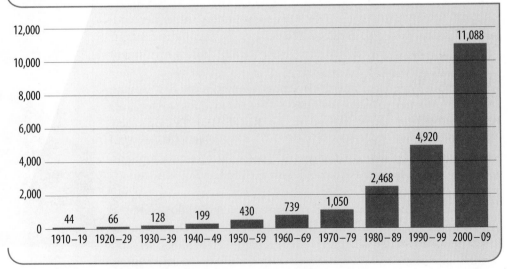

This exhibit shows the number of books and other materials with the subject of "leader" and its derivatives catalogued by Library and Archives Canada and currently listed in its catalogue, by decade that the item was published or produced. Library and Archives Canada is the fourth largest library in the world.

SHARED LEADERSHIP

Leadership isn't restricted to the executive suite. Employees throughout the organization need to informally assume leadership responsibilities in various ways and at various times.[4] This view, known as **shared leadership**, suggests that *leadership* is plural, not singular. It doesn't operate out of one formally assigned position, role, or individual. Instead, employees lead each other as the occasion arises.

shared leadership The view that leadership is broadly distributed, rather than assigned to one person, such that people within the team and organization lead each other.

The late John Gardner, a U.S. government leader who introduced medicare and public broadcasting, wrote that the "vitality" of large organizations depends on shared leadership.[5] Employees across all levels of the organization need to seek out opportunities and solutions to problems rather than rely on formal leaders to serve these roles. Gardner observed, for example, that successful teams consist of individuals other than the formal leader who take responsibility for healing rifts when conflicts arise, and for building confidence in others when events have turned for the worse. Various Canadian studies have also noted that employees step unofficially into leadership positions when they champion the introduction of new ideas and technologies.[6]

Shared leadership flourishes in organizations where the formal leaders are willing to delegate power and encourage employees to take initiative and risks without fear of failure (i.e., a learning orientation culture). Shared leadership also calls for a collaborative rather than internally competitive culture because employees take on shared leadership roles when co-workers support them for their initiative. Furthermore, shared leadership lacks formal authority, so it operates best when employees learn to influence others through their enthusiasm, logical analysis, and involvement of co-workers in their idea or vision.

Consider, for example, the emergence of shared leadership at Rolls-Royce Engine Services in Oakland, California. As part of its employee engagement initiative, the aircraft engine repair facility involved employees directly with clients, encouraged weekly huddles for information sharing, and accepted employee requests for less micromanagement. Employees not only experienced higher levels of engagement and empowerment; they also accepted more leadership responsibilities. "I saw people around me, all front-line employees, who were leaders," says a machine programmer at the Rolls-Royce Oakland plant. "They weren't actually leading the company, but they were people you would listen to and follow. We didn't have titles, but people had respect for what we did."[7] Some organizations, such as Semco SA and W. L. Gore & Associates, have nurtured shared leadership to such an extent that most formal leaders emerge from these shared leadership activities.[8]

As we mentioned earlier, there is probably more writing on leadership than on any other topic in organizational behaviour. Fortunately, most of this enormous volume of leadership literature can be distilled and organized into five perspectives: competency, behavioural, contingency, transformational, and implicit.[9] Although some of these

Shared Leadership at W. L. Gore & Associates

W. L. Gore & Associates has no formal (called vertical) leaders. Instead, the company's 9,000 associates work with champions of projects and other initiatives because they are willing to follow them. "There is no positional power," explains a Gore team leader. "You are only a leader if teams decide to respect and follow you." Diane Davidson discovered this extreme version of shared leadership when the newly hired apparel industry sales executive asked her "starting sponsor" to identify her boss. The sponsor replied that she had no boss and eventually advised her to "stop using the B-word." Davidson initially thought the company must have formal managers who downplayed their position, but she soon realized that Gore really is a shared leadership organization. "Your team is your boss, because you don't want to let them down," says Davidson. "Everyone's your boss, and no one's your boss." In fact, when Gore employees are asked in annual surveys "Are you a leader?" more than 50 percent of them answer "Yes."[10] *Courtesy of W. L. Gore & Associates, Inc.*

perspectives are currently more popular than others, each helps us to more fully understand the complex issue of leadership. This chapter explores each of these five perspectives of leadership. In the final section, we also consider cross-cultural and gender issues in organizational leadership.

COMPETENCY PERSPECTIVE OF LEADERSHIP

LO2

Since the beginning of recorded civilization, people have been interested in the personal characteristics that distinguish great leaders from the rest of us.[11] In the sixth century BCE, the Chinese philosopher Lao-tzu described effective leaders as selfless, honest, fair, and hardworking. The Greek philosopher Plato claimed that great leaders have wisdom and a superior capacity for logical thinking. For the past century, hundreds of leadership studies have tried to empirically identify the traits of effective leaders. However, a major review in the late 1940s concluded that no consistent list of traits could be distilled from this research. This conclusion was revised a decade later, suggesting that a few traits are associated with effective leaders.[12] These nonsignificant findings caused many scholars to give up their search for personal characteristics that distinguish effective leaders.

Over the past two decades, leadership experts have returned to the notion that effective leaders possess specific personal characteristics.[13] The earlier research was apparently plagued by methodological problems, lack of theoretical foundation, and inconsistent definitions of leadership. The emerging work has identified several leadership *competencies,* that is, skills, knowledge, aptitudes, and other personal characteristics that lead to superior performance (see Chapter 2). The main categories of leadership competencies are listed in Exhibit 12.2 and described below:[14]

- *Personality.* Most of the Big Five personality dimensions (see Chapter 2) are associated with effective leadership to some extent, but the strongest predictors are high levels of extroversion (outgoing, talkative, sociable, and assertive) and conscientiousness (careful, dependable, and self-disciplined). With high extroversion, effective leaders are comfortable having an influential role in social settings. With higher conscientiousness, effective leaders set higher goals for themselves (and others) and are more motivated to pursue those goals.

- *Self-concept.* Successful leaders have a complex, internally consistent, and clear self-concept of themselves as a leader (see Chapter 2). This "leader identity" also includes a positive self-evaluation, including high self-esteem, self-efficacy, and internal locus

Canadian Astronaut Named as Commander of International Space Station

Canadian Space Agency astronaut, Chris Hadfield has been promoted to serve as Canada's first commander of the International Space Station (ISS). Hadfield's appointment to lead a team of international astronauts in 2013 was recently announced by NASA and its Space Station partners. An astronaut since 1995, Hadfield has extensive knowledge of the business. He is a former CF-18 and test pilot and is able to fly 70 types of aircraft including the Russian Soyuz capsule, which is the only emergency escape route for the ISS. Hadfield is the first Canadian to perform a space walk, and while serving as a mission specialist, travelled on space shuttle Atlantis to rendezvous with the Russian space station Mir. Motivated to lead others from an early age, Hadfield took part in his first leadership course as a 13-year-old military cadet. He retired as a colonel with the Canadian Forces and is recognized as a confident leader willing to share decision making to solve complex problems. "It's actually a very flat command structure; there are very few decisions I'm going to make unilaterally. It would mainly be when there is a time constraint, such as when we have a fire or a leak," explains Hadfield.[15] *AP Photo/Peter Cosgrove*

Exhibit 12.2 \ COMPETENCIES OF EFFECTIVE LEADERS

Leadership Competency	Description
Personality	The leader's higher levels of extroversion (outgoing, talkative, sociable, and assertive) and conscientiousness (careful, dependable, and self-disciplined).
Self-concept	The leader's self-beliefs and positive self-evaluation about his or her own leadership skills and ability to achieve objectives.
Drive	The leader's inner motivation to pursue goals.
Integrity	The leader's truthfulness and tendency to translate words into deeds.
Leadership motivation	The leader's need for socialized power to accomplish team or organizational goals.
Knowledge of the business	The leader's tacit and explicit knowledge about the company's environment, enabling the leader to make more intuitive decisions.
Cognitive and practical intelligence	The leader's above-average cognitive ability to process information (cognitive intelligence) and ability to solve real-world problems by adapting to, shaping, or selecting appropriate environments (practical intelligence).
Emotional intelligence	The leader's ability to monitor his or her own and others' emotions, discriminate among them, and use the information to guide his or her thoughts and actions.

of control.[16] In short, effective leaders define themselves as leaders and are confident with this self-view.

- *Drive.* Related to their high conscientiousness and positive self-concept, successful leaders have a high need for achievement (see Chapter 5). This drive represents the inner motivation that leaders possess to pursue their goals and encourage others to move forward with theirs. Drive inspires inquisitiveness, an action orientation, and boldness to take the organization or team into uncharted waters. This characteristic, among others, is quite apparent in Moya Greene, who we described at the beginning of this chapter.

 Effective leaders have an inner motivation to pursue their goals and encourage others to move forward with theirs. **"**

- *Integrity.* Integrity involves truthfulness and consistency of words and actions, qualities that are related to honesty and ethical conduct. Leaders have a high moral capacity to judge dilemmas using sound values and to act accordingly. Notice that integrity is ultimately based on the leader's values, which provide an anchor for consistency. Several large-scale studies have reported that integrity and honesty are the most important characteristics of effective leaders.[17] Unfortunately, recent surveys report that employees don't trust their leaders and don't think they have integrity. One global poll reported that only 53 percent of employees in North America and 48 percent in UK/Ireland trust senior management. Another recent survey reported that only 11 percent of the 2,000 American respondents strongly agreed that their managers have consistency between their words and actions.[18]

- *Leadership motivation.* Effective leaders are motivated to lead others. They have a strong need for *socialized power,* meaning that they want power as a means to accomplish organizational objectives and similar good deeds. This contrasts with a need for *personalized power,* which is the desire to have power for personal gain or for the thrill one might experience from wielding power over others (see Chapter 5).[19] Leadership motivation is also necessary because, even in collegial firms, leaders are in contests for positions further up the hierarchy. Effective leaders thrive rather than wither in the face of this competition.[20]

- *Knowledge of the business.* Effective leaders possess tacit and explicit knowledge of the business environment in which they operate. This competency partly explains why Moya Greene may be well suited to lead Britain's Royal Mail. Royal Mail is rated as the least efficient mail service in Europe (partly due to minimal technological innovation), has a massive pension deficit and poor labour relations, and is about to be privatized. Greene has plenty of experience with this type of organization. She dramatically improved productivity at Canada Post due to automation, gained experience as a productivity improvement champion at Bombardier and two Canadian banks, and was a Canadian government senior civil servant responsible for privatizing the Canadian National Railway.

- *Cognitive and practical intelligence.* Leaders have above-average cognitive ability to process enormous amounts of information. Leaders aren't necessarily geniuses; rather, they have a superior ability to analyze a variety of complex alternatives and opportunities. Furthermore, leaders have practical intelligence. Cognitive intelligence is assessed by performance on clearly defined problems with sufficient information and usually one best answer. In contrast, practical intelligence is assessed by performance in real-world settings, where problems are poorly defined, information is missing, and more than one solution may be plausible.[21]

- *Emotional intelligence.* Effective leaders have a high level of emotional intelligence.[22] They are able to perceive and express emotion, assimilate emotion in thought, understand and reason with emotion, and regulate emotion in themselves and others (see Chapter 4).

AUTHENTIC LEADERSHIP

authentic leadership   The view that effective leaders need to be aware of, feel comfortable with, and act consistently with their values, personality, and self-concept.

Several competencies associated with effective leaders relate to another important characteristic, called **authentic leadership** (Exhibit 12.3).[23] Authentic leadership refers to how effective leaders need to be aware of, feel comfortable with, and act consistently with their values, personality, and self-concept. In other words, authenticity is knowing yourself and being yourself. Leaders learn more about their personality, values, thoughts, and habits by reflecting on various situations and personal experiences. They also improve this self-awareness by receiving feedback from trusted people inside and outside the organization. Both self-reflection and receptivity to feedback require high levels of emotional intelligence. As people learn more about themselves, they gain a greater understanding of their inner purpose which, in turn, generates a long-term passion for achieving something worthwhile for the organization or society. Some leadership experts suggest that this inner purpose emerges from a life story, typically a critical event or experience earlier in life that provides guidance for their later career and energy.

Authentic leadership is more than self-awareness; it also involves behaving in ways that are consistent with that self-concept rather than pretending to be someone else. To be themselves, great leaders regulate their decisions and behaviour in several ways. First,

Exhibit 12.3 | **AUTHENTIC LEADERSHIP**

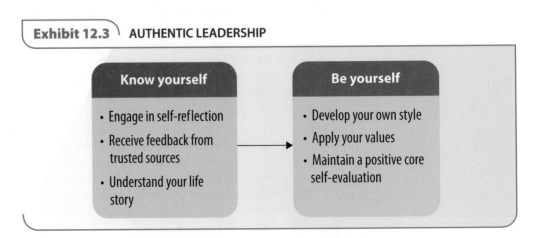

they develop their own style and, where appropriate, place themselves into positions where that style is most effective. Although effective leaders adapt their behaviour to the situation to some extent, they invariably understand and rely on decision methods and interpersonal styles that feel most comfortable to them.

Second, effective leaders continually think about and consistently apply their stable hierarchy of personal values to those decisions and behaviours. Leaders face many pressures and temptations, such as achieving short-term stock price targets at the cost of long-term profitability. Experts note that authentic leaders demonstrate self-discipline by remaining anchored to their values. Third, leaders maintain consistency around their self-concept by having a strong, positive core self-evaluation. They have high self-esteem and self-efficacy as well as an internal locus of control (Chapter 2).

COMPETENCY PERSPECTIVE LIMITATIONS AND PRACTICAL IMPLICATIONS

Although the competency perspective is gaining popularity (again), it has a few limitations.[24] First, it assumes that all effective leaders have the same personal characteristics that are equally important in all situations. This is probably a false assumption; leadership is far too complex to have a universal list of traits that apply to every condition. Some competencies might not be important all the time. Second, alternative combinations of competencies may be equally successful; two people with different sets of competencies might be equally good leaders. Third, the competency perspective views leadership as something within a person, yet experts emphasize that leadership is relational. People are effective leaders because of their favourable relationships with followers, so effective leaders cannot be identified without considering the quality of these relationships.[25]

Several leadership researchers have also warned that some personal characteristics might influence only our perception that someone is a leader, not whether the individual really makes a difference to the organization's success. People who exhibit self-confidence, extroversion, and other traits are called leaders because they fit our prototype of an effective leader. Or we might see a successful person, call that person a leader, and then attribute unobservable traits that we consider essential for great leaders. We will discuss this issue later in the implicit leadership perspective.

The competency perspective of leadership does not necessarily imply that leadership is a talent acquired at birth rather than developed throughout life. On the contrary, competencies indicate only leadership *potential*, not leadership performance. People with these characteristics become effective leaders only after they have developed and mastered the necessary leadership behaviours. People with somewhat lower leadership competencies may become very effective leaders because they have leveraged their potential more fully.

BEHAVIOURAL PERSPECTIVE OF LEADERSHIP

LO3

In the 1940s and 1950s, leadership experts at several universities launched an intensive research investigation to answer the question "What behaviours make leaders effective?" Questionnaires were administered to employees, asking them to rate their supervisors on a large number of behaviours. This study distilled two clusters of leadership behaviours from literally thousands of items (Exhibit 12.4).[26]

One cluster, called directive leadership, includes behaviours that define and structure work roles. Directive leaders assign employees to specific tasks, set goals and deadlines, clarify work duties and procedures, define work procedures, and plan work activities. The other cluster represents supportive behaviours. This cluster includes behaviours such as listening to employees for their opinions and ideas, creating a pleasant physical work environment, showing interest in staff, appreciating and recognizing employees for their effort, and showing consideration of employee needs.

> **Exhibit 12.4**   DIRECTIVE AND SUPPORTIVE LEADERSHIP STYLES

Leaders are directive when they...

- Assign work and clarify responsibilities
- Set goals and deadlines
- Evaluate and provide feedback on work quality
- Establish well-defined best work procedures
- Plan future work activities

Leaders are supportive when they...

- Listen to employees
- Make the workplace more pleasant
- Show interest in others as people
- Recognize employees for their work
- Are considerate of employee needs

CHOOSING DIRECTIVE VERSUS SUPPORTIVE LEADERSHIP

Should leaders be directive or supportive? This is a difficult question to answer because each style has its advantages and disadvantages. Recent evidence suggests that both styles are positively associated with leader effectiveness, but in different ways.[27] Not surprisingly, increasing supportive leadership reduces employee absenteeism, grievances, turnover, and job dissatisfaction, whereas increasing directive leadership results in higher job performance. Research suggests that university students value directive instructors because they want clear objectives and well-prepared lectures that abide by the unit's objectives.[28] Other research indicates that followers have few stress symptoms when leaders show empathy towards employees.[29]

One problem with the behavioural leadership perspective is that the two categories are broad generalizations that mask specific behaviours within each category. For instance, directive leadership includes planning work activities, clarifying roles, and monitoring operations and performance. Each of these clusters of activities are fairly distinct and likely have different effects on employee well-being and performance. A second concern is that the behavioural approach assumes that high levels of both styles are best in all situations. In reality, the best leadership style depends on the situation.[30] On a positive note, the behavioural perspective lays the foundation for two of the main leadership styles—supportive and directive—found in many contemporary leadership theories. As Global Connections 12.1 describes, great leaders apply one leadership style or another, depending on the situation.

SERVANT LEADERSHIP

servant leadership The view that leaders serve followers, rather than vice versa; leaders help employees fulfill their needs and are coaches, stewards, and facilitators of employee performance.

Servant leadership is an extension or variation of the supportive leadership style because it defines leadership as serving others toward their need fulfillment, personal development, and growth.[31] Servant leaders ask, "How can I help you?" rather than expect employees to serve them. People who epitomize servant leadership have been described as selfless, egalitarian, humble, nurturing, empathetic, and ethical coaches. The main objective of servant leadership is to help other stakeholders fulfill their needs and potential, particularly "to become healthier, wiser, freer, more autonomous, more likely themselves to become servants."[32]

Servant leadership research suffers from ambiguous and conflicting definitions, but writers agree on a few features.[33] First, servant leaders have a natural desire or "calling" to serve others. This natural desire is different from a role obligation (it's part of a leader's job to help others) or an instrumental purpose (the leader helps others so they will achieve the leader's objectives). Rather, it is a deep commitment to the growth of others for that purpose alone. Second, servant leaders maintain a relationship with others that is humble, egalitarian, and accepting. Servant leaders do not view leadership as a position of power. Rather, they serve without drawing attention to themselves, without evoking superior status, and without being judgmental about others or defensive of criticisms received. Third, servant leaders anchor their decisions and actions in ethical principles and practices. They display sensitivity to and enactment of moral values and are not swayed by social pressures or expectations to deviate from those values. In this respect, servant leadership overlaps with authentic leadership, which was described a few pages ago.

Servant leadership was introduced four decades ago and has since had a steady following, particularly among practitioners and religious leaders. Scholarly interest in this topic has bloomed over the past few years, but the concept still faces a number of conceptual hurdles. Although there is much agreement on the three features we described above, some servant leadership writers have included various other characteristics that might confound the concept with its predictors and outcomes. Aside from these concerns, the notion of leader as servant has considerable currency and for many centuries has been embedded in leadership principles within most major religions.

CONTINGENCY PERSPECTIVE OF LEADERSHIP

LO4

The contingency perspective of leadership is based on the idea that the most appropriate leadership style depends on the situation. Most (although not all) contingency leadership theories assume that effective leaders must be both insightful and flexible.[34] They must be able to adapt their behaviours and styles to the immediate situation. This isn't easy to do, however. Leaders typically have a preferred style. It takes considerable effort for leaders to choose and enact different styles to match the situation. As we noted earlier, leaders must have high emotional intelligence so that they can diagnose the circumstances and match their behaviours accordingly.

PATH-GOAL THEORY OF LEADERSHIP

path-goal leadership theory A contingency theory of leadership based on the expectancy theory of motivation that relates several leadership styles to specific employee and situational contingencies.

Several contingency theories have been proposed over the years, but **path-goal leadership theory** has withstood scientific critique better than the others. Indeed, one recent study found that the path-goal theory explained more about effective leadership than did another popular perspective of leadership (transformational, which we describe later in this chapter).[35] Path-goal leadership theory has its roots in the expectancy theory of motivation (see Chapter 5) because leaders create paths (expectancies) to effective performance (goals) for their employees.[36] Path-goal theory states that effective leaders ensure that good performers receive more valued rewards than do poor performers. Effective leaders also provide the information, support, and other resources necessary to help employees complete their tasks.[37]

Path-Goal Leadership Styles Exhibit 12.5 presents the path-goal theory of leadership. This model specifically highlights four leadership styles and several contingency factors leading to three indicators of leader effectiveness. The four leadership styles are:[38]

- *Directive.* This leadership style consists of clarifying behaviours that provide a psychological structure for employees. The leader clarifies performance goals, the means to reach those goals, and the standards against which performance will be assessed. It also includes judicious use of rewards and disciplinary actions. Directive leadership is the same as directive leadership, described earlier, and echoes our discussion in Chapter 2 on the importance of clear role perceptions in employee performance.

- *Supportive.* In this style, the leader's behaviours provide psychological support for employees. The leader is friendly and approachable; makes the work more pleasant;

Exhibit 12.5) **PATH-GOAL LEADERSHIP THEORY**

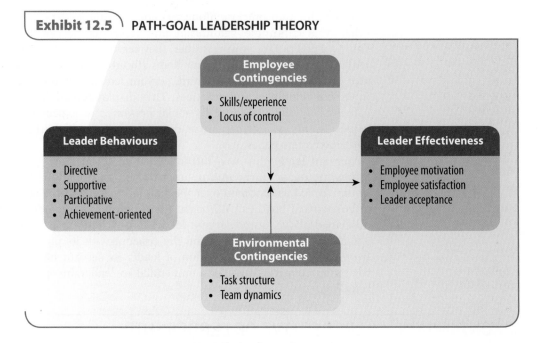

treats employees with equal respect; and shows concern for the status, needs, and well-being of employees. Supportive leadership reflects the benefits of social support to help employees cope with stressful situations.

- *Participative.* Participative leadership behaviours encourage and facilitate subordinate involvement in decisions beyond their normal work activities. The leader consults with employees, asks for their suggestions, and takes these ideas into serious consideration before making a decision. Participative leadership relates to involving employees in decisions.

- *Achievement-oriented.* This leadership style emphasizes behaviours that encourage employees to reach their peak performance. The leader sets challenging goals, expects employees to perform at their highest level, continuously seeks improvement in employee performance, and shows a high degree of confidence that employees will assume responsibility and accomplish challenging goals. Achievement-oriented leadership applies goal-setting theory as well as positive expectations in self-fulfilling prophecy.

The path-goal model contends that effective leaders are capable of selecting the most appropriate behavioural style (or styles) for each situation. Leaders might simultaneously use two or more styles.

Contingencies of Path-Goal Theory   As a contingency theory, path-goal theory states that each of the four leadership styles will be effective in some situations but not in others. The path-goal leadership model specifies two sets of situational variables that moderate the relationship between a leader's style and effectiveness: (1) employee characteristics and (2) characteristics of the employee's work environment. Several contingencies have already been studied within the path-goal framework, and the model is open for more variables in the future.[39] However, only four contingencies are reviewed here.

- *Skill and experience.* A combination of directive and supportive leadership is best for employees who are (or perceive themselves to be) inexperienced and unskilled.[40] Directive leadership gives employees information about how to accomplish the task, whereas supportive leadership helps them cope with the uncertainties of unfamiliar work situations. Directive leadership is detrimental when employees are skilled and experienced because it introduces too much supervisory control.

CONNECTIONS 12.1

Leading With a Steel Fist in a Velvet Glove

Leadership experts have long debated whether great leaders are supportive or directive. Their conclusion? Great leaders apply one style or the other, depending on the situation. Even so, some of the world's most respected leaders have the uncanny ability to keep employees focused on the task while simultaneously being supportive. Anne Sweeney, co-chair of Disney Media Networks and president of Disney/ABC Television Group, is a case in point. News Corporation founder Rupert Murdoch was once quoted as saying that Sweeney has "a steel fist in a velvet glove."

Sweeney is renowned for her empathy and consideration. "She has been incredibly supportive through all the ups and downs of rebuilding a network schedule, which made it possible for us to achieve so much so fast," says one ABC executive. Albert Cheng echoes this view: "Anne makes it a point to engage with everyone," says the Disney Digital Media executive vice-president. "She's very concerned about the people who work for her."

At the same time, Sweeney maintains a sharp focus on the future and ensures that her staff reach their potential. Walt Disney Studios chairman Rich Ross notes that Sweeney avoids micromanaging her staff but applies her analytic skill to challenge managers to think through their ideas. "[She] asks the tough questions. . . . It trains you to anticipate it," says Ross. According to another ABC executive, "Anne draws upon her optimism and her grace in keeping her focus firmly on the future." He adds: "None of us could wish for a better leader, through whatever may come our way."

Anne Sweeney's appropriate application of directive and supportive leadership has undoubtedly been a factor in the

Disney/ABC executive Anne Sweeney is renowned for applying both directive and supportive leadership styles to help staff reach their potential. *AP Photo/ Damian Dovarganes*

company's success. For example, the American television network ABC was floundering in fourth place and employee morale was low before Sweeney took the reins. Yet less than four years later, ABC was competing for the top spot with popular programs. Similar achievements occurred earlier when Sweeney was head of Disney, Nickelodeon, and FX cable networks.[41]

- *Locus of control.* People with an internal locus of control believe that they have control over their work environment (see Chapter 3). Consequently, these employees prefer participative and achievement-oriented leadership styles and may become frustrated with a directive style. In contrast, people with an external locus of control believe that their performance is due more to luck and fate, so they tend to be more satisfied with directive and supportive leadership.

- *Task structure.* Leaders should adopt the directive style when the task is nonroutine, because this style minimizes role ambiguity that tends to occur in complex work situations (particularly for inexperienced employees).[42] The directive style is ineffective when employees have routine and simple tasks because the manager's guidance serves no purpose and may be viewed as unnecessarily close control. Employees in highly routine and simple jobs may require supportive leadership to help them cope with the tedious nature of the work and lack of control over the pace of work. Participative leadership is preferred for employees performing nonroutine tasks because the lack of rules and procedures gives them more discretion to achieve challenging goals. The participative style is ineffective for employees in routine tasks because they lack discretion over their work.

- *Team dynamics.* Cohesive teams with performance-oriented norms act as a substitute for most leader interventions. High team cohesion substitutes for supportive leadership, whereas performance-oriented team norms substitute for directive and possibly achievement-oriented leadership. Thus, when team cohesion is low, leaders should use the supportive style. Leaders should apply a directive style to counteract team norms that oppose the team's formal objectives. For example, the team leader may need to use legitimate power if team members have developed a norm to "take it easy" rather than get a project completed on time.

Path-goal theory has received more research support than other contingency leadership models, but the evidence is far from complete. A few contingencies (e.g., task structure) have limited research support. Other contingencies and leadership styles in the path-goal leadership model haven't been investigated at all.[43] Another concern is that as path-goal theory expands, the model may become too complex for practical use. Few people would be able to remember all the contingencies and the appropriate leadership styles for those contingencies. In spite of these limitations, path-goal theory remains a relatively robust contingency leadership theory.

OTHER CONTINGENCY THEORIES

Many leadership theories have developed over the years, most of which are found in the contingency perspective of leadership. Some overlap with the path-goal model's leadership styles, but most use simpler and more abstract contingencies. We will briefly mention only two here because of their popularity and historical significance to the field.

Situational Leadership Theory   One of the most popular contingency theories among practitioners is the **situational leadership theory (SLT)**, developed by Paul Hersey and Ken Blanchard.[44] SLT suggests that effective leaders vary their style with the ability and motivation (or commitment) of followers. The earliest versions of the model compressed the employee's ability and motivation into a single situational condition called maturity or readiness. The most recent version uses four labels, such as "enthusiastic beginner" (low ability, high motivation) and "disillusioned learner" (moderate ability and low motivation).

> **situational leadership theory (SLT)** A commercially popular but poorly supported leadership model stating that effective leaders vary their style (telling, selling, participating, delegating) with the "readiness" of followers.

The situational leadership model also identifies four leadership styles—telling, selling, participating, and delegating—that Hersey and Blanchard distinguish by the amount of directive and supportive behaviour provided. For example, "telling" has high task behaviour and low supportive behaviour. The situational leadership model has four quadrants, with each quadrant showing the leadership style that is most appropriate under different circumstances.

In spite of its popularity, several studies and at least three reviews have concluded that the situational leadership model lacks empirical support.[45] Only one part of the model apparently works, namely, that leaders should use "telling" (i.e., directive style) when employees lack motivation and ability. This relationship is also documented in path-goal theory. The model's elegant simplicity is attractive and entertaining, but most parts don't represent reality very well.

Fiedler's Contingency Model   **Fiedler's contingency model**, developed by Fred Fiedler and his associates, is the earliest contingency theory of leadership.[46] According to this model, leader effectiveness depends on whether the person's natural leadership style is appropriately matched to the situation. The theory examines two leadership styles that essentially correspond to the previously described supportive and directive styles. Unfortunately, Fiedler's model relies on a questionnaire that does not measure either leadership style very well.

> **Fiedler's contingency model** An early contingency leadership model, developed by Fred Fiedler, which suggests that leader effectiveness depends on whether the person's natural leadership style is appropriately matched to the situation.

Fiedler's model suggests that the best leadership style depends on the level of *situational control*, that is, the degree of power and influence that the leader possesses in a particular situation. Situational control is affected by three factors in the following order of importance: leader-member relations, task structure, and position power.[47] *Leader-member relations* refers to how much employees trust and respect the leader and are willing to follow his or her guidance. *Task structure* refers to the clarity or ambiguity of operating procedures. *Position power* is the extent to which the leader possesses legitimate, reward, and coercive power over subordinates. These three contingencies form the eight possible combinations of *situation favourableness* from the leader's viewpoint. Good leader-member relations, high task structure, and strong position power create the most favourable situation for the leader because he or she has the most power and influence under these conditions.

Fiedler has gained considerable respect for pioneering the first contingency theory of leadership. However, his theory has fared less well. As mentioned, the leadership-style scale used by Fiedler has been widely criticized. There is no scientific justification for placing the three situational control factors in a hierarchy. Furthermore, the concept of leader-member relations is really an indicator of leader effectiveness (as in path-goal theory) rather than a situational factor. Finally, the theory considers only two leadership styles, whereas other models present a more complex and realistic array of behaviour options. These concerns explain why the theory has limited empirical support.[48]

Changing the Situation to Match the Leader's Natural Style   Fiedler's contingency model may have become a historical footnote, but it does make an important and lasting contribution by suggesting that, contrary to most contingency theories, leaders can't change their style very easily to fit the situation. Instead, they tend to rely mainly on one style that is most consistent with their personality and values. Leaders with high agreeableness personality and benevolence values tend to prefer supportive leadership, for example, whereas leaders with high conscientiousness personality and achievement values feel more comfortable with the directive style of leadership.[49] A few scholars have recently proposed that leadership styles are "hardwired" more than most contingency leadership theories assume.[50] Leaders might be able to alter their style temporarily, but they tend to rely mainly on one style that is most consistent with their personality and values.

> ❝ Fiedler's contingency model suggests that leaders can't change their style very easily to fit the situation. ❞

If leadership style is influenced by an individual's personality and values, organizations should engineer the situation to fit the leader's dominant style, rather than expect leaders to change their style with the situation. A directive leader might be assigned inexperienced newcomers who need direction rather than skilled employees who work less effectively under a directive style. Alternatively, companies might transfer supervisors to workplaces where their dominant style fits best. For instance, directive leaders might be parachuted into work teams with counterproductive norms, whereas leaders who prefer a supportive style should be sent to departments in which employees face work pressures and other stressors.

LEADERSHIP SUBSTITUTES

leadership substitutes
A theory identifying contingencies that either limit a leader's ability to influence employees or make a particular leadership style unnecessary.

So far, we have looked at theories that recommend using different leadership styles in various situations. But one theory, called **leadership substitutes**, identifies conditions that either limit a leader's ability to influence employees or make a particular leadership style unnecessary. The literature identifies several conditions that possibly substitute for directive or supportive leadership. Directive leadership might be less important when performance-based reward systems keep employees directed toward organizational goals. Similarly, increasing employee skill and experience might reduce the need for directive leadership. This proposition is consistent with path-goal leadership theory, which states that directive leadership is unnecessary—and may be detrimental—when employees are skilled or experienced.[51]

Some research suggests that effective leaders help team members learn to lead themselves through leadership substitutes; in other words, co-workers substitute for leadership in high-involvement team structures.[52] Co-workers instruct new employees, thereby providing directive leadership. They also provide social support, which reduces stress among fellow employees. Teams with norms that support organizational goals may substitute for achievement-oriented leadership, because employees encourage (or pressure) co-workers to stretch their performance levels.[53] Self-leadership—the process of influencing oneself to establish the self-direction and self-motivation needed to perform a task (see Chapter 6)—might be a substitute for directive and achievement-oriented leadership.[54]

The leadership substitutes model has intuitive appeal, but the evidence so far is mixed. Some studies show that a few substitutes do replace the need for directive or supportive leadership, but others do not. The difficulties of statistically testing for leadership substitutes may account for some problems, but a few writers contend that the limited support is evidence that leadership plays a critical role regardless of the situation.[55] At this point, we can conclude that leadership substitutes might reduce the need for leaders, but they do not completely replace leaders in these situations.

TRANSFORMATIONAL PERSPECTIVE OF LEADERSHIP

L05

transformational leadership A leadership perspective that explains how leaders change teams or organizations by creating, communicating, and modelling a shared vision for the team or organization, and inspiring employees to strive for that vision.

Transformational leadership is by far the most popular perspective of leadership today. Unlike the contingency and behavioural perspectives, which examined how leaders improve employee performance and well-being, transformational leadership views effective leaders as agents of change in the work unit or organization. They create, communicate, and model a shared vision for the team or organization, and they inspire followers to strive for that vision.[56]

TRANSFORMATIONAL VERSUS TRANSACTIONAL LEADERSHIP

transactional leadership Leadership that helps organizations achieve their current objectives more efficiently, such as by linking job performance to valued rewards and ensuring that employees have the resources needed to get the job done.

Leadership experts often contrast transformational leadership with **transactional leadership**.[57] Transactional leaders influence others mainly by using rewards and penalties as well as by negotiating services from employees. James McGregor Burns, who coined the term three decades ago, describes transactional leadership with reference to political leaders who engage in vote buying or making transactional promises (e.g., I'll have a new hospital built in your town if you vote for me).[58] Managers in organizations are rarely elected, yet transactional leadership has become the focus of study in organizational behaviour. The problem is compounded by a confusing and sometimes conflicting array of definitions and measures for transactional leadership. For example, Burns suggests that transactional leaders can appeal to follower wants and convictions about morality and justice, but this is similar to the actions of transformational leadership.[59]

managerial leadership A leadership perspective stating that effective leaders help employees improve their performance and well-being in the current situation.

For these reasons, we will avoid the "transactional leadership" concept. Instead, our focus here will be on transformational leadership. Furthermore, we believe a more appropriate comparison to transformational leadership is **managerial leadership** or managing.[60] Transformational leaders are change agents who energize and direct employees to a new vision and corresponding behaviours. Managerial leadership, on the other hand, refers to helping employees become more proficient and satisfied in the current situation. The contingency and behavioural leadership theories described earlier refer to managerial leadership because they focus on leader behaviours that improve employee performance and well-being rather than on behaviours that move the organization and work unit to a new direction. As leadership expert Warren Bennis noted several years ago, "Managers are people who do things right and leaders are people who do the right thing."[61]

Organizations require both managerial and transformational leadership.[62] Managing improves organizational efficiency, whereas transformational leadership steers companies onto a better course of action. Transformational leadership is particularly important in organizations that require significant alignment with the external environment. Unfortunately, too many leaders get trapped in the daily activities that represent managerial leadership.[63] They lose touch with the transformational aspect of effective leadership. Without transformational leaders, organizations stagnate and eventually become seriously misaligned with their environments.

TRANSFORMATIONAL VERSUS CHARISMATIC LEADERSHIP

Another topic that has generated some confusion and controversy is the distinction between transformational and charismatic leadership. Many researchers either use the words interchangeably, as if they have the same meaning, or view charismatic leadership as an essential ingredient of transformational leadership. Others take this notion further by suggesting that charismatic leadership is the highest degree of transformational leadership.[64]

The emerging view, which this book adopts, comes from a third group of experts who contend that charisma is distinct from transformational leadership. These scholars point out that charisma is a personal trait or relational quality that provides referent power over followers, whereas transformational leadership is a set of behaviours that engage followers toward a better future.[65] This view is most consistent with the original and ongoing scholarly definition of charisma as an inherent characteristic of one's character, not something that can be easily learned or mimicked.[66] Transformational leadership motivates followers through behaviours that persuade and earn trust, whereas charismatic leadership motivates followers directly through existing referent power. Any charisma a leader possesses will amplify follower motivation toward a desired objective beyond the effect of transformational behaviours.

Being charismatic is not inherently good or bad, but several writers have warned that it can have negative consequences in leadership.[67] One concern is that leaders who possess the gift of charisma may become intoxicated by this power, which leads to a greater focus on self-interest than on the common good. "Charisma becomes the undoing of leaders," warns Peter Drucker. "It makes them inflexible, convinced of their own infallibility, unable to change."[68] The late management guru witnessed the destructive effects of charismatic political leaders in Europe a century ago and foresaw that this personal or relational characteristic would create similar problems for organizations.

Another concern is that charismatic leadership tends to produce dependent followers. Transformational leadership has the opposite effect—it builds follower empowerment, which tends to reduce dependence on the leader. One study also found that charismatic leadership has a negative effect on follower self-efficacy, which would further increase dependence on the leader.

The main point here is that transformational leaders are not necessarily charismatic, and charismatic leaders are not necessarily transformational. Furthermore, charisma can have adverse effects. Procter & Gamble CEO Alan G. Lafley is not known for being charismatic, but he has transformed the household goods company like no leader in recent memory. Similarly, IBM CEO Sam Palmisano has guided IBM's success without much inherent charisma. "I don't have much curb appeal," Palmisano admits. "I just try to lead them and get them to come together around a common point of view."[69] In other words, Palmisano and Lafley lead by applying transformational leadership behaviours.

ELEMENTS OF TRANSFORMATIONAL LEADERSHIP

There are several descriptions of transformational leadership, but most include the following four elements: Develop a strategic vision, communicate the vision, model the vision, and build commitment toward the vision (see Exhibit 12.6).

Develop a Strategic Vision   A core element of transformational leadership is strategic vision—a realistic and attractive future that bonds employees together and focuses their energy toward a superordinate organizational goal.[70] Indeed, experts describe vision as the commodity or substance of transformational leadership. Strategic vision represents a "higher purpose" or superordinate goal that energizes and unifies employees and adds

Exhibit 12.6 \ ELEMENTS OF TRANSFORMATIONAL LEADERSHIP

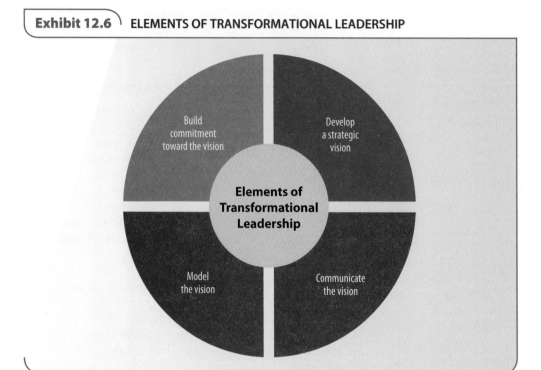

meaning to each person's self-concept.[71] It is typically described in a way that departs from the current situation and is both appealing and achievable. A strategic vision might originate with the leader, but it is just as likely to emerge from employees, clients, suppliers, or other stakeholders. When embraced by employees, a strategic vision plays an important role in organizational effectiveness.[72] It offers the same motivational benefits as goal setting (see Chapter 5), but also serves as a source of common bond that builds employee commitment to this collective purpose.

Communicate the Vision   If vision is the substance of transformational leadership, communicating that vision is the process. CEOs say that the most important leadership quality is being able to build and share their vision for the organization. "Part of a leader's role is to set the vision for the company and to communicate that vision to staff to get their buy-in," explains Dave Anderson, president of WorkSafeBC (the Workers' Compensation Board of British Columbia).[73]

Transformational leaders communicate meaning and elevate the importance of the visionary goal to employees. They frame messages around a grand purpose with emotional appeal that captivates employees and other corporate stakeholders. Framing generates positive emotions and motivation as well as establishes a common mental model so that the group or organization will act collectively toward the desirable goal.[74] Transformational leaders bring their visions to life through symbols, metaphors, stories, and other vehicles that transcend plain language. Metaphors borrow images of other experiences, thereby creating richer meaning of the vision that has not yet been experienced.

The power of metaphors to communicate a strategic vision is apparent in many great Canadian stories of leadership. When George Cohen, the ebullient CEO of McDonald's Canada, faced the difficult challenge of opening restaurants in Moscow, he frequently reminded his team members that they were establishing "hamburger diplomacy." And in the mid-1800s, when ocean transportation was treacherous, Samuel Cunard emphasized that he was creating an "ocean railway." At the time, railroads provided one of the safest forms of transportation, and Cunard's metaphor reinforced the notion to employees and passengers alike that Cunard Steamship Lines, which at the time was based in Halifax, Nova Scotia, would provide equally safe transportation across the Atlantic Ocean."[75]

Vision that Launched a Digital Lifestyle

In 2000, Steve Jobs had just moved from interim to permanent CEO of Apple. Despite fending off bankruptcy, missed revenue targets and plummeting stock prices still threatened Apple's survival. But Steve Jobs, already well-known for his "big-picture vision" was putting in motion the elements that would put Apple on a trajectory to transform music, computing, and telecommunications while generating more than $150 billion in shareholder wealth. "Jobs has this extraordinary ability to see into the future and instinctively see what people want," says a professor at MITS's Sloan School of Management. In a recent technology town hall meeting Bill Gates reflected on Steve Jobs' leadership, "He, of all the leaders in the industry that I've worked with, has shown more inspiration and has saved the company." Under Jobs' leadership, Apple employees have delivered on his demanding vision by bringing the iMac, iPod, iPhone, and iPad to the world. Jobs' ability to generate spontaneous enthusiasm is also legendary. Despite being on medical leave, he recently took to the stage to introduce Apple's newest iPad. "We've been working on this product for awhile, and I didn't want to miss it," said Jobs, who received a standing ovation at the invitation-only event. Steve leaves behind a company that only he could have built, and his spirit will forever be the foundation of Apple.[76] *QI HENG/Xinhua/Landov*

Model the Vision   Transformational leaders not only talk about a vision; they enact it. They "walk the talk" by stepping outside the executive suite and doing things that symbolize the vision.[77] "The example you set at the top is probably the most important thing a CEO does in terms of what you ask people to do," says Calgary-based Suncor CEO Rick George. "You have got to walk that same line yourself."[78]

Leaders walk the talk through significant events such as visiting customers, moving their offices closer to (or further from) employees, and holding ceremonies to destroy outdated policy manuals. However, they also alter mundane activities—meeting agendas, dress codes, executive schedules—so that the activities are more consistent with the vision and its underlying values. Modelling the vision is important because it legitimizes and demonstrates what the vision looks like in practice. Modelling is also important because it builds employee trust in the leader. The greater the consistency between the leader's words and actions, the more employees will believe in and be willing to follow the leader. In fact, one survey reported that leading by example is the most important characteristic of a leader.[79] "As an executive, you're always being watched by employees, and everything you say gets magnified—so you teach a lot by how you conduct yourself," advises Carl Bass, CEO of software company Autodesk.[80]

Build Commitment Toward the Vision   Transforming a vision into reality requires employee commitment, and transformational leaders build this commitment in several ways. Their words, symbols, and stories build a contagious enthusiasm that energizes people to adopt the vision as their own. Leaders demonstrate a "can do" attitude by enacting their vision and staying on course. Their persistence and consistency portray honesty, trust, and integrity. Finally, leaders build commitment by involving employees in the process of shaping the organization's vision.

EVALUATING THE TRANSFORMATIONAL LEADERSHIP PERSPECTIVE

Transformational leaders do make a difference.[81] Employees are more satisfied and have higher affective organizational commitment with transformational leaders. They also perform their jobs better, engage in more organizational citizenship behaviours, and make better or more creative decisions. One study of Canadian bank branches reported that organizational commitment and financial performance seem to increase where the branch manager completed a transformational leadership training program.[82]

Transformational leadership is currently the most popular leadership perspective, but it faces a number of challenges. One problem is that some writers engage in circular logic.[83] They define and measure transformational leadership by how well the leader inspires and engages employees rather than by whether they engage in behaviours we call transformational (e.g., communicating a vision). This approach makes it impossible to evaluate transformational leadership because, by definition and measurement, all transformational leaders are effective!

Another concern is that transformational leadership is usually described as a universal rather than contingency-oriented model. Only very recently have writers begun to explore the idea that transformational leadership is more valuable in some situations than others.[84] For instance, transformational leadership is probably more appropriate when organizations need to adapt than when environmental conditions are stable. Preliminary evidence suggests that the transformational leadership perspective is relevant across cultures. However, there may be specific elements of transformational leadership, such as the way visions are formed and communicated, that are more appropriate in North America than other cultures.

IMPLICIT LEADERSHIP PERSPECTIVE

L06

implicit leadership theory A theory stating that people evaluate a leader's effectiveness in terms of how well that person fits preconceived beliefs about the features and behaviours of effective leaders (leadership prototypes), and that people tend to inflate the influence of leaders on organizational events.

The competency, behavioural, contingency, and transformational leadership perspectives make the basic assumption that leaders "make a difference." Certainly, there is evidence that senior executives do influence organizational performance. However, leadership also involves followers' perceptions about the characteristics and influence of people they call leaders. This perceptual perspective of leadership, called **implicit leadership theory**, has two components: leader prototypes and the romance or attribution of leadership.[85]

PROTOTYPES OF EFFECTIVE LEADERS

One aspect of implicit leadership theory states that everyone has leadership prototypes—preconceived beliefs about the features and behaviours of effective leaders.[86] These prototypes, which develop through socialization within the family and society, shape the follower's expectations and acceptance of others as leaders, and this in turn affects the willingness to remain as a follower. For example, one study reported that inherited personality characteristics significantly influence the perception that someone is a leader in a leaderless situation.[87]

Leadership prototypes not only support a person's role as leader; they also form or influence our perception of the leader's effectiveness. In other words, people are more likely to believe a leader is effective when he or she looks like and acts consistently with their prototype of a leader.[88] This prototype comparison process occurs because people have an inherent need to quickly evaluate individuals as leaders, yet leadership effectiveness is often ambiguous and might not be apparent for a long time.

THE ROMANCE OF LEADERSHIP

Along with relying on implicit prototypes of effective leaders, followers tend to distort their perception of the influence that leaders have on the environment. This "romance of leadership" effect exists because in most cultures people want to believe that leaders make a difference. Consider the experience of Ricardo Semler, the charismatic CEO of Brazilian conglomerate Semco SA:

> At the company, no matter what you do, people will naturally create and nurture a charismatic figure. The charismatic figure, on the other hand, feeds this; it doesn't just happen, and it is very difficult to check your ego at the door. The people at Semco don't look and act like me. They are not yes-men by any means. What is left, however, is a certain feeling that has to do with the cult of personality. They credit me with successes that are not my own, and they don't debit me my mistakes. They give undue importance to what I say, and I think that doesn't go away.[89]

There are two basic reasons why people inflate their perceptions of the leader's influence over the environment.[90] First, leadership is a useful way for us to simplify life events. It is easier to explain organizational successes and failures in terms of the leader's ability than by analyzing a complex array of other forces. Second, there is a strong tendency in Canada and other Western cultures to believe that life events are generated more from people than from uncontrollable natural forces.[91] This illusion of control is satisfied by believing that events result from the rational actions of leaders. In other words, employees feel better believing that leaders make a difference, so they actively look for evidence that this is so.

One way that followers support their perceptions that leaders make a difference is through fundamental attribution error (see Chapter 3). Research has found that (at least in Western cultures) leaders are given credit or blame for the company's success or failure because employees do not readily see the external forces that also influence these events. Leaders reinforce this belief by taking credit for organizational successes.[92]

The implicit leadership perspective provides valuable advice to improve leadership acceptance. It highlights the fact that leadership is a perception of followers as much as the actual behaviours and formal roles of people calling themselves leaders. Potential leaders must be sensitive to this fact, understand what followers expect, and act accordingly. Individuals who do not make an effort to fit leadership prototypes will have more difficulty bringing about necessary organizational change.

CROSS-CULTURAL AND GENDER ISSUES IN LEADERSHIP

LO7

Along with the five perspectives of leadership presented throughout this chapter, cultural values and practices affect what leaders do. Culture shapes the leader's values and norms, which influence his or her decisions and actions. Cultural values also shape the expectations that followers have of their leaders. An executive who acts inconsistently with cultural expectations is more likely to be perceived as an ineffective leader. Furthermore, leaders who deviate from those values may experience various forms of influence to get them to conform to the leadership norms and expectations of the society. In other words, implicit leadership theory, described in the previous section of this chapter, explains differences in leadership practices across cultures.

Over the past decade, 150 researchers from dozens of countries have worked together on Project GLOBE (Global Leadership and Organizational Behaviour Effectiveness) to identify the effects of cultural values on leadership.[93] The project organized countries into 10 regional clusters, of which Canada, the United States, Great Britain, and similar countries are grouped into the "Anglo" cluster. The results of this massive investigation suggest that some features of leadership are universal and some differ across cultures. Specifically, the GLOBE project reports that "charismatic visionary" is a universally recognized concept and that middle managers around the world believe that it is characteristic of effective leaders. *Charismatic visionary* represents a cluster of concepts including visionary, inspirational, performance orientation, integrity, and decisiveness.[94] In contrast, participative leadership is perceived as characteristic of effective leadership in low power distance cultures but less so in high power distance cultures. For instance, one study reported that Mexican employees expect managers to make decisions affecting their work. Mexico is a high power distance culture, so followers expect leaders to apply their authority rather than delegate their power most of the time.[95] In summary, there are similarities and differences in the concept and preferred practice of leadership across cultures.

GENDER AND LEADERSHIP

Studies in field settings have generally found that male and female leaders do not differ in their levels of directive or supportive leadership. The main explanation is that real-world jobs require similar behaviour from male and female job incumbents.[96] However, women do adopt a participative leadership style more readily than their male

Microsoft Germany's Gender Leadership Boom

Europe's population is shrinking and aging, two trends that worried Achim Berg when he was hired as CEO of Microsoft Germany. Fortunately, in a country where men still overwhelmingly dominate the executive suite, the former Deutsche Telekom executive has a straightforward solution: Hire more female managers and create a work environment that motivates them to stay. Berg, who is now head of Windows Phone Marketing, added five women to the 12-person management board and a growing pool of junior female staff members working their way into leadership positions. Berg also welcomes the gender balance because it brings more diverse leadership styles. "Women have a different management style," Berg claims. Dorothee Belz, Microsoft Germany's director of legal and corporate affairs, agrees. She suggests that women look at issues differently and are more willing than men to discuss problems. Berg says that working with more female colleagues has also made him more consultative and less forceful. He has also noticed less politics in executive meetings. "It seems that there is a noticeable decline in territorial behaviour. But perhaps we'd be better off consulting a zoologist," says Berg, laughing. [97] *Photo by Mathias Woltmann*

counterparts. One possible reason is that, compared to boys, girls are often raised to be more egalitarian and less status-oriented, which is consistent with being participative. There is also some evidence that women have somewhat better interpersonal skills than men, and this translates into their relatively greater use of the participative leadership style. A third explanation is that employees, on the basis of their own gender stereotypes, expect female leaders to be more participative, so female leaders comply with follower expectations to some extent.

Several surveys report that women are rated higher than men on the emerging leadership qualities of coaching, teamwork, and empowering employees. [98] Yet research also suggests that women are evaluated negatively when they try to apply the full range of leadership styles, particularly more directive and autocratic approaches. Thus, ironically, women may be well suited to contemporary leadership roles, yet they often continue to face limitations of leadership through the gender stereotypes and prototypes of leaders that are held by followers. [99] Overall, both male and female leaders must be sensitive to the fact that followers have expectations about how leaders should act, and negative evaluations may go to leaders who deviate from those expectations.

CHAPTER SUMMARY

LO1 Define leadership and shared leadership.

Leadership is defined as the ability to influence, motivate, and enable others to contribute toward the effectiveness and success of the organizations of which they are members. Leaders use influence to motivate followers and arrange the work environment so that they do the job more effectively. Shared leadership views leadership as a role rather than a formal position, so employees throughout the organization act informally as leaders as the occasion arises. These situations include serving as champions for specific ideas or changes as well as filling leadership roles where it is needed.

LO2 Identify eight competencies associated with effective leaders and describe authentic leadership.

The competency perspective tries to identify the characteristics of effective leaders. Recent writing suggests that

leaders have specific personality characteristics, positive self-concept, drive, integrity, leadership motivation, knowledge of the business, cognitive and practical intelligence, and emotional intelligence. Authentic leadership refers to how well leaders are aware of, feel comfortable with, and act consistently with their self-concept. This concept consists mainly of two parts: self-awareness and engaging in behaviour that is consistent with one's self-concept.

LO3 Describe the key features of directive, supportive, and servant leadership, and discuss their effects on followers.

The behavioural perspective of leadership identifies two clusters of leader behaviour, supportive and directive. Supportive behaviours include showing mutual trust and respect for employees, demonstrating a genuine concern for their needs, and having a desire to look out for their welfare. Directive behaviours include assigning employees to specific tasks, clarifying their work duties and procedures, ensuring they follow company rules, and pushing them to reach their performance capacity.

Servant leadership defines leadership as serving others toward their need fulfillment and personal development and growth. Servant leaders have a natural desire or "calling" to serve others. They maintain a relationship with others that is humble, egalitarian, and accepting. Servant leaders also anchor their decisions and actions in ethical principles and practices

 LO4   Discuss the key elements of path-goal theory, Fiedler's contingency model, and leadership substitutes.

The contingency perspective of leadership takes the view that effective leaders diagnose the situation and adapt their style to fit that situation. The path-goal model is the prominent contingency theory that identifies four leadership styles—directive, supportive, participative, and achievement-oriented—and several contingencies relating to the characteristics of the employee and of the situation.

Two other contingency leadership theories include the situational leadership theory and Fiedler's contingency theory. Research support is quite weak for both theories. However, a lasting element of Fiedler's theory is the idea that leaders have natural styles and, consequently, companies need to change the leaders' environments to suit their style. Leadership substitutes theory identifies contingencies that either limit the leader's ability to influence subordinates or make a particular leadership style unnecessary.

LO5   Describe the four elements of transformational leadership and distinguish this theory from transactional and charismatic leadership.

Transformational leaders create a strategic vision, communicate that vision through framing and use of

metaphors, model the vision by 'walking the talk' and acting consistently, and build commitment toward the vision. This contrasts with transactional leadership, which has ambiguous meaning, but is usually viewed as an exchange relationship with followers. Transformational leadership is also distinguished from managerial leadership, which relates to the contingency theories of leadership. Some transformational leadership theories view charismatic leadership as an essential ingredient of transformational leadership. However, this view is inconsistent with the meaning of charisma and at odds with research on the dynamics and outcomes of charisma in leader-follower relationships.

 LO6   Describe the implicit leadership perspective.

According to the implicit leadership perspective, people have leadership prototypes, which they use to evaluate the leader's effectiveness. Furthermore, people form a romance of leadership; they want to believe that leaders make a difference, so they engage in fundamental attribution error and other perceptual distortions to support this belief in the leader's impact.

LO7   Discuss cultural and gender similarities and differences in leadership.

Cultural values also influence the leader's personal values, which in turn influence his or her leadership practices. Women generally do not differ from men in the degree of supportive or directive leadership. However, female leaders more often adopt a participative style. Research also suggests that people evaluate female leaders on the basis of gender stereotypes, which may result in higher or lower ratings.

KEY TERMS

authentic leadership, p. 332
Fiedler's contingency model, p. 338
implicit leadership theory, p. 344
leadership, p. 328
leadership substitutes, p. 339

managerial leadership, p. 340
path-goal leadership theory, p. 335
servant leadership, p. 334
shared leadership, p. 329

situational leadership
   theory (SLT), p. 338
transactional leadership, p. 340
transformational leadership, p. 340

CRITICAL-THINKING QUESTIONS

1. Why is it important for top executives to value and support shared leadership?

2. Find two ads for management or executive positions. What leadership competencies are mentioned in these ads? If you were on the selection panel, what methods would you use to identify these competencies in job applicants?

3. Consider your favourite teacher. What supportive and directive leadership behaviours did he or she use effectively? In general, do you think students prefer an

instructor who is more supportive or directive? Explain your preference.

4. Your employees are skilled and experienced customer service representatives who perform nonroutine tasks, such as solving unique customer problems or meeting special needs with the company's equipment. Use path-goal theory to identify the most appropriate leadership style(s) you should use in this situation. Be sure to fully explain your answer, and discuss why other styles are less appropriate.

5. Transformational leadership is the most popular perspective of leadership. However, it is far from perfect. Discuss the limitations of transformational leadership.

6. This chapter distinguished charismatic leadership from transformational leadership. Yet charisma is identified by most employees and managers as a characteristic of effective leaders. Why is charisma commonly related to leadership? In your opinion, are the best leaders charismatic? Why or why not?

7. Identify a current political leader (e.g., prime minister, president, premier, mayor) and his or her recent accomplishments. Now, using the implicit leadership perspective, think of ways that these accomplishments

of the leader may be overstated. In other words, explain why they may be due to factors other than the leader.

8. You hear two people debating the merits of women as leaders. One person claims that women make better leaders than do men because women are more sensitive to their employees' needs and involve them in organizational decisions. The other person counters that although these leadership styles may be increasingly important, most women have trouble gaining acceptance as leaders when they face tough situations in which a more autocratic style is required. Discuss the accuracy of the comments made in this discussion.

 CASE STUDY 12.1

Profitel Inc.

By Steven L. McShane, The University of Western Australia

As a formerly government-owned telephone monopoly, Profitel enjoyed many decades of minimal competition. Even today as a publicly traded enterprise, the company's almost exclusive control over telephone copper wiring across the country keeps its profit margins above 40 percent. Competitors in telephone and DSL broadband continue to rely on Profitel's wholesale business, which generates substantially more profit than similar wholesale services in many other countries. However, Profitel has stiff competition in the cellular (mobile) telephone business, and other emerging technologies (voice-over-Internet) threaten Profitel's dominance. Based on these threats, Profitel's board of directors decided to hire an outsider as the new chief executive.

Although several qualified candidates expressed an interest in Profitel's top job, the board selected Lars Peeters, who had been CEO for six years of a publicly traded European telephone company, followed by a brief stint as CEO of a cellular telephone company in the United States until it was acquired by a larger firm. Profitel's board couldn't believe its good fortune; Peeters brought extensive industry knowledge and global experience, a high-octane energy level, self-confidence, decisiveness, and congenial yet strongly persuasive interpersonal style. He also had a unique "presence," which caused people to pay attention and respect his leadership. The board was also impressed with Peeters strategy to bolster Profitel's profit margins. This included heavy investment in the latest wireless broadband technology (for both cellular telephone and computer Internet) before competitors could gain a foothold, cutting costs through layoffs and reduction of peripheral services, and putting pressure on government to deregulate its traditional and emerging businesses. When Peeters described his strategy to the board, one board member commented that this was the same strategy Peeters used in his previous two CEO postings. Peeters dismissed the comment, saying that each situation is unique.

Peeters lived up to his reputation as a decisive executive. Almost immediately after taking the CEO job at Profitel, he hired two executives from the European company where he previously worked. Together over the next two years they cut the workforce by 5 percent and rolled out the new wireless broadband technology for cellphones and Internet. Costs increased somewhat due to downsizing expenses and the wireless technology rollout. Profitel's wireless broadband subscriber list grew quickly because, in spite of its very high prices, the technology faced limited competition and Profitel was pushing customers off the older technology to the new network. Profitel's customer satisfaction ratings fell, however. A national consumer research group reported that Profitel's broadband offered the country's worst value. Employee morale also declined due to layoffs and the company's public image problems. Some industry experts also noted that Profitel selected its wireless technology without evaluating the alternative emerging wireless technology, which had been gaining ground in other countries. Peeters' aggressive campaign against government regulation also had unintended consequences. Rather than achieving less regulation, criticizing government and its telecommunications regulator made Profitel look even more arrogant in the eyes of both customers and government leaders.

Profitel's board was troubled by the company's lacklustre share price, which had declined 20 percent since Peeters was hired. Some board members also worried that the company had bet on the wrong wireless technology and that subscription levels would stall far below the number necessary to achieve the profits stated in Peeters' strategic plan. This concern came closer to reality when a foreign-owned competitor won a $1 billion government contract to improve broadband services in regional areas of the country. Profitel's proposal for that regional broadband upgrade specified high prices and limited corporate investment, but Peeters was confident Profitel would be awarded the contract because of its market dominance and existing infrastructure with the new wireless network. When the government decided otherwise, Profitel's board fired Peeters along with two executives he had hired from the European company where he previously worked. Now, the board had to figure out what went wrong and how to avoid this problem in the future.

Discussion Questions

1. Which perspective of leadership best explains the problems experienced in this case? Analyze the case using concepts discussed in that leadership perspective.

2. What can organizations do to minimize the leadership problems discussed above?

 CASE STUDY 12.2

The Staff Sergeant's Leadership Dilemma

By James Buchkowsky, Saskatchewan Institute of Applied Science and Technology

Donna Lindsay, staff sergeant and commander of a Canadian regional police force detachment, just learned that she was not getting a replacement for a constable who had recently retired. Lindsay's superintendent said, "Hiring freezes are in effect until the next budget year, so you'll have to figure out a way for the other constables to pick up the work." Donna spent the rest of the day deciding how to divide the work among the other officers in her detachment.

The next morning at the daily briefing session, Donna announced the hiring freeze and that the constable position would not be replaced. She explained how she had divided the job into seven categories so that one constable would be responsible for each. Donna then informed the officers of the additional work that would be added to their duties. During the rest of the session, Donna couldn't help notice that many weren't reacting favourably to the announced assignments.

The next day, one constable, Earl, was waiting for her at her office door. "Why did you assign me to deal with the media?" he asked. "I hate being in front of a camera. Can't you tell someone else they have to do this?"

Before long another staff member, Joe, was at Donna's door. "Can't you reassign the travelling presentations to someone else? I have a wife and young children. This detachment covers a large area with small communities, and asking me to travel all over is really unfair to my family."

By the end of the day, the seven constables had produced seven complaints. Donna re-examined the tasks and duties, attempted to juggle and switch assignments, and considered everyone's concerns but it nearly drove her crazy. She concluded there was nothing she could do to make everyone happy. She called another staff meeting and said, "I've tried to accommodate you, but it can't be done. Take the assignments I've given you and do your best."

The officers didn't take to this decision very well and started taking matters into their own hands. Earl said to Joe, "I know you hate the travelling presentations, so I'll do them if you'll take my assignment." Roz told Linda, "I'll give you my research work if you'll do the evidence cataloguing." When other staff heard about the trading, they joined right in also. With more people making more offers, this wheeling and dealing kept getting louder and louder. Donna came out of her office to see what all the noise was about.

When Donna learned the staff were trading assignments without her consent, she was upset. A few days later, while discussing other matters on the telephone with her immediate supervisor in the regional office, Donna mentioned the events. "Some officers seem happy with their trades, but the ones who didn't get the trade they wanted are unhappy and directing the blame at me. What did I do wrong? How should I have handled this? What am I going to do now?"

Discussion Questions

1. What leadership style did Donna use? Was it appropriate for the situation?

2. Analyze the environmental and employee factors in this case to determine which style she should have adopted.

3. Since her approach did not work, what style should Donna use now?

 TEAM EXERCISE 12.3

Leadership Diagnostic Analysis

Purpose   To help students learn about the different path-goal leadership styles and when to apply each style.

Instructions
- *Step 1:* Students individually write down two incidents in which someone had been an effective manager or leader for them. The leader and situation might be from work, a sports team, a student work group, or any other setting where leadership might emerge. For example, students might describe how their supervisor in a summer job pushed them to reach higher performance goals than they would have done otherwise. Each incident should state the actual behaviours that the leader used, not just general statements (e.g., "My boss sat down with me and we agreed on specific targets and deadlines, then he said several times over the next few weeks that I was capable of reaching those goals"). Each incident requires only two or three sentences.

- *Step 2:* After everyone has written their two incidents, the instructor will form small groups (typically between four or five students). Each team will answer the following questions for each incident presented in that team:

  1. Which path-goal theory leadership style(s)—directive, supportive, participative, or achievement-oriented—did the leader apply in this incident?

  2. Ask the person who wrote the incident about the conditions that made this leadership style (or these styles, if more than one was used) appropriate in this situation. The team should list these contingency factors clearly and, where possible, connect them to the contingencies described in path-goal theory. (Note: the team might identify path-goal leadership contingencies that are not described in the book. These, too, should be noted and discussed.)

- *Step 3:* After the teams have diagnosed the incidents, each team will describe to the entire class the most interesting incidents as well as its diagnosis of that incident. Other teams will critique the diagnosis. Any leadership contingencies not mentioned in the textbook should also be presented and discussed.

SELF-ASSESSMENT EXERCISE 12.4

Do You Think Leaders Make a Difference?

Purpose   This assessment is designed to help you assess your beliefs about the influence of leaders.

Instructions   Read each of the statements below and check the box that best indicates your personal belief about that statement. Then use the scoring key in Appendix B to calculate the results for each leadership dimension. After completing this assessment, be prepared to discuss in class the relevance and level of implicit leadership theory.

Romance of Leadership Scale					
To what extent do you agree or disagree that . . .	Strongly Agree	Agree	Neutral	Disagree	Strongly Disagree
1. Even in an economic recession, a good leader can prevent a company from doing poorly.	☐	☐	☐	☐	☐
2. The quality of leadership is the single most important influence on how well the organization functions.	☐	☐	☐	☐	☐
3. The CEO and executive team have relatively little effect on the company's success or failure.	☐	☐	☐	☐	☐
4. Sooner or later, bad leadership at the top will result in declining organizational performance.	☐	☐	☐	☐	☐
5. The effect of a company's leaders on organizational performance is fairly weak.	☐	☐	☐	☐	☐
6. A company is only as good or as bad as its leaders.	☐	☐	☐	☐	☐
7. Even the best leaders can't help an organization very much when the economy is bad or competition is tough.	☐	☐	☐	☐	☐
8. It is impossible for an organization to do well when its leaders are average.	☐	☐	☐	☐	☐
9. Compared with the economy, competition, and other external forces, leaders have only a small influence on a firm's performance.	☐	☐	☐	☐	☐
10. The company's top executives have the power to make or break the organization.	☐	☐	☐	☐	☐

Source: This instrument is adapted and condensed from B. Schyns, J. R. Meindl, and M. A. Croon, "The Romance of Leadership Scale: Cross-cultural Testing and Refinement," *Leadership* 3, no. 1 (2007), pp. 29–46.

SELF-ASSESSMENT EXERCISE 12.5

What Kind of Leader Are You?

Whether you are the head of a large corporation or an informal leader of a student team, there are several dimensions of leadership that seem to have an effect on the team's or organization's success. This self-assessment estimates your degree of leadership on several important dimensions relevant to both transformational and managerial leadership. This exercise should be completed alone so that you assess yourself honestly, without concerns of social comparison. Class discussion will focus on transformational and managerial leadership, including their dimensions and how they might influence followers in various settings.

Practise and learn online with Connect. Connect resources include additional and interactive study exercises, videos, and practice quizzing, as well as additional material you won't find in the printed text.

CHAPTER 13

Designing Organizational Structures

LEARNING OBJECTIVES

After reading this chapter, you should be able to:

LO1 Describe three types of coordination in organizational structures.

LO2 Discuss the role and effects of span of control, centralization, and formalization, and relate these elements to organic and mechanistic organizational structures.

LO3 Identify and evaluate six types of departmentalization.

LO4 Explain how the external environment, organizational size, technology, and strategy are relevant when designing an organizational structure.

"They've taken decades to be able to get to where handing a Tim Hortons' cup to someone as they get off a plane symbolizes welcoming them to Canada," explains Patricia Cormack, sociology professor at St. Francis Xavier University in Antigonish, Nova Scotia. Have you ever wondered about what type of organizational structure is in place at this iconic brand?

Tim Hortons' coffee blend originated in the kitchen of hockey legend Tim Horton and his wife Lori. His first coffee and doughnuts shop was a former gas station in Hamilton, Ontario. The much loved Tim Hortons' brand has been built on the foundation of consistency, dependability, and a humble approach that mirrors qualities that many Canadians value and see in themselves.

The TDL Group Corp. is the organization that serves as the "operators of the Tim Hortons' chain." TDL's head office, located in the original Tim Hortons' warehouse in Oakville, Ontario, employs more than 700 corporate employees from most major departments. This structure creates specialized areas of talent such as Marketing & Corporate Affairs, Research & Development, Distribution, Operations, Finance & Taxation, Information Technology, Human Resources, Real Estate, and Construction & Store Design. Oakville is also the home of Tim Hortons' National Training Centre where all new restaurant owners engage in seven weeks of intensive training from subject-matter experts in their various fields of expertise.

TDL's functional structure is also supplemented by a geographic divisional structure that consists of regional offices located in Calgary, Alberta; Langley, British Columbia; Debert, Nova Scotia; Kingston, Ontario; Lachine, Quebec; as well as U.S. locations including Dublin, Ohio; West Greenwich, Rhode Island; and Brighton, Michigan. These regional offices employ smaller teams that handle many of the same departmental functions as the Oakville head office and ensure that unique regional needs and customer preferences are managed proactively.

Combining a functional and divisional structure aligned with geographic diversity supports Tim Hortons' success and ability to continue to deliver double-digit growth to its shareholders and the iconic double-double.[1]

What type of organizational structures does Tim Hortons have?
BRENDAN MCDERMID/Reuters/Landov

organizational structure The division of labour as well as the patterns of coordination, communication, workflow, and formal power that direct organizational activities.

This brief summary of Tim Hortons organizational structure reveals how it is an important instrument for guiding and providing resources around the organization's strategy. **Organizational structure** refers to the division of labour as well as the patterns of coordination, communication, workflow, and formal power that direct organizational activities. It formally dictates what activities receive the most attention as well as financial, power, and information resources. For example, Tim Hortons has a combination of functional and geographic structure because the company delivers similar products and services across Canada and into the United States (as well as a few outlets beyond North America). Organizing in this way provides the best arrangement for employees to coordinate and share knowledge effectively with each other.

Tim Hortons organizational chart is only part of its organizational structure. In fact, throughout this chapter, we hope to show that an organization's structure is much more than an organizational chart diagramming which employees report to which managers. Organizational structure includes reporting relationships, but it also relates to job design, information flow, work standards and rules, team dynamics, and power relationships. As such, the organization's structure is an important instrument in an executive's toolkit for organizational change because it establishes new communication patterns and aligns employee behaviour with the corporate vision.[2]

> The organization's structure is an important instrument in an executive's toolkit for organizational change. "

For example, the Toronto Transit Commission's (TTC) customer service advisory panel identified creation of a chief customer service officer position as the top priority for improving the organization's troubled customer service reputation. The TTC followed this advice, with the recently hired executive (a Canadian previously employed with the London Underground) reporting directly to the general manager.[3] Through this organizational structure change, customer focus immediately became a higher priority because the TTC's executive team works continuously with someone who keeps customer service at the forefront of key decisions and actions.

This chapter begins by introducing the two fundamental processes in organizational structure: division of labour and coordination. This is followed by a detailed investigation of the four main elements of organizational structure: span of control, centralization, formalization, and departmentalization. The latter part of this chapter examines the contingencies of organizational design, including external environment, organizational size, technology, and strategy.

DIVISION OF LABOUR AND COORDINATION

LO1

All organizational structures include two fundamental requirements: the division of labour into distinct tasks and the coordination of that labour so that employees are able to accomplish common goals.[4] Organizations are groups of people who work interdependently toward some purpose. To efficiently accomplish their goals, these groups typically divide the work into manageable chunks, particularly when there are many different tasks to perform. They also introduce various coordinating mechanisms to ensure that everyone is working effectively toward the same objectives.

DIVISION OF LABOUR

Division of labour refers to the subdivision of work into separate jobs assigned to different people. Subdivided work leads to job specialization, because each job now includes a narrow subset of the tasks necessary to complete the product or service. Tim Hortons organizes employees into hundreds of specific jobs to more effectively serve customers and manage the purchase and delivery of resources to the restaurants. As companies get larger, this horizontal division of labour is usually accompanied by vertical division of labour: Some people are assigned the task of supervising employees, others are responsible for managing those supervisors, and so on.

Why do companies divide the work of the organization into several jobs? As we described earlier in this book, job specialization increases work efficiency.[5] Job incumbents can master their tasks quickly because work cycles are very short. Less time is wasted changing from one task to another. Training costs are reduced because employees require fewer physical and mental skills to accomplish the assigned work. Finally, job specialization makes it easier to match people with specific aptitudes or skills to the jobs for which they are best suited. Although one person working alone might be able to prepare, serve, and market Tim Hortons food products at each restaurant, doing so would take much longer than having some people prepare the food, others serve it to customers, and still others take care of marketing, purchasing, accounting, and other functions. Some employees are gifted at serving customers, whereas others are more talented at negotiating raw materials or designing interesting marketing campaigns.

COORDINATING WORK ACTIVITIES

When people divide work among themselves, they require coordinating mechanisms to ensure that everyone works in concert. Coordination is so closely connected to division of labour that the optimal level of specialization is limited by the feasibility of coordinating the work. In other words, an organization should divide work among many people only to the extent that those people can coordinate with each other. Otherwise, individual effort is wasted due to misalignment, duplication, and mistiming of tasks. Coordination also tends to become more expensive and difficult as the division of labour increases. Therefore, companies specialize jobs only to the point where it isn't too costly or challenging to coordinate the people in those jobs.[6]

Every organization—from the two-person corner convenience store to the largest corporate entity—uses one or more of the following coordinating mechanisms:[7] informal communication, formal hierarchy, and standardization (see Exhibit 13.1). These forms of coordination align the work of staff within the same department as well as across work units. These coordinating mechanisms are also critical when several organizations work together, such as in joint ventures and humanitarian aid programs.[8]

Exhibit 13.1   COORDINATING MECHANISMS IN ORGANIZATIONS

Form of Coordination	Description	Subtypes/Strategies
Informal communication	Sharing information on mutual tasks; forming common mental models to synchronize work activities	• Direct communication • Liaison roles • Integrator roles • Temporary teams
Formal hierarchy	Assigning legitimate power to individuals, who then use this power to direct work processes and allocate resources	• Direct supervision • Formal communication channels
Standardization	Creating routine patterns of behaviour or output	• Standardized skills • Standardized processes • Standardized output

Sources: Based on information in J. Galbraith, *Designing Complex Organizations* (Reading, MA: Addison-Wesley, 1973), pp. 8–19; H. Mintzberg, *The Structuring of Organizations* (Englewood Cliffs, NJ: Prentice Hall, 1979), Chapter 1; D. A. Nadler and M. L. Tushman, *Competing by Design: The Power of Organizational Architecture* (New York: Oxford University Press, 1997), Chapter 6.

Coordination through Informal Communication   Informal communication is a coordinating mechanism in all organizations. It includes sharing information on mutual tasks as well as forming common mental models so that employees synchronize work activities using the same mental road map.[9] Informal communication is vital in nonroutine and ambiguous situations because employees can exchange a large volume of information through face-to-face communication and other media-rich channels.

Coordination through informal communication is easiest in small firms, although information technologies have further leveraged this coordinating mechanism in large organizations.[10] Companies employing thousands of people also support informal communication by keeping each production site small. Magna International, the Canadian-based global auto-parts manufacturer, keeps its plants to a maximum size of around 200 employees. Magna's leaders believe that employees have difficulty remembering each other's names in plants that are any larger, a situation that makes informal communication more difficult as a coordinating mechanism.[11]

Larger organizations also encourage coordination through informal communication by assigning *liaison roles* to employees, who are expected to communicate and share information with co-workers in other work units. Where coordination is required among several work units, companies create *integrator roles*. These people are responsible for coordinating a work process by encouraging employees in each work unit to share information and informally coordinate work activities. Integrators do not have authority over the people involved in that process, so they must rely on persuasion and commitment. Brand managers at Procter & Gamble have integrator roles because they coordinate work among marketing, production, and design groups.[12]

Another way that larger organizations encourage coordination through informal communication is by organizing employees from several departments into temporary teams. **Concurrent engineering** applies this coordinating strategy for development of products or services. Concurrent engineering typically consists of a cross-functional project team of people from various functional departments, such as design engineering, manufacturing, marketing, and purchasing. By being assigned to a team, rather than working within their usual specialized departments, these employees have more authority and opportunity to coordinate with each other using informal communication. When the design engineer begins to form the product specifications, representatives from manufacturing, engineering, marketing, purchasing, and other departments can offer feedback as well as begin their contribution to the process. By coordinating through information-rich informal communication, concurrent engineering teams tend to produce higher-quality products with dramatically less development time compared to situations where employees work in their own departments and coordinate through other means.[13]

> **concurrent engineering**
> The organization of employees from several departments into a temporary team for the purpose of developing a product or service.

Coordination through Formal Hierarchy   Informal communication is the most flexible form of coordination, but it can become chaotic as the number of employees increases. Consequently, as organizations grow, they rely increasingly on a second coordinating mechanism: formal hierarchy.[14] Hierarchy assigns legitimate power to individuals, who then use this power to direct work processes and allocate resources. In other words, work is coordinated through direct supervision—the chain of command. For instance, Tim Hortons' restaurants have managers and assistant managers who are responsible for ensuring that employees are properly trained and perform their respective tasks as well as coordinate effectively with other staff on each work shift.

A century ago, management scholars applauded the formal hierarchy as the best coordinating mechanism for large organizations. They argued that organizations are most effective when managers exercise their authority and employees receive orders from only one supervisor. The chain of command—in which information flowed across work units only through supervisors and managers—was viewed as the backbone of organizational strength.

Although still important, formal hierarchy is much less popular today. One concern is that it is not as agile for coordination in complex and novel situations. Communicating through the chain of command is rarely as fast or accurate as direct communication between employees. For instance, product development—typically a complex and novel activity—tends to occur more quickly and produce higher-quality results when people coordinate mainly through informal communication rather than formal hierarchy. Another concern with formal hierarchy is that managers are able to closely supervise only a limited number of employees. As the business grows, the number of supervisors and layers of management must increase, resulting in a costly bureaucracy. Finally, today's workforce demands more autonomy over work and more involvement in company decisions. Formal hierarchy coordination processes tend to conflict with employee autonomy and involvement.

Coordination through Standardization   Standardization, the third means of coordination, involves creating routine patterns of behaviour or output. This coordinating mechanism takes three distinct forms:

- *Standardized processes.* Quality and consistency of a product or service can often be improved by standardizing work activities through job descriptions and procedures.[15] This coordinating mechanism is feasible when the work is routine (such as mass production) or simple (such as making pizzas), but it is less effective in nonroutine and complex work such as product design.

- *Standardized outputs.* This form of standardization involves ensuring that individuals and work units have clearly defined goals and output measures (e.g., customer satisfaction, production efficiency). For instance, to coordinate the work of salespeople, companies assign sales targets rather than specific behaviours.

- *Standardized skills.* When work activities are too complex to standardize through processes or goals, companies often coordinate work effort by extensively training employees or hiring people who have learned precise role behaviours from educational programs. This form of coordination is used in hospital operating rooms. Surgeons, nurses, and other operating room professionals coordinate their work more through training than through goals or company rules.

Division of labour and coordination of work represent the two fundamental ingredients of all organizations. But how work is divided, which coordinating mechanisms are emphasized, who makes decisions, and other issues are related to the four elements of organizational structure.

ELEMENTS OF ORGANIZATIONAL STRUCTURE

L02

Organizational structure has four elements that apply to every organization. This section introduces three of them: span of control, centralization, and formalization. The fourth element—departmentalization—is presented in the next section.

SPAN OF CONTROL

span of control The number of people directly reporting to the next level in the hierarchy.

Span of control (also called *span of management*) refers to the number of people directly reporting to the next level in the hierarchy. A narrow span of control exists when very few people report directly to a manager, whereas a wide span exists when a manager has many direct reports.[16] A century ago, French engineer and management scholar Henri Fayol strongly recommended a relatively narrow span of control, typically no more than 20 employees per supervisor and six supervisors per manager. Fayol championed formal hierarchy as the primary coordinating mechanism, so he believed that supervisors should closely monitor and coach employees. His views were similar to those of Napoleon, who declared that five reporting officers is the maximum span of control for more senior leaders. These prescriptions were based on the belief that managers simply could not monitor and control any more employees closely enough.[17]

Today, we know better. The best-performing manufacturing plants currently have an average of 38 production employees per supervisor (see Exhibit 13.2).[18] What's the secret here? Did Fayol, Napoleon, and others miscalculate the optimal span of control? The answer is that those sympathetic to hierarchical control believed that employees should perform the physical tasks, whereas supervisors and other management personnel should make the decisions and monitor employees to make sure they performed their tasks. In contrast, the best-performing manufacturing operations today rely on self-directed teams, so direct supervision (formal hierarchy) is supplemented with other coordinating mechanisms. Self-directed teams coordinate mainly through informal communication and standardization, so formal hierarchy plays more of a supporting role.

Many firms that employ doctors, lawyers, and other professionals also have a wider span of control because these staff members coordinate their work mainly through standardized skills. For example, more than two dozen people report directly to Cindy Zollinger, president of Boston-based litigation-consulting firm Cornerstone Research. Zollinger explains that this large number of direct reports is possible because she leads professional staff who don't require close supervision. "They largely run themselves," Zollinger explains. "I help them in dealing with obstacles they face, or in making the most of opportunities that they find."[19]

A second factor influencing the best span of control is whether employees perform routine tasks. A wider span of control is possible when employees perform routine jobs, because there is less frequent need for direction or advice from supervisors. A narrow span of control is necessary when employees perform novel or complex tasks, because these employees tend to require more supervisory decisions and coaching. This principle

Exhibit 13.2 \ RECOMMENDED, ACTUAL, AND ENFORCED SPANS OF CONTROL[20]

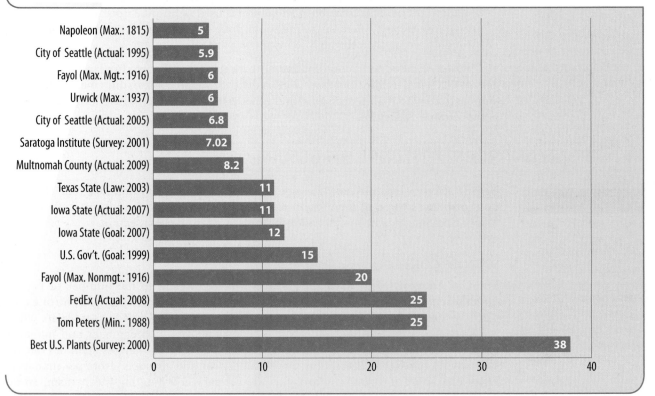

Figures represent the average number of direct reports per manager. "Max." figures represent the maximum spans of control recommended by Napoleon Bonaparte, Henri Fayol, and Lindall Urwick. "Min." figure represents the minimum span of control recommended by Tom Peters. "Goal" figures represent span of control targets that the U.S. Government and the State of Iowa have tried to achieve. The State of Texas figure represents the span of control mandated by law. The Saratoga Institute figure is the average span of control among U.S. companies surveyed. The Best U.S. Plants figure is the average span of control in American manufacturing facilities identified by *Industry Week* magazine as the most effective. "Actual" figures are spans of control at the City of Seattle, Multnomah County (including Portland, Oregon), the State of Iowa, and Fedex Corporation in the years indicated.

is illustrated in a survey of property and casualty insurers. The average span of control in commercial-policy processing departments is around 15 employees per supervisor, whereas the span of control is 6.1 in claims service and 5.5 in commercial underwriting. Staff members in the latter two departments perform more technical work, so they have more novel and complex tasks. Commercial-policy processing, on the other hand, is like production work, where tasks are routine and have few exceptions.[21]

A third influence on span of control is the degree of interdependence among employees within the department or team.[22] Generally, a narrow span of control is necessary where employees perform highly interdependent work with others. More supervision is required for highly interdependent jobs because employees tend to experience more conflict with each other, which requires more of a manager's time to resolve. Also, employees are less clear on their personal work performance in highly interdependent tasks, so supervisors spend more time providing coaching and feedback.

Tall versus Flat Structures   Span of control is interconnected with organizational size (number of employees) and the number of layers in the organizational hierarchy. Consider two companies with the same number of employees. If Company A has a wider span of control (more direct reports per manager) than Company B, then Company A must have fewer layers of management (i.e., a flatter structure) than does Company B. The reason for this relationship is that a company with a wider span of control necessarily has more employees per supervisor, more supervisors for each middle manager, and so on. This larger number of direct reports, compared to a company with a narrower span of control, is possible only by removing layers of management. The interconnection of span of control, organizational size (number of employees), and number of management layers also means that as companies employ more people, they must widen the span of control, build a taller hierarchy, or both. Most companies end up building taller structures because they rely on direct supervision to some extent as a coordinating mechanism and there are limits to how many people each manager can coordinate.

Unfortunately, building a taller hierarchy (more layers of management) creates problems. First, tall structures have higher overhead costs because most layers of hierarchy consist of managers rather than employees who actually make the product or supply the service. Second, senior managers in tall structures often receive lower-quality and less timely information from the external environment because information from front-line employees is transmitted slowly or not at all up the hierarchy. Also, the more layers of management through which information must pass, the higher the probability that managers will filter out information that does not put them in a positive light. Finally, tall hierarchies tend to undermine employee empowerment and engagement because they focus power around managers rather than employees.[23]

These problems have prompted leaders to "delayer"—remove one or more levels in the organizational hierarchy.[24] A recent example is KenGen, Kenya's electricity generation

The Struggle to Stay Flat

When Ken Iverson became CEO of Nucor Corporation in the mid-1960s, he insisted that the American steelmaker have only three layers of management below him: Crew supervisors reported to their functional manager (production, shipping, maintenance), who reported to the plant manager, who reported to Iverson. By allowing each plant to operate as an independent business, this flat structure was manageable even as Nucor grew to more than two dozen plants. But today Nucor is America's largest steelmaker, employing 20,000 people at more than four dozen facilities worldwide (including several in Canada). Managing 50 or more direct reports would itself be a full-time job, so Nucor's current chairman and CEO, Dan DiMicco (shown in this photo), reluctantly added five executive vice-presidents, creating another layer of management. "I needed to be free to make decisions on trade battles," says DiMicco apologetically, adding that he continues to stay involved by checking his own email and meeting with staff at every opportunity. Even with five layers of hierarchy, Nucor is incredibly lean. Many other companies the same size have twice as many levels of management.[25] *AP Photo/Chuck Burton*

company. KenGen had more than 15 layers of hierarchy a few years ago. Today, the company's 1,500 employees work in a hierarchy with only six layers: the chief executive, executive directors, senior managers, chief officers, front-line management, and nonmanagement staff. "This flatter structure has reduced bureaucracy and it has also improved teamwork," explains KenGen executive Simon Ngure.[26] BASF's European Seal Sands plant went even further when it was dramatically restructured around self-directed teams. "Seven levels of management have been cut basically to two," says a BASF executive.[27]

Although many companies enjoy reduced costs and more empowered employees when they delayer the organizational hierarchy, organizational experts warn that there are also negative long-term consequences of cutting out too much middle management.[28] These include undermining necessary managerial functions, increasing workload and stress among management, and restricting managerial career development:

- *Undermines managerial functions.* Critics of delayering point out that all companies need managers to translate corporate strategy into coherent daily operations. "Middle managers are the link between your mission and execution," advises a senior hospital executive. "They turn our strategy into action and get everyone on the same page."[29] Furthermore, managers are needed to make quick decisions, coach employees, and help resolve conflicts. These valuable functions are underserved when the span of control becomes too wide.

- *Increases workload and stress.* Delayering increases the number of direct reports per manager and thus significantly increases management workload and corresponding levels of stress. Managers partly reduce the workload by learning to give employees more autonomy rather than micromanaging them. However, this role adjustment itself is stressful (same responsibility, but less authority or control). Also, many companies increase the span of control beyond the point at which many managers are capable of coaching or leading their direct reports.

- *Restricts managerial career development.* Delayering results in fewer managerial jobs, so companies have less manoeuvrability to develop managerial skills. Promotions are also riskier because they involve a larger jump in responsibility in flatter, compared to taller, hierarchies. Furthermore, having fewer promotion opportunities means that managers experience more career plateauing, which reduces their motivation and loyalty. Chopping back managerial career structures also sends a signal that managers are no longer valued. "Delayering has had an adverse effect on morale, productivity and performance," argues a senior government executive. "Disenfranchising middle management creates negative perceptions and lower commitment to the organization with consequent reluctance to accept responsibility."[30]

CENTRALIZATION AND DECENTRALIZATION

For many years, Barrick Gold Corporation concentrated decision making at its Canadian headquarters even though it was becoming the world's largest gold producer with far flung operations around the world. "Barrick had always been run on this command-and-control model, a centrist approach that saw all the decision making made in Toronto," says Barrick's late CEO Greg Wilkins. "That worked while the company was small and operating only in North America. But all of a sudden we are in four continents and seven countries and it becomes pretty clear that you just can't do it anymore." The solution that Wilkins and his senior leadership team implemented was a more decentralized structure in which Barrick's four regional business units are now responsible for their own operations and business growth. Headquarters provides the strategic guidance and oversight.[31]

> **centralization** The degree to which formal decision making authority is held by a small group of people, typically those at the top of the organizational hierarchy.

This Barrick Gold story illustrates that a key decision in designing organizations is how much to centralize or decentralize decision making power. **Centralization** means that formal decision making authority is held by a small group of people, typically those at the top of the organizational hierarchy. Most organizations begin with centralized structures, as the founder makes most of the decisions and tries to direct the business toward his or her vision. As organizations grow, however, they diversify and their environments become more complex. Senior executives aren't able to process all the decisions that significantly influence the business. Consequently, larger organizations typically *decentralize;* that is, they disperse decision authority and power throughout the organization.

The optimal level of centralization or decentralization depends on several contingencies that we will examine later in this chapter. However, we also need to keep in mind that different degrees of decentralization can occur simultaneously in different parts of an organization. Nestlé, the Swiss-based food company, has decentralized marketing decisions to remain responsive to local markets, but it has centralized production, logistics, and supply chain management activities to improve cost efficiencies and avoid having too much complexity across the organization. "If you are too decentralized, you can become too complicated—you get too much complexity in your production system," explains a Nestlé executive.[32]

Likewise, 7-Eleven relies on both centralization and decentralization in different parts of the organization. The convenience store chain leverages buying power and efficiencies by centralizing decisions about information technology and supplier purchasing. At the same time, it decentralizes local inventory decisions to store managers so that they can adapt quickly to changing circumstances at the local level. Along with receiving ongoing product training and guidance from regional consultants, store managers have the best information about their customers and can respond quickly to local market needs. "We could never predict a busload of football players on a Friday night, but the store manager can," explains a 7-Eleven executive.[33]

formalization The degree to which organizations standardize behaviour through rules, procedures, formal training, and related mechanisms.

FORMALIZATION

Formalization is the degree to which organizations standardize behaviour through rules, procedures, formal training, and related mechanisms.[34] In other words, companies become more formalized as they increasingly rely on various forms of standardization to coordinate work. McDonald's Restaurants and most other efficient fast-food chains typically have a high degree of formalization because they rely on standardization of work processes as a coordinating mechanism. Employees have precisely defined roles, right down to how much mustard should be dispensed, how many pickles should be applied, and how long each hamburger should be cooked.

Older companies tend to become more formalized because work activities become routinized, making them easier to document into standardized practices. Larger companies also tend to have more formalization because direct supervision and informal communication among employees do not operate as easily when large numbers of people are involved. External influences, such as government safety legislation and strict accounting rules, also encourage formalization.

Formalization may increase efficiency and compliance, but it can also create problems.[35] Rules and procedures reduce organizational flexibility, so employees follow prescribed behaviours even when the situation clearly calls for a customized response. High levels of formalization tend to undermine organizational learning and creativity. Some work rules become so convoluted that organizational efficiency would decline if they were actually followed as prescribed. Formalization is also a source of job dissatisfaction and work stress. Finally, rules and procedures have been known to take on a life of their own in some organizations. They become the focus of attention rather than the organization's ultimate objectives of producing a product or service and serving its dominant stakeholders.

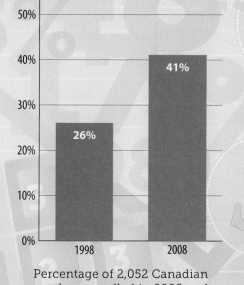

OB BY THE NUMBERS

The Price of Formalization: More Red Tape[36]

Percentage of 2,052 Canadian employees polled in 2008 and 1,200 Canadian employees polled in 1998 who identified "red tape and bureaucracy" as one of the biggest barriers to their work productivity.

1998: 26%
2008: 41%

MECHANISTIC VERSUS ORGANIC STRUCTURES

mechanistic structure
An organizational structure with a narrow span of control and a high degree of formalization and centralization.

organic structure An organizational structure with a wide span of control, little formalization, and decentralized decision making.

We discussed span of control, centralization, and formalization together because they cluster around two broader organizational forms: mechanistic and organic structures (see Exhibit 13.3).[37] A **mechanistic structure** is characterized by a narrow span of control and high degree of formalization and centralization. Mechanistic structures have many rules and procedures, limited decision making at lower levels, tall hierarchies of people in specialized roles, and vertical rather than horizontal communication flows. Tasks are rigidly defined and are altered only when sanctioned by higher authorities. Companies with an **organic structure** have the opposite characteristics. They operate with a wide span of control, little formalization, and decentralized decision making. Tasks are fluid, adjusting to new situations and organizational needs. Connections 13.1 illustrates how TAXI, Canada's top ranked creative agency, relies on an organic structure to remain nimble.

As a general rule, mechanistic structures operate better in stable environments because they rely on efficiency and routine behaviours, whereas organic structures work better in rapidly changing (i.e., dynamic) environments because they are more flexible and responsive to the changes. Organic structures are also more compatible with organizational learning, high-performance workplaces, and quality management because they emphasize information sharing and an empowered workforce rather than hierarchy and status.[38] However, the advantages of organic structures, rather than mechanistic structures, in dynamic environments occur only when employees have developed well-established roles and expertise.[39] Without these conditions, employees are unable to coordinate effectively with each other, resulting in errors and gross inefficiencies.

Start-up companies often face this problem, known as the *liability of newness*. Newness makes start-up firms more organic—they tend to be smaller organizations with few rules and considerable delegation of authority. However, employees in new organizations often lack industry experience, and their teams have not developed sufficiently for peak performance. As a result, the organic structures of new companies cannot compensate for the poorer coordination and significantly lower efficiencies caused by the lack of structure from past experience and team mental models. Fortunately, companies can minimize the liability of newness by launching businesses with existing teams of people or with industry veterans guiding the novices.

Exhibit 13.3 | CONTRASTING MECHANISTIC AND ORGANIC ORGANIZATIONAL STRUCTURES

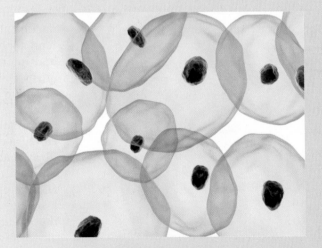

Mechanistic Structure

- Narrow span of control
- High centralization
- High formalization

Organic Structure

- Wide span of control
- High decentralization
- Low formalization

Left: © Kutberk Kargin/iStockphoto; right: Sebastian Kaulitzki/Shutterstock

CONNECTIONS 13.1

Growing an Organic TAXI

With more than 1,200 awards, including recent honours as Canada's creative agency of the decade, TAXI is a company like no other. The agency dreamed up the cute critters in Telus ads and the smiling man skipping to work in Pfizer's famous Viagra ad. Other creative agencies either burn out or become rigid hierarchies over time. TAXI, in contrast, has continued to amaze the world with its creative flair over the past two decades while it also expanded to 350 employees in several offices across Canada, the United States, and the Netherlands.

How has TAXI maintained this momentum? Leadership and talent are key factors, but perhaps equally important is the company's fanatical reliance on an organic organizational structure. This organic structure begins by assigning each client or project to "a nimble, autonomous team that is both empowered and responsible for results" says TAXI's website. The company claims the TAXI name reflects this small-team mandate: "We believe a small team of experts should drive every piece of the business—as many as can fit into a cab."

TAXI's organic structure also accommodates growth. As the company expanded, it deliberately avoided creating work centres that had more than 150 staff members. "Ancient nomadic tribes observed that a population exceeding 150 people had a tendency to form factions, erode group harmony and render it dysfunctional," claims TAXI. Consequently, the company has duplicated itself across several cities, with each office maintaining an organic structure that actively collaborates with other offices. Even when the Toronto business outgrew its

TAXI, Canada's agency of the decade, relies on an organic structure of small flexible teams as well as limited-sized work centres. *Copyright © TAXI Canada Ltd.*

optimal size, TAXI opened a second location, called TAXI 2, within the same city.

TAXI's organic organizational structure contrasts with the rigid departmentalization found in many other creative agencies. "[Other advertising firms] operated on a 19th-century model of many secular departments trying to integrate everything ad hoc. Most cultures were so layered that a great idea was easily crushed," explains TAXI co-founder Paul Lavoie. "We needed a flexible infrastructure, able to move with the pace of change. TAXI started lean and nimble, and remains so today."[40]

FORMS OF DEPARTMENTALIZATION

L03

Span of control, centralization, and formalization are important elements of organizational structure, but most people think about organizational charts when the discussion of organizational structure arises. The organizational chart represents the fourth element in the structuring of organizations, called *departmentalization*. Departmentalization specifies how employees and their activities are grouped together. It is a fundamental strategy for coordinating organizational activities because it influences organizational behaviour in the following ways:[41]

- Departmentalization establishes the chain of command—the system of common supervision among positions and units within the organization. It frames the membership of formal work teams and typically determines which positions and units must share resources. Thus, departmentalization establishes interdependencies among employees and subunits.

- Departmentalization focuses people around common mental models or ways of thinking, such as serving clients, developing products, or supporting a particular skill set. This focus is typically anchored around the common budgets and measures of performance assigned to employees within each departmental unit.

- Departmentalization encourages specific people and work units to coordinate through informal communication. With common supervision and resources, members within each configuration typically work near each other, so they can use frequent and informal interaction to get the work done.

There are almost as many organizational charts as there are businesses, but the six most common pure types of departmentalization are simple, functional, divisional, team-based, matrix, and network.

SIMPLE STRUCTURE

Most companies begin with a *simple structure*.[42] They employ only a few people and typically offer only one distinct product or service. There is minimal hierarchy—usually just employees reporting to the owners. Employees perform broadly defined roles because there are insufficient economies of scale to assign them to specialized jobs. The simple structure is highly flexible and minimizes the walls that form between employees in other structures. However, the simple structure usually depends on the owner's direct supervision to coordinate work activities, so it is very difficult to operate as the company grows and becomes more complex.

FUNCTIONAL STRUCTURE

Growing organizations usually introduce a functional structure at some level of the hierarchy or at some time in their history. A **functional structure** organizes employees around specific knowledge or other resources. For instance, Exhibit 13.4 illustrates a functional structure similar to the one found at Tim Hortons. Employees in that organization are organized around operations (with geographic separation of Canada and U.S./International), marketing, supply chain, finance, and so forth. Organizations with functional structures are typically centralized to more effectively coordinate these diverse activities.

functional structure An organizational structure in which employees are organized around specific knowledge or other resources.

Evaluating the Functional Structure   The functional structure creates specialized pools of talent that typically serve everyone in the organization. This provides more economies of scale than are possible if functional specialists are spread over different parts of the organization. It increases employee identity with the specialization or profession. Direct supervision is easier in functional structures because managers oversee people with common issues and expertise.[43]

The functional structure also has limitations.[44] Grouping employees around their skills tends to focus attention on those skills and related professional needs rather than on the company's product, service, or client needs. Unless people are transferred from one function to the next, they might not develop a broader understanding of the business. Compared with other structures, the functional structure usually produces higher dysfunctional conflict and poorer coordination in serving clients or developing prod-

Exhibit 13.4   A FUNCTIONAL ORGANIZATIONAL STRUCTURE

This organizational chart is similar to the functional organizational structure at Tim Hortons. The two chief operating officer positions are placed above the others due to space limitations. There is no indication that they have higher status on the Tim Hortons executive team.

ucts. These problems occur because employees need to work with co-workers in other departments to complete organizational tasks yet they have different subgoals and mental models of ideal work. Together, these problems require substantial formal controls and coordination when people are organized around functions.

DIVISIONAL STRUCTURE

> **divisional structure** An organizational structure in which employees are organized around geographic areas, outputs (products or services), or clients.

The **divisional structure** (sometimes called the *multidivisional* or *M-form structure*) organizes employees around geographic areas, outputs (products or services), or clients. Exhibit 13.5 illustrates these three variations of divisional structure. The *geographic divisional structure* organizes employees around distinct regions of the country or world. Exhibit 13.5 (*a*) illustrates a geographic divisional structure recently adopted by Barrick Gold Corporation, the world's largest gold-mining company. The *product/service divisional structure* organizes employees around distinct outputs. Exhibit 13.5 (*b*) illustrates a simplified version of this type of structure at Philips. The Dutch electronics company divides its workforce mainly into three divisions: health care products, lighting products, and consumer products. (Philips also has a fourth organizational group consisting of the research and design functions.) The *client divisional structure* organizes employees around specific customer groups. Exhibit 13.5 (*c*) illustrates a client-focused divisional structure similar to one adopted by Bell Canada.[45]

Exhibit 13.5   **THREE TYPES OF DIVISIONAL STRUCTURE**

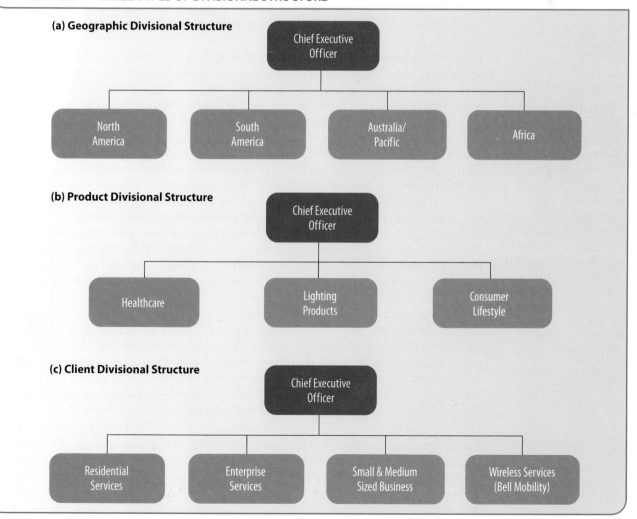

(a) Geographic Divisional Structure

(b) Product Divisional Structure

(c) Client Divisional Structure

Note: Diagram (a) shows a global geographic divisional structure similar to Barrick Gold Corporation; diagram (b) is similar to the product divisions at Philips; diagram (c) is similar to the client-focused structure at Bell Canada.

Which form of divisional structure should large organizations adopt? The answer depends mainly on the primary source of environmental diversity or uncertainty.[46] Suppose an organization has one type of product sold to people across the country. If customers have different needs across regions, or if provincial governments impose different regulations on the product, then a geographic structure would be best to be more vigilant of this diversity. On the other hand, if the company sells several types of products across the country and customer preferences and government regulations are similar everywhere, then a product structure would likely work best.

Coca-Cola, Nestlé, and many other food and beverage companies are organized mainly around geographic regions because consumer tastes and preferred marketing strategies vary considerably around the world. Even though McDonald's makes the same Big Mac throughout the world, the company has more fish products in Hong Kong and more vegetarian products in India, in line with traditional diets in those countries. Philips, on the other hand, is organized around products because consumer preferences around the world are similar within each product group. Hospitals from Geneva, Switzerland, to Santiago, Chile, buy similar medical equipment from Philips, whereas the manufacturing and marketing of these products are quite different from Philips' consumer electronics business.

Many companies are moving away from structures that organize people around geographic clusters.[47] One reason is that clients can purchase products online and communicate with businesses from almost anywhere in the world, so local representation is less critical. Reduced geographic variation is another reason for the shift away from geographic structures; freer trade has reduced government intervention, and consumer preferences for many products and services are becoming more similar (converging) around the world. The third reason is that large companies increasingly have global business customers who demand one global point of purchase, not one in every country or region.

The Globally Integrated Enterprise   The shift away from geographic and toward product or client-based divisional structures reflects the trend toward the **globally integrated enterprise**.[48] As the label implies, a globally integrated enterprise connects work processes around the world, rather than replicating them within each country or region. This type of organization typically organizes people around product or client divisions. Even functional units—production, marketing, design, human resources, and so on—serve the company worldwide rather than within specific geographic clusters. These functions are sensitive to cultural and market differences and have local representation to support that sensitivity, but local representatives are associates of a global function rather than a local subsidiary copied across several regions. Indeed, a globally integrated enterprise is marked by a dramatic increase in virtual teamwork, because employees are assigned global projects and ongoing responsibilities for work units that transcend geographic boundaries.

> **globally integrated enterprise** An organizational structure in which work processes and executive functions are distributed around the world through global centres, rather than developed in a home country and replicated in satellite countries or regions.

The globally integrated enterprise no longer orchestrates its business from a single headquarters in one "home" country. Instead, its divisional and functional operations are led from where the work is concentrated, and this concentration depends on economics (cost of labour, infrastructure, etc.), expertise, and openness (trade, capital flow, knowledge sharing, etc.). For example, IBM has moved toward the globally integrated enterprise structure by locating its global data centres in Colorado, website management in Ireland, back-office finance in Brazil, software in India, and procurement in China. IBM's vice-president of worldwide engineering, responsible for procurement, moved from Armonk, New York, to China, where the procurement centre is located. "These people are not leading teams focused on China or India or Brazil or Ireland—or Colorado or Vermont," says IBM CEO Sam Palmisano. "They are leading integrated global operations."[49]

Evaluating the Divisional Structure   The divisional organizational structure is a building-block structure; it accommodates growth relatively easily and focuses employee attention on products or customers rather than tasks. Different products, services, or clients can be accommodated by sprouting new divisions. These advantages are offset by a number of limitations. First, the divisional structure tends to duplicate resources, such as production equipment and engineering or information technology expertise.

Also, unless the division is quite large, resources are not used as efficiently as they are in functional structures where resources are pooled across the entire organization. The divisional structure also creates silos of knowledge. Expertise is spread across several autonomous business units, and this reduces the ability and perhaps motivation of the people in one division to share their knowledge with counterparts in other divisions. In contrast, a functional structure groups experts together, thereby supporting knowledge sharing.

Finally, the preferred divisional structure depends on the company's primary source of environmental diversity or uncertainty. This principle seems to be applied easily enough at Coca-Cola, McDonald's, and Philips, but many global organizations experience diversity and uncertainty in terms of geography, products, and clients. Consequently, some organizations revise their structures back and forth or create complex structures that attempt to give all three dimensions equal status. This waffling and complexity generates further complications, because organizational structure decisions shift power and status among executives. If the company switches from a geographic to product structure, people who lead the geographic fiefdoms suddenly get demoted under the product chiefs. In short, leaders of global organizations struggle to find the best divisional structure, often resulting in the departure of some executives and frustration among those who remain.

> **"** Leaders of global organizations struggle to find the best divisional structure, often resulting in the departure of some executives and frustration among those who remain. **"**

TEAM-BASED STRUCTURE

team-based organizational structure
An organizational structure built around self-directed teams that complete an entire piece of work.

A **team-based organizational structure** is built around self-directed teams that complete an entire piece of work, such as manufacturing a product or developing an electronic game. This type of structure is usually organic. There is a wide span of control because teams operate with minimal supervision. In extreme situations, there is no formal leader, just someone selected by other team members to help coordinate the work and liaise with top management. Team structures are highly decentralized because almost all day-to-day decisions are made by team members rather than someone further up the organizational hierarchy. Finally, many team-based structures have low formalization because teams are given relatively few rules about how to organize their work. Instead, executives assign quality and quantity output targets and often productivity improvement goals to each team. Teams are then encouraged to use available resources and their own initiative to achieve those objectives.

Team-based structures are usually found within the manufacturing or service operations of larger divisional structures. For example, Pratt & Whitney Canada relies on team-based structures at its operations in Halifax, Lethbridge, and Longueuil, but these plants operate within the company's larger divisional structure. However, a small number of firms apply the team-based structure from top to bottom, including W. L. Gore & Associates and Semco SA, where almost all associates work in teams.

Evaluating the Team-Based Structure   The team-based structure has gained popularity because it tends to be flexible and responsive in turbulent environments.[50] It tends to reduce costs because teams have less reliance on formal hierarchy (direct supervision). A cross-functional team structure improves communication and cooperation across traditional boundaries. With greater autonomy, this structure also allows quicker and more informed decision making.[51] For this reason, some hospitals have shifted from functional departments to cross-functional teams. Teams composed of nurses, radiologists, anesthetists, a pharmacology representative, possibly social workers, a rehabilitation therapist, and other specialists communicate and coordinate more efficiently, thereby reducing delays and errors.[52]

Against these benefits, the team-based structure can be costly to maintain due to the need for ongoing interpersonal skill training. Teamwork potentially takes more time to coordinate than formal hierarchy during the early stages of team development. Employees may experience more stress due to increased ambiguity in their roles. Team leaders also experience more stress due to increased conflict, loss of functional power, and unclear career progression ladders. In addition, team structures suffer from duplication of resources and potential competition (and lack of resource sharing) across teams.[54]

MATRIX STRUCTURE

When physicians Ray Muzyka and Greg Zeschuk and a third partner (who later returned to medical practice) founded BioWare ULC, they initially organized employees at the Edmonton-based electronic games company into a simple structure in which everyone worked together on the first game, *Shattered Steel*. Soon after, Muzyka and Zeschuk decided to create a second game (*Baldur's Gate*), but they weren't sure what organizational structure would be best. Simply creating a second team might duplicate resources, undermine information sharing across teams, and weaken employee loyalty to the overall company. Alternatively, the game developer could adopt a functional structure by assigning employees to specialized departments such as art, programming, audio, quality assurance, and design. A functional structure would encourage employees within each specialization to share information, but it might undermine team dynamics on game projects and reduce employee commitment to the game they were developing.[55]

After carefully weighing the various organizational structure options, Muzyka and Zeschuk adopted a **matrix structure** to gain the benefits of both a functional structure and a project-based (team) structure. BioWare's matrix structure, which is similar to the diagram in Exhibit 13.6, is organized around both functions (art, audio, programming, etc.) and team-based game development projects. Employees are assigned to a cross-functional team responsible for a specific game project, yet they also belong to a permanent functional unit from which they are reassigned when their work is completed on a particular project.[56]

> **matrix structure** An organizational structure that overlays two structures (such as a geographic divisional and a functional structure) in order to leverage the benefits of both.

Muzyka and Zeschuk say the matrix structure focuses employees on the final product yet keeps them organized around their expertise to encourage knowledge sharing. "The matrix structure also supports our overall company culture where BioWare is the team, and everyone is always willing to help each other whether they are on the same project or not," they add. BioWare's matrix structure was a good choice, particularly as the company (which recently became an independent division of Electronic Arts) has grown to almost 800 employees working on numerous game projects in Edmonton, Montreal, Austin (Texas), and Fairfax (Virginia).

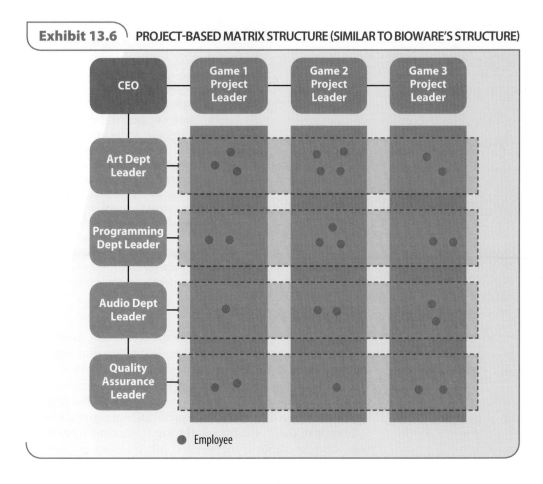

Exhibit 13.6 \ PROJECT-BASED MATRIX STRUCTURE (SIMILAR TO BIOWARE'S STRUCTURE)

• Employee

BioWare's structure, in which project teams overlap with functional departments, is just one form of matrix structure. Another variation, found mainly in large global firms, has geographic divisions on one axis and products/services or client divisions on the other. Nestlé, Procter & Gamble, Shell, and many other global organizations have variations of a matrix structure that attempt to balance geography with products/services. For instance, Nestlé Waters, one of the company's product divisions, markets several brands of bottled water in more than three dozen countries. The brands vary from one country to the next (for example, Montclair is unique to Canada and Santa Maria is unique to Mexico). The manager responsible for Nestlé's bottled water brands in Canada would report to both the country manager and to the Nestlé's waters executive at the company's headquarters in Switzerland. Similarly, the manager responsible for baby foods in Canada would report to the country manager as well as to the headquarter's executive responsible for that product group.[57]

A common error is the belief that everyone in a matrix organizational structure reports to two bosses. This two-boss situation exists for most employees in project-based matrix structures such as at BioWare, but not in global matrix structures such as at Nestlé. In multinational companies with matrix structures, only employees at one level in the organization (typically country-specific brand managers) report to two bosses. For example, the manager responsible for Nestlé's bottled water brands in Canada would report to both Nestlé's Canadian country manager and the world headquarter's executive responsible for Nestlé waters, whereas sales and marketing employees further down the hierarchy report only to a Canadian boss.

Evaluating the Matrix Structure   The matrix structure usually makes very good use of resources and expertise, making it ideal for project-based organizations with fluctuating workloads. When properly managed, it improves communication efficiency, project flexibility, and innovation, compared to purely functional or divisional designs.

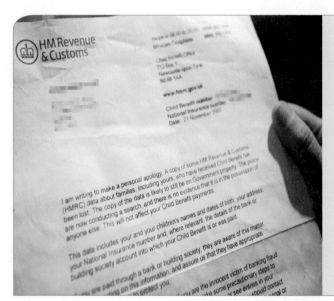

Losing Data in the Matrix

Soon after Britain's Inland Revenue and Customs/Excise departments merged to become HM Revenue & Customs (HMRC), the combined department experienced a series of errors that violated individual privacy rights. The most serious of these incidents occurred when HMRC staff somehow lost two computer discs containing confidential details of 25 million child welfare claimants. The U.K. government's investigation into the security lapse concluded that along with resulting from poor security procedures, the error was partly due to "muddled accountabilities" created by the matrix organizational structure under which the new department operated. The investigator's initial briefing stated that the matrix structure and numerous departments made it "difficult to relate roles and responsibilities amongst senior management to accountability." In fact, responsibility for data security was assigned to no less than five departments, each of which reported to different director generals. The final report concluded that "[HMRC] is not suited to the so-called 'constructive friction' matrix type organization [that was] in place at the time of the data loss." HMRC has since changed to a more traditional, single-command organizational structure. [58] *JEFF MOORE/PA Photos/Landov*

It focuses employees on serving clients or creating products yet keeps people organized around their specialization, so knowledge sharing improves and resources are used more efficiently. The matrix structure is also a logical choice when, as in the case of Procter & Gamble, two different dimensions (regions and products) are equally important. Structures determine executive power and what is important; the matrix structure works when two different dimensions deserve equal attention.

In spite of these advantages, the matrix structure has several well-known problems.[59] One concern is that it increases conflict among managers who equally share power. Employees working at the matrix level have two bosses and, consequently, two sets of priorities that aren't always aligned with each other. Project leaders might squabble with functional leaders regarding the assignment of specific employees to projects as well as regarding the employee's technical competence. For example, Citigroup Inc., recently adopted a geographic-product matrix structure and apparently is already experiencing dysfunctional conflict between the regional and product group executives.[60] Aware of these potential conflicts, BioWare holds several "synchronization meetings" each year involving all department directors (art, design, audio, etc.), producers (i.e., game project leaders), and the human resource manager. These meetings sort out differences and ensure that staff members are properly assigned to each game project.

Another challenge is that the existence of two bosses can dilute accountability. In a functional or divisional structure, one manager is responsible for everything, even the most unexpected issues. But in a matrix structure, the unusual problems don't get resolved because neither manager takes ownership of them.[61] Mark Hurd had just joined Hewlett Packard as CEO when he replaced the technology company's matrix structure because of concerns about accountability. "The more accountable I can make you, the easier it is for you to show you're a great performer," declared Hurd, who is now with Oracle, Inc. "The more I use a matrix, the easier I make it to blame someone else."[62] The combination of dysfunctional conflict and ambiguous accountability in matrix structures also explains why some employees experience more stress and some managers are less satisfied with their work arrangements.

NETWORK STRUCTURE

BMW and Daimler Benz aren't eager to let you know this, but some of their vehicles designed and constructed with Germanic precision are neither designed nor constructed by them or in Germany. Much of BMW's X3, for example, was designed by Canada's Magna Steyr in Austria. Magna also manufactured the vehicle in Austria until BMW transferred this work to its manufacturing plant in the United States.

The contract manufacturer also builds Daimler's off-road G-class Mercedes. Both BMW and Daimler Benz are hub organizations that own and market their respective brands, whereas Magna and other suppliers are spokes around the hub that provide production, engineering, and other services that get the auto firms' luxury products to customers.[63]

network structure An alliance of several organizations for the purpose of creating a product or serving a client.

BMW, Daimler Benz, and many other organizations are moving toward a **network structure** as they design and build a product or serve a client through an alliance of several organizations.[64] As Exhibit 13.7 illustrates, this collaborative structure typically consists of several satellite organizations bee-hived around a hub or core firm. The core firm orchestrates the network process and provides one or two other core competencies, such as marketing or product development. In our example, BMW or Mercedes is the hub that provides marketing and management, whereas other firms perform many other functions. The core firm might be the main contact with customers, but most of the product or service delivery and support activities are farmed out to satellite organizations located anywhere in the world. Extranets (Web-based networks with partners) and other technologies ensure that information flows easily and openly between the core firm and its array of satellites.[65]

One of the main forces pushing toward a network structure is the recognition that an organization has only a few *core competencies*. A core competency is a knowledge base that resides throughout the organization and provides a strategic advantage. As companies discover their core competency, they "unbundle" noncritical tasks to other organizations that have a core competency at performing those tasks. For instance, BMW decided long ago that its core competency is not facilities management, so it outsourced this function at its British engine plant to Dalkia, which specializes in facility maintenance and energy management.[66]

Companies are also more likely to form network structures when technology is changing quickly and production processes are complex or varied.[67] Many firms cannot keep up with the hyperfast changes in information technology, so they have outsourced their entire information system departments to IBM, HP Enterprise Business, and other

Exhibit 13.7   A NETWORK ORGANIZATIONAL STRUCTURE

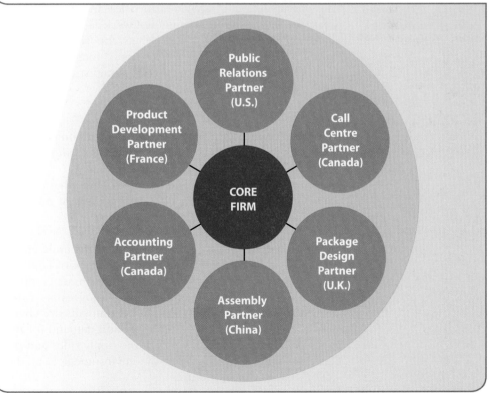

firms that specialize in information system services. Similarly, many high-technology firms form networks with Toronto-based electronic equipment manufacturer Celestica and other companies that have expertise in diverse production processes.

Evaluating the Network Structure   For several years, organizational behaviour theorists have argued that organizational leaders must develop a metaphor of organizations as plasma-like organisms rather than rigid machines.[68] Network structures come close to the organism metaphor because they offer the flexibility to realign their structure with changing environmental requirements. If customers demand a new product or service, the core firm forms new alliances with other firms offering the appropriate resources. For example, by working with Magna International, BMW was probably able to develop and launch the X3 vehicle much sooner than would have been the case if it had performed these tasks on its own. When BMW needs a different type of manufacturing, it isn't saddled with nonessential facilities and resources. Network structures also offer efficiencies because the core firm becomes globally competitive as it shops worldwide for subcontractors with the best people and the best technology at the best price. Indeed, the pressures of global competition have made network structures more vital, and computer-based information technology has made them possible.[69]

A potential disadvantage of network structures is that they expose the core firm to market forces. Other companies may bid up the price for subcontractors, whereas the short-term cost would be lower if the company hired its own employees to perform the same function. Another problem is that although information technology makes worldwide communication much easier, it will never replace the degree of control organizations have when manufacturing, marketing, and other functions are in-house. The core firm can use arm's-length incentives and contract provisions to maintain the subcontractor's quality, but these actions are relatively crude compared to maintaining the quality of work performed by in-house employees.

CONTINGENCIES OF ORGANIZATIONAL DESIGN

LO4

Most organizational behaviour theories and concepts have contingencies: ideas that work well in one situation might not work as well in another situation. This contingency approach is certainly relevant when choosing the most appropriate organizational structure.[70] In this section, we introduce four contingencies of organizational design: external environment, size, technology, and strategy.

EXTERNAL ENVIRONMENT

The best structure for an organization depends on its external environment. The external environment includes anything outside the organization, including most stakeholders (e.g., clients, suppliers, government), resources (e.g., raw materials, human resources, information, finances), and competitors. Four characteristics of external environments influence the type of organizational structure best suited to a particular situation: dynamism, complexity, diversity, and hostility.[71]

Dynamic versus Stable Environments   Dynamic environments have a high rate of change, leading to novel situations and a lack of identifiable patterns. Organic structures are better suited to this type of environment so that the organization can adapt more quickly to changes, but only if employees are experienced and coordinate well in teamwork.[72] In contrast, stable environments are characterized by regular cycles of activity and steady changes in supply and demand for inputs and outputs. Events are more predictable, enabling the firm to apply rules and procedures. Mechanistic structures are more efficient when the environment is predictable, so they tend to work better than organic structures.

Being Big and Small All at Once at Johnson & Johnson

Johnson & Johnson (J&J) may be best known for Band-Aids and baby powder, but the company is really a conglomerate of 250 businesses in 57 countries that manufacture and/or market prescription medicines (accounting for 40 percent of its total business), medical devices and diagnostics (the largest such business in the world), and personal care products (toothbrushes, skin creams, shampoos, etc.). Successful companies decentralize when operating in complex and diversified environments, and J&J is no exception. "J&J is probably the reference company for being decentralized," says William Weldon, J&J's chairman and CEO. Weldon points out that the company's decentralized structure allows it to be more sensitive and responsive to each unique culture and business setting. "The men and women who run our businesses around the world usually are people who grew up in those markets, understand those markets, and develop themselves in those markets," Weldon explains. Decentralization of a large organization has other advantages. "We are big and we are small all at once," says J&J's website. "Each of our operating companies functions as its own small business . . . [yet] they also have access to the know-how and resources of a Fortune 50 company. It's like having dozens of strategic partners at their fingertips." [73] *AP Photo/ Zheng Xi—Imaginechina*

Complex versus Simple Environments   Complex environments have many elements, whereas simple environments have few things to monitor. As an example, a major university library operates in a more complex environment than a small regional public library. The university library's clients require several types of services—book borrowing, online full-text databases, research centres, course reserve collections, and so on. A small regional public library has fewer of these demands placed on it. The more complex the environment, the more decentralized the organization should become. Decentralization is a logical choice in complex environments because decisions are pushed down to people and subunits with the necessary information to make informed choices.

Diverse versus Integrated Environments   Organizations located in diverse environments have a greater variety of products or services, clients, and regions. In contrast, an integrated environment has only one client, product, and geographic area. The more diversified the environment, the more the firm needs to use a divisional structure aligned with that diversity. If it sells a single product around the world, a geographic divisional structure would align best with the firm's geographic diversity, for example.

Hostile versus Munificent Environments   Firms located in a hostile environment face resource scarcity and more competition in the marketplace. Hostile environments are typically dynamic ones because they reduce the predictability of access to resources and demand for outputs. Organic structures tend to be best in hostile environments. However, when the environment is extremely hostile—such as a severe shortage of supplies or lower market share—organizations tend to temporarily centralize so that decisions can be made more quickly and executives feel more comfortable being in control. [74] Ironically, centralization may result in lower-quality decisions during organizational crises, because top management has less information, particularly when the environment is complex.

ORGANIZATIONAL SIZE

Larger organizations should have different structures from smaller organizations. [75] As the number of employees increases, job specialization increases due to a greater division of labour. The greater division of labour requires more elaborate coordinating mechanisms. Thus, larger firms make greater use of standardization (particularly work processes and outcomes) to coordinate work activities. These coordinating mechanisms create an administrative hierarchy and greater formalization. Historically, larger organizations make less use of informal communication as a coordinating mechanism. However, emerging information technologies and increased emphasis on empowerment have caused informal communication to regain its importance in large firms.[76]

Larger organizations also tend to be more decentralized. Executives have neither sufficient time nor expertise to process all the decisions that significantly influence the business as it grows. Therefore, decision-making authority is pushed down to lower levels, where incumbents are able to cope with the narrower range of issues under their control.

TECHNOLOGY

Technology is another factor to consider when designing the best organizational structure for the situation.[77] *Technology* refers to the mechanisms or processes by which an organization produces its product or service. One technological contingency is *variability*—the number of exceptions to standard procedure that tend to occur. In work processes with low variability, jobs are routine and follow standard operating procedures. Another contingency is *analyzability*—the predictability or difficulty of the required work. The less analyzable the work, the more it requires experts with sufficient discretion to address the work challenges. An organic, rather than a mechanistic, structure should be introduced where employees perform tasks with high variety and low analyzability, such as in a research setting. The reason is that employees face unique situations with little opportunity for repetition. In contrast, a mechanistic structure is preferred where the technology has low variability and high analyzability, such as an assembly line. The work is routine and highly predictable, an ideal situation for a mechanistic structure to operate efficiently.

ORGANIZATIONAL STRATEGY

organizational strategy
The way the organization positions itself in its setting in relation to its stakeholders, given the organization's resources, capabilities, and mission.

Organizational strategy refers to the way the organization positions itself in its setting in relation to its stakeholders, given the organization's resources, capabilities, and mission.[78] In other words, strategy represents the decisions and actions applied to achieve the organization's goals. Although size, technology, and environment influence the optimal organizational structure, these contingencies do not necessarily determine structure. Instead, corporate leaders formulate and implement strategies that shape both the characteristics of these contingencies as well as the organization's resulting structure.

This concept is summed up with the simple phrase "structure follows strategy."[79] Organizational leaders decide how large to grow and which technologies to use. They take steps to define and manipulate their environments, rather than let the organization's fate be entirely determined by external influences. Furthermore, organizational structures don't evolve as a natural response to environmental conditions; they result from conscious human decisions. Thus, organizational strategy influences both the contingencies of structure and the structure itself. If a company's strategy is to compete through innovation, a more organic structure would be preferred because it is easier for employees to share knowledge and be creative. If a company chooses a low-cost strategy, a mechanistic structure is preferred because it maximizes production and service efficiency.[80] Overall, it is now apparent that organizational structure is influenced by size, technology, and environment, but the organization's strategy may reshape these elements and loosen their connection to organizational structure.

CHAPTER SUMMARY

LO1   Describe three types of coordination in organizational structures.

Organizational structure is the division of labour as well as the patterns of coordination, communication, workflow, and formal power that direct organizational activities. All organizational structures divide labour into distinct tasks and coordinate that labour to accomplish common goals. The primary means of coordination are informal communication, formal hierarchy, and standardization.

LO2   Discuss the role and effects of span of control, centralization, and formalization, and relate these elements to organic and mechanistic organizational structures.

The four basic elements of organizational structure are span of control, centralization, formalization, and departmentalization. The optimal span of control—the number of people directly reporting to the next level in the hierarchy—depends on the presence of coordinating mechanisms other than formal hierarchy, as well as on whether employees perform routine tasks and how much interdependence there is among employees within the department.

Centralization occurs when formal decision making authority is held by a small group of people, typically senior executives. Many companies decentralize as they become larger and more complex, but some sections of the company may remain centralized while other sections decentralize. Formalization is the degree to which organizations standardize behaviour through rules, procedures, formal training, and related mechanisms. Companies become more formalized as they get older and larger. Formalization tends to reduce organizational flexibility, organizational learning, creativity, and job satisfaction.

Span of control, centralization, and formalization cluster into mechanistic and organic structures. Mechanistic structures are characterized by a narrow span of control and a high degree of formalization and centralization. Companies with an organic structure have the opposite characteristics.

LO3   Identify and evaluate six types of departmentalization.

Departmentalization specifies how employees and their activities are grouped together. It establishes the chain of command, focuses people around common mental models, and encourages coordination through informal communication among people and subunits. A functional structure organizes employees around specific knowledge or other resources. This fosters greater specialization and improves direct supervision, but it weakens the focus on serving clients or developing products.

A divisional structure groups employees around geographic areas, clients, or outputs. This structure accommodates growth and focuses employee attention on products or customers rather than tasks. However, this structure duplicates resources and creates silos of knowledge. Team-based structures are very flat, with low formalization, and organize self-directed teams around work processes rather than functional specialities. The matrix structure combines two structures to leverage the benefits of both types of structure. However, this approach requires more coordination than functional or pure divisional structures, may dilute accountability, and increases conflict. A network structure is an alliance of several organizations for the purpose of creating a product or serving a client.

LO4   Explain how the external environment, organizational size, technology, and strategy are relevant when designing an organizational structure.

The best organizational structure depends on the firm's external environment, size, technology, and strategy. The optimal structure depends on whether the environment is dynamic or stable, complex or simple, diverse or integrated, and hostile or munificent. As organizations increase in size, they become more decentralized and more formalized. The work unit's technology—including variety of work and analyzability of problems—influences whether to adopt an organic or mechanistic structure. These contingencies influence but do not necessarily determine structure. Instead, corporate leaders formulate and implement strategies that shape both the characteristics of these contingencies as well as the organization's resulting structure.

KEY TERMS

centralization, p. 360

concurrent engineering, p. 356

divisional structure, p. 365

formalization, p. 361

functional structure, p. 364

globally integrated enterprise, p. 366

matrix structure, p. 368

mechanistic structure, p. 362

network structure, p. 371

organic structure, p. 362

organizational strategy, p. 374

organizational structure, p. 354

span of control, p. 357

team-based organizational structure, p. 367

CRITICAL-THINKING QUESTIONS

1. Tim Hortons organizational structure was described at the beginning of this chapter. What coordinating mechanism is likely most common within each Tim Hortons restaurant? Describe the extent and form in which the other two types of coordination might be apparent within a Tim Hortons restaurant.

2. Think about the business school or other organizational unit whose classes you are currently attending. What is the dominant coordinating mechanism used to guide or control the instructor? Why is this coordinating mechanism used the most here?

3. Administrative theorists concluded many decades ago that the most effective organizations have a narrow span of control. Yet today's top-performing manufacturing firms have a wide span of control. Why is this possible? Under what circumstances, if any, should manufacturing firms have a narrow span of control?

4. Leaders of large organizations struggle to identify the best level and types of centralization and decentralization. What should companies consider when determining the degree of decentralization?

5. Diversified Technologies Ltd. (DTL) makes four types of products, each type to be sold to different types of clients. For example, one product is sold exclusively to automobile repair shops, whereas another is used mainly in hospitals. Customer expectations and needs are surprisingly similar throughout the world. The company has separate marketing, product design, and manufacturing facilities in Asia, North America, Europe, and South America because, until recently, each jurisdiction had unique regulations governing the production and sales of these products. However, several governments have begun the process of deregulating the products that DTL designs and manufactures, and trade agreements have opened several markets to foreign-made products. Which form of departmentalization might be best for DTL if deregulation and trade agreements occur?

6. IBM is becoming a globally integrated enterprise. What does this organization look like in terms of its departmentalization? What challenges might face companies that try to adopt the globally integrated enterprise model?

7. From an employee perspective, what are the advantages and disadvantages of working in a matrix structure?

8. Suppose that you have been hired as a consultant to diagnose the environmental characteristics of your college or university. How would you describe the school's external environment? Is the school's existing structure appropriate for this environment?

 CASE STUDY 13.1

Nokia's Evolving Organizational Structure

Nokia Corporation has experienced considerable change over the past three decades and its organizational structure has changed just as dramatically. In the early 1990s, the Finnish firm had a product-based organizational structure designed around its diversified businesses: consumer electronics (televisions, audio equipment), cable for construction and power transmission, industrial rubber (tires, footwear), and its recently acquired telecommunications business.

Nokia became the market leader in cellphones by 1998 (overtaking Motorola), so it sold most other divisions and designed a new organizational structure around its cellphone and consumer electronics businesses as well as several function groups (finance, human resources, etc.). The consumer electronics business was not sufficiently profitable, so it was sold and Nokia drew a new organizational chart in 1999 around cellphones, the emerging business of mobile networks, ventures (emerging Internet mobile technology), and communication products (digital terminals).

By 2003, the cellphone market was converging with photography, games, music, and other multimedia content, so Nokia added a new "multimedia" division to keep the company at the forefront of those developments. In 2006, the company's burgeoning network division was spun off as a joint venture with a similar product group at Siemens.

Nokia's earlier organizational structures gave some priority to Internet and multimedia technologies, enough to put the company at the forefront of the quickly emerging "smartphone" market. But with increasing competition from Canada's Research In Motion (which makes the BlackBerry) and Apple (which makes the iPhone), Nokia recently announced a new organizational structure that will focus more power and resources around this segment.

The new chart (a somewhat simplified version is shown here) includes a "Smart Devices" division, mobile phones division, a "Markets" division (responsible for global sales and supply chain operations), and a few functional groups (e.g., finance, human resources). "Nokia's new organizational structure is designed to speed up execution and accelerate innovation, both short-term and longer term," explains Nokia CEO Olli-Pekka Kallasvuo. "We believe that this will allow us to build stronger mobile solutions."

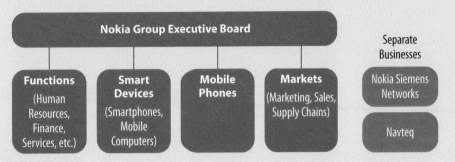

Discussion Questions

1. What form of departmentalization has Nokia relied on throughout most of the past three decades? Why have these forms of departmentalization been adopted?

2. Evaluate Nokia's changing organizational structure against the changing characteristics of the external environment over this time. Has the structure mostly contributed to Nokia's success or been a hindrance to it?

3. Although not explicitly described in this case, in your opinion, in what parts of Nokia would you expect to find the most organic organizational structure, particularly low formalization and high decentralization? What parts of Nokia would be most mechanistic?

Sources: "Nokia in Major Reorganization Plan," *Warren's Consumer Electronics Daily*, September 29, 2003; K. J. O'Brien, "Head of Nokia's Mobile Phone Unit Is Leaving," *New York Times*, May 12, 2010, p. 5; "Nokia Outlines New Strategy, Introduces New Leadership, Operational Structure," *Nokia News Release* (London: February 11, 2011).

 TEAM EXERCISE 13.2

The Club Ed Exercise

By Cheryl Harvey and Kim Morouney, Wilfrid Laurier University

Purpose   This exercise is designed to help you understand the issues to consider when designing organizations at various stages of growth.

Materials   Each student team should have flip chart sheets or other capabilities to display several organizational charts.

Instructions   Each team discusses the scenario presented. The first scenario is presented below. The instructor will facilitate discussion and notify teams when to begin the next step. The exercise and debriefing require approximately 90 minutes, although fewer scenarios can reduce the time somewhat.

1. Students are placed in teams (typically four or five people).

2. After reading the following Scenario 1, each team will design an organizational chart (departmentalization) that is most appropriate for the situation. Students should be able to describe the type of structure chosen and explain why it is appropriate.

The structure should be depicted on flip chart paper or other media for others to see during later class discussion. The instructor will set a fixed time (e.g., 15 minutes) to complete this task.

> *Scenario #1* Determined never to shovel snow again, you are establishing a new resort business on a small Caribbean island. The resort is under construction and is scheduled to open one year from now. You decide it is time to draw up an organizational chart for this new venture, called Club Ed.

3. At the end of the time allowed, the instructor will present Scenario #2, and each team will be asked to draw another organizational chart to suit that situation. Again, students should be able to describe the type of structure chosen and explain why it is appropriate.

4. At the end of the time allowed, the instructor will present Scenario #3, and each team will be asked to create another organizational chart to suit that situation.

5. Depending on the time available, the instructor might present a fourth scenario. The class will gather to present their designs for each scenario. During each presentation, teams should describe the type of structure chosen and explain why it is appropriate.

Source: Adapted from C. Harvey and K. Morouney, *Journal of Management Education* 22 (June 1998), pp. 425–429. Used with permission of the authors.

Go to CONNECT to complete the following interactive self-assessment.

 SELF-ASSESSMENT EXERCISE 13.3

What Organizational Structure Do You Prefer?

Purpose   This exercise is designed to help you understand how an organization's structure influences the personal needs and values of people working in that structure.

Instructions   Personal values influence how comfortable you are working in different organizational structures. You might prefer an organization with clearly defined rules or no rules at all. You might prefer a firm where almost any employee can make important decisions or one where important decisions are screened by senior executives. Read each statement below and indicate the extent to which you would like to work in an organization with that characteristic. When finished, use the scoring key in Appendix B at the end of the book to calculate your results. This self-assessment should be completed alone so that you can assess yourself honestly without concerns of social comparison. Class discussion will focus on the elements of organizational design and their relationship to personal needs and values.

Organizational Structure Preference Scale					
I would like to work in an organization where . . .	Not at All	A Little	Somewhat	Very Much	Score
1. A person's career ladder has several steps toward higher status and responsibility.	☐	☐	☐	☐	_____
2. Employees perform their work with few rules to limit their discretion.	☐	☐	☐	☐	_____
3. Responsibility is pushed down to employees who perform the work.	☐	☐	☐	☐	_____
4. Supervisors have few employees, so they work closely with each person.	☐	☐	☐	☐	_____
5. Senior executives make most decisions to ensure that the company is consistent in its actions.	☐	☐	☐	☐	_____
6. Jobs are clearly defined so that there is no confusion over who is responsible for various tasks.	☐	☐	☐	☐	_____
7. Employees have their say on issues, but senior executives make most of the decisions.	☐	☐	☐	☐	_____
8. Job descriptions are broadly stated or nonexistent.	☐	☐	☐	☐	_____
9. Everyone's work is tightly synchronized around top-management operating plans.	☐	☐	☐	☐	_____
10. Most work is performed in teams without close supervision.	☐	☐	☐	☐	_____
11. Work gets done through informal discussion with co-workers rather than through formal rules.	☐	☐	☐	☐	_____
12. Supervisors have so many employees that they can't monitor anyone very closely.	☐	☐	☐	☐	_____
13. Everyone has clearly understood goals, expectations, and job duties.	☐	☐	☐	☐	_____
14. Senior executives assign overall goals, but leave daily decisions to front-line teams.	☐	☐	☐	☐	_____
15. Even in a large company, there are only three or four levels between the CEO and entry-level positions.	☐	☐	☐	☐	_____

Practise and learn online with Connect. Connect resources include additional and inter-active study exercises, videos, and practice quizzing, as well as additional material you won't find in the printed text.

CHAPTER 14

Organizational Culture

After reading this chapter, you should be able to:

LEARNING OBJECTIVES

LO1 Describe the elements of organizational culture and discuss the importance of organizational subcultures.

LO2 List four categories of artifacts through which corporate culture is deciphered.

LO3 Discuss the importance of organizational culture and the conditions under which organizational culture strength improves organizational performance.

LO4 Compare and contrast four strategies for merging organizational cultures.

LO5 Identify four strategies for changing or strengthening an organization's culture, including the application of attraction-selection-attrition theory.

LO6 Describe the organizational socialization process and identify strategies to improve that process.

WestJet Airlines Ltd.'s award-winning corporate culture has fuelled the airline's success from upstart to Canada's second-largest airline. West-Jet has earned a reputation for its fun-loving, customer-friendly, and entrepreneurial culture. Well known for creating a fun environment for guests, WestJet Airlines Ltd. extends this experience to its own staff. Founder Clive Beddoe was known for his belief that "if you take care of your people, they will take care of guests and the business."

WestJet searches hard for new employees who fit with the culture and WestJet has lots of applicants to pick from. Last year WestJet received more than 118,000 applications for 1,300 advertised jobs. Tyler Matheson, vice-president of people relations says that although unlimited standby flights at a greatly discounted rate is a big attraction to potential employees, "the strong brand recognition and the corporate culture were even higher." The airline looks for applicants who have "fun, friendly, and caring" personalities and then uses mentoring as well as profit-sharing and employee share-ownership to keep employees aligned with WestJet's goals and culture.

Matheson also explains "that a recognized part of the WestJet culture is the accessibility of senior executives and the opportunity for staff to speak their minds on any issues." Each executive takes ownership of one of WestJet's "bases" and provides a visible face and senior contact for staff.

For example, when management gave employees a preview of a new advertising campaign intended to expand business in Eastern Canada, employees felt the ads didn't "reflect the company's culture." The campaign was scrapped in favour of the now-famous slogan, "Why do WestJetters care so much? Because we're also WestJet owners."

WestJet also extends its culture of caring out to the communities it serves by collecting and delivering toys to children in 25 hospitals across Canada, the Bahamas, and Jamaica. Gregg Saretsky, WestJet's president and CEO describes WestJet Cares for Kids. "We've always had a commitment to fun, friendly and caring travel, but over the last few years we've worked hard to bring our caring philosophy to our community."[1]

WestJet's award-winning corporate culture has fuelled the company's growth and success. *Dan Riedlhuber/Reuters/Landov*

organizational culture
The values and assumptions shared within an organization.

WestJet Airlines Ltd. has a distinctive organizational culture that has worked well in the competitive airline business. **Organizational culture** consists of the values and assumptions shared within an organization.[2] It defines what is important and unimportant in the company and, consequently, directs everyone in the organization toward the "right way" of doing things. You might think of organizational culture as the company's DNA—invisible to the naked eye, yet a powerful template that shapes what happens in the workplace.

This chapter begins by identifying the elements of organizational culture and then describing how culture is deciphered through artifacts. This is followed by a discussion of the relationship between organizational culture and performance, including the effects of cultural strength, fit, and adaptability. We then turn our attention to the challenges of and solutions to merging organizational cultures. The latter part of this chapter examines ways to change and strengthen organizational culture, including a closer look at the related topic of organizational socialization.

ELEMENTS OF ORGANIZATIONAL CULTURE

LO1

As its definition states, organizational culture consists of shared values and assumptions. Exhibit 14.1 illustrates how these shared values and assumptions relate to each other and are associated with artifacts, which are discussed later in this chapter. *Values* are stable, evaluative beliefs that guide our preferences for outcomes or courses of action in a variety of situations (see Chapters 1 and 2).[3] They are conscious perceptions about what is good or bad, right or wrong. In the context of organizational culture, values are discussed as *shared values*, which are values that people within the organization or work unit have in common and place near the top of their hierarchy of values.[4] At WestJet, employees generally embrace the shared values of having fun, customer-friendliness, and entrepreneurial spirit.

Organizational culture also consists of *shared assumptions*—a deeper element that some experts believe is the essence of corporate culture. Shared assumptions are unconscious, taken-for-granted perceptions or ideal prototypes of behaviour that are considered the correct way to think and act toward problems and opportunities. Shared assumptions are so deeply ingrained that you probably wouldn't discover them by surveying employees. Only by observing employees, analyzing their decisions, and debriefing them on their actions would these assumptions rise to the surface.

It has become a popular practice for leaders to identify and publicly state their organization's shared values. Vancouver City Savings Credit Union (Vancity) identifies its three core values as integrity (doing what is honest, fair, and trustworthy), innovation (anticipate and respond to challenges and changing needs with creativity, enthusiasm, and determination), and responsibility (being accountable to members, employees, colleagues, and communities). Gap Adventures, the Toronto-based outdoor adventure company, highlights five values: we love changing people's lives, embrace the bizarre, lead with service, do the right thing, and create happiness and community.[5]

Do these values really represent the cultural content of Vancity and Gap Adventures? Very probably in the case of these two organizations, because their cultures are well known and deeply entrenched. However, the values statements of many organizations do not necessarily reflect the values that are widely shared and practised in the organization. The concern is that corporate leaders typically describe *espoused values*—the values that they want others to believe guide the organization's decisions and actions.[6] Espoused values are usually socially desirable, so they present a positive public image. Even if top management acts consistently with the espoused values, lower-level employees might not do so. Employees bring diverse personal values to the organization and, as we discuss later in this chapter, some of these personal values conflict with the organization's espoused values.

Organizational culture is not represented by espoused values. Instead, it consists of shared *enacted values*—the values that most leaders and employees truly rely on to

Exhibit 14.1 \ ORGANIZATIONAL CULTURE ASSUMPTIONS, VALUES, AND ARTIFACTS

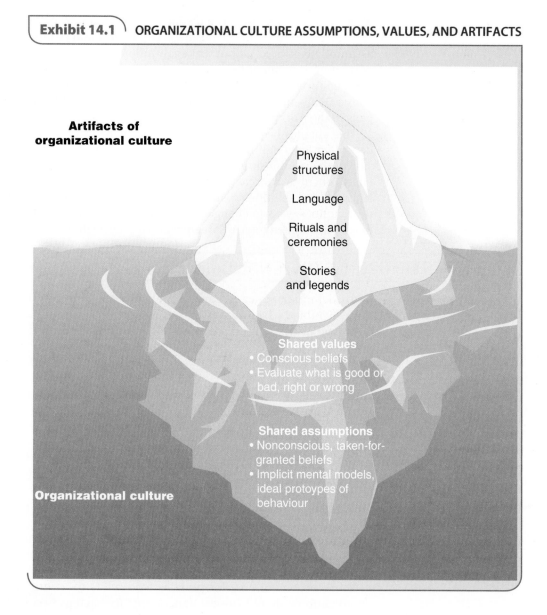

Artifacts of organizational culture

Physical structures

Language

Rituals and ceremonies

Stories and legends

Shared values
- Conscious beliefs
- Evaluate what is good or bad, right or wrong

Shared assumptions
- Nonconscious, taken-for-granted beliefs
- Implicit mental models, ideal protoypes of behaviour

Organizational culture

guide their decisions and behaviour. These "values-in-use" are apparent by watching executives and other employees in action, including their decisions, where they focus their attention and resources, and how they behave toward stakeholders. For example, Global Connections 14.1 describes how BP's stated (espoused) value of responsibility seems to be substantially inconsistent with the decisions, priorities, and behaviour of its leaders and many employees.

CONTENT OF ORGANIZATIONAL CULTURE

Organizations differ in their cultural content, that is, the relative ordering of shared values. For example, contrast the values that dominate WestJet with those at ICICI Bank. India's second-largest bank exudes a competitive, performance-oriented culture focused on growth. Its organizational practices place a premium on training, career development, goal setting, and pay for performance, all with the intent of maximizing employee achievement and customer service. A small percentage of staff receive generous rewards while the bottom 5 percent are cut from the payroll. "Growth happens only when there are differential rewards for differential performers," explains ICICI's head of human resources.[7] No doubt, WestJetters also value

CONNECTIONS 14.1

BP's Espoused vs. Enacted Values

BP, the British energy giant, lists four core values—progressive, responsible, innovative, and performance-driven. The company says that these values "guide us in the conduct of our business." In other words, BP claims these four core values are enacted—they are evident in the company's decisions, allocation of resources, and the daily behaviour of its employees.

Most people around the Gulf of Mexico and in Alaska would quickly dismiss those claims. In particular, BP describes its "responsibility" value as being "committed to the safety and development of our people and the communities and societies in which we operate. We aim for no accidents, no harm to people and no damage to the environment." Yet, the energy company's track record on safety and environmentalism suggests otherwise.

BP is at the centre of the Gulf of Mexico oil spill, now considered the worst environmental disaster in recent history. A few months before the spill occurred, the U.S. government's Occupational Safety and Health Administration (OSHA) penalized BP with the largest fine in OSHA's history for failing to sufficiently improve safety at its Texas City refinery. Four years earlier, 15 employees died in an explosion at that refinery. A U.S. government report on that explosion concluded that BP "did not provide effective safety culture leadership."

BP's "responsibility" value has been around for a few years, yet the company's environmental and safety problems were well known long before the Gulf and Texas disasters. In 2003, the Norwegian government concluded that "a poor HES (Health, Environment, and Safety) culture" contributed to a fatality on a BP oil platform. A few years earlier, a prominent newspaper concluded that a series

One of BP's four core values is "responsibility," yet the energy giant's track record suggests that this value is espoused, not enacted. *AP Photo/Alastair Grant*

of spills, accidents, and alleged hush-ups at the Alaskan operations managed by BP "raises serious questions about BP's safety culture." In short, being safety and environmentally "responsible" is an espoused value at BP, but is not likely part of the company's current or recent culture.[8]

performance and competition, but not as an overriding priority. It would be difficult to maintain WestJet's employee-friendly culture if 5 percent of its staff members were fired each year!

How many corporate cultures are there? Several models and measures classify organizational culture into a handful of easy-to-remember categories. One of these, shown in Exhibit 14.2, identifies seven corporate cultures. Another popular model identifies four organizational cultures organized in a two-by-two table representing internal versus external focus and flexibility versus control. Other models organize cultures around a circle with eight or 12 categories. These circumplex models suggest that some cultures are opposite to others, such as an avoidance culture versus a self-actualization culture, or a power culture versus a collegial culture.[9]

These organizational culture models and surveys are popular with corporate leaders faced with the messy business of diagnosing their company's culture and identifying what kind of culture they want to develop. Unfortunately, they also present a distorted view of organizational culture. One problem is that these models oversimplify the diversity of cultural values in organizations. The fact is, there are dozens of individual values, and many more combinations of values, so the number of organizational cultures that these models describe likely falls considerably short of the full set. A second concern is that organizational culture includes shared assumptions about the right way to do things, not just shared values. Most organizational culture measures ignore assumptions because they represent a more subterranean aspect of culture.

Exhibit 14.2 ORGANIZATIONAL CULTURE PROFILE DIMENSIONS AND CHARACTERISTICS

Organizational culture dimension	Characteristics of the dimension
Innovation	Experimenting, opportunity seeking, risk taking, few rules, low cautiousness
Stability	Predictability, security, rule-oriented
Respect for people	Fairness, tolerance
Outcome orientation	Action-oriented, high expectations, results-oriented
Attention to detail	Precise, analytic
Team orientation	Collaboration, people-oriented
Aggressiveness	Competitive, low emphasis on social responsibility

Source: Based on information in C. A. O'Reilly III, J. Chatman, and D. F. Caldwell, "People and Organizational Culture: A Profile Comparison Approach to Assessing Person-Organization Fit," *Academy of Management Journal* 34, no. 3 (1991), pp. 487–518.

A third concern is that many organizational culture models and measures incorrectly assume that organizations have a fairly clear, unified culture that is easily decipherable.[10] This "integration" perspective, as it is called, further assumes that when an organization's culture changes, it shifts from one unified condition to a new unified condition with only temporary ambiguity or weakness during the transition. These assumptions are probably incorrect or, at best, oversimplified. An organization's culture is usually quite blurry, so much so that it cannot be estimated through employee surveys alone. As we discuss next, organizations consist of diverse subcultures because employees across the organization have different clusters of experiences and backgrounds that have shaped their values and priorities. For example, after BP's Texas refinery explosion a few years ago, an independent panel investigated the energy company's safety culture across the United States. The panel concluded that most of BP's sites required a much stronger safety culture. However, a few already embraced the importance of safety.[11]

Even these subcultural clusters can be ill-defined because values and assumptions ultimately vary from one employee to the next. As long as employees differ, an organization's culture will have noticeable variability. Thus, many of the popular organizational culture models and measures oversimplify the variety of organizational cultures and falsely presume that it is relatively easy to fit organizations within these categories.

ORGANIZATIONAL SUBCULTURES

When discussing organizational culture, we are really referring to the *dominant culture*, that is, the values and assumptions shared most consistently and widely by the organization's members. The dominant culture is usually supported by senior management, but cultures can also persist in spite of senior management's desire for another culture. Furthermore, as mentioned in the previous section, an organization's dominant culture is not as unified or clear as many consultants and business leaders assume. Instead, organizations are composed of *subcultures* located throughout their various divisions, geographic regions, and occupational groups.[12] Some subcultures enhance the dominant culture by espousing parallel assumptions and values. Others differ from but do not oppose the dominant culture. Still others are called *countercultures* because they embrace values or assumptions that directly oppose the organization's dominant culture. It is also possible that some organizations (including some universities, according to one study) operate with subcultures and no decipherable dominant culture at all.[13]

Subcultures maintain the organization's standards of performance and ethical behaviour and are the spawning grounds for emerging values that keep the firm aligned with its environment. **"**

Subcultures, particularly countercultures, potentially create conflict and dissension among employees, but they also serve two important functions.[14] First, they maintain the organization's standards of performance and ethical behaviour. Employees who hold countercultural values are an important source of surveillance and critical review of the dominant order. They encourage constructive conflict and more creative thinking about how the organization should interact with its environment. Subcultures potentially support ethical conduct by preventing employees from blindly following one set of values. Subculture members continually question the "obvious" decisions and actions of the majority, thereby making everyone more mindful of the consequences of their actions.

The second function of subcultures is that they are the spawning grounds for emerging values that keep the firm aligned with the needs of customers, suppliers, society, and other stakeholders. Companies eventually need to replace their dominant values with ones that are more appropriate for the changing environment. If subcultures are suppressed, the organization may take longer to discover and adopt values aligned with the emerging environment.

DECIPHERING ORGANIZATIONAL CULTURE THROUGH ARTIFACTS

LO2

artifacts The observable symbols and signs of an organization's culture.

Shared values and assumptions are not easily measured through surveys and might not be accurately reflected in the organization's values statements. Instead, as Exhibit 14.1 illustrated earlier, an organization's culture needs to be deciphered through a detailed investigation of artifacts. **Artifacts** are the observable symbols and signs of an organization's culture, such as the way visitors are greeted, the organization's physical layout, and how employees are rewarded.[15] A few experts suggest that artifacts are the essence of organizational culture, whereas most others (including the authors of this book) view artifacts as symbols or indicators of culture. In other words, culture is cognitive (values and assumptions inside people's heads) whereas artifacts are observable manifestations of that culture. Either way, artifacts are important because they represent and reinforce an organization's culture.

Artifacts of Protegra's Corporate Culture

One of the first things you might notice when visiting Protegra's offices in Winnipeg is the lack of job titles. Co-founder and CEO Wadood Ibrahim wants the information technology consulting firm to develop a team-oriented, respectful, employee-focused culture, so he refuses to let status differences creep into the organization. "We focus on the employee as a member of a team as opposed to a title," says Ibrahim. A related artifact of the company's culture is its lack of hierarchy; Protegra has only one layer of management, even though it employs more than 50 people. The company's culture is further evident in its share-ownership program, comfortable work environment, fitness centre, staff kitchen, open communications, and fluid assignment of employees to different project teams.[16] *Courtesy of Protegra*

Artifacts provide valuable evidence about a company's culture.[17] An organization's ambiguous (fragmented) culture is best understood by observing workplace behaviour, listening to everyday conversations among staff and with customers, studying written documents and emails, viewing physical structures and settings, and interviewing staff about corporate stories. In other words, to truly understand an organization's culture, we need to sample information from a variety of organizational artifacts.

> To truly understand an organization's culture, we need to sample information from a variety of organizational artifacts. **"**

The Mayo Clinic conducted such an assessment a few years ago. An anthropologist was hired to decipher the medical organization's culture at its headquarters in Minnesota and to identify ways of transferring that culture to its two newer sites in Florida and Arizona. For six weeks, the anthropologist shadowed employees, posed as a patient in waiting rooms, did countless interviews, and accompanied physicians on patient visits. The final report outlined Mayo's dominant culture and how its satellite operations varied from that culture.[18]

In this section, we review the four broad categories of artifacts: organizational stories and legends, rituals and ceremonies, organizational language, and physical structures and symbols.

ORGANIZATIONAL STORIES AND LEGENDS

Cirque du Soleil, the Montreal-based troupe that combines circus with theatre, thrives on a culture of risk and creativity. This is apparent in stories about how the troupe was started and survived during the lean years. In 1980, Gilles Ste-Croix asked the Quebec government for funding to start up a street theatre group in Baie-Saint-Paul, northwest of Quebec City. When the government rejected the application, Ste-Croix walked 90 kilometres from Baie-Saint-Paul to Quebec City . . . on stilts! The gruelling 22-hour trip got the government's attention and financial support. Ste-Croix recalls a Quebec government representative saying, "If you're crazy enough to walk all this way on stilts, we'll give you some money to create jobs." Without that daring event, Cirque du Soleil probably wouldn't exist today, because Ste-Criox's band of 15 performers included Guy Laliberté who founded Cirque du Soleil in 1984 with Ste-Croix and others.

Another story illustrating Cirque du Soleil's culture took place in 1987, when the troupe was invited to perform at the Los Angeles Arts Festival. The festival could not provide funds in advance to cover Cirque du Soleil's costs, so Laliberté took a gamble by literally emptying the troupe's bank account to transport the performers and equipment one way to California. "I bet everything on that one night [at the Los Angeles Arts Festival]," Laliberté recalls. "If we failed, there was no cash for gas to come home." Fortunately, the gamble paid off. Cirque du Soleil was a huge success, which led to more opportunities and successes in the years ahead.[19]

Stories, such as these tales about Cirque du Soleil, permeate strong organizational cultures. Some tales recount heroic deeds, whereas others ridicule past events that deviate from the firm's core values. Organizational stories and legends serve as powerful social prescriptions of the way things should (or should not) be done. They add human realism to corporate expectations, individual performance standards, and the criteria for getting fired. Stories also produce emotions in listeners, and this tends to improve listeners' memory of the lesson within the story.[20] Stories have the greatest effect on communicating corporate culture when they describe real people, are assumed to be true, and are known by employees throughout the organization. Stories are also prescriptive—they advise people what to do or not to do.[21]

rituals The programmed routines of daily organizational life that dramatize the organization's culture.

RITUALS AND CEREMONIES

Rituals are the programmed routines of daily organizational life that dramatize the organization's culture.[22] They include how visitors are greeted, how often senior executives visit front-line staff, how people communicate with each other, how much time employees take for lunch, and so on. These rituals are repetitive, predictable, events that have symbolic meaning of underlying cultural values and assumptions. For instance, BMW's fast-paced culture is quite literally apparent in the way employees walk around the German carmaker's offices. "When you move through the corridors and hallways of other companies' buildings, people kind of crawl, they walk slowly," observes a BMW executive. "But BMW people tend to move faster."[23] **Ceremonies** are more formal artifacts than rituals. Ceremonies are planned activities conducted specifically for the benefit of an audience. This would include publicly rewarding (or punishing) employees or celebrating the launch of a new product or newly won contract.

ceremonies Planned displays of organizational culture, conducted specifically for the benefit of an audience.

ORGANIZATIONAL LANGUAGE

The language of the workplace speaks volumes about the company's culture. How employees talk to each other, describe customers, express anger, and greet stakeholders are all verbal symbols of cultural values. For example, employees at The Container Store compliment each other about "being Gumby," meaning that they are being as flexible as the once-popular green toy to help a customer or another employee.[24] Language also highlights values held by organizational subcultures. Consultants working at Whirlpool kept hearing employees talk about the appliance company's "PowerPoint culture." This phrase, which names Microsoft's presentation software, implied that Whirlpool has a hierarchical culture in which communication is one-way (from executives to employees).[25]

PHYSICAL STRUCTURES AND SYMBOLS

Winston Churchill once said: "We shape our buildings; thereafter, they shape us."[26] The former British prime minister was reminding us that buildings both reflect and influence an organization's culture. The size, shape, location, and age of buildings might suggest a company's emphasis on teamwork, environmental friendliness, flexibility, or any other set of values.[27] An extreme example is the "interplanetary headquarters" of Oakley, Inc. This trend-leading eyewear and apparel firm built a vault-like structure in Foothills Ranch, Calif., complete with towering metallic walls studded with oversize bolts, to represent its secretive and protective culture. "We've always had a fortress mentality," says an Oakley executive. "What we make is gold, and people will do anything to get it, so we protect it."[28]

Even if the building doesn't make much of a statement, there is a treasure trove of physical artifacts inside. Desks, chairs, office space, and wall hangings (or lack of them) are just a few of the items that might convey cultural meaning.[29] Consider the physical artifacts that you might notice when visiting the headquarters of Mother. Housed in a converted warehouse in an artsy district of London, England, the creative agency has a large reception hall with an adjoining casual lounge on one side and a large cafeteria on the other (yes, complete with free snacks). A wide staircase leads to the next floor, which has meeting rooms separated only by dividers made of hanging strips of opaque plastic. The top floor of Mother's offices is one room dominated by a large rectangular concrete table around which dozens of staff work. Each of these physical artifacts alone might not say much, but put enough of them together and you can see how they symbolize Mother's edgy creative culture with a strong team orientation.[30]

IS ORGANIZATIONAL CULTURE IMPORTANT?

L03

Does organizational culture improve organizational effectiveness? Leaders at Cirque du Soleil, The Container Store, Mayo Clinic, and other companies think so. "Culture is one of the most precious things a company has, so you must work harder on it than anything

Lee Kum Kee's Secret Sauce to Success

Guangdong Nanfang Lee Kum Kee Health Products Co., Ltd., a subsidiary of food products company Lee Kum Kee, has a secret sauce that makes it one of the best places to work in Asia. "Two words explain why we are a Best Employer: corporate culture," says human resource vice-president Raymond Lo. "Our unique culture is our competitive edge. It plays a major role in the success of our organization." Lee Kum Kee's core values include pragmatism, integrity, constant entrepreneurship, and sharing the benefits with community. Lo explains that cultural values are so important that leaders must believe in and live them. "The corporate culture must have a soul," he says. "Many companies try to model themselves on successful companies, but unless the chief executive and management truly believe in the culture, it won't work." Lo adds that his company actively works to ensure everyone understands and believes in the company's culture. "We also spend a lot of time in team building in order to nourish our corporate culture."[31] *AP Photo/Vincent Yu*

else," says Herb Kelleher, founder of Southwest Airlines.[32] Many writers of popular-press management books also assert that the most successful companies have strong cultures. In fact, one popular management book, *Built to Last,* suggests that successful companies are "cult-like" (although not actually cults, the authors are careful to point out.)[33]

So, does organizational culture make a difference? The research evidence suggests that companies with strong cultures tend to be more successful, but only under a particular set of conditions.[34] Before discussing these contingencies, let's examine the meaning of a "strong" organizational culture and its potential benefits. The strength of an organization's culture refers to how widely and deeply employees hold the company's dominant values and assumptions. In a strong organizational culture, most employees across all subunits understand and embrace the dominant values. These values and assumptions are also institutionalized through well-established artifacts, thereby making it difficult to change the culture. Furthermore, strong cultures tend to be long-lasting; some can be traced back to the values and assumptions established by the company's founder. In contrast, companies have weak cultures when the dominant values are held mainly by a few people at the top of the organization, are barely discernible, and are in flux.

As mentioned, companies with stronger cultures are potentially more effective, and this occurs through the three important functions listed in Exhibit 14.3 and described below:

1. *Control system.* Organizational culture is a deeply embedded form of social control that influences employee decisions and behaviour.[35] Culture is pervasive and operates nonconsciously. You might think of it as an automatic pilot, directing employees in ways that are consistent with organizational expectations.

2. *Social glue.* Organizational culture is the "social glue" that bonds people together and makes them feel part of the organizational experience.[36] Employees are motivated to internalize the organization's dominant culture because it fulfills their need for social identity. This social glue is increasingly important as a way to attract new staff and retain top performers. It also becomes the common thread that holds together employees in global organizations. "If you're managing a company which has a global footprint, diverse nationalities, diverse clients, diverse all over the place, the values of the company are really the bedrock—the glue which holds the firm together," says Nandan Nilekani, former CEO of India's information technology giant, Infosys.[37]

3. *Sense making.* Organizational culture assists the sense-making process.[38] It helps employees to understand what goes on and why things happen in the company. Corporate culture also makes it easier for employees to understand what is expected of them and to interact with other employees who know the culture and believe in it. For instance, one recent study reported that organizational culture strength increases role clarity, which reduces stress among sales staff.[39]

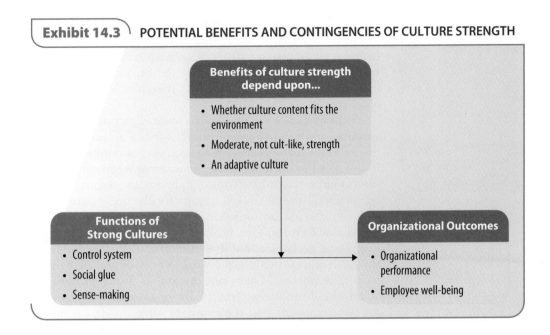

Exhibit 14.3   POTENTIAL BENEFITS AND CONTINGENCIES OF CULTURE STRENGTH

Benefits of culture strength depend upon...

- Whether culture content fits the environment
- Moderate, not cult-like, strength
- An adaptive culture

Functions of Strong Cultures

- Control system
- Social glue
- Sense-making

Organizational Outcomes

- Organizational performance
- Employee well-being

CONTINGENCIES OF ORGANIZATIONAL CULTURE AND EFFECTIVENESS

Studies have found only a modestly positive relationship between culture strength and organizational effectiveness. Why is there such a weak link? The answer is that a strong culture improves organizational effectiveness only under specific conditions (see Exhibit 14.3). Three important contingencies are: (1) whether the culture content fits the environment, (2) whether the culture is moderately strong, not cult-like, and (3) whether the culture incorporates an adaptive culture (see Exhibit 14.3).

Culture Content Alignment with Environment   One contingency between cultural strength and organizational effectiveness is whether the organization's culture content—its dominant values and assumptions—fits the external environment. Consider the situation recently faced by Dell, the computer manufacturer. Dell's culture gave the highest priority to cost efficiency and competitiveness, yet these values and assumptions are no longer sufficient for the marketplace. Low-cost computers are still popular, but consumers increasingly demand computers that are innovative with elegant styling. Dell had a strong culture, but it was no longer the best culture for the external environment. "Dell's culture is not inspirational or aspirational," suggests one industry expert. "[Its] culture only wants to talk about execution."[40]

Avoiding a Corporate Cult   A second contingency is the degree of cultural strength. Various experts suggest that companies with very strong cultures (i.e., corporate "cults") may be less effective than companies with moderately strong cultures.[41] One reason why corporate cults may undermine organizational effectiveness is that they lock people into mental models, which can blind them to new opportunities and unique problems. They overlook or incorrectly dismiss subtle misalignments between the organization's activities and the changing environment.

The other reason why very strong cultures may be dysfunctional is that they suppress dissenting subcultural values. The challenge for organizational leaders is to maintain not only a strong culture but one that allows subcultural diversity. Subcultures encourage constructive conflict, which improves creative thinking and offers some level of ethical watch over the dominant culture. In the long run, a subculture's emerging values could become important dominant values as the environment changes. Corporate cults suppress subcultures, thereby undermining these benefits.

adaptive culture An organizational culture in which employees are receptive to change, including the ongoing alignment of the organization to its environment and continuous improvement of internal processes.

Culture Is an Adaptive Culture   A third contingency determining the influence of cultural strength on organizational effectiveness is whether the culture content includes an **adaptive culture**.[42] An adaptive culture exists when employees are receptive to change—they assume that the organization needs to continuously adapt to its external environment and that they need to be flexible in their roles within the organization.

At companies with an adaptive culture, employees embrace an open-systems perspective, in which the organization's survival and success require ongoing adaptation to the external environment, which itself is continuously changing. They assume that their future depends on monitoring the external environment and serving stakeholders with the resources available. Thus, employees in adaptive cultures have a strong sense of ownership. They take responsibility for the organization's performance and alignment with the external environment.

In an adaptive culture, receptivity to change extends to internal processes and roles. Employees recognize that they need to satisfy stakeholder needs. This occurs by continuously improving internal work processes and by being flexible in their own work roles. The phrase, "That's not my job" is found in nonadaptive cultures. Finally, an adaptive culture has a strong *learning orientation* because being receptive to change necessarily means that the company also supports action-oriented discovery. With a learning orientation, employees welcome new learning opportunities, actively experiment with new ideas and practices, view reasonable mistakes as a natural part of the learning process, and continuously question past practices.[43]

ORGANIZATIONAL CULTURE AND BUSINESS ETHICS

An organization's culture influences the ethical conduct of its employees. This makes sense because good behaviour is driven by ethical values, and ethical values can become embedded into an organization's dominant culture. Michael Dell and his executive team saw this connection between culture and ethics when they launched the 'Soul of Dell' a few years ago. One of the computer maker's revised values was defined as "behaving ethically in every interaction and in every aspect of how we conduct business." Unfortunately, the Soul of Dell initiative probably didn't change the company's culture. Two years after the Soul of Dell cultural change program was launched, the company reported that some executives had manipulated the company books to reach performance targets that would give them a larger bonus.[44]

MERGING ORGANIZATIONAL CULTURES

LO4

4C Corporate Culture Clash and Chemistry is a company with an unusual name and mandate. The Dutch consulting firm helps clients to determine whether their culture is aligned ("chemistry") or incompatible with ("clash") a potential acquisition or merger partner. The firm also analyzes the company's culture with its strategy. There should be plenty of demand for 4C's expertise. One study estimated that only half of the corporate acquisitions adds any value, whereas two other studies report that only 30 percent of these acquisitions produces any financial gains.[45] Meanwhile, mergers have a substantial disruptive effect on the organizations involved, often leading to neglected strategy, employee stress, and customer problems.

Mergers and acquisitions fail partly because corporate leaders are so focused on the financial or marketing logistics of a merger that they do not conduct due-diligence audits on their respective corporate cultures.[46] Some forms of integration (which we discuss later in this section) may allow successful mergers between companies with different cultures. However, research concludes that mergers typically suffer when organizations with significantly divergent corporate cultures merge into a single entity with a high degree of integration.[47]

One recent corporate culture clash occurred when Bank of America (BofA) hastily acquired Merrill Lynch. BofA's "Main Street" culture is about serving middle America with broad-based accessible services, whereas Merrill Lynch had a much more exclusive culture catering to wealthy clients. Consistent with these divergent client orientations, BofA's culture embraces cost efficiencies and penny pinching, whereas Merrill Lynch had more of an "entitlement" culture that encouraged big spending and bigger bonuses. To illustrate, in spite of the company's staggering losses during the previous year, Merrill Lynch's CEO spent more than $1 million renovating his office, hired an executive with a $25 million signing bonus, and handed out billions in bonuses. BofA's culture is also more cautious and bureaucratic, requiring more signatures and higher level authority, whereas Merrill Lynch's "thundering herd" culture was more aggressive, entrepreneurial and, some say, more likely to venture into ethically questionable territory.[48]

BICULTURAL AUDIT

bicultural audit   A process of diagnosing cultural relations between the companies and determining the extent to which cultural clashes will likely occur.

Organizational leaders can minimize these cultural collisions and fulfill their duty of due diligence by conducting a bicultural audit.[49] A **bicultural audit** diagnoses cultural relations between the companies and determines the extent to which cultural clashes will likely occur. The bicultural audit process begins by identifying cultural differences between the merging companies. Next, the bicultural audit data are analyzed to determine which differences between the two firms will result in conflict and which cultural values provide common ground on which to build a cultural foundation in the merged organization. The final stage involves identifying strategies and preparing action plans to bridge the two organizations' cultures.

A classic example of a bicultural audit occurred several years ago when Toronto-based pulp-and-paper conglomerate Abitibi-Price proposed a merger with rival Stone Consolidated. Abitibi developed the Merging Cultures Evaluation Index (MCEI), an evaluation system that helped Abitibi executives compare its culture with other companies in the industry. The MCEI examined several dimensions of corporate culture, such as concentration of power versus diffusion of power, innovation versus tradition, wide versus narrow flow of information, and consensus versus authoritative decision making. Abitibi and Stone executives completed the questionnaire to assess their own culture, and then they compared the results. The MCEI results,

Culture Clash Ends Merger Talks

When Grant Thorton LLP and BDO Dunwoody LLP said their proposed merger would create the second largest accounting and business advisory firm it was described as a "marriage of opportunity." "A combined firm would have enhanced strength, capacity, depth, and market credibility to compete in marketplaces across Canada," announced Gilles Chaput CEO of BDO Dunwoody in announcing the merger plans. However, a month later Chaput announced the wedding was off due to "a number of cultural differences." "The goal was not simply do a merger, but to have a successful implementation," said Mr. Chaput. "We determined that the cultural differences are too large." A merger of Grant Thornton and BDO would have created a national firm second in size only to Deloitte & Touche.[50]
Colin Anderson/Blend Images/Corbis

along with financial and infrastructural information, served as the basis for Abitibi-Price to merge with Stone Consolidated to become Abitibi-Consolidated (now Abitibi Bowater).[51]

STRATEGIES FOR MERGING DIFFERENT ORGANIZATIONAL CULTURES

In some cases, the bicultural audit results in a decision to end merger talks because the two cultures are too different to merge effectively. However, even with substantially different cultures, two companies may form a workable union if they apply the appropriate merger strategy. The four main strategies for merging different corporate cultures are assimilation, deculturation, integration, and separation (see Exhibit 14.4).[52]

Assimilation   Assimilation occurs when employees at the acquired company willingly embrace the cultural values of the acquiring organization. Typically, this strategy works best when the acquired company has a weak, dysfunctional culture and the acquiring company's culture is strong and aligned with the external environment. Culture clash is rare with assimilation because the acquired firm's culture is weak and employees are looking for better cultural alternatives. Research In Motion (RIM), the Waterloo, Ontario, company that produces BlackBerry wireless devices, applies the assimilation strategy by deliberately acquiring only small start-up firms. "Small companies . . . don't have cultural issues," says RIM co-CEO Jim Balsillie, adding that they are typically absorbed into RIM's culture with little fuss or attention.[53]

Deculturation   Assimilation is rare. Employees usually resist organizational change, particularly when they are asked to throw away personal and cultural values. Under these conditions, some acquiring companies apply a *deculturation* strategy by imposing their culture and business practices on the acquired organization. The acquiring firm strips away artifacts and reward systems that support the old culture. People who cannot adopt the acquiring company's culture often lose their jobs. Deculturation may be necessary when the acquired firm's culture doesn't work, even when employees in the acquired company aren't convinced of this. However, this strategy is difficult to apply effectively because the acquired firm's employees resist the cultural intrusions from the buying firm, thereby delaying or undermining the merger process.

Integration   A third strategy is to combine the two or more cultures into a new composite culture that preserves the best features of the previous cultures. Integration is slow and potentially risky because there are many forces preserving the

Exhibit 14.4	STRATEGIES FOR MERGING DIFFERENT ORGANIZATIONAL CULTURES	
Merger strategy	**Description**	**Works best when:**
Assimilation	Acquired company embraces acquiring firm's culture.	Acquired firm has a weak culture.
Deculturation	Acquiring firm imposes its culture on unwilling acquired firm.	Rarely works—may be necessary only when acquired firm's culture doesn't work but employees don't realize it.
Integration	Merging companies combine the two or more cultures into a new composite culture.	Existing cultures can be improved.
Separation	Merging companies remain distinct entities with minimal exchange of culture or organizational practices.	Firms operate successfully in different businesses requiring different cultures.

Sources: Based on ideas in A. R. Malekzedeh and A. Nahavandi, "Making Mergers Work by Managing Cultures," *Journal of Business Strategy* 11 (May–June 1990), pp. 55–57; K. W. Smith, "A Brand-New Culture for the Merged Firm," *Mergers and Acquisitions* 35 (June 2000), pp. 45–50.

existing cultures. Still, this strategy should be considered when the companies have relatively weak cultures or when their cultures include several overlapping values. Integration also works best when people realize that their existing cultures are ineffective and, therefore, the people are motivated to adopt a new set of dominant values.

Separation   A separation strategy occurs when the merging companies agree to remain distinct entities with minimal exchange of culture or organizational practices. This strategy is most appropriate when the two merging companies are in unrelated industries or operate in different countries, because the most appropriate cultural values tend to differ by industry and national culture. This strategy is also relevant advice for the corporate cultures of diversified conglomerates.

Amazon owns several businesses but does not interfere with the cultures of those operations. For example, Amazon acquired Abebooks a few years ago and has allowed the Victoria, B.C. used bookseller to operate independently and maintain its own high-involvement, creative culture. Amazon more recently acquired Zappos, and has followed the same separation strategy. "The Amazon deal got us the best of all worlds," explains Zappos CEO Tony Hsieh. "We can continue to run independently and grow the Zappos brand and culture."[54] Amazon's cultural separation approach is rare, however. Executives in acquiring firms usually have difficulty keeping their hands off the acquired firm. According to one estimate, only 15 percent of mergers leave the acquired company as a stand-alone unit.[55]

CHANGING AND STRENGTHENING ORGANIZATIONAL CULTURE

LO5

Is it possible to change an organization's culture? Yes, but doing so isn't easy, the change rarely occurs quickly, and often the culture ends up changing (or replacing) corporate leaders. A few experts argue that an organization's culture "cannot be managed," so attempting to change the company's values and assumptions is a waste of time.[56] This may be an extreme view, but organizational culture experts generally agree that changing an organization's culture is a considerable challenge. At the same time, it is sometimes necessary to change one or more shared values and assumptions because the alignment of that culture with the external environment can influence the organization's survival and success. Over the next few pages, we will highlight four strategies that have had some success at altering corporate cultures. These strategies, illustrated in Exhibit 14.5, are not exhaustive, but each seems to work well under the right circumstances.

Lululemon's Culture of Health and Wellness Maintains a Loyal Following

With its new-age, self-affirmation culture and a focus on health and wellness, Lululemon Athletica has been a phenomenal success story in the Canadian retail industry. Lululemon has maintained a loyal culture among its employees and customers and has sustained its growth and expansion both in Canada and internationally despite the recent recession. The yoga-inspired clothing retailer opened its first store more than a decade ago and now boasts more than one hundred locations in Canada, the United States, Australia, and Hong Kong. Founder Chip Wilson recognized that Lululemon needed a leader with more corporate experience, but he didn't want that change to undermine the company's culture. He may have found an ideal choice in former Starbucks International Group president, Christine Day. "[Lululemon is] another premium brand with an exceptional product and a tremendous culture," says Day. "I feel quite at home." She adds that the decision to join Lululemon required careful thought about the culture fit with her personal values. "For me that's about really being able to live my values both personally and at work."[57] *Lucas Oleniuk/GetStock.com*

Exhibit 14.5   STRATEGIES FOR CHANGING AND STRENGTHENING
ORGANIZATIONAL CULTURE

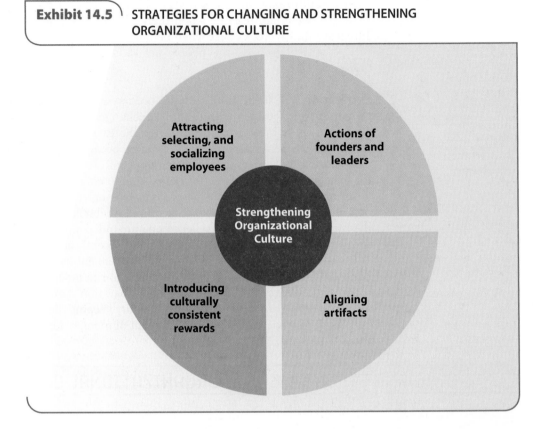

ACTIONS OF FOUNDERS AND LEADERS

In the early 1970s, Four Seasons Hotels & Resorts was a small enterprise with just four properties in Canada and one in London, England. Even so, founder Isadore Sharp believed the Toronto-based company could become "the world's best hotel company." But achieving this lofty goal required mechanisms to build and maintain a strong focus on service, so Sharp searched for these methods in other companies with excellent service. One day, while attending an orientation program for new recruits at McDonald's Restaurants of Canada, Sharp realized that the fast-food chain's ability to maintain quality and service was based on well-entrenched and unwavering values. This was particularly apparent by the fact that the film McDonald's showed to new hires was at least 15 years old. "It struck me then that when you have something people can identify with, you don't have to keep reinventing it," Sharp recalls. "Once it's rooted, it sticks."[58]

Isadore Sharp and other great leaders form their organization's culture during its early stages and introduce ways to make that culture "stick."[59] Founders are often visionaries who provide a powerful role model for others to follow. The company's culture sometimes reflects the founder's personality, and this cultural imprint can remain with the organization for decades. The founder's actions are often the subject of organizational stories that also reinforce the culture. In spite of the founder's cultural imprint, subsequent leaders are sometimes able to reshape that culture by applying transformational leadership and organizational change practices.[60]

ALIGNING ARTIFACTS

Artifacts represent more than just the visible indicators of a company's culture. They are also mechanisms that keep the culture in place. By altering artifacts—or creating new ones—leaders can potentially adjust shared values and assumptions. Corporate culture

Organizational Culture as Part of the Hiring Process[70]

75%
of 500 Canadian executives polled say cultural fit is more important than skills for selecting external candidates.

58%
of 1,500 American job seekers polled, during the hiring process, wanted to know about the company's culture.

61%
of 500 Canadian executives polled say cultural fit is more important than skills for selecting (promoting) internal candidates.

44%
of Fortune 500 companies take steps to describe their corporate culture to job seekers.

is altered and strengthened through the artifacts of stories and behaviours. According to Max De Pree, former CEO of furniture manufacturer Herman Miller Inc., every organization needs "tribal storytellers" to keep the organization's history and culture alive.[61] Leaders play a role by creating memorable events that symbolize the cultural values they want to develop or maintain. Companies also strengthen culture in new operations by transferring current employees who abide by the culture.

INTRODUCING CULTURALLY CONSISTENT REWARDS

Reward systems are artifacts that often have a powerful effect on strengthening or reshaping an organization's culture.[62] Robert Nardelli used rewards to change Home Depot's free-wheeling culture. Nardelli introduced precise measures of corporate performance and drilled managers with weekly performance objectives related to those metrics. A two-hour weekly conference call became a ritual in which Home Depot's top executives were held accountable for the previous week's goals. These actions reinforced a more disciplined (and centralized) performance-oriented culture.[63]

ATTRACTING, SELECTING, AND SOCIALIZING EMPLOYEES

Organizational culture is strengthened by attracting and hiring people who already embrace the cultural values. This process, along with weeding out people who don't fit the culture, is explained by **attraction-selection-attrition (ASA) theory**.[64] ASA theory states that organizations have a natural tendency to attract, select, and retain people with values and personality characteristics that are consistent with the organization's character, resulting in a more homogeneous organization and a stronger culture.

attraction-selection-attrition (ASA) theory
A theory which states that organizations have a natural tendency to attract, select, and retain people with values and personality characteristics that are consistent with the organization's character, resulting in a more homogeneous organization and a stronger culture.

- *Attraction.* Job applicants engage in self-selection by avoiding employment in companies whose values seem incompatible with their own values.[65] Companies often encourage this self-selection by actively describing their cultures, but applicants will look for evidence of the company's culture even when it is not advertised. Applicants also inspect organizational artifacts when visiting the company.

- *Selection.* How well the person "fits" in with the company's culture is often a factor in deciding which job applicants to hire. Companies with strong cultures often put applicants through several interviews and other selection tests, in part to better gauge the applicants' values and their congruence with the company's values.[66] Calgary-based Apex Distribution Inc. is a case in point. "We're an employee-owned company, so it's really important that people who join us are in line with that culture and can support the organizational objectives," says Apex vice-president of finance Linda Wyatt.[67] At Vancouver-based Strangeloop Networks, job applicants are assessed by several employees, not just by the founders. "It is a good feeling to be involved in the hiring process," says Strangeloop software developer Jarrod Connolly. "I think I feel about the culture the same way the CEO of the company does. It will grow the same way everyone here feels and wants it to."[68]

- *Attrition.* People are motivated to seek environments that are sufficiently congruent with their personal values and to leave environments that are a poor fit. This occurs because person-organization value congruence supports their social identity and minimizes internal role conflict. Even if employees aren't forced out, many quit when values incongruence is sufficiently high.[69]

ORGANIZATIONAL SOCIALIZATION

LO6

Over the past half-decade, I Love Rewards has become a leading competitor in the employee incentives industry and one of the best places to work in Canada. Founder Razor Suleman attributes this turnaround to the development of an appealing corporate vision and a strong corporate culture aligned with that vision. Now, as the Toronto-based company expands into the United States, Suleman and his crew are figuring out how to spread that cherished culture to the new location. Their solution has been to move Toronto staff to Boston where they teach and role model the I Love Rewards way of doing things to the local employees. "A few of us came down to Boston to just kind of really implant the culture here," says Suleman.[71]

Along with attracting and selecting people, I Love Rewards and other companies strengthen and maintain the organization's culture through organizational socialization. **Organizational socialization** is the process by which individuals learn the values, expected behaviours, and social knowledge necessary to assume their roles in the organization.[72] Organizational socialization can potentially change employee values to become more aligned with the company's culture, although this is much more difficult than is often assumed. More likely, effective socialization gives newcomers clearer understanding about the company's values and how they are translated into specific on-the-job behaviours.[73] Along with supporting the organization's culture, socialization helps newcomers adjust to co-workers, work procedures, and other corporate realities. Research indicates that when employees are effectively socialized into the organization, they tend to perform better, have higher job satisfaction, and remain longer with the organization.[74]

> **organizational socialization** The process by which individuals learn the values, expected behaviours, and social knowledge necessary to assume their roles in the organization.

ORGANIZATIONAL SOCIALIZATION AS A LEARNING AND ADJUSTMENT PROCESS

Organizational socialization is a process of both learning and adjustment. It is a learning process because newcomers try to make sense of the company's physical workplace, social dynamics, and strategic and cultural environment. They learn about the organization's performance expectations, power dynamics, corporate culture, company history, and jargon. They also need to form successful and satisfying relationships with other people from whom they can learn the ropes.[75] Thus, effective socialization enables new employees to form a cognitive map of the physical, social, strategic, and cultural dynamics of the organization without information overload.

Organizational socialization is also a process of adjustment, because individuals need to adapt to their new work environment. They develop new work roles that reconfigure their social identity, adopt new team norms, and practise new behaviours.[76] Research reports that the adjustment process is fairly rapid for many people, usually occurring within a few months. However, newcomers with diverse work experience seem to adjust better than those with limited previous experience, possibly because they have a larger toolkit of knowledge and skills to make the adjustment possible.[77]

ORGANIZATIONAL SOCIALIZATION AND PSYCHOLOGICAL CONTRACTS

For 14 years, John Kolliopoulos was a loyal employee at Hudson's Bay Co. The information technology expert was proud to be employed at Canada's oldest company and he worked hard to perform his job. Then, one day, he and other IT department employees learned that management had outsourced the entire IT department. "All those feelings of loyalty went away when we were shown the door," recalls Kolliopoulos, who now works for an IT company in Toronto. "Now I no longer have any sense of faith or trust in any employer."[78]

John Kolliopoulos and his co-workers experienced the shock of having their psychological contract violated. The **psychological contract** refers to the individual's beliefs about the terms and conditions of a reciprocal exchange agreement between that person and another party (typically the employer). The psychological contract is a perception formed during recruitment and throughout the organizational socialization process about what the employee is entitled to receive and is obliged to offer the

> **psychological contract** The individual's beliefs about the terms and conditions of a reciprocal exchange agreement between that person and another party (typically the employer).

employer in return.[79] Job applicants form perceptions of what the company will offer them by way of career and learning opportunities, job resources, pay and benefits, quality of management, job security, and so forth. They also form perceptions about what the company expects from them, such as hours of work, continuous skill development, and demonstrated loyalty. For example, John Kolliopoulos believed that his psychological contract included long-term employment in return for hard work and loyalty to his employer. The psychological contract continues to develop and evolve after job applicants become employees, but they are also continuously testing the employer's fulfillment of that exchange relationship.

Types of Psychological Contracts   Psychological contracts vary in the extent that they are transactional or relational.[80] *Transactional contracts* are primarily short-term economic exchanges. Responsibilities are well defined around a fairly narrow set of obligations that do not change over the life of the contract. People hired in temporary positions and as consultants tend to have transactional contracts. To some extent, new employees also form transactional contracts until they develop a sense of continuity with the organization.

Relational contracts, on the other hand, are rather like marriages; they are long-term attachments that encompass a broad array of subjective mutual obligations. Employees with a relational psychological contract are more willing to contribute their time and effort without expecting the organization to pay back this debt in the short term. Relational contracts are also dynamic, meaning that the parties tolerate and expect that mutual obligations are not necessarily balanced in the short-run. Not surprisingly, organizational citizenship behaviours are more likely to prevail under relational than transactional contracts. Permanent employees are more likely to believe they have a relational contract.

STAGES OF ORGANIZATIONAL SOCIALIZATION

Organizational socialization is a continuous process, beginning long before the first day of employment and continuing throughout one's career within the company. However, it is most intense when people move across organizational boundaries, such as when they first join a company or get transferred to an international assignment. Each of these transitions is a process that can be divided into three stages. Our focus here is on the socialization of new employees, so the three stages are called pre-employment socialization, encounter, and role management (see Exhibit 14.6). These stages parallel the individual's transition from outsider to newcomer and then to insider.[81]

Stage 1: Pre-employment Socialization   Think back to the months and weeks before you began working in a new job (or attending a new school). You actively searched for information about the company, formed expectations about working there, and felt some anticipation about fitting into that environment. The pre-employment socialization stage

Exhibit 14.6   STAGES OF ORGANIZATIONAL SOCIALIZATION

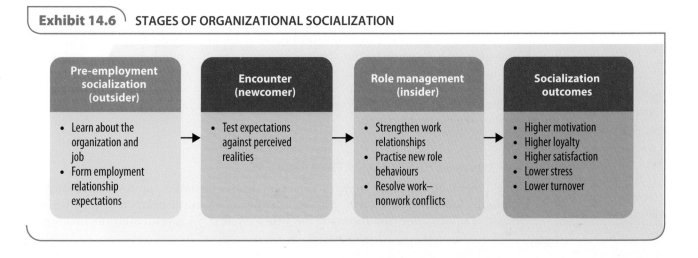

Pre-employment socialization (outsider)	Encounter (newcomer)	Role management (insider)	Socialization outcomes
• Learn about the organization and job • Form employment relationship expectations	• Test expectations against perceived realities	• Strengthen work relationships • Practise new role behaviours • Resolve work–nonwork conflicts	• Higher motivation • Higher loyalty • Higher satisfaction • Lower stress • Lower turnover

encompasses all the learning and adjustment that occurs before the first day of work. In fact, a large part of the socialization adjustment process occurs during this stage.[82]

The main problem with pre-employment socialization is that outsiders rely on indirect information about what it is like to work in the organization. This information is often distorted by inherent conflicts during the mating dance between employer and applicant.[83] One conflict occurs between the employer's need to attract qualified applicants and the applicants' need for complete information to make accurate employment decisions. Many firms use a "flypaper" approach by describing only positive aspects of the job and company, causing applicants to accept job offers from incomplete or false expectations. Another conflict that prevents accurate exchange of information occurs when applicants avoid asking important questions about the company because they don't want to convey an unfavourable image to their prospective employer. For instance, applicants usually don't like to ask about starting salaries and promotion opportunities because it makes them sound greedy or overaggressive. Yet, unless the employer provides this information, applicants might fill in the missing information with false assumptions that produce an inaccurate psychological contract.

Two other types of conflict tend to distort pre-employment information for employers. Applicants engage in impression management when seeking employment, and this tends to motivate them to hide negative information, act out of character, and occasionally embellish information about their past accomplishments. At the same time, employers are sometimes reluctant to ask certain questions or use potentially valuable selection devices because they might scare off applicants. Unfortunately, exaggerated résumés from applicants and reluctance to ask for some information causes employers to form a less accurate opinion of the job candidate's potential as an employee.

reality shock The stress that results when employees perceive discrepancies between their pre-employment expectations and on-the-job reality.

Stage 2: Encounter
The first day on the job typically marks the beginning of the encounter stage of organizational socialization. This is the stage in which newcomers test how well their pre-employment expectations fit reality. Many companies fail the test, resulting in **reality shock**—the stress that results when employees perceive discrepancies between their pre-employment expectations and on-the-job reality.[84] Reality shock doesn't necessarily occur on the first day; it might develop over several weeks or even months as newcomers form a better understanding of their new work environment.

Reality shock is common in many organizations.[85] Unmet expectations sometimes occur because the employer is unable to live up to its promises, such as failing to provide challenging projects or the resources to get the work done. Reality shock also occurs because new hires develop distorted work expectations through the information exchange conflicts described above. Whatever the cause, reality shock impedes the socialization process because the newcomer's energy is directed toward managing the stress rather than learning and accepting organizational knowledge and roles.[86]

Stage 3: Role Management
Role management, the third stage of organizational socialization, really begins during pre-employment socialization, but it is most active as employees make the transition from newcomers to insiders. They strengthen relationships with co-workers and supervisors, practise new role behaviours, and adopt attitudes and values consistent with their new positions and the organization. Role management also involves resolving the conflicts between work and nonwork activities, including resolving discrepancies between their existing values and those emphasized by the organizational culture.

realistic job preview (RJP) A method of improving organizational socialization in which job applicants are provided with a balance of positive and negative information about the job and work context.

IMPROVING THE SOCIALIZATION PROCESS

One potentially effective way to improve the socialization process is through a **realistic job preview (RJP)**—providing applicants with a balance of positive and negative information about the job and work context.[87] Unfortunately, as mentioned earlier, many companies overpromise. They often exaggerate positive features of the job and neglect to mention the undesirable elements in the hope that the best applicants will be attracted to the organization.

In contrast, an RJP helps job applicants to decide for themselves whether their skills, needs, and values are compatible with the job and organization. RJPs scare away some applicants, but they also tend to reduce turnover and increase job performance.[88] This occurs because RJPs help applicants develop more accurate pre-employment expectations, which, in turn, minimize reality shock. RJPs represent a type of vaccination by preparing employees for the more challenging and troublesome aspects of work life. There is also some evidence that RJPs increase organizational loyalty. A possible explanation for this is that companies providing candid information are easier to trust. They also show respect for the psychological contract and concern for employee welfare.[89]

Socialization Agents   Ask new employees what most helped them to adjust to their jobs and chances are they will mention helpful co-workers, bosses, or maybe even friends who work elsewhere in the organization. The fact is, socialization occurs mainly through these socialization agents.[90] Supervisors tend to provide technical information, performance feedback, and information about job duties. They also improve the socialization process by giving newcomers reasonably challenging first assignments, buffering them from excessive demands, and helping them form social ties with co-workers.

Co-workers are important socialization agents because they are easily accessible, can answer questions when problems arise, and serve as role models for appropriate behaviour. New employees tend to receive this information and support when co-workers integrate them into the work team. Co-workers also aid the socialization process by being flexible and tolerant in their interactions with new hires.

The challenge for some companies is helping newcomers to learn from co-workers about the company's culture when opening new offices or stores, or after acquiring another company. Earlier in this section, we described how I Love Rewards addressed this issue by sending employees from Toronto to diffuse its new Boston office with the company's culture. Whole Foods Market goes one step further by transferring many current employees so the new stores acquire the health-oriented retailer's unique culture. "For example, in our Columbus Circle store in New York, about 25 percent of the team members transferred from existing stores," recalls Whole Foods founder John McKey. "They were the starting culture for the fermentation that turned Columbus Circle into a true Whole Foods store."[91]

Lindblad's RJP Keeps Newcomer Expectations Shipshape

Lindblad Expeditions can't afford to have crew members jump ship soon after starting the job. To minimize reality shock, the 500-employee adventure cruise company gives applicants a DVD showing a realistic picture of what it's like to work onboard. The program shows not one, but two scenes where staff members are cleaning toilets. One scene reveals the cramped quarters for crew members. In another scene, a dishwasher talks about washing 5,000 dishes in one day. The video is meant to scare off applicants who cannot adjust easily to the challenges of working onboard a ship. The realistic job preview video does have this effect, says Lindblad human resource manager Kris Thompson, but this attrition is well worth it if it reduces turnover soon after staff are hired. "If [new hires] get on board and say, 'This is not what I expected,' then shame on us," says Thompson.[92] *Courtesy of Lindblad Expeditions*

Several organizations rely on a "buddy system," whereby newcomers are assigned to co-workers for sources of information and social support. Meridian Technology Centre relies on a buddy system in the socialization of new staff members. Buddies introduce new hires to other employees, give them campus tours, and generally familiarize them with the physical layout of the workplace. They have lunch with employees on their first day and meet weekly with them for their first two months. CXtec, the networking and voice technology company in Syracuse, New York, helps new staff meet other employees through food. On the first Friday of each month, new staff members take charge of the doughnut cart, introducing themselves as they distribute the morning snack to the company's 350 employees.[93] Collectively, these practices help newcomers to form social networks, which are powerful means of gaining information and influence in the organization.

CHAPTER SUMMARY

LO1 Describe the elements of organizational culture and discuss the importance of organizational subcultures.

Organizational culture consists of the values and assumptions shared within an organization. Shared assumptions are unconscious, taken-for-granted perceptions or beliefs that have worked so well in the past that they are considered the correct way to think and act toward problems and opportunities. Values are stable, evaluative beliefs that guide our preferences for outcomes or courses of action in a variety of situations.

Organizations differ in their cultural content, that is, the relative ordering of values. There are several classifications of organizational culture, but they tend to oversimplify the wide variety of cultures and completely ignore the underlying assumptions of culture. Organizations have subcultures as well as the dominant culture. Subcultures maintain the organization's standards of performance and ethical behaviour. They are also the source of emerging values that replace aging core values.

LO2 List four categories of artifacts through which corporate culture is deciphered.

Artifacts are the observable symbols and signs of an organization's culture. Four broad categories of artifacts include organizational stories and legends, rituals and ceremonies, language, and physical structures and symbols. Understanding an organization's culture requires assessment of many artifacts because they are subtle and often ambiguous.

LO3 Discuss the importance of organizational culture and the conditions under which organizational culture strength improves organizational performance.

Organizational culture has three main functions: a form of social control, the "social glue" that bonds people together, and a way to help employees make sense of the workplace. Companies with strong cultures generally perform better than those with weak cultures, but only when the cultural content is appropriate for the organization's environment. Also, the culture should not be so strong that it drives out dissenting values, which may form emerging values for the future. Organizations should have adaptive cultures so that employees support ongoing change in the organization and their own roles.

LO4 Compare and contrast four strategies for merging organizational cultures.

Organizational culture clashes are common in mergers and acquisitions. This problem can be minimized by performing a bicultural audit to diagnose the compatibility of the organizational cultures. The four main strategies for merging corporate cultures are integration, deculturation, assimilation, and separation.

LO5 Identify four strategies for changing or strengthening an organization's culture, including the application of attraction-selection-attrition theory.

Organizational culture is very difficult to change, but cultural change is possible and sometimes necessary for a company's continued survival. Four strategies for changing and strengthening an organization's culture are the actions of founders and leaders, aligning artifacts with the desired culture, introducing culturally consistent rewards, and attracting, selecting, and socializing employees.

Attraction-selection-attrition (ASA) theory states that organizations have a natural tendency to attract, select, and retain people with values and personality characteristics that are consistent with the organization's character, resulting in a more homogeneous organization and a stronger culture. Organizational socialization is the process by which individuals learn the values, expected behaviours, and social knowledge necessary to assume their roles in the organization. It is a process of both learning about the work context and adjusting to new work roles, team norms, and behaviours.

LO6 Describe the organizational socialization process and identify strategies to improve that process.

Organizational socialization is the process by which individuals learn the values, expected behaviours, and social knowledge necessary to assume their roles in the organization. It is a process of both learning and adjustment. During this process, job applicants and newcomers develop and test their psychological contract—personal beliefs about the terms and conditions of a reciprocal exchange agreement between that person and another party (the employer).

Employees typically pass through three socialization stages: pre-employment, encounter, and role management. To manage the socialization process, organizations should introduce realistic job previews (RJPs) and recognize the value of socialization agents in the process. RJPs give job applicants a realistic balance of positive and negative information about the job and work context. Socialization agents provide information and social support during the socialization process.

KEY TERMS

adaptive culture, p. 390

artifacts, p. 385

attraction-selection-attrition (ASA) theory, p. 395

bicultural audit, p. 391

ceremonies, p. 387

organizational culture, p. 381

organizational socialization p. 396

psychological contract, p. 396

realistic job preview (RJP), p. 398

reality shock, p. 398

rituals, p. 387

CRITICAL-THINKING QUESTIONS

1. Superb Consultants has submitted a proposal to analyze the cultural values of your organization. The proposal states that Superb has developed a revolutionary new survey to tap the company's true culture. The survey takes just 10 minutes to complete, and the consultants say results can be based on a small sample of employees. Discuss the merits and limitations of this proposal.

2. Some people suggest that the most effective organizations have the strongest cultures. What do we mean by the "strength" of organizational culture, and what possible problems are there with a strong organizational culture?

3. The CEO of a manufacturing firm wants everyone to support the organization's dominant culture of lean efficiency and hard work. The CEO has introduced a new reward system to reinforce this culture and personally interviews all professional and managerial applicants to ensure that they bring similar values to the organization. Some employees who criticized these values had their careers sidelined until they left. Two midlevel managers were fired for supporting contrary values, such as work-life balance. Based on your knowledge of organizational subcultures, what potential problems is the CEO creating?

4. Identify at least two artifacts you have observed in your department or school from each of the four broad categories: (a) organizational stories and legends, (b) rituals and ceremonies, (c) organizational language, (d) physical structures and symbols.

5. "Organizations are more likely to succeed when they have an adaptive culture." What can an organization do to foster an adaptive culture?

6. Suppose you are asked by senior officers of a city government to identify ways to reinforce a new culture of teamwork and collaboration. The senior executive group clearly supports these values, but it wants everyone in the organization to embrace them. Identify four types of activities that would strengthen these cultural values.

7. Socialization is most intense when people pass through organizational boundaries. One example is your entry into the college or university that you are now attending. What learning and adjustment occurred as you moved from outsider to newcomer to insider as a student here?

8. Acme Corp. is planning to acquire Beta Corp., which operates in a different industry. Acme's culture is entrepreneurial and fast-paced, whereas Beta employees value slow, deliberate decision making by consensus. Which merger strategy would you recommend to minimize culture shock when Acme acquires Beta? Explain your answer.

 ## CASE STUDY 14.1

Hillton's Transformation

Twenty years ago, Hillton was a small city (about 70,000 residents) that served as an outer suburb to a large Canadian metropolitan city. Hillton treated employees like family and gave them a great deal of autonomy in their work. Everyone in the organization (including the two labour unions representing employees) implicitly agreed that the leaders and supervisors of the organization should rise through the ranks based on their experience. Few people were ever hired from the outside into middle or senior positions. The rule of employment at Hillton was to learn the job skills, maintain a reasonably good work record, and wait your turn for promotion.

Hillton has grown rapidly since the mid-1970s. As the population grew, so did the municipality's workforce to keep pace with the increasing demand for municipal services. This meant that employees were promoted fairly quickly and were almost assured guaranteed employment. In fact, until recently, Hillton had never laid off any employee. The organization's culture could be described as one of entitlement and comfort. Neither the elected city councillors nor city manager bothered the departmental managers about their work. There were few cost controls because the rapid growth placed more emphasis on keeping up with the population expansion. The public became somewhat more critical of the city's poor service, including road construction at inconvenient times and the apparent lack of respect some employees showed for taxpayers.

During these expansion years, Hillton put most of its money into "outside" (also called "hard") municipal services. These included road building, utility construction and maintenance, fire and police protection, recreational facilities, and land use control. This emphasis occurred because an expanding population demanded more of these services and most of Hillton's senior people came out of the outside services group. For example, Hillton's city manager for many years was a road development engineer. The "inside" workers (taxation, community services, etc.) tended to have less seniority and their departments were given less priority.

As commuter and road systems developed, Hillton attracted more upwardly mobile professionals into the community. Some infrastructure demands continued, but now these suburban dwellers wanted more of the "soft" services, such as libraries, social activities, and community services. They also began complaining about the way the municipality was being run. The population had more than tripled between the 1970s and 2011, and it was increasingly apparent that the organization needed more corporate planning, information systems, organization development, and cost control systems. In various ways, residents voiced their concerns that the municipality was not providing the quality of management that they would expect from a city of its size.

In 2008, a new mayor and council replaced most of the previous incumbents, mainly on the platform of improving the municipality's management structure. The new council gave the city manager, along with two other senior managers, an early retirement buyout package. Rather than promoting from the lower ranks, council decided to fill all three positions with qualified candidates from large municipal corporations in the region. The following year, several long-term managers left Hillton and at least half of those positions were filled by people from outside the organization.

In less than two years, Hillton had eight senior or departmental managers hired from other municipalities who played a key role in changing the organization's value system. These eight managers became known (often with negative connotations) as the "professionals." They worked closely with each other to change the way middle and lower level managers had operated for many years. They brought in a new computer system and emphasized cost controls where managers previously had complete autonomy. Promotions were increasingly based more on merit than seniority.

These managers frequently announced in meetings and newsletters that municipal employees must provide superlative customer service, and that Hillton will become one of the most customer-friendly places for citizens and those who do business with the municipality. To this end, these managers were quick to support the public's increasing demand for more "soft" services, including expanded library services and recreational activities. And when population growth recently flattened out for a few years, the city manager and other professionals gained council support to lay off a few of the outside workers due to lack of demand for hard services.

One of the most significant changes was that the "outside" departments no longer held dominant positions in city management. Most of the "professional" managers had worked exclusively in administrative and related inside jobs. Two had Master of Business Administration degrees. This led to some tension between the professional managers and the older outside managers.

Even before the layoffs, managers of outside departments resisted the changes more than others. These managers complained that their employees with the highest seniority were turned down for promotions. They argued for more budget and warned that infrastructure problems would cause liability problems. Informally, these outside managers were supported by the labour union representing outside workers. The union leaders tried to bargain for more job guarantees whereas the union representing inside workers focused more on improving wages and benefits. Leaders of the outside union made several statements in the local media that the city had "lost its heart" and that the public would suffer from the actions of the new professionals.

Discussion Questions   1. Contrast Hillton's earlier corporate culture with the emerging set of cultural values.

2. Considering the difficulty in changing organizational culture, why does Hillton's management seem to be successful at this transformation?

3. Identify two other strategies that the city might consider to reinforce the new set of corporate values.

Copyright © 2000 Steven L. McShane. This case is a slightly fictionalized account of actual events in a Canadian municipality.

 CASE STUDY 14.2

Separating the Steam from the Haze

"We need more steam mix for our hamburger buns," a veteran employee calls out to the new hire at a McDonald's restaurant. "Get another package of mix, please."

For the newly hired McDonald's employee, this is just another task to learn in the confusing world of fast-food restaurants. For seasoned employees, it is a ritual for newcomers that usually brings hilarity to the otherwise serious work-oriented setting.

Some new employees get the joke immediately, but most scurry to the food storage area in search of the elusive package of steam mix. They check among the stacks of hamburger buns and in the freezer around the boxes of french fries for any package that says "steam mix" on it. After five or ten minutes, the discouraged recruits return empty-handed and ask for further directions.

Sometimes, if it isn't too busy, co-workers might say: "It's the big bag clearly marked 'Steam Mix!'—the one with the picture of a kettle on it." Occasionally, the hazing might go one step further. With a straight face, an employee might reply, "Oh, that's right. We're out of steam mix. Here, take this bucket and go next door to Tim Hortons. We often borrow some of their mix."

Eager to please their fellow employees, newcomers jaunt across the parking lot with a McDonald's bucket in hand and politely ask a Tim Hortons employee for some of their steam mix. A few Tim Hortons staff members have learned to play along with the game by telling the visitor that their steam mix is different than what McDonald's uses. More often, the new McDonald's worker is politely reminded that steam comes from boiled water and doesn't require any other ingredients.

Across the parking lot, co-workers watch the embarrassed (and occasionally angry) newcomer return with the empty McDonald's bucket. Somehow, the hazing ritual never loses its appeal, maybe because it provides a welcome break from the work. No one has quit over the experience, although most newcomers are subsequently cautious whenever co-workers ask them to retrieve anything from the storage area.

Discussion Questions   1. What negative effects, if any, does this hazing activity have on the socialization of new employees? Why? Would this type of hazing have a positive effect on socialization in any way?

2. What hazing rituals are you aware of in organizational settings? Why do they occur? Should they be discouraged or are they of some value?

3. Identify any organizational behaviour topics that would explain why this hazing activity occurs and what consequences it has for the employee, co-workers, and restaurant.

Source: Based on information provided to Steven L. McShane by a student in Vancouver who survived this hazing ritual and watched many others experience it.

TEAM EXERCISE 14.3

Organizational Culture Metaphors

By David L. Luechauer, Butler University and Gary M. Shulman, Miami University

Purpose   Both parts of this exercise are designed to help you understand, assess, and interpret organizational culture using metaphors.

Part A: Assessing Your School's Culture

Instructions   A metaphor is a figure of speech that contains an implied comparison between a word or phrase that is ordinarily used for one thing but can be applied to another. Metaphors also carry a great deal of hidden meaning—they say a lot about what we think and feel about that object. Therefore, this activity asks you to use several metaphors to define the organizational culture of your college or university. (Alternatively, the instructor might ask students to assess another organization that most students know about.)

- *Step 1:* The class will be divided into teams of four to six members.

- *Step 2:* Each team will reach consensus on which words or phrases should be inserted in the blanks of the statements presented below. This information should be recorded on a flip chart or other media for class presentation. The instructor will provide 15 to 20 minutes for teams to determine which words best describe the school's culture.

    If our school was an animal, it would be a _____ because _____.

    If our school was a food, it would be _____ because _____.

    If our school was a place, it would be _____ because _____.

    If our school was a season, it would be _____ because _____.

    If our school was a TV show or movie, it would be _____ because _____.

- *Step 3:* The class will listen to each team present the metaphors that it believes symbolizes the school's culture. For example, a team that picks winter for a season might mean they are feeling cold or distant about the school and its people.

- *Step 4:* The class will discuss the discussion questions stated below.

Discussion Questions for Part A

1. How easy was it for your group to reach consensus regarding these metaphors? What does that imply about the culture of your school?

2. How do you see these metaphors in action? In other words, what are some critical school behaviours or other artifacts that reveal the presence of your culture?

3. Think of another organization to which you belong (e.g., work, religious congregation). What is its dominant cultural values, how do you see them in action, and how do they affect the effectiveness of that organization?

Part B: Analyzing and Interpreting Cultural Metaphors

Instructions   Previously, you completed a metaphor exercise to describe the corporate culture of your school. That exercise gave you a taste of how to administer such a diagnostic tool and draw inferences from the results generated. This activity builds on that experience and is designed to help refine your ability to analyze such data and make suggestions for improvement. Five work teams (four to seven members/mixed gender in all groups) of an organization located in Toronto completed the metaphor exercise similar to the exercise in which you participated in class (see Part A above). Their responses are shown in the following table. Working in teams, analyze the information in this table and answer these questions:

Discussion Questions for Part B

1. In your opinion, what are the dominant cultural values in this organization? Explain your answer.

2. What are the positive aspects of this type of culture?

3. What are the negative aspects of this type of culture?

4. What is this organization's main business, in your opinion? Explain your answer.

5. These groups all reported to one manager. What advice would you give to the manager about this unit?

Metaphor Results of Five Teams in a Toronto Organization					
Team	Animal	Food	Place	TV Show	Season
1	Rabbit	Big Mac	Casino	The Office	Spring
2	Horse	Taco	Racetrack	Hawaii Five-O	Spring
3	Elephant	Ribs	Circus	Big Bang Theory	Summer
4	Eagle	Big Mac	Las Vegas	The Apprentice	Spring
5	Panther	Chinese	New York	Criminal Minds	Racing

Source: Adapted from D. L. Luechauer and G. M. Shulman, "Using A Metaphor Exercise To Explore The Principles of Organizational Culture," *Journal of Management Education* 22 (December 1998), pp. 736–44. Used with permission of the authors.

 CLASS EXERCISE 14.4

Diagnosing Corporate Culture Proclamations

Purpose   This exercise is designed to help you understand the importance and context in which corporate culture is identified and discussed in organizations.

Instructions   This exercise is a take-home activity, although it can be completed in classes where computers and Internet connections are available. The instructor will divide the class into small teams (typically four or five people per team). Each team is assigned a specific industry—such as energy, computers, financial, or automotive.

The team's task is to search the websites of several companies in the selected industry for company statements about their corporate cultures. Use company website search engines (if they exist) to find documents with key phrases such as "corporate culture" or "company values."

In the next class, or at the end of the time allotted in the current class, students will report on their observations by answering the following three discussion questions.

Discussion Questions

1. What values seem to dominate the corporate cultures of the companies you searched? Are these values similar or diverse across companies in the industry?

2. What was the broader content of the Web pages on which these companies described or mentioned their corporate cultures?

3. Do companies in this industry refer to their corporate cultures on their websites more or less than companies in other industries searched by teams in this class?

Go to CONNECT to complete the following interactive self-assessment.

SELF-ASSESSMENT EXERCISE 14.5

Which Corporate Culture Do You Prefer?

Purpose This self-assessment is designed to help you identify the corporate culture that fits most closely with your personal values and assumptions.

Instructions Read each pair of statements in the Corporate Culture Preference Scale and circle the statement that describes the organization you would prefer to work in. Then use the scoring key in Appendix B at the end of the book to calculate your results for each subscale. The scale does not attempt to measure your preference for every corporate culture—just a few of the more common varieties. Also, keep in mind that none of these corporate cultures is inherently good or bad. The focus here is on how well you fit within each of them. This exercise should be completed alone so that you can assess yourself honestly without concerns of social comparison. Class discussion will focus on the importance of matching job applicants to the organization's dominant values.

Corporate Culture Preference Scale		
I would prefer to work in an organization:		
1a. Where employees work well together in teams.	*or*	1b. That produces highly respected products or services.
2a. Where top management maintains a sense of order in the workplace.	*or*	2b. Where the organization listens to customers and responds quickly to their needs.
3a. Where employees are treated fairly.	*or*	3b. Where employees continuously search for ways to work more efficiently.
4a. Where employees adapt quickly to new work requirements.	*or*	4b. Where corporate leaders work hard to keep employees happy.
5a. Where senior executives receive special benefits not available to other employees.	*or*	5b. Where employees are proud when the organization achieves its performance goals.
6a. Where employees who perform the best get paid the most.	*or*	6b. Where senior executives are respected.
7a. Where everyone gets her or his job done efficiently.	*or*	7b. That is on top of innovations in the industry.
8a. Where employees receive assistance to overcome any personal problems.	*or*	8b. Where employees abide by company rules.
9a. That is always experimenting with new ideas in the marketplace.	*or*	9b. That expects everyone to put in 110 percent for peak performance.
10a. That quickly benefits from market opportunities.	*or*	10b. Where employees are always kept informed about what's happening in the organization.
11a. That can quickly respond to competitive threats.	*or*	11b. Where most decisions are made by the top executives.
12a. Where management keeps everything under control.	*or*	12b. Where employees care for each other.

Copyright © 2000 Steven L. McShane

 Practise and learn online with Connect. Connect resources include additional and interactive study exercises, videos, and practice quizzing, as well as additional material you won't find in the printed text.

Organizational Change

LEARNING OBJECTIVES

After reading this chapter, you should be able to:

LO1 Describe the elements of Lewin's force field analysis model.

LO2 Discuss the reasons why people resist organizational change and how change agents should view this resistance.

LO3 Outline six strategies for minimizing resistance to change and debate ways to effectively create an urgency to change.

LO4 Explain the importance of leadership in organizational change and outline the conditions for effectively diffusing change from a pilot project.

LO5 Describe and compare action research, appreciative inquiry, large group interventions, and parallel learning structures as formal approaches to organizational change.

LO6 Discuss two cross-cultural and three ethical issues in organizational change.

"**I** was looking for an environment with a council that wanted change" explains Glen Davies, Regina's City Manager. He was also looking for an organization big enough to have a "high level of sophistication" but "not so big that you can't affect change."

Rather than maintain the status quo that often comes with hiring from within, Davies was hired from outside the organization. Davies was born in southern Ontario and holds undergraduate and graduate degrees from McMaster University. No stranger to a municipal career, Davies worked in four municipalities in Canada before coming to the City of Regina. He also served as the principal consultant for the City's core services review before accepting the City Manager job. He says that review is "a bit of a blueprint for our change agenda."

Davies describes his mandate for change: "I think the earliest, biggest challenge was in developing a senior team that was aligned with my goals and objectives and was loyal to me and that change agenda. It's pretty lonely if you're the only guy in the organization treading down that path."

The City's change agenda includes the goal to become recognized as Canada's best-run municipality. The City of Regina will achieve "Best run" when it is recognized by Excellence Canada with Level 4 certification in the Progressive Excellence Program. Excellence Canada is a not-for-profit organization that is Canada's national authority on quality and healthy workplace practices.

Davies is creating urgency for change at the City through three areas that connect directly to achieving a positive future. These three areas are high-performance, customer-focused, and engaged employees. Some of the milestones already completed include developing a vision for change, corporate strategic plan and workplace business plans, restructuring to make it easier for customers to find and access services and gathering employee feedback to inform the planning process.[1]

Glen Davies, City Manager, City of Regina, is bringing a change agenda to city management, including the goal to have Regina become known as the best-run municipality in Canada. *Courtesy of the City of Regina*

This opening story about Glen Davies' vision for change at the City of Regina reflects many of the topics we will discuss in this chapter. It notes how change is driven by external forces, such as the Canada-wide report card on municipalities. It illustrates the importance of vision and goals, sometimes from change agents brought in from outside. It reveals how the process requires an urgency to change that is felt by employees and leaders alike.

Although the City of Regina's transformation is just beginning, we must remember that most organizational change is difficult and obtuse, not easy and clear-cut. It requires tremendous leadership effort and vigilance. As we will describe throughout this chapter, the challenge of change is not so much in deciding which way to go; the challenge is in the execution of this strategy. When leaders discover the need for change and identify some ideas about the preferred route to a better future, the change process involves navigating around the numerous obstacles and gaining organization-wide support for that change.

This chapter unfolds by introducing Lewin's model of change and its component parts. Our discussion includes sources of resistance to change, ways to minimize this resistance, and ways to stabilize desired behaviours. Next, the chapter examines four approaches to organizational change—action research, appreciative inquiry, large group interventions, and parallel learning structures. The last section of this chapter considers both cross-cultural and ethical issues in organizational change.

LEWIN'S FORCE FIELD ANALYSIS MODEL

LO1

The challenges of organizational change are continuous because, to repeat a well-worn statement, change has become the only constant in organizations. Organizations are, after all, open systems that need to remain compatible with their external environments (see Chapter 1). These environments—such as consumer needs, global competition, technology, community expectations, government (de)regulation, and environmental standards—are constantly changing, so organizations must recognize these shifts and respond accordingly to survive and remain effective. Successful organizations monitor their environments and take appropriate steps to maintain a compatible fit with new external conditions. Rather than resisting change, employees in successful companies embrace change as an integral part of organizational life. "I've always believed that when the rate of change inside an institution becomes slower than the rate of change outside, the end is in sight," says former General Electric CEO Jack Welch. "The only question is when."[2]

It is easy to see that environmental forces push companies to change the way they operate. What is more difficult to see is the complex interplay of these forces on the internal dynamics of organizations. Social psychologist Kurt Lewin developed the force field analysis model to describe this process using the metaphor of a force field (see Exhibit 15.1).[3] Although it was developed more than 50 years ago, recent reviews affirm that Lewin's **force field analysis** model remains one of the most widely respected ways of viewing the change process.[4]

force field analysis Kurt Lewin's model of system-wide change that helps change agents diagnose the forces that drive and restrain proposed organizational change.

One side of the force field model represents the *driving forces* that push organizations toward a new state of affairs. These might include new competitors or technologies, evolving workforce expectations, or a host of other environmental changes. Corporate leaders also produce driving forces even when external forces for change aren't apparent. For instance, some experts call for "divine discontent" as a key feature of successful organizations, meaning that leaders continually urge employees to strive for higher standards or better practices even when the company outshines the competition. "We have a habit of divine discontent with our performance," says creative agency Ogilvy & Mather about its corporate culture. "It is an antidote to smugness."[5]

The other side of Lewin's model represents the *restraining forces* that maintain the status quo. These restraining forces are commonly called "resistance to change" because they appear to block the change process. Stability occurs when the driving and

Exhibit 15.1 ⟩ **LEWIN'S FORCE FIELD ANALYSIS MODEL**

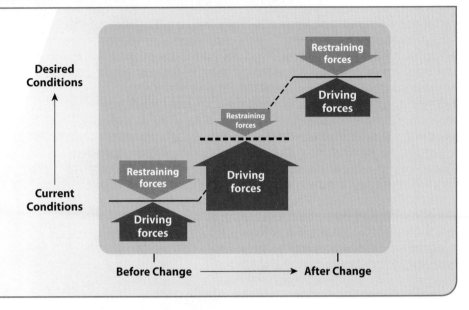

unfreezing The first part of the organizational change process, in which the change agent produces disequilibrium between the driving and restraining forces.

refreezing The latter part of the organizational change process, in which systems and conditions are introduced that reinforce and maintain the desired behaviours.

restraining forces are roughly in equilibrium—that is, they are of approximately equal strength in opposite directions.

Lewin's force field model emphasizes that effective change occurs by **unfreezing** the current situation, moving to a desired condition, and then **refreezing** the system so it remains in the desired state. Unfreezing involves producing disequilibrium between the driving and restraining forces. As we will describe later, this may occur by increasing the driving forces, reducing the restraining forces, or having a combination of both. Refreezing occurs when the organization's systems and structures are aligned with the desired behaviours. They must support and reinforce the new role patterns and prevent the organization from slipping back into the old way of doing things. Over the next few pages, we use Lewin's model to understand why change is blocked and how the process can evolve more smoothly.

 Lewin's force field model emphasizes that effective change occurs by unfreezing the current situation, moving to a desired condition, and then refreezing the system so it remains in the desired state. "

UNDERSTANDING RESISTANCE TO CHANGE

L02

Robert Nardelli pushed hard to transform Home Depot from a loose configuration of fiefdoms to a more performance-oriented operation that delivered a consistent customer experience. Change did occur at the world's largest home improvement retailer, but at a price. A large number of talented managers and employees left the company, and some of those remaining continued to resent Nardelli's transformation. Disenchanted staff referred to the company as "Home Despot" because the changes took away their autonomy. Others named it "Home GEpot," a disparaging reference to the many former GE executives that Nardelli hired into top positions. After five years, the Home Depot board decided to replace Nardelli, partly because he made some unsuccessful strategic decisions and partly because of the after-effects of Nardelli's changes.[6]

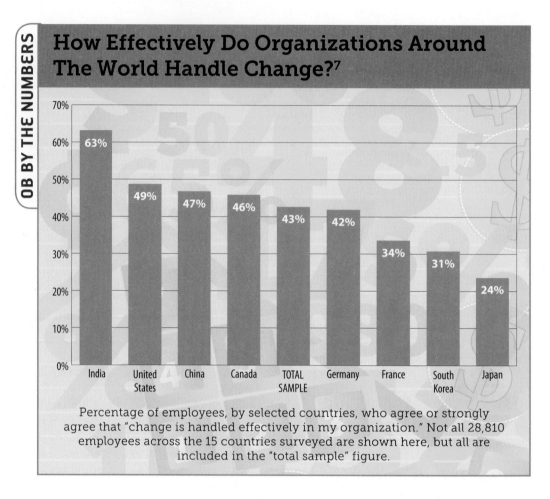

OB BY THE NUMBERS

How Effectively Do Organizations Around The World Handle Change?[7]

Percentage of employees, by selected countries, who agree or strongly agree that "change is handled effectively in my organization." Not all 28,810 employees across the 15 countries surveyed are shown here, but all are included in the "total sample" figure.

Robert Nardelli experienced considerable *resistance to change* at Home Depot. He has plenty of company. A recent survey reported that 71 percent of Canadian human resource managers say employees resist changes put forward by management. This resistance is not short-lived. Twenty-one percent of 1,700 change agents surveyed across more than 40 countries acknowledged that employees still resisted a specific major change one or two years after it was implemented.[8]

Resistance to change takes many forms, ranging from overt work stoppages to subtle attempts to continue the old ways.[9] A study of employees at two Canadian banks reported that subtle resistance is much more common than overt resistance. Some employees in that study avoided the desired changes by moving into different jobs. Others continued to perform tasks the old way as long as management didn't notice. Even when employees complied with the planned changes, they engaged in resistance by performing their work without corresponding cognitive or emotional support for the change.[10] In other words, they resisted by letting customers know that they disapproved of the changes forced on them.

Subtle forms of resistance potentially create the greatest obstacles to change because they are not as visible. In the words of one manager, "[Change efforts] never die because of direct confrontation. Direct confrontation you can work with because it is known. Rather, they die a death of a thousand cuts. People and issues you never confront drain the life out of important [initiatives] and result in solutions that simply do not have the performance impact that they should have."[11] This resistance is not unique to North America. As GLOBAL Connections 15.1 describes, Mina Ishiwatari experienced various forms of resistance to her innovative marketing ideas at Hoppy, the Japanese beverage company.

EMPLOYEE RESISTANCE AS A RESOURCE FOR CHANGE

Although change agents are understandably frustrated by passive or active resistance to change, they need to realize that resistance is a common and natural human response. As

CONNECTIONS 15.1

GLOBAL

Not Hoppy about Change

Hoppy, a carbonated low-alcohol malt-and-hops beverage, was popular around Tokyo after World War II as a cheap alternative to expensive beer, but it fell out of favour as beer became affordable. Mina Ishiwatari (centre in photo), granddaughter of Hoppy Beverage Co.'s founder, was determined to improve Hoppy's image when she joined the company a decade ago. Unfortunately, the company's 30 employees—mostly men in their fifties who were family relatives—didn't want to disturb their cozy jobs.

"It was a turbulent decade of eliminating evils from the company and rebuilding a new organization from scratch," recalls Ishiwatari, who began as a rank-and-file employee and is now the company's executive vice-president. "I tried to take a new marketing approach to change the image of Hoppy . . . but no one would listen to me."

With limited support and budget, Ishiwatari developed a website that informed the public about the product, sold it online, and documented Ishiwatari's views in an early Weblog. As the contemporary marketing caught the attention of health-conscious young people, Ishiwatari pushed for further changes. Most managers who opposed Ishiwatari's radical ideas eventually left the company.

But Ishiwatari experienced resistance even among those who remained. One day, the factory manager presented her with resignations from all of the factory workers. Ishiwatari resolved the dispute, acknowledging that she was pushing

Mina Ishiwatari (centre) faced—and overcame—resistance to change in the company that her grandfather founded. *Yoshiaki Miura Photo/Japan Times*

change through too quickly and without enough consideration of employee feelings.

In the seven years since Ishiwatari began introducing these changes, Hoppy's annual sales have increased fourfold to about CAD$42 million, even though it is sold mainly around Tokyo. The company's workforce has expanded to more than 50 people.[12]

Canadian-born economist John Kenneth Galbraith once quipped: "Faced with the choice between changing one's mind and proving that there is no need to do so, almost everyone gets busy on the proof."[13] Even when people support change, they typically assume that it is others—not themselves—who need to change. The problem, however, isn't so much that resistance to change exists. The main problem is that change agents typically view resistance as an unreasonable, dysfunctional, and irrational response to a desirable initiative. They often form an "us versus them" perspective without considering that the causes of resistance may, in fact, be traced back to their own actions or inaction.[14]

The emerging view among change management experts is that resistance to change needs to be viewed as a resource, rather than as an impediment to change. Resistance is a resource in three ways. First, it is a signal—a warning system—that the change agent has not sufficiently addressed the underlying conditions that support effective organizational change.[15] In some situations, employees may be worried about the *consequences* of change, such as how the new conditions will take away their power and status. In other situations, employees show resistance because of concerns about the *process* of change itself, such as the effort required to break old habits and learn new skills.

Second, resistance should be recognized as a form of constructive conflict. Recall from earlier chapters that constructive conflict can potentially improve decision making, including identifying better ways to improve the organization's success. However, constructive conflict is typically accompanied by dysfunctional relationship conflict. This appears to be the case when change agents see resistance to change as an impediment rather than a resource. They describe the people who resist as the problem, whereas their focus should be on understanding the reasons why these people resist. Thus, by viewing resistance as a form of constructive conflict, change agents may be able to improve the change strategy or change process.

Finally, resistance should be viewed in the context of justice and motivation. Resistance is a form of voice, so it potentially improves procedural justice (see Chapter 5). By redirecting initial forms of resistance into constructive conversations, change agents can increase employee perceptions and feelings of fairness. Furthermore, resistance is motivational; it potentially engages people to think about the change strategy and process. Change agents can harness that motivational force to ultimately strengthen commitment to the change initiative.

WHY EMPLOYEES RESIST CHANGE

Change management experts have developed a long list of reasons why people do not embrace change. Some people resist change because of their personality and values.[16] Aside from these dispositional factors, however, employees often lack the motivation or commitment to change when they believe the change will fail, is the wrong action for the situation, or will be costly to them personally.[17] This cost might be in the form of lost rewards and status, or might represent negative consequences if they attempt to support the change. Another reason for resistance is the person's inability (or perceived inability) to change due to inadequate skills and knowledge. A third reason is that employees lack role clarity about the change. This lack of role clarity occurs when people misunderstand or magnify what is expected of them in the future. These three factors—motivation, ability, and role (mis)perceptions—are the foundations of the six most commonly cited reasons why people resist change, which are summarized below.[18]

Direct Costs   Employees lack commitment to (or even compliance with) a change initiative when their personal cost–benefit analysis calculation is negative rather than positive. They might believe the benefits for them (and possibly for the organization) are trivial (i.e., some pain for little gain). They might anticipate benefits from the change, but also believe that they will be worse off overall. For example, the Malaysian government has introduced sweeping changes in which managers are expected to delegate more power and responsibility to staff. However, many government managers believe these reforms will give them less power and prestige, so they have hindered the change by delegating responsibility slowly.

Saving Face   Several years ago, Goldcorp CEO Rob McEwan decided to post the Canadian mining company's confidential geological data online and offer a handsome reward to anyone who could help find more gold on the property. The Goldcorp Challenge was a huge success, but the firm's geological staff complained just before the event was launched. "We have real concerns," they told McEwen. "You're going to ask the rest of the world to tell you where we're going to find gold in our mine, and we think they're going to think we're really dumb and that you don't have any confidence in us."[19]

Goldcorp's geological staff resisted the global challenge because it threatened their self-esteem. Although McEwan eased those concerns, employees often continue to quietly attack changes that did not originate from them. This "not-invented-here" syndrome sometimes results in staff deliberately inflating problems with externally founded ideas, just to "prove" that those ideas were not superior to their own. This form of resistance is widespread, according to change experts. Says one consultant, "Unless they're scared enough to listen, they'll never forgive you for being right and for knowing something they don't."[20]

Fear of the Unknown   All change includes some degree of uncertainty. This uncertainty puts employees at risk. Their knowledge and skills might become obsolete; their valued workspace, perquisites, or even social relationships might be disrupted and removed. Thus, people resist change out of worry that they cannot adjust to the new work requirements or that they will produce unknown costs. Overall, this uncertainty is usually considered less desirable than the relative certainty of the status quo.

Breaking Routines   People typically resist initiatives that force them out of their comfort zones and require them to invest time and energy in learning new role patterns. Ray Davis, CEO of Umpqua Bank, calls this the rubber band effect. "When you are leading for growth, you know you are going to disrupt comfortable routines and ask for new behaviour, new priorities, new skills," says Davis, whose Oregon-based bank is regarded as one of America's most innovative financial institutions. "Even when we want to change, and *do* change, we tend to relax and the rubber band snaps us back into our comfort zones."[21] Indeed, most employees in one Australian survey admitted they don't follow through with organizational changes because they "like to keep things the way they are" or the changes seem to be too complicated or time wasting.[22]

Incongruent Team Dynamics   Teams develop and enforce conformity to a set of norms that guide behaviour. However, conformity to existing team norms may discourage employees from accepting organizational change. This form of resistance occurred at electronics retailer Best Buy when it introduced the results-only work environment (ROWE). ROWE evaluates employees by their results, not their face time, so employees can come to work and leave when they want. Yet co-workers often responded to deviations from the standard work schedule with half-humorous barbs such as "Forgot to set your alarm clock again?" These jibes supported the old employment model but undermined the ROWE program. Best Buy's consultants eventually set up sessions that warned employees about these taunts, which they called "sludge."[23]

Incongruent Organizational Systems   Rewards, information systems, patterns of authority, career paths, selection criteria, and other systems and structures are both friends and foes of organizational change. When properly aligned, they reinforce desired behaviours. When misaligned, they pull people back into their old attitudes and behaviour. Even enthusiastic employees lose momentum after failing to overcome the structural confines of the past.

UNFREEZING, CHANGING, AND REFREEZING

LO3

According to Lewin's force field analysis model, effective change occurs by unfreezing the current situation, moving to a desired condition, and then refreezing the system so it remains in this desired state. Unfreezing occurs when the driving forces are stronger than the restraining forces. This happens by making the driving forces stronger, weakening or removing the restraining forces, or combining both.

The first option is to increase the driving forces, motivating employees to change through fear or threats (real or contrived). This strategy rarely works, however, because the action of increasing the driving forces alone is usually met with an equal and opposing increase in the restraining forces. A useful metaphor is pushing against the coils of a mattress. The harder corporate leaders push for change, the stronger the restraining forces push back. This antagonism threatens the change effort by producing tension and conflict within the organization.

The second option is to weaken or remove the restraining forces. The problem with this change strategy is that it provides no motivation for change. To some extent, weakening the restraining forces is like clearing a pathway for change. An unobstructed road makes it easier to travel to the destination but does not motivate anyone to go there. The preferred option, therefore, is to both increase the driving forces and reduce or remove the restraining forces. Increasing the driving forces creates an urgency for change, while reducing the restraining forces lessens motivation to oppose the change and removes obstacles such as lack of ability and situational constraints.

CREATING AN URGENCY FOR CHANGE

Organizational change requires employees to have an urgency for change.[24] This typically occurs by informing them about competitors, changing consumer trends, impending

government regulations, and other driving forces in the external environment. These pressures are the main driving forces in Lewin's model. They push people out of their comfort zones, energizing them to face the risks that change creates. In many organizations, however, leaders buffer employees from the external environment to such an extent that these driving forces are hardly felt by anyone below the top executive level. The result is that employees don't understand why they need to change and leaders are surprised when their change initiatives do not have much effect.

Customer-Driven Change   Some companies fuel the urgency to change by putting employees in direct contact with customers. Dissatisfied customers represent a compelling driving force for change because the organization's survival typically depends on having customers who are satisfied with the product or service. Customers also provide a human element that further energizes employees to change current behaviour patterns.[26]

Executives at Shell Europe applied customer-driven change a few years ago. Many middle managers at the energy company seemed blissfully unaware that Shell wasn't achieving either its financial goals or its customer needs; so to create an urgency for change, the European managers were loaded onto buses and taken out to talk with customers and employees who work with customers every day. "We called these 'bus rides.' The idea was to encourage people to think back from the customer's perspective rather than from the head office," explains Shell Europe's vice-president of retailing. "The bus rides were difficult for a lot of people who, in their work history, had hardly ever had to talk to a customer and find out what was good and not so good about Shell from the customer's standpoint."[27]

Creating an Urgency for Change without External Forces   Exposing employees to external forces can strengthen the urgency for change, but leaders often need to begin the change process before problems come knocking at the company's door. "You want to create a burning platform for change even when there isn't a need for one," says Steve Bennett, former CEO of financial software company Intuit.[28] Creating an urgency for change when the organization is riding high requires rare persuasive capability that helps employees visualize future competitive threats and environmental shifts.

For instance, Apple Computer's iPod dominates the digital music market, but Steve Jobs wanted the company to be its own toughest competitor. Just when sales of the iPod Mini were soaring, Jobs challenged a gathering of 100 top executives and engineers to develop a better product to replace it. "Playing it safe is the most dangerous thing we can do," Jobs warned. Nine months later the company launched the iPod Nano, which replaced the still-popular iPod Mini before competitors could offer a better alternative.[29]

Experts warn, however, that employees may see the burning-platform strategy as manipulative—a view that produces cynicism about change and undermines trust in the change agent.[30] Also, the urgency for change doesn't need to originate from problems or threats to the company; this motivation can also develop through a change champion's vision of a more appealing future. By creating a future vision of a better organization, leaders effectively make the current situation less appealing. When the vision connects to employee values and needs, it can be a motivating force for change even when external problems are not strong.

REDUCING THE RESTRAINING FORCES

Employee resistance should be viewed as a resource, but its underlying causes—the restraining forces—need to be addressed. As we explained earlier using the mattress coil metaphor, increasing the driving forces alone will not bring about change because employees often push back harder to offset the opposing forces. Instead, change agents need to address each of the sources of resistance. Six of the main strategies are outlined in Exhibit 15.2. If feasible, communication, learning, employee involvement, and stress management should be attempted first.[31] However, negotiation and coercion are necessary for people who will clearly lose something from the change and in cases where the speed of change is critical.

Communication   Communication is the highest priority and first strategy required for any organizational change. According to one recent survey, communication (together with involvement) is considered the top strategy for engaging employees in the change process.[32] Communication improves the change process in at least two ways.[33] One way, which we described earlier, is by generating an urgency to change. Leaders motivate employees to support the change by candidly telling them about the external threats and opportunities that make change so important. Whether through town hall meetings with senior management or by directly meeting with disgruntled customers, employees become energized to change when they understand and visualize those external forces.

Exhibit 15.2) STRATEGIES FOR MINIMIZING RESISTANCE TO CHANGE

Strategy	Example	When Applied	Problems
Communication	Customer complaints are shown to employees.	When employees don't feel an urgency for change, don't know how the change will affect them, or resist change due to a fear of the unknown.	Time-consuming and potentially costly.
Learning	Employees learn how to work in teams as company adopts a team-based structure.	When employees need to break old routines and adopt new role patterns.	Time-consuming and potentially costly.
Employee involvement	Company forms task force to recommend new customer service practices.	When the change effort needs more employee commitment, some employees need to save face, and/or employee ideas would improve decisions about the change strategy.	Very time-consuming. Might lead to conflict and poor decisions if employees' interests are incompatible with organizational needs.
Stress management	Employees attend sessions to discuss their concerns about the change.	When communication, training, and involvement do not sufficiently ease employee concerns.	Time-consuming and potentially expensive. Some methods may not reduce stress for all employees.
Negotiation	Employees agree to replace strict job categories with multiskilling in return for increased job security.	When employees will clearly lose something of value from the change and would not otherwise support the new conditions. Also necessary when the company must change quickly.	May be expensive, particularly if other employees want to negotiate their support. Also tends to produce compliance but not commitment to the change.
Coercion	Company president tells managers to "get on board" the change or leave.	When other strategies are ineffective and the company needs to change quickly.	Can lead to more subtle forms of resistance, as well as long-term antagonism with the change agent.

Sources: Adapted from J. P. Kotter and L. A. Schlesinger, "Choosing Strategies for Change," *Harvard Business Review* 57 (1979), pp. 106–114; P. R. Lawrence, "How to Deal with Resistance to Change," *Harvard Business Review,* May–June 1954, pp. 49–57.

> Communication is the highest priority and first strategy required for any organizational change. "

The second way that communication minimizes resistance to change is by illuminating the future and thereby reducing fear of the unknown. The more corporate leaders communicate their vision, particularly details about that future and milestones already achieved toward that future, the more easily employees can understand their own roles in that future. Similarly, as the leader communicates the future state more clearly, employees form a clearer picture about how the change relates to their jobs and responsibilities. "No. 1 is to always communicate, communicate, communicate," advises Randall Dearth, CEO of chemical manufacturer Lanxess Corp. "If you're bringing in change, you need to be able to make a very compelling case of what change looks like and why change is necessary."[34]

Learning   Learning is an important process in most change initiatives because employees require new knowledge and skills to fit the organization's evolving requirements. When a company introduces a new sales database, for instance, representatives need to learn how to use the system as well as learn to adapt their previous behaviour patterns to benefit from the new system. Training is time-consuming, but it helps people break routines by learning new role patterns.

Employee Involvement   Unless the change must occur quickly or employee interests are highly incompatible with the organization's needs, employee involvement is almost an essential part of the change process. In the chapter on decision making (Chapter 7), we described several potential benefits of employee involvement, all of which are relevant to organizational change. Employees who participate in decisions about a change tend to feel more personal responsibility for its successful implementation, rather than being disinterested agents of someone else's decisions.[35] This sense of ownership also minimizes the problems of saving face and fear of the unknown. Furthermore, the complexity of today's work environment demands that more people provide ideas regarding the best direction of the change effort. Employee involvement is such an important component of organizational change that special initiatives have been developed to allow participation in large groups. These change interventions are described later in the chapter.

Stress Management   Organizational change is a stressful experience for many people because it threatens self-esteem and creates uncertainty about the future.[36] Communication, learning, and employee involvement can reduce some of the stressors. However, research indicates that companies also need to introduce stress management practices to help employees cope with changes.[37] In particular, stress management minimizes resistance by removing some of the direct costs and fear of the unknown about the change process. Stress also saps energy, so minimizing stress potentially increases employee motivation to support the change process.

Negotiation   As long as people resist change, organizational change strategies will require some influence tactics. Negotiation is a form of influence that involves the promise of benefits or resources in exchange for the target person's compliance with the influencer's request. This strategy potentially gains support from those who would otherwise lose out from the change. However, this support is mostly compliance with, rather than commitment to, the change effort, so it might not be effective in the long term.

Coercion   If all else fails, leaders rely on coercion to change organizations. Coercion can include persistently reminding people of their obligations, frequently monitoring behaviour to ensure compliance, confronting people who do not change, and using threats of sanctions to force compliance. Replacing people who will not support the change is an extreme step, but it is fairly common. For instance, when StandardAero introduced lean management practices during the early 1990s, president Bob Hamaberg threatened to fire senior managers who were resisting these changes. Some eventually supported the change effort; others did not and were dismissed. "You must have senior management commitment," Hamaberg said bluntly at the time. "I had some obstacles. I removed the obstacles." Harsh words and actions, but due to this visionary transformation, StandardAero's Winnipeg business (where the company started) now employs almost 1,400 people and is recognized as a world leader in the aircraft engine repair and overhaul business.[38]

Firing people is the least desirable way to change organizations. However, dismissals and other forms of coercion are sometimes necessary when speed is essential and other tactics are ineffective. For example, it may be necessary to remove several members of an executive team who are unwilling or unable to change their existing mental models of the ideal organization. This is also a radical form of organizational "unlearning" (see Chapter 1) because when executives leave, they take knowledge of the organization's past routines, which potentially opens up opportunities for new practices to take hold.[39] At the same time, coercion is a risky strategy because survivors (employees who do not leave) may have less trust in corporate leaders and engage in more political tactics to protect their own job security.

REFREEZING THE DESIRED CONDITIONS

Unfreezing and changing behaviour won't produce lasting change. People are creatures of habit, so they easily slip back into past patterns. Therefore, leaders need to refreeze the new behaviours by realigning organizational systems and team dynamics with the desired changes.[40] The desired patterns of behaviour can be "nailed down" by changing the physical structure and situational conditions. Organizational rewards are also powerful systems that refreeze behaviours.[41] If the change process is supposed to encourage efficiency, then rewards should be realigned to motivate and reinforce efficient behaviour. Information systems play a complementary role in the change process, particularly as conduits for feedback.[42] Feedback mechanisms help employees learn how well they are moving toward the desired objectives, and they provide a permanent architecture to support the new behaviour patterns in the long term. The adage "What gets measured, gets done" applies here. Employees concentrate on the new priorities when they receive a continuous flow of feedback about how well they are achieving those goals.

CHANGE AGENTS, STRATEGIC VISIONS, AND DIFFUSING CHANGE

LO4

Kurt Lewin's force field analysis model is a useful template to explain the dynamics of organizational change. But it overlooks three ingredients in effective change processes: change agents, strategic visions, and diffusing change.

CHANGE AGENTS AND STRATEGIC VISIONS

The beginning of this chapter described City Manager Glen Davies as a visionary leader who wants Regina to become the best run municipality in Canada. His changes include a workforce that is more engaged as well as performance- and customer-focused. Leadership plays a critical role in organizational change. As we learned in the chapter about leadership (Chapter 12), transformational leaders are agents of change because they develop an appealing vision of the desired future state, communicate that vision in ways that are meaningful to others, make decisions and act in ways that are consistent with that vision, and build commitment to that vision.[43] Change agents come in different forms, and more than one person is often required to fulfill these different roles.[44] In most situations, however, transformational leaders are the primary agents of change.

Transforming The Ottawa Hospital into One of the Most Advanced Medical Facilities in North America

Dale Potter, chief information officer, is the change agent behind the $100 million technology transformation at The Ottawa Hospital. "The mandate set out by the board and our chief executive is to be bold. So, we might as well go big," explains Potter. Potter was hired from the private sector to "shift the large institution onto a new path." One of his revolutionary ideas was to use Nav Canada's air-traffic control system as the model for designing a system to monitor all of the surgeries at the hospital's campuses. Despite some early resistance the "changes are being applauded by hospital staff" because administrative time has been reduced, information is more accessible, and more time is available to attend to patients. One of the most visible changes has been replacing the traditional clipboards that doctors use when they are making their rounds . . . with iPads. Three recent Carleton University grads and their company, Select Start, were commissioned by The Ottawa Hospital to develop the iPad app that is transforming the way doctors access health records, retrieve medical images and records, and change prescriptions.[45] *Chrissie Cloutier/The Ottawa Hospital*

A key element of leading change is a strategic vision. A leader's vision provides a sense of direction and establishes the critical success factors against which the real changes are evaluated. Furthermore, a vision provides an emotional foundation to the change because it links the individual's values and self-concept to the desired change.[46] A strategic vision also minimizes employee fear of the unknown and provides a better understanding of what behaviours employees must learn for the desired future.

DIFFUSION OF CHANGE

Earlier, we mentioned that Best Buy's results-only work environment (ROWE) initiative was introduced to support work-life balance and emerging employment expectations. ROWE evaluates employees by their results, not their face time. This arrangement gives employees at the electronics retailer the freedom to come to work when it suits them. ROWE is a significant departure from the traditional employment relationship, so Best Buy wisely introduced an early version of it as a pilot project. Specifically, the program was first tested with a retail division of 320 employees that suffered from low morale and high turnover. Only after employee engagement scores increased and turnover fell over several months was the ROWE program expanded to other parts of the organization.[47]

As at Best Buy, change agents often test the transformation process with a pilot project and then diffuse what has been learned from this experience to other parts of the organization. Unlike centralized, system-wide changes, pilot projects are more flexible and less risky.[48] The pilot project approach also makes it easier to select organizational groups that are most ready for change, thus increasing the pilot project's success.

But how do we ensure that the change process started in the pilot project is adopted by other segments of the organization? Using the MARS model as a template (see Chapter 2), Exhibit 15.3 outlines several strategies to diffuse pilot projects to other parts of the organization. First, employees are more likely to adopt the practices of a pilot project when they are motivated to do so.[49] This occurs when they see that the pilot project is successful and people in the pilot project receive recognition and rewards for changing their previous work practices. Diffusion also occurs more successfully when managers support and reinforce the desired behaviours. More generally, change agents need to minimize the sources of resistance to change that we discussed earlier in this chapter.

Second, employees must have the ability—the required skills and knowledge—to adopt the practices introduced in the pilot project. According to innovation diffusion

Exhibit 15.3 \ **STRATEGIES FOR DIFFUSING CHANGE FROM A PILOT PROJECT**

Motivation

- Widely communicate and celebrate the pilot project's success.

- Reward and recognize pilot project employees as well as those who work at transferring that change to other parts of the organization.

- Ensure that managers support and reinforce the desired behaviours related to the pilot project's success.

- Identify and address potential sources of resistance to change.

Ability

- Give employees the opportunity to interact with and learn from those in the pilot project.

- Reassign or temporarily second some pilot project employees to other work units, where they can coach and serve as role models.

- Give employees technical training to implement practices identified in the pilot project.

Role Perceptions

- Communicate and support employees to discover how the pilot project practices are relevant for their own functional areas.

- Ensure that the pilot project is described in a way that is neither too specific nor too general.

Situational Factors

- Give staff sufficient time and resources to learn and implement the pilot project practices in their work units.

studies, people adopt ideas more readily when they have an opportunity to interact with and learn from others who have already applied the new practices.[50] Thus pilot projects get diffused when employees in the original pilot are dispersed to other work units as role models and knowledge sources.

Third, pilot projects get diffused when employees have clear role perceptions—that is, when they understand how the practices in a pilot project apply to them even though they are in a completely different functional area. For instance, accounting department employees won't easily recognize how they can adopt quality improvement practices developed by employees in the production department. The challenge here is for change agents to provide guidance that is not too specific (not too narrowly defined around the pilot project environment) because it might not seem relevant to other areas of the organization. At the same time, the pilot project intervention should not be described too broadly or abstractly to other employees because this makes the information and role model too vague. Finally, employees require supportive situational factors, including the resources and time necessary to adopt the practices demonstrated in the pilot project.

FOUR APPROACHES TO ORGANIZATIONAL CHANGE

L05

So far, this chapter has examined the dynamics of change that occur every day in organizations. However, organizational change agents and consultants also apply various structured approaches to organizational change. This section introduces four of the leading approaches: action research, appreciative inquiry, large group interventions, and parallel learning structures.

ACTION RESEARCH APPROACH

action research A problem-focused change process that combines action orientation (changing attitudes and behaviour) and research orientation (testing theory through data collection and analysis).

Along with introducing the force field model, Kurt Lewin recommended an **action research** approach to the change process. The philosophy of action research is that meaningful change is a combination of action orientation (changing attitudes and behaviour) and research orientation (testing theory).[51] On the one hand, the change process needs to be action-oriented because the ultimate goal is to change the workplace.

An action orientation involves diagnosing current problems and applying interventions that resolve those problems. On the other hand, the change process is a research study because change agents apply a conceptual framework (such as team dynamics or organizational culture) to a real situation. As with any good research, the change process involves collecting data to diagnose problems more effectively and to systematically evaluate how well the theory works in practice.[52]

Within this dual framework of action and research, the action research approach adopts an open-systems view. It recognizes that organizations have many interdependent parts, so change agents need to anticipate both the intended and the unintended consequences of their interventions. Action research is also a highly participative process because open-systems change requires both the knowledge and the commitment of members within that system. Indeed, employees are essentially co-researchers as well as participants in the intervention. Overall, action research is a data-based, problem-oriented process that diagnoses the need for change, introduces the intervention, and then evaluates and stabilizes the desired changes. The main phases of action research are illustrated in Exhibit 15.4 and described here:[53]

1. *Form client–consultant relationship.* Action research usually assumes that the change agent originates outside the system (such as a consultant), so the process begins by forming the client–consultant relationship. Consultants need to determine the client's readiness for change, including whether people are motivated to participate in the process, are open to meaningful change, and possess the abilities to complete the process.

2. *Diagnose need for change.* Action research is a problem-oriented activity that carefully diagnoses the problem through systematic analysis of the situation. Organizational diagnosis identifies the appropriate direction for the change effort by gathering and analyzing data about an ongoing system, such as through interviews and surveys of employees and other stakeholders. Organizational diagnosis also includes employee involvement in agreeing on the appropriate change method, the schedule for the actions involved, and the expected standards of successful change.

3. *Introduce intervention.* This stage in the action research model applies one or more actions to correct the problem. It may include any of the prescriptions mentioned in this book, such as building more effective teams, managing conflict, building a better organizational structure, or changing the corporate culture. An important issue is how quickly the changes should occur.[54] Some experts recommend *incremental change,* in which the organization fine-tunes the system and takes small steps toward a desired state. Others claim that *quantum change* is often required, in which the system is overhauled decisively and quickly. Quantum change is usually traumatic to employees and offers little opportunity for correction. But incremental change is also risky when the organization is seriously misaligned with its environment, thereby facing a threat to its survival.

4. *Evaluate and stabilize change.* Action research recommends evaluating the effectiveness of the intervention against the standards established in the diagnostic stage.

Exhibit 15.4   **THE ACTION RESEARCH PROCESS**

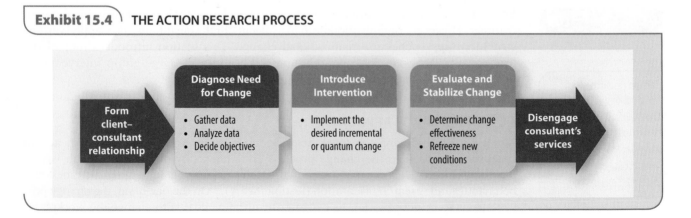

Unfortunately, even when these standards are clearly stated, the effectiveness of an intervention might not be apparent for several years or might be difficult to separate from other factors. If the activity has the desired effect, the change agent and participants need to stabilize the new conditions. This refers to the refreezing process that was described earlier. Rewards, information systems, team norms, and other conditions are redesigned so they support the new values and behaviours.

The action research approach has dominated organizational change thinking since it was introduced in the 1940s. However, some experts are concerned that the problem-oriented nature of action research—in which something is wrong that must be fixed—focuses on the negative dynamics of the group or system rather than its positive opportunities and potential. This concern with action research has led to the development of a more positive approach to organizational change, called *appreciative inquiry.*[55]

APPRECIATIVE INQUIRY APPROACH

appreciative inquiry   An organizational change strategy that directs the group's attention away from its own problems and focuses participants on the group's potential and positive elements.

Appreciative inquiry tries to break out of the problem-solving mentality of traditional change management practices by reframing relationships around the positive and the possible. It searches for organizational (or team) strengths and capabilities and then adapts or applies that knowledge for further success and well-being. Appreciative inquiry is therefore deeply grounded in the emerging philosophy of *positive organizational behaviour,* which suggests that focusing on the positive rather than the negative aspects of life will improve organizational success and individual well-being. In other words, this approach emphasizes building on strengths rather than trying to directly correct problems.[56]

Appreciative inquiry typically examines successful events, organizations, and work units. This focus becomes a form of behavioural modelling, but it also increases open dialogue by redirecting the group's attention away from its own problems. Appreciative inquiry is especially useful when participants are aware of their problems or already suffer from negativity in their relationships. The positive orientation of appreciative inquiry enables groups to overcome these negative tensions and build a more hopeful perspective of their future by focusing on what is possible.[57]

Appreciative inquiry's positive focus is illustrated by the intervention conducted a few years ago by the British Broadcasting Corporation.[58] Almost 40 percent of BBC's workforce attended one of 200 appreciative inquiry meetings held over six months. Participants at each session were organized into pairs, where they asked each other three questions: (1) What has been the most creative/valued experience in your time at the BBC? (2) What were the conditions that made that experience possible?

How Does a Metal Can Company Become Known for Innovation?

Brasilata, a $170 million producer of steel cans, has successfully broken out of the rut of manufacturing in a mature industry to achieve international recognition and awards including Sherwin-Williams "Best Packaging Supplier" and one of "Brazil's Most Innovative Companies." Brasilata management team's goal was to reframe a new organizational identity grounded on the philosophy and positive perspective that employees are "inventors" and the source of the company's innovation, service, and product quality. "The success and growth of Brasilata is achieved on the basis of its inventors who contribute toward this goal to limits of their potential and performance." This identity of "inventor" was introduced to employees by the firm's management team and reinforced through "innovation contracts" signed by all new employees. Brasilata recently reported that it received 205,536 ideas from its employees in one calendar year, an average of 212 ideas forwarded per inventor.[59] *Courtesy of Brasilata*

(3) If those experiences were to become the norm, how would the BBC have to change? These questions focused participants on the positive and the possible rather than on problems. They also produced 98,000 ideas, which were distilled into 15,000 unique suggestions and ultimately 35 concrete initiatives.

Appreciative Inquiry Principles   Appreciative inquiry embraces five key principles (see Exhibit 15.5).[60] One of these is the positive principle, which we describe above. A second principle, called the *constructionist principle*, takes the position that conversations don't describe reality; they shape that reality. In other words, how we come to understand something depends on the questions we ask and the language we use. Thus appreciative inquiry requires sensitivity to and proactive management of the words and language used as well as the thoughts and feelings behind that communication. This relates to a third principle, called the *simultaneity principle*, which states that inquiry and change are simultaneous, not sequential. The moment we ask questions of others, we are changing those people. Furthermore, the questions we ask determine the information we receive, which in turn affects which change intervention we choose. The key learning point from this principle is to be mindful of effects that the inquiry has on the direction of the change process.

A fourth principle, called the *poetic principle*, states that organizations are open books, so we have choices in how they may be perceived, framed, and described. The poetic principle is reflected in the notion that a glass of water can be viewed as half full or half empty. Thus appreciative inquiry actively frames reality in a way that provides constructive value for future development. *The anticipatory principle*, the fifth principle of appreciative inquiry, emphasizes the importance of a positive collective vision of the future state. People are motivated and guided by the vision they see and believe in for the future. Images that are mundane or disempowering will affect current effort and behaviour differently than will images that are inspiring and engaging. We noted the importance of visions earlier in this chapter (change agents) and in our discussion of transformational leadership (Chapter 12).

The Four-D Model of Appreciative Inquiry   Building on these five principles, appreciative inquiry generally follows the "Four-D" process (named after its four stages) shown in Exhibit 15.6. Appreciative inquiry begins with *discovery*—identifying the positive elements of the observed events or organization.[61] This might involve documenting positive customer experiences elsewhere in the organization. Or it might include interviewing members of another organization to discover its fundamental strengths. As participants discuss their findings, they shift into the *dreaming* stage by envisioning what might be possible in an ideal organization. By pointing out a hypothetical ideal organization or situation, participants feel safer revealing their hopes and aspirations than they would if they were discussing their own organization or predicament.

Exhibit 15.5   FIVE PRINCIPLES OF APPRECIATIVE INQUIRY

Appreciative Inquiry Principle	Description
Positive principle	Focusing on positive events and potential produces more positive, effective, and enduring change.
Constructionist principle	How we perceive and understand the change process depends on the questions we ask and language we use throughout that process.
Simultaneity principle	Inquiry and change are simultaneous, not sequential.
Poetic principle	Organizations are open books, so we have choices in how they may be perceived, framed, and described.
Anticipatory principle	People are motivated and guided by the vision they see and believe in for the future.

Sources: Based on D. L. Cooperrider and D. K. Whitney, *Appreciative Inquiry: A Positive Revolution in Change* (San Francisco: Berrett-Koehler, 2005), Chap. 7; D. K. Whitney and A. Trosten-Bloom, *The Power of Appreciative Inquiry: A Practical Guide to Positive Change,* 2nd ed. (San Francisco: Berrett-Koehler Publishers, 2010), Chap. 3.

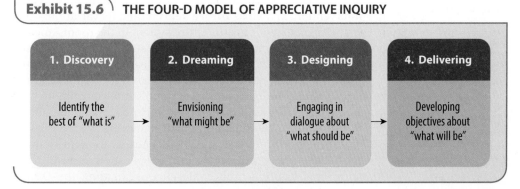

Exhibit 15.6 ⟩ THE FOUR-D MODEL OF APPRECIATIVE INQUIRY

Sources: Based on F. J. Barrett and D. L. Cooperrider, "Generative Metaphor Intervention: A New Approach for Working with Systems Divided by Conflict and Caught in Defensive Perception," *Journal of Applied Behavioural Science* 26 (1990), p. 229; D. Whitney and C. Schau, "Appreciative Inquiry: An Innovative Process for Organization Change," *Employment Relations Today* 25 (Spring 1998), pp. 11–21; D. L. Cooperrider and D. K.Whitney, *Appreciative Inquiry: A Positive Revolution in Change* (San Francisco: Berrett-Koehler, 2005), Chap. 3.

As participants make their private thoughts public to the group, the process shifts into the third stage, called *designing*. Designing involves dialogue in which participants listen with selfless receptivity to each other's models and assumptions and eventually form a collective model for thinking within the team. In effect, they create a common image of what should be. As this model takes shape, group members shift the focus back to their own situation. In the final stage of appreciative inquiry, called *delivering* (also known as *destiny*), participants establish specific objectives and direction for their own organization on the basis of their model of what will be.

Appreciative inquiry was introduced more than two decades ago, but it really gained popularity only within the past few years. Several success stories of organizational change from appreciative inquiry have emerged in a variety of organizational settings, including the British Broadcasting Corporation, Castrol Marine, Canadian Tire, AVON Mexico, American Express, Green Mountain Coffee Roasters, and Hunter Douglas.[62] At Canadian Tire, internal consultants conducted detailed interviews with 377 staff across the organization, asking each to describe occasions where they felt Canadian Tire was working at its best and what they value most about the company. These appreciative incidents were organized around six values, which were affirmed and discussed among middle and senior management in a one-day session. Canadian Tire store managers discussed these values with their staff and participated in an appreciative exercise in which employees visualized a good news story about Canadian Tire's success.[63]

Although appreciative inquiry has much to offer, it is not always the best approach to changing teams or organizations, and, indeed, it has not always been successful. This approach depends on participants' ability to let go of the problem-oriented approach, including the "blame game" of determining who may have been responsible for past failures. It also requires leaders who are willing to accept appreciative inquiry's less structured process.[64] Another concern is that research has not yet examined the contingencies of this approach.[65] In other words, we don't yet know under what conditions appreciative inquiry is a useful approach to organizational change and under what conditions it is less effective. Overall, appreciative inquiry has much to offer the organizational change process, but we are just beginning to understand its potential and limitations.

LARGE GROUP INTERVENTIONS

Appreciative inquiry can occur in small teams, but it is often designed to involve a large number of people, such as the 10,000 employees who participated in the process at the British Broadcasting Corporation. As such, appreciative inquiry is often identified as

future search An organizational change strategy that consists of system-wide group sessions, usually lasting a few days, in which participants identify trends and identify ways to adapt to those changes.

one of several large group organizational change interventions. Another large group intervention, known as **future search** (and its variations—*search conferences* and *open-space technology*), "puts the entire system in the room," meaning that the process tries to involve as many employees and other stakeholders as possible who are associated with the organizational system.[66] Future search conferences are typically held over a few days and involve participants in the search for trends or issues that are emerging. These events also ask participants to develop strategic solutions for those future conditions.

For example, Emerson & Cuming's chemical manufacturing facility relied on a future search conference in which managers, supervisors, and production employees were organized into five stakeholder teams to identify initiatives that would improve the plant's safety, efficiency, and cooperation. Several Canadian school boards have conducted future search conferences, including the Ottawa-Carleton School Board, Toronto School Board, and Lester B. Pearson School Board. The Canadian Nature Federation also held a future search event to assist the change process.[67]

Future search meetings and similar large group change events potentially minimize resistance to change and assist the quality of the change process, but they also have limitations.[68] One problem is that involving so many people invariably limits the opportunity to contribute and increases the risk that a few people will dominate the process. Another concern is that these events focus on finding common ground, and this may prevent the participants from discovering substantive differences that interfere with future progress. A third issue is that these events generate high expectations about an ideal future state that are difficult to satisfy in practice. Employees become even more cynical and resistant to change if they do not see meaningful decisions and actions resulting from these meetings.

parallel learning structures Highly participative arrangements composed of people from most levels of the organization who follow the action research model to produce meaningful organizational change.

PARALLEL LEARNING STRUCTURES APPROACH

Parallel learning structures are highly participative arrangements composed of people from most levels of the organization who follow the action research model to produce meaningful organizational change. They are social structures developed alongside the formal hierarchy with the purpose of increasing the organization's learning.[69] Ideally participants in parallel learning structures are sufficiently free from the constraints of the larger organization that they can effectively solve organizational issues.

Royal Dutch/Shell relied on a parallel learning structure to introduce a more customer-focused organization.[70] Rather than try to change the entire organization at once, executives held week-long "retail boot camps" with six country teams of front-line people (such as gas station managers, truck drivers, and marketing professionals). Participants learned about competitive trends in their regions and were taught powerful marketing tools to identify new opportunities. The teams then returned home to study their markets and develop proposals for improvement. Four months later, boot camp teams returned for a second workshop, at which each proposal was critiqued by Royal/Dutch Shell executives. Each team had 60 days to put its ideas into action; then the teams returned for a third workshop to analyze what worked and what didn't. This parallel learning process did much more than introduce new marketing ideas. It created enthusiasm in participants that spread contagiously to their co-workers, including managers above them, when they returned to their home countries.

CROSS-CULTURAL AND ETHICAL ISSUES IN ORGANIZATIONAL CHANGE

LO6

As we have emphasized throughout this chapter, change is an inevitable and often continuous phenomenon in organizations so they remain aligned with the dynamic external environment. Yet, we also need to be aware of cross-cultural and ethical issues with any change process. Many organizational change practices are built around Western cultural assumptions and values, which may differ from and sometimes conflict with assumptions and values in other cultures.[71] One possible cross-cultural limitation is that Western organizational change models, such as Lewin's force field analysis, often assume that change has a beginning and an ending in a logical linear sequence (that is, a straight line from point A to point B). Yet change is viewed more as a cyclical phenomenon in some cultures, such as the earth's revolution around the sun or a pendulum swinging back and forth. Other cultures have more of an interconnected view of change, whereby one change leads to another (often unplanned) change, which leads to another change, and so on until the change objective is ultimately achieved in a more circuitous way.

Another cross-cultural issue with some organizational change interventions is that they assume effective organizational change is necessarily punctuated by tension and overt conflict. Indeed, some change interventions encourage such conflict. But this direct confrontation view is incompatible with cultures that emphasize harmony and equilibrium. These cross-cultural differences suggest that a more contingency-oriented perspective is required for organizational change to work effectively in a globalized world.

Some organizational change practices also face ethical issues.[72] One ethical concern is the risk of violating individual privacy rights. The action research model is built on the idea of collecting information from organizational members, yet this requires that employees share personal information and emotions that they may not want to divulge.[73] A second ethical concern is that some change activities potentially increase management's power by inducing compliance and conformity in organizational members. For instance, action research is a system-wide activity that requires employee participation rather than allowing individuals to get involved voluntarily. A third concern is that some organizational change interventions undermine the individual's self-esteem. The unfreezing process requires that participants disconfirm their existing beliefs, sometimes including their own competence at certain tasks or interpersonal relations.

Organizational change is usually more difficult than it initially seems. Yet the dilemma is that most organizations operate in hyperfast environments that demand continuous and rapid adaptation. Organizations survive and gain competitive advantage by mastering the complex dynamics of moving people through the continuous process of change as quickly as the external environment is changing.

ORGANIZATIONAL BEHAVIOUR: THE JOURNEY CONTINUES

Nearly 100 years ago American industrialist Andrew Carnegie said, "Take away my people, but leave my factories, and soon grass will grow on the factory floors. Take away my factories, but leave my people, and soon we will have a new and better factory."[74] Carnegie's statement reflects the message woven throughout this textbook: Organizations are not buildings or machinery or financial assets; rather, they are the people in them. Organizations are human entities—full of life, sometimes fragile, and always exciting.

CHAPTER SUMMARY

 Describe the elements of Lewin's force field analysis model.

Lewin's force field analysis model states that all systems have driving and restraining forces. Change occurs through the process of unfreezing, changing, and refreezing. Unfreezing produces disequilibrium between the driving and restraining forces. Refreezing realigns the organization's systems and structures with the desired behaviours.

 Discuss the reasons why people resist organizational change and how change agents should view this resistance.

Restraining forces are manifested as employee resistance to change. The main reasons why people resist change are direct costs, saving face, fear of the unknown, breaking routines, incongruent team dynamics, and incongruent organizational systems. Resistance to change should be viewed as a resource, not an inherent obstacle to change.

Employee resistance is a resource in three ways: (1) it is a signal that the conditions for effective change are not yet in place; (2) it is a form of constructive conflict; and (3) it is a form of voice, so it may improve procedural justice.

LO3 Outline six strategies for minimizing resistance to change and debate ways to effectively create an urgency to change.

Organizational change requires employees to have an urgency for change. This typically occurs by informing them about driving forces in the external environment. Urgency to change also develops by putting employees in direct contact with customers. Leaders often need to create an urgency to change before the external pressures are felt, and this can occur through a vision of a more appealing future.

Resistance to change may be minimized by keeping employees informed about what to expect from the change effort (communicating); teaching employees valuable skills for the desired future (learning); involving them in the change process; helping employees cope with the stress of change; negotiating trade-offs with those who will clearly lose from the change effort; and using coercion (sparingly and as a last resort).

LO4 Explain the importance of leadership in organizational change and outline the conditions for effectively diffusing change from a pilot project.

Every successful change also requires change agents with a clear, well-articulated vision of the desired future state. The success of the pilot project is then diffused to other parts of the organization. This occurs by applying the MARS model, including motivating employees to adopt the pilot project's methods, training people to know how to adopt these practices, helping to clarify how the pilot can be adopted to different areas, and providing time and resources to support this diffusion.

LO5 Describe and compare action research, appreciative inquiry, large group interventions, and parallel learning structures as formal approaches to organizational change.

Action research is a highly participative, open-systems approach to change management that combines an action-orientation (changing attitudes and behaviour) with research orientation (testing theory). It is a data-based, problem-oriented process that diagnoses the need for change, introduces the intervention, and then evaluates and stabilizes the desired changes.

Appreciative inquiry embraces the positive organizational behaviour philosophy by focusing participants on the positive and possible. Along with this positive principle, this approach to change applies the constructionist, simultaneity, poetic, and anticipatory principles. The four stages of appreciative inquiry include discovery, dreaming, designing, and delivering.

Large-group interventions, such as future-search conferences, are highly participative events that typically try to get the entire system into the room. Parallel learning structures rely on social structures developed alongside the formal hierarchy with the purpose of increasing the organization's learning. They are highly participative arrangements, composed of people from most levels of the organization who follow the action research model to produce meaningful organizational change.

LO6 Discuss two cross-cultural and three ethical issues in organizational change.

One significant concern is that organizational change theories developed with a Western cultural orientation potentially conflict with cultural values in some other countries. Also, organizational change practices can raise one or more ethical concerns, including increasing management's power over employees, threatening individual privacy rights, undermining individual self-esteem, and making clients dependent on the change consultant.

KEY TERMS

action research, p. 419
appreciative inquiry, p. 421
force field analysis, p. 408

future search, p. 424
parallel learning
   structures, p. 424

refreezing, p. 409
unfreezing, p. 409

CRITICAL-THINKING QUESTIONS

1. Chances are that the school you are attending is currently undergoing some sort of change to adapt more closely with its environment. Discuss the external forces that are driving the change. What internal drivers for change also exist?

2. Use Lewin's force field analysis to describe the dynamics of organizational change in a typical Canadian municipality. The opening story about the City of Regina provides some information, but think about other forces for and against change in a city or community.

3. Employee resistance is a symptom, not a problem, in the change process. What are some of the real problems that may underlie employee resistance?

4. Senior management of a large multinational corporation is planning to restructure the organization. Currently, the organization is decentralized around geographic areas so that the executive responsible for each area has considerable autonomy over manufacturing and sales. The new structure will transfer power to the executives responsible for different product groups; the executives responsible for each geographic

area will no longer be responsible for manufacturing in their area but will retain control over sales activities. Describe two types of resistance senior management might encounter from this organizational change.

5. Discuss the role of reward systems in organizational change. Specifically, identify where reward systems relate to Lewin's force field model and where they undermine the organizational change process.

6. Web Circuits is a Malaysian-based custom manufacturer for high-technology companies. Senior management wants to introduce lean management practices to reduce production costs and remain competitive. A consultant has recommended that the company start with a pilot project in one department and, when successful, diffuse these practices to other areas of the organization. Discuss the advantages of this recommendation, and identify three ways (other than the pilot project's success) to make diffusion of the change effort more successful.

7. Suppose that you are vice-president of branch services at the Credit Union of Kelowna. You notice that several branches have consistently low customer service ratings even though there are no apparent differences in resources or staff characteristics. Describe an appreciative inquiry process in one of these branches that might help to overcome this problem.

8. This chapter suggests that some organizational change activities face ethical concerns. Yet several consultants actively use these processes because they believe they benefit the organization and do less damage to employees than it seems on the surface. For example, some activities try to open up the employee's hidden area (review the Johari Window discussion in Chapter 3) so that there is better mutual understanding with co-workers. Discuss this argument, and identify where you think organizational change interventions should limit this process.

 CASE STUDY 15.1

TransAct Insurance Corporation

TransAct Insurance Corporation (TIC) provides automobile insurance in parts of Canada that allow private insurers. Last year, a new president was brought in by TIC's board of directors to improve the company's competitiveness and customer service. After spending several months assessing the situation, the new president introduced a strategic plan to improve TIC's competitive position. He also replaced three vice-presidents. Jim Leon was hired as vice-president of Claims, TIC's largest division with 1,500 employees, 50 claims centre managers, and five regional directors.

Jim immediately met with all claims managers and directors, and visited employees at TIC's 50 claims centres. As an outsider, this was a formidable task, but his strong interpersonal skills and uncanny ability to remember names and ideas helped him through the process. Through these visits and discussions, Jim discovered that the claims division had been managed in a relatively authoritarian, top-down manner. He could also see that morale was very low and employee-management relations were guarded. High workloads and isolation (adjusters work in tiny cubicles) were two other common complaints. Several managers acknowledged that the high turnover among claims adjusters was partly due to these conditions.

Following discussions with TIC's president, Jim decided to make morale and supervisory leadership his top priority. He initiated a divisional newsletter with a feedback site for employees to register their comments. He announced an open-door policy in which any claims division employee could speak to him directly and confidentially without going first to the immediate supervisor. Jim also fought organizational barriers to initiate a flex-time program so that employees could design work schedules around their needs. This program later became a model for other areas of TIC.

One of Jim's most pronounced symbols of change was the "Claims Management Credo" outlining the philosophy that every claims manager would follow. At his first meeting with the complete claims management team, Jim presented a list of what he thought were important philosophies and actions of effective managers. The management group was asked to select and prioritize items from this list. They were told that the resulting list would be the division's management philosophy and all managers would be held accountable for abiding by its principles. Most claims managers were uneasy about this process, but they also understood that the organization was under competitive pressure and that Jim was using this exercise to demonstrate his leadership.

The claims managers developed a list of 10 items, such as encouraging teamwork, fostering a trusting work environment, setting clear and reasonable goals, and so on. The list was circulated to senior management in the organization for their comment and approval, and sent back to all claims managers for their endorsement. Once this was done, a copy of the final document was sent to every claims division employee. Jim also announced plans to follow up with an annual survey to evaluate each claims manager's performance. This concerned the managers, but most of them believed that the credo exercise was a result of Jim's initial enthusiasm and that he would be too busy to introduce a survey after settling into the job.

One year after the credo had been distributed, Jim announced that the first annual survey would be conducted. All claims employees would complete the survey and return it confidentially to the human resources department where the survey results would be compiled for each claims centre manager. The survey asked the extent to which the manager had lived up to each of the 10 items in the credo. Each form also provided space for comments.

Claims centre managers were surprised that a survey would be conducted, but they were even more worried about Jim's statement that the results would be shared with employees. What "results" would employees see? Who would distribute these results? What happens if a manager gets poor ratings from his or her employees? "We'll work out the details later," said Jim in response to these questions. "Even if the survey results aren't great, the information will give us a good baseline for next year's survey."

The claims division survey had a high response rate. In some centres, every employee completed and returned a form. Each report showed the claim centre manager's average score for each of the 10 items as well as how many employees rated the manager at each level of the five-point scale. The reports also included every comment made by employees at that centre.

No one was prepared for the results of the first survey. Most managers received moderate or poor ratings on the 10 items. Very few managers averaged above 3.0 (out of a 5-point scale) on more than a couple of items. This suggested that, at best, employees were ambivalent about whether their claims centre manager had abided by the 10 management philosophy items. The comments were even more devastating than the ratings. Comments ranged from mildly disappointed to extremely critical of their claims manager. Employees also described their longstanding frustration with TIC, high workloads, and isolated working conditions. Several people bluntly stated that they were skeptical about the changes that Jim had promised. "We've heard the promises before, but now we've lost faith," responded one claims adjuster.

The survey results were sent to each claims manager, the regional director, and employees at the claims centre. Jim instructed managers to discuss the survey data and comments with their regional manager and directly with employees. The claims centre managers were shocked to learn that the reports included individual comments. They had assumed the reports would exclude comments and only show averaged scores for all employees at the centre. Some managers went to their regional director, complaining that revealing the personal comments would ruin their careers. Many directors sympathized, but the results were already available to employees.

When Jim heard about these concerns, he agreed that the results were lower than expected and that the comments should not have been shown to employees. After discussing the situation with his directors, he decided that the discussion meetings between claims managers and their employees should proceed as planned. To delay or withdraw the reports would undermine the credibility and trust that Jim was trying to develop with employees. However, the regional director attended the meeting in each claims centre to minimize direct conflict between the claims centre manager and employees.

Although many of these meetings went smoothly, a few created harsh feelings between managers and their employees. The source of some comments were easily identified by their content, and this created a few delicate moments in several sessions. A few months after these meetings, two claims centre managers quit and three others asked for transfers back to nonmanagement positions in TIC. Meanwhile, Jim wondered how to manage this process more effectively, particularly since employees expected another survey the following year.

Discussion Questions   1. Identify the forces pushing for change and the forces restraining the change effort in this case.

2. Was Jim Leon successful at bringing about change? Why or why not?

3. What should Jim Leon do now?

 TEAM EXERCISE 15.2

Strategic Change Incidents

Purpose   This exercise is designed to help you identify strategies for facilitating organizational change in various situations.

Instructions   1. The instructor will place students into teams, and each team will be assigned one of the scenarios presented below.

2. Each team will diagnose its assigned scenario to determine the most appropriate set of change management practices. Where appropriate, these practices should (a) create an urgency to change, (b) minimize resistance to change, and (c) refreeze the situation to support the change initiative. Each of these scenarios is based on real events.

3. Each team will present and defend its change management strategy. Class discussion regarding the appropriateness and feasibility of each strategy will occur after all teams assigned the same scenario have presented. The instructor will then describe what the organizations actually did in these situations.

Scenario 1: Latté Troubles

Stock prices have just tumbled to a new 52-week low and the market outlook is weak as consumers look to stretch their paycheques by passing up on $4 lattés. Competitors are rapidly gaining market share in this high-margin industry. Input costs for coffee and dairy products have risen sharply and widespread price increases have been passed on to customers. Performance of the most recently opened stores are lagging behind stores that have been open longer. Executives have been re-shuffled and promises have been made to introduce new beverages to the menu. To cut costs, stores are being closed and employees are being laid off. In the wake of all this, loyal customers are complaining about their in-store experiences citing long line-ups, lengthy wait times, inexperienced baristas, and a loss of the coffee-house ambience the retail chain has been known for. The company founder has just returned as CEO in order to lead a turnaround for his troubled organization. What should he do?

Scenario 2: Greener Telco

The board of directors at a large telecom company wants its executives to make the organization more environmentally friendly by encouraging employees to reduce waste in the workplace. Government and other stakeholders expect the company to take this action and be publicly successful. Consequently, the managing director wants to significantly reduce paper usage, refuse, and other waste throughout the company's many widespread offices. Unfortunately, a survey indicates that employees do not value environmental objectives and do not know how to "reduce, reuse, recycle." As the executive responsible for this change, you have been asked to develop a strategy that might bring about meaningful behavioural change toward this environmental goal. What would you do?

Scenario 3: Go Forward Airline

A major airline had experienced a decade of rough turbulence, including two bouts of bankruptcy protection, 10 managing directors, and morale so low that employees had ripped off company logos from their uniforms out of embarrassment. Service was terrible, and the airplanes rarely arrived or left the terminal on time. This was costing the airline significant amounts of money in passenger layovers. Managers were paralyzed by anxiety, and many had been with the firm so long that they didn't know how to set strategic goals that worked. One-fifth of all flights were losing money, and the company overall was near financial collapse (just three months to defaulting on payroll obligations). The newly hired managing director and you must get employees to quickly improve operational efficiency and customer service. What actions would you take to bring about these changes in time?

Go to CONNECT to complete the following interactive self-assessment.

 SELF-ASSESSMENT EXERCISE 15.3

Are You Tolerant of Change?

Purpose   This exercise is designed to help you understand how people differ in their tolerance of change.

Instructions Read each of the following statements and check the box that best fits your personal belief. Then use the scoring key in Appendix B at the end of this book to calculate your results. This self-assessment should be completed alone so that you can rate yourself honestly without concerns of social comparison. Class discussion will focus on the meaning of the concept measured by this scale and its implications for managing change in organizational settings.

Tolerance of Change Scale							
To what extent does each statement describe you? Indicate your level of agreement by marking the appropriate response on the right.	Strongly Agree	Moderately Agree	Slightly Agree	Neutral	Slightly Disagree	Moderately Disagree	Strongly Disagree
1. I generally prefer the unexpected to the predictable.	☐	☐	☐	☐	☐	☐	☐
2. I am much more comfortable at events where I know most of the people there.	☐	☐	☐	☐	☐	☐	☐
3. I don't consider new situations any more threatening than familiar situations.	☐	☐	☐	☐	☐	☐	☐
4. I prefer solving problems that have only one "best" solution rather than many solutions.	☐	☐	☐	☐	☐	☐	☐
5. I dislike ambiguous situations.	☐	☐	☐	☐	☐	☐	☐
6. I avoid situations that are too complicated for me to easily understand.	☐	☐	☐	☐	☐	☐	☐
7. I like situations that can be interpreted in more than one way.	☐	☐	☐	☐	☐	☐	☐
8. I cope well with unexpected events.	☐	☐	☐	☐	☐	☐	☐
9. Familiar situations are always preferable to me than unfamiliar situations.	☐	☐	☐	☐	☐	☐	☐
10. I enjoy working in ambiguous situations.	☐	☐	☐	☐	☐	☐	☐

Sources: Adapted from D. L. Mclain, "The Mstat-I: A New Measure of an Individual's Tolerance for Ambiguity," *Educational and Psychological Measurement* 53, no. 1 (1993): 183–189; S. Budner, "Intolerance of Ambiguity as a Personality Variable," *Journal of Personality* 30 (1962), pp. 29–50.

 Practise and learn online with Connect. Connect resources include additional and interactive study exercises, videos, and practice quizzing, as well as additional material you won't find in the printed text.

ADDITIONAL CASES

Case 1: **A Mir Kiss?**
Case 2: **Arctic Mining Consultants**
Case 3: **Barrie Super Subs**
Case 4: **Bridging the Two Worlds—The Organizational Dilemma**
Case 5: **Chengdu Bus Group**
Case 6: **Going to the X-Stream**
Case 7: **Keeping Suzanne Chalmers**
Case 8: **Northwest Canadian Forest Products Limited**
Case 9: **The Regency Grand Hotel**
Case 10: **Resonus Corporation**
Case 11: **The Shipping Industry Accounting Team**
Case 12: **Treetop Forest Products**

Case 1   A Mir Kiss?

By Steven L. McShane, The University of Western Australia

A team of psychologists at Moscow's Institute for Biomedical Problems (IBMP) wanted to learn more about the dynamics of long-term isolation in space. This knowledge would be applied to the International Space Station, a joint project of several countries that would send people into space for more than six months. It would eventually include a trip to Mars taking up to three years.

IBMP set up a replica in Moscow of the Mir space station. They then arranged for three international researchers from Japan, Canada, and Austria to spend 110 days isolated in a chamber the size of a train car. This chamber joined a smaller chamber where four Russian cosmonauts had already completed half of their 240 days of isolation. This was the first time an international crew was involved in the studies. None of the participants spoke English as their first language, yet they communicated throughout their stay in English at varying levels of proficiency.

Judith Lapierre, a French-Canadian, was the only female in the experiment. Along with a PhD in public health and social medicine, Lapierre studied space sociology at the International Space University in France and conducted isolation research in the Antarctic. This was her fourth trip to Russia, where she had learned the language. The mission was supposed to have a second female participant from the Japanese space program, but she was not selected by IBMP.

The Japanese and Austrian participants viewed the participation of a woman as a favourable factor, says Lapierre. For example, to make the surroundings more comfortable, they rearranged the furniture, hung posters on the wall, and put a tablecloth on the kitchen table. "We adapted our environment, whereas the Russians just viewed it as something to be endured," she explains. "We decorated for Christmas, because I'm the kind of person who likes to host people."

New Year's Eve Turmoil

Ironically, it was at one of those social events, the New Year's Eve party, where events took a turn for the worse. After drinking vodka (allowed by the Russian space agency), two of the Russian cosmonauts got into a fistfight that left blood splattered on the chamber walls. At one point, a colleague hid the knives in the station's kitchen because of fears that the two Russians were about to stab each other. The two cosmonauts, who generally did not get along, had to be restrained by other men. Soon after that brawl, the Russian commander grabbed Lapierre, dragged her out of view of the television monitoring cameras, and kissed her aggressively—twice. Lapierre fought him off, but the message didn't register. He tried to kiss her again the next morning.

The next day, the international crew complained to IBMP about the behaviour of the Russian cosmonauts. The Russian institute apparently took no action against any of the aggressors. Instead, the institute's psychologists replied that the incidents were part of the experiment. They wanted crew members to solve their personal problems with mature discussion, without asking for outside help. "You have to understand that Mir is an autonomous object, far away from anything," Vadim Gushin, the IBMP psychologist in charge of the project, explained after the experiment had ended in March: "If the crew can't solve problems among themselves, they can't work together."

Following IBMP's response, the international crew wrote a scathing letter to the Russian institute and the space agencies involved in the experiment. "We had never expected such events to take place in a highly controlled scientific experiment where individuals go through a multistep selection process," they wrote. "If we had known . . . we would not have joined it as subjects." The letter also complained about IBMP's response to their concerns.

Informed of the New Year's Eve incident, the Japanese space program convened an emergency meeting on January 2 to address the incidents. Soon after, the Japanese team member quit, apparently shocked by IBMP's inaction. He was replaced with a Russian researcher on the international team. Ten days after the fight—a little over a month after the international team began the mission—the doors between the Russian and international crew's chambers were barred at the request of the international research team. Lapierre later emphasized that this action was taken because of concerns about violence, not the incident involving her.

A Stolen Kiss or Sexual Harassment

By the end of the experiment in March, news of the fistfight between the cosmonauts and the commander's attempts to kiss Lapierre had reached the public. Russian scientists attempted to play down the kissing incident by saying that it was one fleeting kiss, a clash of cultures, and a female participant who was too emotional.

"In the West, some kinds of kissing are regarded as sexual harassment. In our culture it's nothing," said Russian scientist Vadim Gushin in one interview. In another interview, he explained: "The problem of sexual harassment is given a lot of attention in North America but less in Europe. In Russia it is even less of an issue, not because we are more or less moral than the rest of the world; we just have different priorities."

Judith Lapierre says the kissing incident was tolerable compared to this reaction from the Russian scientists who conducted the experiment. "They don't get it at all," she complains. "They don't think anything is wrong. I'm more frustrated than ever. The worst thing is that they don't realize it was wrong."

Norbert Kraft, the Austrian scientist on the international team, also disagreed with the Russian interpretation of events. "They're trying to protect themselves," he says. "They're trying to put the fault on others. But this is not a cultural issue. If a woman doesn't want to be kissed, it is not acceptable."

Sources: G. Sinclair Jr., "If You Scream in Space, Does Anyone Hear?" *Winnipeg Free Press*, May 5, 2000, p. A4; S. Martin, "Reining in the Space Cowboys," *Globe & Mail*, April 19, 2000, p. R1; M. Gray, "A Space Dream Sours," *Maclean's*, April 17, 2000, p. 26; E. Niiler, "In Search of the Perfect Astronaut," *Boston Globe*, April 4, 2000, p. E4; J. Tracy, "110-Day Isolation Ends in Sullen . . . Isolation," *Moscow Times*, March 30, 2000, p. 1; M. Warren, "A Mir Kiss?" *Daily Telegraph (London)*, March 30, 2000, p. 22; G. York, "Canadian's Harassment Complaint Scorned," *Globe & Mail*, March 25, 2000, p. A2; and S. Nolen, "Lust in Space," *Globe & Mail*, March 24, 2000, p. A3.

Case 2 Arctic Mining Consultants

By Steven L. McShane, The University of Western Australia, and Tim Neale

Tom Parker enjoyed working outdoors. At various times in the past, he worked as a ranch hand, high steel rigger, headstone installer, prospector, and geological field technician. Now 43, Parker is a geological field technician and field coordinator with Arctic Mining Consultants. He has specialized knowledge and experience in all nontechnical aspects of mineral exploration, including claim staking, line cutting and grid installation, soil sampling, prospecting, and trenching. He is responsible for hiring, training, and supervising field assistants for all of Arctic Mining Consultants' programs. Field assistants are paid a fairly low daily wage (no matter how long they work, which may be up to 12 hours or more) and are provided meals and accommodation. Many of the programs are operated by a project manager who reports to Parker.

Parker sometimes acts as a project manager, as he did on a job that involved staking 15 claims near Eagle Lake, British Columbia. He selected John Talbot, Greg Boyce, and Brian Millar, all of whom had previously worked with Parker, as the field assistants. To stake a claim, the project team marks a line with flagging tape and blazes along the perimeter of the claim, cutting a claim post every 457 metres (called a "length"). The 15 claims would require almost 96 kilometres of line in total. Parker had budgeted seven days (plus mobilization and demobilization) to complete the job. This meant that each of the four stakers (Parker, Talbot, Boyce, and Millar) would have to complete a little over seven "lengths" each day. The following is a chronology of the project.

Day 1

The Arctic Mining Consultants' crew assembled in the morning and drove to Eagle Lake, from where they were flown by helicopter to the claim site. On arrival, they set up tents at the edge of the area to be staked, and agreed on a schedule for cooking duties. After supper, they pulled out the maps and discussed the job—how long it would take, the order in which the areas were to be staked, possible helicopter landing spots, and areas that might be more difficult to stake.

Parker pointed out that with only a week to complete the job, everyone would have to average seven and a half lengths per day. "I know that is a lot," he said, "but you've all staked claims before and I'm confident that each of you is capable of it. And it's only for a week. If we get the job done in time, there's a $300 bonus for each of you." Two hours later, Parker and his crew members had developed what seemed to be a workable plan.

Day 2

Millar completed six lengths, Boyce six lengths, Talbot eight, and Parker eight. Parker was not pleased with Millar's or Boyce's production. However, he didn't make an issue of it, thinking that they would develop their "rhythm" quickly.

Day 3

Millar completed five and a half lengths, Boyce four, and Talbot seven. Parker, who was nearly twice as old as the other three, completed eight lengths. He also had enough time remaining to walk over and check the quality of stakes that Millar and Boyce had completed, and then walk back to his own area for helicopter pickup back to the tent site.

That night Parker exploded with anger. "I thought I told you that I wanted seven and a half lengths a day!" he shouted at Boyce and Millar. Boyce said that he was slowed down by unusually thick underbrush in his assigned area. Millar said that he had done his best and would try to pick up the pace. Parker did not mention that he had inspected their work. He explained that as far as he was concerned, the field assistants were supposed to finish their assigned area for the day, no matter what.

Talbot, who was sharing a tent with Parker, talked to him later. "I think that you're being a bit hard on them, you know. I know that it has been more by luck than anything else that I've been able to do my quota. Yesterday I only had five lengths done after the first seven hours and there was only an hour before I was supposed to be picked up. Then I hit a patch of really open bush, and was able to do three lengths in 70 minutes. Why don't I take Millar's area tomorrow and he can have mine? Maybe that will help."

"Conditions are the same in all of the areas," replied Parker, rejecting Talbot's suggestion. "Millar just has to try harder."

Day 4

Millar did seven lengths and Boyce completed six and a half. When they reported their production that evening, Parker grunted uncommunicatively. Parker and Talbot did eight lengths each.

Day 5

Millar completed six lengths, Boyce six, Talbot seven and a half, and Parker eight. Once again Parker blew up, but he concentrated his diatribe on Millar. "Why don't you do what you say you are going to do? You know that you have to do seven and a half lengths a day. We went over that when we first got here, so why don't you do it? If you aren't willing to do the job then you never should have taken it in the first place!"

Millar replied by saying that he was doing his best, that he hadn't even stopped for lunch, and that he didn't know how he could possibly do any better. Parker launched into him again: "You have got to work harder! If you put enough effort into it, you will get the area done!"

Later Millar commented to Boyce, "I hate getting dumped on all the time! I'd quit if it didn't mean that I'd have to walk 80 kilometres to the highway. And besides, I need the bonus money. Why doesn't he pick on you? You don't get any more done than me; in fact, you usually get less. Maybe if you did a bit more he wouldn't be so bothered about me."

"I only work as hard as I have to," Boyce replied.

Day 6

Millar raced through breakfast, was the first one to be dropped off by the helicopter, and arranged to be the last one picked up. That evening the production figures were Millar eight and a quarter lengths, Boyce seven, and Talbot and Parker eight each. Parker remained silent when the field assistants reported their performance for the day.

Day 7

Millar was again the first out and last in. That night, he collapsed in an exhausted heap at the table, too tired to eat. After a few moments, he announced in an abject tone, "Six lengths. I worked like a dog all day and I only got a lousy six lengths!" Boyce completed five lengths, Talbot seven, and Parker seven and a quarter.

Parker was furious. "That means we have to do a total of 34 lengths tomorrow if we are to finish this job on time!" With his eyes directed at Millar, he added: "Why is it that you never finish the job? Don't you realize that you are part of a team, and that you are letting the rest of the team down? I've been checking your lines and you're doing too much blazing and wasting too much time making picture-perfect claim posts! If you worked smarter, you'd get a lot more done!"

Day 8

Parker cooked breakfast in the dark. The helicopter dropoffs began as soon as morning light appeared on the horizon. Parker instructed each assistant to complete 8 lengths and, if they finished early, to help the others. Parker said that he would finish the other 10 lengths. Helicopter pickups were arranged for one hour before dark.

By noon, after working as hard as he could, Millar had only completed three lengths. "Why bother," he thought to himself, "I'll never be able to do another five lengths before the helicopter comes, and I'll catch the same amount of abuse from Parker for doing six lengths as for seven and a half." So he sat down and had lunch and a rest. "Boyce won't finish his eight lengths either, so even if I did finish mine, I still wouldn't get the bonus. At least I'll get one more day's pay this way."

That night, Parker was livid when Millar reported that he had completed five and a half lengths. Parker had done ten and a quarter lengths, and Talbot had completed eight. Boyce proudly announced that he finished seven and a half lengths, but sheepishly added that Talbot had helped him with some of it. All that remained were the two and a half lengths that Millar had not completed.

The job was finished the next morning and the crew demobilized. Millar has never worked for Arctic Mining Consultants again, despite being offered work several times by Parker. Boyce sometimes does staking for Arctic, and Talbot works full time with the company.

Case 3   Barrie Super Subs

By Steven L. McShane, The University of Western Australia, based on an earlier case by J. E. Dittrich and R. A. Zawacki

Barrie Super Subs is one of the larger Super Subs restaurants, a chain of 300 restaurants across Canada. This outlet has a restaurant manager, an assistant manager, and several part-time team leaders. The restaurant manager rarely has time to serve customers and head office discourages this activity. The assistant manager serves customers for a couple of hours during the busy lunchtime but otherwise assists the restaurant manager with purchasing, accounts, hiring, and other operations. Most team leaders are university/college students and serve customers alongside other employees, particularly from late afternoon to night closing. Most employees are also students who work part-time; a few are in high school. All regular staff earn minimum wage.

Barrie Super Subs has experienced below average profitability over the past 18 months, which has reduced the monthly bonus paid to the restaurant manager and assistant manager. This bonus is calculated by percentage of "wastage" (unsold, damaged, or unaccounted for food and drinks) relative to sales; the lower the percentage of wastage, the higher the bonus. Wastage occurs when employees drop or spill food, cut up more toppings than are sold, burn heated subs, prepare an order incorrectly, and eat or give away food without permission. When employees make mistakes, the expense is supposed to come out of their paycheque. Eating and giving away food is grounds for immediate dismissal. However, team leaders are reluctant to report any accidental or deliberate wastage, even when confronted by the restaurant manager about the store's high wastage over the previous week and month. One team leader who reported several accidental wastage incidents eventually quit after being snubbed by co-workers who attended the same university classes.

Barrie Super Subs gives employees a food allowance if they work continuously for at least four and one-half hours. Staff complain that the allowance is meagre and that they are often ineligible for the food allowance because many shifts are only three or four hours. Employees who work these shorter shifts sometimes help themselves to food and drinks when the managers aren't around, claiming that they work just as hard as those who have longer shifts. Some also claim the food is a low company expense and makes up for their small paycheque relative to what some of their friends earn elsewhere. Several (but not most) employees give some of their friends generous helpings as well as occasional free soft drinks and chips. Employees say handing out free food to friends makes them more popular to their peers.

Five months ago, the Barrie restaurant's wastage (mainly deliberate wastage) had risen to the point where the two managers no longer received a bonus. The restaurant manager reacted by giving the food allowance only to those who work for six or more hours in a single shift. This action excluded even more staff from receiving the food allowance, but it did not discourage employees from eating or giving away food. However, almost 20 percent of the experienced university/college staff left for other jobs over the next two months. Many of those who stayed discouraged friends from considering jobs at Super Subs. Morale declined, which dampened the fun atmosphere that had been experienced to some extent in past times. Relations between employees and managers, which were already strained, soured further.

With relatively low unemployment, the restaurant manager found it difficult to hire replacements, particularly people with previous work experience of any kind. Temporary staff shortages required the two managers to spend more time working in food preparation and training the new staff. Their increased presence in the restaurant significantly reduced deliberate wastage, but accidental wastage increased somewhat as the larger number of inexperienced staff made more mistakes.

After three months, Barrie Super Subs' manager and assistant manager were confident that the situation had improved, so they spent less time training staff and serving customers. Indeed, they received a moderate bonus after the third month in the store. However, wastage increased again soon after the managers withdrew from daily operations. The experienced staff started eating more food and the new staff soon joined this practice. Exasperated, the restaurant manager took bolder steps. He completely removed the food allowance and threatened to fire any employee caught consuming or giving away food. Wastage dropped somewhat over the next month but is now creeping upward again.

Case 4 Bridging the Two Worlds—The Organizational Dilemma

By William Todorovic, Indiana-Purdue University, Fort Wayne

I had been hired by Aluminum Elements Corp. (AEC), and it was my first day of work. I was 26 years old, and I was now the manager of AEC's customer service group, which looked after customers, logistics, and some of the raw material purchasing. My superior, George, was the vice-president of the company. AEC manufactured most of its products from aluminum, a majority of which were destined for the construction industry.

As I walked around the shop floor, the employees appeared to be concentrating on their jobs, barely noticing me. Management held daily meetings, in which various production issues were discussed. No one from the shop floor was invited to the meeting, unless there was a specific problem. Later I also learned that management had separate washrooms, separate lunchrooms, as well as other perks that floor employees did not have. Most of the floor employees felt that management, although polite on the surface, did not really feel they had anything to learn from the floor employees.

John, who worked on the aluminum slitter, a crucial operation required before any other operations could commence, had a number of unpleasant encounters with George. As a result, George usually sent written memos to the floor in order to avoid a direct confrontation with John. Because the directions in the memos were complex, these memos were often more than two pages in length.

One morning, as I was walking around, I noticed that John was very upset. Feeling that perhaps there was something I could do, I approached John and asked him if I could help. He indicated that everything was just fine. From the looks of the situation, and John's body language, I felt that he was willing to talk, but John knew that this was not the way things were done at AEC. Tony, who worked at the machine next to John's, then cursed and said that the office guys only cared about schedules, not about the people down on the floor. I just looked at him, and then said that I only began working here last week, and thought that I could address some of their issues. Tony gave me a strange look, shook his head, and went back to his machine. I could hear him still swearing as I left. Later I realized that most of the office staff were also offended by Tony's language.

On the way back to my office, Lesley, a recently hired engineer from Russia, approached me and pointed out that the employees were not accustomed to management talking to them. Management only issued orders and made demands. As we discussed the different perceptions between office and floor staff, we were interrupted by a very loud lunch bell, which startled me. I was happy to join Lesley for lunch, but she asked me why I was not eating in the office lunch room. I replied that if I was going to understand how AEC worked, I had to get to know all the people better. In addition, I realized that this was not how things were done, and wondered about the nature of this apparent division between the management and the floor. In the lunchroom, the other workers were amazed to see me there, commenting that I was just new and had not learned the ropes yet.

After lunch, when I asked George, my supervisor, about his recent confrontation with John, George was surprised that John got upset, and exclaimed, "I just wanted John to know that he did a great job, and as a result, we will be able to ship on time one large order to the West Coast. If fact, I thought I was complimenting him."

Earlier, Lesley had indicated that certain behaviour was expected from management, and therefore from me. I reasoned that I do not think that this behaviour works, and besides it is not what I believe or how I care to behave. For the next couple of months, I simply walked around the floor and took every opportunity to talk to the shop floor employees. Often, when the employees related specific information about their workplaces, I felt that it went over my head. Frequently, I had to write down the information and revisit it later. I made a point of listening to them, identifying where they were coming from, and trying to understand them. I needed to keep my mind open to new ideas. Because the shop employees expected me to make requests and demands, I made a point of not doing any of that. Soon enough, the employees became friendly, and started to accept me as one of their own, or at least as a different type of a management person.

During my third month of work, the employees showed me how to improve the scheduling of jobs, especially those on the aluminum slitter. In fact, the greatest contribution was made by John who demonstrated better ways to combine the most common slitting sizes, and reduce waste by retaining some of the "common-sized" material for new orders. Seeing the opportunity, I programmed a spreadsheet to calculate and track inventory. This, in addition to better planning and forecasting, allowed us to reduce our new order turnarounds from four to five weeks to in by 10 a.m. out by 5 p.m. on the same day.

By the time I was employed for four months, I realized that members from other departments came to me and asked me to relay messages to the shop employees. When I asked why they were delegating this task to me, they stated that I spoke the same language as the shop employees. Increasingly, I became the messenger for the office to floor shop communication.

One morning, George called me into his office and complimented me on the levels of customer service and the improvements that have been achieved. As we talked, I mentioned that we could not have done it without John's help. "He really knows his stuff, and he is good," I said. I suggested that we consider him for some type of a promotion. Also, I hoped that this would be a positive gesture that would improve the communication between the office and shop floor.

George turned and pulled a flyer out of his desk; "Here is a management skills seminar. Do you think we should send John to it?"

"That is a great idea," I exclaimed, "Perhaps it would be good if he were to receive the news from you directly, George." George agreed, and after discussing some other issues, we parted company.

That afternoon, John came into my office, upset and ready to quit. "After all my effort and work, you guys are sending me for training seminars. So, am I not good enough for you?"

Case 5 Chengdu Bus Group

By Runtian Jing, The University of Electronic Science and Technology of China

The Chengdu Bus Group (CBG) is a Chinese, state-owned enterprise with more than 4,000 buses and 14,000 employees. A few years ago, CBG encountered serious problems. The primary issue was the company's management systems, but it also faced a considerable financial crisis. Complaints against CBG from its many customers were becoming increasingly common and the operations of the company were in disarray.

At the end of a troubled year, Dr. She Chen was appointed as the director (CEO) of CBG. Dr. Chen had proven himself in previous positions as a thoughtful and insightful manager. He had accumulated not only a wealth of experience on effective leadership in Chinese society, but also in the field of management theory. Additionally, he had earned a PhD—a very rare achievement in the Chinese business community.

Due to the seriousness of CBG's problems, the mayor of Chengdu gave Dr. Chen just three years to reform CBG. This was too short a time to gradually transform the organization, including the critically flawed management system and financial situation. Therefore, Dr. Chen had to implement rapid change and take risks to carry out a successful reform in the required time frame, even though he knew this would be met with great resistance from CBG's employees and many stakeholders.

After taking up his new position, Dr. Chen conducted a careful investigation into the functioning of CBG, after which he formulated a series of reform measures. He then discussed his ideas and proposed changes with the mayor and leaders of Chengdu city, obtaining full support in both authorization and funding before implementing the organizational changes in the company.

Fast-paced Managerial Reform

Because CBG is an old, state-owned enterprise, very complicated working relationships and politics existed among the 14,000 employees. Dr. Chen knew that this would make it very difficult to carry out large-scale organizational reforms within the company. However, after two months of examination, Dr. Chen felt he had accurately grasped the important characteristics of the 533 managers in the company. He then carefully designed a reform plan and schedule for the managers and their positions. To avoid the influence of complicated *guanxi* (special relationships) among the managers, and to avoid the managers forming solid opposition to his changes, Dr. Chen implemented the reforms with a fast, accurate, and ambitious strategy. The changes were made quickly, precisely, and without compromise.

This strategy meant that adjustments to the managerial positions were completed before the managers could effectively react to what was happening and potentially disrupt the process. Nonetheless, when they realized what had happened, they began to protest. Dr. Chen was very calm and simply said to them: "After all these events have passed by you will have many different impressions about me and my reforms. Although such an adjustment may bring some loss to you, in the future the commendation from others will be more than the condemnation. All change must face resistance, complaint, and even rejection. What I have done is not for myself, but for the company."

Simplifying the Branch Company Structure

Another notable reform that Dr. Chen successfully implemented involved the branch companies of CBG. The organization had four branch companies; two were wholly state-owned, while the other two were joint ventures with external investors. In addition to operating bus routes, each company owned buses, bus stations, repair workshops, and other facilities and equipment required to run their bus services. However, this created significant problems and inefficiencies as each company ran its operations independently of the other companies, and did not share their stations or repair workshops—essentially, the four companies were in direct competition with each other.

Furthermore, different routes throughout the city had quite different profit rates. Without any formal authority coordinating the companies, or implementing policies and rules, there was overcompetition for the desirable high-profit routes, resulting in inefficiencies and losses for all of the companies. To rectify this situation, Dr. Chen arranged for CBG to buy back the external equity of the joint ventures, and thereby changed the branch operations to purely state-owned subsidiaries. He then removed the overservicing on the high-profit routes, and redeployed the surplus buses and employees from these routes to develop the potential profitability of other routes under the principle of optimization.

Additionally, all of the routes were rezoned to fall under the operations of four specific areas of the city, forming the eastern, western, southern, and northern bus companies. All of the bus stations were amalgamated into a single station company, and all the repair workshops amalgamated into a single repair company. These reforms made it possible for each of the four bus companies to obtain services from the station company or the repair company anywhere in the city, and thus greatly reduce resource wastage, overcompetition, and operating costs.

Salaries and Rewards

Dr. Chen also found that the salary system of CBG was questionable in both fairness and efficiency. For example, the front-line staff generally worked very hard, however their salaries were lower than the back-up staff who didn't work as hard. This had resulted in low job satisfaction and high turnover rates among the front-line staff. After careful evaluation of the different jobs' tasks and demands, Dr. Chen distinguished the tasks and demands of the front-line and back-up staff. Despite criticism from back-up staff and some managers, he insisted on increasing the wages and bonuses of the front-line staff.

To reduce the frequent accidents by bus drivers, Dr. Chen linked the wage system to each driver's 'safe mileage accumulation program.' If accidents were occurring, the amount of 'safe mileage accumulation' decreased and, as a result, the level of wages. Conversely, if a driver had few accidents, or none at all, wages would increase. This meant that a driver who had not been involved in any accidents could earn an even higher wage than the average middle manager! Such a policy quickly improved the safety awareness and practices of the drivers. Furthermore, Dr. Chen encouraged managers to use rewards instead of punishment to motivate their employees, and abolished more than 50 penalty provisions.

The Results of Reform

After just two years of Dr. She Chen's reforms, Chengdu Bus Group achieved remarkable results. The management was greatly improved, the efficiency and profitability of CBG was enhanced, and the employees were performing better and were significantly happier. Through the safe mileage accumulation system, the drivers' safety awareness and quality of service substantially improved, and the rate of accidents decreased greatly. The public attitude toward the company and its social evaluation also improved significantly. CBG was awarded for its successful reform by the State-owned Assets Supervision and Administration Commission (SASAC) of Chengdu city in 2008.

Case 6   Going to the X-Stream

By Roy Smollan, Auckland University of Technology

Gil Reihana was the chief executive officer of X-Stream, a company he launched in Auckland, New Zealand, six years ago at the age of 25, after graduating with a bachelor's degree in information technology and management. He had inherited $300,000 and had persuaded various family members to invest additional money. X-Stream assembled personal computers for the New Zealand and Australian markets and sold them through a number of chain stores and independent retailers. The company had soon established a reputation for quality hardware, customized products, excellent delivery times, and after-sales service. Six months ago it had started a software division, specializing in Web design and consulting on various applications for the development of electronic business.

Gil was driven by a desire to succeed. He had started working part-time at an electronics retailer at age 16 and in his spare time took apart old computers in his garage to see how they were made. He was extroverted, energetic, and enthusiastic, often arriving at work before 5 a.m. and seldom leaving before 7 p.m. He felt that work should be challenging but fun too. He had initially picked a young senior management team that he thought shared his outlook. A casual, almost irreverent atmosphere developed. However, a poorly organized accounting department led to the demise of the first accountant after two years. Gil believed that major decisions should be made by consensus and that individuals should then be empowered to implement these decisions in their own way. In the beginning he had met with each staff member in January to discuss with them how happy they were in their jobs, what their ambitions were, and what plans they would like to make for the coming year in terms of their own professional development. As the company had grown this had become more difficult and he had left each member of his senior management team to do this with their own staff, but did not monitor whether they were doing it and how well it worked. Now he tried to keep in touch with staff by having lunch with them in the cafeteria occasionally.

Denise Commins (affectionately known to all staff as Dot Com) was the chief financial officer. She and Gil could not be more different. Denise was quiet, methodical, and very patient. Her superb interpersonal skills complemented a highly analytical mind. At 55 she was considerably older than most of the employees and often showed a strong maternal side. Many of her team (and several from other departments as well) frequently consulted her on work issues and personal problems too. She enjoyed the informal relationships she had built up but found that the technical aspects of her role were becoming less rewarding.

Don Head, the marketing manager, was considered to be a rather ruthless operator, often undercutting the competition in terms of price, and, on more than one occasion, by circulating false rumours of defects in their products. He deemed himself "a ladies' man" and was known to flirt with a number of the staff. A case of sexual harassment had been dropped after a 22-year-old secretary had been paid a sizeable sum of money. Gil and the members of the senior management team had been furious but Don had denied any wrongdoing, claiming that she had "led him on." He had been at university with Gil and they spent many hours after work at a pub around the corner from the factory. With sales rising year after year his marketing expertise and cunning were regarded as essential to the company's continuing growth. He had a department of eight whom he had carefully screened as ambitious self-starters. They were required to set and achieve their own targets, as long as they were "big hairy ambitious goals," a phrase he had heard at a seminar.

Jason Palu, the production manager, was a soft-spoken man who had started as a supervisor and who had quickly worked his way to the top position. He set extremely high standards for the production staff and was considered to be a perfectionist. He was highly regarded by his colleagues for his efficiency and reliability. There were very few occasions when an order could not be fulfilled on time and his goal was zero defects.

He tended to be autocratic and some people complained that he never listened to them, allocated work hours that did not suit people, often insisting on (paid) over-time but at very short notice. When one production worker complained he tersely remarked that "we have a job to do and we just have to get on with it. The company depends on us."

Heather Berkowitz was the chief Web designer. She had blue hair, several piercings, and dressed in a variety of exotic clothes that had been sourced from a number of thrift stores. She seldom arrived at work much before 11 a.m. and often left before 4 p.m. She said she did her best work at home, often at night, so why should she "punch the clock like the drones on the assembly line"? Gil and others had often received emails from her that had been sent at all hours of the night. She had established a reputation as a top Web designer, and although her physical appearance did not go down too well with some of the company's clients (or staff) the quality and quantity of her work was extremely high.

On Tuesdays at 9 a.m. the senior staff met to discuss weekly plans and any significant issues that had arisen. All employees were invited to the meeting, an opportunity that some took advantage of by attending. Gil trusted all staff to keep confidential matters within the company. He believed that if the organization shared information with employees they would be more likely to support management decisions. The meetings lacked formality and usually started with some jokes, usually at the expense of some members of staff. By and large the jokes were meant to be inoffensive, but were not always taken that way. Nicknames were often assigned to staff, mostly by Don Head, some quite derogatory. You were thought to be a loser if you objected. Don seemed oblivious to the unflattering nickname he had been given, preferring to call himself Madman, sometimes even signing memos in this fashion.

Although employment agreements referred to a 40-hour week there was an expectation that staff would put in substantially more than that. Only the assembly line workers had to clock in and out but this, Jason had explained, was due to the overtime that assembly staff were required to work to meet deadlines. The overtime pay was welcomed by some production staff and resented by some employees in other departments who believed they should be entitled to the same benefits.

Recently a conflict had arisen between Jason and Don. The company had been developing for some time a top-of-the-line laptop that was scheduled for launching in two weeks' time. Jason had been urging senior management to delay the introduction of the new X-MH until some hitches had been sorted out. A batch of chips acquired from abroad had contained some defective features. He wanted to postpone the new model until these problems had been completely sorted out, a process that he believed would take another month. Don found this to be unacceptable. A former All Black captain had been contracted to attend the launch and market the new model on a roadshow that would travel to New Zealand and Australia's main cities. He would not be available at the time Jason was prepared to release the X-MH. At a heated staff meeting some of the senior staff backed Don, some agreed with Jason. Don had urged all of his department to attend the meeting, to present a united front and convey an image of power.

Heather Berkowitz had arrived half way through the meeting and with a mouthful of muffin proclaimed that there was no rush to get out the "new toy." The company had plenty of other issues to which it could devote its energy. She said she had met the head of information technology of a chain of fast-food restaurants who wanted to revitalize its website. She maintained she needed three extra staff to get this up and running. She exited the meeting five minutes later. Don was fuming at the interruption and demanded that Gil should stick to the original launch date of the X-MH. Gil calmly replied that he understood Don's frustration but that more consultation was necessary. He said that it would be discussed by the parties concerned during the week and a final decision would be made at the following Tuesday's staff meeting.

Don spent the rest of the day lobbying other members of the senior staff. He offered Dorothy the use of his beach cottage if she backed him and promised to support her on the acquisition of expensive new accounting software. She just laughed and said that she was convinced the senior management team would approve the new software.

She also informed Don that a member of her staff had seen one of his sales representatives entering a strip joint the previous week at a time when the sales force had been engaged in a staff meeting.

Other problems had arisen in recent months. Ramesh Patel, the newly recruited head of e-business applications had, with help from a personal contact, developed a software program that would help hotels and restaurants source products and services over the Internet. It was beginning to generate useful revenue. His contact had now billed X-Stream for $25,000 in consultancy fees and development costs. Ramesh claimed that his contact had owed him a favour and that no mention of money had ever been made. X-Stream had referred the matter to its legal counsel.

Les Kong, the research and development manager (hardware) had complained to Gil that he could no longer work under Jason Palu. While he considered him a very pleasant man, and a very capable production manager, he could no longer tolerate his strict control style. "You can't do creative work on command!" was his lament. He loved his job and had spent hours over several weekends developing and refining a new product.

There was considerable resentment from Jason and Don about the resources that had been invested in the software division, partly because they did not see the need for the company to diversify and partly because they claimed that money was being diverted from their departments to fund the new ventures. Ramesh claimed that "a good e-business starts at home—we should open up all our procurement via the Internet." His suggestion did not go down well with Jason and Don.

Gil had been pondering the structure of X-Stream for some time. The old functional structure no longer seemed appropriate. "Silo" mentality and departmental interests seemed to predominate and turf wars took place. The company had grown to 64 staff in New Zealand and eight in Australia. The ongoing development of new hardware and the introduction of the software side of the business had made management somewhat complicated. He missed the old days when he knew every member of staff. The informal decision making that was characteristic of the business might have to give way to more formal processes. Yet he did not want to lose the creativity that underpinned its success. Despite the open invitation to attend the management meetings many staff complained that they never knew what was going on. He expected all senior managers to keep their departmental staff informed of developments. Some had done this admirably while others had virtually ignored his wishes.

A human resources manager, Alkina Bennelong, had been appointed a month previously and reported to Denise Commins. She had been reviewing the company's loosely worded job descriptions and person specifications and the recruitment and selection systems and had suggested more professional but more elaborate approaches. She had also suggested the introduction of a performance management system, including feedback from peers, direct reports, and outsiders, such as suppliers and customers. "Over my dead body!" was the retort of Don Head. "How can you allow subordinates to tell you how to do your job?" queried Jason Palu. "Can't see what the fuss is all about," said Heather Berkowitz. "Everybody keeps telling me what to do anyway, even though they don't understand the first thing about my job! But it doesn't worry me."

Case 7   Keeping Suzanne Chalmers

By Steven L. McShane, The University of Western Australia

Thomas Chan hung up the telephone and sighed. The vice-president of software engineering at Advanced Photonics Inc. (API) had just spoken to Suzanne Chalmers, who called to arrange a meeting with Chan later that day. She didn't say what the meeting was about, but Chan almost instinctively knew that Suzanne was going to quit after working at API for the past four years. Chalmers is a software engineer in Internet Protocol (IP), the software that directs fibre-optic light through API's routers. It is very specialized work, and Suzanne is one of API's top talents in that area.

Thomas Chan had been through this before. A valued employee would arrange a private meeting. The meeting would begin with a few pleasantries, then the employee announces that he or she wants to quit. Some employees say they are leaving because of the long hours and stressful deadlines. They say they need to decompress, get to know the kids again, or whatever. But that's not usually the real reason. Almost every organization in this industry is scrambling to keep up with technological advances and the competition. Employees would just leave one stressful job for another one.

Also, many of the people who leave API join a start-up company a few months later. These start-up firms can be pressure cookers where everyone works 16 hours each day and has to perform a variety of tasks. For example, engineers in these small firms might have to meet customers or work on venture capital proposals rather than focus on specialized tasks related to their knowledge. API now has over 6,000 employees, so it is easier to assign people to work that matches their technical competencies.

No, the problem isn't the stress or long hours, Chan thought. The problem is money—too much money. Most of the people who leave are millionaires. Suzanne Chalmers is one of them. Thanks to generous share options that have skyrocketed on the stock markets, many employees at API have more money than they can use. Most are under 40 years old, so it's too early for them to retire. But their financial independence gives them less reason to remain with API.

The Meeting

The meeting with Suzanne Chalmers took place a few hours after the telephone call. It began like the others, with the initial pleasantries and brief discussion about progress on the latest fibre-optic router project. Then, Suzanne made her well-rehearsed statement: "Thomas, I've really enjoyed working here, but I'm going to leave Advanced Photonics." Suzanne took a breath, then looked at Chan. When he didn't reply after a few seconds, she continued: "I need to take time off. You know, get away to recharge my batteries. The project's nearly done and the team can complete it without me. Well, anyway, I'm thinking of leaving."

Chan spoke in a calm voice. He suggested that Suzanne should take an unpaid leave for two or maybe three months, complete with paid benefits, then return refreshed. Suzanne politely rejected that offer, saying that she needs to get away from work for a while. Thomas then asked Suzanne whether she was unhappy with her work environment—whether she was getting the latest computer technology to do her work and whether there were problems with co-workers. The workplace was fine, Suzanne replied. The job was getting a bit routine, but she had a comfortable workplace with excellent co-workers.

Chan then apologized for the cramped workspace, due mainly to the rapid increase in the number of people hired over the past year. He suggested that if Suzanne took a couple of months off, API would give her special treatment with a larger work space with a better view of the park behind the campus-like building when she returned. She politely thanked Chan for that offer, but it wasn't what she needed. Besides, it wouldn't be fair to have a large work space when other team members work in smaller quarters.

Chan was running out of tactics, so he tried his last hope: money. He asked whether Suzanne had higher offers. Suzanne replied that she regularly received calls from other companies, and some of them offered more money. Most were start-up firms that offered a lower salary but higher potential gains in share options. Chan knew from market surveys that Suzanne was already paid well in the industry. He also knew that API couldn't compete on share option potential. Employees working in start-up firms sometimes saw their shares increase by five or ten times their initial value, whereas shares at API and other large firms increased more slowly. However, Chan promised Suzanne that he would recommend that she receive a significant raise—maybe 25 percent more—and more share options. Chan added that Chalmers was one of API's most valuable employees and that the company would suffer if she left the firm.

The meeting ended with Chalmers promising to consider Chan's offer of higher pay and share options. Two days later, Chan received her resignation in writing. Five months later, Chan learned that after a few months travelling with her husband, Chalmers joined a start-up software firm in the area.

Case 8 Northwest Canadian Forest Products Limited

By Peter Seidl, British Columbia Institute of Technology

Northwest Canadian Forest Products Limited owns and operates five sawmills in British Columbia and Alberta. These mills produce high-quality lumber for use in the manufacture of window frames, doors, and mouldings for markets in the United States and Japan in addition to lower-quality, commodity-type lumber used in the Canadian construction industry. Currently, the president of the company is thinking about the long-term prospects of each of the mills and is paying particular attention to the Jackson Sawmill located in the small town of Jackson, BC.

This mill was originally built in 1950 and was last upgraded in 1986. The president knows she will soon (in 2012) have to decide whether or not to invest substantial sums of money ($50 million) in new plant and equipment at the Jackson Sawmill. New investment is required in order to keep the mill up-to-date and competitive with similar mills throughout North America. However, the mill has consistently been the poorest performer (in terms of productivity and product quality) in the company since 1986 even though its equipment is of similar age, type, and quality as that found in the other mills.

The president would like to invest the money needed because the alternative to re-investing in Jackson would be to downsize the Jackson Sawmill by reducing production capacity and permanently laying off over half the 200-person workforce. The remaining part of the mill would serve the domestic market only. A new mill would then be built in Alberta in order to serve the more demanding, quality-conscious export markets. A new mill in Alberta would cost more than the $50-million investment required at the Jackson Sawmill. However, the president is willing to seriously consider implementing this alternative because she thinks that the labour relations climate in Alberta is much better than the one found at Jackson.

In fact, she attributes most, if not all, of the problems at Jackson to its poor labour-management relations. During the last round of collective bargaining, there was a strike at all four of the company's BC mills. The strike was, however, much more bitter at Jackson than elsewhere. Company buildings suffered minor damage during the strike at the hands of some striking employees. Since then, there were two separate occasions when the entire workforce walked off the job for a day to protest the firings of two employees who were dismissed for insubordination.

The Jackson Sawmill has the worst safety record of all the company's mills. There is a joint labour–management safety committee (as required by law) but it is viewed as a waste of time by both sides. One management member of the safety committee, Des, the production manager and the second highest manager at the mill, has said: "The union guys start each safety committee meeting by complaining about safety but they just can't wait to complain about everything else they can possibly think of. Their whining and complaining is so predictable that I go to every safety meeting ready for a fight on workload and production issues as well as for a fight on safety. Of course, safety is everyone's responsibility but production issues are none of their business. Production is a management responsibility. Plans, budgets, and other management concerns are very definitely not part of the committee's job. Most of what's said at these meetings isn't worth listening to."

The union is also dissatisfied with the functioning of the safety committee. Ivan, the chief union steward who also serves on the committee, observes: "If the safety committee wasn't mandatory by law, management wouldn't even pretend to listen to us. We put forward our safety concerns but management says that we are mixing safety in with workload and production issues. They only want to talk about what they think are safety issues—like serious accidents. Thankfully, we don't have too many of those! But safety is more than just avoiding major accidents. We get far too many 'little accidents' and 'near-accidents' here. At least that's what management calls them. They just want us to work faster and faster. We complain and complain at the meetings but they just say 'that's a production issue and this is a safety committee.' They accuse us of trying to run the company when we ask for better equipment. They say we don't understand things like costs and limited budgets. We don't care about their budgets, we've got work issues to talk about and we'll keep speaking out for the crew no matter what. That's what the union is for."

Big Bad John, one of the mill's toughest and most experienced supervisors, describes his job as follows: "The job of supervisor is to keep a close watch on every move the crew makes. If I look away for a second, some guy is going to be doing something wrong— either with the equipment or with the logs. They're always making mistakes. Lots of mistakes! Some of these guys are just plain dumb. And lazy, too! Any chance they can get to steal some company time, they take. They start work late, they take long lunch breaks, they talk too much during their shifts. A minute here, a minute there—it all adds up. The younger guys are the worst. They always want to talk back to me, they can't follow my orders like most of the older guys can. Lousy attitude, that's what they've got."

Vic, the youngest union steward, gives his view of labour–management relations: "The supervisors and the managers, they know it all. They think they're so smart. They treat the guys on the crew like children. Almost everyone on the crew has a high school education. Some even have college backgrounds. Most are raising families. We're not stupid! Sure, some guys come in late and miss a day of work now and then. Who can blame them? The pace of work is exhausting. How can you do a good job when you're tired and rushing all the time?" He adds: "Of course, we're not perfect. We make mistakes just like everyone else does. But nobody ever explains anything to the crew members. The supervisors just watch everyone like hawks and jump all over them, criticize them, and make them feel stupid when they use a piece of equipment the wrong way. We're always so rushed and busy here that the senior crew members don't have much time to explain things to the newer workers, the younger guys. Also, the equipment could be in better shape, that would help."

The production manager, Des, observes that "the union just doesn't understand—or even care about—the connection between the poor work ethic, the poor attitude on the part of the crew members here, and the mill's mediocre productivity and product quality. The union and the crew only take their very narrow 'employee-view' of how things are done around here. They don't understand the bigger picture. Well, it's very competitive out there. They don't understand what tight budgets, increasing costs, declining quality, missed production targets, and complaining customers mean to a business. They just sit back and complain about our management style. What they don't realize is that their attitude makes our management style necessary. Complaining is easy, no responsibility is needed. Managing, on the other hand, is challenging. And it's especially tough to control and manage this particular crew. We've currently got 30 unresolved grievances—that's a lot of formal complaints for a mill of our size. Some of the union stewards actually go out among the crew and look for grievances just because they're mad they can't run the mill the way they want to. Sometimes I think the stewards want to create grievances where no real problems exist. They want to give us in management headaches."

The president of the company has recently informed Digby, the mill's new general manager (he started at Jackson last month after a career in eastern Canada), of the decision she will soon have to make regarding the mill's future. She told Digby that significant improvements in mill productivity and product quality are required if the mill is to receive the $50-million investment in new plant and equipment. Without such improvements, the mill would be downsized and over half of the workforce would be permanently laid off. Half the supervisory and managerial personnel would also lose their jobs.

Digby has just telephoned Moe (the president of the local union who does not work at the mill but who is very familiar with developments at the mill) to tell him about the message from the company president. Upon hearing of the potential job losses, Moe was troubled and asked to meet with Digby to discuss the situation. However, Moe was also somewhat skeptical because the previous general manager once told him that some permanent layoffs would occur unless productivity was improved. No layoffs subsequently occurred. Therefore, Moe is uncertain if the company is serious about these potential future layoffs or merely bluffing in order to get the employees to work harder.

Case 9   The Regency Grand Hotel

By Lisa Ho, under the supervision of Steven L. McShane, The University of Western Australia

The Regency Grand Hotel is a five-star hotel in Bangkok, Thailand. The hotel was established 15 years ago by a local consortium of investors and has been operated by a Thai general manager throughout this time. The hotel is one of Bangkok's most prestigious hotels and its 700 employees enjoyed the prestige being associated to the hotel. The hotel provides good health benefits, above market rate salary, and job security. In addition, a good year-end bonus amounting to four months' salary was rewarded to employees regardless of the hotel's overall performance during the year.

Recently, the Regency was sold to a large American hotel chain that was very keen to expand its operations into Thailand. When the acquisition was announced, the general manager decided to take early retirement when the hotel changed ownership. The American hotel chain kept all of the Regency employees, although a few were transferred to other positions. John Becker, an American with 10 years of management experience with the hotel chain, was appointed as the new general manager of the Regency Grand Hotel. Becker was selected as the new general manager because of his previous successes in integrating newly acquired hotels in the United States. In most of the previous acquisitions, Becker took over operations with poor profitability and low morale.

Becker is a strong believer in empowerment. He expects employees to go beyond guidelines/standards to consider guest needs on a case by case basis. That is, employees must be guest-oriented at all times so as to provide excellent customer service. From his U.S. experience, Becker has found that empowerment increases employee motivation, performance, and job satisfaction, all of which contribute to the hotel's profitability and customer service ratings. Soon after becoming general manager at the Regency Grand, Becker introduced the practice of empowerment so as to replicate the successes that he had achieved back home.

The Regency Grand Hotel has been very profitable since it opened 15 years ago. The employees have always worked according to management's instructions. Their responsibility was to ensure that the instructions from their managers were carried out diligently and conscientiously. Innovation and creativity were discouraged under the previous management. Indeed, employees were punished for their mistakes and discouraged from trying out ideas that had not been approved by management. As a result, employees were afraid to be innovative and to take risks.

Becker met with the Regency's managers and department heads to explain that empowerment would be introduced in the hotel. He told them that employees must be empowered with decision making authority so that they can use their initiative, creativity, and judgment to satisfy guest needs or handle problems effectively and efficiently. However, he stressed that the more complex issues and decisions were to be referred to superiors, who were to coach and assist rather than provide direct orders. Furthermore, Becker stressed that mistakes were allowed but would not tolerate having the same mistakes made more than twice. He advised his managers and department heads neither to discuss minor issues/problems nor to consult about minor decisions with him . Nevertheless, he told them that they are to discuss important/major issues and decisions with him. He concluded the meeting by asking for feedback. Several managers and department heads told him that they liked the idea and would support it, while others simply nodded their heads. Becker was pleased with the response, and was eager to have his plan implemented.

In the past, the Regency had emphasized administrative control, resulting in many bureaucratic procedures throughout the organization. For example, the front counter employees needed to seek approval from their manager before they could upgrade guests to another category of room. The front counter manager would then have to write and submit a report to the general manager justifying the upgrade. Soon after his meeting with managers, Becker reduced the number of bureaucratic rules at the Regency and allocated more decision making authority to front-line employees. This action upset those who previously had decision making power over these issues. As a result, several of these employees left the hotel.

Becker also began spending a large portion of his time observing and interacting with the employees at the front desk, lobby, restaurants, and various departments. This direct interaction with Becker helped many employees to understand what he wanted and expected of them. However, the employees had much difficulty trying to distinguish between a major and minor issue/decision. More often than not, supervisors would reverse employee decisions by stating that they were major issues requiring management approval. Employees who displayed initiative and made good decisions in satisfying the needs of the guests rarely received any positive feedback from their supervisors. Eventually, most of these employees lost confidence in making decisions, so they once again relied on their superiors for decision making.

Not long after the implementation of the practice of empowerment, Becker realized that his employees were consulting him more frequently than before. Most of them came to him with minor issues and consulted with him about minor decisions. He had to spend most of his time attending to his employees. Soon he began to feel highly frustrated and exhausted, and very often would tell his secretary that "unless the hotel is on fire, don't let anyone disturb me."

Becker thought that the practice of empowerment would benefit the overall performance of the hotel. However, contrary to his expectation, the business and overall performance of the hotel began to deteriorate. There had been an increasing number of guest complaints. In the past, the hotel had minimal guest complaints. Now there has been a significant number of formal written complaints every month. Many other guests voiced their dissatisfaction verbally to hotel employees. The number of mistakes made by employees had been on an increase. Becker was very upset when he realized that two of the local newspapers and an overseas newspaper had published negative feedback on the hotel in terms of service standards. He was most distressed when an international travel magazine had voted the hotel as "one of Asia's nightmare hotels."

The stress levels of the employees were continuously mounting since the introduction of the practice of empowerment. Absenteeism due to illness was increasing at an alarming rate. In addition, the employee turnover rate had reached an all-time high. The good working relationships that were established under the old management had been severely strained. The employees were no longer united and supportive of each other. They were quick to 'point fingers' at or to 'back stab' one another when mistakes were made and when problems occurred.

Note: This case is based on true events, but the industry and names have been changed.

Case 10   Resonus Corporation

By Steven L. McShane, The University of Western Australia, based on an earlier case by John A. Seeger

Frank Choy is normally a quiet person, but his patience has already worn thin by interdepartmental battles. Choy joined Resonus Corporation, a hearing aid designer and manufacturer, eight months ago as director of engineering. Production of the latest product has been delayed by two months and Choy's engineering services department (ESD)—which prepares final manufacturing specifications—is taking the heat as the main culprit for these delays. Similar delays have been occurring at Resonus for the past few years. The previous engineering director was fired after 18 months; the director before him quit after about the same amount of time.

Bill Hunt, CEO of Resonus for the past 15 years, typically responded to these problems by saying "I'm sure we can resolve these differences if we just learn to get along better." Hunt disliked firing anyone, but felt the previous engineering director was too confrontational. Hunt was groomed by the company's founder and took great pride in preserving the organization's family spirit. He also discouraged bureaucracy, believing that Resonus operated best through informal relationships among its managers. Only production director Jacqui Blanc opposed this informality. Hunt tolerated Blanc's formal style because soon after joining Resonus five years ago she discovered and cleaned up fraudulent activity between two production managers and suppliers.

The organizational chart shows that Frank Choy oversees two departments: ESD and research. In reality, "Doc" Kalandry, the research director, informally reports directly to the CEO (Hunt) and has never considered the director of engineering as his boss. Hunt actively supports this informal reporting relationship because of Doc's special status in the organization. "Doc Kalandry is our gold mine," Hunt told Choy soon after he joined the firm. "He's unusual, yes, but he is one of the world's greatest innovators. With Doc in charge of research, this company will continue to keep ahead of the competition." Hunt's first job at Resonus was in the research group and Choy suspected that Hunt still favoured that group.

Everyone at Resonus seems to be enamoured with Doc and his hyper-enthusiasm, but some of Choy's ESD staff are also privately concerned. Says one engineer: "Nothing can stop Doc when he discovers a new technology or design. He has this incredible optimism —too much optimism—about the potential of the idea and perpetually underestimates how long it takes to get that idea into production. Doc has caused us to make almost 200 production change orders already this year. Even if we try to stop him (and we try to, sometimes), Hunt backs him up. Frank really needs to draw the line on new development so we can hit our deadlines for once!"

Soon after joining Resonus, Choy realized that ESD employees get most of the blame and little of the credit for their work. When production staff find a design fault, they directly contact the research design engineer who developed the technology rather than the ESD group who prepare the specifications. Research engineers willingly work with production because they don't want to let go of their project. "The designers are very busy, but they don't want to let go of their design work," Choy explains. "So, when something needs to be corrected, the designer steps in rather than have the clean-up work completed by ESD engineers."

Meanwhile, Choy noted that production supervisors regularly critique ESD staff whereas they tend to accept explanations from the higher-status research department engineers. "Production routinely complains about every little specification error, many of which are due to design changes made by the research group," says one frustrated ESD technician. "ESD engineers and technicians with 10 or 15 years experience shouldn't have to prove that they are capable, but we spend as much time defending ourselves as we do fixing the research group's design errors."

Choy's latest troubles occurred when Doc excitedly told Hunt (Resonus' CEO) about new nano-processor technology that he wanted to install in the forthcoming high-end hearing aid product. As with most of Doc's previous last-minute revisions, Hunt endorsed this change and asked Choy and Blanc (the production director) to show their commitment, even though production was scheduled to begin in less than three weeks. Choy wanted to protest, knowing that his department would have to tackle unexpected incompatibility design errors. Instead, he quietly agreed to Hunt's request to avoid acting like his predecessor and facing similar consequences. Blanc curtly stated that her group was ready if Choy's ESD unit could get accurate production specifications ready on time and if the sales director would stop making wild delivery promises to customers.

When Doc's revised design specs arrived more than a week later, Choy's group discovered numerous incompatibilities that had to be corrected. Even though several ESD staff were assigned to 12-hour days on the revisions, the final production specifications weren't ready until a couple of days after the deadline. Production returned these specs two days later, noting several elements that required revision because they were too costly or difficult to manufacture in their current form. By that time, the production director had to give priority to other jobs and move the new hearing aid product further down the queue. This meant that manufacturing of the new product was delayed by at least two months. The sales director was furious and implied that Frank Choy's incompetence was to blame for this catastrophe.

Case 11   The Shipping Industry Accounting Team

By Steven L. McShane, The University of Western Australia

For the past five years, I have been working at McKay, Sanderson, and Smith Associates, a mid-sized accounting firm in Halifax that specializes in commercial accounting and audits. My particular speciality is accounting practices for shipping companies, ranging from small fishing fleets to a couple of the big firms with ships on the St. Lawrence Seaway.

About 18 months ago, McKay, Sanderson, and Smith Associates became part of a large merger involving two other accounting firms across Canada. These firms have offices in Montreal, Ottawa, Toronto, Calgary, and Vancouver. Although the other two accounting firms were much larger than McKay, all three firms agreed to avoid centralizing the business around one office in Toronto. Instead, the new firm—called Goldberg, Choo, and McKay Associates—would rely on teams across the country to "leverage the synergies of our collective knowledge" (an often-cited statement from the managing partner soon after the merger).

The merger began to affect me a year ago when my boss (a senior partner and vice-president of the merger firm) announced that I would be working more closely with three people from the other two firms to become the firm's new shipping industry accounting team. The other "team members" were Rochelle in Montreal, Thomas in Toronto, and Brad in Vancouver. I had met Rochelle briefly at a meeting in Montreal during the merger. I have never met Thomas or Brad, but was informed during the integration meetings that they were shipping accounting professionals at the other firms.

Initially, the shipping "team" activities involved emailing each other about new contracts and prospective clients. Later, we were asked to submit joint monthly reports on accounting statements and issues. Normally, I submitted my own monthly reports that summarize activities involving my own clients. Coordinating the monthly report with three other people took much more time, particularly since different accounting documentation procedures across the three firms were still being resolved. It took numerous emails and a few telephone calls to work out a reasonable monthly report style.

During this aggravating process, it became apparent—to me at least—that this "teams" business was costing me more time than it was worth. Moreover, Brad in Vancouver didn't have a clue as to how to communicate with the rest of us. He rarely replied to emails. Instead, he often used the telephone voicemail system, which resulted in lots of telephone tag. Brad arrives at work at 9 a.m. in Vancouver (and is often late!), which is early afternoon in Halifax. I typically have a flexible work schedule from 7:30 a.m. to 3:30 p.m. so I can chauffeur my kids after school to sports and music lessons. So Brad and I have a window of less than three hours to share information.

The biggest nuisance with the shipping specialist accounting team started two weeks ago when the firm asked the four of us to develop a new strategy for attracting more shipping firm business. This new strategic plan is a messy business. Somehow, we have to share our thoughts on various approaches, agree on a new plan, and write a unified submission to the managing partner. Already, the project is taking most of my time just writing and responding to emails, and participating in conference calls (which none of us did much before the team formed).

Thomas and Rochelle have already had two or three "misunderstandings" via email about their different perspectives on delicate matters in the strategic plan. The worst of these disagreements required a conference call with all of us to resolve. Except for the most basic matters, it seems that we can't understand each other, let alone agree on key issues. I have come to the conclusion that I would never want Brad to work in my Halifax office (thank goodness, he's on the other side of the country). While Rochelle and I seem to agree on most points, the overall team can't form a common vision or strategy. I don't know how Rochelle, Thomas, or Brad feel, but I would be quite happy to work somewhere that did not require any of these long-distance team headaches.

Case 12   Treetop Forest Products

By Steven L. McShane, The University of Western Australia, and David Lebeter

Treetop Forest Products Ltd. is a sawmill operation in British Columbia, that is owned by a major forest products company, but operates independently of headquarters. It was built 30 years ago, and completely updated with new machinery five years ago. Treetop receives raw logs from the area for cutting and planing into building-grade lumber, mostly 2-by-4 and 2-by-6 pieces of standard lengths. Higher grade logs leave Treetop's sawmill department in finished form and are sent directly to the packaging department. The remaining 40 percent of sawmill output are cuts from lower grade logs, requiring further work by the planing department.

Treetop has one general manager, 16 supervisors and support staff, and 180 unionized employees. The unionized employees are paid an hourly rate specified in the collective agreement, whereas management and support staff are paid a monthly salary. The mill is divided into six operating departments: boom, sawmill, planer, packaging, shipping, and maintenance. The sawmill, boom, and packaging departments operate a morning shift starting at 6 a.m. and an afternoon shift starting at 2 p.m. Employees in these departments rotate shifts every two weeks. The planer and shipping departments operate only morning shifts. Maintenance employees work the night shift (starting at 10 p.m.).

Each department, except for packaging, has a supervisor on every work shift. The planer supervisor is responsible for the packaging department on the morning shift, and the sawmill supervisor is responsible for the packaging department on the afternoon shift. However, the packaging operation is housed in a separate building from the other departments, so supervisors seldom visit the packaging department. This is particularly true for the afternoon shift, because the sawmill supervisor is the furthest distance from the packaging building.

Packaging Quality

Ninety percent of Treetop's product is sold on the international market through Westboard Co., a large marketing agency. Westboard represents all forest products mills owned by Treetop's parent company as well as several other clients in the region. The market for building-grade lumber is very price competitive, because there are numerous mills selling a relatively undifferentiated product. However, some differentiation does occur in product packaging and presentation. Buyers will look closely at the packaging when deciding whether to buy from Treetop or another mill.

To encourage its clients to package their products better, Westboard sponsors a monthly package quality award. The marketing agency samples and rates its clients' packages daily, and the sawmill with the highest score at the end of the month is awarded a plaque. Package quality is a combination of how the lumber is piled (e.g., defects turned in), where the bands and dunnage are placed, how neatly the stencil and seal are applied, the stencil's accuracy, and how neatly and tightly the plastic wrap is attached.

Treetop Forest Products won Westboard's packaging quality award several times over the past five years, and received high ratings in the months that it didn't win. However, the mill's ratings have started to decline over the past year or two, and several clients have complained about the appearance of the finished product. A few large customers switched to competitors' lumber, saying that the decision was based on the substandard appearance of Treetop's packaging when it arrived in their lumber yard.

Bottleneck in Packaging

The planing and sawmilling departments have significantly increased productivity over the past couple of years. The sawmill operation recently set a new productivity record on a single day. The planer operation has increased productivity to the point where last year it reduced operations to just one (rather than two) shifts per day. These productivity improvements are due to better operator training, fewer machine breakdowns, and better selection of raw logs. (Sawmill cuts from high-quality logs usually do not require planing work.)

Productivity levels in the boom, shipping, and maintenance departments have remained constant. However, the packaging department has recorded decreasing productivity over the past couple of years, with the result that a large backlog of finished product is typically stockpiled outside the packaging building. The morning shift of the packaging department is unable to keep up with the combined production of the sawmill and planer departments, so the unpackaged output is left for the afternoon shift. Unfortunately, the afternoon shift packages even less product than the morning shift, so the backlog continues to build. The backlog adds to Treetop's inventory costs and increases the risk of damaged stock.

Treetop has added Saturday overtime shifts as well as extra hours before and after the regular shifts for the packaging department employees to process this backlog. Last month, the packaging department employed 10 percent of the workforce but accounted for 85 percent of the overtime. This is frustrating to Treetop's management, because time and motion studies recently confirmed that the packaging department is capable of processing all of the daily sawmill and planer production without overtime. Moreover, with employees earning one and a half or two times their regular pay on overtime, Treetop's cost competitiveness suffers.

Employees and supervisors at Treetop are aware that people in the packaging department tend to extend lunch by 10 minutes and coffee breaks by 5 minutes. They also typically leave work a few minutes before the end of shift. This abuse has worsened recently, particularly on the afternoon shift. Employees who are temporarily assigned to the packaging department also seem to participate in this time loss pattern after a few days. Although they are punctual and productive in other departments, these temporary employees soon adopt the packaging crew's informal schedule when assigned to that department.

Theory Building and Systematic Research Methods

THEORY BUILDING

theory A general set of propositions that describes interrelationships among several concepts.

People need to make sense of their world, so they form theories about the way the world operates. A **theory** is a general set of propositions that describes interrelationships among several concepts. We form theories for the purpose of predicting and explaining the world around us.[1] What does a good theory look like? First, it should be stated as clearly and simply as possible so that the concepts can be measured and there is no ambiguity regarding the theory's propositions. Second, the elements of the theory must be logically consistent with each other, because we cannot test anything that doesn't make sense. Third, a good theory provides value to society; it helps people understand their world better than they would without the theory.[2]

Theory building is a continuous process that typically includes the inductive and deductive stages shown in Exhibit A.1.[3] The inductive stage draws on personal experience to form a preliminary theory, whereas the deductive stage uses the scientific method to test the theory.

The inductive stage of theory building involves observing the world around us, identifying a pattern of relationships, and then forming a theory from these personal observations. For example, you might casually notice that new employees want their supervisor to give direction, whereas this leadership style irritates long-service employees. From these observations, you form a theory about the effectiveness of directive leadership. (See Chapter 12 for a discussion of this leadership style.)

Exhibit A.1 THEORY BUILDING AND THEORY TESTING

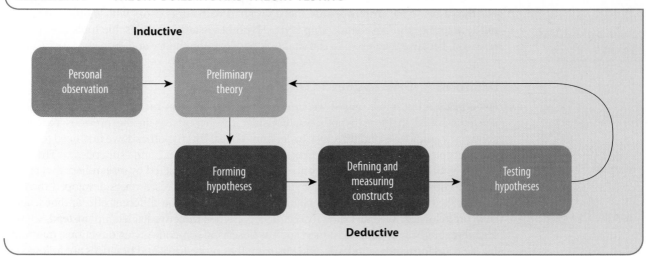

POSITIVISM VERSUS INTERPRETIVISM

positivism A view held in quantitative research in which reality exists independent of the perceptions and interpretations of people.

Research requires an interpretation of reality, and researchers tend to perceive reality in one of two ways. A common view, called **positivism,** is that reality exists independent of the perceptions and interpretations of people. It is "out there" to be discovered and tested. Positivism is the foundation for most quantitative research (statistical analysis). It assumes that we can measure variables and those variables have fixed relationships with other variables. For example, the positivist perspective says that we could study whether a supportive style of leadership reduces stress. If we find evidence that it does, then someone else studying leadership and stress would "discover" the same relationship.

interpretivism The view held in many qualitative studies that reality comes from shared meaning among people in a particular environment.

Interpretivism takes a different view of reality. It suggests that reality comes from shared meaning among people in a particular environment. For example, supportive leadership is a personal interpretation of reality, not something that can be measured across time and people. Interpretivists rely mainly on qualitative data, such as observation and nondirective interviews. They particularly listen to the language people use to understand the common meaning that people have toward various events or phenomena. For example, they might argue that you need to experience and observe supportive leadership to effectively study it. Moreover, you can't really predict relationships because the specific situation shapes reality.[4]

Most OB scholars identify themselves somewhere between the extreme views of positivism and interpretivism. Many believe that inductive research should begin with an interpretivist angle. We should consider a new topic with an open mind and search for shared meaning among people in the situation being studied. In other words, researchers should let the participants define reality rather than let the researcher's preconceived notions shape that reality. This process involves gathering qualitative information and letting this information shape their theory.[5] After the theory emerges, researchers shift to the positivist perspective by quantitatively testing relationships in that theory.

THEORY TESTING: THE DEDUCTIVE PROCESS

hypotheses Statements making empirically testable declarations that certain variables and their corresponding measures are related in a specific way proposed by the theory.

Once a theory has been formed, we shift into the deductive stage of theory building. This process includes forming hypotheses, defining and measuring constructs, and testing hypotheses (see Exhibit A.1). **Hypotheses** make empirically testable declarations that certain variables and their corresponding measures are related in a specific way proposed by the theory. For instance, to find support for the directive leadership theory described earlier, we need to form and then test a specific hypothesis from that theory. One such hypothesis might be: "New employees are more satisfied with supervisors who exhibit a directive rather than nondirective leadership style." Hypotheses are indispensable tools of scientific research, because they provide the vital link between the theory and empirical verification.

DEFINING AND MEASURING CONSTRUCTS

constructs Abstract ideas constructed by researchers that can be linked to observable information.

Hypotheses are testable only if we can define and then form measurable indicators of the concepts stated in those hypotheses. Consider the hypothesis in the previous paragraph about new employees and directive leadership. To test this hypothesis, we first need to define the concepts, such as "new employees," "directive leadership," and "supervisor." These are known as **constructs,** because they are abstract ideas constructed by researchers that can be linked to observable information. Organizational behaviour researchers developed the construct called *directive leadership* to help them understand the different effects that leaders have on followers. We can't directly see, taste, or smell directive leadership; instead, we rely on indirect indicators of its existence, such as observing someone giving directions, maintaining clear performance standards, and ensuring that procedures and practices are followed.

As you can see, defining constructs well is very important because these definitions become the foundation for finding or developing acceptable measures of those constructs. We can't measure directive leadership if we have only a vague idea about what this concept means. The better the construct is defined, the better our chances of finding or developing a good measure of that construct. However, even with a good definition, constructs can be difficult to measure, because the empirical representation must capture several elements in the definition. A measure of directive leadership must be able to identify not only people who give directions, but also those who maintain performance standards and ensure that procedures are followed.

TESTING HYPOTHESES

The third step in the deductive process is to collect data for the empirical measures of the variables. Following our directive leadership example, we might conduct a formal survey in which new employees indicate the behaviour of their supervisors and their attitudes toward their supervisors. Alternatively, we might design an experiment in which people work with someone who applies either a directive or a nondirective leadership style. When the data have been collected, we can use various procedures to statistically test our hypotheses.

A major concern in theory building is that some researchers might inadvertently find support for their theory simply because they use the same information used to form the theory during the inductive stage. Consequently, the deductive stage must collect new data that are completely independent of the data used during the inductive stage. For instance, you might decide to test your theory of directive leadership by studying employees in another organization. Moreover, the inductive process may have relied mainly on personal observation, whereas the deductive process might use survey questionnaires. By studying different samples and using different measurement tools, we minimize the risk of conducting circular research.

USING THE SCIENTIFIC METHOD

scientific method A set of principles and procedures that help researchers to systematically understand previously unexplained events and conditions.

Earlier, we said that the deductive stage of theory building follows the scientific method. The **scientific method** is a systematic, controlled, empirical, and critical investigation of hypothetical propositions about the presumed relationships among natural phenomena.[6] There are several elements to this definition, so let's look at each one. First, scientific research is *systematic and controlled*, because researchers want to rule out all but one explanation for a set of interrelated events. To rule out alternative explanations, we need to control them in some way, such as by keeping them constant or removing them entirely from the environment.

Second, we say that scientific research is *empirical* because researchers need to use objective reality—or as close as we can get to it—to test a theory. They measure observable elements of the environment, such as what a person says or does, rather than relying on their own subjective opinion to draw conclusions. Moreover, scientific research analyzes these data using acceptable principles of mathematics and logic.

Third, scientific research involves *critical investigation*. This means that the study's hypotheses, data, methods, and results are openly described so that other experts in the field can properly evaluate the research. It also means that scholars are encouraged to critique and build on previous research. The scientific method encourages the refinement and eventually the replacement of a particular theory with one that better suits our understanding of the world.

GROUNDED THEORY: AN ALTERNATIVE APPROACH

grounded theory A process of developing knowledge through the constant interplay of data collection, analysis, and theory development.

The scientific method dominates the quantitative approach to systematic research, but another approach, called **grounded theory,** dominates research using qualitative methods.[7] Grounded theory is a process of developing knowledge through the constant interplay of data collection, analysis, and theory development. It relies mainly on qualitative methods to form categories and variables, analyze relationships among these concepts, and form a model based on the observations and analysis. Grounded theory combines the inductive stages of theory development by cycling back and forth between data collection and analysis to converge on a robust explanatory model. This ongoing reciprocal process results in theory that is grounded in the data (thus, the name grounded theory).

Like the scientific method, grounded theory is a systematic and rigorous process of data collection and analysis. It requires specific steps and documentation, and adopts a positivist view by assuming that the results are generalizable to other settings. However, grounded theory also takes an interpretivist view by building categories and variables from the perceived realities of the subjects rather than from an assumed universal truth.[8] It also recognizes that personal biases are not easily removed from the research process.

SELECTED ISSUES IN ORGANIZATIONAL BEHAVIOUR RESEARCH

There are many issues to consider in theory building, particularly when we use the deductive process to test hypotheses. Some of the more important issues are sampling, causation, and ethical practices in organizational research.

SAMPLING IN ORGANIZATIONAL RESEARCH

When finding out why things happen in organizations, we typically gather information from a few sources and then draw conclusions about the larger population. If we survey several employees and determine that older employees are more loyal to their company, then we would like to generalize this statement to all older employees in our population, not just those whom we surveyed. Scientific inquiry generally requires that researchers engage in **representative sampling**—that is, sampling a population in such a way that we can extrapolate the results of the sample to the larger population.

representative sampling
The process of sampling a population in such a way that one can extrapolate the results of that sample to the larger population.

One factor that influences representativeness is whether the sample is selected in an unbiased way from the larger population. Let's suppose that you want to study organizational commitment among employees in your organization. A casual procedure might result in sampling too few employees from the head office and too many located elsewhere in the country. If head office employees actually have higher loyalty than employees located elsewhere, the biased sampling would cause the results to underestimate the true level of loyalty among employees in the company. If you repeat the process again next year but somehow overweight employees from the head office, the results might wrongly suggest that employees have increased their organizational commitment over the past year. In reality, the only change may be the direction of sampling bias.

How do we minimize sampling bias? The answer is to randomly select the sample. A randomly drawn sample gives each member of the population an equal probability of being chosen, so there is less likelihood that a subgroup within that population will dominate the study's results.

The same principle applies to random assignment of subjects to groups in experimental designs. If we want to test the effects of a team development training program, we need to randomly place some employees in the training group and randomly place others in a group that does not receive training. Without this random selection, each group might have different types of employees, so we wouldn't know whether the training explains the differences between the two groups. Moreover, if employees respond differently to the training program, we couldn't be sure that the training program results are representative of the larger population. Of course, random sampling does not necessarily produce a perfectly representative sample, but we do know that it is the best approach to ensure unbiased selection.

The other factor that influences representativeness is sample size. Whenever we select a portion of the population, there will be some error in our estimate of the population values. The larger the sample, the less error will occur in our estimate. Let's suppose that you want to find out how employees in a 500-person firm feel about viewing social media (e.g., Facebook) at work. If you asked 400 of those employees, the information would provide a very good estimate of how the entire workforce in that organization feels. If you survey only

100 employees, the estimate might deviate more from the true population. If you ask only 10 people, the estimate could be quite different from what all 500 employees feel.

Notice that sample size goes hand in hand with random selection. You must have a sufficiently large sample size for the principle of randomization to work effectively. In our example of attitudes toward social media, we would do a poor job of random selection if our sample consisted of only 10 employees from the 500-person organization. The reason is that these 10 people probably wouldn't capture the diversity of employees throughout the organization. In fact, the more diverse the population, the larger the sample size should be, to provide adequate representation through random selection.

CAUSATION IN ORGANIZATIONAL RESEARCH

Theories present notions about relationships among constructs. Often, these propositions suggest a causal relationship, namely, that one variable has an effect on another variable. When discussing causation, we refer to variables as being independent or dependent. *Independent variables* are the presumed causes of *dependent variables,* which are the presumed effects. In our earlier example of directive leadership, the main independent variable (there might be others) would be the supervisor's directive or nondirective leadership style, because we presume that it causes the dependent variable (satisfaction with supervision).

In laboratory experiments (described later), the independent variable is always manipulated by the experimenter. In our research on directive leadership, we might have subjects (new employees) work with supervisors who exhibit directive or nondirective leadership behaviours. If subjects are more satisfied under the directive leaders, we would be able to infer an association between the independent and dependent variables.

Researchers must satisfy three conditions to provide sufficient evidence of causality between two variables.[9] The first condition of causality is that the variables are empirically associated with each other. An association exists whenever one measure of a variable changes systematically with a measure of another variable. This condition of causality is the easiest to satisfy, because there are several well-known statistical measures of association. A research study might find, for instance, that heterogeneous groups (in which members come from diverse backgrounds) produce more creative solutions to problems. This might be apparent because the measure of creativity (such as number of creative solutions produced within a fixed time) is higher for teams that have a high score on the measure of group heterogeneity. They are statistically associated or correlated with each other.

The second condition of causality is that the independent variable precedes the dependent variable in time. Sometimes, this condition is satisfied through simple logic. In our group heterogeneity example, it doesn't make sense to say that the number of creative solutions caused the group's heterogeneity, because the group's heterogeneity existed before the group produced the creative solutions. In other situations, however, the temporal relationship among variables is less clear. One example is the ongoing debate about job satisfaction and organizational commitment. Do companies develop more loyal employees by increasing their job satisfaction, or do changes in organizational loyalty cause changes in job satisfaction? Simple logic does not answer these questions; instead, researchers must use sophisticated longitudinal studies to build up evidence of a temporal relationship between these two variables.

The third requirement for evidence of a causal relationship is that the statistical association between two variables cannot be explained by a third variable. There are many associations that we quickly dismiss as being causally related. For example, there is a statistical association between the number of storks in an area and the birth rate in that area. We know that storks don't bring babies, so something else must cause the association between these two variables. The real explanation is that both storks and birth rates have a higher incidence in rural areas.

In other studies, the third variable effect is less apparent. Many years ago, before polio vaccines were available, a study in the United States reported a surprisingly strong association between consumption of a certain soft drink and the incidence of polio. Was polio caused by drinking this pop, or did people with polio have a unusual craving for this beverage? Neither. Both polio and consumption of the pop drink were caused by a third variable: climate. There was a higher incidence of polio in the summer months and in warmer climates, and people drink more liquids in these climates.[10] As you can see from this example, researchers have a difficult time supporting causal inferences, because third variable effects are sometimes difficult to detect.

ETHICS IN ORGANIZATIONAL RESEARCH

Organizational behaviour researchers need to abide by the ethical standards of the society in which the research is conducted. One of the most important ethical considerations is the individual subject's freedom to participate in the study. For example, it is inappropriate to force employees to fill out a questionnaire or attend an experimental intervention for research purposes only. Moreover, researchers have an obligation to tell potential subjects about any possible risks inherent in the study so that participants can make an informed choice about whether to be involved.

Finally, researchers must be careful to protect the privacy of those who participate in the study. This usually includes letting people know when they are being studied as well as guaranteeing that their individual information will remain confidential (unless publication of identities is otherwise granted). Researchers maintain anonymity through careful security of data. The research results usually aggregate data in numbers large enough that they do not reveal the opinions or characteristics of any specific individual. For example, we would report the average absenteeism of employees in a department rather than state the absence rates of each person. When researchers are sharing data with other researchers, it is usually necessary to specially code each case so that individual identities are not known.

RESEARCH DESIGN STRATEGIES

So far, we have described how to build a theory, including the specific elements of empirically testing the theory within the standards of scientific inquiry. But what are the different ways to design a research study so that we get the data necessary to achieve our research objectives? There are many strategies, but they mainly fall under three headings: laboratory experiments, field surveys, and observational research.

LABORATORY EXPERIMENTS

laboratory experiment
Any research study in which independent variables and variables outside the researcher's main focus of inquiry can be controlled to some extent.

A **laboratory experiment** is any research study in which independent variables and variables outside the researcher's main focus of inquiry can be controlled to some extent. Laboratory experiments are usually located outside the everyday work environment, such as in a classroom, simulation lab, or any other artificial setting in which the researcher can manipulate the environment. Organizational behaviour researchers sometimes conduct experiments in the workplace (called *field experiments*) in which the independent variable is manipulated. However, researchers have less control over the effects of extraneous factors in field experiments than they have in laboratory situations.

Advantages of Laboratory Experiments   There are many advantages of laboratory experiments. By definition, this research method offers a high degree of control over extraneous variables that would otherwise confound the relationships being studied. Suppose we wanted to test the effects of directive leadership on the satisfaction of new employees. One concern might be that employees are influenced by how much leadership is provided, not just the type of leadership style. An experimental design would allow us to control how often the supervisor exhibited this style so that this extraneous variable does not confound the results.

A second advantage of lab studies is that the independent and dependent variables can be developed more precisely than is possible in a field setting. For example, the researcher can ensure that supervisors in a lab study apply specific directive or nondirective behaviours, whereas real-life supervisors would use a more complex mixture of leadership behaviours. By using more precise measures, we are more certain that we are measuring the intended construct. Thus, if new employees are more satisfied with supervisors in the directive leadership condition, we are more confident that the independent variable was directive leadership rather than some other leadership style.

A third benefit of laboratory experiments is that the independent variable can be distributed more evenly among participants. In our directive leadership study, we can ensure that approximately half of the subjects have a directive supervisor, whereas the other half have a nondirective supervisor. In natural settings, we might have trouble finding people who have worked with a nondirective leader and, consequently, we couldn't determine the effects of this condition.

Disadvantages of Laboratory Experiments

With these powerful advantages, you might wonder why laboratory experiments are the least appreciated form of organizational behaviour research.[11] One obvious limitation of this research method is that it lacks realism, and thus the results might be different in the real world. One argument is that laboratory experiment subjects are less involved than their counterparts in an actual work situation. This is sometimes true, although many lab studies have highly motivated participants. Another criticism is that the extraneous variables controlled in the lab setting might produce a different effect of the independent variable on the dependent variables. This might also be true, but remember that the experimental design controls variables in accordance with the theory and its hypotheses. Consequently, this concern is really a critique of the theory, not the lab study.

Finally, there is the well-known problem that participants are aware they are being studied and this causes them to act differently than they normally would. Some participants try to figure out how the researcher wants them to behave and then deliberately try to act that way. Other participants try to upset the experiment by doing just the opposite of what they believe the researcher expects. Still others might act unnaturally simply because they know they are being observed. Fortunately, experimenters are well aware of these potential problems and are usually (although not always) successful at disguising the study's true intent.

FIELD SURVEYS

Field surveys collect and analyze information in a natural environment—an office, a factory, or some other existing location. The researcher takes a snapshot of reality and tries to determine whether elements of that situation (including the attitudes and behaviours of people in that situation) are associated with each other as hypothesized. Everyone does some sort of field research. You might think that people from some provinces are better drivers than others, so you "test" your theory by looking at the way people with out-of-province licence plates drive. Although your methods of data collection might not satisfy scientific standards, this is a form of field research because it takes information from a naturally occurring situation.

Advantages and Disadvantages of Field Surveys

One advantage of field surveys is that the variables often have a more powerful effect than they would in a laboratory experiment. Consider the effect of peer pressure on the behaviour of members within the team. In a natural environment, team members would form very strong cohesive bonds over time, whereas a researcher would have difficulty replicating this level of cohesiveness and corresponding peer pressure in a lab setting.

Another advantage of field surveys is that the researcher can study many variables simultaneously, thereby permitting a fuller test of more complex theories. Ironically, this is also a disadvantage of field surveys because it is difficult for the researcher to contain his or her scientific inquiry. There is a tendency to shift from deductive hypothesis testing to more inductive exploratory browsing through the data. If these two activities become mixed together, the researcher can lose sight of the strict covenants of scientific inquiry.

The main weakness with field surveys is that it is very difficult to satisfy the conditions for causal conclusions. One reason is that the data are usually collected at one point in time, so the researcher must rely on logic to decide whether the independent variable really preceded the dependent variable. Contrast this with the lab study in which the researcher can usually be confident that the independent variable was applied before the dependent variable occurred. Increasingly, organizational behaviour studies use longitudinal research to provide a better indicator of temporal relations among variables, but this is still not as precise as the lab setting. Another reason why causal analysis is difficult in field surveys is that extraneous variables are not controlled as they are in lab studies. Without this control, there is a higher chance that a third variable might explain the relationship between the hypothesized independent and dependent variables.

OBSERVATIONAL RESEARCH

In their study of brainstorming and creativity, Robert Sutton and Andrew Hargadon observed 24 brainstorming sessions at IDEO, a product design firm in Palo Alto, California. They also attended a dozen "Monday morning meetings,"conducted 60 semi-structured interviews with IDEO executives and designers, held hundreds of informal discussions with these people, and read through several dozen magazine articles about the company.[12]

Sutton and Hargadon's use of observational research and other qualitative methods was quite appropriate for their research objectives, which was to re-examine the effectiveness of brainstorming beyond the number of ideas generated. Observational research generates a wealth of descriptive accounts about the drama of human existence in organizations. It is a useful vehicle for learning about the complex dynamics of people and their activities, such as brainstorming. (Sutton and Hargadon's study is cited in Chapter 8 on team dynamics.)

Participant observation takes the observation method one step further by having the observer take part in the organization's activities. This experience gives the researcher a fuller understanding of the activities compared to just watching others participate in those activities.

In spite of its intuitive appeal, observational research has a number of weaknesses. The main problem is that the observer is subject to the perceptual screening and organizing biases that we discuss in Chapter 3 of this textbook. There is a tendency to overlook the routine aspects of organizational life, even though they may prove to be the most important data for research purposes. Instead, observers tend to focus on unusual information, such as activities that deviate from what the observer expects. Because observational research usually records only what the observer notices, valuable information is often lost.

Another concern with the observation method is that the researcher's presence and involvement may influence the people whom he or she is studying. This can be a problem in short-term observations, but in the long term people tend to return to their usual behaviour patterns. With ongoing observations, such as Sutton and Hargadon's study of brainstorming sessions at IDEO, employees eventually forget that they are being studied.

Finally, observation is usually a qualitative process, so it is more difficult to empirically test hypotheses with the data. Instead, observational research provides rich information for the inductive stages of theory building. It helps us to form ideas about the way things work in organizations. We begin to see relationships that lay the foundation for new perspectives and theory. We must not confuse this inductive process of theory building with the deductive process of theory testing.

Scoring Keys for Self-Assessment Exercises

The following pages provide scoring keys for self-assessments that are fully presented in this textbook. These self-assessments, as well as the self-assessments that are only summarized in this book, can also be scored automatically at McGraw-Hill CONNECT.

CHAPTER 2
SCORING KEY FOR THE INTROVERSION-EXTROVERSION SCALE

Scoring Instructions: Use the table below to assign numbers to each box you checked. For example, if you checked "Moderately inaccurate" for statement #1 ("I feel comfortable around people."), you would assign a "1" to that statement. After assigning numbers for all 10 statements, add up the numbers to estimate your introversion-extroversion personality.

For statement items 1, 2, 6, 8, 9:	For statement items 3, 4, 5, 7, 10:
Very accurate description of me = 4	Very accurate description of me = 0
Moderately accurate = 3	Moderately accurate = 1
Neither accurate nor inaccurate = 2	Neither accurate nor inaccurate = 2
Moderately inaccurate = 1	Moderately inaccurate = 3
Very inaccurate description of me = 0	Very inaccurate description of me = 4

Interpreting Your Score: Extroversion characterizes people who are outgoing, talkative, sociable, and assertive. It includes several facets, such as friendliness, gregariousness, assertiveness, activity level, excitement-seeking, and cheerfulness. The opposite of extroversion is introversion, which refers to the personality characteristics of being quiet, shy, and cautious. Extroverts get their energy from the outer world (people and things around them), whereas introverts get their energy from the internal world, such as personal reflection on concepts and ideas. Introverts are more inclined to direct their interests to ideas rather than to social events.

This is the short version of the IPIP Introversion-Extroversion Scale, so it estimates overall introversion-extroversion but not specific facets within the personality dimension. Scores range from 0 to 40. Low scores indicate introversion; high scores indicate extroversion. The norms in the following table are estimated from results of early adults (under 30 years old) in Scotland and undergraduate psychology students in the United States. However, introversion-extroversion norms vary from one group to the next; the best norms are likely based on the entire class you are attending or with past students in this course.

IPIP Introversion-Extroversion Norms	
IPIP Introversion-Extroversion	**Interpretation**
35–40	High extroversion
28–34	Moderate extroversion
21–27	In-between extroversion and introversion
7–20	Moderate introversion
0–6	High introversion

CHAPTER 3
SCORING KEY FOR THE WORK CENTRALITY SCALE

Scoring Instructions: Use the table below to assign numbers to each box you checked. For example, if you checked "Moderately disagree" for statement #3 ("Work should be only a small part of one's life."), you would assign a "5" to that statement. After assigning numbers for all six statements, add up your scores to estimate your level of work centrality.

For statement items 1, 2, 4, 5, 6:	For statement item 3:
Strongly agree = 6	Strongly agree = 1
Moderately agree = 5	Moderately agree = 2
Slightly agree = 4	Slightly agree = 3
Slightly disagree = 3	Slightly disagree = 4
Moderately disagree = 2	Moderately disagree = 5
Strongly disagree = 1	Strongly disagree = 6

Interpreting Your Score: The work centrality scale measures the extent that work is an important part of the individual's self-concept. People with high work centrality define themselves mainly by their work roles and view nonwork roles as much less significant. Consequently, people with a high work centrality score likely have lower complexity in their self-concept. This can be a concern because if something goes wrong with their work role, their nonwork roles are not of sufficient value to maintain a positive self-evaluation. At the same time, work dominates our work lives, so those with very low scores would be more of the exception than the rule in most societies.

Scores range from 6 to 36 with higher scores indicating higher work centrality. The norms in the following table are based on a large sample of Canadian employees (average score was 20.7). However, work centrality norms vary from one group to the next. For example, the average score in a sample of Canadian nurses was around 17 (translated to the scale range used here).

Work Centrality Norms	
Work Centrality Score	**Interpretation**
29–36	High work centrality
24–28	Above average work centrality
18–23	Average work centrality
13–17	Below average work centrality
6–12	Low work centrality

CHAPTER 4

SCORING KEY FOR THE EMOTIONAL INTELLIGENCE SELF-ASSESSMENT

Scoring Instructions: Use the table below to assign numbers to each box you checked. Insert the number for each statement on the appropriate line below the table. For example, if you checked "Moderately disagree" for statement #1 ("I tend to describe my emotions accurately."), you would write a "2" on the line with "(1)" underneath it. After assigning numbers for all 16 statements, add up your scores to estimate your self-assessed emotional intelligence on the four dimensions and overall score.

For statement items 1, 2, 3, 4, 6, 7, 9, 10, 11, 13, 14, 16:	For statement items 5, 8, 12, 15:
Strongly agree = 6	Strongly agree = 1
Moderately agree = 5	Moderately agree = 2
Slightly agree = 4	Slightly agree = 3
Slightly disagree = 3	Slightly disagree = 4
Moderately disagree = 2	Moderately disagree = 5
Strongly disagree = 1	Strongly disagree = 6

Emotional Intelligence Dimension	Calculation	Your Score
Self-awareness of emotions	____ + ____ + ____ + ____ = (1) (7) (9) (12)	_____
Self-management of emotions	____ + ____ + ____ + ____ = (2) (5) (10) (14)	_____
Awareness of others' emotions	____ + ____ + ____ + ____ = (3) (6) (13) (15)	_____
Management of others' emotions	____ + ____ + ____ + ____ = (4) (8) (11) (16)	_____
Emotional intelligence total	Add up all dimension scores =	_____

Interpreting Your Scores: This scale measures the four dimensions of emotional intelligence described in this book. The four dimensions are defined as follows:

- **Self-awareness of emotions:** This is the ability to perceive and understand the meaning of your own emotions.

- **Self-management of emotions:** This is the ability to manage your own emotions. It includes generating or suppressing emotions and displaying behaviours that represent desired emotions in a particular situation.

- **Awareness of others' emotions:** This is the ability to perceive and understand the emotions of other people, including the practices of empathy and awareness of social phenomena such as organizational politics.

- **Management of others' emotions:** This is the ability to manage other people's emotions. It includes generating or suppressing emotions in other people, such as reducing their sadness and increasing their motivation.

Scores on the four Emotional Intelligence Self-Assessment dimensions range from 4 to 20. The overall score ranges from 16 to 80. Norms vary from one group to the next. The following table shows norms from a sample of 75 MBA students in two countries (Australia and Singapore). For example, the top 10 percentile for Self-awareness of emotions is 19, indicating that 10 percent of people score 19 or 20 and 90 percent score below 19 on this dimension. Keep in mind that these scores represent self-perceptions. Evaluations from others (such as through 360-degree feedback) may provide a more accurate estimate of your emotional intelligence on some (not necessarily all) dimensions.

		Emotional Intelligence Self-Assessment Norms			
Percentile	**Self-awareness of emotions**	**Self-management of emotions**	**Awareness of others' emotions**	**Management of others' emotions**	**TOTAL**
Average score	16.3	14.9	14.3	14.6	60.2
Top 10 percentile	19	19	18	18	71
Top 25th percentile	18	17	16	17	64
Median (50th percentile)	16	15	15	15	60
Bottom 25th percentile	15	13	13	13	56
Bottom 10 percentile	14	11	11	10	51

CHAPTER 5
SCORING KEY FOR THE PERSONAL NEEDS QUESTIONNAIRE

Scoring Instructions: Use the table below to assign numbers to each box you checked. Insert the number for each statement on the appropriate line below the table. For example, if you checked "Moderately inaccurate" for statement #1 ("I would rather be myself than be well thought of."), you would write a "3" on the line with "(1)" underneath it. After assigning numbers for all 15 statements, add up your scores to estimate your results for the two learned needs measured by this scale.

For statement items 2, 3, 4, 5, 6, 8, 9, 12, 14, 15:	For statement items 1, 7, 10, 11, 13:
Very accurate description of me = 4	Very accurate description of me = 0
Moderately accurate = 3	Moderately accurate = 1
Neither accurate nor inaccurate = 2	Neither accurate nor inaccurate = 2
Moderately inaccurate = 1	Moderately inaccurate = 3
Very inaccurate description of me = 0	Very inaccurate description of me = 4

Personal Needs Dimension	Calculation	Your Score
Need for achievement	____ + ____ + ____ + ____ + ____ + ____ + ____ = (2) (3) (6) (7) (9) (12) (14)	_____
Need for social approval	____ + ____ + ____ + ____ + ____ + ____ + ____ + ____ = (1) (4) (5) (8) (10) (11) (13) (15)	_____

Although everyone has the same innate drives, our secondary or learned needs vary based on our personality, values, and self-concept. This self-assessment provides an estimate of your need strength on two learned needs: need for achievement and need for social approval.

Interpreting Your Need for Achievement Score: This scale, formally called "achievement striving," estimates the extent to which you are motivated to take on and achieve challenging personal goals. This includes a desire to perform better than others and to reach one's potential. The scale ranges from 0 to 28. How high or low is your need for achievement? The ideal would be to compare your score with the collective results of other students in your class. Otherwise, the following table offers a rough set of norms with which you can compare your score on this scale.

Need for Achievement Norms	
Need for Achievement Score	**Interpretation**
24–28	High need for achievement
18–23	Above average need for achievement
12–17	Average need for achievement
6–11	Below average need for achievement
0–5	Low need for achievement

Interpreting Your Need for Social Approval Score: The need for social approval scale estimates the extent to which you are motivated to seek favourable evaluation from others. Founded on the drive to bond, the need for social approval is a secondary need, because people vary in this need based on their self-concept, values, personality, and possibly social norms. This scale ranges from 0 to 32. How high or low is your need for social approval? The ideal would be to compare your score with the collective results of other students in your class. Otherwise, the following table offers a rough set of norms on which you can compare your score on this scale.

Need for Social Approval Norms	
Need for Social Approval Score	**Interpretation**
28–32	High need for social approval
20–27	Above average need for social approval
12–19	Average need for social approval
6–11	Below average need for social approval
0–5	Low need for social approval

CHAPTER 6
SCORING KEY FOR THE MONEY ATTITUDE SCALE

Scoring Instructions: This instrument presents three dimensions using a smaller number of items from the original Money Attitude Scale. To calculate your score on each dimension, write the number that you circled in the scale to the corresponding item number in the scoring key below. For example, write the number you circled for the scale's first statement ("I sometimes purchase things . . .") on the line above "Item 1." Then add up the numbers for that dimension. The money attitude total score is calculated by adding up all scores and all dimensions.

Money Attitude Dimension	Calculation	Your Score
Money as power/prestige	____ + ____ + ____ + ____ = (1) (4) (7) (10)	_____
Retention time	____ + ____ + ____ + ____ = (2) (5) (8) (11)	_____
Money anxiety	____ + ____ + ____ + ____ = (3) (6) (9) (12)	_____
Total score	Add up all dimension scores =	_____

Interpreting Your Score: The three Money Attitude Scale dimensions measured here, as well as the total score, are defined as follows:

- **Money as power/prestige:** People with higher scores on this dimension tend to use money to influence and impress others.
- **Retention time:** People with higher scores on this dimension tend to be careful financial planners.
- **Money anxiety:** People with higher scores on this dimension tend to view money as a source of anxiety.
- **Money attitude total:** This is a general estimate of how much respect and attention you give to money.

Scores on the three Money Attitude Scale dimensions range from 4 to 20. The overall score ranges from 12 to 60. Norms vary from one group to the next. The following table shows how a sample of MBA students scored on the Money Attitude Scale. The table shows percentiles, that is, the percentage of people with the same or lower score. For example, the table indicates that a score of "13" on the retention scale is quite low because only 25 percent of students would have scored at this level or lower (75 percent scored higher). However, a score of "12" on the prestige scale is quite high because 75 percent of students score at or below this number (only 25 percent scored higher).

Percentile (% with scores at or below this number)	Prestige Score	Retention Score	Anxiety Score	Total Score
Average score	9.89	14.98	12.78	37.64
Top 10 percentile	13	18	16	44
Top 25th percentile	12	17	15	41
Median (50th percentile)	10	15	13	38
Bottom 25th percentile	8	13	11	33
Bottom 10 percentile	7	11	8	29

CHAPTER 7
SCORING KEY FOR THE CREATIVE PERSONALITY SCALE

Scoring Instructions: Assign a positive point (+1) after each of the following words that you checked off in the self-assessment:

Capable _____	Informal _____	Resourceful _____
Clever _____	Insightful _____	Self-confident _____
Confident _____	Intelligent _____	Sexy _____
Egotistical _____	Inventive _____	Snobbish _____
Humorous _____	Original _____	Unconventional _____
Individualistic _____	Reflective _____	Wide interests _____

Assign a negative point (−1) after each of the following words that you checked off in the self-assessment:

Affected _____	Conventional _____	Narrow interests _____
Cautious _____	Dissatisfied _____	Sincere _____
Commonplace _____	Honest _____	Submissive _____
Conservative _____	Mannerly _____	Suspicious _____

Interpreting Your Score: This instrument estimates your creative potential as a personal characteristic. The scale recognizes that creative people are intelligent and persistent and possess an inventive thinking style. Creative personality varies somewhat from one occupational group to the next. The table below provides norms based on undergraduate and graduate university/college students.

Creative Personality Score	Interpretation
Above +9	You have a high creative personality.
+1 to +9	You have an average creative personality.
Below +1	You have a low creative personality.

CHAPTER 8
SCORING KEY FOR THE TEAM ROLES PREFERENCES SCALE

Scoring Instructions: Write the scores circled for each item on the appropriate line below (statement numbers are in parentheses), and add up each scale.

Team Roles Dimension	Calculation	Your Score
Encourager	_____ + _____ + _____ = (6) (9) (11)	_____
Gatekeeper	_____ + _____ + _____ = (4) (10) (13)	_____
Harmonizer	_____ + _____ + _____ = (3) (8) (12)	_____
Initiator	_____ + _____ + _____ = (1) (5) (14)	_____
Summarizer	_____ + _____ + _____ = (2) (7) (15)	_____

Interpreting Your Score: The five team roles measured here are based on scholarship over the years. The following table defines these five roles and presents the range of scores for high, medium, and low levels of each role. These norms are based on results from a sample of MBA students.

Team Roles Preferences Definitions and Norms	
Team Role and Definition	**Interpretation**
Encourager: People who score high on this dimension have a strong tendency to praise and support the ideas of other team members, thereby showing warmth and solidarity to the group.	High: 12 and above Medium: 9 to 11 Low: 8 and below
Gatekeeper: People who score high on this dimension have a strong tendency to encourage all team members to participate in the discussion.	High: 12 and above Medium: 9 to 11 Low: 8 and below
Harmonizer: People who score high on this dimension have a strong tendency to mediate intragroup conflicts and reduce tension.	High: 11 and above Medium: 9 to 10 Low: 8 and below
Initiator: People who score high on this dimension have a strong tendency to identify goals for the meeting, including ways to work on those goals.	High: 12 and above Medium: 9 to 11 Low: 8 and below
Summarizer: People who score high on this dimension have a strong tendency to keep track of what was said in the meeting (i.e., act as the team's memory).	High: 10 and above Medium: 8 to 9 Low: 7 and below

CHAPTER 9
SCORING KEY FOR THE ACTIVE LISTENING SKILLS INVENTORY

Scoring Instructions: Use the first table below to score the response you marked for each statement. Then, in the second table on the next page, write that score on the line corresponding to the statement number (statement numbers are in parentheses) and add up each subscale. For example, if you checked "Seldom" for statement #1 ("I keep an open mind . . ."), you would write a "2" on the line with "(1)" underneath it. Calculate the overall Active Listening Inventory score by summing all subscales.

For statement items 4, 7, 11:	For statement items 1, 2, 3, 5, 6, 8, 9, 10, 12:
Rarely/never = 5	Rarely/never = 1
Seldom = 4	Seldom = 2
Sometimes = 3	Sometimes = 3
Often = 2	Often = 4
Almost always = 1	Almost always = 5

Active Listening Dimension	Calculation	Your Score
Sensing	___ + ___ + ___ + ___ = (1) (4) (7) (10)	_____
Evaluating	___ + ___ + ___ + ___ = (2) (5) (8) (11)	_____
Responding	___ + ___ + ___ + ___ = (3) (6) (9) (12)	_____
Active listening total	Add up all dimension scores =	_____

Interpreting Your Score: The three active listening dimensions are defined below.

- **Sensing:** Sensing is the process of receiving signals from the sender and paying attention to them. Active listeners improve sensing in three ways. They postpone evaluation by not forming an opinion until the speaker has finished, avoid interrupting the speaker's conversation, and remain motivated to listen to the speaker.

- **Evaluating:** This dimension of active listening includes understanding the message meaning, evaluating the message, and remembering the message. To improve their evaluation of the conversation, active listeners empathize with the speaker—they try to understand and be sensitive to the speaker's feelings, thoughts, and situation. Evaluation also improves by organizing the speaker's ideas during the communication episode.

- **Responding:** Responding, the third dimension of active listening, is feedback to the sender, which motivates and directs the speaker's communication. Active listeners show interest through nonverbal cues (eye contact, nodding, symbiotic facial expression) and by sending back channel signals (e.g., "I see"). They also clarify the message, such as by summarizing or rephrasing the speaker's ideas at appropriate breaks ("So you're saying that . . . ?").

Scores on the three Active Listening dimensions range from 4 to 20. The overall score ranges from 12 to 60. Norms vary from one group to the next. The following table shows norms from a sample of 70 MBA students in two countries (Australia and Singapore). For example, the top 10 percentile for Sensing is 17, indicating that 10 percent of people score 17 or above and 90 percent score below 17 on this dimension. Keep in mind that these scores represent self-perceptions. Evaluations from others (such as through 360-degree feedback) may provide a more accurate estimate of your active listening on one or more dimensions, particularly the responding dimension which is visible to others.

Active Listening Norms				
Percentile (% with scores at or below this number)	Sensing Score	Evaluating Score	Responding Score	Total Score
Average score	14.5	14.4	16.7	45.6
Top 10 percentile	17	17	19	53
Top 25th percentile	15	16	18	48
Median (50th percentile)	15	14	17	45
Bottom 25th percentile	13	13	16	43
Bottom 10 percentile	11	12	14	39

CHAPTER 10

SCORING KEY FOR THE CO-WORKER INFLUENCE SCALE

Scoring Instructions: To calculate your scores on the Co-worker Influence Scale, write the number circled for each statement on the appropriate line below (statement numbers are in parentheses), and add up each scale.

Team Roles Dimension	Calculation			Your Score
Persuasion	___ (1)	+ ___ (9)	+ ___ (17) =	_____
Silent authority	___ (2)	+ ___ (10)	+ ___ (18) =	_____
Exchange	___ (3)	+ ___ (11)	+ ___ (19) =	_____
Assertiveness	___ (4)	+ ___ (12)	+ ___ (20) =	_____
Information control	___ (5)	+ ___ (13)	+ ___ (21) =	_____
Coalition formation	___ (6)	+ ___ (14)	+ ___ (22) =	_____
Upward appeal	___ (7)	+ ___ (15)	+ ___ (23) =	_____
Ingratiation	___ (8)	+ ___ (16)	+ ___ (24) =	_____

Interpreting Your Score: Influence refers to any behaviour that attempts to alter someone's attitudes or behaviour. There are several types of influence, including the eight measured by this instrument. This instrument assesses your preference for using each type of influence on co-workers and other people at a similar level as your position in the organization.

- **Persuasion:** Persuasion refers to using logical and emotional appeals to change others' attitudes. This is one of the most widely used influence strategies toward others in any position (e.g., co-workers, bosses, subordinates).

- **Silent authority:** The silent application of authority occurs when someone complies with a request because the target person is aware of the requester's legitimate or expert power. This influence tactic is very subtle, such as making the target person aware of the status or expertise of the person making the request.

- **Exchange:** Exchange involves the promise of benefits or resources in exchange for the target person's compliance with your request. This tactic also includes reminding the target of past benefits or favours with the expectation that the target will now make up for that debt. Negotiation is also part of the exchange strategy.

- **Assertiveness:** Assertiveness involves actively applying legitimate and coercive power to influence others. This tactic includes demanding that the other person comply with your wishes, showing frustration or impatience with the other person, and using threats of sanctions to force compliance.

- **Information control:** Information control involves explicitly manipulating others' access to information for the purpose of changing their attitudes and/or behaviour. It includes screening out information that might oppose your preference and embellishing or highlighting information that supports your position. According to one survey, more than half of employees believe their co-workers engage in this tactic.

- **Coalition formation:** Coalition formation occurs when a group of people with common interests band together to influence others. It also exists as a perception, such as when you convince someone else that several people are on your side and support your position.

- **Upward appeal:** Upward appeal occurs when you rely on support from people higher up the organizational hierarchy. This support may be real (senior management shows support) or logically argued (you explain how your position is consistent with company policy).

- **Ingratiation:** Ingratiation is a special case of impression management in which you attempt to increase the perception of liking or similarity to another person in the hope that they will become more supportive of your ideas. Flattering the co-worker, becoming friendlier with the co-worker, helping the co-worker (with expectation of reciprocity), showing support for the co-worker's ideas, and asking for the co-worker's advice are all examples of ingratiation.

Scores on the eight Co-worker Influence Scale dimensions range from 3 to 15. Higher scores indicate that the person has a higher preference for and use of that particular tactic. Norms vary from one group to the next. The following table shows norms from a sample of 70 MBA students in two countries (Australia and Singapore). For example, the top 10 percentile for Assertiveness is 9, indicating that 10 percent of people score 9 or above and 90 percent score below 9 on this dimension. Keep in mind that these scores represent self-perceptions. Evaluations from others (such as through 360-degree feedback) may provide a more accurate estimate of your preferred influence tactics.

Co-worker Influence Scale Norms				
Percentile	Persuasion	Silent authority	Exchange	Assertiveness
Average score	12.6	10.0	7.3	5.4
Top 10 percentile	15	13	10	9
Top 25th percentile	14	12	9	6
Median (50th percentile)	13	10	8	5
Bottom 25th percentile	12	9	6	4
Bottom 10 percentile	10	7	4	3

Co-worker Influence Scale Norms (cont'd)				
Percentile	Information control	Coalition formation	Upward appeal	Ingratiation
Average score	6.8	7.4	8.1	8.9
Top 10 percentile	10	10	11	13
Top 25th percentile	9	9	10	12
Median (50th percentile)	7	8	8	10
Bottom 25th percentile	5	6	6	7
Bottom 10 percentile	4	4	5	4

CHAPTER 11
SCORING KEY FOR THE CONFLICT HANDLING SCALE

Scoring Instructions: To estimate your preferred conflict handling styles, use the first table below to score the response you marked for each statement. Then, in the second table below, write that score on the line corresponding to the statement number (statement numbers are in parentheses) and add up each subscale. For example, if you checked "Seldom" for statement #1 ("I went along with the other . . ."), you would write a "2" on the line with "(1)" underneath it.

For ALL statement items:
Rarely/never = 1
Seldom = 2
Sometimes = 3
Often = 4
Almost always = 5

Conflict Handling Dimension	Calculation	Your Score
Problem solving	___ + ___ + ___ + ___ = (3) (9) (13) (18)	_____
Forcing	___ + ___ + ___ + ___ = (5) (8) (12) (15)	_____
Avoiding	___ + ___ + ___ + ___ = (4) (6) (14) (19)	_____
Yielding	___ + ___ + ___ + ___ = (1) (7) (16) (20)	_____
Compromising	___ + ___ + ___ + ___ = (2) (10) (11) (17)	_____

Interpreting Your Score: This instrument measures your preference for and use of the five conflict handling dimensions:

- **Problem solving:** Problem solving tries to find a mutually beneficial solution for both parties. Information sharing is an important feature of this style because both parties need to identify common ground and potential solutions that satisfy both (or all) of them.

- **Forcing:** Forcing tries to win the conflict at the other's expense. It includes "hard" influence tactics, particularly assertiveness, to get one's own way.

- **Avoiding:** Avoiding tries to smooth over or avoid conflict situations altogether. It represents a low concern for both self and the other party. In other words, avoiders try to suppress thinking about the conflict.

- **Yielding:** Yielding involves giving in completely to the other side's wishes, or at least cooperating with little or no attention to your own interests. This style involves making unilateral concessions, unconditional promises, and offering help with no expectation of reciprocal help.

- **Compromising:** Compromising involves looking for a position in which your losses are offset by equally valued gains. It involves matching the other party's concessions, making conditional promises or threats, and actively searching for a middle ground between the interests of the two parties.

Scores on the five Conflict Handling Scale dimensions range from 4 to 20. Higher scores indicate that the person has a higher preference for and use of that particular conflict handling style. Norms vary from one group to the next. The following table shows norms from a sample of 70 MBA students in two countries (Australia and Singapore). For example, the top 10 percentile for Yielding is 14, indicating that 10 percent of people score 14 or above and 90 percent score below 14 on this dimension. Keep in mind that these scores represent self-perceptions. Evaluations from others (such as through 360-degree feedback) may provide a more accurate estimate of your preferred conflict handling style.

Conflict Handling Scale Norms					
Percentile	Problem solving	Forcing	Avoiding	Yielding	Compromising
Average score	15.9	13.5	10.2	11.0	13.8
Top 10 percentile	19	17	14	14	17
Top 25th percentile	17	15	12	12	16
Median (50th percentile)	16	13	10	11	14
Bottom 25th percentile	15	12	8	10	12
Bottom 10 percentile	13	10	6	8	10

CHAPTER 12
SCORING KEY FOR THE ROMANCE OF LEADERSHIP SCALE

Scoring Instructions: Use the table below to score the response you marked for each statement. Then, add up the scores to calculate your Romance of Leadership score. For example, if you marked "Disagree" for statement #1 ("Even in an economic . . ."), you would write a "2" on the line with "(1)" underneath it.

For statement items 3, 5, 7, 9:	For statement items 1, 2, 4, 6, 8, 10:
Strongly disagree = 5	Strongly disagree = 1
Disagree = 4	Disagree = 2
Neutral = 3	Neutral = 3
Agree = 2	Agree = 4
Strongly agree = 1	Strongly agree = 5

Total Score: ____ + ____ + ____ + ____ + ____ + ____ + ____ + ____ + ____ + ____ = ____
       (1)   (2)   (3)   (4)   (5)   (6)   (7)   (8)   (9)   (10)

Interpreting Your Score: Romance of leadership is a phenomenon in which followers (and possibly other stakeholders) want to believe that leaders make a difference in the organization's success. People with a high romance of leadership score attribute the causes of organizational events much more to its leaders and much less to the economy, competition, and other factors beyond the leader's short-term control. This ranges from 10 to 50, with higher scores indicating that the person has a higher romance of leadership. The following norms are derived from a large sample of European employees with an average age in the mid 30s and work experience averaging about 15 years. However, these norms should be viewed with caution because the romance of leadership scale is a recent development and norms for any instrument can vary from one group to the next.

Romance of Leadership Norms	
Romance of Leadership Score	**Interpretation**
38–50	Above average romance of leadership
27–37	Average romance of leadership
10–26	Below average romance of leadership

CHAPTER 13
SCORING KEY FOR ORGANIZATIONAL STRUCTURE PREFERENCE SCALE

Scoring Instructions: Use the table below to assign numbers to each response you marked. Insert the number for each statement on the appropriate line below the table. For example, if you checked "Not at all" for item #1 ("A person's career ladder . . ."), you would write a "0" on the line with "(1)" underneath it. After assigning numbers for all 15 statements, add up the scores to estimate your degree of preference for a tall hierarchy, formalization, and centralization. Then calculate the overall score by summing all scales.

For statement items 2, 3, 8, 10, 11, 12, 14, 15	For statement items 1, 4, 5, 6, 7, 9, 13
Not at all = 3	Not at all = 0
A little = 2	A little = 1
Somewhat = 1	Somewhat = 2
Very much = 0	Very much = 3

Conflict Handling Dimension	Calculation	Your Score
Tall Hierarchy (H)	___ + ___ + ___ + ___ + ___ = (1) (4) (10) (12) (15)	___ (H)
Formalization (F)	___ + ___ + ___ + ___ + ___ = (2) (6) (8) (11) (13)	___ (F)
Centralization (C)	___ + ___ + ___ + ___ + ___ = (3) (5) (7) (9) (14)	___ (C)
Total score (Mechanistic)	Add up all dimension scores (H + F + C) =	___ (Total)

Interpreting Your Score: The three organizational structure dimensions and the overall score are defined below, along with the range of scores for high, medium, and low levels of each dimension based on a sample of MBA students:

Organizational Structure Preference Subscale Definitions and Norms	
Organizational Structure Preference Subscale Definition	**Interpretation**
Tall hierarchy: People with high scores on this dimension prefer to work in organizations with several levels of hierarchy and a narrow span of control (few employees per supervisor).	High: 11 to 15 Medium: 6 to 10 Low: Below 6
Formalization: People with high scores on this dimension prefer to work in organizations where jobs are clearly defined with limited discretion.	High: 12 to 15 Medium: 9 to 11 Low: Below 9
Centralization: People with high scores on this dimension prefer to work in organizations where decision making occurs mainly among top management rather than spread out to lower level staff.	High: 10 to 15 Medium: 7 to 9 Low: Below 7
Total Score (Mechanistic): People with high scores on this dimension prefer to work in mechanistic organizations, whereas those with low scores prefer to work in organic organizational structures. Mechanistic structures are characterized by a narrow span of control and high degree of formalization and centralization. Organic structures have a wide span of control, little formalization, and decentralized decision making.	High: 30 to 45 Medium: 22 to 29 Low: Below 22

CHAPTER 14
SCORING KEY FOR THE CORPORATE CULTURE PREFERENCE SCALE

Scoring Instructions: On each line below, write in a "1" if you circled the statement and a "0" if you did not. Then add up the scores for each subscale.

Control culture   ____ + ____ + ____ + ____ + ____ + ____ = _____
                           (2a)   (5a)   (6b)   (8b)   (11b) (12a)

Performance culture   ____ + ____ + ____ + ____ + ____ + ____ = _____
                           (1b)   (3b)   (5b)   (6a)   (7a)   (9b)

Relationship culture ____ + ____ + ____ + ____ + ____ + ____ = _____
                           (1a)   (3a)   (4b)   (8a) (10b) (12b)

Responsive culture   ____ + ____ + ____ + ____ + ____ + ____ = _____
                           (2b)   (4a)   (7b)   (9a) (10a) (11a)

Interpreting Your Score: These corporate cultures may be found in many organizations, but they represent only four of many possible organizational cultures. Also, keep in mind none of these cultures is inherently good or bad. Each is effective in different situations. The four corporate cultures are defined below, along with the range of scores for high, medium, and low levels of each dimension based on a sample of MBA students:

Corporate Culture Preference Subscale Definitions and Norms	
Corporate Culture Dimension and Definition	**Score Interpretation**
Control culture: This culture values the role of senior executives to lead the organization. Its goal is to keep everyone aligned and under control.	High: 3 to 6 Medium: 1 to 2 Low: 0
Performance culture: This culture values individual and organizational performance and strives for effectiveness and efficiency.	High: 5 to 6 Medium: 3 to 4 Low: 0 to 2
Relationship culture: This culture values nurturing and well-being. It considers open communication, fairness, teamwork, and sharing a vital part of organizational life.	High: 6 Medium: 4 to 5 Low: 0 to 3
Responsive culture: This culture values its ability to keep in tune with the external environment, including being competitive and realizing new opportunities.	High: 6 Medium: 4 to 5 Low: 0 to 3

CHAPTER 15

SCORING KEY FOR THE TOLERANCE OF CHANGE SCALE

Scoring Instructions: Use the table below to assign numbers to each box you checked. For example, if you checked "Moderately disagree" for statement #1 ("I generally prefer the unexpected . . ."), you would write a "2" beside that statement. After assigning numbers for all 10 statements, add up your scores to estimate your tolerance for change.

For statement items 1, 3, 7, 8, 10:	For statement items 2, 4, 5, 6, 9 :
Strongly agree = 7	Strongly agree = 1
Moderately agree = 6	Moderately agree = 2
Slightly agree = 5	Slightly agree = 3
Neutral = 4	Neutral = 4
Slightly disagree = 3	Slightly disagree = 5
Moderately disagree = 2	Moderately disagree = 6
Strongly disagree = 1	Strongly disagree = 7

Interpreting Your Score: This instrument is formally known as the "tolerance of ambiguity" scale. The original scale, developed 50 years ago, has since been revised and adapted. The instrument presented here is an adaptation of these revised instruments. People with a high tolerance of ambiguity are comfortable with uncertainty and new situations. These are characteristics of the hyperfast changes occurring in many organizations today. This instrument ranges from 10 to 70, with higher scores indicating a higher tolerance for change (i.e., higher tolerance for ambiguity). The table below indicates the range of scores for high, medium, and low tolerance for change. These norms are estimates from recent studies using some or all of these items.

Tolerance for Change Score	Interpretation
50–70	You seem to have a high tolerance for change.
30–49	You seem to have a moderate level of tolerance for change.
10–29	You seem to have a low degree of tolerance for change. Instead, you prefer stable work environments.

GLOSSARY

The number following each definition indicates the chapter in which the term receives the fullest description.

A

ability   The natural aptitudes and learned capabilities required to successfully complete a task. (2)

absorptive capacity   The ability to recognize the value of new information, assimilate it, and use it for value-added activities. (1)

achievement-nurturing orientation   A cross-cultural value describing the degree to which people in a culture emphasize competitive versus cooperative relations with other people. (2)

action research   A problem-focused change process that combines action orientation (changing attitudes and behaviour) and research orientation (testing theory through data collection and analysis). (15)

adaptive culture   An organizational culture in which employees are receptive to change, including the ongoing alignment of the organization to its environment and continuous improvement of internal processes. (14)

affective (organizational) commitment   The employee's emotional attachment to, identification with, and involvement in a particular organization. (4)

anchoring and adjustment heuristic   A natural tendency for people to be influenced by an initial anchor point such that they do not sufficiently move away from that point as new information is provided. (7)

appreciative inquiry   An organizational change strategy that directs the group's attention away from its own problems and focuses participants on the group's potential and positive elements. (15)

artifacts   The observable symbols and signs of an organization's culture. (14)

attitudes   The cluster of beliefs, assessed feelings, and behavioural intentions toward a person, object, or event (called an *attitude object*). (4)

attraction-selection-attrition (ASA) theory   A theory which states that organizations have a natural tendency to attract, select, and retain people with values and personality characteristics that are consistent with the organization's character, resulting in a more homogeneous organization and a stronger culture. (14)

attribution process   The perceptual process of deciding whether an observed behaviour or event is caused largely by internal or external factors. (3)

authentic leadership   The view that effective leaders need to be aware of, feel comfortable with, and act consistently with their values, personality, and self-concept. (12)

autonomy   The degree to which a job gives employees the freedom, independence, and discretion to schedule their work and to determine the procedures used in completing it. (6)

availability heuristic   A natural tendency to assign higher probabilities to objects or events that are easier to recall from memory, even though ease of recall is also affected by nonprobability factors (e.g., emotional response, recent events). (7)

B

balanced scorecard (BSC)   A goal-setting and reward system that translates the organization's vision and mission into specific, measurable performance goals related to financial, customer, internal, and learning/growth (i.e., human capital processes). (5)

best alternative to a negotiated agreement (BATNA)   The best outcome you might achieve through some other course of action if you abandon the current negotiation. (11)

bicultural audit   A process of diagnosing cultural relations between the companies and determining the extent to which cultural clashes will likely occur. (14)

bounded rationality   The view that people are bounded in their decision-making capabilities, including access to limited information, limited information processing, and tendency toward satisficing rather than maximizing when making choices. (7)

brainstorming   A freewheeling, face-to-face meeting where team members aren't allowed to criticize, but are encouraged to speak freely, generate as many ideas as possible, and build on the ideas of others. (8)

Brooks's law   The principle that adding more people to a late software project only makes it later. Also called the *mythical man-month*. (8)

C

categorical thinking   Organizing people and objects into preconceived categories that are stored in our long-term memory. (3)

centrality   A contingency of power pertaining to the degree and nature of interdependence between the powerholder and others. (10)

centralization   The degree to which formal decision making authority is held by a small group of people, typically those at the top of the organizational hierarchy. (13)

ceremonies   Planned displays of organizational culture, conducted specifically for the benefit of an audience. (14)

charisma   A personal characteristic or special "gift" that serves as a form of interpersonal attraction and referent power over others. (10)

coalition   A group that attempts to influence people outside the group by pooling the resources and power of its members. (10)

cognitive dissonance   A condition that occurs when we perceive an inconsistency between our beliefs, feelings, and behaviour. (4)

collectivism   A cross-cultural value describing the degree to which people in a culture emphasize duty to groups to which they belong, and to group harmony. (2)

communication   The process by which information is transmitted and *understood* between two or more people. (9)

competencies   Skills, knowledge, aptitudes, and other personal characteristics that lead to superior performance. (2)

concurrent engineering   The organization of employees from several departments into a temporary team for the purpose of developing a product or service. (13)

confirmation bias   The tendency to screen out information that is contrary to our decisions, beliefs, values, and assumptions, and to more readily accept confirming information. (3)

conflict   A process in which one party perceives that his or her interests are being opposed or negatively affected by another party. (11)

conscientiousness   A personality dimension describing people who are careful, dependable, and self-disciplined. (2)

constructive conflict   A type of conflict in which people focus their discussion on the issue while maintaining respect for people having other points of view. (8, 11)

constructs   Abstract ideas constructed by researchers that can be linked to observable information. (Appendix A)

contact hypothesis   A theory stating that the more we interact with someone, the less prejudiced or perceptually biased we will be against that person (3)

continuance commitment An employee's calculative attachment to the organization, whereby an employee is motivated to stay only because leaving would be costly. (4)

corporate social responsibility (CSR) Organizational activities intended to benefit society and the environment beyond the firm's immediate financial interests or legal obligations. (1)

counter productive work behaviours (CWBs) Voluntary behaviours that have the potential to directly or indirectly harm the organization. (2)

countervailing power The capacity of a person, team, or organization to keep a more powerful person or group in the exchange relationship. (10)

creativity The development of original ideas that make a socially recognized contribution. (7)

D

decision making The conscious process of making choices among alternatives with the intention of moving toward some desired state of affairs. (7)

deep-level diversity Differences in the psychological characteristics of employees, including personalities, beliefs, values, and attitudes. (1)

distributive justice Perceived fairness in the individual's ratio of outcomes to contributions compared with a comparison to other's ratio of outcomes to contributions. (5)

divergent thinking Reframing a problem in a unique way and generating different approaches to the issue. (7)

divisional structure An organizational structure in which employees are organized around geographic areas, outputs (products or services), or clients. (13)

drives Hardwired characteristics of the brain that correct deficiencies or maintain an internal equilibrium by producing emotions. (5)

E

electronic brainstorming A form of brainstorming that relies on networked computers for submitting and sharing creative ideas. (8)

emotional contagion The nonconscious process of 'catching' or sharing another person's emotions by mimicking that person's facial expressions and other nonverbal behaviour. (9)

emotional dissonance The conflict between required and true emotions. (4)

emotional intelligence (EI) A set of abilities to perceive and express emotion, assimilate emotion in thought, understand and reason with emotion, and regulate emotion in oneself and others. (4)

emotional labour The effort, planning, and control needed to express organizationally desired emotions during interpersonal transactions. (4)

emotions Physiological, behavioural, and psychological episodes experienced toward an object, person, or event that create a state of readiness. (4)

empathy A person's understanding of and sensitivity to the feelings, thoughts, and situation of others. (3)

employee engagement Individual's emotional and cognitive motivation, particularly a focused, intense, persistent, and purposive effort toward work-related goals. (5)

employee involvement The degree to which employees influence how their work is organized and carried out. (7)

employee share ownership plans (ESOPs) Reward systems that encourage employees to buy company shares. (6)

empowerment A psychological concept in which people experience more self-determination, meaning, competence, and impact regarding their role in the organization. (6)

equity sensitivity An individual's outcome/input preferences and reaction to various outcome/input ratios. (5)

equity theory A theory explaining how people develop perceptions of fairness in the distribution and exchange of resources. (5)

escalation of commitment The tendency to repeat an apparently bad decision or allocate more resources to a failing course of action. (7)

ethical sensitivity A personal characteristic that enables people to recognize the presence of an ethical issue and determine its relative importance. (2)

ethics The study of moral principles or values that determine whether actions are right or wrong and outcomes are good or bad. (1)

evaluation apprehension A decision making problem that occurs when individuals are reluctant to mention ideas that seem silly because they believe (often correctly) that other team members are silently evaluating them. (8)

evidence-based managemen The practice of making decisions and taking actions based on research evidence. (1)

exit-voice-loyalty-neglect (EVLN) model The four ways, as indicated in the name, that employees respond to job dissatisfaction. (4)

expectancy theory A motivation theory based on the idea that work effort is directed toward behaviours that people believe will lead to desired outcomes. (5)

extroversion A personality dimension describing people who are outgoing, talkative, sociable, and assertive. (2)

F

false-consensus effect A perceptual error in which we overestimate the extent to which others have beliefs and characteristics similar to our own. (3)

Fiedler's contingency model An early contingency leadership model, developed by Fred Fiedler, which suggests that leader effectiveness depends on whether the person's natural leadership style is appropriately matched to the situation. (12)

field surveys Research design strategies that involve collecting and analyzing information in a natural environment, such as an office, a factory, or other existing location. (Appendix A)

five-factor model (FFM) The five abstract dimensions representing most personality traits: conscientiousness, agreeableness, neuroticism, openness to experience, and extroversion. (2)

force field analysis Kurt Lewin's model of system-wide change that helps change agents diagnose the forces that drive and restrain proposed organizational change. (15)

formalization The degree to which organizations standardize behaviour through rules, procedures, formal training, and related mechanisms. (13)

four-drive theory A motivation theory that is based on the innate drives to acquire, bond, learn, and defend, and that incorporates both emotions and rationality. (5)

functional structure An organizational structure in which employees are organized around specific knowledge or other resources. (13)

fundamental attribution error The tendency to see the person rather than the situation as the main cause of that person's behaviour. (3)

future search An organizational change strategy that consists of system-wide group sessions, usually lasting a few days, in which participants identify trends and identify ways to adapt to those changes. (15)

G

gainsharing plans Team-based rewards that calculate bonuses from the work unit's cost savings and productivity improvement (6)

general adaptation syndrome A model of the stress experience, consisting of three stages: alarm reaction, resistance, and exhaustion. (4)

global mindset An individual's ability to perceive, appreciate, and empathize with people from other cultures and to process complex cross-cultural information. (3)

globalization Economic, social, and cultural connectivity with people in other parts of the world. (1)

globally integrated enterprise An organizational structure in which work processes and executive functions are distributed around the world through global centres, rather than developed in a home country and replicated in satellite countries or regions. (13)

goal setting The process of motivating employees and clarifying their role perceptions by establishing performance objectives. (5)

grapevine An unstructured and informal network founded on social relationships rather than organizational charts or job descriptions. (9)

grounded theory A process of developing knowledge through the constant interplay of data collection, analysis, and theory development. (Appendix A)

groupthink The tendency of highly cohesive groups to value consensus at the price of decision quality. (8)

H

halo effect A perceptual error whereby our general impression of a person, usually based on one prominent characteristic, distorts our perception of other characteristics of that person. (3)

high-performance work practices (HPWP) A perspective which holds that effective organizations incorporate several workplace practices that leverage the potential of human capital. (1)

human capital The stock of knowledge, skills, and abilities among employees that provides economic value to the organization. (1)

hypotheses Statements making empirically testable declarations that certain variables and their corresponding measures are related in a specific way proposed by the theory. (Appendix A)

I

implicit favourite A preferred alternative that the decision maker uses repeatedly as a comparison with other choices. (7)

implicit leadership theory A theory stating that people evaluate a leader's effectiveness in terms of how well that person fits preconceived beliefs about the features and behaviours of effective leaders (leadership prototypes), and that people tend to inflate the influence of leaders on organizational events. (12)

impression management The practice of actively shaping our public images. (10)

individualism A cross-cultural value describing the degree to which people in a culture emphasize independence and personal uniqueness. (2)

influence Any behaviour that attempts to alter someone's attitudes or behaviour. (10)

information overload A condition in which the volume of information received exceeds the person's capacity to process it. (9)

ingratiation Any attempt to increase liking by, or perceived similarity to, some targeted person. (10)

inoculation effect A persuasive communication strategy of warning listeners that others will try to influence them in the future and that they should be wary about the opponent's arguments. (10)

intellectual capital A company's stock of knowledge, including human capital, structural capital, and relationship capital. (1)

interpretivism The view held in many qualitative studies that reality comes from shared meaning among people in a particular environment. (Appendix A)

intuition The ability to know when a problem or opportunity exists and to select the best course of action without conscious reasoning. (7)

J

job burnout The process of emotional exhaustion, cynicism, and reduced personal accomplishment that results from prolonged exposure to stressors. (4)

job characteristics model A job design model that relates the motivational properties of jobs to specific personal and organizational consequences of those properties. (6)

job design The process of assigning tasks to a job, including the interdependency of those tasks with other jobs. (6)

job enlargement The practice of adding more tasks to an existing job. (6)

job enrichment The practice of giving employees more responsibility for scheduling, coordinating, and planning their own work. (6)

job evaluation Systematically rating the worth of jobs within an organization by measuring their required skill, effort, responsibility, and working conditions. (6)

job rotation The practice of moving employees from one job to another. (6)

job satisfaction A person's evaluation of his or her job and work context. (4)

job specialization The result of division of labour in which each job includes a subset of the tasks required to complete the product or service. (6)

Johari Window A model of mutual understanding that encourages disclosure and feedback to increase our own open area and reduce the blind, hidden, and unknown areas. (3)

L

laboratory experiment Any research study in which independent variables and variables outside the researcher's main focus of inquiry can be controlled to some extent. (Appendix A)

leadership Influencing, motivating, and enabling others to contribute toward the effectiveness and success of the organizations of which they are members. (12)

leadership substitutes A theory identifying contingencies that either limit a leader's ability to influence employees or make a particular leadership style unnecessary. (12)

legitimate power An agreement among organizational members that people in certain roles can request certain behaviours of others. (10)

locus of control A person's general belief about the amount of control he or she has over personal life events. (3)

M

Machiavellian values The belief that deceit is a natural and acceptable way to influence others and that getting more than one deserves is acceptable. (10)

management by walking around (MBWA) A ommunication practice in which executives get out of their offices and learn from others in the organization through face-to-face dialogue. (9)

managerial leadership A leadership perspective stating that effective leaders help employees improve their performance and well-being in the current situation. (12)

Maslow's needs hierarchy theory A motivation theory of needs arranged in a hierarchy, whereby people are motivated to fulfill a higher need as a lower one becomes gratified. (5)

matrix structure An organizational structure that overlays two structures (such as a geographic divisional and a functional structure) in order to leverage the benefits of both. (13)

mechanistic structure An organizational structure with a narrow span of control and a high degree of formalization and centralization. (13)

media richness A medium's data-carrying capacity, that is, the volume and variety of information that can be transmitted during a specific time. (9)

mental imagery The process of mentally practising a task and visualizing its successful completion. (6)

mental models Visual or relational images in our mind that represent the external world. (3)

moral intensity The degree to which an issue demands the application of ethical principles. (2)

motivation The forces within a person that affect his or her direction, intensity, and persistence of voluntary behaviour. (2, 5)

motivator-hygiene theory Herzberg's theory stating that employees are primarily motivated by growth and esteem needs, not by lower-level needs. (6)

multisource (360-degree) feedback Information about an employee's performance collected from a full circle of people, including subordinates, peers, supervisors, and customers. (5)

Myers-Briggs Type Indicator (MBTI)   An instrument designed to measure the elements of Jungian personality theory, particularly preferences regarding perceiving and judging information. (2)

N

need for achievement (nAch)   A need in which people want to accomplish reasonably challenging goals, and desire unambiguous feedback and recognition for their success. (5)

need for affiliation (nAff)   A need in which people seek approval from others, conform to their wishes and expectations, and avoid conflict and confrontation. (5)

need for power (nPow)   A need in which people want to control their environment, including people and material resources, to benefit either themselves (personalized power) or others (socialized power). (5)

needs   Goal-directed forces that people experience. (5)

negotiation   The process whereby two or more conflicting parties attempt to resolve their divergent goals by redefining the terms of their interdependence. (11)

network structure   An alliance of several organizations for the purpose of creating a product or serving a client. (13)

neuroticism   A personality dimension describing people with high levels of anxiety, hostility, depression, and self-consciousness. (2)

nominal group technique   A variation of brainstorming consisting of three stages: participants (1) silently and independently document their ideas, (2) collectively describe these ideas to the other team members without critique, and (3) silently and independently evaluate the ideas presented. (8)

norm of reciprocity   A felt obligation and social expectation of helping or otherwise giving something of value to someone who has already helped or given something to you. (10)

norms   The informal rules and shared expectations that groups establish to regulate the behaviour of their members. (8)

O

open systems   A perspective which holds that organizations depend on the external environment for resources, affect that environment through their output, and consist of internal subsystems that transform inputs into outputs. (1)

organic structure   An organizational structure with a wide span of control, little formalization, and decentralized decision making. (13)

organizational (affective) commitment   The employee's emotional attachment to, identification with, and involvement in a particular organization. (4)

organizational behaviour (OB)   The study of what people think, feel, and do in and around organizations. (1)

organizational behaviour modification   A theory that explains employee behaviour in terms of the antecedent conditions and consequences of that behaviour. (5)

organizational citizenship behaviours (OCBs)   Various forms of cooperation and helpfulness to others that support the organization's social and psychological context. (2)

organizational culture   The values and assumptions shared within an organization. (14)

organizational effectiveness   A broad concept represented by several perspectives, including the organization's fit with the external environment, internal-subsystems configuration for high performance, emphasis on organizational learning, and ability to satisfy the needs of key stakeholders. (1)

organizational efficiency   The amount of outputs relative to inputs in the organization's transformation process. (1)

organizational learning   A perspective which holds that organizational effectiveness depends on the organization's capacity to acquire, share, use, and store valuable knowledge. (1)

organizational politics   Behaviours that others perceive as self-serving tactics for personal gain at the expense of other people and possibly the organization. (10)

organizational socialization   The process by which individuals learn the values, expected behaviours, and social knowledge necessary to assume their roles in the organization. (14)

organizational strategy   The way the organization positions itself in its setting in relation to its stakeholders, given the organization's resources, capabilities, and mission. (13)

organizational structure   The division of labour as well as the patterns of coordination, communication, workflow, and formal power that direct organizational activities. (13)

organizations   Groups of people who work interdependently toward some purpose. (1)

P

parallel learning structures   Highly participative arrangements composed of people from most levels of the organization who follow the action research model to produce meaningful organizational change. (15)

path-goal leadership theory   A contingency theory of leadership based on the expectancy theory of motivation that relates several leadership styles to specific employee and situational contingencies. (12)

perception   The process of receiving information about and making sense of the world around us. (3)

personality   The relatively enduring pattern of thoughts, emotions, and behaviours that characterize a person, along with the psychological processes behind those characteristics. (2)

persuasion   The use of facts, logical arguments, and emotional appeals to change another person's beliefs and attitudes, usually for the purpose of changing the person's behaviour. (9, 10)

positive organizational behaviour   A perspective of organizational behaviour that focuses on building positive qualities and traits within individuals or institutions as opposed to focusing on what is wrong with them. (3)

positivism   A view held in quantitative research in which reality exists independent of the perceptions and interpretations of people. (Appendix A)

power   The capacity of a person, team, or organization to influence others. (10)

power distance   A cross-cultural value describing the degree to which people in a culture accept unequal distribution of power in a society. (2)

presenteeism   Attending scheduled work when one's capacity to perform is significantly diminished by illness or other factors. (2)

primacy effect   A perceptual error in which we quickly form an opinion of people on the basis of the first information we receive about them. (3)

procedural justice   Perceived fairness of the procedures used to decide the distribution of resources. (5)

process losses   Resources (including time and energy) expended toward team development and maintenance rather than the task. (8)

production blocking   A time constraint in team decision making due to the procedural requirement that only one person may speak at a time. (8)

profit-sharing plans   A reward system that pays bonuses to employees on the basis of the previous year's level of corporate profits. (6)

prospect theory effect   A natural tendency to feel more dissatisfaction from losing a particular amount than satisfaction from gaining an equal amount. (7)

psychological contract   The individual's beliefs about the terms and conditions of a reciprocal exchange agreement between that person and another party (typically the employer). (14)

psychological harassment   Repeated and hostile or unwanted conduct, verbal comments, actions, or gestures that affect an employee's dignity or psychological or physical integrity and that result in a harmful work environment for the employee. (4)

R

rational choice paradigm   The view in decision making that people should—and typically do—use logic and all available information to choose the alternative with the highest value. (7)

realistic job preview (RJP)   A method of improving organizational socialization in which job applicants are provided with a balance of positive and negative information about the job and work context. (14)

reality shock   The stress that results when employees perceive discrepancies between their pre-employment expectations and on-the-job reality. (14)

recency effect   A perceptual error in which the most recent information dominates our perception of others. (3)

referent power   The capacity to influence others on the basis of an identification with and respect for the powerholder. (10)

refreezing   The latter part of the organizational change process, in which systems and conditions are introduced that reinforce and maintain the desired behaviours. (15)

relationship conflict   Type of conflict in which people focus on the characteristics of other individuals, rather than on the issues, as the source of conflict. (11)

representativeness heuristic   A natural tendency to evaluate probabilities of events or objects by the degree to which they resemble (are representative of) other events or objects rather than on objective probability information. (7)

representative sampling   The process of sampling a population in such a way that one can extrapolate the results of that sample to the larger population. (Appendix A)

rituals   The programmed routines of daily organizational life that dramatize the organization's culture. (14)

role   A set of behaviours that people are expected to perform because of the positions they hold in a team and organization. (8)

role perceptions   The extent to which people understand the job duties (roles) assigned to or expected of them. (2)

S

satisficing   Selecting an alternative that is satisfactory or "good enough" rather than the alternative with the higher value (maximization). (7)

scenario planning   A systematic process of thinking about alternative futures and what the organization should do to anticipate and react to those environments. (7)

scientific management   The practice of systematically partitioning work into its smallest elements and standardizing tasks to achieve maximum efficiency. (6)

scientific method   A set of principles and procedures that help researchers to systematically understand previously unexplained events and conditions. (Appendix A)

selective attention   The process of attending to some information received by our senses and ignoring other information. (3)

self-concept   An individual's self-beliefs and self-evaluations. (3)

self-directed teams (SDTs)   Cross-functional work groups that are organized around work processes, that complete an entire piece of work requiring several interdependent tasks, and that have substantial autonomy over the execution of those tasks. (8)

self-efficacy   A person's belief that he or she has the ability, motivation, correct role perceptions, and favourable situation to complete a task successfully. (3)

self-enhancement   A person's inherent motivation to have a positive self-concept (and to have others perceive him/her favourably), such as being competent, attractive, lucky, ethical, and important. (3)

self-fulfilling prophecy   The perceptual process in which our expectations about another person cause that person to act in a way that is consistent with those expectations. (3)

self-leadership   The process of influencing oneself to establish the self-direction and self-motivation needed to perform a task. (6)

self-reinforcement   Reinforcement that occurs when an employee has control over a reinforcer but doesn't 'take' it until completing a self-set goal. (5)

self-serving bias   The tendency to attribute our favourable outcomes to internal factors and our failures to external factors. (3)

self-talk   The process of talking to ourselves about our own thoughts or actions. (6)

self-verification   A person's inherent motivation to confirm and maintain his/her existing self-concept. (3)

servant leadership   The view that leaders serve followers, rather than vice versa; leaders help employees fulfill their needs and are coaches, stewards, and facilitators of employee performance. (12)

service profit chain model   A theory explaining how employees' job satisfaction influences company profitability indirectly through service quality, customer loyalty, and related factors. (4)

sexual harassment   Unwelcome conduct of a sexual nature that detrimentally affects the work environment or leads to adverse job-related consequences for its victims. (4)

share options   Reward systems that give employees the right to purchase company shares at a future date at a predetermined price. (6)

shared leadership   The view that leadership is broadly distributed, rather than assigned to one person, such that people within the team and organization lead each other. (12)

situational leadership theory (SLT)   A commercially popular but poorly supported leadership model stating that effective leaders vary their style (telling, selling, participating, delegating) with the "readiness" of followers. (12)

skill variety   The extent to which employees must use different skills and talents to perform tasks within their jobs. (6)

social capital   The knowledge and other resources available to people or social units (teams, organizations) from a durable network that connects them to others. (10)

social cognitive theory   A theory that explains how learning and motivation occur by observing and modelling others as well as by anticipating the consequences of our behaviour. (5)

social identity theory   A theory that explains that people define themselves by the groups to which they belong or have an emotional attachment. (3)

social loafing   The problem that occurs when people exert less effort (and usually perform at a lower level) when working in teams than when working alone. (8)

social networks   Social structures of individuals or social units that are connected to each other through one or more forms of interdependence. (10)

span of control   The number of people directly reporting to the next level in the hierarchy. (13)

stakeholders   Individuals, organizations, and other entities who affect, or are affected by, the organization's objectives and actions. (1)

stereotyping   The process of assigning traits to people on the basis of their membership in a social category. (3)

strengths-based coaching   A positive organizational behaviour approach to coaching and feedback that focuses on building and leveraging the employee's strengths rather than trying to correct his or her weaknesses. (5)

stress   An adaptive response to a situation that is perceived as challenging or threatening to a person's well-being. (4)

stressors   Any environmental conditions that place a physical or emotional demand on a person. (4)

structural capital   Knowledge embedded in an organization's systems and structures. (1)

structural hole   An area between two or more dense social network areas that lacks network ties. (10)

subjective expected utility   The probability (expectation) of satisfaction (utility) resulting from choosing a specific alternative in a decision. (7)

substitutability   A contingency of power referring to the availability of alternatives. (10)

superordinate goal   A broad goal that all parties to a dispute value and agree is important. (11)

surface-level diversity   The observable demographic or physiological differences in people, such as their race, ethnicity, gender, age, and physical capabilities. (1)

T

task identity   The degree to which a job requires completion of a whole or an identifiable piece of work. (6)

task interdependence   The extent to which team members must share materials, information, or expertise in order to perform their jobs. (8)

task significance   The degree to which a job has a substantial impact on the organization and/or larger society. (6)

team-based organizational structure   An organizational structure built around self-directed teams that complete an entire piece of work. (13)

team building   A process that consists of formal activities intended to improve the development and functioning of a work team. (8)

team cohesion   The degree of attraction people feel toward the team and their motivation to remain members. (8)

teams   Groups of two or more people who interact and influence each other, are mutually accountable for achieving common goals associated with organizational objectives, and perceive themselves as a social entity within an organization. (8)

theory   A general set of propositions that describes interrelationships among several concepts. (Appendix A)

third-party conflict resolution   Any attempt by a relatively neutral person to help conflicting parties resolve their differences. (11)

transactional leadership   Leadership that helps organizations achieve their current objectives more efficiently, such as by linking job performance to valued rewards and ensuring that employees have the resources needed to get the job done. (12)

transformational leadership   A leadership perspective that explains how leaders change teams or organizations by creating, communicating, and modelling a shared vision for the team or organization, and inspiring employees to strive for that vision. (12)

trust   The positive expectations one person has toward another person or group in situations involving risk. (4, 8)

U

uncertainty avoidance   A cross-cultural value describing the degree to which people in a culture tolerate ambiguity (low uncertainty avoidance) or feel threatened by ambiguity and uncertainty (high uncertainty avoidance). (2)

unfreezing   The first part of the organizational change process, in which the change agent produces disequilibrium between the driving and restraining forces. (15)

upward appeal   A type of influence in which someone with higher authority or expertise is called on (in reality or symbolically) to support the influencer's position. (10)

V

values   Relatively stable, evaluative beliefs that guide a person's preferences for outcomes or courses of action in a variety of situations. (1)

virtual teams   Teams whose members operate across space, time, and organizational boundaries, and are linked through information technologies to achieve organizational tasks. (8)

virtual work   Work performed away from the traditional physical workplace by means of information technology. (1)

W

wikis   Collaborative Web spaces where anyone in a group can write, edit, or remove material from the website. (9)

win–lose orientation   The belief that conflicting parties are drawing from a fixed pie, so the more one party receives, the less the other party will receive. (11)

win–win orientation   The belief that the parties will find a mutually beneficial solution to their disagreement. (11)

work-life balance   The degree to which a person minimizes conflict between work and nonwork demands. (1)

workaholic   A person who is highly involved in work, feels compelled to work, and has a low enjoyment of work. (4)

ENDNOTES

CHAPTER 1

1. S. Houtt, "Everybody Loves an Underdog; Consumers Bond Easily with Stories of Scrappy Upstarts, New research Shows," *The Globe and Mail*, 6 August 2010, B5; K. Laidlaw, "Off to Work They Go; Steam Whistle Staffers Travel by Skateboard and Bicycle," *National Post*, 5 August 2009, A9; R. Mourtada, "Immigrant Talent Adds to Brewer's Bottom Line," *Globe and Mail*, 10 February 2010, B10; P. Quinn, "Full Steam Ahead…with a Passion," *Special Report: Canada's 50 Best, Financial Post*, 2 February 2009, SR22; C Saunders, "Brewing Up Ways to Make Your Beer Greener," *Globe and Mail*, 17 March 2010, L1; E. Wexler, "Full Steam Ahead: Steam Whistle's Sybil Taylor," *Strategy*, September 2009, 19; S. Won, "Microbrewery is Rolling Out the Barrels" *Report on Business, Globe and Mail*, 25 October 2004, B4; P. Evans et al, "Top 40 under 40: 2006 Report on Business: Forty Talents, in Full Bloom," *Globe and Mail*, 8 May 2007; http://www.eluta.ca/young-people-at-steam-whistle-brewing, Retrieved 20 August 2010; www.steamwhistle.ca.

2. M. Warner, "Organizational Behavior Revisited," *Human Relations* 47 (October 1994): 1151–1166; R. Westwood and S. Clegg, "The Discourse of Organization Studies: Dissensus, Politics, and Peradigms," in *Debating Organization: Point-Counterpoint in Organization Studies*, ed. R. Westwood and S. Clegg (Malden, MA: Blackwood, 2003), 1–42.

3. D. Katz and R. L. Kahn, *The Social Psychology of Organizations* (New York: Wiley, 1966), Chap. 2; R. N. Stern and S. R. Barley, "Organizations as Social Systems: Organization Theory's Neglected Mandate," *Administrative Science Quarterly* 41 (1996): 146–162.

4. L. E. Greiner, "A Recent History of Organizational Behavior," in *Organizational Behaviour*, ed. S. Kerr (Columbus, Ohio: Grid, 1979), 3–14; J. Micklethwait and A. Wooldridge, *The Company: A Short History of a Revolutionary Idea* (New York: Random House, 2003); G. Bryce, *The Remarkable History of the Hudson's Bay Company* (London: Sampson, Low, Marston & Company, Ltd., 2005).

5. B. Schlender, "The Three Faces of Steve," *Fortune*, 9 November 1998, 96–101.

6. J. A. Conger, "Max Weber's Conceptualization of Charismatic Authority: Its Influence on Organizational Research," *The Leadership Quarterly* 4, no. 3–4 (1993): 277–288; R. Kanigel, *The One Best Way: Frederick Winslow Taylor and the Enigma of Efficiency* (New York: Viking, 1997); T. Takala, "Plato on Leadership," *Journal of Business Ethics* 17 (May 1998): 785–798; J. A. Fernandez, "The Gentleman's Code of Confucius: Leadership by Values," *Organizational Dynamics* 33, no. 1 (February 2004): 21–31.

7. W. L. M. King, *Industry and Humanity: A Study in the Principles Underlying Industrial Reconstruction* (Toronto: Thomas Allen, 1918); H. C. Metcalf and L. Urwick, *Dynamic Administration: The Collected Papers of Mary Parker Follett* (New York: Harper & Brothers, 1940); J. Smith, "The Enduring Legacy of Elton Mayo," *Human Relations* 51, no. 3 (1998): 221–249; E. O'Connor, "Minding the Workers: The Meaning of, 'Human' and `Human Relations' in Elton Mayo," *Organization* 6, no. 2 (May 1999): 223–246; K. Hallahan, "W.L. Mackenzie King: Rockefeller's 'Other' Public Relations Counselor in Colorado," *Public Relations Review* 29, no. 4 (2003): 401–414.

8. S. L. Rynes *et al.*, "Behavioral Coursework in Business Education: Growing Evidence of a Legitimacy Crisis," *Academy of Management Learning & Education* 2, no. 3 (2003): 269–283; R. P. Singh and A. G. Schick, "Organizational Behavior: Where Does It Fit in Today's Management Curriculum?," *Journal of Education for Business* 82, no. 6 (July 2007): 349.

9. P. R. Lawrence and N. Nohria, *Driven: How Human Nature Shapes Our Choices* (San Francisco: Jossey-Bass, 2002), Chap. 6.

10. J. A. C. Baum, "Companion to Organizations: An Introduction," in *The Blackwell Companion to Organizations*, ed. J. A. C. Baum (Oxford, UK: Blackwell, 2002), 1–34.

11. OB scholars are currently in a heated debate regarding the field's relevance to practitioners. See, for example: P. R. Lawrence "Historical Development of Organizational Behavior," in *Handbook of Organizational Behavior*, ed. L. W. Lorsch (Englewood Cliffs, N. J.: Prentice Hall, 1987), 1–9; S. A. Mohrman, C. B. Gibson, and A. M. Mohrman Jr., "Doing Research That Is Useful to Practice: A Model and Empirical Exploration," *Academy of Management Journal* 44 (April 2001): 357–375; R. Gulati, "Tent Poles, Tribalism, and Boundary Spanning: The Rigor-Relevance Debate in Management Research," *Academy of Management Journal* 50, no. 4 (Aug 2007): 775–782; F. Vermeulen, "'I Shall Not Remain Insignificant': Adding a Second Loop to Matter More," *Academy of Management Journal* 50, no. 4 (2007): 754–761; J. P. Walsh *et al.*, "On the Relationship between Research and Practice: Debate and Reflections," *Journal of Management Inquiry* 16, no. 2 (June 2007): 128–154; D. Palmer, B. Dick, and N. Freiburger, "Rigor and Relevance in Organization Studies," *Journal of Management Inquiry* 18, no. 4 (December 2009): 265–272; A. Nicolai and D. Seidl, "That's Relevant! Different Forms of Practical Relevance in Management Science," *Organization Studies* 31, no. 9–10 (Sept. 2010): 1257–1285. At least one source argues that organizational scholarship does not need to be relevant to practitioners: M. W. Peng and G. G. Dess, "In the Spirit of Scholarship," *Academy of Management Learning & Education* 9, no. 2 (June 2010): 282–298.

12. M. S. Myers, *Every Employee a Manager* (New York: McGraw Hill, 1970).

13. B. N. Pfau and I. T. Kay, *The Human Capital Edge* (New York: McGraw-Hill, 2002); I. S. Fulmer, B. Gerhart, and K. S. Scott, "Are the 100 Best Better? An Empirical Investigation of the Relationship between Being a 'Great Place to Work' and Firm Performance," *Personnel Psychology* 56, no. 4 (Winter 2003): 965–993; Y. H. Ling and B.-S. Jaw, "The Influence of International Human Capital on Global Initiatives and Financial Performance," *The International Journal of Human Resource Management* 17, no. 3 (2006): 379–398; M. A. West *et al.*, "Reducing Patient Mortality in Hospitals: The Role of Human Resource Management," *Journal of Organizational Behavior* 27, no. 7 (2006): 983–1002. However, one study warns that firm performance seems to predict the presence of OB practices as much as vice versa. See P. M. Wright *et al.*, "The Relationship between HR Practices and Firm Performance: Examining Causal Order," *Personnel Psychology* 58, no. 2 (2005): 409–446.

14. Deloitte & Touche, *Human Capital Roi Study: Creating Shareholder Value through People* (Toronto: Deloitte & Touche, 2002); D. Wheeler and J. Thomson, *Human Capital Based Investment Criteria for Total Shareholder Returns: A Canadian and International Perspective* (Toronto: Schulich School of Business, York University, June 2004); P. Shokeen, T. M. Woodward, and

D. Wheeler, "Refining the York Index Investment Criteria," *SSRN eLibrary* (13 December 2006); L. Bassi and D. McMurrer, "Maximizing Your Return on People," *Harvard Business Review* 85, no. 3 (March 2007): 115–123, 144.

15. Mohrman, Gibson, and Mohrman Jr., "Doing Research That Is Useful to Practice: A Model and Empirical Exploration" Walsh *et al.*, "On the Relationship between Research and Practice: Debate and Reflections." Similarly, in 1961, Harvard business professor Fritz Roethlisberger proposed that the field of OB is concerned with human behaviour "from the points of view of both (a) its determination . . . and (b) its improvement." See P. B. Vaill, "F. J. Roethlisberger and the Elusive Phenomena of Organizational Behavior," *Journal of Management Education* 31, no. 3 (June 2007): 321–338.

16. R. H. Hall, "Effectiveness Theory and Organizational Effectiveness," *Journal of Applied Behavioral Science* 16, no. 4 (Oct. 1980): 536–545; K. Cameron, "Organizational Effectiveness: Its Demise and Re-Emergence through Positive Organizational Scholarship," in *Great Minds in Management*, ed. K. G. Smith and M. A. Hitt (New York: Oxford University Press, 2005), 304–330.

17. J. L. Price, "The Study of Organizational Effectiveness," *The Sociological Quarterly* 13 (1972): 3–15.

18. S. C. Selden and J. E. Sowa, "Testing a Multi-Dimensional Model of Organizational Performance: Prospects and Problems," *Journal of Public Administration Research and Theory* 14, no. 3 (July 2004): 395–416.

19. Chester Barnard gives one of the earliest descriptions of organizations as systems interacting with external environments and that are composed of subsystems. See: C. Barnard, *The Functions of the Executive* (Cambridge, MA: Harvard University Press, 1938), esp. Chap. 6. Also see: F. E. Kast and J. E. Rosenzweig, "General Systems Theory: Applications for Organization and Management," *Academy of Management Journal* 15, no. 4 (1972): 447–465; P. M. Senge, *The Fifth Discipline: The Art and Practice of the Learning Organization* (New York: Doubleday Currency, 1990); G. Morgan, *Images of Organization*, 2nd ed. (Newbury Park: Sage, 1996); A. De Geus, *The Living Company* (Boston: Harvard Business School Press, 1997).

20. D. P. Ashmos and G. P. Huber, "The Systems Paradigm in Organization Theory: Correcting the Record and Suggesting the Future," *The Academy of Management Review* 12, no. 4 (1987): 607–621.

21. Katz and Kahn, *The Social Psychology of Organizations*; V. P. Rindova and S. Kotha,

"Continuous 'Morphing': Competing through Dynamic Capabilities, Form, and Function," *Academy of Management Journal* 44 (2001): 1263–1280; J. McCann, "Organizational Effectiveness: Changing Concepts for Changing Environments," *Human Resource Planning* 27, no. 1 (2004): 42–50.

22. A. Bernasek, "The World's Most Admired Companies," *Fortune*, 22 March 2010, 121–126; L. Daniel, "Apple's Shuffle," *Newsweek* 156, no. 11 (13 September 2010); F. Manjoo and J. Caplan, "Apple Nation," *Fast Company*, no. 147 (July-Aug 2010): 69–76; "The World's 50 Most Innovative Companies," *Fast Company*, no. 153 (2011): 67.

23. D. Steinbok, *The Nokia Revolution: The Story of an Extraordinary Company That Transformed an Industry* (New York: AMACOM, 2001).

24. C. Ostroff and N. Schmitt, "Configurations of Organizational Effectiveness and Efficiency," *Academy of Management Journal* 36, no. 6 (1993): 1345.

25. P. S. Adler *et al.*, "Performance Improvement Capability: Keys to Accelerating Performance Improvement in Hospitals," *California Management Review* 45, no. 2 (2003): 12–33; J. Jamrog, M. Vickers, and D. Bear, "Building and Sustaining a Culture That Supports Innovation," *Human Resource Planning* 29, no. 3 (2006): 9–19.

26. K. E. Weick, *The Social Psychology of Organizing* (Reading, MA: Addison-Wesley, 1979); S. Brusoni and A. Prencipe, "Managing Knowledge in Loosely Coupled Networks: Exploring the Links between Product and Knowledge Dynamics," *Journal of Management Studies* 38, no. 7 (Nov. 2001): 1019–1035.

27. G. Huber, "Organizational Learning: The Contributing Processes and Literature," *Organizational Science* 2 (1991): 88–115; D. A. Garvin, *Learning in Action: A Guide to Putting the Learning Organization to Work* (Boston: Harvard Business School Press, 2000); H. Shipton, "Cohesion or Confusion? Towards a Typology for Organizational Learning Research," *International Journal of Management Reviews* 8, no. 4 (2006): 233–252; W. C. Bogner and P. Bansal, "Knowledge Management as the Basis of Sustained High Performance," *Journal of Management Studies* 44, no. 1 (2007): 165–188; D. Jiménez-Jiménez and J. G. Cegarra-Navarro, "The Performance Effect of Organizational Learning and Market Orientation," *Industrial Marketing Management* 36, no. 6 (2007): 694–708.

28. R. Garud and A. Kumaraswamy, "Vicious and Virtuous Circles in the Management of Knowledge: The Case of Infosys Technologies," *MIS Quarterly* 29, no. 1 (March 2005): 9–33; S. L. Hoe and S. L. McShane, "Structural and Informal Knowledge Acquisition and Dissemination

in Organizational Learning: An Exploratory Analysis," *The Learning Organization* 17, no. 4 (2010): 364–386.

29. W. Cohen and D. Levinthal, "Absorptive Capacity: A New Perspective on Learning and Innovation," *Administrative Science Quarterly* 35 (1990): 128–152; G. Todorova and B. Durisin, "Absorptive Capacity: Valuing a Reconceptualization," *Academy of Management Review* 32, no. 3 (2007): 774–786.

30. T. A. Stewart, *Intellectual Capital: The New Wealth of Organizations* (New York: Currency/ Doubleday, 1997); H. Saint-Onge and D. Wallace, *Leveraging Communities of Practice for Strategic Advantage* (Boston: Butterworth-Heinemann, 2003), 9–10; J.-A. Johannessen, B. Olsen, and J. Olaisen, "Intellectual Capital as a Holistic Management Philosophy: A Theoretical Perspective," *International Journal of Information Management* 25, no. 2 (2005): 151–171; L. Striukova, J. Unerman, and J. Guthrie, "Corporate Reporting of Intellectual Capital: Evidence from UK Companies," *British Accounting Review* 40, no. 4 (2008): 297–313.

31. Centre for Education and Work, *The Learning Organization Video* (Winnipeg: Centre for Education and Work, 2009); C. Hawkins, *Duha Colour Group*, Weslat Case Studies (Winnipeg: Centre for Education and Work, 2009).

32. A. Wahl and L. Bogomolny, "Leaders Wanted," *Canadian Business*, 1–14 March 2004, 31–36.

33. M. N. Wexler, "Organizational Memory and Intellectual Capital," *Journal of Intellectual Capital* 3, no. 4 (2002): 393–414.

34. "A Cornerstone for Learning," *T&D*, October 2008, 66–89.

35. M. E. McGill and J. W. Slocum Jr., "Unlearn the Organization," *Organizational Dynamics* 22, no. 2 (1993): 67–79; A. E. Akgün, G. S. Lynn, and J. C. Byrne, "Antecedents and Consequences of Unlearning in New Product Development Teams," *Journal of Product Innovation Management* 23 (2006): 73–88.

36. E. Appelbaum et al., *Manufacturing Advantage: Why High-Performance Work Systems Pay Off* (Ithaca, N. Y.: Cornell University Press, 2000); A. Zacharatos, J. Barling, and R. D. Iverson, "High-Performance Work Systems and Occupational Safety," *Journal of Applied Psychology* 90, no. 1 (2005): 77–93; G. S. Benson, S. M. Young, and E. E. Lawler III, "High-Involvement Work Practices and Analysts' Forecasts of Corporate Earnings," *Human Resource Management* 45, no. 4 (2006): 519–537; L. Sels et al., "Unravelling the HRM-Performance Link: Value-Creating and Cost-Increasing Effects of Small Business HRM," *Journal of Management Studies* 43, no. (2006):319–342.

37. M. A. Huselid, "The Impact of Human Resource Management Practices on Turnover, Productivity, and Corporate," *Academy of Management Journal* 38, no. 3 (1995): 635; B. E. Becker and M. A. Huselid, "Strategic Human Resources Management: Where Do We Go from Here?," *Journal of Management* 32, no. 6 (Dec. 2006): 898–925; J. Combs et al., "How Much Do High-Performance Work Practices Matter? A Meta-Analysis of Their Effects on Organizational Performance," *Personnel Psychology* 59, no. 3 (2006): 501–528.

38. J. Barney, "Firm Resources and Sustained Competitive Advantage," *Journal of Management* 17, no. 1 (1991): 99–120.

39. E. E. Lawler III, S. A. Mohrman, and G. E. Ledford Jr., *Strategies for High Performance Organizations* (San Francisco: Jossey-Bass, 1998); S. H. Wagner, C. P. Parker, and D. Neil, "Employees That Think and Act Like Owners: Effects of Ownership Beliefs and Behaviors on Organizational Effectiveness," *Personnel Psychology* 56, no. 4 (Winter 2003): 847–871; P. J. Gollan, "High Involvement Management and Human Resource Sustainability: The Challenges and Opportunities," *Asia Pacific Journal of Human Resources* 43, no. 1 (April 2005): 18–33; Y. Liu *et al.*, "The Value of Human Resource Management for Organizational Performance," *Business Horizons* 50 (2007): 503–511; P. Tharenou, A. M. Saks, and C. Moore, "A Review and Critique of Research on Training and Organizational-Level Outcomes," *Human Resource Management Review* 17, no. 3 (2007): 251–273.

40. M. Subramony, "A Meta-Analytic Investigation of the Relationship between HRM Bundles and Firm Performance," *Human Resource Management* 48, no. 5 (2009): 745–768.

41. www.eluta.ca/top-employer-pcl. Retrieved July 13, 2010; www.pcl.com/ Careers/CollegeofConstruction.aspx. Retrieved July 13, 2010.

42. S. Fleetwood and A. Hesketh, "HRM-Performance Research: Under-Theorized and Lacking Explanatory Power," *International Journal of Human Resource Management* 17, no. 12 (Dec. 2006): 1977–1993.

43. R. Takeuchi et al., "An Empirical Examination of the Mechanisms Mediating between High-Performance Work Systems and the Performance of Japanese Organizations," *Journal of Applied Psychology* 92, no. 4 (2007): 1069–1083; L.-Q. Wei and C. M. Lau, "High Performance Work Systems and Performance: The Role of Adaptive Capability," *Human Relations* 63, no. 10 (2010): 1487–1511; J. Camps and R. Luna-Arocas, "A Matter of Learning: How Human Resources Affect Organizational Performance," *British Journal of Management* (in press).

44. J. Godard, "High Performance and the Transformation of Work? The Implications of Alternative Work Practices for the Experience and Outcomes of Work," *Industrial and Labor Relations Review* 54, no. 4 (July 2001): 776–805; G. Murray et al., eds., *Work and Employment Relations in the High-Performance Workplace* (London: Continuum, 2002); B. Harley, "Hope or Hype? High Performance Work Systems," in *Participation and Democracy at Work: Essays in Honour of Harvie Ramsay*, ed. B. Harley, J. Hyman, and P. Thompson (Houndsmills, UK: Palgrave Macmillan, 2005), 38–54.

45. A. L. Friedman and S. Miles, *Stakeholders: Theory and Practice* (New York: Oxford University Press, 2006); M. L. Barnett, "Stakeholder Influence Capacity and the Variability of Financial Returns to Corporate Social Responsibility," *Academy of Management Review* 32, no. 3 (2007): 794–816; R. E. Freeman, J. S. Harrison, and A. C. Wicks, *Managing for Stakeholders: Survival, Reputation, and Success* (New Haven, CT: Yale University Press, 2007).

46. C. Eden and F. Ackerman, *Making Strategy: The Journey of Strategic Management* (London: Sage, 1998).

47. G. R. Salancik and J. Pfeffer, *The External Control of Organizations: A Resource Dependence Perspective* (New York: Harper & Row, 1978); T. Casciaro and M. J. Piskorski, "Power Imbalance, Mutual Dependence, and Constraint Absorption: A Closer Look at Dependence Theory," *Administrative Science Quarterly* 50 (2005): 167–199; N. Roome and F. Wijen, "Stakeholder Power and Organizational Learning in Corporate Environmental Management," *Organization Studies* 27, no. 2 (2005): 235–263.

48. R. E. Freeman, A. C. Wicks, and B. Parmar, "Stakeholder Theory and 'the Corporate Objective Revisited'," *Organization Science* 15, no. 3 (May-June 2004): 364–369; Friedman and Miles, *Stakeholders: Theory and Practice*, Chap. 3; B. L. Parmar et al., "Stakeholder Theory: The State of the Art," *Academy of Management Annals* 4, no. 1 (2010): 403–445.

49. B. M. Meglino and E. C. Ravlin, "Individual Values in Organizations: Concepts, Controversies, and Research," *Journal of Management* 24, no. 3 (1998): 351–389; B. R. Agle and C. B. Caldwell, "Understanding Research on Values in Business," *Business and Society* 38, no. 3 (September 1999): 326–387; A. Bardi and S. H. Schwartz, "Values and Behavior: Strength and Structure of Relations," *Personality and Social Psychology Bulletin* 29, no. 10 (October 2003): 1207–1220; S. Hitlin and J. A. Pilavin, "Values: Reviving a Dormant Concept," *Annual Review of Sociology* 30 (2004): 359–393.

50. R. M. Patten, "From Implicit to Explicit: Putting Corporate Values and Personal Accountability Front and Centre," *Ivy Business Journal* (Sept.-Oct. 2004): H1-H4.

51. Aspen Institute, *Where Will They Lead? MBA Student Attitudes About Business & Society* (Washington, DC: Aspen Institute, April 2008).

52. M. van Marrewijk, "Concepts and Definitions of CSR and Corporate Sustainability: Between Agency and Communion," *Journal of Business Ethics* 44 (May 2003): 95–105; Barnett, "Stakeholder Influence Capacity and the Variability of Financial Returns to Corporate Social Responsibility."

53. L. S. Paine, *Value Shift* (New York: McGraw-Hill, 2003); A. Mackey, T. B. Mackey, and J. B. Barney, "Corporate Social Responsibility and Firm Performance: Investor Preferences and Corporate Strategies," *Academy of Management Review* 32, no. 3 (2007): 817–835.

54. S. Zadek, *The Civil Corporation: The New Economy of Corporate Citizenship* (London: Earthscan, 2001); S. Hart and M. Milstein, "Creating Sustainable Value," *Academy of Management Executive* 17, no. 2 (2003): 56–69.

55. M. Friedman, *Capitalism and Freedom*, 40th Anniversary ed. (Chicago: University of Chicago Press, 2002), Chap. 8; N. Vorster, "An Ethical Critique of Milton Friedman, Doctrine on Economics and Freedom," *Journal for the Study of Religions and Ideologies* 9, no. 26 (Summer 2010): 163–188.

56. "George Weston Ltd—Corporate Citizenship Initiatives Earn Top Accolades," Market News news release for Loblaw Companies Limited (Toronto: 22 June 2010); "Loblaw Companies Ltd—Extends Sustainable Seafood Public Awareness Campaign," Market News news release for Loblaw Companies Limited (Toronto: 8 June 2010); *Grocery Stores: Now Stocking Wind Power* (Barre, VT: Northern Power Systems, September 2010); M. Strauss, "Why Loblaw Takes Top Honours for Corporate Social Responsibility," *Globe & Mail*, 20 June 2010.

57. Zadek, *The Civil Corporation: The New Economy of Corporate Citizenship*; "Canadians Inclined to Punish Companies Deemed Socially Irresponsible, Study Suggests," *Canadian Press*, 23 April 2005; M. Johne, "Show Us the Green, Workers Say," *Globe & Mail*, 10 October 2007, C1.

58. R. Martin, "The Virtue Matrix: Calculating the Return on Corporate Responsibility," *Harvard Business Review* 80 (March 2002): 68–85.

59. A. Fox, "Corporate Social Responsibility Pays Off," *HRMagazine* 52, no. 8 (August 2007): 42–47.

60. W. Immen, "On the Move for Work," *Globe & Mail*, 15 May 2010, B16.

61. S. Fischer, "Globalization and Its Challenges," *American Economic Review* (May

2003): 1–29. For discussion of the diverse meanings of *globalization,* see M. F. Guillén, "Is Globalization Civilizing, Destructive or Feeble? A Critique of Five Key Debates in the Social Science Literature," *Annual Review of Sociology* 27 (2001): 235–260.

62. The ongoing debate regarding the advantages and disadvantages of globalization are discussed in Guillén, "Is Globalization Civilizing, Destructive or Feeble?"; D. Doane, "Can Globalization Be Fixed?" *Business Strategy Review* 13, no. 2 (2002): 51–58; J. Bhagwati, *In Defense of Globalization* (New York: Oxford University Press, 2004); M. Wolf, *Why Globalization Works* (New Haven, CT: Yale University Press, 2004).

63. K. Ohmae, *The Next Global Stage* (Philadelphia: Wharton School Publishing, 2005).

64. V. Galt, "Diversity at Work: 77 Employees, 27 Languages," *Globe & Mail*, 3 December 2007.

65. J. Gray, "To Have, not Have Not," *Report on Business, Globe and Mail*, January 2010, 30; M. Sprung, "BNN Market Call Tonight," *Globe and Mail*, 1 July 2010, B7; A. Wahl, "2009 All-Star Execs," *Canadian Business*, Vol. 82 Iss. 82, 23 November 2010, 59–60; "Viterra Acquires Dakota Growers Pasta Company," *Leader-Post*, 5 May 2010; *Viterra 2009 Business Review–Creating Connections*, www.viterra.ca.

66. K. Kelly, *Visible Minorities: A Diverse Group*, Canadian Social Trends (Ottawa: Statistics Canada, 6 February 2004); A. Bélanger and E. C. Malenfant, *Population Projections of Visible Minority Groups, Canada, Provinces, and Regions: 2001–2017* (Ottawa: Statistics Canada, March 2005); "Toronto's Racial Diversity" (Toronto, 2010), http://www.toronto.ca/toronto_facts/diversity.htm (accessed 19 November 2010).

67. D. A. Harrison et al., "Time, Teams, and Task Performance: Changing Effects of Surface- and Deep-Level Diversity on Group Functioning," *Academy of Management Journal* 45, no. 5 (2002): 1029–1046.

68. R. Zemke, C. Raines, and B. Filipczak, *Generations at Work: Managing the Clash of Veterans, Boomers, Xers, and Nexters in Your Workplace* (New York: Amacom, 2000); S. H. Applebaum, M. Serena, and B. T. Shapiro, "Generation X and the Boomers: Organizational Myths and Literary Realities," *Management Research News* 27, no. 11/12 (2004): 1–28; N. Howe and W. Strauss, "The Next 20 Years: How Customer and Workforce Attitudes Will Evolve," *Harvard Business Review* (July-August 2007): 41–52.

69. E. Ng, L. Schweitzer, and S. Lyons, "New Generation, Great Expectations: A Field Study of the Millennial Generation," *Journal of Business and Psychology* 25, no. 2 (2010): 281–292.

70. J. M. Twenge and S. M. Campbell, "Generational Differences in Psychological Traits and Their Impact on the Workplace," *Journal of Managerial Psychology* 23, no. 8 (2008): 862–877; M. Wong et al., "Generational Differences in Personality and Motivation," *Journal of Managerial Psychology* 23, no. 8 (2008): 878–890; J. Deal, D. Altman, and S. Rogelberg, "Millennials at Work: What We Know and What We Need to Do (If Anything)," *Journal of Business and Psychology* 25, no. 2 (2010): 191–199; B. Kowske, R. Rasch, and J. Wiley, "Millennials' (Lack of) Attitude Problem: An Empirical Examination of Generational Effects on Work Attitudes," *Journal of Business and Psychology* 25, no. 2 (2010): 265–279; J. Twenge, "A Review of the Empirical Evidence on Generational Differences in Work Attitudes," *Journal of Business and Psychology* 25, no. 2 (2010): 201–210.

71. Statistics Canada, "Labour Force Characteristics by Age and Sex (2010)," (Ottawa: Statistics Canada, 2011), http://www40.statcan.ca/l01/cst01/labor20a-eng.htm (accessed 9 April 2010).

72. J. M. Twenge et al., "Generational Differences in Work Values: Leisure and Extrinsic Values Increasing, Social and Intrinsic Values Decreasing," *Journal of Management* 36, no. 5 (September 2010): 1117–1142. Another temporal cohort study also reported an increasing preference for leisure, but these differences were not significant. see: J. Meriac, D. Woehr, and C. Banister, "Generational Differences in Work Ethic: An Examination of Measurement Equivalence across Three Cohorts," *Journal of Business and Psychology* 25, no. 2 (2010): 315–324.

73. O. C. Richard, "Racial Diversity, Business Strategy, and Firm Performance: A Resource-Based View," *Academy of Management Journal* 43 (2000): 164–177; T. Kochan et al., "The Effects of Diversity on Business Performance: Report of the Diversity Research Network," *Human Resource Management* 42 (2003): 3–21; R. J. Burke and E. Ng, "The Changing Nature of Work and Organizations: Implications for Human Resource Management," *Human Resource Management Review* 16 (2006): 86–94; M.-E. Roberge and R. van Dick, "Recognizing the Benefits of Diversity: When and How Does Diversity Increase Group Performance?," *Human Resource Management Review* 20, no. 4 (2010): 295–308.

74. D. Porras, D. Psihountas, and M. Griswold, "The Long-Term Performance of Diverse Firms," *International Journal of Diversity* 6, no. 1 (2006): 25–34; R. A. Weigand, "Organizational Diversity, Profits and Returns in U.S. Firms," *Problems & Perspectives in Management*, no. 3 (2007): 69–83.

75. "The Business Case for Diversity," *USBanker* 120, no. 5 (2010): 10–11.

76. R. J. Ely and D. A. Thomas, "Cultural Diversity at Work: The Effects of Diversity Perspectives on Work Group Processes and Outcomes," *Administrative Science Quarterly* 46 (June 2001): 229–273; Kochan et al., "The Effects of Diversity on Business Performance: Report of the Diversity Research Network"; D. van Knippenberg and S. A. Haslam, "Realizing the Diversity Dividend: Exploring the Subtle Interplay between Identity, Ideology and Reality," in *Social Identity at Work: Developing Theory for Organizational Practice*, ed. S. A. Haslam et al. (New York: Taylor and Francis, 2003), 61–80; D. van Knippenberg, C. K. W. De Dreu, and A. C. Homan, "Work Group Diversity and Group Performance: An Integrative Model and Research Agenda," *Journal of Applied Psychology* 89, no. 6 (2004): 1008–1022; E. Molleman, "Diversity in Demographic Characteristics, Abilities and Personality Traits: Do Faultlines Affect Team Functioning?," *Group Decision and Negotiation* 14, no. 3 (2005): 173–193.

77. A. Birritteri, "Workplace Diversity: Realizing the Benefits of an All-Inclusive Employee Base," *New Jersey Business*, November 2005, 36.

78. "Canadians Name Diversity as Key Ingredient in Formula for Innovation Success," Xerox Canada news release for Xerox of Canada (Toronto: 25 September 2007); "Canadians Endorse Multiculturalism but Pick Melting Pot over Mosaic," Angus Reid Public Opinion news release (Vancouver: 8 November 2010); *A Four Country Survey of Opinion on Racism and Prejudice in 2010: Canada, the United States, Germany, and Spain* (Montreal: Association for Canadian Studies; Canadian Race Relations Foundation, 2011); Environics Research Group, "On-Line Survey on Public Perceptions About Career Development and the Workplace," Environics Research Group news release for Canadian Education and Research Institute for Counselling (Toronto: January 2011).

79. W. G. Bennis and R. J. Thomas, *Geeks and Geezers* (Boston: Harvard Business School Press, 2002), 74–79; E. D. Y. Greenblatt, "Work/Life Balance: Wisdom or Whining," *Organizational Dynamics* 31, no. 2 (2002): 177–193.

80. D. Abma, "Staff Cuts Showing Negative Effects," *Montreal Gazette*, September 8, 2010; D. Abma, "Quarter of Employees Want New Jobs," *Vancouver Sun*, 6 October 2010, D7; T. Pearce, "The Time Crunch Takes Its Toll," *Globe & Mail*, 2 November 2010, A10.

81. J. Tattrie, "Half of Canadians Want to Telecommute," *Metro (Toronto)*, 26 October 2010. Also see: L. Duxbury and C. Higgins, "Telecommute: A Primer for the Millennium Introduction," in *The New World of Work: Challenges and Opportunities*, ed. C. L. Cooper and

R. J. Burke (Oxford: Blackwell, 2002), 157–199; S. Raghuram and B. Wiesenfeld, "Work-Nonwork Conflict and Job Stress among Virtual Workers," *Human Resource Management* 43, no. 2/3 (Summer/Fall 2004): 259–277. For historical estimates of telecommuting in Canada, see: E. B. Akyeampong and R. Nadwodny, "Evolution of the Canadian Workplace: Work from Home," *Perspectives on Labour and Income* 13, no. 4 (Winter 2001): 30–36; L. Schweitzer and L. Duxbury, "Benchmarking the Use of Telework Arrangements in Canada," *Canadian Journal of Administrative Sciences* 23, no. 2 (2006): 105–117.

82. "Telus Finds Telecommuting Good for Planet and the Bottom Line," *Vancouver Sun*, 25 June 2007; TELUS 2006 Corporate Social Responsibility Report, 12.

83. A. Bourhis and R. Mekkaoui, "Beyond Work-Family Balance: Are Family-Friendly Organizations More Attractive?" *Relations Industrielles/Industrial Relations* 65, no. 1 (Winter 2010): 98–117; E. J. Hill *et al.*, "Workplace Flexibility, Work Hours, and Work-Life Conflict: Finding an Extra Day or Two," *Journal of Family Psychology* 24, no. 3 (June 2010): 349–358.

84. D. E. Bailey and N. B. Kurland, "A Review of Telework Research: Findings, New Directions, and Lessons for the Study of Modern Work," *Journal of Organizational Behavior* 23 (2002): 383–400; D. W. McCloskey and M. Igbaria, "Does 'out of Sight' Mean 'out of Mind'? An Empirical Investigation of the Career Advancement Prospects of Telecommuters," *Information Resources Management Journal* 16 (April-June 2003): 19–34; Sensis, *Sensis® Insights Report: Teleworking* (Melbourne: Sensis, June 2005).

85. Most of these anchors are mentioned in: J. D. Thompson, "On Building an Administrative Science," *Administrative Science Quarterly* 1, no. 1 (1956): 102–111.

86. D. A. Whetten, T. Felin, and B. G. King, "The Practice of Theory Borrowing in Organizational Studies: Current Issues and Future Directions," *Journal of Management* 35, no. 3 (June 2009): 537–563.

87. On the history of the "culture" concept in organizational behaviour, see: C. Morrill, "Culture and Organization Theory," *The ANNALS of the American Academy of Political and Social Science* 619, no. 1(2008):15–40.

88. M. N. Zald, "More Fragmentation? Unfinished Business in Linking the Social Sciences and the Humanities," *Administrative Science Quarterly* 41 (1996): 251–261; C. Heath and S. B. Sitkin, "Big-B Versus Big-O: What Is Organizational About Organizational Behavior?" *Journal of Organizational Behavior* 22 (2001): 43–58.

89. This anchor has a colourful history dating back to critiques of business schools in

the 1950s. Soon after, systematic research became a mantra by many respected scholars. See, for example: Thompson, "On Building an Administrative Science."

90. J. Pfeffer and R. I. Sutton, *Hard Facts, Dangerous Half-Truths, and Total Nonsense* (Boston: Harvard Business School Press, 2006); D. M. Rousseau and S. McCarthy, "Educating Managers from an Evidence-Based Perspective," *Academy of Management Learning & Education* 6, no. 1 (2007): 84–101.

91. Whetten, Felin, and King, "The Practice of Theory Borrowing in Organizational Studies: Current Issues and Future Directions."

92. D. M. Rousseau and Y. Fried, "Location, Location, Location: Contextualizing Organizational Research," *Journal of Organizational Behavior* 22, no. 1 (2001): 1–13; C. M. Christensen and M. E. Raynor, "Why Hard-Nosed Executives Should Care About Management Theory," *Harvard Business Review* (September 2003): 66–74. For excellent critique of the "one best way" approach in early management scholarship, see P. F. Drucker, "Management's New Paradigms," *Forbes* (October 5 1998): 152–177.

93. H. L. Tosi and J. W. Slocum Jr., "Contingency Theory: Some Suggested Directions," *Journal of Management* 10 (1984): 9–26.

94. D. M. H. Rousseau, R. J. , "Meso Organizational Behavior: Avoiding Three Fundamental Biases," in *Trends in Organizational Behavior*, ed. C. L. Cooper and D. M. Rousseau (Chichester, UK: John Wiley & Sons, 1994), 13–30.

95. "NHS Chief Vows to Cut Waste and Look to Toyota in Efficiency Drive," NHS Federation News release (London, UK: 14 June 2006); D. Jones and A. Mitchell, *Lean Thinking for the NHS* (London: NHS Confederation, 2006); M. McCarthy, "Can Car Manufacturing Techniques Reform Health Care," *Lancet* 367, no. 9507 (28 January 2006): 290–291; "Nissan 'Shot in the Arm' for Healthcare Sector," *Newcarinfo.co.uk*, 13 February 2007; I. Green, "Drive for Success," *Nursing Standard* 21, no. 38 (30 May 2007): 62–63; A.-M. Kelly *et al.*, "Improving Emergency Department Efficiency by Patient Streaming to Outcomes-Based Teams," *Australian Health Review* 31, no. 1 (2007): 16–21.

CHAPTER 2

1. P. Kuitenbrouwer, "Sugar Beach is Sweet and Timely," *National Post*, 8 July 2010, A12; "Corus's Strength Rooted in Employee Teamwork; Strength Came From Sharing Recession Burden," *National Post*, 1 February 2010, JV2; L. Wright, "Who Says Work Can't Be Fun(ny); Corporations Get Creative To Get Their Employees on Board The United Way Fundraising Bandwagon," *Toronto Star*, 3 October 2010, G2; B. Ka-

plan, "Work Perks: A Roof-Top Garden Can Suddenly Make the Office a Preferred Option," 21 August 2010, TO3; "Nurturing A Culture; Corus; In 10 years Media Company Has Become Pervasive," *National Post*, 1 February 2010, JV2.

2. L. L. Thurstone, "Ability, Motivation, and Speed," *Psychometrika* 2, no. 4 (1937): 249–254; N. R. F. Maier, *Psychology in Industry*, 2nd ed. (Boston: Houghton Mifflin Company, 1955); V. H. Vroom, *Work and Motivation* (New York: John Wiley & Sons, 1964); J. P. Campbell *et al.*, *Managerial Behavior, Performance, and Effectiveness* (New York: McGraw-Hill, 1970).

3. U.-C. Klehe and N. Anderson, "Working Hard and Working Smart: Motivation and Ability During Typical and Maximum Performance," *Journal of Applied Psychology* 92, no. 4 (2007): 978–992; J. S. Gould-Williams and M. Gatenby, "The Effects of Organizational Context and Teamworking Activities on Performance Outcomes—A Study Conducted in England Local Government," *Public Management Review* 12, no. 6 (2010): 759–787.

4. E. E. I. Lawler and L. W. Porter, "Antecedent Attitudes of Effective Managerial Performance," *Organizational Behavior and Human Performance* 2 (1967): 122–142; M. A. Griffin, A. Neal, and S. K. Parker, "A New Model of Work Role Performance: Positive Behavior in Uncertain and Interdependent Contexts," *Academy of Management Journal* 50, no. 2 (April 2007): 327–347.

5. Only a few literature reviews have included all four factors. These include J. P. Campbell and R. D. Pritchard, "Motivation Theory in Industrial and Organizational Psychology," in *Handbook of Industrial and Organizational Psychology*, ed. M. D. Dunnette (Chicago: Rand McNally, 1976), 62–130; T. R. Mitchell, "Motivation: New Directions for Theory, Research, and Practice," *Academy of Management Review* 7, no. 1 (Jan. 1982): 80–88; G. A. J. Churchill *et al.*, "The Determinants of Salesperson Performance: A Meta-Analysis," *Journal of Marketing Research (JMR)* 22, no. 2 (1985): 103–118; R. E. Plank and D. A. Reid, "The Mediating Role of Sales Behaviors: An Alternative Perspective of Sales Performance and Effectiveness," *Journal of Personal Selling & Sales Management* 14, no. 3 (Summer 1994): 43–56. The *MARS* acronym was coined by senior officers in the Singapore armed forces. Chris Perryer at the University of Western Australia suggests the full model should be called the "MARS BAR" because the outcomes might be labelled "behaviour and results"!

6. Technically, the model proposes that situation factors moderate the effects of the three within-person factors. For instance, the effect of employee motivation on behaviour and performance depends on (is moderated by) the situation.

7. C. C. Pinder, *Work Motivation in Organizational Behavior* (Upper Saddle River, N. J.: Prentice-Hall, 1998); G. P. Latham and C. C. Pinder, "Work Motivation Theory and Research at the Dawn of the Twenty-First Century," *Annual Review of Psychology* 56 (2005): 485–516.

8. L. M. Spencer and S. M. Spencer, *Competence at Work: Models for Superior Performance* (New York: Wiley, 1993); R. Kurz and D. Bartram, "Competency and Individual Performance: Modelling the World of Work," in *Organizational Effectiveness: The Role of Psychology*, ed. I. T. Robertson, M. Callinan, and D. Bartram (Chichester, UK: John Wiley & Sons, 2002), 227–258; D. Bartram, "The Great Eight Competencies: A Criterion-Centric Approach to Validation," *Journal of Applied Psychology* 90, no. 6 (2005): 1185–1203; H. Heinsman *et al.*, "Competencies through the Eyes of Psychologists: A Closer Look at Assessing Competencies," *International Journal of Selection and Assessment* 15, no. 4 (Dec. 2007): 412–427.

9. P. Tharenou, A. M. Saks, and C. Moore, "A Review and Critique of Research on Training and Organizational-Level Outcomes," *Human Resource Management Review* 17, no. 3 (2007): 251–273; T. W. H. Ng and D. C. Feldman, "How Broadly Does Education Contribute to Job Performance?," *Personnel Psychology* 62, no. 1 (Spring 2009): 89–134.

10. "Canadian Organizations Must Work Harder to Productively Engage Employees," Watson Wyatt Canada news release for Watson Wyatt Canada (Toronto: 25 January 2005).

11. H. Cho, "Super Bowl of Retail Days," *Baltimore Sun*, 23 November 2006; A. Cheng, "Black Friday Kicks Off Retailers' Biggest Selling Season," *Dow Jones Business News*, 24 November 2007; J. Davis, "Training Helps Sales Staff Cope with Black Friday," *Rocky Mountain News (Denver)*, 20 November 2007, Bus3; A. K. Walker, "Stores Looking Hard at Crowd Control for Post-Thanksgiving Rush," *Baltimore Sun*, 26 November 2009. This day is called Black Friday because in theory the typical retailer starts to make a profit (go in the black) around this time of year.

12. J. Becker and L. Layton, "Safety Warnings Often Ignored at Metro," *Washington Post*, 6 June 2005, A01.

13. W. H. Cooper and M. J. Withey, "The Strong Situation Hypothesis," *Personality and Social Psychology Review* 13, no. 1 (February 2009): 62–72; D. C. Funder, "Persons, Behaviors and Situations: An Agenda for Personality Psychology in the Postwar Era," *Journal of Research in Personality* 43, no. 2 (2009): 120–126; R. D. Meyer, R. S. Dalal, and R. Hermida, "A Review and Synthesis of Situational Strength in the Organizational Sciences," *Journal of Management* 36, no. 1 (January 2010): 121–140; R. A. Sherman, C. S. Nave, and D. C. Funder, "Situational Similarity and Personality Predict Behavioral Consistency," *Journal of Personality and Social Psychology* 99, no. 2 (2010): 330–343.

14. K. F. Kane, "Special Issue: Situational Constraints and Work Performance," *Human Resource Management Review* 3 (Summer 1993): 83–175; S. B. Bacharach and P. Bamberger, "Beyond Situational Constraints: Job Resources Inadequacy and Individual Performance at Work," *Human Resource Management Review* 5, no. 2 (1995): 79–102; G. Johns, "Commentary: In Praise of Context," *Journal of Organizational Behavior* 22 (2001): 31–42.

15. Meyer, Dalal, and Hermida, "A Review and Synthesis of Situational Strength in the Organizational Sciences."

16. J. P. Campbell, "The Definition and Measurement of Performance in the New Age," in *The Changing Nature of Performance: Implications for Staffing, Motivation, and Development* ed. D. R. Ilgen and E. D. Pulakos (San Francisco: Jossey-Bass, 1999), 399–429; R. D. Hackett, "Understanding and Predicting Work Performance in the Canadian Military," *Canadian Journal of Behavioural Science* 34, no. 2 (2002): 131–140.

17. O. Varela and R. Landis, "A General Structure of Job Performance: Evidence from Two Studies," *Journal of Business and Psychology* 25, no. 4 (2010): 625–638.

18. D. W. Organ, "Organizational Citizenship Behavior: It's Construct Clean-up Time," *Human Performance* 10 (1997): 85–97; J. A. LePine, A. Erez, and D. E. Johnson, "The Nature and Dimensionality of Organizational Citizenship Behavior: A Critical Review and Meta-Analysis," *Journal of Applied Psychology* 87 (February 2002): 52–65; R. S. Dalal, "A Meta-Analysis of the Relationship between Organizational Citizenship Behavior and Counterproductive Work Behavior," *Journal of Applied Psychology* 90, no. 6 (2005): 1241–1255.

19. K. Lee and N. J. Allen, "Organizational Citizenship Behavior and Workplace Deviance: The Role of Affect and Cognitions," *Journal of Applied Psychology* 87, no. 1 (2002): 131–142.

20. M. Rotundo and P. Sackett, "The Relative Importance of Task, Citizenship, and Counterproductive Performance to Global Ratings of Job Performance: A Policy-Capturing Approach," *Journal of Applied Psychology* 87 (February 2002): 66–80; P. D. Dunlop and K. Lee, "Workplace Deviance, Organizational Citizenship Behaviour, and Business Unit Performance: The Bad Apples Do Spoil the Whole Barrel," *Journal of Organizational Behavior* 25 (2004): 67–80; Dalal, "A Meta-Analysis of the Relationship between Organizational Citizenship Behavior and Counterproductive Work Behavior";

N. A. Bowling and M. L. Gruys, "Overlooked Issues in the Conceptualization and Measurement of Counterproductive Work Behavior," *Human Resource Management Review* 20, no. 1 (2010): 54–61.

21. S. Majumdar, "Meaningful Engagement," *Business Standard (India)*, 5 March 2009, 8.

22. M. Rotundo and J. L. Xie, "Understanding the Domain of Counterproductive Work Behaviour in China," *The International Journal of Human Resource Management* 19, no. 5 (2008): 856–877.

23. C. Sorensen, "Hotels Run out of Workers," *National Post*, 21 June 2006, FP1; J. Skerritt, "Nursing Shortages Plague Reserves," *Winnipeg Free Press*, 13 November 2009, A4; J. Komarnicki, "Tories under Fire for Cancer Centre Delays," *Calgary Herald*, 9 June 2010, A3.

24. "Wanted: Career Monogamy." Towers Watson news release for Towers Watson (Toronto: 16 March 2010); W. Immen, "Employer, Will You Marry Me?," *Globe & Mail*, 24 March 2010, B21.

25. N. Chaudhury *et al.*, "Missing in Action: Teacher and Health Worker Absence in Developing Countries," *The Journal of Economic Perspectives* 20, no. 1 (2006): 91–116; L. Yssaad, "Work Absences in 2009," *Perspectives on Labour and Income* 22, no. 3 (June 2010): 14–23.

26. "Impact of H1N1 and Seasonal Flu on Hours Worked," *The Daily (Statistics Canada)* (15 January 2010); Yssaad, "Work Absences in 2009."

27. A. Furnham and M. Bramwell, "Personality Factors Predict Absenteeism in the Workplace," *Individual Differences Research* 4, no. 2 (2006): 68–77.

28. D. A. Harrison and J. J. Martocchio, "Time for Absenteeism: A 20-Year Review of Origins, Offshoots, and Outcomes," *Journal of Management* 24 (Spring 1998): 305–350; C. M. Mason and M. A. Griffin, "Group Absenteeism and Positive Affective Tone: A Longitudinal Study," *Journal of Organizational Behavior* 24 (2003): 667–687; A. Vaananen *et al.*, "Job Characteristics, Physical and Psychological Symptoms, and Social Support as Antecedents of Sickness Absence among Men and Women in the Private Industrial Sector," *Social Science & Medicine* 57, no. 5 (2003): 807–824.

29. R. Lombardi, "Walking Wounded," *Canadian Occupational Safety*, Nov/Dec 2009, 14–15; G. Johns, "Presenteeism in the Workplace: A Review and Research Agenda," *Journal of Organizational Behavior* 31, no. 4 (2010): 519–542.

30. C. Crawshaw, "Personality Testing Can Be a Sticky Subject," *Edmonton Journal*, 29 March 2008, D14.

31. Personality researchers agree on one point about the definition of personality: It is difficult to pin down. A definition necessarily captures one perspective of the

topic more than others, and the concept of personality is itself very broad. The definition presented here is based on C. S. Carver and M. F. Scheier, *Perspectives on Personality*, 6th ed. (Boston: Allyn & Bacon, 2007); D. C. Funder, *The Personality Puzzle*, 4th ed. (New York: W. W. Norton & Company, 2007).

32. D. P. McAdams and J. L. Pals, "A New Big Five: Fundamental Principles for an Integrative Science of Personality," *American Psychologist* 61, no. 3 (2006): 204–217.

33. B. Reynolds and K. Karraker, "A Big Five Model of Disposition and Situation Interaction: Why a 'Helpful' Person May Not Always Behave Helpfully," *New Ideas in Psychology* 21 (April 2003): 1–13; W. Mischel, "Toward an Integrative Science of the Person," *Annual Review of Psychology* 55 (2004): 1–22.

34. B. W. Roberts and A. Caspi, "Personality Development and the Person-Situation Debate: It's Déjà Vu All over Again," *Psychological Inquiry* 12, no. 2 (2001): 104–109.

35. K. L. Jang, W. J. Livesley, and P. A. Vernon, "Heritability of the Big Five Personality Dimensions and Their Facets: A Twin Study," *Journal of Personality* 64, no. 3 (1996): 577–591; N. L. Segal, *Entwined Lives: Twins and What They Tell Us About Human Behavior* (New York: Plume, 2000); T. Bouchard and J. Loehlin, "Genes, Evolution, and Personality," *Behavior Genetics* 31, no. 3 (May 2001): 243–273; G. Lensvelt-Mulders and J. Hettema, "Analysis of Genetic Influences on the Consistency and Variability of the Big Five across Different Stressful Situations," *European Journal of Personality* 15, no. 5 (2001): 355–371; P. Borkenau *et al.*, "Genetic and Environmental Influences on Person X Situation Profiles," *Journal of Personality* 74, no. 5 (2006): 1451–1480.

36. Segal, *Entwined Lives*, 116–118. For critiques of the genetics perspective of personality, see J. Joseph, "Separated Twins and the Genetics of Personality Differences: A Critique," *American Journal of Psychology* 114, no. 1 (Spring 2001): 1–30; P. Ehrlich and M. W. Feldman, "Genes, Environments & Behaviors," *Daedalus* 136, no. 2 (Spring 2007): 5–12.

37. B. W. Roberts and W. F. DelVecchio, "The Rank-Order Consistency of Personality Traits from Childhood to Old Age: A Quantitative Review of Longitudinal Studies," *Psychological Bulletin* 126, no. 1 (2000): 3–25; A. Terracciano, P. T. Costa, and R. R. McCrae, "Personality Plasticity after Age 30," *Personality and Social Psychology Bulletin* 32, no. 8 (Aug. 2006): 999–1009.

38. M. Jurado and M. Rosselli, "The Elusive Nature of Executive Functions: A Review of Our Current Understanding," *Neuropsychology Review* 17, no. 3 (2007): 213–233.

39. B. W. Roberts and E. M. Pomerantz, "On Traits, Situations, and Their Integration: A Developmental Perspective," *Personality & Social Psychology Review* 8, no. 4 (2004): 402–416; W. Fleeson, "Situation-Based Contingencies Underlying Trait-Content Manifestation in Behavior," *Journal of Personality* 75, no. 4 (2007): 825–862.

40. J. M. Digman, "Personality Structure: Emergence of the Five-Factor Model," *Annual Review of Psychology* 41 (1990): 417–440; O. P. John and S. Srivastava, "The Big Five Trait Taxonomy: History, Measurement, and Theoretical Perspectives," in *Handbook of Personality: Theory and Research*, ed. L. A. Pervin and O. P. John (New York: Guildford Press, 1999), 102–138; A. Caspi, B. W. Roberts, and R. L. Shiner, "Personality Development: Stability and Change," *Annual Review of Psychology* 56, no. 1 (2005): 453–484; McAdams and Pals, "A New Big Five."

41. J. Hogan and B. Holland, "Using Theory to Evaluate Personality and Job-Performance Relations: A Socioanalytic Perspective," *Journal of Applied Psychology* 88, no. 1 (2003): 100–112; D. S. Ones, C. Viswesvaran, and S. Dilchert, "Personality at Work: Raising Awareness and Correcting Misconceptions," *Human Performance* 18, no. 4 (2005): 389–404; I.-S. Oh and C. M. Berry, "The Five-Factor Model of Personality and Managerial Performance: Validity Gains through the Use of 360 Degree Performance Ratings," *Journal of Applied Psychology* 94, no. 6 (2009): 1498–1513.

42. "Grubber, King Hit, Shinboner, Screwie," Retrieved: October 15, 2010 http://www.psychometrics.com/en-us/articles/afl_personality.htm; AFL Canada, Retrieved October 24, 2010 http://www.sportingpulse.com/assoc_page.cgi?c=1-7259-0-0-0&sID=156187.

43. M. R. Barrick and M. K. Mount, "Yes, Personality Matters: Moving on to More Important Matters," *Human Performance* 18, no. 4 (2005): 359–372; S. J. Perry *et al.*, "P = F (Conscientiousness x Ability): Examining the Facets of Conscientiousness," *Human Performance* 23, no. 4 (2010): 343–360.

44. M. R. Barrick, M. K. Mount, and T. A. Judge, "Personality and Performance at the Beginning of the New Millennium: What Do We Know and Where Do We Go Next?," *International Journal of Selection and Assessment* 9, no. 1&2 (2001): 9–30; T. A. Judge and R. Ilies, "Relationship of Personality to Performance Motivation: A Meta-Analytic Review," *Journal of Applied Psychology* 87, no. 4 (2002): 797–807; A. Witt, L. A. Burke, and M. R. Barrick, "The Interactive Effects of Conscientiousness and Agreeableness on Job Performance," *Journal of Applied Psychology* 87 (February 2002): 164–169; J. Moutafi, A. Furnham,

and J. Crump, "Is Managerial Level Related to Personality?," *British Journal of Management* 18, no. 3 (2007): 272–280.

45. R. Ilies, M. W. Gerhardt, and H. Le, "Individual Differences in Leadership Emergence: Integrating Meta-Analytic Findings and Behavioral Genetics Estimates," *International Journal of Selection and Assessment* 12, no. 3 (September 2004): 207–219; Oh and Berry, "The Five-Factor Model of Personality and Managerial Performance: Validity Gains through the Use of 360 Degree Performance Ratings."

46. K. M. DeNeve and H. Cooper, "The Happy Personality: A Meta-Analysis of 137 Personality Traits and Subjective Well-Being," *Psychological Bulletin* 124 (September 1998): 197–229; M. L. Kern and H. S. Friedman, "Do Conscientious Individuals Live Longer? A Quantitative Review," *Health Psychology* 27, no. 5 (2008): 505–512; P. S. Fry and D. L. Debats, "Perfectionism and the Five-Factor Personality Traits as Predictors of Mortality in Older Adults," *Journal of Health Psychology* 14, no. 4 (May 1, 2009): 513–524; F. C. M. Geisler, M. Wiedig-Allison, and H. Weber, "What Coping Tells About Personality," *European Journal of Personality* 23, no. 4 (2009): 289–306; H. S. Friedman, M. L. Kern, and C. A. Reynolds, "Personality and Health, Subjective Well-Being, and Longevity," *Journal of Personality* 78, no. 1 (2010): 179–216.

47. C. G. Jung, *Psychological Types* trans. H. G. Baynes (Princeton, NJ: Princeton University Press, 1971); I. B. Myers, *The Myers-Briggs Type Indicator* (Palo Alto, CA: Consulting Psychologists Press, 1987).

48. M. Gladwell, "Personality Plus," *New Yorker*, 20 September 2004, 42–48; R. B. Kennedy and D. A. Kennedy, "Using the Myers-Briggs Type Indicator in Career Counseling," *Journal of Employment Counseling* 41, no. 1 (March 2004): 38–44.

49. Adapted from an exhibit found at http://www.16-personality-types.com.

50. K. M. Butler, "Using Positive Four-Letter Words," *Employee Benefit News*, April 2007; M. Weinstein, "Personality Assessment Soars at Southwest," *Training*, 3 January 2008.

51. R. M. Capraro and M. M. Capraro, "Myers-Briggs Type Indicator Score Reliability across Studies: A Meta-Analytic Reliability Generalization Study," *Educational and Psychological Measurement* 62 (August 2002): 590–602; J. Michael, "Using the Myers-Briggs Type Indicator as a Tool for Leadership Development? Apply with Caution," *Journal of Leadership & Organizational Studies* 10 (Summer 2003): 68–81; Moutafi, Furnham, and Crump, "Is Managerial Level Related to Personality?"; F. W. Brown and M. D. Reilly, "The Myers-Briggs Type Indicator and Transformational Leadership,"

Journal of Management Development 28, no. 10 (2009): 916–932; B. S. Kuipers *et al.*, "The Influence of Myers-Briggs Type Indicator Profiles on Team Development Processes," *Small Group Research* 40, no. 4 (August 2009): 436–464.

52. R. R. McCrae and P. T. Costa, "Reinterpreting the Myers-Briggs Type Indicator from the Perspective of the Five-Factor Model of Personality," *Journal of Personality* 57 (1989): 17–40; A. Furnham, "The Big Five Versus the Big Four: The Relationship between the Myers-Briggs Type Indicator (MBTI) and NEO-PI Five Factor Model of Personality," *Personality and Individual Differences* 21, no. 2 (1996): 303–307.

53. R. Hogan, "In Defense of Personality Measurement: New Wine for Old Whiners," *Human Performance* 18, no. 4 (2005): 331–341; K. Murphy and J. L. Dzieweczynski, "Why Don't Measures of Broad Dimensions of Personality Perform Better as Predictors of Job Performance?," *Human Performance* 18, no. 4 (2005): 343–357; F. P. Morgeson *et al.*, "Reconsidering the Use of Personality Tests in Personnel Selection Contexts," *Personnel Psychology* 60, no. 3 (2007): 683–729; R. P. Tett and C. N. D., "Personality Tests at the Crossroads: A Response to Morgeson, Campion, Dipboye, Hollenbeck, Murphy, and Schmitt (2007)," *Personnel Psychology* 60, no. 4 (2007): 967–993.

54. L. A. Witt, M. C. Andrews, and D. S. Carlson, "When Conscientiousness Isn't Enough: Emotional Exhaustion and Performance Among Call Center Customer Service Representatives," *Journal of Management* 30, no. 1 (2004): 149–160; J. Stoeber, K. Otto, and C. Dalbert, "Perfectionism and the Big Five: Conscientiousness Predicts Longitudinal Increases in Self-Oriented Perfectionism," *Personality and Individual Differences* 47, no. 4 (2009): 363–368; C. J. Boyce, A. M. Wood, and G. D. A. Brown, "The Dark Side of Conscientiousness: Conscientious People Experience Greater Drops in Life Satisfaction Following Unemployment," *Journal of Research in Personality* 44, no. 4 (2010): 535–539.

55. V. Baker, "Why Men Can't Manage Women," *The Guardian*, 14 April 2007, 1.

56. K. C. Neel, "Abdoulah Sets Wow Apart," *Multichannel News*, 29 January 2007, 2; D. Graham, "She Walks the Talk," *Denver Woman*, April 2009; "Wow! Management Team," (Denver, 2010), http://www.wowway.com/internet-cable-phone-company/wow-management-executive-bios/ (accessed 6 December 2010).

57. B. M. Meglino and E. C. Ravlin, "Individual Values in Organizations: Concepts, Controversies, and Research," *Journal of Management* 24, no. 3 (1998): 351–389; B. R. Agle and C. B. Caldwell, "Understanding Research on Values in Business," *Business and*

Society 38, no. 3 (September 1999): 326–387; S. Hitlin and J. A. Pilavin, "Values: Reviving a Dormant Concept," *Annual Review of Sociology* 30 (2004): 359–393.

58. D. Lubinski, D. B. Schmidt, and C. P. Benbow, "A 20-Year Stability Analysis of the Study of Values for Intellectually Gifted Individuals from Adolescence to Adulthood," *Journal of Applied Psychology* 81 (1996): 443–451.

59. L. Parks and R. P. Guay, "Personality, Values, and Motivation," *Personality and Individual Differences* 47, no. 7 (2009): 675–684.

60. Hitlin and Pilavin, "Values: Reviving a Dormant Concept"; A. Pakizeh, J. E. Gebauer, and G. R. Maio, "Basic Human Values: Inter-Value Structure in Memory," *Journal of Experimental Social Psychology* 43, no. 3 (2007): 458–465.

61. S. H. Schwartz, "Universals in the Content and Structure of Values: Theoretical Advances and Empirical Tests in 20 Countries," *Advances in Experimental Social Psychology* 25 (1992): 1–65; S. H. Schwartz, "Are There Universal Aspects in the Structure and Contents of Human Values?," *Journal of Social Issues* 50 (1994): 19–45; D. Spini, "Measurement Equivalence of 10 Value Types from the Schwartz Value Survey across 21 Countries," *Journal of Cross-Cultural Psychology* 34, no. 1 (January 2003): 3–23; S. H. Schwartz and K. Boehnke, "Evaluating the Structure of Human Values with Confirmatory Factor Analysis," *Journal of Research in Personality* 38, no. 3 (2004): 230–255.

62. G. R. Maio and J. M. Olson, "Values as Truisms: Evidence and Implications," *Journal of Personality and Social Psychology* 74, no. 2 (1998): 294–311; G. R. Maio *et al.*, "Addressing Discrepancies between Values and Behavior: The Motivating Effect of Reasons," *Journal of Experimental Social Psychology* 37, no. 2 (2001): 104–117; B. Verplanken and R. W. Holland, "Motivated Decision Making: Effects of Activation and Self-Centrality of Values on Choices and Behavior," *Journal of Personality and Social Psychology* 82, no. 3 (2002): 434–447; A. Bardi and S. H. Schwartz, "Values and Behavior: Strength and Structure of Relations," *Personality and Social Psychology Bulletin* 29, no. 10 (October 2003): 1207–1220; M. M. Bernard and G. R. Maio, "Effects of Introspection About Reasons for Values: Extending Research on Values-as-Truisms," *Social Cognition* 21, no. 1 (2003): 1–25.

63. N. Mazar, O. Amir, and D. Ariely, "The Dishonesty of Honest People: A Theory of Self-Concept Maintenance," *Journal of Marketing Research* 45 (December 2008): 633–644.

64. K. Hornyak, "Upward Move: Cynthia Schwalm," *Medical Marketing & Media*,

June 2008, 69. For research on the consequences on value congruence, see A. L. Kristof, "Person-Organization Fit: An Integrative Review of Its Conceptualizations, Measurement, and Implications," *Personnel Psychology* 49, no. 1 (Spring 1996): 1–49; M. L. Verquer, T. A. Beehr, and S. H. Wagner, "A Meta-Analysis of Relations between Person-Organization Fit and Work Attitudes," *Journal of Vocational Behavior* 63 (2003): 473–489; J. W. Westerman and L. A. Cyr, "An Integrative Analysis of Person-Organization Fit Theories," *International Journal of Selection and Assessment* 12, no. 3 (September 2004): 252–261; D. Bouckenooghe *et al.*, "The Prediction of Stress by Values and Value Conflict," *Journal of Psychology* 139, no. 4 (2005): 369–382.

65. T. Simons, "Behavioral Integrity: The Perceived Alignment between Managers' Words and Deeds as a Research Focus," *Organization Science* 13, no. 1 (Jan-Feb 2002): 18–35; Watson Wyatt, "Employee Ratings of Senior Management Dip, Watson Wyatt Survey Finds," Watson Wyatt News release (New York: 4 January 2007).

66. M. Johne, "Show Us the Green, Workers Say," *Globe & Mail*, 10 October 2007, C1.

67. Desjardin Financial Security, *Health Is Cool!: 2007 Survey on Canadian Attitudes Towards Physical and Mental Health at Work and Play* (Lévis, Quebec: Desjardin Financial Security, 28 September 2007); "50 Best Employers in Canada Offer Flexibility, Demonstrate Integrity, According to Hewitt Associates," Canadian Newswire news release for Hewitt Associates (Toronto: 3 January 2008); Aspen Institute, *Where Will They Lead?* (New York: Aspen Institute, 17 April 2008).

68. Z. Aycan, R. N. Kanungo, and J. B. P. Sinha, "Organizational Culture and Human Resource Management Practices: The Model of Culture Fit," *Journal of Cross-Cultural Psychology* 30 (July 1999): 501–526; M. Naor, K. Linderman, and R. Schroeder, "The Globalization of Operations in Eastern and Western Countries: Unpacking the Relationship between National and Organizational Culture and Its Impact on Manufacturing Performance," *Journal of Operations Management* 28, no. 3 (2010): 194–205. This type of values incongruence can occur even when the company is founded in that country, that is, when a local company tries to introduce a culture incompatible with the national culture. See for example: A. Danisman, "Good Intentions and Failed Implementations: Understanding Culture-Based Resistance to Organizational Change," *European Journal of Work and Organizational Psychology* 19, no. 2 (2010): 200–220.

69. C. Savoye, "Workers Say Honesty Is Best Company Policy," *Christian Science Monitor*, June 15 2000; J. M. Kouzes and B. Z. Posner,

The Leadership Challenge, 3rd ed. (San Francisco: Jossey-Bass, 2002); J. Schettler, "Leadership in Corporate America," *Training & Development*, September 2002, 66–73; Ekos Politics, *Women See It Differently* (Ottawa: Ekos Politics, 6 May 2010).

70. Ethics Resource Center, *The 2009 National Business Ethics Survey: Ethics in the Recession* (Arlington, VA: Ethics Resource Center, 2009).

71. Transparency International, Transparency International Corruption Perceptions Index 2009 (Berlin, Germany: Transparency International, November 2009).

72. "Quebec Construction Companies Charged with Bid-Rigging Following Competition Bureau Investigation," Marketwire news release for Competition Bureau Canada (Ottawa: 10 November 2008); J. Bagnall, "Canadian Mining Companies Need Tougher Rules," *Montreal Gazette*, 22 October 2010, A21; K. Bolan, "Bush Camp Workers Subjected to Deplorable Conditions, Co-Worker," *Vancouver Sun*, 11 August 2010; R. Elias, "Call to Investigate Forest Camp 'Nightmare'," *The Tyee (Vancouver)*, 11 August 2010; B. Jang, "Airlines Fined $1.1-Billion over Cargo Price-Fixing Cartel," *Globe & Mail*, 10 November 2010, B12; QMI Agency, "Feds to Probe Quebec Construction Industry," *Toronto Sun*, 27 October 2010.

73. P. L. Schumann, "A Moral Principles Framework for Human Resource Management Ethics," *Human Resource Management Review* 11 (Spring-Summer 2001): 93–111; J. Boss, *Analyzing Moral Issues*, 3rd ed. (New York: McGraw-Hill, 2005), Chap. 1; M. G. Velasquez, *Business Ethics: Concepts and Cases*, 6th ed. (Upper Saddle River, NJ: Prentice-Hall, 2006), Chap. 2.

74. Sa, Rachel, "Seems Public Exposure, Not Law, Gets Results," *London Free Press*, 5 June, 2010; "Mississauga Hazing Probe Ends With Suspensions" *CBC News*, 9 June 2010; P. Gombu, "No Grounds For Criminal Charges In Mississauga Hazing, Police Chief Says," *The Toronto Star*, 9 June 2010; R. Sa, "How Mississauga's Reputation Got Thrown Under The Bus," *The Toronto Sun*, 7 June 2010; "Worker at Centre of Abuse Storm Paid More Than Mayor," *CBC News*, 3 June 2010.

75. For a recent analysis of these predictors of ethical conduct, see: J. J. Kish-Gephart, D. A. Harrison, and L. K. Treviño, "Bad Apples, Bad Cases, and Bad Barrels: Meta-Analytic Evidence About Sources of Unethical Decisions at Work," *Journal of Applied Psychology* 95, no. 1 (2010): 1–31.

76. T. J. Jones, "Ethical Decision Making by Individuals in Organizations: An Issue Contingent Model," *Academy of Management Review* 16 (1991): 366–395; B. H. Frey, "The Impact of Moral Intensity on Decision Making in a Business Context," *Journal of*

Business Ethics 26 (August 2000): 181–195; D. R. May and K. P. Pauli, "The Role of Moral Intensity in Ethical Decision Making," *Business and Society* 41 (March 2002): 84–117.

77. J. R. Sparks and S. D. Hunt, "Marketing Researcher Ethical Sensitivity: Conceptualization, Measurement, and Exploratory Investigation," *Journal of Marketing* 62 (April 1998): 92–109.

78. K. F. Alam, "Business Ethics in New Zealand Organizations: Views from the Middle and Lower Level Managers," *Journal of Business Ethics* 22 (November 1999): 145–153; Human Resource Institute, *The Ethical Enterprise: State-of-the-Art* (St. Petersburg, Florida: Human Resource Institute, January 2006).

79. S. J. Reynolds, K. Leavitt, and K. A. DeCelles, "Automatic Ethics: The Effects of Implicit Assumptions and Contextual Cues on Moral Behavior," *Journal of Applied Psychology* 95, no. 4 (2010): 752–760.

80. D. R. Beresford, N. D. Katzenbach, and C. B. Rogers Jr, *Report of Investigation by the Special Investigative Committee of the Board of Directors of Worldcom, Inc.* (31 March 2003).

81. H. Donker, D. Poff, and S. Zahir, "Corporate Values, Codes of Ethics, and Firm Performance: A Look at the Canadian Context," *Journal of Business Ethics* 82, no. 3 (2008): 527–537; L. Preuss, "Codes of Conduct in Organisational Context: From Cascade to Lattice-Work of Codes," *Journal of Business Ethics* 94, no. 4 (2010): 471–487.

82. B. Farrell, D. M. Cobbin, and H. M. Farrell, "Codes of Ethics: Their Evolution, Development and Other Controversies," *Journal of Management Development* 21, no. 2 (2002): 152–163; G. Wood and M. Rimmer, "Codes of Ethics: What Are They Really and What Should They Be?," *International Journal of Value-Based Management* 16, no. 2 (2003): 181.

83. S. Greengard, "Golden Values," *Workforce Management*, March 2005, 52–53; K. Tyler, "Do the Right Thing," *HRMagazine*, Feb. 2005, 99–102.

84. J. Fortier, "Trust in the Workplace," *Ottawa Business Journal*, 4 January 2007.

85. G. Svensson *et al.*, "Ethical Structures and Processes of Corporations Operating in Australia, Canada, and Sweden: A Longitudinal and Cross-Cultural Study," *Journal of Business Ethics* 86, no. 4 (2009): 485–506.

86. E. Aronson, "Integrating Leadership Styles and Ethical Perspectives," *Canadian Journal of Administrative Sciences* 18 (December 2001): 266–276; D. R. May *et al.*, "Developing the Moral Component of Authentic Leadership," *Organizational Dynamics* 32 (2003): 247–260. The Voda-

fone director quotation is from R. Van Lee, L. Fabish, and N. McGaw, "The Value of Corporate Values," *strategy+business*, no. 39 (Summer 2005): 1–13.

87. V. Galt, "A World of Opportunity for Those in Mid-Career," *Globe & Mail*, 7 June 2006, C1.

88. L. Gettler, "The New Global Manager Needs to Understand Different Work Cultures," *The Age*, 6 February 2008.

89. Individual and collectivism information are from the meta-analysis by Oyserman et al., not the earlier findings by Hofstede. See: D. Oyserman, H. M. Coon, and M. Kemmelmeier, "Rethinking Individualism and Collectivism: Evaluation of Theoretical Assumptions and Meta-Analyses," *Psychological Bulletin* 128 (2002): 3–72. Consistent with Oyserman et al., a recent study found high rather than low individualism among Chileans. See: A. Kolstad and S. Horpestad, "Self-Construal in Chile and Norway," *Journal of Cross-Cultural Psychology* 40, no. 2 (March 2009): 275–281.

90. C. P. Earley and C. B. Gibson, "Taking Stock in Our Progress on Individualism-Collectivism: 100 Years of Solidarity and Community," *Journal of Management* 24 (May 1998): 265–304; F. S. Niles, "Individualism-Collectivism Revisited," *Cross-Cultural Research* 32 (November 1998): 315–341; C. L. Jackson *et al.*, "Psychological Collectivism: A Measurement Validation and Linkage to Group Member Performance," *Journal of Applied Psychology* 91, no. 4 (2006): 884–899.

91. Oyserman, Coon, and Kemmelmeier, "Rethinking Individualism and Collectivism," Also see F. Li and L. Aksoy, "Dimensionality of Individualism–Collectivism and Measurement Equivalence of Triandis and Gelfand's Scale," *Journal of Business and Psychology* 21, no. 3 (2007): 313–329. The relationship between individualism and collectivism is still being debated, but most experts now agree that individualism and collectivism have serious problems with conceptualization and measurement.

92. M. Voronov and J. A. Singer, "The Myth of Individualism-Collectivism: A Critical Review," *Journal of Social Psychology* 142 (August 2002): 461–480; Y. Takano and S. Sogon, "Are Japanese More Collectivistic Than Americans?," *Journal of Cross-Cultural Psychology* 39, no. 3 (May 1, 2008 2008): 237–250; D. Dalsky, "Individuality in Japan and the United States: A Cross-Cultural Priming Experiment," *International Journal of Intercultural Relations* 34, no. 5 (2010): 429–435.

93. G. Hofstede, *Culture's Consequences: Comparing Values, Behaviors, Institutions, and Organizations across Nations*, 2nd ed. (Thousand Oaks, CA: Sage, 2001).

94. S. Klie, "Program Breaks Cultural Barriers," *Canadian HR Reporter*, 10 September 2007.

95. Hofstede, *Culture's Consequences: Comparing Values, Behaviors, Institutions, and Organizations across Nations*. Hofstede used the terms *masculinity* and *femininity* for *achievement* and *nurturing orientation*, respectively. We (along with other writers) have adopted the latter two terms to minimize the sexist perspective of these concepts. Also, readers need to be aware that achievement orientation is assumed to be opposite of nurturing orientation, but this opposing relationship might be questioned.

96. V. Taras, J. Rowney, and P. Steel, "Half a Century of Measuring Culture: Review of Approaches, Challenges, and Limitations Based on the Analysis of 121 Instruments for Quantifying Culture," *Journal of International Management* 15, no. 4 (2009): 357–373.

97. R. L. Tung and A. Verbeke, "Beyond Hofstede and GLOBE: Improving the Quality of Cross-Cultural Research," *Journal of International Business Studies* 41, no. 8 (2010): 1259–1274.

98. S. S. Sarwono and R. W. Armstrong, "Microcultural Differences and Perceived Ethical Problems: An International Business Perspective," *Journal of Business Ethics* 30 (March 2001): 41–56; R. L. Tung and C. Baumann, "Comparing the Attitudes toward Money, Material Possessions and Savings of Overseas Chinese Vis-À-Vis Chinese in China: Convergence, Divergence or Cross-Vergence, Vis-À-Vis, 'One Size Fits All' Human Resource Management Policies and Practices," *International Journal of Human Resource Management* 20, no. 11 (2009): 2382–2401.

99. W. K. W. Choy, A. B. E. Lee, and P. Ramburuth, "Multinationalism in the Workplace: A Myriad of Values in a Singaporean Firm," *Singapore Management Review* 31, no. 1 (January 2009).

100. N. Jacob, "Cross-Cultural Investigations: Emerging Concepts," *Journal of Organizational Change Management* 18, no. 5 (2005): 514–528; V. Taras, B. L. Kirkman, and P. Steel, "Examining the Impact of Culture's Consequences: A Three-Decade, Multilevel, Meta-Analytic Review of Hofstede's Cultural Value Dimensions," *Journal of Applied Psychology* 95, no. 3 (2010): 405–439.

101. M. Adams, "New Canadians, Old Values?," *Globe & Mail*, 2 March 2005, A17.

102. Z. Wu and D. Baer, "Attitudes toward Family and Gender Roles: A Comparison of English and French Canadian Women," *Journal of Comparative Family Studies* 27 (Autumn 1996): 437–452. The reference to "two solitudes" comes from: H. McLennan, *Two Solitudes* (Toronto: MacMillan of Canada, 1945).

103. M. Major *et al.*, "Meanings of Work and Personal Values of Canadian Anglophone and Francophone Middle Managers," *Canadian Journal of Administrative Sciences* 11 (September 1994): 251–263; M. Laroche *et al.*, "The Influence of Culture on Pro-Environmental Knowledge, Attitudes, and Behavior: A Canadian Perspective," *Advances In Consumer Research* 23 (1996): 196–202.

104. I. Chapman, D. McCaskill, and D. Newhouse, "Management in Contemporary Aboriginal Organizations," *Canadian Journal of Native Studies* 11, no. 2 (1991): 333–349; L. Redpath and M. O. Nielsen, "A Comparison of Native Culture, Non-Native Culture and New Management Ideology," *Canadian Journal of Administrative Sciences* 14, no. 3 (September 1997): 327–339; M. Julien, B. Wright, and D. M. Zinni, "Stories from the Circle: Leadership Lessons Learned from Aboriginal Leaders," *The Leadership Quarterly* 21, no. 1 (2010): 114–126.

105. M. Adams, *Fire and Ice: The United States, Canada, and the Myth of Converging Values* (Toronto: Penguin Canada, 2004), 142.

106. J. Laxer, *The Border: Canada, the U.S. And Dispatches from the 49th Parallel* (Toronto: Anchor Canada, 2004).

107. C. Cobb, "Canadians Want a Diverse Society: Poll," *Ottawa Citizen*, 18 February 2002, A5; K. May, "Canadian Nationalism Growing: Study," *Ottawa Citizen*, 5 June 2002, A8; C. Boucher, "Canada-Us Values: Distinct, Inevitably Carbon Copy, or Narcissism of Small Differences?," *Horizons: Policy Research Initiative* 7, no. 1 (June 2004): 42–49.

108. Adams, *Fire and Ice*. For earlier research, see: M. Adams, *Sex in the Snow* (Toronto: Penguin Canada, 1998); M. Adams, "What Makes Us Different," *Globe & Mail*, 4 July 2001, A11; M. Adams, *Better Happy Than Rich?* (Toronto: Viking, 2001).

109. D. Baer, E. Grabb, and W. Johnston, "National Character, Regional Culture, and the Values of Canadians and Americans," *Canadian Review of Sociology and anthropology* 30, no. 1 (1993): 13–36; E. Grabb and J. Curtis, *The Four Societies of Canada and the United States* (New York: Oxford University Press, 2005). Evidence of small differences in Canadian-American culture is also reported in: Boucher, "Canada-US Values."

CHAPTER 3

1. "Mediator Finds Women Fire Fighters in Richmond Endured Harassment at Work," November 2006, http://www.firefightingincanada.com/content/view/1549/132/. Retrieved October 8, 2010; "Female Firefighters All Off the Job," *The Vancouver Province*, March 22, 2006; "Firefighters," *Service Canada*, http://www.servicecanada.gc.ca/eng/qc/job_futures/statistics/6262.shtml. Retrieved October 8,

2010; Ellen Mauro, "Girls Test their Firefighting Mettle," *The Ottawa Citizen*, August 18, 2010, C1.

2. "Kate's Just One of a Growing Number of Female Firefighters," *Express & Echo (Exeter, UK)*, 28 April 2008, 24; C. Foran, "It's Not Just a Man's Job," *Odessa American (Texas)*, 13 March 2008.

3. J. D. Campbell, S. Assanand, and A. Di Paula, "The Structure of the Self-Concept and Its Relation to Psychological Adjustment," *Journal of Personality* 71, no. 1 (2003): 115–140; M. J. Constantino *et al.*, "The Direct and Stress-Buffering Effects of Self-Organization on Psychological Adjustment: The Direct and Stress-Buffering Effects of Self-Organization on Psychological Adjustment," *Journal of Social & Clinical Psychology* 25, no. 3 (2006): 333–360.

4. E. J. Koch and J. A. Shepperd, "Is Self-Complexity Linked to Better Coping? A Review of the Literature," *Journal of Personality* 72, no. 4 (2004): 727–760; A. R. McConnell, R. J. Rydell, and C. M. Brown, "On the Experience of Self-Relevant Feedback: How Self-Concept Organization Influences Affective Responses and Self-Evaluations," *Journal of Experimental Social Psychology* 45, no. 4 (2009): 695–707.

5. J. Lodi-Smith and B. W. Roberts, "Getting to Know Me: Social Role Experiences and Age Differences in Self-Concept Clarity During Adulthood," *Journal of Personality* 78, no. 5 (2010): 1383–1410.

6. Koch and Shepperd, "Is Self-Complexity Linked to Better Coping? A Review of the Literature"; A. R. McConnell *et al.*, "The Simple Life: On the Benefits of Low Self-Complexity," *Personality and Social Psychology Bulletin* 35, no. 7 (July 2009): 823–835. On the process of self-concept repair, see: S. Chen and H. C. Boucher, "Relational Selves as Self-Affirmational Resources," *Journal of Research in Personality* 42, no. 3 (2008): 716–733.

7. A. T. Brook, J. Garcia, and M. A. Fleming, "The Effects of Multiple Identities on Psychological Well-Being," *Personality and Social Psychology Bulletin* 34, no. 12 (December 2008): 1588–1600.

8. J. D. Campbell, "Self-Esteem and Clarity of the Self-Concept," *Journal of Personality and Social Psychology* 59, no. 3 (1990).

9. T. W. H. Ng, K. L. Sorensen, and D. C. Feldman, "Dimensions, Antecedents, and Consequences of Workaholism: A Conceptual Integration and Extension," *Journal of Organizational Behavior* 28 (2007): 111–136; S. Pachulicz, N. Schmitt, and G. Kuljanin, "A Model of Career Success: A Longitudinal Study of Emergency Physicians," *Journal of Vocational Behavior* 73, no. 2 (2008): 242–253.

10. B. George, *Authentic Leadership* (San Francisco: Jossey-Bass, 2004); S. T. Hannah

and B. J. Avolio, "Ready or Not: How Do We Accelerate the Developmental Readiness of Leaders?," *Journal of Organizational Behavior* 31, no. 8 (2010): 1181–1187.

11. C. Sedikides and A. P. Gregg, "Portraits of the Self," in *The Sage Handbook of Social Psychology*, ed. M. A. Hogg and J. Cooper (London: Sage Publications, 2003), 110–138; M. D. Alicke and C. Sedikides, "Self-Enhancement and Self-Protection: What They Are and What They Do," *European Review of Social Psychology* 20 (2009): 1–48; C. L. Guenther and M. D. Alicke, "Deconstructing the Better-Than-Average Effect," *Journal of Personality and Social Psychology* 99, no. 5 (2010): 755–770; S. Loughnan *et al.*, "Universal Biases in Self-Perception: Better and More Human Than Average," *British Journal of Social Psychology* 49 (2010): 627–636.

12. K. P. Cross, "Not Can, but *Will* College Teaching Be Improved?," *New Directions for Higher Education*, no. 17 (Spring 1977): 1–15; U.S. Merit Systems Protection Board, *Accomplishing Our Mission: Results of the 2005 Merit Principles Survey* (Washington, DC: U.S. Merit Systems Protection Board, 6 December 2007).

13. D. A. Moore, "Not So above Average after All: When People Believe They Are Worse Than Average and Its Implications for Theories of Bias in Social Comparison," *Organizational Behavior and Human Decision Processes* 102, no. 1 (2007): 42–58.

14. M. S. Horswill, A. E. Waylen, and M. I. Tofield, "Drivers' Ratings of Different Components of Their Own Driving Skill: A Greater Illusion of Superiority for Skills That Relate to Accident Involvement1," *Journal of Applied Social Psychology* 34, no. 1 (2004): 177–195; N. J. Hiller and D. C. Hambrick, "Conceptualizing Executive Hubris: The Role of (Hyper-) Core Self-Evaluations in Strategic Decision-Making," *Strategic Management Journal* 26, no. 4 (2005): 297–319; U. Malmendier and G. Tate, "CEO Overconfidence and Corporate Investment," *The Journal of Finance* 60, no. 6 (2005): 2661–2700; J. A. Doukas and D. Petmezas, "Acquisitions, Overconfident Managers and Self-Attribution Bias," *European Financial Management* 13, no. 3 (2007): 531–577; N. Harrè and C. G. Sibley, "Explicit and Implicit Self-Enhancement Biases in Drivers and Their Relationship to Driving Violations and Crash-Risk Optimism," *Accident Analysis & Prevention* 39, no. 6 (2007): 1155–1161; D. A. Moore and P. J. Healy, "The Trouble with Overconfidence," *Psychological Review* 115, no. 2 (2008): 502–517.

15. W. B. Swann Jr, "To Be Adored or to Be Known? The Interplay of Self-Enhancement and Self-Verification," in *Foundations of Social Behavior*, ed. R. M. Sorrentino and E. T. Higgins (New York: Guildford, 1990), 408–448; W. B. Swann

Jr, P. J. Rentfrow, and J. S. Guinn, "Self-Verification: The Search for Coherence," in *Handbook of Self and Identity*, ed. M. R. Leary and J. Tagney (New York: Guildford, 2002), 367–383.

16. F. Anseel and F. Lievens, "Certainty as a Moderator of Feedback Reactions? A Test of the Strength of the Self-Verification Motive," *Journal of Occupational & Organizational Psychology* 79, no. 4 (2006): 533–551; T. Kwang and W. B. Swann, "Do People Embrace Praise Even When They Feel Unworthy? A Review of Critical Tests of Self-Enhancement Versus Self-Verification," *Personality and Social Psychology Review* 14, no. 3 (August 2010): 263–280.

17. M. R. Leary, "Motivational and Emotional Aspects of the Self," *Annual Review of Psychology* 58, no. 1 (2007): 317–344.

18. T. A. Judge and J. E. Bono, "Relationship of Core Self-Evaluations Traits—Self-Esteem, Generalized Self-Efficacy, Locus of Control, and Emotional Stability—with Job Satisfaction and Job Performance: A Meta-Analysis," *Journal of Applied Psychology* 86, no. 1 (2001): 80–92; T. A. Judge and C. Hurst, "Capitalizing on One's Advantages: Role of Core Self-Evaluations," *Journal of Applied Psychology* 92, no. 5 (2007): 1212–1227. We have described the three most commonly noted components of self-evaluation. The full model also includes emotional stability (low neuroticism). However, the core self-evaluation model has received limited research and its dimensions are being debated. For example, see T. W. Self, "Evaluating Core Self-Evaluations: Application of a Multidimensional, Latent-Construct, Evaluative Framework to Core Self-Evaluations Research" (Ph.D., University of Houston, 2007); R. E. Johnson, C. C. Rosen, and P. E. Levy, "Getting to the Core of Core Self-Evaluation: A Review and Recommendations," *Journal of Organizational Behavior* 29 (2008): 391–413.

19. R. F. Baumeister and J. M. Twenge, *The Social Self, Handbook of Psychology* (New York: John Wiley & Sons, Inc., 2003); W. B. Swann Jr, C. Chang-Schneider, and K. L. McClarty, "Do People's Self-Views Matter?: Self-Concept and Self-Esteem in Everyday Life," *American Psychologist* 62, no. 2 (2007): 84–94.

20. R. Langlois, "Fairmont Hotels: Business Strategy Starts with People," *Canadian HR Reporter*, 5 November 2001, 19; V. Galt, "A World of Opportunity for Those in Mid-Careers," *The Globe and Mail*, 7 June 2006, C1; M. T. Bitti, "Rewards of Hard Work," *National Post*, 17 October 2007, WK2; I. Amed, "Carolyn Clark: Creating Memories Through Exceptional Service," *LuxurySociety*, 10 September 2009, Retrieved October 24, 2010 http://luxury-society.com/articles/2009/09/carolyn-clark-creating-memories-through-exceptional-

service; "Fairmont Toastmasters Members Newsletter," January 2010, 3.

21. A. Bandura, *Self-Efficacy: The Exercise of Control* (New York: W. H. Freeman, 1997). However, one recent review found that self-efficacy's effect on task and job performance is much lower when also including the effects of personality traits on performance. See: T. A. Judge *et al.*, "Self-Efficacy and Work-Related Performance: The Integral Role of Individual Differences," *Journal of Applied Psychology* 92, no. 1 (2007): 107–127.

22. G. Chen, S. M. Gully, and D. Eden, "Validation of a New General Self-Efficacy Scale," *Organizational Research Methods* 4, no. 1 (Jan. 2001): 62–83.

23. J. B. Rotter, "Generalized Expectancies for Internal Versus External Control of Reinforcement," *Psychological Monographs* 80, no. 1 (1966): 1–7.

24. P. E. Spector, "Behavior in Organizations as a Function of Employee's Locus of Control," *Psychological Bulletin* 91 (1982): 482–497; K. Hattrup, M. S. O'Connell, and J. R. Labrador, "Incremental Validity of Locus of Control after Controlling for Cognitive Ability and Conscientiousness," *Journal of Business and Psychology* 19, no. 4 (2005): 461–481; T. W. H. Ng, K. L. Sorensen, and L. T. Eby, "Locus of Control at Work: A Meta-Analysis," *Journal of Organizational Behavior* 27 (2006): 1057–1087; Kwang and Swann, "Do People Embrace Praise Even When They Feel Unworthy?"

25. J. M. Twenge, L. Zhang, and C. Im, "It's Beyond My Control: A Cross-Temporal Meta-Analysis of Increasing Externality in Locus of Control, 1960–2002," *Personality and Social Psychology Review* 8, no. 3 (August 2004): 308–319.

26. H. Tajfel, *Social Identity and Intergroup Relations* (Cambridge: Cambridge University Press, 1982); B. E. Ashforth and F. Mael, "Social Identity Theory and the Organization," *Academy of Management Review* 14 (1989): 20–39; M. A. Hogg and D. J. Terry, "Social Identity and Self-Categorization Processes in Organizational Contexts," *Academy of Management Review* 25 (January 2000): 121–140; L. L. Gaertner *et al.*, "The "I," The "We," And The "When": A Meta-Analysis of Motivational Primacy in Self-Definition," *Journal of Personality and Social Psychology* 83, no. 3 (2002): 574; S. A. Haslam, R. A. Eggins, and K. J. Reynolds, "The Aspire Model: Actualizing Social and Personal Identity Resources to Enhance Organizational Outcomes," *Journal of Occupational and Organizational Psychology* 76 (2003): 83–113.

27. Sedikides and Gregg, "Portraits of the Self." The history of the social self in human beings is described in M. R. Leary and N. R. Buttermore, "The Evolution of

the Human Self: Tracing the Natural History of Self-Awareness," *Journal for the Theory of Social Behaviour* 33, no. 4 (2003): 365–404.

28. M. R. Edwards, "Organizational Identification: A Conceptual and Operational Review," *International Journal of Management Reviews* 7, no. 4 (2005): 207–230; D. A. Whetten, "Albert and Whetten Revisited: Strengthening the Concept of Organizational Identity," *Journal of Management Inquiry* 15, no. 3 (Sept. 2006): 219–234.

29. M. B. Brewer, "The Social Self: On Being the Same and Different at the Same Time," *Personality and Social Psychology Bulletin* 17, no. 5 (October 1991): 475–482; R. Imhoff and H.-P. Erb, "What Motivates Nonconformity? Uniqueness Seeking Blocks Majority Influence," *Personality and Social Psychology Bulletin* 35, no. 3 (March 1, 2009 2009): 309–320; M. G. Mayhew, J. Gardner, and N. M. Ashkanasy, "Measuring Individuals' Need for Identification: Scale Development and Validation," *Personality and Individual Differences* 49, no. 5 (2010): 356–361; K. R. Morrison and S. C. Wheeler, "Nonconformity Defines the Self: The Role of Minority Opinion Status in Self-Concept Clarity," *Personality and Social Psychology Bulletin* 36, no. 3 (March 2010): 297–308.

30. See, for example: W. B. Swann Jr, R. E. Johnson, and J. K. Bosson, "Identity Negotiation at Work," *Research in Organizational Behavior* 29 (2009): 81–109; M. N. Bechtoldt *et al.*, "Self-Concept Clarity and the Management of Social Conflict," *Journal of Personality* 78, no. 2 (2010): 539–574; Hannah and Avolio, "Ready or Not: How Do We Accelerate the Developmental Readiness of Leaders?"; H.-L. Yang and C. Y. Lai, "Motivations of Wikipedia Content Contributors," *Computers in Human Behavior* 26, no. 6 (2010): 1377–1383.

31. The effect of the target in selective attention is known as "bottom-up selection"; the effect of the perceiver's psychodynamics on this process is known as "top-down selection." See C. E. Connor, H. E. Egeth, and S. Yantis, "Visual Attention: Bottom-up Versus Top-Down," *Current Biology* 14, no. 19 (2004): R850-R852; E. I. Knudsen, "Fundamental Components of Attention," *Annual Review of Neuroscience* 30, no. 1 (2007): 57–78.

32. A. Mack *et al.*, "Perceptual Organization and Attention," *Cognitive Psychology* 24, no. 4 (1992): 475–501; A. R. Damasio, *Descartes' Error: Emotion, Reason, and the Human Brain* (New York: Putnam Sons, 1994); C. Frith, "A Framework for Studying the Neural Basis of Attention," *Neuropsychologia* 39, no. 12 (2001): 1367–1371; N. Lavie, "Distracted and Confused?: Selective

Attention under Load," *Trends in Cognitive Sciences* 9, no. 2 (2005): 75–82; M. Shermer, "The Political Brain," *Scientific American* 295, no. 1 (July 2006): 36; D. Westen, *The Political Brain: The Role of Emotion in Deciding the Fate of the Nation* (Cambridge, MA: PublicAffairs, 2007).

33. Plato, *The Republic*, trans. D. Lee (Harmondsworth, England: Penguin, 1955).

34. D. J. Simons and C. F. Chabris, "Gorillas in Our Midst : Sustained Inattentional Blindness for Dynamic Events," *Perception* 28 (1999): 1059–1074.

35. Confirmation bias is defined as "unwitting selectivity in the acquisition and use of evidence." R. S. Nickerson, "Confirmation Bias: A Ubiquitous Phenomenon in Many Guises," *Review of General Psychology* 2, no. 2 (1998): 175–220. This occurs in a variety of ways, including overweighting positive information, perceiving only positive information, and restricting cognitive attention to a favoured hypothesis. Research has found that confirmation bias is typically nonconscious and driven by emotions.

36. K. A. Lane, J. Kang, and M. R. Banaji, "Implicit Social Cognition and Law," *Annual Review of Law and Social Science* 3, no. 1 (2007).

37. K. A. Findley and M. Scott, "The Multiple Dimensions of Tunnel Vision in Criminal Cases," *Wisconsin Law Review* 2 (2006): 291–397; I. Bailey, "Maintenance Man among Murder Victims," *Globe & Mail*, 22 October 2007, A1; V. Geberth, "10 Most Common Errors in Death Investigations: Part 1," *Law & Order* 55, no. 11 (November 2007): 84–89. The Sherlock Holmes quotation is from S. A. Conan Doyle, "A Study in Scarlet," in *The Complete Sherlock Holmes* (New York: Fine Creative Media, 2003), 3–96. Sherlock Holmes offers similar advice in "A Scandal in Bohemia," 189.

38. A. Cromer, "Pathological Science: An Update," *The Skeptical Inquirer* 17, no. 4 (Summer 1993): 400–407.

39. C. N. Macrae and G. V. Bodenhausen, "Social Cognition: Thinking Categorically About Others," *Annual Review of Psychology* 51 (2000): 93–120. For literature on the automaticity of the perceptual organization and interpretation process, see J. A. Bargh, "The Cognitive Monster: The Case against the Controllability of Automatic Stereotype Effects," in *Dual Process Theories in Social Psychology*, ed. S. Chaiken and Y. Trope (New York: Guilford, 1999), 361–382; J. A. Bargh and M. J. Ferguson, "Beyond Behaviorism: On the Automaticity of Higher Mental Processes," *Psychological Bulletin* 126, no. 6 (2000): 925–945; M. Gladwell, *Blink: The Power of Thinking without Thinking* (New York: Little, Brown, 2005).

40. E. M. Altmann and B. D. Burns, "Streak Biases in Decision Making: Data and a Memory Model," *Cognitive Systems Research* 6, no. 1 (2005): 5–16. For a discussion of cognitive closure and perception, see A. W. Kruglanski, *The Psychology of Closed Mindedness* (New York: Psychology Press, 2004).

41. N. Ambady and R. Rosenthal, "Half a Minute: Predicting Teacher Evaluations from Thin Slices of Nonverbal Behavior and Physical Attractiveness," *Journal of Personality and Social Psychology* 64, no. 3 (March 1993): 431–441. For other research on thin slices, see N. Ambady and R. Rosenthal, "Thin Slices of Expressive Behavior as Predictors of Interpersonal Consequences: A Meta-Analysis," *Psychological Bulletin* 111, no. 2 (1992): 256–274; N. Ambady *et al.*, "Surgeons' Tone of Voice: A Clue to Malpractice History," *Surgery* 132, no. 1 (July 2002): 5–9.

42. P. M. Senge, *The Fifth Discipline: The Art and Practice of the Learning Organization* (New York: Doubleday Currency, 1990), Chap. 10; P. N. Johnson-Laird, "Mental Models and Deduction," *Trends in Cognitive Sciences* 5, no. 10 (2001): 434–442; A. B. Markman and D. Gentner, "Thinking," *Annual Review of Psychology* 52 (2001): 223–247; T. J. Chermack, "Mental Models in Decision Making and Implications for Human Resource Development," *Advances in Developing Human Resources* 5, no. 4 (2003): 408–422.

43. G. W. Allport, *The Nature of Prejudice* (Reading, MA: Addison-Wesley, 1954); J. C. Brigham, "Ethnic Stereotypes," *Psychological Bulletin* 76, no. 1 (1971): 15–38; D. J. Schneider, *The Psychology of Stereotyping* (New York: Guilford, 2004); S. Kanahara, "A Review of the Definitions of Stereotype and a Proposal for a Progressional Model," *Individual Differences Research* 4, no. 5 (2006): 306–321.

44. C. N. Macrae, A. B. Milne, and G. V. Bodenhausen, "Stereotypes as Energy-Saving Devices: A Peek inside the Cognitive Toolbox," *Journal of Personality and Social Psychology* 66 (1994): 37–47; J. W. Sherman *et al.*, "Stereotype Efficiency Reconsidered: Encoding Flexibility under Cognitive Load," *Journal of Personality and Social Psychology* 75 (1998): 589–606; Macrae and Bodenhausen, "Social Cognition: Thinking Categorically About Others."

45. S. N. Cory, "Quality and Quantity of Accounting Students and the Stereotypical Accountant: Is There a Relationship?," *Journal of Accounting Education* 10, no. 1 (1992): 1–24; P. D. Bougen, "Joking Apart: The Serious Side to the Accountant Stereotype," *Accounting, Organizations and Society* 19, no. 3 (1994): 319–335; A. L. Friedman and S. R. Lyne, "The Beancounter Stereotype: Towards a

General Model of Stereotype Generation," *Critical Perspectives on Accounting* 12, no. 4 (2001): 423–451; T. Dimnik and S. Felton, "Accountant Stereotypes in Movies Distributed in North America in the Twentieth Century," *Accounting, Organizations and Society* 31, no. 2 (2006): 129–155; Mark Freebairn, "Accountants Aren't Boring: Breaking the Stereotype," *Accountancy Age*, 29 June 2006; "Dynamic, Colourful Logo Symbolizes Value Provided by Canada's CAs," *CA Magazine*, June/July 2007, Vol. 140, Iss. 5, 18–21; Lorie Murdoch, "Destination CA," *CA Magazine*, March 2010, Vol. 143, Iss. 2, 27–33; "Public Appreciates Your Hard Work," *CA Magazine*, June/July 2010, Vol. 143, Iss. 5, 6.

46. J. C. Turner and S. A. Haslam, "Social Identity, Organizations, and Leadership," in *Groups at Work: Theory and Research*, ed. M. E. Turner (Mahwah, NJ: Lawrence Erlbaum Associates, 2001), 25–65; M. A. Hogg *et al.*, "The Social Identity Perspective: Intergroup Relations, Self-Conception, and Small Groups," *Small Group Research* 35, no. 3 (June 2004): 246–276; J. Jetten, R. Spears, and T. Postmes, "Intergroup Distinctiveness and Differentiation: A Meta-Analytic Integration," *Journal of Personality and Social Psychology* 86, no. 6 (2004): 862–879; K. Hugenberg and D. F. Sacco, "Social Categorization and Stereotyping: How Social Categorization Biases Person Perception and Face Memory," *Social and Personality Psychology Compass* 2, no. 2 (2008): 1052–1072.

47. J. W. Jackson and E. R. Smith, "Conceptualizing Social Identity: A New Framework and Evidence for the Impact of Different Dimensions," *Personality & Social Psychology Bulletin* 25 (January 1999): 120–135.

48. S. Hayward, "Discrimination Troubles," *Metro-Toronto*, 21 March 2005; "Workplace Discrimination the Biggest Hurdle for Older and Younger Canadians," Kelly Global Workforce Index News release (Toronto: 17 October 2006).

49. "Employers Face New Danger: Accidental Age Bias," *Omaha World-Herald*, 10 October 2005, D1; "Tiptoeing through the Employment Minefield of Race, Sex, and Religion? Here's Another One," *North West Business Insider (Manchester, UK)*, February 2006.

50. S. O. Gaines and E. S. Reed, "Prejudice: From Allport to Dubois," *American Psychologist* 50 (February 1995): 96–103; S. T. Fiske, "Stereotyping, Prejudice, and Discrimination," in *Handbook of Social Psychology*, ed. D. T. Gilbert, S. T. Fiske, and G. Lindzey, 4th ed. (New York: McGraw-Hill, 1998), 357–411; M. Hewstone, M. Rubin, and H. Willis, "Intergroup Bias," *Annual Review of Psychology* 53 (2002): 575–604.

51. M. Patriquin, "Quebec Farm Segregated Black Workers," *Globe & Mail*, 30 April 2005, A1.

52. E. Cediey and F. Foroni, *Discrimination in Access to Employment on Grounds of Foreign Origin in France* (Geneva: International Labour Organization, 2008). Also see: P. Gumbel, "The French Exodus," *Time International*, 16 April 2007, 18.

53. J. A. Bargh and T. L. Chartrand, "The Unbearable Automaticity of Being," *American Psychologist* 54, no. 7 (July 1999): 462–479; S. T. Fiske, "What We Know Now About Bias and Intergroup Conflict, the Problem of the Century," *Current Directions in Psychological Science* 11, no. 4 (August 2002): 123–128. For recent evidence that shows that intensive training can minimize stereotype activation, see K. Kawakami *et al.*, "Just Say No (to Stereotyping): Effects of Training in the Negation of Stereotypic Associations on Stereotype Activation," *Journal of Personality and Social Psychology* 78, no. 5 (2000): 871–888; E. A. Plant, B. M. Peruche, and D. A. Butz, "Eliminating Automatic Racial Bias: Making Race Non-Diagnostic for Responses to Criminal Suspects," *Journal of Experimental Social Psychology* 41, no. 2 (2005): 141. On the limitations of some stereotype training, see: B. Gawronski *et al.*, "When 'Just Say No' Is Not Enough: Ayrmation Versus Negation Training and the Reduction of Automatic Stereotype Activation," *Journal of Experimental Social Psychology* 44 (2008): 370–377.

54. H. H. Kelley, *Attribution in Social Interaction* (Morristown, N.J.: General Learning Press, 1971).

55. J. M. Feldman, "Beyond Attribution Theory: Cognitive Processes in Performance Appraisal," *Journal of Applied Psychology* 66 (1981): 127–148.

56. J. M. Crant and T. S. Bateman, "Assignment of Credit and Blame for Performance Outcomes," *Academy of Management Journal* 36 (1993): 7–27; B. Weiner, "Intrapersonal and Interpersonal Theories of Motivation from an Attributional Perspective," *Educational Psychology Review* 12 (2000): 1–14; N. Bacon and P. Blyton, "Worker Responses to Teamworking: Exploring Employee Attributions of Managerial Motives," *International Journal of Human Resource Management* 16, no. 2 (February 2005): 238–255.

57. Fundamental attribution error is part of a larger phenomenon known as correspondence bias. See D. T. Gilbert and P. S. Malone, "The Correspondence Bias," *Psychological Bulletin* 117, no. 1 (1995): 21–38.

58. I. Choi, R. E. Nisbett, and A. Norenzayan, "Causal Attribution across Cultures: Variation and Universality," *Psychological Bulletin* 125, no. 1 (1999): 47–63; D. S.

Krull *et al.*, "The Fundamental Fundamental Attribution Error: Correspondence Bias in Individualist and Collectivist Cultures," *Personality and Social Psychology Bulletin* 25, no. 10 (October 1999): 1208–1219; R. E. Nisbett, *The Geography of Thought: How Asians and Westerners Think Differently—and Why* (New York: Free Press, 2003), Chap. 5.

59. D. T. Miller and M. Ross, "Self-Serving Biases in the Attribution of Causality: Fact or Fiction?," *Psychological Bulletin* 82, no. 2 (1975): 213–225; J. Shepperd, W. Malone, and K. Sweeny, "Exploring Causes of the Self-Serving Bias," *Social and Personality Psychology Compass* 2, no. 2 (2008): 895–908. The Philo Vance quotation is from: S. S. Van Dine (Willard Huntington Wright), *The Benson Murder Mystery* (New York: Charles Scribner's Sons, 1926), Chap. 6.

60. E. W. K. Tsang, "Self-Serving Attributions in Corporate Annual Reports: A Replicated Study," *Journal of Management Studies* 39, no. 1 (January 2002): 51–65; N. J. Roese and J. M. Olson, "Better, Stronger, Faster: Self-Serving Judgment, Affect Regulation, and the Optimal Vigilance Hypothesis," *Perspectives on Psychological Science* 2, no. 2 (2007): 124–141; R. Hooghiemstra, "East–West Differences in Attributions for Company Performance: A Content Analysis of Japanese and U.S. Corporate Annual Reports," *Journal of Cross-Cultural Psychology* 39, no. 5 (September 1, 2008 2008): 618–629; M. Franco and H. Haase, "Failure Factors in Small and Medium-Sized Enterprises: Qualitative Study from an Attributional Perspective," *International Entrepreneurship and Management Journal* 6, no. 4 (2010): 503–521.

61. Similar models are presented in D. Eden, "Self-Fulfilling Prophecy as a Management Tool: Harnessing Pygmalion," *Academy of Management Review* 9 (1984): 64–73; R. H. G. Field and D. A. Van Seters, "Management by Expectations (Mbe): The Power of Positive Prophecy," *Journal of General Management* 14 (Winter 1988): 19–33; D. O. Trouilloud *et al.*, "The Influence of Teacher Expectations on Student Achievement in Physical Education Classes: Pygmalion Revisited," *European Journal of Social Psychology* 32 (2002): 591–607.

62. D. Eden, "Interpersonal Expectations in Organizations," in *Interpersonal Expectations: Theory, Research, and Applications* (Cambridge, UK: Cambridge University Press, 1993), 154–178.

63. D. Eden, "Pygmalion Goes to Boot Camp: Expectancy, Leadership, and Trainee Performance," *Journal of Applied Psychology* 67 (1982): 194–199; R. P. Brown and E. C. Pinel, "Stigma on My Mind: Individual Differences in the Experience of Stereotype Threat," *Journal of*

Experimental Social Psychology 39, no. 6 (2003): 626–633.

64. S. Madon, L. Jussim, and J. Eccles, "In Search of the Powerful Self-Fulfilling Prophecy," *Journal of Personality and Social Psychology* 72, no. 4 (April 1997): 791–809; A. E. Smith, L. Jussim, and J. Eccles, "Do Self-Fulfilling Prophecies Accumulate, Dissipate, or Remain Stable over Time?," *Journal of Personality and Social Psychology* 77, no. 3 (1999): 548–565; S. Madon *et al.*, "Self-Fulfilling Prophecies: The Synergistic Accumulative Effect of Parents' Beliefs on Children's Drinking Behavior," *Psychological Science* 15, no. 12 (2005): 837–845.

65. W. H. Cooper, "Ubiquitous Halo," *Psychological Bulletin* 90 (1981): 218–244; K. R. Murphy, R. A. Jako, and R. L. Anhalt, "Nature and Consequences of Halo Error: A Critical Analysis," *Journal of Applied Psychology* 78 (1993): 218–225; T. H. Feeley, "Comment on Halo Effects in Rating and Evaluation Research," *Human Communication Research* 28, no. 4 (October 2002): 578–586. For a variation of the classic halo effect in business settings, see P. Rosenzweig, *The Halo Effect...And the Eight Other Business Delusions That Deceive Managers* (New York: Free Press, 2007).

66. B. Mullen *et al.*, "The False Consensus Effect: A Meta-Analysis of 115 Hypothesis Tests," *Journal of Experimental Social Psychology* 21, no. 3 (1985): 262–283; G. Marks and N. Miller, "Ten Years of Research on the False-Consensus Effect: An Empirical and Theoretical Review," *Psychological Bulletin* 102, no. 1 (1987): 72–90; R. L. Cross and S. E. Brodt, "How Assumptions of Consensus Undermine Decision Making," *MIT Sloan Management Review* 42, no. 2 (Winter 2001): 86–94; F. J. Flynn and S. S. Wiltermuth, "Who's with Me? False Consensus, Brokerage, and Ethical Decision Making in Organizations," *Academy of Management Journal* 53, no. 5 (October 2010): 1074–1089; S. Goel, W. Mason, and D. J. Watts, "Real and Perceived Attitude Agreement in Social Networks," *Journal of Personality and Social Psychology* 99, no. 4 (2010): 611–621.

67. C. L. Kleinke, *First Impressions: The Psychology of Encountering Others* (Englewood Cliffs, N.J.: Prentice Hall, 1975); E. A. Lind, L. Kray, and L. Thompson, "Primacy Effects in Justice Judgments: Testing Predictions from Fairness Heuristic Theory," *Organizational Behavior and Human Decision Processes* 85 (July 2001): 189–210; O. Ybarra, "When First Impressions Don't Last: The Role of Isolation and Adaptation Processes in the Revision of Evaluative Impressions," *Social Cognition* 19 (October 2001): 491–520; S. D. Bond *et al.*, "Information Distortion in the Evaluation of a Single Option," *Organizational Behavior and Human Decision Processes* 102, no. 2 (2007): 240–254.

68. D. D. Steiner and J. S. Rain, "Immediate and Delayed Primacy and Recency Effects in Performance Evaluation," *Journal of Applied Psychology* 74 (1989): 136–142; K. T. Trotman, "Order Effects and Recency: Where Do We Go from Here?," *Accounting & Finance* 40 (2000): 169–182; W. Green, "Impact of the Timing of an Inherited Explanation on Auditors' Analytical Procedures Judgements," *Accounting and Finance* 44 (2004): 369–392.

69. L. Roberson, C. T. Kulik, and M. B. Pepper, "Using Needs Assessment to Resolve Controversies in Diversity Training Design," *Group & Organization Management* 28, no. 1 (March 2003): 148–174; D. E. Hogan and M. Mallott, "Changing Racial Prejudice through Diversity Education," *Journal of College Student Development* 46, no. 2 (March/April 2005): 115–125; Gawronski *et al.*, "When 'Just Say No' Is Not Enough: Ayrmation Versus Negation Training and the Reduction of Automatic Stereotype Activation."

70. Eden, "Self-Fulfilling Prophecy as a Management Tool: Harnessing Pygmalion"; S. S. White and E. A. Locke, "Problems with the Pygmalion Effect and Some Proposed Solutions," *Leadership Quarterly* 11 (Autumn 2000): 389–415.

71. T. W. Costello and S. S. Zalkind, *Psychology in Administration: A Research Orientation* (Englewood Cliffs, N.J.: Prentice Hall, 1963), 45–46; J. M. Kouzes and B. Z. Posner, *The Leadership Challenge*, 4th ed. (San Francisco: Jossey-Bass, 2007), Chap. 3.

72. George, *Authentic Leadership*; W. L. Gardner *et al.*, "'Can You See the Real Me?' a Self-Based Model of Authentic Leader and Follower Development," *Leadership Quarterly* 16 (2005): 343–372; B. George, *True North* (San Francisco: Jossey-Bass, 2007).

73. For a discussion of the Implicit Association Test, including critique, see H. Blanton *et al.*, "Decoding the Implicit Association Test: Implications for Criterion Prediction," *Journal of Experimental Social Psychology* 42, no. 2 (2006): 192–212; A. G. Greenwald, B. A. Nosek, and N. Sriram, "Consequential Validity of the Implicit Association Test: Comment on Blanton and Jaccard (2006)," *American Psychologist* 61, no. 1 (2006): 56–61; W. Hofmann *et al.*, "Implicit and Explicit Attitudes and Interracial Interaction: The Moderating Role of Situationally Available Control Resources," *Group Processes Intergroup Relations* 11, no. 1 (Jan. 2008): 69–87.

74. Hofmann *et al.*, "Implicit and Explicit Attitudes and Interracial Interaction: The Moderating Role of Situationally Available Control Resources"; J. T. Jost *et al.*, "The Existence of Implicit Bias Is Beyond Reasonable Doubt: A Refutation of Ideological and Methodological Objections and Executive Summary of Ten Studies That No Manager Should Ignore," *Research in Organizational Behavior* 29 (2009): 39–69.

75. J. Luft, *Group Processes* (Palo Alto, Calif: Mayfield Publishing, 1984). For a variation of this model, see J. Hall, "Communication Revisited," *California Management Review* 15 (Spring 1973): 56–67.

76. L. C. Miller and D. A. Kenny, "Reciprocity of Self-Disclosure at the Individual and Dyadic Levels: A Social Relations Analysis," *Journal of Personality and Social Psychology* 50 (1986): 713–719.

77. J. Dixon and K. Durrheim, "Contact and the Ecology of Racial Division: Some Varieties of Informal Segregation," *British Journal of Social Psychology* 42 (March 2003): 1–23; P. J. Henry and C. D. Hardin, "The Contact Hypothesis Revisited: Status Bias in the Reduction of Implicit Prejudice in the United States and Lebanon," *Psychological Science* 17, no. 10 (2006): 862–868; T. F. Pettigrew and L. R. Tropp, "A Meta-Analytic Test of Intergroup Contact Theory," *Journal of Personality and Social Psychology* 90, no. 5 (2006): 751–783; C. Tredoux and G. Finchilescu, "The Contact Hypothesis and Intergroup Relations 50 Years On: Introduction to the Special Issue," *South African Journal of Psychology* 37, no. 4 (2007): 667–678; T. F. Pettigrew, "Future Directions for Intergroup Contact Theory and Research," *International Journal of Intercultural Relations* 32, no. 3 (2008): 187–199.

78. W. Frey, "Rubbish Boy Doing Well as Junk Man," *Metro-Vancouver*, 25 April 2005, 11; "Domino's Pizza Named One of Michigan's 'Cool Places to Work'," PR Newswire News release (Ann Arbor: 10 September 2007); K. C. Neel, "Abdoulah Sets Wow Apart," *Multichannel News*, 29 January 2007, 2; G. Thomas, "Fye Rewrites the Tune at ANZ," *Air Transport World*, September 2007, 61; "Too Many Signatures," *McKinsey Quarterly*, no. 4 (2009); J. Campbell, "She Delivers," *Ottawa Citizen*, 3 July 2010; J. Manby, "A CEO Goes Undercover," *HBS Alumni Bulletin*, September 2010.

79. C. Duan and C. E. Hill, "The Current State of Empathy Research," *Journal of Counseling Psychology* 43 (1996): 261–274; W. G. Stephen and K. A. Finlay, "The Role of Empathy in Improving Intergroup Relations," *Journal of Social Issues* 55 (Winter 1999): 729–743; S. K. Parker and C. M. Axtell, "Seeing Another Viewpoint: Antecedents and Outcomes of Employee Perspective Taking," *Academy of Management Journal* 44 (December 2001): 1085–1100; G. J. Vreeke and I. L. van der Mark, "Empathy, an Integrative Model," *New Ideas in Psychology* 21, no. 3 (2003): 177–207.

80. D. Calderwood-Smith, "Degroote Grad Uses MBA Training to Aid a Developing

Economy," *McMaster Daily News (Hamilton, Ont.)*, 15 June 2010.

81. S. J. Black, W. H. Mobley, and E. Weldon, "The Mindset of Global Leaders: Inquisitiveness and Duality," in *Advances in Global Leadership* (JAI, 2006), 181–200; O. Levy *et al.*, "What We Talk About When We Talk About 'Global Mindset': Managerial Cognition in Multinational Corporations," *Journal of International Business Studies* 38, no. 2 (2007): 231–258; S. Beechler and D. Baltzley, "Creating a Global Mindset," *Chief Learning Officer* 7, no. 6 (2008): 40–45.

82. A. K. Gupta and V. Govindarajan, "Cultivating a Global Mindset," *Academy of Management Executive* 16, no. 1 (2002): 116–126.

83. M. Jackson, "Corporate Volunteers Reaching Worldwide," *Boston Globe*, 4 May 2008, 3.

84. IBM, Sam Palmisano Discusses IBM's New Corporate Service Corps, Armonk, N.Y., IBM, 25 July, 2007; "Bringing Business Smarts to Africa," *Ottawa Business Journal*, 16 April 2008; "IBM's Corporate Service Corps Heading to Six Emerging Countries to Spark Socio-Economic Growth While Developing Global Leaders," IBM News release (Armonk, N.Y.: 26 March 2008); C. Hymowitz, "IBM Combines Volunteer Service, Teamwork to Cultivate Emerging Markets," *Wall Street Journal*, 4 August 2008, B6.

CHAPTER 4

1. Andy Newman and Ray Rivera J. Gray, "Flight Attendant Snaps, Swears, Pulls The Chute On His Career," *Toronto Star*, August 10, 2010, A3; Dakshana Bascaramurty, "Quitters Sometimes Prosper" *Globe and Mail*, August 11, 2010, A3; Mary Vallis, "Was JetBlue Flight Attendant Steven Slater's Outlandish Freakout Justified?" *National Post*, August 11, 2010; Anjali Khosla Mullany, "Facebook Fans Raise Thousands of Dollars for JetBlue Flight Attendant Steven Slater," *New York Daily News*, August 11, 2010; Cathal Kelly, "Flight Attendant 'Hero' Started Fight: Report," *Toronto Star*, August 12, 2010.

2. Emotions are also cognitive processes. However, we use the narrow definition of cognition as a well-used label referring only to reasoning processes. Also, this and other chapters emphasizes that emotional and cognitive processes are intertwined.

3. For discussion of emotions in marketing, economics, sociology, and political science, see: G. Loewenstein, "Emotions in Economic Theory and Economic Behavior," *American Economic Review* 90, no. 2 (May 2000): 426–432; D. S. Massey, "A Brief History of Human Society: The Origin and Role of Emotion in Social Life," *American Sociological Review* 67 (February 2002): 1–29; J. O'Shaughnessy and N. J. O'Shaughnessy, *The Marketing Power of*

Emotion (New York: Oxford University Press, 2003); J. Druckman and R. McDermott, "Emotion and the Framing of Risky Choice," *Political Behavior* 30, no. 3 (2008): 297–321; E. Petit, "The Role of Affects in Economics," *Revue d'économie politique* 119, no. 6 (2009): 859–897; M. Hubert, "Does Neuroeconomics Give New Impetus to Economic and Consumer Research?," *Journal of Economic Psychology* 31, no. 5 (2010): 812–817.

4. The definition presented here is constructed from the following sources: N. M. Ashkanasy, W. J. Zerbe, and C. E. J. Hartel, "Introduction: Managing Emotions in a Changing Workplace," in *Managing Emotions in the Workplace* ed. N. M. Ashkanasy, W. J. Zerbe, and C. E. J. Hartel (Armonk, N. Y.: M. E. Sharpe, 2002), 3–18; H. M. Weiss, "Conceptual and Empirical Foundations for the Study of Affect at Work," in *Emotions in the Workplace* ed. R. G. Lord, R. J. Klimoski, and R. Kanfer (San Francisco: Jossey-Bass, 2002), 20–63. However, the meaning of emotions is still being debated. See, for example, M. Cabanac, "What Is Emotion?," *Behavioral Processes* 60 (2002): 69–83; J. Gooty, M. Gavin, and N. M. Ashkanasy, "Emotions Research in Ob: The Challenges That Lie Ahead," *Journal of Organizational Behavior* 30, no. 6 (2009): 833–838.

5. R. Kanfer and R. J. Klimoski, "Affect and Work: Looking Back to the Future," in *Emotions in the Workplace* ed. R. G. Lord, R. J. Klimoski, and R. Kanfer (San Francisco: Jossey-Bass, 2002), 473–490; J. A. Russell, "Core Affect and the Psychological Construction of Emotion," *Psychological Review* 110, no. 1 (2003): 145–172.

6. R. B. Zajonc, "Emotions," in *Handbook of Social Psychology*, ed. D. T. Gilbert, S. T. Fiske, and L. Gardner (New York: Oxford University press, 1998), 591–634.

7. N. A. Remington, L. R. Fabrigar, and P. S. Visser, "Reexamining the Circumplex Model of Affect," *Journal of Personality and Social Psychology* 79, no. 2 (2000): 286–300; R. J. Larson, E. Diener, and R. E. Lucas, "Emotion: Models, Measures, and Differences," in *Emotions in the Workplace* ed. R. G. Lord, R. J. Klimoski, and R. Kanfer (San Francisco: Jossey- Bass, 2002), 64–113; L. F. Barrett *et al.*, "The Experience of Emotion," *Annual Review of Psychology* 58, no. 1 (2007): 373–403.

8. A. H. Eagly and S. Chaiken, *The Psychology of Attitudes* (Orlando, FL: Harcourt Brace Jovanovich, 1993); A. P. Brief, *Attitudes in and around Organizations* (Thousand Oaks, CA: Sage, 1998). There is an amazing lack of consensus on the definition of attitudes. This book adopts the three-component model, whereas some experts define attitude as only the "feelings" component, with "beliefs" as a predictor

and "intentions" as an outcome. Some writers specifically define attitudes as an "evaluation" of an attitude object, whereas others distinguish attitudes from evaluations of an attitude object. Some even define specific attitudes as "affects" (emotions), although there is also confusion whether affect is emotion as well as cognitive feelings. For some of these definitional variations, see I. Ajzen, "Nature and Operation of Attitudes," *Annual Review of Psychology* 52 (2001): 27–58; D. Albarracín *et al.*, "Attitudes: Introduction and Scope," in *The Handbook of Attitudes*, ed. D. Albarracín, B. T. Johnson, and M. P. Zanna (Mahwah, NJ: Lawrence Erlbaum Associates, 2005), 3–20; W. A. Cunningham and P. D. Zelazo, "Attitudes and Evaluations: A Social Cognitive Neuroscience Perspective," *TRENDS in Cognitive Sciences* 11, no. 3 (2007): 97–104.

9. C. D. Fisher, "Mood and Emotions While Working: Missing Pieces of Job Satisfaction?," *Journal of Organizational Behavior* 21 (2000): 185–202; Cunningham and Zelazo, "Attitudes and Evaluations"; M. D. Lieberman, "Social Cognitive Neuroscience: A Review of Core Processes," *Annual Review of Psychology* 58, no. 1 (2007): 259–289; M. Fenton-O'Creevy *et al.*, "Thinking, Feeling and Deciding: The Influence of Emotions on the Decision Making and Performance of Traders," *Journal of Organizational Behavior* (2010): n/a-n/a. The dual emotion-cognition processes are likely the same as the implicit-explicit attitude processes reported by a few scholars. See: W. J. Becker and R. Cropanzano, "Organizational Neuroscience: The Promise and Prospects of an Emerging Discipline," *Journal of Organizational Behavior* 31, no. 7 (2010): 1055–1059.

10. S. Orbell, "Intention-Behavior Relations: A Self-Regulation Perspective," in *Contemporary Perspectives on the Psychology of Attitudes*, ed. G. Haddock and G. R. Maio (East Sussex, UK: Psychology Press, 2004), 145–168.

11. H. M. Weiss and R. Cropanzano, "Affective Events Theory: A Theoretical Discussion of the Structure, Causes and Consequences of Affective Experiences at Work," *Research in Organizational Behavior* 18 (1996): 1–74; H. A. Elfenbein, "Chapter 7: Emotion in Organizations," *The Academy of Management Annals.* 1 (2007): 315–386.

12. J. A. Bargh and M. J. Ferguson, "Beyond Behaviorism: On the Automaticity of Higher Mental Processes," *Psychological Bulletin* 126, no. 6 (2000): 925–945; P. Winkielman and K. C. Berridge, "Unconscious Emotion," *Current Directions in Psychological Science* 13, no. 3 (2004): 120–123; J. M. George, "The Illusion of Will in Organizational Behavior Research: Nonconscious Processes and Job Design," *Journal of Management* 35, no. 6

(December 1, 2009 2009): 1318–1339; K. I. Ruys and D. A. Stapel, "The Unconscious Unfolding of Emotions," *European Review of Social Psychology* 20 (2009): 232–271.

13. A. R. Damasio, *Descartes' Error: Emotion, Reason, and the Human Brain* (New York: Putnam Sons, 1994); A. Damasio, *The Feeling of What Happens* (New York: Harcourt Brace and Co., 1999); P. Ekman, "Basic Emotions," in *Handbook of Cognition and Emotion*, ed. T. Dalgleish and M. Power (San Francisco: Jossey-Bass, 1999), 45–60; J. E. LeDoux, "Emotion Circuits in the Brain," *Annual Review of Neuroscience* 23 (2000): 155–184; R. J. Dolan, "Emotion, Cognition, and Behavior," *Science* 298, no. 5596 (8 November 2002): 1191–1194.

14. N. Schwarz, "Emotion, Cognition, and Decision Making," *Cognition and Emotion* 14, no. 4 (2000): 433–440; M. T. Pham, "The Logic of Feeling," *Journal of Consumer Psychology* 14, no. 4 (2004): 360–369.

15. G. R. Maio, V. M. Esses, and D. W. Bell, "Examining Conflict between Components of Attitudes: Ambivalence and Inconsistency Are Distinct Constructs," *Canadian Journal of Behavioural Science* 32, no. 2 (2000): 71–83.

16. P. C. Nutt, *Why Decisions Fail* (San Francisco, CA: Berrett-Koehler, 2002); S. Finkelstein, *Why Smart Executives Fail* (New York: Viking, 2003); P. C. Nutt, "Search During Decision Making," *European Journal of Operational Research* 160 (2005): 851–876.

17. http://www.eluta.ca/top-employer-hill-%26-knowlton Retrieved August 17, 2009; http://www.hillandknowlton.ca/index.php/news/press_releases/79.html Retrieved November 1, 2010.

18. C. Foster, "Turning Ha-Ha into a-Ha!," *Employee Benefit News Canada*, December 2007; S. Davies, "Razer Employees Wear Shorts, T-Shirts and Flip-Flops to Work," *Straits Times (Singapore)*, 10 May 2008.

19. D. L. Collinson, "Managing Humour," *Journal of Management Studies* 39, no. 3 (2002): 269–288; K. Owler, R. Morrison, and B. Plester, "Does Fun Work? The Complexity of Promoting Fun at Work," *Journal of Management and Organization* 16, no. 3 (2010): 338–352.

20. C. Cooper, "Elucidating the Bonds of Workplace Humor: A Relational Process Model," *Human Relations* 61, no. 8 (August 1, 2008 2008): 1087–1115; B. Plester and M. Orams, "Send in the Clowns: The Role of the Joker in Three New Zealand IT Companies," *Humor: International Journal of Humor Research* 21, no. 3 (2008): 253–281.

21. Weiss and Cropanzano, "Affective Events Theory."

22. L. Festinger, *A Theory of Cognitive Dissonance* (Evanston, Ill.: Row, Peterson, 1957); G. R. Salancik, "Commitment and the Control of Organizational Behavior

and Belief," in *New Directions in Organizational Behavior*, ed. B. M. Staw and G. R. Salancik (Chicago: St. Clair, 1977), 1–54; A. D. Galinsky, J. Stone, and J. Cooper, "The Reinstatement of Dissonance and Psychological Discomfort Following Failed Affirmation," *European Journal of Social Psychology* 30, no. 1 (2000): 123–147.

23. J. Cooper, *Cognitive Dissonance: Fifth Years of a Classic Theory* (London: Sage, 2007); A. R. McConnell and C. M. Brown, "Dissonance Averted: Self-Concept Organization Moderates the Effect of Hypocrisy on Attitude Change," *Journal of Experimental Social Psychology* 46, no. 2 (2010): 361–366; J. M. Jarcho, E. T. Berkman, and M. D. Lieberman, "The Neural Basis of Rationalization: Cognitive Dissonance Reduction During Decision-Making," *Social Cognitive and Affective Neuroscience* (2011): in press.

24. T. A. Judge, E. A. Locke, and C. C. Durham, "The Dispositional Causes of Job Satisfaction: A Core Evaluations Approach," *Research in Organizational Behavior* 19 (1997): 151–188; T. W. H. Ng and K. L. Sorensen, "Dispositional Affectivity and Work-Related Outcomes: A Meta-Analysis," *Journal of Applied Social Psychology* 39, no. 6 (2009): 1255–1287.

25. C. M. Brotheridge and A. A. Grandey, "Emotional Labor and Burnout: Comparing Two Perspectives of 'People Work,'" *Journal of Vocational Behavior* 60 (2002): 17–39; P. G. Irving, D. F. Coleman, and D. R. Bobocel, "The Moderating Effect of Negative Affectivity in the Procedural Justice-Job Satisfaction Relation," *Canadian Journal of Behavioural Science* 37, no. 1 (January 2005): 20–32.

26. J. Schaubroeck, D. C. Ganster, and B. Kemmerer, "Does Trait Affect Promote Job Attitude Stability?," *Journal of Organizational Behavior* 17 (1996): 191–196; C. Dormann and D. Zapf, "Job Satisfaction: A Meta-Analysis of Stabilities," *Journal of Organizational Behavior* 22 (2001): 483–504.

27. R. Corelli, "Dishing out Rudeness," *Maclean's*, 11 January 1999, 44–47; D. Matheson, "A Vancouver Cafe Where Rudeness Is Welcomed," *Canada AM, CTV Television* (11 January 2000); A. Crossan, "Get Abused in the Elbow Room Café," *PRI's The World (Boston)*, 23 February 2010.

28. B. E. Ashforth and R. H. Humphrey, "Emotional Labor in Service Roles: The Influence of Identity," *Academy of Management Review* 18 (1993): 88–115. For a recent review of the emotional labour concept, see T. M. Glomb and M. J. Tews, "Emotional Labor: A Conceptualization and Scale Development," *Journal of Vocational Behavior* 64, no. 1 (2004): 1–23.

29. "Reach for the Sky," *New Sunday Times (Kuala Lumpur)*, 16 November 2008, 4; C. Platt, "Inside Flight Attendant School," *WA Today (Perth)*, 24 February 2009.

30. J. A. Morris and D. C. Feldman, "The Dimensions, Antecedents, and Consequences of Emotional Labor," *Academy of Management Review* 21 (1996): 986–1010; D. Zapf, "Emotion Work and Psychological Well-Being: A Review of the Literature and Some Conceptual Considerations," *Human Resource Management Review* 12 (2002): 237–268.

31. L. Pivot, "Objectif Canada: A Vos Marques, Prêts... Partez !," *L'Express*, 4 June 2008; P. O'Neil, "Canada a Top Draw for French Seeking Jobs," *Montreal Gazette*, 18 November 2010, B2.

32. A. E. Raz and A. Rafaeli, "Emotion Management in Cross-Cultural Perspective: 'Smile Training' in Japanese and North American Service Organizations," *Research on Emotion in Organizations* 3 (2007): 199–220; D. Matsumoto, Seung Hee Yoo, and J. Fontaine, "Mapping Expressive Differences around the World," *Journal of Cross-Cultural Psychology* 39, no. 1 (January 1, 2008 2008): 55–74; S. Ravid, A. Rafaeli, and A. Grandey, "Expressions of Anger in Israeli Workplaces: The Special Place of Customer Interactions," *Human Resource Management Review* 20, no. 3 (2010): 224–234. Emotional display norms might also explain differences in aggression across cultures. See: N. Bergeron and B. H. Schneider, "Explaining Cross-National Differences in Peer-Directed Aggression: A Quantitative Synthesis," *Aggressive Behavior* 31, no. 2 (2005): 116–137.

33. F. Trompenaars and C. Hampden-Turner, *Riding the Waves of Culture*, 2nd ed. (New York: McGraw-Hill, 1998), Chap. 6. For a similar example of Canadian and Japanese students, see: S. Safdar *et al.*, "Variations of Emotional Display Rules within and across Cultures: A Comparison between Canada, USA, and Japan," *Canadian Journal of Behavioural Science* 41, no. 1 (2009): 1–10.

34. This relates to the automaticity of emotion, which is summarized in Winkielman and Berridge, "Unconscious Emotion"; K. N. Ochsner and J. J. Gross, "The Cognitive Control of Emotions," *TRENDS in Cognitive Sciences* 9, no. 5 (May 2005): 242–249.

35. W. J. Zerbe, "Emotional Dissonance and Employee Well-Being," in *Managing Emotions in the Workplace* ed. N. M. Ashkanasy, W. J. Zerbe, and C. E. J. Hartel (Armonk, N.Y.: M. E. Sharpe, 2002), 189–214; R. Cropanzano, H. M. Weiss, and S. M. Elias, "The Impact of Display Rules and Emotional Labor on Psychological Well-Being at Work," *Research in Occupational Stress and Well Being* 3 (2003): 45–89.

36. Brotheridge and Grandey, "Emotional Labor and Burnout: Comparing Two Perspectives of 'People Work'"; Zapf, "Emotion Work and Psychological Well-Being"; J. M. Diefendorff, M. H. Croyle, and R. H.

Gosserand, "The Dimensionality and Antecedents of Emotional Labor Strategies," *Journal of Vocational Behavior* 66, no. 2 (2005): 339–357.

37. D. McGinn, "The Emotional Workplace," *National Post*, 18 August 2007, FW3.

38. J. D. Mayer, P. Salovey, and D. R. Caruso, "Models of Emotional Intelligence," in *Handbook of Human Intelligence*, ed. R. J. Sternberg, 2nd ed. (New York: Cambridge University Press, 2000), 396–420. This definition is also recognized in C. Cherniss, "Emotional Intelligence and Organizational Effectiveness," in *The Emotionally Intelligent Workplace* ed. C. Cherniss and D. Goleman (San Francisco: Jossey-Bass, 2001), 3–12; M. Zeidner, G. Matthews, and R. D. Roberts, "Emotional Intelligence in the Workplace: A Critical Review," *Applied Psychology: An International Review* 53, no. 3 (2004): 371–399.

39. This model is very similar to Goleman's revised emotional intelligence model. See R. Boyatzis, D. Goleman, and K. S. Rhee, "Clustering Competence in Emotional Intelligence," in *The Handbook of Emotional Intelligence* ed. R. Bar-On and J. D. A. Parker (San Francisco: Jossey-Bass, 2000), 343–362; D. Goleman, "An EI-Based Theory of Performance," in *The Emotionally Intelligent Workplace* ed. C. Cherniss and D. Goleman (San Francisco: Jossey-Bass, 2001), 27–44; D. Goleman, R. Boyatzis, and A. McKee, *Primal Leadership* (Boston: Harvard Business School Press, 2002), Chap. 3. Goleman's revised model received a cool reception by most scholars. Yet recent studies indicate that variations of this model (when properly framed as a set of abilities) provide a better fit than other models. See, in particular: C.-S. Wong and K. S. Law, "The Effects of Leader and Follower Emotional Intelligence on Performance and Attitude: An Exploratory Study," *Leadership Quarterly* 13 (2002): 243–274; R. P. Tett and K. E. Fox, "Confirmatory Factor Structure of Trait Emotional Intelligence in Student and Worker Samples," *Personality and Individual Differences* 41 (2006): 1155–1168; P. J. Jordan and S. A. Lawrence, "Emotional Intelligence in Teams: Development and Initial Validation of the Short Version of the Workgroup Emotional Intelligence Profile (Weip-S)," *Journal of Management & Organization* 15 (2009): 452–469; D. L. Joseph and D. A. Newman, "Emotional Intelligence: An Integrative Meta-Analysis and Cascading Model," *Journal of Applied Psychology* 95, no. 1 (2010): 54–78.

40. H. A. Elfenbein and N. Ambady, "Predicting Workplace Outcomes from the Ability to Eavesdrop on Feelings," *Journal of Applied Psychology* 87, no. 5 (2002): 963–971.

41. The hierarchical nature of the four EI dimensions is discussed by Goleman, but it is more explicit in the Salovey and Mayer model. See D. R. Caruso and P. Salovey, *The Emotionally Intelligent Manager* (San Francisco: Jossey-Bass, 2004). This hierarchy is also identified (without the self-other distinction) as a sequence in: Joseph and Newman, "Emotional Intelligence."

42. P. N. Lopes *et al.*, "Emotional Intelligence and Social Interaction," *Personality and Social Psychology Bulletin* 30, no. 8 (August 2004): 1018–1034; C. S. Daus and N. M. Ashkanasy, "The Case for the Ability-Based Model of Emotional Intelligence in Organizational Behavior," *Journal of Organizational Behavior* 26 (2005): 453–466; J. E. Barbuto Jr and M. E. Burbach, "The Emotional Intelligence of Transformational Leaders: A Field Study of Elected Officials," *Journal of Social Psychology* 146, no. 1 (2006): 51–64; M. A. Brackett *et al.*, "Relating Emotional Abilities to Social Functioning: A Comparison of Self-Report and Performance Measures of Emotional Intelligence," *Journal of Personality and Social Psychology* 91, no. 4 (2006): 780–795; D. L. Reis *et al.*, "Emotional Intelligence Predicts Individual Differences in Social Exchange Reasoning," *NeuroImage* 35, no. 3 (2007): 1385–1391; S. K. Singh, "Role of Emotional Intelligence in Organisational Learning: An Empirical Study," *Singapore Management Review* 29, no. 2 (2007): 55–74.

43. Some studies have reported situations where EI has a limited effect on individual performance. For example, see A. L. Day and S. A. Carroll, "Using an Ability-Based Measure of Emotional Intelligence to Predict Individual Performance, Group Performance, and Group Citizenship Behaviors," *Personality and Individual Differences* 36 (2004): 1443–1458; Z. Ivcevic, M. A. Brackett, and J. D. Mayer, "Emotional Intelligence and Emotional Creativity," *Journal of Personality* 75, no. 2 (2007): 199–236; J. C. Rode *et al.*, "Emotional Intelligence and Individual Performance: Evidence of Direct and Moderated Effects," *Journal of Organizational Behavior* 28, no. 4 (2007): 399–421.

44. R. Johnson, "Can You Feel It?," *People Management*, 23 August 2007, 34–37; K. K. Spors, "Top Small Workplaces 2007," *Wall Street Journal*, 1 October 2007, R1.

45. Goleman, Boyatzis, and McKee, *Primal Leadership*; S. C. Clark, R. Callister, and R. Wallace, "Undergraduate Management Skills Courses and Students' Emotional Intelligence," *Journal of Management Education* 27, no. 1 (February 2003): 3–23; Lopes *et al.*, "Emotional Intelligence and Social Interaction"; H. A. Elfenbein, "Learning in Emotion Judgments: Training and the Cross-Cultural Understanding of Facial Expressions," *Journal of Nonverbal Behavior* 30, no. 1 (2006): 21–36; C.-S. Wong *et al.*, "The Feasibility of Training and Development of EI: An Exploratory Study in Singapore, Hong Kong and Taiwan," *Intelligence* 35, no. 2 (2007): 141–150.

46. V. Galt, "Emotional Intelligence Trumps Technical Know-How," *Globe & Mail*, 2 June 2010.

47. E. A. Locke, "Why Emotional Intelligence Is an Invalid Concept," *Journal of Organizational Behavior* 26 (2005): 425–431; J. Antonakis, "Emotional Intelligence: What Does It Measure and Does It Matter for Leadership?," in *Lmx Leadership—Game-Changing Designs: Research-Based Tools*, ed. G. B. Graen (Greenwich, CT: Information Age Publishing, 2009), 163–192; J. Antonakis, N. M. Ashkanasy, and M. T. Dasborough, "Does Leadership Need Emotional Intelligence?," *Leadership Quarterly* 20 (2009): 247–261; M. Fiori and J. Antonakis, "The Ability Model of Emotional Intelligence: Searching for Valid Measures," *Personality and Individual Differences* 50, no. 3 (2011): 329–334.

48. D. A. Harrison, D. A. Newman, and P. L. Roth, "How Important Are Job Attitudes? Meta-Analytic Comparisons of Integrative Behavioral Outcomes and Time Sequences," *Academy of Management Journal* 49, no. 2 (2006): 305–325. Another recent study concluded that job satisfaction and organizational commitment are so highly correlated that they represent the same construct. See: H. Le *et al.*, "The Problem of Empirical Redundancy of Constructs in Organizational Research: An Empirical Investigation," *Organizational Behavior and Human Decision Processes* 112, no. 2 (2010): 112–125. They are also considered the two central work-related variables in the broader concept of happiness at work. see: C. D. Fisher, "Happiness at Work," *International Journal of Management Reviews* 12, no. 4 (2010): 384–412.

49. E. A. Locke, "The Nature and Causes of Job Satisfaction," in *Handbook of Industrial and Organizational Psychology*, ed. M. Dunnette (Chicago: Rand McNally, 1976), 1297–1350; H. M. Weiss, "Deconstructing Job Satisfaction: Separating Evaluations, Beliefs and Affective Experiences," *Human Resource Management Review*, no. 12 (2002): 173–194. Some definitions still include emotion as an element of job satisfaction, whereas the definition presented in this book views emotion as a cause of job satisfaction. Also, this definition views job satisfaction as a "collection of attitudes," not several "facets" of job satisfaction.

50. Ipsos-Reid, "Ipsos-Reid Global Poll Finds Major Differences in Employee Satisfaction around the World,"News release (Toronto: 8 January 2001); International Survey Research, *Employee Satisfaction in the World's 10 Largest Economies: Globalization or Diversity?* (Chicago: International Survey Research, 2002); Watson Wyatt Worldwide, "Malaysian Workers

More Satisfied with Their Jobs Than Their Companies' Leadership and Supervision Practices," Watson Wyatt Worldwide News release (Kuala Lumpur: 30 November 2004); Kelly Global Workforce Index, *American Workers Are Happy with Their Jobs and Their Bosses* (Troy, Michigan: Kelly Services, November 2006).

51. T. W. Smith, *Job Satisfaction in America: Trends and Socio-Demographic Correlates* (Chicago: National Opinion Research Center/University of Chicago, August 2007); G. Langer, "Happy at Work? Depends Who's Asking," *ABC News*, 5 January 2010, http://blogs.abcnews.com/thenumbers/2010/01/happy-at-work-depends-whos-asking.html. Recent Canadian job satisfaction results are reported in: D. Abma, "Canadian among World's Happiest Workers," *Vancouver Sun*, 6 September 2007, C4; W. Immen, "Not Enthusiastic About Work?," *Globe & Mail*, 27 October 2010, B17.

52. W. Immen, "Employer, Will You Marry Me?," *Globe & Mail*, 24 March 2010, B21.

53. The problems with measuring attitudes and values across cultures is discussed in: G. Law, "If You're Happy & You Know It, Tick the Box," *Management-Auckland*, no. 45 (March 1998): 34–37; P. E. Spector et e. al., "Do National Levels of Individualism and Internal Locus of Control Relate to Well-Being: An Ecological Level International Study," *Journal of Organizational Behavior*, no. 22 (2001): 815–832; L. Saari and T. A. Judge, "Employee Attitudes and Job Satisfaction," *Human Resource Management* 43, no. 4 (Winter 2004): 395–407.

54. H. Rao and R. I. Sutton, "Innovation Lessons from Pixar: An Interview with Oscar-Winning Director Brad Bird," *McKinsey Quarterly* (April 2008): 1–9.

55. M. J. Withey and W. H. Cooper, "Predicting Exit, Voice, Loyalty, and Neglect," *Administrative Science Quarterly*, no. 34 (1989): 521–539; W. H. Turnley and D. C. Feldman, "The Impact of Psychological Contract Violations on Exit, Voice, Loyalty, and Neglect," *Human Relations*, no. 52 (July 1999): 895–922. Subdimensions of silence and voice also exist. See L. van Dyne, S. Ang, and I. C. Botero, "Conceptualizing Employee Silence and Employee Voice as Multidimensional Constructs," *Journal of Management Studies* 40, no. 6 (Sept. 2003): 1359–1392.

56. T. R. Mitchell, B. C. Holtom, and T. W. Lee, "How to Keep Your Best Employees: Developing an Effective Retention Policy," *Academy of Management Executive* 15 (November 2001): 96–108; C. P. Maertz and M. A. Campion, "Profiles of Quitting: Integrating Process and Content Turnover Theory," *Academy of Management Journal* 47, no. 4 (2004): 566–582; K. Morrell, J. Loan-Clarke, and A. Wilkinson, "The Role of

Shocks in Employee Turnover," *British Journal of Management* 15 (2004): 335–349; B. C. Holtom, T. R. Mitchell, and T. W. Lee, "Increasing Human and Social Capital by Applying Job Embeddedness Theory," *Organizational Dynamics* 35, no. 4 (2006): 316–331.

57. A. A. Luchak, "What Kind of Voice Do Loyal Employees Use?," *British Journal of Industrial Relations* 41 (March 2003): 115–134. For a critique and explanation for historical errors in the EVLN model's development, see: S. L. McShane, "Reconstructing the Meaning and Dimensionality of Voice in the Exit-Voice-Loyalty-Neglect Model (Paper Presented in the Voice and Loyalty" Symposium)," Paper presented at Annual Conference of the Administrative Sciences Association of Canada, Organizational Behaviour Division, Halifax, 21 May 2008

58. A. O. Hirschman, *Exit, Voice, and Loyalty: Responses to Decline in Firms, Organizations, and States* (Cambridge, Mass.: Harvard University Press, 1970); E. A. Hoffmann, "Exit and Voice: Organizational Loyalty and Dispute Resolution Strategies," *Social Forces* 84, no. 4 (June 2006): 2313–2330.

59. J. D. Hibbard, N. Kumar, and L. W. Stern, "Examining the Impact of Destructive Acts in Marketing Channel Relationships," *Journal of Marketing Research* 38 (February 2001): 45–61; J. Zhou and J. M. George, "When Job Dissatisfaction Leads to Creativity: Encouraging the Expression of Voice," *Academy of Management Journal* 44 (August 2001): 682–696.

60. M. J. Withey and I. R. Gellatly, "Situational and Dispositional Determinants of Exit, Voice, Loyalty and Neglect," *Proceedings of the Administrative Sciences Association of Canada, Organizational Behaviour Division* (June 1998); D. C. Thomas and K. Au, "The Effect of Cultural Differences on Behavioral Responses to Low Job Satisfaction," *Journal of International Business Studies* 33, no. 2 (2002): 309–326; S. F. Premeaux and A. G. Bedeian, "Breaking the Silence: The Moderating Effects of Self-Monitoring in Predicting Speaking up in the Workplace," *Journal of Management Studies* 40, no. 6 (2003): 1537–1562.

61. T. A. Judge *et al.*, "The Job Satisfaction-Job Performance Relationship: A Qualitative and Quantitative Review," *Psychological Bulletin* 127, no. 3 (2001): 376–407; C. D. Fisher, "Why Do Lay People Believe That Satisfaction and Performance Are Correlated? Possible Sources of a Commonsense Theory," *Journal of Organizational Behavior* 24, no. 6 (2003): 753–777; Saari and Judge, "Employee Attitudes and Job Satisfaction." Other studies report stronger correlations with job performance when both the belief and feeling components of job satisfaction are consistent with each other and when overall job attitude (satisfaction

and commitment combined) is being measured. See D. J. Schleicher, J. D. Watt, and G. J. Greguras, "Reexamining the Job Satisfaction-Performance Relationship: The Complexity of Attitudes," *Journal of Applied Psychology* 89, no. 1 (2004): 165–177; Harrison, Newman, and Roth, "How Important Are Job Attitudes?" The positive relationship between job satisfaction and employee performance is also consistent with emerging research on the outcomes of positive organizational behaviour. For example, see: J. R. Sunil, "Enhancing Employee Performance through Positive Organizational Behavior," *Journal of Applied Social Psychology* 38, no. 6 (2008): 1580–1600.

62. However, panel studies suggest that satisfaction has a stronger effect on performance than the other way around. For a summary, see: Fisher, "Happiness at Work."

63. "The Greatest Briton in Management and Leadership," *Personnel Today* (18 February 2003): 20; J. Bonasia, "When Employees Occupy the Top Spot at Work," *Investor's Business Daily*, 5 November 2007; S. R. Ezzedeen, C. M. Hyde, and K. R. Laurin, "Is Strategic Human Resource Management Socially Responsible? The Case of Wegman's Food Markets, Inc.," *Employee Rights and Responsibilities Journal* 18 (2007): 295–307.

64. "CCW-Update," Customer Contact Management Association News release (Australia: 7 December 2007); E. G. Brown and J. Lubahn, "We Need 'to Talk'," *Bank Marketing* 39, no. 7 (2007): 32–36; J. Penman, "Clydesdale Rings the Changes," *Sunday Times (London)*, 4 February 2007, 13; T. Russell, "Centres of Excellence," *Personnel Today*, 23 January 2007, 24–25.

65. J. I. Heskett, W. E. Sasser, and L. A. Schlesinger, *The Service Profit Chain* (New York: Free Press, 1997); A. J. Rucci, S. P. Kirn, and R. T. Quinn, "The Employee-Customer-Profit Chain at Sears," *Harvard Business Review* 76 (January-February 1998): 83–97; G. A. Gelade and S. Young, "Test of a Service Profit Chain Model in the Retail Banking Sector," *Journal of Occupational & Organizational Psychology* 78 (2005): 1–22; S. P. Brown and S. K. Lam, "A Meta-Analysis of Relationships Linking Employee Satisfaction to Customer Responses," *Journal of Retailing* 84, no. 3 (2008): 243–255; C. G. Chi and D. Gursoy, "Employee Satisfaction, Customer Satisfaction, and Financial Performance: An Empirical Examination," *International Journal of Hospitality Management* 28, no. 2 (2009): 245–253; R. W. Y. Yee *et al.*, "The Service-Profit Chain: A Review and Extension," *Total Quality Management & Business Excellence* 20, no. 6 (2009): 617–632.

66. W.-C. Tsai and Y.-M. Huang, "Mechanisms Linking Employee Affective Delivery and Customer Behavioral Intentions,"

Journal of Applied Psychology 87, no. 5 (2002): 1001–1008; P. Guenzi and O. Pelloni, "The Impact of Interpersonal Relationships on Customer Satisfaction and Loyalty to the Service Provider," *International Journal Of Service Industry Management* 15, no. 3–4 (2004): 365–384; S. J. Bell, S. Auh, and K. Smalley, "Customer Relationship Dynamics: Service Quality and Customer Loyalty in the Context of Varying Levels of Customer Expertise and Switching Costs," *Journal of the Academy of Marketing Science* 33, no. 2 (Spring 2005): 169–183; P. B. Barger and A. A. Grandey, "Service with a Smile and Encounter Satisfaction: Emotional Contagion and Appraisal Mechanisms," *Academy of Management Journal* 49, no. 6 (2006): 1229–1238.

67. R. T. Mowday, L. W. Porter, and R. M. Steers, *Employee Organization Linkages: The Psychology of Commitment, Absenteeism, and Turnover* (New York: Academic Press, 1982); J. P. Meyer, "Organizational Commitment," *International Review of Industrial and Organizational Psychology* 12 (1997): 175–228 Along with affective and continuance commitment, Meyer identifies "normative commitment," which refers to employee feelings of obligation to remain with the organization. This commitment has been excluded so that students focus on the two most common perspectives of commitment. Also, there is some question whether continuance and normative commitment are comparable to affective commitment; they are attitudes toward quitting and repaying a debt, respectively, rather than toward the organization. See: O. N. Solinger, W. van Olffen, and R. A. Roe, "Beyond the Three-Component Model of Organizational Commitment," *Journal of Applied Psychology* 93, no. 1 (2008): 70–83.

68. R. D. Hackett, P. Bycio, and P. A. Hausdorf, "Further Assessments of Meyer and Allen's (1991) Three-Component Model of Organizational Commitment," *Journal of Applied Psychology* 79 (1994): 15–23.

69. J. P. Meyer *et al.*, "Affective, Continuance, and Normative Commitment to the Organization: A Meta-Analysis of Antecedents, Correlates, and Consequences," *Journal of Vocational Behavior* 61 (2002): 20–52; M. Riketta, "Attitudinal Organizational Commitment and Job Performance: A Meta-Analysis," *Journal of Organizational Behavior* 23 (2002): 257–266; J. P. Meyer, T. E. Becker, and C. Vandenberghe, "Employee Commitment and Motivation: A Conceptual Analysis and Integrative Model," *Journal of Applied Psychology* 89, no. 6 (2004): 991–1007; J. P. Meyer and E. R. Maltin, "Employee Commitment and Well-Being: A Critical Review, Theoretical Framework and Research Agenda," *Journal of Vocational Behavior* 77, no. 2 (2010): 323–337.

70. J. P. Meyer *et al.*, "Organizational Commitment and Job Performance: It's the Nature of the Commitment That Counts," *Journal of Applied Psychology* 74 (1989): 152–156; A. A. Luchak and I. R. Gellatly, "What Kind of Commitment Does a Final-Earnings Pension Plan Elicit?," *Relations Industrielles* 56 (Spring 2001): 394–417; Z. X. Chen and A. M. Francesco, "The Relationship between the Three Components of Commitment and Employee Performance in China," *Journal of Vocational Behavior* 62, no. 3 (2003): 490–510; D. M. Powell and J. P. Meyer, "Side-Bet Theory and the Three-Component Model of Organizational Commitment," *Journal of Vocational Behavior* 65, no. 1 (2004): 157–177.

71. J. E. Finegan, "The Impact of Person and Organizational Values on Organizational Commitment," *Journal of Occupational and Organizational Psychology* 73 (June 2000): 149–169; A. Panaccio and C. Vandenberghe, "Perceived Organizational Support, Organizational Commitment and Psychological Well-Being: A Longitudinal Study," *Journal of Vocational Behavior* 75, no. 2 (2009): 224–236.

72. Data provided in several country-specific news releases from Kelly Services. For a white paper summary of the survey, see: Kelly Services, *Employee Loyalty Rises During Global Economic Recession, Kelly International Workforce Survey Finds* (Troy, MI: Kelly services, 8 March 2010).

73. J. W. Westerman and L. A. Cyr, "An Integrative Analysis of Person-Organization Fit Theories," *International Journal of Selection and Assessment* 12, no. 3 (September 2004): 252–261; A. L. Kristof-Brown, R. D. Zimmerman, and E. C. Johnson, "Consequences of Individuals' Fit at Work: A Meta-Analysis of Person-Job, Person-Organization, Person-Group, and Person-Supervisor Fit," *Personnel Psychology* 58, no. 2 (2005): 281–342; J. R. Edwards, "Chapter 4: Person-Environment Fit in Organizations: An Assessment of Theoretical Progress," *The Academy of Management Annals* 2 (2008): 167–230.

74. D. M. Rousseau *et al.*, "Not So Different after All: A Cross-Discipline View of Trust," *Academy of Management Review* 23 (1998): 393–404.

75. A. Travaglione and B. Cross, "Diminishing the Social Network in Organizations: Does There Need to Be Such a Phenomenon as 'Survivor Syndrome' after Downsizing?," *Strategic Change* 15 (Jan-Feb 2006): 1–13; D. K. Datta *et al.*, "Causes and Effects of Employee Downsizing: A Review and Synthesis," *Journal of Management* 36, no. 1 (January 2010): 281–348.

76. Similar concepts on information acquisition are found in socialization and organizational change research. See, for example: P. Bordia *et al.*, "Uncertainty During Organizational Change: Types, Consequences, and Management Strategies," *Journal of Business and Psychology* 18, no. 4 (2004): 507–532; H. D. Cooper-Thomas and N. Anderson, "Organizational Socialization: A Field Study into Socialization Success and Rate," *International Journal of Selection and Assessment* 13, no. 2 (2005): 116–128; T. N. Bauer, "Newcomer Adjustment During Organizational Socialization: A Meta-Analytic Review of Antecedents, Outcomes, and Methods," *Journal of Applied Psychology* 92, no. 3 (2007): 707–721.

77. T. S. Heffner and J. R. Rentsch, "Organizational Commitment and Social Interaction: A Multiple Constituencies Approach," *Journal of Vocational Behavior* 59 (2001): 471–490.

78. J. Pierce, L. , T. Kostova, and K. T. Dirks, "Toward a Theory of Psychological Ownership in Organizations," *Academy of Management Review* 26, no. 2 (2001): 298–310; M. Mayhew *et al.*, "A Study of the Antecedents and Consequences of Psychological Ownership in Organizational Settings," *The Journal of Social Psychology* 147, no. 5 (2007): 477–500; T.-S. Han, H.-H. Chiang, and A. Chang, "Employee Participation in Decision Making, Psychological Ownership and Knowledge Sharing: Mediating Role of Organizational Commitment in Taiwanese High-Tech Organizations," *The International Journal of Human Resource Management* 21, no. 12 (2010): 2218–2233.

79. H. Samuel, "Why Have 24 France Telecom Workers Killed Themselves in the Past 19 Months?," *The Telegraph (UK) (London)*, 4 October 2009; "Doctor or Decorator?," *Economist*, 8 April 2010; F. Aizicovici, "France Télécom: La Lutte Contre Le Stress Au Travail Se Met En Place Lentement," *Le Monde (Paris)*, 26 January 2010; R. Tomlinson and G. Viscusi, "Suicides inside France Telecom Prompting Sarkozy Stress Testing," *BusinessWeek*, 25 January 2010.

80. J. C. Quick *et al.*, *Preventive Stress Management in Organizations* (Washington, D.C.: American Psychological Association, 1997), 3–4; R. S. DeFrank and J. M. Ivancevich, "Stress on the Job: An Executive Update," *Academy of Management Executive* 12 (August 1998): 55–66; A. L. Dougall and A. Baum, "Stress, Coping, and Immune Function," in *Handbook of Psychology*, ed. M. Gallagher and R. J. Nelson (Hoboken, N. J.: John Wiley & Sons, 2003), 441–455. There are at least three schools of thought regarding the meaning of stress, and some reviews of the stress literature describe these schools without pointing to any one as

the preferred definition. One reviewer concluded that the stress concept is so broad that it should be considered an umbrella concept, capturing a broad array of phenomena and providing a simple term for the public to use. See T. A. Day, "Defining Stress as a Prelude to Mapping Its Neurocircuitry: No Help from Allostasis," *Progress in Neuro-Psychopharmacology and Biological Psychiatry* 29, no. 8 (2005): 1195–1200; R. Cropanzano and A. Li, "Organizational Politics and Workplace Stress," in *Handbook of Organizational Politics*, ed. E. Vigoda-Gadot and A. Drory (Cheltenham, UK: Edward Elgar, 2006), 139–160; R. L. Woolfolk, P. M. Lehrer, and L. A. Allen, "Conceptual Issues Underlying Stress Management," in *Principles and Practice of Stress Management*, ed. P. M. Lehrer, R. L. Woolfolk, and W. E. Sime (New York: Guilford Press, 2007), 3–15.

81. Finegan, "The Impact of Person and Organizational Values on Organizational Commitment"; Dougall and Baum, "Stress, Coping, and Immune Function"; R. S. Lazarus, *Stress and Emotion: A New Synthesis* (New York: Springer Publishing, 2006); L. W. Hunter and S. M. B. Thatcher, "Feeling the Heat: Effects of Stress, Commitment, and Job Experience on Job Performance," *Academy of Management Journal* 50, no. 4 (2007): 953–968.

82. W. Lester, "Poll: Stress Knows Few Boundaries for People in Industrial Democracies," *USA Today*, 20 December 2006; "Hungarians Say Work Conditions Contribute to Poor Health." news release for Kelly Services (Budapest: 2008).

83. Quick *et al.*, *Preventive Stress Management in Organizations*, 5–6; B. L. Simmons and D. L. Nelson, "Eustress at Work: The Relationship between Hope and Health in Hospital Nurses," *Health Care Management Review* 26, no. 4 (October 2001): 7ff.

84. H. Selye, "A Syndrome Produced by Diverse Nocuous Agents," *Nature* 138, no. 1 (4 July 1936): 32; H. Selye, *Stress without Distress* (Philadelphia: J. B. Lippincott, 1974). The earliest use of the word *stress* is reported in R. M. K. Keil, "Coping and Stress: A Conceptual Analysis," *Journal of Advanced Nursing* 45, no. 6 (2004): 659–665.

85. S. E. Taylor, R. L. Repetti, and T. Seeman, "Health Psychology: What Is an Unhealthy Environment and How Does It Get under the Skin?," *Annual Review of Psychology* 48 (1997): 411–447.

86. D. Ganster, M. Fox, and D. Dwyer, "Explaining Employees' Health Care Costs: A Prospective Examination of Stressful Job Demands, Personal Control, and Physiological Reactivity," *Journal of Applied Psychology* 86 (May 2001): 954–964; M. Kivimaki *et al.*, "Work Stress and Risk of Cardiovascular Mortality: Prospective Cohort Study

of Industrial Employees," *British Medical Journal* 325 (19 October 2002): 857–860; S. Andrew and S. Ayers, "Stress, Health, and Illness," in *The Sage Handbook of Health Psychology*, ed. S. Sutton, A. Baum, and M. Johnston (London: Sage, 2004), 169–196; A. Rosengren *et al.*, "Association of Psychosocial Risk Factors with Risk of Acute Myocardial Infarction in 11 119 Cases and 13 648 Controls from 52 Countries (the Interheart Study): Case-Control Study," *The Lancet* 364, no. 9438 (11 September 2004): 953–962.

87. R. C. Kessler, "The Effects of Stressful Life Events on Depression," *Annual Review of Psychology* 48 (1997): 191–214; L. Greenburg and J. Barling, "Predicting Employee Aggression against Coworkers, Subordinates and Supervisors: The Roles of Person Behaviors and Perceived Workplace Factors," *Journal of Organizational Behavior* 20 (1999): 897–913; M. Jamal and V. V. Baba, "Job Stress and Burnout among Canadian Managers and Nurses: An Empirical Examination," *Canadian Journal of Public Health* 91, no. 6 (Nov-Dec 2000): 454–458; L. Tourigny, V. V. Baba, and T. R. Lituchy, "Job Burnout among Airline Employees in Japan: A Study of the Buffering Effects of Absence and Supervisory Support," *International Journal of Cross Cultural Management* 5, no. 1 (April 2005): 67–85; M. S. Hershcovis *et al.*, "Predicting Workplace Aggression: A Meta-Analysis," *Journal of Applied Psychology* 92, no. 1 (2007): 228–238.

88. C. Maslach, W. B. Schaufeli, and M. P. Leiter, "Job Burnout," *Annual Review of Psychology* 52 (2001): 397–422; J. R. B. Halbesleben and M. R. Buckley, "Burnout in Organizational Life," *Journal of Management* 30, no. 6 (2004): 859–879.

89. K. Danna and R. W. Griffin, "Health and Well-Being in the Workplace: A Review and Synthesis of the Literature," *Journal of Management* (Spring 1999): 357–384.

90. This is a slight variation of the definition in the Quebec anti-harassment legislation. See www.cnt.gouv.qc.ca. For related definitions and discussion of workplace incivility, see H. Cowiea and e. al., "Measuring Workplace Bullying," *Aggression and Violent Behavior* 7 (2002): 33–51; C. M. Pearson and C. L. Porath, "On the Nature, Consequences and Remedies of Workplace Incivility: No Time for 'Nice'? Think Again," *Academy of Management Executive* 19, no. 1 (February 2005): 7–18.

91. Pearson and Porath, "On the Nature, Consequences and Remedies of Workplace Incivility"; J. Scott, C. Blanshard, and S. Child, "Workplace Bullying of Junior Doctors: A Cross-Sectional Questionnaire Survey," *New Zealand Medical Journal* 121, no. 1282 (19 September 2008): 10–14; A. Yeung and B. Griffin, "Workplace Incivilty:

Does It Matter in Asia," *People & Strategy* 31, no. 1 (December 2008): 14–19.

92. For a legal discussion of types of sexual harassment, see: B. Lindemann and D. D. Kadue, *Sexual Harassment in Employment Law* (Washington: BNA Books, 1999), 7–9.

93. "Let's Slow Down!," *The Royal Bank of Canada Monthly Letter*, September 1949.

94. E. Galinsky *et al.*, *Overwork in America: When the Way We Work Becomes Too Much* (New York: Families and Work Institute, March 2005); J. MacBride-King, *Wrestling with Workload: Organizational Strategies for Success* (Ottawa: Conference Board of Canada, 2005); "Canadian Workers Feel More Stressed and Less Appreciated, Desjardins Financial Security National Survey on Canadian Health Finds." Canada NewsWire news release for Desjardins Financial Security (Toronto: 8 September 2010).

95. S. DuBois, "Addicted to Bits; Smartphones are Our New Drug of Choice," 20 October 2010, Retrieved: http://tech.fortune.cnn.com/2010/10/20/addicted-to-bits-smartphones-are-our-new-drug-of-choice/; "BlackBerry still a Favorite Tasty Treat," *Strategic Direction*, Vol. 25 No. 5 (2009), 5–7; N. Mokey, "Top 10 Signs of Cell Phone Addiction," 25 January 2010, Retrieved: http://www.digitaltrends.com/mobile/top-10-signs-of-cell-phone-addiction/; S. Davis, "Addicted to Your Smartphone? Here's What to Do," WebMD, http://www.webmd.com/balance/features/addicted-your-smartphone-what-to-do; N. Chesley, "Blurring Boundaries? Linking Technology Use, Spillover, Individual Distress, and Family Satisfaction," *Journal of Marriage and Family* 67, no. 5 (2005): 1237–1248.; T. Taylor, "Hard-Working Canadians Find It Tough to Disconnect," *Calgary Herald*, 18 May 2005, A10.; R. Parloff, "Secrets of Greatness—How I Work: Amy W. Schulman," *Fortune*, 20 March 2006, 66; F.C.J. Morris, "Technology Addicted Employees," *New Jersey Law Journal* (2 March 2007).

96. R. Drago, D. Black, and M. Wooden, *The Persistence of Long Work Hours*, Melbourne Institute Working Paper Series (Melbourne: Melbourne Institute of Applied Economic and Social Research, University of Melbourne, August 2005); L. Golden, "A Brief History of Long Work Time and the Contemporary Sources of Overwork," *Journal of Business Ethics* 84, supp. 2 (2009): 217–227.

97. C. B. Meek, "The Dark Side of Japanese Management in the 1990s: Karoshi and Ijime in the Japanese Workplace," *Journal of Managerial Psychology* 19, no. 3 (2004): 312–331; "Nagoya Court Rules Toyota Employee Died from Overwork," *Japan Times*, 1 December 2007; Y. Kageyama, "Questions Rise About Temps, Overwork at Toyota," *Associated Press Newswires*, 10

September 2008; Y. Kawanishi, "On Karo-Jisatsu (Suicide by Overwork)," *International Journal of Mental Health* 37, no. 1 (Spring2008 2008): 61–74; P. Novotny, "Overwork a Silent Killer in Japan," *Agence France Presse*, 11 January 2009.

98. A. Bakker, E. Demerouti, and W. Verbeke, "Using the Job Demands-Resources Model to Predict Burnout and Performance," *Human Resources Management* 43, no. 1 (2004): 83–104; W. B. Schaufeli, "Job Demands, Job Resources, and Their Relationship with Burnout and Engagement: A Multisample Study," *Journal of Organizational Behavior* 25 (2004): 293–315; A. Bakker and E. Demerouti, "The Job Demands-Resources Model: State of the Art," *Journal of Managerial Psychology* 22, no. 3 (2007): 309.

99. R. Karasek and T. Theorell, *Healthy Work: Stress, Productivity, and the Reconstruction of Working Life* (New York: Basic Books, 1990); N. Turner, N. Chmiel, and M. Walls, "Railing for Safety: Job Demands, Job Control, and Safety Citizenship Role Definition," *Journal of Occupational Health Psychology* 10, no. 4 (2005): 504–512.

100. Lazarus, *Stress and Emotion: A New Synthesis*, Chap. 5.

101. M. Zuckerman and M. Gagne, "The Cope Revised: Proposing a 5-Factor Model of Coping Strategies," *Journal of Research in Personality* 37 (2003): 169–204; S. Folkman and J. T. Moskowitz, "Coping: Pitfalls and Promise," *Annual Review of Psychology* 55 (2004): 745–774; C. A. Thompson et al., " On the Importance of Coping: A Model and New Directions for Research on Work and Family," *Research in Occupational Stress and Well-Being* 6 (2007): 73–113.

102. S. E. Taylor et al., "Psychological Resources, Positive Illusions, and Health," *American Psychologist* 55, no. 1 (January 2000): 99–109; F. Luthans and C. M. Youssef, "Emerging Positive Organizational Behavior," *Journal of Management* 33, no. 3 (June 1, 2007 2007): 321–349; P. Steel, J. Schmidt, and J. Shultz, "Refining the Relationship between Personality and Subjective Well-Being," *Psychological Bulletin* 134, no. 1 (2008): 138–161; G. Alarcon, K. J. Eschleman, and N. A. Bowling, "Relationships between Personality Variables and Burnout: A Meta-Analysis," *Work & Stress* 23, no. 3 (2009): 244–263; R. Kotov et al., "Linking "Big" Personality Traits to Anxiety, Depressive, and Substance Use Disorders: A Meta-Analysis," *Psychological Bulletin* 136, no. 5 (2010): 768–821.

103. G. A. Bonanno, "Loss, Trauma, and Human Resilience: Have We Underestimated the Human Capacity to Thrive after Extremely Aversive Events?," *American Psychologist* 59, no. 1 (2004): 20–28; F. Luthans, C. M. Youssef, and B. J. Avolio, *Psychological Capital: Developing the Human*

Competitive Edge (New York: Oxford University Press, 2007).

104. J. T. Spence and A. S. Robbins, "Workaholism: Definition, Measurement and Preliminary Results," *Journal of Personality Assessment* 58 (1992): 160–178; R. J. Burke, "Workaholism in Organizations: Psychological and Physical Well-Being Consequences," *Stress Medicine* 16, no. 1 (2000): 11–16; I. Harpaz and R. Snir, "Workaholism: Its Definition and Nature," *Human Relations* 56 (2003): 291–319; R. J. Burke, A. M. Richardson, and M. Martinussen, "Workaholism among Norwegian Senior Managers: New Research Directions," *International Journal of Management* 21, no. 4 (December 2004): 415–426; T. W. H. Ng, K. L. Sorensen, and D. C. Feldman, "Dimensions, Antecedents, and Consequences of Workaholism: A Conceptual Integration and Extension," *Journal of Organizational Behavior* 28 (2007): 111–136.

105. M. Siegall and L. L. Cummings, "Stress and Organizational Role Conflict," *Genetic, Social, and General Psychology Monographs* 12 (1995): 65–95.

106. L. T. Eby et al., "Work and Family Research in IO/OB: Content Analysis and Review of the Literature (1980–2002)," *Journal of Vocational Behavior* 66, no. 1 (2005): 124–197.

107. N. Davidson, "Vancouver Developer Looks to Make Video Games without Burning out Staff," *Canadian Press*, 21 February 2006; F. Jossi, "Clocking Out," *HRMagazine*, June 2007, 46–50.

108. S. R. Madsen, "The Effects of Home-Based Teleworking on Work-Family Conflict," *Human Resource Development Quarterly* 14, no. 1 (2003): 35–58; S. Raghuram and B. Wiesenfeld, "Work-Nonwork Conflict and Job Stress among Virtual Workers," *Human Resource Management* 43, no. 2/3 (Summer/Fall 2004): 259–277.

109. Organization for Economic Co-operation and Development, *Babies and Bosses: Reconciling Work and Family Life*, vol. 4 (Canada, Finland, Sweden and the United Kingdom) (Paris: OECD Publishing, 2005); J. Heymann et al., *The Work, Family, and Equity Index: How Does the United States Measure Up?*, Project on Global Working Families (Montreal: Institute for Health and Social Policy, June 2007).

110. M. Secret, "Parenting in the Workplace: Child Care Options for Consideration," *The Journal of Applied Behavioral Science* 41, no. 3 (September 2005): 326–347.

111. V. Bland, "Sabbaticals Ideal Refresher," *New Zealand Herald*, 31 August 2005; A. E. Carr and T. L.-P. Tang, "Sabbaticals and Employee Motivation: Benefits, Concerns, and Implications," *Journal of Education for Business* 80, no. 3 (Jan/Feb 2005): 160–164;

S. Overman, "Sabbaticals Benefit Companies as Well as Employees," *Employee Benefit News*, 15 April 2006; O. B. Davidson et al., "Sabbatical Leave: Who Gains and How Much?," *Journal of Applied Psychology* 95, no. 5 (2010): 953–964. For discussion of psychological detachment and stress management, see: C. Fritz et al., "Happy, Healthy, and Productive: The Role of Detachment from Work During Nonwork Time," *Journal of Applied Psychology* 95, no. 5 (2010): 977–983.

112. M. H. Abel, "Humor, Stress, and Coping Strategies," *Humor: International Journal of Humor Research* 15, no. 4 (2002): 365–381; N. A. Kuiper et al., "Humor Is Not Always the Best Medicine: Specific Components of Sense of Humor and Psychological Well-Being," *Humor: International Journal of Humor Research* 17, no. 1/2 (2004): 135–168; E. J. Romero and K. W. Cruthirds, "The Use of Humor in the Workplace," *Academy of Management Perspectives* 20, no. 2 (2006): 58–69; M. McCreaddie and S. Wiggins, "The Purpose and Function of Humor in Health, Health Care and Nursing: A Narrative Review," *Journal of Advanced Nursing* 61, no. 6 (2008): 584–595.

113. W. M. Ensel and N. Lin, "Physical Fitness and the Stress Process," *Journal of Community Psychology* 32, no. 1 (January 2004): 81–101.

114. S. Armour, "Rising Job Stress Could Affect Bottom Line," *USA Today*, 29 July 2003; V. A. Barnes, F. A. Treiber, and M. H. Johnson, "Impact of Transcendental Meditation on Ambulatory Blood Pressure in African-American Adolescents," *American Journal of Hypertension* 17, no. 4 (2004): 366–369; P. Manikonda et al., "Influence of Non-Pharmacological Treatment (Contemplative Meditation and Breathing Technique) on Stress Induced Hypertension a Randomized Controlled Study," *American Journal of Hypertension* 18, no. 5, Supplement 1 (2005): A89-A90.

115. K. MacQueen, "Dealing with the Stressed," *Maclean's*, 15 October 2007, 52–58.

116. W. Leung, "Till Layoffs Do Us Part," *Globe & Mail*, 9 March 2010; J. Myers, "Good Company," *Globe & Mail*, 13 March 2010, B15.

117. C. Viswesvaran, J. I. Sanchez, and J. Fisher, "The Role of Social Support in the Process of Work Stress: A Meta-Analysis," *Journal of Vocational Behavior* 54, no. 2 (1999): 314–334; S. E. Taylor et al., "Biobehavioral Responses to Stress in Females: Tend-and-Befriend, Not Fight-or-Flight," *Psychological Review* 107, no. 3 (July 2000): 411–429; R. Eisler and D. S. Levine, "Nurture, Nature, and Caring: We Are Not Prisoners of Our Genes," *Brain and Mind* 3 (2002): 9–52; T. A. Beehr, N. A. Bowling, and M. M. Bennett, "Occupational Stress and Failures of Social Support: When Helping Hurts," *Journal of Occupational Health Psychology*

15, no. 1 (Jan 2010): 45–59; B. A. Scott *et al.*, "A Daily Investigation of the Role of Manager Empathy on Employee Well-Being," *Organizational Behavior and Human Decision Processes* 113, no. 2 (2010): 127–140.

CHAPTER 5

1. P. Brent, "Packaging Loyalty," *National Post*, 22 October 2005, WK2; M. Andrews, "Richmond Manufacturer Ties up Neat Package Deal," *Vancouver Sun*, 6 September 2007, C1; R. Colman, "Packing the Perfect Punch," *CMA Management*, March 2007, 40–43, "Great Little Box Company: Employer Review," www.eluta.ca/top-employer-great-little-box-company, Retrieved September 22, 2010; "Great Little Box Company: A Team Approach to Success," www.ic.gc.ca/.../..%5Cvwapj%5Cgreatlittlebox_company_eng.pdf%5C$file%5Cgreatlittlebox_company_eng.pdf, Retrieved August 18, 2010; M. MacIsaac "Best Companies to Work for in B.C.," *BCBusiness*, 3 December 2009.

2. C. C. Pinder, *Work Motivation in Organizational Behavior* (Upper Saddle River, NJ: Prentice-Hall, 1998); R. M. Steers, R. T. Mowday, and D. L. Shapiro, "The Future of Work Motivation Theory," *Academy of Management Review* 29 (2004): 379–387.

3. A. B. Bakker and W. B. Schaufeli, "Positive Organizational Behavior: Engaged Employees in Flourishing Organizations," *Journal of Organizational Behavior* 29, no. 2 (2008): 147–154; W. H. Macey and B. Schneider, "The Meaning of Employee Engagement," *Industrial and Organizational Psychology* 1 (2008): 3–30.

4. M. Millar, "Getting the Measure of Its People," *Personnel Today*, 14 December 2004, 6; A. M. Saks, "Antecedents and Consequences of Employee Engagement," *Journal of Managerial Psychology* 21, no. 7 (2006): 600–619; Scottish Executive Social Research, *Employee Engagement in the Public Sector: A Review of the Literature* (Edinburgh: Scottish Executive Social Research, May 2007); J. Engen, "Are Your Employees Truly Engaged?," *Chief Executive*, March 2008, 42; S. Flander, "Terms of Engagement," *Human Resource Executive Online*, January 2008.

5. Corporate Research Forum, *Workshop Review: Using Strengths-Based Approaches to Improve Individual and Organisational Performance* (London: Corporate Research Forum, 10 July 2007); H. Syedain, "A Talent for Numb3rs," *People Management*, 14 June 2007; P. Flade, "Employee Engagement Drives Shareholder Value," *Director of Finance Online*, 13 February 2008; Standard Chartered, *Sustainability Review 2007: Leading the Way in Asia, Africa, and the Middle East* (London: Standard Chartered Bank, 17 March 2008).

6. "Gallup Study: Feeling Good Matters in the Workplace," *Gallup Management Journal*, 12 January 2006; "Few Workers Are 'Engaged' at Work and Most Want More from Execs," *Dow Jones Business News (San Francisco)*, 22 October 2007; M. Weinstein, "The Young and the Engage-Less," *Training*, October 2008, 6; BlessingWhite, *The State of Employee Engagement 2008: Asia Pacific Overview* (Princeton, NJ: BlessingWhite, 3 March 2009); Gallup Consulting, *The Gallup Q12-Employee Engagement-Poll 2008 Results* (Gallup Consulting, February 2009).

7. Several sources attempt to identify and organize the drivers of employee engagement. See, for example: D. Robinson, S. Perryman, and S. Hayday, *The Drivers of Employee Engagement* (Brighton, UK: Institute for Employment Studies., 2004); W. H. Macey *et al.*, *Employee Engagement: Tools for Analysis, Practice, and Competitive Advantage* (Malden, MA: Wiley-Blackwell, 2009); M. Stairs and M. Galpin, "Positive Engagement: From Employee Engagement to Workplace Happiness," in *Oxford Handbook of Positive Psychology of Work*, ed. P. A. Linley, S. Harrington, and N. Garcea (New York: Oxford University Press, 2010), 155–172.

8. The confusing array of definitions about drives and needs has been the subject of criticism for a half century. See, for example, R. S. Peters, "Motives and Motivation," *Philosophy* 31 (1956): 117–130; H. Cantril, "Sentio, Ergo Sum: 'Motivation' Reconsidered," *Journal of Psychology* 65, no. 1 (Jan. 1967): 91–107; G. R. Salancik and J. Pfeffer, "An Examination of Need-Satisfaction Models of Job Attitudes," *Administrative Science Quarterly* 22, no. 3 (Sep. 1977): 427–456.

9. A. Blasi, "Emotions and Moral Motivation," *Journal for the Theory of Social Behaviour* 29, no. 1 (1999): 1–19; D. W. Pfaff, *Drive: Neurobiological and Molecular Mechanisms of Sexual Motivation* (Cambridge, MA: MIT Press, 1999); T. V. Sewards and M. A. Sewards, "Fear and Power-Dominance Drive Motivation: Neural Representations and Pathways Mediating Sensory and Mnemonic Inputs, and Outputs to Premotor Structures," *Neuroscience and Biobehavioral Reviews* 26 (2002): 553–579; K. C. Berridge, "Motivation Concepts in Behavioral Neuroscience," *Physiology & Behavior* 81, no. 2 (2004): 179–209. We distinguish drives from emotions, but future research may find that the two concepts are not so different as is stated here. Woodworth is credited with either coining or popularizing the term "drives" in the context of human motivation. His classic book is certainly the first source to discuss the concept in detail. See: R. S. Woodworth, *Dynamic Psychology* (New York: Columbia University Press, 1918).

10. G. Loewenstein, "The Psychology of Curiosity: A Review and Reinterpretation," *Psychological Bulletin* 116, no. 1 (1994): 75–98; R. E. Baumeister and M. R. Leary, "The Need to Belong: Desire for Interpersonal Attachments as a Fundamental Human Motivation," *Psychological Bulletin* 117 (1995): 497–529; A. E. Kelley, "Neurochemical Networks Encoding Emotion and Motivation: An Evolutionary Perspective," in *Who Needs Emotions? The Brain Meets the Robot*, ed. J.-M. Fellous and M. A. Arbib (New York: Oxford University Press, 2005), 29–78; L. A. Leotti, S. S. Iyengar, and K. N. Ochsner, "Born to Choose: The Origins and Value of the Need for Control," *Trends in Cognitive Sciences* 14, no. 10 (2010): 457–463.

11. K. Passyn and M. Sujan, "Self-Accountability Emotions and Fear Appeals: Motivating Behavior," *Journal of Consumer Research* 32, no. 4 (2006): 583–589; S. G. Barsade and D. E. Gibson, "Why Does Affect Matter in Organizations?," *Academy of Management Perspectives* 21, no. 2 (Feb. 2007): 36–59.

12. A. R. Damasio, *The Feeling of What Happens: Body and Emotion in the Making of Consciousness* (New York: Harcourt Brace & Company, 1999), 286.

13. S. Hitlin, "Values as the Core of Personal Identity: Drawing Links between Two Theories of Self," *Social Psychology Quarterly* 66, no. 2 (2003): 118–137; D. D. Knoch and E. E. Fehr, "Resisting the Power of Temptations. The Right Prefrontal Cortex and Self-Control," *Annals of the New York Academy of Sciences* 1104, no. 1 (2007): 123; B. Monin, D. A. Pizarro, and J. S. Beer, "Deciding Versus Reacting: Conceptions of Moral Judgment and the Reason-Affect Debate," *Review of General Psychology* 11, no. 2 (2007): 99–111.

14. A. H. Maslow, "A Theory of Human Motivation," *Psychological Review* 50 (1943): 370–396; A. H. Maslow, *Motivation and Personality* (New York Harper & Row, 1954).

15. D. T. Hall and K. E. Nougaim, "An Examination of Maslow's Need Hierarchy in an Organizational Setting," *Organizational Behavior and Human Performance* 3, no. 1 (1968): 12; M. A. Wahba and L. G. Bridwell, "Maslow Reconsidered: A Review of Research on the Need Hierarchy Theory," *Organizational Behavior and Human Performance* 15 (1976): 212–240; E. L. Betz, "Two Tests of Maslow's Theory of Need Fulfillment," *Journal of Vocational Behavior* 24, no. 2 (1984): 204–220; P. A. Corning, "Biological Adaptation in Human Societies: A 'Basic Needs' Approach," *Journal of Bioeconomics* 2, no. 1 (2000): 41–86. For a recent proposed revision of the model, see: D. T. Kenrick *et al.*, "Renovating the Pyramid of Needs: Contemporary Extensions Built Upon Ancient

Foundations," *Perspectives on Psychological Science* 5, no. 3 (May 2010): 292–314.

16. K. Dye, A. J. Mills, and T. G. Weatherbee, "Maslow: Man Interrupted—Reading Management Theory in Context," *Management Decision* 43, no. 10 (2005): 1375–1395.

17. A. H. Maslow, "A Preface to Motivation Theory," *Psychsomatic Medicine* 5 (1943): 85–92.

18. S. Kesebir, J. Graham, and S. Oishi, "A Theory of Human Needs Should Be Human-Centered, Not Animal-Centered," *Perspectives on Psychological Science* 5, no. 3 (May 2010): 315–319.

19. A. H. Maslow, *Maslow on Management* (New York: John Wiley & Sons, 1998).

20. F. F. Luthans, "Positive Organizational Behavior: Developing and Managing Psychological Strengths," *The Academy of Management Executive* 16, no. 1 (2002): 57–72; S. L. Gable and J. Haidt, "What (and Why) Is Positive Psychology?," *Review of General Psychology* 9, no. 2 (2005): 103–110; M. E. P. Seligman *et al.*, "Positive Psychology Progress: Empirical Validation of Interventions," *American Psychologist* 60, no. 5 (2005): 410–421.

21. L. Parks and R. P. Guay, "Personality, Values, and Motivation," *Personality and Individual Differences* 47, no. 7 (2009): 675–684.

22. B. A. Agle and C. B. Caldwell, "Understanding Research on Values in Business," *Business and Society* 38 (September 1999): 326–387; B. Verplanken and R. W. Holland, "Motivated Decision Making: Effects of Activation and Self-Centrality of Values on Choices and Behavior," *Journal of Personality and Social Psychology* 82, no. 3 (2002): 434–447; S. Hitlin and J. A. Pilavin, "Values: Reviving a Dormant Concept," *Annual Review of Sociology* 30 (2004): 359–393.

23. D. C. McClelland, *The Achieving Society* (New York: Van Nostrand Reinhold, 1961); D. C. McClelland and D. H. Burnham, "Power Is the Great Motivator," *Harvard Business Review* 73 (January- February 1995): 126–139; D. Vredenburgh and Y. Brender, "The Hierarchical Abuse of Power in Work Organizations," *Journal of Business Ethics* 17 (September 1998): 1337–1347; S. Shane, E. A. Locke, and C. J. Collins, "Entrepreneurial Motivation," *Human Resource Management Review* 13, no. 2 (2003): 257–279.

24. McClelland, *The Achieving Society.*

25. Shane, Locke, and Collins, "Entrepreneurial Motivation."

26. McClelland and Burnham, "Power Is the Great Motivator"; J. L. Thomas, M. W. Dickson, and P. D. Bliese, "Values Predicting Leader Performance in the U.S. Army Reserve Officer Training Corps Assessment Center: Evidence for a Personality-Mediated Model," *The Leadership Quarterly* 12, no. 2 (2001): 181–196.

27. Vredenburgh and Brender, "The Hierarchical Abuse of Power in Work Organizations."

28. D. Miron and D. C. McClelland, "The Impact of Achievement Motivation Training on Small Business," *California Management Review* 21 (1979): 13–28.

29. P. R. Lawrence and N. Nohria, *Driven: How Human Nature Shapes Our Choices* (San Francisco: Jossey-Bass, 2002). On the application of four-drive theory to leadership, see: P. R. Lawrence, *Driven to Lead* (San Francisco: Jossey-Bass, 2010).

30. The drive to acquire is likely associated with research on getting ahead, desire for competence, the selfish gene, and desire for social distinction. See R. H. Frank, *Choosing the Right Pond: Human Behavior and the Quest for Status* (New York: Oxford University Press, 1985); L. Gaertner *et al.*, "The "I," The "We," And The "When": A Meta-Analysis of Motivational Primacy in Self-Definition," *Journal of Personality and Social Psychology* 83, no. 3 (2002): 574–591; J. Hogan and B. Holland, "Using Theory to Evaluate Personality and Job-Performance Relations: A Socioanalytic Perspective," *Journal of Applied Psychology* 88, no. 1 (2003): 100–112; R. Dawkins, *The Selfish Gene*, 30th Anniversary Edition ed. (Oxford, UK: Oxford University Press, 2006); B. S. Frey, "Awards as Compensation," *European Management Journal* 4 (2007): 6–14; M. R. Leary, "Motivational and Emotional Aspects of the Self," *Annual Review of Psychology* 58, no. 1 (2007): 317–344.

31. Baumeister and Leary, "The Need to Belong."

32. J. Litman, "Curiosity and the Pleasures of Learning: Wanting and Liking New Information," *Cognition and Emotion* 19, no. 6 (2005): 793–814; T. G. Reio Jr *et al.*, "The Measurement and Conceptualization of Curiosity," *Journal of Genetic Psychology* 167, no. 2 (2006): 117–135.

33. W. H. Bexton, W. Heron, and T. H. Scott, "Effects of Decreased Variation in the Sensory Environment," *Canadian Journal of Psychology* 8 (1954): 70–76; Loewenstein, "The Psychology of Curiosity."

34. A. R. Damasio, *Descartes' Error: Emotion, Reason, and the Human Brain* (New York: Putnam sons, 1994); J. E. LeDoux, "Emotion Circuits in the Brain," *Annual Review of Neuroscience* 23 (2000): 155–184; P. Winkielman and K. C. Berridge, "Unconscious Emotion," *Current Directions in Psychological Science* 13, no. 3 (2004): 120–123.

35. Lawrence and Nohria, *Driven*, 145–147.

36. S. H. Schwartz, B. A. Hammer, and M. Wach, "Les Valeurs De Base De La Personne: Théorie, Mesures et Applications," *Revue franc—aise de sociologie* 47, no. 4 (Oct-Dec 2006): 929–968.

37. Lawrence and Nohria, *Driven*, Chap. 11.

38. D. Nebenzahl, "At Radialpoint, Innovation is Key," *Montreal Gazette*, 17 October 2009, F16; D. Jermyn, "Polish These Resumes: Here Are the Top 50," *Globe and Mail*, 2 June 2010, B6; A. Willis, "IPO Window Opening For Private Canadian Tech Companies," *Globe and Mail*, 21 August 2009, B8; Radialpoint, "Where Careers Happen" website, http://jobs.radialpoint.com/en/home/index.php.

39. Expectancy theory of motivation in work settings originated in V. H. Vroom, *Work and Motivation* (New York: Wiley, 1964). The version of expectancy theory presented here was developed by Edward Lawler. Lawler's model provides a clearer presentation of the model's three components. P-to-O expectancy is similar to "instrumentality" in Vroom's original expectancy theory model. The difference is that instrumentality is a correlation whereas P-to-O expectancy is a probability. See J. P. Campbell *et al.*, *Managerial Behavior, Performance, and Effectiveness* (New York: McGraw-Hill, 1970); E. E. Lawler III, *Motivation in Work Organizations* (Monterey, CA: Brooks-Cole, 1973); D. A. Nadler and E. E. Lawler, "Motivation: A Diagnostic Approach," in *Perspectives on Behavior in Organizations*, ed. J. R. Hackman, E. E. Lawler III, and L. W. Porter, 2nd ed. (New York: McGraw-Hill, 1983), 67–78.

40. M. Zeelenberg *et al.*, "Emotional Reactions to the Outcomes of Decisions: The Role of Counterfactual Thought in the Experience of Regret and Disappointment," *Organizational Behavior and Human Decision Processes* 75, no. 2 (1998): 117–141; B. A. Mellers, "Choice and the Relative Pleasure of Consequences," *Psychological Bulletin* 126, no. 6 (November 2000): 910–924; R. P. Bagozzi, U. M. Dholakia, and S. Basuroy, "How Effortful Decisions Get Enacted: The Motivating Role of Decision Processes, Desires, and Anticipated Emotions," *Journal of Behavioral Decision Making* 16, no. 4 (October 2003): 273–295.

41. Nadler and Lawler, "Motivation: A Diagnostic Approach."

42. B. Moses, "Time to Get Serious About Rewarding Employees," *Globe & Mail*, 28 April 2010, B16.

43. T. Matsui and T. Terai, "A Cross-Cultural Study of the Validity of the Expectancy Theory of Motivation," *Journal of Applied Psychology* 60 (1975): 263–265; D. H. B. Welsh, F. Luthans, and S. M. Sommer, "Managing Russion Factory Workers: The Impact of U.S.-Based Behavioral and Participative Techniques," *Academy of Management Journal* 36 (1993): 58–79.

44. This limitation was recently acknowledged by Victor Vroom, who had introduced expectancy theory in his 1964 book. See G. P. Latham, *Work Motivation: History, Theory, Research, and Practice* (Thousand Oaks, CA: Sage, 2007), 47–48.

45. J. B. Watson, *Behavior: An Introduction to Comparative Psychology* (New York: Henry Holt & Co., 1914).

46. B. F. Skinner, *About Behaviorism* (New York: Alfred A. Knopf, 1974); J. Komaki, T. Coombs, and S. Schepman, "Motivational Implications of Reinforcement Theory," in *Motivation and Leadership at Work*, ed. R. M. Steers, L. W. Porter, and G. A. Bigley (New York: McGraw-Hill, 1996), 34–52; R. G. Miltenberger, *Behavior Modification: Principles and Procedures* (Pacific Grove, CA: Brooks/Cole, 1997).

47. T. K. Connellan, *How to Improve Human Performance* (New York: Harper & Row, 1978), 48–57; F. Luthans and R. Kreitner, *Organizational Behavior Modification and Beyond* (Glenview, Ill.: Scott, Foresman, 1985), 85–88.

48. B. F. Skinner, *Science and Human Behavior* (New york: The Free Press, 1965); Miltenberger, *Behavior Modification: Principles and Procedures*, Chap. 4–6.

49. T. R. Hinkin and C. A. Schriesheim, "If You Don't Hear from Me You Know You Are Doing Fine," *Cornell Hotel & Restaurant Administration Quarterly* 45, no. 4 (November 2004): 362–372.

50. L. K. Trevino, "The Social Effects of Punishment in Organizations: A Justice Perspective," *Academy of Management Review* 17 (1992): 647–676; L. E. Atwater *et al.*, "Recipient and Observer Reactions to Discipline: Are Managers Experiencing Wishful Thinking?," *Journal of Organizational Behavior* 22, no. 3 (May 2001): 249–270.

51. G. P. Latham and V. L. Huber, "Schedules of Reinforcement: Lessons from the Past and Issues for the Future," *Journal of Organizational Behavior Management* 13 (1992): 125–149; B. A. Williams, "Challenges to Timing-Based Theories of Operant Behavior," *Behavioural Processes* 62 (April 2003): 115–123.

52. T. Grant, "Thanking Staff without a Fistful of Dollars," *Globe & Mail*, 21 March 2009, B15; C. Prete, "Big Steel Weighs In," *Hamilton Spectator*, 22 January 2009, G01.

53. D. Gibson, "Investing in Employees' Health," *Lane Report (Kentucky)*, December 2007, 28; "10,000 Steps in the Right Direction," *Our City (Stoke-on-Trent magazine)*, January 2009, 11; D. Blackhurst, "£1m Bill to Get Council and NHS Staff Walking," *The Sentinel (Staffordshire)*, 2 February 2009, 13.

54. J. A. Bargh and M. J. Ferguson, "Beyond Behaviorism: On the Automaticity of Higher Mental Processes," *Psychological Bulletin* 126, no. 6 (2000): 925–945. Some writers argue that behaviourists long ago accepted the relevance of cognitive processes in behaviour modification. See I. Kirsch *et al.*, "The Role of Cognition in Classical and Operant Conditioning," *Journal of Clinical Psychology* 60, no. 4 (April 2004): 369–392.

55. A. Bandura, *Social Foundations of Thought and Action: A Social Cognitive Theory* (Englewood Cliffs, N.J: Prentice Hall, 1986); A. Bandura, "Social Cognitive Theory of Self-Regulation," *Organizational Behavior and Human Decision Processes* 50, no. 2 (1991): 248–287; A. Bandura, "Social Cognitive Theory: An Agentic Perspective," *Annual Review of Psychology* 52, no. 1 (2001): 1–26.

56. M. E. Schnake, "Vicarious Punishment in a Work Setting," *Journal of Applied Psychology* 71 (1986): 343–345; Trevino, "The Social Effects of Punishment in Organizations: A Justice Perspective"; J. Malouff *et al.*, "Effects of Vicarious Punishment: A Meta-Analysis," *Journal of General Psychology* 136, no. 3 (2009): 271–286.

57. A. Pescuric and W. C. Byham, "The New Look of Behavior Modeling," *Training & Development* 50 (July 1996): 24–30.

58. A. Bandura, "Self-Reinforcement: Theoretical and Methodological Considerations," *Behaviorism* 4 (1976): 135–155; C. A. Frayne and J. M. Geringer, "Self-Management Training for Improving Job Performance: A Field Experiment Involving Salespeople," *Journal of Applied Psychology* 85, no. 3 (June 2000): 361–372; J. B. Vancouver and D. V. Day, "Industrial and Organisation Research on Self-Regulation: From Constructs to Applications," *Applied Psychology: an International Journal* 54, no. 2 (April 2005): 155–185.

59. S. Zeller, "Good Calls," *Government Executive*, 15 May 2005; C. Bailor, "Checking the Pulse of the Contact Center," *Customer Relationship Management*, November 2007, 24–29.

60. A. Shin, "What Customers Say and How They Say It," *Washington Post*, 18 October 2006, D01; D. Ververidis and C. Kotropoulos, "Emotional Speech Recognition: Resources, Features, and Methods," *Speech Communication* 48, no. 9 (2006): 1162–1181.

61. G. P. Latham, "Goal Setting: A Five-Step Approach to Behavior Change," *Organizational Dynamics* 32, no. 3 (2003): 309–318; E. A. Locke and G. P. Latham, *A Theory of Goal Setting and Task Performance* (Englewood Cliffs, N.J: Prentice Hall, 1990). The acronym *SMART* refers to goals that are specific, measurable, acceptable, relevant, and timely. However, this list duplicates some characteristics (e.g., specific goals *are* measurable and timely) and overlooks the characteristics of challenging and feedback-related.

62. A. Li and A. B. Butler, "The Effects of Participation in Goal Setting and Goal Rationales on Goal Commitment: An Exploration of Justice Mediators," *Journal of Business and Psychology* 19, no. 1 (Fall 2004): 37–51.

63. Locke and Latham, *A Theory of Goal Setting and Task Performance* Chap. 6 and 7; J. Wegge, "Participation in Group Goal Setting: Some Novel Findings and a Comprehensive Model as a New Ending to an Old Story," *Applied Psychology: An International Review* 49 (2000): 498–516.

64. M. London, E. M. Mone, and J. C. Scott, "Performance Management and Assessment: Methods for Improved Rater Accuracy and Employee Goal Setting," *Human Resource Management* 43, no. 4 (Winter 2004): 319–336; G. P. Latham and C. C. Pinder, "Work Motivation Theory and Research at the Dawn of the Twenty-First Century," *Annual Review of Psychology* 56 (2005): 485–516.

65. K. Hendricks, L. Menor, and C. Wiedman, "The Balanced Scorecard: To Adopt or Not to Adopt?," *Ivey Business Journal* (Nov/Dec 2004): 1–9; City of Edmonton, *Drainage Services Branch: Business Plan 2008–2010* (Edmonton: City of Edmonton, Drainage Services Branch, October 2007); E. Weir *et al.*, "Applying the Balanced Scorecard to Local Public Health Performance Measurement: Deliberations and Decisions," *BMC Public Health* 9, no. 1 (2009): 127; Children's Aid Society of Brant, *Child and Performance Outcomes for Fiscal Year April 1, 2009 to March 31, 2010* (Brantford, Ont.: Children's Aid Society of Brant, 22 October 2010); R. Mostray, "The Rcmp's Experience with the Balanced Scorecard: 8 Years+," Paper presented at Centre of Excellence on Performance Management & Accountability, Ottawa, 10 March 2010.

66. S. P. Brown, S. Ganesan, and G. Challagalla, "Self-Efficacy as a Moderator of Information-Seeking Effectiveness," *Journal of Applied Psychology* 86, no. 5 (2001): 1043–1051; P. A. Heslin and G. P. Latham, "The Effect of Upward Feedback on Managerial Behaviour," *Applied Psychology: An International Review* 53, no. 1 (2004): 23–37; D. Van-Dijk and A. N. Kluger, "Feedback Sign Effect on Motivation: Is It Moderated by Regulatory Focus?," *Applied Psychology: An International Review* 53, no. 1 (2004): 113–135; J. E. Bono and A. E. Colbert, "Understanding Responses to Multi-Source Feedback: The Role of Core Self-Evaluations," *Personnel Psychology* 58, no. 1 (Spring 2005): 171–203.

67. P. Drucker, *The Effective Executive* (Oxford, UK: Butterworth-Heinemann, 2007), 22.

68. M. Buckingham, *Go Put Your Strengths to Work* (New York: Free Press, 2007); S. L. Orem, J. Binkert, and A. L. Clancy, *Appreciative Coaching: A Positive Process for Change* (San Francisco: Jossey-Bass, 2007);

S. Gordon, "Appreciative Inquiry Coaching," *International Coaching Psychology Review* 3, no. 2 (March 2008): 19–31.

69. R. White, "Building on Employee Strengths at Sony Europe," *Strategic HR Review* 5, no. 5 (2006): 28–31.

70. A. Terracciano, P. T. Costa, and R. R. McCrae, "Personality Plasticity after Age 30," *Personality and Social Psychology Bulletin* 32, no. 8 (Aug. 2006): 999–1009; Leary, "Motivational and Emotional Aspects of the Self."

71. D. Hendry, "Game-Playing: The Latest Business Tool," *Globe & Mail*, 17 November 2006, C11.

72. L. Hollman, "Seeing the Writing on the Wall," *Call Center* (August 2002): 37; S. E. Ante, "Giving the Boss the Big Picture," *Business Week*, 13 February 2006, 48.

73. F. P. Morgeson, T. V. Mumford, and M. A. Campion, "Coming Full Circle: Using Research and Practice to Address 27 Questions About 360-Degree Feedback Programs," *Consulting Psychology Journal* 57, no. 3 (2005): 196–209; J. W. Smither, M. London, and R. R. Reilly, "Does Performance Improve Following Multisource Feedback? A Theoretical Model, Meta-Analysis, and Review of Empirical Findings," *Personnel Psychology* 58, no. 1 (2005): 33–66; L. E. Atwater, J. F. Brett, and A. C. Charles, "Multisource Feedback: Lessons Learned and Implications for Practice," *Human Resource Management* 46, no. 2 (Summer 2007): 285–307.

74. A. S. DeNisi and A. N. Kluger, "Feedback Effectiveness: Can 360-Degree Appraisals Be Improved?," *Academy of Management Executive* 14 (February 2000): 129–139; M. A. Peiperl, "Getting 360 Degree Feedback Right," *Harvard Business Review* 79 (January 2001): 142–147; M.-G. Seo, L. F. Barrett, and J. M. Bartunek, "The Role of Affective Experience in Work Motivation," *Academy of Management Review* 29 (2004): 423–449.

75. S. J. Ashford and G. B. Northcraft, "Conveying More (or Less) Than We Realize: The Role of Impression Management in Feedback Seeking," *Organizational Behavior and Human Decision Processes* 53 (1992): 310–334; J. R. Williams *et al.*, "Increasing Feedback Seeking in Public Contexts: It Takes Two (or More) to Tango," *Journal of Applied Psychology* 84 (December 1999): 969–976.

76. J. B. Miner, "The Rated Importance, Scientific Validity, and Practical Usefulness of Organizational Behavior Theories: A Quantitative Review," *Academy of Management Learning and Education* 2, no. 3 (2003): 250–268. Also see Pinder, *Work Motivation in Organizational Behavior*, 384.

77. P. M. Wright, "Goal Setting and Monetary Incentives: Motivational Tools That Can Work Too Well," *Compensation and Benefits Review* 26 (May- June 1994): 41–49; E. A. Locke and G. P. Latham, "Building a Practically Useful Theory of Goal Setting and Task Motivation: A 35-Year Odyssey," *American Psychologist* 57, no. 9 (2002): 705–717.

78. Latham, *Work Motivation*, 188.

79. R. Colman, "Packing the Perfect HR Punch," *CMA Management*, March 2007, 40–43.

80. J. Greenberg and E. A. Lind, "The Pursuit of Organizational Justice: From Conceptualization to Implication to Application," in *Industrial and Organizational Psychology: Linking Theory with Practice* ed. C. L. Cooper and E. A. Locke (London: Blackwell, 2000), 72–108; R. Cropanzano and M. Schminke, "Using Social Justice to Build Effective Work Groups," in *Groups at Work: Theory and Research* ed. M. E. Turner (Mahwah, N.J.: Lawrence Erlbaum Associates, 2001), 143–171; D. T. Miller, "Disrespect and the Experience of Injustice," *Annual Review of Psychology* 52 (2001): 527–553.

81. J. S. Adams, "Toward an Understanding of Inequity," *Journal of Abnormal and Social Psychology* 67 (1963): 422–436; R. T. Mowday, "Equity Theory Predictions of Behavior in Organizations," in *Motivation and Work Behavior*, ed. L. W. Porter and R. M. Steers, 5th ed. (New York: McGraw-Hill, 1991), 111–131; R. G. Cropanzano, J., "Progress in Organizational Justice: Tunneling through the Maze," in *International Review of Industrial and Organizational Psychology* ed. C. L. Cooper and I. T. Robertson (New York: Wiley, 1997), 317–372; L. A. Powell, "Justice Judgments as Complex Psychocultural Constructions: An Equity-Based Heuristic for Mapping Two- and Three-Dimensional Fairness Representations in Perceptual Space ", *Journal of Cross-Cultural Psychology* 36, no. 1 (January 2005): 48–73.

82. C. T. Kulik and M. L. Ambrose, "Personal and Situational Determinants of Referent Choice," *Academy of Management Review* 17 (1992): 212–237; G. Blau, "Testing the Effect of Level and Importance of Pay Referents on Pay Level Satisfaction," *Human Relations* 47 (1994): 1251–1268.

83. T. P. Summers and A. S. DeNisi, "In Search of Adams' Other: Reexamination of Referents Used in the Evaluation of Pay," *Human Relations* 43 (1990): 497–511.

84. Y. Cohen-Charash and P. E. Spector, "The Role of Justice in Organizations: A Meta-Analysis," *Organizational Behavior and Human Decision Processes* 86 (November 2001): 278–321.

85. R. Boswell, "Nearly Half of Canadians Think They're Underpaid: Poll," *Canada. com*, 7 September 2010; Robert Half, *Banking and Financial Services: Asia Pacific Salary Guide 2010/2011* (Tokyo: Robert Half, Financial services Group, 21 June 2010); L. Saad, "More Workers Ok with Their Pay in 2010," *Gallup Daily News*, 19 August 2010.

86. Canadian Press, "Pierre Berton, Canadian Cultural Icon, Enjoyed Long and Colourful Career," *Times Colonist (Victoria, B.C.)*, 30 November 2004.

87. K. S. Sauleya and A. G. Bedeian, "Equity Sensitivity: Construction of a Measure and Examination of Its Psychometric Properties," *Journal of Management* 26 (September 2000): 885–910; G. Blakely, M. Andrews, and R. Moorman, "The Moderating Effects of Equity Sensitivity on the Relationship between Organizational Justice and Organizational Citizenship Behaviors," *Journal of Business and Psychology* 20, no. 2 (2005): 259–273.

88. M. Ezzamel and R. Watson, "Pay Comparability across and within UK Boards: An Empirical Analysis of the Cash Pay Awards to CEOs and Other Board Members," *Journal of Management Studies* 39, no. 2 (March 2002): 207–232; J. Fizel, A. C. Krautman, and L. Hadley, "Equity and Arbitration in Major League Baseball," *Managerial and Decision Economics* 23, no. 7 (Oct-Nov 2002): 427–435.

89. "Nova Scotia Quiznos Offers Job To Good Sub Samaritan Fired By Rival Chain," *National Post*, 12 June 2010, A15; "Woman Fired for Giving Away Subs to Fire Victims," *CTV Canada AM*, 11 June 2010.

90. Greenberg and Lind, "The Pursuit of Organizational Justice: From Conceptualization to Implication to Application"; K. Roberts and K. S. Markel, "Claiming in the Name of Fairness: Organizational Justice and the Decision to File for Workplace Injury Compensation," *Journal of Occupational Health Psychology* 6 (October 2001): 332–347; J. B. Olson-Buchanan and W. R. Boswell, "The Role of Employee Loyalty and Formality in Voicing Discontent," *Journal of Applied Psychology* 87, no. 6 (2002): 1167–1174.

91. R. Hagey *et al.*, "Immigrant Nurses' Experience of Racism," *Journal of Nursing Scholarship* 33 (Fourth Quarter 2001): 389–395; Roberts and Markel, "Claiming in the Name of Fairness: Organizational Justice and the Decision to File for Workplace Injury Compensation"; D. A. Jones and D. P. Skarlicki, "The Effects of Overhearing Peers Discuss an Authority's Fairness Reputation on Reactions to Subsequent Treatment," *Journal of Applied Psychology* 90, no. 2 (2005): 363–372.

92. Miller, "Disrespect and the Experience of Injustice."

93. M. L. Ambrose, M. A. Seabright, and M. Schminke, "Sabotage in the Workplace: The Role of Organizational Injustice," *Organizational Behavior and Human Decision Processes* 89, no. 1 (2002): 947–965.

CHAPTER 6

1. B. Sass, "Top-ranked Employers Listen To Their Workers," *Edmonton Journal*, 24 October 2009, K1; B. Mah, "Forestry Workers Sought; New Industry Strategy Sets Sights On Immigrants, Mature Workers and The Disabled To Attract Labourers," *Edmonton Journal*, 31 July 2008, F1; http://www.eluta.ca/top-employer-spruceland Retrieved 10 October 2010; P. Koven, "The Making of A Score Card for Job Seekers," *National Post*, 18 October 2006, WK11; D. Finlayson, "Top Employers—Premium Perks," *Edmonton Journal*, 22 October 2005, I1; "Keeping in Good Company" *Edmonton Journal*, 14 October 2006; L. Young, "Spruceland Millworks Benefits from Generosity," *Canadian HR Reporter*, 22 October 2007, 12.

2. M. C. Bloom and G. T. Milkovich, "Issues in Managerial Compensation Research," in *Trends in Organizational Behavior*, ed. C. L. Cooper and D. M. Rousseau (Chicester, UK: John Wiley & Sons, 1996), 23–47. For an excellent review of the history of money, see: N. Ferguson, *The Ascent of Money: A Financial History of the World* (New York: Penguin, 2008).

3. S. E. G. Lea and P. Webley, "Money as Tool, Money as Drug: The Biological Psychology of a Strong Incentive," *Behavioral and Brain Sciences* 29 (2006): 161–209; D. Valenze, *The Social Life of Money in the English Past* (New York: Cambridge University Press, 2006); G. M. Rose and L. M. Orr, "Measuring and Exploring Symbolic Money Meanings," *Psychology and Marketing* 24, no. 9 (2007): 743–761.

4. D. W. Krueger, "Money, Success, and Success Phobia," in *The Last Taboo: Money as Symbol and Reality in Psychotherapy and Psychoanalysis*, ed. D. W. Krueger (New York: Brunner/Mazel, 1986), 3–16.

5. P. F. Wernimont and S. Fitzpatrick, "The Meaning of Money," *Journal of Applied Psychology* 56, no. 3 (1972): 218–226; T. R. Mitchell and A. E. Mickel, "The Meaning of Money: An Individual-Difference Perspective," *Academy of Management Review* (July 1999): 568–578; R. Trachtman, "The Money Taboo: Its Effects in Everyday Life and in the Practice of Psychotherapy," *Clinical Social Work Journal* 27, no. 3 (1999): 275–288; S. Lea, "Money: Motivation, Metaphors, and Mores," *Behavioral and Brain Sciences* 29, no. 2 (2006): 196–209; Lea and Webley, "Money as Tool, Money as Drug"; T. L.-P. Tang *et al.*, "The Love of Money and Pay Level Satisfaction: Measurement and Functional Equivalence in 29 Geopolitical Entities around the World," *Management and Organization Review* 2, no. 3 (2006): 423–452.

6. A. Furnham and R. Okamura, "Your Money or Your Life: Behavioral and Emotional Predictors of Money Pathology," *Human Relations* 52 (September 1999): 1157–1177.

7. Tang *et al.*, "The Love of Money and Pay Level Satisfaction: Measurement and Functional Equivalence in 29 Geopolitical Entities around the World"; T. Tang *et al.*, "To Help or Not to Help? The Good Samaritan Effect and the Love of Money on Helping Behavior," *Journal of Business Ethics* (2007); T. Tang and Y.-J. Chen, "Intelligence vs. Wisdom: The Love of Money, Machiavellianism, and Unethical Behavior across College Major and Gender," *Journal of Business Ethics* 82, no. 1 (2008): 1–26.

8. R. Lynn, *The Secret of the Miracle Economy* (London: SAE, 1991), cited in Furnham and Okamura, "Your Money or Your Life: Behavioral and Emotional Predictors of Money Pathology."

9. A. Furnham, B. D. Kirkcaldy, and R. Lynn, "National Attitudes to Competitiveness, Money, and Work among Young People: First, Second, and Third World Differences," *Human Relations* 47 (January 1994): 119–132; G. Dell'Orto and K. O. Doyle, "Poveri Ma Belli: Meanings of Money in Italy and in Switzerland," *American Behavioral Scientist* 45, no. 2 (October 1, 2001 2001): 257–271; K. O. Doyle, "Introduction: Ethnicity and Money," *American Behavioral Scientist* 45, no. 2 (October 1, 2001 2001): 181–190; V. K. G. Lim, "Money Matters: An Empirical Investigation of Money, Face and Confucian Work Ethic," *Personality and Individual Differences* 35 (2003): 953–970; T. L.-P. Tang, A. Furnham, and G. M.-T. Davis, "A Cross-Cultural Comparison of the Money Ethic, the Protestant Work Ethic, and Job Satisfaction: Taiwan, the USA, and the UK," *International Journal of Organization Theory and Behavior* 6, no. 2 (Summer 2003): 175–194; R. Tung and C. Baumann, "Comparing the Attitudes toward Money, Material Possessions and Savings of Overseas Chinese Vis-À-Vis Chinese in China: Convergence, Divergence or Cross-Vergence, Vis-À-Vis 'One Size Fits All' Human Resource Management Policies and Practices," *International Journal of Human Resource Management* 20, no. 11 (2009): 2382–2401.

10. D. Gardner, G., V. D. Linn, and J. L. Pierce, "The Effects of Pay Level on Organization-Based Self-Esteem and Performance: A Field Study," *Journal of Occupational and Organizational Psychology* 77 (2004): 307–322; S. L. Rynes, B. Gerhart, and K. A. Minette, "The Importance of Pay in Employee Motivation: Discrepancies between What People Say and What They Do," *Human Resource Management* 43, no. 4 (Winter 2004): 381–394; B. S. Frey, "Awards as Compensation," *European Management Journal* 4 (2007): 6–14.

11. J. S. Mill, *Utilitarianism*, Seventh ed. (London: Longmans, Green, and Co., 1879; Project Gutenberg EBook), Chap. 4.

12. "Seniority Pay System Seeing Revival," *Kyodo News (Tokyo)*, 29 March 2004; R. J. Palabrica, "13th Month Pay," *Philippine Daily Inquirer*, 30 November 2007.

13. D. M. Figart, "Equal Pay for Equal Work: The Role of Job Evaluation in an Evolving Social Norm," *Journal of Economic Issues* 34 (March 2000): 1–19.

14. E. E. Lawler III, *Rewarding Excellence: Pay Strategies for the New Economy* (San Francisco: Jossey-Bass, 2000), 30–35, 109–119; R. McNabb and K. Whitfield, "Job Evaluation and High Performance Work Practices: Compatible or Conflictual?," *Journal of Management Studies* 38 (March 2001): 293–312.

15. R. J. Long, "Paying for Knowledge: Does It Pay?," *Canadian HR Reporter*, 28 March 2005, 12–13; N. Le Pan, *Enhancing Integrated Market Enforcement Teams, Acheiving Results in Fighting Capital Markets* (Ottawa: RCMP, 25 October 2007).

16. P. K. Zingheim and J. R. Schuster, "Competencies and Rewards: Substance or Just Style?," *Compensation Benefits Review* 35, no. 5 (2003): 40–44.

17. Long, "Paying for Knowledge: Does It Pay?"; J. D. Shaw *et al.*, "Success and Survival of Skill-Based Pay Plans," *Journal of Management* 31, no. 1 (February 2005): 28–49; E. C. Dierdorff and E. A. Surface, "If You Pay for Skills, Will They Learn? Skill Change and Maintenance under a Skill-Based Pay System," *Journal of Management* 34, no. 4 (August 2008): 721–743.

18. Zingheim and Schuster, "Competencies and Rewards"; F. Giancola, "Skill-Based Pay—Issues for Consideration," *Benefits & Compensation Digest* 44, no. 5 (2007): 1–15.

19. S. Clarke, *Compensation Planning Outlook 2008* (Ottawa: Conference Board of Canada, October 2007). The history of performance-based pay is described in: E. B. Peach and D. A. Wren, "Pay for Performance from Antiquity to the 1950s," *Journal of Organizational Behavior Management* (1992): 5–26.

20. G. G. Nasmith, *Timothy Eaton* (Toronto: McClelland & Stewart, 1923), 91; C. Newman, *Caesars of the Wilderness* (Toronto: Viking, 1987), 121.

21. N. Stewart & A. Cowan, "Compensation Planning Outlook 2011," *The Conference Board of Canada*, October 2010, p. 7; D. Easton, "Prepaid Incentives Rewarding Experience," *Canadian HR Reporter*, Vol. 23, Iss. 9, 3 May 2010, 23.

22. N. Byrnes and M. Arndt, "The Art of Motivation," *BusinessWeek*, 1 May 2006, 56; M. Bolch, "Rewarding the Team," *HR-Magazine*, February 2007, 91–93.

23. G. Hamel, *The Future of Management* (Boston: Harvard Business School Press, 2007), 73–75.

24. J. D. Ketcham and M. F. Furukawa, "Hospital-Physician Gainsharing in Cardiology," *Health Affairs* 27, no. 3 (2008): 803–812.

25. L. R. Gomez-Mejia, T. M. Welbourne, and R. M. Wiseman, "The Role of Risk Sharing and Risk Taking under Gainsharing," *Academy of Management Review* 25 (July 2000): 492–507; K. M. Bartol and A. Srivastava, "Encouraging Knowledge Sharing: The Role of Organizational Reward System," *Journal of Leadership & Organizational Studies* 9 (Summer 2002): 64–76.

26. K. Brady, W. Thomas, and J. Clipsham, *CSR Case Study: Syncrude Canada Ltd.* (Ottawa: Government of Canada. Natural Resources Canada, November 2003).

27. G. Pitts, "PCL Finds a Way to Keep Things Private," *CTV News* (Toronto), 4 January 2011.

28. O. Hammarström, *Handelsbanken, Sweden: Make Work Pay–Make Work Attractive*, Attractive workplace for all: company cases (Dublin, Ireland: Eurofound, October 2007).

29. J. Chelius and R. S. Smith, "Profit Sharing and Employment Stability," *Industrial and Labor Relations Review* 43 (1990): 256s–273s; S. H. Wagner, C. P. Parkers, and N. D. Christiansen, "Employees That Think and Act Like Owners: Effects of Ownership Beliefs and Behaviors on Organizational Effectiveness," *Personnel Psychology* 56, no. 4 (Winter 2003): 847–871; G. Ledford, M. Lucy, and P. Leblanc, "The Effects of Stock Ownership on Employee Attitudes and Behavior: Evidence from the Rewards at Work Studies," *Perspectives (Sibson)*, January 2004; C. Rosen, J. Case, and M. Staubus, "Every Employee an Owner [Really]," *Harvard Business Review* 83, no. 6 (June 2005): 122–130.

30. A. J. Maggs, "Enron, Esops, and Fiduciary Duty," *Benefits Law Journal* 16, no. 3 (Autumn 2003): 42–52; C. Brodzinski, "ESOP's Fables Can Make Coverage Risky," *National Underwriter. P & C*, 13 June 2005, 16–17.

31. J. Pfeffer, *The Human Equation* (Boston: Harvard Business School Press, 1998); B. N. Pfau and I. T. Kay, *The Human Capital Edge* (New York: McGraw-Hill, 2002); D. Guest, N. Conway, and P. Dewe, "Using Sequential Tree Analysis to Search for 'Bundles' of HR Practices," *Human Resource Management Journal* 14, no. 1 (2004): 79–96. The problems with performance-based pay are discussed in W. C. Hammer, "How to Ruin Motivation with Pay," *Compensation Review* 7, no. 3 (1975): 17–27; A. Kohn, *Punished by Rewards* (Boston: Houghton Mifflin, 1993); M. O'Donnell and J. O' Brian, "Performance-Based Pay

in the Australian Public Service," *Review of Public Personnel Administration* 20 (Spring 2000): 20–34; M. Beer and M. D. Cannon, "Promise and Peril of Implementing Pay-for-Performance," *Human Resource Management* 43, no. 1 (Spring 2004): 3–48.

32. Watson Wyatt, *WorkCanada 2004/2005—Pursuing Productive Engagement* (Toronto: Watson Wyatt, January 2005); Kelly Services, "Majority of Canada's Workers Happy, Bosses among Best in World," Kelly Services News release (Toronto: 28 November 2006).

33. S. Kerr, "Organization Rewards: Practical, Cost-Neutral Alternatives That You May Know, but Don't Practice," *Organizational Dynamics* 28 (Summer 1999): 61–70.

34. J. S. DeMatteo, L. T. Eby, and E. Sundstrom, "Team-Based Rewards: Current Empirical Evidence and Directions for Future Research," *Research in Organizational Behavior* 20 (1998): 141–183; S. Rynes, B. Gerhart, and L. Parks, "Personnel Psychology: Performance Evaluation and Pay for Performance," *Annual Review of Psychology* 56 (2005): 571–600.

35. B. Moses, "Time to Get Serious About Rewarding Employees," *Globe & Mail*, 28 April 2010, B16.

36. "Dream Teams," *Human Resources Professional* (November 1994): 17–19.

37. D. R. Spitzer, "Power Rewards: Rewards That Really Motivate," *Management Review* (May 1996): 45–50. For a classic discussion on the unintended consequences of pay, see S. Kerr, "On the Folly of Rewarding a, While Hoping for B," *Academy of Management Journal* 18 (1975): 769–783.

38. D. MacDonald, "Good Managers Key to Buffett's Acquisitions," *The Gazette (Montreal)*, 16 November 2001. The recent poll is reported in "Survey Shows What Matters Most to Canadian Workers When Deciding on the Right Choice of Job." news release for Kelly Services (Toronto: 25 February 2009).

39. J. R. Edwards, J. A. Scully, and M. D. Brtek, "The Nature and Outcomes of Work: A Replication and Extension of Interdisciplinary Work-Design Research," *Journal of Applied Psychology* 85, no. 6 (2000): 860–868; F. P. Morgeson and M. A. Campion, "Minimizing Tradeoffs When Redesigning Work: Evidence from a Longitudinal Quasi-Experiment," *Personnel Psychology* 55, no. 3 (Autumn 2002): 589–612.

40. R. M. Johnson, D. Lucking-Reiley, and J. C. Munos, "'The War for the Fare': How Driver Compensation Affects Bus System Performance" (SSRN, 2005); M. Munger, "Planning Order, Causing Chaos: Transantiago," *Library of Economics and Liberty*

(1 September 2008); R. Banick, *Bus Rapid Transit and the Latin American City: Successes to Date, but Miles to Go* (Washington: Council on Hemispheric Affairs, December 2009).

41. "There's Only One Lesson to Learn from UBS," *Euromoney*, May 2008, 9; *Shareholder Report on Ubs's Write-Downs* (Zurich, Switzerland: UBS, 18 April 2008); U. Harnischfeger, "UBS Says Excess of Ambition Led to Its Miscues on Subprime Loans," *New York Times*, 22 April 2008, C3; S. Reed, "Behind the Mess at UBS," *Business Week*, no. 4073 (3 March 2008): 30–31.

42. H. Connon, "Overhyped, Overpaid and Overextended," *The Observer (London)*, 20 March 2005, 4; J. Harris and P. Bromiley, "Incentives to Cheat: The Influence of Executive Compensation and Firm Performance on Financial Misrepresentation," *Organization Science* 18, no. 3 (May 2007): 350–367.

43. A. Holecek, "Griffith, Ind., Native Takes over as Steel Plant Manager," *Northwest Indiana Times (Munster, Ind.)*, 25 May 2003.

44. E. E. Lawler III, *Strategic Pay* (San Francisco: Jossey-Bass, 1990), 120.

45. E. Clark, "The Cost of Fun," *The Telegraph (London)*, 26 March 2007; "Grads Find Job-Hopping Is Not a Career-Stopper," *Shanghai Daily*, 23 June 2008.

46. S. Leroy, "Why Is It So Hard to Do My Work? The Challenge of Attention Residue When Switching between Work Tasks," *Organizational Behavior and Human Decision Processes* 109, no. 2 (2009): 168–181.

47. H. Fayol, *General and Industrial Management*, trans. C. Storrs (London: Pitman, 1949); E. E. Lawler III, *Motivation in Work Organizations* (Monterey, Calif.: Brooks/Cole, 1973), Chap. 7; M. A. Campion, "Ability Requirement Implications of Job Design: An Interdisciplinary Perspective," *Personnel Psychology* 42 (1989): 1–24.

48. F. C. Lane, *Venice: A Maritime Republic* (Baltimore: Johns Hopkins University Press, 1973), 361–364; R. C. Davis, "Arsenal and *Arsenalotti*: Workplace and Community in Seventeenth-Century Venice," in *The Workplace before the Factory*, ed. T. M. Safley and L. N. Rosenband (Ithaca, N.Y.: Cornell University Press, 1993), 180–203.

49. A. Smith, *An Inquiry into the Nature and Causes of the Wealth of Nations* 5th ed. (London: Methuen and Co., 1904), 8–9.

50. F. W. Taylor, *The Principles of Scientific Management* (New York: Harper & Row, 1911); R. Kanigel, *The One Best Way: Frederick Winslow Taylor and the Enigma of Efficiency* (NY: Viking, 1997).

51. C. R. Walker and R. H. Guest, *The Man on the Assembly Line* (Cambridge, MA: Harvard University Press, 1952); W. F. Dowling, "Job Redesign on the Assembly Line: Farewell to Blue-Collar Blues?," *Organizational*

Dynamics (Autumn 1973): 51–67; E. E. Lawler III, *High-Involvement Management* (San Francisco: Jossey-Bass, 1986).

52. M. Keller, *Rude Awakening* (New York: Harper Perennial, 1989), 128.

53. F. Herzberg, B. Mausner, and B. B. Snyderman, *The Motivation to Work* (New York: Wiley, 1959).

54. S. K. Parker, T. D. Wall, and J. L. Cordery, "Future Work Design Research and Practice: Towards an Elaborated Model of Work Design," *Journal of Occupational and Organizational Psychology* 74 (November 2001): 413–440. For a decisive critique of motivator-hygiene theory, see N. King, "Clarification and Evaluation of the Two Factor Theory of Job Satisfaction," *Psychological Bulletin* 74 (1970): 18–31.

55. J. R. Hackman and G. Oldham, *Work Redesign* (Reading, MA: Addison-Wesley, 1980).

56. Hosford, "Flying High"; Hosford, "Training Programs Benefit Rolls-Royce."

57. J. E. Champoux, "A Multivariate Test of the Job Characteristics Theory of Work Motivation," *Journal of Organizational Behavior* 12, no. 5 (September 1991): 431–446; R. B. Tiegs, L. E. Tetrick, and Y. Fried, "Growth Need Strength and Context Satisfactions as Moderators of the Relations of the Job Characteristics Model," *Journal of Management* 18, no. 3 (September 1992): 575–593.

58. "Region Positioned among Dcx Leaders in Advanced Manufacturing," *Toledo Business Journal*, August 2004, 1; M. Connelly, "Chrysler Boosts Belvidere Flexibility," *Automotive News*, 13 February 2006, 44.

59. Data provided in several country-specific news releases from Kelly Services. For a white paper summary of the survey, see: Kelly Services, *Employee Loyalty Rises During Global Economic Recession, Kelly International Workforce Survey Finds* (Troy, MI: Kelly Services, 8 March 2010). Percentage of employees in India choosing higher salary/benefits and employees in China choosing meaningful responsibility are inferred (i.e., they were not stated in available sources, but received a lower percentage than the other two identified categories).

60. M. A. Campion and C. L. McClelland, "Follow-up and Extension of the Interdisciplinary Costs and Benefits of Enlarged Jobs," *Journal of Applied Psychology* 78 (1993): 339–351; N. G. Dodd and D. C. Ganster, "The Interactive Effects of Variety, Autonomy, and Feedback on Attitudes and Performance," *Journal of Organizational Behavior* 17 (1996): 329–347.

61. J. R. Hackman *et al.*, "A New Strategy for Job Enrichment," *California Management Review* 17, no. 4 (1975): 57–71; R. W. Griffin, *Task Design: An Integrative Approach* (Glenview, IL: Scott Foresman, 1982).

62. P. E. Spector and S. M. Jex, "Relations of Job Characteristics from Multiple Data Sources with Employee Affect, Absence, Turnover Intentions, and Health," *Journal of Applied Psychology* 76 (1991): 46–53; P. Osterman, "How Common Is Workplace Transformation and Who Adopts It?," *Industrial and Labor Relations Review* 47 (1994): 173–188; R. Saavedra and S. K. Kwun, "Affective States in Job Characteristics Theory," *Journal of Organizational Behavior* 21 (2000): 131–146.

63. Hackman and Oldham, *Work Redesign*, 137–138.

64. S. Wong, "Open Communication Gives Better Connection," *South China Morning Post (Hong Kong)*, 19 January 2008, 4.

65. R. Bostelaar, "Call Centres, Unscripted," *Ottawa Citizen*, 28 August 2010, F1 & F2; D. Holman *et al.* "Work Design Variation and Outcomes in Call Centres: Strategic Choice and Institutional Explanations," *Industrial & Labor Relations Review*, Vol. 62, No. 4 (July 2009), 510–532.

66. E. Stoessel, "Winning Corporate Culture at Fairmont," *Penton Insight*, 13 January 2010.

67. This definition is based mostly on G. M. Spreitzer and R. E. Quinn, *A Company of Leaders: Five Disciplines for Unleashing the Power in Your Workforce* (San Francisco: Jossey-Bass, 2001). However, most elements of this definition appear in other discussions of empowerment. See, for example, R. Forrester, "Empowerment: Rejuvenating a Potent Idea," *Academy of Management Executive* 14 (August 2000): 67–80; W. A. Randolph, "Re-Thinking Empowerment: Why Is It So Hard to Achieve?," *Organizational Dynamics* 29 (November 2000): 94–107; S. T. Menon, "Employee Empowerment: An Integrative Psychological Approach," *Applied Psychology: An International Review* 50 (2001): 153–180.

68. The positive relationship between these structural empowerment conditions and psychological empowerment is reported in H. K. S. Laschinger *et al.*, "A Longitudinal Analysis of the Impact of Workplace Empowerment on Work Satisfaction," *Journal of Organizational Behavior* 25, no. 4 (June 2004): 527–545.

69. C. S. Koberg *et al.*, "Antecedents and Outcomes of Empowerment," *Group and Organization Management* 24 (1999): 71–91; Y. Melhem, "The Antecedents of Customer-Contact Employees' Empowerment," *Employee Relations* 26, no. 1/2 (2004): 72–93.

70. B. J. Niehoff *et al.*, "The Influence of Empowerment and Job Enrichment on Employee Loyalty in a Downsizing Environment," *Group and Organization Management* 26 (March 2001): 93–113; J. Yoon, "The Role of Structure and Motivation for Workplace Empowerment: The Case of Korean Employees," *Social Psychology Quarterly* 64 (June 2001): 195–206; T. D. Wall, J. L. Cordery, and C. W. Clegg, "Empowerment, Performance, and Operational Uncertainty: A Theoretical Integration," *Applied Psychology: An International Review* 51 (2002): 146–169.

71. "Running a Business: Managing a Handelsbanken Branch," *A View from the Top (Handelsbanken Maidstone Newsletter)*, Winter 2007, 1; Hammarström, *Handelsbanken, Sweden: Make Work Pay—Make Work Attractive*; R. M. Lindsay and T. Libby, "Svenska Handelsbanken: Controlling a Radically Decentralized Organization without Budgets," *Issues in Accounting Education* 22, no. 4 (November 2007): 625–640; "The Sunday Times 100 Best Companies to Work for 2008," (Chester, UK: Svenska Handelsbanken, 10 March 2008), www.handelsbanken.co.uk (accessed 11 September 2008).

72. G. M. Spreitzer, "Social Structural Characteristics of Psychological Empowerment," *Academy of Management Journal* 39 (April 1996): 483–504; J. Godard, "High Performance and the Transformation of Work? The Implications of Alternative Work Practices for the Experience and Outcomes of Work," *Industrial & Labor Relations Review* 54 (July 2001): 776–805; P. A. Miller, P. Goddard, and H. K. Spence Laschinger, "Evaluating Physical Therapists' Perception of Empowerment Using Kanter's Theory of Structural Power in Organizations," *Physical Therapy* 81 (December 2001): 1880–1888.

73. J.-C. Chebat and P. Kollias, "The Impact of Empowerment on Customer Contact Employees' Role in Service Organizations," *Journal of Service Research* 3 (August 2000): 66–81; H. K. S. Laschinger, J. Finegan, and J. Shamian, "The Impact of Workplace Empowerment, Organizational Trust on Staff Nurses' Work Satisfaction and Organizational Commitment," *Health Care Management Review* 26 (Summer 2001): 7–23.

74. "Bosses Love Team Workers," *Lancashire Evening Post (U.K.)*, 25 May 2006; C. P. Parkhill, "Region's Top Employers Offer Career Satisfaction," *Waterloo Region Record*, 17 October 2009, C1.

75. C. P. Neck and C. C. Manz, "Thought Self-Leadership: The Impact of Mental Strategies Training on Employee Cognition, Behavior, and Affect," *Journal of Organizational Behavior* 17 (1996): 445–467.

76. D. Finlayson, "Noodle chain sprouts a franchise plan," *Edmonton Journal*, 28 August 2010, G1.

77. C. C. Manz, "Self-Leadership: Toward an Expanded Theory of Self-Influence Processes in Organizations," *Academy of Management Review* 11 (1986): 585–600; C. C. Manz and C. Neck, *Mastering Self-Leadership*,

3rd ed. (Upper Saddle River, NJ: Prentice Hall, 2004); C. P. Neck and J. D. Houghton, "Two Decades of Self-Leadership Theory and Research," *Journal of Managerial Psychology* 21, no. 4 (2006): 270–295.

78. O. J. Strickland and M. Galimba, "Managing Time: The Effects of Personal Goal Setting on Resource Allocation Strategy and Task Performance," *Journal of Psychology* 135 (July 2001): 357–367.

79. R. M. Duncan and J. A. Cheyne, "Incidence and Functions of Self-Reported Private Speech in Young Adults: A Self-Verbalization Questionnaire," *Canadian Journal of Behavioral Science* 31 (April 1999): 133–136.

80. A. Hatzigeorgiadis *et al.*, "Mechanisms Underlying the Self-Talk–Performance Relationship: The Effects of Motivational Self-Talk on Self-Confidence and Anxiety," *Psychology of Sport and Exercise* 10 (2009): 186–192.

81. J. E. Driscoll, C. Copper, and A. Moran, "Does Mental Practice Enhance Performance?," *Journal of Applied Psychology* 79 (1994): 481–492; C. P. Neck, G. L. Stewart, and C. C. Manz, "Thought Self-Leadership as a Framework for Enhancing the Performance of Performance Appraisers," *Journal of Applied Behavioral Science* 31 (September 1995): 278–302. Some research separates mental imagery from mental practice, whereas most studies combine both into one concept.

82. A. Joyce, "Office Parks: Re-Energize to Get through the Blahs," *Washington Post*, 28 August 2005, F05.

83. A. Wrzesniewski and J. E. Dutton, "Crafting a Job: Revisioning Employees as Active Crafters of Their Work," *Academy of Management Review* 26 (April 2001): 179–201.

84. "Steve Collier Profile," *CCMA Case Study*, 1st Quarter 2008.

85. M. I. Bopp, S. J. Glynn, and R. A. Henning, *Self-Management of Performance Feedback During Computer-Based Work by Individuals and Two-Person Work Teams*, Paper presented at the APA-NIOSH conference (March 1999).

86. A. W. Logue, *Self-Control: Waiting until Tomorrow for What You Want Today* (Englewood Cliffs, NJ: Prentice-Hall, 1995).

87. Neck and Manz, "Thought Self-Leadership: The Impact of Mental Strategies Training on Employee Cognition, Behavior, and Affect"; A. M. Saks and B. E. Ashforth, "Proactive Socialization and Behavioral Self-Management," *Journal of Vocational Behavior* 48 (1996): 301–323; L. Morin and G. Latham, "The Effect of Mental Practice and Goal Setting as a Transfer of Training Intervention on Supervisors' Self-Efficacy and Communication Skills: An Exploratory Study," *Applied Psychology: An International Review* 49 (July 2000): 566–578; J. S. Hickman and

E. S. Geller, "A Safety Self-Management Intervention for Mining Operations," *Journal of Safety Research* 34 (2003): 299–308.

88. S. Ming and G. L. Martin, "Single-Subject Evaluation of a Self-Talk Package for Improving Figure Skating Performance," *Sport Psychologist* 10 (1996): 227–238; J. Bauman, "The Gold Medal Mind," *Psychology Today* 33 (May 2000): 62–69; L. J. Rogerson and D. W. Hrycaiko, "Enhancing Competitive Performance of Ice Hockey Goaltenders Using Centering and Self-Talk," *Journal of Applied Sport Psychology* 14, no. 1 (2002): 14–26; A. Papaioannou *et al.*, "Combined Effect of Goal Setting and Self-Talk in Performance of a Soccer-Shooting Task," *Perceptual and Motor Skills* 98, no. 1 (February 2004): 89–99; R. A. Hamilton, D. Scott, and M. P. MacDougall, "Assessing the Effectiveness of Self-Talk Interventions on Endurance Performance," *Journal of Applied Sport Psychology* 19, no. 2 (2007): 226–239. For a review of the self-talk research, including limitations of this self-leadership strategy, see J. Hardy, "Speaking Clearly: A Critical Review of the Self-Talk Literature," *Psychology of Sport and Exercise* 7 (2006): 81–97.

89. S. Williams, "Personality and Self-Leadership," *Human Resource Management Review* 7, no. 2 (1997): 139–155; J. Houghton, D. *et al.*, "The Relationship between Self-Leadership and Personality: A Comparison of Hierarchical Factor Structures," *Journal of Managerial Psychology* 19, no. 4 (2004): 427–441; R. W. Renn *et al.*, "The Roles of Personality and Self-Defeating Behaviors in Self-Management Failure," *Journal of Management* 31, no. 5 (2005): 659–679.

90. J. D. Houghton and S. K. Yoho, "Toward a Contingency Model of Leadership and Psychological Empowerment: When Should Self-Leadership Be Encouraged?," *Journal of Leadership & Organizational Studies* 11, no. 4 (2005): 65–83; J. D. Houghton and D. L. Jinkerson, "Constructive Thought Strategies and Job Satisfaction: A Preliminary Examination," *Journal of Business and Psychology* 22 (2007): 45–53.

CHAPTER 7

1. J. Carroll & E. Klump, "BP Offshore Engineer Had 'Huge Responsibility,'" *Calgary Herald*, 28 August 2010, D4; C. Tait, "New CEO Fires BP Exploration Unit Head," *National Post*, 30 September 2010, FP6; S. McCarthy, "A Disaster of Gargantuan Proportions," *The Globe and Mail*, 20 September, 2010, A13; R. Colvin *et al.*, "BP and Partners Trade Blame For Oil Spill," *Reuters*, 8 September 2010; J. Snyder, "Halliburton Defends Its Cement Work, Blaming BP for Gulf Spill," *BusinessWeek*, 26 September 2010; J. Carroll & K. Klimasinska, "BP's Wells Says He Doesn't Know Who Was in Charge," *BusinessWeek*, 26 August 2010.

2. F. A. Shull Jr., A. L. Delbecq, and L. L. Cummings, *Organizational Decision Making* (New York: McGraw-Hill, 1970), p. 31.

3. M. V. White, "Jevons in Australia: A Reassessment," *The Economic Record* 58 (1982): 32–45; R. E. Nisbett, *The Geography of Thought: How Asians and Westerners Think Differently—and Why* (New York: Free Press, 2003); R. Hanna, "Kant's Theory of Judgment" (Stanford Encyclopedia of Philosophy, 2004), http://plato.stanford.edu/entries/kant-judgment/ (accessed 31 March 2008); D. Baltzly, "Stoicism," (Stanford Encyclopedia of Philosophy, 2008), http://plato.stanford.edu/entries/stoicism/ (accessed 30 March 2008).

4. J. G. March and H. A. Simon, *Organizations* (New York: John Wiley & Sons, 1958).

5. This model is adapted from several sources, including H. A. Simon, *The New Science of Management Decision* (New York: Harper & Row, 1960); H. Mintzberg, D. Raisinghani, and A. Théorét, "The Structure of, 'Unstructured' Decision Processes," *Administrative Science Quarterly* 21 (1976): 246–275; W. C. Wedley and R. H. G. Field, "A Predecision Support System," *Academy of Management Review* 9 (1984): 696–703.

6. P. F. Drucker, *The Practice of Management* (New York: Harper & Brothers, 1954), 353–357; B. M. Bass, *Organizational Decision Making* (Homewood, Ill: Irwin, 1983), Chap. 3.

7. L. R. Beach and T. R. Mitchell, "A Contingency Model for the Selection of Decision Strategies," *Academy of Management Review* 3 (1978): 439–449; I. L. Janis, *Crucial Decisions* (New York: The Free Press, 1989), 35–37; W. Zhongtuo, "Meta-Decision Making: Concepts and Paradigm," *Systematic Practice and Action Research* 13, no. 1 (February 2000): 111–115.

8. N. Schwarz, "Social Judgment and Attitudes: Warmer, More Social, and Less Conscious," *European Journal of Social Psychology* 30 (2000): 149–176; N. M. Ashkanasy and C. E. J. Hartel, "Managing Emotions in Decision-Making," in *Managing Emotions in the Workplace*, ed. N. M. Ashkanasy, W. J. Zerbe, and C. E. J. Hartel (Armonk, N.Y: M. E. Sharpe, 2002); S. Maitlis and H. Ozcelik, "Toxic Decision Processes: A Study of Emotion and Organizational Decision Making," *Organization Science* 15, no. 4 (July-August 2004): 375–393.

9. A. Howard, "Opinion," *Computing* (8 July 1999): 18.

10. For a recent discussion on problem finding in organizations, see: M. A. Roberto, *Know What You Don't Know: How Great Leaders Prevent Problems Before They Happen* (Saddle River, NJ: Wharton School Publishing, 2009).

11. T. K. Das and B. S. Teng, "Cognitive Biases and Strategic Decision Processes: An Integrative Perspective," *Journal Of*

Management Studies 36, no. 6 (Nov 1999): 757–778; P. Bijttebier, H. Vertommen, and G. V. Steene, "Assessment of Cognitive Coping Styles: A Closer Look at Situation-Response Inventories," *Clinical Psychology Review* 21, no. 1 (2001): 85–104; P. C. Nutt, "Expanding the Search for Alternatives During Strategic Decision-Making," *Academy of Management Executive* 18, no. 4 (November 2004): 13–28.

12. W. Ocasio, "Toward an Attention-Based View of the Firm," *Strategic Management Journal* 18, no. S1 (1997): 187–206; S. Kaplan, "Framing Contests: Strategy Making under Uncertainty," *Organization Science* 19, no. 5 (September 2008): 729–752; J. S. McMullen, D. A. Shepherd, and H. Patzelt, "Managerial (in)Attention to Competitive Threats," *Journal of Management Studies* 46, no. 2 (2009): 157–181.

13. P. C. Nutt, *Why Decisions Fail* (San Francisco, CA: Berrett-Koehler, 2002); S. Finkelstein, *Why Smart Executives Fail* (New York: Viking, 2003).

14. E. Witte, "Field Research on Complex Decision-Making Processes—the Phase Theorum," *International Studies of Management and Organization*, no. 56 (1972): 156–182; J. A. Bargh and T. L. Chartrand, "The Unbearable Automaticity of Being," *American Psychologist* 54, no. 7 (July 1999): 462–479.

15. A. H. Maslow, *The Psychology of Science: A Reconnaissance* (Chapel Hill, NC: Maurice Bassett Publishing, 2002).

16. J. Brandtstadter, A. Voss, and K. Rothermund, "Perception of Danger Signals: The Role of Control," *Experimental Psychology* 51, no. 1 (2004): 24–32; M. Hock and H. W. Krohne, "Coping with Threat and Memory for Ambiguous Information: Testing the Repressive Discontinuity Hypothesis," *Emotion* 4, no. 1 (2004): 65–86.

17. "NASA Managers Differed over Shuttle Strike," *Reuters* (22 July 2003); Columbia Accident Investigation Board, *Report, Volume 1* (Washington, DC: Government Printing Office, August 2003); C. Gibson, "Columbia: The Final Mission," *NineMSN* (13 July 2003); S. Jefferson, "NASA Let Arrogance on Board," *Palm Beach Post*, 30 August 2003; R. J. Smith, "NASA Culture, Columbia Probers Still Miles Apart," *Washington Post* (22 August 2003): A3.

18. R. Collison, "How Bata Rules Its World," *Canadian Business*, September 1990, 28; J. Portman, "Harry Potter Was Almost a Yankee," *Vancouver Sun*, 5 July 2007.

19. Collison, "How Bata Rules Its World."

20. M. McCarthy, "Top 20 in 20 Years: Apple Computer—1984," (2003), www.adweek.com/adweek/creative/top20_20years/index.jsp (accessed 16 January 2003); O. W. Linzmayer, *Apple Confidential 2.0: The Definitive Story of the World's Most Colorful*

Company (San Francisco: No Starch Press, 2004), 109–114.

21. T. Jones, *Innovating at the Edge* (San Francisco: Butterworth-Heinemann, 2002),59–62; R. K. Sawyer, *Explaining Creativity: The Science of Human Innovation* (New York: Oxford University Press, 2006), chap. 15.

22. R. Rothenberg, "Ram Charan: The Thought Leader Interview," *strategy + business* (Fall 2004).

23. H. A. Simon, *Administrative Behavior*, 2nd ed. (New York: The Free Press, 1957); H. A. Simon, "Rational Decision Making in Business Organizations," *American Economic Review* 69, no. 4 (September 1979): 493–513.

24. Simon, *Administrative Behavior*, xxv, 80–84.

25. S. Sacchi and M. Burigo, "Strategies in the Information Search Process: Interaction among Task Structure, Knowledge, and Source," *Journal of General Psychology* 135, no. 3 (2008): 252–270.

26. P. O. Soelberg, "Unprogrammed Decision Making," *Industrial Management Review* 8 (1967): 19–29; J. E. Russo, V. H. Medvec, and M. G. Meloy, "The Distortion of Information During Decisions," *Organizational Behavior & Human Decision Processes* 66 (1996): 102–110; K. H. Ehrhart and J. C. Ziegert, "Why Are Individuals Attracted to Organizations?," *Journal of Management* 31, no. 6 (December 2005): 901–919. This is consistent with the observations by Milton Rokeach, who famously stated, "Life is ipsative, because decisions in everyday life are inherently and phenomenologically ipsative decisions." M. Rokeach, "Inducing Changes and Stability in Belief Systems and Personality Structures," *Journal of Social Issues* 41, no. 1 (1985): 153–171.

27. A. L. Brownstein, "Biased Predecision Processing," *Psychological Bulletin* 129, no. 4 (2003): 545–568.

28. T. Gilovich, D. Griffin, and D. Kahneman, *Heuristics and Biases: The Psychology of Intuitive Judgment* (Cambridge: Cambridge University Press, 2002); D. Kahneman, "Maps of Bounded Rationality: Psychology for Behavioral Economics," *American Economic Review* 93, no. 5 (December 2003): 1449–1475; F. L. Smith *et al.*, "Decision-Making Biases and Affective States: Their Potential Impact on Best Practice Innovations," *Canadian Journal of Administrative Sciences / Revue Canadienne des Sciences de l'Administration* 27, no. 4 (2010): 277–291.

29. A. Tversky and D. Kahneman, "Judgment under Uncertainty: Heuristics and Biases," *Science* 185, no. 4157 (27 September 1974): 1124–1131; I. Ritov, "Anchoring in Simulated Competitive Market Negotiation," *Organizational Behavior and Human Decision Processes* 67, no. 1 (1996): 16; D.

Ariely, G. Loewenstein, and A. Prelec, "'Coherent Arbitrariness': Stable Demand Curves without Stable Preferences," *The Quarterly Journal of Economics* 118 (2003): 73; N. Epley and T. Gilovich, "Are Adjustments Insufficient?," *Personality and Social Psychology Bulletin* 30, no. 4 (April 2004): 447–460; J. D. Jasper and S. D. Christman, "A Neuropsychological Dimension for Anchoring Effects," *Journal of Behavioral Decision Making* 18 (2005): 343–369; S. D. Bond *et al.*, "Information Distortion in the Evaluation of a Single Option," *Organizational Behavior & Human Decision Processes* 102 (2007): 240–254.

30. A. Tversky and D. Kahneman, "Availability: A Heuristic for Judging Frequency and Probability," *Cognitive Psychology* 5 (1973): 207–232.

31. D. Kahneman and A. Tversky, "Subjective Probability: A Judgment of Representativeness," *Cognitive Psychology* 3, no. 3 (1972): 430; T. Gilovich, *How We Know What Isn't So: The Fallibility of Human Reason in Everyday Life* (New York: Free Press, 1991); B. D. Burns, "Heuristics as Beliefs and as Behaviors: The Adaptiveness of the 'Hot Hand'," *Cognitive Psychology* 48 (2004): 295–331; E. M. Altmann and B. D. Burns, "Streak Biases in Decision Making: Data and a Memory Model," *Cognitive Systems Research* 6, no. 1 (2005): 5.

32. H. A. Simon, "Rational Choice and the Structure of Environments," *Psychological Review* 63 (1956): 129–138.

33. S. Botti and S. S. Iyengar, "The Dark Side of Choice: When Choice Impairs Social Welfare," *Journal of Public Policy and Marketing* 25, no. 1 (2006): 24–38; K. D. Vohs *et al.*, "Making Choices Impairs Subsequent Self-Control: A Limited-Resource Account of Decision Making, Self-Regulation, and Active Initiative," *Journal of Personality and Social Psychology* 94, no. 5 (2008): 883–898.

34. S. S. Iyengar, G. Huberman, and W. Jiang, "How Much Choice Is Too Much?: Contributions to 401 (K) Retirement Plans," in *Pension Design and Structure: New Lessons from Behavioral Finance*, ed. O. Mitchell and S. Utkas (Oxford, UK: Oxford University Press, 2004), 83–95; J. Beshears *et al.*, "Simplification and Saving," 2006, http://ssrn.com/paper=1086462; J. Choi, D. Laibson, and B. Madrian, *Reducing the Complexity Costs of 401(K) Participation through Quick Enrollment* (National Bureau of Economic Research, Inc, Jan 2006).

35. A. Tofler, *Future Shock* (New York: Random House, 1970), p. 264.

36. P. C. Nutt, "Search During Decision Making," *European Journal of Operational Research* 160 (2005): 851–876.

37. P. Winkielman *et al.*, "Affective Influence on Judgments and Decisions: Moving Towards

Core Mechanisms," *Review of General Psychology* 11, no. 2 (2007): 179–192.

38. A. R. Damasio, *Descartes' Error: Emotion, Reason, and the Human Brain* (New York: Putnam Sons, 1994); P. Winkielman and K. C. Berridge, "Unconscious Emotion," *Current Directions in Psychological Science* 13, no. 3 (2004): 120–123; A. Bechara and A. R. Damasio, "The Somatic Marker Hypothesis: A Neural Theory of Economic Decision," *Games and Economic Behavior* 52, no. 2 (2005): 336–372.

39. J. P. Forgas and J. M. George, "Affective Influences on Judgments and Behavior in Organizations: An Information Processing Perspective," *Organizational Behavior and Human Decision Processes* 86 (September 2001): 3–34; G. Loewenstein and J. S. Lerner, "The Role of Affect in Decision Making," in *Handbook of Affective Sciences*, ed. R. J. Davidson, K. R. Scherer, and H. H. Goldsmith (New York: Oxford University Press, 2003), 619–642; M. T. Pham, "Emotion and Rationality: A Critical Review and Interpretation of Empirical Evidence," *Review of General Psychology* 11, no. 2 (2007): 155–178; J. P. Forgas, L. Goldenberg, and C. Unkelbach, "Can Bad Weather Improve Your Memory? An Unobtrusive Field Study of Natural Mood Effects on Real-Life Memory," *Journal of Experimental Social Psychology* 45 (2009): 254–257; H. J. M. Kooij-de Bode, D. Van Knippenberg, and W. P. Van Ginkel, "Good Effects of Bad Feelings: Negative Affectivity and Group Decision-Making," *British Journal of Management* 21, no. 2 (2010): 375–392.

40. D. Miller, *The Icarus Paradox* (New York: HarperBusiness, 1990); D. Miller, "What Happens after Success: The Perils of Excellence," *Journal of Management Studies* 31, no. 3 (1994): 325–368; A. C. Amason and A. C. Mooney, "The Icarus Paradox Revisited: How Strong Performance Sows the Seeds of Dysfunction in Future Strategic Decision-Making," *Strategic Organization* 6, no. 4 (November 2008): 407–434.

41. M. T. Pham, "The Logic of Feeling," *Journal of Consumer Psychology* 14 (September 2004): 360–369; N. Schwarz, "Metacognitive Experiences in Consumer Judgment and Decision Making," *Journal of Consumer Psychology* 14 (September 2004): 332–349.

42. L. Sjöberg, "Intuitive vs. Analytical Decision Making: Which Is Preferred?," *Scandinavian Journal of Management* 19 (2003): 17–29.

43. M. Lyons, "Cave-in Too Close for Comfort, Miner Says," *Saskatoon StarPhoenix*, 6 May 2002.

44. W. H. Agor, "The Logic of Intuition," *Organizational Dynamics* (Winter 1986): 5–18; H. A. Simon, "Making Management Decisions: The Role of Intuition and Emotion," *Academy of Management Executive* (February 1987): 57–64; O. Behling and N. L. Eckel, "Making Sense out of Intuition," *Academy of Management Executive* 5 (February 1991): 46–54. This process is also known as naturalistic decision making. For a discussion of research on naturalistic decision making, see the special issue in *Organization Studies:* R. Lipshitz, G. Klein, and J. S. Carroll, "Introduction to the Special Issue: Naturalistic Decision Making and Organizational Decision Making: Exploring the Intersections," *Organization Studies* 27, no. 7 (2006): 917–923.

45. M. D. Lieberman, "Intuition: A Social Cognitive Neuroscience Approach," *Psychological Bulletin* 126 (2000): 109–137; G. Klein, *Intuition at Work* (New York: Currency/Doubleday, 2003); E. Dane and M. G. Pratt, "Exploring Intuition and Its Role in Managerial Decision Making," *Academy of Management Review* 32, no. 1 (2007): 33–54.

46. Klein, *Intuition at Work*, 12–13, 16–17.

47. *What if… Edition: Shipping* (Harstad, Norway: Dreyer Kompetense, 16 July 2009); Z. A. Wahab, "Norwegian Firm Offers Board Game as Training Tool," *Bernama Daily Malaysian News (Kuala Lumpur)*, 25 March 2010.

48. Y. Ganzach, A. H. Kluger, and N. Klayman, "Making Decisions from an Interview: Expert Measurement and Mechanical Combination," *Personnel Psychology* 53 (Spring 2000): 1–20; A. M. Hayashi, "When to Trust Your Gut," *Harvard Business Review* 79 (February 2001): 59–65. Evidence of high failure rates from quick decisions is reported in Nutt, *Why Decisions Fail*; Nutt, "Search During Decision Making"; P. C. Nutt, "Investigating the Success of Decision Making Processes," *Journal of Management Studies* 45, no. 2 (March 2008): 425–455.

49. P. Goodwin and G. Wright, "Enhancing Strategy Evaluation in Scenario Planning: A Role for Decision Analysis," *Journal of Management Studies* 38 (January 2001): 1–16; R. Bradfield *et al.*, "The Origins and Evolution of Scenario Techniques in Long Range Business Planning," *Futures* 37, no. 8 (2005): 795–812; G. Wright, G. Cairns, and P. Goodwin, "Teaching Scenario Planning: Lessons from Practice in Academe and Business," *European Journal of Operational Research* 194, no. 1 (April 2009): 323–335.

50. J. Pfeffer and R. I. Sutton, "Knowing 'What' to Do Is Not Enough: Turning Knowledge into Action," *California Management Review* 42, no. 1 (Fall 1999): 83–108; R. Charan, C. Burke, and L. Bossidy, *Execution: The Discipline of Getting Things Done* (New York: Crown Business, 2002).

51. R. S. Nickerson, "Confirmation Bias: A Ubiquitous Phenomenon in Many Guises," *Review of General Psychology* 2, no. 2 (1998): 175–220; O. Svenson, I. Salo, and T. Lindholm, "Post-Decision Consolidation and Distortion of Facts," *Judgment and decision making* 4, no. 5 (2009): 397–407.

52. G. Whyte, "Escalating Commitment to a Course of Action: A Reinterpretation," *Academy of Management Review* 11 (1986): 311–321; J. Brockner, "The Escalation of Commitment to a Failing Course of Action: Toward Theoretical Progress," *Academy of Management Review* 17, no. 1 (January 1992): 39–61.

53. H. Drummond, *Escalation in Decision-Making: The Tragedy of Taurus* (Oxford: Oxford University Press, 1996); M. Keil and R. Montealegre, "Cutting Your Losses: Extricating Your Organization When a Big Project Goes Awry," *Sloan Management Review*, no. 41 (Spring 2000): 55–68.

54. J. Lorinc, "Power Failure," *Canadian Business*, November 1992, 50–58; L. Solomon, "An $87-Billion Grave," *National Post (Toronto)*, 27 November 2010, FP19. An advisor on the Darlington plant explains some of the project's cost increases. See: A. Frame, "Darlington the Backbone of Ontario's Power System," *Toronto Star*, 20 June 2008, AA06.

55. F. D. Schoorman and P. J. Holahan, "Psychological Antecedents of Escalation Behavior: Effects of Choice, Responsibility, and Decision Consequences," *Journal of Applied Psychology* 81 (1996): 786–793; N. Sivanathan *et al.*, "The Promise and Peril of Self-Affirmation in De-Escalation of Commitment," *Organizational Behavior and Human Decision Processes* 107, no. 1 (2008): 1–14.

56. G. Whyte, "Escalating Commitment in Individual and Group Decision Making: A Prospect Theory Approach," *Organizational Behavior and Human Decision Processes* 54 (1993): 430–455; D. Kahneman and J. Renshon, "Hawkish Biases," in *American Foreign Policy and the Politics of Fear: Threat Inflation since 9/11*, ed. T. Thrall and J. Cramer (New York: Routledge, 2009), 79–96.

57. M. Keil, G. Depledge, and A. Rai, "Escalation: The Role of Problem Recognition and Cognitive Bias," *Decision Sciences* 38, no. 3 (August 2007): 391–421.

58. S. McKay, "When Good People Make Bad Decisions," *Canadian Business*, February 1994, 52–55.

59. J. D. Bragger *et al.*, "When Success Breeds Failure: History, Hysteresis, and Delayed Exit Decisions ," *Journal of Applied Psychology* 88, no. 1 (2003): 6–14. A second logical reason for escalation, called the Martingale strategy, is described in J. A. Aloysius, "Rational Escalation of Costs by Playing a Sequence of Unfavorable Gambles: The Martingale," *Journal of Economic Behavior & Organization* 51 (2003): 111–129.

60. I. Simonson and B. M. Staw, "De-Escalation Strategies: A Comparison of Techniques for Reducing Commitment to

Losing Courses of Action," *Journal of Applied Psychology* 77 (1992): 419–426; W. Boulding, R. Morgan, and R. Staelin, "Pulling the Plug to Stop the New Product Drain," *Journal of Marketing Research*, no. 34 (1997): 164–176; B. M. Staw, K. W. Koput, and S. G. Barsade, "Escalation at the Credit Window: A Longitudinal Study of Bank Executives' Recognition and Write-Off of Problem Loans," *Journal of Applied Psychology*, no. 82 (1997): 130–142; M. Keil and D. Robey, "Turning around Troubled Software Projects: An Exploratory Study of the Deescalation of Commitment to Failing Courses of Action," *Journal of Management Information Systems* 15 (Spring 1999): 63–87; B. C. Gunia, N. Sivanathan, and A. D. Galinsky, "Vicarious Entrapment: Your Sunk Costs, My Escalation of Commitment," *Journal of Experimental Social Psychology* 45, no. 6 (2009): 1238–1244.

61. D. Ghosh, "De-Escalation Strategies: Some Experimental Evidence," *Behavioral Research in Accounting*, no. 9 (1997): 88–112.

62. J. Zhou and C. E. Shalley, "Research on Employee Creativity: A Critical Review and Directions for Future Research," *Research in Personnel and Human Resources Management* 22 (2003): 165–217; M. A. Runco, "Creativity," *Annual Review of Psychology* 55 (2004): 657–687.

63. V. Khanna, "The Voice of Google," *Business Times Singapore*, 12 January 2008.

64. G. Wallas, *The Art of Thought* (London: Jonathan Cape, 1926). For recent applications of Wallas's classic model, see T. Kristensen, "The Physical Context of Creativity," *Creativity and Innovation Management* 13, no. 2 (June 2004): 89–96; U.-E. Haner, "Spaces for Creativity and Innovation in Two Established Organizations," *Creativity and Innovation Management* 14, no. 3 (2005): 288–298.

65. R. S. Nickerson, "Enhancing Creativity," in *Handbook of Creativity* ed. R. J. Sternberg (New York: Cambridge University Press, 1999), 392–430.

66. E. Oakes, *Notable Scientists: A to Z of STS Scientists* (New York: Facts on File, 2002), 207–209.

67. For a thorough discussion of insight, see R. J. Sternberg and J. E. Davidson, *The Nature of Insight* (Cambridge, MA: MIT Press, 1995). Helmholtz and Wallas called this stage "illumination," but "insight" is used here because it is more widely adopted today.

68. R. J. Sternberg and L. A. O' Hara, "Creativity and Intelligence," in *Handbook of Creativity* ed. R. J. Sternberg (New York: Cambridge University Press, 1999), 251–272; S. Taggar, "Individual Creativity and Group Ability to Utilize Individual Creative Resources: A Multilevel Model," *Academy of Management Journal* 45 (April 2002): 315–330.

69. G. J. Feist, "The Influence of Personality on Artistic and Scientific Creativity," in *Handbook of Creativity*, ed. R. J. Sternberg (New York: Cambridge University Press, 1999), 273–296; R. I. Sutton, *Weird Ideas That Work* (New York: Free Press, 2002), 8–9, Chap. 10; T. Åsterbro, S. A. Jeffrey, and G. K. Adomdza, "Inventor Perseverance after Being Told to Quit: The Role of Cognitive Biases," *Journal of Behavioral Decision Making* 20 (2007): 253–272.

70. R. W. Weisberg, "Creativity and Knowledge: A Challenge to Theories," in *Handbook of Creativity*, ed. R. J. Sternberg (New York: Cambridge University Press, 1999), 226–250.

71. Sutton, *Weird Ideas That Work*, 121, 153–154; E. Dane, "Reconsidering the Trade-Off between Expertise and Flexibility: A Cognitive Entrenchment Perspective," *Academy of Management Review* 35, no. 4 (2010): 579–603.

72. T. Koppell, *Powering the Future* (New York: Wiley, 1999), p. 15.

73. J. Ross, "Interactive Design," *North Shore Outlook (North Vancouver)*, 1 December 2010; L. Sin, "Ideas, Passion Drive Inspired Designer," *Vancouver Province*, 19 October 2010.

74. R. J. Sternberg and T. I. Lubart, *Defying the Crowd: Cultivating Creativity in a Culture of Conformity* (New york: Free Press, 1995); Feist, "The Influence of Personality on Artistic and Scientific Creativity"; S. J. Dollinger, K. K. Urban, and T. A. James, "Creativity and Openness to Experience: Validation of Two Creative Product Measures," *Creativity Research Journal* 16, no. 1 (2004): 35–47; C. E. Shalley, J. Zhou, and G. R. Oldham, "The Effects of Personal and Contextual Characteristics on Creativity: Where Should We Go from Here?," *Journal of Management* 30, no. 6 (2004): 933–958; T. S. Schweizer, "The Psychology of Novelty-Seeking, Creativity and Innovation: Neurocognitive Aspects within a Work-Psychological Perspective," *Creativity and Innovation Management* 15, no. 2 (2006): 164–172.

75. T. M. Amabile *et al.*, "Leader Behaviors and the Work Environment for Creativity: Perceived Leader Support," *The Leadership Quarterly* 15, no. 1 (2004): 5–32; Shalley, Zhou, and Oldham, "The Effects of Personal and Contextual Characteristics on Creativity"; S. T. Hunter, K. E. Bedell, and M. D. Mumford, "Climate for Creativity: A Quantitative Review," *Creativity Research Journal* 19, no. 1 (2007): 69–90; T. C. DiLiello and J. D. Houghton, "Creative Potential and Practised Creativity: Identifying Untapped Creativity in Organizations," *Creativity and Innovation Management* 17, no. 1 (2008): 37–46.

76. R. Westwood and D. R. Low, "The Multicultural Muse: Culture, Creativity and Innovation," *International Journal of Cross Cultural Management* 3, no. 2 (2003): 235–259.

77. "Samsung CEO Yun Picks Google as New Role Model," *Korea Times*, 1 October 2007.

78. T. M. Amabile, "Motivating Creativity in Organizations: On Doing What You Love and Loving What You Do," *California Management Review* 40 (Fall 1997): 39–58; A. Cummings and G. R. Oldham, "Enhancing Creativity: Managing Work Contexts for the High Potential Employee," *California Management Review*, no. 40 (Fall 1997): 22–38; F. Coelho and M. Augusto, "Job Characteristics and the Creativity of Frontline Service Employees," *Journal of Service Research* 13, no. 4 (November 2010): 426–438.

79. T. M. Amabile, "Changes in the Work Environment for Creativity During Downsizing," *Academy of Management Journal* 42 (December 1999): 630–640.

80. J. Moultrie *et al.*, "Innovation Spaces: Towards a Framework for Understanding the Role of the Physical Environment in Innovation," *Creativity & Innovation Management* 16, no. 1 (2007): 53–65.

81. M. Strauss, "Retailers Tap into War-Room Creativity of Employees," *Globe & Mail*, 12 March 2007, B1.

82. J. M. Howell and K. Boies, "Champions of Technological Innovation: The Influence of Contextual Knowledge, Role Orientation, Idea Generation, and Idea Promotion on Champion Emergence," *The Leadership Quarterly* 15, no. 1 (2004): 123–143; Shalley, Zhou, and Oldham, "The Effects of Personal and Contextual Characteristics on Creativity"; S. Powell, "The Management and Consumption of Organisational Creativity," *Journal of Consumer Marketing* 25, no. 3 (2008): 158–166.

83. A. Hiam, "Obstacles to Creativity—and How You Can Remove Them," *Futurist* 32 (October 1998): 30–34.

84. M. A. West, *Developing Creativity in Organizations* (Leicester, UK: BPS Books, 1997), 33–35.

85. S. Hemsley, "Seeking the Source of Innovation," *Media Week*, 16 August 2005, 22.

86. A. Hargadon and R. I. Sutton, "Building an Innovation Factory," *Harvard Business Review* 78 (May-June 2000): 157–166; T. Kelley, *The Art of Innovation* (New York: Currency Doubleday, 2001), 158–162; P. F. Skilton and K. J. Dooley, "The Effects of Repeat Collaboration on Creative Abrasion," *Academy of Management Review* 35, no. 1 (2010): 118–134.

87. M. Burton, "Open Plan, Open Mind," *Director* (March 2005): 68–72; A. Benady, "Mothers of Invention," *The Independent (London)*, 27 November 2006; B. Murray, "Agency Profile: Mother London," *Ihaveanidea*, 28 January 2007, http://www.ihaveanidea.org.

88. "John Collee-Biography," (IMDB (Internet Movie Database), 2009), http://www.imdb.com/name/nm0171722/bio (accessed 27 April 2009).

89. N. Desai, "Management by Trust in a Democratic Enterprise: A Law Firm Shapes Organizational Behavior to Create Competitive Advantage," *Global Business and Organizational Excellence* 28, no. 6 (2009): 7–21.

90. M. Fenton-O'Creevy, "Employee Involvement and the Middle Manager: Saboteur or Scapegoat?," *Human Resource Management Journal*, no. 11 (2001): 24–40. Also see V. H. Vroom and A. G. Jago, *The New Leadership: Managing Participation in Organizations* (Englewood Cliffs, N.J.: Prentice Hill, 1988).

91. Vroom and Jago, *The New Leadership*.

92. Some of the early OB writing on employee involvement includes C. Argyris, *Personality and Organization* (New York: Harper & Row, 1957); D. McGregor, *The Human Side of Enterprise* (New York: McGraw-Hill, 1960); R. Likert, *New Patterns of Management* (New York: McGraw-Hill, 1961).

93. A. G. Robinson and D. M. Schroeder, *Ideas Are Free* (San Francisco: Berrett-Koehler, 2004).

94. R. J. Ely and D. A. Thomas, "Cultural Diversity at Work: The Effects of Diversity Perspectives on Work Group Processes and Outcomes," *Administrative Science Quarterly* 46 (June 2001): 229–273; E. Mannix and M. A. Neale, "What Differences Make a Difference?: The Promise and Reality of Diverse Teams in Organizations," *Psychological Science in the Public Interest* 6, no. 2 (2005): 31–55.

95. D. Berend and J. Paroush, "When Is Condorcet's Jury Theorem Valid?," *Social Choice and Welfare* 15, no. 4 (1998): 481–488.

96. D. Kloster, "High Tech Firms Take to the Track for Cancer Research," *Times Colonist* (Victoria) 2007; D. Meissner, "Hack Day Not a Slack Day," *Globe & Mail*, 19 July 2007; D. Kloster, "Personal Growth Is the Name of the Game," *British Columbia Biolinks*, 18 March 2008, www.lifesciencebc.ca; D. De veau, "Online Collaboration Tools Replace Business Travel," *Times Colonist*, 17 June 2010, C7; "Rix was a Giant In Life Sciences," *Times Colonist*, 18 November 2009, B5; Doris McCooey & Dawn McCooey, *Keeping Good Employees on Board: Employee Retention Strategies to Navigate any Economic Storm* (New York, NY: Morgan James Publishing, 2009), 46–47.

97. K. T. Dirks, L. L. Cummings, and J. L. Pierce, "Psychological Ownership in Organizations: Conditions under Which Individuals Promote and Resist Change," *Research in Organizational Change and Development*, no. 9 (1996): 1–23; J. P. Walsh and S.-F. Tseng, "The Effects of Job Characteristics on Active Effort at Work," *Work & Occupations*, no. 25 (February 1998): 74–96; B. Scott-

Ladd and V. Marshall, "Participation in Decision Making: A Matter of Context?," *Leadership & Organization Development Journal* 25, no. 8 (2004): 646–662.

98. T. Fenton, "Inside the Worldblu List: 1–800-Got-Junk?'s CEO on Why 'Being Democratic Is Extremely Important to Maintaining Our Competitive Advantage,'" (Atlanta: WorldBlu, 3 January 2008).

99. Vroom and Jago, *The New Leadership*.

100. S. Litt, "Church's Transformation into Business Offers Answer to Many People's Prayers," *Plain Dealer (Cleveland)*, 12 September 2003, E1; K. Palmer, "Design of the Times," *Smart Business Cleveland*, September 2003, 37; M. Smith, "A New Class: They're Creative, Driven and They're Here," *Inside Business*, April 2003, 48; D. Trattner, "Old Church Provides Inspiration for Designers," *Plain Dealer (Cleveland)*, 2 January 2006, E3; A. Fisher, "Ideas Made Here," *Fortune*, 11 June 2007, 35; M. R. Kropko, "Designing Men," *Charleston Gazette*, 5 November 2007, P2C; J. Morgan, Lewis, "Wizards of Wal-Mart," *Inside Business*, March 2007, 34; L. Taxel, "It Takes Two," *Continental In-Flight Magazine*, April 2007.

CHAPTER 8

1. B. Bowes, "Team Players," *Winnipeg Free Press*, 29 May 2010, I1; M. McNeill, "Adapting is the name of this game," *Winnipeg Free Press*, 24 March 2010, B5; "Precision Metalcraft Retires Lunch Table with 5S," *Canadian Manufacturers & Exporters Manitoba Newsletter*, June 2009, 1; http://precisionmetal.hepcom.ca/.

2. "Trends: Are Many Meetings a Waste of Time? Study Says So," MeetingsNet news release (1 November 1998); "Teamwork and Collaboration Major Workplace Trends," *Ottawa Business Journal*, 18 April 2006; "Go Teams! Firms Can't Do without Them," (American Management Association, 2008), http://amalearning.com (accessed 21 April 2010).

3. S. Wuchty, B. F. Jones, and B. Uzzi, "The Increasing Dominance of Teams in Production of Knowledge," *Science* 316 (18 May 2007): 1036–1039.

4. M. E. Shaw, *Group Dynamics*, 3 ed. (New York: McGraw-Hill, 1981), 8; S. A. Mohrman, S. G. Cohen, and A. M. Mohrman Jr., *Designing Team-Based Organizations: New Forms for Knowledge Work* (San Francisco: Jossey-Bass, *1995*), 39–40; E. Sundstrom, "The Challenges of Supporting Work Team Effectiveness," in *Supporting Work Team Effectiveness* ed. E. Sundstrom and Associates (San Francisco, CA: Jossey-Bass, 1999), 6–9.

5. R. A. Guzzo and M. W. Dickson, "Teams in Organizations: Recent Research on Performance and Effectiveness," *Annual Review of Psychology* 47 (1996): 307–338; D. A. Nadler, "From Ritual to Real Work: The Board as a

Team," *Directors and Boards* 22 (Summer 1998): 28–31; L. R. Offerman and R. K. Spiros, "The Science and Practice of Team Development: Improving the Link," *Academy of Management Journal* 44 (April 2001): 376–392.

6. B. D. Pierce and R. White, "The Evolution of Social Structure: Why Biology Matters," *Academy of Management Review* 24 (October 1999): 843–853; P. R. Lawrence and N. Nohria, *Driven: How Human Nature Shapes Our Choices* (San Francisco: Jossey-Bass, 2002); J. R. Spoor and J. R. Kelly, "The Evolutionary Significance of Affect in Groups: Communication and Group Bonding," *Group Processes & Intergroup Relations* 7, no. 4 (2004): 398–412. For a critique of this view, see: G. Sewell, "What Goes Around, Comes Around," *Journal of Applied Behavioural Science* 37, no. 1 (March 2001): 70–91.

7. M. A. Hogg *et al.*, "The Social Identity Perspective: Intergroup Relations, Self-Conception, and Small Groups," *Small Group Research* 35, no. 3 (June 2004): 246–276; N. Michinov, E. Michinov, and M.-C. Toczek-Capelle, "Social Identity, Group Processes, and Performance in Synchronous Computer-Mediated Communication," *Group Dynamics: Theory, Research, and Practice* 8, no. 1 (2004): 27–39; M. Van Vugt and C. M. Hart, "Social Identity as Social Glue: The Origins of Group Loyalty," *Journal of Personality and Social Psychology* 86, no. 4 (2004): 585–598.

8. S. Schacter, *The Psychology of Affiliation* (Stanford, CA: Stanford University Press, 1959), 12–19; R. Eisler and D. S. Levine, "Nurture, Nature, and Caring: We Are Not Prisoners of Our Genes," *Brain and Mind* 3 (2002): 9–52; A. C. DeVries, E. R. Glasper, and C. E. Detillion, "Social Modulation of Stress Responses," *Physiology & Behavior* 79, no. 3 (August 2003): 399–407; S. Cohen, "The Pittsburgh Common Cold Studies: Psychosocial Predictors of Susceptibility to Respiratory Infectious Illness," *International Journal of Behavioral Medicine* 12, no. 3 (2005): 123–131.

9. Cohen, "The Pittsburgh Common Cold Studies: Psychosocial Predictors of Susceptibility to Respiratory Infectious Illness"; M. T. Hansen, M. L. Mors, and B. Løvås, "Knowledge Sharing in Organizations: Multiple Networks, Multiple Phases," *Academy of Management Journal* 48, no. 5 (2005): 776–793; R. Cross *et al.*, "Using Social Network Analysis to Improve Communities of Practice," *California Management Review* 49, no. 1 (2006): 32–60; P. Balkundi *et al.*, "Demographic Antecedents and Performance Consequences of Structural Holes in Work Teams," *Journal of Organizational Behavior* 28, no. 2 (2007): 241–260; W. Verbeke and S. Wuyts, "Moving in Social Circles: Social Circle Membership and Performance Implications," *Journal of Organizational Behavior* 28, no. 4 (2007): 357–379.

10. G. Macaluso, "Hotel Dieu Grace Gets New Critical Care Team," *Windsor Star*, 10 September 2007; "Transformational Business Project and Top Professionals among HR Awards Winners," Mediacom News release (Auckland: 3 March 2009); Rackspace Hosting, *Rackspace Hosting, Inc.—Form 10-K* (San Antonio, Texas: 26 February 2010).

11. M. Moldaschl and W. Weber, "The 'Three Waves' of Industrial Group Work: Historical Reflections on Current Research on Group Work," *Human Relations* 51 (March 1998): 347–388. Several popular books in the 1980s encouraged teamwork, based on the Japanese economic miracle. These books include W. Ouchi, *Theory Z: How American Management Can Meet the Japanese Challenge* (Reading, Mass.: Addison-Wesley, 1981); R. T. Pascale and A. G. Athos, *Art of Japanese Management* (New York: Simon and Schuster, 1982).

12. C. R. Emery and L. D. Fredenhall, "The Effect of Teams on Firm Profitability and Customer Satisfaction," *Journal of Service Research* 4 (February 2002): 217–229; G. S. Van der Vegt and O. Janssen, "Joint Impact of Interdependence and Group Diversity on Innovation," *Journal of Management* 29 (2003): 729–751.

13. R. E. Baumeister and M. R. Leary, "The Need to Belong: Desire for Interpersonal Attachments as a Fundamental Human Motivation," *Psychological Bulletin* 117 (1995): 497–529; S. Chen, H. C. Boucher, and M. P. Tapias, "The Relational Self Revealed: Integrative Conceptualization and Implications for Interpersonal Life," *Psychological Bulletin* 132, no. 2 (2006): 151–179; J. M. Feinberg and J. R. Aiello, "Social Facilitation: A Test of Competing Theories," *Journal of Applied Social Psychology* 36, no. 5 (2006): 1087–1109; A. M. Grant, "Relational Job Design and the Motivation to Make a Prosocial Difference," *Academy of Management Review* 32, no. 2 (2007): 393–417; N. L. Kerr *et al.*, "Psychological Mechanisms Underlying the Kohler Motivation Gain," *Personality & Social Psychology Bulletin* 33, no. 6 (2007): 828–841.

14. "Cactus Restaurants Ltd.," *BC Business*, December 2009, 81; "Cactus Club the Third Best Company to Work for in Bc." Cactus Restaurants Ltd. news release for Cactus Restaurants Ltd. (Vancouver: November 2009); M. Purvis, "What Makes a True Team? Desire to Collaborate," *National Post (Toronto)*, 24 November 2009, FE4.

15. "Powerhouse Team Switched on by Pride," *The Australian*, 23 August 2008, 4.

16. E. A. Locke et al, "The Importance of the Individual in an Age of Groupism," in *Groups at Work: Theory and Research* ed. M. E. Turner (Mahwah, N. J.: Lawrence Erbaum Associates, 2001), 501–528; N. J. Allen and T. D. Hecht, "The 'Romance of Teams': Toward an Understanding of Its Psychological Underpinnings and Implications," *Journal of Occupational and Organizational Psychology* 77 (2004): 439–461.

17. I. D. Steiner, *Group Process and Productivity* (New York: Academic Press, 1972); N. L. Kerr and S. R. Tindale, "Group Performance and Decision Making," *Annual Review of Psychology* 55 (2004): 623–655.

18. D. Dunphy and B. Bryant, "Teams: Panaceas or Prescriptions for Improved Performance?," *Human Relations* 49 (1996): 677–699. For a discussion of Brooks' Law, see F. P. Brooks, ed., *The Mythical Man-Month: Essays on Software Engineering*, 2nd ed. (Reading, Mass.: Addison-Wesley, 1995).

19. "Empowering Canadians in an Evolving World of Work," Microsoft Canada news release (Mississauga, Ont.: 18 April 2006); "Canadians Name Diversity as Key Ingredient in Formula for Innovation Success." Canada News Wire news release for Xerox of Canada (Toronto: 25 September 2007); "Virtual Teams Now a Reality." Institute for Corporate Productivity news release for Institute for Corporate Productivity (Seattle: 4 September 2008).

20. J. Gruber, "More Aperture Dirt," (Daring Fireball, 4 May 2006), http://daringfireball.net/2006/05/more_aperture_dirt (accessed 7 June 2006); J. Gruber, "Aperture Dirt," (Daring Fireball, 28 April 2006), http://daringfireball.net/2006/04/aperture_dirt (accessed 30 April 2006).

21. S. J. Karau and K. D. Williams, "Social Loafing: A Meta-Analytic Review and Theoretical Integration," *Journal of Personality and Social Psychology* 65 (1993): 681–706; R. C. Liden *et al.*, "Social Loafing: A Field Investigation," *Journal of Management* 30 (2004): 285–304; L. L. Chidambaram, "Is out of Sight, out of Mind? An Empirical Study of Social Loafing in Technology-Supported Groups," *Information Systems Research* 16, no. 2 (2005): 149–168; U.-C. Klehe and N. Anderson, "The Moderating Influence of Personality and Culture on Social Loafing in Typical Versus Maximum Performance Situations," *International Journal of Selection and Assessment* 15, no. 2 (2007): 250–262.

22. J. R. Engen, "Tough as Nails," *Bank Director*, July 2009, 24.

23. M. Erez and A. Somech, "Is Group Productivity Loss the Rule or the Exception? Effects of Culture and Group-Based Motivation," *Academy of Management Journal* 39 (1996): 1513–1537; Kerr and Tindale, "Group Performance and Decision Making"; A. Jassawalla, H. Sashittal, and A. Malshe, "Students' Perceptions of Social Loafing: Its Antecedents and Consequences in Undergraduate Business Classroom Teams," *Academy of Management Learning and Education* 8, no. 1 (March 2009): 42–54.

24. G. P. Shea and R. A. Guzzo, "Group Effectiveness: What Really Matters?," *Sloan Management Review* 27 (1987): 33–46; J. R. Hackman *et al.*, "Team Effectiveness in Theory and in Practice," in *Industrial and Organizational Psychology: Linking Theory with Practice*, ed. C. L. Cooper and E. A. Locke (Oxford, UK: Blackwell, 2000), 109–129.

25. M. A. West, C. S. Borrill, and K. L. Unsworth, "Team Effectiveness in Organizations," *International Review of Industrial and Organizational Psychology* 13 (1998): 1–48; R. Forrester and A. B. Drexler, "A Model for Team-Based Organization Performance," *Academy of Management Executive* 13 (August 1999): 36–49; J. E. McGrath, H. Arrow, and J. L. Berdahl, "The Study of Groups: Past, Present, and Future," *Personality & Social Psychology Review* 4, no. 1 (2000): 95–105; M. A. Marks, J. E. Mathieu, and S. J. Zaccaro, "A Temporally Based Framework and Taxonomy of Team Processes," *Academy of Management Review* 26, no. 3 (July 2001): 356–376.

26. J. S. DeMatteo, L. T. Eby, and E. Sundstrom, "Team-Based Rewards: Current Empirical Evidence and Directions for Future Research," *Research in Organizational Behavior* 20 (1998): 141–183; E. E. Lawler III, *Rewarding Excellence: Pay Strategies for the New Economy* (San Francisco: Jossey-Bass, 2000), 207–214; G. Hertel, S. Geister, and U. Konradt, "Managing Virtual Teams: A Review of Current Empirical Research," *Human Resource Management Review* 15 (2005): 69–95.

27. These and other environmental conditions for effective teams are discussed in R. Wageman, "Case Study: Critical Success Factors for Creating Superb Self-Managing Teams at Xerox," *Compensation and Benefits Review* 29 (September-October 1997): 31–41; Sundstrom, "The Challenges of Supporting Work Team Effectiveness"; J. N. Choi, "External Activities and Team Effectiveness: Review and Theoretical Development," *Small Group Research* 33 (April 2002): 181–208; T. L. Doolen, M. E. Hacker, and E. M. Van Aken, "The Impact of Organizational Context on Work Team Effectiveness: A Study of Production Team," *IEEE Transactions on Engineering Management* 50, no. 3 (August 2003): 285–296; S. D. Dionne *et al.*, "Transformational Leadership and Team Performance," *Journal Of Organizational Change Management* 17, no. 2 (2004): 177–193; G. L. Stewart, "A Meta-Analytic Review of Relationships between Team Design Features and Team Performance," *Journal of Management* 32, no. 1 (February 2006): 29–54.

28. D. McCutcheon, "Chipping Away: Celestica's Toronto Plant Cuts Waste Blitz by Blitz," *Advanced Manufacturing*, Nov/Dec 2004, 23.

29. M. A. Campion, E. M. Papper, and G. J. Medsker, "Relations between Work Team Characteristics and Effectiveness: A Replication and Extension," *Personnel Psychology* 49 (1996): 429–452; D. C. Man and S. S. K. Lam, "The Effects of Job Complexity and Autonomy on Cohesiveness in Collectivistic and Individualistic Work Groups: A Cross-Cultural Analysis," *Journal of Organizational Behavior* 24 (2003): 979–1001.

30. L. Hirsh, "Manufacturing in Action," *Press-Enterprise (Riverside, Calif.)*, 21 June 2008, E01.

31. G. S. Van der Vegt, J. M. Emans, and E. Van de Vliert, "Patterns of Interdependence in Work Teams: A Two-Level Investigation of the Relations with Job and Team Satisfaction," *Personnel Psychology* 54 (Spring 2001): 51–69; R. Wageman, "The Meaning of Interdependence," in *Groups at Work: Theory and Research* ed. M. E. Turner (Mahwah, N. J.: Lawrence Erlbaum Associates, 2001), 197–217; S. M. Gully *et al.*, "A Meta-Analysis of Team-Efficacy, Potency, and Performance: Interdependence and Level of Analysis as Moderators of Observed Relationships," *Journal of Applied Psychology* 87, no. 5 (Oct 2002): 819–832; M. R. Barrick *et al.*, "The Moderating Role of Top Management Team Interdependence: Implications for Real Teams and Working Groups," *Academy of Management Journal* 50, no. 3 (2007): 544–557.

32. A. Deutschman, "Inside the Mind of Jeff Bezos," *Fast Company*, August 2004, 52–58; L. Gratton and T. J. Erickson, "Ways to Build Collaborative Teams," *Harvard Business Review* (November 2007): 100–109.

33. G. Stasser, "Pooling of Unshared Information During Group Discussion," in *Group Process and Productivity*, ed. S. Worchel, W. Wood, and J. A. Simpson (Newbury Park, California: Sage, 1992); J. R. Katzenbach and D. K. Smith, *The Wisdom of Teams: Creating the High-Performance Organization* (Boston: Harvard University Press, 1993), 45–47.

34. J. O'Toole, "The Power of Many: Building a High-Performance Management Team," *ceoforum.com.au* (March 2003).

35. C. Fishman, "The Anarchist's Cookbook," *Fast Company*, July 2004, 70.

36. F. P. Morgeson, M. H. Reider, and M. A. Campion, "Selecting Individuals in Team Setting: The Importance of Social Skills, Personality Characteristics, and Teamwork Knowledge," *Personnel Psychology* 58, no. 3 (2005): 583–611; V. Rousseau, C. Aubé, and A. Savoie, "Teamwork Behaviors: A Review and an Integration of Frameworks," *Small Group Research* 37,

no. 5 (2006): 540–570. For a detailed examination of the characteristics of effective team members, see M. L. Loughry, M. W. Ohland, and D. D. Moore, "Development of a Theory-Based Assessment of Team Member Effectiveness," *Educational and Psychological Measurement* 67, no. 3 (June 2007): 505–524.

37. P. Wise, "How Shell Finds Student World's Brightest Sparks," *Financial Times (London)*, 8 January 2004, 12; "Shell Oil Introduces Undergrads to Gourami Business Challenge," University of Texas at Austin News release (Austin, TX: 15 August 2005); S. Ganesan, "Talent Quest," *Malaysia Star*, 28 January 2007; J. Porretto, "Wanted: Engineers," *The Commercial Appeal*, 4 September 2007, B3; S. McNulty, "Oil Groups Seek a Burst of Energy," *Financial Times (London)*, 17 January 2008, 16.

38. C. O. L. H. Porter *et al.*, "Backing up Behaviors in Teams: The Role of Personality and Legitimacy of Need," *Journal of Applied Psychology* 88, no. 3 (2003): 391–403; C. E. Härtel and D. Panipucci, "How 'Bad Apples' Spoil the Bunch: Faultlines, Emotional Levers, and Exclusion in the Workplace," *Research on Emotion in Organizations* 3 (2007): 287–310. The bad apple phenomenon is also identified in executive teams as "derailers." See: R. Wageman *et al.*, *Senior Leadership Teams* (Boston: Harvard Business School Press, 2008), 97–102.

39. D. van Knippenberg, C. K. W. De Dreu, and A. C. Homan, "Work Group Diversity and Group Performance: An Integrative Model and Research Agenda," *Journal of Applied Psychology* 89, no. 6 (2004): 1008–1022; E. Mannix and M. A. Neale, "What Differences Make a Difference?: The Promise and Reality of Diverse Teams in Organizations," *Psychological Science in the Public Interest* 6, no. 2 (2005): 31–55. For a positive view of team diversity, see: G. K. Stahl *et al.*, "A Look at the Bright Side of Multicultural Team Diversity," *Scandinavian Journal of Management* 26, no. 4 (2010): 439–447.

40. D. C. Lau and J. K. Murnighan, "Interactions within Groups and Subgroups: The Effects of Demographic Faultlines," *Academy of Management Journal* 48, no. 4 (August 2005): 645–659; R. Rico *et al.*, "The Effects of Diversity Faultlines and Team Task Autonomy on Decision Quality and Social Integration," *Journal of Management* 33, no. 1 (Feb. 2007): 111–132.

41. B. W. Tuckman and M. A. C. Jensen, "Stages of Small-Group Development Revisited," *Group and Organization Studies* 2 (1977): 419–442; B. W. Tuckman, "Developmental Sequence in Small Groups," *Group Facilitation* (Spring 2001): 66–81.

42. G. R. Bushe and G. H. Coetzer, "Group Development and Team Effectiveness: Using Cognitive Representations to Measure

Group Development and Predict Task Performance and Group Viability," *Journal of Applied Behavioral Science* 43, no. 2 (June 2007): 184–212.

43. J. E. Mathieu and G. F. Goodwin, "The Influence of Shared Mental Models on Team Process and Performance," *Journal of Applied Psychology* 85 (April 2000): 273–284; J. Langan-Fox and J. Anglim, "Mental Models, Team Mental Models, and Performance: Process, Development, and Future Directions," *Human Factors and Ergonomics in Manufacturing* 14, no. 4 (2004): 331–352; B.C. Lim and K. J. Klein, "Team Mental Models and Team Performance: A Field Study of the Effects of Team Mental Model Similarity and Accuracy," *Journal of Organizational Behavior* 27 (2006): 403–418; R. Rico, M. Sánchez-Manzanares, and C. Gibson, "Team Implicit Coordination Processes: A Team Knowledge-Based Approach," *Academy of Management Review* 33, no. 1 (2008): 163–184, 163–184.

44. L. A. DeChurch and J. R. Mesmer-Magnus, "The Cognitive Underpinnings of Effective Teamwork: A Meta-Analysis," *Journal of Applied Psychology* 95, no. 1 (2010): 32–53.

45. A. P. Hare, "Types of Roles in Small Groups: A Bit of History and a Current Perspective," *Small Group Research* 25 (1994): 443–448; A. Aritzeta, S. Swailes, and B. Senior, "Belbin's Team Role Model: Development, Validity and Applications for Team Building," *Journal of Management Studies* 44, no. 1 (Jan. 2007): 96–118.

46. S. H. N. Leung, J. W. K. Chan, and W. B. Lee, "The Dynamic Team Role Behavior: The Approaches of Investigation," *Team Performance Management* 9 (2003): 84–90; G. L. Stewart, I. S. Fulmer, and M. R. Barrick, "An Exploration of Member Roles as a Multilevel Linking Mechanism for Individual Traits and Team Outcomes," *Personnel Psychology* 58, no. 2 (2005): 343–365.

47. W. G. Dyer, *Team Building: Current Issues and New Alternatives*, 3rd ed. (Reading, MA: Addison-Wesley, 1995); C. A. Beatty and B. A. Barker, *Building Smart Teams: Roadmap to High Performance* (Thousand Oaks, CA: Sage Publications, 2004).

48. "The Amazing Chase," http://www.calgaryteambuilding.com/teambuilding_chase.php Retrieved January, 15, 2011; "Recent Client Feedback," http://www.calgaryteambuilding.com/teambuilding_chase.php Retrieved January 15, 2011.

49. Langan-Fox and Anglim, "Mental Models, Team Mental Models, and Performance: Process, Development, and Future Directions"; J. E. Mathieu *et al.*, "Scaling the Quality of Teammates' Mental Models: Equifinality and Normative Comparisons," *Journal of Organizational Behavior* 26 (2005): 37–56.

50. "German Businesswoman Demands End to Fun at Work," *Reuters*, 9 July 2003.

51. R. W. Woodman and J. J. Sherwood, "The Role of Team Development in Organizational Effectiveness: A Critical Review," *Psychological Bulletin* 88 (1980): 166–186.

52. L. Mealiea and R. Baltazar, "A Strategic Guide for Building Effective Teams," *Personnel Management* 34, no. 2 (Summer 2005): 141–160.

53. G. E. Huszczo, "Training for Team Building," *Training and Development Journal* 44 (February 1990): 37–43; P. McGraw, "Back from the Mountain: Outdoor Management Development Programs and How to Ensure the Transfer of Skills to the Workplace," *Asia Pacific Journal of Human Resources* 31 (Spring 1993): 52–61.

54. D. C. Feldman, "The Development and Enforcement of Group Norms," *Academy of Management Review* 9 (1984): 47–53; E. Fehr and U. Fischbacher, "Social Norms and Human Cooperation," *Trends in Cognitive Sciences* 8, no. 4 (2004): 185–190.

55. N. Ellemers and F. Rink, "Identity in Work Groups: The Beneficial and Detrimental Consequences of Multiple Identities and Group Norms for Collaboration and Group Performance," *Advances in Group Processes* 22 (2005): 1–41.

56. J. J. Dose and R. J. Klimoski, "The Diversity of Diversity: Work Values Effects on Formative Team Processes," *Human Resource Management Review* 9, no. 1 (Spring 1999): 83–108.

57. S. Taggar and R. Ellis, "The Role of Leaders in Shaping Formal Team Norms," *Leadership Quarterly* 18, no. 2 (2007): 105–120.

58. D. J. Beal *et al.*, "Cohesion and Performance in Groups: A Meta-Analytic Clarification of Construct Relations," *Journal of Applied Psychology* 88, no. 6 (2003): 989–1004; S. W. J. Kozlowski and D. R. Ilgen, "Enhancing the Effectiveness of Work Groups and Teams," *Psychological Science in the Public Interest* 7, no. 3 (2006): 77–124.

59. K. A. Jehn, G. B. Northcraft, and M. A. Neale, "Why Differences Make a Difference: A Field Study of Diversity, Conflict, and Performance in Workgroups," *Administrative Science Quarterly* 44, no. 4 (1999): 741–763; van Knippenberg, De Dreu, and Homan, "Work Group Diversity and Group Performance: An Integrative Model and Research Agenda," For evidence that diversity/similarity does not always influence cohesion, see S. S. Webber and L. M. Donahue, "Impact of Highly and Less Job-Related Diversity on Work Group Cohesion and Performance: A Meta-Analysis," *Journal of Management* 27, no. 2 (2001): 141–162.

60. E. Aronson and J. Mills, "The Effects of Severity of Initiation on Liking for a Group," *Journal of Abnormal and Social Psychology* 59 (1959): 177–181; J. E. Hautaluoma and R. S. Enge, "Early Socialization into a Work Group: Severity of Initiations Revisited," *Journal of Social Behavior & Personality* 6 (1991): 725–748.

61. B. Mullen and C. Copper, "The Relation between Group Cohesiveness and Performance: An Integration," *Psychological Bulletin* 115 (1994): 210–227; C. J. Fullagar and D. O. Egleston, "Norming and Performing: Using Microworlds to Understand the Relationship between Team Cohesiveness and Performance," *Journal of Applied Social Psychology* 38, no. 10 (October 2008): 2574–2593.

62. Wageman *et al.*, *Senior Leadership Teams*, 69–70.

63. M. Rempel and R. J. Fisher, "Perceived Threat, Cohesion, and Group Problem Solving in Intergroup Conflict," *International Journal of Conflict Management* 8 (1997): 216–234; M. E. Turner and T. Horvitz, "The Dilemma of Threat: Group Effectiveness and Ineffectiveness under Adversity," in *Groups at Work: Theory and Research* ed. M. E. Turner (Mahwah, N. J.: Lawrence Erlbaum Associates, 2001), 445–470.

64. F. Piccolo, "Brownie Points," Atlantic Business, Oct/Nov 2004, 22; http://www.southshorenow.ca/about/lighthouse/index.php Retrieved January 14, 2010.

65. W. Piper *et al.*, "Cohesion as a Basic Bond in Groups," *Human Relations* 36 (1983): 93–108; C. A. O'Reilly, D. E. Caldwell, and W. P. Barnett, "Work Group Demography, Social Integration, and Turnover," *Administrative Science Quarterly* 34 (1989): 21–37.

66. Mullen and Copper, "The Relation between Group Cohesiveness and Performance"; A. V. Carron *et al.*, "Cohesion and Performance in Sport: A Meta-Analysis," *Journal of Sport and Exercise Psychology* 24 (2002): 168–188; Beal *et al.*, "Cohesion and Performance in Groups"; Fullagar and Egleston, "Norming and Performing: Using Microworlds to Understand the Relationship between Team Cohesiveness and Performance"; DeChurch and Mesmer-Magnus, "The Cognitive Underpinnings of Effective Teamwork: A Meta-Analysis."

67. C. Langfred, "Is Group Cohesiveness a Double-Edged Sword? An Investigation of the Effects of Cohesiveness on Performance," *Small Group Research* 29 (1998): 124–143; K. L. Gammage, A. V. Carron, and P. A. Estabrooks, "Team Cohesion and Individual Productivity: The Influence of the Norm for Productivity and the Identifiablity of Individual Effort," *Small Group Research* 32 (February 2001): 3–18.

68. S. L. Robinson, "Trust and Breach of the Psychological Contract," *Administrative Science Quarterly* 41 (1996): 574–599; D. M. Rousseau *et al.*, "Not So Different after All: A Cross-Discipline View of Trust," *Academy of Management Review* 23 (1998): 393–404; D. L. Duarte and N. T. Snyder, *Mastering Virtual Teams: Strategies, Tools, and Techniques That Succeed*, 2nd ed. (San Francisco, CA: Jossey-Bass, 2000), 139–155. For the importance of trust in virtual teams, see: L. M. Peters and C. C. Manz, "Getting Virtual Teams Right the First Time," in *The Handbook of High-Performance Virtual Teams: A Toolkit for Collaborating across Boundaries*, ed. J. Nemiro and M. M. Beyerlein (San Francisco: Jossey Bass, 2008), 105–130.

69. Rousseau *et al.*, "Not So Different after All: A Cross-Discipline View of Trust."

70. D. J. McAllister, "Affect- and Cognition-Based Trust as Foundations for Interpersonal Cooperation in Organizations," *Academy of Management Journal* 38, no. 1 (February 1995): 24–59; M. Williams, "In Whom We Trust: Group Membership as an Affective Context for Trust Development," *Academy of Management Review* 26, no. 3 (July 2001): 377–396.

71. O. E. Williamson, "Calculativeness, Trust, and Economic Organization," *Journal of Law and Economics* 36, no. 1 (1993): 453–486.

72. E. M. Whitener *et al.*, "Managers as Initiators of Trust: An Exchange Relationship Framework for Understanding Managerial Trustworthy Behavior," *Academy of Management Review* 23 (July 1998): 513–530; J. M. Kouzes and B. Z. Posner, *The Leadership Challenge*, 3rd ed. (San Francisco: Jossey-Bass, 2002), Chap. 2; T. Simons, "Behavioral Integrity: The Perceived Alignment between Managers' Words and Deeds as a Research Focus," *Organization Science* 13, no. 1 (Jan-Feb 2002): 18–35.

73. S. L. Jarvenpaa and D. E. Leidner, "Communication and Trust in Global Virtual Teams," *Organization Science* 10 (1999): 791–815; M. M. Pillutla, D. Malhotra, and J. Keith Murnighan, "Attributions of Trust and the Calculus of Reciprocity," *Journal of Experimental Social Psychology* 39, no. 5 (2003): 448–455.

74. K. T. Dirks and D. L. Ferrin, "The Role of Trust in Organizations," *Organization Science* 12, no. 4 (July-August 2004): 450–467.

75. Fishman, "The Anarchist's Cookbook"; J. Mackey, "Open Book Company," *Newsweek*, 28 November 2005, 42; D. Jacobson, "Best-Kept Secrets of the World's Best Companies: Gainsharing," *Business 2.0*, April 2006, 82; A. Kimball-Stanley, "Bucking the Trend in Benefits," *Providence Journal (Rhode Island)*, 14 May 2006, H01; K. Zimbalist, "Green Giant," *Time*, 24 April 2006, 24.

76. Mohrman, Cohen, and Mohrman Jr., *Designing Team-Based Organizations: New Forms for Knowledge Work*; D. E. Yeatts and C. Hyten, *High-Performing Self-Managed Work Teams: A Comparison of Theory and*

Practice (Thousand Oaks, CA: Sage, 1998); E. E. Lawler, *Organizing for High Performance* (San Francisco: Jossey-Bass, 2001); R. J. Torraco, "Work Design Theory: A Review and Critique with Implications for Human Resource Development," *Human Resource Development Quarterly* 16, no. 1 (Spring 2005): 85–109.

77. P. Panchak, "Production Workers Can Be Your Competitive Edge," *Industry Week*, October 2004, 11; S. K. Muthusamy, J. V. Wheeler, and B. L. Simmons, "Self-Managing Work Teams: Enhancing Organizational Innovativeness," *Organization Development Journal* 23, no. 3 (Fall 2005): 53–66.

78. Emery and Fredenhall, "The Effect of Teams on Firm Profitability and Customer Satisfaction"; A. Krause and H. Dunckel, "Work Design and Customer Satisfaction: Effects of the Implementation of Semi-Autonomous Group Work on Customer Satisfaction Considering Employee Satisfaction and Group Performance (Translated Abstract)," *Zeitschrift Fur Arbeits-Und Organisationspsychologie* 47, no. 4 (2003): 182–193; H. van Mierlo *et al.*, "Self-Managing Teamwork and Psychological Well-Being: Review of a Multilevel Research Domain," *Group & Organization Management* 30, no. 2 (April 2005): 211–235.

79. Moldaschl and Weber, "The 'Three Waves' of Industrial Group Work: Historical Reflections on Current Research on Group Work"; W. Niepce and E. Molleman, "Work Design Issues in Lean Production from Sociotechnical System Perspective: Neo-Taylorism or the Next Step in Sociotechnical Design?," *Human Relations* 51, no. 3 (March 1998): 259–287.

80. E. Ulich and W. G. Weber, "Dimensions, Criteria, and Evaluation of Work Group Autonomy," in *Handbook of Work Group Psychology* ed. M. A. West (Chichester, UK: John Wiley and Sons, 1996), 247–282.

81. "Medical Marvel," *Works Management (Best Factory Awards Supplement)*, October 2007, 21–22.

82. K. P. Carson and G. L. Stewart, "Job Analysis and the Sociotechnical Approach to Quality: A Critical Examination," *Journal of Quality Management* 1 (1996): 49–65; C. C. Manz and G. L. Stewart, "Attaining Flexible Stability by Integrating Total Quality Management and Socio-Technical Systems Theory," *Organization Science* 8 (1997): 59–70.

83. K. Marron, "Close Encounters of the Faceless Kind," *Globe & Mail*, 9 February 2005, C1.

84. J. Lipnack and J. Stamps, *Virtual Teams: People Working across Boundaries with Technology* (New York: John Wiley and Sons, 2001); Hertel, Geister, and Konradt, "Managing Virtual Teams"; L. Schweitzer and L. Duxbury, "Conceptualizing and Measuring the Virtuality of Teams," *Information Systems Journal* 20, no. 3 (2010): 267–295.

85. "Virtual Teams Now a Reality," news release.

86. G. Gilder, *Telecosm: How Infinite Bandwidth Will Revolutionize Our World* (New York: Free Press, 2001); L. L. Martins, L. L. Gilson, and M. T. Maynard, "Virtual Teams: What Do We Know and Where Do We Go Form Here?," *Journal of Management* 30, no. 6 (2004): 805–835.

87. N. Weil, "Global Team Management: Continental Divides," *CIO*, 23 January 2008.

88. Martins, Gilson, and Maynard, "Virtual Teams"; G. Hertel, U. Konradt, and K. Voss, "Competencies for Virtual Teamwork: Development and Validation of a Web-Based Selection Tool for Members of Distributed Teams," *European Journal of Work and Organizational Psychology* 15, no. 4 (2006): 477–504.

89. *Long-Distance Loathing (Summary and Data)* (Provo, Utah: VitalSmarts, March 2009).

90. G. G. Harwood, "Design Principles for Successful Virtual Teams," in *The Handbook of High-Performance Virtual Teams: A Toolkit for Collaborating across Boundaries*, ed. J. Nemiro and M. M. Beyerlein (San Francisco: Jossey-Bass, 2008), 59–84. Also see: H. Duckworth, "How TRW Automotive Helps Global Virtual Teams Perform at the Top of Their Game," *Global Business and Organizational Excellence* 28, no. 1 (2008): 6–16.

91. V. H. Vroom and A. G. Jago, *The New Leadership* (Englewood Cliffs, NJ: Prentice-Hall, 1988), 28–29.

92. M. Diehl and W. Stroebe, "Productivity Loss in Idea-Generating Groups: Tracking Down the Blocking Effects," *Journal of Personality and Social Psychology* 61 (1991): 392–403; R. B. Gallupe *et al.*, "Blocking Electronic Brainstorms," *Journal of Applied Psychology* 79 (1994): 77–86; B. A. Nijstad, W. Stroebe, and H. F. M. Lodewijkx, "Production Blocking and Idea Generation: Does Blocking Interfere with Cognitive Processes?," *Journal of Experimental Social Psychology* 39, no. 6 (November 2003): 531–548; B. A. Nijstad and W. Stroebe, "How the Group Affects the Mind: A Cognitive Model of Idea Generation in Groups," *Personality & Social Psychology Review* 10, no. 3 (2006): 186–213.

93. B. E. Irmer, P. Bordia, and D. Abusah, "Evaluation Apprehension and Perceived Benefits in Interpersonal and Database Knowledge Sharing," *Academy of Management Proceedings* (2002): B1-B6.

94. I. L. Janis, *Groupthink: Psychological Studies of Policy Decisions and Fiascoes*, 2nd ed. (Boston: Houghton Mifflin, 1982); J. K. Esser, "Alive and Well after 25 Years: A Review of Groupthink Research," *Organizational Behavior and Human Decision Processes* 73, no. 2–3 (1998): 116–141.

95. J. N. Choi and M. U. Kim, "The Organizational Application of Groupthink and Its Limitations in Organizations," *Journal of Applied Psychology* 84, no. 2 (April 1999): 297–306; W.-W. Park, "A Comprehensive Empirical Investigation of the Relationships among Variables of the Groupthink Model," *Journal of Organizational Behavior* 21, no. 8 (Dec 2000): 873–887; D. D. Henningsen *et al.*, "Examining the Symptoms of Groupthink and Retrospective Sensemaking," *Small Group Research* 37, no. 1 (Feb. 2006): 36–64.

96. D. Miller, *The Icarus Paradox: How Exceptional Companies Bring About Their Own Downfall* (New York: HarperBusiness, 1990); S. Finkelstein, *Why Smart Executives Fail* (New York: Viking, 2003); K. Tasa and G. Whyte, "Collective Efficacy and Vigilant Problem Solving in Group Decision Making: A Non-Linear Model," *Organizational Behavior and Human Decision Processes* 96, no. 2 (March 2005): 119–129.

97. B. Frisch, "When Teams Can't Decide," *Harvard Business Review* 86, no. 11 (2008): 121–126.

98. H. Collingwood, "Best-Kept Secrets of the World's Best Companies: Outside-in R&D," *Business 2.0*, April 2006, 82.

99. K. M. Eisenhardt, J. L. Kahwajy, and L. J. Bourgeois III, "Conflict and Strategic Choice: How Top Management Teams Disagree," *California Management Review* 39 (1997): 42–62; R. Sutton, *Weird Ideas That Work* (New York: Free Press, 2002); C. J. Nemeth *et al.*, "The Liberating Role of Conflict in Group Creativity: A Study in Two Countries," *European Journal of Social Psychology* 34, no. 4 (2004): 365–374. For a discussion on how all conflict is potentially detrimental to teams, see C. K. W. De Dreu and L. R. Weingart, "Task Versus Relationship Conflict, Team Performance, and Team Member Satisfaction: A Meta-Analysis," *Journal of Applied Psychology* 88 (August 2003): 587–604; P. Hinds and D. E. Bailey, "Out of Sight, out of Sync: Understanding Conflict in Distributed Teams," *Organization Science* 14, no. 6 (2003): 615–632.

100. Advertising executive Alex Osborn (the "O" in BBDO, the world's second largest creative agency) first described brainstorming in the little-known 1942 booklet *How to Think Up*. He originally called them "brain-storm suppers" (29) because the company initially held these events in the evening after a meal in the company dining room. Osborn gave a fuller description of the brainstorming process in his popular 1948 (*Your Creative Power*) and 1953 (*Applied Imagination*) books. See: A. F. Osborn, *How to Think Up* (New York: McGraw-Hill, 1942), Chap. 4; A. F. Osborn, *Your Creative Power* (New York: Charles Scribner's Sons, 1948); A. F. Osborn, *Applied Imagination* (New York: Charles Scribner's Sons, 1953).

101. Rachel Pulfer, "Brainstorming: Funny Business," *Canadian Business*, 27 April 2009: 27–28.

102. B. S. Benson, "Let's Toss This Idea Up," *Fortune*, October 1957, 145–146.

103. B. Mullen, C. Johnson, and E. Salas, "Productivity Loss in Brainstorming Groups: A Meta-Analytic Integration," *Basic and Applied Psychology* 12 (1991): 2–23.

104. R. I. Sutton and A. Hargadon, "Brainstorming Groups in Context: Effectiveness in a Product Design Firm," *Administrative Science Quarterly* 41 (1996): 685–718; T. Kelley, *The Art of Innovation* (New York: Currency Doubleday, 2001); V. R. Brown and P. B. Paulus, "Making Group Brainstorming More Effective: Recommendations from an Associative Memory Perspective," *Current Directions in Psychological Science* 11, no. 6 (2002): 208–212; K. Leggett Dugosh and P. B. Paulus, "Cognitive and Social Comparison Processes in Brainstorming," *Journal of Experimental Social Psychology* 41, no. 3 (2005): 313–320.

105. R. B. Gallupe, L. M. Bastianutti, and W. H. Cooper, "Unblocking Brainstorms," *Journal of Applied Psychology* 76 (1991): 137–142; W. H. Cooper *et al.*, "Some Liberating Effects of Anonymous Electronic Brainstorming," *Small Group Research* 29, no. 2 (April 1998): 147–178; A. R. Dennis, B. H. Wixom, and R. J. Vandenberg, "Understanding Fit and Appropriation Effects in Group Support Systems Via Meta-Analysis," *MIS Quarterly* 25, no. 2 (June 2001): 167–193; D. M. DeRosa, C. L. Smith, and D. A. Hantula, "The Medium Matters: Mining the Long-Promised Merit of Group Interaction in Creative Idea Generation Tasks in a Meta-Analysis of the Electronic Group Brainstorming Literature," *Computers in Human Behavior* 23, no. 3 (2007): 1549–1581.

106. A. L. Delbecq, A. H. Van de Ven, and D. H. Gustafson, *Group Techniques for Program Planning: A Guide to Nominal Group and Delphi Processes* (Middleton, Wis: Green Briar Press, 1986).

107. J. W. Colton and G. Bissix, "Developing Agritourism in Nova Scotia: Issues and Challenges," *Journal of Sustainable Agriculture* 27, no. 1 (2005): 91–112.

108. S. Frankel, "NGT + MDS: An Adaptation of the Nominal Group Technique for Ill-Structured Problems," *Journal of Applied Behavioral Science* 23 (1987): 543–551; H. Barki and A. Pinsonneault, "Small Group Brainstorming and Idea Quality: Is Electronic Brainstorming the Most Effective Approach?," *Small Group Research* 32, no. 2 (April 2001): 158–205.

109. P. P. Lago *et al.*, "Structuring Group Decision Making in a Web-Based Environment by Using the Nominal Group Technique," *Computers & Industrial Engineering* 52, no. 2 (2007): 277–295.

110. D. W. Johnson and F. P. Johnson, *Joining Together: Group Theory and Group Skills* (Upper Saddle River, NJ: Merrill, 2009).

CHAPTER 9

1. Dr. J. McFerran, "Home Game: Comfortable Employees Put Guests At Ease," *Winnipeg Free Press*, 1 May 2010, I1; "Bayer Inc. Recognized as One of North America's 50 Most Engaged Workplaces," *Canada NewsWire*, 17 August 2010. Retrieved January 15, 2011. http://www.newswire.ca/en/releases/archive/August2010/17/c3075.html; J. Kavur, "Social Networking Unveils Tacit Knowledge: PwC," ComputerWorld Canada, 16 February 2010. Retrieved January 16, 2011 http://www.itworldcanada.com/news/social-networking-unveils-tacit-knowledge-says-pwc/139993-pg2; "Case Study: Driving Collaboration in a Multi-Generational Environment: Cisco Systems," Retrieved January 10, 2011 www.cisco.com/.../DeLong-CiscoCollaborativeCultureCase3–09.pdf.

2. A. H. Van de Ven, A. L. Delbecq, and R. Koenig, Jr., "Determinants of Coordination Modes within Organizations," *American Sociological Review* 41, no. 2 (1976): 322–338; R. Foy *et al.*, "Meta-Analysis: Effect of Interactive Communication between Collaborating Primary Care Physicians and Specialists," *Annals of Internal Medicine* 152, no. 4 (16 February 2010): 247–258; J. H. Gittell, R. Seidner, and J. Wimbush, "A Relational Model of How High-Performance Work Systems Work," *Organization Science* 21, no. 2 (March 2010): 490–506.

3. C. Barnard, *The Functions of the Executive* (Cambridge, MA: Harvard University Press, 1938), 82. Barnard's entire statement also refers to the other features of organizations that we describe in Chapter 1, namely that (a) people are willing to contribute their effort to the organization and (b) they have a common purpose.

4. M. T. Hansen, M. L. Mors, and B. Løvås, "Knowledge Sharing in Organizations: Multiple Networks, Multiple Phases," *Academy of Management Journal* 48, no. 5 (2005): 776–793; S. R. Murray and J. Peyrefitte, "Knowledge Type and Communication Media Choice in the Knowledge Transfer Process," *Journal of Managerial Issues* 19, no. 1 (Spring 2007): 111–133; S. L. Hoe and S. L. McShane, "Structural and Informal Knowledge Acquisition and Dissemination in Organizational Learning: An Exploratory Analysis," *Learning Organization* 17, no. 4 (2010): 364–386.

5. J. O'Toole and W. Bennis, "What's Needed Next: A Culture of Candor," *Harvard Business Review* 87, no. 6 (2009): 54–61.

6. N. Ellemers, R. Spears, and B. Doosje, "Self and Social Identity," *Annual Review of Psychology* 53 (2002): 161–186; S. A. Haslam and S. Reicher, "Stressing the Group: Social Identity and the Unfolding Dynamics of Responses to Stress," *Journal of Applied Psychology* 91, no. 5 (2006): 1037–1052; M. T. Gailliot and R. F. Baumeister, "Self-Esteem, Belongingness, and Worldview Validation: Does Belongingness Exert a Unique Influence Upon Self-Esteem?," *Journal of Research in Personality* 41, no. 2 (2007): 327–345.

7. A. M. Saks, K. L. Uggerslev, and N. E. Fassina, "Socialization Tactics and Newcomer Adjustment: A Meta-Analytic Review and Test of a Model," *Journal of Vocational Behavior* 70, no. 3 (2007): 413–446.

8. S. Cohen, "The Pittsburgh Common Cold Studies: Psychosocial Predictors of Susceptibility to Respiratory Infectious Illness," *International Journal of Behavioral Medicine* 12, no. 3 (2005): 123–131; B. N. Uchino, "Social Support and Health: A Review of Physiological Processes Potentially Underlying Links to Disease Outcomes," *Journal of Behavioral Medicine* 29, no. 4 (2006): 377–387.

9. C. E. Shannon and W. Weaver, *The Mathematical Theory of Communication* (Urbana, Il: University of Illinois Press, 1949); R. M. Krauss and S. R. Fussell, "Social Psychological Models of Interpersonal Communication," in *Social Psychology: Handbook of Basic Principles*, ed. E. T. Higgins and A. Kruglanski (New York: Guilford Press, 1996), 655–701.

10. J. R. Carlson and R. W. Zmud, "Channel Expansion Theory and the Experiential Nature of Media Richness Perceptions," *Academy of Management Journal* 42 (April 1999): 153–170.

11. P. Shachaf and N. Hara, "Behavioral Complexity Theory of Media Selection: A Proposed Theory for Global Virtual Teams," *Journal of Information Science* 33 (2007): 63–75.

12. M. Hauben and R. Hauben, "Netizens: On the History and Impact of Usenet and the Internet," *First Monday* 3, no. 8 (August 1998); J. Abbate, (Cambridge, MA: MIT Press, 1999).

13. N. B. Ducheneaut and L. A. Watts, "In Search of Coherence: A Review of E-Mail Research," *Human-Computer Interaction* 20, no. 1–2 (2005): 11–48.

14. W. Lucas, "Effects of E-Mail on the Organization," *European Management Journal* 16, no. 1 (February 1998): 18–30; D. A. Owens, M. A. Neale, and R. I. Sutton, "Technologies of Status Management Status Dynamics in E-Mail Communications," *Research on Managing Groups and Teams* 3 (2000): 205–230; N. B. Ducheneaut, "Ceci N'est Pas Un Objet? Talking About Objects in E-Mail," *Human-Computer Interaction* 18, no. 1–2 (2003): 85–110.

15. N. B. Ducheneaut, "The Social Impacts of Electronic Mail in Organizations: A Case Study of Electronic Power Games Using Communication Genres," *Information,*

Communication, & Society 5, no. 2 (2002): 153–188; N. Panteli, "Richness, Power Cues and Email Text," *Information & Management* 40, no. 2 (2002): 75–86.

16. N. Epley and J. Kruger, "When What You Type Isn't What They Read: The Perseverance of Stereotypes and Expectancies over E-Mail," *Journal of Experimental Social Psychology* 41, no. 4 (2005): 414–422.

17. J. Kruger *et al.*, "Egocentrism over E-Mail: Can We Communicate as Well as We Think?," *Journal of Personality and Social Psychology* 89, no. 6 (2005): 925–936.

18. "Russia Has World's Most Engaged Social Networking Audience." comScore news release for comScore (London: 2 July 2009); "Twitter Usage up 33% over the Summer," (pingdom, 2010) (accessed 16 March 2011); *Email Statistics Report, 2010* (Palo Alto, CA: Radicati Group, 14 April 2010); *2010 Canada Digital Year in Review* (Reston, VA: comScore, 8 March 2011); "Facebook Statistics by Country," (Czech Republic: socialbakers, 2011) (accessed 16 March 2011); Canadian Wireless Telecommunications Association, "Wireless Facts & Figures," (Ottawa: CTWA, 2011) (accessed 16 March 2011).

19. J. B. Walther, "Language and Communication Technology: Introduction to the Special Issue," *Journal of Language and Social Psychology* 23, no. 4 (December 2004): 384–396; J. B. Walther, T. Loh, and L. Granka, "Let Me Count the Ways: The Interchange of Verbal and Nonverbal Cues in Computer-Mediated and Face-to-Face Affinity," *Journal of Language and Social Psychology* 24, no. 1 (March 2005): 36–65; K. Byron, "Carrying Too Heavy a Load? The Communication and Miscommunication of Emotion by Email," *Academy of Management Review* 33, no. 2 (2008): 309–327; J. M. Whalen, P. M. Pexman, and A. J. Gill, "'Should Be Fun—Not!': Incidence and Marking of Nonliteral Language in E-Mail," *Journal of Language and Social Psychology* 28, no. 3 (September 2009): 263–280.

20. Byron, "Carrying Too Heavy a Load? The Communication and Miscommunication of Emotion by Email."

21. G. Hertel, S. Geister, and U. Konradt, "Managing Virtual Teams: A Review of Current Empirical Research," *Human Resource Management Review* 15 (2005): 69–95; H. Lee, "Behavioral Strategies for Dealing with Flaming in an Online Forum," *The Sociological Quarterly* 46, no. 2 (2005): 385–403.

22. D. D. Dawley and W. P. Anthony, "User Perceptions of E-Mail at Work," *Journal of Business and Technical Communication* 17, no. 2 (April 2003): 170–200; G. F. Thomas and C. L. King, "Reconceptualizing E-Mail Overload," *Journal of Business and Technical Communication* 20, no. 3 (July 2006): 252–287; S. Carr, "Email Overload Menace Growing," *Silicon.com*, 12 July 2007.

23. R. D. Waters *et al.*, "Engaging Stakeholders through Social Networking: How Nonprofit Organizations Are Using Facebook," *Public Relations Review* 35, no. 2 (2009): 102–106; J. Cunningham, "New Workers, New Workplace? Getting the Balance Right," *Strategic Direction* 26, no. 1 (2010): 5; A. M. Kaplan and M. Haenlein, "Users of the World, Unite! The Challenges and Opportunities of Social Media," *Business Horizons* 53, no. 1 (2010): 59–68.

24. J. H. Kietzmann *et al.*, "Social Media? Get Serious! Understanding the Functional Building Blocks of Social Media," *Business Horizons* In Press, Corrected Proof (in press).

25. "Atos Origin Abandoning Email," *Computerworld UK*, 9 February 2011; G. Nairn, "The Trouble with Office Email," *Financial Times (London)*, 17 February 2011.

26. S. Holtz, "Open the Door," *Communication World*, September 2010, 26.

27. Towers Watson, *Capitalizing on Effective Communication* (New York: Towers Watson, 4 February 2010).

28. S. Humphries, "Companies Warm up to Social Networks," *Christian Science Monitor*, 8 September 2008, 13; R. Weston, "Facebook: Your Company's Intranet?," *Forbes*, 20 March 2009.

29. L. Z. Tiedens and A. R. Fragale, "Power Moves: Complementarity in Dominant and Submissive Nonverbal Behavior," *Journal of Personality and Social Psychology* 84, no. 3 (2003): 558–568.

30. P. Ekman and E. Rosenberg, *What the Face Reveals: Basic and Applied Studies of Spontaneous Expression Using the Facial Action Coding System* (Oxford, England: Oxford University Press, 1997); P. Winkielman and K. C. Berridge, "Unconscious Emotion," *Current Directions in Psychological Science* 13, no. 3 (2004): 120–123.

31. W. J. Becker and R. Cropanzano, "Organizational Neuroscience: The Promise and Prospects of an Emerging Discipline," *Journal of Organizational Behavior* 31, no. 7 (2010): 1055–1059.

32. E. Hatfield, J. T. Cacioppo, and R. L. Rapson, *Emotional Contagion* (Cambridge, UK: Cambridge University Press, 1993); S. G. Barsade, "The Ripple Effect: Emotional Contagion and Its Influence on Group Behavior," *Administrative Science Quarterly* 47 (December 2002): 644–675; M. Sonnby-Borgstrom, P. Jonsson, and O. Svensson, "Emotional Empathy as Related to Mimicry Reactions at Different Levels of Information Processing," *Journal of Nonverbal Behavior* 27 (Spring 2003): 3–23; S. G. Barsade and D. E. Gibson, "Why Does Affect Matter in Organizations?," *Academy of Management Perspectives* (February 2007): 36–59; S. K. Johnson, "I Second That Emotion: Effects of Emotional Contagion and Affect at Work on Leader and Follower Outcomes," *Leadership Quarterly* 19, no. 1 (2008): 1–19.

33. J. R. Kelly and S. G. Barsade, "Mood and Emotions in Small Groups and Work Teams," *Organizational Behavior and Human Decision Processes* 86 (September 2001): 99–130.

34. J. Fulk, "Social Construction of Communication Technology," *Academy of Management Journal* 36, no. 5 (1993): 921–950; L. K. Treviño, J. Webster, and E. W. Stein, "Making Connections: Complementary Influences on Communication Media Choices, Attitudes, and Use," *Organization Science* 11, no. 2 (2000): 163–182; B. van den Hooff, J. Groot, and S. de Jonge, "Situational Influences on the Use of Communication Technologies," *Journal of Business Communication* 42, no. 1 (January 1, 2005 2005): 4–27; J. W. Turner *et al.*, "Exploring the Dominant Media: How Does Media Use Reflect Organizational Norms and Affect Performance?," *Journal of Business Communication* 43, no. 3 (July 2006): 220–250; M. B. Watson-Manheim and F. Bélanger, "Communication Media Repertoires: Dealing with the Multiplicity of Media Choices," *MIS Quarterly* 31, no. 2 (2007): 267–293.

35. Z. Lee and Y. Lee, "Emailing the Boss: Cultural Implications of Media Choice," *IEEE Transactions on Professional Communication* 52, no. 1 (March 2009): 61–74.

36. R. C. King, "Media Appropriateness: Effects of Experience on Communication Media Choice," *Decision Sciences* 28, no. 4 (1997): 877–910.

37. M. Madden and S. Jones, *Networked Workers*, Pew Internet & American Life Project (Washington, D.C.: Pew Research Center, 24 September 2008).

38. K. Griffiths, "KPMG Sacks 670 Employees by E-Mail," *The Independent (London)*, 5 November 2002, 19; "Shop Worker Sacked by Text Message," *The Post (Claremont/Nedlands, Western Australia)*, 28 July 2007, 1, 78.

39. R. L. Daft and R. H. Lengel, "Information Richness: A New Approach to Managerial Behavior and Organization Design," *Research in Organizational Behavior* 6 (1984): 191–233; R. H. Lengel and R. L. Daft, "The Selection of Communication Media as an Executive Skill," *Academy of Management Executive* 2 (1988): 225–232.

40. R. E. Rice, "Task Analyzability, Use of New Media, and Effectiveness: A Multi-Site Exploration of Media Richness," *Organization Science* 3 (1992): 475–500.

41. J. W. Turner and N. L. Reinsch Jr, "The Business Communicator as Presence Allocator," *Journal of Business Communication* 44, no. 1 (2007): 36–58; N. L. Reinsch Jr., J. W. Turner, and C. H. Tinsley, "Multicommunicating: A Practice Whose Time

Has Come?," *Academy of Management Review* 33, no. 2 (2008): 391–403.

42. "Employer Snapshots: 2008," *Toronto Star*, 13 October 2007; H. Schachter, "Strange but True: Some Staff Meetings Are Actually Efficient," *Globe & Mail*, 23 July 2007.

43. Carlson and Zmud, "Channel Expansion Theory and the Experiential Nature of Media Richness Perceptions"; N. Kock, "Media Richness or Media Naturalness? The Evolution of Our Biological Communication Apparatus and Its Influence on Our Behavior toward E-Communication Tools," *IEEE Transactions on Professional Communication* 48, no. 2 (June 2005): 117–130.

44. V. W. Kupritz and E. Cowell, "Productive Management Communication: Online and Face-to-Face," *Journal of Business Communication* 48, no. 1 (January 2011): 54–82.

45. D. Muller, T. Atzeni, and F. Butera, "Coaction and Upward Social Comparison Reduce the Illusory Conjunction Effect: Support for Distraction-Conflict Theory," *Journal of Experimental Social Psychology* 40, no. 5 (2004): 659–665; L. P. Robert and A. R. Dennis, "Paradox of Richness: A Cognitive Model of Media Choice," *IEEE Transactions on Professional Communication* 48, no. 1 (2005): 10–21.

46. E. V. Wilson, "Perceived Effectiveness of Interpersonal Persuasion Strategies in Computer-Mediated Communication," *Computers in Human Behavior* 19, no. 5 (2003): 537–552; K. Sassenberg, M. Boos, and S. Rabung, "Attitude Change in Face-to-Face and Computer-Mediated Communication: Private Self-Awareness Ad Mediator and Moderator," *European Journal of Social Psychology* 35 (2005): 361–374; P. Di Blasio and L. Milani, "Computer-Mediated Communication and Persuasion: Peripheral vs. Central Route to Opinion Shift," *Computers in Human Behavior* 24, no. 3 (2008): 798–815.

47. Kruger *et al.*, "Egocentrism over E-Mail: Can We Communicate as Well as We Think?".

48. D. Woodruff, "Crossing Culture Divide Early Clears Merger Paths," *Asian Wall Street Journal*, 28 May 2001, 9.

49. R. M. Krauss, "The Psychology of Verbal Communication," in *International Encyclopedia of the Social and Behavioral Sciences*, ed. N. Smelser and P. Baltes (London: Elsevier, 2002), 16161–16165.

50. H. Tsoukas, "The Missing Link: A Transformational View of Metaphors in Organizational Science," *The Academy of Management review* 16, no. 3 (1991): 566–585; G. Morgan, *Images of Organization*, 2nd ed. (Thousand Oaks, CA: Sage, 1997); J. Amernic, R. Craig, and D. Tourish, "The Transformational Leader as Pedagogue, Physician, Architect, Commander, and Saint: Five Root Metaphors in Jack

Welch's Letters to Stockholders of General Electric," *Human Relations* 60, no. 12 (Dec. 2007): 1839–1872.

51. M. Rubini and H. Sigall, "Taking the Edge Off of Disagreement: Linguistic Abstractness and Self-Presentation to a Heterogeneous Audience," *European Journal of Social Psychology* 32 (2002): 343–351.

52. T. Walsh, "Nardelli Brags on Vip Recruits, Game Plan," *Detroit Free Press*, 8 September 2007.

53. D. Goleman, R. Boyatzis, and A. McKee, *Primal Leaders* (Boston: Harvard Business School Press, 2002), 92–95.

54. O'Toole and Bennis, "What's Needed Next: A Culture of Candor."

55. T. Koski, "Reflections on Information Glut and Other Issues in Knowledge Productivity," *Futures* 33 (August 2001): 483–495.

56. A. G. Schick, L. A. Gordon, and S. Haka, "Information Overload: A Temporal Approach," *Accounting, Organizations & Society* 15 (1990): 199–220; A. Edmunds and A. Morris, "The Problem of Information Overload in Business Organisations: A Review of the Literature," *International Journal of Information Management* 20 (2000): 17–28; R. Pennington, "The Effects of Information Overload on Software Project Risk Assessment," *Decision Sciences* 38, no. 3 (August 2007): 489–526.

57. D. C. Thomas and K. Inkson, *Cultural Intelligence: People Skills for Global Business* (San Francisco: Berrett-Koehler, 2004), Chap. 6; D. Welch, L. Welch, and R. Piekkari, "Speaking in Tongues," *International Studies of Management & Organization* 35, no. 1 (Spring 2005): 10–27.

58. S. Ohtaki, T. Ohtaki, and M. D. Fetters, "Doctor-Patient Communication: A Comparison of the USA and Japan," *Family Practice* 20 (June 2003): 276–282; M. Fujio, "Silence During Intercultural Communication: A Case Study," *Corporate Communications* 9, no. 4 (2004): 331–339.

59. T. Hasegawa and W. B. Gudykunst, "Silence in Japan and the United States," *Journal of Cross-Cultural Psychology* 29, no. 5 (Sept. 1998): 668–684.

60. D. C. Barnlund, *Communication Styles of Japanese and Americans: Images and Realities* (Belmont, Calif.: Wadsworth, 1988); H. Yamada, *American and Japanese Business Discourse: A Comparison of Interaction Styles* (Norwood, NJ: Ablex, 1992), Chap. 2.

61. P. Harris and R. Moran, *Managing Cultural Differences* (Houston: Gulf, 1987); H. Blagg, "A Just Measure of Shame?," *British Journal of Criminology* 37 (Autumn 1997): 481–501; R. E. Axtell, *Gestures: The Do's and Taboos of Body Language around the World*, Revised ed. (New York: Wiley, 1998).

62. D. Tannen, *You Just Don't Understand: Men and Women in Conversation* (New

York: Ballentine Books, 1990); D. Tannen, *Talking from 9 to 5* (New York: Avon, 1994); M. Crawford, *Talking Difference: On Gender and Language* (Thousand Oaks, CA: Sage, 1995), 41–44; L. L. Namy, L. C. Nygaard, and D. Sauerteig, "Gender Differences in Vocal Accommodation: The Role of Perception," *Journal of Language and Social Psychology* 21, no. 4 (December 2002): 422–432; H. Itakura and A. B. M. Tsui, "Gender and Conversational Dominance in Japanese Conversation," *Language in Society* 33, no. 2 (2004): 223–248.

63. A. Mulac *et al.*, "Uh-Huh. What's That All About?' Differing Interpretations of Conversational Backchannels and Questions as Sources of Miscommunication across Gender Boundaries," *Communication Research* 25 (December 1998): 641–668; N. M. Sussman and D. H. Tyson, "Sex and Power: Gender Differences in Computer-Mediated Interactions," *Computers in Human Behavior* 16 (2000): 381–394; D. R. Caruso and P. Salovey, *The Emotionally Intelligent Manager* (San Francisco: Jossey-Bass, 2004), p. 23; D. Fallows, *How Women and Men Use the Internet* (Washington, D.C.: Pew Internet and American Life Project, 28 December 2005).

64. M. Hartley, "Women Lead Way in Digital Revolution," *Times-Colonist (Victoria, BC)*, 29 July 2010, B10; A. Abraham, M. Mörn & A. Vollman, "Women on the Web: How Women are Shaping the Internet," June 2010. Retrieved January 17, 2011 http://www.comscore.com/Press_Events/Presentations_Whitepapers/2010/Women_on_the_Web_How_Women_are_Shaping_the_Internet.

65. This quotation is varied slightly from the original translations by: E. Carter, *All the Works of Epictetus, Which Are Now Extant*, 3rd ed., 2 vols., vol. 2 (London: J. and F. Rivington, 1768), 333; T. W. Higginson, *The Works of Epictetus* (Boston: Little, Brown, and Company, 1866), 428.

66. The three components of listening discussed here are based on several recent studies in the field of marketing, including: S. B. Castleberry, C. D. Shepherd, and R. Ridnour, "Effective Interpersonal Listening in the Personal Selling Environment: Conceptualization, Measurement, and Nomological Validity," *Journal of Marketing Theory and Practice* 7 (Winter 1999): 30–38; L. B. Comer and T. Drollinger, "Active Empathetic Listening and Selling Success: A Conceptual Framework," *Journal of Personal Selling & Sales Management* 19 (Winter 1999): 15–29; K. de Ruyter and M. G. M. Wetzels, "The Impact of Perceived Listening Behavior in Voice-to-Voice Service Encounters," *Journal of Service Research* 2 (February 2000): 276–284.

67. A. Leaman and B. Bordass, "Productivity in Buildings: The Killer Variables," *Building Research & Information* 27, no. 1 (1999): 4–19; T. J. Allen, "Architecture and

Communication among Product Development Engineers," *California Management Review* 49, no. 2 (Winter 2007): 23–41; F. Becker, "Organizational Ecology and Knowledge Networks," *California Management Review* 49, no. 2 (Winter 2007): 42–61.

68. M. Gardner, "Democratic Principles Make Businesses More Transparent," *Christian Science Monitor*, 19 March 2007, 13.

69. G. Evans and D. Johnson, "Stress and Open-Office Noise," *Journal of Applied Psychology* 85 (2000): 779–783; F. Russo, "My Kingdom for a Door," *Time Magazine*, 23 October 2000, B1.

70. D. Waisberg, "Quiet Please!...We're Working," *National Post*, 30 May 2007.

71. S. P. Means, "Playing at Pixar," *Salt Lake Tribune (Utah)*, 30 May 2003, D1; G. Whipp, "Swimming against the Tide," *Daily News of Los Angeles*, 30 May 2003, U6.

72. C. Wagner and A. Majchrzak, "Enabling Customer-Centricity Using Wikis and the Wiki Way," *Journal of Management Information Systems* 23, no. 3 (2006): 17–43; R. B. Ferguson, "Build a Web 2.0 Platform and Employees Will Use It," *eWeek*, 20 June 2007; C. Karena, "Working the Wiki Way," *Sydney Morning Herald*, 6 March 2007.

73. T. Fenton, "Inside the Worldblu List: 1–800-Got-Junk?'s CEO on Why 'Being Democratic Is Extremely Important to Maintaining Our Competitive Advantage,'" (Atlanta: WorldBlu, 3 January 2008). The original term is "management by *wandering* around, but this has been replaced with "walking around" over the years. See: W. Ouchi, *Theory Z* (New York: Avon Books, 1981), 176–177; T. Peters and R. Waterman, *In Search of Excellence* (New York: Harper and Row, 1982), p. 122.

74. T. Hsieh, "How Twitter Can Make You a Better (and Happier) Person," (Las Vegas, 2009), http://blogs.zappos.com/blogs/ceo-and-coo-blog (accessed 17 March 2011); J. Vijayan, "Staying on Message," *Computerworld*, 19 October 2009; "Social Media Training Programs: Different Approaches, Common Goals," *PR News*, 4 January 2010; A. Bryant, "On a Scale of 1 to 10, How Weird Are You?," *New York Times*, 10 January 2010.

75. R. Rousos, "Trust in Leaders Lacking at Utility," *The Ledger (Lakeland, Fl)*, 29 July 2003, B1; B. Whitworth and B. Riccomini, "Management Communication: Unlocking Higher Employee Performance," *Communication World*, Mar-Apr 2005, 18–21.

76. K. Davis, "Management Communication and the Grapevine," *Harvard Business Review* 31 (September-October 1953): 43–49; W. L. Davis and J. R. O'Connor, "Serial Transmission of Information: A Study of the Grapevine," *Journal of Applied Communication Research* 5 (1977): 61–72.

77. H. Mintzberg, *The Structuring of Organizations* (Englewood Cliffs, N.J.: Prentice Hall, 1979), 46–53; D. Krackhardt and J. R. Hanson, "Informal Networks: The Company Behind the Chart," *Harvard Business Review* 71 (July-August 1993): 104–111.

78. C. J. Walker and C. A. Beckerle, "The Effect of State Anxiety on Rumor Transmission," *Journal of Social Behaviour & Personality* 2 (August 1987): 353–360; R. L. Rosnow, "Inside Rumor: A Personal Journey," *American Psychologist* 46 (May 1991): 484–496; M. Noon and R. Delbridge, "News from Behind My Hand: Gossip in Organizations," *Organization Studies* 14 (1993): 23–36.

79. N. Nicholson, "Evolutionary Psychology: Toward a New View of Human Nature and Organizational Society," *Human Relations* 50 (September 1997): 1053–1078; R. F. Baumeister, L. Zhang, and K. D. Vohs, "Gossip as Cultural Learning," *Review of General Psychology* 8, no. 2 (2004): 111–121; E. K. Foster, "Research on Gossip: Taxonomy, Methods, and Future Directions," *Review of General Psychology* 8, no. 2 (2004): 78–99.

CHAPTER 10

1. Douglas Quan, "RCMP Making Strides Toward Reform: Elliott," *Ottawa Citizen*, 8 January 2011, A3; L. Stone, "Elliott Adjusting Leadership Style," *Leader-Post*, 26 November 2010, B12; J. O'Neill, "RCMP Boss Claims Support," *Leader-Post*, 22 October 2010, C11; L. Corbella, "A Cure Much Worse Than The Disease," Leader-Post, 12 October 2010, B6; J. Wingrove, "Defiant RCMP Chief Says He Won't Quit," *The Globe and Mail*, 21 August 2010, A7.

2. J. R. P. French and B. Raven, "The Bases of Social Power," in *Studies in Social Power*, ed. D. Cartwright (Ann Arbor, Mich: University of Michigan Press, 1959), 150–167; A. D. Galinsky *et al.*, "Power and Perspectives Not Taken," *Psychological Science* 17, no. 12 (2006): 1068–1074. Also see: H. Mintzberg, *Power in and around Organizations* (Englewood Cliffs, NJ: Prentice Hall, 1983), Chap. 1; J. Pfeffer, *Managing with Power* (Boston: Harvard Business University Press, 1992), 17, 30; A. Guinote and T. K. Vescio, "Introduction: Power in Social Psychology," in *The Social Psychology of Power*, ed. A. Guinote and T. K. Vescio (New York: Guilford Press, 2010), 1–18.

3. R. A. Dahl, "The Concept of Power," *Behavioral Science* 2 (1957): 201–218; R. M. Emerson, "Power-Dependence Relations," *American Sociological Review* 27 (1962): 31–41; A. M. Pettigrew, *The Politics of Organizational Decision-Making* (London: Tavistock, 1973).

4. J. Pfeffer and G. R. Salancik, *The External Control of Organizations* (New York: Harper & Row, 1978), 52–54; R. Gulati and M. Sytch, "Dependence Asymmetry and Joint Dependence in Interorganizational Relationships: Effects of Embeddedness on a Manufacturer's Performance in Pro-

curement Relationships," *Administrative Science Quarterly* 52, no. 1 (2007): 32–69.

5. French and Raven, "The Bases of Social Power"; P. Podsakoff and C. Schreisheim, "Field Studies of French and Raven's Bases of Power: Critique, Analysis, and Suggestions for Future Research," *Psychological Bulletin* 97 (1985): 387–411; P. P. Carson and K. D. Carson, "Social Power Bases: A Meta-Analytic Examination of Interrelationships and Outcomes," *Journal of Applied Social Psychology* 23 (1993): 1150–1169. The alternative models of power bases are reviewed in a recent dissertation by Heinemann, who points out that most of them parallel French and Raven's list. See: P. Heinemann, *Power Bases and Informational Influence Strategies: A Behavioral Study on the Use of Management Accounting Information* (Wiesbaden, Germany: Deutscher Universitäts-Verlag, 2008). Raven subsequently proposed information power as a sixth source of power. We present this later as a derivation of the five sources of power rather than as a distinct sixth power base.

6. C. Barnard, *The Function of the Executive* (Cambridge, MA: Harvard University Press, 1938), 167–170; C. Hardy and S. R. Clegg, "Some Dare Call It Power," in *Handbook of Organization Studies*, ed. S. R. Clegg, C. Hardy, and W. R. Nord (London: Sage, 1996), 622–641.

7. B. Crumley, "Game of Death: France's Shocking Tv Experiment," *Time*, 17 March 2010; R. L. Parry, "Contestants Turn Torturers in French Tv Experiment," *Yahoo! News*, 16 March 2010.

8. A. I. Shahin and P. L. Wright, "Leadership in the Context of Culture: An Egyptian Perspective," *Leadership & Organization Development Journal* 25, no. 5/6 (2004): 499–511; Y. J. Huo *et al.*, "Leadership and the Management of Conflicts in Diverse Groups: Why Acknowledging Versus Neglecting Subgroup Identity Matters," *European Journal of Social Psychology* 35, no. 2 (2005): 237–254.

9. B. H. Raven, "Kurt Lewin Address: Influence, Power, Religion, and the Mechanisms of Social Control," *Journal of Social Issues* 55 (Spring 1999): 161–186.

10. A. W. Gouldner, "The Norm of Reciprocity: A Preliminary Statement," *American Sociological Review* 25 (1960): 161–178.

11. G. Yukl and C. M. Falbe, "Importance of Different Power Sources in Downward and Lateral Relations," *Journal of Applied Psychology* 76 (1991): 416–423; Raven, "Kurt Lewin Address: Influence, Power, Religion, and the Mechanisms of Social Control."

12. P. L. Dawes, D. Y. Lee, and G. R. Dowling, "Information Control and Influence in Emergent Buying Centers," *Journal Of Marketing* 62, no. 3 (July 1998): 55–68; D. Willer, "Power-at-a-Distance," *Social*

Forces 81, no. 4 (2003): 1295–1334; D. J. Brass *et al.*, "Taking Stock of Networks and Organizations: A Multilevel Perspective," *Academy of Management Journal* 47, no. 6 (December 2004): 795–817.

13. L. S. Sya, "Flying to Greater Heights," *New Sunday Times (Kuala Lumpur)*, 31 July 2005, 14; M. Bolch, "Rewarding the Team," *HRMagazine*, February 2007, 91–93.

14. J. M. Peiro and J. L. Melia, "Formal and Informal Interpersonal Power in Organisations: Testing a Bifactorial Model of Power in Role-Sets," *Applied Psychology* 52, no. 1 (2003): 14–35.

15. C. R. Hinings *et al.*, "Structural Conditions of Intraorganizational Power," *Administrative Science Quarterly* 19 (1974): 22–44. Also see: C. S. Saunders, "The Strategic Contingency Theory of Power: Multiple Perspectives," *The Journal of Management Studies* 27 (1990): 1–21.

16. C. Russo, "Dodge Charger Case Study," *iMediaConnection*, 17 January 2006; D. Brady, "The It Girl," *Canadian Business*, 5 November 2007, 43–46; A. McMains, "TBWA Confirms DeCourcy Hire," *AdWeek*, 21 August 2007, www.adweek.com/aw/national/article_display, jsp?vnu_content_id=1003628468; Maureen Morrison, "Havas Takes Majority Stake in Colleen DeCourcy's Startup," *Advertising Age*, 24 January 2011.

17. R. B. Cialdini and N. J. Goldstein, "Social Influence: Compliance and Conformity," *Annual Review of Psychology* 55 (2004): 591–621.

18. C. Perkel, "It's Not Csi," *Canadian Press*, 10 November 2007. The doctor-nurse study is reported in: C. K. Hofling *et al.*, "An Experimental Study in Nurse-Physician Relationships," *Journal of Nervous and Mental Disease* 143, no. 2 (1966): 171–177. Writing on evidence-based management also warns against blindly following the advice of management gurus. See: J. Pfeffer and R. I. Sutton, *Hard Facts, Dangerous Half-Truths, and Total Nonsense* (Boston: Harvard Business School Press, 2006), 45–46.

19. K. Miyahara, "Charisma: From Weber to Contemporary Sociology," *Sociological Inquiry* 53, no. 4 (Fall 1983): 368–388; J. D. Kudisch and M. L. Poteet, "Expert Power, Referent Power, and Charisma: Toward the Resolution of a Theoretical Debate," *Journal of Business & Psychology* 10 (Winter 1995): 177–195; D. Ladkin, "The Enchantment of the Charismatic Leader: Charisma Reconsidered as Aesthetic Encounter," *Leadership* 2, no. 2 (May 2006): 165–179.

20. D. J. Hickson *et al.*, "A Strategic Contingencies' Theory of Intraorganizational Power," *Administrative Science Quarterly* 16 (1971): 216–227; Hinings *et al.*, "Struc-

tural Conditions of Intraorganizational Power"; R. M. Kanter, "Power Failure in Management Circuits," *Harvard Business Review* (July-August 1979): 65–75.

21. Hickson *et al.*, "A Strategic Contingencies' Theory of Intraorganizational Power"; J. D. Hackman, "Power and Centrality in the Allocation of Resources in Colleges and Universities," *Administrative Science Quarterly* 30 (1985): 61–77; D. J. Brass and M. E. Burkhardt, "Potential Power and Power Use: An Investigation of Structure and Behavior," *Academy of Management Journal* 36 (1993): 441–470.

22. S. D. Harrington and B. Ivry, "For Commuters, a Day to Adapt," *The Record (Bergen, N.J.)*, 21 December 2005, A1; S. McCarthy, "Transit Strike Cripples New York," *Globe & Mail (Toronto)*, 21 December 2005, A17.

23. Kanter, "Power Failure in Management Circuits"; B. E. Ashforth, "The Experience of Powerlessness in Organizations," *Organizational Behavior and Human Decision Processes* 43 (1989): 207–242; L. Holden, "European Managers: HRM and an Evolving Role," *European Business Review* 12 (2000).

24. D. Hambrick, C. and E. Abrahamson, "Assessing Managerial Discretion across Industries: A Multimethod Approach," *Academy of Management journal* 38, no. 5 (1995): 1427–1441; M. A. Carpenter and B. R. Golden, "Perceived Managerial Discretion: A Study of Cause and Effect," *Strategic Management Journal* 18, no. 3 (1997): 187–206.

25. R. Madell, "Ground Floor," *Pharmaceutical Executive (Women in Pharma Supplement)*, June 2000, 24–31.

26. S. Wasserman and K. Faust, *Social Network Analysis: Methods and Applications, Structural Analysis in the Social Sciences* (Cambridge, UK: Cambridge University Press, 1994), Chap. 1; Brass *et al.*, "Taking Stock of Networks and Organizations: A Multilevel Perspective."

27. M. Grossetti, "Where Do Social Relations Come From?: A Study of Personal Networks in the Toulouse Area of France," *Social Networks* 27, no. 4 (2005): 289–300.

28. Y. Fan, "Questioning Guanxi: Definition, Classification, and Implications," *International Business Review* 11 (2002): 543–561; W. R. Vanhonacker, "When Good Guanxi Turns Bad," *Harvard Business Review* 82, no. 4 (April 2004): 18–19; R. J. Taormina and J. H. Gao, "A Research Model for Guanxi Behavior: Antecedents, Measures, and Outcomes of Chinese Social Networking," *Social Science Research* 39, no. 6 (November 2010): 1195–1212.

29. D. Krackhardt and J. R. Hanson, "Informal Networks: The Company Behind the Chart," *Harvard Business Review* 71 (July-August 1993): 104–111; A. Portes,

"Social Capital: Its Origins and Applications in Modern Society," *Annual Review of Sociology* 24 (1998): 1–24.

30. P. S. Adler and S.-W. Kwon, "Social Capital: Prospects for a New Concept," *Academy of Management Review* 27, no. 1 (2002): 17–40.

31. R. F. Chisholm, *Developing Network Organizations: Learning from Practice and Theory* (Reading MA: Addison Wesley Longman, 1998); W. S. Chow and L. S. Chan, "Social Network, Social Trust and Shared Goals in Organizational Knowledge Sharing," *Information & Management* 45, no. 7 (2008): 458–465.

32. R. S. Burt, *Structural Holes: The Social Structure of Competition* (Cambridge, MA: Harvard University Press, 1992).

33. M. T. Rivera, S. B. Soderstrom, and B. IUzzi, "Dynamics of Dyads in Social Networks: Assortative, Relational, and Proximity Mechanisms," *Annual Review of Sociology* 36 (2010): 91–115.

34. R. Cross and R. J. Thomas, *Driving Results through Social Networks: How Top Organizations Leverage Networks for Performance and Growth* (San Francisco: Jossey-Bass, 2009); R. McDermott and D. Archibald, "Harnessing Your Staff's Informal Networks," *Harvard Business Review* 88, no. 3 (2010): 82–89.

35. M. Kilduff and D. Krackhardt, *Interpersonal Networks in Organizations: Cognition, Personality, Dynamics, and Culture* (New York: Cambridge University Press, 2008).

36. D. Bushey and M. Joll, "Social Network Analysis Comes to Raytheon," *The Monitor (Raytheon news magazine)* 2006; J. McGregor, "The Office Chart That Really Counts," *BusinessWeek*, 27 February 2006, 48; J. Reingold, "What's Your Oq?," *Fortune*, 23 July 2007, 98–106; t. Cox, "Map Quest," *Quality Progress*, May 2008, 44.

37. N. B. Ellison, C. Steinfield, and C. Lampe, "The Benefits of Facebook "Friends:" Social Capital and College Students' Use of Online Social Network Sites," *Journal of Computer-Mediated Communication* 12, no. 4 (2007): 1143–1168.

38. M. S. Granovetter, "The Strength of Weak Ties," *American Journal of Sociology* 78 (1973): 1360–1380; B. Erickson, "Social Networks," in *The Blackwell Companion to Sociology*, ed. J. R. Blau (Malden, MA: Blackwell Publishing, 2004), 314–326.

39. B. Uzzi and S. Dunlap, "How to Build Your Network," *Harvard Business Review* 83, no. 12 (2005): 53–60.

40. S. C. de Janasz and M. L. Forret, "Learning the Art of Networking: A Critical Skill for Enhancing Social Capital and Career Success," *Journal of Management Education* 32, no. 5 (October 1, 2008): 629–650.

41. A. Mehra, M. Kilduff, and D. J. Brass, "The Social Networks of High and Low Self-Monitors: Implications for Workplace Performance," *Administrative Science Quarterly* 46 (March 2001): 121–146.

42. Burt, *Structural Holes: The Social Structure of Competition.*

43. B. R. Ragins and E. Sundstrom, "Gender and Power in Organizations: A Longitudinal Perspective," *Psychological Bulletin* 105 (1989): 51–88; M. Linehan, "Barriers to Women's Participation in International Management," *European Business Review* 13 (2001).

44. A. DeFelice, "Climbing to the Top," *Accounting Technology* 24, no. 1 (2008): 12–18.

45. D. M. McCracken, "Winning the Talent War for Women: Sometimes It Takes a Revolution," *Harvard Business Review* (November-December 2000): 159–167.

46. J. Lammers, J. I. Stoker, and D. A. Stapel, "Differentiating Social and Personal Power: Opposite Effects on Stereotyping, but Parallel Effects on Behavioral Approach Tendencies," *Psychological Science* 20, no. 12 (2009): 1543–1549.

47. D. Keltner, D. H. Gruenfeld, and C. Anderson, "Power, Approach, and Inhibition," *Psychological Review* 110, no. 2 (2003): 265–284; B. Simpson and C. Borch, "Does Power Affect Perception in Social Networks? Two Arguments and an Experimental Test," *Social Psychology Quarterly* 68, no. 3 (2005): 278–287; Galinsky *et al.*, "Power and Perspectives Not Taken."

48. K. Atuahene-Gima and H. Li, "Marketing's Influence Tactics in New Product Development: A Study of High Technology Firms in China," *Journal of Product Innovation Management* 17 (2000): 451–470; A. Somech and A. Drach-Zahavy, "Relative Power and Influence Strategy: The Effects of Agent/Target Organizational Power on Superiors' Choices of Influence Strategies," *Journal of Organizational Behavior* 23 (2002): 167–179.

49. D. Kipnis, S. M. Schmidt, and I. Wilkinson, "Intraorganizational Influence Tactics: Explorations in Getting One's Way," *Journal of Applied Psychology* 65 (1980): 440–452; A. Rao and K. Hashimoto, "Universal and Culturally Specific Aspects of Managerial Influence: A Study of Japanese Managers," *Leadership Quarterly* 8 (1997): 295–312; L. A. McFarland, A. M. Ryan, and S. D. Kriska, "Field Study Investigation of Applicant Use of Influence Tactics in a Selection Interview," *Journal of Psychology* 136 (July 2002): 383–398.

50. Cialdini and Goldstein, "Social Influence: Compliance and Conformity."

51. Rao and Hashimoto, "Universal and Culturally Specific Aspects of Managerial Influence." Silent authority as an influ-

ence tactic in non-Western cultures is also discussed in: S. F. Pasa, "Leadership Influence in a High Power Distance and Collectivist Culture," *Leadership & Organization Development Journal* 21 (2000): 414–426.

52. "Be Part of the Team If You Want to Catch the Eye," *Birmingham Post (UK)*, 31 August 2000, 14; S. Maitlis, "Taking It from the Top: How CEOs Influence (and Fail to Influence) Their Boards," *Organization Studies* 25, no. 8 (2004): 1275–1311.

53. A. T. Cobb, "Toward the Study of Organizational Coalitions: Participant Concerns and Activities in a Simulated Organizational Setting," *Human relations* 44 (1991): 1057–1079; E. A. Mannix, "Organizations as Resource Dilemmas: The Effects of Power Balance on Coalition Formation in Small Groups," *Organizational Behavior and Human Decision Processes* 55 (1993): 1–22; D. J. Terry, M. A. Hogg, and K. M. White, "The Theory of Planned Behavior: Self-Identity, Social Identity and Group Norms," *British Journal of Social Psychology* 38 (September 1999): 225–244.

54. A. P. Brief, *Attitudes in and around Organizations* (Thousand Oaks, CA: Sage, 1998), 69–84; D. J. O'Keefe, *Persuasion: Theory and Research* (Thousand Oaks, CA: Sage Publications, 2002).

55. These and other features of message content in persuasion are detailed in: R. Petty and J. Cacioppo, *Attitudes and Persuasion: Classic and Contemporary Approaches* (Dubuque, Iowa: W. C. Brown, 1981); M. Pfau, E. A. Szabo, and J. Anderson, "The Role and Impact of Affect in the Process of Resistance to Persuasion," *Human Communication Research* 27 (April 2001): 216–252; O'Keefe, *Persuasion: Theory and Research*, Chap. 9; R. Buck *et al.*, "Emotion and Reason in Persuasion: Applying the Ari Model and the Casc Scale," *Journal of Business Research* 57, no. 6 (2004): 647–656; W. D. Crano and R. Prislin, "Attitudes and Persuasion," *Annual Review of Psychology* 57 (2006): 345–374.

56. N. Rhodes and W. Wood, "Self-Esteem and Intelligence Affect Influenceability: The Mediating Role of Message Reception," *Psychological Bulletin* 111, no. 1 (1992): 156–171.

57. D. Strutton and L. E. Pelton, "Effects of Ingratiation on Lateral Relationship Quality within Sales Team Settings," *Journal of Business Research* 43 (1998): 1–12; R. Vonk, "Self-Serving Interpretations of Flattery: Why Ingratiation Works," *Journal of Personality and Social Psychology* 82 (2002): 515–526.

58. C. A. Higgins, T. A. Judge, and G. R. Ferris, "Influence Tactics and Work Outcomes: A Meta-Analysis," *Journal of Organizational Behavior* 24 (2003): 90–106.

59. D. Strutton, L. E. Pelton, and J. Tanner, J. F., "Shall We Gather in the Garden: The

Effect of Ingratiatory Behaviors on Buyer Trust in Salespeople," *Industrial Marketing Management* 25 (1996): 151–162; J. O' Neil, "An Investigation of the Sources of Influence of Corporate Public Relations Practitioners," *Public Relations Review* 29 (June 2003): 159–169.

60. M. C. Bolino and W. H. Tunley, "More Than One Way to Make an Impression: Exploring Profiles of Impression Management," *Journal of Management* 29 (2003): 141–160.

61. T. Peters, "The Brand Called You," *Fast Company*, August 1997, http://www.fastcompany.com/magazine/10/brandyou.html; J. Sills, "Becoming Your Own Brand," *Psychology Today* 41, no. 1 (February 2008): 62–63.

62. W. Immen, "Employer, Will You Marry Me?," *Globe & Mail (Toronto)*, 24 March 2010, B21.

63. S. L. McShane, "Applicant Misrepresentations in Résumés and Interviews in Canada," *Labor Law Journal* (January 1994): 15–24; S. Romero and M. Richtel, "Second Chance," *New York Times*, 5 March 2001, C1; P. Sabatini, "Fibs on Résumés Commonplace," *Pittsburgh Post-Gazette*, 24 February 2006.

64. J. Laucius, "Internet Guru's Credentials a True Work of Fiction," *Ottawa Citizen*, 12 June 2001.

65. C. M. Falbe and G. Yukl, "Consequences for Managers of Using Single Influence Tactics and Combinations of Tactics," *Academy of Management Journal* 35 (1992): 638–652.

66. R. C. Ringer and R. W. Boss, "Hospital Professionals' Use of Upward Influence Tactics," *Journal of Managerial Issues* 12 (2000): 92–108.

67. G. Blickle, "Do Work Values Predict the Use of Intraorganizational Influence Strategies?," *Journal of Applied Social Psychology* 30, no. 1 (January 2000): 196–205; P. P. Fu *et al.*, "The Impact of Societal Cultural Values and Individual Social Beliefs on the Perceived Effectiveness of Managerial Influence Strategies: A Meso Approach," *Journal Of International Business Studies* 35, no. 4 (July 2004): 284–305.

68. This definition of organizational politics has become the dominant perspective over the past 15 years. See: G. R. Ferris and K. M. Kacmar, "Perceptions of Organizational Politics," *Journal of Management* 18 (1992): 93–116; R. Cropanzano *et al.*, "The Relationship of Organizational Politics and Support to Work Behaviors, Attitudes, and Stress," *Journal of Organizational Behavior* 18 (1997): 159–180; E. Vigoda, "Stress-Related Aftermaths to Workplace Politics: The Relationships among Politics, Job Distress, and Aggressive Behavior in Organizations," *Journal of Organizational Behavior* 23 (2002): 571–591. However, organizational politics was previously viewed as influence tactics outside

the formal role that could be either selfish or altruistic. This older definition is less common today, possibly because it is incongruent with popular views of politics and because it overlaps too much with the concept of influence. For the older perspective of organizational politics, see: J. Pfeffer, *Power in Organizations* (Boston: Pitman, 1981); Mintzberg, *Power in and around Organizations*.

69. K. M. Kacmar and R. A. Baron, "Organizational Politics: The State of the Field, Links to Related Processes, and an Agenda for Future Research," in *Research in Personnel and Human Resources Management*, ed. G. R. Ferris (Greenwich, CT: JAI Press, 1999), 1–39; Vigoda, "Stress-Related Aftermaths to Workplace Politics: The Relationships among Politics, Job Distress, and Aggressive Behavior in Organizations"; C.-H. Chang, C. C. Rosen, and P. E. Levy, "The Relationship between Perceptions of Organizational Politics and Employee Attitudes, Strain, and Behavior: A Meta-Analytic Examination," *Academy of Management Journal* 52, no. 4 (2009): 779–801.

70. C. Hardy, *Strategies for Retrenchment and Turnaround: The Politics of Survival* (Berlin: Walter de Gruyter, 1990), Chap. 14; M. C. Andrews and K. M. Kacmar, "Discriminating among Organizational Politics, Justice, and Support," *Journal of Organizational Behavior* 22 (2001): 347–366.

71. "The 2008 Wasting Time at Work Survey Reveals a Record Number of People Waste Time at Work." Salary.com news release (2008); "When It Comes to Red Tape, Many Canadian Employers Might Just Need to Cut It: RBC Study," CNW news release for RBC (Toronto: 23 January 2008); "Survey: More Than One-Quarter of Employees Have Had Ideas Stolen at Work," PR Newswire news release for OfficeTeam (8 October 2009); "Survey: Majority of Employees Have Had Ideas Stolen at Work," Canada NewsWire news release for OfficeTeam (Toronto: 10 November 2009); J. Gifford *et al.*, *The Management Agenda 2009* (Horsham, UK: Roffey Park Institute, 13 January 2009).

72. "Dark Theory of Alycia E-Mail," *New York Post*, 5 June 2008, 12; M. Klein, "Lane Suit Details Mendte Gossip," *Philadelphia Inquirer*, 24 September 2008, B01; M. Klein, "Alycia Lane Sues Cbs3," *Philadelphia Inquirer*, 20 June 2008, B01; M. Klein, "Mendte Could Push Either Way," *Philadelphia Inquirer*, 13 July 2008, A01; P. Walters, "Fired Phillu Tv Anchor Charged in E-Mail Scandal," *Associated Press Newswires*, 22 July 2008.

73. S. Blazejewski and W. Dorow, "Managing Organizational Politics for Radical Change: The Case of Beiersdorf-Lechia S.A., Poznan," *Journal of World Business* 38 (August 2003): 204–223.

74. L. W. Porter, R. W. Allen, and H. L. Angle, "The Politics of Upward Influence in Organizations," *Research in Organizational Behavior* 3 (1981): 120–122; R. J. House, "Power and Personality in Complex Organizations," *Research in Organizational Behavior* 10 (1988): 305–357.

75. R. Christie and F. Geis, *Studies in Machiavellianism* (New York: Academic Press, 1970); S. M. Farmer *et al.*, "Putting Upward Influence Strategies in Context," *Journal of Organizational Behavior* 18 (1997): 17–42; K. S. Sauleya and A. G. Bedeian, "Equity Sensitivity: Construction of a Measure and Examination of Its Psychometric Properties," *Journal of Management* 26 (September 2000): 885–910.

76. G. R. Ferris *et al.*, "Perceptions of Organizational Politics: Prediction, Stress-Related Implications, and Outcomes," *Human Relations* 49 (1996): 233–263.

CHAPTER 11

1. A. Morrow, "Deal Reached in 18-month Labrador Nickel Strike," *Globe & Mail*, 27 January 2011, A8; "Ontario Vale Workers Vote To Approve New Contract," *The Canadian Press*, 8 July 2010; T. Van Alphen, "Clash of Cultures Blamed In Vale Inco Strike," *Toronto Star*, 27 March 2010; Sudbury Northern Life Staff, "Vale Inco Strike—The Sounds Of Silence," *Northern Life.ca*, 20 January 2010; N. Stewart, Effects of Lengthy Vale Inco Strike Felt Through the North," *Northern Ontario Business*, 11 December 2009; "Vale Inco Retraining Workers To Replace Striking Colleagues," *CBC News*, 11 November 2009; A. Hoffman, "Strike Caps Restructuring at Vale Inco," *Globe & Mail*, 26 August 2009; B. Bouw, "Vale Inco Nickel Workers To Vote On Contract," *Globe & Mail*, 8 July 2010, B3.

2. D. Tjosvold, *Working Together to Get Things Done* (Lexington, Mass.: Lexington, 1986), 114–115; J. A. Wall and R. R. Callister, "Conflict and Its Management," *Journal of Management*, 21 (1995): 515–558; D. Tjosvold, "Defining Conflict and Making Choices About Its Management," *International Journal of Conflict Management* 17, no. 2 (2006): 87–95; M. A. Rahim, *Managing Conflict in Organizations*, 4th ed. (New Brunswick, NJ: Transaction Publishers, 2011), 15–17.

3. For example, see: L. Urwick, *The Elements of Administration*, 2nd ed. (London: Pitman, 1947); C. Argyris, "The Individual and Organization: Some Problems of Mutual Adjustment," *Administrative Science Quarterly* 2, no. 1 (1957): 1–24; K. E. Boulding, "Organization and Conflict," *Conflict Resolution* 1, no. 2 (June 1957): 122–134; R. R. Blake, H. A. Shepard, and J. S. Mouton, *Managing Intergroup Conflict in Industry* (Houston: Gulf Publishing, 1964).

4. Rahim, *Managing Conflict in Organizations*.

5. C. K. W. De Dreu and L. R. Weingart, "A Contingency Theory of Task Conflict and Performance in Groups and Organizational Teams," in *International Handbook of Organizational Teamwork and Cooperative Working*, ed. M. A. West, D. Tjosvold, and K. G. Smith (Chicester, UK: John Wiley & Sons, 2003), 151–166; K. A. Jehn and C. Bendersky, "Intragroup Conflict in Organizations: A Contingency Perspective on the Conflict-Outcome Relationship," *Research in Organizational Behavior* 25 (2003): 187–242.

6. *Workplace Conflict and How Businesses Can Harness It to Thrive*, CPP Global Human Capital Report (Mountain View, CA: CPP, Inc, July 2008).

7. Rahim, *Managing Conflict in Organizations*, 6–7.

8. J. Dewey, *Human Nature and Conduct: An Introduction to Social Psychology* (New York: Holt, 1922), 300.

9. M. P. Follett, "Constructive Conflict," in *Dynamic Administration: The Collected Papers of Mary Parker Follett*, ed. H. C. Metcalf and L. Urwick (Bath, UK: Management Publications Trust, 1941), 30–49.

10. M. A. Rahim, "Toward a Theory of Managing Organizational Conflict," *International Journal of Conflict Management* 13, no. 3 (2002): 206–235; M. Duarte and G. Davies, "Testing the Conflict-Performance Assumption in Business-to-Business Relationships," *Industrial Marketing Management* 32 (2003): 91–99. Although the 1970s marked a point when the benefits conflict became widely acknowledged, this view was expressed earlier by some writers. See: L. A. Coser, *The Functions of Social Conflict* (New York: Free Press, 1956); J. A. Litterer, "Conflict in Organization: A Re-Examination," *Academy of Management Journal* 9 (1966): 178–186; H. Assael, "Constructive Role of Interorganizational Conflict," *Administrative Science Quarterly* 14, no. 4 (1969): 573–582.

11. P. J. Carnevale, "Creativity in the Outcomes of Conflict," in *The Handbook of Conflict Resolution: Theory and Practice*, ed. M. Deutsch, P. T. Coleman, and E. C. Marcus, 2nd ed. (San Francisco: Jossey-Bass, 2006), 414–435.

12. K. M. Eisenhardt, J. L. Kahwajy, and L. J. Bourgeois III, "How Management Teams Can Have a Good Fight," *Harvard Business Review* (July-August 1997): 77–85; K. M. Eisenhardt, J. L. Kahwajy, and L. J. Bourgeois III, "Conflict and Strategic Choice: How Top Management Teams Disagree," *California Management Review* 39 (Winter 1997): 42–62; T. Greitemeyer *et al.*, "Information Sampling and Group Decision Making: The Effects of an Advocacy Decision Procedure and Task Experience," *Journal of Experimental Psychology-Applied* 12, no. 1 (Mar 2006): 31–42; U. Klocke,

"How to Improve Decision Making in Small Groups: Effects of Dissent and Training Interventions," *Small Group Research* 38, no. 3 (June 2007): 437–468.

13. H. Guetzkow and J. Gyr, "An Analysis of Conflict in Decision-Making Groups," *Human Relations* 7, no. 3 (Aug. 1954): 367–382; L. H. Pelled, K. M. Eisenhardt, and K. R. Xin, "Exploring the Black Box: An Analysis of Work Group Diversity, Conflict, and Performance," *Administrative Science Quarterly* 44 (March 1999): 1–28; Jehn and Bendersky, "Intragroup Conflict in Organizations." The notion of two types of conflict dates back to Georg Simmel, who described two types of conflict: one with a personal and subjective goal, the other which has an impersonal and objective quality. See: Coser, *The Functions of Social Conflict*, 112. Contemporary scholars use various labels for constructive and relationship conflict. We have avoided the "cognitive" and "affective" conflict labels because cognitions and emotions are interconnected processes in all human activity.

14. C. K. W. De Dreu, "When Too Little or Too Much Hurts: Evidence for a Curvilinear Relationship between Task Conflict and Innovation in Teams," *Journal of Management* 32, no. 1 (Feb. 2006): 83–107.

15. R. S. Lau and A. T. Cobb, "Understanding the Connections between Relationship Conflict and Performance: The Intervening Roles of Trust and Exchange," *Journal of Organizational Behavior* 31, no. 6 (2010): 898–917.

16. A. Grove, "How to Make Confrontation Work for You," in *The Book of Management Wisdom*, ed. P. Krass (New York: John Wiley & Sons, 2000), 83–89; J. Detar, "Andy Grove, Intel's Inside Man," *Investor's Business Daily*, 24 July 2007; D. Senor and S. Singer, *Start-up Nation: The Story of Israel's Economic Miracle* (New York: Hachette Book Group, 2009).

17. C. K. W. De Dreu and L. R. Weingart, "Task Versus Relationship Conflict, Team Performance, and Team Member Satisfaction: A Meta-Analysis," *Journal of Applied Psychology* 88 (August 2003): 587–604; A. C. Mooney, P. J. Holahan, and A. C. Amason, "Don't Take It Personally: Exploring Cognitive Conflict as a Mediator of Affective Conflict," *Journal of Management Studies* 44, no. 5 (2007): 733–758.

18. J. Yang and K. W. Mossholder, "Decoupling Task and Relationship Conflict: The Role of Intergroup Emotional Processing," *Journal of Organizational Behavior* 25 (2004): 589–605.

19. A. C. Amason and H. J. Sapienza, "The Effects of Top Management Team Size and Interaction Norms on Cognitive and Affective Conflict," *Journal of Management* 23, no. 4 (1997): 495–516.

20. L. Pondy, "Organizational Conflict: Concepts and Models," *Administrative Science Quarterly* 2 (1967): 296–320; K. W. Thomas, "Conflict and Negotiation Processes in Organizations," in *Handbook of Industrial and Organizational Psychology*, ed. M. D. Dunnette and L. M. Hough, 2nd ed. (Palo Alto, CA: Consulting Psychologists Press, 1992), 651–718.

21. H. Barki and J. Hartwick, "Conceptualizing the Construct of Interpersonal Conflict," *International Journal of Conflict Management* 15, no. 3 (2004): 216–244.

22. M. A. Von Glinow, D. L. Shapiro, and J. M. Brett, "Can We Talk, and Should We? Managing Emotional Conflict in Multicultural Teams," *Academy of Management Review* 29, no. 4 (2004): 578–592.

23. G. E. Martin and T. J. Bergman, "The Dynamics of Behavioral Response to Conflict in the Workplace," *Journal of Occupational & Organizational Psychology* 69 (December 1996): 377–387; J. M. Brett, D. L. Shapiro, and A. L. Lytle, "Breaking the Bonds of Reciprocity in Negotiations," *Academy of Management Journal* 41 (August 1998): 410–424.

24. R. E. Walton and J. M. Dutton, "The Management of Conflict: A Model and Review," *Administrative Science Quarterly* 14 (1969): 73–84; S. M. Schmidt and T. A. Kochan, "Conflict: Toward Conceptual Clarity," *Administrative Science Quarterly* 17, no. 3 (Sept. 1972): 359–370.

25. V. Murphy, "Microsoft's Midlife Crisis," *Forbes*, 3 October 2005, 88; D. Brass, "Microsoft's Creative Destruction," *New York Times*, 4 February 2010.

26. J. A. McMullin, T. Duerden Comeau, and E. Jovic, "Generational Affinities and Discourses of Difference: A Case Study of Highly Skilled Information Technology Workers," *British Journal of Sociology* 58, no. 2 (2007): 297–316.

27. http://ca.linkedin.com/pub/tennyson-cho/12/B59/981 Retrieved February 12, 2011; L.Belkin, "When Herbert Met Matthew: The Generation Clash," *Globe & Mail*, 27 July 2007; C. Silverman, "Attack of the Fresh-Faced Go-Getters," *Globe & Mail*, 25 June 2007; T.E. Winchell Sr. "Ten Principles for Coalescing the Generations," *Public Manager*, 36, no. 3 (Fall 2007), 87–88; M. Gabriel and P. Robitaille, "Sustaining High Performance with Generation-Y Employees," *Canadian HR Reporter*, 14 January 2008, 13; L.S. Rikleen, "Office Politics: Solve Generational Conflict in the Workplace," *Nova Scotia Business Journal*, 19 March 2008.

28. R. Wageman and G. Baker, "Incentives and Cooperation: The Joint Effects of Task and Reward Interdependence on Group Performance," *Journal of Organizational Behavior* 18, no. 2 (1997): 139–158; G. S. van der Vegt, B. J. M. Emans, and E. van der Vliert, "Patterns of Interdependence in Work Teams: A Two-Level Investigation of the Relations with Job and Team Satisfaction," *Personnel Psychology* 54, no. 1 (2001): 51–69.

29. P. C. Earley and G. B. Northcraft, "Goal Setting, Resource Interdependence, and Conflict Management," in *Managing Conflict: An Interdisciplinary Approach*, ed. M. A. Rahim (New York: Praeger, 1989), 161–170; K. Jehn, "A Multimethod Examination of the Benefits and Detriments of Intragroup Conflict," *Administrative Science Quarterly* 40 (1995): 245–282.

30. Data are from the 2009 Kelly Global Workforce Index, based on information published in news releases in each country by Kelly Services in September 2009.

31. A. Risberg, "Employee Experiences of Acquisition Processes," *Journal of World Business* 36 (March 2001): 58–84.

32. Jehn and Bendersky, "Intragroup Conflict in Organizations."

33. M. Hewstone, M. Rubin, and H. Willis, "Intergroup Bias," *Annual Review of Psychology* 53 (2002): 575–604; J. Jetten, R. Spears, and T. Postmes, "Intergroup Distinctiveness and Differentiation: A Meta-Analytic Integration," *Journal of Personality and Social Psychology* 86, no. 6 (2004): 862–879.

34. Follett, "Constructive Conflict"; Blake, Shepard, and Mouton, *Managing Intergroup Conflict in Industry*; T. Ruble and K. Thomas, "Support for a Two-Dimensional Model of Conflict Behavior," *Organizaiotnal Behavior and Human Performance* 16 (1976): 143–155; C. K. W. De Dreu *et al.*, " A Theory-Based Measure of Conflict Management Strategies in the Workplace," *Journal of Organizational Behavior* 22 (2001): 645–668; Rahim, "Toward a Theory of Managing Organizational Conflict."

35. Jehn, "A Multimethod Examination of the Benefits and Detriments of Intragroup Conflict."

36. *Workplace Conflict and How Businesses Can Harness It to Thrive.*

37. D. W. Johnson *et al.*, "Effects of Cooperative, Competitive, and Individualistic Goal Structures on Achievement: A Meta-Analysis," *Psychological Bulletin* 89 (1981): 47–62; Rahim, "Toward a Theory of Managing Organizational Conflict"; G. A. Callanan, C. D. Benzing, and D. F. Perri, "Choice of Conflict-Handling Strategy: A Matter of Context," *Journal of Psychology* 140, no. 3 (2006): 269–288.

38. R. A. Friedman *et al.*, "What Goes around Comes Around: The Impact of Personal Conflict Style on Work Conflict and Stress," *International Journal of Conflict Management* 11, no. 1 (2000): 32–55; X. M. Song, J. Xile, and B. Dyer, "Antecedents and Consequences of Marketing Managers' Conflict-Handling Behaviors," *Journal of*

Marketing 64 (January 2000): 50–66; M. Song, B. Dyer, and R. J. Thieme, "Conflict Management and Innovation Performance: An Integrated Contingency Perspective," *Academy of Marketing Science* 34, no. 3 (2006): 341–356; L. A. DeChurch, K. L. Hamilton, and C. Haas, "Effects of Conflict Management Strategies on Perceptions of Intragroup Conflict," *Group Dynamics* 11, no. 1 (2007): 66–78.

39. G. A. Chung-Yan and C. Moeller, "The Psychosocial Costs of Conflict Management Styles," *International Journal of Conflict Management* 21, no. 4 (2010): 382–399.

40. C. K. W. De Dreu and A. E. M. Van Vianen, "Managing Relationship Conflict and the Effectiveness of Organizational Teams," *Journal of Organizational Behavior* 22 (2001): 309–328; R. J. Lewicki *et al.*, *Negotiation*, 4th ed. (New York: McGraw-Hill/Irwin, 2003), 35–36.

41. M. W. Morris and H.-Y. Fu, "How Does Culture Influence Conflict Resolution? Dynamic Constructivist Analysis," *Social Cognition* 19 (June 2001): 324–349; C. H. Tinsley, "How Negotiators Get to Yes: Predicting the Constellation of Strategies Used across Cultures to Negotiate Conflict," *Journal of Applied Psychology* 86, no. 4 (2001): 583–593; J. L. Holt and C. J. DeVore, "Culture, Gender, Organizational Role, and Styles of Conflict Resolution: A Meta-Analysis," *International Journal of Intercultural Relations* 29, no. 2 (2005): 165–196.

42. D. A. Cai and E. L. Fink, "Conflict Style Differences between Individualists and Collectivists," *Communication Monographs* 69 (March 2002): 67–87; C. H. Tinsley and E. Weldon, "Responses to a Normative Conflict among American and Chinese Managers," *International Journal of Conflict Management* 3, no. 2 (2003): 183–194; F. P. Brew and D. R. Cairns, "Styles of Managing Interpersonal Workplace Conflict in Relation to Status and Face Concern: A Study with Anglos and Chinese," *International Journal of Conflict Management* 15, no. 1 (2004): 27–57.

43. N. Brewer, P. Mitchell, and N. Weber, "Gender Role, Organizational Status, and Conflict Management Styles," *International Journal of Conflict Management* 13 (2002): 78–95; N. B. Florea *et al.*, "Negotiating from Mars to Venus: Gender in Simulated International Negotiations," *Simulation & Gaming* 34 (June 2003): 226–248; Holt and DeVore, "Culture, Gender, Organizational Role, and Styles of Conflict Resolution."

44. C. Cattaneo, "Asia's Influence Rising in Alberta; Wild West Adjusting to Far East Mentality," *National Post*, 15 January 2011, FP1; C. Malek, "Face," University of Colorado, Retrieved http://www.crinfo.org/CK_Essays/ck_face.jsp. Retrieved February 12, 2011.

45. K. Lewin, *Resolving Social Conflicts* (New York: Harper, 1948).

46. J. D. Hunger and L. W. Stern, "An Assessment of the Functionality of the Superordinate Goal in Reducing Conflict," *Academy of Management Journal* 19, no. 4 (1976): 591–605 M. Sherif, "Superordinate Goals in the Reduction of Intergroup Conflict," *The American Journal of Sociology* 63, no. 4 (1958): 349–356.

47. Sherif, "Superordinate Goals in the Reduction of Intergroup Conflict"; Eisenhardt, Kahwajy, and Bourgeois III, "How Management Teams Can Have a Good Fight"; Song, Xile, and Dyer, "Antecedents and Consequences of Marketing Managers' Conflict-Handling Behaviors"; O. Doucet, J. Poitras, and D. Chenevert, "The Impacts of Leadership on Workplace Conflicts," *International Journal of Conflict Management* 20, no. 4 (2009): 340–354.

48. Lau and Cobb, "Understanding the Connections between Relationship Conflict and Performance: The Intervening Roles of Trust and Exchange."

49. H. C. Triandis, "The Future of Workforce Diversity in International Organisations: A Commentary," *Applied Psychology: An International Journal* 52, no. 3 (2003): 486–495.

50. "Can the New CEO End a Culture Clash after a Merger?," *Financial Times*, 10 September 2008, 16.

51. T. F. Pettigrew, "Intergroup Contact Theory," *Annual Review of Psychology* 49 (1998): 65–85; S. Brickson, "The Impact of Identity Orientation on Individual and Organizational Outcomes in Demographically Diverse Settings," *Academy of Management Review* 25 (January 2000): 82–101; J. Dixon and K. Durrheim, "Contact and the Ecology of Racial Division: Some Varieties of Informal Segregation," *British Journal of Social Psychology* 42 (March 2003): 1–23.

52. D. Nebenzahl, "Managing the Generation Gap," *Montreal Gazette*, 28 February 2009, G1; D. Deveau, "L'Oréal Canada Discovers the Beauty of Motivation," *Postmedia News (Toronto)*, 24 January 2011.

53. Triandis, "The Future of Workforce Diversity in International Organisations."

54. Von Glinow, Shapiro, and Brett, "Can We Talk, and Should We?".

55. M. Cash, "CN Chief Builds Bridges with Prairie Clientele," *Winnipeg Free Press*, 18 February 2011, B4; E. White, "Railways Improved, but Regulation Needed, Says CWB," *Western Producer*, 24 February 2011.

56. E. Horwitt, "Knowledge, Knowledge, Who's Got the Knowledge," *Computerworld* (April 8 1996): 80, 81, 84.

57. L. L. Putnam, "Beyond Third Party Role: Disputes and Managerial Interven-

tion," *Employee Responsibilities and Rights Journal* 7 (1994): 23–36; A. R. Elangovan, "The Manager as the Third Party: Deciding How to Intervene in Employee Disputes," in *Negotiation: Readings, Exercises, and Cases*, ed. R. J. Lewicki, J. A. Litterer, and D. Saunders, 3rd ed. (New York: McGraw-Hill, 1999), 458–469. For a somewhat different taxonomy of managerial conflict intervention, see: P. G. Irving and J. P. Meyer, "A Multidimensional Scaling Analysis of Managerial Third-Party Conflict Intervention Strategies," *Canadian Journal of Behavioural Science* 29, no. 1 (January 1997): 7–18. A recent review describes 10 species of third-party intervention, but these consist of variations of the three types described here. See: D. E. Conlon *et al.*, "Third Party Interventions across Cultures: No 'One Best Choice'," in *Research in Personnel and Human Resources Management* (JAI, 2007), 309–349.

58. B. H. Sheppard, "Managers as Inquisitors: Lessons from the Law," in *Bargaining inside Organizations*, ed. M. H. Bazerman and R. J. Lewicki (Beverly Hills, CA: Sage, 1983); N. H. Kim, D. W. Sohn, and J. A. Wall, "Korean Leaders' (and Subordinates') Conflict Management," *International Journal of Conflict Management* 10, no. 2 (April 1999): 130–153; D. J. Moberg, "Managers as Judges in Employee Disputes: An Occasion for Moral Imagination," *Business Ethics Quarterly* 13, no. 4 (2003): 453–477.

59. R. Karambayya and J. M. Brett, "Managers Handling Disputes: Third Party Roles and Perceptions of Fairness," *Academy of Management Journal* 32 (1989): 687–704; R. Cropanzano *et al.*, "Disputant Reactions to Managerial Conflict Resolution Tactics," *Group & Organization Management* 24 (June 1999): 124–153.

60. This information is found at: RBC Corporate Responsibility: Workplace: Engagement (http://www.rbc.com/responsibility/workplace/engagement.html). Accessed 30 April 2008.

61. A. R. Elangovan, "Managerial Intervention in Organizational Disputes: Testing a Prescriptive Model of Strategy Selection," *International Journal of Conflict Management* 4 (1998): 301–335; P. S. Nugent, "Managing Conflict: Third-Party Interventions for Managers," *Academy Of Management Executive* 16, no. 1 (February 2002): 139–154.

62. J. P. Meyer, J. M. Gemmell, and P. G. Irving, "Evaluating the Management of Interpersonal Conflict in Organizations: A Factor-Analytic Study of Outcome Criteria," *Canadian Journal of Administrative Sciences* 14 (1997): 1–13; L. B. Bingham, "Employment Dispute Resolution: The Case for Mediation," *Conflict Resolution Quarterly* 22, no. 1–2 (2004): 145–174;

M. Hyde *et al.*, "Workplace Conflict Resolution and the Health of Employees in the Swedish and Finnish Units of an Industrial Company," *Social Science & Medicine* 63, no. 8 (2006): 2218–2227.

63. W. H. Ross and D. E. Conlon, "Hybrid Forms of Third-Party Dispute Resolution: Theoretical Implications of Combining Mediation and Arbitration," *Academy of Management Review* 25, no. 2 (2000): 416–427; W. H. Ross, C. Brantmeier, and T. Ciriacks, "The Impact of Hybrid Dispute-Resolution Procedures on Constituent Fairness Judgments," *Journal of Applied Social Psychology* 32, no. 6 (Jun 2002): 1151–1188.

64. R. Stagner and H. Rosen, *Psychology of Union—Management Relations* (Belmont, Calif.: Wadsworth, 1965), 95–96, 108–110; R. E. Walton and R. B. McKersie, *A Behavioral Theory of Labor Negotiations: An Analysis of a Social Interaction System* (New York: McGraw-Hill, 1965), 41–46; L. Thompson, *The Mind and Heart of the Negotiator* (Upper Saddle River, NJ: Prentice-Hall, 1998), Chap. 2.

65. K. G. Allred, "Distinguishing Best and Strategic Practices: A Framework for Managing the Dilemma between Creating and Claiming Value," *Negotiation Journal* 16 (2000): 287–397.

66. S. Doctoroff, "Reengineering Negotiations," *Sloan Management Review* 39 (March 1998): 63–71; D. C. Zetik and A. F. Stuhlmacher, "Goal Setting and Negotiation Performance: A Meta-Analysis," *Group Processes & Intergroup Relations* 5 (January 2002): 35–52.

67. B. McRae, *The Seven Strategies of Master Negotiators* (Toronto: McGraw-Hill Ryerson, 2002), 7–11.

68. A. F. Stuhlmacher, T. L. Gillespie, and M. V. Champagne, "The Impact of Time Pressure in Negotiation: A Meta-Analysis," *International Journal of Conflict Management* 9, no. 2 (April 1998): 97–116; C. K. W. De Dreu, "Time Pressure and Closing of the Mind in Negotiation," *Organizational Behavior and Human Decision Processes* 91 (July 2003): 280–295. However, one recent study reported that speeding up these concessions leads to better negotiated outcomes. See: D. A. Moore, "Myopic Prediction, Self-Destructive Secrecy, and the Unexpected Benefits of Revealing Final Deadlines in Negotiation," *Organizational Behavior and Human Decision Processes* 94, no. 2 (2004): 125–139.

69. R. J. Robertson, "Defusing the Exploding Offer: The Farpoint Gambit," *Negotiation Journal* 11, no. 3 (1995): 277–285.

70. A. Tversky and D. Kahneman, "Judgment under Uncertainty: Heuristics and Biases," *Science* 185, no. 4157 (27 September 1974): 1124–1131; J. D. Jasper and S. D. Christman, "A Neuropsychological Dimension for Anchoring Effects," *Journal of Behavioral Decision Making* 18 (2005): 343–369.

71. Lewicki *et al.*, *Negotiation*, 90–96; S. Kwon and L. R. Weingart, "Unilateral Concessions from the Other Party: Concession Behavior, Attributions, and Negotiation Judgments," *Journal of Applied Psychology* 89, no. 2 (2004): 263–278.

72. D. Malhotra, "The Fine Art of Making Concessions," *Negotiation* (January 2006): 3–5.

73. J. Z. Rubin and B. R. Brown, *The Social Psychology of Bargaining and Negotiation* (New York: Academic Press, 1976), Chap. 9.

74. For a critical view of the problem solving style in negotiation, see: J. M. Brett, "Managing Organizational Conflict," *Professional Psychology: Research and Practice* 15 (1984): 664–678.

75. L. L. Thompson, "Information Exchange in Negotiation," *Journal of Experimental Social Psychology* 27 (1991): 161–179.

76. S. R. Covey, *The 7 Habits of Highly Effective People* (New York: Free Press, 1989), 235–260.

77. Lewicki *et al.*, *Negotiation*, p. 95; M. Olekalns and P. L. Smith, "Testing the Relationships among Negotiators' Motivational Orientations, Strategy Choices, and Outcomes," *Journal of Experimental Social Psychology* 39, no. 2 (Mar 2003): 101–117.

78. M. Olekalns and P. L. Smith, "Moments in Time: Metacognition, Trust, and Outcomes in Dyadic Negotiations," *Personality and Social Psychology Bulletin* 31, no. 12 (Dec 2005): 1696–1707.

79. D. W. Choi, "Shared Metacognition in Integrative Negotiation," *International Journal of Conflict Management* 21, no. 3 (2010): 309–333.

80. J. M. Brett *et al.*, "Sticks and Stones: Language, Face, and Online Dispute Resolution," *Academy of Management Journal* 50, no. 1 (Feb 2007): 85–99; D. Druckman and M. Olekalns, "Emotions in Negotiation," *Group Decision and Negotiation* 17, no. 1 (2008): 1–11; D. Pietroni *et al.*, "Emotions as Strategic Information: Effects of Other's Emotional Expressions on Fixed-Pie Perception, Demands, and Integrative Behavior in Negotiation," *Journal of Experimental Social Psychology* 44, no. 6 (2008): 1444–1454; M. J. Boland and W. H. Ross, "Emotional Intelligence and Dispute Mediation in Escalating and De-Escalating Situations," *Journal of Applied Social Psychology* 40, no. 12 (2010): 3059–3105.

81. "Shanghai, Disney Reach Agreement to Build Theme Park: Mayor." Xinhua's China Economic Information Service news release (19 January 2009).

82. P. J. Carnevale and A. M. Isen, "The Influence of Positive Affect and Visual Access on the Discovery of Integrative Solutions in Bilateral Negotiation," *Organizational Behavior and Human Decision Processes* 37 (1986): 1–13; Thompson, *The Mind and Heart of the Negotiator.*

83. J. W. Salacuse and J. Z. Rubin, "Your Place or Mine? Site Location and Negotiation," *Negotiation Journal* 6 (January 1990): 5–10; J. Mayfield *et al.*, "How Location Impacts International Business Negotiations," *Review of Business* 19 (December 1998): 21–24.

84. J. Margo, "The Persuaders," *Boss Magazine*, 29 December 2000, 38. For a full discussion of the advantages and disadvantages of face-to-face and alternative negotiations situations, see: M. H. Bazerman *et al.*, "Negotiation," *Annual Review of Psychology* 51 (2000): 279–314.

85. Lewicki *et al.*, *Negotiation*, 298–322.

CHAPTER 12

1. S. Silcoff, "Delivering a New Canada Post," *National Post*, 17 September 2007; S. Klie, "Canada Post CEO Walks in Employees' Shoes," *Canadian HR Reporter*, 23 October 2006; K. Moore, "Canada Post Boss Sees Balanced Team as Crucial," *Globe & Mail*, 7 August 2006, B10; J. Campbell, "She Delivers," *Ottawa Citizen*, 3 July 2010, B3; N. Van Praet, "The Best Woman For Job," *Ottawa Citizen*, 29 May 2010, D10; F. Mihlar, "Time for Women To Widen Their Vision," *Ottawa Citizen*, 8 February 2010, A10; K. May, "More than 500 of Federal Payroll Top $200K, *Ottawa Citizen*, 29 October 2010, A1.

2. R. House, M. Javidan, and P. Dorfman, "Project GLOBE: An Introduction," *Applied Psychology: An International Review* 50 (2001): 489–505; R. House *et al.*, "Understanding Cultures and Implicit Leadership Theories across the Globe: An Introduction to Project GLOBE," *Journal of World Business* 37 (2002): 3–10.

3. Data were calculated directly from the Library and Archives Canada library search site in April 2011 for the decades from 1910–1919 to 2000–2009. The data represent the number of items published in that decade where the subject of those items is recorded as "leader" or its derivatives (leaders, leadership, etc). See: http://www.collectionscanada.gc.ca/lac-bac/search/lib_adv.

4. J. A. Raelin, "We the Leaders: In Order to Form a Leaderful Organization," *Journal of Leadership & Organizational Studies* 12, no. 2 (2005): 18–30; C. L. Pearce, J. A. Conger, and E. A. Locke, "Shared Leadership Theory," *Leadership Quarterly* 19, no. 5 (2008): 622–628; E. Engel Small and J. R. Rentsch, "Shared Leadership in Teams: A Matter of Distribution," *Journal of Personnel Psychology* 9, no. 4 (2010): 203–211.

5. J. W. Gardner, *On Leadership* (New York: Free Press, 1990), 138–155.

6. C. A. Beatty, "Implementing Advanced Manufacturing Technologies: Rules of the Road," *Sloan Management Review* (Summer 1992): 49–60; J. M. Howell, "The Right Stuff: Identifying and Developing Effective Champions of Innovation," *The Academy of Management Executive* 19, no. 2 (2005): 108–119; J. M. Howell and C. M. Shea, "Effects of Champion Behavior, Team Potency, and External Communication Activities on Predicting Team Performance," *Group & Organization Management* 31, no. 2 (April 2006): 180–211.

7. "Powered by Frontline People," *Employee Engagement Today*, September 2007; C. Hosford, "Flying High," *Incentive* 181, no. 12 (December 2007): 14–20.

8. J. A. Raelin, *Creating Leaderful Organizations: How to Bring out Leadership in Everyone* (San Francisco: Berret-Koehler, 2003).

9. Many of these perspectives are summarized in R. N. Kanungo, "Leadership in Organizations: Looking Ahead to the 21st Century," *Canadian Psychology* 39 (Spring 1998): 71–82; G. A. Yukl, *Leadership in Organizations*, 6th ed. (Upper Saddle River, NJ: Pearson Education, 2006).

10. A. Deutschman, "The Fabric of Creativity," *Fast Company*, December 2004, 54–; P. J. Kiger, "Power to the Individual," *Workforce Management*, 27 Feb. 2006, 1–7; G. Hamel, *The Future of Management* (Boston: Harvard Business School Press, 2007), Chap. 5.

11. The history of the trait perspective of leadership, as well as current research on this topic, is nicely summarized in S. J. Zaccaro, C. Kemp, and P. Bader, "Leader Traits and Attributes," in *The Nature of Leadership*, ed. J. Antonakis, A. T. Cianciolo, and R. J. Sternberg (Thousand Oaks, CA: Sage, 2004), 101–124.

12. R. M. Stogdill, *Handbook of Leadership* (New York: The Free Press, 1974), Chap. 5.

13. J. Intagliata, D. Ulrich, and N. Smallwood, "Leveraging Leadership Competencies to Produce Leadership Brand: Creating Distinctiveness by Focusing on Strategy and Results," *Human Resources Planning* 23, no. 4 (2000): 12–23; J. A. Conger and D. A. Ready, "Rethinking Leadership Competencies," *Leader to Leader* (Spring 2004): 41–47; Zaccaro, Kemp, and Bader, "Leader Traits and Attributes." For a recent discussion on leadership traits and evolutionary psychology, see: T. A. Judge, R. F. Piccolo, and T. Kosalka, "The Bright and Dark Sides of Leader Traits: A Review and Theoretical Extension of the Leader Trait Paradigm," *Leadership Quarterly* 20 (2009): 855–875.

14. This list is based on S. A. Kirkpatrick and E. A. Locke, "Leadership: Do Traits Matter?," *Academy of Management Executive* 5 (May 1991): 48–60; R. M. Aditya,

R. J. House, and S. Kerr, "Theory and Practice of Leadership: Into the New Millennium," in *Industrial and Organizational Psychology: Linking Theory with Practice*, ed. C. L. Cooper and E. A. Locke (Oxford, UK: Blackwell, 2000), 130–165; D. Goleman, R. Boyatzis, and A. McKee, *Primal Leaders* (Boston: Harvard Business School Press, 2002); T. A. Judge *et al.*, "Personality and Leadership: A Qualitative and Quantitative Review," *Journal Of Applied Psychology* 87, no. 4 (August 2002): 765–780; T. A. Judge, A. E. Colbert, and R. Ilies, "Intelligence and Leadership: A Quantitative Review and Test of Theoretical Propositions," *Journal Of Applied Psychology* 89, no. 3 (June 2004): 542–552; Zaccaro, Kemp, and Bader, "Leader Traits and Attributes."

15. "Canada's Final Frontier," *The Globe and Mail*, 7 September 2010, A. 16; L. Perreaux, "A Step Up For Hadfield And A Giant Leap for Canada," *The Globe and Mail*, 3 September 2010, A4; "Biography of Col. Chris A. Hadfield," http://www.asc-csa.gc.ca/eng/astronauts/biohadfield.asp Retrieved February 20, 2011; "NASA and Partners Name Upcoming Space Station Crew Members," http://www.nasa.gov/home/hqnews/2011/feb/HQ_11-044_ISS_Crews.html Retrieved March 3, 2011.

16. M. Popper *et al.*, "The Capacity to Lead: Major Psychological Differences between Leaders and Nonleaders," *Military Psychology* 16, no. 4 (2004): 245–263; R. G. Lord and R. J. Hall, "Identity, Deep Structure and the Development of Leadership Skill," *Leadership Quarterly* 16, no. 4 (August 2005): 591–615; D. V. Day, M. M. Harrison, and S. M. Halpin, *An Integrative Approach to Leader Development: Connecting Adult Development, Identity, and Expertise* (New York: Routledge, 2009); D. S. DeRue and S. J. Ashford, "Who Will Lead and Who Will Follow? A Social Process of Leadership Identity Construction in Organizations," *Academy of Management Review* 35, no. 4 (2010): 627–647.

17. The large-scale studies are reported in C. Savoye, "Workers Say Honesty Is Best Company Policy," *Christian Science Monitor*, June 15 2000; J. M. Kouzes and B. Z. Posner, *The Leadership Challenge*, 3rd ed. (San Francisco: Jossey-Bass, 2002), Chap. 2; J. Schettler, "Leadership in Corporate America," *Training & Development*, September 2002, 66–73.

18. BlessingWhite, *The State of Employee Engagement 2008: Asia Pacific Overview* (Princeton, NJ: BlessingWhite, 3 March 2008); "Managing in an Era of Mistrust: Maritz Poll Reveals Employees Lack Trust in Their Workplace." news release for Maritz Research (St. Louis: 14 April 2010).

19. R. Davidovitz *et al.*, "Leaders as Attachment Figures: Leaders' Attachment Orientations Predict Leadership-Related Mental Representations and Followers' Perfor-

mance and Mental Health," *Journal of Personality and Social Psychology* 93, no. 4 (2007): 632–650.

20. J. B. Miner, "Twenty Years of Research on Role Motivation Theory of Managerial Effectiveness," *Personnel Psychology* 31 (1978): 739–760; R. J. House and R. N. Aditya, "The Social Scientific Study of Leadership: Quo Vadis?," *Journal of Management* 23 (1997): 409–473.

21. J. Hedlund *et al.*, "Identifying and Assessing Tacit Knowledge: Understanding the Practical Intelligence of Military Leaders," *Leadership Quarterly* 14, no. 2 (2003): 117–140; R. J. Sternberg, "A Systems Model of Leadership: WICS," *American Psychologist* 62, no. 1 (2007): 34–42.

22. J. George, "Emotions and Leadership: The Role of Emotional Intelligence," *Human Relations* 53 (August 2000): 1027–1055; Goleman, Boyatzis, and McKee, *Primal Leaders*; Lord and Hall, "Identity, Deep Structure and the Development of Leadership Skill"; C. Skinner and P. Spurgeon, "Valuing Empathy and Emotional Intelligence in Health Leadership: A Study of Empathy, Leadership Behaviour and Outcome Effectiveness," *Health Services Management Research* 18, no. 1 (February 2005): 1–12.

23. B. George, *Authentic Leadership* (San Francisco: Jossey-Bass, 2004); W. L. Gardner *et al.*, "'Can You See the Real Me?' a Self-Based Model of Authentic Leader and Follower Development," *Leadership Quarterly* 16 (2005): 343–372; B. George, *True North* (San Francisco: Jossey-Bass, 2007), Chap. 4; M. E. Palanski and F. J. Yammarino, "Integrity and Leadership: Clearing the Conceptual Confusion," *European Management Journal* 25, no. 3 (2007): 171–184; F. O. Walumbwa *et al.*, "Authentic Leadership: Development and Validation of a Theory-Based Measure," *Journal of Management* 34, no. 1 (February 2008): 89–126.

24. R. Jacobs, "Using Human Resource Functions to Enhance Emotional Intelligence," in *The Emotionally Intelligent Workplace* ed. C. Cherniss and D. Goleman (San Francisco: Jossey-Bass, 2001), 161–163; Conger and Ready, "Rethinking Leadership Competencies."

25. R. G. Lord and D. J. Brown, *Leadership Processes and Self-Identity: A Follower-Centered Approach to Leadership* (Mahwah, NJ: Lawrence Erlbaum Associates, 2004); R. Bolden and J. Gosling, "Leadership Competencies: Time to Change the Tune?," *Leadership* 2, no. 2 (May 2006): 147–163.

26. E. A. Fleishman, "The Description of Supervisory Behavior," *Journal of Applied Psychology* 37, no. 1 (1953): 1–6. For discussion on methodological problems with the development of these people vs. task-oriented leadership constructs, see: C. A. Schriesheim, R. J. House, and S. Kerr, "Leader Initiating Structure: A Reconciliation of Discrepant

Research Results and Some Empirical Tests," *Organizational Behavior and Human Performance* 15, no. 2 (1976): 297–321; L. Tracy, "Consideration and Initiating Structure: Are They Basic Dimensions of Leader Behavior?," *Social Behavior and Personality* 15, no. 1 (1987): 21–33.

27. A. K. Korman, "Consideration, Initiating Structure, and Organizational Criteria—A Review," *Personnel Psychology* 19 (1966): 349–362; E. A. Fleishman, "Twenty Years of Consideration and Structure," in *Current Developments in the Study of Leadership*, ed. E. A. Fleishman and J. C. Hunt (Carbondale, Ill.: Southern Illinois University Press, 1973), 1–40; T. A. Judge, R. F. Piccolo, and R. Ilies, "The Forgotten Ones?: The Validity of Consideration and Initiating Structure in Leadership Research," *Journal of Applied Psychology* 89, no. 1 (2004): 36–51; Yukl, *Leadership in Organizations*, 62–75; D. S. Derue *et al.*, "Trait and Behavioral Theories of Leadership: An Integration and Meta-Analytic Test of Their Relative Validity," *Personnel Psychology* 64, no. 1 (2011): 7–52.

28. V. V. Baba, "Serendipity in Leadership: Initiating Structure and Consideration in the Classroom," *Human Relations* 42 (1989): 509–525.

29. B. A. Scott *et al.*, "A Daily Investigation of the Role of Manager Empathy on Employee Well-Being," *Organizational Behavior and Human Decision Processes* 113, no. 2 (2010): 127–140.

30. S. Kerr *et al.*, "Towards a Contingency Theory of Leadership Based Upon the Consideration and Initiating Structure Literature," *Organizational Behavior and Human Performance* 12 (1974): 62–82; L. L. Larson, J. G. Hunt, and R. N. Osbom, "The Great Hi—Hi Leader Behavior Myth: A Lesson from Occam's Razor," *Academy of Management Journal* 19 (1976): 628–641.

31. R. K. Greenleaf, *Servant Leadership: A Journey into the Nature of Lergitimate Power & Greatness* (Mahwah, NJ: Paulist Press, 1977; 2002); D. van Dierendonck and K. Patterson, "Servant Leadership: An Introduction," in *Servant Leadership: Developments in Theory and Research*, ed. D. van Dierendonck and K. Patterson (Houndmills UK: Palgrave Macmillan, 2010), 3–11.

32. Greenleaf, *Servant Leadership*, 27.

33. J. E. Barbuto, Jr. and D. W. Wheeler, "Scale Development and Construct Clarification of Servant Leadership," *Group & Organization Management* 31, no. 3 (June 2006): 300–326; R. C. Liden *et al.*, "Servant Leadership: Development of a Multidimensional Measure and Multi-Level Assessment," *Leadership Quarterly* 19, no. 2 (2008): 161–177; S. Sendjaya, J. C. Sarros, and J. C. Santora, "Defining and Measuring Servant Leadership Behaviour in Organizations," *Journal of Management Studies* 45, no. 2 (2008): 402–424; K.-Y. Ng

and C. S.-K. Koh, "Motivation to Serve: Understanding the Heart of the Servant-Leader and Servant Leadership Behaviours," in *Servant Leadership: Developments in Theory and Research*, ed. D. van Dierendonck and K. Patterson (Houndmills UK: Palgrave Macmillan, 2010), 90–104.

34. R. Tannenbaum and W. H. Schmidt, "How to Choose a Leadership Pattern," *Harvard Business Review* (May-June 1973): 162–180.

35. R. P. Vecchio, J. E. Justin, and C. L. Pearce, "The Utility of Transactional and Transformational Leadership for Predicting Performance and Satisfaction within a Path-Goal Theory Framework," *Journal of Occupational and Organizational Psychology* 81 (2008): 71–82.

36. For a thorough study of how expectancy theory of motivation relates to leadership, see R. G. Isaac, W. J. Zerbe, and D. C. Pitt, "Leadership and Motivation: The Effective Application of Expectancy Theory," *Journal of Managerial Issues* 13 (Summer 2001): 212–226.

37. R. J. House, "A Path-Goal Theory of Leader Effectiveness," *Administrative Science Quarterly* 16 (1971): 321–338; M. G. Evans, "Extensions of a Path-Goal Theory of Motivation," *Journal of Applied Psychology* 59 (1974): 172–178; R. J. House and T. R. Mitchell, "Path-Goal Theory of Leadership," *Journal of Contemporary Business* (Autumn 1974): 81–97; M. G. Evans, "Path Goal Theory of Leadership," in *Leadership*, ed. L. L. Neider and C. A. Schriesheim (Greenwich, CT: Information Age Publishing, 2002), 115–138.

38. R. J. House, "Path-Goal Theory of Leadership: Lessons, Legacy, and a Reformulated Theory," *Leadership Quarterly* 7 (1996): 323–352.

39. J. Indvik, "Path-Goal Theory of Leadership: A Meta-Analysis," *Academy of Management Proceedings* (1986): 189–192; J. C. Wofford and L. Z. Liska, "Path-Goal Theories of Leadership: A Meta-Analysis," *Journal of Management* 19 (1993): 857–876.

40. J. D. Houghton and S. K. Yoho, "Toward a Contingency Model of Leadership and Psychological Empowerment: When Should Self-Leadership Be Encouraged?," *Journal of Leadership & Organizational Studies* 11, no. 4 (2005): 65–83.

41. "Driving the Engine," *Broadcasting & Cable* 133, no. 16 (21 April 2003): 6A; S. Pappu, "The Queen of Tween," *Atlantic Monthly*, November 2004, 118–125; A. Becker, "The Wonderful World of Sweeney," *Broadcasting & Cable*, 25 February 2008, 19; J. R. Littlejohn, "Distinguished Vanguard Award for Leadership," *Multichannel News*, 19 May 2008.

42. R. T. Keller, "A Test of the Path-Goal Theory of Leadership with Need for Clar-

ity as a Moderator in Research and Development Organizations," *Journal of Applied Psychology* 74 (1989): 208–212.

43. C. A. Schriesheim and L. L. Neider, "Path-Goal Leadership Theory: The Long and Winding Road," *Leadership Quarterly* 7 (1996): 317–321.

44. P. Hersey and K. H. Blanchard, *Management of Organizational Behavior: Utilizing Human Resources*, 5th ed. (Englewood Cliffs, N.J.: Prentice Hall, 1988).

45. R. P. Vecchio, "Situational Leadership Theory: An Examination of a Prescriptive Theory," *Journal of Applied Psychology* 72 (1987): 444–451; W. Blank, J. R. Weitzel, and S. G. Green, "A Test of the Situational Leadership Theory," *Personnel Psychology* 43 (1990): 579–597; C. L. Graeff, "Evolution of Situational Leadership Theory: A Critical Review," *Leadership Quarterly* 8 (1997): 153–170; G. Thompson and R. P. Vecchio, "Situational Leadership Theory: A Test of Three Versions," *Leadership Quarterly* 20, no. 5 (2009): 837–848.

46. F. E. Fiedler, *A Theory of Leadership Effectiveness* (New York: McGraw-Hill, 1967); F. E. Fiedler and M. M. Chemers, *Leadership and Effective Management* (Glenview, Ill.: Scott, Foresman, 1974).

47. F. E. Fiedler, "Engineer the Job to Fit the Manager," *Harvard Business Review* 43, no. 5 (1965): 115–122.

48. For a summary of criticisms, see Yukl, *Leadership in Organizations*, 217–218.

49. Judge, Piccolo, and Ilies, "The Forgotten Ones?: The Validity of Consideration and Initiating Structure in Leadership Research"; Judge, Piccolo, and Kosalka, "The Bright and Dark Sides of Leader Traits: A Review and Theoretical Extension of the Leader Trait Paradigm."

50. N. Nicholson, *Executive Instinct* (New York: Crown, 2000).

51. This observation has also been made by C. A. Schriesheim, "Substitutes-for-Leadership Theory: Development and Basic Concepts," *Leadership Quarterly* 8 (1997): 103–108.

52. D. F. Elloy and A. Randolph, "The Effect of Superleader Behavior on Autonomous Work Groups in a Government Operated Railway Service," *Public Personnel Management* 26 (Summer 1997): 257–272; C. C. Manz and H. Sims Jr., *The New Super-Leadership: Leading Others to Lead Themselves* (San Francisco: Berrett-Koehler, 2001).

53. M. L. Loughry, "Coworkers Are Watching: Performance Implications of Peer Monitoring," *Academy of Management Proceedings* (2002): O1-O6.

54. C. C. Manz and C. Neck, *Mastering Self-Leadership*, 3rd ed. (Upper Saddle River, NJ: Prentice Hall, 2004).

55. P. M. Podsakoff and S. B. MacKenzie, "Kerr and Jermier's Substitutes for

Leadership Model: Background, Empirical Assessment, and Suggestions for Future Research," *Leadership Quarterly* 8 (1997): 117–132; S. D. Dionne *et al.*, "Neutralizing Substitutes for Leadership Theory: Leadership Effects and Common-Source Bias," *Journal Of Applied Psychology* 87, no. 3 (June 2002): 454–464; J. R. Villa *et al.*, "Problems with Detecting Moderators in Leadership Research Using Moderated Multiple Regression," *Leadership Quarterly* 14, no. 1 (February 2003): 3–23; S. D. Dionne *et al.*, "Substitutes for Leadership, or Not," *Leadership Quarterly* 16, no. 1 (2005): 169–193.

56. J. M. Burns, *Leadership* (New York: Harper & Row, 1978); B. J. Avolio and F. J. Yammarino, eds., *Transformational and Charismatic Leadership: The Road Ahead* (Greenwich, CT: JAI Press, 2002); B. M. Bass and R. E. Riggio, *Transformational Leadership*, 2nd ed. (Mahwah, N. J.: Lawrence Erlbaum Associates, 2006).

57. V. L. Goodwin, J. C. Wofford, and J. L. Whittington, "A Theoretical and Empirical Extension to the Transformational Leadership Construct," *Journal of Organizational Behavior* 22 (November 2001): 759–774.

58. Burns, *Leadership*, 19–20. Burns also describes transactional and "transforming leadership" in his more recent book: J. M. Burns, *Transforming Leadership* (New York: Grove Press, 2004). In both books, Burns describes both leadership concepts in complex and occasionally confounding ways.

59. For Burns's discussion on the ethics of transactional leadership, see: Burns, *Transforming Leadership*, 28. Regarding transactional leadership and appealing to needs, justice, and morality, see: Burns, *Leadership*, 258.

60. A. Zaleznik, "Managers and Leaders: Are They Different?," *Harvard Business Review* 55, no. 5 (1977): 67–78; W. Bennis and B. Nanus, *Leaders: The Strategies for Taking Charge* (New York: Harper & Row, 1985). For a recent discussion regarding managing versus leading, see G. Yukl and R. Lepsinger, "Why Integrating the Leading and Managing Roles Is Essential for Organizational Effectiveness," *Organizational Dynamics* 34, no. 4 (2005): 361–375.

61. Bennis and Nanus, *Leaders*, 20. Peter Drucker is also widely cited as the source of this quotation. The closest passage we could find, however, is in the first two pages of *The Effective Executive* (1966) where Drucker states that effective executives "get the right things done". On the next page, he states that manual workers only need efficiency, "that is, the ability to do things right rather than the ability to get the right things done." See: P. F. Drucker, *The Effective Executive* (New York: Harper Business, 1966), 1–2.

62. B. M. Bass *et al.*, "Predicting Unit Performance by Assessing Transformational and Transactional Leadership," *Journal of Applied Psychology* 88 (April 2003): 207–218; Yukl and Lepsinger, "Why Integrating the Leading and Managing Roles Is Essential for Organizational Effectiveness."

63. For a discussion on the tendency to slide from transformational to transactional leadership, see W. Bennis, *An Invented Life: Reflections on Leadership and Change* (Reading, MA: Addison-Wesley, 1993).

64. R. J. House, "A 1976 Theory of Charismatic Leadership," in *Leadership: The Cutting Edge*, ed. J. G. Hunt and L. L. Larson (Carbondale, IL.: Southern Illinois University Press, 1977), 189–207; J. A. Conger, "Charismatic Leadership," in *The Sage Handbook of Leadership*, ed. A. Bryman *et al.* (London: Sage, 2011), 86–102.

65. J. E. Barbuto Jr., "Taking the Charisma out of Transformational Leadership," *Journal of Social Behavior & Personality* 12 (September 1997): 689–697; Y. A. Nur, "Charisma and Managerial Leadership: The Gift That Never Was," *Business Horizons* 41 (July 1998): 19–26; M. D. Mumford and J. R. Van Doorn, "The Leadership of Pragmatism—Reconsidering Franklin in the Age of Charisma," *Leadership Quarterly* 12, no. 3 (Fall 2001): 279–309; A. Fanelli, "Bringing out Charisma: CEO Charisma and External Stakeholders," *The Academy of Management Review* 31, no. 4 (2006): 1049–1061; M. J. Platow *et al.*, "A Special Gift We Bestow on You for Being Representative of Us: Considering Leader Charisma from a Self-Categorization Perspective," *British Journal of Social Psychology* 45, no. 2 (2006): 303–320.

66. L. Greenfeld, "Reflections on Two Charismas," *British Journal of Sociology* 36, no. 1 (1985): 117–132.

67. B. Shamir *et al.*, "Correlates of Charismatic Leader Behavior in Military Units: Subordinates' Attitudes, Unit Characteristics, and Superiors' Appraisals of Leader Performance," *Academy of Management Journal* 41, no. 4 (1998): 387–409; R. E. De Vries, R. A. Roe, and T. C. B. Taillieu, "On Charisma and Need for Leadership," *European Journal of Work and Organizational Psychology* 8 (1999): 109–133; R. Khurana, *Searching for a Corporate Savior: The Irrational Quest for Charismatic CEOs* (Princeton, NJ: Princeton University Press, 2002). The effect of charismatic leadership on follower dependence was also noted earlier by American government leader John Gardner. See: Gardner, *On Leadership*, 34–36.

68. J. Lipman-Blumen, "A Pox on Charisma: Why Connective Leadership and Character Count," in *The Drucker Difference: What the World's Greatest Management Thinker Means to Today's Business Leaders*, ed. C. L. Pearce,

J. A. Maciariello, and H. Yamawaki (New York: McGraw-Hill, 2010), 149–174.

69. D. Olive, "The 7 Deadly Chief Executive Sins," *Toronto Star*, 17 February 2004, D01.

70. Y. Berson *et al.*, "The Relationship between Vision Strength, Leadership Style, and Context," *The Leadership Quarterly* 12, no. 1 (2001): 53–73. Collective vision has been identified as a key factor in leadership since Chester Barnard's seminal book in organizational behaviour. see: C. Barnard, *The Functions of the Executive* (Cambridge, MA: Harvard University Press, 1938), 86–89.

71. Bennis and Nanus, *Leaders*, 27–33, 89; I. M. Levin, "Vision Revisited," *Journal of Applied Behavioral Science* 36 (March 2000): 91–107; R. E. Quinn, *Building the Bridge as You Walk on It: A Guide for Leading Change* (San Francisco: Jossey-Bass, 2004), Chap. 11; J. M. Strange and M. D. Mumford, "The Origins of Vision: Effects of Reflection, Models, and Analysis," *Leadership Quarterly* 16, no. 1 (2005): 121–148; D. Ulrich and W. Ulrich, *The Why of Work: How Great Leaders Build Abundant Organizations That Win* (New York: McGraw-Hill, 2010), Chap. 1.

72. J. R. Baum, E. A. Locke, and S. A. Kirkpatrick, "A Longitudinal Study of the Relation of Vision and Vision Communication to Venture Growth in Entrepreneurial Firms," *Journal of Applied Psychology* 83 (1998): 43–54; S. L. Hoe and S. L. McShane, "Leadership Antecedents of Informal Knowledge Acquisition and Dissemination," *International Journal of Organisational Behaviour* 5 (2002): 282–291.

73. "Canadian CEOs Give Themselves Top Marks for Leadership!," *Canada NewsWire*, 9 September 1999; L. Manfield, "Creating a Safety Culture from Top to Bottom," *WorkSafe Magazine*, February 2005, 8–9.

74. J. A. Conger, "Inspiring Others: The Language of Leadership," *Academy of Management Executive* 5 (February 1991): 31–45; G. T. Fairhurst and R. A. Sarr, *The Art of Framing: Managing the Language of Leadership* (San Francisco, CA: Jossey-Bass, 1996); A. E. Rafferty and M. A. Griffin, "Dimensions of Transformational Leadership: Conceptual and Empirical Extensions," *Leadership Quarterly* 15, no. 3 (2004): 329–354; D. A. Waldman, P. A. Balthazard, and S. J. Peterson, "Leadership and Neuroscience: Can We Revolutionize the Way That Inspirational Leaders Are Identified and Devedloped?," *Academy of Mnagement Perspectives* 25, no. 1 (2011): 60–74.

75. S. Franklin, *The Heroes: A Saga of Canadian Inspiration* (Toronto: McClelland and Stewart, 1967); L. Black, "Hamburger Diplomacy," *Report on Business Magazine* August 1988, 30–36.

76. A. Lashinsky and D. Burke, "The Decade of Steve," *Fortune*, 23 November

2009, p. 92; A. Senwer, "Jobs Hunting," *Fortune*, 23 November 2009, p. 12; P. Newcomb, "Business-Person of the Year," *Fortune*, 6 December 2010, p. 134; J. Castaldo, "The Game-Changer," *Canadian Business*, 9 November 2010, p. 30; J. Hempel, B. Kowitt, and J.P. Mangalinan, "10 Smartest People in Tech," *Fortune*, 26 July 2010, p. 82; "Do Innovations Die With People?" *The CTO Forum*, 28 February 2011; B. Stone and P. Burrows, "Apple, With or Without Steve Jobs, "*Business Week*, 24 January 2011, p. 1.

77. D. E. Berlew, "Leadership and Organizational Excitement," *California Management Review* 17, no. 2 (Winter 1974): 21–30; Bennis and Nanus, *Leaders*, 43–55; T. Simons, "Behavioral Integrity: The Perceived Alignment between Managers' Words and Deeds as a Research Focus," *Organization Science* 13, no. 1 (Jan-Feb 2002): 18–35.

78. S. Ewart, "Unique Suncor Boasts Unique CEO," *Calgary Herald*, 11 September 1999, 1. For discussion of trust in leadership, see: C. S. Burke *et al.*, "Trust in Leadership: A Multi-Level Review and Integration," *Leadership Quarterly* 18, no. 6 (2007): 606–632.

79. M. Webb, "Executive Profile: Peter C. Farrell," *San Diego Business Journal*, 24 March 2003, 32; P. Benesh, "He Likes Them Breathing Easy," *Investor's Business Daily*, 13 September 2005, A04. For a discussion of trust in leadership, see Burke *et al.*, "Trust in Leadership: A Multi-Level Review and Integration." The survey on leading by example is reported in J. C. Maxwell, "People Do What People See," *BusinessWeek*, 19 November 2007, 32.

80. C. Hymowitz, "Today's Bosses Find Mentoring Isn't Worth the Time and Risks," *Wall Street Journal*, 13 March 2006, B1.

81. A. Mackey, "The Effect of CEOs on Firm Performance," *Strategic Management Journal* 29, no. 12 (2008): 1357–1367.

82. J. Barling, T. Weber, and E. K. Kelloway, "Effects of Transformational Leadership Training on Attitudinal and Financial Outcomes: A Field Experiment," *Journal of Applied Psychology* 81 (1996): 827–832.

83. A. Bryman, "Leadership in Organizations," in *Handbook of Organization Studies*, ed. S. R. Clegg, C. Hardy, and W. R. Nord (Thousand Oaks, CA: Sage, 1996), 276–292.

84. B. S. Pawar and K. K. Eastman, "The Nature and Implications of Contextual Influences on Transformational Leadership: A Conceptual Examination," *Academy of Management Review* 22 (1997): 80–109; C. P. Egri and S. Herman, "Leadership in the North American Environmental Sector: Values, Leadership Styles, and Contexts of Environmental Leaders and Their Organizations," *Academy of Management Journal* 43, no. 4 (2000): 571–604.

85. J. R. Meindl, "On Leadership: An Alternative to the Conventional Wisdom," *Research in Organizational Behavior* 12 (1990): 159–203; L. R. Offermann, J. J. K. Kennedy, and P. W. Wirtz, "Implicit Leadership Theories: Content, Structure, and Generalizability," *Leadership Quarterly* 5, no. 1 (1994): 43–58; R. J. Hall and R. G. Lord, "Multi-Level Information Processing Explanations of Followers' Leadership Perceptions," *Leadership Quarterly* 6 (1995): 265–287; O. Epitropaki and R. Martin, "Implicit Leadership Theories in Applied Settings: Factor Structure, Generalizability, and Stability over Time," *Journal of Applied Psychology* 89, no. 2 (2004): 293–310. For a broader discussion of the social construction of leadership, see: G. T. Fairhurst and D. Grant, "The Social Construction of Leadership: A Sailing Guide," *Management Communication Quarterly* 24, no. 2 (May 2010): 171–210.

86. R. G. Lord *et al.*, "Contextual Constraints on Prototype Generation and Their Multilevel Consequences for Leadership Perceptions," *Leadership Quarterly* 12, no. 3 (2001): 311–338; K. A. Scott and D. J. Brown, "Female First, Leader Second? Gender Bias in the Encoding of Leadership Behavior," *Organizational Behavior and Human Decision Processes* 101 (2006): 230–242; S. J. Shondrick, J. E. Dinh, and R. G. Lord, "Developments in Implicit Leadership Theory and Cognitive Science: Applications to Improving Measurement and Understanding Alternatives to Hierarchical Leadership," *Leadership Quarterly* 21, no. 6 (2010): 959–978.

87. R. Ilies, M. W. Gerhardt, and H. Le, "Individual Differences in Leadership Emergence: Integrating Meta-Analytic Findings and Behavioral Genetics Estimates," *International Journal of Selection and Assessment* 12, no. 3 (September 2004): 207–219.

88. S. F. Cronshaw and R. G. Lord, "Effects of Categorization, Attribution, and Encoding Processes on Leadership Perceptions," *Journal of Applied Psychology* 72 (1987): 97–106; J. L. Nye and D. R. Forsyth, "The Effects of Prototype-Based Biases on Leadership Appraisals: A Test of Leadership Categorization Theory," *Small Group Research* 22 (1991): 360–379.

89. L. M. Fisher, "Ricardo Semler Won't Take Control," *strategy+business*, no. 41 (Winter 2005): 1–11.

90. Meindl, "On Leadership: An Alternative to the Conventional Wisdom"; J. Felfe and L.-E. Petersen, "Romance of Leadership and Management Decision Making," *European Journal of Work and Organizational Psychology* 16, no. 1 (2007): 1–24; B. Schyns, J. R. Meindl, and M. A. Croon, "The Romance of Leadership Scale: Cross-Cultural Testing and Refinement," *Leadership* 3, no. 1 (February 2007): 29–46.

91. J. Pfeffer, "The Ambiguity of Leadership," *Academy of Management Review* 2 (1977): 102–112.

92. R. Weber *et al.*, "The Illusion of Leadership: Misattribution of Cause in Coordination Games," *Organization Science* 12, no. 5 (2001): 582–598; N. Ensari and S. E. Murphy, "Cross-Cultural Variations in Leadership Perceptions and Attribution of Charisma to the Leader," *Organizational Behavior and Human Decision Processes* 92 (2003): 52–66; M. L. A. Hayward, V. P. Rindova, and T. G. Pollock, "Believing One's Own Press: The Causes and Consequences of CEO Celebrity," *Strategic Management Journal* 25, no. 7 (July 2004): 637–653.

93. Six of the Project GLOBE clusters are described in a special issue of the *Journal of World Business*, 37 (2000). For an overview of Project GLOBE, see House, Javidan, and Dorfman, "Project GLOBE: An Introduction"; House *et al.*, "Understanding Cultures and Implicit Leadership Theories across the Globe: An Introduction to Project GLOBE."

94. J. C. Jesiuno, "Latin Europe Cluster: From South to North," *Journal of World Business* 37 (2002): 88. Another GLOBE study, of Iranian managers, also reported that "charismatic visionary" stands out as a primary leadership dimension. See A. Dastmalchian, M. Javidan, and K. Alam, "Effective Leadership and Culture in Iran: An Empirical Study," *Applied Psychology: An International Review* 50 (2001): 532–558.

95. D. N. Den Hartog *et al.*, "Culture Specific and Cross-Cultural Generalizable Implicit Leadership Theories: Are Attributes of Charismatic/Transformational Leadership Universally Endorsed?," *Leadership Quarterly* 10 (1999): 219–256; F. C. Brodbeck and e. al., "Cultural Variation of Leadership Prototypes across 22 European Countries," *Journal of Occupational and Organizational Psychology* 73 (2000): 1–29; E. Szabo and e. al., "The Europe Cluster: Where Employees Have a Voice," *Journal of World Business* 37 (2002): 55–68. The Mexican study is reported in C. E. Nicholls, H. W. Lane, and M. B. Brechu, "Taking Self-Managed Teams to Mexico," *Academy of Management Executive* 13 (August 1999): 15–25.

96. G. N. Powell, "One More Time: Do Female and Male Managers Differ?," *Academy of Management Executive* 4 (1990): 68–75; M. L. van Engen and T. M. Willemsen, "Sex and Leadership Styles: A Meta-Analysis of Research Published in the 1990s," *Psychological Reports* 94, no. 1 (February 2004): 3–18.

97. R. Fend, "Wir Sind Die Firma (We Are the Company)," *Financial Times Deutschland*, 2 October 2008, 31; N. Klawitter *et al.*, "Die Natur Der Macht (the Nature of Power)," *Der Spiegel*, 22 September 2008, 52; M. Schiessl, "Microsoft Reaps the

Rewards of Female Managers," *Spiegel Online*, 8 February 2008, http://www.spiegel.de/international/business/0,1518,533852,00.html.

98. R. Sharpe, "As Leaders, Women Rule," *BusinessWeek*, 20 November 2000, 74; M. Sappenfield, "Women, It Seems, Are Better Bosses," *Christian Science Monitor*, 16 January 2001; A. H. Eagly and L. L. Carli, "The Female Leadership Advantage: An Evaluation of the Evidence," *The Leadership Quarterly* 14, no. 6 (December 2003): 807–834; A. H. Eagly, M. C. Johannesen-Schmidt, and M. L. van Engen, "Transformational, Transactional, and Laissez-Faire Leadership Styles: A Meta-Analysis Comparing Women and Men," *Psychological Bulletin* 129 (July 2003): 569–591.

99. A. H. Eagly, S. J. Karau, and M. G. Makhijani, "Gender and the Effectiveness of Leaders: A Meta-Analysis," *Psychological Bulletin* 117 (1995): 125–145; J. G. Oakley, "Gender-Based Barriers to Senior Management Positions: Understanding the Scarcity of Female CEOs," *Journal of Business Ethics* 27 (2000): 821–834; N. Z. Stelter, "Gender Differences in Leadership: Current Social Issues and Future Organizational Implications," *Journal of Leadership Studies* 8 (2002): 88–99; M. E. Heilman *et al.*, "Penalties for Success: Reactions to Women Who Succeed at Male Gender-Typed Tasks," *Journal of Applied Psychology* 89, no. 3 (2004): 416–427; A. H. Eagly, "Achieving Relational Authenticity in Leadership: Does Gender Matter?," *The Leadership Quarterly* 16, no. 3 (June 2005): 459–474.

CHAPTER 13

1. www.timhortons.com Retrieved March 7, 2011; M. McCleam, "On a First-Name Basis," *Canadian Business*, 27 April–10 May, 2010, p. 31.

2. S. Ranson, R. Hinings, and R. Greenwood, "The Structuring of Organizational Structure," *Administrative Science Quarterly* 25 (1980): 1–14; J.-E. Johanson, "Intraorganizational Influence," *Management Communication Quarterly* 13 (February 2000): 393–435; K. Walsh, "Interpreting the Impact of Culture on Structure," *Journal of Applied Behavioral Science* 40, no. 3 (Sept. 2004): 302–322.

3. N. Alcoba, "TTC Told How to Improve Customer Service 78 Different Ways," *National Post*, 23 August 2010; "Listening Is Job One," *Toronto Star*, 23 March 2011.

4. H. Mintzberg, *The Structuring of Organizations* (Englewood Cliffs, N.J.: Prentice Hall, 1979), 2–3.

5. E. E. Lawler III, *Motivation in Work Organizations* (Monterey, Calif.: Brooks/Cole, 1973); M. A. Campion, "Ability Requirement Implications of Job Design: An Interdisciplinary Perspective," *Personnel Psychology* 42 (1989): 1–24.

6. G. S. Becker and K. M. Murphy, "The Division-of-Labor, Coordination Costs and Knowledge," *Quarterly Journal of Economics* 107, no. 4 (Nov 1992): 1137–1160; L. Borghans and B. Weel, "The Division of Labour, Worker Organisation, and Technological Change," *The Economic Journal* 116, no. 509 (2006): F45-F72.

7. Mintzberg, *The Structuring of Organizations* Chap. 1; D. A. Nadler and M. L. Tushman, *Competing by Design: The Power of Organizational Architecture* (N. Y.: Oxford University Press, 1997), Chap. 6; J. R. Galbraith, *Designing Organizations: An Executive Guide to Strategy, Structure, and Process* (San Francisco: Jossey-Bass, 2002), Chap. 4.

8. J. Stephenson, Jr., "Making Humanitarian Relief Networks More Effective: Operational Coordination, Trust and Sense Making," *Disasters* 29, no. 4 (2005): 337.

9. A. Willem, M. Buelens, and H. Scarbrough, "The Role of Inter-Unit Coordination Mechanisms in Knowledge Sharing: A Case Study of a British MNC," *Journal of Information Science* 32, no. 6 (2006): 539–561; R. R. Gulati, "Silo Busting," *Harvard Business Review* 85, no. 5 (2007): 98–108.

10. Borghans and Weel, "The Division of Labour, Worker Organisation, and Technological Change."

11. T. Van Alphen, "Magna in Overdrive," *Toronto Star*, 24 July 2006.

12. For a discussion of the role of brand manager at Proctor & Gamble, see C. Peale, "Branded for Success," *Cincinnati Enquirer* (20 May 2001): A1. Details about how to design integrator roles in organizational structures are presented in Galbraith, *Designing Organizations*, 66–72.

13. M. Hoque, M. Akter, and Y. Monden, "Concurrent Engineering: A Compromise Approach to Develop a Feasible and Customer-Pleasing Product," *International Journal of Production Research* 43, no. 8 (2005): 1607–1624; S. M. Sapuan, M. R. Osman, and Y. Nukman, "State of the Art of the Concurrent Engineering Technique in the Automotive Industry," *Journal of Engineering Design* 17, no. 2 (2006): 143–157; D. H. Kincade, C. Regan, and F. Y. Gibson, "Concurrent Engineering for Product Development in Mass Customization for the Apparel Industry," *International Journal of Operations & Production Management* 27, no. 6 (2007): 627–649.

14. A. H. Van De Ven, A. L. Delbecq, and R. J. Koenig Jr., "Determinants of Coordination Modes within Organizations," *American Sociological Review* 41, no. 2 (1976): 322–338.

15. Y.-M. Hsieh and A. Tien-Hsieh, "Enhancement of Service Quality with Job Standardisation," *Service Industries Journal* 21 (July 2001): 147–166.

16. For recent discussion of span of control, see N. A. Theobald and S. Nicholson-Crotty, "The Many Faces of Span of Control: Organizational Structure across Multiple Goals," *Administration Society* 36, no. 6 (January 2005): 648–660; R. M. Meyer, "Span of Management: Concept Analysis," *Journal of Advanced Nursing* 63, no. 1 (2008): 104–112.

17. H. Fayol, *General and Industrial Management*, trans. C. Storrs (London: Pitman, 1949); D. D. Van Fleet and A. G. Bedeian, "A History of the Span of Management," *Academy of Management Review* 2 (1977): 356–372; D. A. Wren, A. G. Bedeian, and J. D. Breeze, "The Foundations of Henri Fayol's Administrative Theory," *Management Decision* 40, no. 9 (2002): 906–918.

18. D. Drickhamer, "Lessons from the Leading Edge," *Industry Week*, 21 February 2000, 23–26.

19. G. Anders, "Overseeing More Employees—with Fewer Managers—Consultants Are Urging Companies to Loosen Their Supervising Views," *Wall Street Journal*, 24 March 2008, B6.

20. D. D. Van Fleet and A. G. Bedeian, "A History of the Span of Management," *Academy of Management Review* 2 (July 1977): 356–372; B. Davison, "Management Span of Control: How Wide Is Too Wide?," *Journal of Business Strategy* 24, no. 4 (2003): 22–29; S. Nix *et al.*, *Span of Control in City Government Increases Overall* (Seattle, WA: Office of City Auditor, City of Seattle, 19 September 2005); "Fedex 2008 Shareowners Meeting" (Memphis, TN: Fedex, 29 September 2008); S. O. Iowa, "Results Iowa: Operational Scan" (1 February 2008) (accessed 23 May 2010); J. McLellan, *Administrative Review: An Agenda for Business Improvement* (Portland, OR: Multnomah County, 19 May 2009).

21. J. Greenwald, "Ward Compares the Best with the Rest," *Business Insurance*, 26 August 2002, 16.

22. J. H. Gittell, "Supervisory Span, Relational Coordination and Flight Departure Performance: A Reassessment of Postbureaucracy Theory," *Organization Science* 12, no. 4 (July-August 2001): 468–483.

23. T. D. Wall, J. L. Cordery, and C. W. Clegg, "Empowerment, Performance, and Operational Uncertainty: A Theoretical Integration," *Applied Psychology: An International Review* 51 (2002): 146–169.

24. J. Morris, J. Hassard, and L. McCann, "New Organizational Forms, Human Resource Management and Structural Convergence? A Study of Japanese Organizations," *Organization Studies* 27, no. 10 (2006): 1485–1511.

25. P. Glader, "It's Not Easy Being Lean," *Wall Street Journal*, 19 June 2006, B1;

"About Us," (Charlotte, N. C.: Nucor Corporation, 2008), http://www.nucor.com/indexinner.aspx?finpage=aboutus (accessed 2 September 2008).

26. J. Denby, "Leaders in African Electricity," *African Business Review*, 11 May 2010.

27. "BASF Culling Saves (GBP) 4m," *Personnel Today* 19 February 2002, 3; A. Lashinsky, "The Hurt Way," *Fortune*, 17 April 2006, 92.

28. Q. N. Huy, "In Praise of Middle Managers," *Harvard Business Review* 79 (September 2001): 72–79; C. R. Littler, R. Wiesner, and R. Dunford, "The Dynamics of Delayering: Changing Management Structures in Three Countries," *Journal of Management Studies* 40, no. 2 (2003): 225–256; H. J. Leavitt, *Top Down: Why Hierarchies Are Here to Stay and How to Manage Them More Effectively* (Cambridge: Harvard Business School Press, 2005); L. McCann, J. Morris, and J. Hassard, "Normalized Intensity: The New Labour Process of Middle Management," *Journal of Management Studies* 45, no. 2 (2008): 343–371.

29. K. Tyler, "The Strongest Link," *HRMagazine* 2011, 51–53.

30. Littler, Wiesner, and Dunford, "The Dynamics of Delayering: Changing Management Structures in Three Countries."

31. W. Stueck, "Revamped Barrick Keeps Eyes on the Hunt for the Golden Prize," *Globe & Mail*, 17 September 2005, B4; Barrick Gold Corporation, *Annual Report 2007* (Toronto: Barrick Gold Corporation, April 2008).

32. S. Wetlaufer, "The Business Case against Revolution: An Interview with Nestle's Peter Brabeck," *Harvard Business Review* 79, no. 2 (February 2001): 112–119; H. A. Richardson *et al.*, "Does Decentralization Make a Difference for the Organization? An Examination of the Boundary Conditions Circumscribing Decentralized Decision-Making and Organizational Financial Performance," *Journal of Management* 28, no. 2 (2002): 217–244; G. Masada, "To Centralize or Decentralize?," *Optimize*, May 2005, 58–61.

33. J. G. Kelley, "Slurpees and Sausages: 7-Eleven Holds School," *Richmond (Va.) Times-Dispatch*, 12 March 2004, C1; S. Marling, "The 24-Hour Supply Chain," *InformationWeek*, 26 January 2004, 43.

34. Mintzberg, *The Structuring of Organizations* Chap. 5.

35. W. Dessein and T. Santos, "Adaptive Organizations," *Journal of Political Economy* 114, no. 5 (2006): 956–995; A. A. M. Nasurdin *et al.*, "Organizational Structure and Organizational Climate as Potential Predictors of Job Stress: Evidence from Malaysia," *International Journal of Commerce and Management* 16, no. 2 (2006): 116–129; C.-J. Chen and J.-W. Huang, "How Organizational Climate and Structure Affect Knowledge Management—the Social Interaction Perspective," *International Journal of Information Management* 27, no. 2 (2007): 104–118.

36. "Royal Bank Survey Finds Canadian Workplaces Buoyed by Optimism and High Level of Satisfaction." Canada NewsWire news release for R. B. of Canada (Toronto: 8 October 1998); "When It Comes to Red Tape, Many Canadian Employers Might Just Need to Cut It: RBC Study." CNW news release for RBC (Toronto: 23 January 2008).

37. T. Burns and G. Stalker, *The Management of Innovation* (London Tavistock: 1961).

38. J. Tata, S. Prasad, and R. Thom, "The Influence of Organizational Structure on the Effectiveness of TQM Programs," *Journal of Managerial Issues* 11, no. 4 (Winter 1999): 440–453; A. Lam, "Tacit Knowledge, Organizational Learning and Societal Institutions: An Integrated Framework," *Organization Studies* 21 (May 2000): 487–513.

39. W. D. Sine, H. Mitsuhashi, and D. A. Kirsch, "Revisiting Burns and Stalker: Formal Structure and New Venture Performance in Emerging Economic Sectors," *Academy of Management Journal* 49, no. 1 (2006): 121–132.

40. P. Lavoie, "TAXI," *Campaign*, 12 October 2007, 15; L. Sylvain, "Taxi Deconstructed," *Strategy*, June 2007, 50; S. Vranica, "For Small Agency, a Battle to Shed 'Boutique Stigma'," *Wall Street Journal*, 8 August 2007, B2D; E. Wexler, "There's No Stopping TAXI," *Strategy*, January 2011, 40–42. Although it was recently acquired by WPP, the world's largest creative holding company, TAXI will apparently remain an autonomous business and use WPP's resources for European and further international expansion.

41. Mintzberg, *The Structuring of Organizations* 106.

42. Mintzberg, *The Structuring of Organizations* Chap. 17.

43. Galbraith, *Designing Organizations*, 23–25.

44. E. E. Lawler III, *Rewarding Excellence: Pay Strategies for the New Economy* (San Francisco: Jossey-Bass, 2000), 31–34.

45. These structures were identified from corporate websites and annual reports. These organizations typically rely on a mixture of other structures, so the charts shown have been adapted for learning purposes.

46. M. Goold and A. Campbell, "Do You Have a Well-Designed Organization," *Harvard Business Review* 80 (March 2002): 117–124.

47. J. R. Galbraith, "Structuring Global Organizations," in *Tomorrow's Organization* ed. S. A. Mohrman *et al.* (San Francisco: Jossey-Bass, 1998), 103–129; C. Homburg, J. P. Workman Jr., and O. Jensen, "Fundamental Changes in Marketing Organization: The Movement toward a Corganizational Structure," *Academy of Marketing Science. Journal* 28 (Fall 2000): 459–478; T. H. Davenport, J. G. Harris, and A. K. Kohli, "How Do They Know Their Customers So Well?," *Sloan Management Review* 42 (Winter 2001): 63–73; J. R. Galbraith, "Organizing to Deliver Solutions," *Organizational Dynamics* 31 (2002): 194–207.

48. S. J. Palmisano, "The Globally Integrated Enterprise," *Foreign Affairs* 85, no. 3 (May/June 2006): 127–136; S. Palmisano, "The Globally Integrated Enterprise," *Vital Speeches of the Day* 73, no. 10 (2007): 449–453.

49. "IBM Moves Engineering Vp to China as Part of Global Focus," *Manufacturing Business Technology*, September 2007, 13; J. Bonasia, "Globalization: Learning to Close the Continental Divide," *Investor's Business Daily*, 7 September 2007.

50. J. R. Galbraith, E. E. Lawler III, and Associates, *Organizing for the Future: The New Logic for Managing Complex Organizations* (San Francisco, CA: Jossey-Bass, 1993); R. Bettis and M. Hitt, "The New Competitive Landscape," *Strategic Management Journal* 16 (1995): 7–19.

51. P. C. Ensign, "Interdependence, Coordination, and Structure in Complex Organizations: Implications for Organization Design," *Mid-Atlantic Journal of Business* 34 (March 1998): 5–22.

52. M. M. Fanning, "A Circular Organization Chart Promotes a Hospital-Wide Focus on Teams," *Hospital & Health Services Administration* 42 (June 1997): 243–254; L. Y. Chan and B. E. Lynn, "Operating in Turbulent Times: How Ontario's Hospitals Are Meeting the Current Funding Crisis," *Health Care Management Review* 23 (June 1998): 7–18.

53. D. Deveau, "Rapid-Response Team; HRSDC Staff Brought 'Laser-Sharp Focus' to Assisting Canadians Caught in the Downturn," *The Ottawa Citizen*, 12 October 2010, D7.

54. R. Cross, "Looking before You Leap: Assessing the Jump to Teams in Knowledge-Based Work," *Business Horizons* (September 2000); M. Fenton-O'Creevy, "Employee Involvement and the Middle Manager: Saboteur or Scapegoat?," *Human Resource Management Journal* 11 (2001): 24–40; G. Garda, K. Lindstrom, and M. Dallnera, "Towards a Learning Organization: The Introduction of a Client-Centered Team-Based Organization in Administrative Surveying Work," *Applied Ergonomics* 34 (2003): 97–105; C. Douglas and W. L. Gardner, "Transition to Self-Directed Work Teams: Implications of Transition Time and Self-Monitoring for Managers' Use of Influence Tactics," *Journal of Organizational Behavior* 25 (2004): 47–65.

55. R. Muzyka and G. Zeschuk, "Managing Multiple Projects," *Game Developer*, March 2003, 34–42; M. Saltzman, "The

Ex-Doctors Are In," *National Post*, 24 March 2004, AL4; R. McConnell, "For Edmonton's Bioware, Today's the Big Day," *Edmonton Journal*, 14 April 2005, C1; D. Gladstone and s. Molloy, "Doctors & Dragons," *Computer Gaming World*, Dec 2006.

56. R. C. Ford and W. A. Randolph, "Cross-Functional Structures: A Review and Integration of Matrix Organization and Project Management," *Journal of Management* 18 (1992): 267–294.

57. Nestlé's geographic and product structure is somewhat more complex than is described here, and its matrix is not as balanced as described. For discussion of these variations, see: J. R. Galbraith, *Designing Matrix Organizations That Actually Work* (San Francisco: Jossey-Bass, 2009).

58. K. Poynter, *Data Security at HMRC* (Progress Report to Chancellor of the Exchequer anf HM Treasury, 14 December 2007); V. Houlder, "The Merger That Exposed a Taxing Problem for Managers," *Financial Times*, 11 July 2008, 12; K. Poynter, *Review of Information Security at HM Revenue and Customs* (London: HM Treasury, Government of the United Kingdom, June 2008).

59. G. Calabrese, "Communication and Co-Operation in Product Development: A Case Study of a European Car Producer," *R & D Management* 27 (July 1997): 239–252; T. Sy and L. S. D'Annunzio, "Challenges and Strategies of Matrix Organizations: Top-Level and Mid-Level Managers' Perspectives," *Human Resource Planning* 28, no. 1 (2005): 39–48.

60. D. Enrich, "Citigroup Will Revamp Capital-Markets Group," *Wall Street Journal*, 23 August 2008, B7.

61. Nadler and Tushman, *Competing by Design*, Chap. 6; M. Goold and A. Campbell, "Structured Networks: Towards the Well-Designed Matrix," *Long Range Planning* 36, no. 5 (October 2003): 427–439.

62. D. Ciampa and M. Watkins, "Rx for New CEOs," *Chief Executive*, January 2008.

63. P. Siekman, "This Is Not a BMW Plant," *Fortune*, 18 April 2005, 208; "Magna's Austria Plant to Lose Production of BMW X3," *Reuters*, 16 May 2007.

64. R. F. Miles and C. C. Snow, "The New Network Firm: A Spherical Structure Built on a Human Investment Philosophy," *Organizational Dynamics* 23, no. 4 (1995): 5–18; C. Baldwin and K. Clark, "Managing in an Age of Modularity," *Harvard Business Review* 75 (September-October 1997): 84–93.

65. J. Hagel III and M. Singer, "Unbundling the Corporation," *Harvard Business Review* 77 (March-April 1999): 133–141; R. Hacki and J. Lighton, "The Future of the Networked Company," *McKinsey Quarterly* 3 (2001): 26–39.

66. J. Dwyer, "Mind How You Go," *Facilities Management*, May 2008, 22–25.

67. M. A. Schilling and H. K. Steensma, "The Use of Modular Organizational Forms: An Industry-Level Analysis," *Academy of Management Journal* 44 (December 2001): 1149–1168.

68. G. Morgan, *Images of Organization*, 2nd ed. (Newbury Park: Sage, 1996); G. Morgan, *Imagin-I-Zation: New Mindsets for Seeing, Organizing and Managing* (Thousand Oaks, CA: Sage, 1997).

69. H. Chesbrough and D. J. Teece, "When Is Virtual Virtuous? Organizing for Innovation," *Harvard Business Review* (January-February 1996): 65–73; P. M. J. Christie and R. Levary, "Virtual Corporations: Recipe for Success," *Industrial Management* 40 (July 1998): 7–11.

70. L. Donaldson, *The Contingency Theory of Organizations* (Thousand Oaks, CA: Sage, 2001); J. Birkenshaw, R. Nobel, and J. Ridderstrâle, "Knowledge as a Contingency Variable: Do the Characteristics of Knowledge Predict Organizational Structure?," *Organization Science* 13, no. 3 (May-June 2002): 274–289.

71. P. R. Lawrence and J. W. Lorsch, *Organization and Environment* (Homewood, Ill.: Irwin, 1967); Mintzberg, *The Structuring of Organizations* Chap. 15.

72. Burns and Stalker, *The Management of Innovation*; Lawrence and Lorsch, *Organization and Environment*.

73. S. Warner, "From Band-Aids to Biotech," *New York Times*, 10 April 2005, 1; "Johnson & Johnson CEO William Weldon: Leadership in a Decentralized Company," *Knowledge@Wharton*, 25 June 2008; "Our Management Approach," (New Brunswick, N. J.: Johnson & Johnson, 2008), http://www.jnj.com/connect/about-jnj/management-approach/ (accessed 2 September 2008).

74. Mintzberg, *The Structuring of Organizations* p. 282.

75. D. S. Pugh and C. R. Hinings, *Organizational Structure: Extensions and Replications* (Farnborough, England: Lexington Books, 1976); Mintzberg, *The Structuring of Organizations* Chap. 13.

76. Galbraith, *Designing Organizations*, 52–55; G. Hertel, S. Geister, and U. Konradt, "Managing Virtual Teams: A Review of Current Empirical Research," *Human Resource Management Review* 15 (2005): 69–95.

77. C. Perrow, "A Framework for the Comparative Analysis of Organizations," *American Sociological Review* 32 (1967): 194–208; D. Gerwin, "The Comparative Analysis of Structure and Technology: A Critical Appraisal," *Academy of Management Review* 4, no. 1 (1979): 41–51; C. C. Miller *et al.*, "Understanding Technology-Structure Relationships: Theory Development and Meta-Analytic Theory

Testing," *Academy of Management Journal* 34, no. 2 (1991): 370–399.

78. R. H. Kilmann, *Beyond the Quick Fix* (San Francisco: Jossey-Bass, 1984), p. 38.

79. A. D. Chandler, *Strategy and Structure* (Cambridge, Mass.: MIT Press, 1962).

80. D. Miller, "Configurations of Strategy and Structure," *Strategic Management Journal* 7 (1986): 233–249.

CHAPTER 14

1. S. Brearton, "2009 Fifty Best Employers in Canada," *Report on Business Magazine*, December 2009, 47; G. Teel, "Air Canada Overhauls Image; CEO Building Bridges With Customers," *Calgary Herald*, 29 September 2009, D1; D. Parker, "WestJetters Work Hard For Culture Of Teamwork," *Calgary Herald*, 23 January 2010, H3; G. Saretsky, "Incredible Spirit Of Giving Is In The Air," *Calgary Herald*, 12 December 2010, A2; K. Guttomson, "WestJet CEO Took Airline To New Heights in 2010; Ready to Soar in 2011; Company Seeks Global Partnerships," *Calgary Herald*, 30 December 2010, E1.

2. A. Williams, P. Dobson, and M. Walters, *Changing Culture: New Organizational Approaches* (London: Institute of Personnel Management, 1989); E. H. Schein, "What Is Culture?," in *Reframing Organizational Culture*, ed. P. J. Frost *et al.* (Newbury Park, CA: Sage, 1991), 243–253.

3. B. M. Meglino and E. C. Ravlin, "Individual Values in Organizations: Concepts, Controversies, and Research," *Journal of Management* 24, no. 3 (1998): 351–389; B. R. Agle and C. B. Caldwell, "Understanding Research on Values in Business," *Business and Society* 38, no. 3 (September 1999): 326–387; S. Hitlin and J. A. Pilavin, "Values: Reviving a Dormant Concept," *Annual Review of Sociology* 30 (2004): 359–393.

4. N. M. Ashkanasy, "The Case for Culture," in *Debating Organization*, ed. R. Westwood and S. Clegg (Malden, MA: Blackwell, 2003), 300–310.

5. Information about the corporate values of Vancity and Gap Adventures were found at their company websites: http://www.vancitycareers.com/aboutus/values/ourvalues/ (retrieved 5 May 2011); http://www.gapadventures.com/about-us/gap-adventures/ (retrieved 5 May 2011).

6. B. Kabanoff and J. Daly, "Espoused Values in Organisations," *Australian Journal of Management* 27, no. Special issue (2002): 89–104.

7. S. Shrinate, "Performance Appraisal: The 10% Rule," *Business Today (India)*, 5 December 2004, 160; G. S. Alexander, "Expert Hand to Help Pick Kamath's Successor at ICICI," *Economic Times (India)*, 3 October 2008; A. Dhall, "ICICI Bank: Measuring

Success in Global Standards," *Economics Times (India)*, 14 September 2008.

8. "Norway Criticizes BP, Smedvig over Safety," *Energy Compass*, 3 January 2003; J. A. Lozano, "BP Refinery Had History of Dangerous Releases, Report Finds," *Associated Press*, 28 October 2005; S. McNulty, "A Corroded Culture?," *Financial Times (London)*, 18 December 2006, 17; U.S. Chemical Safety and Hazard Investigation Board, *Investigation Report: Refinery Explosion and Fire (BP, Texas City, Texas, March 23, 2005)* (Washington, DC: U.S. Chemical Safety Board, March 2007); S. Greenhouse, "BP Faces Record Fine for '05 Refinery Explosion," *New York Times*, 30 October 2009; L. C. Steffy, *Drowning in Oil: BP and the Reckless Pursuit of Profit* (New York: McGraw-Hill, 2011).

9. C. A. O'Reilly III, J. Chatman, and D. F. Caldwell, "People and Organizational Culture: A Profile Comparison Approach to Assessing Person–Organization Fit," *Academy of Management Journal* 34 (1991): 487–516; J. J. van Muijen, "Organizational Culture," in *A Handbook of Work and Organizational Psychology: Organizational Psychology*, ed. P. J. D. Drenth, H. Thierry, and C. J. de Wolff, 2nd ed. (East Sussex, UK: Psychology Press, 1998), 113–132; P. A. Balthazard, R. A. Cooke, and R. E. Potter, "Dysfunctional Culture, Dysfunctional Organization: Capturing the Behavioral Norms That Form Organizational Culture and Drive Performance," *Journal of Managerial Psychology* 21, no. 8 (2006): 709–732; C. Helfrich *et al.*, "Assessing an Organizational Culture Instrument Based on the Competing Values Framework: Exploratory and Confirmatory Factor Analyses," *Implementation Science* 2, no. 1 (2007): 13. For recent reviews of organizational culture survey instruments, see T. Scott *et al.*, "The Quantitative Measurement of Organizational Culture in Health Care: A Review of the Available Instruments," *Health Services Research* 38, no. 3 (2003): 923–945; D. E. Leidner and T. Kayworth, "A Review of Culture in Information Systems Research: Toward a Theory of Information Technology Culture Conflict," *MIS Quarterly* 30, no. 2 (2006): 357–399; S. Scott-Findlay and C. A. Estabrooks, "Mapping the Organizational Culture Research in Nursing: A Literature Review," *Journal of Advanced Nursing* 56, no. 5 (2006): 498–513.

10. J. Martin, P. J. Frost, and O. A. O'Neill, "Organizational Culture: Beyond Struggles for Intellectual Dominance," in *Handbook of Organization Studies*, ed. S. Clegg *et al.*, 2nd ed. (London: Sage, 2006), 725–753; N. E. Fenton and S. Inglis, "A Critical Perspective on Organizational Values," *Nonprofit Management and Leadership* 17, no. 3 (2007): 335–347; K. Haukelid, "Theories of (Safety) Culture Revisited—an An-

thropological Approach," *Safety Science* 46, no. 3 (2008): 413–426.

11. J. A. Baker III et al, *The Report of the BP U.S. Refineries Independent Safety Review Panel* (Houston: The BP U.S. Refineries Independent Safety Review Panel, February 2007).

12. J. Martin and C. Siehl, "Organizational Culture and Counterculture: An Uneasy Symbiosis," *Organizational Dynamics* (Autumn 1983): 52–64; G. Hofstede, "Identifying Organizational Subcultures: An Empirical Approach," *Journal of Management Studies* 35, no. 1 (1990): 1–12; E. Ogbonna and L. C. Harris, "Organisational Culture in the Age of the Internet: An Exploratory Study," *New Technology, Work and Employment* 21, no. 2 (2006): 162–175.

13. H. Silver, "Does a University Have a Culture?," *Studies in Higher Education* 28, no. 2 (2003): 157–169.

14. A. Sinclair, "Approaches to Organizational Culture and Ethics," *Journal of Business Ethics* 12 (1993); T. E. Deal and A. A. Kennedy, *The New Corporate Cultures* (Cambridge, MA: Perseus Books, 1999), Chap. 10; A. Boisnier and J. Chatman, "The Role of Subcultures in Agile Organizations," in *Leading and Managing People in Dynamic Organizations*, ed. R. Petersen and E. Mannix (Mahwah, NJ: Lawrence Erlbaum Associates, 2003), 87–112; C. Morrill, M. N. Zald, and H. Rao, "Covert Political Conflict in Organizations: Challenges from Below," *Annual Review of Sociology* 29, no. 1 (2003): 391–415.

15. J. S. Ott, *The Organizational Culture Perspective* (Pacific Grove, CA: Brooks/Cole, 1989), Chap. 2; J. S. Pederson and J. S. Sorensen, *Organizational Cultures in Theory and Practice* (Aldershot, England: Gower, 1989), 27–29; M. O. Jones, *Studying Organizational Symbolism: What, How, Why?* (Thousand Oaks, CA: Sage, 1996).

16. W. Immen, "The 50 Best Employers to Work For," *Globe & Mail*, 14 January 2009, C1; B. Travica, *Challenges of Growth at Protegra* (London, Ont.: Richard Ivey School of Business, University of Western Ontario, 2010); C. Atchison, "Secrets of Canada's Best Bosses," *Profit (Profitguide.com)*, 16 February 2011.

17. E. H. Schein, "Organizational Culture," *American Psychologist* (February 1990): 109–119; A. Furnham and B. Gunter, "Corporate Culture: Definition, Diagnosis, and Change," *International Review of Industrial and Organizational Psychology* 8 (1993): 233–261; E. H. Schein, *The Corporate Culture Survival Guide* (San Francisco: Jossey-Bass, 1999), Chap. 4.

18. M. Doehrman, "Anthropologists—Deep in the Corporate Bush," *Daily Record (Kansas City, MO)*, 19 July 2005, 1.

19. M. Miller, "The Acrobat," *Forbes*, 15 March 2004, 100–103; R. Ouzounian, "Cirque's Dream Factory," *Toronto Star*, 1 August 2004.

20. T. E. Deal and A. A. Kennedy, *Corporate Cultures* (Reading, Mass.: Addison-Wesley, 1982), chap. 5; C. J. Boudens, "The Story of Work: A Narrative Analysis of Workplace Emotion," *Organization Studies* 26, no. 9 (2005): 1285–1306; S. Denning, *The Leader's Guide to Storytelling* (San Francisco: Jossey-Bass, 2005).

21. A. L. Wilkins, "Organizational Stories as Symbols Which Control the Organization," in *Organizational Symbolism*, ed. L. R. Pondy *et al.* (Greenwich, CT: JAI Press, 1984), 81–92; R. Zemke, "Storytelling: Back to a Basic," *Training* 27 (March 1990): 44–50; J. C. Meyer, "Tell Me a Story: Eliciting Organizational Values from Narratives," *Communication Quarterly* 43 (1995): 210–224; W. Swap *et al.*, "Using Mentoring and Storytelling to Transfer Knowledge in the Workplace," *Journal of Management Information Systems* 18 (Summer 2001): 95–114.

22. A. C. T. Smith and B. Stewart, "Organizational Rituals: Features, Functions and Mechanisms," *International Journal of Management Reviews* (2011): in press.

23. "The Ultimate Chairman," *Business Times Singapore*, 3 September 2005.

24. D. Roth, "My Job at the Container Store," *Fortune* (10 January 2000): 74–78.

25. R. E. Quinn and N. T. Snyder, "Advance Change Theory: Culture Change at Whirlpool Corporation," in *The Leader's Change Handbook* ed. J. A. Conger, G. M. Spreitzer, and E. E. Lawler III (San Francisco: Jossey-Bass, 1999), 162–193.

26. Churchill apparently made this statement on October 28, 1943 in the British House of Commons, when London, damaged by bombings in World War II, was about to be rebuilt.

27. G. Turner and J. Myerson, *New Workspace New Culture: Office Design as a Catalyst for Change* (Aldershot, UK: Gower, 1998).

28. P. Roberts, "The Empire Strikes Back," *Fast Company*, no. 22 (February-March 1999): 122–131; H. Nguyen, "Oakley Shades for Her Eyes Only," *Orange County Register (Santa Ana, CA)*, 11 May 2006. Details and photos are also found at: www.oakley.com; and americahurrah.com/Oakley/Entry.htm.

29. K. D. Elsbach and B. A. Bechky, "It's More Than a Desk: Working Smarter through Leveraged Office Design," *California Management Review* 49, no. 2 (Winter 2007): 80–101.

30. M. Burton, "Open Plan, Open Mind," *Director* (March 2005): 68–72; B. Murray, "Agency Profile: Mother London," *Ihaveanidea*, 28 January 2007, www.ihaveanidea.org.

31. A. Krishnan, "CEOs from the Best Provide Insights Gained from Hewitt Best Employers Study," *the Edge (Malaysia)*, 21 July 2008.

32. K. Frieberg and J. Frieberg, *Nuts!* (N.Y.: Bantam Doubleday Dell, 1998), p. 144.

33. J. C. Collins and J. I. Porras, *Built to Last: Successful Habits of Visionary Companies* (London: Century, 1994); Deal and Kennedy, *The New Corporate Cultures*; R. Barrett, *Building a Values-Driven Organization: A Whole System Approach to Cultural Transformation* (Burlington, MA: Butterworth-Heinemann, 2006); J. M. Kouzes and B. Z. Posner, *The Leadership Challenge*, 4th ed. (San Francisco: Jossey-Bass, 2007), Chap. 3.

34. C. Siehl and J. Martin, "Organizational Culture: A Key to Financial Performance?," in *Organizational Climate and Culture*, ed. B. Schneider (San Francisco, CA: Jossey-Bass, 1990), 241–281; G. G. Gordon and N. DiTomasco, "Predicting Corporate Performance from Organizational Culture," *Journal of Management Studies* 29 (1992): 783–798; J. P. Kotter and J. L. Heskett, *Corporate Culture and Performance* (New York: Free Press, 1992); C. P. M. Wilderom, U. Glunk, and R. Maslowski, "Organizational Culture as a Predictor of Organizational Performance," in *Handbook of Organizational Culture and Climate*, ed. N. M. Ashkanasy, C. P. M. Wilderom, and M. F. Peterson (Thousand Oaks, CA: Sage, 2000), 193–210; A. Carmeli and A. Tishler, "The Relationships between Intangible Organizational Elements and Organizational Performance," *Strategic Management Journal* 25 (2004): 1257–1278; S. Teerikangas and P. Very, "The Culture-Performance Relationship in M&A: From Yes/No to How," *British Journal of Management* 17, no. S1 (2006): S31-S48.

35. J. C. Helms Mills and A. J. Mills, "Rules, Sensemaking, Formative Contexts, and Discourse in the Gendering of Organizational Culture," in *International Handbook of Organizational Climate and Culture*, ed. N. Ashkanasy, C. Wilderom, and M. Peterson (Thousand Oaks, CA: Sage, 2000), 55–70; J. A. Chatman and S. E. Cha, "Leading by Leveraging Culture," *California Management Review* 45 (Summer 2003): 20–34.

36. B. Ashforth and F. Mael, "Social Identity Theory and the Organization," *Academy of Management Review* 14 (1989): 20–39.

37. Heidrick & Struggles, *Leadership Challenges Emerge as Asia Pacific Companies Go Global* (Melbourne: Heidrick & Struggles, August 2008).

38. M. R. Louis, "Surprise and Sensemaking: What Newcomers Experience in Entering Unfamiliar Organizational Settings," *Administrative Science Quarterly* 25 (1980): 226–251; S. G. Harris, "Organizational Culture and Individual Sensemaking: A Schema-Based Perspective," *Organization Science* 5 (1994): 309–321.

39. J. W. Barnes *et al.*, "The Role of Culture Strength in Shaping Sales Force Outcomes," *Journal of Personal Selling & Sales Management* 26, no. 3 (Summer 2006): 255–270.

40. N. Byrnes, P. Burrows, and L. Lee, "Dark Days at Dell," *BusinessWeek*, 4 September 2006, 26; S. Lohr, "Can Michael Dell Refocus His Namesake?," *New York Times*, 9 September 2007, 1.

41. C. A. O'Reilly III and J. A. Chatman, "Culture as Social Control: Corporations, Cults, and Commitment," *Research in Organizational Behavior* 18 (1996): 157–200; B. Spector and H. Lane, "Exploring the Distinctions between a High Performance Culture and a Cult," *Strategy & Leadership* 35, no. 3 (2007): 18–24.

42. Kotter and Heskett, *Corporate Culture and Performance*; J. P. Kotter, "Cultures and Coalitions," *Executive Excellence* 15 (March 1998): 14–15; B. M. Bass and R. E. Riggio, *Transformational Leadership*, 2nd ed. (New York: Routledge, 2006), Chap. 7. The term *adaptive culture* has a different meaning in organizational behaviour than it has in cultural anthropology, where it refers to nonmaterial cultural conditions (such as ways of thinking) that lag the material culture (physical artifacts). For the anthropological perspective, see W. Griswold, *Cultures and Societies in a Changing World*, 3rd ed. (Thousand Oaks, Calif.: Pine Forge Press (Sage), 2008), p. 66.

43. W. E. Baker and J. M. Sinkula, "The Synergistic Effect of Market Orientation and Learning Orientation on Organizational Performance," *Academy of Marketing Science Journal* 27, no. 4 (Fall 1999): 411–427; Z. Emden, A. Yaprak, and S. T. Cavusgil, "Learning from Experience in International Alliances: Antecedents and Firm Performance Implications," *Journal of Business Research* 58, no. 7 (2005): 883–892.

44. D. Ho, "Michael Dell Says He Had No Role in Accounting Scandal," *Cox News Service*, 6 September 2007.

45. M. L. Sirower, *The Synergy Trap: How Companies Lose the Acquisition Game* (New York: The Free Press, 1997); C. Cook and D. Spitzer, *World Class Transactions* (London: KPMG, 2001); J. P. Daly *et al.*, "The Effects of Initial Differences in Firms' Espoused Values on Their Postmerger Performance," *Journal of Applied Behavioral Science* 40, no. 3 (2004): 323–343; J. Krug, *Mergers and Acquisitions: Turmoil in Top Management Teams* (Williston, VT: Business Expert Press, 2009).

46. M. L. Marks, "Adding Cultural Fit to Your Diligence Checklist," *Mergers & Acquisitions* 34, no. 3 (Nov-Dec 1999): 14–20; Schein, *The Corporate Culture Survival Guide* Chap. 8; M. L. Marks, "Mixed Signals," *Across the Board* (May 2000): 21–26.

47. Teerikangas and Very, "The Culture-Performance Relationship in M&A: From Yes/No to How"; G. K. Stahl and A. Voigt, "Do Cultural Differences Matter in Mergers and Acquisitions? A Tentative Model and Examination," *Organization Science* 19, no. 1 (January 2008): 160–176.

48. R. Smith and D. Fitzpatrick, "Cultures Clash as Merrill Herd Meets 'Wal-Mart of Banking'," *Wall Street Journal*, 14 November 2008, C1; "Bank of America-Merrill Lynch: A $50 Billion Deal from Hell," *Deal Journal (Wall Street Journal Blog)*, 22 January 2009; M. Read, "Wall Street's Entitlement Culture Hard to Shake," *Associated Press*, 23 January 2009; D. Sarch, "Merrill Lynch: Culture Change or Just the Latest Innovation?," *Investment News*, 27 May 2010.

49. C. A. Schorg, C. A. Raiborn, and M. F. Massoud, "Using a 'Cultural Audit' to Pick M&A Winners," *Journal of Corporate Accounting & Finance* (May/June 2004): 47–55; W. Locke, "Higher Education Mergers: Integrating Organisational Cultures and Developing Appropriate Management Styles," *Higher Education Quarterly* 61, no. 1 (2007): 83–102.

50. D. Mavin, "Grant Thornton, BDO call off wedding," *National Post*, 12 May 2007, FP7; S. Won, "Big accounting firms talk 'marriage of opportunity'," *Globe & Mail*, 14 April 2007, B6; "Grant Thornton, BDO set to merge," *Financial Post*, 13 April 2007.

51. S. Greengard, "Due Diligence: The Devil in the Details," *Workforce* (October 1999): 68; Marks, "Adding Cultural Fit to Your Diligence Checklist."

52. A. R. Malekazedeh and A. Nahavandi, "Making Mergers Work by Managing Cultures," *Journal of Business Strategy* (May-June 1990): 55–57; K. W. Smith, "A Brand-New Culture for the Merged Firm," *Mergers and Acquisitions* 35 (June 2000): 45–50.

53. T. Hamilton, "RIM on a Roll," *Toronto Star*, 22 February 2004, C01.

54. M. Andrews, "Amazon Looks to Fill Niche with Abebooks Purchase," *Vancouver Sun*, 2 August 2008; A. A. Duffy, "Add 'Business Incubator' to Abebooks's Achievements," *Vancouver Sun*, 3 December 2008, D4; E. Frauenheim, "Jungle Survival," *Workforce Management*, 14 September 2009, 19; B. Lennox and W. Nie, "The Case Study: Creating a Distinct Corporate Culture," *Financial Times (London)*, 17 February 2011, 14.

55. Hewitt Associates, "Mergers and Acquisitions May Be Driven by Business Strategy—But Often Stumble Over People and Culture Issues," PR Newswire News release (Lincolnshire, IL: 3 August 1998).

56. J. Martin, "Can Organizational Culture Be Managed?," in *Organizational Culture*, ed. P. J. Frost *et al.* (Beverly Hills, CA: Sage, 1985), 95–98.

57. J. Wells, "Now It's Her Chance to Stretch," *Globe & Mail*, 3 April 2008; D. Flavelle, "Yoga-Wear Icon Brews up New Top Executive," *Toronto Star*, 3 April 2008; B. Bouw, "Zen and the Art of Retailing," *Globe & Mail*, 30 November 2007; D. Law, "From Coffee Beans to Yoga; Christine Day on the Retail Environment," *The Commerce Times*, 7 October 2009; D. Jermyn, "Be an Ember, Lululemon's Leader Says," *Special to The Globe & Mail*, 12 November 2009.

58. I. Sharp, *Four Seasons: The Story of a Business Philosophy* (New York: Portfolio, 2009), Chaps. 10 and 11.

59. E. H. Schein, "The Role of the Founder in Creating Organizational Culture," *Organizational Dynamics* 12, no. 1 (Summer 1983): 13–28; R. House, M. Javidan, and P. Dorfman, "Project GLOBE: An Introduction," *Applied Psychology: An International Review* 50 (2001): 489–505; R. House *et al.*, "Understanding Cultures and Implicit Leadership Theories across the Globe: An Introduction to Project GLOBE," *Journal of World Business* 37 (2002): 3–10.

60. A. S. Tsui *et al.*, "Unpacking the Relationship between CEO Leadership Behavior and Organizational Culture," *Leadership Quarterly* 17 (2006): 113–137; Y. Berson, S. Oreg, and T. Dvir, "CEO Values, Organizational Culture and Firm Outcomes," *Journal of Organizational Behavior* 29, no. 5 (July 2008): 615–633.

61. M. De Pree, *Leadership Is an Art* (East Lansing, MI: Michigan State University Press, 1987).

62. J. Kerr and J. W. Slocum Jr., "Managing Corporate Culture through Reward Systems," *Academy of Management Executive* 1 (May 1987): 99–107; J. M. Higgins *et al.*, "Using Cultural Artifacts to Change and Perpetuate Strategy," *Journal of Change Management* 6, no. 4 (2006): 397–415.

63. R. Charan, "Home Depot's Blueprint for Culture Change," *Harvard Business Review* (April 2006): 61–70.

64. B. Schneider, "The People Make the Place," *Personnel Psychology* 40, no. 3 (1987): 437–453; B. Schneider *et al.*, "Personality and Organizations: A Test of the Homogeneity of Personality Hypothesis," *Journal of Applied Psychology* 83, no. 3 (Jun 1998): 462–470; T. R. Giberson, C. J. Resick, and M. W. Dickson, "Embedding Leader Characteristics: An Examination of Homogeneity of Personality and Values in Organizations," *Journal of Applied Psychology* 90, no. 5 (2005): 1002–1010.

65. T. A. Judge and D. M. Cable, "Applicant Personality, Organizational Culture, and Organization Attraction," *Personnel Psychology* 50, no. 2 (1997): 359–394; D. S. Chapman *et al.*, "Applicant Attraction to Organizations and Job Choice: A Meta-Analytic Review of the Correlates of Recruit- ing Outcomes," *Journal of Applied Psychology* 90, no. 5 (2005): 928–944; A. L. Kristof-Brown, R. D. Zimmerman, and E. C. Johnson, "Consequences of Individuals' Fit at Work: A Meta-Analysis of Person-Job, Person-Organization, Person-Group, and Person-Supervisor Fit," *Personnel Psychology* 58, no. 2 (2005): 281–342; C. Hu, H.-C. Su, and C.-I. B. Chen, "The Effect of Person-Organization Fit Feedback Via Recruitment Web Sites on Applicant Attraction," *Computers in Human Behavior* 23, no. 5 (2007): 2509–2523.

66. A. Kristof-Brown, "Perceived Applicant Fit: Distinguishing between Recruiters' Perceptions of Person-Job and Person-Organization Fit," *Personnel Psychology* 53, no. 3 (Autumn 2000): 643–671; A. E. M. Van Vianen, "Person-Organization Fit: The Match between Newcomers' and Recruiters' Preferences for Organizational Cultures," *Personnel Psychology* 53 (Spring 2000): 113–149.

67. S. Brimble, "Apex Distribution Enters Next Level of Growth through Product Diversification," *On Stream*, Summer 2006, 12–16; D. Sankey, "Avoiding a Culture Clash in New Job," *Calgary Herald*, 25 August 2007.

68. P. Mitham, "Hiring a Stellar Staff," *BC Business*, December 2010.

69. D. M. Cable and J. R. Edwards, "Complementary and Supplementary Fit: A Theoretical and Empirical Integration," *Journal of Applied Psychology* 89, no. 5 (2004): 822–834.

70. "WestJet, Tim Hortons and RBC Financial Group." CNW news release for Waterstone Human Capital and National Post (Toronto: 13 October 2005); Y. Lermusi, "The No. 1 Frustration of Your Job Candidates," (15 August 2006), www.ere.net (accessed 2 June 2010); S. Singleton, "Starbucks, Goodlife Fitness among Most Admired Companies," *Money.Canoe.ca (Toronto)*, 12 November 2009; Taleo Research, "Talent Management Processes," (Dublin, CA: Taleo, 2010), www.taleo.com (accessed 2 June 2010).

71. P. Brent, "Practising What It Preaches," *Toronto Star*, 16 November 2010, B7.

72. J. Van Maanen, "Breaking In: Socialization to Work," in *Handbook of Work, Organization, and Society*, ed. R. Dubin (Chicago: Rand McNally, 1976).

73. S. L. McShane, G. O'Neill, and T. Travaglione, "Managing Employee Values in Values-Driven Organizations: Contradiction, Façade, and Illusions" in *21st Annual ANZAM Conference* (Sydney, Australia, December, 2007); S. L. McShane, G. O'Neill, and T. Travaglione, "Rethinking the Values-Driven Organization Process: From Values Engineering to Behavioral Domain Training," Paper presented at Academy of Management 2008 Annual Meeting, Anaheim, Calif., August 2008.

74. D. G. Allen, "Do Organizational Socialization Tactics Influence Newcomer Embeddedness and Turnover?," *Journal of Management* 32, no. 2 (April 2006): 237–256; A. M. Saks, K. L. Uggerslev, and N. E. Fassina, "Socialization Tactics and Newcomer Adjustment: A Meta-Analytic Review and Test of a Model," *Journal of Vocational Behavior* 70, no. 3 (2007): 413–446.

75. G. T. Chao *et al.*, "Organizational Socialization: Its Content and Consequences," *Journal of Applied Psychology* 79 (1994): 450–463; H. D. Cooper-Thomas and N. Anderson, "Organizational Socialization: A Field Study into Socialization Success and Rate," *International Journal of Selection and Assessment* 13, no. 2 (2005): 116–128.

76. N. Nicholson, "A Theory of Work Role Transitions," *Administrative Science Quarterly* 29 (1984): 172–191; B. E. Ashforth, D. M. Sluss, and A. M. Saks, "Socialization Tactics, Proactive Behavior, and Newcomer Learning: Integrating Socialization Models," *Journal of Vocational Behavior* 70, no. 3 (2007): 447–462; T. N. Bauer, "Newcomer Adjustment During Organizational Socialization: A Meta-Analytic Review of Antecedents, Outcomes, and Methods," *Journal of Applied Psychology* 92, no. 3 (2007): 707–721; A. Elfering *et al.*, "First Years in Job: A Three-Wave Analysis of Work Experiences," *Journal of Vocational Behavior* 70, no. 1 (2007): 97–115.

77. J. M. Beyer and D. R. Hannah, "Building on the Past: Enacting Established Personal Identities in a New Work Setting," *Organization Science* 13 (November/December 2002): 636–652; H. D. C. Thomas and N. Anderson, "Newcomer Adjustment: The Relationship between Organizational Socialization Tactics, Information Acquisition and Attitudes," *Journal of Occupational and Organizational Psychology* 75 (December 2002): 423–437.

78. M. Johne, "Workplace Loyalty a Two-Way Street," *Globe & Mail*, 5 August 2009, B13.

79. S. L. Robinson and E. Wolfe Morrison, "The Development of Psychological Contract Breach and Violation: A Longitudinal Study," *Journal of Organizational Behavior* 21, no. 5 (2000): 525–546; K. J. McInnis, J. P. Meyer, and S. Feldman, "Psychological Contracts and Their Implications for Commitment: A Feature-Based Approach," *Journal of Vocational Behavior* 74, no. 2 (2009): 165–180; M.-È. Lapalme, G. Simard, and M. Tremblay, "The Influence of Psychological Contract Breach on Temporary Workers' Commitment and Behaviors: A Multiple Agency Perspective," *Journal of Business and Psychology* (2011): in press.

80. S. L. Robinson and D. M. Rousseau, "Violating the Psychological Contract: Not the Exception but the Norm," *Journal of Organizational Behavior* 15 (1994): 245–259;

E. W. Morrison and S. L. Robinson, "When Employees Feel Betrayed: A Model of How Psychological Contract Violation Develops," *Academy of Management Review* 22 (1997): 226–256; S. D. Montes and P. G. Irving, "Disentangling the Effects of Promised and Delivered Inducements: Relational and Transactional Contract Elements and the Mediating Role of Trust," *Journal of Applied Psychology* 93, no. 6 (2008): 1367–1381.

81. L. W. Porter, E. E. Lawler III, and J. R. Hackman, *Behavior in Organizations* (New York: McGraw-Hill, 1975), 163–167; Van Maanen, "Breaking In: Socialization to Work"; D. C. Feldman, "The Multiple Socialization of Organization Members," *Academy of Management Review* 6 (1981): 309–318.

82. B. E. Ashforth and A. M. Saks, "Socialization Tactics: Longitudinal Effects on Newcomer Adjustment," *Academy of Management Journal* 39 (1996): 149–178; J. D. Kammeyer-Mueller and C. R. Wanberg, "Unwrapping the Organizational Entry Process: Disentangling Multiple Antecedents and Their Pathways to Adjustment," *Journal of Applied Psychology* 88, no. 5 (2003): 779–794.

83. Porter, Lawler III, and Hackman, *Behavior in Organizations* Chap. 5.

84. Louis, "Surprise and Sensemaking: What Newcomers Experience in Entering Unfamiliar Organizational Settings."

85. Robinson and Rousseau, "Violating the Psychological Contract: Not the Exception but the Norm."

86. D. L. Nelson, "Organizational Socialization: A Stress Perspective," *Journal of Occupational Behavior* 8 (1987): 311–324; Elfering *et al.*, "First Years in Job."

87. J. P. Wanous, *Organizational Entry* (Reading, Mass.: Addison-Wesley, 1992); J. A. Breaugh and M. Starke, "Research on Employee Recruitment: So Many Studies, So Many Remaining Questions," *Journal of Management* 26, no. 3 (2000): 405–434.

88. J. M. Phillips, "Effects of Realistic Job Previews on Multiple Organizational Outcomes: A Meta-Analysis," *Academy of Management Journal* 41 (December 1998): 673–690.

89. Y. Ganzach *et al.*, "Social Exchange and Organizational Commitment: Decision-Making Training for Job Choice as an Alternative to the Realistic Job Preview," *Personnel Psychology* 55 (Autumn 2002): 613–637.

90. C. Ostroff and S. W. J. Koslowski, "Organizational Socialization as a Learning Process: The Role of Information Acquisition," *Personnel Psychology* 45 (1992): 849–874; Cooper-Thomas and Anderson, "Organizational Socialization: A Field Study into Socialization Success and Rate"; A. Baber and L. Waymon, "Uncovering the Unconnected Employee," *T&D* (May 2008): 60–66.

91. C. Fishman, "The Anarchist's Cookbook," *Fast Company*, July 2004, 70;

"World's Finest Food Retailers: Whole Foods, Not Holy Food," *The Grocer*, 12 November 2005, 32.

92. E. Simon, "Employers Study Applicants' Personalities," *Associated Press*, 5 November 2007. Also see the Lindblad RJP video at: http://www.expeditions.com/Theater17.asp?Media=475.

93. L. Buchanan *et al.*, "That's Chief Entertainment Officer," *Inc.* 29, no. 8 (August 2007): 86–94; P. Burkes Erickson, "Welcoming Employees: Making That First Day a Great Experience," *Daily Oklahoman*, 15 July 2007.

CHAPTER 15

1. A. Coyne, "Our Best (and Worst) Run Cities," *Macleans*, 22 July 2009, 14; J. Couture, "Bringing Change to the City," *Leader Post (Regina)*, 12 July 2010, A3; "Meet the City Manager," www.regina.ca/Page233.aspx Retrieved March 11, 2011. The authors gratefully acknowledge the contributions provided by: Jim Nicol, Chief of Staff to the City Manager, Linda Allen-Hardisty, Manager Strategy & Performance, and Sylvia Lee, Director of Human Resources, City of Regina.

2. J. Welch, *Jack: Straight from the Heart* (New York: Warner Business books, 2001), 432.

3. K. Lewin, *Field Theory in Social Science* (New York: Harper & Row, 1951).

4. D. Coghlan and T. Brannick, "Kurt Lewin: The 'Practical Theorist' for the 21st Century," *Irish Journal of Management* 24, no. 2 (2003): 31–37; B. Burnes, "Kurt Lewin and the Planned Approach to Change: A Re-Appraisal," *Journal of Management Studies* 41, no. 6 (Sept. 2004): 977–1002.

5. "Ogilvy & Mather Corporate Culture" (New York, 2011), http://www.ogilvy.com/About/Our-History/Corporate-Culture.aspx (accessed 17 May 2011).

6. D. Howell, "Nardelli Nears Five-Year Mark with Riveting Record," *DSN Retailing Today*, 9 May 2005, 1, 38; R. Charan, "Home Depot's Blueprint for Culture Change," *Harvard Business Review* (April 2006): 61–70; R. DeGross, "Five Years of Change: Home Depot's Results Mixed under Nardelli," *Atlanta Journal-Constitution*, 1 January 2006, F1; B. Grow, D. Brady, and M. Arndt, "Renovating Home Depot," *BusinessWeek*, 6 March 2006, 50–57.

7. M. Haid *et al.*, *Ready, Get Set...Change!: The Impact of Change on Workforce Productivity and Engagement*, Leadership Insights (Philadelphia, PA: Right Management, 2009).

8. D. Miller, "Building Commitment to Major Change—What 1700 Change Agents Told Us Really Works," *Developing HR Strategy*, no. 22 (September 2008): 5–8; W. Immen, "When Leaders Become Glory Hounds," *Globe & Mail (Toronto)*, 5 March 2010, B15.

9. Some experts suggest that resistance to change should be restated in a more positive way by its opposite: readiness for change. See: M. Choi and W. E. A. Ruona, "Individual Readiness for Organizational Change and Its Implications for Human Resource and Organization Development," *Human Resource Development Review* 10, no. 1 (March 2011): 46–73.

10. S. Chreim, "Postscript to Change: Survivors' Retrospective Views of Organizational Changes," *Personnel Review* 35, no. 3 (2006): 315–335.

11. M. Johnson-Cramer, S. Parise, and R. Cross, "Managing Change through Networks and Values," *California Management Review* 49, no. 3 (Spring 2007): 85–109.

12. K. Shimizu, "Hoppy Enjoying Comeback after Radical Shift in Management," *Japan Times*, 15 August 2007; S. K. S. Kotaka, "Hoppy Beverage's Heir Is Bubbling with Enthusiasm," *Kyodo News (Tokyo)* 2009.

13. J. K. Galbraith, *Economics, Peace, and Laughter* (Boston: Houghton Mifflin, 1971), 50.

14. B. J. Tepper *et al.*, "Subordinates' Resistance and Managers' Evaluations of Subordinates' Performance," *Journal of Management* 32, no. 2 (April 2006): 185–209; J. D. Ford, L. W. Ford, and A. D'Amelio, "Resistance to Change: The Rest of the Story," *Academy of Management Review* 33, no. 2 (2008): 362–377.

15. E. B. Dent and S. G. Goldberg, "Challenging 'Resistance to Change'," *Journal of Applied Behavioral Science* 35 (March 1999): 25–41; D. B. Fedor, S. Caldwell, and D. M. Herold, "The Effects of Organizational Changes on Employee Commitment: A Multilevel Investigation," *Personnel Psychology* 59, no. 1 (2006): 1–29.

16. S. Oreg *et al.*, "Dispositional Resistance to Change: Measurement Equivalence and the Link to Personal Values across 17 Nations," *Journal of Applied Psychology* 93, no. 4 (2008): 935–944.

17. R. R. Sharma, *Change Management: Concepts and Applications* (New Delhi: Tata McGraw-Hill, 2007), Chap. 4; A. A. Armenakis and S. G. Harris, "Reflections: Our Journey in Organizational Change Research and Practice," *Journal of Change Management* 9, no. 2 (2009): 127–142; I. Cinite, L. E. Duxbury, and C. Higgins, "Measurement of Perceived Organizational Readiness for Change in the Public Sector," *British Journal of Management* 20, no. 2 (2009): 265–277; S. Jaros, "Commitment to Organizational Change: A Critical Review," *Journal of Change Management* 10, no. 1 (March 2010): 79–108.

18. D. A. Nadler, "The Effective Management of Organizational Change," in *Handbook of Organizational Behavior*, ed. J. W. Lorsch (Englewood Cliffs, N.J.: Prentice

Hall, 1987), 358–369; R. Maurer, *Beyond the Wall of Resistance: Unconventional Strategies to Build Support for Change* (Austin, TX: Bard Books, 1996); P. Strebel, "Why Do Employees Resist Change?," *Harvard Business Review* (May-June 1996): 86–92; D. A. Nadler, *Champions of Change* (San Francisco, CA: Jossey-Bass, 1998).

19. L. Brody and D. Raffa, *Everything I Need to Know About Business...I Learned from a Canadian*, 2nd ed. (Mississauga, Ont.: John Wiley & Sons Canada, 2009), 201–202.

20. V. Newman, "The Psychology of Managing for Innovation," *KM Review* 9, no. 6 (2007): 10–15.

21. R. Davis, *Leading for Growth: How Umpqua Bank Got Cool and Created a Culture of Greatness* (San Francisco, Calif.: Jossey-Bass, 2007), 40.

22. *Bosses Want Change but Workers Want More of the Same!* (Sydney: Talent2, 29 June 2005).

23. C. Ressler and J. Thompson, *Why Work Sucks and How to Fix It* (New York: Portfolio, 2008), Chapter 2.

24. T. G. Cummings, "The Role and Limits of Change Leadership," in *The Leader's Change Handbook*, ed. J. A. Conger, G. M. Spreitzer, and E. E. Lawler III (San Francisco: Jossey-Bass, 1999), 301–320; J. P. Kotter and D. S. Cohen, *The Heart of Change* (Boston: Harvard Business School Press, 2002), 15–36; J. P. Kotter, *A Sense of Urgency* (Boston: Harvard Business School Press, 2008).

25. S. Simpson, "White Spot Restaurants Keep Iconic Brand Sizzling," *Vancouver Sun*, 24 March 2011, C3.

26. L. D. Goodstein and H. R. Butz, "Customer Value: The Linchpin of Organizational Change," *Organizational Dynamics* 27 (June 1998): 21–35.

27. I. J. Bozon and P. N. Child, "Refining Shell's Position in Europe," *McKinsey Quarterly*, no. 2 (2003): 42–51.

28. D. Darlin, "Growing Tomorrow," *Business 2.0*, May 2005, 126.

29. L. Grossman and S. Song, "Stevie's Little Wonder," *Time*, 19 September 2005, 63; S. Levy, "Honey, I Shrunk the iPod. A Lot," *Newsweek*, 19 September 2005, 58.

30. T. F. Cawsey and G. Deszca, *Toolkit for Organizational Change* (Los Angeles: Sage, 2007), 104.

31. J. P. Kotter and L. A. Schlesinger, "Choosing Strategies for Change," *Harvard Business Review* (March-April 1979): 106–114.

32. M. Meaney and C. Pung, "Creating Organizational Transformations: McKinsey Global Survey Results," *McKinsey Quarterly*, July 2008, 1–7.

33. B. Nanus and S. M. Dobbs, *Leaders Who Make a Difference* (San Francisco: Jossey-

Bass, 1999); Kotter and Cohen, *The Heart of Change*, 83–98; J. Allen *et al.*, "Uncertainty During Organizational Change: Managing Perceptions through Communication," *Journal of Change Management* 7, no. 2 (2007): 187–210; T. L. Russ, "Communicating Change: A Review and Critical Analysis of Programmatic and Participatory Implementation Approaches," *Journal of Change Management* 8, no. 3 (2008): 199–211.

34. G. Jones, "Chemical Reaction," *Smart Business Pittsburgh*, February 2011, 10.

35. K. T. Dirks, L. L. Cummings, and J. L. Pierce, "Psychological Ownership in Organizations: Conditions under Which Individuals Promote and Resist Change," *Research in Organizational Change and Development* 9 (1996): 1–23; A. Cox, S. Zagelmeyer, and M. Marchington, "Embedding Employee Involvement and Participation at Work," *Human Resource Management Journal* 16, no. 3 (2006): 250–267.

36. N. T. Tan, "Maximising Human Resource Potential in the Midst of Organisational Change," *Singapore Management Review* 27, no. 2 (2005): 25–35.

37. M. McHugh, "The Stress Factor: Another Item for the Change Management Agenda?," *Journal of Organizational Change Management* 10 (1997): 345–362; D. Buchanan, T. Claydon, and M. Doyle, "Organisation Development and Change: The Legacy of the Nineties," *Human Resource Management Journal* 9 (1999): 20–37.

38. T. Wakefield, "No Pain, No Gain," *Canadian Business*, January 1993, 50–54; M. Cash, "StandardAero Back on the Sale Block," *Winnipeg Free Press*, 14 December 2010.

39. D. Nicolini and M. B. Meznar, "The Social Construction of Organizational Learning: Conceptual and Practical Issues in the Field," *Human Relations* 48 (1995): 727–746.

40. E. E. Lawler III, "Pay Can Be a Change Agent," *Compensation & Benefits Management* 16 (Summer 2000): 23–26; Kotter and Cohen, *The Heart of Change*, 161–177; M. A. Roberto and L. C. Levesque, "The Art of Making Change Initiatives Stick," *MIT Sloan Management Review* 46, no. 4 (Summer 2005): 53–60.

41. Lawler III, "Pay Can Be a Change Agent."

42. Goodstein and Butz, "Customer Value: The Linchpin of Organizational Change"; R. H. Miles, "Leading Corporate Transformation: Are You Up to the Task?," in *The Leader's Change Handbook* ed. J. A. Conger, G. M. Spreitzer, and E. E. Lawler III (San Francisco: Jossey-Bass, 1999), 221–267.

43. R. E. Quinn, *Building the Bridge as You Walk on It: A Guide for Leading Change* (San Francisco: Jossey-Bass, 2004), Chap. 11.

44. R. Caldwell, "Models of Change Agency: A Fourfold Classification," *British Journal of Management* 14 (June 2003): 131–142.

45. H. Paterson, "Trio Helps Pad Hospital's Results, Three Carleton Grads have Produced an Ipad App to Help Doctors with Their Bedside Manner," *Ottawa Citizen*, 3 November 2010, D1; "The Changing Business of Saving Lives: Telus Bets Big on Paperless Care," *Globe & Mail*, 21 October 2010, B1; V. Pilieci, "Ottawa Hospital Boss Urges Staff to 'Be Bold...Go Big'; Information Technology Systems at the Ottawa Hospital were On Life Support Before Dale Potter Signed On. The IT Expert's Revolutionary Ideas have Transformed the Institution," *Ottawa Citizen*, 2 May 2010, A1; "Five Steps Toward High-Tech Health Care," *Ottawa Citizen*, 2 May 2010, A1.

46. Kotter and Cohen, *The Heart of Change*, 61–82; D. S. Cohen and J. P. Kotter, *The Heart of Change Field Guide* (Boston: Harvard Business School Press, 2005).

47. J. Thottam, "Reworking Work," *Time*, 25 July 2005, 50; Ressler and Thompson, *Why Work Sucks and How to Fix It*, 20, 45–48.

48. M. Beer, R. A. Eisenstat, and B. Spector, *The Critical Path to Corporate Renewal* (Boston, Mass.: Harvard Business School Press, 1990).

49. R. E. Walton, "Successful Strategies for Diffusing Work Innovations," *Journal of Contemporary Business* (Spring 1977): 1–22; R. E. Walton, *Innovating to Compete: Lessons for Diffusing and Managing Change in the Workplace* (San Francisco: Jossey-Bass, 1987); Beer, Eisenstat, and Spector, *The Critical Path to Corporate Renewal*, Chap. 5.

50. E. M. Rogers, *Diffusion of Innovations*, 4th ed. (New York: Free Pree, 1995).

51. P. Reason and H. Bradbury, *Handbook of Action Research*, London (Sage: 2001); Coghlan and Brannick, "Kurt Lewin: The 'Practical Theorist' for the 21st Century"; C. Huxham and S. Vangen, "Researching Organizational Practice through Action Research: Case Studies and Design Choices," *Organizational Research Methods* 6 (July 2003): 383–403.

52. V. J. Marsick and M. A. Gephart, "Action Research: Building the Capacity for Learning and Change," *Human Resource Planning* 26 (2003): 14–18.

53. L. Dickens and K. Watkins, "Action Research: Rethinking Lewin," *Management Learning* 30 (June 1999): 127–140; J. Heron and P. Reason, "The Practice of Co-Operative Inquiry: Research 'with' Rather Than 'on' People," in *Handbook of Action Research*, ed. P. Reason and H. Bradbury (Thousand Oaks, CA: Sage, 2001), 179–188.

54. D. A. Nadler, "Organizational Frame Bending: Types of Change in the Complex Organization," in *Corporate Transformation: Revitalizing Organizations for a Competitive World*, ed. R. H. Kilmann, T. J. Covin, and Associates (San Francisco: Jossey-Bass, 1988), 66–83; K. E. Weick and R. E. Quinn, "Organizational Change

and Development," *Annual Review of Psychology* 50 (1999): 361–386.

55. T. M. Egan and C. M. Lancaster, "Comparing Appreciative Inquiry to Action Research: OD Practitioner Perspectives," *Organization Development Journal* 23, no. 2 (Summer 2005): 29–49.

56. F. F. Luthans, "Positive Organizational Behavior: Developing and Managing Psychological Strengths," *The Academy of Management Executive* 16, no. 1 (2002): 57–72; N. Turner, J. Barling, and A. Zacharatos, "Positive Psychology at Work," in *Handbook of Positive Psychology*, ed. C. R. Snyder and S. Lopez (Oxford, UK: Oxford University Press, 2002), 715–730; K. Cameron, J. E. Dutton, and R. E. Quinn, eds., *Positive Organizational Scholarship: Foundation of a New Discipline* (San Francisco: Berrett Koehler Publishers, 2003); J. I. Krueger and D. C. Funder, "Towards a Balanced Social Psychology: Causes, Consequences, and Cures for the Problem-Seeking Approach to Social Behavior and Cognition," *Behavioral and Brain Sciences* 27, no. 3 (June 2004): 313–327; S. L. Gable and J. Haidt, "What (and Why) Is Positive Psychology?," *Review of General Psychology* 9, no. 2 (2005): 103–110; M. E. P. Seligman *et al.*, "Positive Psychology Progress: Empirical Validation of Interventions," *American Psychologist* 60, no. 5 (2005): 410–421.

57. D. K. Whitney and D. L. Cooperrider, "The Appreciative Inquiry Summit: Overview and Applications," *Employment Relations Today* 25 (Summer 1998): 17–28; J. M. Watkins and B. J. Mohr, *Appreciative Inquiry: Change at the Speed of Imagination* (San Francisco: Jossey-Bass, 2001).

58. S. Berrisford, "Using Appreciative Inquiry to Drive Change at the BBC," *Strategic Communication Management* 9, no. 3 (2005): 22–25; M.-Y. Cheung-Judge and E. H. Powley, "Innovation at the BBC," in *The Handbook of Large Group Methods*, ed. B. B. Bunker and B. T. Alban (New York: Wiley, 2006), 45–61.

59. "Make the Emotional Case for Change: An Interview with Chip Heath," *McKinsey Quarterly*, March 2010; www.brasilata.com Retrieved March 11, 2010.

60. D. L. Cooperrider and D. K. Whitney, *Appreciative Inquiry: A Positive Revolution in Change* (San Francisco: Berrett-Koehler, 2005) Recent writing has extended this list to eight principles. see: D. K. Whitney and A. Trosten-Bloom, *The Power of Appreciative Inquiry: A Practical Guide to Positive Change*, 2nd ed. (San Francisco: Berrett-Koehler Publishers, 2010).

61. F. J. Barrett and D. L. Cooperrider, "Generative Metaphor Intervention: A New Approach for Working with Systems Divided by Conflict and Caught in Defensive Perception," *Journal of Applied Behavioral Science* 26 (1990): 219–239; Whitney and

Cooperrider, "The Appreciative Inquiry Summit: Overview and Applications"; Watkins and Mohr, *Appreciative Inquiry: Change at the Speed of Imagination*, 15–21.

62. M. Schiller, "Case Study: Avon Mexico" in *Appreciative Inquiry: Change at the Speed of Imagination* ed. J. M. Watkins and B. J. Mohr (San Francisco: Jossey-Bass, 2001), 123–126; P. Babcock, "Seeing a Brighter Future," *HRMagazine* 50, no. 9 (September 2005): 48; D. S. Bright, D. L. Cooperrider, and W. B. Galloway, "Appreciative Inquiry in the Office of Research and Development: Improving the Collaborative Capacity of Organization," *Public Performance & Management Review* 29, no. 3 (2006): 285; D. Gilmour and A. Radford, "Using OD to Enhance Shareholder Value: Delivering Business Results in BP Castrol Marine," *Organization Development Journal* 25, no. 3 (2007): P97-P102; Whitney and Trosten-Bloom, *The Power of Appreciative Inquiry*.

63. Canadian Tire, *Team Values Development Process (Powerpoint File)* (Toronto: Canadian Tire, 24 September 2001); Canadian Tire, *Leadership Guide* (Toronto: Canadian Tire, 2002).

64. T. F. Yaeger, P. F. Sorensen, and U. Bengtsson, "Assessment of the State of Appreciative Inquiry: Past, Present, and Future," *Research in Organizational Change and Development* 15 (2004): 297–319; G. R. Bushe and A. F. Kassam, "When Is Appreciative Inquiry Transformational? A Meta-Case Analysis," *Journal of Applied Behavioral Science* 41, no. 2 (June 2005): 161–181.

65. G. R. Bushe, "Five Theories of Change Embedded in Appreciative Inquiry" in *18th Annual World Congress of Organization Development* (Dublin, Ireland, July 14–18, 1998).

66. M. Weisbord and S. Janoff, *Future Search: An Action Guide to Finding Common Ground in Organizations and Communities* (San Francisco: Berrett-Koehler, 2000); R. M. Lent, M. T. McCormick, and D. S. Pearce, "Combining Future Search and Open Space to Address Special Situations," *Journal of Applied Behavioral Science* 41, no. 1 (March 2005): 61–69; S. Janoff and M. Weisbord, "Future Search as 'Real-Time' Action Research," *Futures* 38, no. 6 (2006): 716–722.

67. J. Pratt, "Naturalists Deserve More Credit," *St. John's Telegram*, 22 June 2002, B3; C. Chowaniec, R. Gordezky, and J. Grieve, "Supporting the Merger of Two School Boards in Ottawa, Ontario, Canada: The Ottawa-Carleton Community and Public Education to 2015," in *Future Search in School District Change*, ed. R. Schweitz, K. Martens, and N. Aronson (Lanham, Maryland: ScarecrowEducation, 2005), 56–70; P. Deans, K. Martens, and R. Gordezky, "Success and System Readiness: Lester B. Pearson School Board and Its Commitment to Educational Excellence, Montreal, Quebec,"

in *Future Search in School District Change*, ed. R. Schweitz, K. Martens, and N. Aronson (Lanham, Maryland: Scarecrow Education, 2005), 192–208; R. Lent, J. Van Patten, and T. Phair, "Creating a World-Class Manufacturer in Record Time," in *The Handbook of Large Group Methods*, ed. B. B. Bunker and B. T. Alban (New York: Wiley, 2006), 112–124.

68. For a critique of future search conferences and similar whole-system events, see A. Oels, "Investigating the Emotional Roller-Coaster Ride: A Case Study-Based Assessment of the Future Search Conference Design," *Systems Research and Behavioral Science* 19 (July-August 2002): 347–355; M. F. D. Polanyi, "Communicative Action in Practice: Future Search and the Pursuit of an Open, Critical and Non-Coercive Large-Group Process," *Systems Research and Behavioral Science* 19 (July 2002): 357–366; A. De Grassi, "Envisioning Futures of African Agriculture: Representation, Power, and Socially Constituted Time," *Progress in Development Studies* 7, no. 2 (2007): 79–98.

69. G. R. Bushe and A. B. Shani, *Parallel Learning Structures* (Reading, Mass.: Addison-Wesley, 1991); E. M. Van Aken, D. J. Monetta, and D. S. Sink, "Affinity Groups: The Missing Link in Employee Involvement," *Organization Dynamics* 22 (Spring 1994): 38–54.

70. D. J. Knight, "Strategy in Practice: Making It Happen," *Strategy & Leadership* 26 (July-August 1998): 29–33; R. T. Pascale, 'Grass-roots Leadership—Royal Dutch/Shell," *Fast Company*, no. 14 (April-May 1998): 110–120; R. T. Pascale, "Leading from a Different Place," in *The Leader's Change Handbook* ed. J. A. Conger, G. M. Spreitzer, and E. E. Lawler III (San Francisco: Jossey-Bass, 1999), 301–320; R. Pascale, M. Millemann, and L. Gioja, *Surfing on the Edge of Chaos* (London: Texere, 2000).

71. T. C. Head and P. F. Sorenson, "Cultural Values and Organizational Development: A Seven-Country Study," *Leadership and Organization Development Journal* 14 (1993): 3–7; R. J. Marshak, "Lewin Meets Confucius: A Review of the OD Model of Change," *Journal of Applied Behavioral Science* 29 (1993): 395–415; C.-M. Lau, "A Culture-Based Perspective of Organization Development Implementation," *Research in Organizational Change and Development* 9 (1996): 49–79; C. M. Lau and H. Y. Ngo, "Organization Development and Firm Performance: A Comparison of Multinational and Local Firms," *Journal Of International Business Studies* 32, no. 1 (2001): 95–114.

72. M. McKendall, "The Tyranny of Change: Organizational Development Revisited," *Journal of Business Ethics* 12 (February 1993): 93–104; C. M. D. Deaner, "A Model of Organization Development Ethics," *Public Administration Quarterly* 17 (1994): 435–446.

73. G. A. Walter, "Organization Development and Individual Rights," *Journal of Applied Behavioral Science* 20 (1984): 423–439.

74. The source of this often-cited quotation was not found. It does not appear, even in rough form, in the books that Andrew Carnegie wrote (such as *Gospel of Wealth,* 1900; *Empire of Business,* 1902; and *Autobiography,* 1920). However, Carnegie may have stated these words (or similar ones) in other places. He gave a multitude of speeches and wrote many articles, and his words are reported by numerous other authors.

Appendix A

1. F. N. Kerlinger, *Foundations of Behavioral Research* (New York: Holt, Rinehart, & Winston, 1964), 11.

2. J. B. Miner, *Theories of Organizational Behavior* (Hinsdale, IL.: Dryden, 1980), 7–9.

3. Ibid., 6–7.

4. J. Mason, *Qualitative Researching* (London: Sage, 1996).

5. A. Strauss and J. Corbin (eds.), *Grounded Theory in Practice* (London: Sage Publications, 1997); B. G. Glaser and A. Strauss. *The Discovery of Grounded Theory: Strategies for Qualitative Research* (Chicago, IL: Aldine Publishing Co, 1967).

6. Kerlinger, *Foundations of Behavioral Research*, 13.

7. A. Strauss and J. Corbin (eds.), *Grounded Theory in Practice* (London: Sage Publications, 1997); B. G. Glaser and A. Strauss. *The Discovery of Grounded Theory: Strategies for Qualitative Research* (Chicago, IL: Aldine Publishing Co, 1967).

8. W. A. Hall and P. Callery, "Enhancing the Rigor of Grounded Theory: Incorporating Reflexivity and Relationality," *Qualitative Health Research*, 11 (March 2001), 257–72.

9. P. Lazarsfeld, *Survey Design and Analysis* (New York: The Free Press, 1955).

10. This example is cited in D. W. Organ and T. S. Bateman, *Organizational Behavior*, 4th ed. (Homewood, IL.: Irwin, 1991), 42.

11. Ibid., p. 45.

12. R. I. Sutton and A. Hargadon, "Brainstorming Groups in Context: Effectiveness in a Product Design Firm," *Administrative Science Quarterly* 41 (1996), 685–718.

NAME AND ORGANIZATION INDEX

A

ABB Grain, 15
ABC, 337
Abdoulah, Colleen, 41
Abebooks, 393
Abitibi-Price, 391–392
Accenture, 230
Adams, Lisa, 230
Adams, Michael, 52
Adidas Group, 186
Air Canada, 5, 99–100, 101
Air New Zealand, 81, 81f
AirAsia, 276
Albi, Frank, 266
Algonquin Park, 1
Amazon, 219, 393
American Express (AmEx), 423
American Express (AmEx) Canada, w169, 169f
AmOil, 85
Anderson, Dave, 342
Apex Distribution Inc., 395
Apple Inc., 3, 6, 6f, 7, 186, 215, 291, 343, 343f, 414
Armstrong World Industries, Inc., 311
Arunski, Karl, 280
Ashton, M.C., 61n, 152n
Atlantic Superstore, 13, 13f
Atos Origin, 250–251, 251f
AT&T, 131
Aubé, C., 221n
Australian Rules Football (ARL), 38, 38f
AVON Mexico, 423

B

Bachman, Greg, 218
Bailey, Kate, 64
Baiocco, Maja, 14–15
Ballard, Geoffrey, 196
Ballard Power Systems, 196
Ballmer, Steve, 140
Balsillie, Jim, 392
Bandura, Albert, 136
Bank of America (BofA), 391
Bank of America New Jersey, 17
Bank of Montreal (BMO), 13
Barak, Eran, 280
Barnard, Chester, 3, 246
Barret, F.J., 423f
Barrick Gold Corporation, 360–361, 365
BASF, 360
Bass, Carl, 343
Bata, Thomas, 186
Bata Ltd., 186
Bayer Inc., 245–246
BDO Dunwoody LLP, 391

Beauport, Rochelle, 86
Beddoe, Clive, 380
Beersma, B., 306n, 326n
Beim, Alex, 197, 197f
Bell Canada, 131, 365
Belz, Dorothee, 346
Bennett, Lucie, 215
Bennett, Steve, 414
Bennis, Warren, 340
Bentall Capital, 224
Berbee, 266
Berg, Achim, 346
Best Buy, 31, 31f, 112, 123, 413, 418
Better Beef Ltd., 156
Beveridge, Brad, 101
BHP Billiton, 160
Billing, Sean, 48
BioWare ULC, 368–370
Bird, Brad, 102
Blake, Phillip, 245
Blake, R.R., 326n
Blake, Sherri, 28
Blanchard, 338
BMW, 370–371, 372, 387
Bogyo, Terrance J., 429n
Boland, Linda, 260
Bolton Hospitals NHS Trust, 24
Bombardier, Inc., 315, 332
Bossidy, Larry, 192
Bower, Mark, 245
Bowes, Kingsley, 211
Boyce, Kevin, 238
BP, 181–182, 181f, 382, 383–384, 383f
Branson, Richard, 104
Brasilata, 421, 421f
Breton, Thierry, 251
Brigham Young University, 236, 319
British Broadcasting Corporation (BBC), 421–422, 423
British Columbia Ferry Services, 193
Brown, Alex, 262
Brown, S.P., 104n
Brydon, Donald, 327
BT, 266
Buchkowsky, James, 349
Budner, S., 431
Buffalo Bills, 116
Burns, James McGregor, 340
Burton, Pierre, 144
Business Objects, 309
Butler, Katie, 211, 211f
Butler University, 404

C

Cactus Club Café, 214, 214f
Calcraft, Stef, 198

Caldwell, D.F., 384n
Callanan, Gerard A., 319, 324n
Campbell, Robert, 327
Campbell Soup, 161
Canada Post, 81, 327–328, 332
Canadian Council of Criminal Defence Lawyers, 277
Canadian National Railways (CN), 301, 301f, 315, 332
Canadian Nature Federation, 424
Canadian Outback Adventures & Events, 224, 224f
Canadian Space Agency, 330
Canadian Tire, 6, 197, 423
Canadian Union of Postal Workers, 327
Canadian Wheat Board (CWB), 301, 301f
CanOil, 85
Canpages, 158
Capgemini, 14
Cara Operations Ltd., 136
Card, Shannon, 293
Carleton University, 418
Carlton, Andrew, 169
Carnegie, Andrew, 425
Carroll, Tom, 276
Carter, Maurice, 166
Cassady, John, 28
Celestica, Inc., 217, 372
CERN, 71
Chamberland, Denis, 230
Chaput, Gilles, 391
Chartered Accountants of Ontario, 73
Chatman, J., 384n
Cheliak, Marty, 271
Cheng, Albert, 337
Cherrington, David J., 236, 319
Children's Aid Society of Brant, 138
Cho, Tennyson, 303, 303f
Chrysler, 166–167, 256
Churchill, Winston, 387
Cirque du Soleil, 386, 387
Cisco Systems, 19, 245–246
Citigroup Inc., 370
City of Edmonton, 138
City of Mississauga, 46
City of Regina, 407–408, 426
City of Toronto, 16
City Telecom, 168
Clark, Carolyn, 67
Cloniger, C.R., 61n, 152n
Clydesdale Bank, 105, 105f
Coates, Michael, 96
Coca-Cola, 366
Cohen, George, 342

Collee, John, 198
Collier, Steve, 172
Colliers, 113
Columbus Circle, 219, 399
comScore.Inc, 260
Conestoga-Rovers and Associates, 116
Conference Board of Canada, 158
Connectegrity, 245
Connellan, T.K., 135*n*
Connelly, Anne, 81–82
Connolly, Jarrod, 395
The Container Store, 387
Continuum, 261
Cooper, J.T., 119*n*
Cooperrider, D.L., 422*n*, 423*f*
Cormack, Patricia, 353
Cornerstone Research, 358
Corning Inc., 233
Corus Entertainment, 28–29, 28*f*, 34
Covey, Stephen, 316
Cramer, K.L., 87*n*
Cromwell, Gregory, 1
Croon, M.A., 351*n*
CSIS (Canadian Security Intelligence Services), 271
Cunard, Samuel, 342
Cunard Steamship Lines, 342
Currie, Richard, 161
Customs/Excise, 370
CXtec, 400

D

Dabu, Jovie, 217
Daffern, Gillean, 242*n*
Daft, R., 254*n*
Daimler Benz, 370–371
Dakota Growers Pasta Company, 15
Davidson, Diane, 329
Davies, Glen, 407–408, 407*f*, 417
Davis, Ray, 413
Day, Christine, 393
de Dreu, C.K.W., 306*n*, 326*n*
de Hooge, John, 63
de Mestral, Georges, 195
De Pree, Max, 395
Dearth, Randall, 416
Deck, Philip, 170
DeCourcy, Colleen, 276, 276*f*
Dell, 389, 390
Dell, Michael, 390
Deloitte Touche Tohmatsu, 282, 391
Delta Hotels and Resorts, 245–246, 245*f*, 250
Dennison, Richard, 266, 267*n*
Despotes, Marc-Henri, 251
Deutsche Telekom, 346
Dewey, John, 299
Dickie, Mary, 177*n*
Diener, E., 94*n*
Digh, P., 59*n*
Dillon, Gary, 291
DiMicco, Dan, 359, 359*f*
Direct Energy Marketing Ltd., 286
Disney, 337
Disney Media Networks, 337
Disney/ABC Television Group, 337

Dominguez, Maria, 64
Domino's, 81
Donnelly Mirrors, 162
Dornheim, L., 119*n*
Drucker, Peter, 139, 236, 341
Duffy, Luke, 291–292
Duha Group, 7, 9, 9*f*
Duke University, 249
Dunnette, M.D., 326*n*

E

Eaton, Timothy, 158
Eaton's, 158
eBay Canada, 262, 262*f*
Eber, H.W., 61*n*, 152*n*
Einstein, Albert, 184, 195
Eisai Co. Ltd., 44
Elbow Room Café, 98
Elliott, Meagan, 63*f*
Elliott, William, 271–272, 271*f*, 274
Emerson & Cuming's, 424
Encore Avenue, 28
Enron, 48
Ergon Energy, 215
Erhart, Warren, 414
Ernst & Young, 81
Ernst & Young America, 81
Ernst & Young Canada, 82
Euro RSCG Worldwide, 276
Evans, Elizabeth, 234
Evers, A., 306*n*, 326*n*
Ewart, Scott, 238
Exactech Inc., 101
Excellence Canada, 407

F

Facebook, 92, 111, 203, 214, 245–246, 251, 260, 263, 266, 274, 280
Fairmont Hotels & Resorts, 48, 67, 169
Families and Work Institute, 110
Fayol, Henri, 298, 357–358
FBI, 289
Ferguson, Becky, 28
Fernandes, Tony, 276
Fernando, Sean, 49
Ferrara, Gerard, 38
Field, Richard, 240, 242*n*
Fieldler, Fred, 338–339, 347
Fire Service Women of Ontario, 63
First Bank Korea, 124
Fleming, Anne, 24
Flickr, 260
Flinders Medical Centre, 24
Follett, Mary Parker, 3, 299, 305
Foothills Provincial General Hospital, 3
Ford, 141
Forsythe, Meredith, 18, 18*f*
4C Corporate Culture Clash and Chemistry, 390
Four Seasons Hotels & Resorts, 98, 394
France Telecom, 108
Freeman, Dianne, 116
French, John, 273
Friedman, Milton, 13
Frohman, Dov, 300

Frost, Harriet, 198
FX, 337
Fyfe, Rob, 81, 81*f*

G

Galbraith, J., 355*n*
Galbraith, John Kenneth, 411
Gander, Mary, 267
Gap Adventures, 381
Gardner, John, 329
Gates, Bill, 343
Geberth, Vernon, 70
General Electric, 408
Genologics, 200, 200*f*
Gentilin, Dennis, 291–292
George, Rick, 343
Gilman, Syd, 85–86
Global Container Terminals, 315
GLOBE (Global Leadership and Organizational Behaviour Effectiveness), 345
Gluyas, R., 292*n*
Goldberg, L.R., 61*n*, 152*n*
Goldcorp, 412
Golden, C.J., 119*n*
Goleman, D., 100*n*
Google, 194, 203, 245, 328
Gough, H.C., 61*n*, 152*n*, 209*n*
Gould, Claire, 220
Grace, S.L., 87*n*
Grant Thorton LLP, 391
Great Little Box Company Ltd. (GLBC), 122–123, 122*f*, 131, 141, 159
Green, I., 24*n*
Green Mountain Coffee Roasters, 423
Greene, Moya, 81, 327–328, 327*f*, 331, 332
Grove, Andy, 300
Guangdong Nanfang Lee Kum Kee Health Products Co., Ltd., 388
Guide, John, 181

H

Habitat for Humanity, 238
Hackman, J.R., 165*n*
Hadfield, Chris, 330, 330*f*
Haggerty, D.J., 119*n*
Haliburton, 181–182
Hall, L.E., 119*n*
Hall, Shawn, 18
Hammer, Allen L., 40*n*
Hanaberg, Bob, 417
Harvard Business School, 129
Harvard University, 3, 298
Harvey, Cheryl, 377, 378*n*
Hassell, Jim, 219
HBO Canada, 28
HBOG, 85
HCL Technologies, 104
Heaps, Cameron, 1
Heilbrun, A.B., 209*n*
Heise, Heidi, 144, 144*f*
Hennigar, Lynn, 226
Henry, Trent, 82
Herman Miller Inc., 395
Hermkens, K., 252*n*

Herschend Family Entertainment, 81
Hersey, Paul, 338
Herzberg, Frederick, 164
Heskett, J.I., 104*n*
Hewlett Packard, 370
Hill, Hamnett, 131
Hill & Knowlton Canada, 96
Hill & Knowlton (H&K), 96, 96*f*
Hine-Schmidt, Louise, 63
HM Revenue & Customs (HMRC), 370, 370*f*
Hoeft, Steve, 266
Hofstede, G., 50*n*
Hogan, R., 61*n*
Holmes, Deborah K., 83
Home Depot, 395, 409–410
Honeywell and Allied Signal, 192
Hoppy Beverage Co., 410–411
Horton, Lori, 353
Horton, Tim, 353
Hotel Dieu Grace Hospital, 214
Hough, L.M., 326*n*
Houlden, Gordon, 308
House, Robert, J., 325*n*
HP Enterprise Business, 371
Hsieh, Tony, 263, 263*f*, 393
Hudson's Bay Company, 2, 14, 158, 396
Human Resources and Skills Development Canada (HRSDC), 368, 368*f*
Human Resources Development Canada, 327
Human Rights Tribunal (Quebec), 74
Hunt, Chad, 44
Hunter Douglas, 423
Hurd, Mark, 370
Husky Injection Molding Systems Ltd., 44, 44*f*
Hy Dairies, Ltd., 85–86
Hydro One, 193

I

I Love Rewards, 255, 255*f*, 263, 396, 399
IBM, 6, 19, 51, 81, 186, 219, 230, 262, 341, 366, 371
IBM Canada, 81, 234
Ibrahim, Wadood, 385
ICICI Bank, 382
Imperial College, 220
Inacom, 266
Infosys Technologies, 49, 49*f*, 388
Ingram, Harry, 79
Inland Revenue, 370
Intel Israel, 300, 300*f*
Intuit, 414
Intuit Canada, 137
Ishiwatari, Mina, 410–411, 411*f*
Israeli Defence Force, 77
Iverson, Ken, 359

J

Jaffray, Richard, 214
Jago, A.G., 204*n*
Jar-Hoon, Hur, 54–55
JC Penny, 123
JetBlue, 92–93

Jobs, Steve, 3, 6, 291, 343, 343*f*, 414
Johnson, J.A., 61*n*, 152*n*
Johnson & Johnson (J&J), 373, 373*f*
Johnston, E., 292*n*
Jones, D., 24*n*
Jones, David, 276
Jones, T.J., 47*n*
Jong-yong, Yun, 197
Jordan, Peter J., 100*n*, 119*n*
Juani, Alex, 46*f*
Jung, Carl, 39–40

K

Kahneman, Daniel, 188
Kaizen Blitzes, 9, 9*f*
Kallasvuo, Olli-Pekka, 377
Kananaskis Provincial Park, 240
Kanungo, R.N., 89*n*
Kariel, Patricia E., 242*n*
Kelleher, Herb, 388
Kelly, A.-M., 24*n*
Kelly Services, 107*n*
Kemmelmeier, M., 50*n*
KenGen, 359–360
Ketchum Public Relations Canada, 114
Kids Can Press, 28
Kietzmenn, J.H., 252*n*
Kim, S.P., 104*n*
King, William Lyon Mackenzie, 3
Kluwer, E.S., 306*n*, 326*n*
Knightbridge Human Capital Solutions, 101
Kolliopoulos, John, 396–397
Kotter, J.P., 415*n*
Kreitner, R., 135*n*
Krug, Dan, 276
Krywulak, Tim, 25*n*
Kuhn, M.H., 87*n*

L

Labossiere, Leah, 211, 211*f*
Lafley, Alan G., 341
Laird, Chris, 176–177
Laliberté, Guy, 386
Lam, S.K., 104*n*
Lane, Alycia, 289
Lanxess, Corp, 414
Larson, J., 94*n*
Larson, J.R.Jr., 56*n*
Latchford, Andrew, 214
Lavoie, Paul, 363
Law, K.S., 119*n*
Lawrence, Paul, 129, 130*n*
Lawrence, P.R., 415*n*
Lawrence, Sandra A., 100*n*, 119*n*
Lay, C., 87*n*
La-Z-Boy, Inc., 217–218
Lee Fong, Choong, 98
Lee Kum Kee, 388
Leiter, John, 83*f*
Lenger, R., 254*n*
Lepp, Annalee, 63
Lester B. Pearson School Board, 424
Lewin, Kurt, 408, 409, 413, 414, 417, 419, 425, 426, 427

Lewis, Jim, 37
L'Express, 99
LG Electronics Co., 55
Library and Archives Canada, 328
Lighthouse Publishing, 226, 226*f*
LinkedIn, 203, 214, 246, 280, 303
Lo, Raymond, 388
Loblaw Companies Limited, 13, 13*f*, 161
Lochhead, Christopher, 110
London Drugs, 4
London School of Economics, 195
London Stock Exchange, 193
L'Oréal Canada, 310
Los Angeles Arts Festival, 386
Loughridge, Ken, 280
Loughry, M.L., 221*n*
Lowy, Frank, 317
Lucas, R.E., 94*n*
Lucent Technologies, 286
Luechauer, David L., 404
Luft, Joseph, 79, 80*n*
Lululemon Athletica, 393, 393*f*
Luthans, F., 135*n*

M

Machiavelli, Niccolò, 289
Mackey, John, 229
Magna International, 162, 356, 372
Magna Steyr, 370–371
Major League Baseball Players Association (MLBPA), 291
Malaysia Airlines, 98, 98*f*
Malekzedeh, A.R., 392*n*
Malouff, J.M., 119*n*
Manby, Joel, 81
Manning, Erin, 114
Marks & Spencer, 123
Martin, H.J., 152*n*
Maslow, Abraham, 123, 126–128, 126*f*, 126*n*, 130, 145, 152–153, 185
Matheson, Tyler, 380
Matzek, MaryBeth, 267*n*
Mayo, Elton, 3, 298
Mayo Clinic, 386, 387
McAdam, Peter, 18
McAusland, David, 271
McCallum, Vanessa, 292
McCarthy, I.P., 252*n*
McCarthy, M., 24*n*
McClelland, David, 123, 128, 145
McDonald, Greg, 191
McDonald's, 98, 361, 366, 403
McDonald's Canada, 342, 394
McDougall, Barbara, 327
McEwan, Rob, 412
McKey, John, 399
Mclain, D.L., 431
McMaster University, 82, 407
McNair, Kathleen, 29
McParlland, T.S., 87*n*
McPhee, Cory, 297
McShane, Steven L., 119*n*, 147, 148*n*, 149, 151*n*, 175, 176*n*, 206*n*, 243*n*, 269*n*, 270*n*, 295*n*, 326*n*, 348, 379*n*, 403*n*, 406*n*, 429*n*
Meals of Wheels, 1

Médecins Sans Frontières (Doctors Without Borders), 81
Meggy, Robert, 122, 141
Mei, Li, 163
Meindl, J.R., 351*n*
Mendte, Larry, 289
Meridian Technology Centre, 400
Merrill Lynch, 391
Merritt, Samantha, 73*f*
Metropolitan Transit Authority (New York City), 278
Miami University, 404
Microsoft, 140, 302–303, 387
Microsoft Germany, 346, 346*f*
Milgram, Stanley, 275
Miller, Tim, 124
Mills, Deborah, 233
Mills, John Stuart, 155
Mintzberg, H., 355*n*
MIT, 286
Mitchell, A., 24*n*
Mitchell, T.R., 56*n*
MKS, 170
Moir, Miranda, 63
Molson Canada, 238
Molson Coors, 48, 238
Mongeau, Claude, 310
Montana's Cookhouse, 135–136
Moore, D.D., 221*n*
Moore, Graham, 211
Morden, Reid, 271
Morgon, Gill, 24
Morouney, Kim, 377, 378*n*
Mother, 198
Motorola, 96, 376
Mount Allison University, 327
Mouton, J.S., 306*n*, 326*n*
Movie Central, 28
Muhammed, Nura, 169
Murdoch, Rupert, 337
Muzyka, Ray, 368
MWH Global, 280

N

Nadler, D.A., 355*n*
Nahavandi, A., 392*n*
Nardelli, Robert, 256, 395, 409–410
NASA, 185, 330
National Australian Bank (NAB), 172, 291–292
National Health System (Britain), 278
National Hockey League, 38
Nauta, A., 306*n*, 326*n*
NBN, 219
Nestlé, 361, 366, 369
New Zealand Post, 214
Ng, Ellis, 168
Ngure, Simon, 360
Nickelodeon, 28, 337
Nilekani, Nandan, 388
Nishith Desai Associates (NDA), 198–199
Nissan, 23–24
Nogueira, Linsey, 114
Nohria, Nitim, 129, 130*n*

Nokia Corporation, 6–7, 376–377
Nottingham, John, 205
Nottingham-Spirk Design Associates, Inc., 204–205
Nova Chemicals, 140
Nucor Inc., 159, 276, 359
Nyp, Gary, 116*n*

O

Oakley, Inc., 387
O'Brien, Andy, 136
O'Brien, Dave, 266
O'Brien, K.J., 377
Occupational Safety and Health Administration (OSHA), 383
Odoardi, Maria, 101
Ogilvy & Mather, 408
Ohland, M.W., 221*n*
Oktoberfest, 1
Oldham, G., 165*n*
OMD, 198
Omnicom Group, 276
1-800-GOT-JUNK?, 81, 200, 262
Ontario Hydro, 193
Ontario Power Generation, 9, 193
Oodle Noodle, 171, 171*f*
Oracle, Inc., 370
O'Reilly, C.A.III., 384*n*
Orzech, Josh, 286
Osborn, Alex, 233
Ossi, Nita, 114
Ottawa Fire Service, 63
The Ottawa Hospital, 418, 418*f*
Ottawa-Carelton Scolle Board, 424
Oyserman, D., 50*n*

P

Page, Kevin, 105
Palmisano, Sam, 83, 341, 366
Park Nicollet Health Services, 24
PCL, 11, 11*f*, 159
Peeters, Lars, 348–349
Perri, David F., 319, 324*n*
Perron, Felice, 63*f*
Pfeffer, J., 21*n*
Pfizer, 363
Pham, Sonny, 171, 171*f*
Philips, 365, 366
Phillips, C., 59*n*
Pincaré, Henri, 195
Pivot, Laurence, 99
Pixar Animation Studios, 102, 262
Potash Corp., 68, 191
Potter, Dale, 418
Precision Metalcraft, 211–212, 211*f*, 221
PricewaterhouseCoopers LLP (PwC), 14–15, 41
Proctor & Gamble (P&G), 34, 34*f*, 341, 356, 369, 370
Proctor & Gamble (P&G) Canada, 176–177
Profitel, 348–349
ProMation Engineering Ltd., 15

Propaganda Games, 112
Protegra, 385, 385*f*

Q

Queen's University, 303
Quinn, R.T., 104*n*
Quiznos, 144

R

Rackspace Hosting, Inc., 214
Radialpoint, 131, 131*f*
Rahim, M.A., 306*n*, 326*n*
Ramstad, E., 55*n*
Raven, Bertrand, 273
Raytheon, 280
Razer, 97
Ready, Vince, 63
Reckitt Benkiser Healthcare, 229–230, 230*f*
Reebok International Ltd., 186
Reliance Industries, 10
Research In Motion (RIM), 68, 376, 392
RFRD (Richmond Fire Rescue Department), 63
Richard, Stephane, 108
Richardson, Ian, 116
Richardson Capital Partners, 303
Roberts, Ed, 116
Roberts, J.A., 179*n*
Roberts, Martha, 25*n*
Robitaille, Dave, 83
Rocky Mountain Engineering, 280
Rodgerson, Dave, 234
Rogers Cable Communications Inc., 48, 137
Rokeach, Milton, 42
Rolls Royce Engine Services, 165, 166*f*, 329
Rompré, Marjolaine, 310
Rosen, R., 59*n*
Ross, Rich, 337
Roth, Thomas, 181
Rousseau, V., 221*n*
Royal Bank of Canada (RBC), 17, 110, 138, 312, 313, 313*f*
Royal Canadian Mint, 81, 96
Royal Canadian Mounted Police (RCMP), 70, 138, 157, 271–272, 274, 284
Royal Dutch/Shell, 219–220, 220*f*, 424
Royal Mail (Britain), 327, 332
Ruble, T.L., 306*n*
Rucci, A.J., 104*n*
Russell, J.A., 94*n*
Ryanair, 74

S

Sage Software, 282
Salaysay, Nick, 111
Salesforce.com, 251
Samsung Electronics, 54, 197
Sanford, Aaron, 31*f*
SAP, 309

Saskatchewan Institute of Applied Science and Technology, 349
Sasser, W.E., 104*n*
Saunders, Craig, 205
Savoie, A., 221*n*
Savoie, Patrick, 98
Sawatzky, Ben, 154
SC First Bank, 124
Schau, C., 423*f*
Schlesinger, L.A., 104*n*, 415*n*
Schmidt, Mayo, 15
Schutte, N.S., 119*n*
Schwartz, Shalom, 42, 43*f*, 43*n*, 53, 130
Schwarz, John, 309
Schyns, B., 351*n*
Scope International-India, 124
ScotiaBank, 33
Scudamore, Brian, 81, 200, 262
Second City, 234, 234*f*
Selye, Hans, 109, 109*n*
Semco SA, 329, 344
Semler, Ricardo, 344
Sepulveda, C.J., 179*n*
Serena Software, 251
7-Eleven, 361
Shah, Arpan, 220
Shanghai Municipal Government, 317
Sharp, Isadore, 394
Shaw, Beorge Bernard, 256
Shaw Communications, 28
Shell, 369
Shell Canada, 220, 312
Shell Europe, 414
Shepard, H.A., 306*n*, 326*n*
Sherwin-Williams, 205, 421
Shin-bae, Kim, 55
Shulman, Gary M., 404
Sidoryk, Mike, 211, 211*f*
Silvestre, B.S., 252*n*
Simon, Herbert, 187, 190
Sims, David, 181
Singer, M., 59*n*
SK Telecom, 54–55
Skype, 265
Slater, Steve, 92–93, 92*f*
Smart, Lee, 234
Smith, Adam, 3, 163
Smith, K.W., 392*n*
Smith, Mark, 230
Smith, Nina, 282
Softchoice Corp., 101, 101*f*
Sony Europe, 101, 139, 139*f*
Souccar, Raf, 271
Southern Alberta Institute of Technology, 68
Southwest Airlines, 39–40, 388
Spirks, John, 205
Springer, Jim, 37
Spruceland Millworks, 154–155, 154*f*, 156, 158, 159, 160
St. Francis Xavier University, 353
Stadnyk, Sandy, 211, 211*f*
Standard Chartered Bank, 123–124, 124*f*, 139
StandardAero, 417
Stanford University, 286

Starbucks International Group, 393*f*
Startegic Investments & Holdings Inc., 216
Statistics Canada, 16*n*, 35, 74
Steam Whistle Brewing Co., 1–2, 1*f*, 3, 4, 7, 17
Ste-Croix, Gilles, 386
Steen, Sandra L., 204*n*
Stoke-on-Trent, 136, 136*f*
Stone Consolidated, 391–392
Strangeloop Networks, 395
Subway, 144
Suleman, Razor, 255, 396
Sun, 219
Suncor, 343
Sunderland Royal Hospital, 23–24
Suntech Optics, 96–97
Sutton, Nicola, 240, 242*n*
Sutton, R.I., 21*n*
Svenska Handelsbanken AB, 159, 170, 170*f*
Sweeney, Anne, 337, 337*f*
Syncrude Canada, 159
Synott, Mark, 113

T

Taft, John, 17
Tangible Interaction Design, 197
TAXI, 362–363, 363*f*
Taylor, Frederick Winslow, 3, 163–164
Taylor, Greg, 1
TBWA, 276
TD Bank, 18
TD Canada Trust, 312
TDL Group Corp., 353
Ted Rogers of Retail Management (Ryerson University), 234
TELETOON, 28
Tellier, Paul, 315
TELUS, 18, 363
Templer, D., 179*n*
Texas Instruments, 48
Thomas, K., 306*n*
Thomas, K.W., 326*n*
Thomson Reuters, 280
3M, 275
Tim Hortons', 353–355, 353*f*, 364, 376, 403
Time Warner Cable, 266
Toffler, Alvin, 189
Tokai Rubber Industries Ltd., 157
Toronto School Board, 424
Toronto Transit Commission (TTC), 354
Transocean Ltd., 181
Transportation and Works Department (Mississauga), 46
TreeHouse, 28
Trosten-Bloom, A., 422*n*
Tushman, M.I., 355*n*
Tversky, Amos, 188
Twitter, 111, 203, 245, 248, 260

U

UBS AG, 162

Umpqua, Bank, 413
United Nations, 15
United Steelworkers Local 6500, 297
United Way, 28–29
University of Alberta, 308
University of New Brunswick, 161
University of Texas, 220
University of Victoria, 63
University of Waterloo, 92
University of Western Australia, 147, 149, 175, 348
University of Western Ontario, 48
U.S. Department of Defense, 249

V

Vale Inco, 297–298, 297*f*, 303, 305
Vance, Philo, 76
Vancouver City Savings Credit Union (Vancity), 113, 381
Verizon, 131
Verkuyten, M., 87*n*
Vêtements Ltée, 147–148
Virgin Group, 104
Virgin Mobile, 96, 131
Virginia Mason Medical Center, 24
Visa, 158*f*
Viterra, 15, 15*f*
Vodafone, 48
von Helmholtz, Hermann, 195
Vroom, V.H., 204*n*

W

Walker, Smauel D., 238
Wallas, Graham, 195, 195*n*
Walt Disney Co., 317, 317*f*
Walt Disney Studios, 337
Wang, Tony, 172
Webber, Steve, 144
Weber, Max, 3, 298
Wegmans Food Market, 104
Weisensel, Ward, 310
Welch, Jack, 408
Weldon, William, 373
West Chester University of Pennsylvania, 319
Westfield Group, 317
Westhues, Kenneth, 92
WestJet Airlines Ltd., 159, 380–381, 380*f*, 382–383
Whirlpool, 387
White, Ray, 139
White Spot, 414, 414*f*
Whitney, D.K., 422*n*, 423*f*
Whole Foods Market, 159, 219, 229, 399
Wide Open West, 41, 81
Wilfred Laurier University, 377
Wilkins, Greg, 360
Wilson, Chip, 393
Wilson, Laura, 124
Winona State University, 267
W.L. Gore & Associates, 329, 329*f*
Wong, C.-S., 119*n*
Woods, Dustin, 124

WorkSafeBC (Workers' Compensation Board of British Columbia), 342
Wyatt, Linda, 395

X

Xerox PARC, 186

Y

Yakka Tech Ltd., 175–176

Yamauchi, K., 179n
Yarish, Brandi, 200
Youssef, Tasmeen, 67f
YouTube, 245
YTV, 28

Z

Zappos, 263, 393
Zebro, David, 216
Zeschuk, Greg, 368

Zheng, Han, 317
Zimny, Mark, 15
Zollinger, Cindy, 358
Zomma, Mostafa, 368
Zou, Melody, 163

SUBJECT INDEX

A

A-B-C model of OB Mod, 134–135, 135*f*
ability, 30–31
Aboriginal peoples, 52
absenteeism, 35, 65, 105
absorption, 276
absorptive capacity, 8
achievement, 42, 128
achievement-nurturing orientation, 51
achievement-oriented leadership, 336
acquisition (drive), 129
action research, 419–421, 420*f*
action scripts, 191
active listening, 260–261, 261*f*
adaptive culture, 390
adaptive transformation process, 7
adjourning stage, 223
Advanced Research Projects Agency
    Network (ARPANET), 249
advisory teams, 213*t*
affective commitment, 106–108
age discrimination, 74
agreeableness, 38, 39
alarm reaction, 109
alternatives, 187–192, 187*f*, 277
ambiguity, 51
ambiguous rules, 305
analyzability, 374
anchoring and adjustment heuristic, 188
anchors of OB knowledge, 19–21, 19*f*
and workplace behaviours and
    outcomes, 39
Anglophones, 52
antecedents, 134
anti-harassment legislation, 110
anticipatory principle, 422, 422*t*
applied performance practices
    empowerment practices, 169–170
    financial reward practices, 156–161
    job design practices, 161–168
    money in the workplace, meaning of,
        155–156
    self-leadership practices, 170–173
appreciative coaching, 139–140
appreciative inquiry, 421–423, 422*t*, 423*f*
aptitudes, 30
arbitration, 311
artifacts, 385–387, 394–395
assertiveness, 51, 283*t*, 284
assimilation, 392, 392*t*
associative play, 198
assumptions, 69–70
attitude object, 94
attitudes, 94–98
    job satisfaction, 102–106
    organizational commitment, 106–108
attraction, 395

attraction-selection-attrition (ASA)
    theory, 395
attribution errors, 75–76
attribution process, 74
attribution rules, 74–75, 75*f*
attribution theory, 74–76
attrition, 395
Austria, 50*f*, 51, 155
authentic leadership, 332–333, 332*f*
authority, deference to, 52
autonomy, 52, 165, 166
availability heuristic, 188
avoidance style, 306, 307, 307*f*
awareness training, 79

B

Baby Boomers, 16
balanced scorecard (BSC), 138
bargaining zone model of negotiations,
    314, 314*f*
barriers to communication, 256–257
behaviour, individual. *See* individual
    behaviour
behaviour modelling, 137
behavioural intentions, 95–96
behavioural perspective of leadership, 333–335
behaviourism, 134
Belgium, 50*f*, 51
beliefs, 95
belonginess/love, 127
benevolence, 42
best alternative to a negotiated agreement
    (BATNA), 315
biases
    biased decision heuristics, 188–189
    confirmation bias, 70–71, 192–193
    perceptual biases, 69–70, 72–78, 79
    self-serving bias, 76
bicultural audit, 391–392
"Big Five" personality dimensions, 37–39,
    37*f*, 330
blind area, 79
bonding (drive), 129
bounded rationality, 187
brainstorming, 233–234
Brazil, 50*f*, 125
breaking routines, 413
Brooks's law, 215–216
buddy system, 400
buffers, 310–311
bundles of organizational practices, 10–11

C

calculus-based trust, 228, 228*f*
Canada
    absenteeism, 35

achievement orientation, 50*f*, 51
Anglophones, 52
Canadian *vs.* American values, 52
cultural diversity, 52
diversity advantage, 17
employee engagement in, 123–124
ethical standards in, 45
Francophones, 52
individualism, 50*f*
job satisfaction, 102
low collectivism, 49, 50*f*
multigenerational workforce,
    16–17, 16*f*
power distance, 50, 50*f*
silence, 258
uncertainty avoidance, 50*f*, 51
CANOE, 37–38, 37*f*
capital
    human capital, 8–9, 10
    intellectual capital, 8–9, 34
    relationship capital, 9
    social capital, 279
    structural capital, 9
case studies
    And the Award for Best Commercial
        Goes To..., 176–177
    Communicating with the Millennials,
        266–267
    employee involvement cases, 203–204
    Going for WOW at Nottingham-Spirk,
        204–205
    Hilton's Transformation, 401–403
    Hospitals Driving Toward Leaner
        Organization, 23–24
    Hy Dairies, Ltd., 85–86
    NAB's Rogue Trader, 291–292
    Nokia's Evolving Organizational
        Structure, 376–377
    Outstanding Faculty Award, 236–237
    Philanthropic Team-Builder, 238
    Profitel Inc., 348–349
    Pushing Papers Can Be Fun, 55–56
    Separating the Steam from
        the Haze, 403
    South Korea's SK Telecom Goes
        Egalitarian, 54–55
    The Staff Sergeant's Leadership
        Dilemma, 349–350
    Tamarack Industries, 319–320
    TransAct Insurance Corporation,
        427–429
    Vêtements Ltée, 147–148
    YakkaTech Ltd., 175–176
categorical thinking, 71
categorization, 73
centrality, 278
centralization, 360–361

ceremonies, 387
challenges for organizations, 14–19
challenging goals, 138
change. *See* organizational change
change agents, 417–418
channel proficiency, 248
channels of communication. *See* communication channels
charisma, 277
charismatic leadership, 341
child care support, 113
China, 102, 110, 111, 125, 155, 279
claiming value, 314–315
claiming value (in negotiations), 314–315
clarity, 64–65
client-consultant relationship, 420
client divisional structure, 365
client relationships, establishing, 168
closed systems, 5
closing costs, 194
clustering illusion, 189
coalition, 283t, 284
code of ethics, 48
codebooks", 248, 256
coercion, 415t, 416–417
coercive power, 276
cognition, 93
cognitive dissonance, 97–98
cognitive-emotional attitude process, 96–97
cognitive intelligence, 196, 331t, 332
cognitive reasoning, 96
collective rights, 52
collectivism, 49–50
combining jobs, 311
commissions, 158
commitment, 286–287, 343
communication
    active listening, 260–261, 261f
    barriers (noise), 256–257
    channel proficiency, 248
    channels, 248–253
    choice of communication channel, 253–256
    codebooks", 248, 256
    communication process model, 247–248, 247f
    and conflict resolution, 309–310
    cross-cultural communication, 258
    decoding, 247–248
    defined, 246
    email, 249–250
    emotional contagion, 252–253
    encoding, 247–248
    functions of, 246
    gender differences, 258–259, 259f, 260
    grapevine, 263–264
    importance of, 246–247
    improvement of interpersonal communication, 259–261
    improvement throughout the hierarchy, 261–263
    informal communication, 355t, 356
    information overload, 257, 257f
    media richness, 253–255, 254f
    mental models, 248
    multi-communication, 254–255

nonverbal communication, 251–253, 258
persuasion, 255–256
problems, and conflict, 305
proficiency, 255
resistance to change, minimizing, 415–416, 415t
social acceptance, 253
social media, 250–251, 252f
social presence effects, 255
teams, 220
top management, direct communication with, 262–263
of vision, 342
Web-based communication, 249, 260, 262
workspace design, 261–262
communication barriers, 256–257
communication channels, 248–253
    channel proficiency, 248
    choice of channel, 253–256
    persuasion, 255–256
communication process model, 247–248, 247f
communities of practice, 213t
comparison other, 142
compensation. *See* financial reward practices
competence, 169
competencies, 30–31
competency-based rewards, 156t, 157–158
competency perspective of leadership, 330–333, 331t
competitive advantage, 10
competitiveness, 51
complex environment, 373
complex self-concept, 64, 65
compliance, 286
compromising, 306, 307f
concessions, 315, 316
concurrent engineering, 356
confirmation bias, 70–71, 192–193
conflict
    "conflict-is-bad" perspective, 298–299
    conflict process model, 301–302, 302f
    consequences of, 298–301, 299t
    constructive conflict, 300–301, 411
    defined, 298
    interpersonal conflict handling styles, 305–308, 306f, 307f
    management of. *See* conflict resolution
    meaning of conflict, 298–301
    optimal conflict perspective, 299–300
    relationship conflict, 300–301
    socioemotional conflict, 300–301
    structural sources, 302–305
    task-related conflict, 300–301
conflict episodes, 301
conflict handling styles, 305–308, 306f, 307f
conflict management. *See* conflict resolution
conflict process model, 301–302, 302f
conflict resolution
    clarifying rules and procedures, 311
    communication, improving, 309–310
    effective teams, 220

interdependence, reducing, 310–311
mutual understanding, 309–310
negotiation, 313–317
reducing differentiation, 309
resources, increasing, 311
structural approaches, 309–311
superordinate goals, 309
third party conflict resolution, 311–313, 312f
conformity, 42
congruent values, 43–45
conscientiousness, 38, 39
consensus, 74–75, 75f
consequences, 134
consequential principle, 45–46
conservation, 42
consistency, 64, 65, 74–75, 75f
constructionist principle, 422, 422t
constructive conflict, 233, 300–301, 411
constructive thought patterns, 171
contact hypothesis, 80
contemporary challenges for organizations, 14–19
contingencies of power, 277–278
contingency anchor, 20–21
contingency perspective of leadership, 335–340
continuance commitment, 106
continuous reinforcement, 135
control system, 388
convergent thinking, 195
cooperation, 219
coordination, 7, 220, 246, 249, 355–357, 355t
coping mechanisms, 111–112
core affect, 93
core competencies, 371
core job characteristics, 164–165
corporate code of ethics, 48
corporate cult, 389
corporate culture. *See* organizational culture
corporate scandals, 45
corporate social responsibility (CSR), 13–14
corporate social responsibility audits, 48
counterproductive work behaviours (CWBs), 33–34
countervailing power, 272
creating value, 315–317
creative process, 195, 195f
creativity, 194–198
    activities encouraging creativity, 198
    characteristics of creative people, 196–197, 196f
    creative process, 195, 195f
    defined, 194
    learning orientation, 197
    organizational conditions supporting creativity, 197–198
cross-cultural communication, 258
cross-cultural values. *See* cultural values
cross-pollination, 198
cultural values, 41, 48–52
    achievement-nurturing orientation, 51
    Canadian *vs.* American values, 52
    caveats about cross-cultural knowledge, 51

collectivism, 49–50
diversity of Canadian cultural values, 52
five cross-cultural values, 50*f*
individualism, 49–50
and job satisfaction, 102
power distance, 50–51
uncertainty avoidance, 51
culture
communication and, 258
conflict handling styles, 308
display norms, 99
job design, 167
and leadership, 345
money, meaning of, 155
and organizational change, 424–425
organizational culture. *See* organizational culture
values. *See* cultural values
culture shock, 48
customer-driven change, 414
customer satisfaction, 104–105
cycle time, 163
cynicism, 110

D

"death from overwork," 111
decentralization, 360–361
decision heuristics, 188–189
decision making
alternatives, 187–192, 187*f*
bounded rationality, 187
creativity, 194–198
defined, 182
effective choices, 191–192
emotions, 190–191
employee involvement, 198–201, 201*f*
escalation of commitment, 193–194
evaluation of decision outcomes, 192–194
implementation of decisions, 192
and intuition, 191
problem identification, 184–187
rational choice decision making process, 183–184, 183*f*
rational choice paradigm, 182–184, 187–192, 187*f*
team decision making, 231–235
decisive leadership, 185
decoding, 247–248
deculturation, 392, 392*t*
deep acting, 99
deep-level diversity, 16
defend (drive), 129
delegating leadership style, 338
delivering stage, 423
demographics, 16, 68
Denmark, 50, 50*f*, 51, 102, 155
departmental teams, 213*t*
departmentalization, 363–372
divisional structure, 365–367, 365*f*
functional structure, 364–365, 364*f*
M-form structure, 365–367, 365*f*
matrix structure, 368–370, 369*f*
multidivisional structure, 365–367, 365*f*
network structure, 370–372, 371*f*

simple structure, 364
team-based organizational structure, 367–368
dependence, 272–273, 273*f*
depersonalization, 110
designing stage, 423
destiny stage, 423
differentiation, 73, 303–304, 309
diffusion of change, 418–419, 419*f*
direct costs, 412
direction, 29
directive leadership, 333–334, 334*f*, 335
disclosure, 80
discovery, 422
discretion, 278
discrimination, 74
display norms, 99
display rules, 98
distinctiveness, 74–75, 75*f*
distress, 108, 109–110
distributive justice, 46, 141
divergent thinking, 195
diverse environment, 373
diversity. *See* workforce diversity
divine discontent, 186–187
division of labour, 354–355
divisional structure, 365–367, 365*f*
dominant culture, 384
dreaming stage, 422
drive, and leadership, 331, 331*t*
drives, 125–131
see also motivation
and behaviour, 125*f*
defined, 125
four-drive theory, 129–131, 130*f*
motivation, influence on, 129–130
dynamic environment, 372
dysfunctional team norms, 225

E

E-to-P expectancy, 132, 133, 133*f*
e-zines, 262
effective teams, 216–217, 217*f*, 229
efficiency, 163
effort-to-performance (E-to-P) expectancy, 132, 133, 133*f*
electronic brainstorming, 234
email, 249–250
emotional contagion, 252–253
emotional dissonance, 99
emotional exhaustion, 109–110
emotional intelligence (EI), 99–102, 100*f*, 301, 331*t*, 332
emotional labour, 98–99
emotional stability, 38, 39
emotions, 93–99
and attitudes, 94–98
awareness of others' emotions, 100
and behaviour, 94–98
circumplex model, 94*f*
cognitive-emotional attitude process, 96–97
conflict-generated emotions, 301–302
core affect, 93
and decision making, 190–191
defined, 93

display norms, 99
from early preferences, 190
emotional dissonance, 99
emotional labour, 98–99
management of, at work, 98–99
management of others' emotions, 101
vs. moods, 93
and nonverbal communication, 252–253
and personality, 98
positive emotions at work, 96–97
prospect theory effect, 193
self-awareness, 100
self-management, 100
types of emotions, 93–94
empathy, 80–81, 100, 260
employee assistance programs (EAPs), 113
employee competence, 10
employee engagement, 123–124
see also motivation
employee involvement, 10, 107–108, 198–201, 201*f*, 203–204, 415*t*, 416
employee motivation. *See* motivation
employee retention, 34
employee share ownership plans (ESOPs), 159, 160
employees
see also individual behaviour
attraction-selection-attrition (ASA) theory, 395
emerging employment relationships, 18–19
organizational commitment, 106–108
resistance to change, 410–413
roundtable forums, 263
work-at-home employees, 18–19
and workforce diversity. *See* workforce diversity
employment relationships, 18–19
empowerment, 169–170, 282
enacted values, 381–382
encoding, 247–248
encounter stage, 398
environment. *See* external environment; internal environment
equality principle, 142
equity principle, 142
equity sensitivity, 144
equity theory, 141–142, 142*f*
escalation of commitment, 193–194
espoused-enacted values congruence, 44
establishing client relationships, 168
esteem needs, 127
ethical codes, 48
ethical sensitivity, 47
ethics
audits, 48
code of ethics, 48
consequential principle, 45–46
corporate scandals, 45
defined, 13, 45
distributive justice, 46
ethical sensitivity, 47
and individual behaviour, 45–48
individual rights, 46
and job satisfaction, 105–106
moral intensity, 46, 47*f*
and organizational change, 424–425

ethics *(continued)*
and organizational culture, 390
organizational support for ethical behaviour, 48
situational influences, 47
training, 48
utilitarianism, 45–46
eustress, 108
evaluating, 260–261
evaluation apprehension, 232
evidence-based management, 20, 21*f*
exchange, 283*t*, 286
executive function, 37
exhaustion, 109
exit, 103
exit-voice-loyalty-neglect (EVLN) model, 103
expectancy theory, 132–134, 132*f*, 133*f*
expectations, 69–70, 76–77
experience, 196
experienced meaningfulness, 165
experienced responsibility, 166
experiences, 94
expert power, 276–277
exploding offer, 315
external attribution, 74
external environment
complex environment, 373
diverse environment, 373
dynamic environment, 372
effect of, 14
hostile environment, 373
integrated environment, 373
munificent environment, 373
and open systems, 5–6
organization-environment fit, 6–7
and organizational design, 372–373
simple environment, 373
stable environment, 372
and stakeholders, 11
external locus of control, 67
external self-concept, 68
extinction, 135
extroversion, 38, 39

F

false-consensus effect, 78
fear of the unknown, 412
feedback
balanced scorecard (BSC), 138
effective feedback, 138–139
evaluation of, 141
goal feedback, 138
job feedback, 165
and Johari Window, 80
multisource (360-degree) feedback, 140
sources of, 140–141
strengths-based coaching, 139–140
feeling (F), 39
feelings, 95
see also emotions
Fiedler's contingency model, 338–339
fight-or-flight response, 129
filtering, 257
financial reward practices, 156–161
advantages, 156*t*

competency-based rewards, 156*t*, 157–158
disadvantages, 156*t*
individual rewards, 158
job status-based rewards, 156*t*, 157
membership-based rewards, 156–157, 156*t*
money in the workplace, meaning of, 155–156
objectives, 156*t*
and organizational culture, 395
organizational rewards, 159–160
performance-based rewards, 156*t*, 158–160
seniority-based rewards, 156–157, 156*t*
team rewards, 158–159, 160–161
unintended consequences, 161, 162
Finland, 102
firefighting, 63, 64
first offers, 315
five-factor model (FFM), 37–39, 37*f*
flat structures, 359–360
flexible work time, 112
force field analysis, 408–409, 409*f*
forcing, 306, 307–308, 307*f*
forecasting, 276
formal groups. *See* teams
formal hierarchy, 355*t*, 356–357
formalization, 361
forming stage, 222–223
Four-D model of appreciative inquiry, 422–423, 423*f*
four-drive theory, 129–131, 130*f*
France, 125
Francophones, 52
friendly compliance, 38
functional structure, 364–365, 364*f*
fundamental attribution error, 75–76, 81
future search, 424

G

gainsharing plans, 159, 162
gender
and communication, 258–259, 259*f*, 260
and conflict handling styles, 308
and leadership, 345–346
general adaptation syndrome, 108–109, 109*f*
Generation-X, 16
Generation-Y, 16
generational cohorts, 16
generational conflicts, 303, 304
genetics, and personality, 36–37
geographic divisional structure, 365
Germany, 49
global corruption index, 45
global mindset, 81–83
globalization, 14–15, 51, 110, 258
globally integrated enterprise, 366
goal commitment, 138
goal feedback, 138
goal incompatibility, 302–303
goal participation, 138
goal setting, 137–138, 141, 171, 315
goals
challenging goals, 138
incompatible goals, 302–303

rational choice paradigm, 187, 187*f*
relevant goals, 138
SMART goals, 137–138
specific goals, 137
superordinate goals, 309
grapevine, 263–264
Greece, 50*f*, 51
groupthink, 232–233
guanxi, 279

H

halo effect, 77–78
harassment, 110
hard influence tactics, 283, 287, 287*f*
hedonism, 42
heredity, and personality, 36–37
hidden area, 79
high-performance work practices (HPWP), 10–11
historical foundations of organizational behaviour, 3
holistic perspective to motivation, 127
homogenization, 73
Hong Kong, 102
hostile environment, 373
hostile noncompliance, 38
hostile work environment harassment, 110
human capital, 8–9, 10
human interaction, 51
human motivation. *See* motivation
human rights, 46
humanistic perspective to motivation, 127
Hungary, 102
hygienes, 164

I

identification-based trust, 228
illumination, 195
imagination, 196–197
impact, 169
implementation of decisions, 192
implicit favourite, 188
implicit leadership theory, 344–345
impression management, 283*t*, 286
incivility, 110
incompatible goals, 302–303
incubation, 195
independent imagination, 196–197
India, 35, 50, 50*f*, 102, 125
individual behaviour
ability, 30–31
absenteeism, 35
and behavioural intentions, 95–96
counterproductive work behaviours (CWBs), 33–34
and emotions, 94–98
and ethics, 45–48
joining the organization, 34
MARS model, 29–32, 30*f*
motivation, 29–30
and needs, 125*f*
organizational citizenship behaviours (OCBs), 33, 34
presenteeism, 35

role perceptions, 31–32
situational factors, 32
staying with the organization, 34
task performance, 32–33
types of individual behaviour, 32–35, 33*f*
and values, 42–43
work attendance, 35
individual rewards, 158
individual rights, 46, 52
individualism, 49–50
Indonesia, 35
inequity, and motivation, 142–144
influence, 283–288
consequences, 286–288, 287*f*
contingencies of, 286–288
defined, 283
and organizational politics, 288–289
types of influence tactics, 283–286, 283*f*
informal communication, 355*t*, 356
informal groups, 212–214
informal roles, 223
information control, 283*t*, 284
information overload, 250, 257, 257*f*
information processing, 188–189
information processing capacity, 257
ingratiation, 283*t*, 285
initial offer point, 314
innovative transformation process, 7
inoculation effect, 285
inquisition, 312
integrated environment, 373
integration, 392–393, 392*t*
integrator roles, 356
integrators, 311
integrity, 331, 331*t*
intellectual capital, 8–9, 34
intelligence, 196
intensity, 30
intentional discrimination, 74
interdependence, 304, 310–311
intergenerational conflicts, 303, 304
internal attribution, 74
internal consistency, 64, 65
internal environment, 11
internal locus of control, 67
internal self-concept, 68
interpersonal conflict handling styles,
305–308, 306*f*, 307*f*
introversion, 38
intuition, 39, 191
Israel, 49, 50, 50*f*, 155
Italy, 125

J

Japan, 49–50, 50*f*, 51, 102, 111, 125, 155,
157, 258
jargon, 256
job, 161
job autonomy, 10
job burnout, 109–110
job characteristics model, 164–165, 165*f*
job demands, 111
job design, 161–168
defined, 161
and efficiency, 163
individual differences, 166

job characteristics model, 164–165, 165*f*
job enlargement, 167, 168*f*
job enrichment, 168
job rotation, 166–167
job specialization, 163–164
and motivation, 164–168
motivator-hygiene theory, 164
job enlargement, 167, 168*f*
job enrichment, 168, 311
job evaluation, 157
job feedback, 165
job resources, 111
job rotation, 166–167
job satisfaction, 102–106
and customer satisfaction, 104–105
defined, 102
and ethics, 105–106
exit-voice-loyalty-neglect (EVLN)
model, 103
and performance, 103–104
service profit chain model,
104–105, 104*f*
and work behaviour, 102–106
job sharing, 112
job specialization, 163–164, 354–355
job status-based rewards, 156*t*, 157
Johari Window, 79–80, 80*f*
joining the organization, 34
judging orientation, 39
judgments, 94
Jungian personality theory, 39–40, 40*f*
justice, 106
see also organizational justice

K

key performance indicators (KPIs), 137
knowledge, 196
knowledge acquisition, 7
knowledge-based trust, 228, 228*f*
knowledge management, 7–10
knowledge of results, 166
knowledge of the business, 331*t*, 332
knowledge sharing, 7
knowledge storage, 8
knowledge transfer, 10
knowledge use, 7–8
Korea, 110

L

labour efficiency, 162
language
issues, 256
organizational language, 387
leader identity, 330–331
leader-member relations, 338
leadership
achievement-oriented leadership, 336
authentic leadership, 332–333, 332*f*
behavioural perspective, 333–335
charismatic leadership, 341
competency perspective, 330–333, 331*t*
contingency perspective, 335–340
cross-cultural issues, 345
decisive leadership, 185
defined, 328

directive leadership, 333–334, 334*f*, 335
and evidence-based management, 20
Fiedler's contingency model, 338–339
and gender, 345–346
implicit leadership theory, 344–345
leadership substitutes, 339–340
managerial leadership, 340–341
motivation, 331, 331*t*
organizational culture, changing, 394
participative leadership, 336
path-goal leadership theory, 335–338,
336*f*
prototypes of effective leaders, 344
research on, 328, 328*f*
romance of, 344–345
servant leadership, 334–335
shared leadership, 329–330
situational leadership theory (SLT), 338
supportive leadership, 333–334, 334*f*,
335–336
transactional leadership, 340
transformational leadership, 340–344,
342*f*, 417
leadership substitutes, 339–340
leadership teams, 213*t*
learned capabilities, 30
learned helplessness, 110
learned needs theory, 128–129
learning, 415*t*, 416
learning behaviour consequences,
136–137
learning (drive), 129
learning orientation, 197, 390
legends, 386
legitimate power, 273–275
Lewin's force field analysis model,
408–409, 409*f*
liability of newness, 362
liaison roles, 356
locus of control, 67, 337
low task control, 111
loyalty, 103

M

M-form structure, 365–367, 365*f*
Machiavellian values, 289
making choices. *See* decision making
Malaysia, 50, 50*f*
management by walking
around (MBWA), 262
managerial leadership, 340–341
MARS model, 29–32, 30*f*, 67, 125, 418
Maslow's needs hierarchy theory,
126–128, 126*f*
materialism, 51
maternity leave, 113
matrix structure, 368–370, 369*f*
maximization, 189
meaning, 169
meaningful interaction, 80–81
mechanistic structure, 362, 362*f*, 372
media richness, 253–255, 254*f*
mediation, 312
membership-based rewards, 156–157, 156*t*
men. *See* gender
mental imagery, 172

mental models, 71–72, 185, 248
merging organizational cultures, 390–393
Millennials, 16, 266–267
mimicry, 252–253
mindless behaviour, 47
money, 155–156
money ethic, 155
moods, 93
moral intensity, 46, 47*f*
moral permissiveness, 52
moral principles. *See* ethics
morphological analysis, 198
motivation, 29–30
  defined, 123
  direction, 29
  drives, 125–131
  employee engagement, 123–124
  equity theory, 141–142, 142*f*
  expectancy theory, 132–134, 132*f*, 133*f*
  feedback, 138–141
  four-drive theory, 129–131, 130*f*
  goal setting, 137–138, 141
  holistic perspective, 127
  humanistic perspective, 127
  and inequity, 142–144
  intensity, 30
  and job design, 164–168
  leadership motivation, 331, 331*t*
  learned needs theory, 128–129
  Maslow's needs hierarchy theory,
    126–128, 126*f*
  motivator-hygiene theory, 164
  needs, 125–131
  organizational behaviour modification
    (OB Mod), 134–136
  organizational justice, 141–145
  persistence, 30
  and personality dimensions, 38
  positive perspective, 127
  social cognitive theory, 136–137
motivator-hygiene theory, 164
motivators, 164
multi-communication, 254–255
multiculturalism, 51
multidisciplinary anchor, 19–20
multidivisional structure, 365–367, 365*f*
multigenerational workforce, 16–17, 16*f*
multisource (360-degree) feedback, 140
mutual understanding, 309–310
Myers-Briggs Type Indicator (MBTI),
  39–40, 40*f*
mythical man-month, 215

N

natural grouping approach, 168
natural rewards, 172
natural task groups, 168
nature *vs.* nurture, 36–38
need for achievement (nAch), 128
need for affiliation (nAff), 128
need for power (nPow), 128
need principle, 142
needs, 125–131
  see also motivation
  and behaviour, 125*f*
  belonginess/love, 127

defined, 125
  esteem needs, 127
  individual differences, 125–126
  learned needs theory, 128–129
  Maslow's needs hierarchy theory,
    126–128, 126*f*
  physiological needs, 127
  safety needs, 127
  self-actualization, 127
needs hierarchy theory, 126–128, 126*f*
negative reinforcement, 135
neglect, 103
negotiation, 313–317
  audience characteristics, 317
  bargaining zone model of negotiations,
    314, 314*f*
  best alternative to a negotiated
    agreement (BATNA), 315
  claiming value, 314–315
  creating value, 315–317
  defined, 313
  location, 317
  physical setting, 317
  resistance to change, minimizing,
    415*t*, 416
  situational influences, 317
Netherlands, 50*f*, 51, 125
network structure, 370–372, 371*f*
neuroticism, 38, 39
new economy, 7
noise, 256–257
nominal group technique, 234–235
nonprogrammed decisions, 183, 200
nonsubstitutability, 277–278
nonverbal communication, 251–253, 258
norm of reciprocity, 275
norming stage, 223
norms, 224–225, 301
Norway, 50*f*, 51, 102
nurture *vs.* nature, 36–38

O

OB Mod, 134–136
office politics, 288–289
open area, 79
open systems, 5–7, 5*f*
openness to change, 42
openness to experience, 38, 39, 197
openspace technology, 424
opportunities, 183
  evaluation, 189–190
  identification, 184–187
  missed, 186
organic structure, 362, 362*f*
organization-community values
  congruence, 45
organization-environment fit, 6–7
organizational (affective) commitment,
  106–108
organizational behaviour modification
  (OB Mod), 134–136
organizational behaviour (OB)
  anchors of OB knowledge, 19–21, 19*f*
  contingency anchor, 20–21
  defined, 2
  field of organizational behaviour, 2–4

  historical foundations, 3
  importance of, 4
  multidisciplinary anchor, 19–20
  and organizational effectiveness, 14
  and organization's financial health, 4
  positive organizational behaviour,
    77, 127
  and self-concept, 68
  study of, 3–4
  systematic research anchor, 20
organizational change
  action research approach, 419–421, 420*f*
  appreciative inquiry approach, 421–423,
    422*t*, 423*f*
  change agents, 417–418
  coercion, 415*t*, 416–417
  communication, 415–416, 415*t*
  cross-cultural issues, 424–425
  customer-driven change, 414
  diffusion of change, 418–419, 419*f*
  employee involvement, 415*t*, 416
  ethical issues, 424–425
  global perspective, 410
  learning, 415*t*, 416
  Lewin's force field analysis model,
    408–409, 409*f*
  negotiation, 415*t*, 416
  parallel learning structures
    approach, 424
  refreezing, 409, 417
  resistance to change, 409–413, 415*f*
  resistance to change, minimizing,
    415–417, 415*t*
  restraining forces, reducing,
    415–417, 415*t*
  strategic visions, 417–418
  stress management, 415*t*, 416
  unfreezing, 409, 413–417
  urgency for change, 413–415
organizational chart, 363
organizational citizenship behaviours
  (OCBs), 33, 34
organizational comprehension, 107
organizational culture
  adaptive culture, 390
  alignment with environment, 389
  artifacts, 382*f*, 385–387, 394–395
  assimilation, 392, 392*t*
  assumptions, 381, 382*f*
  attraction-selection-attrition (ASA)
    theory, 395
  bicultural audit, 391–392
  ceremonies, 387
  changing organizational culture,
    393–395, 394*f*
  characteristics, 384*f*
  content of, 382–384
  contingencies, 389–390, 389*f*
  control system, 388
  corporate cult, 389
  deculturation, 392, 392*t*
  defined, 381
  elements of, 381–385
  and ethics, 390
  importance of, 387–390
  integration, 392–393, 392*t*
  integration perspective, 384

merging organizational cultures, 390–393
organizational language, 387
organizational stories and legends, 386
physical structures and symbols, 387
profile dimensions, 384*f*
reward systems, 395
rituals, 387
sense-making process, 388
separation, 392*t*, 393
social glue, 388
strength of, 389*f*
strengthening, 393–395, 394*f*
subcultures, 384–385
and values, 381–382, 382*f*
organizational design
contingencies of, 372–374
external environment, 372–373
organizational size, 373–374
organizational strategy, 374
technology, 374
organizational effectiveness, 4–14
corporate social responsibility (CSR), 13–14
defined, 4
ethics, 13
"goal attainment" definition, 4
high-performance work practices (HPWP) perspective, 10–11
open systems perspective, 5–7, 5*f*
and organizational behaviour, 14
organizational learning perspective, 7–10, 8*f*
stakeholder perspective, 11–14
values, 12–13
organizational efficiency, 7
organizational justice, 141–145
distributive justice, 141
equity theory, 141–142, 142*f*
procedural justice, 141, 145
organizational language, 387
organizational learning, 7–10, 8*f*
organizational loyalty, 107
organizational memory, 9–10
organizational politics, 288–289
organizational rewards, 159
organizational size, 373–374
organizational socialization, 396–400
as adjustment process, 396
defined, 396
encounter, 398
improvement of socialization process, 398–400
as learning process, 396
pre-employment socialization, 397–398
psychological contract, 396–397
reality shock, 398
role management, 398
socialization agents, 399–400
stages of, 397–398, 397*f*
organizational stories and legends, 386
organizational strategy, 374
organizational structure
centralization, 360–361
coordination, 355–357, 355*t*
decentralization, 360–361
defined, 354
departmentalization, 363–372

division of labour, 354–355
divisional structure, 365–367, 365*f*
elements of, 357–362
flat structures, 359–360
formalization, 361
functional structure, 364–365, 364*f*
M-form structure, 365–367, 365*f*
matrix structure, 368–370, 369*f*
mechanistic structure, 362, 362*f*
multidivisional structure, 365–367, 365*f*
network structure, 370–372, 371*f*
organic structure, 362, 362*f*
simple structure, 364
span of control, 357–360, 358*f*
tall structures, 359–360
team-based organizational structure, 367–368
organizational subsystems, 6, 7
organizational values, 41
organizations
contemporary challenges, 14–19
defined, 2
key features, 2–3
outcome/input ratio, 142, 142*f*
outcome valences, 132, 133–134, 133*f*

P

P-to-O expectancy, 132, 133, 133*f*
parallel learning structures, 424
participating leadership style, 338
participative leadership, 336
participative management. *See* employee involvement
paternity leave, 113
path-goal leadership theory, 335–338, 336*f*
perceiving orientation, 39
perception, 69–72
attribution theory, 74–76
defined, 69
of equity or inequity, 142–143
false-consensus effect, 78
global mindset, 81–83
halo effect, 77–78
improving perceptions, 79–81
meaningful interaction, 80–81
mental models, 71–72
model of perceptual process, 70*f*
perceptual biases, 72–78, 79
perceptual organization and interpretation, 71–72
and power, 272
primacy effect, 78
recency effect, 78
selective attention, 69
self-awareness, 79–80
self-fulfilling prophecy, 76–77, 76*f*, 79
similar-to-me effect, 78
specific perceptual processes and problems, 72–78
stereotyping, 72–74, 79
stress perceptions, 113
perceptual biases, 69–70, 72–78, 79
perceptual blinders, 193
perceptual defence, 185
perceptual interpretation, 71–72
perceptual organization, 71–72

perfectionism, 41
performance
ability, 30–31
applied performance practices. *See* applied performance practices
and job satisfaction, 103–104
key performance indicators (KPIs), 137
MARS model, 29–32, 30*f*
motivation, 29–30
and rewards, 160
role perceptions, 31–32
situational factors, 32
performance-based rewards, 156*t*, 158–161
improvement of reward effectiveness, 160–161
individual rewards, 158
organizational rewards, 159–160
relevance of rewards, 160
rewards, and performance, 160
team rewards, 158–159, 160–161
unintended consequences, 161, 162
performance-to-outcome (P-to-O) expectancy, 132, 133, 133*f*
performing stage, 223
persistence, 30, 196
person-organization values congruence, 44
personal identity, 68
personal leave, 113
personal values, 41
personality, 35–41
agreeableness, 38, 39
"Big Five" personality dimensions, 37–39, 37*f*, 330
clashes, 300
conscientiousness, 38, 39
defined, 36
determinants, 36–38
emotional stability, 38, 39
and emotions, 98
extroversion, 38, 39
five-factor model (FFM), 37–39, 37*f*
Jungian personality theory, 39–40, 40*f*
and leadership, 330, 331*t*
Myers-Briggs Type Indicator (MBTI), 39–40, 40*f*
nature *vs.* nurture, 36–38
neuroticism, 38, 39
openness to experience, 38, 39
personality testing, caveats about, 40–41
and stress, 112
vs. values, 41–42
personality tests, 40–41
personality theory, 36
personality traits, 36
persuasion, 255–256, 283*t*, 284, 285*f*
physical structures, 387
physiological needs, 127
poetic principle, 422, 422*t*
politics, organizational, 288–289
pooled interdependence, 218
position power, 338–339
positive organizational behaviour, 77, 127, 421, 422*t*
positive perspective to motivation, 127
positive reinforcement, 135
positive self-talk, 171
post-decisional justification, 192

power
 centrality, 278
 coercive power, 276
 consequences of, 282
 contingencies of, 274f, 277–278
 countervailing power, 272
 defined, 272
 dependence, 272–273, 273f
 discretion, 278
 expert power, 276–277
 influence. *See* influence
 legitimate power, 273–275
 meaning of power, 272–273
 need for power (nPow), 128
 position power, 338–339
 referent power, 277
 reward power, 275
 social capital, 279
 social networks, 279–282
 sources of, 273–277, 274f
 substitutability, 277–278
 trust, 272–273
 as value category, 42
 visibility, 278
power distance, 50–51, 155
practical intelligence, 196, 331t, 332
pre-employment socialization,
  397–398
preferred behaviours, 32
prejudice, 74
preparation, 195
presenteeism, 35
prevention, 276
primacy effect, 78
primary needs. *See* drives
priority, 32
privacy rights, 46
problem identification, 184–187
problem solving, 306, 307, 307f
problems, 183
procedural justice, 141, 145
process losses, 215
product/service divisional structure, 365
production blocking, 232
production teams, 213t
productivity. *See* organizational efficiency
profit-sharing plans, 159
programmed decisions, 183, 200
project teams, 213t
prospect theory effect, 193
psychological comfort, 220
psychological contract, 396–397
psychological harassment, 110
psychological states, 165–166
psychology, 19
punishment, 135

Q

quid pro quo harassment, 110

R

racial discrimination, 74
rapport talk, 259
rational choice decision making process,
  183–184, 183f

rational choice paradigm, 182–184
 goals, 187, 187f
 information processing, 188
 maximization, 189
realistic job preview (RJP), 398–399
reality shock, 398
recency effect, 78
reciprocal interdependence, 218
reduced personal accomplishment, 110
referent power, 277
refreezing, 409, 417
reinforcement, 126, 135
reinforcement contingencies, 135
reinforcement schedules, 135
relational contracts, 397
relationship capital, 9
relationship conflict, 300–301
relevant goals, 138
report talk, 259
representativeness heuristic, 188–189
resistance, 109, 286
resistance point, 314
resistance to change, 409–413
resource scarcity, 305
responding, 261
reverse engineering, 9
reward power, 275
rewards. *See* financial reward practices
rights, individual, 46
rituals, 387
role, 223
role clarity, 38
role definition team building, 224
role management, 398
role obligations, 31–32
role perceptions, 31–32
rubber band effect, 413

S

sabbaticals, 113
safety needs, 127
satisficing, 189
saving face, 412
scarce resources, 305
scenario planning, 192
schedules of reinforcement, 135
Schwartz's values circumplex, 42, 43f
scientific management, 163–164
search conferences, 424
security, 42
selection, 395
selective attention, 69
self-actualization, 127
self-awareness
 emotions, 100
 perception, 79–80
self-concept, 37, 64–68
 clarity, 64–65
 cognitive dissonance, 98
 complexity, degrees of, 64, 65
 defined, 64
 dimension of, 64–65, 65f
 external self-concept, 68
 internal consistency, 64, 65
 internal self-concept, 68
 and leadership, 330, 331t

and motivation, 126
 and organizational behaviour, 68
 self-enhancement, 65–66, 73
 self-evaluation, 66–67
 self-verification, 66
 social identity theory, 68, 69f, 73
 social self, 67–68
 and stress, 112
self-determination, 169
self-directed teams (SDTs), 213t, 229–230
self-direction, 42
self-efficacy, 66
self-enhancement, 42, 65–66, 73
self-esteem, 66
self-evaluation, 66–67
self-fulfilling prophecy, 76–77, 76f, 79
self-justification, 193
self-leadership, 170–173
 contingencies, 173
 defined, 170
 effectiveness of, 172–173
 elements of, 172f
 strategies, 171–172
self-monitoring, 172
self-regulation, 137
self-reinforcement, 137, 172
self-serving bias, 76
self-talk, 171
self-transcendence, 42
self-verification, 66
selling leadership style, 338
seniority-based rewards, 156–157, 156t
sense-making process, 388
sensing, 39, 260
separation, 392t, 393
sequential interdependence, 218
servant leadership, 334–335
service profit chain model, 104–105, 104f
service teams, 213t
sexual harassment, 110
share options, 159, 162
shared assumptions, 381
shared leadership, 329–330
shared mental models, 248
shared values, 12, 41, 106–107, 381
silence, 258
silent authority, 283, 283t
similar-to-me effect, 78
simple environment, 373
simple structure, 364
simultaneity principle, 422, 422t
Singapore, 50f, 51
situation favourableness, 339
situational control, 338
situational factors, 32, 47
situational leadership theory (SLT), 338
skill-and-will model, 29
skill-based pay plans, 157
skill variety, 164
skunkworks, 213t
SMART goals, 137–138
social acceptance, 253
social capital, 279
social cognitive theory, 136–137
social glue, 388
social identity, 68, 73
social identity theory, 68, 69f

social loafing, 216
social media, 250–251, 252*f*
social network centrality, 281–282, 281*f*
social networks, 214, 279–282
social norms, 126
social presence effects, 255
social sciences, 19–20
social self, 67–68
social support, 113–114
socialization, 126
 see also organizational socialization
socialization agents, 399–400
socioemotional conflict, 300–301
sociology, 19
soft influence tactics, 283, 287, 287*f*
solution-focused problems, 185
South Africa, 50*f*
South Korea, 102, 125
span of control, 357–360, 358*f*
span of management, 357–360
specific goals, 137
stable environment, 372
stakeholder framing, 184–185
stakeholders, 12*f*
 corporate social responsibility (CSR),
  13–14
 defined, 11
 dynamic relations, 11
 ethics, 13
 and organizational effectiveness, 11–14
 values, 12–13
standardization, 355*t*, 357
start-up companies, 362
staying with the organization, 34
stereotyping, 72–74, 79
stimulation, 42
stock of organizational knowledge, 8–9
stories, 386
storming stage, 223
strategic vision, 341–343, 417–418
strengths-based coaching, 139–140
stress, 108–114
 control of stress consequences, 113
 coping mechanisms, 111–112
 cynicism, 110
 defined, 108
 depersonalization, 110
 distress, 108, 109–110
 emotional exhaustion, 109–110
 eustress, 108
 general adaptation syndrome,
  108–109, 109*f*
 harassment, 110
 incivility, 110
 individual differences, 111–112
 job burnout, 109–110
 management of work-related stress,
  112–114
 perceptions, 113
 reduced personal accomplishment, 110
 stressors, 110–111, 112–113
 work overload, 110–111
stress management, 112–114, 415*t*, 416
stressors, 110–111, 112–113
structural capital, 9
structural hole, 282
study of organizational behaviour, 3–4

subcultures, 384–385
subjective expected utility, 182–183
substitutability, 277–278
subsystems, 6, 7
superordinate goals, 309
support, 106
supportive leadership, 333–334, 334*f*,
 335–336
surface acting, 99
surface-level diversity, 16
Sweden, 50*f*, 51, 102
swift trust, 228
symbols, 387
systematic research anchor, 20
systemic discrimination, 74

T

Taiwan, 49, 50*f*
tall structures, 359–360
target point, 314
task control, 111
task force teams, 213*t*
task identity, 164
task interdependence, 218, 218*f*
task performance, 32–33
task-related conflict, 300–301
task significance, 165
task structure, 337, 338
team-based organizational structure,
 367–368
team building, 223–224
team cohesion, 225–227, 227*f*, 232, 301
team competence, 223
team decision making, 231–235
 brainstorming, 233–234
 constraints on, 231–233
 constructive conflict, 233
 electronic brainstorming, 234
 evaluation apprehension, 232
 groupthink, 232–233
 nominal group technique, 234–235
 pressure to conform, 232
 team structures to improve decision
  making, 233–235
 time constraints, 232
team identity, 223
team processes, 222–229
 norms, 224–225, 301
 team building, 223–224
 team cohesion, 225–227, 227*f*,
  232, 301
 team development, 222–223, 222*f*
 team roles, 223
 trust, 227–229, 228*f*
team rewards, 158–159, 160–161
teams
 advantages, 214–215
 Brooks's law, 215–216
 challenges of, 215–216
 composition, 219–222
 decision making. *See* team decision
  making
 defined, 212
 disadvantages, 215–216
 diversity, 221–222
 dynamics, and leadership, 337–338

effective teams, 216–217, 217*f*, 229
five C's of team member competency, 221*f*
incongruent team dynamics, 413
organizational environment, 216–217
process losses, 215
self-directed teams (SDTs), 213*t*,
 229–230
size, 219, 226
social loafing, 216
task characteristics, 217–219
task interdependence, 218, 218*f*
team design elements, 217–222
team environment, 216–217
team players, 38
team processes, 222–229
types of teams in organizations, 213*t*
virtual teams, 230–231
technology, 374
telecommuting, 18–19
teleworking, 18–19, 112–113
telling leadership style, 338
"thin slice" studies, 71
thinking (T), 39
third party conflict resolution,
 311–313, 312*f*
360-degree feedback, 140
time constraints, 232
time-limited offers, 315
tolerance, 52
town hall meetings, 263
tradition, 42
training
 awareness training, 79
 ethics training, 48
 learning needs, 128–129
transactional contracts, 397
transactional leadership, 340
transformational leadership, 340–344,
 342*f*, 417
trust, 107, 227–229, 228*f*, 272–273, 316, 331
trustworthiness, 316–317
turnover, 65, 105
twins, 37

U

Uganda, 35
uncertainty, 412
uncertainty avoidance, 51
unfreezing, 409, 413–417
unintentional discrimination, 74
United Kingdom, 35
United States
 absenteeism, 35
 Canadian *vs.* American values, 52
 employee engagement, 125
 employee share ownership plans
  (ESOPs), 160
 job satisfaction, 102
 low collectivism, 49
 silence, 258
universalism, 42
unknown area, 80
unlearning, 9–10
upward appeal, 283*t*, 284
urgency for change, 413–415
user-generated content, 250

utilitarianism, 45–46
utility, 189

V

valence, 132, 133–134, 133*f*
value system, 41
values, 12–13
    across cultures, 48–52
    cultural values, 41
    defined, 12, 41
    enacted values, 381–382
    and individual behaviour, 42–43
    and organizational culture, 381–382
    organizational values, 41
    personal values, 41
    vs. personality, 41–42
    Schwartz's values circumplex, 42, 43*f*
    shared values, 12, 41, 106–107, 381
    types of values, 42
    values congruence, 43–45
    in the workplace, 41–45
values congruence, 43–45

values-driven organization model, 13
values hierarchy, 43
variability, 374
variable ratio schedule, 135
Venezuela, 50*f*
verification, 195
virtual teams, 213*t*, 230–231
virtual work, 18–19
voice, 103

W

Web-based communication, 249, 260, 262
wikis, 262
win-lose orientation, 306, 307
win-win orientation, 306
women
    see also gender
    and firefighting, 63, 64
    and social networks, 282
work addict, 112
work-at-home employees, 18–19
work attendance, 35

work efficiency, 163
work-life balance, 18, 112
work overload, 110–111
work-related stress. *See* stress
work spouses, 114
workaholic, 112
workforce diversity
    Canada's diversity advantage, 17
    challenges of, 15–17
    consequences of diversity, 17
    deep-level diversity, 16
    multigenerational workforce, 16–17, 16*f*
    surface-level diversity, 16
    team diversity, 221–222
workspace design, 261–262

Y

yielding, 306, 307*f*, 308

Z

zone of indifference, 274